A-Z LONDON Street Atlas

CONTENTS

REFERENCE

Motorway	M1	Disabled Toilet National Key Scheme	♿
Dual Carriageway		Fire Station	■
'A' Road	A40	Hospital	🄷
'B' Road	B106	House Numbers 'A' and 'B' Roads only	2 45
One Way Street One Way traffic flow on 'A' Roads is indicated by a heavy line on drivers left	traffic flow ➡	Information Centre	🄸
Map Continuation	130	National Grid Reference	578
Docklands Light Railway Station	DLR	Place of Worship	✛
British Rail line Level Crossing Station		Police Station	▲
Underground Station	●	Post Office	★

SCALE

Map Pages 4—137
1:22,000 (2.88 inches to 1 mile)

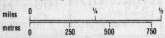

Central Area pages 138—149
1:14,080 (4½ inches to 1 mile)

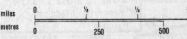

Geographers' A-Z Map Co. Ltd.

Head Office :
Vestry Road, Sevenoaks, Kent, TN14 5EP
Telephone 0732-451152

Showrooms :
44 Gray's Inn Road, London, WC1X 8LR
Telephone 071-242 9246

© Edition 13 1990
    Edition 13A (part revision) 1990

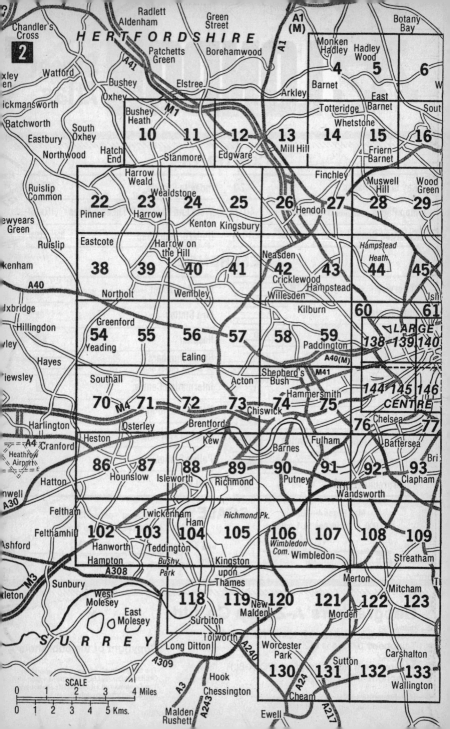

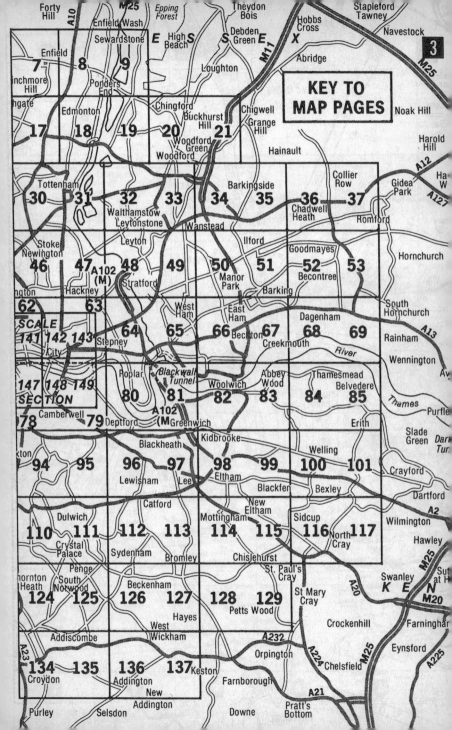

Forty Hill
A10
M25
Epping Forest
Theydon Bois
Stapleford Tawney
Navestock
Enfield Wash
Sewardstone
High Beach
S
Debden Green
Hobbs Cross
Abridge
M11
X
M25
Enfield
7
8
9
Ponders End
Loughton
Chigwell Grange Hill
Noak Hill

KEY TO MAP PAGES

3

inchmore Hill
ngate
Edmonton
17
18
19
Chingford
Buckhurst Hill
Woodford Green
Woodford
20
21
Hainault
Harold Hill
A12
Ha W
A127

Tottenham
30
31
Walthamstow
Leytonstone
32
33
Wanstead
34
Barkingside
35
36
Chadwell Heath
Romford
Collier Row
37
Gidea Park
Ha W
A127

Stoke Newington
46
47
A102 (M)
48
Stratford
Leyton
49
Ilford
50
Manor Park
51
Goodmayes
52
Becontree
53
Hornchurch

ngton
Hackney
62
63
West Ham
64
65
East Ham
Barking
66
Beckton
67
Dagenham
68
69
South Hornchurch
A13

SCALE
141 **142** **143**
City
Stepney
Creekmouth
River
Rainham
Wennington
Av

147 **148** **149**
SECTION
Poplar
80
Blackwall Tunnel
81
Woolwich
82
Abbey Wood
83
Thamesmead
84
Belvedere
85
Thames
Purfle

78 Camberwell **79** Deptford
A102 (M)
Greenwich
Erith
Slade Green
Dar Tur.

Blackheath
Kidbrooke
Welling
94 **95** **96** **97** **98** **99** **100** **101**
Lewisham
Lee
Eltham
Blackfen
Bexley
Crayford
Dartford

Catford
New Eltham
Sidcup
A2

Dulwich
110 **111**
112 **113**
Mottingham
114 **115**
116 North Cray
117
Wilmington
Hawley

Crystal Palace
Sydenham
Bromley
Chislehurst
M25

Penge
thornton Heath
South Norwood
124 **125**
Beckenham
126 **127**
St. Paul's Cray
128 **129**
St Mary Cray
Swanley
K E N
M20
Sut at H

Hayes
West Wickham
Crockenhill
Farningha

Addiscombe
A232
Orpington
A224
Chelsfield
Eynsford
A225

134 **135**
Croydon
136 **137**
Keston
Addington
New Addington
Farnborough
Downe
A21
Pratt's Bottom
Purley
Selsdon
A23
A20

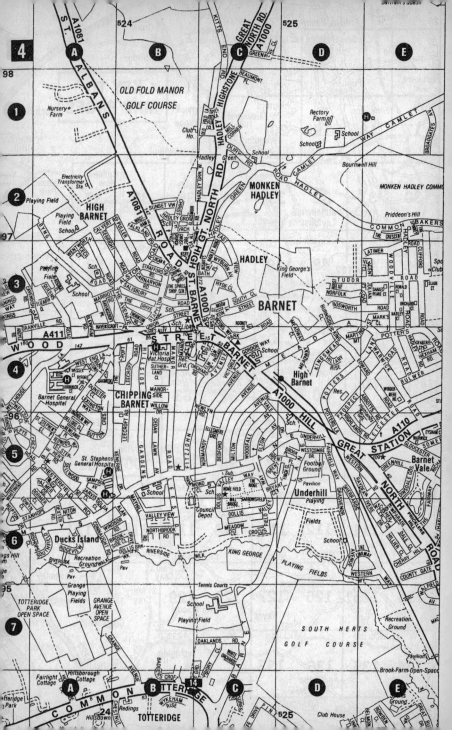

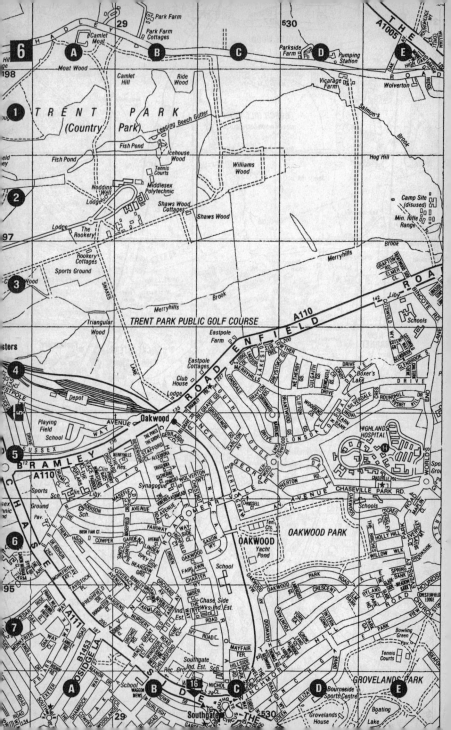

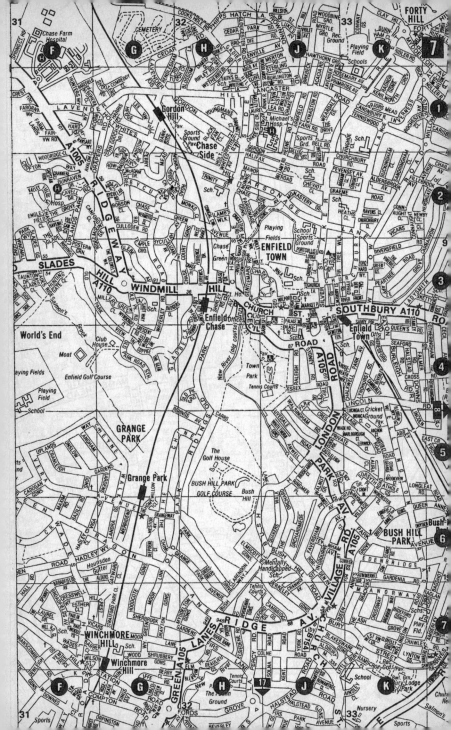

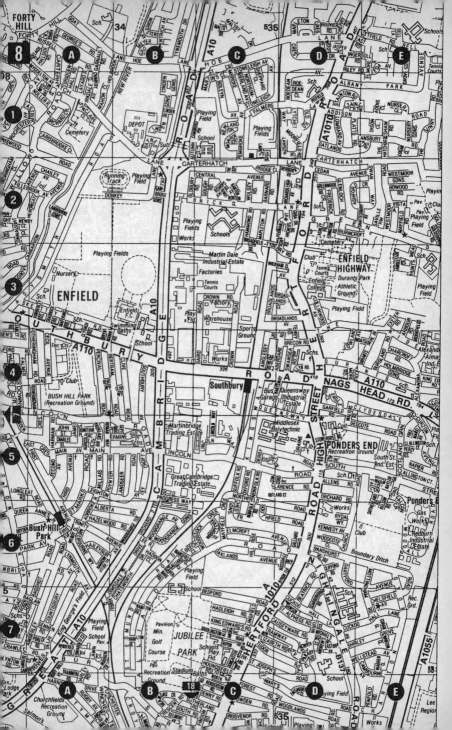

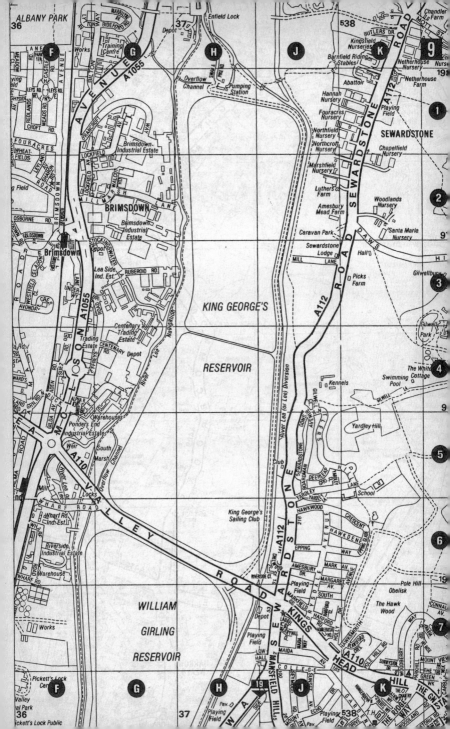

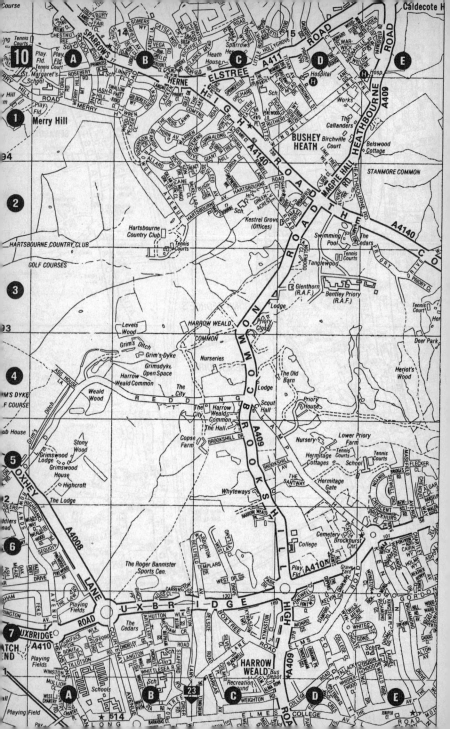

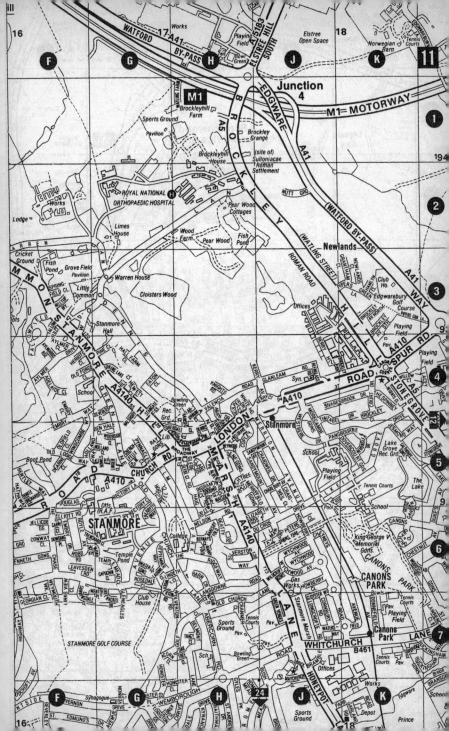

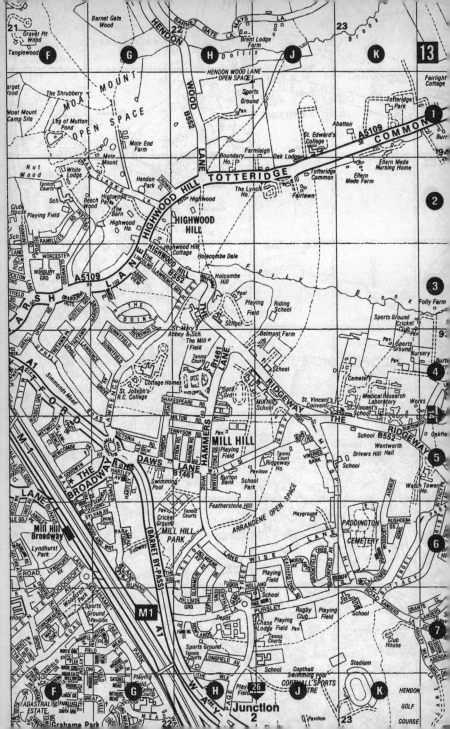

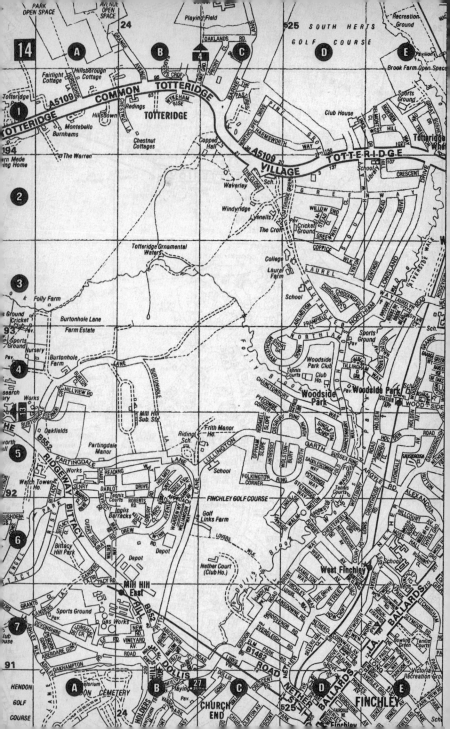

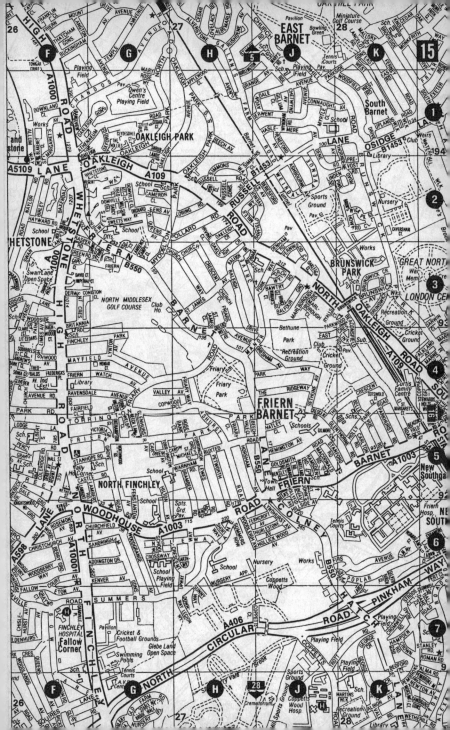

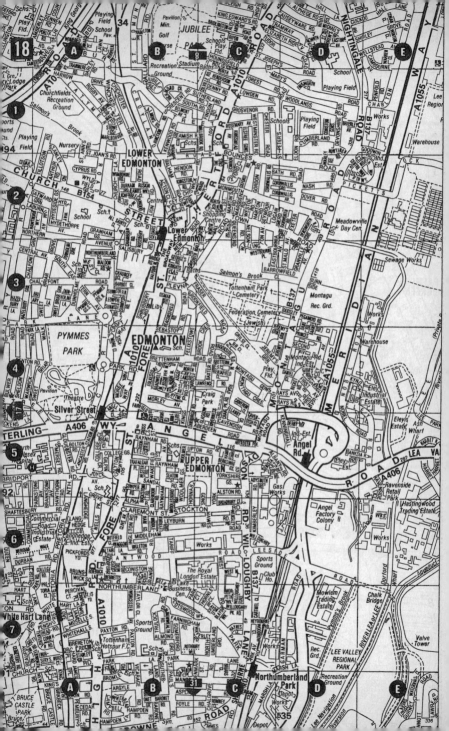

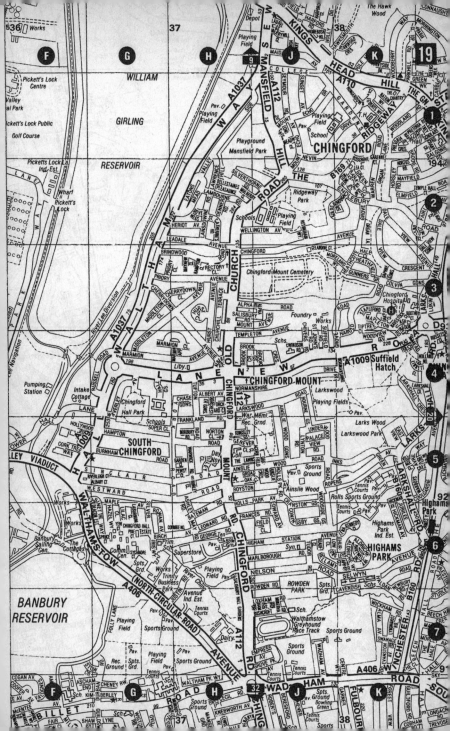

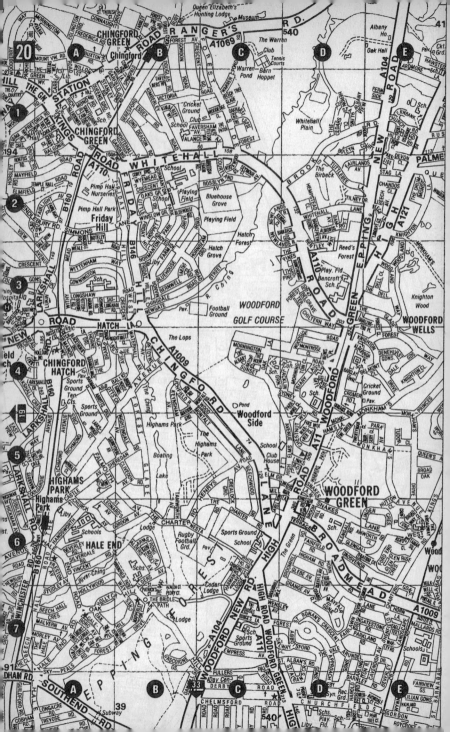

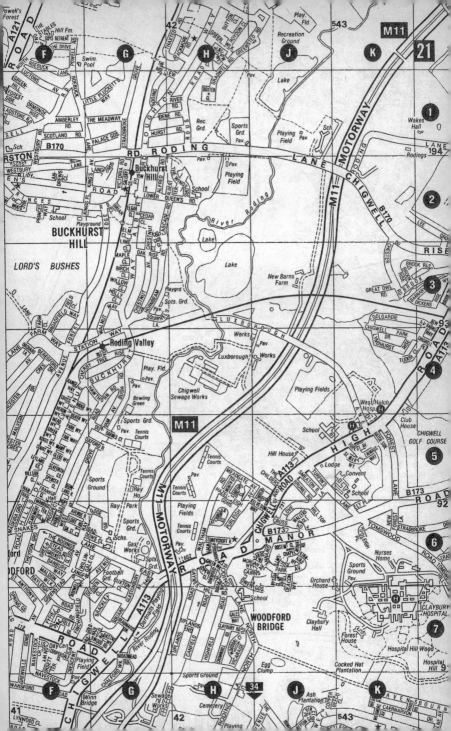

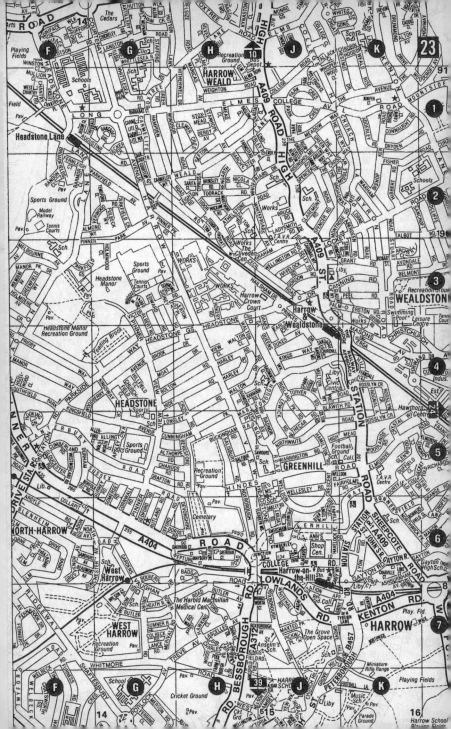

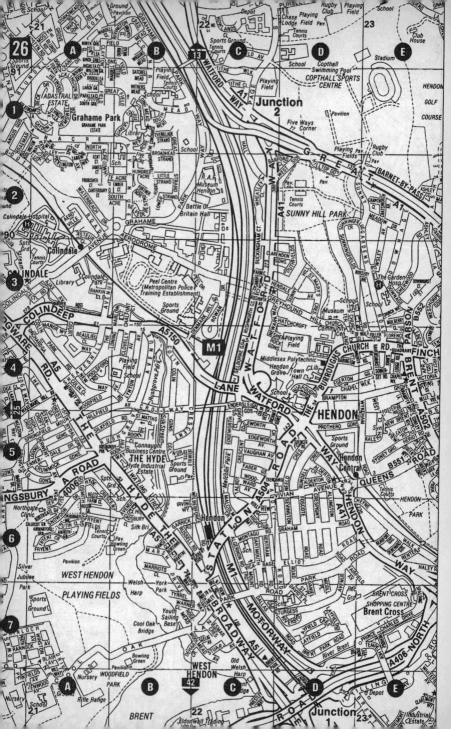

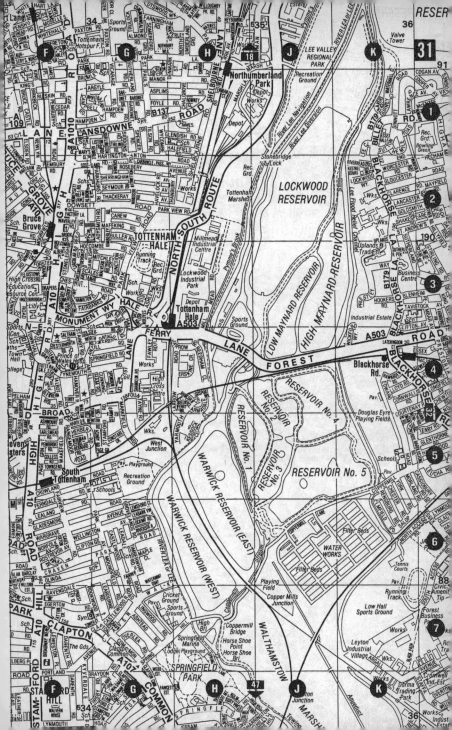

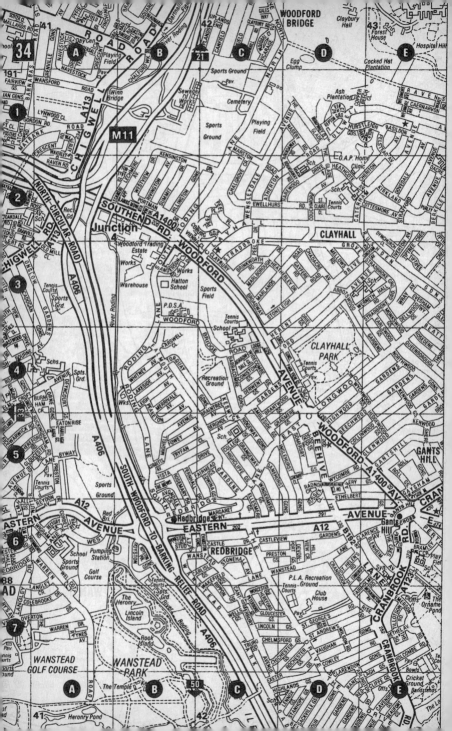

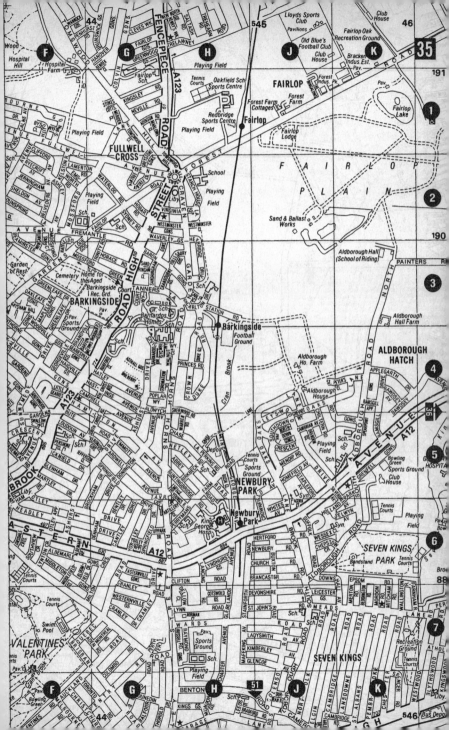

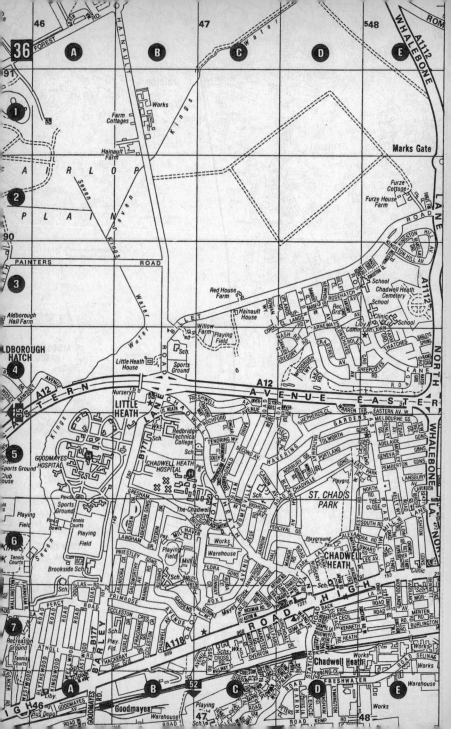

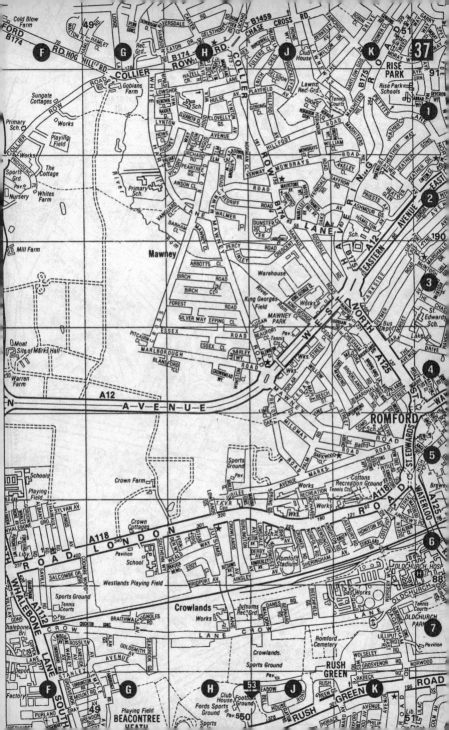

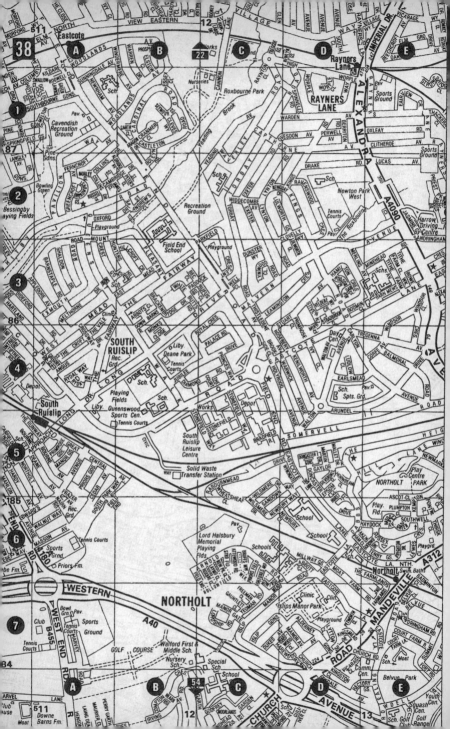

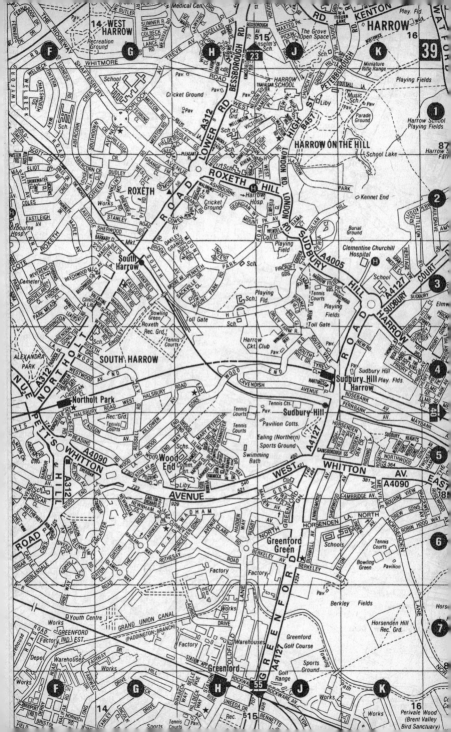

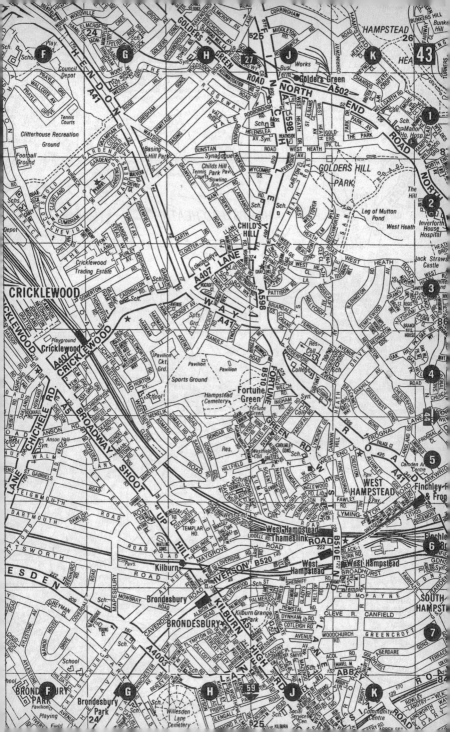

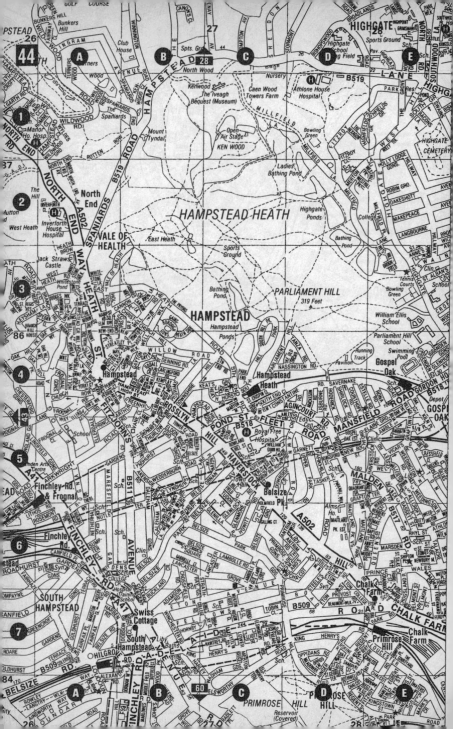

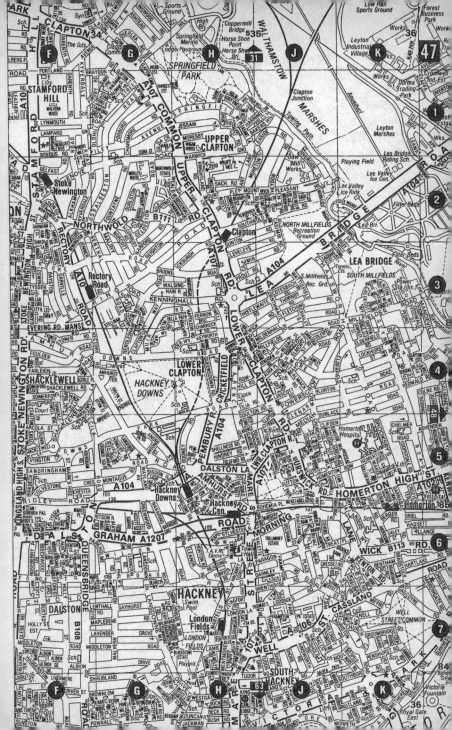

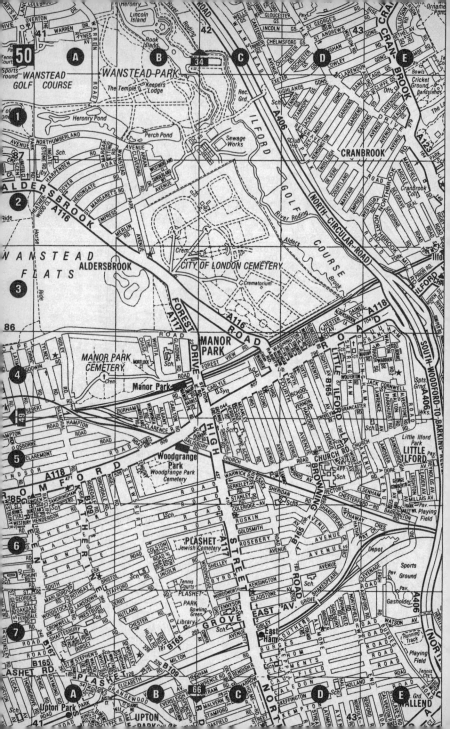

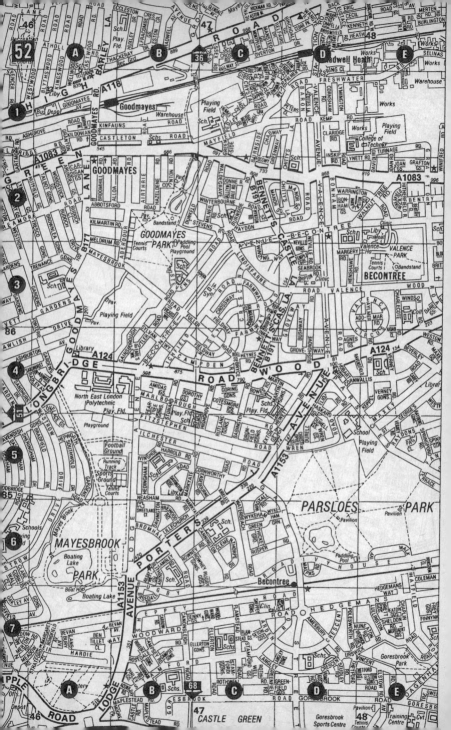

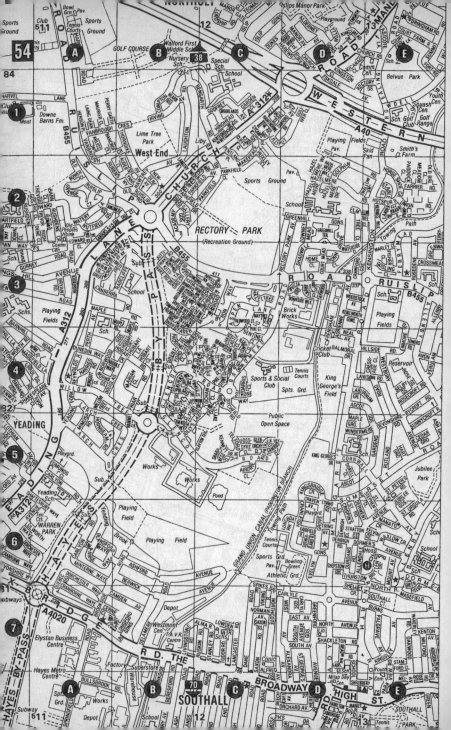

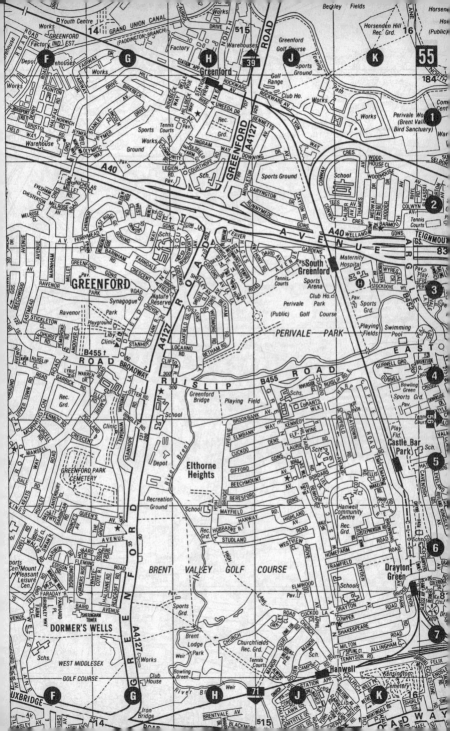

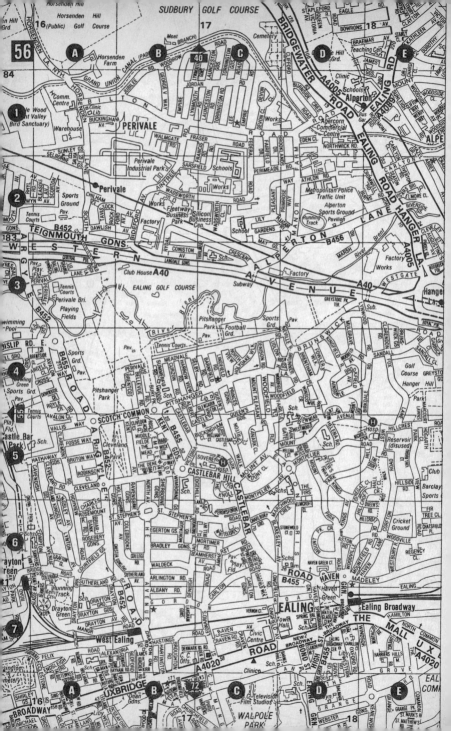

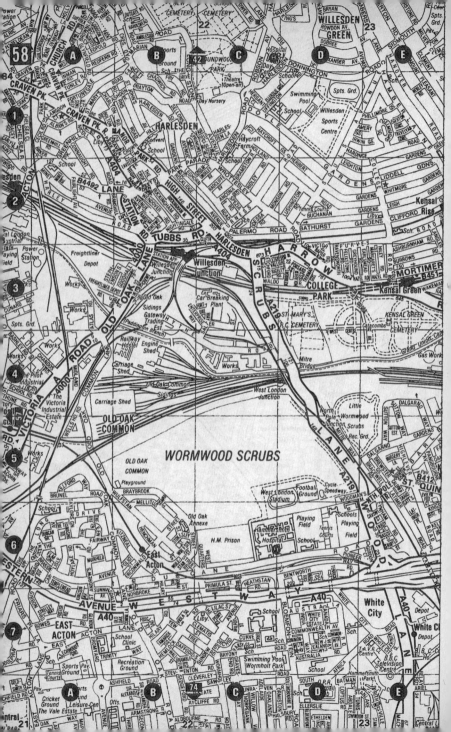

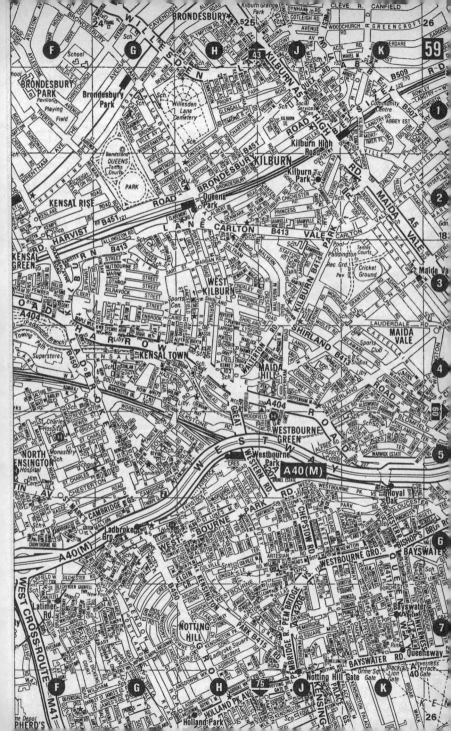

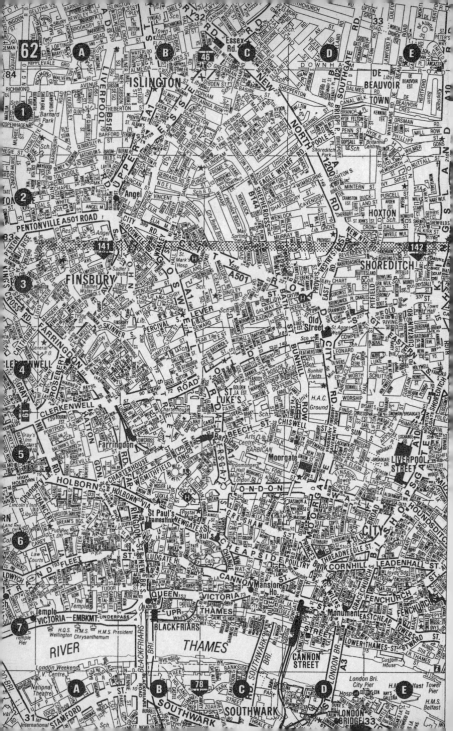

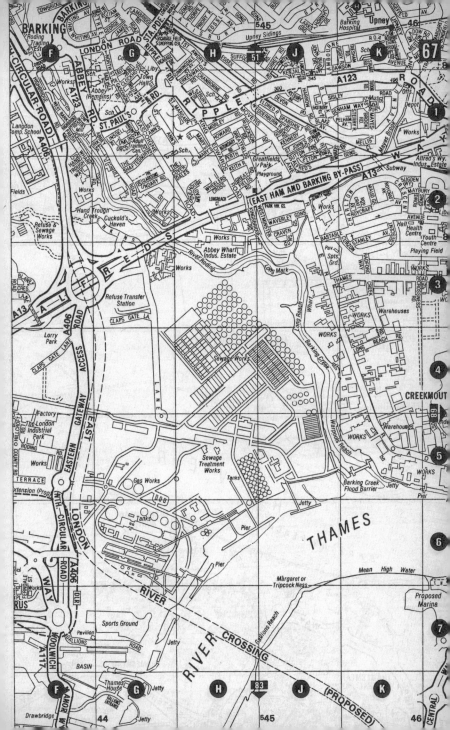

BARKING

F   G   H   51   J   K

LONDON ROAD STA.PDE.
BARKING RIPPLE RD.

Upney Sidings

Barking Hospital

Upney   46

545

A123

ROAD

1

RIPPLE ROAD

EAST HAM AND BARKING BY-PASS

A13   Subway

Alfred's Wy. Indus. Estate

2

AVENUE

Hall
Health
Centre

Youth
Centre
Playing Field

8

CREEKMOUT

3

Warehouses

WORKS

Long Reach Rd.

4

Warpoints Reach

68

5

Barking Creek
Flood Barrier

WORKS

Jetty
Pier

Jetty

Refuse Transfer
Station

CLAPS GATE LA.

Lorry
Park

Sewage Works

EAST GATEWAY ACCESS ROAD

The London
Industrial
Park

Sewage
Treatment
Works

Gas Works

Tanks

Tanks

Pier

Jetty

Pier

THAMES

6

RIVER

Mean High Water

Màrgaret or
Tripcock Ness

Proposed
Marina

7

Sports Ground

Pavilion

Jetty

RIVER   CROSSING   (PROPOSED)

Galions Reach

Thames
House

Jetty

Jetty

F   G   H   83   J   K

Drawbridge

44   545   46

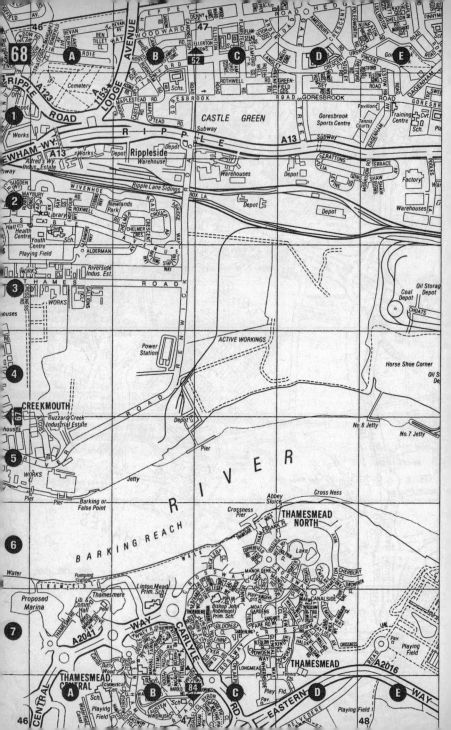

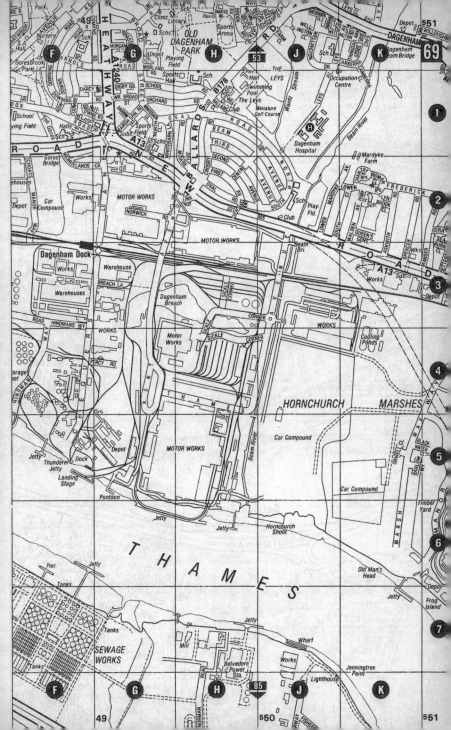

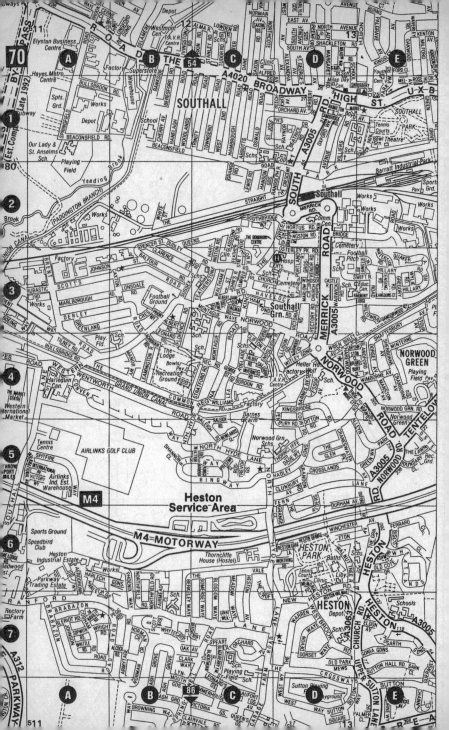

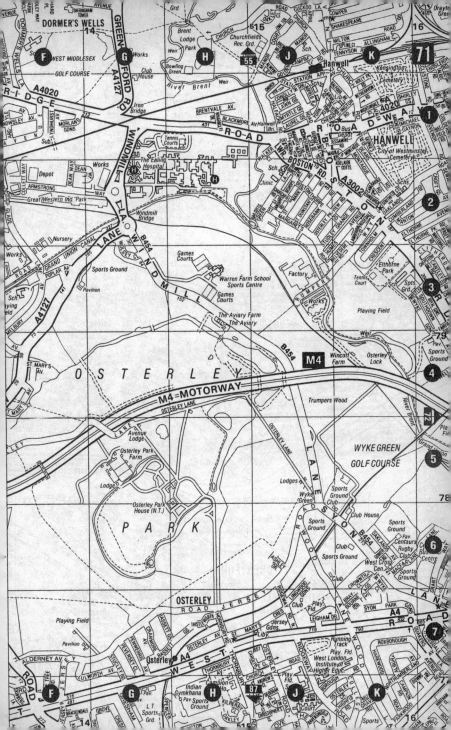

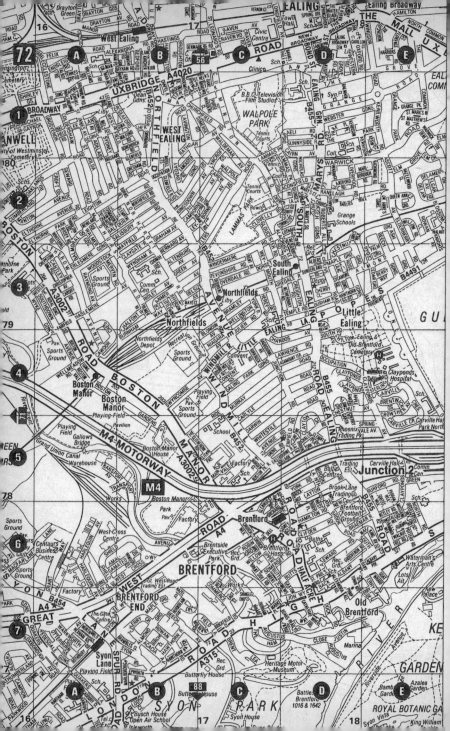

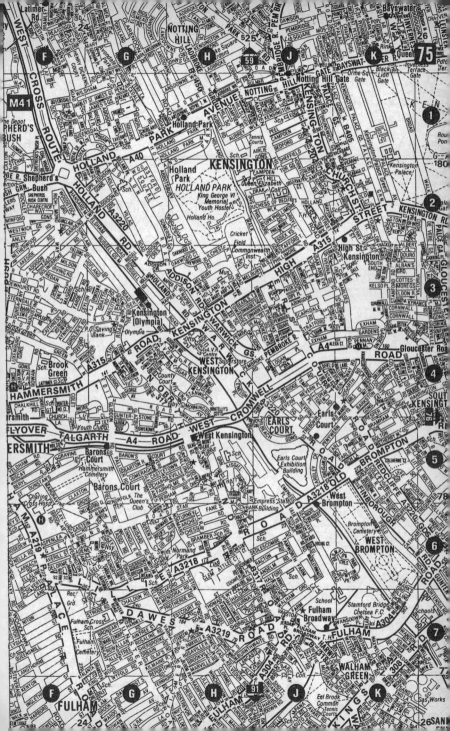

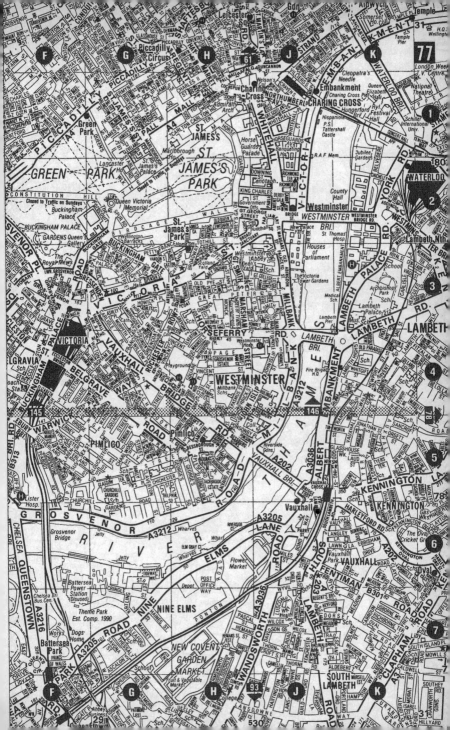

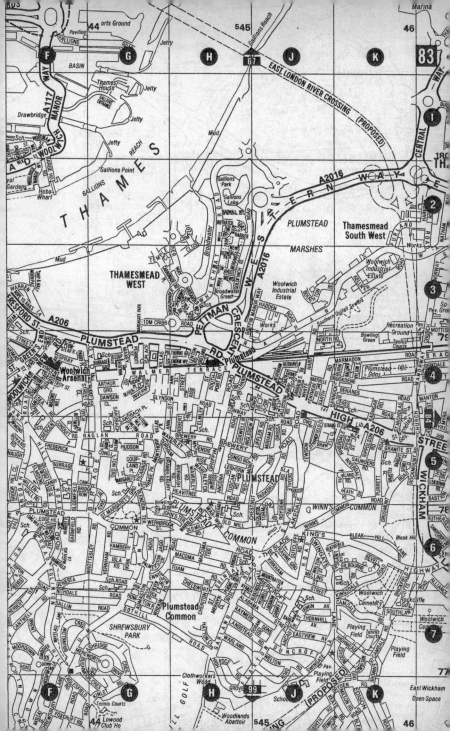

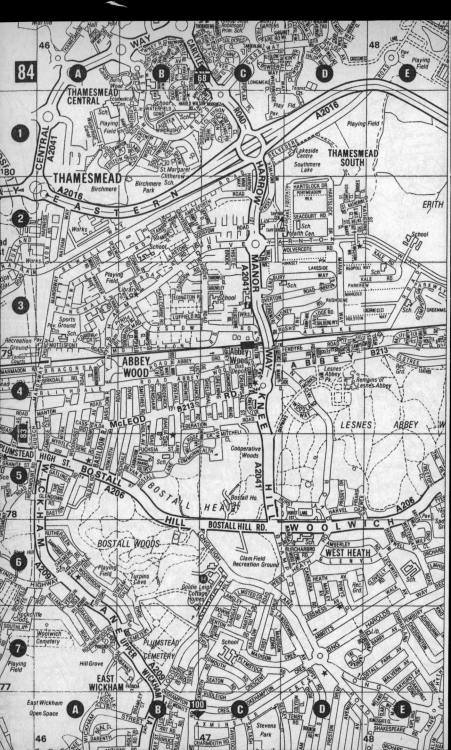

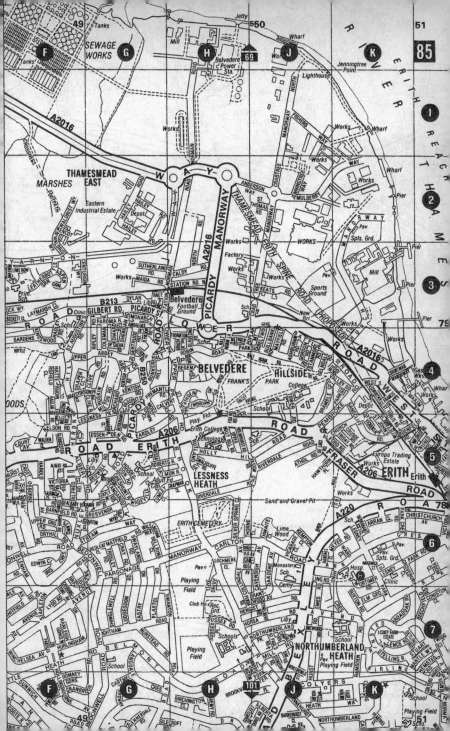

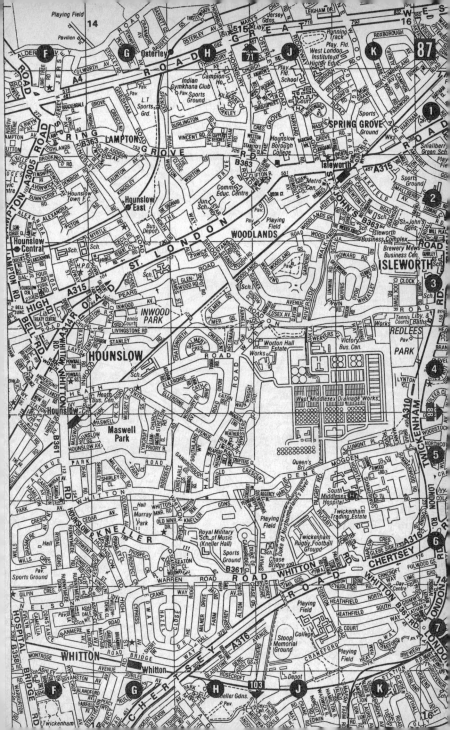

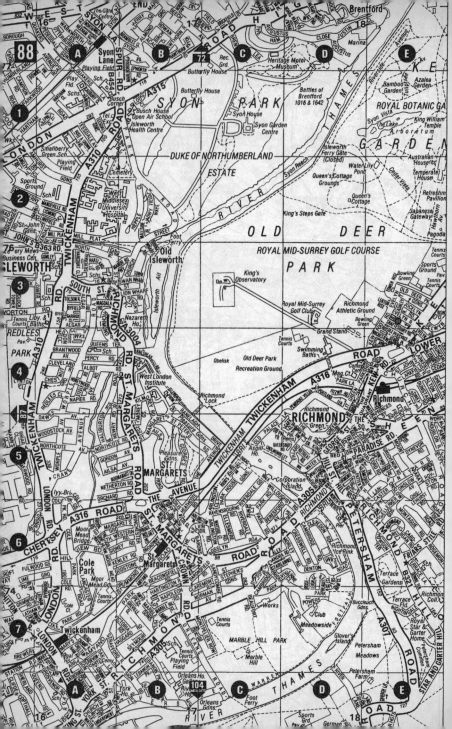

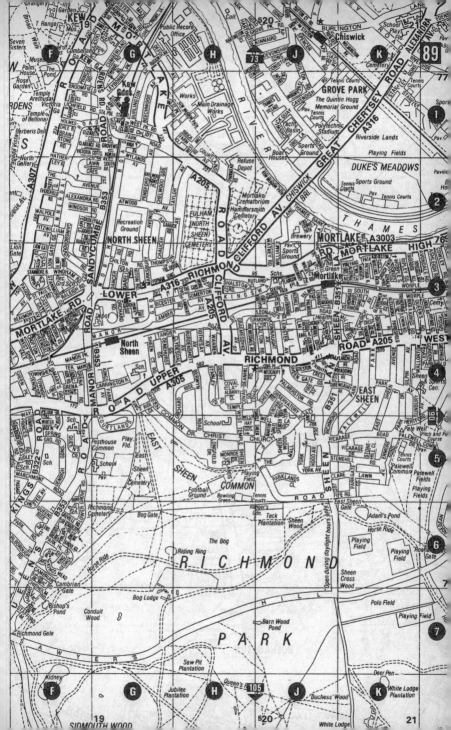

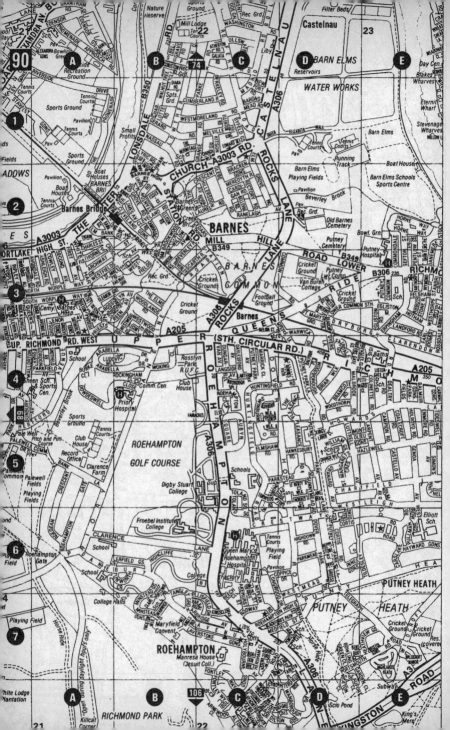

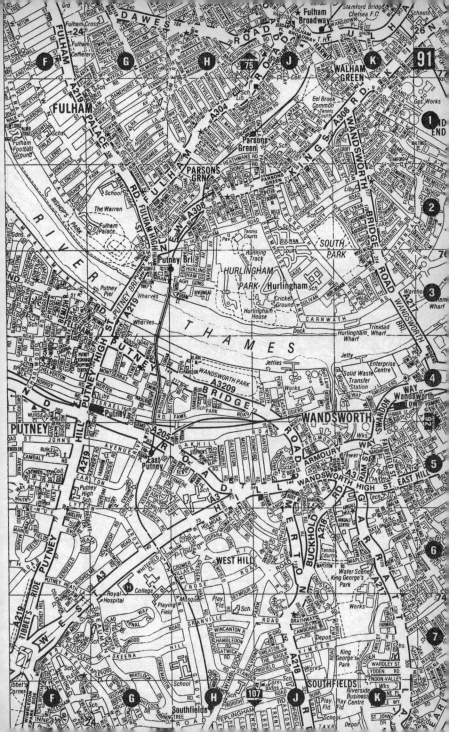

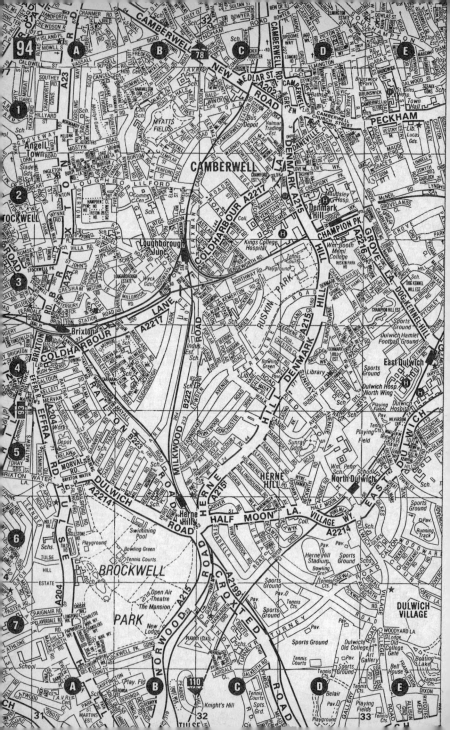

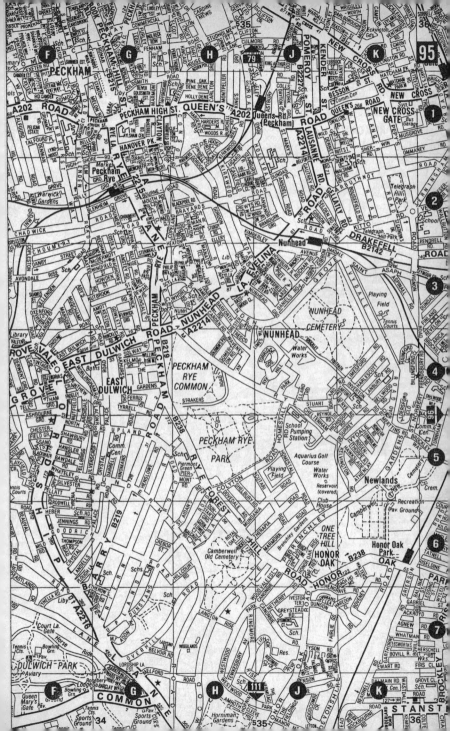

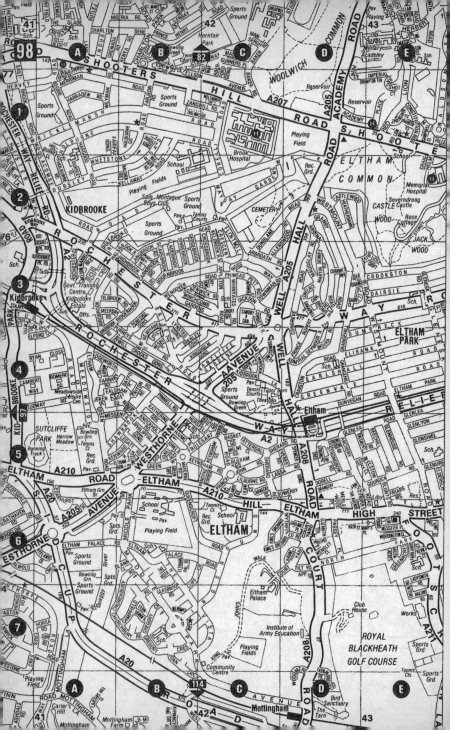

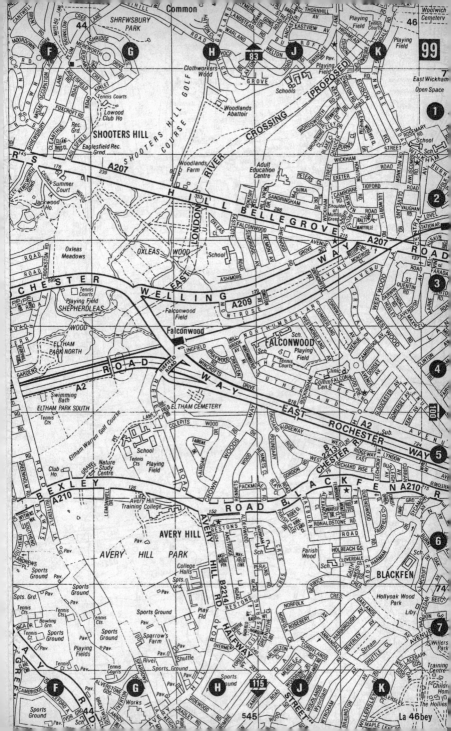

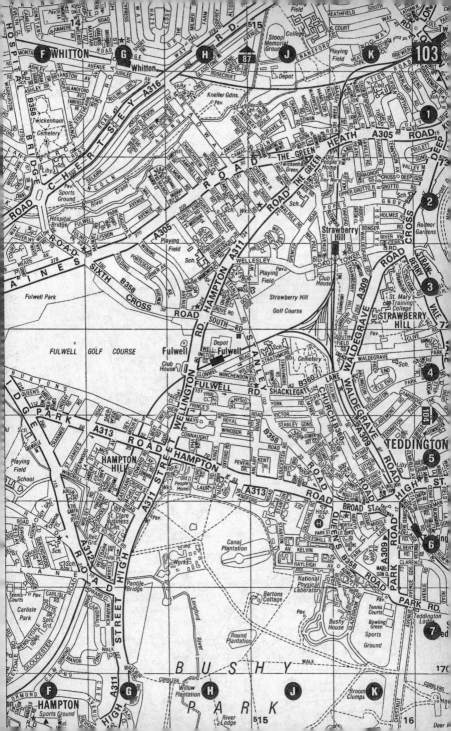

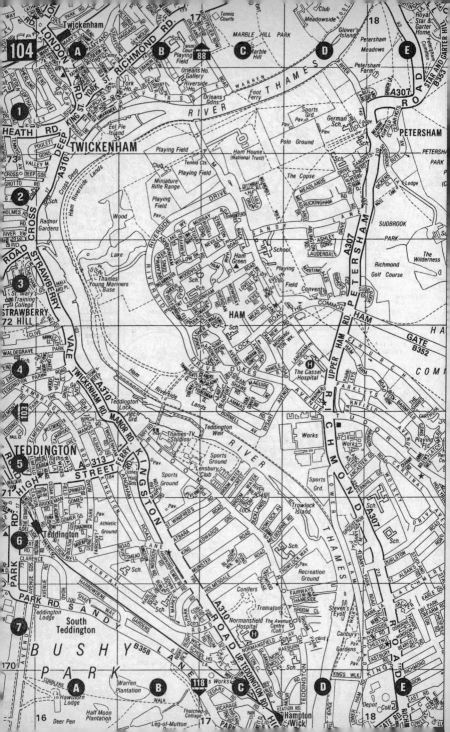

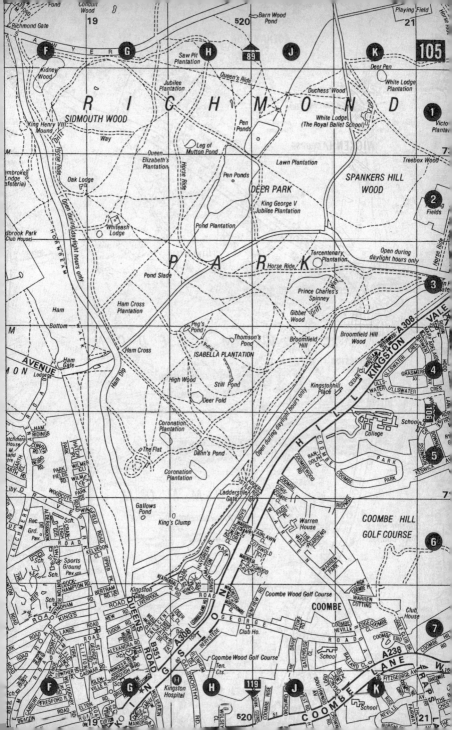

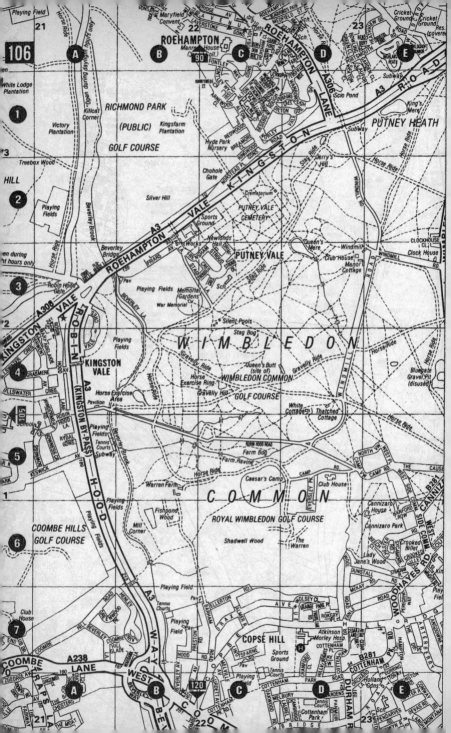

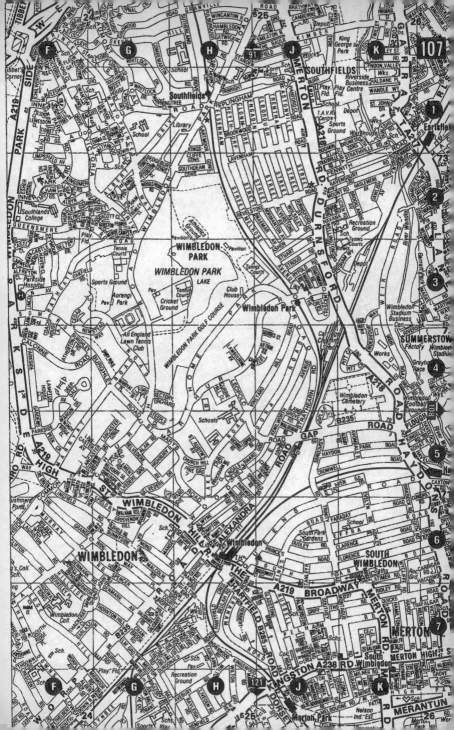

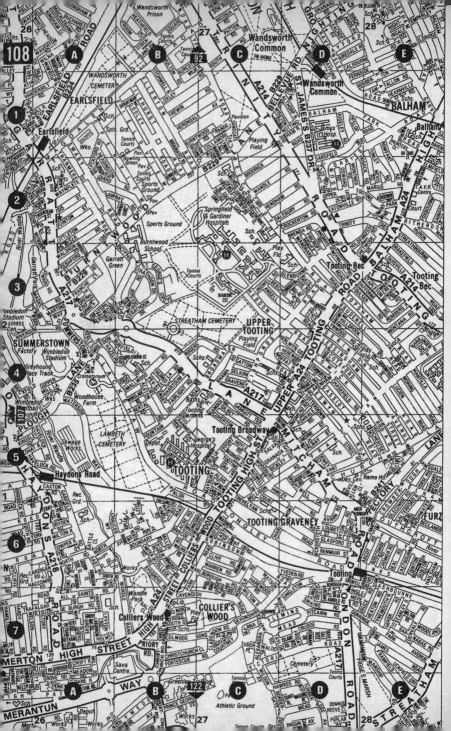

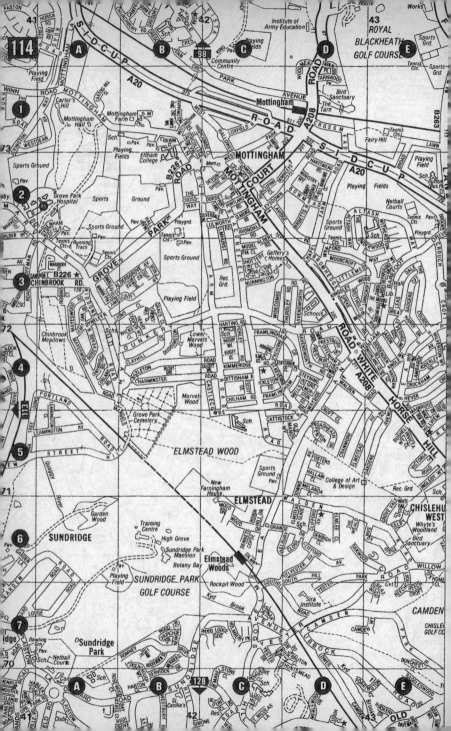

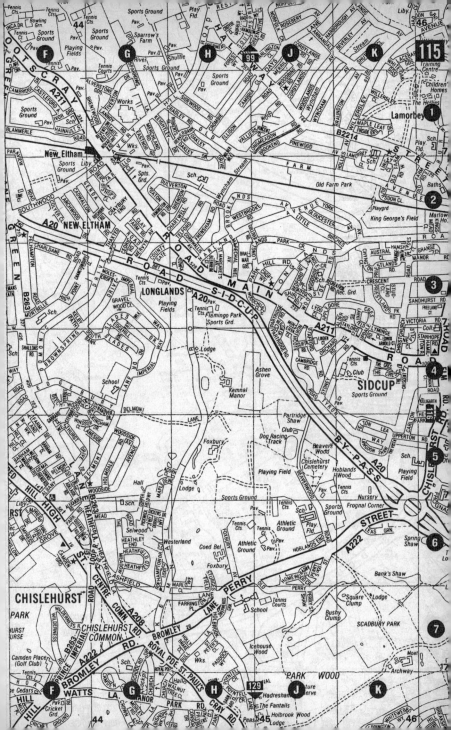

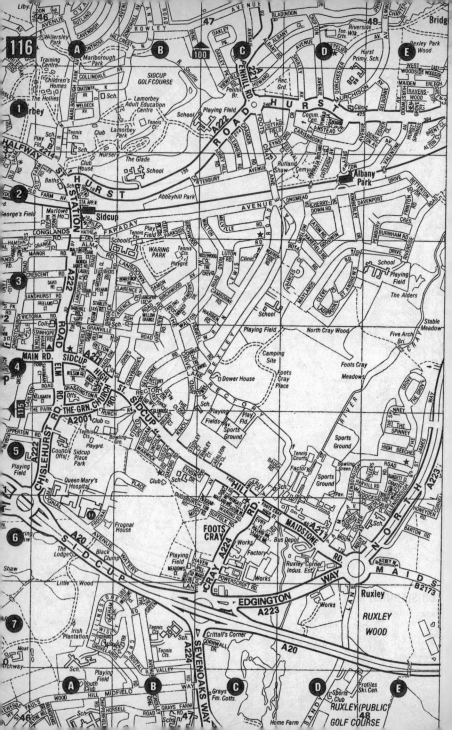

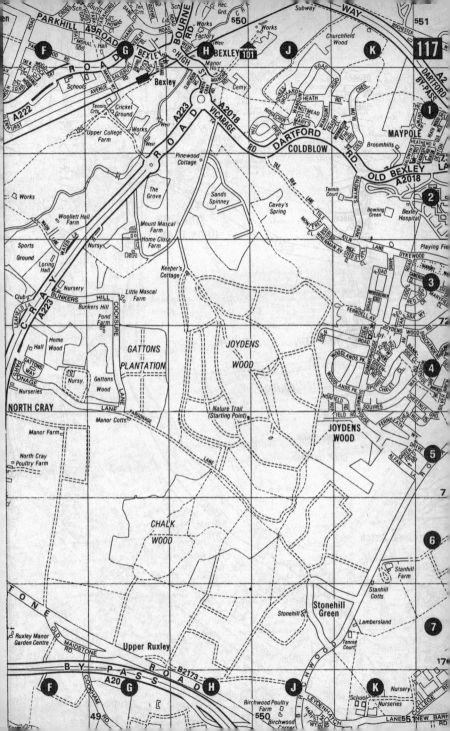

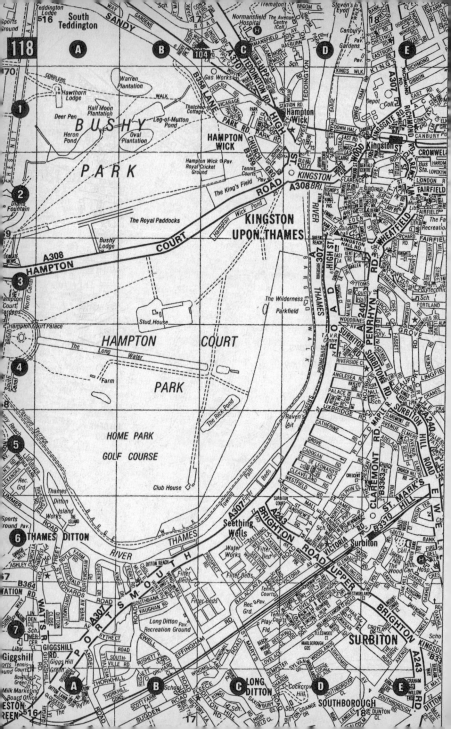

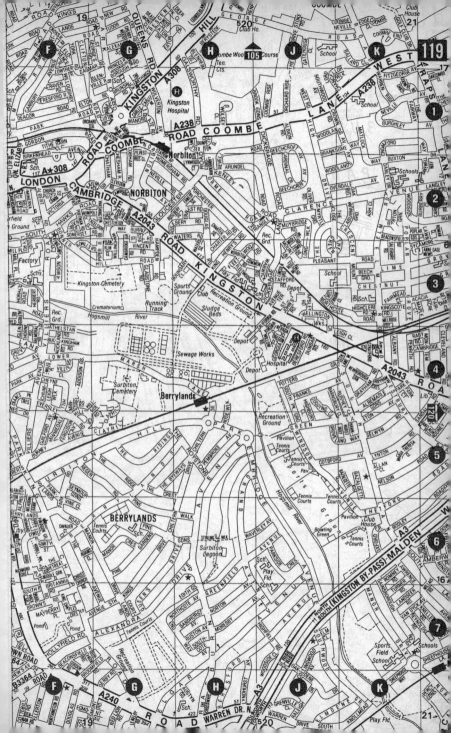

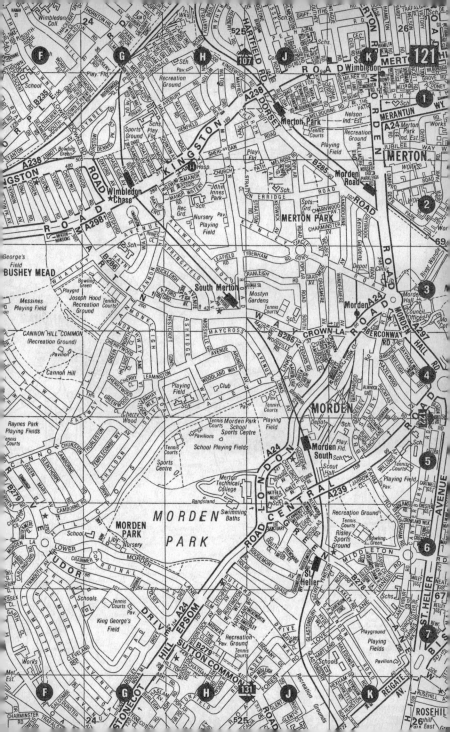

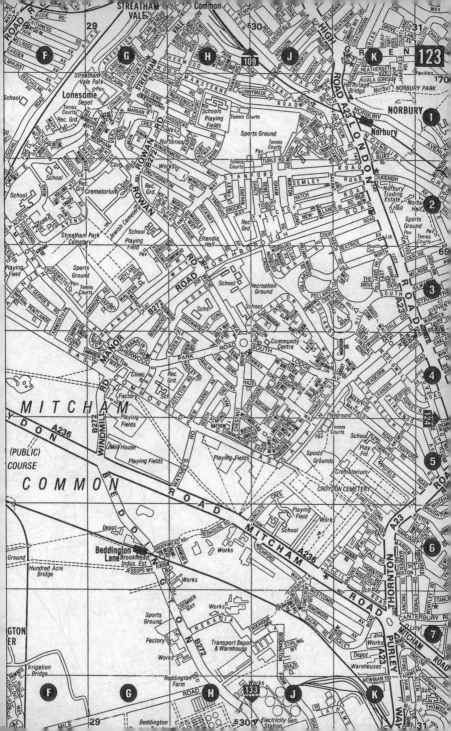

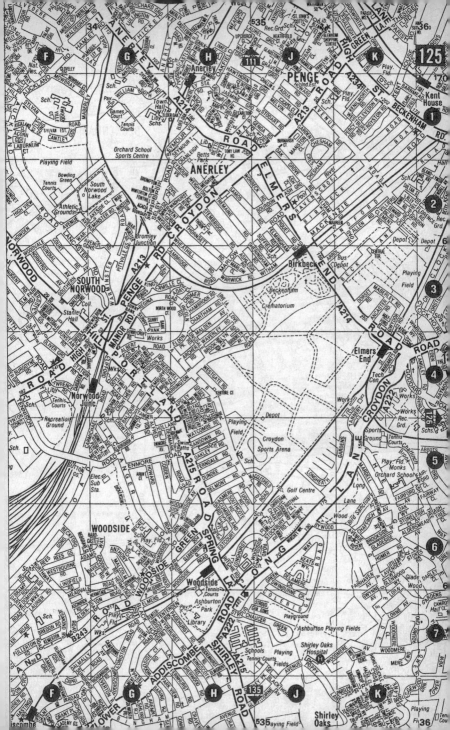

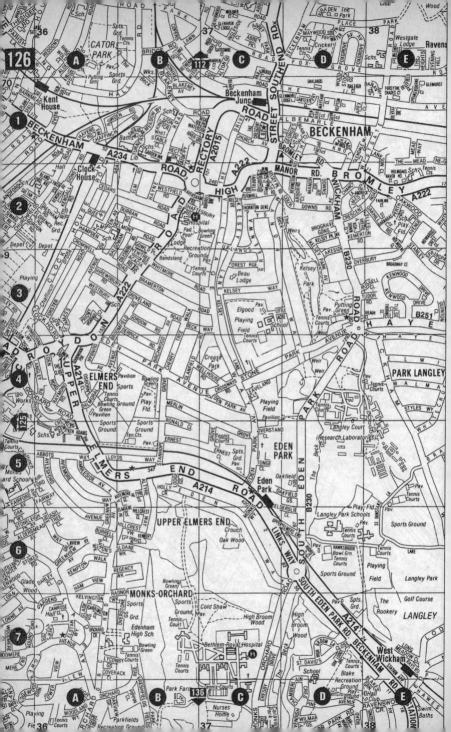

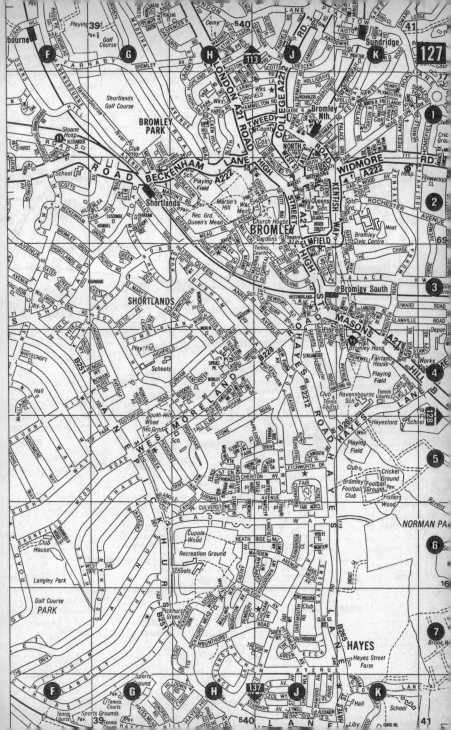

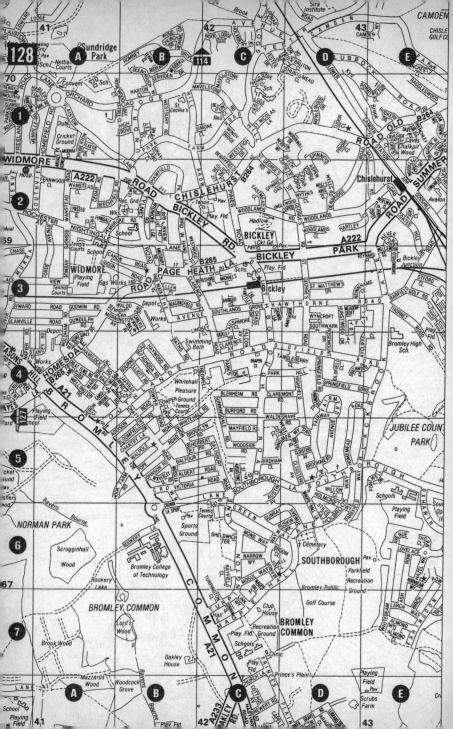

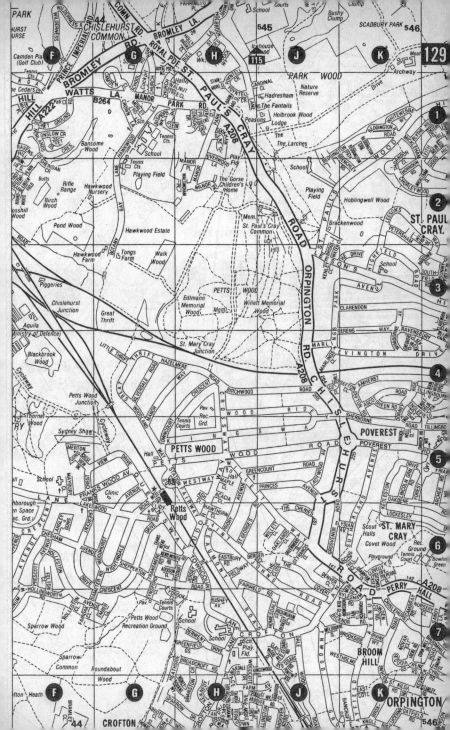

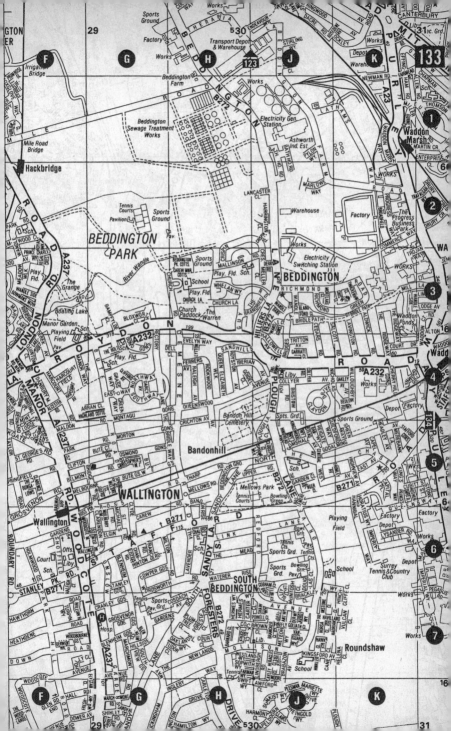

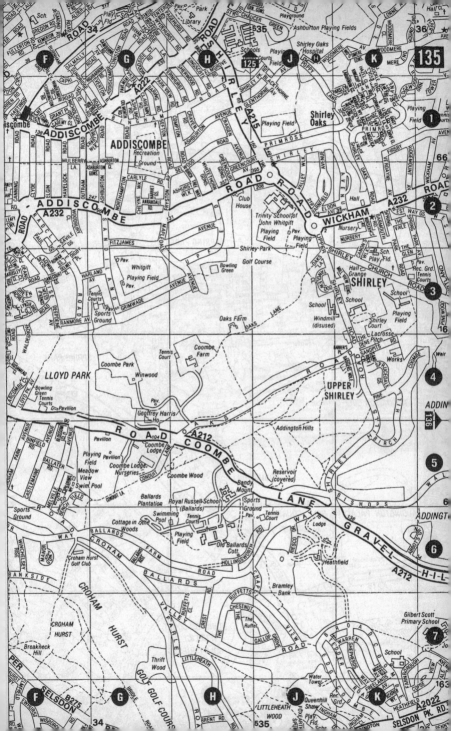

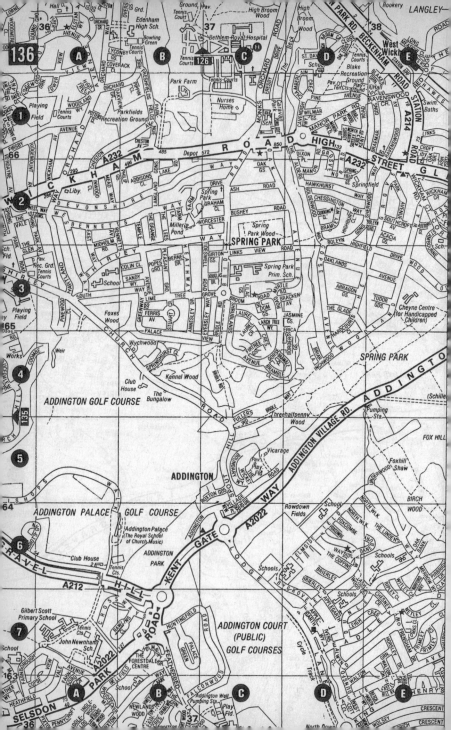

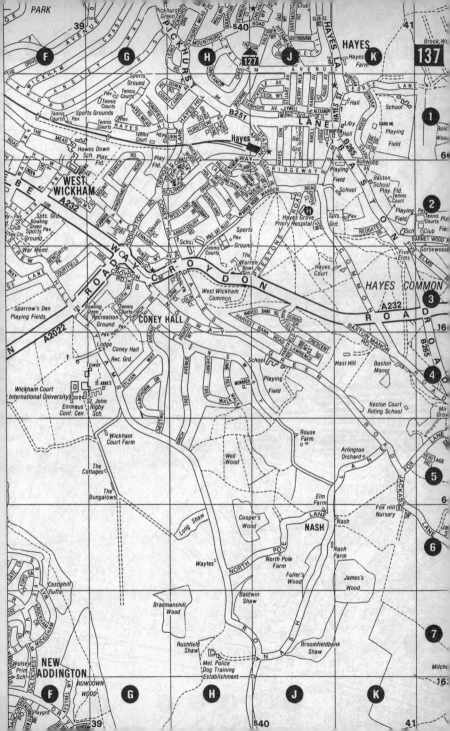

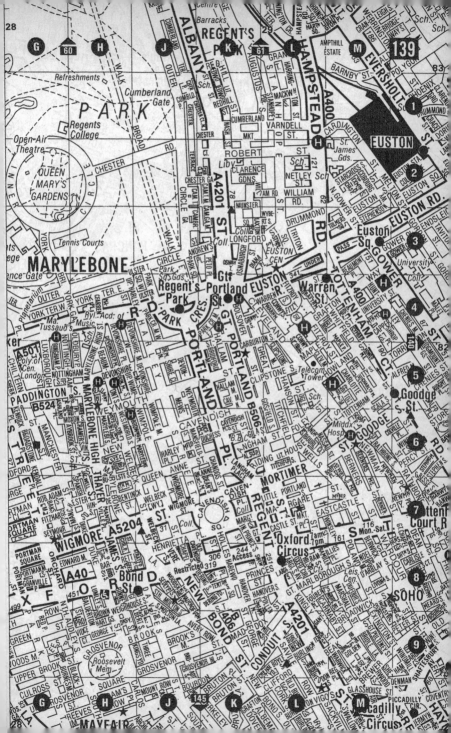

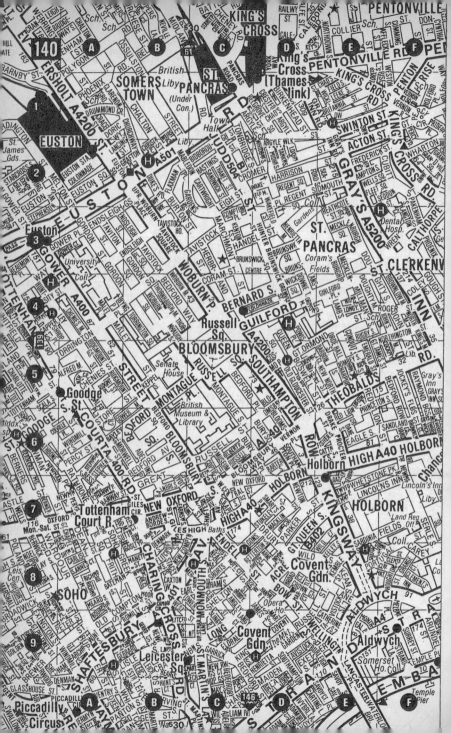

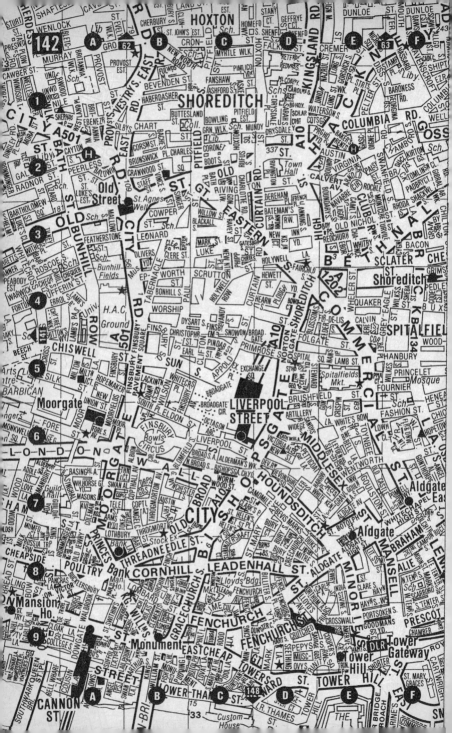

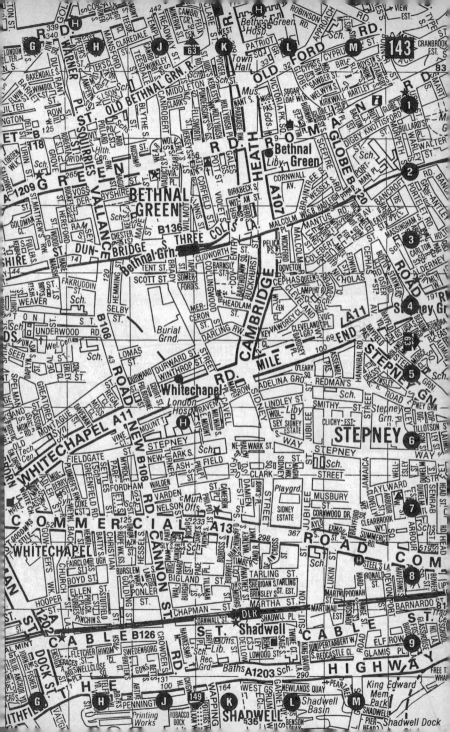

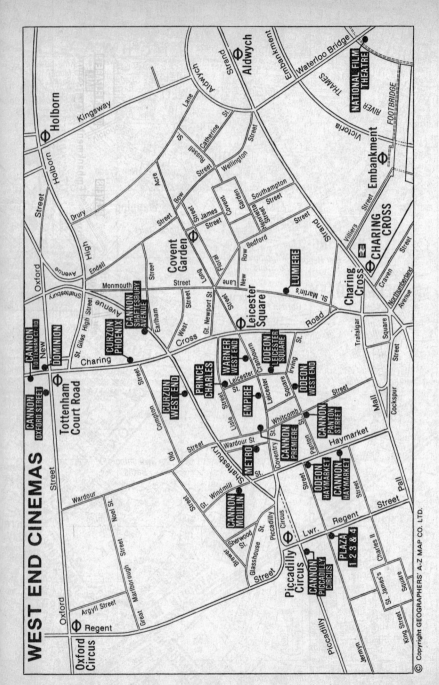

WEST END CINEMAS

Oxford Circus

Regent

CANNON OXFORD STREET

DOMINION

CANNON TOTTENHAM CT. RD.

Tottenham Court Road

Holborn

CURZON PHOENIX

CANNON SHAFTESBURY AVENUE

Covent Garden

Aldwych

CURZON WEST END

PRINCE CHARLES

WARNER WEST END

ODEON LEICESTER SQUARE

LUMIERE

Leicester Square

Charing Cross

CHARING CROSS

Embankment

NATIONAL FILM THEATRE

EMPIRE

ODEON WEST END

METRO

CANNON PREMIERE

CANNON PANTON STREET

CANNON MOULIN

ODEON HAYMARKET

CANNON HAYMARKET

Piccadilly Circus

CANNON PICCADILLY CIRCUS

PLAZA 1 2 3 & 4

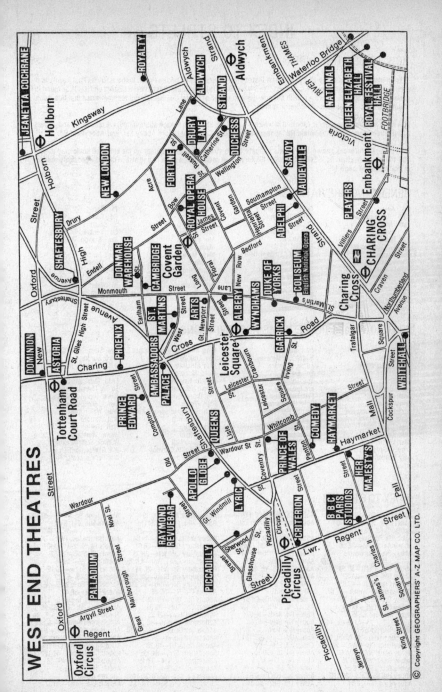

WEST END THEATRES

ROYALTY
JEANETTA COCHRANE
Holborn
Kingsway
Aldwych
Strand
Aldwych
ALDWYCH
STRAND
DRURY LANE
DUCHESS
Waterloo Bridge
Embankment
RIVER THAMES
NATIONAL
QUEEN ELIZABETH HALL
ROYAL FESTIVAL HALL
FOOTBRIDGE
NEW LONDON
FORTUNE
ROYAL OPERA HOUSE
SAVOY
VAUDEVILLE
ADELPHI
PLAYERS
Embankment
CHARING CROSS
SHAFTESBURY
DONMAR WAREHOUSE
Covent Garden
CAMBRIDGE
Charing Cross
COLISEUM
English National Opera
DOMINION
ASTORIA
PHOENIX
ST. MARTINS
ARTS
AMBASSADORS
PALACE
ALBERY
WYNDHAMS
DUKE OF YORKS
GARRICK
Leicester Square
WHITEHALL
Tottenham Court Road
PRINCE EDWARD
QUEENS
COMEDY
HAYMARKET
Haymarket
PRINCE OF WALES
HER MAJESTY'S
APOLLO
GLOBE
LYRIC
RAYMOND REVUEBAR
CRITERION
B.B.C PARIS STUDIOS
PALLADIUM
PICCADILLY
Piccadilly Circus
Regent
Oxford Circus

151

© Copyright GEOGRAPHERS' A-Z MAP CO. LTD.

INDEX TO STREETS

HOW TO USE THIS INDEX

1. Each street name is followed by its Postal District (or, if outside the London Postal Districts, by its Post Town), and then by its map page reference; e.g. Abbess Clo. SW2—1B 110 is in the South West 2 Postal District and it is to be found in square 1B on page 110. However, with the now general usage of Postal Coding, it is not recommended that this index should be used as a means of addressing mail.

2. A strict alphabetical order is followed in which Av., Rd., St. etc. (even though abbreviated) are read in full and as part of the street name; e.g. Abbeydale Rd. appears after Abbey Cres., but before Abbey Est. and Abbeyfield Rd.

3. The page references shown in brackets indicate those streets that also appear on the enlarged scale map pages 138-149; e.g. Abbeyfield Rd. SE16—4J 79 (8L 149) appears in square 4J on page 79 and also in the enlarged scale section in square 8L on page 149

GENERAL ABBREVIATIONS

All : Alley
App : Approach
Arc : Arcade
Av : Avenue
Bk : Back
Boulevd : Boulevard
Bri : Bridge
B'way : Broadway
Bldgs : Buildings
Chu : Church
Chyd : Churchyard
Circ : Circle
Cir : Circus
Clo : Close

Comn : Common
Cotts : Cottages
Ct : Court
Cres : Crescent
Dri : Drive
E : East
Embkmt : Embankment
Est : Estate
Gdns : Gardens
Ga : Gate
Gt : Great
Grn : Green
Gro : Grove
Ho : House

Junct : Junction
La : Lane
Lit : Little
Lwr : Lower
Mnr : Manor
Mans : Mansions
Mkt : Market
M : Mews
Mt : Mount
N : North
Pal : Palace
Pde : Parade
Pk : Park
Pas : Passage

Pl : Place
Rd : Road
S : South
Sq : Square
Sta : Station
St : Street
Ter : Terrace
Up : Upper
Vs : Villas
Wlk : Walk
W : West
Yd : Yard

POST TOWN and PLACE NAME ABBREVIATIONS

Bark: Barking
Barn: Barnet
Beck: Beckenham
Belv: Belvedere
Bex: Bexley
Bexh: Bexleyheath
Bren: Brentford
Brom: Bromley
Buck H: Buckhurst Hill
Bush: Bushey
Cars: Carshalton
Chig: Chigwell
Chst: Chislehurst
Croy: Croydon
Dag: Dagenham

Dart: Dartford
E Mol: Eas Molesey
Edgw: Edgware
Enf: Enfield
Eps: Epsom
Eri: Erith
Felt: Feltham
Gnfd: Greenford
Hmptn: Hampton
Harr: Harrow
Hay: Hayes (Middlesex)
Houn: Hounslow
Ilf: Ilford
Iswth: Isleworth
Kes: Keston

King: Kingston upon Thames
Lou: Loughton
Mitc: Mitcham
Mord: Morden
N Mald: New Malden
N'holt: Northolt
Orp: Orpington
Pinn: Pinner
Rich: Richmond upon Thames
Romf: Romford
Ruis: Ruislip
Sidc: Sidcup
S'hall: Southall
S Croy: South Croydon
Stan: Stanmore

Sun: Sunbury-on-Thames
Surb: Surbiton
Sutt: Sutton
Swan: Swanley
Tedd: Teddington
Th Dit: Thames Ditton
T Hth: Thornton Heath
Twic: Twickenham
Wall: Wallington
Wat: Watford
Well: Welling
Wemb: Wembley
W Wick: West Wickham
Wfd G: Woodford Green
Wor Pk: Worcester Park

INDEX TO STREETS

Abbotts Cres. E4—4A 20
Abbotts Cres. Enf—2G 7
Abbotts Dri. Wemb—2B 40
Abbotts Pk. Rd. E10—7E 32
Abbotts Rd. Barn—4E 4
Abbotts Rd. Mitc—4G 123
Abbotts Rd. S'hall—1C 70
Abbotts Rd. Sutt—4G 131
(in two parts)
Abbott's Wlk. Bexh—7D 84
Abchurch La. EC4
—7D 62 (9B 142)
Abdale Rd. W12—1D 74
Aberavon Rd. E3—3A 64
Abercairn Rd. SW16—7G 109
Aberconway Rd. Mord—4K 121
Abercorn Clo. NW7—7B 14
Abercorn Clo. NW8—3A 60
Abercorn Commercial Centre.
Wemb—1D 56
Abercorn Cres. Harr—1F 39
Abercorn Gdns. Harr—7D 24
Abercorn Gdns. Romf—6B 36
Abercorn Pl. NW8
—3A 60 (1A 138)
Abercorn Rd. NW7—7B 14
Abercorn Rd. Stan—7H 11
Abercrombie St. SW11—2C 92
Aberdare Clo. W Wick—2E 136
Aberdare Gdns. NW6—7K 43
Aberdare Gdns. NW7—7A 14
Aberdare Rd. Enf—4D 8
Aberdeen La. N5—5C 46
Aberdeen Pde. N18—5C 18
Aberdeen Pk. N5—5C 46
Aberdeen Pl. NW8
—4B 60 (3A 138)
Aberdeen Rd. N5—4C 46
Aberdeen Rd. N18—5C 18
Aberdeen Rd. NW10—5B 42
Aberdeen Rd. Croy—4D 134
Aberdeen Rd. Harr—2K 23
Aberdeen Ter. SE3—2F 97
Aberdour Rd. Ilf—3B 52
Aberdour St. SE1
—4E 78 (8C 148)
Aberfeldy St. E14—6E 64
(in two parts)
Aberford Gdns. SE18—1C 98
Aberfoyle Rd. SW16—7H 109
Abergeldie Rd. SE12—6K 97
Abernethy Rd. SE13—4G 97
Abersham Rd. E8—5F 47
Abery St. SE18—4J 83
Abingdon Clo. NW1—6H 45
Abingdon Clo. SW19—6A 108
Abingdon Rd. N3—2A 28
Abingdon Rd. SW16—2J 123
Abingdon Rd. W8—3J 75
Abingdon St. SW1
—3J 77 (6C 146)
Abingdon Vs. W8—3J 75
Abinger Clo. Bark—4A 52
Abinger Clo. Brom—3C 128
Abinger Clo. Wall—5J 133
Abinger Gdns. Iswth—3J 87
Abinger Gro. SE8—6B 80
Abinger M. W9—4J 59
Abinger Rd. W4—3A 74
Ablett St. SE16—5J 79
Aboyne Dri. SW20—2C 120
Aboyne Rd. NW10—3A 42
Aboyne Rd. SW17—3B 108
Abridge Way. Bark—2B 68
Abyssinia Clo. SW11—4C 92
Acacia Av. N17—7J 17
Acacia Av. Bren—7B 72
Acacia Av. Rich—2F 89
Acacia Av. Wemb—5E 40
Acacia Clo. SE20—2G 125
Acacia Clo. Orp—5H 129
Acacia Clo. Stan—6D 10
Acacia Dri. Sutt—1J 131
Acacia Gdns. NW8—2B 60
Acacia Gdns. W Wick—2E 136
Acacia Gro. SE21—2D 110
Acacia Gro. N Mald—3A 120

Acacia Pl. NW8—2B 60
Acacia Rd. E11—2G 49
Acacia Rd. E17—6A 32
Acacia Rd. N22—1A 30
Acacia Rd. NW8—2B 60
Acacia Rd. SW16—1J 123
Acacia Rd. W3—7J 57
Acacia Rd. Beck—3B 126
Acacia Rd. Enf—1J 7
Acacia Rd. Hmptn—6E 102
Acacia Rd. Mitc—2E 122
Acacias, The. Barn—5G 5
Academy Gdns. Croy—1F 135
Academy Gdns. N'holt—2B 54
Academy Pl. SE18—1D 98
Academy Rd. SE18—1D 98
Acanthus Rd. SW11—3E 92
Accommodation Rd. NW11
—1H 43
A. C. Court. Th Dit—6A 118
Acfold Rd. SW6—1K 91
Achilles Rd. NW6—5J 43
Achilles St. SE14—7B 80
Achilles Way. W1
—1E 76 (3H 145)
Acklam Rd. W10—5G 59
Acklington Dri. NW9—1A 26
Ackmar Rd. SW6—1J 91
Ackroyd Dri. E3—5B 64
Ackroyd Rd. SE23—7K 95
Acland Cres. SE5—3D 94
Acland Rd. NW2—6D 42
Acol Cres. Ruis—5A 38
Acol Rd. NW6—7K 43
Aconbury Rd. Dag—1B 68
Acorn Clo. E4—5J 19
Acorn Clo. Chst—5G 115
Acorn Clo. Enf—1G 7
Acorn Clo. Stan—7G 11
Acorn Ct. Ilf—6J 35
Acorn Gdns. SE19—1F 125
Acorn Gdns. W3—5K 57
Acorn Pde. SE15—7H 79
Acorn Wlk. SE16—1A 80
Acorn Way. SE23—3K 111
Acre La. SW2—4J 93
Acre La. SW19—6B 108
Acre Rd. Dag—7H 53
Acre Rd. King—1E 118
Acris St. SW18—5A 92
Acton Clo. N9—2B 18
Acton La. NW10—2J 57
Acton La.—2J to 4J 73
W4 1-287 & 2-288
W3 remainder
Acton M. E8—1F 63
Acton Pk. Industrial Est. W3
—2K 73
Acton St. WC1—3K 61 (2E 140)
Acton Vale Industrial Pk. W3
—1B 74
Acuba Rd. SW18—2K 107
Acworth Clo. N9—7D 8
Ada Gdns. E14—6F 65
Ada Gdns. E15—1H 65
Adair Clo. SE25—3H 125
Adair Rd. W10—4G 59
Adam & Eve M. W8—3J 75
Adams Clo. N3—7D 14
Adams Clo. NW9—2H 41
Adams Clo. Surb—6F 119
Adams Ct. EC2—6E 62 (7C 142)
Adams Gdns. Est. SE16
—2J 79 (5L 149)
Adamson Rd. E16—6J 65
Adamson Rd. NW3—7B 44
Adams Pl. N7—5K 45
Adamsrill Clo. Enf—6J 7
Adamsrill Rd. SE26—4K 111
Adams Rd. N17—2D 30
Adams Rd. Beck—5A 126
Adam's Row. W1
—7E 60 (1H 145)
Adams Sq. Bexh—3E 100
Adam St. WC2—7J 61 (1D 146)
Adams Way. SE25—2G 135

Ada Pl. E2—1G 63
Adare Wlk. SW16—3K 109
Ada Rd. SE5—7E 78
Ada Rd. Wemb—3D 40
Adastral Est. NW9—1A 26
Ada St. E8—1H 63
Adderley Gdns. SE9—4E 114
Adderley Gro. SW11—5E 92
Adderley Rd. Harr—1K 23
Adderley St. E14—6E 64
Addington Ct. SW14—3K 89
Addington Dri. N12—6G 15
Addington Gro. SE26—4A 112
Addington Rd. E3—3C 64
Addington Rd. E16—4G 65
Addington Rd. N4—6A 30
Addington Rd. Croy—1A 134
Addington Rd. S Croy—7K 135
Addington Rd. W Wick—4E 136
Addington Sq. SE5—6D 78
Addington St. SE1
—2K 77 (5F 146)
Addington Village Rd. Croy
—6B & 5D 136
Addis Clo. Enf—1E 8
Addiscombe Av. Croy—1G 135
Addiscombe Clo. Harr—5C 24
Addiscombe Ct. Rd. Croy
—1E 134
Addiscombe Gro. Croy—2E 134
Addiscombe Rd. Croy—2E 134
Addison Av. N14—6A 6
Addison Av. W11—1G 75
Addison Av. Houn—1G 87
Addison Bri. Pl. W14—4H 75
Addison Clo. Orp—6G 129
Addison Cres. W14—3G 75
Addison Dri. SE12—5K 97
Addison Gdns. W14—3F 75
Addison Gdns. Surb—4F 119
Addison Gro. W4—3A 74
Addison Pl. SE25—4G 125
Addison Pl. W11—1G 75
Addison Pl. S'hall—7E 54
Addison Rd. E11—6J 33
Addison Rd. E17—5D 32
Addison Rd. SE25—4G 125
Addison Rd. W14—2G 75
Addison Rd. Brom—5B 128
Addison Rd. Enf—1D 8
Addison Rd. Ilf—1G 35
Addison Rd. Tedd—6B 104
Addisons Clo. Croy—2B 136
Addison Way. NW11—4H 27
Addle Hill. EC4—6B 62 (8K 141)
Addle St. EC2—6C 62 (7M 141)
Adela Av. N Mald—5D 120
Adelaide Av. SE4—4B 96
Adelaide Clo. Enf—1K 7
Adelaide Clo. Stan—4F 11
Adelaide Cotts. W7—2K 71
Adelaide Ct. Beck—7C 112
Adelaide Gdns. Romf—5E 36
Adelaide Gro. W12—1C 74
Adelaide Rd. E10—3E 48
Adelaide Rd. NW3—7B 44
Adelaide Rd. W13—1A 72
Adelaide Rd. Chst—5F 115
Adelaide Rd. Houn—1C 86
Adelaide Rd. Ilf—2F 51
Adelaide Rd. Rich—4F 89
Adelaide Rd. S'hall—4C 70
Adelaide Rd. Surb—5E 118
Adelaide Rd. Tedd—6K 103
Adelaide Rd. WC2
—7J 61 (1C 146)
Adelaide Ter. Bren—5D 72
Adelaide Wlk. SW9—4A 94
Adela St. W10—4G 59
Adelina Gro. E1—5J 63 (5L 143)
Adeline Pl. WC1—5H 61 (6B 140)
Adelphi Ter. WC2
—7J 61 (1D 146)
Adeney Clo. W6—6F 75
Aden Gro. N16—4D 46
Adenmore Rd. SE6—7C 96
Aden Rd. Enf—4F 9

Aden Rd. Ilf—7G 35
Aden Ter. N16—4D 46
Adie Rd. W6—3E 74
Adine Rd. E13—4K 65
Adler St. E1—6G 63 (7G 143)
Adley St. E5—5A 48
Admaston Rd. SE18—7G 83
Admiral Hyson Industrial Est.
SE16—5H 79 (9K 149)
Admiral M. W10—4F 59
Admiral Pl. SE16—1A 80
Admirals Clo. E18—4K 33
Admiral Seymour Rd. SE9
—4D 98
Admiral Sq. SW10—1A 92
Admiral St. SE8—1C 96
Admirals Wlk. NW3—3A 44
Admirals Way. E14—2C 80
Admiralty Rd. Tedd—6K 103
Adolf St. SE6—4D 112
Adolphus Rd. N4—1B 46
Adolphus St. SE8—7B 80
Adomar Rd. Dag—3E 52
Adpar St. W2—5B 60 (5A 138)
Adrian Av. NW2—1D 42
Adrian M. SW10—5K 75
Adrienne Av. S'hall—3D 54
Ady's Rd. SE15—3F 95
Aerodrome Rd. NW9 & NW4
—3B 26
Aerodrome Way. Houn—6A 70
Aeroville. NW9—2A 26
Affleck St. N1—2K 61 (1F 140)
Afghan Rd. SW11—2C 92
Agamemnon Rd. NW6—5H 43
Agar Gro. NW1—7H 45
Agar Gro. Est. NW1—7H 45
Agar Pl. NW1—7G 45
Agar St. WC2—7J 61 (1D 146)
Agate Clo. E16—6B 66
Agate Rd. W6—3E 74
Agatha Clo. E1—1H 79 (2K 149)
Agaton Rd. SE9—2G 115
Agave Rd. NW2—4E 42
Agdon St. EC1—4B 62 (3J 141)
Agincourt Rd. NW3—4D 44
Agnes Av. Ilf—4E 50
Agnes Clo. E6—7E 66
Agnes Gdns. Dag—4D 52
Agnes Rd. W3—1B 74
Agnes St. E14—6B 64
Agnew Rd. SE23—7K 95
Agricola Pl. Enf—5A 8
Aidan Clo. Dag—4E 52
Aileen Wlk. E15—7H 49
Ailsa Av. Twic—5A 88
Ailsa Rd. Twic—5B 88
Ailsa St. E14—5E 64
Ainger Rd. NW3—7D 44
Ainsdale Cres. Pinn—3E 22
Ainsdale Rd. W5—4D 56
Ainsley Av. Romf—6H 37
Ainslie Clo. N9—1K 17
Ainsley St. E2—3H 63 (2K 143)
Ainslie Wlk. SW12—7F 93
Ainslie Wood Cres. E4—5J 19
Ainslie Wood Gdns. E4—5J 19
Ainslie Wood Rd. E4—5H 19
Ainsty Est. SE16
—2K 79 (5M 149)
Ainsty St. SE16—2J 79 (4M 149)
Ainsworth Clo. NW2—3C 42
Ainsworth Rd. E9—7J 47
Ainsworth Rd. Croy—2B 134
Ainsworth Way. NW8—1A 60
Aintree Av. E6—1C 66
Aintree Cres. Ilf—2G 35
Aintree Est. SW6—7G 75
Airdrie Clo. N1—7K 45
Airdrie Clo. Hay—5C 54
Airedale Av. W4—4B 74
Airedale Av. S. W4—5B 74
Airedale Rd. SW12—7D 92
Airedale Rd. W5—3D 72
Airlie Gdns. W8—1J 75
Airlie Gdns. Ilf—1F 51

154

Alexandra Pl. NW8—1A 60
Alexandra Pl. SE25—5D 124
Alexandra Pl. Croy—1E 134
Alexandra Rd. E6—3E 66
Alexandra Rd. E10—3E 48
Alexandra Rd. E17—7B 32
Alexandra Rd. E18—3K 33
Alexandra Rd. N8—3A 30
Alexandra Rd. N9—7C 8
Alexandra Rd. N10—1F 29
Alexandra Rd. N15—5D 30
Alexandra Rd. NW4—4F 27
Alexandra Rd. NW8—1A 60
Alexandra Rd. SE26—6K 111
Alexandra Rd. SW14—3K 89
Alexandra Rd. SW19—6H 107
Alexandra Rd. W4—2K 73
Alexandra Rd. Bren—6D 72
Alexandra Rd. Croy—1E 134
Alexandra Rd. Enf—4E 8
Alexandra Rd. Houn—2F 87
Alexandra Rd. King—7G 105
Alexandra Rd. Mitc—7C 108
Alexandra Rd. Rich—2F 89
Alexandra Rd. Romf—6D 36
 (Chadwell Heath)
Alexandra Rd. Th Dit—5A 118
Alexandra Rd. Twic—6C 88
Alexandra Rd. / Alma Rd.
     Industrial Est. Enf—4E 8
Alexandra Sq. Mord—5J 121
Alexandra St. E16—5J 65
Alexandra St. SE14—7A 80
Alexandra Wlk. SE19—6E 110
Alexandria Rd. W13—7B 56
Alexis St. SE16—4G 79 (8H 149)
Alfan La. Dart—5K 117
Alfearn Rd. E5—4J 47
Alford Grn. Croy—6F 137
Alford Pl. N1—2C 62 (1M 141)
Alford Rd. SW8—1H 93
Alford Rd. Eri—5J 85
Alfoxton Av. N15—4B 30
Alfreda St. SW11—1F 93
Alfred M. W1—5H 61 (5A 140)
Alfred Pl. WC1—5H 61 (5A 140)
Alfred Rd. E15—5H 49
Alfred Rd. SE25—5G 125
Alfred Rd. W2—5J 59
Alfred Rd. W3—1J 73
Alfred Rd. Belv—5F 85
Alfred Rd. Buck H—2G 21
Alfred Rd. Felt—2A 102
Alfred Rd. King—3F 119
Alfred Rd. Sutt—5A 132
Alfred's Gdns. Bark—2J 67
Alfred St. E3—3B 64
Alfreds Way. Bark—3F 67
Alfreds Way Industrial Est.
     Bark—1A 68
Alfreton Clo. SW19—3F 107
Alfriston. Surb—6F 119
Alfriston Av. Croy—7J 123
Alfriston Av. Harr—6E 22
Alfriston Clo. Surb—6F 119
Alfriston Rd. SW11—5D 92
Algar Clo. SW19—5F 107
Algar Clo. Stan—5E 10
Algar Rd. Iswth—3A 88
Algarve Rd. SW18—1K 107
Algernon Rd. NW4—6C 26
Algernon Rd. NW6—1J 59
Algernon Rd. SE13—4D 96
Algiers Rd. SE13—4C 96
Alibon Gdns. Dag—5G 53
Alibon Rd. Dag—5G 53
Alice St. SE1—3E 78 (7C 148)
Alice Way. Houn—4F 87
Alicia Av. Harr—4B 24
Alicia Clo. Harr—5C 24
Alicia Gdns. Harr—4B 24
Alie St. E1—6F 63 (8F 142)
Alington Cres. NW9—7J 25
Alington Gro. Wall—7G 133
Alison Clo. E6—6E 66
Alison Clo. Croy—1K 135

Aliwal Rd. SW11—4C 92
Alkerden Rd. W4—5A 74
Alkham Rd. N16—2F 47
Allan Clo. N Mald—5K 119
Allandale Av. N3—3G 27
Allan Way. W3—5J 57
Allard Cres. Bush, Wat—2B 10
Allardyce St. SW4—4K 93
Allbrook Clo. Tedd—5J 103
Allcroft Rd. NW5—5E 44
Allenby Clo. Gnfd—3E 54
Allenby Rd. SE23—3A 112
Allenby Rd. S'hall—6E 54
Allendale Av. S'hall—6E 54
Allendale Clo. SE5—2D 94
 (in two parts)
Allendale Clo. SE26—5K 111
Allendale Rd. Gnfd—6B 40
Allen Edwards Dri. SW8—1J 93
Allen Pl. Twic—1A 104
Allen Rd. E3—1B 64
Allen Rd. N16—4E 46
Allen Rd. Beck—2K 125
Allen Rd. Croy—1A 134
Allensbury Pl. NW1—7H 45
Allens Rd. Enf—5D 8
Allen St. W8—3J 75
Allenswood Rd. SE9—3C 98
Allerford Rd. SE6—3D 112
Allerton Rd. N16—2C 46
Allerton Wlk. N7—2K 45
Allestree Rd. SW6—7G 75
Alleyn Cres. SE21—2D 110
Alleyndale Rd. Dag—2C 52
Alleyn Pk. SE21—2D 110
Alleyn Pk. S'hall—5E 70
Alleyn Rd. SE21—3D 110
Allfarthing La. SW18—6K 91
Allgood Clo. Mord—6F 121
Allgood St. E2—2F 63 (1F 142)
Allhallows La. EC4
                    —7D 62 (1A 148)
Allhallows Rd. E6—5B 66
All Hallows Rd. N17—1E 30
Alliance Clo. Wemb—4D 40
Alliance Rd. E13—5A 66
Alliance Rd. SE18—6A 84
Alliance Rd. W3—4H 57
Allingham Clo. W7—7K 55
Allingham St. N1—2C 62
Allington Av. N17—6K 17
Allington Clo. SW19—5F 107
Allington Ct. Enf—5E 8
 (in two parts)
Allington Rd. NW4—6D 26
Allington Rd. W10—2G 59
Allington Rd. Harr—5G 23
Allington Rd. Orp—7J 129
Allington St. SW1
                    —3F 77 (7K 145)
Allison Clo. SE10—1E 96
Allison Gro. SE21—1E 110
Allison Rd. N8—5A 30
Allison Rd. W3—6J 57
Allitsen Rd. NW8—2C 60
Allnutt Way. SW4—5H 93
Alloa Rd. SE8—5A 80
Alloa Rd. Ilf—2A 52
Allonby Gdns. Wemb—1C 40
Alloway Rd. E3—3A 64
All Saints Clo. N9—2B 18
All Saints Dri. SE3—2G 97
All Saints M. Harr—6D 10
All Saints Pas. SW18—5J 91
All Saint's Rd. SW19—7A 108
All Saints Rd. W3—3J 73
All Saints Rd. W11—5H 59
All Saints Rd. Sutt—3K 131
All Saints St. N1—2K 61
Allsop Pl. NW1—4D 60 (4F 138)
All Souls Av. NW10—2D 58
All Soul's Pl. W1
                    —5F 61 (6K 139)
Allum Way. N20—1F 15
Allwood Clo. SE26—4A 112
Alma Av. E4—7K 19

Almack Rd. E5—4J 47
Alma Cres. Sutt—5G 131
Alma Gro. SE1—4F 79 (9F 148)
Alma Pl. NW10—3D 58
Alma Pl. SE19—7F 111
Alma Pl. T Hth—5A 124
Alma Rd. N10—7A 16
Alma Rd. SW18—4A 92
Alma Rd. Cars—5C 132
Alma Rd. Enf—5F 9
Alma Rd. Sidc—3A 116
Alma Rd. S'hall—7C 54
Alma Row. Harr—1H 23
Alma Sq. NW8—2A 60 (1A 138)
Alma St. E15—6F 49
Alma St. NW5—6F 45
Alma Ter. SW18—7B 92
Alma Ter. W8—3J 75
Almeida St. N1—1B 62
Almer Rd. SW20—7C 106
Almington St. N4—1K 45
Almond Av. W5—3E 72
Almond Av. Cars—2D 132
Almond Clo. SE15—2G 95
Almond Clo. Brom—7E 128
Almond Gro. Bren—7B 72
Almond Rd. N17—7B 18
Almond Rd. SE16
                    —4H 79 (9K 149)
Almonds Av. Buck H—2D 20
Almond Way. Brom—7E 128
Almond Way. Harr—2G 23
Almond Way. Mitc—5H 123
Almorah Rd. N1—7D 46
Almorah Rd. Houn—1B 86
Alnwick Gro. Mord—4K 121
Alnwick Rd. E16—6A 66
Alnwick Rd. SE12—7K 97
Alperton La. Gnfd—3C 56
Alperton St. W10—4H 59
Alpha Clo. NW1—4C 60 (3D 138)
Alpha Gro. E14—2C 80
Alpha Pl. NW6—2J 59
Alpha Pl. SW3—6C 76
Alpha Rd. E4—3H 19
Alpha Rd. N18—6B 18
Alpha Rd. SE14—1B 96
Alpha Rd. Croy—1E 134
Alpha Rd. Enf—4F 9
Alpha Rd. Surb—6F 119
Alpha Rd. Tedd—5H 103
Alpha St. SE15—2G 95
Alphea Clo. SW19—7C 108
Alpine Business Centre. E6
                    —5E 66
Alpine Clo. Croy—3E 134
Alpine Copse. Brom—2E 128
Alpine Rd. SE16
                    —4J 79 (9M 149)
Alpine Wlk. Stan—2D 10
Alpine Way. E6—5E 66
Alric Av. NW10—7K 41
Alric Av. N Mald—3A 120
Alroy Rd. N4—7A 30
Alsace Rd. SE17—5E 78
Alscot Rd. SE1—4F 79 (8E 148)
 (in two parts)
Alscot Way. SE1
                    —4F 79 (8E 148)
Alsike Rd. SE2 & Eri—3D 84
Alsom Av. Wor Pk—4C 130
Alston Clo. Surb—7B 118
Alston Rd. N18—5C 18
Alston Rd. SW17—4B 108
Alston Rd. Barn—3B 4
Altair Clo. N17—6A 18
Altash Way. SE9—2D 114
Altenburg Av. W13—3B 72
Altenburg Gdns. SW11—4D 92
Alt Gro. SW19—7H 107
Altham Rd. Pinn—1C 22
Althea St. SW6—2K 91
Althorne Gdns. E18—4H 33
Althorne Way. Dag—2G 53
Althorpe M. SW11—1B 92
 (in two parts)

Althorpe Rd. Harr—5G 23
Althorp Rd. SW17—1D 108
Altmore Av. E6—7D 50
Alton Av. Stan—7E 10
Alton Clo. Bex—1E 116
Alton Clo. Iswth—2K 87
Alton Gdns. Beck—7C 112
Alton Gdns. Twic—7H 87
Alton Rd. N17—3D 30
Alton Rd. SW15—1C 106
Alton Rd. Croy—3A 134
Alton Rd. Rich—4E 88
Alton St. E14—6D 64
Altyre Clo. Beck—5B 126
Altyre Rd. Croy—2D 134
Altyre Way. Beck—5B 126
Alvanley Gdns. NW6—5K 43
Alverstone Av. SW19—2J 107
Alverstone Av. Barn—7H 5
Alverstone Gdns. SE9—1G 115
Alverstone Rd. E12—4E 50
Alverstone Rd. NW2—7E 42
Alverstone Rd. N Mald—4B 120
Alverstone Rd. Wemb—1F 41
Alverston Gdns. SE25—5E 124
Alverton St. SE8—5B 6 & 6B 80
Alveston Av. Harr—3B 24
Alvey St. SE17—5E 78 (9C 148)
Alvia Gdns. Sutt—4A 132
Alvington Cres. E8—5F 47
Alwold Cres. SE12—6K 97
Alwyn Av. W4—5K 73
Alwyn Clo. Croy—7D 136
Alwyne La. N1—7B 46
Alwyne Pl. N1—6C 46
Alwyne Rd. N1—7C 46
Alwyne Rd. SW19—6H 107
Alwyne Rd. W7—7J 55
Alwyne Sq. N1—6C 46
Alwyne Vs. N1—7B 46
Alwyn Gdns. W3—H 57
Alyth Gdns. NW11—6J 27
Amalgamated Dri. Bren—6B 72
Amazon St. E1—6G 63 (8H 143)
Ambassador Clo. Houn—2C 86
Ambassador Gdns. E6—5D 66
Ambassador Sq. E14—4D 80
Amber Av. E17—1A 32
Amberden Av. N3—3J 27
Ambergate St. SE17—5B 78
Amberley Clo. Pinn—3D 22
Amberley Ct. Sidc—5C 116
Amberley Gdns. Enf—7K 7
Amberley Gdns. Eps—4B 130
Amberley Gro. SE26—5H 111
Amberley Gro. Croy—7F 125
Amberley Rd. E10—7D 32
Amberley Rd. N13—2E 16
Amberley Rd. SE2—6D 84
Amberley Rd. W9—5J 59
Amberley Rd. Buck H—1F 21
Amberley Rd. Enf—7A 8
Amberley Way. Houn—5A 86
Amberley Way. Mord—7H 121
Amberley Way. Romf—4H 37
Amber St. E15—6F 49
Amberwood Rise. N Mald
                    —6A 120
Amblecote Clo. SE12—3K 113
Amblecote Rd. SE12—3K 113
Ambler Rd. N4—3B 46
Ambleside. Brom—6F 113
Ambleside Av. SW16—4H 109
Ambleside Av. Beck—5A 126
Ambleside Clo. E9—5J 47
Ambleside Cres. Enf—3E 8
Ambleside Gdns. SW16
                    —5H 109
Ambleside Gdns. Ilf—5C 34
Ambleside Gdns. Sutt—6A 132
Ambleside Gdns. Wemb—1D 40
Ambleside Rd. NW10—7B 42
Ambleside Rd. Bexh—2G 101
Ambrooke Rd. Belv—3G 85
Ambrosden Av. SW1
                    —3G 77 (7M 145)
Ambrose Av. NW11—6H 27

Ambrose Clo. E6—5D 66
Ambrose M. SW11—2D 92
Ambrose St. SE16
—4H 79 (9J 149)
Ambrose Wlk. E3—2C 64
Amelia St. SE17—5C 78 (9L 147)
Amen Corner. EC4
—6B 62 (8K 141)
Amen Corner. SW17—6D 108
Amen Ct. EC4—6B 62 (7K 141)
America Sq. EC3
—7F 63 (9E 142)
America St. SE1
—1C 78 (3L 147)
Amerland Rd. SW18—6H 91
Amersham Av. N18—6J 17
Amersham Gro. SE14—1B 80
Amersham Rd. SE14—1B 96
Amersham Rd. Croy—6C 124
Amersham Rd. Harr—6J 23
Amersham Vale. SE14—7B 80
Amery Gdns. NW10—1D 58
Amery Rd. Harr—2A 40
Amesbury Av. SW2—2J 109
Amesbury Clo. Wor Pk—1E 130
Amesbury Dri. E4—6J 9
Amesbury Rd. Brom—3B 128
Amesbury Rd. Dag—7D 52
Amesbury Rd. Felt—2B 102
Amethyst Rd. E15—4F 49
Amhen Way. SE22—5E 94
Amherst Av. W13—6C 56
Amherst Dri. Orp—4K 129
Amherst Rd. W13—6C 56
Amhurst Gdns. Iswth—2A 88
Amhurst Pk. N16—7D 30
Amhurst Pas. E8—5G 47
Amhurst Rd.—4F 47
E8 1-233 & 2-240
N16 remainder
Amhurst Ter. E8—4G 47
Amhurst Wlk. SE28—1A 84
Amidas Gdns. Dag—4B 52
Amiel St. E1—4J 63 (3M 143)
Amies St. SW11—3D 92
Amina Way. SE16
—3G 79 (7G 149)
Amity Gro. SW20—1E 120
Amity Rd. E15—7H 49
Ammanford Grn. NW9—6A 26
Amner Rd. SW11—6E 92
Amor Rd. W6—3E 74
Amos Est. SE16—1K 79
Amoy Pl. E14—7C 64
Ampleforth Rd. SE2—2B 84
Ampthill Est. NW1
—2G 61 (1M 139)
Ampton Pl. WC1
—3K 61 (2E 140)
Ampton St. WC1
—3K 61 (2E 140)
Amroth Clo. SE23—1H 111
Amroth Grn. NW9—6A 26
Amsterdam Rd. E14—3E 80
Amwell Clo. Enf—5J 7
Amwell Ct. Est. N4—1C 46
Amwell St. EC1—3A 62 (1G 141)
Amyand Cotts. Twic—6B 88
Amyand La. Twic—7B 88
Amyand Pk. Gdns. Twic—7B 88
Amyand Pk. Rd. Twic—7A 88
Amyruth Rd. SE4—5C 96
Anatola Rd. N19—2G 45
Ancaster Cres. N Mald—6C 120
Ancaster Rd. Beck—3K 125
Ancaster St. SE18—7J 83
Anchorage Clo. SW19—5J 107
Anchor & Hope La. SE7—3K 81
Anchor Ct. Enf—5K 7
Anchor M. SW12—6F 93
Anchor St. SE16
—4H 79 (9J 149)
Anchor Yd. EC1—4C 62 (3L 141)
Ancill Clo. W6—6F 75
Ancona Rd. NW10—2C 58
Ancona Rd. SE18—5H 83

Andace Pk. Gdns. Brom
—1A 128
Andalus Rd. SW9—3J 93
Ander Clo. Wemb—4D 40
Anderson Rd. E9—6K 47
Anderson Rd. Wfd G—3B 34
Anderson St. SW3
—5D 76 (9F 144)
Anderson Way. Belv—2H 85
Anderton Clo. SE5—3D 94
Andorra Ct. Brom—1A 128
Andover Clo. Gnfd—4F 55
Andover Pl. NW6—2K 59
Andover Rd. N7—2K 45
Andover Rd. Orp—7J 129
Andover Rd. Twic—1H 103
Andreck Ct. Beck—2E 126
Andre St. E8—5G 47
Andrew Borde St. WC2
—6H 61 (7B 140)
Andrew Clo. Bex—5K 101
Andrewes Clo. E6—6C 66
Andrew Pl. SW8—7H 77
Andrews Clo. Buck H—2F 21
Andrews Clo. Harr—7H 23
Andrews Clo. Wor Pk—2F 131
Andrews Pl. SE9—6F 99
Andrew's Rd. E8—1H 63
Andrew St. E14—6E 64
Andrews Wlk. SE17—6B 78
Androse Gdns. Brom—1A 128
Andwell Clo. SE2—2B 84
Anerley Gro. SE19—7F 111
Anerley Hill. SE19—6F 111
Anerley Pk. SE20—7G 111
Anerley Pk. Rd. SE20—7H 111
Anerley Rd.—7G 111
SE19 19-69 & 54-120
SE20 remainder
Anerley Sta. Rd. SE20—1H 125
Anerley St. SW11—2D 92
Anerley Vale. SE19—7F 111
Aneurin Bevan Ho. N11—7C 16
Anfield Clo. SW12—7G 93
Angel All. E1—6F 63 (7F 142)
Angel Centre, The. N1 & EC1
—1H 61 (1H 140)
Angel Clo. N18—4A 18
Angel Ct. EC2—6D 62 (7B 142)
Angel Ct. SW1—1G 77 (3M 145)
Angelfield. Houn—4F 87
Angel Hill. Sutt—3K 131
Angel Hill Dri. Sutt—3K 131
Angelica Gdns. Croy—1K 135
Angel La. E15—6F 49
Angell Pk. Gdns. SW9—3A 94
Angell Rd. SW9—3A 94
Angel M. N1—2A 62
Angel Pas. EC4—7D 62 (1A 148)
Angel Pl. N18—5B 18
Angel Pl. SE1—2D 78 (4A 148)
Angel Rd. N18—5B 18
Angel Rd. Harr—6J 23
(in two parts)
Angel Rd. Th Dit—7A 118
Angel Sq. N1—2A 62
Angel St. EC1—6C 62 (7L 141)
Angel Wlk. W6—4E 74
Angel Way. Romf—5K 37
Angerstein La. SE3—1H 97
Angle Grn. Dag—1C 52
Anglers Clo. Rich—4C 104
Angler's La. NW5—6F 45
Anglesea Av. SE18—4F 83
Anglesea Rd. SE18—4F 83
Anglesea Rd. King—4D 118
Anglesey Ct. Rd. Cars—6E 132
Anglesey Gdns. Cars—6E 132
Anglesey Rd. Enf—4C 8
Anglesmede Cres. Pinn—3E 22
Anglesmede Way. Pinn—3E 22
Angles Rd. SW16—4J 109
Anglo Rd. E3—2B 64
Angus Dri. Ruis—4A 38
Angus Gdns. NW9—1K 25
Angus Rd. E13—3A 66

Angus St. SE14—7A 80
Anhalt Rd. SW11—7C 76
Ankerdine Cres. SE18—7F 83
Anlaby Rd. Tedd—5J 103
Anley Rd. W14—2F 75
Anmersh Gro. Stan—1D 24
Annabel Clo. E14—6D 64
Anna Clo. E8—1F 63
Annandale Rd. SE10—6H 81
Annandale Rd. W4—5A 74
Annandale Rd. Croy—2G 135
Annandale Rd. Sidc—7J 99
Anna Neagle Clo. E7—4J 49
Annan Way. Romf—1K 37
Anne Boleyn's Wlk. King
—5E 104
Anne Boleyn's Wlk. Sutt
—7F 131
Anne Case M. N Mald—3A 120
Annesley Av. NW9—3K 25
Annesley Clo. NW10—3A 42
Annesley Dri. Croy—3B 136
Annesley Rd. SE3—1K 97
Annesley Wlk. N19—2G 45
Anne St. E13—4J 65
Annette Clo. Harr—2J 23
Annette Rd. N7—3K 45
Annett's Cres. N1—7C 46
Annie Besant Clo. E3—1B 64
Anning St. EC2—4E 62 (3D 142)
Annington Rd. N2—3D 28
Annis Rd. E9—6A 48
Ann La. SW10—6B 76
Ann St. SE18—5G 83
(in two parts)
Annsworthy Av. T Hth—3D 124
Annsworthy Cres. SE25
—2D 124
Ansdale Clo. Orp—7H 129
Ansdell Rd. SE15—2J 95
Ansdell St. W8—3K 75
Ansdell Ter. W8—3K 75
Ansell Gro. Cars—1D 132
Ansell Rd. SW17—3C 108
Anselm Clo. Croy—3F 135
Anselm Rd. SW6—6J 75
Anselm Rd. Pinn—1D 22
Ansford Rd. Brom—5E 112
Anson Clo. Romf—2H 37
Anson Rd. N7—4H 45
Anson Rd. NW2—5D 42
Anson Ter. N'holt—6F 39
Anstey Rd. SE15—3G 95
Anstey Wlk. N15—4B 30
Anstice Clo. W4—7A 74
Anstridge Path. SE9—6H 99
Anstridge Rd. SE9—6H 99
Antelope Rd. SE18—3D 82
Anthony Rd. SE25—6G 125
Anthony Rd. Gnfd—3J 55
Anthony Rd. Well—1A 100
Anthony St. E1—6H 63 (7K 143)
Antill Rd. E3—3A 64
Antill Rd. N15—4G 31
Antill Ter. E1—6K 63 (7M 143)
Antlers Hill. E4—5J 9
Anton Cres. Sutt—3J 131
Antoneys Clo. Pinn—2B 22
Anton St. E8—5G 47
Antrim Gro. NW3—6D 44
Antrim Rd. NW3—6D 44
Antrobus Clo. Sutt—5H 131
Antrobus Rd. W4—4J 73
Anworth Clo. Wfd G—6E 20
Apeldoorn Dri. Wall—7J 133
Apex Clo. Beck—1D 126
Apex Corner. NW7—4F 13
Aplin Way. Iswth—1J 87
Apollo Av. Brom—1K 127
Apollo Industrial Business
Centre. SE8—6A 80
Apollo Pl. SW10—7B 76
Apollo Way. SE28—3H 83
Apothecary St. EC4
—6B 62 (8J 141)
Appach Rd. SW2—6A 94
Appleby Clo. E4—6K 19

Appleby Clo. N15—5D 30
Appleby Clo. Twic—2H 103
Appleby Rd. E8—7G 47
Appleby Rd. E16—6H 65
Appleby St. E2—2F 63
Appledore Av. Bexh—1J 101
Appledore Av. Ruis—3A 38
Appledore Clo. SW17—2D 108
Appledore Clo. Brom—5J 127
Appledore Clo. Edgw—1G 25
Appledore Cres. Sidc—3J 115
Appleford Rd. W10—4G 59
Apple Garth. Bren—4D 72
Applegarth. Croy—7D 136
(in two parts)
Applegarth Dri. Ilf—4K 35
Applegarth Rd. SE28—1B 84
Applegarth Rd. W14—3F 75
Apple Gro. Enf—3K 7
Apple Mkt. King—2D 118
Appleton Gdns. N Mald—6C 120
Appleton Rd. SE9—3C 98
Apple Tree Yd. SW1
—1G 77 (2M 145)
Applewood Clo. N20—1H 15
Applewood Clo. NW2—3D 42
Appold St. EC2—5E 62 (5C 142)
Apprentice Way. E5—4H 47
Approach Rd. E2
—2J 63 (1M 143)
Approach Rd. SW20—2E 120
Approach Rd. Barn—4G 5
Approach, The. NW4—5F 27
Approach, The. W3—6K 57
Approach, The. Enf—2C 8
Aprey Gdns. NW4—4E 26
April Clo. W7—7J 55
April Glen. SE23—3K 111
April St. E8—4F 47
Apsley Clo. Harr—5G 23
Apsley Rd. E17—5B 32
Apsley Rd. SE25—4H 125
Apsley Rd. N Mald—3J 119
Apsley Way. W1
—2E 76 (4H 145)
Aquila St. NW8—2B 60
Aquinas St. SE1
—1A 78 (3H 147)
Arabella Dri. SW15—4A 90
Arabia Clo. E4—7K 9
Arabin Rd. SE4—4B 96
Aragon Av. Th Dit—5A 118
Aragon Clo. Brom—7D 128
Aragon Clo. Enf—1E 6
Aragon Dri. Ruis—1B 38
Aragon Rd. King—5E 104
Aragon Rd. Mord—6F 121
Arandora Cres. Romf—6B 36
Aran Dri. Stan—4H 11
Arbery Rd. E3—3A 64
Arbor Clo. Beck—2D 126
Arbor Rd. E4—3A 20
Arbour Rd. Enf—3E 8
Arbroath Rd. SE9—3C 98
Arbuthnot La. Bex—6E 100
Arbuthnot Rd. SE14—2K 95
Arbutus St. E8—1F 63
Arcadia Av. N3—2J 27
Arcadian Av. Bex—6E 100
Arcadian Clo. Bex—6E 100
Arcadian Gdns. N22—7E 16
Arcadian Rd. Bex—6E 100
Arcadia St. E14—6C 64
Archangel St. SE16—2K 79
Archbishop's Pl. SW2—7K 93
Archdale Rd. SE22—4F 95
Archel Rd. W14—6H 75
Archer Clo. King—7E 104
Archer Rd. SE25—4H 125
Archer Rd. Orp—5K 129
Archers Dri. Enf—2D 8
Archer St. W1—7H 61 (9A 140)
Archery Clo. W2
—6C 60 (8D 138)
Archery Clo. Harr—3K 23
Archery Rd. SE9—5D 98

Arches, The. Harr—2F 39
Archibald Cres. NW2—6D 42
Archibald M. W1
　　　—7E 60 (1H 145)
Archibald Rd. N7—4H 45
Archibald St. E3—3C 64
Arch St. SE1—3C 78 (7L 147)
Archway Clo. N19—2G 45
Archway Clo. SW19—3K 107
Archway Mall. N19—2G 45
Archway Rd.—6E 28
　　N19 1-43 & 2-92
　　N6 remainder
Archway St. SW13—3A 90
Arcola St. E8—5F 47
Arctic St. NW5—5F 45
Arcus Rd. Brom—6G 113
Ardbeg Rd. SE24—5D 94
Arden Clo. Bush, Wat—1E 10
Arden Clo. Harr—3H 39
Arden Ct. Gdns. N2—6B 28
Arden Cres. E14—4C 80
Arden Cres. Dag—7C 52
Arden Est. N1—2E 62
Arden M. E17—5D 32
Arden Mhor. Pinn—4A 22
Arden Rd. N3—3H 27
Arden Rd. W13—7C 56
Ardent Clo. SE25—3E 124
Ardfern Av. SW16—3A 124
Ardfillan Rd. SE6—1F 113
Ardgowan Rd. SE6—7G 97
Ardilaun Rd. N5—4C 46
Ardleigh Gdns. Sutt—7J 121
Ardleigh M. Ilf—3F 51
Ardleigh Rd. E17—1B 32
Ardleigh Rd. N1—6E 46
Ardleigh Ter. E17—1B 32
Ardley Clo. NW10—3A 42
Ardley Clo. SE6—3A 112
Ardlui Rd. SE27—2C 110
Ardmay Gdns. Surb—5E 118
Ardmere Rd. SE13—6F 97
Ardmore La. Buck H—1E 20
Ardoch Rd. SE6—2F 113
Ardrossan Gdns. Wor Pk
　　　—3C 130
Ardshiel Clo. SW15—3F 91
Ardwell Av. Ilf—5G 35
Ardwell Rd. SW2—2J 109
Ardwick Rd. NW2—4J 43
Argall Av. E10—7K 31
Argon M. SW6—7J 75
Argus Clo. Romf—1H 37
Argus Way. W3—3H 73
Argus Way. N'holt—3C 54
Argyle Av. Houn—6E 86
Argyle Clo. W13—4A 56
Argyle Pl. W6—4D 74
Argyle Rd. E1—4K 63 (3M 143)
Argyle Rd. E15—4G 49
Argyle Rd. E16—6A 66
Argyle Rd. N12—5E 14
Argyle Rd. N17—1G 31
Argyle Rd. N18—4B 18
Argyle Rd. Barn—4A 4
Argyle Rd. Gnfd & W13—3K 55
Argyle Rd. Harr—6F 23
Argyle Rd. Houn—5F 87
Argyle Rd. Ilf—2E 50
Argyle Rd. Tedd—5K 103
Argyle Sq. WC1—3J 61 (1D 140)
Argyle St. WC1—3J 61 (1C 140)
Argyle Wlk. WC1
　　　—3J 61 (2D 140)
Argyll Clo. SW9—3K 93
Argyll Gdns. Edgw—2H 25
Argyll Rd. W8—2J 75
Argyll St. W1—6G 61 (8L 139)
Arica Rd. SE4—4A 96
Ariel Rd. NW6—6J 43
Ariel Way. W12—1E 74
Aristotle Rd. SW4—3H 93
Arkell Gro. SE19—7B 110
Arkindale Rd. SE6—3E 112
Arkley Cres. E17—5B 32

Arkley Rd. E17—5B 32
Arklow Rd. SE14—6B 80
Arkwright Rd. NW3—5A 44
Arkwright Rd. S Croy—7F 135
Arlesey Clo. SW15—5G 91
Arlesford Rd. SW9—3J 93
Arlingford Rd. SW2—5A 94
Arlington. N12—3D 14
Arlington Av. N1—1C 62
Arlington Clo. Sidc—7J 99
Arlington Clo. Sutt—2J 131
Arlington Clo. Twic—6C 88
Arlington Dri. Cars—2D 132
Arlington Gdns. W4—5J 73
Arlington Gdns. Ilf—1E 50
Arlington Rd. N14—2A 16
Arlington Rd. NW1—1F 61
Arlington Rd. W13—6B 56
Arlington Rd. Rich—2D 104
Arlington Rd. Surb—6D 118
Arlington Rd. Tedd—4K 103
Arlington Rd. Twic—6C 88
Arlington Rd. Wfd G—7E 20
Arlington Sq. N1—1C 62
Arlington St. SW1
　　　—1G 77 (2L 145)
Arlington Way. EC1
　　　—3A 62 (1H 141)
Arliss Way. N'holt—1A 54
Arlow Rd. N21—1F 17
Armada Ct. SE8—6C 80
Armadale Clo. N17—4H 31
Armadale Rd. SW6—6J 75
Armagh Rd. E3—1B 64
Armfield Cres. Mitc—2D 122
Armfield Rd. Enf—1J 7
Arminger Rd. W12—1D 74
Armitage Rd. NW11—1G 43
Armitage Rd. SE10—5H 81
Armour Clo. N7—6K 45
Armoury Way. SW18—5J 91
Armstead Wlk. Dag—7G 53
Armstrong Clo. Wfd G—6B 20
Armstrong Clo. E6—6D 66
Armstrong Clo. Dag—1C 52
Armstrong Cres. Barn—3G 5
Armstrong Rd. SW7
　　　—3B 76 (7A 144)
Armstrong Rd. W3—1B 74
Armstrong Rd. Felt—5C 102
Armstrong Way. S'hall—2F 71
Armytage Rd. Houn—7B 70
Arnal Cres. SW18—7G 91
Arndale Centre. SW18—6K 91
Arndale Wlk. SW18—5K 91
Arne St. WC2—6J 61 (8D 140)
Arne Wlk. SE3—4H 97
Arneways Av. Romf—3D 36
Arneway St. SW1
　　　—3H 77 (7B 146)
Arnewood Clo. SW15—1C 106
Arneys La. Mitc—6E 122
Arngask Rd. SE6—7F 97
Arnhem Wharf Development.
　　　E14—3C 80
Arnold Cir. E2—3F 63 (2E 142)
Arnold Rd. Harr—7F 25
Arnold Cres. Iswth—5H 87
Arnold Est. SE1—2F 79 (5F 148)
Arnold Gdns. N13—5G 17
Arnold Rd. E3—3C 64
Arnold Rd. N15—3F 31
Arnold Rd. SW17—7D 108
Arnold Rd. Dag—7F 53
Arnold Rd. N'holt—6C 38
Arnos Gro. N14—4C 16
Arnos Rd. N11—4B 16
Arnott Clo. SE28—1C 84
Arnott Clo. W4—4K 73
Arnould Av. SE5—4D 94
Arnsberg Way. Bexh—4G 101
Arnside Gdns. Wemb—1D 40
Arnside Rd. Bexh—1G 101
Arnside St. SE17—6D 78
Arnulf St. SE6—4D 112

Arnulls Rd. SW16—6B 110
Arodene Rd. SW2—6K 93
Arragon Gdns. SW16—7J 109
Arragon Gdns. W Wick—3D 136
Arragon Rd. E6—1B 66
Arragon Rd. Twic—7A 88
Arran Clo. Eri—6K 85
Arran Clo. Wall—4G 133
Arran Dri. E12—2B 50
Arran M. W5—1F 73
Arran Rd. SE6—2D 112
Arran Wlk. N1—7C 46
Arras Av. Mord—5A 122
Arrol Rd. Beck—3J 125
Arrow Rd. E3—3D 64
Arrowscout Wlk. N'holt—3C 54
Arsenal Rd. SE9—2D 98
Arterberry Rd. SW20—7E 106
Artesian Rd. W2—6J 59
Arthingworth St. E15—1G 65
Arthurdon Rd. SE4—5C 96
Arthur Gro. SE18—4G 83
Arthur Rd. E6—2D 66
Arthur Rd. N7—4K 45
Arthur Rd. N9—2A 18
Arthur Rd. SW19—4H 107
Arthur Rd. King—7G 105
Arthur Rd. N Mald—5D 120
Arthur Rd. Romf—6D 36
Arthur St. EC4—7D 62 (9B 142)
Artichoke Hill. E1
　　　—7H 63 (1J 149)
Artichoke Pl. SE5—1D 94
Artillery Clo. Ilf—6G 35
Artillery La. E1—5E 62 (6D 142)
Artillery Pl. SE18—4E 82
Artillery Pl. SW1
　　　—3H 77 (7A 146)
Artillery Pl. Harr—7B 10
Artillery Row. SW1
　　　—3H 77 (7A 146)
Arun Ct. SE25—5G 125
Arundel Av. Mord—4H 121
Arundel Clo. E15—4G 49
Arundel Clo. SW11—5C 92
Arundel Clo. Bex—6F 101
Arundel Clo. Croy—3B 134
Arundel Clo. Hmptn—6F 103
Arundel Ct. N12—6H 15
Arundel Ct. Brom—2G 127
Arundel Dri. Harr—4D 38
Arundel Dri. Wfd G—7D 20
Arundel Gdns. N21—1F 17
Arundel Gdns. W11—7H 59
Arundel Gdns. Edgw—7E 12
Arundel Gdns. Ilf—2A 52
Arundel Gro. N16—5E 46
Arundel Pl. N1—6A 46
Arundel Rd. Barn—3H 5
Arundel Rd. Croy—6D 124
Arundel Rd. Houn—3A 86
Arundel Rd. King—2H 119
Arundel Rd. Sutt—7H 131
Arundel Sq. N7—6A 46
Arundel St. WC2
　　　—7K 61 (9F 140)
Arundel Ter. SW13—6D 74
Arvon Rd. N5—5A 46
Ascalon St. SW8—7G 77
Ascham Dri. E4—7J 19
Ascham End. E17—1A 32
Ascham St. NW5—5G 45
Aschurch Rd. Croy—7F 125
Ascot Clo. N'holt—5E 38
Ascot Gdns. S'hall—5D 54
Ascot Pl. Stan—5H 11
Ascot Rd. E6—3D 66
Ascot Rd. N15—5D 30
Ascot Rd. N18—4B 18
Ascot Rd. SW17—6E 108
Ascot Rd. Orp—4K 129
Ascott Av. W5—2E 72
Aseing Clo. E6—7E 66
Ashbourne Av. E18—4K 33
Ashbourne Av. N20—2J 15
Ashbourne Av. NW11—5H 27
Ashbourne Av. Bexh—7E 84

Ashbourne Av. Harr—2H 39
Ashbourne Clo. N12—4E 14
Ashbourne Clo. W5—5G 57
Ashbourne Gro. NW7—5E 12
Ashbourne Gro. SE22—4F 95
Ashbourne Gro. W4—5A 74
Ashbourne Rd. W5—4F 57
Ashbourne Rd. Mitc—7E 108
Ashbourne Ter. SW19—7J 107
Ashbourne Way. NW11—4H 27
Ashbridge Rd. E11—7H 33
Ashbridge St. NW8
　　　—4C 60 (4C 138)
Ashbrook Rd. N19—1H 45
Ashbrook Rd. Dag—3H 53
Ashburn Gdns. SW7—4A 76
Ashburnham Av. Harr—6K 23
Ashburnham Clo. N2—3B 28
Ashburnham Gdns. Harr
　　　—6K 23
Ashburnham Gro. SE10—7D 80
Ashburnham Pl. SE10—7D 80
Ashburnham Retreat. SE10
　　　—7D 80
Ashburnham Rd. NW10—3E 58
Ashburnham Rd. SW10—7A 76
Ashburnham Rd. Belv—4J 85
Ashburnham Rd. Rich—3B 104
Ashburn M. SW7—4A 76
Ashburn Pl. SW7—4A 76
Ashburton Av. Croy—1H 135
Ashburton Av. Ilf—5J 51
Ashburton Clo. Croy—1G 135
Ashburton Ct. Pinn—3B 22
Ashburton Gdns. Croy—2G 135
Ashburton Gro. N7—4A 46
Ashburton Rd. E16—6J 65
Ashburton Rd. Croy—2G 135
Ashburton Ter. E13—2J 65
Ashbury Gdns. Romf—5D 36
Ashbury Rd. SW11—3D 92
Ashby Gro. N1—7C 46
Ashby Rd. N15—5G 31
Ashby Rd. SE4—2B 96
Ashby St. EC1—3B 62 (2K 141)
Ashby Wlk. Croy—6C 124
Aschurch Gro. W12—3C 74
Aschurch Pk. Vs. W12—3C 74
Aschurch Ter. W12—3C 74
Ash Clo. SE20—2J 125
Ash Clo. Cars—2D 132
Ash Clo. Edgw—4D 12
Ash Clo. N Mald—2K 119
Ash Clo. Orp—5H 129
Ash Clo. Romf—1H 37
Ash Clo. Sidc—3B 116
Ash Clo. Stan—6F 11
Ashcombe Av. Surb—7D 118
Ashcombe Gdns. Edgw—4B 12
Ashcombe Pk. NW2—3A 42
Ashcombe Rd. SW19—5J 107
Ashcombe Rd. Cars—6E 132
Ashcombe Sq. N Mald—3J 119
Ashcombe St. SW6—2K 91
Ash Ct. SW19—7G 107
Ash Croft. Pinn—6A 10
Ashcroft Av. Sidc—6A 100
Ashcroft Cres. Sidc—6A 100
Ashcroft Rd. E3—3A 64
Ashcroft Sq. W6—4E 74
Ashdale Clo. Twic—7G 87
Ashdale Gro. Stan—6E 10
Ashdale Rd. SE12—1K 113
Ashdale Way. Twic—7F 87
Ashdene. Pinn—3A 22
Ashdon Clo. Wfd G—6E 20
Ashdon Rd. NW10—1B 58
Ashdown Clo. Beck—2D 126
Ashdown Cres. NW5—5E 44
Ashdown Est. E11—4F 49
Ashdown Rd. Enf—2D 8
Ashdown Rd. King—2E 118
Ashdown Wlk. Romf—1H 37
Ashdown Way. SW17—2E 108
Ashenden Rd. E5—5A 48
Ashen Gro. SW19—3J 107
Asher Way. E1—7G 63 (1H 149)

Ashfield Av. Bush, Wat—1B 10
Ashfield Av. Felt—1A 102
Ashfield Clo. Rich—1E 104
Ashfield La. Chst—6G 115
Ashfield Pde. N14—1C 16
Ashfield Rd. N4—6C 30
Ashfield Rd. N14—3B 16
Ashfield Rd. W3—1B 74
Ashfield St. E1—5H 63 (6J 143)
Ashford Av. N8—4J 29
Ashford Av. Hay—6B 54
Ashford Clo. E17—6B 32
Ashford Cres. Enf—2D 8
Ashford Pas. NW2—4F 43
Ashford Rd. E6—7E 50
Ashford Rd. E18—2K 33
Ashford Rd. NW2—4F 43
Ashford St. N1—3E 62 (1C 142)
  (in two parts)
Ash Gro. N13—3H 17
Ash Gro. NW2—4F 43
Ash Gro. SE20—2J 125
Ash Gro. W5—2E 72
Ash Gro. Enf—7K 7
Ash Gro. Houn—1B 86
Ash Gro. S'hall—5E 54
Ash Gro. Wemb—4A 40
Ash Gro. W Wick—2E 136
Ashgrove Rd. Brom—6F 113
Ashgrove Rd. Ilf—1K 51
Ash Hill Clo. Bush, Wat—1A 10
Ash Hill Dri. Pinn—3A 22
Ashingdon Clo. E4—3K 19
Ashington Rd. SW6—2H 91
Ashlake Rd. SW16—4J 109
Ashland Pl. W1—5E 60 (5G 139)
Ashleigh Gdns. Sutt—2K 131
Ashleigh Rd. SE20—3H 125
Ashleigh Rd. SW14—3A 90
Ashley Av. Ilf—2F 35
Ashley Av. Mord—5J 121
Ashley Clo. NW4—2E 26
Ashley Cres. N22—2A 30
Ashley Cres. SW11—3E 92
Ashley Dri. Iswth—6J 71
Ashley Dri. Twic—1F 103
Ashley Gdns. N13—4H 17
Ashley Gdns. SW1
                —3G 77 (7M 145)
Ashley Gdns. Rich—2D 104
Ashley Gdns. Wemb—2E 40
Ashley La. NW4—2E 26
Ashley La. Croy—4B 134
Ashley Pl. SW1—3G 77 (7L 145)
Ashley Rd. E4—6H 19
Ashley Rd. E7—7A 50
Ashley Rd. N17—3G 31
Ashley Rd. N19—1J 45
Ashley Rd. SW19—6K 107
Ashley Rd. Enf—2D 8
Ashley Rd. Hmptn—7E 102
Ashley Rd. Rich—3E 88
Ashley Rd. Th Dit—6A 118
Ashley Rd. T Hth—4K 123
Ashley Wlk. NW7—7K 13
Ashling Rd. Croy—1G 135
Ashlin Rd. E15—4F 49
Ashlone Rd. SW15—3F 91
Ashmead. N14—5B 6
Ashmead Rd. SE8—2C 96
Ashmere Av. Beck—2F 127
Ashmere Clo. Sutt—5F 131
Ashmere Gro. SW2—4J 93
Ashmill St. NW1
                —5C 60 (5C 138)
Ashmole Pl. SW8—6K 77
Ashmole St. SW8—6K 77
Ashmore Ct. Houn—6E 70
Ashmore Gro. Well—3H 99
Ashmore Rd. W9—3H 59
Ashmount Rd. N15—5F 31
Ashmount Rd. N19—7G 29
Ashmount Ter. W5—4D 72
Ashmour Gdns. Romf—2K 37
Ashneal Gdns. Harr—3H 39
Ashness Gdns. Gnfd—6B 40

Ashness Rd. SW11—5D 92
Ashridge Clo. Harr—6C 24
Ashridge Cres. SE18—7G 83
Ashridge Gdns. N13—5C 16
Ashridge Gdns. Pinn—4C 22
Ashridge Way. Mord—4H 121
Ash Rd. E15—5G 49
Ash Rd. Croy—2C 136
Ash Rd. Sutt—1H 131
Ash Row. Brom—7E 128
Ashstead Rd. E5—7G 31
Ashton Clo. Sutt—4J 131
Ashton Gdns. Houn—4D 86
Ashton Gdns. Romf—6E 36
Ashton Rd. E15—5F 49
Ashton St. E14—7E 64
Ash Tree Clo. Croy—6A 126
Ashtree Dell. NW9—5K 25
Ash Tree Way. Croy—5K 125
Ashurst Clo. SE20—1H 125
Ashurst Dri. Ilf—6F 35
Ashurst Rd. N12—5H 15
Ashurst Rd. Barn—5J 5
Ashurst Wlk. Croy—2H 135
Ashvale Rd. SW17—5D 108
Ashville Rd. E11—2F 49
Ashwater Rd. SE12—1J 113
Ashwin St. E8—6F 47
Ashwood Gdns. Croy—6D 136
Ashwood Rd. E4—3A 20
Ashworth Clo. SE5—2D 94
Ashworth Industrial Est. Croy
                —1J 133
Ashworth Rd. W9—3K 59
Askern Clo. Bexh—4D 100
Aske St. N1—3E 62 (1C 142)
Askew Cres. W12—2B 74
Askew Rd. W12—2B 74
Askham Ct. W12—1C 74
Askham Rd. W12—1C 74
Askill Dri. SW15—5G 91
Askwith Rd. Rain—3K 69
Asland Rd. E15—1G 65
Aslett St. SW18—7K 91
Asmara Rd. NW2—5G 43
Asmuns Hill. NW11—5J 27
Asmuns Pl. NW11—5H 27
Aspen Clo. N19—2G 45
Aspen Clo. W5—2F 73
Aspen Copse. Brom—2D 128
Aspen Dri. Wemb—3A 40
Aspen Gdns. W6—5D 74
Aspen Gdns. Mitc—5E 122
Aspen Grn. Eri—3F 85
Aspen La. N'holt—3C 54
Aspenlea Rd. W6—6F 75
Aspen Way. E14—7D 64
Aspern Gro. NW3—5C 44
Aspinall Rd. SE4—3K 95
Aspinden Rd. SE16
                —4H 79 (8K 149)
Aspley Rd. SW18—5K 91
Asplins Rd. N17—1G 31
Asquith Clo. Dag—1C 52
Assam St. E1—6G 63 (7G 143)
Assembly Pas. E1
                —5J 63 (5M 143)
Assembly Wlk. Cars—7C 122
Ass Ho. La. Harr—4A 10
Astall Clo. Harr—1J 23
Astbury Rd. SE15—1J 95
Astell St. SW3—5C 76 (9D 144)
Aste St. E14—2E 80
Astey's Row. N1—7C 46
Asthall Gdns. Ilf—4G 35
Astle St. SW11—2E 92
Astley Av. NW2—5E 42
Aston Av. Harr—7C 24
Aston Clo. Sidc—3A 116
Aston Grn. Houn—2A 86
Aston M. Romf—7C 36
Aston Rd. SW20—2E 120
Aston Rd. W5—6D 56
Aston St. E14—5A 64
Astonville St. SW18—1J 107

Astor Av. Romf—6J 37
Astor Clo. King—6H 105
Astoria Wlk. SW9—3A 94
Astrop M. W6—3E 74
Astrop Ter. W6—2E 74
Astwood M. SW7—4A 76
Asylum Rd. SE15—7H 79
Atalanta St. SW6—7F 75
Atbara Rd. Tedd—6B 104
Atcham Rd. Houn—4G 87
Atcost Rd. Bark—5A 68
Atheldene Rd. SW18—1A 108
Athelney St. SE6—3C 112
Athelstane Gro. E3—2B 64
Athelstane Rd. N4—1A 46
Athelstan Rd. King—4F 119
Athelstone Rd. Harr—2H 23
Athena Clo. Harr—2H 23
Athenaeum Pl. N10—3F 29
Athenaeum Rd. N20—1F 15
Athenlay Rd. SE15—5K 95
Athens Gdns. W9—4J 59
Atherden Rd. E5—4J 47
Atherfold Rd. SW9—3J 93
Atherley Way. Houn—7D 86
Atherstone M. SW7
                —4A 76 (8A 144)
Atherton Dri. SW19—4F 107
Atherton Heights. Wemb
                —6C 40
Atherton M. E7—6H 49
Atherton Pl. Harr—3H 23
Atherton Pl. S'hall—7E 54
Atherton Rd. E7—6H 49
Atherton Rd. SW13—7C 74
Atherton Rd. Ilf—2C 34
Atherton St. SW11—2C 92
Athlone Clo. E5—5H 47
Athlone Rd. SW2—7K 93
Athlone St. NW5—6E 44
Athlon Rd. Wemb—2D 56
Athol Clo. Pinn—1A 22
Athol Gdns. Pinn—1A 22
Atholl Rd. Ilf—7A 36
Athol Rd. Eri—5J 85
Athol Sq. E14—6E 64
Atkinson Rd. E16—5A 66
Atkins Rd. E10—6D 32
Atkins Rd. SW12—7G 93
Atlantic Rd. SW9—4A 94
Atlas Business Centre. NW2
                —2D 42
Atlas Gdns. SE7—4A 82
Atlas M. N7—6K 45
Atlas Rd. E13—2J 65
Atlas Rd. NW10—3A 58
Atlas Rd. Wemb—4J 41
Atley Rd. E3—1C 64
Atney Rd. SW15—4G 91
Atterbury Rd. N4—6B 30
Atterbury St. SW1
                —4J 77 (9C 146)
Attewood Av. NW10—3A 42
Attewood Rd. N'holt—6C 38
Attfield Clo. N20—2G 15
Attlee Rd. SE28—7B 68
Attneave St. WC1
                —3A 62 (2G 141)
Atwater Clo. SW2—1A 110
Atwell Clo. E10—6D 32
Atwell Rd. SE15—2G 95
Atwood Av. Rich—2G 89
Atwood Rd. W6—4D 74
Atwoods All. Rich—1G 89
Aubert Ct. N5—4B 46
Aubert Pk. N5—4B 46
Aubert Rd. N5—4B 46
Aubrey Pl. NW8—2A 60
Aubrey Rd. E17—3C 32
Aubrey Rd. N8—5J 29
Aubrey Rd. W8—1H 75
Aubrey Wlk. W8—1H 75
Aubyn Hill. SE27—4C 110
Aubyn Sq. SW15—5C 90
Auckland Clo. SE19—1F 125
Auckland Gdns. SE19—1E 124

Auckland Hill. SE27—4C 110
Auckland Rise. SE19—1E 124
Auckland Rd. E10—3D 48
Auckland Rd. SE19—1F 125
Auckland Rd. SW11—4C 92
Auckland Rd. Ilf—1F 51
Auckland Rd. King—4F 119
Auckland St. SE11—5K 77
Auden Pl. NW1—1E 60
Audleigh Pl. Chig—6K 21
Audley Clo. SW11—3E 92
Audley Ct. E18—4H 33
Audley Ct. Pinn—2A 22
Audley Gdns. Ilf—2K 51
Audley Pl. Sutt—7K 131
Audley Rd. NW4—6C 26
Audley Rd. W5—5F 57
Audley Rd. Enf—2G 7
Audley Rd. Rich—5F 89
Audley Sq. W1—1E 76 (2H 145)
Audrey Clo. Beck—6D 126
Audrey Gdns. Wemb—2B 40
Audrey Rd. Ilf—3F 51
Audrey St. E2—2G 63
Audric Clo. King—1G 119
Augurs La. E13—3K 65
Augusta Rd. Twic—2G 103
Augusta St. E14—6D 64
Augustine Rd. Harr—1G 23
Augustine Rd. W14—3F 75
Augustus Clo. Bren—7C 72
Augustus Ct. SW16—2H 109
Augustus Rd. SW19—1G 107
Augustus St. NW1
                —2F 61 (1K 139)
Aultone Way. Cars—3D 132
Aultone Way. Sutt—2K 131
Aulton Pl. SE11—5A 78
Aurelia Gdns. Croy—5K 123
Aurelia Rd. Croy—6J 123
Auriel Av. Dag—6K 53
Auriga M. N1—6D 46
Auriol Clo. Wor Pk—3A 130
Auriol Dri. Gnfd—7H 39
Auriol Pk. Rd. Wor Pk—3A 130
Auriol Rd. W14—4G 75
Austell Gdns. NW7—3F 13
Austen Clo. SE28—1B 84
Austen Rd. Harr—2F 39
Austin Av. Brom—5C 128
Austin Clo. SE23—7B 96
Austin Clo. Twic—5C 88
Austin Ct. E6—1A 66
Austin Friars. EC2
                —6D 62 (7B 142)
Austin Rd. SW11—1E 92
Austin Rd. SE2—3F 63 (2E 142)
Austral Clo. Sidc—3K 115
Australia Rd. W12—7D 58
Austral St. SE11
                —4B 78 (8J 147)
Austyn Gdns. Surb—7H 119
Autumn Clo. Enf—1B 8
Autumn St. E3—1C 64
Avalon Clo. W13—5A 56
Avalon Clo. Enf—2F 7
Avalon Rd. SW6—1K 91
Avalon Rd. W13—4A 56
Avarn Rd. SW17—6D 108
Avebury Pk. Surb—7D 118
Avebury Rd. E11—1F 49
Avebury Rd. SW19—1H 121
Avebury St. N1—1D 62
Aveley Rd. Romf—4K 37
Aveline St. SE11—5A 78
Aveling Pk. Rd. E17—2C 32
Ave Maria La. EC4
                —6B 62 (8K 141)
Avenell Rd. N5—3B 46
Avening Rd. SW18—7J 91
Avening Ter. SW18—7J 91
Avenons Rd. E13—4J 65
Avenue Clo. N14—6B 6
Avenue Clo. NW8—1C 60
Avenue Ct. N14—6B 6
Avenue Ct. NW2—3H 43

Balgowan St. SE18—4K 83
Balham Gro. SW12—7E 92
Balham High Rd.—3E 108
  SW12 1-197 & 2-222
  SW17 remainder
Balham Hill. SW12—7F 93
Balham New Rd. SW12—7F 93
Balham Pk. Rd. SW12—1D 108
Balham Rd. N9—2B 18
Balham Sta. Rd. SW12—1F 109
Baling Downs Ct. Gnfd—3A 56
Balkan Wlk. E1—7H 63 (1K 149)
Ballamore Rd. Brom—3J 113
Ballance Rd. E9—6K 47
Ballantine St. SW18—4A 92
Ballard Clo. King—7K 105
Ballards Clo. Dag—1H 69
Ballards Farm Rd. S Croy &
  Croy—6G 135
Ballards La.—1J 27
  N3 1-265 & 2-240
  N12 remainder
Ballards M. Edgw—6B 12
Ballards Rise. S Croy—6G 135
Ballards Rd. NW2—2C 42
Ballards Rd. Dag—1H 69
Ballards Way. S Croy & Croy
  —6G 135
Ballast Quay. SE10—5F 81
Ballater Rd. SW2—4J 93
Ballater Rd. S Croy—5F 135
Ballina St. SE23—7K 95
Ballingdon Rd. SW11—6E 92
Balliol Av. E4—4B 20
Balliol Rd. N17—1E 30
Balliol Rd. W10—6E 58
Balliol Rd. Well—2B 100
Balloch Rd. SE6—1F 113
Ballogie Av. NW10—4A 42
Ballow Clo. SE5—7E 78
Balls Pond Rd. N1—6D 46
Balmain Clo. W5—1D 72
Balmer Rd. E3—2B 64
Balmes Rd. N1—1D 62
Balmoral Av. Beck—4A 126
Balmoral Clo. SW15—6F 91
Balmoral Ct. Wemb—3F 41
Balmoral Dri. S'hall—4D 54
Balmoral Gdns. W13—3A 72
Balmoral Gdns. Bex—7F 101
Balmoral Gdns. IIf—1K 51
Balmoral Gro. N7—6K 45
Balmoral M. W12—3B 74
Balmoral Rd. E7—4A 50
Balmoral Rd. E10—2D 48
Balmoral Rd. NW2—6D 42
Balmoral Rd. Harr—4E 38
Balmoral Rd. King—4F 119
Balmoral Rd. Wor Pk—2D 130
Balmore Cres. Barn—5K 5
Balmore St. N19—2F 45
Balmuir Gdns. SW15—4E 90
Balnacraig Av. NW10—4A 42
Balniel Ga. SW1—5H 77
Baltic Centre. Bren—5D 72
Baltic Clo. SW19—7B 108
Baltic Ct. SE16—2K 79
Baltic St. EC1—4C 62 (4L 141)
Baltimore Pl. Well—2K 99
Balvaird Pl. SW1—5H 77
Balvernie Gro. SW18—7H 91
Bamborough Gdns. W12—2E 74
Bamford Av. Wemb—1F 57
Bamford Rd. Bark—6G 51
Bamford Rd. Brom—5E 112
Bampfylde Clo. Wall—3G 133
Bampton Rd. SE23—3K 111
Banavie Gdns. Beck—1E 126
Banbury Ct. Sutt—7J 131
Banbury Rd. E9—7K 47
Banbury St. SW11—2C 92
Banchory Rd. SE3—7K 81
Bancroft Av. N2—5C 28
Bancroft Ct. N'holt—1A 54
Bancroft Gdns. Harr—1G 23
Bancroft Gdns. Orp—7K 129

Bancroft Rd. E1
  —3K 63 (2M 143)
Bancroft Rd. Harr—2G 23
Bandon Rise. Wall—5H 133
Bangalore St. SW15—3F 91
Bangor Clo. N'holt—5F 39
Banim St. W6—4D 74
Banister Rd. W10—3F 59
Bank Av. Mitc—2B 122
Bank End. SE1—1C 78 (2M 147)
Bankfoot Rd. Brom—4G 113
Bankhurst Rd. SE6—7B 96
Bank La. SW15—5A 90
Bank La. King—7E 104
Bank M. Sutt—6A 132
Banksian Wlk. Iswth—1J 87
Banksia Rd. N18—5D 18
Bankside. SE1—7C 62 (1L 147)
Bankside. Enf—1G 7
Bankside. S'hall—1B 70
Bankside. S Croy—6F 135
Bankside Clo. Bex—4K 117
Bankside Clo. Cars—6C 132
Bankside Way. SE19—6E 110
Banks La. Bexh—4F 101
Bank, The. N6—1F 45
Bankton Rd. SW2—4A 94
Bankwell Rd. SE13—4G 97
Banner St. EC1—4C 62 (3M 141)
Banning St. SE10—5G 81
Bannister Clo. Gnfd—5H 39
Bannister Rd. SW2—1A 110
Bannockburn Rd. SE18—4J 83
Banstead Gdns. N9—3K 17
Banstead Rd. Cars—7B 132
Banstead Rd. S. Sutt—7B 132
Banstead St. SE15—3J 95
Banstead Way. Wall—5J 133
Banstock Rd. Edgw—6C 12
Banton Clo. Enf—2C 8
Bantry St. SE5—7D 78
Banwell Rd. Bex—6D 100
Banyard Rd. SE16
  —3H 79 (7K 149)
Baptist Gdns. NW5—6E 44
Barandon Wlk. W11—7F 59
Barbara Brosnan Ct. NW8
  —2B 60 (1A 138)
Barbauld St. N16—3E 46
Barber Clo. N21—7F 7
Barbers All. E13—3K 65
Barbers Rd. E15—2D 64
Barbican. EC2—5C 62 (5M 141)
Barbican Rd. Gnfd—6F 55
Barb M. W6—3E 74
Barbon Clo. WC1
  —5K 61 (5E 140)
Barbot Clo. N9—3B 18
Barchard St. SW18—5K 91
Barchester Clo. W7—1K 71
Barchester Rd. Harr—2H 23
Barchester St. E14—5D 64
Barclay Clo. SW6—7J 75
Barclay Oval. Wfd G—4D 20
Barclay Rd. E11—1H 49
Barclay Rd. E13—4A 66
Barclay Rd. E17—5E 32
Barclay Rd. N18—6J 17
Barclay Rd. SW6—7J 75
Barclay Rd. Croy—3D 134
Barclay Way. SE22—1G 111
Barcombe Av. SW2—2J 109
Barcombe Clo. Orp—3K 129
Barden St. SE18—7J 83
Bardfield Av. Romf—3D 36
Bardney Rd. Mord—4K 121
Bardolph Av. Croy—7B 136
Bardolph Rd. N7—4J 45
Bardolph Rd. Rich—3F 89
Bard Rd. W10—7F 59
Bardsey Pl. E1—4J 63 (4L 143)
Bardsey Wlk. N1—6C 46
Bardsley Clo. Croy—3F 135
Bardsley La. SE10—6E 80
Barfett St. W10—4H 59
Barfield Av. N20—2J 15
Barfield Rd. E11—1H 49

Barfield Rd. Brom—3E 128
Barford Clo. NW4—2C 26
Barford St. N1—1A 62
Barforth Rd. SE15—3H 95
Barfreston Way. SE20—1H 125
Bargate Clo. SE18—5K 83
Bargate Clo. N Mald—7C 120
Barge Ho. Rd. E16—2F 83
Barge Ho. St. SE1
  —1A 78 (2H 147)
Bargery Rd. SE6—1D 112
Barge Wlk. E Mol & King
  —6A 118
Barge Wlk. King—1D 118
Bargrove Clo. SE20—7G 111
Bargrove Cres. SE6—2B 112
Barham Clo. Brom—7C 128
Barham Clo. Chst—5F 115
Barham Clo. Romf—2H 37
Barham Clo. Wemb—6B 40
Barham Rd. SW20—7C 106
Barham Rd. Chst—5F 115
Barham Rd. S Croy—5C 134
Baring Clo. SE12—2J 113
Baring Rd. SE12—7J 97
Baring Rd. Barn—3G 5
Baring Rd. Croy—1G 135
Baring St. N1—1D 62
Barker Dri. NW1—7G 45
Barker St. SW10—6A 76
Barker Wlk. SW16—3H 109
Barker Way. SE22—7G 95
Barkham Rd. N17—7K 17
Barking Rd.—5H 65
  E16 1-233 & 2-242
  E13 remainder
Barkis Way. SE16—5H 79
Bark Pl. W2—7K 59
Barkston Gdns. SW5—4K 75
Barkwood Clo. Romf—5J 37
Barkworth Rd. SE16—5J 79
Barlborough St. SE14—7K 79
Barlby Gdns. W10—4F 59
Barlby Rd. W10—5E 58
Barleycorn Way. E14—7B 64
Barleyfields Clo. Romf—7B 36
Barley La. IIf & Romf—7A 36
Barley Mow Pas. W4—5K 73
Barlow Clo. Wall—6J 133
Barlow Rd. NW6—6H 43
Barlow Rd. W3—1H 73
Barlow Rd. Hmptn—7E 102
Barlow St. SE17
  —4D 78 (9B 148)
Barlow Way. Rain—5K 69
Barmeston Rd. SE6—2D 112
Barmor Clo. Harr—2F 23
Barmouth Av. Gnfd—2K 55
Barmouth Rd. SW18—6A 92
Barmouth Rd. Croy—2K 135
Barnabas Rd. E9—5K 47
Barnaby Clo. Harr—2G 39
Barnaby Way. Chig—3K 21
Barnard Clo. SE18—3E 82
Barnard Clo. Chst—1H 129
Barnard Clo. Wall—7H 133
Barnard Gdns. Hay—4A 54
Barnard Gdns. N Mald—4C 120
Barnard Gro. E15—7H 49
Barnard Hill. N10—1F 29
Barnard M. SW11—4C 92
Barnardo Dri. IIf—4G 35
Barnardo St. E1
  —6K 63 (8M 143)
Barnard Rd. SW11—4C 92
Barnard Rd. Enf—2C 8
Barnard Rd. Mitc—3E 122
Barnby Sq. E15—1G 65
Barnby St. E15—1G 65
Barnby St. NW1
  —2G 61 (1M 139)
Barn Clo. N'holt—2A 54
Barn Cres. Stan—6H 11
Barnehurst Av. Eri & Bexh
  —1J 101
Barnehurst Clo. Eri—1J 101
Barnehurst Rd. Bexh—2J 101

Barn Elms Pk. SW15—3E 90
Barnes Av. SW13—7C 74
Barnes Av. S'hall—4D 70
Barnes Clo. E12—4B 50
Barnes Ct. E16—5A 66
Barnes Ct. Wfd G—5G 21
Barnes End. N Mald—5C 120
Barnes High St. SW13—2B 90
Barnes Pikle. W5—7D 56
Barnes Rd. N18—4D 18
Barnes Rd. IIf—5G 51
Barnes St. E14—6A 64
Barnet By-Pass. NW7 & NW4
  —6G 13
Barnet Ga. La. Barn—1H 13
Barnet Gro. E2—3G 63 (1G 143)
Barnet Hill. Barn—4C 4
Barnet La. N20 & Barn—1C 14
Barnetts Ct. Harr—3F 39
Barnett St. E1—6H 63 (8J 143)
Barnet Way. NW7—3E 12
Barnet Wood Rd. Brom—2K 137
Barney Clo. SE7—5A 82
Barnfield. N Mald—6A 120
Barnfield Av. Croy—2J 135
Barnfield Av. King—4D 104
Barnfield Av. Mitc—3F 123
Barnfield Clo. N4—7J 29
Barnfield Gdns. King—4E 104
Barnfield Pl. E14—4C 80
Barnfield Rd. SE18—6F 83
  (in two parts)
Barnfield Rd. W5—4C 56
Barnfield Rd. Belv—6F 85
Barnfield Rd. Edgw—1J 25
Barnfield Rd. S Croy—7E 134
Barnfield Wood Clo. Beck
  —6F 127
Barnfield Wood Rd. Beck
  —6F 127
Barnham Rd. Gnfd—3G 55
Barnham St. SE1
  —2E 78 (4D 148)
Barnhill. Pinn—5A 22
Barn Hill. Wemb—1G 41
Barnhill Av. Brom—5H 127
Barnhill La. Hay—4A 54
Barnhill Rd. Hay—4A 54
Barnhill Rd. Wemb—3J 41
Barningham Way. NW9—6K 25
Barnlea Clo. Felt—2C 102
Barnmead Gdns. Dag—5F 53
Barnmead Rd. Beck—1K 125
Barnmead Rd. Dag—5F 53
Barn M. Harr—3E 38
Barn Rise. Wemb—1G 41
Barnsbury Clo. N Mald—4J 119
Barnsbury Gro. N7—7K 45
Barnsbury M. N1—7A 46
Barnsbury Pk. N1—7A 46
Barnsbury Rd. N1—1A 62
Barnsbury Sq. N1—7A 46
Barnsbury St. N1—7A 46
Barnsbury Ter. N1—7K 45
Barnscroft. SW20—3D 120
Barnsdale Av. E14—4D 80
Barnsdale Rd. W9—4H 59
Barnsley St. E1—4H 63 (3K 143)
Barnstaple Rd. Ruis—3A 38
Barn St. N16—2E 46
Barn Way. Wemb—1G 41
Barnwell Rd. SW2—5A 94
Barnwood Clo. W9—4K 59
Barnwood Ct. E16—1K 81
Baron Clo. N1—2A 62
Baroness Rd. E2
  —3F 63 (1F 142)
Baronet Gro. N17—1G 31
Baronet Rd. N17—1G 31
Baron Gdns. IIf—3G 35
Baron Gro. Mitc—4C 122
Baron Rd. Dag—1D 52
Baronsclere Ct. N6—7H 29
Baron's Ct. Rd. W14—5G 75
Baronsfield Rd. Twic—6B 88
Barons Ga. Barn—6H 5
Barons Keep. W14—5G 75

Barons Mead. Harr—4J 23
Baronsmead Rd. SW13—1C 90
Baronsmede. W5—2F 73
Baronsmere Rd. N2—4C 28
Baron's Pl. SE1—2A 78 (5H 147)
Barons, The. Twic—6B 88
Baron St. N1—2A 62
Baron Wlk. E16—5H 65
Baron Wlk. Mitc—4C 122
Barque M. SE8—6C 80
Barrack Rd. Houn—4B 86
Barratt Av. N22—2K 29
Barratt Industrial Pk. S'hall
—1E 70
Barratt Way. Harr—3H 23
Barrenger Rd. N10—1D 28
Barrets Grn. Rd. NW10—3J 57
Barrett Rd. E17—4E 32
Barrett's Gro. N16—5E 46
Barrett St. W1—6E 60 (8H 139)
Barrhill Rd. SW2—2J 109
Barriedale. SE14—2A 96
Barrie Est. W2—7B 60 (9A 138)
Barrier App. SE7—3B 82
Barringer Sq. SW17—4E 108
Barrington Clo. NW5—5E 44
Barrington Rd. E12—6E 50
Barrington Rd. N8—5H 29
Barrington Rd. SW9—3B 94
Barrington Rd. Bexh—2D 100
Barrington Rd. Sutt—2J 131
Barrington Vs. SE18—1E 98
Barrow Av. Cars—7D 132
Barrow Clo. N21—3G 17
Barrowdene Clo. Pinn—2C 22
Barrowell Grn. N21—2G 17
Barrowfield Clo. N9—3C 18
Barrowfield La. N9—3C 18
Barrowgate Rd. W4—5J 73
Barrow Hedges Clo. Cars
—7C 132
Barrow Hedges Way. Cars
—7C 132
Barrow Hill. Wor Pk—2A 130
Barrow Hill Clo. Wor Pk
—2A 130
Barrow Hill Rd. NW8
—2C 60 (1C 138)
Barrow Point Av. Pinn—2C 22
Barrow Point La. Pinn—2C 22
Barrs Rd. NW10—7K 41
Barry Av. N15—6F 31
Barry Av. Bexh—7E 84
Barry Rd. E6—6C 66
Barry Rd. NW10—7J 41
Barry Rd. SE22—6G 95
Barset Rd. SE15—3J 95
(in three parts)
Barsons Clo. SE20—7J 111
Barston Rd. SE27—3C 110
Barstow Cres. SW2—1K 109
Barter St. WC1—5J 61 (6D 140)
Barters Wlk. Pinn—3C 22
Bartholomew Clo. EC1
—5C 62 (6L 141)
Bartholomew Clo. SW18
—4A 92
Bartholomew La. EC2
—6D 62 (8B 142)
Bartholomew Rd. NW5—6G 45
Bartholomew Sq. E1
—4H 63 (3K 143)
Bartholomew Sq. EC1
—4C 62 (3M 141)
Bartholomew St. SE1
—3D 78 (7B 148)
Bartholomew Vs. NW5—6G 45
Barth Rd. SE18—4J 83
Bartle Av. E6—2C 66
Bartle Rd. W11—6G 59
Bartlett Clo. E14—6C 64
Bartlett Ct. EC4—6A 62 (7H 141)

Bartlett St. S Croy—5D 134
Bartlow Gdns. Romf—1K 37
Barton Av. Romf—1H 53
Barton Clo. E6—6D 66
Barton Clo. E9—5J 47
Barton Clo. SE15—3H 95
Barton Clo. Bexh—5E 100
Barton Ct. W14—5G 75
Barton Grn. N Mald—2K 119
Barton Meadows. Ilf—4F 35
Barton Rd. W14—5G 75
Barton Rd. Sidc—6E 116
Barton St. SW1—3J 77 (6C 146)
Bartram Rd. SE4—5A 96
Bartrams La. Barn—1F 5
Barwick Rd. E7—4K 49
Barwood Av. W Wick—1D 136
Basden Gro. Felt—2E 102
Basedale Rd. Dag—7B 52
Baseing Clo. E6—7E 66
Bashley Rd. NW10—4K 57
Basil Av. E6—3C 66
Basildene Rd. Houn—3B 86
Basildon Av. Ilf—1E 34
Basildon Clo. Sutt—7K 131
Basildon Rd. SE2—5A 84
Basil Gdns. Croy—1K 135
Basilon Rd. Bexh—2E 100
Basil St. SW3—3D 76 (6E 144)
Basing Clo. Th Dit—7A 118
Basing Ct. SE15—1F 95
Basingdon Way. SE5—4D 94
Basing Dri. Bex—6F 101
Basinghall Av. EC2
—6D 62 (7A 142)
Basinghall Gdns. Sutt—7K 131
Basinghall St. EC2
—6D 62 (7A 142)
Basing Hill. NW11—1H 43
Basing Hill. Wemb—2F 41
Basing Ho. Yd. E2
—3E 62 (1D 142)
Basing Pl. E2—3E 62 (1D 142)
Basing St. W11—6H 59
Basing Way. N3—3J 27
Basing Way. Th Dit—7A 118
Basire St. N1—1C 62
Baskerville Rd. SW18—7C 92
Basket Gdns. SE9—5C 98
Baslow Clo. Harr—1H 23
Baslow Wlk. E5—4K 47
Basnett Rd. SW11—3E 92
Bassano St. SE22—5F 95
Bassant Rd. SE18—6K 83
Bassein Pk. Rd. W12—2B 74
Bassett Gdns. Iswth—7G 71
Bassett Rd. W10—6F 59
Bassett St. NW5—6E 44
Bassett Way. Gnfd—6F 55
Bassingham Rd. SW18—7A 92
Bassingham Rd. Wemb—6D 40
Basswood Clo. SE15—3H 95
Bastable Av. Bark—2K 67
Bastion Rd. SE2—5A 84
Baston Mnr. Rd. Brom—4K 137
Baston Rd. Brom—2K 137
Bastwick St. EC1
—4C 62 (3L 141)
Basuto Rd. SW6—1J 91
Batavia M. SE14—7A 80
Batavia Rd. SE14—7A 80
Batchelor St. N1—1A 62
Bateman Clo. Bark—6G 51
Bateman Rd. E4—6H 19
Bateman's Row. EC2
—4E 62 (3D 142)
Bateman St. W1
—6H 61 (8A 140)
Bates Cres. Croy—5A 134
Bateson St. SE18—4J 83
Bate St. E14—7B 64
Bath Clo. SE15—1J 95
Bathgate Rd. SW19—3F 107
Bath Ho. Rd. Croy—1J 133
Bathhurst Rd. Ilf—1F 51
Bath Pas. King—2D 118
Bath Pl. EC1—3E 62 (2C 142)

Bath Pl. Barn—3C 4
Bath Rd. E7—6B 50
Bath Rd. N9—2D 18
Bath Rd. W4—4A 74
Bath Rd. Mitc—3B 122
Bath Rd. Romf—6E 36
Bath Rd. Houn—1A 86
Baths Rd. Brom—4B 128
Bath St. EC1—3C 62 (2M 141)
Bath Ter. SE1—3C 78 (6M 147)
Bathurst Av. SW19—1K 121
Bathurst Gdns. NW10—2D 58
Bathurst M. W2—7B 60 (9B 138)
Bathurst St. W2—7B 60 (9A 138)
Bathway. SE18—4E 82
Batley Pl. N16—3F 47
Batley Rd. N16—3F 47
Batley Rd. Enf—1H 7
Batman Clo. W12—1D 74
Batoum Gdns. W6—3E 74
Batson St. W12—2C 74
Batsworth Rd. Mitc—3B 122
Battenberg Wlk. SE19—6E 110
Batten Clo. E6—6D 66
Batten St. SW11—3C 92
Battersby Rd. SE6—2F 113
Battersea Bri. SW3 & SW11
—7B 76
Battersea Bri. Rd. SW11—7C 76
Battersea Chu. Rd. SW11
—1B 92
Battersea High St. SW11
—1B 92
Battersea Pk. Rd.—2C 92
SW8 1-179 & 2-18
SW11 remainder
Battersea Rise. SW11—5C 92
Battishill St. N1—7B 46
Battis, The. Romf—6K 37
Battle Bri. La. SE1
—1E 78 (2C 148)
Battle Bri. Rd. NW1—2J 61
Battle Clo. SW19—6A 108
Battledean Rd. N5—5B 46
Battle Rd. Belv & Eri—4J 85
Batty St. E1—6G 63 (7H 143)
Baudwin Rd. SE6—2G 113
Baugh Rd. Sidc—5C 116
Baulk, The. SW18—7J 91
Bavant Rd. SW16—2J 123
Bavaria Rd. N19—2J 45
Bavent Rd. SE5—2C 94
Bawdale Rd. SE22—5F 95
Bawdsey Av. Ilf—4K 35
Bawtree Rd. SE14—7A 80
Bawtry Rd. N20—3J 15
Baxendale. N20—2F 15
Baxendale St. E2
—3G 63 (1G 143)
Baxter Rd. E16—6A 66
Baxter Rd. N1—6D 46
Baxter Rd. N18—4C 18
Baxter Rd. Ilf—5F 51
Bayard Ct. Bexh—4H 101
Bayes Clo. SE26—5J 111
Bayfield Rd. SE9—4B 98
Bayford Rd. NW10—3F 59
Bayford St. E8—7H 47
Bayham Pl. NW1—2G 61
Bayham Rd. W4—3K 73
Bayham Rd. W13—7B 56
Bayham Rd. Mord—4K 121
Bayham St. NW1—1G 61
Bayley St. WC1—5H 61 (6A 140)
Bayley Wlk. SE2—5E 84
Baylin Rd. SW18—6K 91
Baylis Rd. SE1—2A 78 (5G 147)
Baylis Av. SE28—7D 68
Bayne Clo. E6—6D 66
Baynes Clo. Enf—1B 8
Baynes M. NW3—6B 44
Baynes St. NW1—7G 45
Bayonne Rd. SW6—6G 75
Bays Ct. Edgw—5C 12
Bayston Rd. N16—3F 47
Bayswater Rd. W2
—7K 59 (1A 144)

Baythorne St. E3—5B 64
(in two parts)
Bay Tree Clo. Brom—1A 128
Baytree Rd. SW2—4K 93
Bazalgette Clo. N Mald—5K 119
Bazalgette Gdns. N Mald
—5K 119
Bazely St. E14—7E 64
Bazile Rd. N21—6F 7
Beacham Clo. SE7—6B 82
Beachborough Rd. Brom
—4E 112
Beachcroft Rd. E11—3G 49
Beachcroft Way. N19—1H 45
Beach Gro. Felt—2E 102
Beachy Rd. E3—7C 48
Beacon Gro. Cars—4E 132
Beacon Hill. N7—5J 45
Beacon Rd. SE13—6F 97
Beacons Clo. E6—5C 66
Beaconsfield Clo. N11—5K 15
Beaconsfield Clo. SE3—6J 81
Beaconsfield Clo. W4—5J 73
Beaconsfield Rd. E10—3E 48
Beaconsfield Rd. E16—4H 65
Beaconsfield Rd. E17—6B 32
Beaconsfield Rd. N9—3B 18
Beaconsfield Rd. N11—3K 15
Beaconsfield Rd. N15—4E 30
Beaconsfield Rd. NW10—6B 42
Beaconsfield Rd. SE3—7H 81
Beaconsfield Rd. SE9—2C 114
Beaconsfield Rd. SE17—5E 78
Beaconsfield Rd. W4—3K 73
Beaconsfield Rd. W5—2D 72
Beaconsfield Rd. Bex—2K 117
Beaconsfield Rd. Brom—3B 128
Beaconsfield Rd. Croy—6D 124
Beaconsfield Rd. Hay—1A 54
Beaconsfield Rd. N Mald
—2K 119
Beaconsfield Rd. S'hall—1B 70
Beaconsfield Rd. Surb—7F 119
Beaconsfield Rd. Twic—6B 88
Beaconsfield Ter. Romf—6D 36
Beaconsfield Ter. Rd. W14
—3G 75
Beaconsfield Wlk. SW6—1J 91
Beacontree Av. E17—1F 33
Beacontree Rd. E11—7H 33
Beadlow Clo. Cars—6B 122
Beadman St. SE27—4B 110
Beadnell Rd. SE23—1K 111
Beadon Rd. W6—4E 74
Beadon Rd. Brom—4J 127
Beaford Gro. SW20—3G 121
Beak St. W1—7G 61 (9M 139)
Beal Clo. Well—1A 100
Beale Clo. N13—5G 17
Beale Pl. E3—2B 64
Beal Rd. Ilf—2E 50
Beam Av. Dag—1H 69
Beaminster Gdns. Ilf—3F 35
Beamish Dri. Bush, Wat—1B 10
Beamish Ga. NW1—7H 45
Beamish Rd. N9—1B 18
Beamway. Dag—7K 53
Beanacre Clo. E9—6B 48
Bean Rd. Bexh—4D 100
Beanshaw. SE9—4E 114
Beansland Gro. Romf—3E 36
Bear All. EC4—6B 62 (7J 141)
Beardell St. SE19—6F 111
Beardow Gro. N14—6B 6
Beard Rd. King—5F 105
Beardsfield. E13—2J 65
Beardsley Way. W3—2K 73
Bearfield Rd. King—7E 104
Bear Gdns. SE1—1C 78 (2L 147)
Bear Rd. Felt—4B 102
Bearstead Rise. SE4—5B 96
Bearsted Ter. Beck—1C 126
Bear St. WC2—7H 61 (9B 140)
Beatrice Av. SW16—2K 123
Beatrice Av. Wemb—5E 40

Beatrice Clo. E13—4J 65
Beatrice Rd. E17—5C 32
Beatrice Rd. N4—7A 30
Beatrice Rd. N9—7D 8
Beatrice Rd. SE1
　　　　　　—4G 79 (9H 149)
Beatrice Rd. Rich—5F 89
Beatson Wlk. SE16—1A 80
Beattock Rise. N10—4F 29
Beatty Rd. N16—4E 46
Beatty Rd. Stan—6H 11
Beatty St. NW1—2G 61
Beattyville Gdns. Ilf—4E 34
Beauchamp Clo. W4—3J 73
Beauchamp Pl. SW3
　　　　　　—3C 76 (7D 144)
Beauchamp Rd. E7—7K 49
Beauchamp Rd. SE19—1D 124
Beauchamp Rd. SW11—4C 92
Beauchamp Rd. Sutt—4J 131
Beauchamp Rd. Twic—7A 88
Beauchamp St. EC1
　　　　　　—5A 62 (5G 141)
Beauchamp Ter. SW15—3D 90
Beauclerc Rd. W6—3E 74
Beauclerk Clo. Felt—1A 102
Beaufort Av. Harr—4A 24
Beaufort Clo. E4—6J 19
Beaufort Clo. SW15—7D 90
Beaufort Clo. W5—5F 57
Beaufort Clo. Romf—4J 37
Beaufort Ct. Rich—4C 104
Beaufort Dri. NW11—4J 27
Beaufort Gdns. NW4—6E 26
Beaufort Gdns. SW3
　　　　　　—3C 76 (7D 144)
Beaufort Gdns. SW16—7K 109
Beaufort Gdns. Houn—1C 86
Beaufort Gdns. Ilf—1E 50
Beaufort Rd. W5—5F 57
Beaufort Rd. King—4E 118
Beaufort Rd. Rich—4C 104
Beaufort Rd. Twic—7C 88
Beaufort St. SW3—6B 76
Beaufort Way. Eps—7C 130
Beaufoy Rd. N17—7K 17
Beaufoy Wlk. SE11
　　　　　　—4K 77 (9F 146)
Beaulieu Av. SE26—4H 111
Beaulieu Clo. NW9—4A 26
Beaulieu Clo. SE5—3D 94
Beaulieu Clo. Mitc—1E 122
Beaulieu Clo. Twic—6D 88
Beaulieu Gdns. N21—7H 7
Beaulieu Pl. W4—3J 73
Beaumanor Gdns. SE9—4E 114
Beaumaris Dri. Wfd G—7G 21
Beaumont Av. W14—5H 75
Beaumont Av. Harr—6F 23
Beaumont Av. Rich—3F 89
Beaumont Av. Wemb—5C 40
Beaumont Clo. King—7G 105
Beaumont Ct. W4—5J 73
Beaumont Cres. W14—5H 75
Beaumont Gdns NW3—2J 43
Beaumont Gro. E1
　　　　　　—4K 63 (4M 143)
Beaumont M. W1
　　　　　　—5E 60 (5H 139)
Beaumont Pl. W1
　　　　　　—4G 61 (3M 139)
Beaumont Pl. Barn—1C 4
Beaumont Pl. Iswth—6C 87
Beaumont Rise. N19—1H 45
Beaumont Rd. E10—7D 32
(in two parts)
Beaumont Rd. E13—3K 65
Beaumont Rd. SE19—6C 110
Beaumont Rd. SW19—7G 91
Beaumont Rd. W4—3J 73
Beaumont Rd. Orp—6H 129
Beaumont Sq. E1
　　　　　　—5K 63 (5M 143)
Beaumont St. W1
　　　　　　—5E 60 (5H 139)

Beaumont Wlk. NW3—7D 44
Beauvais Ter. N'holt—3B 54
Beauval Rd. SE22—6F 95
Beaverbank Rd. SE9—1H 115
Beaver Clo. SE20—7G 111
Beaver Clo. Hmptn—7F 103
Beavercote Wlk. Belv—5F 85
Beaver Gro. N'holt—3C 54
Beavers Cres. Houn—4A 86
Beavers La. Houn—3A 86
Beaverwood Rd. Chst—5J 115
Beavor La. W6—4C 74
Bebbington Rd. SE18—4J 83
Beccles Dri. Bark—6J 51
Beccles St. E14—7B 64
Bec Clo. Ruis—3B 38
Beck Clo. SE13—1D 96
Beckenham Business Centre.
　　　　　　Beck—6A 112
Beckenham Gdns. N9—3K 17
Beckenham Gro. Brom—2F 127
Beckenham Hill Est. Beck
　　　　　　—5D 112
Beckenham Hill Rd.—6D 112
　　SE6 1-95 & 2-62
　　Beck remainder
Beckenham La. Brom—2G 127
Beckenham Pl. Pk. Beck
　　　　　　—7D 112
Beckenham Rd. Beck—1K 125
Beckenham Rd. W Wick
　　　　　　—7E 126
Becket Av. E6—3E 66
Becket Clo. SE25—6G 125
Becket Rd. N18—4D 18
Becket St. SE1—3D 78 (6A 148)
Beckett Clo. NW10—6A 42
Beckett Clo. SW16—2H 109
Beckett Clo. Belv—3F 85
Becketts Clo. Felt—6A 86
Becketts Pl. Tedd—1D 118
Beckett Wlk. Beck—6A 112
Beckford Pl. SE17—5C 78
Beckford Rd. Croy—6F 125
Beck La. Beck—3K 125
Becklow Rd. W12—2B 74
Beck River Pk. Beck—1C 126
Beck Rd. E8—1H 63
Becks Rd. Sidc—3A 116
Beckton Rd. E16—5H 65
Beck Way. Beck—3B 126
Beckway Rd. SW16—2H 123
Beckway St. SE17
　　(in two parts)—4E 78 (9C 148)
Beckwith Rd. SE24—5D 94
Beclands Rd. SW17—6E 108
Becmead Av. SW16—4H 109
Becmead Av. Harr—5B 24
Becondale Rd. SE19—5E 110
Becontree Av. Dag—4B 52
Bective Pl. SW15—4H 91
Bective Rd. E7—4J 49
Bective Rd. SW15—4H 91
Becton Pl. Eri—1H 101
Becton Retail Pk. E6—5E 66
Bedale Rd. Enf—1H 7
Bedale St. SE1—1D 78 (3A 148)
Beddington Farm Rd Croy
　　　　　　—7J 123
Beddington Gdns. Cars—6E 132
Beddington Gdns. Wall—6F 133
Beddington Grn. Orp—1K 129
Beddington Gro Wall—5H 133
Beddington La. Croy—6G 123
Beddington Pk. Cotts. Wall
　　　　　　—3H 133
Beddington Path. Orp—1K 129
Beddington Rd. Ilf—7K 35
Beddington Rd. Orp—1J 129
Bede Clo. Pinn—1B 22
Bedens Rd. Sidc—6E 116
Bede Rd. Romf—6C 36
Bedfont Clo. Mitc—2E 122
Bedford Av. WC1
　　　　　　—5H 61 (6B 140)
Bedford Av Barn—5C 4

Bedford Av. Hay—6A 54
Bedfordbury. WC2
　　　　　　—7J 61 (1C 146)
Bedford Clo. N10—7K 15
Bedford Ct. WC2
　　　　　　—7J 61 (1C 146)
Bedford Gdns. W8—1J 75
Bedford Hill—1F 109
　　SW12 1-203 & 2-210
　　SW16 remainder
Bedford Pk. Croy—1C 134
Bedford Pk. Corner. W4—4A 74
Bedford Pas. W1
　　　　　　—5G 61 (5M 139)
Bedford Pl. WC1—5J 61 (5C 140)
Bedford Pl. Croy—1D 134
Bedford Rd. E6—1E 66
Bedford Rd. E17—2C 32
Bedford Rd. E18—2J 33
Bedford Rd. N2—3C 28
Bedford Rd. N8—6H 29
Bedford Rd. N9—7C 8
Bedford Rd. N15—4E 30
Bedford Rd. N22—2J 29
Bedford Rd. NW7—2F 13
Bedford Rd. SW4—4J 93
Bedford Rd. W4—3K 73
Bedford Rd. W13—7B 56
Bedford Rd. Harr—6G 23
Bedford Rd. Ilf—3F 51
Bedford Rd. Sidc—3J 115
Bedford Rd. Twic—3H 103
Bedford Rd. Wor Pk—2E 130
Bedford Row. WC1
　　　　　　—5K 61 (5F 140)
Bedford Sq. WC1
　　　　　　—5H 61 (6B 140)
Bedford St. WC2
　　　　　　—7J 61 (9C 140)
Bedford Way. WC1
　　　　　　—4H 61 (4B 140)
Bedgebury Gdns. SW19
　　　　　　—2G 107
Bedgebury Rd. SE9—4B 98
Bedivere Rd. Brom—3J 113
Bedlow Way. Croy—4K 133
Bedonwell Rd.—4D 84
　　SE2 365-397 & 402-434
　　Belv & Bexh remainder
Bedser Dri. Gnfd—5H 39
Bedwardine Rd. SE19—7E 110
Bedwell Rd. N17—1E 30
Bedwell Rd. Belv—5G 85
Bedwin Way. SE16—5H 79
Beeby Rd. E16—5K 65
Beech Av. N20—1H 15
Beech Av. W3—1A 74
Beech Av. Bren—7B 72
Beech Av. Buck H—2E 20
Beech Av. Ruis—1A 38
Beech Av. Sidc—7A 100
Beech Clo. N9—6C 8
Beech Clo. SE8—6C 80
Beech Clo. SW15—7C 90
Beech Clo. SW19—6E 106
Beech Clo. Cars—2D 132
Beech Copse. Brom—2D 128
Beech Copse. S Croy—5E 134
Beech Ct. E17—3F 33
Beech Ct. Surb—7D 118
Beechcroft. Chst—7E 114
Beechcroft Av. NW11—7H 27
Beechcroft Av. Bexh—1K 101
Beechcroft Av. Harr—7E 22
Beechcroft Av. N Mald—2J 119
Beechcroft Av. S'hall—1D 70
Beechcroft Clo SW16—5K 109
Beechcroft Clo Houn—7C 70
Beechcroft Rd. N5—4B 46
Beech Croft Dr. N5—4B 46
Beechcroft Gdns. Wemb—3F 41
Beechcroft Rd. E18—2K 33
Beechcroft Rd. SW14—3J 89
Beechcroft Rd. SW17—2C 108
Beechdale N21—2E 16
Beechdale Rd. SW2—6K 93
Beech Dri N2—2D 28

Beechen Cliff Way. Iswth
　　　　　　—2K 87
Beechen Gro. Pinn—3D 22
Beechen Pl. SE23—2K 111
Beeches Av. Cars—7C 132
Beeches Clo. SE20—1J 125
Beeches Rd. SW17—3C 108
Beeches Rd. Sutt—1G 131
Beeches, The. S Croy—5D 134
Beeches Wlk. Cars—7B 132
Beechfield Gdns. Romf—7J 37
Beechfield Rd. N4—6C 30
Beechfield Rd. SE6—1B 112
Beechfield Rd. Brom—2A 128
Beechfield Rd. Eri—7K 85
Beech Gdns. W5—2E 72
Beech Gro. Mitc—5H 123
Beech Gro. N Mald—3K 119
Beech Hall Cres. E4—7A 20
Beech Hall Rd. E4—7K 19
Beech Hill. Barn—1G 5
Beech Hill Av. Barn—1F 5
Beech Ho. Rd. Croy—3D 134
Beechill Rd. SE9—5E 98
Beech La. Buck H—2E 20
Beech Lawns. N12—5G 15
Beechmont Clo. Brom—5G 113
Beechmore Gdns. Sutt—2F 131
Beechmore Rd. SW11—1D 92
Beechmount Av. W7—5A 55
Beecholme Av. Mitc—1F 123
Beech Rd. N11—6D 16
Beech Rd. SW16—3K 123
Beechrow. King—4E 104
Beech St. EC2—5C 62 (5L 141)
Beech St. Romf—4J 37
Beechtree Clo. Stan—5H 11
Beech Tree Glade. E4—1C 20
Beech Tree Pl. Sutt—5K 131
Beechvale Clo. N12—5H 15
Beech Wlk. NW7—6F 13
Beech Way. NW10—7K 41
Beechway. Bex—6D 100
Beech Way. Twic—3E 102
Beechwood Av. N3—3H 27
Beechwood Av. Gnfd—3F 55
Beechwood Av. Harr—3F 39
Beechwood Av. Rich—1G 89
Beechwood Av. T Hth—4B 124
Beechwood Circ. Harr—3G 39
Beechwood Clo. NW7—5F 13
Beechwood Clo. Surb—7D 118
Beechwood Cres. Bexh—3E 100
Beechwood Dri. Wfd G—5C 20
Beechwood Gdns. NW10—3F 57
Beechwood Gdns. Harr—3F 39
Beechwood Gdns. Ilf—5D 34
Beechwood Gro. W3—7A 58
Beechwood Gro. Surb—7C 118
Beechwood M. N9—2B 18
Beechwood Pk. E18—3J 33
Beechwood Rise. Chst—4F 115
Beechwood Rd. E8—6F 47
Beechwood Rd. N8—3H 29
Beechwood Rd. S Croy—7E 134
Beechwoods Ct. SE19—6F 111
Beechworth Clo. NW3—2K 43
Beecroft Rd. SE4—5A 96
Beehive La. Ilf—5D 34
Beehive Pl. SW9—3A 94
Beeleigh Rd. Mord—4K 121
Beeston Clo. E8—5G 47
Beeston Pl. SW1
　　　　　　—3F 77 (6K 145)
Beeston Rd. Barn—6G 5
Beeston Way. Felt—6A 86
Beethoven St. W10—3G 59
Beeton Clo. Pinn—1E 22
Begbie Rd. SE3—1A 98
Beggars Hill. Eps—7B 130
Begonia Pl. Hmptn—6E 102
Begonia Wlk. W12—6B 58
Beira St. SW12—7F 93
Bekesbourne St. E14—6A 64
Belasis Av. SW2—2J 109
Belcroft Clo Brom—7H 113

162

Belfairs Dri. Romf—7C 36
Belfast Gdns. SE3—6H 81
Belfast Rd. N16—2F 47
Belfast Rd. SE25—4H 125
Belfield Rd. Eps—7A 130
Belfont Wlk. N7—4J 45
Belford Gro. SE18—4E 82
Belfort Rd. SE15—2J 95
Belgrade Rd. N16—4E 46
Belgrave Clo. N14—5B 6
Belgrave Clo. W3—2H 73
Belgrave Ct. W4—5J 73
Belgrave Cres. Sun—7A 102
Belgrave Gdns. N14—4C 6
Belgrave Gdns. NW8—1K 59
Belgrave Gdns. Stan—5H 11
Belgrave M. N. SW1
—2E 76 (5G 145)
Belgrave M. S. SW1
—3E 76 (6H 145)
Belgrave M. W. SW1
—3E 76 (6G 145)
Belgrave Pl. SW1
—3E 76 (7H 145)
Belgrave Rd. E10—1E 48
Belgrave Rd. E11—2J 49
Belgrave Rd. E13—4A 66
Belgrave Rd. E17—5C 32
Belgrave Rd. SE25—4F 125
Belgrave Rd. SW1
—4F 77 (8K 145)
Belgrave Rd. SW13—7B 74
Belgrave Rd. Houn—3D 86
Belgrave Rd. Ilf—1D 50
Belgrave Rd. Mitc—3B 122
Belgrave Rd. Sun—7A 102
Belgrave Sq. SW1
—3E 76 (6G 145)
Belgrave St. E1—6K 63
Belgrave Ter. Wfd G—3D 20
Belgrave Wlk. Mitc—3B 122
Belgravia Gdns. Brom—6B 113
Belgravia M. King—4D 118
Belgrove St. WC1
—3J 61 (1C 140)
Belinda Rd. SW9—3B 94
Belitha Vs. N1—7K 45
Bellamy Clo. W14—5H 75
Bellamy Dri. Stan—1B 24
Bellamy Rd. E4—6J 19
Bellamy Rd. Ent—2J 7
Bellamy St. SW12—7F 93
Bell Clo. Pinn—3A 22
Bell Dri. SW18—7G 91
Bellefields Rd. SW9—3K 93
Bellegrove Clo. Well—2K 99
Bellegrove Pde. Well—3K 99
Bellegrove Rd. Well—2J 99
Bellenden Rd. SE15—2F 95
Bellestaines Pleasaunce. E4
—2H 19
Belleville Rd. SW11—5C 92
Belle Vue La. Bush, Wat—1C 10
Bellevue Pk. T Hth—3C 124
Bellevue Pl. E1—4J 63 (4L 143)
Belle Vue Rd. E17—2F 33
Bellevue Rd. N11—4K 15
Belle Vue Rd. NW4—4E 26
Bellevue Rd. SW13—2C 90
Bellevue Rd. SW17—1C 108
Bellevue Rd. W13—4B 56
Bellevue Rd. Bexh—5F 101
Bellevue Rd. King—4E 118
Bellew St. SW17—3A 108
Bell Farm Av. Dag—3J 53
Bellfield. Croy—7A 136
Bellfield Av. Harr—6C 10
Bellflower Clo. E6—5C 66
Bellgate M. NW5—4F 45
Bell Grn. SE26—4B 112
Bell Grn. La. SE26—5B 112
Bell Hill. Croy—2C 134
Bell Ho. Rd. Romf—1J 53
Bellingham Grn. SE6—3C 112
Bellingham Rd. SE6—3D 112
Bell Inn Yd EC3—6D 62 (8B 142)

Bell Junct. Houn—3F 87
Bell La. E1—5F 63 (6E 142)
Bell La. E16—1J 81
Bell La. NW4—4E 26
Bell La. Enf—1E 8
Bell La. Twic—1A 104
Bell Meadow. SE19—5E 110
Bellot St. SE10—5G 81
Bellring Clo. Belv—6G 85
Bell Rd. Enf—1J 7
Bell Rd. Houn—3F 87
Bells All. SW6—2J 91
Bells Hill. Barn—5A 4
Bell St. NW1—5C 60 (5C 138)
Bell Trees Gro. SW16—5K 109
Bell Water Ga. SE18—3E 82
Bell Wharf La. EC4
—7C 62 (1M 147)
Bellwood Rd. SE15—4K 95
Bell Yd. WC2—6A 62 (8G 141)
Belmont Av. N9—1B 18
Belmont Av. N13—5E 16
Belmont Av. N17—3E 30
Belmont Av. Barn—5J 5
Belmont Av. N Mald—5C 120
Belmont Av. S'hall—3C 70
Belmont Av. Well—3J 99
Belmont Av. Wemb—1F 57
Belmont Circ. Harr—1B 24
Belmont Clo. E4—5A 20
Belmont Clo. N20—1E 14
Belmont Clo. SW4—3G 93
Belmont Clo. Barn—4J 5
Belmont Clo. Wfd G—4E 20
Belmont Ct. NW11—5H 27
Belmont Gro. SE13—3F 97
Belmont Hill. SE13—3F 97
Belmont La. Chst—5G 115
Belmont La. Stan—7H 11
Belmont Pk. SE13—4F 97
Belmont Pk. Clo. SE13—4G 97
Belmont Pk. Rd. E10—6D 32
Belmont Rise. Sutt—7H 131
Belmont Rd.—4C 30
N15 1-47 & 2-46
N17 remainder
Belmont Rd. SE25—5H 125
Belmont Rd. SW4—3G 93
Belmont Rd. W4—4K 73
Belmont Rd. Beck—2B 126
Belmont Rd. Chst—5F 115
Belmont Rd. Eri—7G 85
Belmont Rd. Harr—4K 23
Belmont Rd. Ilf—3G 51
Belmont Rd. Twic—2H 103
Belmont Rd. Wall—5F 133
Belmont St. NW1—7E 44
Belmont Ter. W4—4K 73
Belmore La. N7—5H 45
Belmore St. SW8—1H 93
Beloe Clo. SW13—3C 90
Belsham St. E9—6J 47
Belsize Av. N13—6E 16
Belsize Av. NW3—5B 44
Belsize Av. W13—3B 72
Belsize Ct. NW3—5B 44
Belsize Cres. NW3—5B 44
Belsize Gdns. Sutt—4K 131
Belsize Gro. NW3—6C 44
Belsize La. NW3—5B 44
Belsize M. NW3—6B 44
Belsize Pk. NW3—6B 44
Belsize Pk. Gdns. NW3—6C 44
Belsize Pk. M. NW3—6B 44
Belsize Pl. NW3—5B 44
Belsize Rd. NW6—1K 59
Belsize Rd. Harr—7C 10
Belsize Sq. NW3—6B 44
Belsize Ter. NW3—6B 44
Belson Rd. SE18—4D 82
Beltane Dri. SW19—3F 107
Beltham Wlk. SE5—1D 94
Belthorn Cres. SW12—7G 93
Belton Rd. E7—7K 49
Belton Rd. E11—4G 49
Belton Rd. N17—3E 30

Belton Rd. NW2—6C 42
Belton Rd. Sidc—4A 116
Belton Way. E3—5C 64
Beltran Rd. SW6—2K 91
Beltwood Rd. Belv—4J 85
Belvedere Av. SW19—5G 107
Belvedere Av. Ilf—2F 35
Belvedere Bldgs. SE1
—2B 78 (5K 147)
Belvedere Clo. Tedd—5J 103
Belvedere Dri. SW19—5G 107
Belvedere Gro. SW19—5G 107
Belvedere Pl. SE1
—2B 78 (5K 147)
Belvedere Rd. E10—1A 48
Belvedere Rd. SE1
—2K 77 (4F 146)
Belvedere Rd. SE2—1C 84
Belvedere Rd. SE19—7F 111
Belvedere Rd. W7—3K 71
Belvedere Rd. Bexh—8F 101
Belvedere Sq. SW19—5G 107
Belvedere Strand NW9—2B 26
Belvedere Way. Harr—6E 24
Belvoir Clo. SE9—3C 114
Belvoir Rd. SE22—7G 95
Belvue Clo. N'holt—7E 38
Belvue Rd. N'holt—7E 38
Bembridge Clo. NW6—7G 43
Bemerton Est. N1—7J 45
Bemerton St. N1—1K 61
Bemish Rd. SW15—3F 91
Bemsted Rd. E17—3B 32
Benares Rd. SE18—4K 83
Benbow Rd. W6—3D 74
Benbow St. SE8—6C 80
Benbury Clo. Brom—5E 112
Bench Field. S Croy—5F 135
Bench, The. Rich—3C 104
Bencroft Rd. SW16—7G 109
Bencurtis Pk. W Wick—3F 137
Bendemeer Rd. SW15—3F 91
Bendish Rd. E6—7C 50
Bendmore Av. SE2—5A 84
Bendon Valley. SW18—7K 91
Benedict Clo. Belv—3E 84
Benedict Rd. SW9—3K 93
Benedict Rd. Mitc—3B 122
Benedict Way. N2—3A 28
Benenden Grn. Brom—5J 127
Benett Gdns. SW16—2J 123
Benfleet Clo. Sutt—3A 132
Bengal Rd. Ilf—3F 51
Bengarth Dri. Harr—2H 23
Bengarth Rd. N'holt—1C 54
Bengeworth Rd. SE5—3C 94
Bengeworth Rd. Harr—3A 40
Ben Hale Clo. Stan—5G 11
Benham Clo. SW11—3B 92
Benham Gdns. Houn—5D 86
Benham Rd. W7—5J 55
Benhill Av. Sutt—4K 131
(in two parts)
Benhill Rd. SE5—7D 78
Benhill Rd. Sutt—3A 132
Benhill Wood Rd. Sutt—3A 132
Benhilton Gdns. Sutt—3K 131
Benhurst Ct. SW16—5A 110
Benhurst La. SW16—5A 110
Benin St. SE13—7F 97
Benjafield Clo. N18—4C 18
Benjamin Clo. E8—1G 63
Benjamin Clo. Horn—6F 85
Benjamin St. EC1
—5B 62 (5J 141)
Ben Jonson Rd. E1—5A 64
Benledi St. E14—6F 65
Bennerley Rd. SW11—5C 92
Bennets Copse. Chst—6C 114
Bennet's Hill. EC4
—7C 62 (9L 141)
Bennet St. SW1—1G 77 (2L 145)
Bennett Clo. King—1C 118
Bennett Clo. Well—2A 100
Bennett Gro. SE13—1D 96
Bennett Pk. SE3—3H 97
Bennett Rd. E13—4A 66

Bennett Rd. Romf—7E 36
Bennetts Av. Croy—2A 136
Bennetts Av. Gnfd—1J 55
Bennett's Castle La. Dag
—2C 52
Bennetts Clo. N17—6B 18
Bennett St. N16—4E 46
Bennett St. W4—6A 74
Bennetts Way. Croy—2A 136
Bennett's Yd. SW1
—3H 77 (7B 146)
Benningholme Rd. Edgw
—6F 13
Bennington Rd. N17—1E 30
Bennington Rd. Wfd G—7B 20
Benn St. E9—6A 48
Benns Wlk. Rich—4E 88
Benrek Clo. Ilf—1G 35
Bensbury Clo. SW15—7D 90
Bensham Clo. T Hth—4C 124
Bensham Gro. T Hth—2C 124
Bensham La. Croy & T Hth
—7B 124
Bensham Mnr. Rd. T Hth
—4C 124
Bensley Clo. N11—5J 15
Ben Smith Way. SE16
—3G 79 (6H 149)
Benson Av. E6—2B 66
Benson Clo. Houn—4E 86
Benson Quay. E1
—7J 63 (1L 149)
Benson Rd. SE23—1J 111
Benson Rd. Croy—3A 134
Bentall Centre, The. King
—2E 118
Bentfield Gdns. SE9—3B 114
Benthal Rd. N16—3G 47
Bentham Rd. E9—6K 47
Bentham Rd. SE28—1B 84
Bentham Wlk. NW10—5J 41
Ben Tillet Clo. Bark—7A 52
Bentinck M. W1—6E 60 (7H 139)
Bentinck St. W1—6E 60 (7H 139)
Bentley Dri. Ilf—6G 35
Bentley Rd. N1—6E 46
Bentley Way. Stan—5F 11
Bentley Way. Wfd G—3D 20
Benton Rd. Ilf—1H 51
Bentons La. SE27—4C 110
Bentons Rise. SE27—5D 110
Bentry Clo. Dag—2E 52
Bentry Rd. Dag—2E 52
Bentworth Rd. W12—6D 58
Benwell Rd. N7—5A 46
Benwick Clo. SE16
—4H 79 (8K 149)
Benworth St. E3—3B 64
Berber Rd. SW11—5D 92
Bercta Rd. SE9—2G 115
Berens Rd. NW10—3F 59
Berens Way. Chst—4K 129
Beresford Av. N20—2J 15
Beresford Av. W7—5H 55
Beresford Av. Surb—7H 119
Beresford Av. Twic—6C 88
Beresford Av. Wemb—1F 57
Beresford Dri. Brom—3C 128
Beresford Dri. Wfd G—4F 21
Beresford Gdns. Enf—4K 7
Beresford Gdns. Houn—5D 86
Beresford Gdns. Romf—5E 36
Beresford Rd. E4—1B 20
Beresford Rd. E17—1D 32
Beresford Rd. N2—3C 28
Beresford Rd. N5—5D 46
Beresford Rd. N8—5A 30
Beresford Rd. Harr—5H 23
Beresford Rd. King—1F 119
Beresford Rd. N Mald—4J 119
Beresford Rd. S'hall—1B 70
Beresford Rd. Sutt—7H 131
Beresford Sq. SE18—4F 83
Beresford St. SE18—3D 83
Beresford Ter. N5—5C 46
Berestede Rd. W6—5B 74

163

Bere St. E1—7K 63
Berger Clo. Orp—6H 129
Berger Rd. E9—6K 47
Bergholt Av. Ilf—5C 34
Bergholt Cres. N16—7E 30
Bergholt M. NW1—7G 45
Bering Wlk. E16—6B 66
Berkeley Av. Bexh—1D 100
Berkeley Av. Gnfd—6G 39
Berkeley Av. Ilf—2E 34
Berkeley Av. Romf—1J 37
Berkeley Clo. Bren—6A 72
Berkeley Clo. King—7E 104
Berkeley Clo. Orp—7J 129
Berkeley Ct. N14—6B 6
Berkeley Ct. Surb—7D 118
Berkeley Cres. Barn—5G 5
Berkeley Gdns. N21—7J 7
Berkeley Gdns. W8—1J 75
Berkeley M. W1—6D 60 (8F 138)
Berkeley Pl. SW19—6F 107
Berkeley Rd. E12—5C 50
Berkeley Rd. N8—5H 29
Berkeley Rd. N15—6D 30
Berkeley Rd. NW9—4G 25
Berkeley Rd. SW13—1C 90
Berkeley Sq. W1
              —7F 61 (1K 145)
Berkeley St. W1—1F 77 (2K 145)
Berkeley Waye. Houn—6B 70
Berkhampstead Rd. Belv
              —5G 85
Berkhamsted Av. Wemb—6F 41
Berkley Gro. NW1—7E 44
Berkley Rd. NW1—7D 44
Berkshire Gdns. N13—6F 17
Berkshire Gdns. N18—5C 18
Berkshire Rd. E9—6B 48
Berkshire Way. Mitc—4J 123
Bermans Way. NW10—4A 42
Bermondsey Sq. SE1
              —3E 78 (6D 148)
Bermondsey St. SE1
              —2E 78 (4C 148)
Bermondsey Wall E. SE16
              —2H 79 (5J 149)
Bermondsey Wall W. SE16
              —2G 79 (4G 149)
Bernal Clo. SE28—7D 68
Bernard Av. W13—3B 72
Bernard Cassidy St. E16—5H 65
Bernard Gdns. SW19—5H 107
Bernard Rd. N15—5F 31
Bernard Rd. Romf—7J 37
Bernard Rd. Wall—4F 133
Bernard St. WC1
              —4J 61 (4C 140)
Bernays Clo. Stan—6H 11
Bernay's Gro. SW9—4K 93
Bernel Dri. Croy—3B 136
Berne Rd. T Hth—5C 124
Berners Dri. W13—7A 56
Berners M. W1—5G 61 (6M 139)
Berners Pl. W1—6G 61 (7M 139)
Berners Rd. N1—1B 62
Berners Rd. N22—2A 30
Berners St. W1—5G 61 (6M 139)
Berney Rd. Croy—7D 124
Bernville Way. Harr—5F 25
Bernwell Rd. E4—3B 20
Berridge Grn. Edgw—7B 12
Berridge Rd. SE19—5D 110
Berriman Rd. N7—3K 45
Berriton Rd. Harr—1D 38
Berrybank Clo. E4—2K 19
Berry Clo. N21—1G 17
Berry Clo. NW10—7A 42
Berry Ct. Houn—5D 86
Berrydale Rd. Hay—4C 54
Berry Field Clo. E17—4D 32
Berryfield Clo. Brom—2C 128
Berryfield Rd. SE17—5B 78
Berryhill. SE9—4F 99
Berry Hill. Stan—4J 11
Berryhill Gdns. SE9—4F 99
Berrylands. SW20—3E 120
Berrylands. Surb—6F 119

Berry La. SE21—4D 110
Berryman Clo. Dag—3C 52
Berryman's La. SE26—4K 111
Berrymead Gdns. W3—2J 73
Berrymede Rd. W4—3K 73
Berry Pl. EC1—3B 62 (2K 141)
Berry St. EC1—4B 62 (3K 141)
Berry Way. W5—3E 72
Bertal Rd. SW17—4B 108
Berthon St. SE8—7C 80
Bertie Rd. NW10—6C 42
Bertie Rd. SE26—6K 111
Bertram Cotts. SW19—7J 107
Bertram Rd. NW4—6C 26
Bertram Rd. Enf—4B 8
Bertram Rd. King—7G 105
Bertrand St. SE13—3D 96
Bertrand Way. SE28—7C 68
Bert Rd. T Hth—5C 124
Berwick Av. Hay—6B 54
Berwick Clo. Stan—6E 10
Berwick Cres. Sidc—7J 99
Berwick Rd. E16—6K 65
Berwick Rd. N22—1B 30
Berwick Rd. Well—1B 100
Berwick St. W1—6G 61 (8M 139)
Berwyn Av. Houn—1F 87
Berwyn Rd. SE24—1B 110
Berwyn Rd. Rich—4H 89
Beryl Av. E6—5C 66
Beryl Rd. W6—5F 75
Berystede. King—7H 105
Besant Rd. NW2—4G 43
Besant Wlk. N7—2K 45
Besant Way. NW10—5J 41
Besley St. SW16—6G 109
Bessborough Gdns. SW1
              —5H 77 (9B 146)
Bessborough Pl. SW1—5H 77
Bessborough Rd. SW15
              —1C 106
Bessborough Rd. Harr—7H 23
Bessborough St. SW1
              —5H 77 (9A 146)
Bessemer Rd. SE5—2C 94
Bessie Landsbury Clo. E6
              —6E 66
Besson St. SE14—1K 95
Bessy St. E2—3J 63 (1L 143)
Bestwood St. SE8—4K 79
Beswick M. NW6—5K 43
Betchworth Clo. Sutt—5B 132
Betchworth Rd. Ilf—2J 51
Betchworth Way. Croy—7E 136
Betham Rd. Gnfd—4H 55
Bethecar Rd. Harr—5J 23
Bethel Av. Ilf—7E 34
Bethell Av. E16—4H 65
Bethel Rd. Well—3C 100
Bethersden Clo. Beck—7B 112
Bethnal Grn. Rd.
              —4F 63 (3E 142)
E1 1-99 & 2-94
E2 remainder
Bethune Av. N11—4J 15
Bethune Clo. N16—1E 46
Bethune Rd. N16—7D 30
Bethune Rd. NW10—4K 57
Bethwin Rd. SE5—7B 78
Betjeman Clo. Pinn—4E 22
Betony Clo. Croy—1K 135
Betoyne Av. E4—4B 20
Betstyle Cir. N11—4A 16
Betstyle Rd. N11—4A 16
Betterton Dri. Sidc—2E 116
Betterton Rd. Rain—3K 69
Betterton St. WC2
              —6J 61 (8D 140)
Bettons Pk. E15—1G 65
Bettridge Rd. SW6—2H 91
Betts Clo. Beck—2A 126
Betts Rd. E16—7K 65
Betts St. E1—7H 63 (9J 143)
Betts Way. SE20—1H 125
Betts Way. Surb—7B 118

Beulah Av. T Hth—2C 124
Beulah Clo. Edgw—3C 12
Beulah Cres. T Hth—2C 124
Beulah Gro. Croy—6C 124
Beulah Hill. SE19—7B 110
Beulah Rd. E17—5D 32
Beulah Rd. SW19—7H 107
Beulah Rd. Sutt—4J 131
Beulah Rd. T Hth—3C 124
Bevan Av. Bark—7A 52
Bevan Ct. Croy—5A 134
Bevan Rd. SE2—5B 84
Bevan Rd. Barn—4J 5
Bevan St. N1—1C 62
Bevenden St. N1
              —3D 62 (1B 142)
Beveridge Rd. NW10—7A 42
Beverley Av. SW20—1B 120
Beverley Av. Houn—4D 86
Beverley Av. Sidc—7K 99
Beverley Clo. SW11—4B 92
Beverley Clo. SW13—2C 90
Beverley Clo. Enf—4K 7
Beverley Ct. N14—7B 6
Beverley Ct. SE4—3B 96
Beverley Ct. SW4—5J 73
Beverley Cres. Wfd G—1K 33
Beverley Dri. Edgw—3G 25
Beverley Gdns. NW11—7G 27
Beverley Gdns. SW13—3B 90
Beverley Gdns. Stan—1A 24
Beverley Gdns. Wemb—1F 41
Beverley Gdns. Wor Pk—1C 130
Beverley La. SW15—3B 106
Beverley La. King—7A 106
Beverley Path. SW13—2B 90
Beverley Rd. E4—6A 20
Beverley Rd. E6—3B 66
Beverley Rd. SE20—2H 125
Beverley Rd. SW13—3B 90
Beverley Rd. W4—5B 74
Beverley Rd. Bexh—2J 101
Beverley Rd. Dag—4E 52
Beverley Rd. King—1C 118
Beverley Rd. Mitc—4H 123
Beverley Rd. N Mald—4C 120
Beverley Rd. Ruis—3A 38
Beverley Rd. S'hall—4C 70
Beverley Rd. Sun—3A 38
Beverley Rd. Wor Pk—2E 130
Beverley Way. King & SW20
              —1B 120
Beversbrook Rd. N19—3H 45
Beverstone Rd. SW2—5K 93
Beverstone Rd. T Hth—4A 124
Bevill Allen Clo. SW17—5D 108
Bevin Clo. SE16—1A 80
Bevington Rd. W10—5G 59
Bevington Rd. Beck—2D 126
Bevington St. SE16
              —2G 79 (5H 149)
Bevin Way. WC1
              —2A 62 (1G 141)
Bevis Marks. EC3
              —6E 62 (7D 142)
Bewcastle Gdns. Enf—4D 6
Bewdley St. N1—7A 46
Bewick St. SW8—2F 93
Bewley St. E1—7J 63 (9L 143)
Bewlys Rd. SE27—5B 110
Bexhill Clo. Felt—2C 102
Bexhill Rd. N11—5C 16
Bexhill Rd. SE4—6B 96
Bexhill Rd. SW14—3J 89
Bexhill Wlk. E15—1G 65
Bexley Gdns. N9—3J 17
Bexley High St. Bex—7G 101
Bexley La. Dart—5K 101
Bexley La. Sidc—4C 116
Bexley Rd. SE9—5F 99
Bexley Rd. Eri—7J 85
(in two parts)
Beynon Rd. Cars—5D 132
Bianca Rd. SE15—6G 79
Bibsworth Rd. N3—2H 27
Bibury Clo. SE15—6E 78

Bicester Rd. Rich—3G 89
Bickenhall St. W1
              —5D 60 (5F 138)
Bickersteth Rd. SW17—6D 108
Bickerton Rd. N19—2G 45
Bickley Cres. Brom—4C 128
Bickley Pk. Rd. Brom—3C 128
Bickley Rd. E10—7D 32
Bickley Rd. Brom—2B 128
Bickley St. SW17—5C 108
Bicknell Rd. SE5—3C 94
Bicknoller Rd. Enf—1A 8
Bicknor Rd. Orp—7K 129
Bidborough Clo. Brom—5H 127
Bidborough St. WC1
              —3J 61 (2C 140)
Biddenden Way. SE9—4E 114
Bidder St. E16—5G 65
(in two parts)
Biddestone Rd. N7—4K 45
Biddulph Rd. W9—3K 59
Bideford Av. Gnfd—2B 56
Bideford Clo. Edgw—1G 25
Bideford Clo. Felt—3D 102
Bideford Gdns. Enf—7K 7
Bideford Rd. Brom—3H 113
Bideford Rd. Enf—1G 9
Bideford Rd. Ruis—3A 38
Bideford Rd. Well—7B 84
Bidwell Gdns. N11—7B 16
Bidwell St. SE15—1H 95
Bigbury Clo. N17—7K 17
Biggerstaff Rd. E15—1E 64
Biggerstaff St. N4—2A 46
Biggin Av. Mitc—1D 122
Biggin Hill. SE19—7B 110
Biggin Way. SE19—7B 110
Bigginwood Rd. SW16—7B 110
Biggs Row. SW15—3F 91
Big Hill. E5—1H 47
Bigland Est. E1—6H 63 (8J 143)
Bigland St. E1—6H 63 (8J 143)
Bignell Rd. SE18—5F 83
Bignold Rd. E7—4J 49
Bigwood Ct. NW11—5K 27
Bigwood Rd. NW11—5K 27
Billet Clo. Romf—3D 36
Billet Rd. E17—1K 31
Billet Rd. Romf—3B 36
Bill Hamling Clo. SE9—2D 114
Billingford Clo. SE4—4K 95
Billing Pl. SW10—7K 75
Billing St. SW10—7K 75
Billing Rd. SW10—7K 75
Billingsgate. E14—7C 64
Billington Rd. SE14—7K 79
Billiter St. EC3—6E 62 (8D 142)
Billson St. E14—4E 80
Bilsby Gro. SE9—4B 114
Bilton Rd. Gnfd—1A 56
Bilton Way. Enf—1F 9
Bina Gdns. SW5—4A 76
Bincote Rd. Enf—3E 6
Binden Rd. W12—3B 74
Bindon Grn. Mord—4K 121
Binfield Rd. SW4—1J 93
Binfield Rd. S Croy—5F 135
Bingfield St. N1—1J 61
(in two parts)
Bingham Pl. W1—5E 60 (5G 139)
Bingham Rd. Croy—1G 135
Bingham St. N1—6D 46
Bingley Rd. E16—6A 66
Bingley Rd. Gnfd—4G 55
Binney St. W1—6E 60 (8H 139)
Binns Rd. W4—5A 74
Binsey Wlk. SE2—2C 84
Binyon Cres. Stan—5E 10
Birbetts Rd. SE9—2D 114
Birchanger Rd. SE25—5G 125
Birch Av. N13—3H 17
Birch Clo. E16—5G 65
Birch Clo. N19—2G 45
Birch Clo. SE15—2G 95
Birch Clo. Bren—7B 72
Birch Clo. Buck H—3G 21
Birch Clo. Romf—3H 37

Birch Clo. Tedd—5A 104
Birchdale Gdns. Romf—7D 36
Birchdale Rd. E7—5A 50
Birchdene Dri. SE28—1A 84
Birchen Clo. NW9—2K 41
Birchend Clo. S Croy—6D 134
Birchen Gro. NW9—2K 41
Birches Clo. Mitc—3D 122
Birches Clo. Pinn—5C 22
Birches, The. N21—6E 6
Birches, The. SE7—6K 81
Birchfield St. E14—7C 64
Birch Gdns. Dag—3J 53
Birch Grn. NW9—7F 13
Birch Gro. SE12—7H 97
Birch Gro. W3—1G 73
Birch Gro. Well—4A 100
Birch Hill. Croy—5K 135
Birchington Clo. Bexh—1H 101
Birchington Rd. N8—6H 29
Birchington Rd. NW6—1J 59
Birchington Rd. Surb—7F 119
Birchin La. EC3—6D 62 (8B 142)
Birchlands Av. SW12—7D 92
Birchmead Av. Pinn—4A 22
Birchmere Row. SE3—2H 97
Birchmore Wlk. N5—3C 46
(in two parts)
Birch Pk. Harr—7B 10
Birch Rd. Felt—5B 102
Birch Rd. Romf—3H 37
Birch Row. Brom—7E 128
Birch Tree Av. W Wick—5H 137
Birch Tree Way. Croy—2H 135
Birch Wlk. Eri—6J 85
Birch Wlk. Mitc—1F 123
Birchwood Av. N10—3E 28
Birchwood Av. Beck—4B 126
Birchwood Av. Sidc—3B 116
Birchwood Av. Wall—3E 132
Birchwood Clo. Mord—4K 121
Birchwood Ct. N13—5G 17
Birchwood Ct. Edgw—2J 25
Birchwood Dri. NW3—3K 43
Birchwood Dri. Dart—4K 117
Birchwood Gro. Hmptn—6E 102
Birchwood Rd. SW17—5F 109
Birchwood Rd. Orp—4H 129
Birchwood Rd. Swan & Dart
—7J 117
Birdbrook Clo. Dag—7J 53
Birdbrook Rd. SE3—3A 98
Birdcage Wlk. SW1
—2G 77 (5M 145)
Birdham Clo. Brom—5C 128
Birdhurst Av. S Croy—4D 134
Birdhurst Gdns. S Croy—4D 134
Birdhurst Rise. S Croy—5E 134
Birdhurst Rd. SW18—5A 92
Birdhurst Rd. SW19—6C 108
Birdhurst Rd. S Croy—5E 134
Bird-in-Bush Rd. SE15—7G 79
Bird in Hand La. Brom—2B 128
Bird-in-Hand Pas. SE23—2J 111
Birdlip Clo. SE15—6E 78
Birds Farm Av. Romf—1H 37
Bird St. W1—6E 60 (8H 139)
Bird Wlk. Twic—1D 102
Birdwood Clo. Tedd—4J 103
Birkbeck Av. W3—7J 57
Birkbeck Av. Gnfd—1G 55
Birkbeck Gdns. Wfd G—2D 20
Birkbeck Gro. W3—2K 73
Birkbeck Hill. SE21—1B 110
Birkbeck Pl. SE21—2C 110
Birkbeck Rd. E8—5F 47
Birkbeck Rd. N8—4J 29
Birkbeck Rd. N12—5F 15
Birkbeck Rd. N17—1F 31
Birkbeck Rd. NW7—5G 13
Birkbeck Rd. SW19—5K 107
Birkbeck Rd. W3—1K 73
Birkbeck Rd. W5—4C 72
Birkbeck Rd. Beck—2J 125
Birkbeck Rd. Enf—1J 7
Birkbeck Rd. Ilf—5H 35
Birkbeck Rd. Romf—1K 53

Birkbeck Rd. Sidc—3A 116
Birkbeck St. E2—3H 63 (2K 143)
Birkbeck Way. Gnfd—1H 55
Birkdale Av. Pinn—3E 22
Birkdale Clo. Orp—7H 129
Birkdale Rd. SE2—4A 84
Birkdale Rd. W5—4E 56
Birkenhead Av. King—2F 119
Birkenhead St. WC1
—3J 61 (1D 140)
Birkhall Rd. SE6—1F 113
Birkwood Clo. SW12—7H 93
Birley Rd. N20—2F 15
Birley St. SW11—2E 92
Birling Rd. Eri—7K 85
Birnam Rd. N4—2K 45
Birnbeck Ct. NW11—5H 27
Birnbeck Ct. Barn—4A 4
Birse Cres. NW10—3A 42
Birstall Rd. N15—5E 30
Biscay Rd. W6—5F 75
Biscoe Clo. Houn—6E 70
Biscoe Way. SE13—3F 97
Bisenden Rd. Croy—2E 134
Bisham Clo. Cars—1D 132
Bisham Gdns. N6—1E 44
Bishop Clo. W4—5J 73
Bishop Ken Rd. Harr—2K 23
Bishop King's Rd. W14—4G 75
Bishop Rd. N14—7A 6
Bishop's Av. E13—1K 65
Bishop's Av. SW6—2F 91
Bishops Av. Brom—2A 128
Bishops Av. Romf—6C 36
Bishops Av., The. N2—6B 28
Bishop's Bri. Rd. W2—6K 59
Bishops Clo. E17—4D 32
Bishop's Clo. SE9—2G 115
Bishops Clo. Barn—6A 4
Bishops Clo. Enf—2C 8
Bishops Clo. Rich—3D 104
Bishop's Clo. Sutt—3J 131
Bishops Ct. Rich—3E 88
Bishopsford Rd. Mord—7A 122
Bishopsgate. EC2
—6E 62 (7C 142)
Bishopsgate Chu. Yd. EC2
—6E 62 (7C 142)
Bishops Gro. N2—6C 28
Bishop's Gro. Hmptn—4D 102
Bishop's Hall. King—2D 118
Bishop's Pk. Rd. SW6—2F 91
Bishop's Pk. Rd. SW16—1J 123
Bishops Rd. N6—6E 28
Bishop's Rd. SW6—1H 91
Bishop's Rd. SW11—7C 76
Bishop's Rd. W7—2J 71
Bishop's Rd. Croy—7B 124
Bishop's Ter. SE11
—4A 78 (8H 147)
Bishopsthorpe Rd. SE26
—4K 111
Bishop St. N1—1C 62
Bishops Wlk. Chst—1G 129
Bishops Wlk. Croy—5K 135
Bishops Wlk. Pinn—3C 22
Bishop's Way. E2
—2H 63 (1J 143)
Bishops Way. NW10—7A 42
Bishopswood Rd. N6—7D 28
Bisley Clo. Wor Pk—1E 130
Bispham Rd. NW10—3F 57
Bisson Rd. E15—2E 64
Bisterne Av. E17—3F 33
Bittacy Clo. NW7—6A 14
Bittacy Hill. NW7—6A 14
Bittacy Pk. Av. NW7—5A 14
Bittacy Rise. NW7—6K 13
Bittacy Rd. NW7—6A 14
Bittern Pl. N22—2K 29
Bittern St. SE1—2C 78 (5L 147)
Bittoms, The. King—3D 118
Bixley Clo. S'hall—4D 70
Blackall St. EC2—4E 62 (3C 142)
Blackberry Farm Clo. Houn
—7C 70
Blackbird Hill. NW9—2J 41

Blackborne Rd. Dag—6G 53
Black Boy La. N15—5C 30
Blackbrook La. Brom—5E 128
Blackburne's M. W1
—7E 60 (9G 139)
Blackburn Rd. NW6—6K 43
Blackbush Av. Romf—5D 36
Blackbush Clo. Sutt—7K 131
Blackett St. SW15—3F 91
Black Fan Clo. Enf—1H 7
Blackfen Rd. Sidc—5J 99
Blackford Clo. S Croy—7B 134
Blackford's Path. SW15—7C 90
Blackfriars Bri. SE1 & EC4
—7B 62 (1J 147)
Black Friars La. EC4
—6B 62 (8J 141)
Blackfriars Pas. EC4
—7B 62 (9J 141)
Blackfriars Rd. SE1
—2B 78 (5J 147)
Black Gates. Pinn—3D 22
Blackheath Av. SE10—7F 81
Blackheath Gro. SE3—2H 97
Blackheath Hill. SE10—1E 96
Blackheath Pk. SE3—3H 97
Blackheath Rise. SE13—2E 96
Blackheath Rd. SE10—1D 96
Blackheath Vale. SE3—2G 97
Blackheath Village. SE3—3H 97
Blackhorse La. E17—2K 31
Black Horse La. Croy—7G 125
Blackhorse Rd. E17—4K 31
Blackhorse Rd. SE8—6A 80
Blackhorse Rd. Sidc—4A 116
Blacklands Rd. SE6—4E 112
Blacklands Ter. SW3
—4D 76 (9F 144)
Black Lion La. W6—4C 74
Blackmore Av. S'hall—1H 71
Blackmore Rd. Buck H—1H 21
Blackmore's Gro. Tedd—6A 104
Black Path. E10—7K 31
Blackpool Rd. SE15—2H 95
Black Prince Rd. SE1 & SE11
—4K 77 (9E 146)
Blackshaw Pl. N1—7E 46
Blackshaw Rd. SW17—4A 108
Blacksmiths Clo. Romf—6C 36
Blacks Rd. W6—4E 74
Blackstock M. N4—2B 46
Blackstock Rd.—2B 46
N4 3-175 & 2-158a
N5 remainder
Blackstone Est. E8—7H 47
Blackstone Rd. NW2—5E 42
Black Swan Yd. SE1
—2E 78 (4D 148)
Blackthorn Ct. Houn—7C 70
Blackthorne Av. Croy—1J 135
Blackthorne Dri. E4—4A 20
Blackthorn Gro. Bexh—3E 100
Blackthorn St. E3—4C 64
Blacktree M. SW9—3A 94
Blackwall La. SE10—5G 81
Blackwall Tunnel—1F 81
Blackwall Tunnel App. E14
—7E 64
Blackwall Tunnel Northern
App. E3 & E14—2D 64
Blackwall Tunnel Southern
App. SE10—3G 81
Blackwall Way. E14—7E 64
(in two parts)
Blackwater Clo. Rain—5K 69
Blackwater Rd. Sutt—4K 131
Blackwater St. SE22—5F 95
Blackwell Clo. E5—4K 47
Blackwell Clo. Harr—7C 10
Blackwell Gdns. Edgw—4B 12
Blackwood St. SE17
—5D 78 (9A 148)
Blade M. SW15—4H 91
Bladindon Dri. Bex—7C 100
Bladon Gdns. Harr—6F 23
Blagdens Clo. N14—2C 16
Blagdens La. N14—2C 16

Blagdon Rd. SE13—6D 96
Blagdon Rd. N Mald—4B 120
Blagdon Wlk. Tedd—6C 104
Blagrove Rd. W10—5G 59
Blair Av. NW9—7A 26
Blair Clo. N1—6C 46
Blair Clo. Sidc—5J 99
Blair Ct. Beck—1D 126
Blairderry Rd. SW2—2J 109
Blair St. E14—6E 64
Blake Av. Bark—1J 67
Blake Clo. Well—1J 99
Blake Gdns. SW6—1K 91
Blake Hall Cres. E11—1J 49
Blake Hall Rd. E11—7J 33
Blakehall Rd. Cars—6D 132
Blakeley Cotts. SE10—2F 81
Blakemore Rd. SW16—3J 109
Blakemore Rd. T Hth—5K 123
Blakemore Way. Belv—3E 84
Blakeney Av. Beck—1B 126
Blakeney Clo. E8—5G 47
Blakeney Clo. N20—1F 15
Blakeney Rd. NW1—7H 45
Blakeney Rd. Beck—7B 112
Blakenham Rd. SW17—4D 108
Blake Rd. E16—4H 65
Blake Rd. N11—7B 16
Blake Rd. Croy—2E 134
Blake Rd. Mitc—3C 122
Blaker Rd. E15—1E 64
Blakes Av. N Mald—5B 120
Blakes Grn. W Wick—1E 136
Blakes La. N Mald—5B 120
Blakesley Av. W5—5C 56
Blakesley Wlk. SW20—2H 121
Blake's Rd. SE15—7E 78
Blakes Ter. N Mald—5C 120
Blakesware Gdns. N9—7J 7
Blakewood Clo. Felt—4A 102
Blanchard Clo. SE9—3C 114
Blanchard Way. E8—6G 47
Blanch Clo. SE15—7J 79
Blanchedowne. SE5—4D 94
Blanche St. E16—4H 65
Blanchland Rd. Mord—5K 121
Blandfield Rd. SW12—7E 92
Blandford Av. Beck—2A 126
Blandford Av. Twic—1F 103
Blandford Clo. N2—4A 28
Blandford Clo. Croy—3J 133
Blandford Clo. Romf—4G 37
Blandford Cres. E4—7K 9
Blandford Rd. W4—3A 74
Blandford Rd. W5—2D 72
Blandford Rd. Beck—2K 125
Blandford Rd. S'hall—4E 70
Blandford Rd. Tedd—5H 103
Blandford Sq. NW1
—4C 60 (4D 138)
Blandford St. W1
—5E 60 (6G 139)
Bland St. SE9—4B 98
Blaney Cres. E6—3F 67
Blanmerle Rd. SE9—1F 115
Blann Clo. SE9—6B 98
Blantyre St. SW10—7B 76
Blashford St. SE13—7F 97
Blasker Wlk. E14—5D 80
Blawith Rd. Harr—4J 23
Blaydon Clo. N17—7C 18
Blaydon Wlk. N17—7C 18
Bleak Hill La. SE18—6K 83
Blean Gro. SE20—7J 111
Bleasdale Av. Gnfd—2A 56
Blechynden St. W10—7F 59
Bleddyn Clo. Sidc—6C 100
Bledlow Clo. SE28—7C 68
Bledlow Rise. Gnfd—2G 55
Blegborough Rd. SW16—6G 109
Blendon Dri. Bex—6D 100
Blendon Path. Brom—7H 113
Blendon Rd. Bex—6D 100
Blendon Ter. SE18—5G 83
Blendworth Way. SE15—7E 78
Blenheim Av. Ilf—6E 34

Blenheim Clo. N21—1H 17
Blenheim Clo. SW20—3E 120
Blenheim Clo. Gnfd—2H 55
Blenheim Clo. Romf—4J 37
Blenheim Clo. Wall—7G 133
Blenheim Ct. N19—2J 45
Blenheim Ct. Sidc—3H 115
Blenheim Cres. W11—7G 59
Blenheim Cres. S Croy—7C 134
Blenheim Dri. Well—1K 99
Blenheim Gdns. NW2—6E 42
Blenheim Gdns. SW2—6K 93
Blenheim Gdns. King—7H 105
Blenheim Gdns. Wall—7G 133
Blenheim Gdns. Wemb—3E 40
Blenheim Gro. SE15—2G 95
Blenheim Pk. Rd. S Croy
　　　　　　　　—7C 134
Blenheim Pas. NW8—2A 60
Blenheim Rise. N15—4F 31
Blenheim Rd. E6—3B 66
Blenheim Rd. E15—4G 49
Blenheim Rd. E17—3K 31
Blenheim Rd. NW8—2A 60
Blenheim Rd. SE20—7J 111
Blenheim Rd. SW20—3E 120
Blenheim Rd. W4—3A 74
Blenheim Rd. Barn—3A 4
Blenheim Rd. Brom—4C 128
Blenheim Rd. Harr—6F 23
Blenheim Rd. N'holt—6F 39
Blenheim Rd. Sidc—1C 116
Blenheim Rd. Sutt—3K 131
Blenheim Shopping Centre.
　　　　　　　　SE20—7J 111
Blenheim St. W1
　　　　　　　　—6F 61 (8J 139)
Blenheim Ter. NW8—2A 60
Blenkarne Rd. SW11—6D 92
Bleriot Rd. Houn—7A 70
Blessbury Rd. Edgw—1J 25
Blessington Clo. SE13—3F 97
Blessington Rd. SE13—3F 97
Bletchingley Clo. T Hth—4B 124
Bletchley St. N1
　　　　　　　　—2C 62 (1M 141)
Bletsoe Wlk. N1—2C 62
Blincoe Clo. SW19—2F 107
Bliss Cres. SE13—2D 96
Blissett St. SE10—1E 96
Blisworth Clo. Hay—4C 54
Blithbury Rd. Dag—6B 52
Blithdale Rd. SE2—4A 84
Blithfield St. W8—3K 75
Blockley Rd. Wemb—2B 40
Bloemfontein Av. W12—1D 74
Bloemfontein Rd. W12—7D 58
Blomfield Rd. W9
　　　　　　　　—5K 59 (4A 138)
Blomfield St. EC2
　　　　　　　　—5D 62 (6B 142)
Blomfield Vs. W2—5K 59
Blomville Rd. Dag—3F 53
Blondel St. SW11—2E 92
Blondin Av. W5—4C 72
Blondin St. E3—2C 64
Bloomburg St. SW1
　　　　　　　　—4H 77 (9A 146)
Bloomfield Cres. Ilf—6F 35
Bloomfield Rd. N6—6E 28
Bloomfield Rd. SE18—5F 83
Bloomfield Rd. Brom—5B 128
Bloomfield Rd. King—3E 118
Bloomfield Ter. SW1
　　　　　　　　—5E 76 (9H 145)
Bloom Gro. SE27—3B 110
Bloomhall Rd. SE19—5D 110
Bloom Pk. Rd. SW6—7H 75
Bloomsbury Clo. W5—7F 57
Bloomsbury Ct. Pinn—3D 22
Bloomsbury Pl. SW18—5A 92
Bloomsbury Pl. WC1
　　　　　　　　—5J 61 (5D 140)
Bloomsbury Sq. WC1
　　　　　　　　—5J 61 (6D 140)
Bloomsbury St. WC1
　　　　　　　　—5H 61 (6B 140)

Bloomsbury Way.WC1
　　　　　　　　—5J 61 (6C 140)
Blore Clo. SW8—1H 93
Blossom Clo. W5—2E 72
Blossom Clo. S Croy—5F 135
Blossom La. Enf—1H 7
Blossom St. E1—4E 62 (4D 142)
Blossom Waye. Houn—6C 70
Blount St. E14—6A 64
Bloxam Gdns. SE9—5C 98
Bloxhall Rd. E10—1B 48
Bloxham Cres. Hmptn—7D 102
Bloxworth Clo. Wall—3G 133
Blucher Rd. SE5—7C 78
Blue Anchor All. Rich—4E 88
Blue Anchor La. SE16
　　　　　　　　—4G 79 (8H 149)
Blue Anchor Yd. E1
　　　　　　　　—7G 63 (9G 143)
Blue Ball Yd. SW1
　　　　　　　　—1G 77 (3L 145)
Bluebell Clo. SE26—4F 111
Bluebell Clo. Wall—1F 133
Bluefield Clo. Hmptn—5E 102
Bluehouse Rd. E4—3B 20
Blue Riband Est. Croy—2B 134
Blundell Rd. Edgw—1K 25
Blundell St. N7—7J 45
Blunden Clo. Dag—1C 52
Blunt Rd. S Croy—5D 134
Blunts Rd. SE9—5E 98
Blurton Rd. E5—4J 47
Blyth Clo. E14—4F 81
Blyth Clo. Twic—7K 87
Blythe Clo. SE6—7B 96
Blythe Hill. SE6—7B 96
Blythe Hill. Orp—1K 129
Blythe Hill La. SE6—7B 96
Blythe Rd. W14—3F 75
Blythe St. E2—3H 63 (1J 143)
Blyth Rd. E17—7B 32
Blyth Rd. SE28—7C 68
Blyth Rd. Brom—1H 127
Blythswood Rd. Ilf—1A 52
Blythwood Rd. N4—7J 29
Blythwood Rd. Pinn—1B 22
Boade's M. NW3—4B 44
Boadicea St. N1—1K 61
Boakes Clo. NW9—4J 25
Boardman Av. E4—5J 9
Boars Head Yd. Bren—7D 72
Boathouse Wlk. SE15—7G 79
Bob Anker Clo. E13—3J 65
Bobbin Clo. SW4—3G 93
Bob Marley Way. SW4—4A 94
Bockhampton Rd. King—7F 105
Bocking St. E8—1H 63
Boddicott Clo. SW19—2G 107
Bodiam Clo. Enf—2K 7
Bodiam Rd. SW16—7H 109
Bodley Clo. N Mald—5A 120
Bodley Mnr. Way. SW2—7A 94
Bodley Rd. N Mald—6K 119
Bodmin Clo. Harr—3D 38
Bodmin Gro. Mord—5K 121
Bodmin St. SW18—1J 107
Bodnant Gdns. SW20—3C 120
Bodney Rd. E8—5H 47
Boeing Way. S'hall—3A 70
Boevey Path. Belv—5F 85
Bognor Rd. Well—1D 100
Bohemia Pl. E8—6J 47
Bohun Gro. Barn—6H 5
Boileau Rd. SW13—7C 74
Boileau Rd. W5—6F 57
Bolden St. SE8—2D 96
Bolderwood Way. W Wick
　　　　　　　　—2D 136
Boldmore Rd. Pinn—7A 22
Boleyn Av. Enf—1C 8
Boleyn Clo. E17—4C 32
Boleyn Ct. Buck H—1D 20
Boleyn Dri. Ruis—2B 38
Boleyn Gdns. Dag—7J 53
Boleyn Gdns. W Wick—2D 136
Boleyn Gro. W Wick—2E 136

Boleyn Rd. E6—2B 66
Boleyn Rd. E7—7J 49
Boleyn Rd. N16—5E 46
Boleyn Way. Barn—3F 5
Bolina Rd. SE16—5J 79
Bolingbroke Gro. SW11—5C 92
Bolingbroke Rd. W14—3F 75
Bolingbroke Wlk. SW11—1C 92
Bollo Bri. Rd. W3—3H 73
Bollo La.—2H 73
　　W4 1-95 & 2-100
　　W3 remainder
Bolney Ga. SW7—2C 76 (5C 144)
Bolney St. SW8—7K 77
Bolney Way. Felt—3C 102
Bolsover St. W1—4F 61 (4K 139)
Bolstead Rd. Mitc—1F 123
Bolt Ct. EC4—6A 62 (8H 141)
Boltmore Clo. NW4—3F 27
Bolton Clo. SE20—2G 125
Bolton Cres. SE5—7B 78
Bolton Gdns. NW10—7F 59
Bolton Gdns. SW5—5K 75
Bolton Gdns. Brom—6H 113
Bolton Gdns. Tedd—6A 104
Bolton Gdns. M. SW10—5A 76
Bolton Rd. E15—6H 49
Bolton Rd. N18—5A 18
Bolton Rd. NW8—1K 59
Bolton Rd. NW10—1A 58
Bolton Rd. W4—7J 73
Bolton Rd. Harr—4G 23
Boltons, The. SW10—5A 76
Boltons, The. Wemb—4K 39
Bolton St. W1—1F 77 (2K 145)
Bombay St. SE16
　　　　　　　　—4H 79 (8J 149)
Bomore Rd. W11—7G 59
Bonar Pl. Chst—7C 114
Bonar Rd. SE15—7G 79
Bonchester Clo. Chst—7E 114
Bonchurch Clo. Sutt—7K 131
Bonchurch Rd. W10—5G 59
Bonchurch Rd. W13—1B 72
Bondfield Rd. E6—5D 66
Bond Gdns. Wall—4G 133
Bonding Yd. Wlk. SE16—3A 80
Bond Rd. Mitc—2C 122
Bond St. E15—5G 49
Bond St. (New) W1
　　　　　　　　—6F 61 (8J 139)
Bond St. (Old) W1
　　　　　　　　—7G 61 (1L 145)
Bond Way. SW8—6J 77
Boneta Rd. SE18—3D 82
Bonfield Rd. SE13—4E 96
Bonham Gdns. Dag—2D 52
Bonham Rd. SW2—5K 93
Bonham Rd. Dag—2D 52
Bonheur Rd. W4—2G 73
Bonhill St. EC2—4D 62 (4B 142)
Boniface Gdns. Harr—7A 10
Boniface Wlk. Harr—7A 10
Bon Marche Ter. SE27—4E 110
Bonner Hill Rd. King—2F 119
Bonner Rd. E2—2J 63
Bonnersfield Clo. Harr—6K 23
Bonnersfield La. Harr—6K 23
Bonner St. E2—2J 63 (1M 143)
Bonneville Gdns. SW4—6G 93
Bonnington Sq. SW8—6K 77
Bonny St. NW1—7G 45
Bonser Rd. Twic—2K 103
Bonsor St. SE5—7E 78
Bonville Rd. Brom—5H 113
Booker Clo. E14—5B 64
Booker Rd. N18—5B 18
Boone Ct. N9—3D 18
Boones Rd. SE13—4G 97
Boone St. SE13—4G 97
Boord St. SE10—3G 81
Boothby Ct. E4—3K 19
Boothby Rd. N19—1H 45
Booth Clo. SE28—1B 84
Booth Rd. NW9—2K 25

Booth Rd. Croy—2B 134
Booth's Pl. W1—5G 61 (6M 139)
Boot St. N1—3E 62 (2C 142)
Bordars Rd. W7—5J 55
Bordars Wlk. W7—5J 55
Borden Av. Enf—6J 7
Border Cres. SE26—5H 111
Border Gdns. Croy—4D 136
Bordergate. Mitc—1D 122
Border Rd. SE26—5H 111
Bordesley Rd. Mord—4K 121
Bordon.Wlk. SW15—7C 90
Boreham Av. E16—6J 65
Boreham Clo. E11—1E 48
Boreham Rd. N22—2C 30
Borgard Rd. SE18—4D 82
Borland Rd. SE15—4J 95
Borland Rd. Tedd—7B 104
Borneo St. SW15—3E 90
Borough High St. SE1
　　　　　　　　—2C 78 (5M 147)
Borough Hill. Croy—3B 134
Borough Rd. SE1
　　　　　　　　—3B 78 (6K 147)
Borough Rd. Iswth—1J 87
Borough Rd. King—1G 119
Borough Rd. Mitc—2C 122
Borrett Clo. SE17—5C 78
Borrodaile Rd. SW18—6K 91
Borrowdale Av. Harr—2A 24
Borrowdale Clo. Ilf—4C 34
Borrowdale Ct. Enf—1H 7
Borthwick M. E15—4G 49
Borthwick Rd. E15—4G 49
Borthwick Rd. NW9—6B 26
Borthwick St. SE8—5C 80
Borwick Av. E17—3B 32
Bosbury Rd. SE6—3E 112
Boscastle Rd. NW5—3F 45
Boscobel Pl. SW1
　　　　　　　　—4E 76 (8H 145)
Boscobel St. NW8
　　　　　　　　—4B 60 (4B 138)
Boscombe Av. E10—7F 33
Boscombe Clo. E5—5A 48
Boscombe Gdns. SW16—6J 109
Boscombe Rd. SW17—6E 108
Boscombe Rd. SW19—1K 121
Boscombe Rd. W12—2C 74
Boscombe Rd. Wor Pk—1E 130
Bosgrove. E4—2K 19
Boss St. SE1—2F 79 (4E 148)
Bostall Hill. SE2—5A 84
Bostall Hill Rd. SE2—6C 84
Bostall La. SE2—5B 84
Bostall Mnr. Way. SE2—4B 84
Bostall Pk. Av. Bexh—7E 84
Bostall Rd. Orp—7B 116
Bostal Row. Bexh—3F 101
Boston Gdns. W4—6A 74
Boston Gdns. W7—4A 72
Boston Gdns. Bren—4A 72
Boston Mnr. Rd. Bren—4B 72
Boston Pk. Rd. Bren—5C 72
Boston Pl. NW1—4D 60 (4E 138)
Boston Rd. E6—3C 66
Boston Rd. E17—6C 32
Boston Rd. W7—2K 71
Boston Rd. Croy—6K 123
Boston Rd. Edgw—7D 12
Boston St. E2—2G 63
Bostonthorpe Rd. W7—2J 71
Boston Vale. W7—4A 72
Boswell Ct. WC1
　　　　　　　　—5J 61 (5D 140)
Boswell Rd. T Hth—4C 124
Boswell St. WC1
　　　　　　　　—5J 61 (5D 140)
Bosworth Clo. E17—1B 32
Bosworth Rd. N11—6C 16
Bosworth Rd. W10—4G 59
Bosworth Rd. Barn—3D 4
Bosworth Rd. Dag—3G 53
Botany Bay La. Chst—2G 129
Boteley Clo. E4—2A 20
Botham Clo. Edgw—7D 12
Botha Rd. E13—5K 65

Bothwell Clo. E16—5H 65
Bothwell St. W6—6F 75
Botol ph La. EC3—7E 62 (9C 142)
Botsford Rd. SW20—2G 121
Botts M. W2—6J 59
Boucher Clo. Tedd—5K 103
Boughton Av. Brom—7H 127
Boughton Rd. SE28—3J 83
Boulcott St. E1—6K 63 (9G 143)
Boulevard, The. SW17—2E 108
Boulevard, The. Pinn—4E 22
Boulogne Rd. Croy—6C 124
Boulton Rd. Dag—3F 53
Boultwood Rd. E6—6D 66
Bounces La. N9—2C 18
Bounces Rd. N9—2C 18
Boundaries Rd. SW12—2D 108
Boundaries Rd. Felt—1A 102
Boundary Av. E17—7B 32
Boundary Clo. SE20—2G 125
Boundary Clo. Ilf—4J 51
Boundary Clo. King—3H 119
Boundary Clo. S'hall—5E 70
Boundary La. E13—4B 66
Boundary La. SE17—6C 78
Boundary Pas. E2
—4F 63 (3E 142)
Boundary Rd. E13—2A 66
Boundary Rd. E17—7B 32
Boundary Rd. N9—6D 8
Boundary Rd. N22—3B 30
Boundary Rd. NW8—1A 60
Boundary Rd. SW19—6B 108
Boundary Rd. Bark—2G 67
(in two parts)
Boundary Rd. Pinn—7B 22
Boundary Rd. Sidc—5J 99
Boundary Rd. Wall & Cars
—6F 133
Boundary Row. SE1
—2B 78 (4J 147)
Boundary St. E2—3F 63 (2E 142)
(in two parts)
Boundary Way. Croy—5C 124
Boundfield Rd. SE6—3G 113
Bounds Grn. Industrial Est. N11
—6B 16
Bounds Grn. Rd.—6B 16
N22 1-107
N11 remainder
Bourbon Ho. SE6—4E 112
Bourchier St. W1
—7H 61 (9A 140)
Bourdon Rd. SE20—2J 125
Bourdon St. W1—7F 61 (1J 145)
Bourke Clo. NW10—6A 42
Bourke Clo. SW4—6J 93
Bourlet Clo. W1—5G 61 (6L 139)
Bournbrook Rd. SE3—3B 98
Bourne Av. N14—2D 16
Bourne Av. N15—4D 30
Bourne Av. Barn—5G 5
Bourne Ct. Ruis—5A 38
Bourne Dri. Mitc—2B 122
Bourne Est. EC1
—5A 62 (5G 141)
Bourne Hill. N13—2E 16
Bourne Hill Clo. N13—2E 16
Bourne Industrial Pk. Dart
—5K 101
Bourne Mead. Bex—5K 101
Bournemouth Rd. SE15—2G 95
Bournemouth Rd. SW19
—1J 121
Bourne Pl. W4—5K 73
Bourne Rd. E7—3H 49
Bourne Rd. N8—6J 29
Bourne Rd. Bex—7H 101
Bourne Rd. Brom—4B 128
Bourneside Cres. N14—1C 16
Bourneside Gdns. SE6—5E 112
Bourne St. SW1—4E 76 (9G 145)
Bourne St. Croy—2B 134
Bourne Ter. W2—5K 59
Bourne, The. N14—2D 16

Bourne Vale. Brom—1H 137
Bournevale Rd. SW16—4J 109
Bourne View. Gnfd—5K 39
Bourneville Rd. SE6—7C 96
Bourne Way. Brom—2H 137
Bourne Way. Sutt—5H 131
Bournwood Rd. SE18—7A 84
Bournwell Clo. Barn—3J 5
Bousefield Rd. SE14—2K 95
Boutflower Rd. SW11—4C 92
Bouverie Gdns. Harr—6D 24
Bouverie M. N16—2E 46
Bouverie Pl. W2—6B 60 (7B 138)
Bouverie Rd. N16—2E 46
Bouverie Rd. Harr—6G 23
Bouverie St. EC4
—6A 62 (8H 141)
Bouvier Rd. Enf—1D 8
Boveney Rd. SE23—7K 95
Bovill Rd. SE23—7K 95
Bovingdon Av. Wemb—6G 41
Bovingdon Clo. N19—2G 45
Bovingdon La. NW9—1A 26
Bovingdon Rd. SW6—1K 91
Bowater Clo. NW9—5K 25
Bowater Clo. SW2—6J 93
Bowater Pl. SE3—7K 81
Bowater Rd. SE18—3B 82
Bow Bri. Est. E3—3D 64
Bow Comn. La. E3—4A 64
Bowden St. SE11—5A 78
Bowditch. SE8—5B 80
Bowdon Rd. E17—7C 32
Bowen Dri. SE21—3E 110
Bowen Rd. Harr—7G 23
Bowen St. E14—6D 64
Bower Av. SE10—1G 97
Bower Clo. N'holt—2A 54
Bower Clo. Romf—1K 37
Bowerdean St. SW6—1K 91
Bowerman Av. SE14—6A 80
Bowerman Rd. E6—6K 63 (8M 143)
Bowers Wlk. E6—5D 66
Bowes Clo. Sidc—6B 100
Bowes Rd.—5B 16
N13 1-153 & 2-138
N11 remainder
Bowes Rd. W3—7A 58
Bowes Rd. Dag—4C 52
Bowfell Rd. W6—6E 74
Bowford Av. Bexh—1E 100
Bowie Clo. SW4—7H 93
Bowland Rd. SW4—4H 93
Bowland Rd. Wfd G—5F 21
Bow La. EC4—6C 62 (8M 141)
Bow La. N12—7F 15
Bow La. Mord—6G 121
Bowl Ct. EC2—4E 62 (4D 142)
Bowles Rd. SE1—6G 79
Bowley La. SE19—5F 111
Bowley St. E14—7B 64
Bowling Grn. Clo. SW15—7D 90
Bowling Grn. La. EC1
—4A 62 (3H 141)
Bowling Grn. Pl. SE1
—2D 78 (4A 148)
Bowling Grn. Row. SE18—3C 82
Bowling Grn. St. SE11—6A 78
Bowling Grn. Wlk. N1
—3E 62 (1C 142)
Bowls Clo. Stan—5G 11
Bowman Av. E16—7H 65
Bowman M. SW18—1H 107
Bowmans Clo. W13—1B 72
Bowmans Lea. SE23—7J 95
Bowmans Meadow. Wall
—3F 133
Bowman's Pl. N7—3J 45
Bowmans Trading Est. NW9
—4G 25
Bowmead. SE9—2D 114
Bowmore Wlk. NW1—7H 45
Bowness Cres. SW15—5A 106
Bowness Dri. Houn—4C 86
Bowness Rd. SE6—7D 96
Bowness Rd. Bexh—2H 101

Bowood Rd. SW11—5E 92
Bowood Rd. Enf—2E 8
Bow Rd. E3—3B 64
Bowrons Av. Wemb—7D 40
Bow St. E15—5G 49
Bow St. WC2—6J 61 (8D 140)
Bowyer Clo. E6—5D 66
Bowyer Pl. SE5—7C 78
Bowyer St. SE5—7C 78
Boxall Rd. SE21—6E 94
Boxgrove Rd. SE2—3C 84
Box La. Bark—2B 68
Boxley Rd. Mord—4A 122
Boxley St. E16—1K 81
Boxmoor Rd. Harr—4B 24
Boxoll Rd. Dag—4F 53
Boxted Clo. Buck H—1H 21
Boxtree La. Harr—1G 23
Boxtree Rd. Harr—7C 10
Boxworth Gro. N1—1K 61
Boyard Rd. SE18—5F 83
Boyce Way. E13—4J 65
Boycroft Av. NW9—6J 25
Boyd Av. S'hall—1D 70
Boyd Clo. King—7G 105
Boydell Ct. NW8—7B 44
Boyd Rd. SW19—6B 108
Boyd St. E1—6G 63 (8H 143)
Boyfield St. SE1
—2B 78 (5K 147)
Boyland Rd. Brom—5H 113
Boyle Av. Stan—6F 11
Boyle Farm Rd. Th Dit—6A 118
Boyle St. W1—7G 61 (9L 139)
Boyne Av. NW4—4F 27
Boyne Rd. SE13—3E 96
Boyne Rd. Dag—3G 53
Boyne Ter. M. W11—1H 75
Boyseland Ct. Edgw—2D 12
Boyson Rd. SE17—6C 78
Boythorn Rd. SE16—5H 79
Boythorn Way. SE16—5H 79
Boyton Clo. E1—4J 63 (3M 143)
Boyton Clo. N8—3J 29
Boyton Rd. N8—3J 29
Brabant Rd. N22—2K 29
Brabazon Av. Wall—7J 133
Brabazon Rd. Houn—7A 70
Brabazon Rd. N'holt—2E 54
Brabazon St. E14—5D 64
Brabourne Clo. SE19—5E 110
Brabourne Cres. Bexh—6F 85
Brabourne Heights. NW7
—3F 13
Brabourne Rise. Beck—5E 126
Braburn Gro. SE15—2J 95
Braburn Rd. W10—5E 58
Bracewood Gdns. Croy—3F 135
Bracey St. N4—2J 45
Bracken Av. SW12—7E 92
Bracken Av. Croy—3D 136
Brackenbridge Dri. Ruis—3B 38
Brackenbury Gdns. W6—3D 74
Brackenbury Rd. N2—3A 28
Brackenbury Rd. W6—3D 74
Bracken Clo. E6—5D 66
Bracken Clo. Twic—7E 86
Brackendale. N21—2E 16
Brackendale Clo. Houn—1F 87
Brackendene. Dart—4K 117
Bracken End. Iswth—5H 87
Brackenfield Clo. E5—3H 47
Bracken Gdns. SW13—2C 90
Bracken Hill Clo. Brom—1H 127
Bracken Hill La. Brom—1H 127
Bracken Industrial Est. Ilf
—1K 35
Bracken M. Romf—6H 37
Brackens. Beck—7C 112
Brackens, The. Enf—7K 7
Brackley Clo. Wall—7J 133
Brackley Rd. W4—5A 74
Brackley Rd. Beck—7B 112
Brackley Sq. Wfd G—7G 21
Brackley St. EC1
—4C 62 (4M 141)

Brackley Ter. W4—5A 74
Bracklyn St. N1—2D 62
Bracknell Clo. N22—1A 30
Bracknell Gdns. NW3—4K 43
Bracknell Way. NW3—4K 43
Bracondale SE2—4A 84
Bradbourne Rd. Bex—7G 101
Bradbourne St. SW6—2J 91
Bradbury St. N16—5E 46
Braddon Rd. Rich—3F 89
Braddyll St. SE10—5G 81
Bradenham Av. Well—4A 100
Bradenham Rd. Harr—4B 24
Braden St. W9—4K 59
Bradfield Dri. Bark—5A 52
Bradfield Rd. E16—2J 81
Bradfield Rd. Ruis—5C 38
Bradford Clo. SE26—6D 110
Bradford Dri. Eps—6B 130
Bradford Rd. W3—2A 74
Bradford Rd. Ilf—1H 51
Bradgate Rd. SE6—6D 96
Brading Cres. E11—2K 49
Brading Rd. SW2—7K 93
Brading Rd. Croy—6K 123
Bradiston Rd. W9—3H 59
Bradley Clo. N7—6J 45
Bradley Gdns. W13—6B 56
Bradley M. SW17—1D 108
Bradley Rd. N22—2K 29
Bradley Rd. SE19—6C 110
Bradley's Clo. N1—2A 62
Bradman Row. Edgw—7D 12
Bradmead. SW8—7F 77
Bradmore Pk. Rd. W6—4D 74
Bradshaws Clo. SE25—3G 125
Bradstock Rd. E9—6K 47
Bradstock Rd. Eps—5C 130
Brad St. SE1—1A 78 (3H 147)
Bradwell Av. Dag—2G 53
Bradwell Clo. E18—4H 33
Bradwell M. N18—4B 18
Bradwell Rd. Buck H—1H 21
Brady St. E1—4H 63 (3J 143)
Braemar Av. N22—1J 29
Braemar Av. NW10—3K 41
Braemar Av. SW19—2J 107
Braemar Av. Bexh—4J 101
Braemar Av. S Croy—7C 134
Braemar Av. T Hth—3B 124
Braemar Av. Wemb—7D 40
Braemar Gdns. NW9—1K 25
Braemar Gdns. Sidc—3H 115
Braemar Gdns. S Wick—1E 136
Braemar Rd. E13—4H 65
Braemar Rd. N15—5E 30
Braemar Rd. Bren—6D 72
Braemar Rd. Wor Pk—3D 130
Braeside. Beck—5C 112
Braeside Av. SW19—1G 121
Braeside Cres. Bexh—4J 101
Braeside Rd. SW16—7G 109
Braes St. N1—7B 46
Braesyde Clo. Belv—4F 85
Brafferton Rd. Croy—4C 134
Braganza St. SE17—5B 78
Braham St. E1—6F 63 (8F 142)
Braid Av. W3—6A 58
Braid Clo. Felt—2D 102
Braidwood Rd. SE6—1F 113
Braidwood St. SE1
—1E 78 (3C 148)
Brailsford Rd. SW2—6A 94
Brainton Av. Felt—7A 86
Braintree Av. Ilf—4C 34
Braintree Rd. Dag—3G 53
Braintree Rd. Ruis—4A 38
Braintree St. E2—3J 63 (2L 143)
Braithwaite Av. Romf—7G 37
Braithwaite Gdns. Stan—1C 24
Bramah Grn. SW9—1A 94
Bramalea Clo. N6—6E 28
Bramall Clo. E15—5H 49
Bramber Ct. W5—4E 72
Bramber Rd. N12—5H 15
Bramber Rd. W14—6H 75
Bramblebury Rd. SE18—5G 83

Bramble Clo. Croy—4C 136
Bramble Clo. Stan—7J 11
Bramble Croft. Eri—4J 85
Brambledown Clo. W Wick
—5G 127
Brambledown Rd. Cars & Wall
—7E 132
Brambledown Rd. S Croy
—1C 132
Bramble Gdns. W12—7B 58
Brambles Clo. Bren—7B 72
Bramblewood Clo. Cars
—1C 132
Bramblings, The. E4—4A 20
Bramcote Av. Mitc—4D 122
Bramcote Gro. SE16—5J 79
Bramcote Rd. SW15—4D 90
Bramdean Cres. SE12—1J 113
Bramdean Gdns. SE12—1J 113
Bramerton Rd. Beck—3B 126
Bramerton St. SW3—6C 76
Bramfield Rd. SW11—6C 92
Bramford Rd. SW18—4A 92
Bramham Gdns. SW5—5K 75
Bramhope La. SE7—6K 81
Bramlands Clo. SW11—3C 92
Bramley Clo. E17—2A 32
Bramley Clo. N14—5A 6
Bramley Clo. Orp—7F 129
Bramley Clo. S Croy—5C 134
Bramley Clo. Twic—6G 87
Bramley Ct. Well—1B 100
Bramley Cres. Ilf—6E 34
Bramley Hill. S Croy—5B 134
Bramley Pde. N14—4C 6
Bramley Rd. N14—5A 6
Bramley Rd. W5—3C 72
Bramley Rd. W10—7F 59
Bramley Rd. Sutt—5B 132
Bramley Rd. Sutt—7F 131
(East Ewell)
Bramley St. W10—6F 59
Bramley Way. Houn—5D 86
Bramley Way. W Wick—2D 136
Brampton Clo. E5—2H 47
Brampton Gdns. N15—5C 30
Brampton Gro. NW4—2D 26
Brampton Gro. Harr—4A 24
Brampton Gro. Wemb—1G 41
Brampton La. NW4—4E 26
Brampton Pk. Rd. N8—3A 30
Brampton Rd. E6—3B 66
Brampton Rd. N15—5C 30
Brampton Rd. NW9—4G 25
Brampton Rd. Bexh & SE2
—3D 100
Brampton Rd. Croy—6F 125
Bramshaw Rise. N Mald
—6A 120
Bramshaw Rd. E9—6K 47
Bramshill Gdns. NW5—3F 45
Bramshill Rd. NW10—2A 58
Bramshot Av. SE7—6J 81
Bramston Rd. NW10—2C 58
Brancaster Rd. E12—4D 50
Brancaster Rd. SW16—3J 109
Brancaster Rd. Ilf—6J 35
Brancepeth Gdns. Buck H
—2D 20
Branch Hill. NW3—3A 44
Branch Hill Ho. NW3—3K 43
Branch Pl. N1—1D 62
Branch Rd. E14—7A 64
Brancker Clo. Wall—7J 133
Brancker Rd. Harr—3D 24
Brancroft Way. Enf—1F 9
Brandbury Clo. S'hall—4E 70
Brandlehow Rd. SW15—4H 91
Brandon Est. SE17—6B 78
Brandon Rd. E17—4E 32
Brandon Rd. N7—7J 45
Brandon Rd. S'hall—5D 70
Brandon Rd. Sutt—4K 131
Brandon St. SE17
(in two parts)—4C 78 (9M 147)
Brandram Rd. SE13—3G 97
Brandreth Rd. E6—6D 66

Brandreth Rd. SW17—2F 109
Brandries, The. Wall—3H 133
Brand St. SE10—7E 80
Brandville Gdns. Ilf—4F 35
Brandy Way. Sutt—7J 131
Brangbourne Rd. Brom—5E 112
Brangton Rd. SE11—5K 77
Branksea St. SW6—7G 75
Branksome Av. N18—5A 18
Branksome Rd. SW2—5J 93
Branksome Rd. SW19—1J 121
Branksome Way. Harr—6F 25
Branksome Way. N Mald
—1J 119
Branscombe Gdns. N21—7F 7
Branscombe St. SE13—3D 96
Bransdale Clo. NW6—1J 59
Bransgrove Rd. Edgw—1F 25
Branston Cres. Orp—7H 129
Branstone Rd. Rich—1F 89
Brants Wlk. W7—4J 55
Brantwood Av. Eri—7J 85
Brantwood Av. Iswth—4A 88
Brantwood Clo. E17—3E 32
Brantwood Gdns. Enf—4D 6
Brantwood Gdns. Ilf—4C 34
Brantwood Rd. N17—6B 18
Brantwood Rd. SE24—5C 94
Brantwood Rd. Bexh—2H 101
Brantwood Rd. S Croy—7C 134
Brasher Clo. Gnfd—5H 39
Brassey Rd. NW6—6H 43
Brassey Sq. SW11—3E 92
Brassie Av. W3—6A 58
Brasted Clo. SE26—4J 111
Brasted Clo. Bexh—5D 100
Brathway Rd. SW18—7J 91
Bratley St. E1—4G 63 (4G 143)
Bratten Ct. Croy—6D 124
Braund Av. Gnfd—4F 55
Braundton Av. Sidc—1K 115
Braunston Dri. Hay—4C 54
Bravington Pl. W9—4H 59
Bravington Rd. W9—3H 59
Braxfield Rd. SE4—4A 96
Braxted Pk. SW16—6K 109
Brayards Rd. SE15—2H 95
Braybourne Dri. Iswth—7K 71
Braybrooke Gdns. SE19
—7E 110
Braybrook St. W12—5B 58
Brayburne Av. SW4—2G 93
Bray Cres. SE16—2K 79
Bray Dri. E16—7H 65
Brayfield Ter. N1—7A 46
Brayford Sq. E1
—6J 63 (7M 143)
Bray Pas. E16—7J 65
Bray Pl. SW3—4D 76 (9E 144)
Bray Rd. NW7—5A 14
Brayton Gdns. Enf—4C 6
Braywood Rd. SE9—4H 99
Brazil Clo. Croy—7J 123
Breach La. Dag—3G 69
Bread St. EC4—6C 62 (8M 141)
Breakspears Dri. Orp—1K 129
Breakspears Rd. SE4—4B 96
Bream Gdns. E6—3E 66
Breamore Clo. SW15—1C 106
Breamore Rd. Ilf—2K 51
Bream's Bldgs. EC4
—6A 62 (7G 141)
Bream St. E3—7C 48
Breamwater Gdns. Rich
—3B 104
Brearly Clo. Edgw—7D 12
Breasley Clo. SW15—4D 90
Brechin Pl. SW7
—4A 76 (9A 144)
Brecknock Rd. —4G 45
N7 1-113 & 2-142
N19 remainder
Brecknock Rd. Est. N7—4H 45
Brecon Clo. Mitc—3J 123
Brecon Grn. NW9—6A 26

Brecon Rd. W6—6G 75
Brecon Rd. Enf—4D 8
Brede Clo. E6—3E 66
Bredgar Rd. N19—2G 45
Bredhurst Clo. SE20—6J 111
Bredon Rd. SE5—3C 94
Bredon Rd. Croy—7F 125
Breer St. SW6—3K 91
Breezer's Hill. E1
—7G 63 (1H 149)
Brember Rd. Harr—2G 39
Bremner Rd. SW7
—3A 76 (6A 144)
Brenchley Clo. Brom—6H 127
Brenchley Clo. Chst—1E 128
Brenchley Gdns. SE23—6J 95
Brenchley Rd. Orp—2K 129
Brenda Rd. SW17—2D 108
Brendon Av. NW10—5A 42
Brendon Gdns. Harr—4F 39
Brendon Gdns. Ilf—5J 35
Brendon Rd. SE9—2H 115
Brendon Rd. Dag—1G 53
Brendon St. W1—6C 60 (7D 138)
Brendon Way. Enf—7K 7
Brenley Clo. Mitc—3E 122
Brenley Gdns. SE9—4B 98
Brennand Ct. N19—3G 45
Brent Clo. Bex—1E 116
Brentcot Clo. W13—4B 56
Brent Cres. NW10—2F 57
Brent Cross Fly-Over. NW2
—7F 27
Brent Cross Shopping Centre.
NW4—7E 26
Brentfield. NW10—7H 41
Brentfield Clo. NW10—6K 41
Brentfield Gdns. NW2—7F 27
Brentfield Rd. NW10—6K 41
Brentford Clo. Hay—4B 54
Brent Grn. NW4—5F 27
Brent Grn. Wlk. Wemb—3J 41
Brentham Way. W5—4D 56
Brenthouse Rd. E9—6J 47
Brenthurst Rd. NW10—6B 42
Brent Lea. Bren—7C 72
Brentmead Clo. W7—7J 55
Brentmead Gdns. NW10—2F 57
Brentmead Pl. NW11—6F 27
Brenton St. E14—6A 64
Brent Pk. Rd. NW4—7D 26
(in two parts)
Brent Pl. Barn—5C 4
(in two parts)
Brent Rd. E16—6J 65
Brent Rd. SE18—7F 83
Brent Rd. Bren—6C 72
Brent Rd. S'hall—3A 70
Brent Rd. S Croy—7H 135
Brent Side. Bren—6C 72
Brentside Clo. W13—4A 56
Brentside Executive Pk. Bren
—6B 72
Brent St. NW4—4E 26
Brent Ter. NW2—1E 42
Brent Trading Centre. NW10
—5A 42
Brentvale Av. S'hall—1H 71
Brentvale Av. Wemb—1F 57
Brent View Rd. NW9—7C 26
Brent Way. N3—6D 14
Brent Way. Bren—7D 72
Brent Way. Wemb—6H 41
Brentwick Gdns. Bren—4E 72
Brentwood Clo. SE9—1G 115
Brereton Rd. N17—7A 18
Bressenden Pl. SW1
—3G 77 (6L 145)
Bressey Gro. E18—2H 33
Brett Clo. N16—2E 46
Brett Clo. N'holt—3B 54
Brett Ct. N9—2D 18
Brett Cres. NW10—1K 57
Brettell St. SE17—5D 78
Brettenham Av. E17—1C 32
Brettenham Rd. E17—2C 32

Brettenham Rd. N18—4B 18
Brettenham Rd. Industrial Est.
N18—4C 18
Brett Gdns. Dag—7E 52
Brett Ho. Clo. SW15—7F 91
Brett Rd. E8—5H 47
Brett St. SW6—7G 61 (9M 139)
Brewer St. W1—7G 61 (9M 139)
Brewery Clo. Wemb—4A 40
Brewery La. Twic—7K 87
Brewery M. Business Centre.
Iswth—3K 87
Brewery Rd. N7—7J 45
Brewery Rd. SE18—5H 83
Brewery Rd. Brom—7C 128
Brewhouse La. E1
—1H 79 (3K 149)
Brewhouse Rd. SE18—4D 82
Brewhouse St. SW15—3G 91
Brewhouse Wlk. SE16—1A 80
Brewhouse Yd. EC1
—4B 62 (3J 141)
Brewood Rd. Dag—6B 52
Brewster Gdns. W10—5G 59
Brewster Rd. E10—1D 48
Brian Rd. Romf—5C 36
Briants Clo. Pinn—2D 22
Briant St. SE14—1K 95
Briar Av. SW16—7K 109
Briarbank Rd. W13—6A 56
Briar Clo. N2—3K 27
Briar Clo. N13—3H 17
Briar Clo. Buck H—2G 21
Briar Clo. Hmptn—5D 102
Briar Clo. Iswth—5K 87
Briar Ct. Sutt—4E 130
Briar Cres. N'holt—6F 39
Briardale Gdns. NW3—3J 43
Briarfield Av. N3—2K 27
Briar Gdns. Brom—1H 137
Briar La. Croy—4D 136
Briar Rd. NW2—4E 42
Briar Rd. SW16—3J 123
Briar Rd. Bex—3K 117
Briar Rd. Harr—5C 24
Briar Rd. Twic—1J 103
Briars Clo. N17—5F 18
Briars, The. Bush. Wat—1D 10
Briar Wlk. SW15—4D 90
Briar Wlk. W10—4G 59
Briar Wlk. Edgw—7D 12
Briar Wood Clo. NW9—6J 25
Briarwood Rd. SW4—5H 93
Briarwood Rd. Eps—6C 130
Briary Clo. NW3—7C 44
Briary Ct. Sidc—5B 116
Briary Gdns. Brom—5K 113
Briary Gro. Edgw—2H 25
Briary La. N9—3A 18
Brick Ct. EC4—6A 62 (8G 141)
Brick Farm Clo. Rich—1H 89
Brickfield Clo. Bren—7C 72
Brickfield Rd. E3—4D 64
Brickfield Rd. SW19—4K 107
Brickfield Rd. T'hth—1B 124
Brickfields. Harr—2H 39
Brick La. —4F 63 (3F 142)
E1 1-165 & 2-226
E2 remainder
Brick La. Enf—2C 8
Brick La. Stan—7J 11
Brick St. W1—1F 77 (3J 145)
Brickwood Clo. SE26—3H 111
Brickwood Rd. Croy—2E 134
Bride La. EC4—6B 62 (8J 141)
Bride St. N7—6K 45
Bridewell Pl. E1—1H 79 (3K 149)
Bridewell Pl. EC4
—6B 62 (8J 141)
Bridford M. W1—5F 61 (5K 139)
Bridge App. NW1—7E 44
Bridge Av. W6—4E 74
Bridge Av. W7—5H 55
Bridge Clo. Enf—2C 8
Bridge End. E17—1E 32
Bridgefield Rd. Sutt—6J 131

Bridge Foot. SE1
—5J 77 (9E 146)
Bridgeford St. SW18—3A 108
Bridge Ga. N21—7H 7
Bridge Ho. Quay. E14—1E 80
Bridgeland Rd. E16—6J 65
Bridge La. NW11—5G 27
Bridge La. SW11—1C 92
Bridgeman Rd. N1—7K 45
Bridgeman Rd. Tedd—6A 104
Bridgeman St. NW8—2C 60
Bridgend Rd. SW18—4A 92
Bridgenhall Rd. Enf—1A 8
Bridgen Rd. Bex—7E 100
Bridge Pk. SW18—5J 91
Bridge Pl. Croy—1D 134
Bridgeport Pl. E1
—1G 79 (2H 149)
Bridge Rd. E6—7D 50
Bridge Rd. E15—1F 65
Bridge Rd. E17—7B 32
Bridge Rd. N9—3B 18
Bridge Rd. N22—1J 29
Bridge Rd. NW10—6A 42
Bridge Rd. Beck—7B 112
Bridge Rd. Bexh—2E 100
Bridge Rd. Houn & Iswth
—3H 87
Bridge Rd. S'hall—2D 70
Bridge Rd. Sutt—6K 131
Bridge Rd. Twic—6B 88
Bridge Rd. Wall—5G 133
Bridge Rd. Wemb—3G 41
Bridge Row. Croy—1D 134
Bridges Ct. SW11—3B 92
Bridges La. Croy—4J 133
Bridges Pl. SW6—1H 91
Bridges Rd. SW19—6K 107
Bridges Rd. Stan—5E 10
Bridges Rd. M. SW19—6K 107
Bridge St. SW1—2J 77 (5C 146)
Bridge St. W4—4K 73
Bridge St. Pinn—3C 22
Bridge St. Rich—5D 88
Bridge Ter. E15—7F 49
Bridge, The. Harr—4K 23
Bridgetown Clo. SE19—5E 110
Bridge View. W6—5E 74
Bridgewater Clo. Chst—3J 129
Bridgewater Gdns. Edgw
—2F 25
Bridgewater Rd. E15—1E 64
Bridgewater Rd. Wemb—6C 40
Bridgewater Sq. EC2
—5C 62 (5L 141)
Bridgewater St. EC2
—5C 62 (5L 141)
Bridge Way. N11—3B 16
Bridge Way. NW11—5H 27
Bridgeway. Bark—7K 51
Bridge Way. Twic—7G 87
Bridge Way. Wemb—7F 41
Bridgeway St. NW1
—2H 61 (1A 140)
Bridge Wharfe Rd. Iswth
—3B 88
Bridgewood Clo. SE20—7H 111
Bridgewood Rd. SW16—7H 109
Bridgewood Rd. Wor Pk
—4C 130
Bridge Yd. SE1—1D 78 (2B 148)
Bridgman Rd. W4—3J 73
Bridle Clo. King—4D 118
Bridle La. W1—7G 61 (9M 139)
Bridle Path. Croy—3J 133
Bridle Path, The. Wfd G—7B 20
Bridle Rd. Croy—3C 136
(in two parts)
Bridle Rd. Pinn—6A 22
Bridle Rd. S Croy—7G 135
Bridle Way. Croy—4C 136
Bridle Way, The. Wall—5G 133
Bridlington Rd. N9—7C 8
Bridport Av. Romf—6H 37
Bridport Pl. N1—1D 62
(in two parts)
Bridport Rd. N18—5K 17

Bridport Rd. Gnfd—1F 55
Bridport Rd. T Hth—3A 124
Bridport Ter. SW8—1H 93
Bridstow Pl. W2—6J 59
Brief St. SE5—1B 94
Brierley. Croy—6D 136
(in two parts)
Brierley Av. N9—1D 18
Brierley Clo. SE25—4G 125
Brierley Rd. E11—4F 49
Brierley Rd. SW12—2G 109
Brierly Gdns. E2
—3J 63 (1M 143)
Brigade Clo. Harr—2H 39
Brigade St. SE3—2H 97
Brigadier Av. Enf—1H 7
Brigadier Hill. Enf—1H 7
Briggeford Clo. E5—2G 47
Bright Clo. Belv—4D 84
Brightfield Rd. SE13—5G 97
Brightling Rd. SE4—6B 96
Brightlingsea Pl. E14—7B 64
Brightman Rd. SW18—1B 108
Brighton Av. E17—5B 32
Brighton Dri. N'holt—6E 38
Brighton Gro. SE14—1A 96
Brighton Rd. E6—3E 66
Brighton Rd. N2—2A 28
Brighton Rd. N16—4E 46
Brighton Rd. Red, Coul, Purl, &
S Croy—7C 134
Brighton Rd. Surb—6C 118
Brighton Rd. Tad, Bans & Sutt
—7K 131
Brighton Ter. SW9—4K 93
Brightside Rd. SE13—6F 97
Brightside, The. Enf—1F 9
Bright St. E14—6D 64
Brightwell Cres. SW17—5D 108
Brig M. SE8—6C 80
Brigstock Rd. Belv—4H 85
Brigstock Rd. T Hth—5A 124
Brill Pl. NW1—2H 61 (1B 140)
Brim Hill. N2—4A 28
Brimpsfield Clo. SE2—3B 84
(in two parts)
Brimsdown Av. Enf—2F 9
Brimsdown Industrial Est. Enf
—2G & 1G 9
Brindley St. SE14—1B 96
Brindley Way. Brom—5J 113
Brindley Way. S'hall—7F 55
Brindwood Rd. E4—3H 19
Brinkburn Clo. SE2—4A 84
Brinkburn Clo. Edgw—3H 25
Brinkburn Gdns. Edgw—3G 25
Brinkley Rd. Wor Pk—2D 130
Brinklow Cres. SE18—7F 83
Brinkworth Rd. Ilf—3C 34
Brinkworth Way. E9—6B 48
Brinsdale Rd. NW4—3F 27
Brinsley Rd. Harr—2H 23
Brinsley St. E1—6H 63 (8K 143)
Brinsworth Clo. Twic—2H 103
Brion Pl. E14—5E 64
Brisbane Av. SW19—1K 121
Brisbane Rd. E10—2D 48
Brisbane Rd. W13—2A 72
Brisbane Rd. Ilf—7F 35
Brisbane St. SE5—7D 78
Briscoe Clo. E11—3H 49
Briscoe Rd. SW19—6B 108
Briset Rd. SE9—3B 98
Briset St. EC1—5B 62 (5J 141)
Briset Way. N7—2K 45
Bristol Gdns. SW15—7E 90
Bristol Gdns. W9—4K 59
Bristol M. W9—4K 59
Bristol Pk. Rd. E17—4A 32
Bristol Rd. E7—6A 50
Bristol Rd. Gnfd—1F 55
Bristol Rd. Mord—5A 122
Briston Gro. N8—6J 29
Bristow Rd. SE19—5E 110
Bristow Rd. Bexh—1E 100
Bristow Rd. Croy—4J 133
Bristow Rd. Houn—3G 87

Britannia Clo. SW4—4H 93
Britannia Clo. N'holt—3B 54
Britannia La. Twic—7G 87
Britannia Rd. N12—3F 15
Britannia Rd. SW6—7K 75
Britannia Rd. Ilf—3F 51
Britannia Rd. Surb—7F 119
Britannia Row. N1—1B 62
Britannia St. WC1
—3K 61 (1E 140)
Britannia Wlk. N1
(in two parts)—3D 62 (1A 142)
Britannia Way. NW10—4H 57
British Gro. W4—5B 74
British Gro. S. W6—5B 74
British Gro. Pas. W6—5B 74
British Legion Rd. E4—2C 20
British St. E3—3B 64
Brittain Rd. Dag—3E 52
Britten Clo. NW11—1K 43
Britten Dri. S'hall—6E 54
Britten's Ct. E1—7G 63 (9H 143)
Britten St. SW3—5C 76
Britton St. EC1—4B 62 (4J 141)
Brixham Gdns. Ilf—5J 51
Brixham Rd. Well—1D 100
Brixham St. E16—1E 82
Brixton Est. Edgw—2H 25
Brixton Hill. SW2—7J 93
Brixton Hill Pl. SW2—7J 93
Brixton Rd. SW9—3A 94
Brixton Sta. Rd. SW9—3A 94
Brixton Water La. SW2—5A 94
Broadbent Clo. N6—1F 45
Broadbent St. W1
—7F 61 (9J 139)
Broadbridge Clo. SE3—7J 81
Broadbury Ct. N18—6C 18
Broadcoombe. S Croy—7K 135
Broad Ct. WC2—6J 61 (8D 140)
Broadcroft Av. Stan—2D 24
Broadcroft Rd. Orp—7H 129
Broadfield Clo. NW2—3E 42
Broadfield Clo. Croy—2K 133
Broadfield Ct. Bush, Wat
—2D 10
Broadfield Heights. Edgw
—4C 12
Broadfield La. NW1—7H 45
Broadfield Rd. SE6—7G 97
Broadfields. Harr—2F 23
Broadfields Av. N21—7F 7
Broadfields Av. Edgw—4C 12
Broadfields Centre. Edgw
—2C 12
Broadfield Sq. Enf—2C 8
Broadfield Way. Buck H—3F 21
Broadgate. EC2—5E 62 (6C 142)
Broadgate Circle. EC2
—5E 62 (6D 142)
Broadgate Rd. SE16—6B 66
Broadgates Av. Barn—1E 4
Broadgates Rd. SW18—1B 108
Broad Grn. Av. Croy—7B 124
Broadhead Strand. NW9
—2B 26
Broadheath Dri. Chst—5D 114
Broadhinton Rd. SW4—3F 93
Broadhurst Av. Edgw—4C 12
Broadhurst Av. Ilf—4K 51
Broadhurst Clo. NW6—6A 44
Broadhurst Clo. Rich—5F 89
Broadhurst Gdns. NW6—6K 43
Broadhurst Gdns. Ruis—2A 38
Broadlands Av. SW16—2J 109
Broadlands Av. Enf—3C 8
Broadlands Clo. N6—7E 28
Broadlands Clo. SW16—2J 109
Broadlands Clo. Enf—3D 8
Broadlands Rd. N6—7D 28
Broadlands Rd. Brom—4K 113
Broadlands, The. Felt—3E 102
Broadlands Way. N Mald
—6B 120
Broad La. N8—5K 29
Broad La. N15—4F 31
Broad La. Hmptn—7D 102

Broad Lawn. SE9—2E 114
Broad Lawns Ct. Harr—1K 23
Broadley St. NW8
—5B 60 (5B 138)
Broadley Ter. NW1
—4C 60 (4D 138)
Broadmead. SE6—3C 112
Broadmead Av. N Mald
—7C 120
Broadmead Clo. Hmptn
—6E 102
Broadmead Clo. Pinn—1C 22
Broadmead Rd. Hay & N'holt
—4C 54
Broadmead Rd. Wfd G—6D 20
Broad Oak. Wfd G—5E 20
Broad Oak Clo. E4—5H 19
Broadoak Rd. Eri—7K 85
Broadoaks Way. Brom—5H 127
Broad Sanctuary. SW1
—2H 77 (5B 146)
Broadstone Pl. W1
—5E 60 (6G 139)
Broad St. Dag—7G 53
Broad St. Tedd—6K 103
Broad St. Av. EC2
—5E 62 (6C 142)
Broad View. NW9—6G 25
Broadview Rd. SW16—7H 109
Broadwalk. E18—3H 33
Broad Wlk. N21—2E 16
Broad Wlk. NW1
—2E 60 (1H 139)
Broad Wlk. SE3—2A 98
Broadwalk. Harr—5E 22
Broad Wlk. Houn—1B 86
Broad Wlk. Rich—7F 73
Broad Wlk. La. NW11—7H 27
Broadwalk Shopping Centre.
Edgw—6C 12
Broad Wlk., The. W8—1K 75
Broadwall. SE1—1A 78 (2H 147)
Broadwater Rd. N17—2E 30
Broadwater Rd. SE28—3H 83
Broadwater Rd. SW17—4C 108
Broadway. E13—2K 65
Broadway. E15—7F 49
Broadway. SW1
—3H 77 (6A 146)
Broadway. W7 & W13—1K 71
Broadway. Bexh—4E 100
Broadway. Gnfd—4G 55
Broadway Av. Croy—5D 124
Broadway Av. Twic—6B 88
Broadway Clo. Wfd G—6E 20
Broadway Ct. SW19—6J 107
Broadway Ct. Beck—3E 126
Broadway Gdns. Mitc—4C 122
Broadway Mkt. E8—1H 63
Broadway M. E5—7F 31
Broadway M. N13—5E 16
Broadway M. N21—1G 17
Broadway Pde. N8—6J 29
Broadway Pde. Harr—5F 23
Broadway Pl. SW19—6H 107
Broadway Shopping Centre
Bexh—4G 101
Broadway, The. E4—6A 20
Broadway, The. N8—6J 29
Broadway, The. N9—3B 18
Broadway, The. N22—2A 30
Broadway, The. NW7—5F 13
Broadway, The. NW9—6B 26
Broadway, The. SW19—7J 107
Broadway, The. W5—7D 56
Broadway, The. Croy—4J 133
Broadway, The. Dag—2G 53
Broadway, The. Eps—5C 130
Broadway, The. Harr—2J 23
Broadway, The. Pinn—1D 22
Broadway, The. S'hall—1C 70
Broadway, The. Stan—5H 11
Broadway, The. Sutt—4A 132
Broadway, The. Sutt—6G 131
(Cheam)
Broadway, The. Wemb—3F 40
Broadway, The. Wfd G—6E 20

169

Broadwick St. W1
—7G 61 (9M 139)
Broad Yd. EC1—4B 62 (4J 141)
Brocas Clo. NW3—7C 44
Brockdish Av. Bark—5K 51
Brockenhurst Av. Wor Pk
—1A 130
Brockenhurst Gdns. NW7
—6F 13
Brockenhurst Gdns. Ilf—5G 51
Brockenhurst Rd. Croy—7H 125
Brockenhurst Way. SW16
—2H 123
Brockham Clo. SW19—5H 107
Brockham Cres. Croy—7F 137
Brockham Dri. SW2—7K 93
Brockham Dri. Ilf—5G 35
Brockham St. SE1
—3C 78 (6M 147)
Brockhurst Clo. Stan—6E 10
Brockill Cres. SE4—4A 96
Brocklebank Rd. SE7—4K 81
Brocklebank Rd. SW18—7A 92
Brocklebank Rd. Industrial Est.
SE7—4K 81
Brocklehurst St. SE14—7K 79
Brocklesby Rd. SE25—4H 125
Brockley Av. N. Stan—3K 11
Brockley Av. S. Stan—3K 11
Brockley Clo. Stan—4K 11
Brockley Cres. Romf—1J 37
Brockley Cross. SE4—3A 96
Brockley Footpath. SE4—5A 96
Brockley Footpath. SE15
—4J 95
Brockley Gdns. SE4—2B 96
Brockley Gro. SE4—5B 96
Brockley Hall Rd. SE4—5A 96
Brockley Hill. Stan—1H 11
Brockley Pk. SE23—7A 96
Brockley Rise. SE23—1A 112
Brockley Rd. SE4—5A 96
Brockleyside. Stan—4K 11
Brockley View. SE23—7A 96
Brockley Way. SE4—5A 96
Brockman Rise. Brom—4F 113
Brock Pl. E3—4D 64
Brock Rd. E13—5K 65
Brocks Dri. Sutt—3G 131
Brockshot Clo. Bren—5D 72
Brock St. SE15—3J 95
Brockway Clo. E11—2G 49
Brockwell Clo. Orp—5K 129
Brockwell Pk. Gdns. SE24
—7B 94
Brockworth Clo. SE15—6E 78
Broderick Gro. SE2—4B 84
Brodia Rd. N16—3E 46
Brodie Rd. E4—1K 19
Brodie Rd. Enf—1H 7
Brodie St. SE1—5F 79 (9F 148)
Brodlove La. E1
—7K 63 (9M 143)
Brodrick Rd. SW17—2C 108
Brograve Gdns. Beck—2D 126
Broken Wharf. EC4
—7C 62 (9L 141)
Brokesley St. E3—3B 64
Broke Wlk. E8—1G 63
Bromar Rd. SE5—3E 94
Bromefield. Stan—1C 24
Bromells Rd. SW4—4G 93
Brome Rd. SE9—3D 98
Bromfelde Rd. SW4—3H 93
Bromfelde Wlk. SW4—2J 93
Bromfield St. N1—2A 62
Bromhall Rd. Dag—6B 52
Bromhedge. SE9—3D 114
Bromholm Rd. SE2—3B 84
Bromley Av. Brom—7G 113
Bromley Comn. Brom—4A 128
Bromley Cres. Brom—3H 127
Bromley Gdns. Brom—3H 127
Bromley Gro. Brom—2F 127
Bromley Hall Rd. E14—5E 64
Bromley High St. E3—3D 64
Bromley Hill. Brom—6G 113

Bromley Industrial Centre.
Brom—3B 128
Bromley La. Chst—7G 115
Bromley Pl. W1—5G 61 (5L 139)
Bromley Rd. E10—6D 32
Bromley Rd. E17—3C 32
Bromley Rd. N17—1G 31
Bromley Rd. N18—3J 17
Bromley Rd.—1D 112
SE6 1-427 & 2-394
Brom remainder
Bromley Rd. Beck—1D 126
Bromley Rd. Beck & Brom
—2D 126
Bromley Rd. Chst—1F 129
Bromley St. E1—6K 63
Brompton Clo. SE20—2G 125
Brompton Clo. Houn—5D 86
Brompton Gro. N2—4C 28
Brompton Pk. Cres. SW6
—6K 75
Brompton Pl. SW3
—3D 76 (6E 144)
Brompton Rd. SW3 & SW1
—4C 76 (8C 144)
Brompton Sq. SW3
—3C 76 (6C 144)
Brompton Ter. SE18—1E 98
Bromwich Av. N6—2E 44
Bromyard Av. W3—7A 58
Brondesbury M. NW6—7J 43
Brondesbury Pk.—7E 42
NW6 1-97 & 2-64
NW2 remainder
Brondesbury Rd. NW6—2H 59
Brondesbury Vs. NW6—2H 59
Bronsart Rd. SW6—7G 75
Bronson Rd. SW20—2F 121
Bronte Clo. E7—4J 49
Bronte Clo. Ilf—4E 34
Bronti Clo. SE17—5C 78
Bronze St. SE8—7C 80
Brook Av. Dag—7H 53
Brook Av. Edgw—5C 12
Brook Av. Wemb—3G 41
Brookbank Av. W7—4H 55
Brookbank Rd. SE13—3C 96
Brook Clo. NW7—7B 14
Brook Clo. SW20—3D 120
Brook Cres. E4—4H 19
Brook Cres. N9—4C 18
Brookdale. N11—4B 16
Brookdale Rd. E17—3C 32
Brookdale Rd. SE6—7D 96
Brookdale Rd. Bex—6E 100
Brookdene Rd. SE18—4K 83
Brook Dri. SE11—3A 78 (7H 147)
Brook Dri. Harr—4G 23
Brooke Av. Harr—3G 39
Brooke Clo. Bush, Wat—1B 10
Brookehowse Rd. SE6—2C 112
Brookend Rd. Sidc—1J 115
Brooke Rd. E17—4E 32
Brooke Rd.—3F 47
N16 1-147 & 6-160
E5 remainder
Brooke's Ct. EC1
—5A 62 (5G 141)
Brooke St. EC1—5A 62 (6G 141)
Brooke Way. Bush, Wat—1B 10
Brookfield. N6—3E 44
Brookfield Av. E17—4E 32
Brookfield Av. NW7—6J 13
Brookfield Av. W5—4D 56
Brookfield Av. Sutt—3C 132
Brookfield Clo. NW7—6J 13
Brookfield Ct. Gnfd—3G 55
Brookfield Cres. NW7—6J 13
Brookfield Cres. Harr—5E 24
Brookfield Pk. NW5—3F 45
Brookfield Path. Wfd G—6B 20
Brookfield Rd. E9—6A 48
Brookfield Rd. N9—3B 18
Brookfield Rd. W4—2K 73
Brookfields. Enf—4E 8
Brookfields Av. Mitc—5C 122
Brook Gdns. E4—4J 19

Brook Gdns. SW13—3B 90
Brook Gdns. King—1J 119
Brook Ga. W1—7D 60 (1F 144)
Brook Grn. W6—3F 75
Brook Hill Clo. SE18—5F 83
Brookhill Clo. Barn—5H 5
Brookhill Rd. SE18—5F 83
Brookhill Rd. Barn—5H 5
Brook Ho. Gdns. E4—4B 20
Brooking Rd. E7—5J 49
Brookland Clo. NW11—4K 27
Brookland Garth. NW11—4K 27
Brookland Hill. NW11—4K 27
Brookland Rise. NW11—4J 27
Brooklands App. Romf—4K 37
Brooklands Av. SW19—2K 107
Brooklands Av. Sidc—2H 115
Brooklands Clo. Romf—4K 37
Brooklands Ct. N21—5J 7
Brooklands Ct. Mitc—2B 122
Brooklands Dri. Gnfd—1C 56
Brooklands La. Romf—4K 37
Brooklands Pk. SE3—3J 97
Brooklands Rd. Romf—4K 37
Brooklands St. SW8—1H 93
Brook La. SE3—2K 97
Brook La. Bex—6D 100
Brook La. Brom—6J 113
Brook La. Trading Centre. Bren
—5D 72
Brook La. N. Bren—5D 72
(in two parts)
Brooklea Clo. NW9—1A 26
Brooklyn Av. SE25—4H 125
Brooklyn Gro. SE25—4H 125
Brooklyn Rd. SE25—4H 125
Brooklyn Rd. Brom—5B 128
Brook Mead. Eps—6A 130
Brookmead Av. Brom—5B 128
Brookmead Industrial Est. Croy
—6G 123
Brook Meadow. N12—3E 14
Brookmead Rd. Croy—6G 123
Brook M. N. W2—7A 60 (9A 138)
Brookmill Rd. SE8—1C 96
Brook Pde. Chig—3K 21
Brook Pas. SW6—7J 75
Brook Pl. Barn—5D 4
Brook Rise. Chig—3K 21
Brook Rd. N8—4J 29
Brook Rd. N22—2K 29
Brook Rd. NW2—2B 42
Brook Rd. Buck H—2D 20
Brook Rd. Ilf—6J 35
Brook Rd. T Hth—4C 124
Brook Rd. Twic—6A 88
Brook Rd. S. Bren—6D 72
Brooks Av. E6—4D 66
Brooksbank St. E9—6J 47
Brooksby M. N1—7A 46
Brooksby St. N1—7A 46
Brooksby's Wlk. E9—5K 47
Brooks Clo. SE9—2E 114
Brookscroft Rd. E17—1D 32
Brookshill. Harr—5C 10
Brookshill Av. Harr—5C 10
Brookshill Dri. Harr—5C 10
Brookside. N21—6E 6
Brookside. Barn—6H 5
Brookside. Cars—5E 132
Brookside. Orp—7K 129
Brookside Clo. Barn—5D 4
Brookside Clo. Harr—5D 24
(Kenton)
Brookside Clo. Harr—4C 38
(South Harrow)
Brookside Cres. Wor Pk
—1C 130
Brookside Rd. N9—4C 18
Brookside Rd. N19—2G 45
Brookside Rd. NW11—6G 27
Brookside Rd. Hay—7A 54
Brookside S. Barn—7K 5
Brookside Wlk. N3—3G 27
Brookside Wlk. N12—6D 14
Brookside Wlk. NW11—4H 27
Brookside Way. Croy—6K 125

Brooks La. W4—6G 73
Brook's M. W1—7F 61 (9J 139)
Brooks Rd. E13—1J 65
Brooks Rd. W4—5G 73
Brook St. N17—2F 31
Brook St. W1—7F 61 (9J 139)
Brook St. W2—7B 60 (9B 138)
Brook St. Belv & Eri—5H 85
Brook St. King—2E 118
Brooksville Av. NW6—1G 59
Brookvale. Eri—1H 101
Brookview Ct. Enf—5K 7
Brookview Rd. SW16—5G 109
Brookville Rd. SW6—7H 75
Brook Wlk. N2—1B 28
Brook Wlk. Edgw—6E 12
Brookway. SE3—3J 97
Brook Way. Chig—3K 21
Brookwood Av. SW13—2B 90
Brookwood Clo. Brom—4H 127
Brookwood Rd. SW18—1H 107
Brookwood Rd. Houn—2F 87
Broom Clo. Brom—6C 128
Broom Clo. Tedd—7D 104
Broomcroft Av. N'holt—3A 54
Broome Rd. Hmptn—7D 102
Broome Way. SE5—7D 78
Broomfield. E17—7B 32
Broomfield Av. N13—5E 16
Broomfield La. N13—4D 16
Broomfield Pl. W13—1B 72
Broomfield Rd. N13—5D 16
Broomfield Rd. W13—1B 72
Broomfield Rd. Beck—3B 126
Broomfield Rd. Bexh—5G 101
Broomfield Rd. Rich—1F 89
Broomfield Rd. Romf—7D 36
Broomfield Rd. Surb—7F 119
Broomfield Rd. Tedd—6C 104
Broomfield St. E14—5D 64
Broom Gdns. Croy—3C 136
Broomgrove Gdns. Edgw
—1G 25
Broomgrove Rd. SW9—2K 93
Broomhall Rd. S Croy—7D 134
Broomhill Rise. Bexh—5G 101
Broomhill Rd. SW18—5J 91
Broomhill Rd. Ilf—2A 52
Broomhill Rd. Orp—7K 129
Broomhill Rd. Wfd G—6D 20
(in two parts)
Broomhill Wlk. Wfd G—7C 20
Broomhouse La. Sutt—2J 131
Broomhouse Rd. SW6—2J 91
Broomloan La. Sutt—2J 131
Broom Lock. Tedd—6C 104
Broom Mead. Bexh—5G 101
Broom Pk. Tedd—7D 104
Broom Rd. Croy—3C 136
Broom Rd. Tedd—5B 104
Broomsleigh St. NW6—5H 43
Broom Water. Tedd—6C 104
Broom Water W. Tedd—5C 104
Broomwood Rd. SW11—6D 92
Broseley Gro. SE26—5A 112
Broster Gdns. SE25—3F 125
Brougham Rd. E8—1G 63
Brougham Rd. W3—6J 57
Brough Clo. SW8—7J 77
Brough St. SW8—7J 77
Broughton Av. N3—3G 27
Broughton Av. Rich—3B 104
Broughton Dri. SW9—4B 94
Broughton Gdns. N6—6G 29
Broughton Rd. SW6—2K 91
Broughton Rd. W13—7B 56
Broughton Rd. T Hth—6A 124
Broughton St. SW8—2F 93
Brouncker Rd. W3—2J 73
Browells La. Felt—2A 102
Brown Clo. Wall—7J 133
Brownfield St. E14—6E 64
Brown Hart Gdns. W1
—7E 60 (9H 139)
Brownhill Rd. SE6—7D 96
Browning Av. W7—6K 55
Browning Av. Sutt—4C 132

Browning Av. Wor Pk—1D 130
Browning Clo. W9
—4A 60 (4A 138)
Browning Clo. Hmptn—4D 102
Browning Clo. Well—1J 99
Browning M. W1
—5E 60 (6H 139)
Browning Rd. E11—7H 33
Browning Rd. E12—5D 50
Browning Rd. Enf—1J 7
Browning St. SE17
—5C 78 (9M 147)
Browning Way. Houn—1B 86
Brownlea Gdns. Ilf—2A 52
Brownlow M. WC1
—4K 61 (4F 140)
Brownlow Rd. E7—4J 49
Brownlow Rd. E8—1G 63
Brownlow Rd. N3—7E 14
Brownlow Rd. N11—6D 16
Brownlow Rd. NW10—7A 42
Brownlow Rd. W13—1A 72
Brownlow Rd. Croy—4E 134
Brownlow St. WC1
—5K 61 (6F 140)
Brown's Bldgs. EC3
—6E 62 (8D 142)
Browns La. NW5—5F 45
Brownspring Dri. SE9—4F 115
Browns Rd. E17—3C 32
Brown's Rd. Surb—7F 119
Brown St. W1—6D 60 (7E 138)
Brownswell Rd. N2—2B 28
Brownswood Rd. N4—2B 46
Broxash Rd. SW11—6E 92
Broxbourne Av. E18—4K 33
Broxbourne Rd. E7—3J 49
Broxbourne Rd. Orp—7K 129
Broxholm Rd. SE27—3A 110
Broxted Rd. SE6—2B 112
Broxwood Way. NW8—1C 60
Bruce Castle Rd. N17—1F 31
Bruce Clo. W10—5F 59
Bruce Clo. Well—1B 100
Bruce Gdns. N20—3J 15
Bruce Gro. N17—2F 31
Bruce Hall M. SW17—4E 108
Bruce Rd. E3—3D 64
Bruce Rd. NW10—7K 41
Bruce Rd. Barn—3B 4
Bruce Rd. Harr—2J 23
Bruce Rd. Mitc—7E 108
Brudenell Rd. SW17—3D 108
Bruffs Meadow. N'holt—6C 38
Bruges Pl. NW1—7G 45
Brummel Clo. Bexh—3J 101
Brunel Clo. SE19—6F 111
Brunel Clo. N'holt—3D 54
Brunel Est. W2—5J 59
Brunel Pl. S'hall—6F 55
Brunel Rd. SE16—2J 79 (5L 149)
Brunel Rd. Wfd G—5J 21
Brunel Rd. W3—5A 58
Brunel St. E16—6H 65
Brunel Wlk. N15—4E 30
Brune St. E1—5F 63 (6E 142)
Brunner Clo. NW11—5A 28
Brunner Ho. SE6—4E 112
Brunner Rd. E17—5A 32
Brunner Rd. W5—4D 56
Bruno Pl. NW9—2J 41
Brunswick Av. N11—3K 15
Brunswick Centre. WC1
—4J 61 (3C 140)
Brunswick Clo. Bexh—4D 100
Brunswick Clo. Pinn—6C 22
Brunswick Clo. Twic—3H 103
Brunswick Ct. SE1
—2E 78 (5D 148)
Brunswick Ct. Barn—5G 5
Brunswick Cres. N11—3K 15
Brunswick Gdns. W5—4E 56
Brunswick Gdns. W8—1J 75
Brunswick Gdns. Ilf—1G 35
Brunswick Gro. N11—3K 15

Brunswick M. W1
—6D 60 (7F 138)
Brunswick Pk. SE5—1E 94
Brunswick Pk. Gdns. N11
—2K 15
Brunswick Pk. Rd. N11—2K 15
Brunswick Pl. N1
—3D 62 (2B 142)
Brunswick Pl. SE19—7G 111
Brunswick Quay. SE16—3K 79
Brunswick Rd. E10—1E 48
Brunswick Rd. E14—6E 64
Brunswick Rd. N15—5E 30
(in two parts)
Brunswick Rd. W5—4D 56
Brunswick Rd. Bexh—4D 100
Brunswick Rd. King—1G 119
Brunswick Rd. Sutt—4K 131
Brunswick Sq. N17—6A 18
Brunswick Sq. WC1
—4J 61 (3D 140)
Brunswick St. E17—5E 32
Brunswick Vs. SE5—1E 94
Brunswick Way. N11—4A 16
Brunton Pl. E14—6A 64
Brushfield St. E1
—5E 62 (5D 142)
Brussels Rd. SW11—4B 92
Bruton Clo. Chst—7D 114
Bruton La. W1—7F 61 (1K 145)
Bruton Pl. W1—7F 61 (1K 145)
Bruton Rd. Mord—4A 122
Bruton St. W1—7F 61 (1K 145)
Bruton Way. W13—5A 56
Bryan Av. NW10—7D 42
Bryan Rd. SE16—2B 80
Bryanston Av. Twic—1F 103
Bryanston Clo. S'hall—4D 70
Bryanstone Rd. N8—6H 29
Bryanston M. E. W1
—5D 60 (6E 138)
Bryanston M. W. W1
—6D 60 (7E 138)
Bryanston Pl. W1
—5D 60 (6E 138)
Bryanston Sq. W1
—6D 60 (7E 138)
Bryanston St. W1
—6D 60 (8F 138)
Bryant Clo. Barn—5C 4
Bryant Rd. N'holt—3A 54
Bryant St. E15—7F 49
Bryantwood Rd. N7—5A 46
Brycedale Cres. N14—3C 16
Bryce Rd. Dag—4C 52
Bryden Clo. SE26—5A 112
Brydges Pl. WC2
—7J 61 (1C 146)
Brydges Rd. E15—5F 49
Brydon Wlk. N1—1J 61
Bryett Rd. N7—3J 45
Brymaer Rd. SW11—1D 92
Brynmawr Rd. Enf—4A 8
Bryony Rd. W12—7C 58
Buchanan Gdns. NW10—2D 58
Buchan Rd. SE15—3J 95
Bucharest Rd. SW18—7A 92
Buckden Clo. SE12—6J 97
Buckfast Rd. Mord—4K 121
Buckfast St. E2—3G 63 (2H 143)
Buck Hill Wlk. W2
—7B 60 (1B 144)
Buckhold Rd. SW18—6J 91
Buckhurst Av. Cars—1C 132
Buckhurst St. E1
—4H 63 (4K 143)
Buckhurst Way. Buck H—4G 21
Buckingham Av. N20—7F 5
Buckingham Av. Gnfd—1A 56
Buckingham Av. T Hth—1A 124
Buckingham Av. Well—4J 99
Buckingham Clo. W5—5C 56
Buckingham Clo. Enf—2B 7
Buckingham Clo. Hmptn
—5D 102
Buckingham Clo. Orp—7J 129

Buckingham Ct. NW4—3C 26
Buckingham Dri. Chst—5G 115
Buckingham Gdns. Edgw
—7K 11
Buckingham Gdns. T Hth
—2A 124
Buckingham Ga. SW1
—2G 77 (5L 145)
Buckingham La. SE23—7A 96
Buckingham M. NW10—2B 58
Buckingham Pal. Rd. SW1
—4F 77 (9J 145)
Buckingham Pde. Stan—5H 11
Buckingham Pl. SW1
—3G 77 (6L 145)
Buckingham Rd. E10—3D 48
Buckingham Rd. E11—5A 34
Buckingham Rd. E15—5H 49
Buckingham Rd. E18—1H 33
Buckingham Rd. N1—6E 46
Buckingham Rd. N22—1J 29
Buckingham Rd. NW10—2B 58
Buckingham Rd. Edgw—7A 12
Buckingham Rd. Hmptn
—5D 102
Buckingham Rd. Harr—5H 23
Buckingham Rd. Ilf—2H 51
Buckingham Rd. King—4F 119
Buckingham Rd. Mitc—5J 123
Buckingham Rd. Rich—2D 104
Buckingham St. WC2
—7J 61 (1D 146)
Buckingham Way. Wall
—7G 133
Buckland Cres. NW3—6B 44
Buckland Rise. Pinn—1A 22
Buckland Rd. E10—2E 48
Bucklands Rd. Tedd—6C 104
Buckland St. N1—2D 62
Buckland's Wharf. King
—2D 118
Buckland Wlk. W3—2J 73
Buckland Wlk. Mord—4A 122
Buckland Way. Wor Pk—1E 130
Buck La. NW9—5K 25
Buckleigh Av. SW20—3H 121
Buckleigh Rd. SW16—6H 109
Buckleigh Way. SE19—1F 125
Buckler Gdns. SE9—3D 114
Bucklers All. SW6—6H 75
Bucklersbury. EC4
—6D 62 (8A 142)
Buckler's Way. Cars—1D 132
Buckles Ct. Belv—4D 84
Buckle St. E1—6F 63 (8F 142)
Buckley Rd. NW6—7H 43
Buckmaster Rd. SW11—5C 92
Bucknall St. WC2
—6J 61 (7C 140)
Bucknall Rd. SW2—4K 93
Buckner Rd. SW2—4K 93
Buckrell Rd. E4—2A 20
Buckstone Clo. SE23—6J 95
Buckstone Rd. N18—5B 18
Buck St. NW1—7F 45
Buckters Rents. SE16—1A 80
Buckthorne Rd. SE4—5A 96
Buck Wlk. E17—4F 33
Buddings Circ. Wemb—3J 41
Budd's All. Twic—5C 88
Budge Row. EC4
—7D 62 (9A 142)
Budleigh Cres. Well—1C 100
Budoch Ct. Ilf—2A 52
Budoch Dri. Ilf—2A 52
Buer Rd. SW6—2G 91
Bugsby's Way. SE10 & SE7
—4H 81
Bulganak Rd. T Hth—4C 124
Bulinga St. SW1—4J 77 (9C 146)
Bull All. SE1—7A 62 (1H 147)
Bull All. Well—3B 100
Bullard's Pl. E2—3K 63 (1M 143)
Bullbanks Rd. Belv—4J 85
Bullen St. SW11—2C 92
Buller Clo. SE15—7G 79
Buller Rd. N17—2G 31

Buller Rd. N22—2A 30
Buller Rd. NW10—3F 59
Buller Rd. Bark—7J 51
Buller Rd. T Hth—2D 124
Bullers Clo. Sidc—5E 116
Bullers Wood Dri. Chst—7D 114
Bullescroft Rd. Edgw—3C 12
Bullivant St. E14—7E 64
Bull La. N18—5K 17
Bull La. Chst—7H 115
Bull La. Dag—3H 53
Bull Rd. E15—2H 65
Bull's All. SW14—2K 89
Bulls Bri. Industrial Est. S'hall
—4A 70
Bullsbridge Rd. S'hall—4A 70
Bullsbrook Rd. Hay—1A 70
Bull's Gdns. SW3
—4C 76 (8D 144)
Bull Wharf La. EC4
—7C 62 (9M 141)
Bull Yd. SE15—1G 95
Bulmer Gdns. Harr—7D 24
Bulmer M. W11—1J 75
Bulmer Pl. W11—1J 75
Bulstrode Av. Houn—2D 86
Bulstrode Gdns. Houn—3E 86
Bulstrode Pl. W1
—5E 60 (6H 139)
Bulstrode Rd. Houn—3E 86
Bulstrode St. W1
—6E 60 (7H 139)
Bulwer Ct. Rd. E11—1F 49
Bulwer Gdns. Barn—4F 5
Bulwer Rd. E11—1F 49
Bulwer Rd. N18—4K 17
Bulwer Rd. Barn—4E 4
Bulwer St. W12—1E 74
Bunce's La. Wfd G—7C 20
Bungalow Rd. SE25—4E 124
Bungalows, The. E10—6E 32
Bungalows, The. SW16—7F 109
Bungalows, The. Ilf—1J 35
Bungalows, The. Wall—5F 133
Bunhill Row. EC1
—4D 62 (3A 142)
Bunhouse Pl. SW1
—5E 76 (9H 145)
Bunkers Hill. NW11—7A 28
Bunkers Hill. Belv—4G 85
Bunkers Hill. Sidc—3F 117
Bunns La. NW7—6F 13
Bunsen St. E3—2A 64
Buntingbridge Rd. Ilf—5H 35
Bunting Clo. Mitc—5D 122
Bunton St. SE18—3E 82
Bunyan Rd. E17—3A 32
Burbage Clo. SE1
—3D 78 (7A 148)
Burbage Rd.—6C 94
SE24 1-105 & 2-118
SE21 remainder
Burberry Clo. N Mald—2A 120
Burbridge Way. N17—2G 31
Burcham St. E14—6E 64
Burcharbro Rd. SE2—6D 84
Burchell Ct. Bush, Wat—1B 10
Burchell Rd. E10—1D 48
Burchell Rd. SE15—1H 95
Burchett Way. Romf—6F 37
Burchwall Clo. Romf—1J 37
Burcote Rd. SW18—7B 92
Burden Clo. Bren—5C 72
Burdenshott Av. Rich—4H 89
Burden Way. E11—2K 49
Burder Clo. N1—6E 46
Burder Rd. N1—6E 46
Burdett Av. SW20—1C 120
Burdett Clo. Sidc—5E 116
Burdett M. NW3—6B 44
Burdett M. W2—6K 59
Burdett Rd.—4A 64
E3 1-207 & 2-230
E14 remainder
Burdett Rd. Croy—6D 124
Burdett Rd. Rich—2F 89
Burdett St. SE1—3A 78 (6G 147)

Burdock Clo. Croy—1K 135
Burdon La. Sutt—7H 131
Burfield Clo. SW17—4B 108
Burford Clo. IIf—4G 35
Burford Gdns. N13—3E 16
Burford Rd. E6—3C 66
Burford Rd. E15—1F 65
Burford Rd. SE6—2B 112
Burford Rd. Bren—5E 72
Burford Rd. Brom—4C 128
Burford Rd. N Mald—7C 120
Burford Rd. Sutt—2J 131
Burford Wlk. SW6—7A 76
Burford Way. Croy—6E 136
Burges Rd. E6—7C 50
Burgess Av. NW9—6K 25
Burgess Clo. Felt—4C 102
Burgess Hill. NW2—4J 43
Burgess Pk. Industrial Est. SE5
—7D 78
Burgess Rd. E15—4G 49
Burgess Rd. Sutt—4K 131
Burgess St. E14—5C 64
Burge St. SE1—3D 78 (7B 148)
Burghhill Rd. SE26—4A 112
Burghley Av. N Mald—1K 119
Burghley Pl. Mitc—5D 122
Burghley Rd. E11—1G 49
Burghley Rd. N8—3A 30
Burghley Rd. NW5—4F 45
Burghley Rd. SW19—4G 107
Burgh St. N1—2B 62
Burgos Gro. SE10—1D 96
Burgoyne Rd. N4—6B 30
Burgoyne Rd. SE25—4F 125
Burgoyne Rd. SW9—3K 93
Burham Clo. SE20—7J 111
Burhill Gro. Pinn—2C 22
Burke Clo. SW15—4A 90
Burke St. E16—5H 65
Burland Rd. SW11—5D 92
Burleigh Av. Sidc—5K 99
Burleigh Av. Wall—3E 132
Burleigh Gdns. N14—1B 16
Burleigh Pl. SW15—5F 91
Burleigh Rd. Enf—4K 7
Burleigh Rd. Sutt—1G 131
Burleigh St. WC2
—7K 61 (9E 140)
Burleigh Way. Enf—3J 7
Burley Clo. E4—5H 19
Burley Clo. SW16—2H 123
Burley Rd. E16—6A 66
Burlington Arc. W1
—7G 61 (1L 145)
Burlington Av. Rich—1G 89
Burlington Av. Romf—6H 37
Burlington Clo. E6—6C 66
Burlington Clo. W9—4J 59
Burlington Gdns. W1
—7G 61 (1L 145)
Burlington Gdns. W3—1J 73
Burlington Gdns. W4—5J 73
Burlington Gdns. Romf—7E 36
Burlington La. W4—7K 73
Burlington M. W3—1J 73
Burlington Pl. SW6—2G 91
Burlington Pl. Wfd G—3E 20
Burlington Rise. Barn—1H 15
Burlington Rd. N10—3E 28
Burlington Rd. N17—1G 31
Burlington Rd. SW6—2G 91
Burlington Rd. W4—5J 73
Burlington Rd. Enf—1J 7
Burlington Rd. N Mald—4B 120
Burlington Rd. Iswth—1H 87
Burlington Rd. T Hth—2C 124
Burma M. N16—4D 46
Burma Rd. N16—4D 46
Burmarsh Ct. SE20—1J 125
Burma Ter. SE19—5E 110
Burmester Rd. SW17—3A 108
Burnaby Cres. W4—6J 73
Burnaby Gdns. W4—6H 73
Burnaby St. SW10—7A 76
Burnage Ct. SE19—4J 111

Burnbrae Clo. N12—6E 14
Burnbury Rd. SW12—1G 109
Burncroft Av. Enf—2D 8
Burnell Av. Rich—5C 104
Burnell Av. Well—2A 100
Burnell Gdns. Stan—2D 24
Burnell Rd. Sutt—4K 131
Burnels Av. E6—3E 66
Burness Clo. N7—6K 45
Burne St. NW1—5C 60 (5C 138)
Burnett Clo. E9—5J 47
Burney Av. Surb—5F 119
Burney St. SE10—7E 80
Burnfoot Av. SW6—1G 91
Burnham Clo. Enf—1K 7
Burnham Cres. E11—4A 34
Burnham Dri. Wor Pk—2F 131
Burnham Gdns. Croy—7F 125
Burnham Rd. E4—5G 19
Burnham Rd. Dag—7B 52
Burnham Rd. Mord—4K 121
Burnham Rd. Romf—3K 37
Burnham Rd. Sidc—2E 116
Burnham St. E2—3J 63 (1L 143)
Burnham St. King—1G 119
Burnham Way. W13—4B 72
Burnhill Rd. Beck—2C 126
Burnley Rd. NW10—5B 42
Burnley Rd. SW9—2K 93
Burnsall St. SW3—5C 76
Burns Av. Sidc—6B 100
Burns Av. S'hall—7E 54
Burns Clo. SW19—6B 108
Burns Clo. Well—1K 99
Burn Side. N9—3D 18
Burnside Clo. Barn—3D 4
Burnside Clo. Twic—6A 88
Burnside Cres. Wemb—1D 56
Burnside Rd. Dag—2C 52
Burns Rd. NW10—1B 58
Burns Rd. SW11—2D 92
Burns Rd. W13—2B 72
Burns Rd. Wemb—2E 56
Burns Way. Houn—2B 86
Burnt Ash Hill. SE12—6H 97
Burnt Ash La. Brom—6J 113
Burnt Ash Rd. SE12—5H 97
Burnthwaite Rd. SW6—7H 75
Burnt Oak B'way. Edgw—7C 12
Burnt Oak Fields. Edgw—1J 25
Burnt Oak La. Sidc—6A 100
Burntwood Clo. SW18—1C 108
Burntwood Grange Rd. SW18
—1C 108
Burntwood La. SW17—3A 108
Buross St. E1—6H 63 (7K 143)
Burrage Gro. SE18—4G 83
Burrage Pl. SE18—5F 83
Burrage Rd. SE18—5G 83
Burrard Rd. E16—6K 65
Burrard Rd. NW6—4J 43
Burr Clo. E1—1G 79 (2G 149)
Burrell Clo. Edgw—2C 12
Burrell Clo. Croy—6A 126
Burrell Row. Beck—2C 126
Burrell St. SE1—1B 78 (2J 147)
Burrell's Wharf Development.
E14—5D 80
Burritt Rd. King—2G 119
Burroughs Gdns. NW4—4D 26
Burroughs, The. NW4—4D 26
Burrows M. SE1—2B 78 (4J 147)
Burrows Rd. NW10—3E 58
Burrow Wlk. SE21—7C 94
Burr Rd. SW18—1J 107
Bursdon Clo. Sidc—2K 115
Bursland Rd. Enf—4E 8
Burslem St. E1—6G 63 (8H 143)
Burstock Rd. SW15—4G 91
Burston Rd. SW15—5F 91
Burstow Rd. SW20—1G 121
Burtenshaw Rd. Th Dit—6A 118
Burtley Clo. N4—1C 46
Burton Clo. NW7—4A 14
Burton Gdns. Houn—1D 86
Burton Gro. SE17—5D 78

Burtonhole La. NW7—5K 13
Burtonhole La. Farm Est. NW7
—4A 14
Burton La. SW9—2A 94
Burton M. SW1—4E 76 (9H 145)
Burton Pl. WC1—4H 61 (3B 140)
Burton Rd. E18—3K 33
Burton Rd. NW6—7H 43
Burton Rd. SW9—2A & 2B 94
(in two parts)
Burton Rd. King—7E 104
Burtons Ct. E15—7F 49
Burton's Rd. Hmptn—4F 103
Burt Rd. E16—1A 82
Burtwell La. SE27—4D 110
Burwash Rd. SE18—5H 83
Burwell Av. Gnfd—6J 39
Burwell Clo. E1—6H 63 (8K 143)
Burwell Rd. E10—1A 48
Burwell Rd. Industrial Est. E10
—1A 48
Burwell Wlk. E3—4C 64
Burwood Av. Brom—2K 137
Burwood Av. Pinn—5A 22
Burwood Pl. W2—6C 60 (7D 138)
Bury Ct. EC3—6E 62 (7D 142)
Bury Gro. Mord—5K 121
Bury Hall Vs. N9—7A 8
Bury Pl. WC1—5J 61 (6C 140)
Bury Rd. E4—1B 20
Bury Rd. N22—3A 30
Bury Rd. Dag—5H 53
Bury St. EC3—6E 62 (7D 142)
Bury St. N9—7A 8
Bury St. SW1—1G 77 (2M 145)
Bury St. W. N9—7J 7
Bury Wlk. SW3—4C 76 (9C 144)
Busby M. NW5—6H 45
Busby Pl. NW5—6H 45
Busby St. E2—4F 63 (3F 142)
Bushberry Rd. E9—6A 48
Bush Clo. IIf—5H 35
Bush Cotts. SW18—5J 91
Bushell Clo. SW2—2K 109
Bushell Grn. Bush, Wat—2C 10
Bushell St. E1—1G 79 (3H 149)
Bushell Way. Chst—5E 114
Bushey Av. E18—3H 33
Bushey Av. Orp—7H 129
Bushey Ct. SW20—2D 120
Bushey Hill Rd. SE5—1E 94
Bushey La. Sutt—4J 131
Bushey Rd. E13—2A 66
Bushey Rd. N15—6E 30
Bushey Rd. SW20—3D 120
Bushey Rd. Croy—2C 136
Bushey Rd. Sutt—4J 131
Bushey Way. Beck—6F 127
Bush Fair Ct. N14—6A 6
Bushfield Clo. Edgw—2C 12
Bushfield Cres. Edgw—2C 12
Bush Gro. NW9—7J 25
Bush Gro. Stan—7J 11
Bushgrove Rd. Dag—4D 52
Bush Hill. N21—7H 7
Bush Hill Pde. N9—7J 7
Bush Hill Rd. N21—6J 7
Bush Hill Rd. Harr—6F 25
Bush Industrial Est. N19—3H 45
Bush La. EC4—7D 62 (9A 142)
Bushmoor Cres. SE18—7F 83
Bushnell Rd. SW17—3F 109
Bush Rd. E8—1H 63
Bush Rd. E11—7H 33
Bush Rd. SE8—4K 79
Bush Rd. Buck H—4G 21
Bush Rd. Rich—6F 73
Bushway. Dag—4D 52
Bushwood. E11—1H 49
Bushwood Rd. Rich—6G 73
Bushy Down. SW12—2F 109
Bushy Lees. Sidc—6K 99
Bushy Pk. Gdns. Tedd—5H 103
Bushy Pk. Rd. Tedd—7B 104
Bushy Rd. Tedd—6K 103

Butcher Row—7K 63
E1 4-12
E14 remainder
Butchers Rd. E16—6J 65
Bute Av. Rich—2E 104
Bute Ct. Wall—5G 133
Bute Gdns. W6—4F 75
Bute Gdns. Wall—5G 133
Bute Gdns. W. Wall—5G 133
Bute Rd. Croy—1A 134
Bute Rd. IIf—5F 35
Bute Rd. Wall—4G 133
Bute St. SW7—4B 76
Bute Wlk. N1—6D 46
Butler Av. Harr—7H 23
Butler Rd. NW10—7A 42
Butler Rd. Dag—4B 52
Butler Rd. Harr—7G 23
Butlers Dri. E4—1K 9
Butler St. E2—3J 63 (1M 143)
Butterfield Clo. Twic—6K 87
Butterfields. E17—5E 32
Butterfield Sq. E6—6D 66
Butterfly La. SE9—6F 99
Butter Hill. Wall & Cars—3E 132
Buttermere Clo. Mord—6F 121
Buttermere Dri. SW15—5G 91
Buttermere Wlk. E8—6F 47
Butterwick. W6—4F 75
Buttesland St. N1
—3D 62 (1B 142)
Buttfield Clo. Dag—6H 53
Buttmarsh Clo. SE18—5F 83
Buttsbury Rd. IIf—5G 51
Butts Cotts. Felt—3C 102
Butts Cres. Felt—3E 102
Butts Rd. Brom—5G 113
Butts, The. Bren—6D 72
Buxted Clo. E8—7F 47
Buxted Rd. N12—5H 15
Buxton Clo. Wfd G—6G 21
Buxton Cres. Sutt—4G 131
Buxton Dri. E11—4G 33
Buxton Dri. N Mald—2K 119
Buxton Gdns. W3—7H 57
Buxton Rd. E4—1A 20
Buxton Rd. E6—3C 66
Buxton Rd. E15—5G 49
Buxton Rd. E17—4A 32
Buxton Rd. N19—1H 45
Buxton Rd. NW2—6D 42
Buxton Rd. SW14—3A 90
Buxton Rd. Eri—7K 85
Buxton Rd. IIf—6J 35
Buxton Rd. T Hth—5B 124
Buxton St. E1—4F 63 (4F 142)
Buzzard Creek Industrial Est.
Bark—5A 68
Byam St. SW6—2A 92
Byards Croft. SW16—1H 123
Byatt Wlk. Hmptn—6C 102
Bycroft Rd. S'hall—4E 54
Bycroft St. SE20—7K 111
Bycullah Av. Enf—3G 7
Bycullah Rd. Enf—2G 7
Byegrove Rd. SW19—6B 108
Bye, The. W3—6A 58
Bye Ways. Twic—3F 103
Byeways, The. Surb—5G 119
Byeway, The. SW14—3J 89
Byeway, The. Eps—4B 130
Bye Way, The. Harr—1K 23
Byfeld Gdns. SW13—1C 90
Byfield Pas. Iswth—3A 88
Byfield Rd. Iswth—3A 88
Byford Clo. E15—7G 49
Byford Ho. Barn—4A 4
Bygrove. Croy—7D 136
Bygrove St. E14—6D 64
Byland Clo. N21—7F 7
Bylands Clo. SE2—3B 84
Byne Rd. SE26—6J 111
Byne Rd. Cars—2C 132
Bynes Rd. S Croy—7D 134
Byng Pl. WC1—4H 61 (4A 140)
Byng Rd. Barn—2A 4
Byng St. E14—2C 80

Bynon Av. Bexh—3F 101
Byre Rd., The. N14—6A 6
(in two parts)
Byrne St. SW12—1F 109
Byron Av. E12—6C 50
Byron Av. E18—3H 33
Byron Av. NW9—4H 25
Byron Av. N Mald—5C 120
Byron Av. Sutt—4B 132
Byron Av. E. Sutt—4B 132
Byron Clo. E8—1G 63
Byron Clo. N2—6B 28
Byron Clo. SE28—1C 84
Byron Clo. Hmptn—4D 102
Byron Ct. Enf—2G 7
Byron Gdns. Sutt—4B 132
Byron Hill Rd. Harr—1H 39
Byron Rd. E10—1D 48
Byron Rd. E17—3C 32
Byron Rd. NW2—2D 42
Byron Rd. NW7—5H 13
Byron Rd. W5—1F 73
Byron Rd. Harr—6J 23
(Greenhill)
Byron Rd. Harr—2K 23
(Wealdstone)
Byron Rd. Wemb—2C 40
Byron St. E14—6E 64
Byron Ter. N9—6D 8
Byron Way. N'holt—3C 54
Bysouth Clo. Ilf—1F 35
Bythorn St. SW9—3K 93
Byton Rd. SW17—6D 108
Byward Av. Felt—6A 86
Byward St. EC3—7E 62 (1D 148)
Bywater Pl. SE16—1A 80
Bywater St. SW3
—5D 76 (9E 144)
Byway. E11—5A 34
Byway, The. Sutt—7B 132
Bywood Av. Croy—6J 125
Byworth Wlk. N19—1J 45

Cabbell St. NW1
—5C 60 (6C 138)
Cabinet Way. E4—5G 19
Cable Pl. SE10—1E 96
Cable St. E1—7G 63 (9H 143)
Cabot Way. E6—1B 66
Cabul Rd. SW11—2C 92
Cactus Wlk. W12—6B 58
Cadbury Clo. Iswth—1A 88
Cadbury Wlk. SE16
—4F 79 (8F 148)
Cadbury Way. SE16
—4G 79 (8F 148)
Caddington Clo. Barn—5H 5
Caddington Rd. NW2—3G 43
Caddis Clo. Stan—7E 10
Cadell Clo. E2—2F 63 (1F 142)
Cade Rd. SE10—1F 97
Cader Rd. SW18—6A 92
Cadet Pl. SE10—5G 81
Cadiz Rd. Dag—7J 53
Cadiz St. SE17—5C 78
Cadley Ter. SE23—2J 111
Cadmer Clo. N Mald—4A 120
Cadogan Clo. E9—7B 48
Cadogan Clo. Beck—1F 127
Cadogan Clo. Harr—4F 39
Cadogan Clo. Tedd—5J 103
Cadogan Ct. Sutt—6K 131
Cadogan Gdns. E18—3K 33
Cadogan Gdns. N3—1K 27
Cadogan Gdns. N21—5F 7
Cadogan Gdns. SW3
—4D 76 (8F 144)
Cadogan Ga. SW1
—4D 76 (8F 144)
Cadogan La. SW1
—3E 76 (7G 145)
Cadogan Pl. SW1
—3D 76 (6F 144)
Cadogan Rd. Surb—5D 118
Cadogan Sq. SW1
—3D 76 (7E 144)

Cadogan St. SW3
—4D 76 (9E 144)
Cadogan Ter. E9—6B 48
Cadoxton Av. N15—6F 31
Cadwallon Rd. SE9—2F 115
Caedmon Rd. N7—4K 45
Caerleon Clo. Sidc—5C 116
Caerleon Ter. SE2—4B 84
Caernarvon Clo. Mitc—3J 123
Caernarvon Dri. Ilf—1E 34
Caesars Wlk. Mitc—5D 122
Cahill St. EC1—4C 62 (4M 141)
Cahir St. E14—4D 80
Caird St. W10—3G 59
Cairn Av. W5—1D 72
Cairndale Clo. Brom—7H 113
Cairnfield Av. NW2—3A 42
Cairngorm Clo. Tedd—5A 104
Cairns Av. Wfd G—6J 21
Cairns Rd. SW11—5C 92
Cairn Way. Stan—6E 10
Cairo New Rd. Croy—2B 134
Cairo Rd. E17—4C 32
Caistor M. SW12—7F 93
Caistor Pk. Rd. E15—1H 65
Caistor Rd. SW12—7F 93
Caithness Gdns. Sidc—6K 99
Caithness Rd. W14—3F 75
Caithness Rd. Mitc—7F 109
Calabria Rd. N5—6B 46
Calais Ga. SE5—1B 94
Calais St. SE5—1B 94
Calbourne Rd. SW12—7D 92
Calcott Wlk. SE9—4C 114
Caldbeck Av. Wor Pk—1D 130
Caldecote Gdns. Bush, Wat
—1D 10
Caldecot Rd. SE5—2C 94
Caldecott Way. E5—3K 47
Calder Av. Gnfd—2K 55
Calder Clo. Enf—3K 7
Calder Gdns. Edgw—3G 25
Calderon Pl. W10—5E 58
Calderon Rd. E11—4E 48
Caldervale Rd. SW4—5H 93
Calderwood St. SE18—4E 82
Caldew St. SE5—6D 78
Caldicot Grn. NW9—6A 26
Caldwell St. SW9—7K 77
Caldwell Yd. EC4
—7C 62 (9L 141)
Caldy Rd. Belv—3H 85
Caldy Wlk. N1—6C 46
Caleb St. SE1—2C 78 (4M 147)
Caledonian Rd.—2J 61 (1D 140)
N1 1-351 & 2-400
N7 remainder
Caledonian Wharf. E14—4F 81
Caledonia St. N1
—2J 61 (1D 140)
Caledon Rd. E6—1D 66
Caledon Rd. Wall—4E 132
Cale St. SW3—5C 76 (9C 144)
Caletock Way. SE10—5H 81
Calico Row. SW11—3A 92
California La. Bush, Wat
—1C 10
California Rd. N Mald—3J 119
Callaghan Clo. SE13—4G 97
Callander Rd. SE6—2D 112
Callard Av. N13—4G 17
Callcott Rd. NW6—7H 43
Callcott St. W8—1J 75
Callender Rd. SW7
—3B 76 (6A 144)
Callingham Clo. E14—5B 64
Callis Rd. E17—6B 32
Callow St. SW3—6B 76
Calmington Rd. SE5—6E 78
Calmont Rd. Brom—6F 113
Calne Av. Ilf—1F 35
Calonne Rd. SW19—4F 107
Calshot Rd. N1—2K 61 (1E 140)
Calshot Way. Enf—3G 7
Calthorpe Gdns. Edgw—5K 11
Calthorpe Gdns. Sutt—3A 132

Calthorpe St. WC1
—4K 61 (3F 140)
Calton Av. SE21—6E 94
Calton Rd. Barn—6F 5
Calverley Clo. Beck—6D 112
Calverley Cres. Dag—2G 53
Calverley Gdns. Harr—7D 24
Calverley Gro. N19—1H 45
Calverley Rd. Eps—6C 130
Calvert Av. E2—3F 63 (2E 142)
Calvert Clo. Belv—4G 85
Calvert Clo. Sidc—6E 116
Calverton Rd. E6—1E 66
Calvert Rd. SE10—5H 81
Calvert Rd. Barn—2A 4
Calvert St. NW1—1E 60
Calvin St. E1—4F 63 (4E 142)
Calydon Rd. SE7—5K 81
Calypso Way. SE16—4B 80
Camac Rd. Twic—1H 103
Cambalt Rd. SW15—5F 91
Camberley Av. SW20—2D 120
Camberley Av. Enf—4K 7
Camberley Clo. Sutt—3F 131
Cambert Way. SE3—4K 97
Camberwell Chu. St. SE5
—1D 94
Camberwell Glebe. SE5—1E 94
Camberwell Grn. SE5—1D 94
Camberwell Gro. SE5—1D 94
Camberwell New Rd. SE5
—7A 78
Camberwell Pas. SE5—1C 94
Camberwell Rd. SE5—6C 78
Camberwell Sta. Rd. SE5
—1C 94
Cambeys Rd. Dag—5H 53
Camborne Av. W13—2B 72
Camborne Rd. SW18—7J 91
Camborne Rd. Croy—7G 125
Camborne Rd. Mord—5F 121
Camborne Rd. Sidc—3C 116
Camborne Rd. Sutt—7K 131
Camborne Rd. Well—2K 99
Camborne Way. Houn—1E 86
Cambourne Av. N9—7E 8
Cambourne M. W11—6G 59
Cambourne Wlk. Rich—6D 88
Cambray Rd. SW12—1G 109
Cambray Rd. Orp—7K 129
Cambria Clo. Houn—4E 86
Cambria Clo. Sidc—1H 115
Cambria Ct. Felt—7A 86
Cambria Rd. SE5—3C 94
Cambria St. SW6—7K 75
Cambridge Av. NW6—2J 59
Cambridge Av. Gnfd—5K 39
Cambridge Av. N Mald—2A 120
Cambridge Av. Well—4K 99
Cambridge Barracks Rd. SE18
—4D 82
Cambridge Cir. WC2
—6H 61 (8B 140)
Cambridge Clo. SW20—1D 120
Cambridge Clo. Houn—4C 86
Cambridge Cotts. Rich—6G 73
Cambridge Cres. E2—2H 63
Cambridge Cres. Tedd—5A 104
Cambridge Dri. SE12—5J 97
Cambridge Dri. Ruis—2A 38
Cambridge Gdns. N10—1F 29
Cambridge Gdns. N17—7J 17
Cambridge Gdns. N21—7J 7
Cambridge Gdns. NW6—2J 59
Cambridge Gdns. W10—6F 59
Cambridge Gdns. Enf—2B 8
Cambridge Gdns. King—2G 119
Cambridge Ga. NW1
—4F 61 (3J 139)
Cambridge Ga. M. NW1
—4F 61 (3K 139)
Cambridge Grn. SE9—1F 115
Cambridge Gro. SE20—1H 125

Cambridge Gro. W6—4D 74
Cambridge Gro. Rd. King
(in two parts)   —3G 119
Cambridge Heath Rd.
—4H 63 (4K 143)
E1 1-183 & 2-154a
E2 remainder
Cambridge Lodge Vs. E8
—1H 63
Cambridge Pde. Enf—1B 8
Cambridge Pk. E11—7J 33
Cambridge Pk. Twic—6C 88
Cambridge Pk. Rd. E11—7H 33
Cambridge Pl. NW6—3J 59
Cambridge Pl. W8—2K 75
Cambridge Rd. E4—1A 20
Cambridge Rd. E11—6H 33
Cambridge Rd. NW6—3J 59
(in two parts)
Cambridge Rd. SE20—3H 125
Cambridge Rd. SW11—1D 92
Cambridge Rd. SW13—2B 90
Cambridge Rd. SW20—1C 120
Cambridge Rd. W7—2K 71
Cambridge Rd. Bark—7G 51
Cambridge Rd. Brom—7J 113
Cambridge Rd. Cars—6C 132
Cambridge Rd. Hmptn—7D 102
Cambridge Rd. Harr—5E 22
Cambridge Rd. Houn—4C 86
Cambridge Rd. Ilf—1J 51
Cambridge Rd. King—2F 119
Cambridge Rd. Mitc—3G 123
Cambridge Rd. N Mald—4A 120
Cambridge Rd. Rich—7G 73
Cambridge Rd. Sidc—4J 115
Cambridge Rd. S'hall—1D 70
Cambridge Rd. Tedd—4A 104
Cambridge Rd. Twic—6D 88
Cambridge Rd. N. W4—5H 73
Cambridge Rd. S. W4—5H 73
Cambridge Row. SE18—5F 83
Cambridge Sq. W2
—6C 60 (7C 138)
Cambridge St. SW1
—4F 77 (9K 145)
Cambridge Ter. N9—7A 8
Cambridge Ter. NW1
—3F 61 (2J 139)
Cambridge Ter. M. NW1
—3F 61 (2K 139)
Cambus Clo. Hay—5C 54
Cambus Rd. E16—5J 65
Camdale Rd. SE18—7K 83
Camden Av. Felt—1A 102
Camden Av. Hay—7B 54
Camden Clo. Chst—1G 129
Camden Est. SE15—1F 95
Camden Gdns. NW1—7F 45
Camden Gdns. Sutt—5K 131
Camden Gdns. T Hth—3B 124
Camden Gro. Chst—6F 115
Camden High St. NW1—1F 61
Camden Hill Rd. SE19—6E 110
Camdenhurst St. E14—6A 64
Camden La. N7—5H 45
Camden Lock Pl. NW1—7F 45
Camden M. NW1—6H 45
Camden Pk. Rd. NW1—6H 45
Camden Pk. Rd. Chst—7D 114
Camden Pas. N1—1B 62
Camden Rd. E11—6K 33
Camden Rd. E17—6B 32
Camden Rd.—7G 45
NW1 1-227 & 2a-282
N7 remainder
Camden Rd. Bex—1F 117
Camden Rd. Cars—4D 132
Camden Rd. Sutt—5K 131
Camden Row. SE3—2G 97
Camden Row. Pinn—3A 22
Camden Sq. NW1—6H 45
Camden Sq. SE15—1F 95
Camden Ter. NW1—6H 45
Camden Wlk. N1—1B 62
Camden Way. Chst—7E 114

Carlisle Av. W3—6A 58
Carlisle Clo. King—1G 119
Carlisle Gdns. Harr—7D 24
Carlisle Gdns. Ilf—6C 34
Carlisle La. SE1—3K 77 (7F 146)
Carlisle M. NW8
—5B 60 (5B 138)
Carlisle Pl. N11—4A 16
Carlisle Pl. SW1—3G 77 (7L 145)
Carlisle Rd. E10—1C 48
Carlisle Rd. N4—7A 30
Carlisle Rd. NW6—1G 59
Carlisle Rd. NW9—3J 25
Carlisle Rd. Hmptn—7F 103
Carlisle Rd. Sutt—6H 131
Carlisle St. W1—6H 61 (8A 140)
Carlisle Wlk. E8—6F 47
Carlisle Way. SW17—5E 108
Carlos Pl. W1—7E 60 (1H 145)
Carlow St. NW1—2G 61
Carlton Av. N14—5C 6
Carlton Av. Felt—6A 86
Carlton Av. Harr—5B 24
Carlton Av. S Croy—7E 134
Carlton Av. E. Wemb—2D 40
Carlton Av. W. Wemb—2B 40
Carlton Clo. NW3—2J 43
Carlton Clo. Edgw—5B 12
Carlton Clo. N'holt—5G 39
Carlton Ct. SE20—1H 125
Carlton Ct. Ilf—3H 35
Carlton Cres. Sutt—4G 131
Carlton Dri. SW15—5G 91
Carlton Dri. Ilf—3H 35
Carlton Gdns. SW1
—1H 77 (3A 146)
Carlton Gdns. W5—6C 56
Carlton Grn. SW9—1B 94
Carlton Gro. SE15—1H 95
Carlton Hill. NW8—2K 59
Carlton Ho. Ter. SW1
—1H 77 (3A 146)
Carlton Pk. Av. SW20—2F 121
Carlton Rd. E11—1H 49
Carlton Rd. E12—4B 50
Carlton Rd. E17—1A 32
Carlton Rd. N4—7A 30
Carlton Rd. N11—5K 15
Carlton Rd. SW14—4J 89
Carlton Rd. W4—2K 73
Carlton Rd. W5—7C 56
Carlton Rd. Eri—6H 85
Carlton Rd. N Mald—2A 120
Carlton Rd. Sidc—5K 115
Carlton Rd. S Croy—7D 134
Carlton Rd. Well—3B 100
Carlton Sq. E1—4K 63 (3M 143)
(in two parts)
Carlton St. SW1
—7H 61 (1A 146)
Carlton Ter. E11—5K 33
Carlton Ter. N18—3J 17
Carlton Ter. SE26—3J 111
Carlton Vale. NW6—2H 59
Carlwell St. SW17—5C 108
Carlyle Av. Brom—3B 128
Carlyle Av. S'hall—7D 54
Carlyle Clo. N2—6A 28
Carlyle Clo. NW10—1K 57
Carlyle Gdns. S'hall—7D 54
Carlyle Pl. SW15—4F 91
Carlyle Rd. E12—4C 50
Carlyle Rd. SE28—7B 68
Carlyle Rd. W4—4C 72
Carlyle Rd. Croy—2G 135
Carlyle Sq. SW3—5B 76
Carlyon Av. Harr—4D 38
Carlyon Clo. Wemb—1E 56
Carlyon Rd. Hay—5A 54
(in two parts)
Carlyon Rd. Wemb—2E 56
Carmalt Gdns. SW15—4E 90
Carmarthen Pl. SE1
—2E 78 (4C 148)
Carmelite Clo. Harr—1G 23
Carmelite Rd. Harr—1G 23

Carmelite St. EC4
—7A 62 (9H 141)
Carmelite Wlk. Harr—1G 23
Carmelite Way. Harr—2G 23
Carmen St. E14—6D 64
Carmichael Clo. SW11—3B 92
Carmichael M. SW18—6B 92
Carmichael Rd. SE25—5G 125
Carminia Rd. SW17—2F 109
Carnaby St. W1—6G 61 (8L 139)
Carnac St. SE27—4D 110
Carnanton Rd. E17—1F 33
Carnarvon Av. Enf—3A 8
Carnarvon Rd. E10—5E 32
Carnarvon Rd. E15—6H 49
Carnarvon Rd. E18—1H 33
Carnarvon Rd. Barn—3B 4
Carnation St. SE2—5B 84
Carnbrook Rd. SE3—3B 98
Carnecke Gdns. SE9—5C 98
Carnegie Pl. SW19—3F 107
Carnegie St. N1—1K 61
Carnforth Rd. SW16—7H 109
Carnie Hall. SW17—3F 109
Carnoustie Dri. N1—7K 45
Carnwath Rd. SW6—3J 91
Carolina Rd. T Hth—2B 124
Caroline Clo. N10—2F 29
Caroline Clo. SW16—3K 109
Caroline Clo. Croy—4E 134
Caroline Clo. Iswth—7J 71
Caroline Ct Stan—6F 11
Caroline Gdns. E2
—3E 62 (1D 142)
Caroline Pl. SW11—2E 92
Caroline Pl. M. W2—7K 59
Caroline Rd. SW19—7H 107
Caroline St. E1—6K 63
Caroline Ter. SW1
—4E 76 (9G 145)
Caroline Wlk. W6—6G 75
Carol St. NW1—1G 61
Carpenter Gdns. N21—2G 17
Carpenters Pl. SW4—4H 93
Carpenter's Rd. E15—6C 48
Carpenter St. W1
—7F 61 (1J 145)
Carrara Wlk. SW9—4A 94
Carriage Dri. E. SW11—7E 76
Carriage Dri. N. SW11—7D 76
Carriage Dri. S. SW11—1D 92
Carriage Dri. W. SW11—7D 76
Carrick Gdns. N17—7K 17
Carrick M. SE8—6C 80
Carrill Way. Belv—3F 84
Carrington Av. Houn—5F 87
Carrington Clo. Croy—7A 126
Carrington Gdns. E7—4J 49
Carrington Rd. Rich—4G 89
Carrington Sq. Harr—7B 10
Carrington St. W1
—1F 77 (3J 145)
Carrol Clo. NW5—4F 45
Carroll Clo. E15—5H 49
Carroun Rd. SW8—7K 77
Carroway La. Gnfd—3H 55
Carrow Clo. E14—6D 64
Carrow Rd. Dag—7B 52
Carr Rd. E17—2C 32
Carr Rd. N'holt—6E 38
Carrs La. N21—5H 7
Carr St. E14—5A 64
(in two parts)
Carshalton Gro. Sutt—5B 132
Carshalton Pk. Rd. Cars
—6D 132
Carshalton Pl. Cars—5E 132
Carshalton Rd. Mitc—5E 122
Carshalton Rd. Sutt & Cars
—5A 132
Carslake Rd. SW15—6E 90
Carson Rd. E16—4J 65
Carson Rd. SE21—2D 110
Carson Rd. Barn—4J 5
Carstairs Rd. SE6—3E 112
Carston Clo. SE12—5H 97
Carswell Clo. Ilf—4B 34

Carswell Rd. SE6—7E 96
Carter Clo. Wall—7H 133
Carter Dri. Romf—1H 37
Carteret St. SW1
—2H 77 (5A 146)
Carteret Way. SE8—4A 80
Carterhatch La. Enf—1A 8
Carterhatch Rd. Enf—2D 8
Carter La. EC4—6B 62 (8K 141)
Carter Pl. SE17—5C 78
Carter Rd. E13—1K 65
Carter Rd. SW19—6B 108
Carters Clo. Wor Pk—1F 131
Carters Hill Clo. SE9—1A 114
Carters La. SE23—2A 112
Carter St. SE17—6C 78
Carthew Rd. W6—3D 74
Carthew Vs. W6—3D 74
Carthusian St. EC1
—5C 62 (5L 141)
Carting La. WC2
—7K 61 (1E 146)
Cart La. E4—1B 20
Cartmel Clo. N17—7C 18
Cartmel Gdns. Mord—5A 122
Cartmel Rd. Bexh—1G 101
Cartwright Gdns. WC1
—3J 61 (2C 140)
Cartwright Rd. Dag—7F 53
Cartwright St. E1
—7F 63 (1F 148)
Carver Rd. SE24—6C 94
Carville Cres. Bren—4E 72
Cary Rd. E11—4G 49
Carysfort Rd. N8—5H 29
Carysfort Rd. N16—3D 46
Cascade Av. N10—4G 29
Cascade Clo. Buck H—2G 21
Cascade Rd. Buck H—2G 21
Cascades Tower. E14—1C 80
Casella Rd. SE14—7K 79
Casewick Rd. SE27—5A 110
Casimir Rd. E5—3H 47
Casino Av. SE24—5D 94
Caspian St. SE5—7D 78
Caspian Wlk. E16—6B 66
Casselden Rd. NW10—7K 41
Cassidy Rd. SW6—7J 75
(in two parts)
Cassilda Rd. SE2—4A 84
Cassilis Rd. Twic—6B 88
Cassiobury Rd. E17—5A 32
Cassland Rd. E9—7K 47
Cassland Rd. T Hth—4D 124
Casslee Rd. SE6—7B 96
Casson St. E1—5G 63 (6G 143)
Castalia Sq. E14—2E 80
Castellain Rd. W9—4K 59
Castellane Clo. Stan—7E 10
Castello Av. SW15—5E 90
Castelnau. SW13—1C 90
Castelnau Gdns. SW13—6D 74
Castelnau Pl. SW13—6D 74
Castelnau Row. SW13—6D 74
Casterbridge Rd. SE3—3J 97
Castile Rd. SE18—4E 82
Castillon Rd. SE6—2G 113
Castlands Rd. SE6—2B 112
Castle Av. E4—5A 20
Castle Av. Eps—7D 130
Castlebar Ct. W5—5C 56
Castlebar Hill. W5—5C 56
Castlebar M. W5—5C 56
Castlebar Pk. W5—5B 56
Castlebar Rd. W5—6C 56
Castle Baynard St. EC4
—7B 62 (9K 141)
Castle Clo. E9—5A 48
Castle Clo. SW19—3F 107
Castle Clo. Brom—3G 127
Castlecombe Dri. SW19—7F 91
Castlecombe Rd. SE9—4C 114
Castledine Rd. SE20—7H 111
Castle Dri. Ilf—6C 34
Castleford Av. SE9—1F 115
Castlegate. Rich—3F 89

Castlehaven Rd. NW1—7F 45
Castle Hill Av. Croy—7D 136
Castle Industrial Est. SE17
—4C 78 (8L 147)
Castleleigh Ct. Enf—5J 7
Castlemaine Av. Eps—7D 130
Castlemaine Av. S Croy
—5F 135
Castle M. NW1—6F 45
Castle Pde. Eps—7C 130
Castle Pl. W4—4A 74
Castlereagh St. W1
—6D 60 (7E 138)
Castle Rd. N12—5F 15
Castle Rd. NW1—6F 45
Castle Rd. Dag—1B 68
Castle Rd. Enf—1F 9
Castle Rd. Iswth—2K 87
Castle Rd. N'holt—6F 39
Castle Rd. S'hall—3D 70
Castle St. E6—2B 66
Castle St. King—2E 118
Castleton Av. Bexh—1K 101
Castleton Av. Wemb—4E 40
Castleton Gdns. Wemb—3E 40
Castleton Rd. E17—2F 33
Castleton Rd. SE9—4B 114
Castleton Rd. Ilf—1A 52
Castleton Rd. Mitc—4H 123
Castleton Rd. Ruis—1B 38
Castletown Rd. W14—5G 75
Castleview Gdns. Ilf—6C 34
Castle Way. SW19—3F 107
Castle Way. Felt—4A 102
Castlewood Dri. SE9—2D 98
Castlewood Rd.—7G 31
N16 1-121 & 2-102
N15 remainder
Castlewood Rd. Barn—3G 5
Castle Yd. N6—7E 28
Castle Yd. SE1—1B 78 (2K 147)
Castle Yd. Rich—5D 88
Castor La. E14—7D 64
Caterham Av. Ilf—2D 34
Caterham Rd. SE13—3F 97
Catesby St. SE17
—4D 78 (9B 148)
Catford B'way. SE6—7D 96
Catford Hill. SE6—1B 112
Catford M. SE6—7D 96
Catford Rd. SE6—7C 96
Cathall Rd. E11—2F 49
Cathay St. SE16
—2H 79 (5K 149)
Cathcart Dri. Orp—7J 129
Cathcart Hill. N19—3G 45
Cathcart Rd. SW10—6K 75
Cathcart St. NW5—6F 45
Cathedral Piazza. SW1
—3G 77 (7L 145)
Cathedral St. SE1
—1D 78 (2A 148)
Catherall Rd. N5—3C 46
Catherine Gdns. Houn—4H 87
Catherine Gro. SE10—1D 96
Catherine Pl. SW1
—3G 77 (6L 145)
Catherine Rd. Surb—5D 118
Catherine St. WC2
—7K 61 (9E 140)
Catherine Wheel All. E1
—5E 62 (6D 142)
Catherine Wheel Rd. Bren
—7D 72
Cat Hill. Barn—5H 5
Cathles Rd. SW12—6F 93
Cathnor Hall Ct. W12—2D 74
Cathnor Rd. W12—2D 74
Catling Clo. SE23—3J 111
Catlins La. Pinn—3A 22
Catlin St. SE16—5G 79
Cator La. Beck—1B 126
Cator Rd. SE26—6K 111
Cator Rd. Cars—5D 132

Cator St. SE15—6F 79
(in two parts)
Cato St. W1—6C 60 (7D 138)
Catsey La. Bush, Wat—1B 10
Catsey Woods. Bush, Wat
—1B 10
Cattistock Rd. SE9—5C 114
Catton St. WC1—5K 61 (6E 140)
Caudwell Ter. SW18—6B 92
Caulfield Rd. E6—7D 50
Caulfield Rd SE15—2H 95
Causeway, The. N2—4C 28
Causeway, The. SW18—4K 91
Causeway, The. SW15—5E 106
Causeway, The. Cars—2E 132
Causeway, The Felt & Houn
—3A 86
Causeway, The. Sutt—7A 132
Causeway, The. Tedd—6K 103
Causeyware Rd. N9—7D 8
Causton Rd N6—7F 29
Causton St SW1
—4H 77 (9B 146)
Cautley Av. SW4—5G 93
Cavalier Clo Wemb—4D 36
Cavalier Ct. Surb—6F 119
Cavalry Cres. Houn—4B 86
Cavalry Gdns. SW15—5H 91
Cavaye Pl SW10—5A 76
Cavell Dri Enf—2F 7
Cavell Rd N17—7J 17
Cavell St. E1—5H 63 (6K 143)
Cavendish Av N3—2J 27
Cavendish Av NW8
—2B 60 (1B 138)
Cavendish Av W13—5A 56
Cavendish Av Eri—6J 85
Cavendish Av Harr—4H 39
Cavendish Av N Mald—4D 120
Cavendish Av Ruis—3A 38
Cavendish Av Sidc—7A 100
Cavendish Av Well—3K 99
Cavendish Av Wfd G—7E 20
Cavendish Clo N18—5C 18
Cavendish Clo NW6—6H 43
Cavendish Clo NW8
—3B 60 (1B 138)
Cavendish Dri. E11—1F 49
Cavendish Dri Edgw—6A 12
Cavendish Gdns Bark—5J 51
Cavendish Gdns Ilf—1E 50
Cavendish Gdns Romf—5E 36
Cavendish M N W1
—5F 61 (5K 139)
Cavendish M S W1
—5F 61 (6K 139)
Cavendish Pl W1
—6F 61 (7K 139)
Cavendish Rd E4—6K 19
Cavendish Rd N4—6B 30
Cavendish Rd N18—5C 18
Cavendish Rd NW6—7G 43
Cavendish Rd SW12—6G 93
Cavendish Rd SW19—7B 108
Cavendish Rd W4—1J 89
Cavendish Rd Barn—3A 4
Cavendish Rd Croy—1B 134
Cavendish Rd N Mald—4B 120
Cavendish Rd Sutt—7A 132
Cavendish Sq W1
—6F 61 (7K 139)
Cavendish St. N1—2D 62
Cavendish Way W Wick
—1D 136
Cavenham Gdns Ilf—3H 51
Caverleigh Way Wor Pk
—1C 130
Cave Rd. E13—3K 65
Cave Rd. Rich—4C 104
Caversham Av N13—3F 17
Caversham Av Sutt—2G 131
Caversham Ct. N11—2K 15
Caversham M. SW3—6D 76
Caversham Rd N15—4C 30
Caversham Rd NW5—6G 45
Caversham Rd King—2F 119
Caversham St SW3—6D 76

Caverswall St. W12—6E 58
Caveside Clo. Chst—1E 128
Cawdor Cres. W7—4A 72
Cawnpore St. SE19—5E 110
Caxton Gro. E3—3C 64
Caxton M. Bren—6D 72
Caxton Rd. N22—2K 29
Caxton Rd. SW19—5A 108
Caxton Rd. W12—2F 75
Caxton Rd. S'hall—3B 70
Caxton St. SW1—3H 77 (6A 146)
Caxton St. N. E16—6H 65
Caxton St. S. E16—7H 65
Caxton Wlk. WC2
—6H 61 (8B 140)
Caygill Clo. Brom—4H 127
Cayley Clo. Wall—7J 133
Cayton Rd. Gnfd—2J 55
Cayton St. EC1—3D 62 (2A 142)
Cazenove Rd. E17—1C 32
Cazenove Rd. N16—2F 47
Cearns Ho. E6—1B 66
Cecil Av. Bark—7H 51
Cecil Av. Enf—4A 8
Cecil Av. Wemb—5F 41
Cecil Ct. WC2—7J 61 (1C 146)
Cecil Ct. Barn—3A 4
Cecile Pk. N8—6J 29
Cecilia Clo. N2—3A 28
Cecilia Rd. E8—5F 47
Cecil Pk. Pinn—4C 22
Cecil Rd. E11—3H 49
Cecil Rd. E13—1J 65
Cecil Rd. E17—1C 32
Cecil Rd. N10—2F 29
Cecil Rd. N14—1B 16
Cecil Rd. NW9—3A 26
Cecil Rd. NW10—1A 58
Cecil Rd. SW19—7K 107
Cecil Rd. W3—5J 57
Cecil Rd Croy—6K 123
Cecil Rd Enf—4H 7
Cecil Rd Harr—3H 23
Cecil Rd Houn—2G 87
Cecil Rd Ilf—4F 51
Cecil Rd Romf—7D 36
Cecil Rd Sutt—6H 131
Cecil Way Brom—1J 137
Cedar Av Barn—7H 5
Cedar Av Enf—2D 8
Cedar Av Romf—5E 36
Cedar Av Ruis—5A 38
Cedar Av Sidc—7A 100
Cedar Av Twic—6F 87
Cedar Clo SE21—1C 110
Cedar Clo SW15—4K 105
Cedar Clo Buck H—2G 21
Cedar Clo Cars—6D 132
Cedar Clo Romf—4J 37
Cedar Copse. Brom—2D 128
Cedar Ct. N1—7C 46
Cedar Ct. N11—5B 16
Cedar Ct. N20—1G 15
Cedar Ct. SW19—3F 107
Cedar Dri. N2—4C 28
Cedar Dri. Pinn—6A 10
Cedar Gdns. Sutt—6A 132
Cedar Grange. Enf—5K 7
Cedar Gro W5—3E 72
Cedar Gro Bex—6D 100
Cedar Gro S'hall—5E 54
Cedar Heights. Rich—1E 104
Cedarhurst Dri SE9—5A 98
Cederland Ter SW20—7D 106
Cedar Lawn Av Barn—5B 4
Cedar Mt SE9—1B 114
Cedarne Rd SW6—7K 75
Cedar Pk Gdns. Romf—7D 36
Cedar Pk. Rd. Enf—1H 7
Cedar Rise N14—7K 5
Cedar Rd N17—1F 31
Cedar Rd NW2—4E 42
Cedar Rd Brom—2A 128
Cedar Rd Croy—2E 134
Cedar Rd Enf—1G 7
Cedar Rd Houn—2A 86

Cedar Rd. Romf—4J 37
Cedar Rd. Sutt—6A 132
Cedar Rd. Tedd—5A 104
Cedars Av. E17—5C 32
Cedars Av. Mitc—4E 122
Cedars Ct. N9—2K 17
Cedars M. SW4—4F 93
Cedars Rd. E15—6G 49
Cedars Rd. N9—2B 18
Cedars Rd. N21—2G 17
Cedars Rd. SW4—3F 93
Cedars Rd. SW13—2C 90
Cedars Rd. W4—6J 73
Cedars Rd. Beck—2A 126
Cedars Rd. Croy—3J 133
Cedars Rd. King—1C 118
Cedars Rd. Mord—4J 121
Cedars, The. Buck H—1D 20
Cedars, The. Tedd—6K 103
Cedar Ter. Rich—4F 89
Cedar Tree Gro. SE27—5B 110
Cedarville Gdns. SW16—6K 109
Cedar Vista. Rich—2E 88
(in two parts)
Cedar Way. NW1—7H 45
Cedra Ct. N16—1G 47
Cedric Rd. SE9—3G 115
Celadon Clo. Enf—3F 9
Celandine Clo. E3—5C 64
Celandine Ct. E4—3J 19
Celandine Dri. SE28—1B 84
Celandine Way. E15—3G 65
Celestial Gdns. SE13—4F 97
Celia Rd. N19—4G 45
Celtic Av. Brom—3G 127
Celtic St. E14—5D 64
Cemetery La. SE7—6C 82
Cemetery Rd. E7—4H 49
Cemetery Rd. N17—7K 17
Cemetery Rd SE2—7B 84
Cenacle Clo. NW3—3J 43
Centaurs Business Centre.
Iswth—6A 72
Centaur St SE1—3K 77 (6F 146)
Centenary Rd. Enf—4G 9
Centenary Trading Est Enf
—3G 9
Central Av E11—2F 49
Central Av N2—2B 28
Central Av N9—3K 17
Central Av SW11—7D 76
Central Av Enf—2C 8
Central Av Houn—4G 87
Central Av Pinn—6D 22
Central Av Wall—5J 133
Central Av Well—2K 99
Central Cir. NW4—5D 26
Central Hill. SE19—5D 110
Central Pde Gnfd—3A 56
Central Av. Dag—3H 53
Central Pk. Est. Houn—5B 86
Central Pk. Rd. E6—2B 66
Central Rd. Mord—6J 121
Central Rd. Wemb—5B 40
Central Rd. Wor Pk—1C 130
Central School Path SW14
—3J 89
Central Sq. NW11—6K 27
Central Sq Wemb—6E 40
Central St. EC1—3C 62 (1L 141)
Central Ter Beck—3C 125
Central Way SE28—1A 84
Central Way Felt—5A 86
Centre Av W3—1K 73
Centre Comn. Rd Chst—7G 115
Centre Rd. E11 & E7—2J 49
Centre Rd Dag—2H 69
Centre St. E2—2H 63 (1K 143)
Centre Way E17—7K 19
Centre Way N9—2D 18
Centreway Ilf—2G 51
Centric Clo NW1—1F 61
Centurion Clo. N7—7K 45
Centurion Way. Eri—3F 85
Century Rd E17—3A 32

Cephas Av. E1—4J 63 (3M 143)
Cephas St. E1—4J 63 (4L 143)
Ceres Rd. SE18—4K 83
Cerise Rd. SE15—2G 95
Cerne Clo. Hay—7A 54
Cerne Rd. Mord—6A 122
Cervantes Ct. W2—6K 59
Cester St. E2—1G 63
Ceylon Rd. W14—3F 75
Chadacre Av. Ilf—3D 34
Chadacre Rd. Eps—6D 130
Chadbourn St. E14—5D 64
Chadd Dri. Brom—3C 128
Chad Grn. E13—1J 65
Chad St. E3—2B 64
Chadville Gdns. Romf—5D 36
Chadway. Dag—1C 52
Chadwell Av. Romf—7B 36
Chadwell Heath La. Romf
—4B 36
Chadwell St. EC1
—3A 62 (1H 141)
Chadwick Av. E4—4A 20
Chadwick Dri. Tedd—6A 104
Chadwick Rd. E11—7G 33
Chadwick Rd. NW10—1B 58
Chadwick Rd. SE15—2F 95
Chadwick Rd. Ilf—3F 51
Chadwick St. SW1
—3H 77 (7A 146)
Chadwick Way. SE28—7D 68
Chadwin Rd. E13—5K 65
Chaffinch Av. Croy—6K 125
Chaffinch Clo. Croy—6K 125
Chaffinch Rd. Beck—1A 126
Chafford Way. Romf—4C 36
Chagford St. NW1
—4D 60 (4E 138)
Chailey Av. Enf—2A 8
Chailey Clo. Houn—1B 86
Chailey St. E5—3J 47
Chalbury Wlk. N1—2K 61
Chalcombe Rd. SE2—3B 84
Chalcot Clo. Sutt—7J 131
Chalcot Cres. NW1—1D 60
Chalcot Gdns. NW3—6D 44
Chalcot Rd. NW1—7E 44
Chalcot Sq. NW1—7E 44
Chalcroft Rd SE13—5G 97
Chaldon Ct. SE19—1D 124
Chaldon Rd. SW6—7G 75
Chale Rd. SW2—6J 93
Chalet Clo. Bex—4K 117
Chalfont Av. Wemb—6H 41
Chalfont Ct. NW9—3B 26
Chalfont Grn. N9—3K 17
Chalfont Rd. N9—3K 17
Chalfont Rd. SE25—3F 125
Chalfont Wlk. Pinn—2A 22
Chalfont Way. W13—3B 72
Chalford Rd. SE21—4D 110
Chalford Wlk. Wfd G—1B 34
Chalgrove Av. Mord—5J 121
Chalgrove Cres. Ilf—2C 34
Chalgrove Gdns. N3—3G 27
Chalgrove Rd. E9—6J 47
Chalgrove Rd. N17—1H 31
Chalgrove Rd. Sutt—7B 132
Chalice Clo. Wall—6H 133
Chalise Ct. N2—4C 28
Chalkenden Clo. SE20—7H 111
Chalk Farm Rd. NW1—7E 44
Chalkhill Rd. W6—4F 75
Chalkhill Rd Wemb—3H 41
Chalklands. Wemb—3J 41
Chalk La. Barn—3J 5
Chalk Pit Way. Sutt—5A 132
Chalk Rd. E13—5K 65
Chalkstone Clo. Well—1A 100
Chalkwell Pk. Av. Enf—4E 8
Challice Way. SW2—1K 109
Challin St. SE20—1J 125
Challis Rd Bren—5D 72
Challoner Clo. N2—2B 28
Challoner Cres. W14—5H 75
Challoner St. W14—5H 75
Chalsey Rd SE4—4B 96

Chalton Dri. N2—6B 28
Chalton St. NW1
—2H 61 (1A 140)
Chamberlain Clo. SE28—3H 83
Chamberlain Cotts. SE5—1D 94
Chamberlain Cres. W Wick
—1D 136
Chamberlain Rd. N2—2A 28
Chamberlain Rd. N9—3B 18
Chamberlain Rd. W13—2A 72
Chamberlain St. NW1—7D 42
Chamberlain Wlk. Felt—4C 102
Chamberlain Way. Pinn—3A 22
Chamberlain Way. Surb
—7E 118
Chamberlayne Rd. NW10
—1E 58
Chambers Gdns. N2—1B 28
Chambers La. NW10—7D 42
Chambers Rd. N7—4J 45
Chambers St. SE16
—2G 79 (5G 149)
Chambers Wharf. SE16
—2G 79 (4H 149)
Chambord St. E2
—3F 63 (2F 142)
Champion Gro. SE5—3D 94
Champion Hill. SE5—3D 94
Champion Hill Est. SE5—3E 94
Champion Pk. SE5—2D 94
Champion Rd. SE26—4A 112
Champness Clo. SE27—4D 110
Champneys Clo. Sutt—7H 131
Chancel Industrial Est. NW10
—6B 42
Chancellor Gdns. S Croy
—7B 134
Chancellor Gro. SE21—3C 110
Chancellor's Rd. W6—5E 74
Chancellor's St. W6—5E 74
Chancelot Rd. SE2—4B 84
Chancel St. SE1—1B 78 (3J 147)
Chancery La. WC2
—6A 62 (7G 141)
Chancery La. Beck—2D 126
Chance St. E2 & E1
—4F 63 (3E 142)
Chanctonbury Clo. SE9—3F 115
Chanctonbury Gdns. Sutt
—7K 131
Chanctonbury Way. N12
—4C 14
Chandler Av. E16—5J 65
Chandler Clo. Hmptn—7E 102
Chandler St. E1—1H 79 (2K 149)
Chandlers Way. SW2—7A 94
Chandos Av. E17—2C 32
Chandos Av. N14—3B 16
Chandos Av. N20—1F 15
Chandos Av. W5—4C 72
Chandos Clo. Buck H—2E 20
Chandos Ct. N14—3C 16
Chandos Cres. Edgw—7A 12
Chandos Pl. WC2
—7J 61 (1C 146)
Chandos Rd. E15—5F 49
Chandos Rd. N2—2B 28
Chandos Rd. N17—2E 30
Chandos Rd. NW2—5C 42
Chandos Rd. NW10—4A 58
Chandos Rd. Harr—5G 23
Chandos Rd. Pinn—7B 22
Chandos St. W1—5F 61 (6K 139)
Chandos Way. NW11—1K 43
Change All. EC3—6D 62 (8B 142)
Channel Clo. Houn—1E 86
Channelsea Rd. E15—1F 65
Chantrey Rd. SW9—3K 93
Chantry Clo. Enf—1H 7
Chantry Clo. Harr—5E 26
Chantry Clo. Sidc—5E 116
Chantry La. Brom—5B 128
Chantry Pl. Harr—1F 23
Chantry Rd. Harr—1F 23
Chantry St. N1—1B 62
Chantry, The. E4—1K 19

Chantry Way. Rain—2K 69
Chant Sq. E15—7F 49
Chant St. E15—7F 49
Chapel Clo. Dart—5K 101
Chapel Ct. N2—3C 28
Chapel Ct. SE1—2D 78 (4A 148)
Chapel Farm Rd. SE9—3D 114
Chapel Hill. Dart—5K 101
Chapel Ho. St. E14—5D 80
Chapel La. Pinn—3B 22
Chapel La. Romf—7D 36
Chapel Mkt. N1—2A 62
Chapelmount Rd. Wfd G—6J 21
Chapel Pl. N1—2A 62
Chapel Pl. N17—7A 18
Chapel Pl. W1—6F 61 (8J 139)
Chapel Rd. SE27—4B 110
Chapel Rd. W13—1B 72
Chapel Rd. Bexh—4G 101
Chapel Rd. Houn—3F 87
Chapel Rd. Ilf—3E 50
Chapel Rd. Twic—7B 88
Chapel Side. W2—7K 59
Chapel St. E15—7F 49
Chapel St. NW1—5C 60 (6C 138)
Chapel St. SW1—3E 76 (6H 145)
Chapel St. Enf—3J 7
Chapel View. S Croy—6J 135
Chapel Wlk. NW4—4D 26
(in two parts)
Chapel Wlk. Croy—2C 134
Chapel Way. N7—3K 45
Chaplin Clo. SE1
—2B 78 (4J 147)
Chaplin Rd. E15—2H 65
Chaplin Rd. N17—3F 31
Chaplin Rd. NW2—6C 42
Chaplin Rd. Dag—7E 52
Chaplin Rd. Wemb—6C 40
Chapman Cres. Harr—6E 24
Chapman Rd. E9—6B 48
Chapman Rd. Belv—5H 85
Chapman Rd. Croy—1A 134
Chapman's La. SE2 & Belv
—4D 84
Chapman St. E1—7H 63 (9J 143)
Chapter Clo. W4—3J 73
Chapter Rd. NW2—5C 42
Chapter Rd. SE17—5B 78
Chapter St. SW1
—4H 77 (9A 146)
Chapter Ter. SE17—6B 78
Chapter Way. Hmptn—4E 102
Chara Pl. W4—6K 73
Charcroft Gdns. Enf—4E 8
Chardin Rd. W4—4A 74
Chardmore Rd. N16—1G 47
Chardwell Clo. E6—6D 66
Charecroft Way. W12—2F 75
Charford Rd. E16—5J 65
Chargeable La. E13—4H 65
Chargeable St. E16—4H 65
Chargrove Clo. SE16—2K 79
Charing Cross Rd. WC2
—6H 61 (8B 140)
Charlbert St. NW8—2C 60
Charlbury Av. Stan—5J 11
Charlbury Gdns. Ilf—2K 51
Charlbury Gro. W5—6C 56
Charldane Rd. SE9—3F 115
Charlecote Gro. SE26—3H 111
Charlecote Rd. Dag—3E 52
Charlemont Rd. E6—3D 66
Charles Barry Clo. SW4—3G 93
Charles Clo. Sidc—4B 116
Charles Cres. Harr—7H 23
(in two parts)
Charle Sevright Dri. NW7
—5A 14
Charlesfield. SE9—3A 114
Charles Grinling Wlk. SE18
—4E 82
Charles La. NW8—2C 60
Charles Pl. NW1
—3G 61 (2M 139)
Charles Rd. E7—7A 50
Charles Rd. SW19—1J 121

Charles Rd. W13—6A 56
Charles Rd. Dag—6K 53
Charles Rd. Romf—6D 36
Charles II St. SW1
—1H 77 (2A 146)
Charles Sq. N1—3D 62 (2B 142)
Charles St. E16—1A 82
Charles St. SW13—2A 90
Charles St. W1—1F 77 (2J 145)
Charles St. Enf—5A 8
Charles St. Houn—2D 86
Charles St. Trading Est. E16
—1A 82
Charleston St. SE17
—4C 78 (9M 147)
Charles Utton Ct. E8—4G 47
Charleville Cir. SE26—5G 111
Charleville Rd. W14—5G 75
Charlieville Rd. Eri—7J 85
Charlmont Rd. SW17—6C 108
Charlotte Ct. N8—6H 29
Charlotte Despard Av. SW11
—1E 92
Charlotte M. W1
—5G 61 (5M 139)
Charlotte M. W14—4G 75
Charlotte M. NW9—5J 25
Charlotte Pl. SW1
—4G 77 (8L 145)
Charlotte Pl. W1
—5G 61 (6M 139)
Charlotte Rd. EC2
—3E 62 (2C 142)
Charlotte Rd. SW13—1B 90
Charlotte Rd. Dag—6H 53
Charlotte Rd. Wall—6G 133
Charlotte Row. SW4—3G 93
Charlotte Sq. Rich—6F 89
Charlotte St. W1
—5G 61 (5M 139)
Charlotte Ter. N1—1K 61
Charlton Chu. La. SE7—5A 82
Charlton Cres. Bark—2K 67
Charlton Dene. SE7—7A 82
Charlton King's Rd. NW5
—5H 45
Charlton La. SE7—4B 82
Charlton Pk. La. SE7—7B 82
Charlton Pk. Rd. SE7—6B 82
Charlton Pl. N1—2B 62
Charlton Rd. N9—1E 18
Charlton Rd. NW10—1A 58
Charlton Rd. SE7—7J 81
Charlton Rd. Harr—4D 24
Charlton Rd. Wemb—1F 41
Charlton Way. SE3—1G 97
Charlwood. Croy—7B 136
Charlwood Clo. Harr—6D 10
Charlwood Pl. SW1
—4G 77 (9M 145)
Charlwood Rd. SW15—4F 91
Charlwood St. SW1
—5G 61 (9M 145)
Charlwood Ter. SW15—4F 91
Charmian Av. Stan—3D 24
Charminster Av. SW19—2J 121
Charminster Ct. Surb—7D 118
Charminster Rd. SE9—4B 114
Charminster Rd. Wor Pk
—1F 131
Charmouth Rd. Well—1C 100
Charnock Rd. E5—3H 47
Charnwood Av. SW19—2J 121
Charnwood Clo. N Mald
—4A 120
Charnwood Dri. E18—3K 33
Charnwood Gdns. E14—4C 80
Charnwood Pl. N20—3F 15
Charnwood Rd. SE25—5D 124
Charnwood St. E5—2H 47
Charrington Rd. Croy—2C 134
Charrington St. NW1—2H 61
Charsley Rd. SE6—2D 112
Chart Clo. Brom—1G 127
Chart Clo. Croy—6J 125

Charter Av. Ilf—1H 51
Charter Ct. New Mald—3A 120
Charter Cres. Houn—4C 86
Charter Dri. Bex—7E 100
Charterhouse Av. Wemb
—5C 40
Charterhouse Bldgs. EC1
—4C 62 (4L 141)
Charterhouse M. EC1
—5B 62 (5K 141)
Charterhouse Sq. EC1
—5B 62 (5K 141)
Charterhouse St. EC1
—5B 62 (6J 141)
Charteris Rd. N4—1A 46
Charteris Rd. NW6—1H 59
Charteris Rd. Wfd G—7E 20
Charter Rd. King—3H 119
Charter Rd., The. Wfd G—6B 20
Charters Clo. SE19—5E 110
Charter Sq. King—2H 119
Charter Way. N3—4H 27
Charter Way. N14—6C 6
Chartfield Av. SW15—5D 90
Chartfield Sq. SW15—5F 91
Chartham Gro. SE23—3B 110
Chartham Rd. SE25—3H 125
Chartley Av. NW2—3A 42
Chartley Av. Stan—6E 10
Charton Clo. Belv—6G 85
Chart St. N1—3D 62 (1B 142)
Chartwell Clo. SE9—2H 115
Chartwell Pl. Sutt—3H 131
Chartwell Way. SE20—1H 125
Charville Ct. Harr—6K 23
Charwood. SW16—4A 110
Chase Ct. Gdns. Enf—3H 7
Chase Cross Rd. Romf—1J 37
Chasefield Rd. SW17—4D 108
Chase Gdns. E4—4H 19
Chase Gdns. Twic—7H 87
Chase Grn. Enf—3H 7
Chase Grn. Av. Enf—2G 7
Chase Hill. Enf—3H 7
Chase La. Ilf—5H 35
(in two parts)
Chaseley Dri. W4—5H 73
Chaseley St. E14—6A 64
Chasemore Gdns. Croy
—5A 134
Chase Ridings. Enf—2F 7
Chase Rd. N14—5B 6
Chase Rd. W3 & NW10—5K 57
Chase Side. N14—6K 5
Chase Side. Enf—3H 7
Chaseside Av. SW20—2G 121
Chase Side Av. Enf—2H 7
Chase Side Cres. Enf—1H 7
Chase Side Pl. Enf—3H 7
Chase Side Works. N14—7C 6
Chase, The. E12—4B 50
Chase, The. SW4—4F 93
Chase, The. SW16—7A 110
Chase, The. SW20—1G 121
Chase, The. Bexh—3H 101
Chase, The. Brom—3K 127
Chase, The. Edgw—1H 25
Chase, The. Pinn—4D 22
Chase, The. Pinn—6A 22
(Eastcote)
Chase, The. Romf—3K 37
Chase, The. Romf—6E 36
(Chadwell Heath)
Chase, The. Stan—6F 11
Chase, The. Sun—7A 102
Chase, The. Wall—5K 133
Chaseville Pde. N21—5E 6
Chaseville Pk. Rd. N21—5D 6
Chase Way. N14—2A 16
Chasewood Av. Enf—2G 7
Chasewood Pk. Harr—3K 39
Chatfield Rd. SW11—3A 92
Chatfield Rd. Croy—1B 134
Chatham Av. Brom—7J 127
Chatham Clo. NW11—5J 27
Chatham Clo. Sutt—7H 121
Chatham Pl. E9—6J 47

Chatham Rd. E17—3A 32
Chatham Rd. E18—2H 33
Chatham Rd. SW11—5D 92
Chatham Rd. King—2G 119
Chatham St. SE17
—4D 78 (8A 148)
Chatsfield Pl. W5—6E 56
Chatsworth Av. NW4—2E 26
Chatsworth Av. SW20—1G 121
Chatsworth Av. Brom—4K 113
Chatsworth Av. Sidc—1A 116
Chatsworth Av. Wemb—5F 41
Chatsworth Clo. NW4—2E 26
Chatsworth Clo. W Wick
—2H 137
Chatsworth Cres. Houn—4H 87
Chatsworth Dri. Enf—7B 8
Chatsworth Gdns. W3—1H 73
Chatsworth Gdns. Harr—1F 39
Chatsworth Gdns. N Mald
—5B 120
Chatsworth Pl. Mitc—3D 122
Chatsworth Pl. Tedd—4A 104
Chatsworth Rise. W5—4F 57
Chatsworth Rd. E5—3J 47
Chatsworth Rd. E15—5H 49
Chatsworth Rd. NW2—6F 43
Chatsworth Rd. W4—6J 73
Chatsworth Rd. W5—4F 57
Chatsworth Rd. Croy—4D 134
Chatsworth Rd. Hay—4A 54
Chatsworth Rd. Sutt—5F 131
Chatsworth Way. SE27—3B 110
Chatterton Rd. N4—3B 46
Chatterton Rd. Brom—4B 128
Chatto Rd. SW11—5D 92
Chaucer Av. Rich—3G 89
Chaucer Clo. N11—5B 16
Chaucer Gdns. Sutt—3J 131
Chaucer Grn. Croy—7J 125
Chaucer Rd. E7—6J 49
Chaucer Rd. E11—6J 33
Chaucer Rd. E17—2E 32
Chaucer Rd. SE24—5A 94
Chaucer Rd. W3—1J 73
Chaucer Rd. Sidc—1C 116
Chaucer Rd. Sutt—4J 131
Chaucer Rd. Well—1J 99
Chaucer Way. SW19—6B 108
Chauncey Clo. N9—3B 18
Chaundrye Clo. SE9—6D 98
—2D 130
Cheam Comn. Rd. Wor Pk
Cheam Pk. Way. Sutt—6G 131
Cheam Rd. Eps & Sutt—7F 131
Cheam Rd. Sutt—6H 131
Cheam St. SE15—3H 95
Cheapside. EC2—6C 62 (8L 141)
Cheapside. N13—4H 17
Cheddington Rd. N18—4K 17
Chedworth Clo. E16—6H 65
Cheeseman Clo. Hmptn
—6C 102
Cheeseman's Ter. W14—5H 75
Chelford Rd. Brom—5F 113
Chelmer Cres. Bark—2B 68
Chelmer Rd. E9—5K 47
Chelmsford Clo. E6—6D 66
Chelmsford Clo. W6—6F 75
Chelmsford Gdns. Ilf—7C 34
Chelmsford Rd. E11—1F 49
Chelmsford Rd. E17—6C 32
Chelmsford Rd. E18—1H 33
Chelmsford Rd. N14—7B 6
Chelmsford Sq. NW10—1E 58
Chelsea Bri. SW1 & SW8—6F 77
Chelsea Bri. Rd. SW1—5E 76
Chelsea Clo. NW10—1K 57
Chelsea Clo. Edgw—2G 25
Chelsea Clo. Hmptn—5G 103
Chelsea Cres. SW10—1A 92
Chelsea Embkmt. SW6—6C 76
Chelsea Garden Mkt. SW10
—1A 92
Chelsea Gdns. Sutt—4G 131
Chelsea Harbour Dri. SW10
—1A 92

Chelsea Mnr. Gdns. SW3
—5C 76
Chelsea Mnr. St. SW3—5C 76
Chelsea Pk. Gdns. SW3—6B 76
Chelsea Sq. SW3—5B 76
Chelsfield Av. N9—7E 8
Chelsfield Gdns. SE26—3J 111
Chelsham Rd. SW4—3H 93
Chelsham Rd. S Croy—6D 134
Chelsworth Dri. SE18—6H 83
Cheltenham Av. Twic—7A 88
Cheltenham Clo. N Mald
—3J 119
Cheltenham Clo. N'holt—6F 39
Cheltenham Gdns. E6—2C 66
Cheltenham Pl. W3—1H 73
Cheltenham Pl. Harr—4E 24
Cheltenham Rd. E10—6E 32
Cheltenham Rd. SE15—4J 95
Cheltenham Ter. SW3
—5D 76 (9F 144)
Chelverton Rd. SW15—4F 91
Chelwood Clo. E4—6J 9
Chelwood Gdns. Rich—2G 89
Chelwood Gdns. Pas. Rich
—2G 89
Chelwood Wlk. SE4—4A 96
Chenappa Clo. E13—3J 65
Chenduit Way. Stan—5E 10
Cheney Ct. SE23—1K 111
Cheney Rd. NW1
—2J 61 (1C 140)
Cheney Row. E17—1B 32
Cheneys Rd. E11—3G 49
Cheney St. Pinn—5A 22
Chenies M. WC1
—4H 61 (4A 140)
Chenies Pl. NW1—2H 61
Chenies St. WC1
—5H 61 (5A 140)
Chenies, The. Orp—6J 129
Cheniston Gdns. W8—3K 75
Chepstow Clo. SW15—6G 91
Chepstow Cres. W11—7J 59
Chepstow Cres. Ilf—6J 35
Chepstow Gdns. S'hall—6D 54
Chepstow Pl. W2—7J 59
Chepstow Rise. Croy—3E 134
Chepstow Rd. W2—6J 59
Chepstow Rd. W7—3A 72
Chepstow Rd. Croy—3E 134
Chepstow Vs. W11—7H 59
Chepstow Way. SE15—1F 95
Chequers Clo. Orp—4K 129
Chequers La. Dag—4F 69
Chequer St. EC1
—4C 62 (4M 141)
Chequers Way. N13—5G 17
Cherbury Clo. SE28—6D 68
Cherbury St. N1—2D 62 (1B 142)
Cherchefelle M. Stan—5G 11
Cherington Rd. W7—1K 71
Cheriton Av. Brom—5H 127
Cheriton Av. Ilf—2E 34
Cheriton Clo. W5—5C 56
Cheriton Ct. SE12—7J 97
Cheriton Dri. SE18—7H 83
Cheriton Sq. SW17—2E 108
Cherry Av. S'hall—1B 70
Cherry Clo. W5—3D 72
Cherry Clo. Cars—2D 132
Cherry Clo. Mord—4G 121
Cherry Cres. Bren—7B 72
Cherry Croft Gdns. Pinn—1D 22
Cherrydown Av. E4—3G 19
Cherrydown Clo. E4—3H 19
Cherrydown Rd. Sidc—2D 116
Cherrydown Wlk. Romf—2H 37
Cherry Gdns. Dag—5F 53
Cherry Garden St. SE16
—2H 79 (5J 149)
Cherry Garth. Bren—5D 72
Cherry Hill. Barn—6E 4
Cherry Hill Gdns. Croy—4K 133
Cherry Laurel Wlk. SW2—6K 93
Cherry Orchard. SE7—6A 82

Cherry Orchard Gdns. Croy
—1D 134
Cherry Orchard Rd. Croy
—2D 134
Cherry Rd. Enf—1D 8
Cherry St. Romf—5K 37
Cherry Tree Clo. Wemb—4A 40
Cherry Tree Ct. NW9—4J 25
Cherrytree Dri. SW16—3J 109
Cherry Tree Hill. N2—5C 28
Cherry Tree Rise. Buck H
—4F 21
Cherry Tree Rd. E15—5G 49
Cherry Tree Rd. N2—4D 28
Cherry Tree Wlk. EC1
—4C 62 (4M 141)
Cherry Tree Wlk. Beck—4B 126
Cherry Tree Wlk. W Wick
—4H 137
Cherrytree Way. Stan—6G 11
Cherry Wlk. Brom—1J 137
Cherrywood Clo. King—7G 105
Cherrywood Dri. SW15—5F 91
Cherrywood La. Mord—4G 121
Cherry Wood Way. W5—5G 57
Chertsey Dri. Sutt—2G 131
Chertsey Rd. E11—2F 49
Chertsey Rd. Ilf—4H 51
Chertsey Rd. Twic—2F 103
Chertsey Rd. SW17—5E 108
Chervil M. SE28—1B 84
Cheryls Clo. SW6—1K 91
Cheseman St. SE26—3H 111
Chesfield Rd. King—7E 104
Chesham Av. Orp—6F 129
Chesham Clo. Romf—4K 37
Chesham Cres. SE20—1J 125
Chesham Pl. SW1
—3E 76 (7G 145)
Chesham Rd. SE20—2J 125
Chesham Rd. SW19—6B 108
Chesham Rd. King—2G 119
Chesham Rd. NW10—3K 41
Chesham St. SW1
—3E 76 (7G 145)
Chesham Ter. W13—2B 72
Cheshire Clo. SE4—2B 96
Cheshire Clo. Mitc—3J 123
Cheshire Rd. N22—7E 16
Cheshire St. E2—4G 63 (3G 143)
Chesholm Rd. N16—3E 46
Cheshunt Rd. E7—6K 49
Cheshunt Rd. Belv—5G 85
Chesilton Rd. SW6—1H 91
Chesley Gdns. E6—2B 66
Chesney Cres. Croy—7E 136
Chesney St. SW11—1E 92
Chesnut Gro. N17—3F 31
Chesnut Rd. N17—3F 31
Chessington Av. N3—3G 27
Chessington Av. Bexh—7E 84
Chessington Clo. N16—5E 46
Chessington Ct. Pinn—4D 22
Chessington Rd. Eps—7A &
7B 130
Chessington Way. W Wick
—2D 136
Chesson Rd. W14—6H 75
Chesswood Way. Pinn—2B 22
Chester Av. Rich—6F 89
Chester Av. Twic—1D 102
Chester Clo. SW1
—2F 77 (5J 145)
Chester Clo. SW15—3D 90
Chester Clo. Sutt—2J 131
Chester Clo. N. NW1
—3F 61 (1K 139)
Chester Clo. S. NW1
—3F 61 (2K 139)
Chester Ct. NW1
—3F 61 (2K 139)
Chester Cres. E8—6F 47
Chester Dri. Harr—6D 22
Chesterfield Clo. SE13—3F 97
Chesterfield Gdns. N4—5B 30
Chesterfield Gdns W1
—1F 77 (2J 145)

Chesterfield Gro. SE22—5F 95
Chesterfield Hill. W1
—1F 77 (2J 145)
Chesterfield Lodge. N21—7E 6
Chesterfield Rd. E10—6E 32
Chesterfield Rd. N3—6D 14
Chesterfield Rd. W4—6J 73
Chesterfield Rd. Barn—5A 4
Chesterfield St. W1
—1F 77 (2J 145)
Chesterfield Wlk. SE10—1F 97
Chesterfield Way. SE15—7J 79
Chesterford Rd. E12—5D 50
Chester Gdns. W13—6B 56
Chester Gdns. Enf—6C 8
Chester Gdns. Mord—6A 122
Chester Ga. NW1
—3F 61 (2J 139)
Chester M. SW1—3F 77 (6J 145)
Chester Pl. NW1—3F 61 (1J 139)
Chester Rd. E7—7B 50
Chester Rd. E11—6K 33
Chester Rd. E16—4G 65
Chester Rd. E17—5K 31
Chester Rd. N9—1C 18
Chester Rd. N17—3E 30
Chester Rd. N19—2F 45
Chester Rd. NW1
—3F 60 (2H 139)
Chester Rd. SW19—6E 106
Chester Rd. Chig—3K 21
Chester Rd. Houn—3A 86
Chester Rd. Ilf—1K 51
Chester Rd. Sidc—5J 99
Chester Row. SW1
—4E 76 (9H 145)
Chester Sq. SW1
—4E 76 (8H 145)
Chesters, The. N Mald—1A 120
Chester St. E2—4G 63 (3H 143)
Chester St. SW1
—3E 76 (6H 145)
Chester Ter. NW1
—3F 61 (1J 139)
Chesterton Clo. SW18—5J 91
Chesterton Clo. Gnfd—2F 55
Chesterton Rd. E13—3J 65
Chesterton Rd. W10—5F 59
Chesterton Ter. E13—3J 65
Chesterton Ter. King—2G 119
Chester Way. SE11
—4A 78 (9H 147)
Chesthunte Rd. N17—1C 30
Chestnut All. SW6—6H 75
Chestnut Av. E7—4K 49
Chestnut Av. N8—5J 29
Chestnut Av. SW14—3K 89
Chestnut Av. Bren—4D 72
Chestnut Av. Buck H—3G 21
Chestnut Av. Edgw—6K 11
Chestnut Av. Eps—4A 130
Chestnut Av. Hmptn—7E 102
Chestnut Av. Tedd—2A 118
Chestnut Av. Wemb—5B 40
Chestnut Av. W Wick—5G 137
Chestnut Av. N. E17—4E 32
Chestnut Av. S. E17—4E 32
Chestnut Clo. N14—5C 6
Chestnut Clo. N16—2D 46
Chestnut Clo. SE6—5E 112
Chestnut Clo. Buck H—2G 21
Chestnut Clo. Cars—1D 132
Chestnut Ct. SW6—6H 75
Chestnut Dri. E11—6J 33
Chestnut Dri. Bexh—3D 100
Chestnut Dri. Harr—7E 10
Chestnut Dri. Pinn—6B 22
Chestnut Gro. SW12—7E 92
Chestnut Gro. W5—3D 72
Chestnut Gro. Barn—5J 5
Chestnut Gro. Dart—5K 117
Chestnut Gro. Iswth—4A 88
Chestnut Gro. Mitc—5H 123
Chestnut Gro. N Mald—3K 119
Chestnut Gro S Croy—7H 135
Chestnut Gro Wemb—5B 40

Chestnut La. N20—1B 14
Chestnut Rise. SE18—6H 83
Chestnut Rise. Bush, Wat
　　　　　　　　　　　—1A 10
Chestnut Rd. SE27—3C 110
Chestnut Rd. SW20—2F 121
Chestnut Rd. King—7E 104
Chestnut Rd. Twic—2J 103
Chestnuts, The. SW16—4A 110
Chestnut Ter. Sutt—4K 131
Chestnut Wlk. Wfd G—5D 20
Chestnut Way. Felt—3A 102
Cheston Av. Croy—2A 136
Chettle Ct. N8—6A 30
Chetwode Rd. SW17—3E 108
Chetwynd Av. Barn—1J 15
Chetwynd Rd. NW5—4F 45
Cheval Pl. SW7—3C 76 (6D 144)
Chevening Rd. NW6—2F 59
Chevening Rd. SE10—5H 81
Chevening Rd. SE19—6D 110
Chevenings, The. Sidc—3C 116
Cheverton Rd. N19—1H 45
Chevet St. E9—5A 48
Cheviot Clo. Bexh—2K 101
Cheviot Clo. Enf—2J 7
Cheviot Gdns. NW2—2F 43
Cheviot Ga. NW2—2G 43
Cheviot Rd. SE27—5A 110
Cheviot Way. Ilf—4J 35
Chewton Rd. E17—4A 32
Cheyne Av. E18—3H 33
Cheyne Av. Twic—1D 102
Cheyne Ct. SW3—6D 76
Cheyne Gdns. SW3—6C 76
Cheyne Hill. Surb—4F 119
Cheyne M. SW3—6C 76
Cheyne Path. W7—6K 55
Cheyne Row. SW3—6C 76
Cheyne Wlk. N21—5G 7
Cheyne Wlk. NW4—6E 26
Cheyne Wlk.—7B 76
　SW3 1-90
　SW10 remainder
Cheyne Wlk. Croy—2G 135
Cheyneys Av. Edgw—6J 11
Chichele Gdns. Croy—4E 134
Chichele Rd. NW2—5F 43
Chicheley Gdns. Harr—7B 10
Chicheley Rd. Harr—7B 10
Chicheley St. SE1
　　　　　　—2K 77 (4F 146)
Chichester Clo. E6—6C 66
Chichester Clo. SE3—1A 98
Chichester Ct. Eps—7B 130
Chichester Ct. Stan—3E 24
Chichester Gdns. Ilf—7D 34
Chichester Rd. E11—3G 49
Chichester Rd. N9—1B 18
Chichester Rd. NW6—2J 59
Chichester Rd. W02—5K 59
Chichester Rd. Croy—3E 134
Chichester St. SW1—5G 77
Chichester Way. E14—4F 81
Chichester Way. Felt—7A 86
Chicksand St. E1
　　　　　　—5G 63 (6G 143)
Chiddingfold. N12—3D 14
Chiddingstone Av. Bexh—7F 85
Chiddingstone St. SW6—2J 91
Chieveley Rd. Bexh—4H 101
Chignell Pl. W13—1A 72
Chigwell Hill. E1
　　　　　　—7H 63 (1J 149)
Chigwell Pk. Chig—4K 21
Chigwell Pk. Dri. Chig—4K 21
Chigwell Rise. Chig—2K 21
Chigwell Rd.—3K 33 to 5J 21
　E18 1-179 & 2-234
　Wfd G remainder
Childebert Rd. SW17—2F 109
Childeric Rd. SE14—7A 80
Childerley St. SW6—1G 91
Childers St. SE8—6A 80
Childers, The. Wfd G—5J 21

Child's La. SE19—6E 110
Child's Pl. SW5—4J 75
Child's St. SW5—4J 75
Child's Wlk. SW5—4J 75
Childs Way. NW11—5H 27
Chilham Clo. Gnfd—2A 56
Chilham Rd. SE9—4C 114
Chilham Way. Brom—7J 127
Chiliot Clo. E14—6D 64
Chillerton Rd. SW17—5F 109
Chillingworth Gdns. Twic
　　　　　　　　　　　—2K 103
Chillingworth Rd. N7—5A 46
Chilmark Gdns. N Mald—6C 120
Chilmark Rd. SW16—1H 123
Chiltern Av. Twic—1E 102
Chiltern Clo. Bexh—1K 101
Chiltern Clo. Croy—3E 134
Chiltern Ct. N10—2E 28
Chiltern Dene. Enf—4E 6
Chiltern Dri. Surb—6H 119
Chiltern Gdns. NW2—3F 43
Chiltern Gdns. Brom—4H 127
Chiltern Rd. E3—4C 64
Chiltern Rd. Ilf—5J 35
Chiltern Rd. Pinn—5A 22
Chiltern St. W1—5E 60 (5G 139)
Chiltern Way. Wfd G—3D 20
Chilthorne Clo. SE6—7B 96
Chilton Av. W5—4D 72
Chilton Gro. SE8—4A 80
Chilton Rd. Edgw—6B 12
Chilton Rd. Rich—3G 89
Chiltons, The. E18—2J 33
Chilton St. E2—4F 63 (3F 142)
Chilver St. SE10—5H 81
Chilworth Ct. SW19—1F 107
Chilworth Gdns. Sutt—3A 132
Chilworth M. W2
　　　　　　—6B 60 (8A 138)
Chilworth St. W2
　　　　　　—6A 60 (8A 138)
Chimes Av. N13—5F 17
Chinbrook Cres. SE12—3K 113
Chinbrook Rd. SE12—3K 113
Chinchilla Dri. Houn—2A 86
Chine, The. N10—4G 29
Chine, The. N21—6G 7
Chine, The. Wemb—5C 40
Chingdale Rd. E4—3B 20
Chingford Av. E4—3H 19
Chingford Hall Est. E4—6G 19
Chingford La. Wfd G—4B 20
Chingford Mt. Rd. E4—4H 19
Chingford Rd.—6H 19
　E17 1-425 & 2-290
　E4 remainder
Chingley Clo. Brom—6G 113
Chinnery Clo. Enf—1A 8
Chinnor Cres. Gnfd—2F 55
Chipka St. E14—2E 80
　(in two parts)
Chipley St. SE14—6A 80
Chipmunk Gro. N'holt—3C 54
Chippendale St. E5—3K 47
Chippenham Av. Wemb—5H 41
Chippenham Gdns. NW6—3J 59
Chippenham M. W9—4J 59
Chippenham Rd. W9—4J 59
Chipperfield Rd. Orp—7A 116
　(in two parts)
Chipping Clo. Barn—3B 4
Chipstead Av. T Hth—4B 124
Chipstead Clo. SE19—7F 111
Chipstead Gdns. NW2—2D 42
Chipstead St. SW6—2J 91
Chip St. SW4—4H 93
Chirk Clo. Hay—4C 54
Chisenhale Rd. E3—2A 64
Chisholm Rd. Croy—2E 134
Chisholm Rd. Rich—6F 89
Chislehurst Av. N12—7F 15
Chislehurst Rd. Brom & Chst
　　　　　　　　　　　—2B 128
Chislehurst Rd. Orp—4J 129
Chislehurst Rd. Rich—5E 88
Chislehurst Rd. Sidc—5A 116

Chislet Clo. Beck—7C 112
Chisley Rd. N15—6E 30
Chiswell Sq. SE3—2K 97
Chiswell St. EC1
　　　　　　—5D 62 (5A 142)
Chiswick Bri. SW14 & W4
　　　　　　　　　　　—2J 89
Chiswick Clo. Croy—3K 133
Chiswick Comn. Rd. W4—4K 73
Chiswick Ct. Pinn—3D 22
Chiswick High Rd. Bren & W4
　　　　　　—5G 73 to 4B 74
Chiswick La. N. W4—5A 74
Chiswick La. S. W4—6B 74
Chiswick Mall. W4 & W6—6B 74
Chiswick Quay. W4—1J 89
Chiswick Rd. N9—2B 18
Chiswick Rd. W4—4J 73
Chiswick Sq. W4—6A 74
Chiswick Staithe. W4—1H 89
Chiswick Village. W4—6H 73
Chiswick Wharf. W4—6B 74
Chitty's La. Dag—2D 52
Chitty St. W1—5G 61 (5M 139)
Chivalry Rd. SW11—5C 92
Chive Clo. Croy—1K 135
Chivers Rd. E4—4J 19
Choats Mnr. Way. Dag—2F 69
Choats Rd. Dag—3E 68
Chobham Gdns. SW19—2F 107
Chobham Rd. E15—5F 49
Cholmeley Cres. N6—7F 29
Cholmeley Pk. N6—1F 45
Cholmley Gdns. NW6—5J 43
Cholmley Rd. Th Dit—6B 118
Cholmondeley Av. NW10
　　　　　　　　　　　—2C 58
Cholmondeley Wlk. Rich
　　　　　　　　　　　—5C 88
Choppin's Ct. E1
　　　　　　—1H 79 (2K 149)
Chorleywood Cres. Orp
　　　　　　　　　　　—2K 129
Choumert Gro. SE15—2G 95
Choumert Rd. SE15—3F 95
Choumert Sq. SE15—2G 95
Chrisp St. E14—6D 64
Christchurch Av. N12—6F 15
Christchurch Av. NW6—1F 59
Christchurch Av. Eri—6K 85
Christchurch Av. Harr—4K 23
Christchurch Av. Tedd—5A 104
Christchurch Av. Wemb—6E 40
Christchurch Clo. SW19
　　　　　　　　　　　—7B 108
Christchurch Gdns. Harr
　　　　　　　　　　　—4A 24
Christchurch Grn. Wemb
　　　　　　　　　　　—6E 40
Christchurch Hill. NW3—3B 44
Christchurch La. Barn—2B 4
Christchurch Pk. Sutt—7A 132
Christchurch Pas. NW3—3A 44
Christchurch Pas. Barn—2B 4
Christchurch Pl. SW8—2H 93
Christchurch Rd. N8—6J 29
Christchurch Rd. SW2—1K 109
Christ Chu. Rd. SW14—5H 89
Christchurch Rd. SW19
　　　　　　　　　　　—1B 122
Christ Chu. Rd. Beck—2C 126
Christchurch Rd. Ilf—1F 51
Christchurch Rd. Sidc—4K 115
Christchurch Rd. Surb—6F 119
Christchurch St. SW3—6D 76
Christchurch Way. SE10
　　　　　　　　　　　—5G 81
Christian Fields. SW16—7G 111
Christian St. E1—6G 63 (8H 143)
Christie Ct. N19—2J 45
Christie Gdns. Romf—6B 36
Christie Rd. E9—6A 48
Christina Sq. N4—1B 46
Christina St. EC2
　　　　　　—4E 62 (3C 142)
Christopher Av. W7—3A 72
Christopher Clo. Sidc—6K 99

Christopher Gdns. Dag—5D 52
Christopher Pl. NW1
　　　　　　—3H 61 (2B 140)
Christopher Rd. S'hall—4A 70
Christopher St. EC2
　　　　　　—4D 62 (4B 142)
Chryssell Rd. SW9—7A 78
Chubworthy St. SE14—6A 80
Chudleigh Cres. Ilf—4J 51
Chudleigh Gdns. Sutt—3A 132
Chudleigh Rd. NW6—7F 43
Chudleigh Rd. SE4—5B 96
Chudleigh Rd. Twic—6J 87
Chudleigh St. E1—6K 63
Chulsa Rd. SE26—5H 111
Chumleigh St. SE5—6E 78
Chumleigh Wlk. Surb—4F 119
Church All. Croy—1A 134
Church App. SE21—3D 110
Church Av. E4—6A 20
Church Av. NW1—6F 45
Church Av. SW14—3K 89
Church Av. Beck—1C 126
Church Av. N'holt—7D 38
Church Av. Pinn—6C 22
Church Av. Sidc—5A 116
Church Av. S'hall—3C 70
Churchbury Clo. Enf—2K 7
Churchbury La. Enf—3J 7
Churchbury Rd. SE9—7B 98
Churchbury Rd. Enf—2K 7
Church Clo. N20—3H 15
Church Clo. Edgw—5D 12
Church Ct. Rich—5D 88
Church Ct. Wdf G—6F 21
Church Cres. E9—7K 47
Church Cres. N3—1H 27
Church Cres. N10—4F 29
Church Cres. N20—3H 15
Churchcroft Clo. SW12—7E 92
Church Dri. NW9—1K 41
Church Dri. Harr—6E 22
Church Dri. W Wick—3G 137
Church Elm La. Dag—6G 53
Church End. E17—4D 32
Church End. NW4—3D 26
Church Farm La. Sutt—6G 131
Churchfield Av. N12—6G 15
Churchfield Clo. Harr—4G 23
Churchfield Rd. W3—1J 73
Churchfield Rd. W7—2J 71
Churchfield Rd. W13—1B 72
Churchfield Rd. Well—3A 100
Churchfields. E18—1J 33
Churchfields. SE10—6E 80
Churchfields Av. Felt—3D 102
Churchfields Rd. Beck—2K 125
Church Gdns. W5—2D 72
Church Gdns. Wemb—4A 40
Church Ga. SW6—3G 91
Church Gro. SE13—5D 96
Church Gro. King—1C 118
Church Hill. E17—4C 32
Church Hill. N21—7E 6
Church Hill. SE18—3D 82
Church Hill. SW19—5H 107
Church Hill. Cars—5D 132
Church Hill. Dart—4K 101
　(Crayford)
Church Hill. Harr—1J 39
Church Hill Rd. E17—4D 32
Church Hill Rd. Barn—6H 5
Church Hill Rd. Surb—5E 118
Church Hill Rd. Sutt—3F 131
Church Hill Wood. Orp—5K 129
Church Hyde. SE18—6J 83
Churchill Av. Harr—6B 24
Churchill Ct. W5—4F 57
Churchill Gdns. SW1—5G 77
Churchill Gdns. W3—6G 57
Churchill Gdns. Rd. SW1—5F 77
Churchill Pl. Harr—4J 23
Churchill Rd. E16—6A 66
Churchill Rd. NW2—6D 42
Churchill Rd. NW5—4F 45
Churchill Rd. Edgw—6A 12

179

Churchill Rd. S Croy—7C 134
Churchills M. Wfd G—6C 20
Churchill Ter. E4—3H 19
Churchill Wlk. E9—5J 47
Church La. E11—1G 69
Church La. E17—4D 32
Church La. N2—3B 28
Church La. N8—4K 29
Church La. N9—2B 18
Church La. N17—1E 30
Church La. NW9—6J 25
Church La. SW17—5D 108
Church La. SW19—1J 121
Church La. W5—2C 72
Church La. Brom—7C 128
Church La. Chst—1G 129
Church La. Dag—7J 53
Church La. Enf—3J 7
Church La. Harr—1K 23
Church La. Pinn—3C 22
Church La. Rich—1E 104
Church La. Tedd—5K 103
Church La. Th Dit—6A 118
Church La. Twic—1A 104
Church La. Wall—3H 133
Churchley Rd. SE26—4H 111
Church Manorway. SE2—4A 84
Church Manorway. Eri—3K 85
Churchmead Clo. Barn—6H 5
Churchmead Rd. NW10—6C 42
Churchmore Rd. SW16—1G 123
Church Mt. N2—5B 28
Church Pas. Barn—4B 4
Church Pas. Surb—5E 118
Church Pas. Twic—1B 104
Church Path. E11—5J 33
Church Path. E17—4D 32
Church Path. N5—5B 46
Church Path. N12—4F 15
Church Path. N17—1E 30
Church Path. NW10—7A 42
Church Path. SW14—3K 89
(in two parts)
Church Path. SW19—2H 121
Church Path. W4—3J 73
Church Path. W7—1J 71
Church Path. Bark—1E 67
Church Path. Croy—2C 134
Church Path. Mitc—3C 122
(in two parts)
Church Path. Romf—5K 37
Church Path. S'hall—1E 70
Church Path. S'hall—3D 70
(in three parts)
Church Pl. SW1—7G 61 (1M 145)
Church Pl. W5—2D 72
Church Pl. Mitc—3C 122
Church Rise. SE23—2K 111
Church Rd. E10—1C 48
Church Rd. E12—5C 50
Church Rd. E17—2A 32
Church Rd. N6—6E 28
Church Rd. N17—1E 30
Church Rd. NW4—4D 26
Church Rd. NW10—7A 42
Church Rd. SE19—1E 124
Church Rd. SW13—2B 90
Church Rd. SW19—5G 107
Church Rd.—1B 122
  SW19 311-413 & 338-406
  Mitc remainder
Church Rd. W3—1J 73
Church Rd. W7—7H 55
Church Rd. Bark—6G 51
Church Rd. Bexh—2F 101
Church Rd. Brom—2J 127
Church Rd. Brom—3G 127
  (Shortlands)
Church Rd. Buck H—1E 20
Church Rd. Croy—3C 134
  (in two parts)
Church Rd. Enf—6D 8
Church Rd. Eps—7A 130
  (West Ewell)
Church Rd. Eri—5K 85
Church Rd. Felt—5B 102

Church Rd. Houn—6A 70
  (Cranford)
Church Rd. Houn—7E 70
  (Heston)
Church Rd. Ilf—6J 35
Church Rd. Iswth—7J 71
Church Rd. King—2F 119
Church Rd. N'holt—2B 54
Church Rd. Rich—4E 88
Church Rd. Rich—4E 104
  (Ham)
Church Rd. Sidc—4A 116
Church Rd. S'hall—3D 70
Church Rd. Stan—5G 11
Church Rd. Sutt—6G 131
Church Rd. Tedd—4J 103
Church Rd. Wall—3H 133
Church Rd. Well—2B 100
Church Rd. Wor Pk—1A 130
Church Row. NW3—4A 44
Church Row. Chst—1G 129
Church Sq. E9—1J 63
Church St. E15—1G 65
Church St. E16—1F 83
Church St.—5B 60 (5B 138)
  NW8 1-127 & 2-142
  W2 remainder
Church St. W4—6B 74
Church St. Croy—2C 134
Church St. Dag—6H 53
Church St. Enf—3H 7
Church St. Eps—7C 130
  (Ewell)
Church St. Hmptn—7G 103
Church St. Iswth—3B 88
Church St. King—2D 118
Church St. Sutt—5K 131
Church St. Twic—1A 104
Church St. N. E15—1G 65
Church St. Pas. E15—1G 65
Church Stretton Rd. Houn
  —5G 87
Church Ter. NW4—3D 26
Church Ter. SE13—3G 97
Church Ter. Rich—5D 88
Church Vale. N2—3D 28
Church Vale. SE23—2K 111
Church View. Rich—5E 88
Churchview Rd. Twic—1H 103
Church Wlk. N6—3E 44
Church Wlk. N16—4D 46
Church Wlk. NW2—3H 43
Church Wlk. NW4—3E 26
Church Wlk. NW9—2K 41
Church Wlk. SW13—1C 90
Church Wlk. SW15—5D 90
Church Wlk. SW16—2G 123
Church Wlk. SW20—3E 120
Church Wlk. Bren—6C 72
Church Wlk. Rich—5D 88
Church Wlk. Th Dit—6A 118
Church Way. N20—3H 15
Churchway. NW1
  —3H 61 (1B 140)
Church Way. Barn—4J 5
Church Way. Edgw—6B 12
Churchwell Path. E9—5J 47
Churchyard Row. SE11
  —4B 78 (8K 147)
Churston Av. E13—1K 65
Churston Clo. SW2—1A 110
Churston Dri. Mord—5F 121
Churston Gdns. N11—6B 16
Churton Pl. SW1
  —4G 77 (9M 145)
Churton St. SW1
  —4G 77 (9M 145)
Chusan Pl. E14—6B 64
Chyngton Clo. Sidc—3K 115
Cibber Rd. SE23—2K 111
Cicada Rd. SW18—6A 92
Cicely Rd. SE15—1G 95
Cinderford Way. Brom—4G 113
Cinema Pde. W5—4F 57
Cinnamon Row. SW11—3A 92

Cinnamon St. E1
  (in two parts)—1H 79 (3K 149)
Cintra Pk. SE19—7F 111
Circle Gdns. SW19—2J 121
Circle, The. NW2—3A 42
Circle, The. NW7—6E 12
Circuits, The. Pinn—4A 22
Circular Rd. N17—3F 31
Circular Way. SE18—6D 82
Circus Pl. EC2—5D 62 (6B 142)
Circus Rd. NW8—3B 60 (1A 138)
Circus St. SE10—7E 80
Cirencester St. W2—5K 59
Cissbury Ho. SE26—3G 111
Cissbury Ring N. N12—5C 14
Cissbury Ring S. N12—5C 14
Cissbury Rd. N15—5D 30
Citizen Rd. N7—4A 46
City Garden Row. N1
  —2B 62 (1K 141)
City Rd. EC1—2B 62 (1J 141)
Civic Way. Ilf—4G 35
Civic Way. Ruis—5B 38
Clabon M. SW1—3D 76 (7E 144)
Clack St. SE16—2J 79 (5M 149)
Clacton Rd. E6—3B 66
Clacton Rd. E17—6A 32
Clacton Rd. N17—2F 31
Claigmar Gdns. N3—1K 27
Claire Ct. N12—4F 15
Claire Ct. Bush, Wat—1C 10
Claire Ct. Pinn—1D 22
Claire Pl. E14—3C 80
Clairvale Rd. Houn—1C 86
Clairvale Rd. SW16—5F 109
Clairville Gdns. W7—1J 71
Clamp Hill. Stan—4C 10
Clancarty Rd. SW6—2J 91
Clandon Clo. W3—2H 73
Clandon Clo. Eps—6B 130
Clandon Gdns. N3—3J 27
Clandon Rd. Ilf—2J 51
Clandon St. SE8—2C 96
Clanfield Way. SE15—7F 79
Clanricarde Gdns. W2—7J 59
Clapham Comn. N. Side. SW4
  —4E 92
Clapham Comn. S. Side. SW4
  —6F 93
Clapham Comn. W. Side. SW4
  (in three parts)—4D 92
Clapham Cres. SW4—4H 93
Clapham High St. SW4—4H 93
Clapham Junct. Est. SW11
  —4C 92
Clapham Junct. App. SW11
  —4C 92
Clapham Mnr. St. SW4—3G 93
Clapham Pk. Est. SW4—6H 93
Clapham Pk. Rd. SW4—4H 93
Clapham Rd. SW9—3J 93
Clapham Rd. Est. SW4—3J 93
Claps Ga. La. Bark—4F 67
Clapton Comn. E5—7F 31
Clapton Comn. N16—1G 47
Clapton Pk. Est. E5—4K 47
Clapton Pas. E5—5J 47
Clapton Sq. E5—5J 47
Clapton Ter. N16—1G 47
Clapton Way. E5—4G 47
Clara Pl. SE18—4E 82
Clare Clo. N2—3A 28
Clare Corner. SE9—7F 99
Claredale St. E2
  —2G 63 (1H 143)
Clare Gdns. E7—4J 49
Clare Gdns. W11—6G 59
Clare Gdns. Bark—6K 51
Clare Gdns. Stan—5H 11
Clare La. N1—7C 46
Clare Lawn Av. SW14—5K 89
Clare Mkt. WC2—6K 61 (8F 140)
Claremont Av. Harr—5E 24
Claremont Av. N Mald—5D 120
Claremont Clo. E16—1E 82

Claremont Clo. N1
  —2A 62 (1H 141)
Claremont Clo. SW2—1J 109
Claremont Gdns. Ilf—2J 51
Claremont Gdns. Surb—5E 118
Claremont Gro. W4—7A 74
Claremont Gro. Wfd G—6F 21
Claremont Pk. N3—1G 27
Claremont Rd. E7—5K 49
Claremont Rd. E11—3F 49
Claremont Rd. E17—2A 32
Claremont Rd. N6—7G 29
Claremont Rd. NW2—1F 43
Claremont Rd. W9—2H 59
Claremont Rd. W13—5A 56
Claremont Rd. Brom—4C 128
Claremont Rd. Croy—1G 135
Claremont Rd. Harr—2J 23
Claremont Rd. Surb—5E 118
Claremont Rd. Tedd—5K 103
Claremont Rd. Twic—6C 88
Claremont Sq. N1
  —2A 62 (1G 141)
Claremont St. E16—1E 82
Claremont St. N18—6B 18
Claremont St. SE10—6D 80
Claremont Way. NW2—1E 42
Clarence Av. SW4—7H 93
Clarence Av. Brom—4C 128
Clarence Av. Ilf—6E 34
Clarence Av. N Mald—2J 119
Clarence Clo. Bush, Wat—1E 10
Clarence Cres. SW4—6H 93
Clarence Cres. Sidc—3B 116
Clarence Gdns. NW1
  —3F 61 (2K 139)
Clarence La. SW15—6A 90
Clarence M. E5—5H 47
Clarence Pas. NW1
  —2J 61 (1C 140)
Clarence Pl. E5—5H 47
Clarence Rd. E5—4H 47
Clarence Rd. E12—5B 50
Clarence Rd. E16—4G 65
Clarence Rd. E17—2K 31
Clarence Rd. N15—5C 30
Clarence Rd. N22—7D 16
Clarence Rd. NW6—7H 43
Clarence Rd. SE9—2C 114
Clarence Rd. SW19—6K 107
Clarence Rd. W4—5G 73
Clarence Rd. Bexh—4E 100
Clarence Rd. Brom—3B 128
Clarence Rd. Croy—7D 124
Clarence Rd. Enf—5D 8
Clarence Rd. Rich—1F 89
Clarence Rd. Sidc—3B 116
Clarence Rd. Sutt—5K 131
Clarence Rd. Tedd—6K 103
Clarence Rd. Wall—5F 133
Clarence St. King—2D 118
Clarence St. Rich—4E 88
Clarence St. S'hall—3B 70
Clarence Ter. NW1
  —4D 60 (3F 138)
Clarence Ter. Houn—4F 87
Clarence Wlk. SW4—2J 93
Clarence Way. NW1—7F 45
Clarendon Clo. E9
  —7C 60 (9C 138)
Clarendon Clo. Orp—3K 129
Clarendon Cres. Twic—3H 103
Clarendon Cross. W11—7G 59
Clarendon Dri. SW15—4E 90
Clarendon Gdns. NW4—3D 26
Clarendon Gdns. W9
  —4A 60 (4A 138)
Clarendon Gdns. Ilf—7D 34
Clarendon Gdns. Wemb—3D 40
Clarendon Grn. Orp—4K 129
Clarendon Gro. NW1
  —3H 61 (1A 140)
Clarendon Gro. Mitc—3D 122
Clarendon M. W2
  —7C 60 (9C 138)
Clarendon M. Bex—1H 117

Clarendon Path. Orp—3K 129
(in two parts)
Clarendon Pl. W2
　　　　　—7C 60 (9C 138)
Clarendon Rise. SE13—4E 96
Clarendon Rd. E11—1F 49
Clarendon Rd. E17—6D 32
Clarendon Rd. E18—3J 33
Clarendon Rd. N8—3K 29
Clarendon Rd. N15—4C 30
Clarendon Rd. N18—6B 18
Clarendon Rd. N22—2K 29
Clarendon Rd. SW19—7C 108
Clarendon Rd. W5—4E 56
Clarendon Rd. W11—7G 59
Clarendon Rd. Croy—2G 134
Clarendon Rd. Harr—6J 23
Clarendon Rd. Wall—6G 133
Clarendon St. SW1
　　　　　—5F 77 (9K 145)
Clarendon Ter. W9
　　　　　—4A 60 (3A 138)
Clarendon Wlk. W11—6G 59
Clarendon Way. N21—6H 7
Clarendon Way. Chst & Orp
　　　　　—3K 129
Clarens St. SE6—2B 112
Clare Pl. SW15—7B 90
Clare Rd. E11—6F 33
Clare Rd. NW10—7C 42
Clare Rd. SE14—2B 96
Clare Rd. Gnfd—6H 39
Clare Rd. Houn—3D 86
Clare St. E2—2H 63 (1K 143)
Claret Gdns. SE25—3E 124
Clareville Gro. SW7
　　　　　—4A 76 (9A 144)
Clareville St. SW7
　　　　　—4A 76 (9A 144)
Clare Way. Bexh—1E 100
Clarewood Wlk. SW9—4A 94
Clarges M. W1—1F 77 (2J 145)
Clarges St. W1—1F 77 (2K 145)
Claribel Rd. SW9—2B 94
Clarice Way. Wall—7J 123
Claridge Rd. Dag—1D 52
Clarissa Rd. Romf—7D 36
Clarissa St. E8—1F 63
Clarke Path. N16—1G 47
Clarkes Av. Wor Pk—1F 131
Clarks Mead. Bush, Wat—1B 10
Clarkson Rd. E16—6H 65
Clarksons, The. Bark—2G 67
Clarkson St. E2—3H 63 (1J 143)
Clarks Rd. Ilf—2H 51
Clark St. E1—5J 63 (6L 143)
Clark Way. Houn—7B 70
Claude Rd. E10—1E 48
Claude Rd. E13—1K 65
Claude Rd. SE15—2H 95
Claude St. E14—4C 80
Claudia Jones Way. SW2
　　　　　—6J 93
Claudia Pl. SW19—1G 107
Claughton Rd. E13—2A 66
Clauson Av. N'holt—5F 39
Clavell St. SE10—6E 80
Claverdale Rd. SW2—7K 93
Clavering Av. SW13—6D 74
Clavering Clo. Twic—4A 104
Clavering Rd. E12—2B 50
Claverings Industrial Est. N9
　　　　　—2D 18
Claverley Gro. N3—1K 27
Claverley Vs. N3—1K 27
Claverton St. SW1—5G 77
Clave St. E1—1J 79 (3L 149)
Claxton Gro. W6—5F 75
Clay Av. Mitc—2F 123
Claybank Gro. SE13—3D 96
Claybourne M. SE19—7F 111
Claybridge Rd. SE12—4A 114
Claybrook Clo. N2—3B 28
Claybrook Rd. W6—6F 75
Claybury. Bush, Wat—1A 10
Claybury B'way. Ilf—3C 34

Claybury Rd. Wfd G—7H 21
Claydon Dri. Croy—4J 133
Clay Farm Rd. SE9—2G 115
Claygate Cres. Croy—6E 136
Claygate La. Esh & Th Dit
　　　　　—7A 118
Claygate Rd. W13—3B 72
Clayhall Av. Ilf—2C 34
Clay Hill. Enf—1K 7
Clayhill. Surb—5G 119
Clayhill Cres. SE9—4B 114
Claylands Pl. SW8—7A 78
Claylands Rd. SW8—6K 77
Clay La. Bush, Wat—1D 10
Clay La. Edgw—2B 12
Claymore Clo. Mord—7J 121
Claypole Rd. E15—2E 64
Clayponds Av. W5 & Bren
　　　　　—4E 72
Clayponds Gdns. W5—4D 72
Clayponds La. Bren—5E 72
Clays La. E15—5D 48
Clays La. E15—5D 48
Clay St. W1—5D 60 (6F 138)
Clayton Av. Wemb—7E 40
Clayton Clo. E6—6D 66
Clayton Cres. Bren—5D 72
Clayton Field. NW9—7F 13
Clayton Rd. SE15—1G 95
Clayton Rd. Iswth—3J 87
Clayton Rd. Romf—1J 53
Clayton St. SE11—6A 78
Clayton Ter. Hay—5C 54
Claywood Clo. Orp—7J 129
Clayworth Clo. Sidc—6B 100
Cleanthus Clo. SE18—1F 99
Cleanthus Rd. SE18—1F 99
Clearbrook Way. E1
　　　　　—6J 63 (7M 143)
Clearwell Dri. W9—4K 59
Cleaveland Rd. Surb—5D 118
Cleaverholme Clo. Croy
　　　　　—6H 125
Cleaver Sq. SE11—5A 78
Cleaver St. SE11—5A 78
Cleeve Hill. SE23—1H 111
Cleeve Pk. Gdns. Sidc—2B 116
Clegg St. E1—1H 79 (2K 149)
Clegg St. E13—2J 65
Clematis St. W12—7C 58
Clem Attlee Ct. SW6—6H 75
Clemence St. E14—5B 64
Clement Clo. NW6—7E 42
Clement Clo. W4—4K 73
Clementhorpe Rd. Dag—6C 52
Clementina Rd. E10—1B 48
Clementine Clo. W13—2B 72
Clement Rd. SW19—5G 107
Clement Rd. Beck—2K 125
Clement's Av. E16—7J 65
Clements Ct. Houn—4B 86
Clement's Inn. WC2
　　　　　—6K 61 (8F 140)
Clement's La. EC4
　　　　　—7D 62 (9B 142)
Clements La. Ilf—3F 51
Clements Pl. Bren—5D 72
Clements Rd. E6—7D 50
Clement's Rd. SE16
　　　　　—3G 79 (7H 149)
Clements Rd. Ilf—3F 51
Clendon Way. SE18—4H 83
Clennam St. SE1
　　　　　—2C 78 (4M 147)
Clensham La. Sutt—2J 131
Clenston M. W1—6D 60 (7E 138)
Clephane Rd. N1—6C 46
Clere Pl. EC2—4D 62 (3B 142)
Clere St. EC2—4D 62 (3B 142)
Clerkenwell Clo. EC1
　　　　　—4A 62 (4H 141)
Clerkenwell Grn. EC1
　　　　　—4B 62 (4J 141)
Clerkenwell Rd. EC1
　　　　　—4A 62 (4G 141)
Clermont Rd. E9—1J 63
Clevedon Clo. N16—3F 47

Clevedon Rd. SE20—1K 125
Clevedon Rd. King—2G 119
Clevedon Rd. Twic—6D 88
Cleveland Av. SW20—2H 121
Cleveland Av. W4—4B 74
Cleveland Av. Hmptn—7D 102
Cleveland Gdns. N4—5C 30
Cleveland Gdns. NW2—2F 43
Cleveland Gdns. SW13—2B 90
Cleveland Gdns. W2—6A 60
Cleveland Gdns. Wor Pk
　　　　　—2A 130
Cleveland Gro. E1
　　　　　—4J 63 (4L 143)
Cleveland M. W1
　　　　　—5G 61 (5L 139)
Cleveland Pk. Av. E17—4C 32
Cleveland Pk. Cres. E17—4C 32
Cleveland Pl. SW1
　　　　　—1G 77 (2M 145)
Cleveland Rise. Mord—7F 121
Cleveland Rd. E18—3J 33
Cleveland Rd. N1—7D 46
Cleveland Rd. N9—7C 8
Cleveland Rd. SW13—2B 90
Cleveland Rd. W4—3J 73
Cleveland Rd. W13—5A 56
Cleveland Rd. Ilf—3F 51
Cleveland Rd. Iswth—4A 88
Cleveland Rd. N Mald—4A 120
Cleveland Rd. Well—2K 99
Cleveland Rd. Wor Pk—2A 130
Cleveland Row. SW1
　　　　　—1G 77 (3M 145)
Cleveland Sq. W2—6A 60
Cleveland St. W1
　　　　　—4F 61 (4K 139)
Cleveland Ter. W2
　　　　　—6A 60 (7A 138)
Cleveland Way. E1
　　　　　—4J 63 (4L 143)
Cleveley Clo. SE7—4B 82
Cleveley Cres. W5—2E 56
Cleveleys Rd. E5—3H 47
Cleverley Est. W12—1C 74
Cleve Rd. NW6—7K 43
Cleve Rd. Sidc—3D 116
Cleves Av. Eps—7D 130
Cleves Rd. E6—1B 66
Cleves Rd. Rich—3C 104
Cleves Wlk. Ilf—1G 35
Cleves Way. Hmptn—7D 102
Cleves Way. Ruis—1B 38
Clewer Cres. Harr—1H 23
Clichy Est. E1—5J 63 (6M 143)
Clifden Rd. E5—5J 47
Clifden Rd. Bren—6D 72
Clifden Rd. Twic—1K 103
Cliffe Rd. S Croy—5D 134
Clifford Av. SW14—3H 89
Clifford Av. Chst—6D 114
Clifford Av. Ilf—2F 35
Clifford Av. Wall—4G 133
Clifford Clo. N'holt—1C 54
Clifford Dri. SW9—4B 94
Clifford Gdns. NW10—2E 58
Clifford Rd. E16—4H 65
Clifford Rd. E17—2E 32
Clifford Rd. N9—6D 8
Clifford Rd. SE25—4G 125
Clifford Rd. Barn—3E 4
Clifford Rd. Houn—3B 86
Clifford Rd. Rich—2D 104
Clifford Rd. Wemb—7D 40
Clifford's Inn Pas. EC4
　　　　　—6A 62 (8G 141)
Clifford St. W1—7G 61 (1L 145)
Clifford Way. NW10—4B 42
Cliff Rd. NW1—6H 45
Cliff Ter. SE8—2C 96
Cliffview Rd. SE13—3C 96
Cliff Vs. NW1—6H 45
Cliff Wlk. E16—5H 65
Clifton Av. E17—3K 31
Clifton Av. N3—1H 27
Clifton Av. W12—1B 74
Clifton Av. Felt—3A 102

Clifton Av. Stan—2B 24
Clifton Av. Wemb—6F 41
Clifton Cres. SE15—7J 79
(in two parts)
Clifton Est. SE15—1H 95
Clifton Gdns. N15—6F 31
Clifton Gdns. NW11—6H 27
Clifton Gdns. W4—4K 73
Clifton Gdns. W9
　　　　　—4A 60 (4A 138)
Clifton Gdns. Enf—4D 6
Clifton Gro. E8—6G 47
Clifton Hill. NW8—2A 59
Clifton Ho. E11—3G 49
Clifton Pk. Av. SW20—2E 120
Clifton Pl. SE16—2J 79 (4M 149)
Clifton Pl. W2—6B 60 (8B 138)
Clifton Rise. SE14—7A 80
Clifton Rd. E7—6B 50
Clifton Rd. E16—5G 65
Clifton Rd. N3—1A 28
Clifton Rd. N8—6H 29
Clifton Rd. N22—1G 29
Clifton Rd. NW10—2C 58
Clifton Rd. SE25—4E 124
Clifton Rd. SW19—6F 107
Clifton Rd. W9—4A 60 (3A 138)
Clifton Rd. Gnfd—4G 55
Clifton Rd. Harr—4F 25
Clifton Rd. Ilf—6H 35
Clifton Rd. Iswth—2J 87
Clifton Rd. King—7F 105
Clifton Rd. Sidc—4J 115
Clifton Rd. S'hall—4C 70
Clifton Rd. Tedd—4J 103
Clifton Rd. Wall—5F 133
Clifton Rd. Well—3C 100
Clifton St. EC2—5E 62 (5C 142)
Clifton Ter. N4—2A 46
Clifton Vs. W9—5A 60
Cliftonville Ct. SE12—1J 113
Clifton Way. SE15—7J 79
Clifton Way. Wemb—1E 56
Cline Rd. N11—6B 16
Clinger Ct. N1—1E 62
Clink St. SE1—1D 78 (2A 148)
Clinton Av. Well—4A 100
Clinton Rd. E3—3A 64
Clinton Rd. E7—4J 49
Clinton Rd. N15—4D 30
Clipper Clo. SE16
　　　　　—2K 79 (4M 149)
Clipper Way. SE13—4E 96
Clipstone M. W1
　　　　　—5G 61 (5L 139)
Clipstone Rd. Houn—3E 86
Clipstone St. W1
　　　　　—5G 61 (5L 139)
Clissold Clo. N2—3D 28
Clissold Ct. N4—2C 46
Clissold Cres. N16—3D 46
Clissold Rd. N16—3D 46
Clitheroe Av. Harr—1E 38
Clitheroe Rd. SW9—2J 93
Clitherow Av. W7—3A 72
Clitherow Pas. Bren—5C 72
Clitherow Rd. Bren—5B 72
Clitterhouse Cres. NW2—1E 42
Clitterhouse Rd. NW2—1E 42
Clive Av. N18—6B 18
Cliveden Clo. N12—4F 15
Cliveden Pl. SW1
　　　　　—4E 76 (8G 145)
Cliveden Rd. SW19—1H 121
Clivedon Ct. W13—5B 56
Clivedon Rd. E4—5B 20
Clive Pas. SE21—3D 110
Clive Rd. SE21—3D 110
Clive Rd. SW19—6C 108
Clive Rd. Belv—4G 85
Clive Rd. Enf—4B 8
Clive Rd. Twic—4K 103
Clive Way. Enf—4B 8
Cloak La. EC4—7C 62 (9M 141)
Clockhouse Av. Bark—1G 67
Clockhouse Clo. SW19—2E 106
Clockhouse La. Romf—1H 37

Clockhouse Pde. N13—5F 17
Clock Ho. Rd. Beck—3A 126
Clock Pde. Enf—5J 7
Clock Tower M. N1—1C 62
Clock Tower Pl. N7—6J 45
Clock Tower Rd. Iswth—3K 87
Cloister Gdns. Croy—6H 125
Cloister Gdns. Edgw—5D 12
Cloister Rd. NW2—3H 43
Cloister Rd. W3—5J 57
Cloisters Av. Brom—5D 128
Cloisters Mall. King—2E 118
Cloisters, The. SW9—1A 94
Clonard Way. Pinn—6A 10
Clonbrook Rd. N16—4E 46
Cloncurry St. SW6—2F 91
Clonmel Clo. Harr—2H 39
Clonmel Rd. SW6—1H 91
Clonmel Rd. Tedd—4H 103
Clonmore St. SW18—1H 107
Clorane Gdns. NW3—3J 43
Close, The. E4—7K 19
Close, The. N14—2C 16
Close, The. N20—2C 14
Close, The. Barn—6J 5
Close, The. Beck—4A 126
Close, The. Bex—6G 101
Close, The. Cars—7C 132
Close, The. Harr—2G 23
Close, The. Iswth—2H 87
Close, The. Mitc—4D 122
Close, The. N Mald—2J 119
Close, The. Orp—6J 129
Close, The. Pinn—7A 22
(Eastcote)
Close, The. Pinn—7D 22
(Rayners Lane)
Close, The. Rich—3H 89
Close, The. Romf—6E 36
Close, The. Sidc—4B 116
Close, The. Sutt—7H 121
Close, The. Wemb—3J 41
(Barnhill Rd.)
Close, The. Wemb—6E 40
(Lyon Pk. Av.)
Cloth Fair. EC1—5B 62 (6K 141)
Cloth St. EC1—5C 62 (5L 141)
Cloudesdale Rd. SW17—2F 109
Cloudesley Pl. N1—1A 62
Cloudesley Rd. Bexh—1F 101
Cloudesley Sq. N1—1A 62
Cloudesley St. N1—1A 62
Clouston Clo. Wall—5J 133
Clova Rd. E7—6H 49
Clove Hitch Quay. SW11—3A 92
Clovelly Av. NW9—4B 26
Clovelly Gdns. SE19—7F 111
Clovelly Gdns. Enf—7K 7
Clovelly Gdns. Romf—1H 37
Clovelly Rd. N8—4H 29
Clovelly Rd. W4—2K 73
Clovelly Rd. W5—2C 72
Clovelly Rd. Bexh—6E 84
Clovelly Rd. Houn—2E 86
Clovelly Way. E1
　　　　　—6J 63 (7M 143)
Clovelly Way. Harr—2D 38
Clovelly Way. Orp—6K 129
Clover Clo. E11—2F 49
Cloverdale Gdns. Sidc—6K 99
Clover M. SW3—6D 76
Clover Way. Wall—1E 132
Clove St. E13—4J 65
Clowders Rd. SE6—3B 112
Clowser Clo. Sutt—5A 132
Cloysters Grn. E1
　　　　　—1G 79 (2G 149)
Cloyster Wood. Edgw—7J 11
Club Gdns. Rd. Brom—7J 127
Club Row. E1—4F 63 (3E 142)
E1 1-11 & 2-10
E2 remainder
Clunbury Av. S'hall—5D 70
Clunbury St. N1—2D 62
Cluny Est. SE1—3E 78 (6C 148)

Cluny M. SW5—4J 75
Cluny Pl. SE1—3E 78 (6C 148)
Clutton St. E14—5D 64
Clydach Rd. Enf—4A 8
Clyde Cir. N15—4E 30
Clyde Pl. E10—7D 32
Clyde Rd. N15—4E 30
Clyde Rd. N22—1H 29
Clyde Rd. Croy—2F 135
Clyde Rd. Sutt—5J 131
Clyde Rd. Wall—6G 133
Clydesdale. Enf—4E 8
Clydesdale Av. Stan—3D 24
Clydesdale Clo. Iswth—3K 87
Clydesdale Ct. N20—1G 15
Clydesdale Gdns. Rich—4H 89
Clydesdale Rd. W11—6H 59
Clyde St. SE8—6B 80
Clyde Ter. SE23—2J 111
Clyde Vale. SE23—2J 111
Clyde Way. Romf—1K 37
Clydon Clo. Eri—6K 85
Clyston St. SW8—2G 93
Coach & Horses Yd. W1
　　　　　—7G 61 (9L 139)
Coach Ho. La. N5—4B 46
Coach Ho. La. SW19—4F 107
Coachhouse M. SE20—7H 111
Coach Ho. M. SE23—6K 95
Coaldale Wlk. SE21—7C 94
Coalecroft Rd. SW15—4E 90
Coal Wharf Rd. W12—2F 75
Coates Hill Rd. Brom—2E 128
Coate St. E2—2G 63
Coates Wlk. Bren—5E 72
Cobbett Rd. SE9—3C 98
Cobbett Rd. Twic—1E 102
Cobbetts Av. Ilf—5B 34
Cobbett St. SW8—7K 77
Cobble M. N5—4B 46
Cobbold Est. NW10—6B 42
Cobbold Rd. NW10—6B 42
Cobbold Rd. W12—2A 74
Cobb's Rd. Houn—4D 86
Cobb St. E1—5F 63 (6E 142)
Cobden Rd. E11—3G 49
Cobden Rd. SE25—5G 125
Cobden St. E14—5D 64
Cobham Av. N Mald—5C 120
Cobham Clo. SW11—6C 92
Cobham Clo. Brom—7C 128
Cobham Clo. Wall—6J 133
Cobham Ct. Mitc—2B 122
Cobham Rd. E17—1E 32
Cobham Rd. N22—3B 30
Cobham Rd. Houn—7A 70
Cobham Rd. Ilf—2J 51
Cobham Rd. King—2G 119
Cobland Rd. SE12—4A 114
Coborn Rd. E3—3B 64
Coborn St. E3—3B 64
Cobourg Rd. SE5—6F 79
Cobourg St. NW1
　　　　　—3G 61 (2M 139)
Coburg Cres. SW2—1K 109
Coburg Gdns. Ilf—2C 34
Coburg Rd. N22—3K 29
Cochrane M. NW8
　　　　　—2B 60 (1B 138)
Cochrane Rd. SW19—7H 107
Cochrane St. NW8
　　　　　—2B 60 (1B 138)
Cockayne Way. SE8—4A 80
Cockerell Rd. E17—6K 31
Cockfosters Pde. Barn—4K 5
Cockfosters Rd. Barn—3J 5
Cockfosters Rd. Pot B & Barn
　　　　　—1J 5
Cock Hill. E1—5E 62 (6D 142)
Cock La. EC1—5B 62 (6K 141)
Cockpit Yd. WC1
　　　　　—5K 61 (5F 140)
Cocks Cres. N Mald—4B 120
Cockspur Ct. SW1
　　　　　—1H 77 (2B 146)
Cockspur St. SW1
　　　　　—1H 77 (2B 146)

Cocksure La. Sidc—3G 117
Code St. E1—4F 63 (4F 142)
Codling Clo. E1—1G 79 (2H 149)
Codling Way. Wemb—4D 40
Codrington Hill. SE23—7A 96
Codrington M. W11—6G 59
Cody Clo. Harr—3D 24
Cody Clo. Wall—7H 133
Cody Rd. E16—4G 65
Coe Av. Croy—6G 125
Coe's All. Barn—4B 4
Cofers Circ. Wemb—3H 41
Cogan Av. E17—1A 32
Coin St. SE1—1A 78 (2G 147)
Coity Rd. NW5—6E 44
Cokers La. SE21—1D 110
Coke St. E1—6G 63 (7H 143)
Colas M. NW6—1J 59
Colbeck M. SW7—4K 75
Colbeck Rd. Harr—7G 23
Colberg Pl. N16—7F 31
Colborne Way. Wor Pk—3E 130
Colburn Way. Sutt—3B 132
Colby M. SE19—5E 110
Colby Rd. SE19—5E 110
Colchester Av. E12—3D 50
Colchester Dri. Pinn—5B 22
Colchester Rd. E10—7E 32
Colchester Rd. E17—6C 32
Colchester Rd. Edgw—7D 12
Coldbath Sq. EC1
　　　　　—4A 62 (3G 141)
Coldbath St. SE13—1D 96
Cold Blow Cres. Bex—1K 117
Cold Blow La. SE14—7K 79
Cold Blows. Mitc—3D 122
Coldershaw Rd. W13—1A 72
Coldfall Av. N10—2E 28
Coldham Ct. N22—1B 30
Coldharbour. E14—1E 80
Coldharbour La.—4A 94
SE5 1-199 & 2-200
SW9 remainder
Coldharbour Pl. SE5—2D 94
Coldharbour Rd. Croy—5A 134
Coldharbour Way. Croy
　　　　　—5A 134
Coldstream Gdns. SW18
　　　　　—6H 91
Colebeck M. N1—6B 46
Colebert Av. E1—4J 63 (3L 143)
Colebrook Clo. SW15—7F 91
Colebrook Av. W13—6B 56
Colebrooke Dri. E11—7A 34
Colebrooke Pl. N1—1B 62
Colebrooke Rise. Brom—2G 127
Colebrooke Rd. SW16—1J 123
Colebrooke Row. N1
　　　　　—2B 62 (1J 141)
Colebrook Way. N11—5A 16
Coleby Path. SE5—7D 78
Cole Clo. SE28—1B 84
Coledale Dri. Stan—1C 24
Coleford Rd. SW18—5A 92
Colegrave Rd. E15—5F 49
Colegrove Rd. SE15—6F 79
Coleherne Ct. SW5—5K 75
Coleherne M. SW10—5K 75
Coleherne Rd. SW10—5K 75
Colehill Gdns. SW6—1G 91
Colehill La. SW6—1G 91
Coleman Fields. N1—1C 62
Coleman Rd. SE5—7E 78
Coleman Rd. Belv—4G 85
Coleman Rd. Dag—6E 52
Colemans Heath. SE9—3F 115
Coleman St. EC2
　　　　　—6D 62 (7A 142)
Colenso Rd. E5—4J 47
Colenso Rd. Ilf—1J 51
Cole Pk. Gdns. Twic—5A 88
Cole Pk. Rd. Twic—6A 88
Cole Pk. View. Twic—6A 88
Colepits Wood Rd. SE9—5H 99
Coleraine Rd. N8—3A 30
Coleraine Rd. SE3—6H 81
Coleridge Av. E12—6C 50

Coleridge Av. Sutt—4C 132
Coleridge Clo. SW8—2F 93
Coleridge Gdns. NW6—7A 44
Coleridge La. N8—6J 29
Coleridge Rd. E17—4B 32
Coleridge Rd. N4—2A 46
Coleridge Rd. N8—6H 29
Coleridge Rd. N12—5F 15
Coleridge Rd. Croy—7J 125
Coleridge Sq. W13—6A 56
Coleridge Wlk. NW11—4J 27
Cole Rd. Twic—6A 88
Colesburg Rd. Beck—3B 126
Coles Cres. Harr—2F 39
Coles Grn. Bush, Wat—1B 10
Coles Grn. Rd. NW2—1C 42
Coleshill Rd. Tedd—6J 103
Colestown St. SW11—2C 92
Cole St. SE1—2C 78 (5M 147)
Colet Gdns. W14—4F 75
Coley St. WC1—4K 61 (4F 140)
Colfe Rd. SE23—1A 112
Colina M. N15—4B 30
Colina Rd. N15—5B 30
Colin Clo. NW9—4A 26
Colin Clo. Croy—3B 136
Colin Clo. W Wick—3H 137
Colin Cres. NW9—4B 26
Colindale Av. NW9—3K 25
Colindale Business Pk. NW9
　　　　　—3J 25
Colindeep Gdns. NW4—4C 26
Colindeep La.—3A 26
NW4 2-28
NW9 remainder
Colin Dri. NW9—5B 26
Colinette Rd. SW15—4E 90
Colin Gdns. NW9—4B 26
Colin Pk. Rd. NW9—4A 26
Colin Rd. NW10—6C 42
Colinton Rd. Ilf—2B 52
Coliston Rd. SW18—7J 91
Collamore Av. SW18—1C 108
Collapit Clo. Harr—6F 23
College App. SE10—6E 80
College Av. Harr—1J 23
College Clo. E9—5J 47
College Clo. N18—5A 18
College Clo. Harr—7D 10
College Clo. Twic—1H 103
College Cres. NW3—6B 44
College Cross. N1—7A 46
College Gdns. E4—7J 9
College Gdns. N18—5B 18
College Gdns. SE21—1E 110
College Gdns. SW17—2C 108
College Gdns. Ilf—5C 34
College Gdns. N Mald—5B 120
College Gdns. Rd. Enf—1J 7
College Grn. SE19—7E 110
College Gro. NW1—1H 61
College Hill. EC4
　　　　　—7C 62 (9M 141)
College Hill Rd. Harr—7D 10
College La. NW5—4F 45
College Pk. Clo. SE13—4F 97
College Pk. Rd. N17—6A 18
College Pl. E17—4G 33
College Pl. NW1—1G 61
College Rd. E17—5E 32
College Rd. N17—6A 18
College Rd. N21—2F 17
College Rd. NW10—2E 58
College Rd.—7E 94
SE21 1-111 & 2-120
SE19 remainder
College Rd. SW19—6B 108
College Rd. W13—6B 56
College Rd. Brom—1J 127
College Rd. Croy—2D 134
College Rd. Harr—6J 23
College Rd. Harr—1J 23
(Harrow Weald)
College Rd. Iswth—1K 87
College Rd. Swan—7K 117
College Rd. Wemb—1D 40

Connaught St. W2
—6C 60 (8D 138)
Connaught Way. N13—4G 17
Connell Cres. W5—4F 57
Connington Cres. E4—3A 20
Connor Rd. Dag—4F 53
Connor St. E9—1K 63
Conolly Rd. W7—1J 71
Conrad Dri. Wor Pk—1E 130
Consfield Av. N Mald—5C 120
Consort M. Iswth—5H 87
Consort Rd. SE15—1H 95
Cons St. SE1—2A 78 (4H 147)
Constable Clo. NW11—6K 27
Constable Cres. N15—5G 31
Constable Gdns. Edgw—1G 25
Constable Gdns. Iswth—5H 87
Constable Wlk. SE21—3E 110
Constance Cres. Brom—7H 127
Constance Rd. Enf—6K 7
Constance Rd. Croy—7B 124
Constance Rd. Sutt—4A 132
Constance Rd. Twic—7F 87
Constance St. E16—1C 82
Constantine Rd. NW3—4D 44
Constitution Hill. SW1
—2F 77 (4J 145)
Constitution Rise. Sutt—1E 98
Content St. SE17
—4D 78 (9A 148)
Convair Wlk. N'holt—3B 54
Convent Gdns. W5—4C 72
Convent Gdns. W11—6G 59
Convent Hill. SE19—6C 110
Convent Way. S'hall—4A 70
Conway Clo. Stan—6F 11
Conway Cres. Gnfd—2J 55
Conway Cres. Romf—6C 36
Conway Gdns. Enf—1K 7
Conway Gdns. Mitc—4J 123
Conway Gdns. Wemb—7C 24
Conway Gro. W3—5K 57
Conway Rd. N14—3D 16
Conway Rd. N15—5B 30
Conway Rd. NW2—2E 42
Conway Rd. SE18—4H 83
Conway Rd. SW20—1E 120
Conway Rd. Felt—5B 102
Conway Rd. Houn—7D 86
Conway St. W1—4G 61 (4L 139)
(in two parts)
Conway Wlk. Hmptn—6D 102
Conybeare. NW3—1C 60
Conyers Clo. Wfd G—6B 20
Conyer's Rd. SW16—5H 109
Conyer St. E3—2A 64
Cooden Clo. Brom—7K 113
Cookes Clo. E11—2H 49
Cookes La. Sutt—6G 131
Cookham Cres. SE16—2K 79
Cookham Dene Clo. Chst
—1H 129
Cookham Rd. Sidc, Orp & Swan
—7F 117
Cookhill Rd. SE2—3B 84
Cook's Clo. Romf—1J 37
Cooks Hole Rd. Enf—1H 7
Cook's Rd. E15—2D 64
Cook's Rd. SE17—6B 78
Coolfin Rd. E16—6J 65
Coolgardie Av. E4—5A 20
Coolgardie Av. Chig—3K 21
Coolhurst Rd. N8—6H 29
Cooling Way. Wemb—4D 40
Cool Oak La. NW9—1A 42
Coomassie Rd. W9—4H 59
Coombe Av. Croy—4E 134
Coombe Bank. King—1A 120
Coombe Clo. Edgw—2F 25
Coombe Clo. Houn—4E 86
Coombe Corner. N21—1G 17
Coombe Cres. Hmptn—7D 102
Coombe Dri. Ruis—1A 38
Coombe End. King—7K 105
Coombefield Clo. N Mald
—5A 120
Coombe Gdns. SW20—2C 120

Coombe Gdns. N Mald—4B 120
Coombe Hill Glade. King
—7A 106
Coombe Hill Rd. King—7A 106
Coombe Ho. E4—6H 19
Coombe Ho. Chase. N Mald
—1K 119
Coombehurst Clo. Barn—2J 5
Coombe La. SW20—1C 120
Coombe La. Croy—5H 135
Coombe La. W. King—1H 119
Coombe Lea. Brom—3C 128
Coombe Neville. King—7K 105
Coombe Pk. King—5J 105
Coombe Ridings. King—5J 105
Coombe Rise. King—1J 119
Coombe Rd. N22—2A 30
Coombe Rd. NW10—3K 41
Coombe Rd. SE26—4H 111
Coombe Rd. W4—5A 74
Coombe Rd. W13—3B 72
Coombe Rd. Croy—4D 134
Coombe Rd. Hmptn—6D 102
Coombe Rd. King—1G 119
Coombe Rd. N Mald—2A 120
Coomber Way. Croy—7H 123
Coombes Rd. Dag—1F 69
Coombe Wlk. Sutt—3K 131
Coombe Wood Dri. Romf
—6F 37
Coombewood Rd. King—5J 105
Coombs St. N1—2B 62 (1K 141)
Coomer M. SW6—6H 75
Coomer Pl. SW6—6H 75
Coomer Rd. SW6—6H 75
Cooms Wlk. Edgw—1J 25
Cooperage Clo. N17—6A 18
Cooper Av. E17—1A 32
Cooper Clo. SE1
—2A 78 (5H 147)
Cooper Ct. E15—5D 48
Cooper Cres. Cars—3D 132
Cooper Mead Clo. NW2—3E 42
Cooper Rd. NW4—6F 27
Cooper Rd. NW10—5C 42
Cooper Rd. Croy—4B 134
Coopersale Clo. Wfd G—7F 21
Coopersale Rd. E9—5K 47
Coopers Clo. E1
—4J 63 (4M 143)
Coopers La. E10—1D 48
Coopers La. NW1
—2H 61 (1B 140)
Cooper's La. SE12—2K 113
Cooper's Rd. SE1
—5F 79 (9F 148)
Cooper's Row. EC3
—7F 63 (9E 142)
Cooper St. E16—5H 65
Cooper's Yd. SE19—6E 110
Coote Gdns. Dag—3F 53
Coote Rd. Bexh—1F 101
Coote Rd. Dag—3F 53
Copeland Dri. E14—4C 80
Copeland Rd. E17—6D 32
Copeland Rd. SE15—2G 95
Copeman Clo. SE26—5J 111
Copenhagen Gdns. W4—2K 73
Copenhagen Pl. E14—6B 64
Copenhagen St. N1—1J 61
Cope Pl. W8—3J 75
Copers Cope Rd. Beck—7B 112
Cope St. SE16—4K 79 (8M 143)
Copford Clo. Wfd G—6H 21
Copinger Wlk. Edgw—1H 25
Copland Av. Wemb—5D 40
Copland Clo. Wemb—5C 40
Copland Rd. Wemb—6E 40
Copleston Pas. SE15—2E 94
Copleston Rd. SE15—3F 95
Copley Clo. SE17—6C 78
Copley Clo. W7—4K 55
Copley Dene. Brom—1B 128
Copley Pk. SW16—6K 109
Copley Rd. Stan—5H 11
Copley St. E1—5K 63 (6M 143)
Copner Way. SE15—7F 79

Coppelia Rd. SE3—4H 97
Coppen Rd. Dag—7F 37
Copperas St. SE8—6D 80
Copperbeech Clo. NW3—5B 44
Copper Beech Clo. Ilf—1D 34
Copper Beeches Ct. Iswth
—1H 87
Copper Clo. SE19—7F 111
Copperfield M. N18—5K 17
Copperfield Rd. E3—5A 64
Copperfield Rd. SE28—6C 68
Copperfields Ct. W3—2G 73
Copperfield St. SE1
—2B 78 (4K 147)
Copper Field Way. Chst
—6G 115
Copperfield Way. Pinn—4D 22
Coppergate Clo. Brom—1K 127
Coppermill La. E17—5K 45
Copper Mill La. SW17—4A 108
Coppetts Clo. N12—7H 15
Coppetts Rd. N10—7J 15
Coppice Clo. SW20—3E 120
Coppice Clo. Stan—6E 10
Coppice Dri. SW15—6D 90
Coppice, The. Enf—4G 7
Coppice Wlk. N20—3D 14
Coppies Gro. N11—4A 16
Copping Clo. Croy—4E 134
Coppins, The. Croy—6D 136
Coppins, The. Harr—6D 10
Coppock Clo. SW11—2C 92
Copse Av. W Wick—3D 136
Copse Clo. SE7—6K 81
Copse Glade. Surb—7D 118
Copse Hill. SW20—1C 120
Copse Hill. Sutt—7K 131
Copse, The. E4—2C 20
Copse View. S Croy—7K 135
Coptefield Dri. Belv—3D 84
Copthall Av. EC2
(in two parts)—6D 62 (7B 142)
Copthall Clo. EC2
—6D 62 (7A 142)
Copthall Dri. NW7—7H 13
Copthall Gdns. NW7—7H 13
Copthall Gdns. Twic—1K 103
Copthorne Av. SW12—7H 93
Coptic St. WC1—5J 61 (6C 140)
Copwood Clo. N12—4H 15
Coral Clo. Romf—4C 36
Coralline Wlk. SE2—2C 84
Coral Row. SW11—3A 92
Coral St. SE1—2A 78 (5H 147)
Coram St. WC1—4J 61 (4C 140)
Coran Clo. N9—7E 8
Corban Rd. Houn—3E 86
Corbar Clo. Barn—1G 5
Corbet Clo. Wall—1E 132
Corbet Ct. EC3—6D 62 (8B 142)
Corbet Pl. E1—5F 63 (5E 142)
Corbett Ct. SE26—4B 112
Corbett Gro. N22—7D 16
Corbett Rd. E11—6A 34
Corbett Rd. E17—3E 32
Corbett's La. SE16
—4J 79 (9L 149)
Corbett's Pas. SE16
—4J 79 (9L 149)
Corbicum. E11—7G 33
Corbiere Ct. SW19—6F 107
Corbins La. Harr—3F 39
Corbridge Cres. E2—2H 63
Corby Cres. Enf—4D 6
Corbylands Rd. Sidc—1J 115
Corbyn St. N4—1J 45
Corby Rd. NW10—2K 57
Corby Way. E3—4C 64
Cordelia Clo. SE24—4B 94
Cordelia St. E14—6D 64
Cording St. E14—5D 64
Cordova Rd. E3—3A 64
Cordwainers Wlk. E13—2J 65
Cord Way. E14—3C 80
Cordwell Rd. SE13—5G 97
Corelli Rd. SE3—2C 98
Corfe Av. Harr—4E 38

Corfield St. E2—3H 63 (2K 143)
Corfton Rd. W5—6E 56
Corinium Clo. Wemb—4F 41
Corinne Rd. N19—4G 45
Corinthian Manorway. Eri
—4K 85
Corinthian Rd. Eri—4K 85
Corkers Path. Ilf—2G 51
Corker Wlk. N7—2K 45
Corkran Rd. Surb—7D 118
Corkscrew Hill. W Wick
—2E 136
Cork Sq. E1—1H 79 (2J 149)
Cork St. W1—7G 61 (1L 145)
Cork Tree Way. E4—5F 19
Corlett St. NW1—5C 60 (5C 138)
Cormont Rd. SE5—1B 94
Cornbury Rd. Edgw—7J 11
Cornelia St. N7—6K 45
Cornell Clo. Sidc—6E 116
Corner Grn. SE3—2J 97
Corner Mead. NW9—7G 13
Corney Rd. W4—6A 74
Cornflower La. Croy—1K 135
Cornflower Ter. SE22—6H 95
Cornford Clo. Brom—5J 127
Cornford Gro. SW12—2F 109
Cornhill. EC3—6D 62 (8B 142)
Cornish Gro. SE20—1H 125
Corn Mill Dri. Orp—7K 129
Cornmill La. SE13—3E 96
Cornshaw Rd. Dag—1D 52
Cornthwaite Rd. E5—3J 47
Cornwall Av. E2—3J 63 (2L 143)
Cornwall Av. N3—7D 14
Cornwall Av. N22—1J 29
Cornwall Av. S'hall—5D 54
Cornwall Av. Well—3J 99
Cornwall Clo. Bark—6K 51
Cornwall Cres. W11—6G 59
Cornwall Dri. Orp—7C 116
Cornwall Gdns. NW10—6D 42
Cornwall Gdns. SW7—3K 75
Cornwall Gdns. Wlk.
—3K 75
Cornwall Gro. W4—5A 74
Cornwallis Av. N9—2D 18
Cornwallis Av. SE9—3H 115
Cornwallis Gro. N9—2D 18
Cornwallis Rd. E17—4K 31
Cornwallis Rd. N9—2C 18
Cornwallis Rd. N19—2J 45
Cornwallis Rd. Dag—4D 52
Cornwallis Wlk. SE9—3D 98
Cornwall M. S. SW7—3A 76
Cornwall M. W. SW7—3K 75
Cornwall Rd. N4—7A 30
Cornwall Rd. N15—5D 30
Cornwall Rd. N18—5B 18
Cornwall Rd. SE1
—1A 78 (2G 147)
Cornwall Rd. Croy—2B 134
Cornwall Rd. Harr—6G 23
Cornwall Rd. Pinn—1D 22
Cornwall Rd. Sutt—7H 131
Cornwall Rd. Twic—1A 104
Cornwall St. E1—7H 63 (9K 143)
Cornwall Ter. NW1
—4D 60 (4F 138)
Cornwood Clo. N2—4B 28
Cornwood Dri. E1
—6J 63 (7M 143)
Cornworthy Rd. Dag—5C 52
Corona Rd. SE12—7J 97
Coronation Av. N16—4F 47
Coronation Clo. Bex—6D 100
Coronation Clo. Ilf—4G 35
Coronation Rd. E13—3A 66
Coronation Rd. NW10—3F 57
Coronation Wlk. Twic—1E 102
Coronet St. N1—3E 62 (2C 142)
Corporation Av. Houn—4C 86
Corporation Row. EC1
—4A 62 (3H 141)
Corporation St. E15—2G 65
Corporation St. N7—5J 45
Corrance Rd. SW2—4J 93

Corri Av. N14—4C 16
Corrib Dri. Sutt—5C 132
Corringham Rd. NW11—7J 27
Corringham Rd. Wemb—2G 41
Corringway. NW11—7K 27
Corringway. W5—4G 57
Corronade Pl. SE28—3H 83
Corscombe Clo. King—5J 105
Corsehill St. SW16—6G 109
Corsham St. N1—3D 62 (2B 142)
Corsica St. N5—6B 46
Corsley Way. E9—6B 48
Cortayne Rd. SW6—2H 91
Cortis Rd. SW15—6D 90
Cortis Ter. SW15—6D 90
Corunna Rd. SW8—1G 93
Corunna Ter. SW8—1G 93
Corvette Sq. SE10—6F 81
Coryton Path. W9—4H 59
Cosbycote Av. SE24—5C 94
Cosdach Av. Wall—7H 133
Cosedge Cres. Croy—5A 134
Cosgrove Clo. N21—2H 17
Cosgrove Clo. Hay—4C 54
Cosmo Pl. WC1—5J 61 (5D 140)
Cosmur Clo. W12—3B 74
Cossall Wlk. SE15—2H 95
Cosser St. SE1—3A 78 (7G 147)
Costa St. SE15—2G 95
Costons Av. Gnfd—3H 55
Costons La. Gnfd—3H 55
Cosway St. NW1
　　　　　—5C 60 (5D 138)
Cotall St. E14—5C 64
Coteford St. SW17—4D 108
Cotelands. Croy—3E 134
Cotesbach Rd. E5—3J 47
Cotesmore Gdns. Dag—4C 52
Cotford Rd. T Hth—4C 124
Cotham St. SE17
　　　　　—4C 78 (9M 147)
Cotherstone Rd. SW2—1K 109
Cotleigh Av. Bex—2D 116
Cotleigh Rd. NW6—7J 43
Cotleigh Rd. Romf—6K 37
Cotman Clo. NW11—6A 28
Cotman Clo. SW15—6F 91
Cotman Gdns. Edgw—2G 25
Coton Rd. Well—3A 100
Cotsford Av. N Mald—5J 119
Cotswold Clo. Bexh—2K 101
Cotswold Clo. King—6J 105
Cotswold Ct. N11—4K 15
Cotswold Gdns. E6—3B 66
Cotswold Gdns. NW2—2F 43
Cotswold Gdns. Ilf—7H 35
Cotswold Ga. NW2—1G 43
Cotswold Grn. Enf—4E 6
Cotswold M. SW11—1B 92
Cotswold Rise. Orp—6K 129
Cotswold Rd. Hmptn—6E 102
Cotswold St. SE27—4B 110
Cotswold Way. Enf—3E 6
Cottage Av. Brom—7C 128
Cottage Field Clo. Sidc—1C 116
Cottage Grn. SE5—7D 78
Cottage Gro. SW9—3J 93
Cottage Gro. Surb—6D 118
Cottage Pl. SW3
　　　　　—3C 76 (7C 144)
Cottage Rd. Eps—7A 130
Cottage St. E14—7D 64
Cottage Wlk. SE15—1F 95
Cottage Wlk. SW1
　　　　　—3D 76 (6F 144)
Cottenham Dri. SW20—7D 106
Cottenham Pk. Rd. SW20
(in two parts)　　　—1C 120
Cottenham Pl. SW20—7D 106
Cottenham Rd. E17—4B 32
Cotterill Rd. Surb—7F 119
Cottesbrook St. SE14—7A 80
Cottesmore Av. Ilf—2E 34
Cottesmore Gdns. W8—3K 75
Cottingham Rd. SE20—7K 111
Cottingham Rd. SW8—7K 77

Cottington Clo. SE11
　　　　　—5B 78 (9J 147)
Cottington Rd. Felt—4B 102
Cottington St. SE11
　　　　　—5B 78 (9J 147)
Cotton Av. W3—6K 57
Cottongrass Clo. Croy—1K 135
Cotton Hill. Brom—4E 112
Cotton Row. SW11—3B 92
Cottons App. Romf—5K 37
Cottons Centre. SE1
　　　　　—1E 78 (2C 148)
Cottons Ct. Romf—5K 37
Cotton's Gdns. E2
　　　　　—3E 62 (1D 142)
Cottons La. SE1—1E 78 (2C 148)
Cotton St. E14—7E 64
Couchmore Av. Ilf—2D 34
Coulgate St. SE4—3A 96
Coulson Clo. Dag—1C 52
Coulson St. SW3
　　　　　—5D 76 (9E 144)
Coulston Rd. SW18—7J 91
Coulter Clo. Hay—4C 54
Coulter Rd. W6—3D 74
Councillor St. SE5—7C 78
Countess Rd. NW5—5G 45
Countisbury Av. Enf—7A 8
Country Way. Felt—6A 102
County Gdns. Bark—2J 67
County Ga. SE9—3G 115
County Ga. Barn—6E 4
County Gro. SE5—1C 94
County Rd. E6—5F 67
County Rd. T Hth—2B 124
County St. SE1—3C 78 (7M 147)
Coupland Pl. SE18—5G 83
Courcy Rd. N8—3A 30
Courland Gro. SW8—1H 93
Courland St. SW8—1H 93
(in two parts)
Course, The. SE9—3E 114
Courtauld Clo. SE28—1A 84
Courtauld Rd. N19—1J 45
Court Av. Belv—5F 85
Court Clo. Harr—3E 24
Court Clo. Twic—3F 103
Court Clo. Wall—7H 133
Court Clo. Av. Twic—3F 103
Court Downs Rd. Beck—2D 126
Court Dri. Croy—4K 133
Court Dri. Stan—4K 11
Court Dri. Sutt—4C 132
Courtenay Av. N6—7C 28
Courtenay Av. Harr—7B 10
Courtenay Av. Sutt—7J 131
Courtenay Gdns. Harr—2G 23
Courtenay M. E17—5A 32
Courtenay Pl. E17—5A 32
Courtenay Rd. E11—3H 49
Courtenay Rd. E17—4K 31
Courtenay Rd. SE20—6K 111
Courtenay Rd. Wor Pk—3E 130
Courtenay Sq. SE11—5A 78
Courtenay St. SE11
　　　　　—5A 78 (9G 147)
Court Farm Av. Eps—5A 130
Court Farm La. N'holt—7E 38
Court Farm Rd. SE9—2B 114
Court Farm Rd. N'holt—7E 38
Courtfield. W5—5C 56
Courtfield Av. Harr—5K 23
Courtfield Cres. Harr—5K 23
Courtfield Gdns. SW5—4K 75
Courtfield Gdns. W13—6A 56
Courtfield M. SW7—4A 76
Courtfield Rise. W Wick
　　　　　—3F 137
Courtfield Rd. SW7—4A 76
Courthill Rd. SE13—4E 96
Courthope Rd. NW3—4D 44
Courthope Rd. SW19—5G 107
Courthope Rd. Gnfd—2H 55
Courthope's. SW19—7G 107
Court Ho. Gdns. N3—6D 14
Courthouse Rd. N12—6E 14
Courtland Av. E4—2C 20

Courtland Av. NW7—3F 13
Courtland Av. SW16—7K 109
Courtland Av. Ilf—2D 50
Courtland Gro. SE28—7D 68
Courtland Rd. E6—1C 66
Courtlands. Rich—5G 89
Courtlands Av. SE12—5K 97
Courtlands Av. Brom—1H 137
Courtlands Av. Hmptn—6D 102
Courtlands Av. Rich—2H 89
Courtlands Dri. Eps—6A 130
Courtlands Rd. Surb—7G 119
Court La. SE21—6E 94
Court La. Gdns. SE21—7E 94
Courtleet Dri. Eri—1H 101
Courtleigh Gdns. NW11—4G 27
Courtman Rd. N17—7H 17
Court Mead. N'holt—3D 54
Courtmead Clo. SE24—6C 94
Courtnell St. W2—6J 59
Courtney Clo. SE19—6E 110
Courtney Cres. Cars—7D 132
Courtney Pl. Croy—3A 134
Courtney Rd. N7—5A 46
Courtney Rd. SW19—7C 108
Courtney Rd. Croy—3A 134
Courtrai Rd. SE23—6A 96
Court Rd. SE9—6D 98
Court Rd. SE25—2F 125
Court Rd. S'hall—5D 70
Courtside. N8—6H 29
Courtside. SE26—3H 111
Court St. E1—5H 63 (5J 143)
Court St. Brom—2J 127
Court, The. Ruis—4C 38
Court Way. NW4—2A 26
Court Way. W3—5J 57
Court Way. Ilf—3G 35
Court Way. Twic—7K 87
Court Way. Wfd G—5F 21
Court Wood La. Croy—7B 136
Court Yd. SE9—6D 98
Courtyard, The. N1—7K 45
Courtyard, The. NW1—7E 44
Cousin La. EC4—7D 62 (1A 148)
Couthurst Rd. SE3—7K 81
Coutt's Cres. NW5—3E 44
Coval Gdns. SW14—4H 89
Coval La. SW14—4H 89
Coval Pas. SW14—4J 89
Coval Rd. SW14—4J 89
Covent Garden. WC2
　　　　　—7J 61 (9D 140)
Coventry Clo. E6—6D 66
Coventry Clo. NW6—2J 59
Coventry Rd. E1 & E2
　　　　　—4H 63 (3K 143)
Coventry Rd. SE25—4G 125
Coventry Rd. Ilf—2F 51
Coventry St. W1
　　　　　—7H 61 (1A 146)
Coverack Clo. N14—6B 6
Coverack Clo. Croy—7A 126
Coverdale Clo. Stan—5G 11
Coverdale Gdns. Croy—3F 135
Coverdale Rd. NW2—7F 43
Coverdale Rd. W12—2D 74
Coverdales, The. Bark—2H 67
Coverley Clo. E1
　　　　　—5G 63 (5G 143)
Coverton Rd. SW17—5C 108
Covert, The. Orp—6J 129
Covert Way. Barn—2F 5
Covington Gdns. SW16—7B 110
Covington Way. SW16—6K 109
(in two parts)
Cowan Clo. E6—5C 66
Cowbridge La. Bark—7F 51
Cowbridge Rd. Harr—4F 25
Cowcross St. EC1
　　　　　—5B 62 (5J 141)
Cowdenbeath Path. N1—1K 61
Cowden Rd. Orp—7K 129
Cowden St. SE6—4C 112
Cowdrey Clo. Enf—2K 7
Cowdrey Rd. SW19—5A 108
Cowdry Rd. E9—6A 48

Cowen Av. Harr—2H 39
Cowgate Rd. Gnfd—3H 55
Cowick Rd. SW17—4D 108
Cowings Mead. N'holt—6C 38
Cowland Av. Enf—4D 8
Cow La. Gnfd—2H 55
Cowleaze Rd. King—1E 118
Cowley La. E11—3G 49
Cowley Pl. NW4—5E 26
Cowley Rd. E11—5K 33
Cowley Rd. SW9—1A 94
Cowley Rd. SW14—3A 90
Cowley Rd. W3—1B 74
Cowley Rd. Ilf—7D 34
Cowley St. SW1—3J 77 (6C 146)
Cowling Clo. W11—1G 75
Cowper Av. E6—7C 50
Cowper Av. Sutt—4B 132
Cowper Clo. Brom—4B 128
Cowper Clo. Well—5A 100
Cowper Gdns. N14—6A 6
Cowper Gdns. Wall—6G 133
Cowper Rd. N14—1A 16
Cowper Rd. N16—5E 46
(in two parts)
Cowper Rd. N18—5B 18
Cowper Rd. SW19—6A 108
Cowper Rd. W3—1K 73
Cowper Rd. W7—7K 55
Cowper Rd. Belv—4G 85
Cowper Rd. Brom—4B 128
Cowper Rd. King—5F 105
Cowper St. EC2—4D 62 (3B 142)
Cowper Ter. W10—5F 59
Cowslip Rd. E18—2K 33
Cowthorpe Rd. SW8—1H 93
Coxmount Rd. SE7—5B 82
Coxson Pl. SE1—2F 79 (5E 148)
Cox's Wlk. SE21 & SE26
　　　　　—1G 111
Coxwell Rd. SE18—5H 83
Coxwell Rd. SE19—7E 110
Crab Hill. Beck—7F 113
Crabtree Av. Romf—4D 36
Crabtree Av. Wemb—2F 57
Crabtree Ct. E15—5D 48
Crabtree La. SW6—7E 74
(in two parts)
Crabtree Manorway. Belv
　　　　　—3J 85
Crabtree Manorway N. Belv
　　　　　—2J 85
Crabtree Wlk. Croy—1G 135
Crace St. NW1—3H 61 (1A 140)
Craddock Rd. Enf—3A 8
Craddock St. NW5—6E 44
Cradley Rd. SE9—1H 115
Craigen Av. Croy—1H 135
Craigerne Rd. SE3—7K 81
Craig Gdns. E18—2H 33
Craigholm. SE18—2E 98
Craigmuir Pk. Wemb—1F 57
Craignair Rd. SW2—7A 94
Craignish Av. SW16—2K 123
Craig Pk. Rd. N18—5C 18
Craig Rd. Rich—4C 104
Craig's Ct. SW1—1J 77 (2C 146)
Craigton Rd. SE9—4D 98
Craigweil Clo. Stan—5J 11
Craigweil Dri. Stan—5J 11
Crail Row. SE17—4D 78 (9B 148)
Cramer St. W1—5E 60 (6H 139)
Cramond Clo. W6—6G 75
Crampton Rd. SE20—6J 111
Crampton St. SE17
　　　　　—4C 78 (9L 147)
Cranberry Clo. N'holt—2B 54
Cranborne Av. S'hall—4E 70
Cranborne Rd. Bark—1H 67
Cranbourne Av. E11—4K 33
Cranbourne Clo. SW16—3J 123
Cranbourne Dri. Pinn—5B 22
Cranbourne Gdns. NW11
　　　　　—5G 27
Cranbourne Gdns. Ilf—3G 35
Cranbourne Rd. E12—5C 50
Cranbourne Rd. E15—4E 48

Cranbourne Rd. N10—2F 29
Cranbourn Pas. SE16
   —2H 79 (5J 149)
Cranbourn St. WC2
   —7H 61 (9B 140)
Cranbrook Clo. Brom—6J 127
Cranbrook Dri. Twic—1F 103
Cranbrook Est. E2
   —2K 63 (1M 143)
Cranbrook M. E17—5B 32
Cranbrook Pk. N22—1A 30
Cranbrook Point. E16—1K 81
Cranbrook Rise. Ilf—6D 34
Cranbrook Rd. SE8—1C 96
Cranbrook Rd. SW19—7G 107
Cranbrook Rd. W4—5A 74
Cranbrook Rd. Barn—6G 5
Cranbrook Rd. Bexh—1F 101
Cranbrook Rd. Houn—4D 86
Cranbrook Rd. Ilf—7E 34
Cranbrook Rd. T Hth—2C 124
Cranbrook St. E2—2K 63
Cranbury Rd. SW6—2K 91
Crane Av. W3—7J 57
Crane Av. Iswth—5A 88
Cranebrook. Twic—2G 103
Crane Clo. Dag—6G 53
Crane Ct. EC4—6A 62 (8H 141)
Craneford Clo. Twic—7K 87
Craneford Way. Twic—7J 87
Crane Gro. N7—6A 46
Crane Lodge Rd. Houn—6A 70
Cranemead. SE16
   —4K 79 (9M 149)
Crane Pk. Rd. Twic—2F 103
Crane Rd. Twic—1J 103
Cranes Dri. Surb—4E 118
Cranes Pk. Surb—4E 118
Cranes Pk. Av. Surb—4E 118
Cranes Pk. Cres. Surb—4F 119
Crane St. SE10—5F 81
Craneswater Pk. S'hall—5D 70
Crane Way. Twic—7G 87
Cranfield Clo. SE27—3C 110
Cranfield Dri. NW9—7F 13
Cranfield Rd. SE4—3B 96
Cranfield Rd. E. Cars—7E 132
Cranfield Rd. W. Cars—7E 132
Cranford Av. N13—5D 16
Cranford Clo. SW20—7D 106
Cranford La. Houn—7A 70
   (Heston)
Cranford St. E1—7K 63
Cranford Way. N8—4K 29
Cranhurst Rd. NW2—5E 42
Cranleigh Clo. SE20—2H 125
Cranleigh Clo. Bex—6H 101
Cranleigh Gdns. N21—5F 7
Cranleigh Gdns. SE25—3E 124
Cranleigh Gdns. Bark—7H 51
Cranleigh Gdns. Harr—5E 24
Cranleigh Gdns. King—6F 105
Cranleigh Gdns. S'hall—6D 54
Cranleigh Gdns. Sutt—2K 131
Cranleigh M. SW11—3E 92
Cranleigh Rd. N15—5C 30
Cranleigh Rd. SW19—3J 121
Cranleigh St. NW1—2G 61
Cranley Dene Ct. N10—4F 29
Cranley Dri. Ilf—7G 35
Cranley Gdns. N10—4F 29
Cranley Gdns. N13—3E 16
Cranley Gdns. SW7
   —5A 76 (9A 144)
Cranley Gdns. Wall—7G 133
Cranley M. SW7
   —5A 76 (9A 144)
Cranley Pl. SW7
   —4B 76 (9A 144)
Cranley Rd. E13—5K 65
Cranley Rd. Ilf—6G 35
Cranmer Av. W13—3B 72
Cranmer Clo. Mord—6F 121
Cranmer Clo. Ruis—1B 38
Cranmer Clo. Stan—7H 11
Cranmer Ct. SW3
   —4C 76 (9D 144)

Cranmer Ct. SW4—3H 93
Cranmere Ct. Enf—2F 7
Cranmer Farm Clo. Mitc
   —4D 122
Cranmer Gdns. Dag—4J 53
Cranmer Rd. E7—4K 49
Cranmer Rd. SW9—7A 78
Cranmer Rd. Croy—3B 134
Cranmer Rd. Edgw—3C 12
Cranmer Rd. Hmptn—5F 103
Cranmer Rd. King—5E 104
Cranmer Rd. Mitc—4D 122
Cranmer Ter. SW17—5B 108
Cranmore Av. Iswth—7G 71
Cranmore Rd. Brom—3H 113
Cranmore Rd. Chst—5D 114
Cranmore Way. N10—4G 29
Cranston Clo. Houn—2C 86
Cranston Est. N1—2D 62
Cranston Gdns. E4—6J 19
Cranston Rd. SE23—1A 112
Cranswick Rd. SE16—5H 79
Crantock Rd. SE6—2D 112
Cranwell Clo. E3—4D 64
Cranwich Av. N21—7J 7
Cranwich Rd. N16—7D 30
Cranwood St. EC1
   —3D 62 (2B 142)
Cranworth Cres. E4—1A 20
Cranworth Gdns. SW9—1A 94
Craster Rd. SW2—7K 93
Crathie Rd. SE12—6K 97
Crathorn St. SE13—3E 96
Craven Av. W5—7C 56
Craven Av. S'hall—5D 54
Craven Clo. N16—7G 31
Craven Gdns. SW19—5K 107
Craven Gdns. Bark—2J 67
Craven Gdns. Ilf—2H 35
Craven Hill. W2—7A 60 (9A 138)
Craven Hill Gdns. W2—7A 60
Craven Hill. W2
   —7A 60 (9A 138)
Craven M. SW11—3E 92
Craven Pk. NW10—1K 57
Craven Pk. M. NW10—1A 58
Craven Pk. Rd. N15—6F 31
Craven Pk. Rd. NW10—1A 58
Craven Rd. NW10—1K 57
Craven Rd. W2—6B 60 (8A 138)
Craven Rd. W5—7C 56
Craven Rd. Croy—1H 135
Craven Rd. King—1F 119
Craven St. WC2—1J 77 (2C 146)
Craven Ter. W2—7A 60 (9A 138)
Craven Wlk. N16—7G 31
Crawford Av. Wemb—5D 40
Crawford Clo. Iswth—2J 87
Crawford Est. SE5—2C 94
Crawford Gdns. N13—3G 17
Crawford Gdns. N'holt—3D 54
Crawford M. W1
   —5D 60 (6E 138)
Crawford Pas. EC1
   —4A 62 (4G 141)
Crawford Pl. W1
   —6C 60 (7D 138)
Crawford Rd. SE5—1C 94
Crawford St. W1
   —5D 60 (6E 138)
Crawley Rd. E10—1D 48
Crawley Rd. N22—2C 30
Crawley Rd. Enf—7K 7
Crawshay Ct. SW9—1A 94
Crawthew Gro. SE22—4F 95
Craybrooke Rd. Sidc—4B 116
Craybury End. SE9—2G 115
Crayford Industrial Pk. Orp
   —7C 116
Crayford Clo. E6—5C 66
Crayford Rd. N7—4J 45
Craymill Sq. Dart—2D 92
Cray Rd. Belv—6G 85
Cray Rd. Sidc—6C 116
Cray Valley Rd. Orp—5K 129
Crealock Gro. Wfd G—5C 20
Crealock St. SW18—6K 91

Creasy St. SE1—3E 78 (7C 148)
Crebor St. SE22—6G 95
Credenhall Dri. Brom—7D 129
Credenhill St. SW16—6G 109
Credenhill Way. SE15—7H 79
Crediton Hill. NW6—5K 43
Crediton Rd. E16—6J 65
Crediton Rd. NW10—1F 59
Credon Rd. E13—2A 66
Credon Rd. SE16—5H 79
Creechurch La. EC3
   —6E 62 (8D 142)
Creed La. EC4—6B 62 (8K 141)
Creek Rd.—6C 80
   SE8 1-201 & 2-194
   SE10 remainder
Creek Rd. Bark—3K 67
Creekside. SE8—7D 80
Creeland Gro. SE6—1B 112
Crefeld Clo. W6—6G 75
Creffield Rd.—7F 57
   W5 1-51 & 2-56
   W3 remainder
Creighton Av. E6—2B 66
Creighton Av.—3C 28
   N10 1-79 & 2-78
   N2 remainder
Creighton Rd. N17—7K 17
Creighton Rd. NW6—2F 59
Creighton Rd. W5—3D 72
Cremer St. E2—2F 63 (1E 142)
Cremorne Est. SW10—6B 76
Cremorne Rd. SW10—7B 76
Crescent Ct. Surb—5D 118
Crescent Dri. Orp—6F 129
Crescent E. Barn—1F 5
Crescent Gdns. SW19—3J 107
Crescent Gdns. Ruis—7A 22
Crescent Gro. SW4—4G 93
Crescent Gro. Mitc—5C 122
Crescent La. SW4—4G 93
Crescent Pl. SW3
   —4C 76 (8D 144)
Crescent Rise. N22—1H 29
Crescent Rise. Barn—5H 5
Crescent Rd. E4—1B 20
Crescent Rd. E6—1A 66
Crescent Rd. E10—2D 48
Crescent Rd. E13—1J 65
Crescent Rd. E18—1A 34
Crescent Rd. N3—1H 27
Crescent Rd. N8—6H 29
Crescent Rd. N9—1B 18
Crescent Rd. N11—4J 15
Crescent Rd. N15—3B 30
Crescent Rd. N22—1H 29
Crescent Rd. SW20—1F 121
Crescent Rd. Barn—4G 5
Crescent Rd. Beck—2D 126
Crescent Rd. Brom—7J 113
Crescent Rd. Dag—3H 53
Crescent Rd. Enf—4G 7
Crescent Rd. King—7G 105
Crescent Rd. Sidc—3K 115
Crescent Row. EC1
   —4C 62 (4L 141)
Crescent Stables. SW15—5G 91
Crescent St. N1—7K 45
Crescent Ter. E6—5E 66
Crescent, The. E17—5A 32
Crescent, The. N9—2C 18
Crescent, The. N11—4K 15
Crescent, The. NW2—3D 42
Crescent, The. SW13—2C 90
Crescent, The. SW19—3J 107
Crescent, The. W3—6A 58
Crescent, The. Barn—2E 4
Crescent, The. Beck—1C 126
Crescent, The. Bex—7C 100
Crescent, The. Croy—6D 124
Crescent, The. Harr—1G 39
Crescent, The. Ilf—6E 34
Crescent, The. N Mald—2K 119
Crescent, The. Sidc—4K 115
Crescent, The. S'hall—2D 70
Crescent, The. Surb—5E 118

Crescent, The. Sutt—5B 132
Crescent, The. Wemb—2B 40
Crescent, The. W Wick—6G 127
Crescent Way. N12—6H 15
Crescent Way. SE4—3C 96
Crescent Way. SW16—7K 109
Crescent W. Barn—1F 5
Crescent Wood Rd. SE26
   —3G 111
Cresford Rd. SW6—1K 91
Crespigny Rd. NW4—6D 26
Cressage Clo. S'hall—4E 54
Cresset Rd. E9—6J 47
Cresset St. SW4—3H 93
Cresswell Gdns. SW5—5A 76
Cresswell Pk. SE3—3H 97
Cresswell Pl. SW10—5A 76
Cresswell Rd. SE25—4G 125
Cresswell Rd. Felt—3C 102
Cresswell Rd. Twic—6D 88
Cresswell Way. N21—7F 7
Cressy Ct. E1—5J 63 (5M 143)
Cressy Ct. W6—3D 74
Cressy Pl. E1—5J 63 (5M 143)
Cressy Rd. NW3—5D 44
Crestbrook Av. N13—3G 17
Crest Dri. Enf—1D 8
Crestfield St. WC1
   —3J 61 (1D 140)
Crest Gdns. Ruis—3A 38
Creston Way. Wor Pk—1F 131
Crest Rd. NW2—2C 42
Crest Rd. Brom—7H 127
Crest Rd. S Croy—7H 135
Crest, The. N13—4F 17
Crest, The. NW4—5E 26
Crest, The. Surb—5G 119
Crest View. Pinn—4B 22
Crest View Dri. Orp—5F 129
Crestway. SW15—6C 90
Crestwood Way. Houn—5D 86
Creswick Rd. W3—7H 57
Creswick Rd. SW18—6A 92
Creswick Wlk. E3—3C 64
Creswick Wlk. NW11—4H 27
Creton St. SE18—3E 82
Crewdson Rd. SW9—7A 78
Crewe Pl. NW10—3B 58
Crews St. E14—4C 80
Crewys Rd. NW2—2H 43
Crewys Rd. SE15—2H 95
Crichton Av. Wall—5H 133
Crichton Rd. Cars—7D 132
Cricketers Arms Rd. Enf—2H 7
Cricketers Clo. Eri—5K 85
Cricketfield Rd. E5—4H 47
Cricket Grn. Mitc—4D 122
Cricket Ground Rd. Chst
   —1F 129
Cricklade Av. SW2—2J 109
Cricklewood B'way. NW2
   —3F 43
Cricklewood La. NW2—4F 43
Cricklewood Trading Est. NW2
   —3G 43
Cridland St. E15—1H 65
Crieff Ct. Tedd—7C 104
Crieff Rd. SW18—6A 92
Criffel Av. SW2—2H 109
Crimscott St. SE1
   —3E 78 (7D 148)
Crimsworth Rd. SW8—7H 77
Crinan St. N1—2J 61
Cringle St. SW8—7G 77
Cripplegate St. EC2
   —5C 62 (5L 141)
Crispen Rd. Felt—4C 102
Crispian Clo. NW10—4A 42
Crispin Clo. Croy—2J 133
Crispin Cres. Croy—3H 133

Crispin Rd. Edgw—6D 12
Crispin St. E1—5F 63 (6E 142)
Crisp Rd. W6—5E 74
Cristowe Rd. SW6—2H 91
Criterion M. N19—2H 45
Crockerton Rd. SW17—2D 108
Crockham Way. SE9—4E 114
Crocus Clo. Croy—1K 135
Crocus Field. Barn—6C 4
Croft Av. W Wick—1E 136
Croft Clo. NW7—3F 13
Croft Clo. Belv—5F 85
Croft Clo. Chst—5D 114
Croftdown Rd. NW5—3E 44
Crofters Clo. Iswth—5H 87
Crofters Mead. Croy—7B 136
Crofters Way. NW1—1H 61
Croft Gdns. W7—2A 72
Croft Lodge Clo. Wfd G—6E 20
Croft M. Enf—5K 7
Crofton Av. Bex—7D 100
Crofton La. Orp—7H 129
Croftongate Way. SE4—5A 96
Crofton Pk. Rd. SE4—6B 96
Crofton Rd. E13—4K 65
Crofton Rd. SE5—1E 94
Crofton Ter. E5—5A 48
Crofton Ter. Rich—4F 89
Crofton Way. Barn—6E 4
Crofton Way. Enf—2F 7
Croft Rd. SW16—1A 124
Croft Rd. SW19—7A 108
Croft Rd. Brom—6J 113
Croft Rd. Enf—1F 9
Croft Rd. Sutt—5C 132
Crofts Rd. Harr—6A 24
Crofts St. E1—7G 63 (1G 149)
Croft St. SE8—4A 80
Croft, The. NW10—2B 58
Croft, The. W5—5E 56
Croft, The. Barn—4B 4
Croft, The. Houn—7C 70
Croft, The. Pinn—7D 22
Croft, The. Ruis—4A 38
Croft, The. Wemb—5C 40
Croftway. NW3—4J 43
Croftway. Rich—3B 104
Croft Way. Sidc—3J 115
Crogsland Rd. NW1—7E 44
Croham Clo. S Croy—6E 134
—7E 134
Croham Mt. S Croy—7E 134
Croham Pk. Av. S Croy—5F 135
Croham Rd. S Croy—5D 134
Croham Valley Rd. S Croy
—6G 135
Croindene Rd. SW16—1J 123
Cromartie Rd. N19—7H 29
Crombie Clo. Ilf—5D 34
Crombie Rd. Sidc—1H 115
Cromer Pl. Orp—7H 129
Cromer Rd. E10—7F 33
Cromer Rd. N17—2G 31
Cromer Rd. SE25—3H 125
Cromer Rd. SW17—6E 108
Cromer Rd. Barn—4F 5
Cromer Rd. Romf—6J 37
Cromer Rd. Romf—6E 36
(Chadwell Heath)
Cromer Rd. Wfd G—4D 20
Cromer St. WC1—3J 61 (2D 140)
Cromer Ter. E8—5G 47
Cromer Vs. Rd. SW18—6H 91
Cromford Path. E5—4K 47
Cromford Rd. SW18—5J 91
Cromford Way. N Mald—1K 119
Cromlix Clo. Chst—2F 129
Crompton St. W2
—4B 60 (4A 138)
Cromwell Av. N6—1F 45
Cromwell Av. Brom—4K 127
Cromwell Av. N Mald—5B 120
Cromwell Centre. NW10—3K 57
Cromwell Clo. E1
—1G 79 (2H 149)
Cromwell Clo. N2—4B 28

Cromwell Clo. W3—1J 73
Cromwell Clo. Brom—4K 127
Cromwell Cres. SW5—4J 75
Cromwell Gdns. SW7
—3B 76 (7B 144)
Cromwell Gro. W6—3E 74
Cromwell Industrial Est. E10
—1A 48
Cromwell La. W6—5D 74
Cromwell M. SW7
—4B 76 (8B 144)
Cromwell Pl. N6—1F 45
Cromwell Pl. SW7
—4B 76 (8B 144)
Cromwell Pl. SW14—3J 89
Cromwell Rd. E7—7A 50
Cromwell Rd. E17—5E 32
Cromwell Rd. N3—1A 28
Cromwell Rd. N10—7K 15
(in two parts)
Cromwell Rd. E—4K 75 (8A 144)
SW7 1-147 & 2-156
SW5 remainder
Cromwell Rd. SW9—1B 94
Cromwell Rd. SW19—5J 107
Cromwell Rd. Beck—2A 126
Cromwell Rd. Croy—7D 124
Cromwell Rd. Felt—1A 102
Cromwell Rd. Houn—4E 86
Cromwell Rd. King—1E 118
Cromwell Rd. Tedd—6A 104
Cromwell Rd. Wemb—2E 56
Cromwell Rd. Wor Pk—3A 130
Cromwell St. Houn—4E 86
Crondace Rd. SW6—1J 91
Crondall St. N1—2E 62 (1C 142)
Crooked Billet. SW19—6E 106
Crooked Billet Yd. E2
—3E 62 (1D 142)
Crooked Usage. N3—3G 27
Crooke Rd. SE8—5B 79
Crookham Rd. SW6—1H 91
Crook Log. Bexh—3D 100
Crookston Rd. SE9—3E 98
Croombs Rd. E16—5A 66
Croom's Hill. SE10—7E 80
Croom's Hill Gro. SE10—7E 80
Cropath Rd. Dag—4G 53
Cropley St. N1—2D 62 (1A 142)
Crosby Clo. Felt—3C 102
Crosby Rd. E7—6J 49
Crosby Rd. Dag—2H 69
Crosby Row. SE1
—2D 78 (4A 148)
Crosby Sq. EC3—6E 62 (8C 142)
Crosby Wlk. E8—6F 47
Crosby Wlk. SW2—7A 94
Crosland Pl. SW11—3F 92
Cross Av. SE10—6G 81
Crossbrook Rd. SE3—3C 98
Cross Deep. Twic—2K 103
Cross Deep Gdns. Twic—2K 103
Crossfield Rd. N17—3C 30
Crossfield Rd. NW3—6B 44
Crossfield St. SE8—7C 80
Crossford St. SW9—2K 93
Cross Ga. Edgw—3B 12
Crossgate. Gnfd—6B 40
Crossharbour. E14—3D 80
Cross Keys Clo. W1
—5E 60 (6H 139)
Cross Lances Rd. Houn—4F 87
Crossland Rd. T Hth—6B 124
Crosslands Av. W5—1F 73
Crosslands Av. S'hall—5D 70
Cross La. EC3—7E 62 (1C 148)
Cross La. N8—3K 29
(in two parts)
Cross La. Bex—7F 101
Crosslet St. SE17
—4D 78 (9B 148)
Crossley St. N7—6A 46
Crossmead. SE9—1D 114
Crossmead Av. Gnfd—3E 54
Crossness Footpath. Eri—2F 85
Crossness La. SE28—7D 68
Crossness Rd. Bark—3K 67

Cross Rd. E4—1B 20
Cross Rd. N8—3J 29
Cross Rd. N11—5A 16
Cross Rd. N22—7F 17
Cross Rd. SE5—2E 94
Cross Rd. SW19—7J 107
Cross Rd. Croy—1D 134
Cross Rd. Enf—4K 7
Cross Rd. Felt—4C 102
Cross Rd. Harr—4H 23
(Headstone)
Cross Rd. Harr—3F 39
(South Harrow)
Cross Rd. King—7F 105
Cross Rd. Romf—3G 37
Cross Rd. Romf—7C 36
(Chadwell Heath)
Cross Rd. Sidc—4B 116
Cross Rd. Stan—2A 24
Cross Rd. Sutt—5B 132
Cross Rd. Wfd G—6J 21
Cross St. N1—1B 62
Cross St. N18—5B 18
Cross St. SW13—2A 90
Cross St. Hmptn—5G 103
Crossthwaite Av. SE5—4D 94
Crosswall. EC3—7F 63 (9E 142)
Crossway. N12—6G 15
Crossway. N16—5E 46
Crossway. NW9—4B 26
Crossway. SE28—7C 68
Crossway. SW20—4E 120
Crossway. W13—4A 56
Crossway. Dag—3C 52
Crossway. Enf—7K 7
Crossway. Orp—4H 129
Cross Way. Pinn—2A 22
Crossway. Ruis—4A 38
Cross Way. Wfd G—4F 21
Crossways. N21—6H 7
Crossways. S Croy—7A 136
Crossways. Sutt—7B 132
Crossways Rd. Beck—4C 126
Crossways. Mitc—3F 123
Crossways, The. Houn—7D 70
Crossways, The. Surb—7H 119
Crossways, The. Wemb—2G 41
Crossway, The. N22—7G 17
Crossway, The. SE9—2B 114
Cross Way, The. Harr—2J 23
Croston Rd. E8—1G 63
Crothall Clo. N13—3E 16
Crouch Av. Bark—2B 68
Crouch Clo. Beck—6C 112
Crouch Croft. SE9—3E 114
Crouch End Hill. N8—7H 29
Crouch Hall Rd. N8—6H 29
Crouch Hill. N4—6J 29
N4 1-75 & 2-58
N8 remainder
Crouchman's Clo. SE26
—3F 111
Crouch Rd. NW10—7K 41
Crowborough Rd. SW17
—6E 108
Crowden Way. SE28—7C 68
Crowder St. E1—7H 63 (9J 143)
Crowhurst Clo. SW9—2A 94
Crowland Gdns. N14—7D 6
Crowland Rd. N15—5F 31
Crowland Rd. T Hth—4D 124
Crowlands Av. Romf—6H 37
Crowland Ter. N1—7D 46
Crowland Wlk. Mord—6A 122
Crow La. Romf—7F 37
Crowley Cres. Croy—5A 134
Crowlin Wlk. N1—6D 46
Crowmarsh Gdns. SE23—7J 95
Crown Arc. King—2D 118
Crown Clo. E3—1C 64
Crown Clo. NW6—6K 43
Crown Clo. NW7—2G 13
Crown Ct. SE12—6K 97
Crown Ct. WC2—6J 61 (8D 140)
Crown Dale. SE19—6B 110
Crowndale Rd. NW1—2G 61
Crownfield Av. Ilf—6J 35

Crownfield Rd. E15—4F 49
Crown Hill. Croy—2C 134
Crown Hill Rd. NW10—1B 58
Crownhill Rd. Wfd G—7H 21
Crown La. N14—1H 15
Crown La. SW16—5A 110
Crown La. Brom—5B 128
Crown La. Chst—1G 129
Crown La. Mord—4J 121
Crown La. Gdns. SW16—5A 110
Crown La. Spur. Brom—6B 128
Crownmead Way. Romf—4H 37
Crown Office Row. EC4
—7A 62 (9G 141)
Crown Pas. SW1
—1G 77 (3M 145)
Crown Pas. King—2D 118
Crown Pl. NW5—6F 45
Crown Rd. N10—7K 15
Crown Rd. Enf—4C 8
Crown Rd. Ilf—4H 35
Crown Rd. Mord—4K 121
Crown Rd. N Mald—1J 119
Crown Rd. Sutt—4K 131
Crown Rd. Twic—6B 88
Crownstone Rd. SW2—5A 94
Crown St. SE5—7C 78
Crown St. W3—1H 73
Crown St. Dag—6J 53
(in two parts)
Crown St. Harr—1H 39
Crown Ter. Rich—4F 89
Crowntree Clo. Iswth—6K 71
Crown Wlk. Wemb—3F 41
Crown Woods La. SE18—2F 99
Crown Woods Way. SE9—5H 99
Crown Yd. Houn—3G 87
Crowshott Av. Stan—2C 24
Crows Rd. E15—3F 65
Crowther Av. Bren—4E 72
Crowther Rd. SE25—4G 125
Crowthorne Clo. SW18—1H 107
Crowthorne Rd. W10—6F 59
Croxden Clo. Edgw—3G 25
Croxden Wlk. Mord—6A 122
Croxford Gdns. N22—7G 17
Croxford Way. Romf—1K 53
Croxley Grn. Orp—7B 116
Croxley Rd. W9—3H 59
Croxted Clo. SE21—7C 94
Croxted Rd.—7C 94
SE21 1-293 & 2-198
SE24 remainder
Croyde Av. Gnfd—3G 55
Croyde Clo. Sidc—7H 99
Croydon Flyover, The. Croy
—3C 134
Croydon Gro. Croy—1B 134
Croydon Rd. E13—4H 65
Croydon Rd. SE20—2H 125
Croydon Rd. Beck—4K 125
Croydon Rd. Mitc—4E 122
Croydon Rd. Wall & Croy
—4F 133
Croydon Rd. W Wick, Brom,
Kes & Orp—3G 137
Croyland Rd. N9—1B 18
Croylands Dri. Surb—7E 118
Crozier Ter. E9—5K 47
Crucifix La. SE1—2E 78 (4C 148)
Cruden St. N1—1B 62
Cruikshank Rd. E15—4G 49
Cruikshank St. WC1
—3A 62 (1G 141)
Crummock Gdns. NW9—5A 26
Crumpsall St. SE2—4C 84
Crundale Av. NW9—5G 25
Crunden Rd. S Croy—7D 134
Crusader Gdns. Croy—3E 134
Crusoe Rd. Eri—5K 85
Crusoe Rd. Mitc—7D 108
Crutched Friars. EC3
—7E 62 (9D 142)
Crutchley Rd. SE6—2G 113
Crystal Pal. Pde. SE19—6F 111
Crystal Pal. Pk. Rd. SE26
—5G 111

Dell Clo. E15—1F 65
Dell Clo. Wall—4H 133
Dell Clo. Wfd G—3E 20
Dellfield Clo. Beck—1E 126
Dell La. Eps—5C 130
Dellors Clo. Barn—5A 4
Dellow Clo. Ilf—7H 35
Dellow St. E1—7H 63 (9K 143)
Dell Rd. Eps—6C 130
Dell, The. SE2—5A 84
Dell, The. SE19—1F 125
Dell, The. Bex—1K 117
Dell, The. Bren—6C 72
Dell, The. Pinn—2B 22
Dell, The. Wemb—5B 40
Dell, The. Wfd G—3E 20
Dell Wlk. N Mald—2A 120
Dell Way. W13—6C 56
Dellwood Gdns. Ilf—3E 34
Delmare Clo. SW9—4K 93
Delme Cres. SE3—2K 97
Delmey Clo. Croy—3F 135
Delorme St. W6—6F 75
Delta Clo. Wor Pk—3B 130
Delta Rd. Wor Pk—3A 130
Delta St. E2—3G 63 (1G 143)
De Luci Rd. Eri—5J 85
De Lucy St. SE2—4B 84
Delvan Clo. SE18—7E 82
Delvers Mead. Dag—4J 53
Delverton Rd. SE17—5B 78
Delvino Rd. SW6—1J 91
Demesne Rd. Wall—4H 133
Demeta Clo. Wemb—3J 41
De Montfort Rd. SW16—2J 109
De Morgan Rd. SW6—3K 91
Dempster Rd. Surb—7C 118
Dempster Rd. SW18—5A 92
Denberry Dri. Sidc—3B 116
Denbigh Clo. NW10—7A 42
Denbigh Clo. W11—7H 59
Denbigh Clo. Chst—6D 114
Denbigh Clo. S'hall—6D 54
Denbigh Gdns. Sutt—5H 131
Denbigh Gdns. Rich—5F 89
Denbigh Pl. SW1
—5G 77 (9L 145)
Denbigh Rd. E6—3B 66
Denbigh Rd. W11—7H 59
Denbigh Rd. W13—7B 56
Denbigh Rd. Houn—2F 87
Denbigh Rd. S'hall—6D 54
Denbigh St. SW1
—4G 77 (9L 145)
Denbigh Ter. W11—7H 59
Denbridge Rd. Brom—2D 128
Den Clo. Beck—3F 127
Dendy St. SW12—1E 108
Dene Av. Houn—3D 86
Dene Av. Sidc—7B 100
Dene Clo. SE4—3A 96
Dene Clo. Brom—1H 137
Dene Clo. Dart—4K 117
Dene Clo. Wor Pk—2B 130
Dene Gdns. Stan—5H 11
Denehurst Gdns. NW4—6E 26
Denehurst Gdns. W3—1H 73
Denehurst Gdns. Rich—4G 89
Denehurst Gdns. Twic—7H 87
Denehurst Gdns. Wfd G—4E 20
Dene Rd. Buck H—1H 21
Dene, The. W13—5B 56
Dene, The. Croy—4K 135
Dene, The. Wemb—4E 40
Denewood. Barn—5F 5
Denewood Rd. N6—6D 28
Denham Clo. Well—3C 100
Denham Cres. Mitc—4D 122
Denham Dri. Ilf—6G 35
Denham Rd. N20—3J 15
Denham Rd. Felt—7A 86
Denham St. SE10—5H 81
Denham Way. Bark—1K 67
Denholme Rd. W9—3H 59
Denison Clo. N2—3A 28

Denison Rd. SW19—6B 108
Denison Rd. W5—4C 56
Deniston Av. Bex—1E 116
Denleigh Gdns. N21—7F 7
Denman Dri. NW11—5J 27
Denman Dri. N. NW11—5J 27
Denman Dri. S. NW11—5J 27
Denman Rd. SE15—1F 95
Denman St. W1—7H 61 (1A 146)
Denmark Av. SW19—7G 107
Denmark Ct. Mord—6J 121
Denmark Gdns. Cars—3D 132
Denmark Hill. SE5—4D 94
Denmark Hill Dri. NW9—3C 26
Denmark Hill Est. SE5—4D 94
Denmark Path. SE25—5H 125
Denmark Pl. WC2
—6H 61 (7B 140)
Denmark Rd. N8—4A 30
Denmark Rd. NW6—2H 59
(in two parts)
Denmark Rd. SE5—1C 94
Denmark Rd. SE25—5G 125
Denmark Rd. SW19—6F 107
Denmark Rd. W13—7B 56
Denmark Rd. Brom—1K 127
Denmark Rd. Cars—3D 132
Denmark Rd. King—3E 118
Denmark Rd. Twic—3H 103
Denmark St. E11—3G 49
Denmark St. E13—5K 65
Denmark St. N17—7C 18
Denmark St. WC2
—6H 61 (7B 140)
Denmark Wlk. SE27—4C 110
Denmead Rd. Croy—1B 134
Dennan Rd. Surb—7F 119
Denner Rd. E4—2H 19
Denne Ter. E8—1F 63
Dennett Rd. Croy—7A 124
Dennett's Gro. SE14—1J 95
Dennett's Rd. SE14—2K 95
Denning Av. Croy—4A 134
Denning Clo. NW8
—3A 60 (2A 138)
Denning Clo. Hmptn—5D 102
Denning Rd. NW3—4B 44
Dennington Clo. E5—2J 47
Dennington Pk. Rd. NW6—6J 43
Dennis Av. Wemb—5F 41
Dennis Gdns. Stan—5H 11
Dennis La. Stan—3G 11
Dennison M. E10—7D 32
Dennis Pde. N14—1C 16
Dennis Pk. Cres. SW20—1G 121
Dennis Reeve Clo. Mitc—1D 122
Denny Clo. E6—5C 66
Denny Cres. SE11
—5A 78 (9H 147)
Denny Gdns. Dag—7B 52
Denny Rd. N9—1C 18
Denny St. SE11—5A 78 (9G 147)
Den Rd. Brom—3F 127
Densham Rd. E15—1G 65
Densole Clo. Beck—1A 126
Densworth Gro. N9—2D 18
Denton Rd. N8—5K 29
Denton Rd. N18—4K 17
Denton Rd. NW10—7J 41
Denton Rd. Bex—2K 117
Denton Rd. Twic—6D 88
Denton Rd. Well—7C 84
Denton St. SW18—6K 91
Denton Ter. Bex—2K 117
Denton Way. E5—3K 47
Dents Rd. SW11—6D 92
Denver Clo. Orp—6J 129
Denver Rd. N16—7E 30
Denyer St. SW3—4C 76 (8D 144)
Denzil Rd. NW10—5B 42
Deodara Clo. N20—3H 15
Deodar Rd. SW15—4G 91
Depot App. N3—1K 27
Depot Rd. Houn—3H 87
Deptford Bri. SE8—1C 96
Deptford B'way. SE8—1C 96
Deptford Chu. St. SE8—7C 80

Deptford Ferry Rd. E14—4C 80
Deptford Grn. SE8—6C 80
Deptford High St. SE8—6C 80
Deptford Strand. SE8—4B 80
Deptford Wharf. SE8—4B 80
De Quincey Rd. N17—1D 30
Derby Av. N12—5F 15
Derby Av. Harr—1H 23
Derby Av. Romf—6J 37
Derby Est. Houn—4F 87
Derby Ga. SW1—2J 77 (4C 146)
Derby Hill. SE23—2J 111
Derby Hill Cres. SE23—2J 111
Derby Rd. E7—7B 50
Derby Rd. E9—1K 63
Derby Rd. E18—1H 33
Derby Rd. N18—5D 18
Derby Rd. SW14—4H 89
Derby Rd. SW19—7J 107
Derby Rd. Croy—1B 134
Derby Rd. Enf—5C 8
Derby Rd. Gnfd—1F 55
Derby Rd. Houn—4F 87
Derby Rd. Sutt—6H 131
Derbyshire St. E2
—3G 63 (2H 143)
Derby St. W1—1E 76 (3H 145)
Dereham Pl. EC2
—3E 62 (2D 142)
Dereham Rd. Bark—5K 51
Derek Av. Wall—4F 133
Derek Av. Wemb—7H 41
Dericote St. E8—1H 63
Derifall Clo. E6—5D 66
Dering Pl. Croy—4C 134
Dering Rd. Croy—4C 134
Dering St. W1—6F 61 (8K 139)
Dering Yd. W1—6F 61 (8K 139)
Derinton Rd. SW17—4D 108
Derley Rd. S'hall—3A 70
Dermody Gdns. SE13—5F 97
Dermody Rd. SE13—5F 97
Deronda Est. SW2—1B 110
Deronda Rd. SE24—1B 110
Deroy Clo. Cars—6D 132
Derrick Gdns. SE7—4A 82
Derrick Rd. Beck—3B 126
Derry Rd. Croy—3J 133
Derry St. W8—2K 75
Dersingham Av. E12—4D 50
Dersingham Rd. NW2—3G 43
Derwent Av. N18—5J 17
Derwent Av. NW7—6E 12
Derwent Av. NW9—5A 26
Derwent Av. SW15—4A 106
Derwent Av. Barn—1J 15
Derwent Cres. N20—3F 15
Derwent Cres. Bexh—2G 101
Derwent Cres. Stan—2C 24
Derwent Dri. Orp—7H 129
Derwent Gdns. Ilf—4C 34
Derwent Gdns. Wemb—7C 24
Derwent Gro. SE22—4F 95
Derwent Rise. NW9—6A 26
Derwent Rd. N13—4E 16
Derwent Rd. SE20—2G 125
Derwent Rd. SW20—5F 121
Derwent Rd. W5—3C 72
Derwent Rd. S'hall—6E 54
Derwent Rd. Twic—6F 87
Derwent St. SE10—5G 81
Derwent Wlk. Wall—7F 133
Derwentwater Rd. W3—1J 73
Desenfans Rd. SE21—6E 94
Desford Rd. E16—4G 65
Desmond St. SE14—7A 80
Despard Rd. N19—1G 45
Detling Rd. Brom—5J 113
Detling Rd. Eri—7K 85
Detmold Rd. E5—2J 47
Devalls Clo. E6—7F 67
Devana End. Cars—3D 132
Devas Rd. SW20—1E 120
Devas St. E3—4D 64
Devenay Rd. E15—7H 49
Devenish Rd. SE2—2A 84
Deventer Cres. SE22—5E 94

De Vere Gdns. W8—2A 76
De Vere Gdns. Ilf—2D 50
Deverell St. SE1
—3D 78 (7A 148)
Devereux Rd. SW11—6D 92
Deveron Way. Romf—1K 37
Devon Av. Twic—1G 103
Devon Clo. N17—3F 31
Devon Clo. Buck H—2E 20
Devon Clo. Gnfd—1C 56
Devoncroft Gdns. Twic—7A 88
Devon Gdns. N4—6B 30
Devonhurst Pl. W4—5K 73
Devonia Gdns. N18—6H 17
Devonia Rd. N1—2B 62
Devonport Gdns. Ilf—6D 34
Devonport M. W12—1D 74
Devonport Rd. W12—2D 74
Devonport St. E1
—6J 63 (8M 143)
Devon Rise. N2—4B 28
Devon Rd. Bark—1J 67
Devon Rd. Sutt—7G 131
Devons Est. E3—3D 64
Devonshire Av. Sutt—7A 132
Devonshire Clo. E15—4G 49
Devonshire Clo. N13—3F 17
Devonshire Clo. W1
—5F 61 (5J 139)
Devonshire Cres. NW7—7A 14
Devonshire Dri. SE10—7D 80
Devonshire Gdns. N17—6H 17
Devonshire Gdns. N21—7H 7
Devonshire Gdns. W4—7J 73
Devonshire Gro. SE15—6H 79
Devonshire Hill La. N17—6H 17
Devonshire M. N13—4F 17
Devonshire M. W4—5A 74
Devonshire M. N. W1
—5F 61 (5J 139)
Devonshire M. S. W1
—5F 61 (5J 139)
Devonshire M. W. W1
—4E 60 (4H 139)
Devonshire Pas. W4—5A 74
Devonshire Pl. NW2—3J 43
Devonshire Pl. W1
—4E 60 (4H 139)
Devonshire Pl. M. W1
—5E 60 (5H 139)
Devonshire Rd. E15—4G 49
Devonshire Rd. E16—6K 65
Devonshire Rd. E17—6C 32
Devonshire Rd. N9—1D 18
Devonshire Rd. N13—4F 17
Devonshire Rd. N17—6H 17
Devonshire Rd. NW7—7A 14
Devonshire Rd. SE9—2C 114
Devonshire Rd. SE23—2J 111
Devonshire Rd. SW19—7C 108
Devonshire Rd. W4—5A 74
Devonshire Rd. W5—3C 72
Devonshire Rd. Bexh—4E 100
Devonshire Rd. Cars—4E 132
Devonshire Rd. Croy—7D 124
Devonshire Rd. Felt—3C 102
Devonshire Rd. Harr—6H 23
Devonshire Rd. Ilf—7J 35
Devonshire Rd. Orp—7K 129
Devonshire Rd. Pinn—7A 22
(Eastcote)
Devonshire Rd. Pinn—1D 22
(Hatch End)
Devonshire Rd. S'hall—5E 54
Devonshire Rd. Sutt—7A 132
Devonshire Row. EC2
—5E 62 (6D 142)
Devonshire Sq. EC2
—6E 62 (7D 142)
Devonshire Sq. Brom—4K 127
Devonshire St. W1
—5E 60 (5H 139)
Devonshire St. W4—5A 74
Devonshire Ter. W2
—6A 60 (8A 138)
Devonshire Way. Croy—2A 136

190

Devonshire Way. Hay—6A 54
Devons Rd. E3—5C 64
Devon St. SE15—6H 79
Devon Waye. Houn—7D 70
De Walden St. W1
—5E 60 (6H 139)
Dewar St. SE15—3G 95
Dewberry Gdns. E6—5C 66
Dewey Rd. N1—2A 62
Dewey Rd. Dag—6H 53
Dewey St. SW17—5D 108
Dewhurst Rd. W14—3F 75
Dewsberry St. E14—5E 64
Dewsbury Clo. Pinn—6C 22
Dewsbury Ct. W4—4J 73
Dewsbury Gdns. Wor Pk
—3C 130
Dewsbury Rd. NW10—5C 42
Dewsbury Ter. NW1—1F 61
Dexter Rd. Barn—6A 4
Deyncourt Gdns. E11—4A 34
Deyncourt Rd. N17—1C 30
D'Eynsford Rd. SE5—1D 94
Diameter Rd. Orp—6G 129
Diamond Clo. Dag—1C 52
Diamond Est. SW17—3C 108
Diamond Rd. Ruis—4B 38
Diamond Ter. SE10—1E 96
Diana Clo. E18—1K 33
Diana Ho. SW13—1B 90
Diana Pl. NW1—4F 61 (3K 139)
Diana Rd. E17—3B 32
Dianthus Clo. SE2—5B 84
Dibden St. N1—1C 62
Dibdin Clo. Sutt—3J 131
Dibdin Rd. Sutt—3J 131
Dibdin Row. SE1
—3A 78 (6H 147)
Dicey Av. NW2—4E 42
Dickens Av. N3—1A 28
Dickens Clo. Harr—2F 39
Dickens Clo. Rich—2E 104
Dickens Dri. Chst—6G 115
Dickens Est. SE16
—3G 79 (6G 149)
Dickens La. N18—5K 17
Dickenson Rd. N8—7J 29
Dickenson Rd. Felt—5B 102
Dickensons La. SE25—6G 125
Dickensons Pl. SE25—6G 125
Dickenson St. NW5—6F 45
Dickens Rise. Chig—3K 21
Dickens Rd. E6—2B 66
Dickens Sq. SE1
—3C 78 (6M 147)
Dickens St. SW8—2F 93
Dickerage La. N Mald—3J 119
Dickerage Rd. King—1J 119
Dickson Fold. Pinn—4B 22
Dickson Rd. SE9—3C 98
Didsbury Clo. E6—1D 66
Digby Cres. N4—2C 46
Digby Gdns. Dag—1G 69
Digby Pl. Croy—3F 135
Digby Rd. E9—6K 47
Digby Rd. Bark—7K 51
Digby St. E2—3J 63 (1M 143)
Diggon St. E1—5K 63 (6M 143)
Dighton Rd. SW18—5A 92
Dignum St. N1—2A 62
Digswell St. N7—6A 46
Dilhorne Clo. SE12—3K 113
Dilke St. SW3—6D 76
Dillon Ho. N7—3K 45
Dillwyn Clo. SE26—4A 112
Dilston Clo. N'holt—3A 54
Dilton Gdns. SW15—1D 106
Dimes Pl. W6—4D 74
Dimmock Dri. Gnfd—5H 39
Dimond Clo. E7—4J 49
Dimsdale Dri. NW9—1J 41
Dimsdale Dri. Enf—6B 8
Dimsdale Wlk. E13—2J 65
Dingle Gdns. E14—7C 64
Dingles Ct. Pinn—1B 22
Dingley La. SW16—2H 109

Dingley Pl. EC1—3C 62 (2M 141)
Dingley Rd. EC1—3C 62 (2L 141)
Dingwall Av. Croy—2C 134
Dingwall Gdns. NW11—6J 27
Dingwall Rd. SW18—7A 92
Dingwall Rd. Cars—7D 132
Dingwall Rd. Croy—2D 134
Dinsdale Gdns. SE25—5E 124
Dinsdale Gdns. Barn—5E 4
Dinsdale Rd. SE3—6H 81
Dinsmore Rd. SW12—7F 93
Dinton Rd. SW19—6B 108
Dinton Rd. King—7F 105
Diploma Av. N2—4C 28
Dirleton Rd. E15—1H 65
Disbrowe Rd. W6—6G 75
—7H 63 (1J 149)
Dishforth La. NW9—1A 26
Disney Pl. SE1—2C 78 (4M 147)
Disney St. SE1—2C 78 (4M 147)
Dison Clo. Enf—1E 8
Disraeli Clo. SE28—1C 84
Disraeli Clo. W4—4K 73
Disraeli Rd. E7—6J 49
Disraeli Rd. NW10—2K 57
Disraeli Rd. SW15—4G 91
Disraeli Rd. W5—1D 72
Diss St. E2—3F 63 (1E 142)
Distaff La. EC4—7C 62 (9L 141)
Distillery La. W6—5E 74
Distillery Rd. W6—5E 74
Distillery Wlk. Bren—6E 72
Distin St. SE11—4A 78 (8G 147)
District Rd. Wemb—5B 40
Ditch All. SE10—1D 96
Ditchburn St. E14—7E 64
Ditchfield Rd. Hay—4C 54
Dittisham Rd. SE9—4C 114
Ditton Clo. Th Dit—7A 118
Ditton Grange Dri. Surb
—7D 118
Ditton Lawn. Th Dit—7A 118
Ditton Pl. SE20—1H 125
Ditton Reach. Th Dit—6E 118
Ditton Rd. Bexh—5E 100
Ditton Rd. S'hall—5D 70
Divis Way. SW15—6D 90
Dixon Clo. E6—6D 66
Dixon Pl. W Wick—1D 136
Dixon Rd. SE14—1A 96
Dixon Rd. SE25—3E 124
Dixon's All. SE16
—2H 79 (5J 149)
Dobbin Clo. Harr—2A 24
Dobell Rd. SE9—5D 98
Dobree Av. NW10—7D 42
Dobson Clo. NW6—7B 44
Dockhead. SE1—2F 79 (5F 148)
Dockland St. E16—1E 82
Dockley Rd. SE16
—3G 79 (7G 149)
Dock Rd. E16—7H 65
Dock Rd. Bren—7D 72
Dock St. E1—7G 63 (9G 143)
Doctor Johnson Av. SW17
—3F 109
Doctors Clo. SE26—5J 111
Docwra's Bldgs. N1—6E 46
Dodbrooke Rd. SE27—3A 110
Doddington Gro. SE17—5B 78
Doddington Pl. SE17—6B 78
Dodsley Pl. N9—3D 18
Dodson St. SE1—2A 78 (5H 147)
Dod St. E14—6C 64
Doel Clo. SW19—7A 108
Doggett Rd. SE6—7C 96
Doggetts Courts. Barn—5H 5
Dog Kennel Hill. SE22—3E 94
Dog Kennel Hill Est. SE22
—3E 94
Dog La. NW10—4A 42
Doherty Rd. E13—4J 65

Dolben St. SE1—1B 78 (3J 147)
(in two parts)
Dolby Rd. SW6—2H 91
Dolland St. SE11—5K 77
Dollis Av. N3—1H 27
Dollis Brook Wlk. Barn—6E 4
Dollis Cres. Ruis—1A 38
Dollis Hill Av. NW2—3D 42
Dollis Hill La. NW2—4B 42
Dollis Pk. N3—1H 27
Dollis Rd.—7B 14
N3 1-89 & 2-66
NW7 remainder
Dollis Valley Way. Barn—6C 4
Dolman Rd. W4—4K 73
Dolman St. SW4—4K 93
Dolphin Clo. SE16
—2K 79 (4M 149)
Dolphin Clo. SE28—6D 68
Dolphin Clo. Surb—5D 118
Dolphin Ct. NW11—6G 27
Dolphin La. E14—7D 64
Dolphin Rd. N'holt—2D 54
Dolphin Sq. SW1—5G 77
Dolphin St. King—2E 118
Dombey St. WC1
—5K 61 (5E 140)
Dome Hill Pk. SE26—4F 111
Domett Clo. SE5—4D 94
Domfe Way. E5—4J 47
Domingo St. EC1
—4C 62 (4L 141)
Dominion Centre, The. S'hall
—3C 70
Dominion Rd. Croy—7F 125
Dominion Rd. S'hall—3C 70
Dominion St. EC2
—5D 62 (5B 142)
Domitian Pl. Enf—5A 8
Domonic Dri. SE9—4F 115
Domville Clo. N20—2G 15
Domville Gro. SE5—7F 79
Donald Dri. Romf—5C 36
Donald Rd. E13—1K 65
Donald Rd. Croy—7K 123
Donaldson Rd. NW6—1H 59
Donaldson Rd. SE18—1E 98
Doncaster Dri. N'holt—5D 38
Doncaster Gdns. N4—6C 30
Doncaster Gdns. N'holt—5D 38
Doncaster Rd. N9—7C 8
Donegal St. N1—2K 61
Doneraile St. SW6—2F 91
Dongola Rd. E13—3K 65
Dongola Rd. N17—3E 30
Dongola Rd. W. E13—3K 65
Donington Av. Ilf—5G 35
Donkey La. Enf—2B 8
Donne Ct. SE24—6C 94
Donnefield Av. Edgw—7K 11
Donne Pl. SW3—4C 76 (8D 144)
Donne Rd. Dag—2C 52
Donnington Rd. NW10—7D 42
Donnington Rd. Harr—5C 24
Donnington Rd. Wor Pk
—2C 130
Donnybrook Rd. SW16—7G 109
Donovan Av. N10—2G 29
Don Phelan Clo. SE5—1D 94
Doone Clo. Tedd—6A 104
Doon St. SE1—1A 78 (2G 147)
Doral Way. Cars—5D 132
Doran Gro. SE18—7J 83
Doran Wlk. E15—7E 48
Dora Rd. SW19—5J 107
Dora St. E14—6B 64
Dorchester Av. N13—4H 17
Dorchester Av. Bex—1D 116
Dorchester Av. Harr—6G 23
Dorchester Clo. N'holt—5F 39
Dorchester Clo. Orp—7B 116
Dorchester Ct. N14—7A 6
Dorchester Dri. SE24—5C 94
Dorchester Gdns. E4—4H 19
Dorchester Gdns. NW11—4J 27
Dorchester Gro. W4—5A 74

Dorchester M. N Mald—4K 119
Dorchester Rd. Mord—7K 121
Dorchester Rd. N'holt—5F 39
Dorchester Rd. Wor Pk—1E 130
Dorchester Way. Harr—6F 25
Dorcis Av. Bexh—2E 100
Dordrecht Rd. W3—2A 74
Dore Av. E12—5E 50
Doreen Av. NW9—1K 41
Dore Gdns. Mord—7K 121
Dorell Clo. S'hall—5D 54
Doria Rd. SW6—2H 91
Doric Way. NW1
—3H 61 (1A 140)
Dorien Rd. SW20—2F 121
Dorinda St. N7—6A 46
Doris Av. Eri—1J 101
Doris Emmerton Ct. SW11
—4A 92
Doris Rd. E7—7J 49
Doritt M. N18—5K 17
Dorking Clo. SE8—6B 80
Dorking Clo. Wor Pk—2F 131
Dorlcote Rd. SW18—7C 92
Dorman Pl. N9—2B 18
Dorman Wlk. NW10—5K 41
Dorman Way. NW8—1B 60
Dorma Trading Pk. E10—1K 47
Dormay St. SW18—5K 91
Dormer Clo. E15—6H 49
Dormer Clo. Barn—5A 4
Dormer's Av. S'hall—6E 54
Dormers Rise. S'hall—6F 55
Dormer's Wells La. S'hall
—6E 54
Dornberg Clo. SE3—7J 81
Dorncliffe Rd. SW6—2G 91
Dorney Rise. Orp—4K 129
Dorney Way. Houn—5C 86
Dornfell St. NW6—5H 43
Dornton Rd. SW12—7F 109
Dornton Rd. S Croy—5D 134
Dorothy Av. Wemb—7E 40
Dorothy Evans Clo. Bexh
—4H 101
Dorothy Gdns. Dag—4B 52
Dorothy Rd. SW11—3D 92
Dorrell Pl. SW9—4A 94
Dorrien Wlk. SW16—2H 109
Dorrington Ct. SE25—2E 124
Dorrington St. EC1
—5A 62 (5G 141)
Dorrit Way. Chst—6G 115
Dorryn Ct. SE26—5K 111
Dors Clo. NW9—1K 41
Dorset Av. Romf—3K 37
Dorset Av. S'hall—4E 70
Dorset Av. Well—4K 99
Dorset Bldgs. EC4
—6B 62 (8J 141)
Dorset Clo. NW1
—5D 60 (5E 138)
Dorset Dri. Edgw—6A 12
Dorset Gdns. Mitc—4K 123
Dorset M. SW1—3F 77 (6J 145)
Dorset Pl. E15—6F 49
Dorset Rise. EC4
—6B 62 (8J 141)
Dorset Rd. E7—7A 50
Dorset Rd. N15—4D 30
Dorset Rd. N22—1J 29
Dorset Rd. SE9—2C 114
Dorset Rd. SW8—7J 77
Dorset Rd. SW19—1J 121
Dorset Rd. W5—3C 72
Dorset Rd. Beck—3K 125
Dorset Rd. Harr—6G 23
Dorset Rd. Mitc—2C 122
Dorset Sq. NW1—4D 60 (4E 138)
Dorset St. W1—5D 60 (6F 138)
Dorset Way. Twic—1H 103
Dorset Waye. Houn—7D 70
Dorville Cres. W6—3D 74
Dorville Rd. SE12—5H 97
Dothill Rd. SE18—7G 83
Douai Gro. Hmptn—7G 103

Doughty M. WC1
—4K 61 (4E 140)
Doughty St. WC1
—4K 61 (3E 140)
Douglas Av. E17—1B 32
Douglas Av. N Mald—4D 120
Douglas Av. Wemb—7E 40
Douglas Clo. Stan—5F 11
Douglas Clo. Wall—6J 133
Douglas Cres. Hay—4A 54
Douglas Dri. Croy—3C 136
Douglas Pl. E14—5E 80
Douglas Rd. E4—1B 20
Douglas Rd. E16—5J 65
Douglas Rd. N1—7C 46
Douglas Rd. N22—1A 30
Douglas Rd. NW6—1H 59
Douglas Rd. Houn—3F 87
Douglas Rd. Ilf—7A 36
Douglas Rd. King—2H 119
Douglas Rd. Surb—7F 119
Douglas Rd. Well—1B 100
Douglas Sq. Mord—6J 121
Douglas St. SW1
—4H 77 (9A 146)
Douglas Way. SE8—7B 80
Dounesforth Gdns. SW18
—1K 107
Douro Pl. W8—3K 75
Douro St. E3—2C 64
Douthwaite Sq. E1
—1G 79 (2H 149)
Dove App. E6—5C 66
Dove Clo. N'holt—4B 54
Dove Commercial Centre. NW5
—5G 45
Dovecote Av. N22—3A 30
Dovecott Gdns. SW14—3K 89
Dovedale Av. Harr—6C 24
Dovedale Av. Ilf—2E 36
Dovedale Clo. Well—2A 100
Dovedale Rise. Mitc—7D 108
Dovedale Rd. SE22—5H 95
Dovedon Clo. N14—2D 16
Dove Ho. Gdns. E4—2H 19
Dovehouse Mead. Bark—2H 67
Dovehouse St. SW3
—5B 76 (9B 144)
Dove M. SW5—4A 76
Dove Pk. Pinn—1E 22
Dover Clo. Romf—2J 37
Dovercourt Av. T Hth—5A 124
Dovercourt Est. N1—6D 46
Dovercourt Gdns. Stan—5K 11
Dovercourt La. Sutt—3A 132
Dovercourt Rd. SE22—6E 94
Doverfield Rd. SW2—7J 93
Dover Ho. Rd. SW15—4C 90
Doveridge Gdns. N13—4G 17
Dove Rd. N1—6D 46
Dove Row. E2—1G 63
Dover Pk. Dri. SW15—6D 90
Dover Rd. E12—2A 50
Dover Rd. N9—2D 18
Dover Rd. SE19—6D 110
Dover Rd. Romf—6E 36
Dover St. W1—7F 61 (1K 145)
Doveton Rd. S Croy—5D 134
Doveton St. E1—4J 63 (3L 143)
Dove Wlk. SW1—5E 76 (9G 145)
Dowanhill Rd. SE6—1F 113
Dowdeswell Clo. SW15—4A 90
Dowding Pl. Stan—6F 11
Dower Av. Wall—7F 133
Dowgate Hill. EC4
—7D 62 (9A 142)
Dowland St. W10—3G 59
Dowlas St. SE5—7E 78
Dowman Clo. SW19—7K 107
Downage. NW4—3E 26
Downalong. Bush, Wat—1C 10
Downbank Av. Bexh—1K 101
Down Barns Rd. Ruis—3B 38
Down Clo. N'holt—2A 54
Downderry Rd. Brom—3F 113
Downe Clo. Well—7C 84
Down End. SE18—7F 83
Downe Rd. Mitc—2D 122

Downers Cotts. SW4—4G 93
Downes Clo. Twic—6B 88
Downes Ct. N21—1F 17
Downes Pl. SE15—6G 79
Downe Ter. Rich—6E 88
Downfield. Wor Pk—1B 130
Downfield Clo. W9—4K 59
Down Hall Rd. King—1D 118
Downham Clo. Romf—1G 37
Downham Rd. N1—7D 46
Downham Way. Brom—5F 113
Downhills Av. N17—3D 30
Downhills Pk. Rd. N17—3C 30
Downhills Way. N17—3C 30
Downhurst Av. NW7—5E 12
Downhurst Ct. NW4—3E 26
Downing Clo. Harr—3G 23
Downing Dri. Gnfd—1J 55
Downing Rd. Dag—7F 53
Downing St. SW1
—2J 77 (4C 146)
Downland Clo. N20—1F 15
Downleys Clo. SE9—2D 114
Downman Rd. SE9—3C 98
Down Pl. W6—4D 74
Down Rd. Tedd—6B 104
Downs Av. Chst—5D 114
Downs Av. Pinn—6D 22
Downsbridge Rd. Beck—1F 127
Downsell Rd. E15—4F 49
Downsfield Rd. E17—6A 32
Downshall Av. Ilf—6J 35
Downs Hill. Beck—7F 113
Downshire Hill. NW3—4B 44
Downside. Twic—3K 103
Downside Clo. SW19—6A 108
Downside Cres. NW3—5C 44
Downside Cres. W13—4A 56
Downside Rd. Sutt—6B 132
Downside Wlk. N'holt—3D 54
Downs La. E5—4H 47
Downs Pk. Rd.—5F 47
E8 1-73 & 2-90
E5 remainder
Downs Rd. E5—4G 47
Downs Rd. Beck—2D 126
Downs Rd. Enf—4K 7
Downs Rd. T Hth—1C 124
Downs, The. SW20—7F 107
Down St. W1—1F 77 (3J 145)
Down St. M. W1—1F 77 (3J 145)
Downs View. Iswth—1K 87
Downsview Gdns. SE19
—7B 110
Downsview Rd. SE19—7C 110
Downsway, The. Sutt—7A 132
Downton Av. SW2—2J 109
Downtown Rd. SE16—2A 80
Downway. N12—7H 15
Dowrey St. N1—1A 62
Dowsett Rd. N17—2F 31
Dowson Clo. SE5—4D 94
Doyce St. SE1—2C 78 (4L 147)
Doyle Gdns. NW10—1C 58
Doyle Rd. SE25—4G 125
D'Oyley St. SW1—4E 76 (8G 145)
Doynton St. N19—2F 45
Draco St. SE17—6C 78
Dragmire La. Mitc—3B 122
Dragoon Rd. SE8—5B 80
Dragor Rd. NW10—4J 57
Drake Clo. SE16—2K 79
Drake Cres. SE28—6C 68
Drakefell Rd.—2K 95
SE14 1-87 & 2-134
SE4 remainder
Drakefield Rd. SW17—3E 108
Drakeley Ct. N5—4B 46
Drake Rd. SE4—3C 96
Drake Rd. Croy—7K 123
Drake Rd. Harr—2D 38
Drake Rd. Mitc—6E 122
Drakes Courtyard. NW6—7H 43
Drake St. WC1—5K 61 (6E 140)
Drake St. Enf—1J 7
Drakes Wlk. E6—2D 66
Drakewood Rd. SW16—7H 109

Draper Clo. Belv—4F 85
Draper Ct. Brom—4C 128
Draper's Gdns. EC2
—6D 62 (7B 142)
Drapers Rd. E15—4F 49
Drapers Rd. N17—3F 31
Drapers Rd. Enf—2G 7
Drappers Way. SE16
—4G 79 (8H 149)
Drawdock Rd. SE10—2F 81
Drawell Clo. SE18—5J 83
Drax Av. SW20—7C 106
Draxmont App. SW19—6G 107
Draycot Rd. E11—6K 33
Draycott Av. SW3
—4C 76 (9D 144)
Draycott Av. Harr—6B 24
Draycott Clo. Harr—6B 24
Draycott Pl. SW3
—4D 76 (9E 144)
Draycott Ter. SW3
—4D 76 (9F 144)
Drayford Clo. W9—4H 59
Dray Gdns. SW2—5K 93
Drayside M. S'hall—2D 70
Drayson M. W8—2J 75
Drayton Av. W13—7A 56
Drayton Bri. Rd. W7 & W13
—7K 55
Drayton Clo. Houn—5D 86
Drayton Gdns. N21—7G 7
Drayton Gdns. SW10
—5A 76 (9A 144)
Drayton Gdns. W13—7A 56
Drayton Grn. W13—7A 56
Drayton Grn. Rd. W13—7B 56
Drayton Gro. W13—7A 56
Drayton Pk. N5—4A 46
Drayton Rd. E11—1F 49
Drayton Rd. N17—2E 30
Drayton Rd. NW10—1B 58
Drayton Rd. W13—7B 56
Drayton Rd. Croy—2B 134
Drayton Waye. Harr—6B 24
Dreadnought St. SE10—3G 81
Dresden Clo. NW6—6K 43
Dresden M. NW6—6K 43
Dresden Rd. N19—1H 45
Dressington Av. SE4—6C 96
Drew Av. NW7—6B 14
Drew Gdns. Gnfd—6K 39
Drew Rd. E16—1C 82
(in three parts)
Drewstead Rd. SW16—2H 109
Driffield Rd. E3—2A 64
Driftway, The. Mitc—1E 122
Drinkwater Rd. Harr—2F 39
Drive, The. E4—1A 20
Drive, The. E17—3D 32
Drive, The. E18—3J 33
Drive, The. N3—7D 14
Drive, The. N7—6K 45
Drive, The. N11—6C 16
Drive, The. NW10—1B 58
Drive, The. NW11—7G 27
Drive, The. SW16—3K 123
Drive, The. SW20—7E 106
Drive, The. W3—6J 57
Drive, The. Bark—7K 51
Drive, The. Barn—3B 4
(High Barnet)
Drive, The. Barn—6F 5
(New Barnet)
Drive, The. Beck—2C 126
Drive, The. Bex—7D 100
Drive, The. Buck H—1F 21
Drive, The. Chst—3K 129
Drive, The. Edgw—5B 12
Drive, The. Enf—1J 7
Drive, The. Eps—6B 130
Drive, The. Eri—6H 85
Drive, The. Felt—7A 86
Drive, The. Harr—7E 22
Drive, The. Houn & Iswth
—2H 87
Drive, The. Ilf—7D 34
Drive, The. King—7J 105

Drive, The. Mord—5B 122
Drive, The. Romf—1K 37
(Collier Row)
Drive, The. Sidc—4B 116
Drive, The. Surb—7E 118
Drive, The. T Hth—4D 124
Drive, The. Wemb—2J 41
Drive, The. W Wick—7F 127
Droitwich Clo. SE26—3G 111
Dromey Gdns. Harr—7E 10
Dromore Rd. SW15—6G 91
Dronfield Gdns. Dag—5C 52
Droop St. W10—3G 59
Drovers Rd. S Croy—5D 134
Druce Rd. SE21—6E 94
Druid St. SE1—2E 78 (4D 148)
Druids Way. Brom—4F 127
Drumaline Ridge. Wor Pk
—2A 130
Drummond Av. Romf—4K 37
Drummond Centre. Croy
—2C 134
Drummond Cres. NW1
—3H 61 (1A 140)
Drummond Dri. Stan—7E 10
Drummond Ga. SW1
—5H 77 (9B 146)
Drummond Pl. Twic—6B 88
Drummond Rd. E11—6A 34
Drummond Rd. SE16
—3H 79 (6J 149)
Drummond Rd. Croy—2C 134
Drummond Rd. Romf—4K 37
Drummonds, The. Buck H
—2E 20
Drummond St. NW1
—4G 61 (3L 139)
Drum St. E1—6F 63 (7F 142)
Drury Cres. Croy—2A 134
Drury Industrial Est. NW10
—5J 41
Drury La. WC2—6J 61 (8D 140)
Drury Rd. Harr—7G 23
Drury Way. NW10—5K 41
Dryad St. SW15—3F 91
Dryburgh Gdns. NW9—3G 25
Dryburgh Rd. SW15—3D 90
Dryden Av. W7—6K 55
Dryden Ct. SE11—4B 78 (9J 147)
Dryden Rd. SW19—6A 108
Dryden Rd. Enf—6K 7
Dryden Rd. Harr—1K 23
Dryden Rd. Well—1K 99
Dryden St. WC2—6J 61 (8D 140)
Dryfield Clo. NW10—6J 41
Dryfield Rd. Edgw—6D 12
Dryfield Wlk. SE8—6C 80
Dryhill Rd. Belv—6F 85
Drylands Rd. N8—6J 29
Drysdale Av. E4—7J 9
Drysdale Pl. N1—3E 62 (1D 142)
Drysdale St. N1—3E 62 (1D 142)
Du Burstow Ter. W7—2J 71
Ducal St. E2—3F 63 (2F 142)
Du Cane Ct. SW12—1E 108
Du Cane Rd. W12—6B 58
Duchess M. W1—5F 61 (6K 139)
Duchess of Bedford's Wlk. W8
—2J 75
Duchess St. W1—5F 61 (6K 139)
Duchy Pl. SE1—1A 78 (2H 147)
Duchy Rd. Barn—1G 5
Duchy St. SE1—1A 78 (2H 147)
Ducie St. SW4—4K 93
Duckett Rd. N4—6B 30
Duckett St. E1—4K 63
Duck Lees La. Enf—4F 9
Ducks Wlk. Twic—5C 88
Du Cros Dri. Stan—6J 11
Du Cros Rd. W3—1A 74
Dudden Hill La. NW10—4B 42
Duddington Clo. SE9—4B 114
Dudley Av. Harr—3C 24
Dudley Dri. Mord—1G 131
Dudley Dri. Ruis—5A 38
Dudley Gdns. W13—2B 72
Dudley Gdns. Harr—1H 39

Dudley Rd. E17—2C 32
Dudley Rd. N3—2K 27
Dudley Rd. NW6—2G 59
Dudley Rd. SW19—6J 107
Dudley Rd. Harr—2G 39
Dudley Rd. Ilf—4F 51
Dudley Rd. King—3F 119
Dudley Rd. Rich—2F 89
Dudley Rd. S'hall—2B 70
Dudley St. W2—5B 60 (6A 138)
Dudlington Rd. E5—2J 47
Dudsbury Rd. Sidc—6B 116
Dufferin St. EC1
    —4C 62 (4M 141)
Duffield Clo. Harr—5K 23
Duff St. E14—6D 64
Dufour's Pl. W1—6G 61 (8M 139)
Dufton Business Pk. SE9
    —2E 114
Duke Gdns. Ilf—4H 35
Duke Humphrey Rd. SE3—1G 97
Duke of Cambridge Clo. Twic
    —6H 87
Duke of Edinburgh Rd. Sutt
    —2B 132
Duke of Wellington Pl. SW1
    —2E 76 (4H 145)
Duke of York St. SW1
    —1G 77 (2M 145)
Duke Rd. W4—5K 73
Duke Rd. Ilf—4H 35
Dukes Av. N3—1K 27
Duke's Av. N10—3F 29
Duke's Av. W4—5K 73
Duke's Av. Edgw—6A 12
Dukes Av. Harr—6D 22
  (North Harrow)
Dukes Av. Harr—4J 23
  (Wealdstone)
Dukes Av. Houn—4C 86
Dukes Av. N Mald—3B 120
Dukes Av. N'holt—7C 38
Dukes Av. Rich & King—4C 104
Dukes Clo. Hmptn—5D 102
Dukes Ct. E6—1E 66
Dukes Head Pas. Hmptn
    —7G 103
Duke Shore Pl. E14—7B 64
Duke's La. W8—2K 75
Dukes M. N10—3F 29
Dukes Orchard. Bex—1J 117
Duke's Pl. EC3—6E 62 (8D 142)
Dukes Rd. E6—1E 66
Dukes Rd. W3—4G 57
Duke's Rd. WC1—3H 61 (2B 140)
Dukesthorpe Rd. SE26—4K 111
Duke St. W1—6E 60 (7H 139)
Duke St. Rich—5D 88
Duke St. Sutt—4B 132
Duke St. Hill. SE1
    —1D 78 (2B 148)
Duke St. Saint James's. SW1
    —1G 77 (2M 145)
Dukes Way. Brom—3H 127
Dukes Way. W Wick—3G 137
Duke's Yd. W1—7E 60 (9H 139)
Dulas St. N4—1K 45
Dulford St. W11—7G 59
Dulka Rd. SW11—5D 92
Dulverton Rd. SE9—2H 115
Dulwich Comn. SE21—1E 110
Dulwich Rd. SE24—5A 94
Dulwich Village. SE21—6E 94
Dulwich Wood Av. SE19
    —4E 110
Dulwich Wood Pk. SE19
    —4E 110
Dumbarton Rd. SW2—6J 93
Dumbleton Clo. King—1H 119
Dumbreck Rd. SE9—4D 98
Dumont Rd. N16—3E 46
Dumpton Pl. NW1—7E 44
Dunbar Av. SW16—2A 124
Dunbar Av. Beck—4A 126
Dunbar Av. Dag—3G 53
Dunbar Ct. Sutt—5B 132
Dunbar Gdns. Dag—5H 53

Dunbar Rd. E7—6J 49
Dunbar Rd. N22—1A 30
Dunbar Rd. N Mald—4J 119
Dunbar St. SE27—3C 110
Dunblane Rd. SE9—2C 98
Dunboyne Rd. NW3—5D 44
Dunbridge St. E2
    —4G 63 (3H 143)
Duncan Clo. Barn—4F 5
Duncan Grn. W3—6A 58
Duncannon St. WC2
    —7J 61 (1C 146)
Duncan Rd. E8—1H 63
Duncan Rd. Rich—4E 88
Duncan St. N1—2B 62
Duncan Ter. N1—2B 62 (1J 141)
Dunch St. E1—6H 63 (8K 143)
Duncombe Hill. SE23—7A 96
Duncombe Rd. N19—1H 45
Duncrievie Rd. SE13—6F 97
Duncroft. SE18—7J 83
Dundalk Rd. SE4—3A 96
Dundas Rd. SE15—2J 95
Dundee Rd. E13—2K 65
Dundee Rd. SE25—5H 125
Dundee St. E1—1H 79 (3J 149)
Dundela Gdns. Wor Pk—4D 130
Dundonald Clo. E6—6C 66
Dundonald Rd. NW10—1F 59
Dundonald Rd. SW19—7G 107
Dundry Ho. SE26—3G 111
Dunedin Rd. E10—3D 48
Dunedin Rd. Ilf—1G 51
Dunedin Way. Hay—4A 54
Dunelm St. E1—6K 63 (7M 143)
Dunfield Gdns. SE6—5D 112
Dunfield Rd. SE6—5D 112
  (in two parts)
Dunford Rd. N7—4K 45
Dungarvan Av. SW15—4C 90
Dunheved Clo. T Hth—6A 124
Dunheved Rd. N. T Hth—6A 124
Dunheved Rd. S. T Hth—6A 124
Dunheved Rd. W. T Hth—6A 124
Dunholme Grn. N9—3A 18
Dunholme La. N9—3A 18
Dunholme Rd. N9—3A 18
Dunkeld Rd. SE25—4D 124
Dunkeld Rd. Dag—2B 52
Dunkery Rd. SE9—4B 114
Dunkirk St. SE27—4C 110
Dunlace Rd. E5—4J 47
Dunleary Clo. Houn—7D 86
Dunlem Gro. SE27—3C 110
Dunley Dri. Croy—7D 136
Dunloe Av. N17—3D 30
Dunloe St. E2—2F 63
Dunlop Pl. SE16—3F 79 (7F 148)
Dunlop Point. E16—1K 81
Dunmore Rd. NW6—1G 59
Dunmore Rd. SW20—1E 120
Dunmow Clo. Felt—4C 102
Dunmow Rd. E15—4F 49
Dunn Mead. NW9—7G 13
Dunnock Rd. E6—6C 66
Dunnow Clo. Romf—5C 36
Dunn St. E8—5F 47
Dunollie Pl. NW5—5G 45
Dunollie Rd. NW5—5G 45
Dunoon Rd. SE23—7J 95
Dunraven Dri. Enf—2F 7
Dunraven Rd. W12—1C 74
Dunraven St. W1
    —7D 60 (9F 138)
Dunsany Rd. W14—3F 75
Dunsfold Way. Croy—7D 136
Dunsmore Clo. Hay—4C 54
Dunsmure Rd. N16—1E 46
Dunspring La. Ilf—2F 35
Dunstable M. W1
    —5E 60 (5H 139)
Dunstable Rd. Rich—4E 88
Dunstall Rd. SW20—6D 106
Dunstall Welling Est. Well
    —2B 100
Dunstan Clo. N2—3A 28
Dunstan Rd. NW11—1H 43

Dunstan's Gro. SE22—6H 95
Dunstan's Rd. SE22—7G 95
Dunster Av. Mord—1F 131
Dunster Clo. Barn—4A 4
Dunster Clo. Romf—2J 37
Dunster Ct. EC3—7E 62 (9D 142)
Dunster Dri. NW9—1J 41
Dunster Gdns. NW6—7H 43
Dunster Ho. SE6—3D 112
Dunsterville Way. SE1
    —2D 78 (5B 148)
Dunster Way. Harr—3C 38
Dunston Rd. E8—1F 63
Dunston Rd. SW11—3E 92
Dunston St. E8—1F 63
Dunton Clo. Surb—7E 118
Dunton Rd. E10—7D 32
Dunton Rd. SE1—4F 79 (9E 148)
Dunton Rd. Romf—4K 37
Duntshill Rd. SW18—1K 107
Dunvegan Rd. SE9—4D 98
Dunwich Rd. Bexh—1F 101
Dunworth M. W11—6H 59
Duplex Ride. SW1
    —2D 76 (5F 144)
Dupont Rd. SW20—2F 121
Dupont St. E14—5A 64
Duppas Av. Croy—4B 134
Duppas Hill La. Croy—4B 134
Duppas Hill Rd. Croy—4A 134
Duppas Hill Ter. Croy—3B 134
Duppas Rd. Croy—3A 134
Dupree Rd. SE7—5K 81
Dura Den Clo. Beck—7D 112
Durand Clo. Cars—1D 132
Durand Gdns. SW9—1K 93
Durands Wlk. SE16—2A 80
Durand Way. NW10—7J 41
Durants Pk. Av. Enf—4E 8
Durants Rd. Enf—4D 8
Durant St. E2—3G 63 (1G 143)
Durban Gdns. Dag—7J 53
Durban Rd. E15—3G 65
Durban Rd. E17—1B 32
Durban Rd. N17—6K 17
Durban Rd. SE27—4C 110
Durban Rd. Beck—2B 126
Durban Rd. Ilf—1J 51
Durdans Rd. S'hall—6D 54
Durell Gdns. Dag—5D 52
Durell Rd. Dag—5D 52
Durford Cres. SW15—1D 106
Durham Av. Brom—4H 127
Durham Av. Houn—5D 70
Durham Av. Wfd G—5G 21
Durham Clo. SW20—2D 120
Durham Hill. Brom—4H 113
Durham Rise. SE18—5G 83
Durham Rd. E12—4B 50
Durham Rd. E16—4G 65
Durham Rd. N2—3C 28
Durham Rd. N7—2K 45
Durham Rd. N9—2B 18
Durham Rd. SW20—1D 120
Durham Rd. W5—3D 72
Durham Rd. Brom—3H 127
Durham Rd. Dag—5J 53
Durham Rd. Felt—7A 86
Durham Rd. Harr—5F 23
Durham Rd. Sidc—5B 116
Durham Row. E1—5K 63
Durham St. SE11—6K 77
Durham Ter. W2—6K 59
Durham Wharf. Bren—7C 72
Durley Av. Pinn—7C 22
Durley Rd. N16—7E 30
Durlston Rd. E5—2G 47
Durlston Rd. King—6E 104
Durnford Ho. SE6—3D 112
Durnford St. N15—5E 30
Durnford St. SE10—6E 80
Durning Rd. SE19—5D 110
Durnsford Av. SW19—2J 107
Durnsford Rd. N11—1H 29
Durnsford Rd. SW19—2J 107
Durre'' Rd. SW6—1H 91
Durrington Av. SW20—7E 106

Durrington Pk. Rd. SW20
    —1E 120
Durrington Rd. E5—4A 48
Dursley Clo. SE3—2A 98
Dursley Gdns. SE3—1B 98
Dursley Rd. SE3—2A 98
Durward St. E1—5H 63 (5J 143)
  (in two parts)
Durweston St. W1
    —5D 60 (6F 138)
Dury Rd. Barn—1C 4
Dutch Gdns. King—6H 105
Dutch Yd. SW18—5J 91
Duthie St. E14—7E 64
Dutton St. SE10—1E 96
Dye Ho. La. E3—1C 64
Dyer's Bldgs. EC1
    —5A 62 (6G 141)
Dyers Hall Rd. E11—2G 49
Dyers La. SW15—3D 90
Dykewood Clo. Bex—3K 117
Dylan Rd. Belv—3G 85
Dylways. SE5—4D 94
Dymchurch Clo. Ilf—2E 34
Dymes Path. SW19—2F 107
Dymock St. SW6—3K 91
Dyneley Rd. SE12—3A 114
Dyne Rd. NW6—7G 43
Dynevor Rd. N16—3E 46
Dynevor Rd. Rich—5E 88
Dynham Rd. NW6—7J 43
Dyott St. WC1—6H 61 (7B 140)
Dysart Av. King—5C 104
Dysart St. EC2—4E 62 (4C 142)
Dyson Rd. E11—6G 33
Dyson Rd. E15—6H 49
Dysons Rd. N18—5C 18

Eade Rd. N4—7C 30
Eagans Clo. N2—3B 28
Eagle Av. Romf—6E 36
Eagle Clo. Enf—4D 8
Eagle Ct. EC1—5B 62 (5J 141)
Eagle Hill. SE19—6D 110
Eagle La. E11—4J 33
Eagle Lodge. NW11—7H 27
Eagle Rd. Wemb—7D 40
Eaglesfield Rd. SE18—1F 99
Eagle St. WC1—5K 61 (6E 140)
Eagle Ter. Wfd G—7E 20
Eagle Wharf Rd. N1—2C 62
Ealdham Sq. SE9—4A 98
Ealing B'way Centre. W5
    —7D 56
Ealing Grn. W5—1D 72
Ealing Pk. Gdns. W5—4C 72
Ealing Rd. Bren—5D 72
Ealing Rd. N'holt—1E 54
Ealing Rd. Trading Est. Bren
    —5D 72
Ealing Rd. Wemb—6D 40
Ealing Village. W5—6E 56
Eamont St. NW8—2C 60
Eardley Cres. SW5—5J 75
Eardley Rd. SW16—5G 109
Eardley Rd. Belv—5G 85
Eardoom Rd. SW15—4E 90
Earle Gdns. King—7E 104
Earlham Gro. E7—5H 49
Earlham Gro. N22—7E 16
Earlham St. WC2
    —6J 61 (8C 140)
Earl Rise. SE18—4H 83
Earl Rd. SE1—5F 79 (9E 148)
Earl Rd. SW14—4J 89
Earls Ct. Gdns. SW5—4K 75
Earls Ct. Rd.—3J 75
  W8 1-109 & 4-138
  SW5 remainder
Earls Ct. Sq. SW5—5K 75
Earls Cres. Harr—4J 23
Earlsferry Way. N1—7K 45
Earlsfield Rd. SW18—1A 108
Earlshall Rd. SE9—4D 98
Earlsmead. Harr—4D 38
Earlsmead Rd. N15—5F 31

Earlsmead Rd. NW10—3E 58
Earls Ter. W8—3H 75
Earlsthorpe M. SW12—6E 92
Earlsthorpe Rd. SE26—4K 111
Earlstoke St. EC1
　　　　　—3B 62 (1J 141)
Earlston Gro. E1—1H 63
Earl St. EC2—5D 62 (5B 142)
Earls Wlk. W8—3J 75
Earl's Wlk. Dag—4B 52
Earlswood Av. T Hth—5A 124
Earlswood Clo. SE10—5G 81
Earlswood Gdns. Ilf—3E 34
Earlswood St. SE10—5G 81
Early M. NW1—1F 61
Earnshaw St. WC2
　　　　　—6H 61 (7B 140)
Earsby St. W14—4G 75
Easby Cres. Mord—6K 121
Easebourne Rd. Dag—5C 52
E. Acton La. W3—1A 74
E. Arbour St. E1
　　　　　—6K 63 (7M 143)
East Av. E12—7C 50
East Av. E17—4D 32
East Av. S'hall—7D 54
East Av. Wall—5K 133
East Bank. N16—7E 30
Eastbank Rd. Hmptn—5G 103
E. Barnet Rd. Barn—4M 5
Eastbourne Av. W3—6K 57
Eastbourne Gdns. SW14—3J 89
Eastbourne M. W2
　　　　　—6A 60 (7A 138)
Eastbourne Rd. E6—3E 66
Eastbourne Rd. E15—1G 65
Eastbourne Rd. N15—6E 30
Eastbourne Rd. SW17—6E 108
Eastbourne Rd. W4—6J 73
Eastbourne Rd. Bren—5D 72
Eastbourne Rd. Felt—2B 102
Eastbourne Ter. W2
　　　　　—6A 60 (7A 138)
Eastbournia Av. N9—3C 18
Eastbrook Av. N9—7D 8
Eastbrook Av. Dag—4J 53
Eastbrook Dri. Romf—3K 53
Eastbrook Rd. SE3—1K 97
Eastbury Av. Bark—1J 67
Eastbury Av. Enf—1A 8
Eastbury Ct. Bark—1J 67
Eastbury Gro. W4—5A 74
Eastbury Rd. E6—4E 66
Eastbury Rd. King—7E 104
Eastbury Rd. Orp—6H 129
Eastbury Rd. Romf—6K 37
Eastbury Sq. Bark—1K 67
Eastbury Ter. E1—4K 63
Eastcastle St. W1
　　　　　—6G 61 (7M 139)
Eastcheap. EC3—7E 62 (9C 142)
E. Churchfield Rd. W3—1K 73
East Clo. W5—4G 57
East Clo. Barn—4K 5
East Clo. Gnfd—2G 55
Eastcombe Av. SE7—6K 81
Eastcote. Orp—7K 129
Eastcote Av. Gnfd—5A 40
Eastcote Av. Harr—2F 39
Eastcote High Rd. Pinn—4A 22
Eastcote La. Harr—4D 38
Eastcote La. N'holt—5D 38
Eastcote La. N. N'holt—6E 38
Eastcote Rd. Harr—3G 39
Eastcote Rd. Pinn—5B 22
Eastcote Rd. Well—2H 99
Eastcote St. SW9—2K 93
Eastcote View. Pinn—4A 22
East Ct. Wemb—2C 40
East Cres. N11—4J 15
East Cres. Enf—5A 8
Eastcroft Rd. Eps—7A 130
Eastdown Pk. SE13—4F 97
East Dri. Cars—7C 132
E. Dulwich Gro. SE22—5E 94
E. Dulwich Rd. SE22—4F 95
(in two parts)

East End Rd.—2J 27
　　N3 1-55 & 2-120
　　N2 remainder
E. End Way. Pinn—3C 22
E. Entrance. Dag—2H 69
Eastern Av.—6K 33 to 4D 36
　　E11 61-75 & 48-120
　　Ilf & Romf remainder
Eastern Av. Pinn—7B 22
Eastern Av. E. Romf—3K 37
Eastern Av. W. Romf—4E 36
Eastern Gateway Access Rd.
　　　　　Bark & E6—3F 67
Eastern Industrial Est. Eri
　　　　　—2G 85
Eastern Rd. E13—2K 65
Eastern Rd. E17—5E 32
Eastern Rd. N2—4D 28
Eastern Rd. N22—1J 29
Eastern Rd. SW13—7D 74
Eastern Way. SE28—2A 84
E. Ferry Rd. E14—3D 80
(in two parts)
Eastfield Gdns. Dag—4G 53
Eastfield Rd. E17—4C 32
Eastfield Rd. N8—3J 29
Eastfield Rd. Bexh—3J 101
Eastfield Rd. Dag—4F 53
Eastfield Rd. Enf—1E 8
Eastfields. Pinn—5A 22
Eastfields Rd. W3—5J 57
Eastfields Rd. Mitc—2E 122
East Gdns. SW17—6C 108
Eastgate Clo. SE28—6D 68
Eastglade. Pinn—3D 22
East Ham and Barking
　　By-Pass. Bark—2J 67
East Ham Mnr. Way. E6—6E 66
E. Harding St. EC4
　　　　　—6A 62 (7H 141)
E. Heath Rd. NW3—3A 44
East Hill. SW18—5K 91
East Hill. Wemb—2G 41
Eastholm. NW11—4K 27
East Holme. Eri—1K 101
E. India Dock Rd. E14—6C 64
E. India Dock Wall Rd. E14
　　　　　—7F 65
Eastlake Rd. SE5—2C 94
Eastlands Cres. SE21—6F 95
East La. SE16—2G 79 (5G 149)
East La. King—3D 118
East La. Wemb—3B 40
Eastleigh Av. Harr—2F 39
Eastleigh Clo. NW2—3A 42
Eastleigh Clo. Sutt—7K 131
Eastleigh Rd. Bexh—3J 101
Eastleigh Wlk. SW15—7C 90
Eastman Rd. W3—2K 73
East Mead. Ruis—3B 38
Eastmead Av. Gnfd—3F 55
Eastmead Clo. Brom—2C 128
Eastmearn Rd. SE21—2C 110
Eastmoor Pl. SE7—3B 82
Eastmoor St. SE7—3B 82
E. Mount St. E1—5H 63 (6K 143)
Eastney Rd. Croy—1B 134
Eastney St. SE10—5F 81
Eastnor Rd. SE9—1G 115
Easton St. WC1—4A 62 (3G 141)
E. Park Clo. Romf—5E 36
East Pier. E1—1H 79 (3J 149)
East Pl. SE27—4C 110
E. Poultry Av. EC1
　　　　　—5B 62 (6J 141)
East Rd. E15—1J 65
East Rd. N1—3D 62 (2A 142)
East Rd. SW19—6A 108
East Rd. Barn—1K 15
East Rd. Edgw—1H 25
East Rd. Enf—1D 8
East Rd. King—1E 118
East Rd. Romf—5E 36
　　(Chadwell Heath)
East Rd. Romf—7K 37
　　(Rush Green)

East Rd. Well—2B 100
E. Rochester Way. Sidc & Bex
　　　　　—4J 99
East Row. E11—6J 33
East Row. W10—4G 59
Eastry Av. Brom—6H 127
Eastry Rd. Eri—7G 85
E. Sheen Av. SW14—5K 89
Eastside Rd. NW11—4H 27
E. Smithfield. E1
　　　　　—7F 63 (1F 148)
East St. SE17—5C 78 (9A 148)
East St. Bark—1G 67
East St. Bexh—4G 101
East St. Bren—7C 72
East St. Brom—2J 127
E. Surrey Gro. SE15—7F 79
E. Tenter St. E1—6F 63 (8F 142)
East Towers. Pinn—5B 22
East View. E4—5K 19
East View. Barn—2C 4
Eastview Av. SE18—7J 83
Eastville Av. NW11—6H 27
East Wlk. Barn—7K 5
Eastway. E9—6B 48
East Way. E11—5K 33
East Way. Brom—7J 127
East Way. Croy—2A 136
Eastway. Mord—5F 121
Eastway. Wall—4G 133
Eastway Commercial Centre
　　　　　E15—5C 48
Eastwell Clo. Beck—7A 112
Eastwood Clo. E18—2J 33
Eastwood Rd. E18—2J 33
Eastwood Rd. N10—2E 28
Eastwood Rd. Ilf—7A 36
E. Woodside. Bex—1E 116
Eastwood St. SW16—6G 109
Eatington Rd. E10—5F 33
Eaton Clo. SW1—4E 76 (8G 145)
Eaton Clo. Stan—4G 11
Eaton Dri. SW9—4B 94
Eaton Dri. King—7G 105
Eaton Dri. Romf—1H 37
Eaton Gdns. Dag—7E 52
Eaton Ga. SW1—4E 76 (8G 145)
Eaton La. SW1—3F 77 (7K 145)
Eaton M. N. SW1
　　　　　—3E 76 (7G 145)
Eaton M. S. SW1
　　　　　—3F 77 (7J 145)
Eaton M. W. SW1
　　　　　—4E 76 (8H 145)
Eaton Pk. Rd. N13—2F 17
Eaton Pl. SW1—3E 76 (7G 145)
Eaton Rise. E11—5A 34
Eaton Rise. W5—5D 56
Eaton Rd. NW4—5E 26
Eaton Rd. Enf—4K 7
Eaton Rd. Houn—4H 87
Eaton Rd. Sidc—2D 116
Eaton Rd. Sutt—6B 132
Eaton Row. SW1
　　　　　—3F 77 (7J 145)
Eatons Mead. E4—2H 19
Eaton Sq. SW1—4E 76 (8H 145)
Eaton Ter. SW1—4E 76 (8G 145)
Eatonville Rd. SW17—2D 108
Eatonville Vs. SW17—2D 108
Ebbisham Dri. SW8—6K 77
Ebbisham Rd. Wor Pk—2E 130
Ebbsfleet Rd. NW2—5G 43
Ebdon Way. SE3—3K 97
Ebenezer St. N1—3D 62 (1A 142)
Ebenezer Wlk. SW16—1G 123
Ebley Clo. SE15—6F 79
Ebner St. SW18—5K 91
Ebor Cotts. SW18—3A 106
Ebor St. E1—4F 63 (3E 142)
Ebrington Rd. Harr—6D 24
Ebsworth St. SE23—7K 95
Eburne Rd. N7—3J 45
Ebury Bri. SW1—5F 77 (9J 145)
Ebury Bri. Rd. SW1
　　　　　—5E 76 (9J 145)

Ebury M. SW1—4F 77 (8J 145)
Ebury M. E. SW1
　　　　　—3F 77 (7J 145)
Ebury Sq. SW1—4F 77 (9J 145)
Ebury St. SW1—4F 76 (9H 145)
Ecclesbourne Clo. N13—5F 17
Ecclesbourne Gdns. N13—5F 17
Ecclesbourne Rd. N1—7C 46
Ecclesbourne Rd. T Hth
　　　　　—5C 124
Eccles Rd. SW11—4D 92
Eccleston Bri. SW1
　　　　　—4F 77 (8K 145)
Eccleston Clo. Barn—4J 5
Eccleston Cres. Romf—7B 36
Ecclestone Ct. Wemb—5E 40
Ecclestone Ho. SW2—6A 94
Ecclestone M. Wemb—5E 40
Ecclestone Pl. Wemb—5FF 41
Ecclestone Rd. W13—1A 72
Eccleston M. SW1
　　　　　—3E 76 (7H 145)
Eccleston Pl. SW1
　　　　　—4F 77 (8J 145)
Eccleston Sq. SW1
　　　　　—4F 77 (9K 145)
Eccleston Sq. M. SW1
　　　　　—4G 77 (9L 145)
Eccleston St. SW1
　　　　　—3F 77 (7J 145)
Echo Heights. E4—1J 19
Eckersley St. E1—4F 63 (4F 142)
Eckford St. N1—2A 62
Eckstein Rd. SW11—4C 92
Eclipse Rd. E13—5K 65
Ector Rd. SE6—2G 113
Edam Ct. Sidc—3A 116
Edbrooke Rd. W9—4J 59
Eddington St. N4—1A 46
Eddisbury Ho. SE26—3G 111
Eddiscombe Rd. SW6—2H 91
Eddy Clo. Romf—6H 37
Eddystone Rd. SE4—5A 96
Ede Clo. Houn—3D 86
Edenbridge Rd. E9—7K 47
Edenbridge Rd. Enf—6K 7
Eden Clo. Bex—4K 117
Eden Clo. Wemb—1D 56
Edencourt Rd. SW16—6F 109
Edendale Rd. Bexh—1K 101
Edenfield Gdns. Wor Pk
　　　　　—3B 130
Eden Gro. E17—5D 32
Eden Gro. N7—5K 45
Edenham Way. W10—4H 59
Edenhurst Av. SW6—3H 91
Eden M. SW17—3A 108
Eden Pk. Av. Beck—4B 126
Eden Rd. E17—5D 32
Eden Rd. SE27—5B 110
Eden Rd. Beck—4A 126
Eden Rd. Bex—4J 117
Eden Rd. Croy—4D 134
Edensor Gdns. W4—7A 74
Edensor Rd. W4—7A 74
Eden St. King—2D 118
Edenvale Rd. Mitc—7E 108
Edenvale St. SW6—2A 92
Eden Wlk. King—2E 118
Eden Way. Beck—5B 126
Ederline Av. SW16—3K 123
Edgar Ho. E11—7J 33
Edgarley Ter. SW6—1G 91
Edgar Rd. E3—3D 64
Edgar Rd. Houn—7D 86
Edgar Rd. Romf—7D 36
Edgeborough Way. Brom
　　　　　—1B 128
Edgebury. Chst—4F 115
Edgebury Wlk. Chst—4G 115
Edgecombe. E11—1H 49
Edgecoombe. S Croy—7J 135
Edgecombe Clo. King—7K 105
Edgecote Clo. W3—1J 73
Edgecot Gro. N15—5E 30
Edgefield Av. Bark—7K 51
Edge Hill. SE18—6F 83

Ellesmere Rd. E3—2A 64
Ellesmere Rd. NW10—5C 42
Ellesmere Rd. W4—6K 73
Ellesmere Rd. Gnfd—4G 55
Ellesmere Rd. Twic—6C 88
Ellesmere St. E14—6D 64
Elleswood Ct. Surb—7D 118
Ellingfort Rd. E8—7H 47
Ellingham Rd. E15—4F 49
Ellingham Rd. W12—2C 74
Ellington Rd. N10—4F 29
Ellington Rd. Houn—2F 87
Ellington St. N7—6A 46
Elliot Clo. E15—7G 49
Elliot Rd. NW4—6D 26
Elliot Rd. Brom—4B 128
Elliot Clo. Wemb—3G 41
Elliott Rd. SW9—7B 78
Elliott Rd. W4—4A 74
Elliott Rd. Stan—6F 11
Elliott Rd. T Hth—4B 124
Elliott's Pl. N1—1B 62
Elliott Sq. NW3—7C 44
Elliotts Row. SE11
—4B 78 (8K 147)
Ellis Clo. SE9—2G 115
Elliscombe Rd. SE7—6A 82
Ellis Ct. W7—5K 55
Ellisfield Dri. SW15—7C 90
Ellis M. SE7—6A 82
Ellison Gdns. S'hall—4D 70
Ellison Rd. SW13—2B 90
Ellison Rd. SW16—7H 109
Ellison Rd. Sidc—1H 115
Ellis Rd. Mitc—6D 122
Ellis St. SW1—4E 76 (8G 145)
Ellora Rd. SW16—5H 109
Ellsworth St. E2
—3H 63 (1K 143)
Elmar Rd. N15—4D 30
Elm Av. W5—1E 72
Elm Av. Ruis—7A 22
Elm Bank. N14—7D 6
Elmbank Av. Barn—4A 4
Elm Bank Gdns. SW13—2A 90
Elmbank Way. W7—5H 55
Elmbourne Dri. Belv—4H 85
Elmbourne Rd. SW17—3F 109
Elmbridge Av. Surb—5H 119
Elmbridge Wlk. E8—7G 47
Elmbrook Gdns. SE9—4C 98
Elmbrook Rd. Sutt—4H 131
Elm Clo. E11—6K 33
Elm Clo. N19—2G 45
Elm Clo. NW4—5F 27
Elm Clo. SW20—4E 120
Elm Clo. Buck H—2G 21
Elm Clo. Cars—1D 132
Elm Clo. Harr—6F 23
Elm Clo. Romf—1H 37
Elm Clo. S Croy—6E 134
Elm Clo. Surb—7J 119
Elm Clo. Twic—2F 103
Elmcourt Rd. SE27—2B 110
Elm Cres. W5—1E 72
Elm Cres. King—1E 118
Elmcroft. N6—7G 29
Elmcroft Av. E11—5K 33
Elmcroft Av. N9—6C 8
Elmcroft Av. NW11—7H 27
Elmcroft Av. Sidc—6A 100
Elmcroft Clo. E11—4K 33
Elmcroft Clo. W5—6D 56
Elmcroft Cres. NW11—7G 27
Elmcroft Cres. Harr—3E 22
Elmcroft Gdns. NW9—5G 25
Elmcroft St. E5—4J 47
Elmdale Rd. N13—5E 16
Elmdene. Surb—7J 119
Elmdene Clo. Beck—6B 126
Elmdene Rd. SE18—5F 83
Elmdon Rd. Houn—2C 86
Elm Dri. Harr—6F 23
Elmer Clo. Enf—3E 6
Elmer Gdns. Edgw—7C 12
Elmer Gdns. Iswth—3H 87
Elmer Rd. SE6—7E 96

Elmers Dri. Tedd—6B 104
Elmers End Rd.—2J 125
SE20 1-81 & 2-82
Beck remainder
Elmerside Rd. Beck—4A 126
Elmers Rd. SE25—7G 125
Elmfield Av. N8—5J 29
Elmfield Av. Mitc—1E 122
Elmfield Av. Tedd—5K 103
Elmfield Clo. Harr—2J 39
Elmfield Pk. Brom—3J 127
Elmfield Rd. E4—2K 19
Elmfield Rd. E17—6K 31
Elmfield Rd. N2—3B 28
Elmfield Rd. SW17—2E 108
Elmfield Rd. Brom—3J 127
Elmfield Rd. S'hall—3C 70
Elmfield Way. S Croy—7F 135
Elm Friars Wlk. NW1—7H 45
Elm Gdns. N2—3A 28
Elm Gdns. Mitc—4H 123
Elmgate Av. Felt—3A 102
Elmgate Gdns. Edgw—5D 12
Elm Grn. W3—6A 58
Elm Grn. Clo. E15—1G 65
Elm Gro. N8—6J 29
Elm Gro. NW2—4F 43
Elm Gro. SE15—2F 95
Elm Gro. SW19—7G 107
Elm Gro. Eri—7K 85
Elm Gro. Harr—7E 22
Elm Gro. King—1E 118
Elm Gro. Sutt—4K 131
Elm Gro. Wfd G—5C 20
Elmgrove Cres. Harr—5A 24
Elmgrove Gdns. Harr—5A 24
Elm Gro. Pde. Wall—3E 132
Elm Gro. Rd. SW13—2C 90
Elm Gro. Rd. W5—2E 72
Elmgrove Rd. Croy—7H 125
Elmgrove Rd. Harr—5K 23
(in two parts)
Elmhall Gdns. E11—6K 33
Elmhurst. Belv—6E 84
Elmhurst Av. N2—3B 28
Elmhurst Av. Mitc—7F 109
Elmhurst Dri. E18—2J 33
Elmhurst Rd. E7—7K 49
Elmhurst Rd. N17—2F 31
Elmhurst Rd. SE9—2C 114
Elmhurst St. SW4—3H 93
Elmington Clo. Bex—6H 101
Elmington Est. SE5—7D 78
Elmington Rd. SE5—7D 78
Elmira St. SE13—3D 96
Elm La. SE6—2B 112
Elmlee Clo. Chst—6D 114
Elmley Clo. E6—5C 66
Elmley St. SE18—4H 83
Elm Lodge. SW6—1F 91
Elm M. Rich—6F 89
Elm Pk. SW2—6K 93
Elm Pk. Stan—5G 11
Elm Pk. Av. N15—5F 31
Elm Pk. Gdns. NW4—5F 27
Elm Pk. Gdns. SW10—5B 76
Elm Pk. La. SW3—5B 76
Elm Pk. Rd. E10—1A 48
Elm Pk. Rd. N3—7C 14
Elm Pk. Rd. N21—7H 7
Elm Pk. Rd. SE25—3F 125
Elm Pk. Rd. SW3—6B 76
Elm Pk. Rd. Pinn—2A 22
Elm Pas. Barn—4C 4
Elm Pl. SW7—5B 76
Elm Rd. E7—6H 49
Elm Rd. E11—2F 49
Elm Rd. E17—5E 32
Elm Rd. N22—1B 30
Elm Rd. SW14—3J 89
Elm Rd. Barn—4C 4
Elm Rd. Beck—2B 126
Elm Rd. Eps—6B 130

Elm Rd. King—1F 119
Elm Rd. N Mald—3K 119
Elm Rd. Romf—2H 37
Elm Rd. Sidc—4A 116
Elm Rd. T Hth—4D 124
Elm Rd. Wall—1E 132
Elm Rd. Wemb—5E 40
Elm Rd. W. Sutt—7H 121
Elm Row. NW3—3A 44
Elms Av. N10—3F 29
Elms Av. NW4—5F 27
Elmscott Gdns. N21—6H 7
Elmscott Rd. Brom—5H 113
Elms Ct. Wemb—4A 40
Elms Cres. SW4—6G 93
Elmsdale Rd. E17—4B 32
Elms Gdns. Dag—4F 53
Elms Gdns. Wemb—4A 40
Elmshaw Rd. SW15—5C 90
Elmshurst Cres. N2—4B 28
Elmside. Croy—6D 136
Elmside Rd. Wemb—3G 41
Elms La. Wemb—3A 40
Elmsleigh Av. Harr—4B 24
Elmsleigh Rd. Twic—2H 103
Elmslie Clo. Wfd G—6J 21
Elms M. W2—7B 60 (9A 138)
Elmsmead Rd. E17—4B 32
Elms Pk. Av. Wemb—4A 40
Elms Rd. SW4—5G 93
Elms Rd. Harr—7D 10
Elmstead Av. Chst—5D 114
Elmstead Av. Wemb—1E 40
Elmstead Clo. N20—2D 14
Elmstead Clo. Eps—5A 130
Elmstead Gdns. Wor Pk
—3C 130
Elmstead Glade. Chst 5D 114
Elmstead La. Chst—7C 114
Elmstead Rd. Ilf—2J 51
Elmstead Rd. Eri—7K 85
Elms, The. SW13—3B 90
Elmstone Rd. SW6—1J 91
Elm St. WC1—4K 61 (4F 140)
Elmsworth Av. Houn—2F 87
Elm Ter. NW2—3J 43
Elm Ter. NW3—4C 44
Elm Ter. SE9—6E 98
Elm Ter. Harr—1H 23
Elm Ter. Stan—5H 11
Elmton Way. E5—3G 47
Elm Tree Clo. NW8
—3B 60 (1A 138)
Elm Tree Clo. N'holt—2D 54
Elm Tree Rd. NW8
—3B 60 (1A 138)
Elmtree Rd. Tedd—4J 103
Elm Wlk. NW3—2J 43
Elm Wlk. SW20—4E 120
Elm Way. N11—6K 15
Elm Way. NW10—4A 42
Elm Way. Wor Pk—3E 130
Elmwood Av. N13—5D 16
Elmwood Av. Felt—3A 102
Elmwood Av. Harr—5A 24
Elmwood Clo. Eps—7C 130
Elmwood Clo. Wall—2F 133
Elmwood Ct. Wemb—3A 40
Elmwood Cres. NW9—4J 25
Elmwood Dri. Bex—7E 100
Elmwood Dri. Eps—6C 130
Elmwood Gdns. W7—5J 55
Elmwood Rd. SE24—5D 94
Elmwood Rd. W4—6J 73
Elmwood Rd. Croy—7B 124
Elmwood Rd. Mitc—3D 122
Elmworth Gro. SE21—2D 110
Elnathan M. W9—4K 59
Elphinstone Rd. E17—2B 32
Elphinstone St. N5—4B 46
Elrington Rd. E8—6G 47
Elsa Rd. Well—2B 100
Elsa St. E1—5A 64
Elsdale St. E9—6J 47
Elsden M. E2—2J 63 (1M 143)
Elsden Rd. N17—1F 31
Elsenham Rd. E12—5E 50
Elsenham St. SW18—1H 107

Elsham Rd. E11—4G 49
Elsham Rd. W14—2G 75
Elsiedene Rd. N21—7H 7
Elsiemaud Rd. SE4—5B 96
Elsie Rd. SE22—4F 95
Elsinore Rd. SE23—1A 112
Elsinore Way. Rich—3H 89
Elsley Rd. SW11—3D 92
Elspeth Rd. SW11—4D 92
Elspeth Rd. Wemb—5E 40
Elsrick Av. Mord—5J 121
Elstan Way. Croy—7A 126
Elsted St. SE17—4D 78 (9B 148)
Elstow Clo. SE9—5E 98
(in two parts)
Elstow Clo. Ruis—7B 22
Elstow Gdns. Dag—1E 68
Elstow Rd. Dag—1E 68
Elstree Gdns. N9—1C 18
Elstree Gdns. Belv—4E 84
Elstree Gdns. Ilf—5G 51
Elstree Hill. Brom—7G 113
Elstree Hill S. Borwd—1J 11
Elstree Rd. Bush, Wat & Borwd
—1C 10
Elswick Rd. SE13—2D 96
Elswick St. SW6—2A 92
Elsworthy Rise. NW3—7C 44
Elsworthy Rd. NW3—1C 60
Elsworthy Ter. NW3—7C 44
Elsynge Rd. SW18—5B 92
Eltham Grn. SE9—5B 98
Eltham Grn. Rd. SE9—4A 98
Eltham High St. SE9—6D 98
Eltham Hill. SE9—5B 98
Eltham Pal. Rd. SE9—6A 98
Eltham Pk. Gdns. SE9—4E 98
Eltham Rd.—5J 97
SE12 1-101 & 2-120
SE9 remainder
Elthiron Rd. SW6—1J 91
Elthorne Av. W7—2K 71
Elthorne Ct. Felt—1A 102
Elthorne Pk. Rd. W7—2A 72
Elthorne Rd. N19—2H 45
Elthorne Rd. NW9—7K 25
Elthorne Way. NW9—6K 25
Elthruda Rd. SE13—6F 97
Eltisley Rd. Ilf—4F 51
Elton Av. Barn—5C 4
Elton Av. Gnfd—6K 39
Elton Av. Wemb—5B 40
Elton Clo. Tedd—7C 104
Elton Pl. N16—5E 46
Elton Rd. King—1F 119
Eltringham St. SW18—4A 92
Elvaston M. SW7
—3A 76 (7A 144)
Elvaston Pl. SW7
—3A 76 (7A 144)
Elveden Pl. NW10—2G 57
Elveden Rd. NW10—2G 57
Elvendon Rd. N13—6D 16
Elverson Rd. SE8—2D 96
Elverton St. SW1
—4H 77 (8A 146)
Elvington Grn. Brom—5H 127
Elvington La. NW9—1A 26
Elvino Rd. SE26—5A 112
Elvis Rd. NW2—6E 42
Elwill Way. Beck—4E 126
Elwin St. E2—3G 63 (1G 143)
Elwood St. N5—3B 46
Elwyn Gdns. SE12—7J 97
Ely Clo. N Mald—2B 120
Ely Gdns. Dag—3J 53
Ely Gdns. Ilf—7C 34
Elyne Rd. N4—6A 30
Ely Pl. EC1—5A 62 (6H 141)
Ely Pl. Wfd G—6K 21
Ely Rd. E10—7E 32
Ely Rd. Croy—5D 124
Ely Rd. Houn—3A 86
Elysian Av. Orp—6K 129
Elysium St. SW6—2H 91
Elystan Business Centre Hay
—7A 54

Etta St. SE8—6A 80
Etton Clo. Horn—2J 45
Ettrick St. E14—6E 64
(in two parts)
Etwell Pl. Surb—6F 119
Eugenia Rd. SE16
—4J 79 (9M 149)
Eureka Rd. King—2G 119
Europa Pl. EC1—3C 62 (2L 141)
Europa Trading Est. Eri—5K 85
Europe Rd. SE18—3D 82
Eustace Rd. E6—3C 66
Eustace Rd. SW6—7J 75
Eustace Rd. Romf—7D 36
Euston Rd. NW1
—3H 61 (2A 140)
Euston Rd. Croy—1A 134
Euston Sq. NW1
—3H 61 (2A 140)
Euston Sta. Colonnade. NW1
—3H 61 (2A 140)
Euston St. NW1
—3G 61 (2M 139)
Evandale Rd. SW9—2A 94
Evangelist Rd. NW5—4F 45
Evans Clo. E8—6F 47
Evans Gro. Felt—2E 102
Evans Rd. SE6—2G 113
Evanston Av. E4—7K 19
Evanston Gdns. Ilf—6C 34
Eva Rd. Romf—7C 36
Evelina Rd. SE15—3J 95
Evelina Rd. SE20—7J 111
Eveline Rd. Mitc—1D 122
Evelyn Av. NW9—4K 25
Evelyn Clo. Twic—7F 87
Evelyn Ct. E8—4G 47
Evelyn Denington Rd. E6
—5D 66
Evelyn Dri. Pinn—1B 22
Evelyn Fox Ct. W10—5E 58
Evelyn Gdns. SW7—5B 76
Evelyn Gdns. Rich—4E 88
Evelyn Gro. W5—1F 73
Evelyn Gro. S'hall—6D 54
Evelyn Lowe Est. SE16
—4G 79 (8G 149)
Evelyn Rd. E17—4E 32
Evelyn Rd. SW19—6K 107
Evelyn Rd. W4—3K 73
Evelyn Rd. Barn—4J 5
Evelyn Rd. Rich—3E 88
Evelyn Rd. Rich—3C 104
(Ham)
Evelyn St. SE8—5A 80
Evelyn Ter. Rich—3E 88
Evelyn Wlk. N1—2D 62 (1A 142)
Evelyn Way. Wall—4H 133
Evelyn Yd. W1—6H 61 (7A 140)
Evening Hill. Beck—7E 112
Evenwood Clo. SW15—5G 91
Everard Av. Brom—1J 137
Everard Way. Wemb—3E 40
Everatt Clo. SW18—6H 91
Everdon Rd. SW13—6C 74
Everest Pl. E14—5E 64
Everest Rd. SE9—5D 98
Everett Wlk. Belv—5F 85
Everglade Strand. NW9—1B 26
Everilda St. N1—1K 61
Evering Rd.—3F 47
    N16 1-183 & 2-158
    E5 remainder
Everington Rd. N10—2D 28
Everington St. W6—6F 75
Everitt Rd. NW10—3K 57
Everleigh St. N4—1K 45
Eve Rd. E11—4G 49
Eve Rd. E15—2G 65
Eve Rd. N17—3E 30
Eve Rd. Iswth—4A 88
Eversfield Gdns. NW7—6F 13
Eversfield Rd. Rich—2F 89
Evershot St. NW1
—2G 61 (1M 139)
Evershot Rd. N4—1K 45
Eversleigh Rd. E6—1B 66

Eversleigh Rd. N3—7C 14
Eversleigh Rd. SW11—3D 92
Eversleigh Rd. Barn—5F 5
Eversley Av. Bexh—2K 101
Eversley Av. Wemb—2G 41
Eversley Clo. N21—6E 6
Eversley Cres. N21—6F 7
Eversley Cres. Iswth—1H 87
Eversley Mt. N21—6E 6
Eversley Pk. SW19—5D 106
Eversley Pk. Rd. N21—6E 6
Eversley Rd. SE7—6K 81
Eversley Rd. SE19—7D 110
Eversley Rd. Surb—4F 119
Eversley Way. Croy—3C 136
Everthorpe Rd. SE15—3F 95
Everton Dri. Stan—3E 24
Everton Rd. Croy—1G 135
Evesham Av. E17—2C 32
Evesham Clo. Gnfd—2F 55
Evesham Clo. Sutt—7J 131
Evesham Grn. Mord—6K 121
Evesham Rd. E15—7H 49
Evesham Rd. N11—5B 16
Evesham Rd. W11—7F 59
Evesham Rd. Mord—6K 121
Evesham Wlk. SE5—2D 94
Evesham Wlk. SW9—2A 94
Evesham Way. SW11—3E 92
Evesham Way. Ilf—3E 34
Evry Rd. Sidc—6C 116
Ewald Rd. SW6—2H 91
Ewanrigg Ter. Wfd G—5F 21
Ewart Gro. N22—1A 30
Ewart Rd. SE23—7K 95
Ewe Clo. N7—6J 45
Ewell By-Pass. Eps—7C 130
Ewell Ct. Av. Eps—5B 130
Ewellhurst Rd. Ilf—2C 34
Ewell Pk. Way. Eps—6C 130
Ewell Rd. Surb—7B 118
Ewell Rd. Surb—6E 118
    (Long Ditton)
Ewell Rd. Sutt—7F 131
Ewelme Rd. SE23—1J 111
Ewen Cres. SW2—1A 110
Ewer St. SE1—1C 78 (3L 147)
Ewhurst Av. S Croy—7F 135
Ewhurst Rd. SE4—6B 96
Exbury Rd. SE6—2C 112
Excelsior Clo. King—2G 119
Excelsior Gdns. SE13—2E 96
Exchange Ct. WC2
—7J 61 (1D 146)
Exchange Pl. EC2
—5E 62 (5C 142)
Exchange Sq. EC2
—5E 62 (5C 142)
Exchange St. Romf—5K 37
Exeter Clo. E6—6D 66
Exeter Gdns. Ilf—1C 50
Exeter M. NW6—6K 43
Exeter Rd. E16—5J 65
Exeter Rd. E17—5C 32
Exeter Rd. N9—2D 18
Exeter Rd. N14—1A 16
Exeter Rd. NW2—5G 43
Exeter Rd. SE15—1F 95
Exeter Rd. Croy—7E 124
Exeter Rd. Dag—6H 53
Exeter Rd. Enf—3E 8
Exeter Rd. Felt—3D 102
Exeter Rd. Harr—2C 38
Exeter Rd. Well—2K 99
Exeter St. WC2—7J 61 (9D 140)
Exeter Way. SE14—7B 80
Exford Gdns. SE12—1K 113
Exford Rd. SE12—2K 113
Exhibition Clo. W12—7E 58
Exhibition Rd. SW7
—2B 76 (5B 144)
Exmoor St. W10—5F 59
Exmouth Mkt. EC1
—4A 62 (3G 141)
Exmouth M. NW1
—3G 61 (2M 139)
Exmouth Pl. E8—7H 47

Exmouth Rd. E17—5B 32
Exmouth Rd. Brom—3K 127
Exmouth Rd. Ruis—3A 38
Exmouth Rd. Well—1C 100
Exmouth St. E1—6J 63 (7M 143)
Exning Rd. E16—4H 65
Exon St. SE17—5E 78 (9C 148)
Exton Cres. NW10—7J 41
Exton Gdns. Dag—5C 52
Exton St. SE1—1A 78 (3G 147)
Eyebright Clo. Croy—1K 135
Eyhurst Clo. NW2—2D 42
Eylewood Rd. SE27—5C 110
Eynella Rd. SE22—7F 95
Eynham Rd. W12—6E 58
Eynsford Clo. Orp—7G 129
Eynsford Cres. Sidc—1C 116
Eynsford Rd. Ilf—2J 51
Eynsham Dri. SE2—4A 84
Eynswood Dri. Sidc—5B 116
Eyot Gdns. W6—5B 74
Eyot Grn. W4—5B 74
Eyre Ct. NW8—2B 60
Eyre St. Hill. EC1
—4A 62 (4G 141)
Eysham Ct. Barn—5E 4
Eythorne Rd. SW9—1A 94
Ezra St. E2—3F 63 (1F 142)

Faber Gdns. NW4—5C 26
Fabian Rd. SW6—7H 75
Fabian St. E6—4D 66
Factory La. N17—2F 31
Factory La. Croy—1A 134
Factory Pl. E14—5D 80
Factory Rd. E16—1C 82
Factory Sq. SW16—6J 109
Factory W. W7—1J 71
Fairacre. N Mald—3A 120
Fairacres. SW15—4C 90
Fairacres. Croy—7B 136
Fairbairn Grn. SW9—1B 94
Fairbanks Rd. N17—3G 31
Fairbourne Rd. N17—3E 30
Fairbridge Rd. N19—2H 45
Fairbrook Clo. N13—5F 17
Fairbrook Rd. N13—6F 17
Fairburn Ct. SW15—5G 91
Fairby Rd. SE12—5K 97
Fairchild Ho. N3—1J 27
Fairchild St. EC2
—4E 62 (4D 142)
Fair Clo. Bush. Wat—1A 10
Fairclough St. E1
—6G 63 (8H 143)
Faircroft Ct. Tedd—6A 104
Faircross Av. Bark—6G 51
Faircross Av. Romf—1K 37
Fairdale Gdns. SW15—4D 90
Fairfax Av. Eps—7D 130
Fairfax Gdns. SE3—1A 98
Fairfax Pl. NW6—7A 44
Fairfax Rd. N8—4A 30
Fairfax Rd. NW6—7A 44
Fairfax Rd. W4—3A 74
Fairfax Rd. Tedd—6A 104
Fairfield Av. NW4—6D 26
Fairfield Av. Edgw—6C 12
Fairfield Av. Twic—1F 103
Fairfield Clo. N12—4F 15
Fairfield Clo. Enf—4F 9
Fairfield Clo. Eps—5A 130
Fairfield Clo. Sidc—6K 99
Fairfield Ct. NW10—1C 58
Fairfield Cres. Edgw—6C 12
Fairfield Dri. SW18—5K 91
Fairfield Dri. Gnfd—1C 56
Fairfield Dri. Harr—3G 23
Fairfield E. King—2E 118
Fairfield Gdns. N8—5J 29
Fairfield Gro. SE7—6B 82
Fairfield N. King—2E 118
Fairfield Path. Croy—3E 134
Fairfield Pl. King—3E 118
Fairfield Rd. E3—2C 64

Fairfield Rd. E17—2A 32
Fairfield Rd. N8—5J 29
Fairfield Rd. N18—4B 18
Fairfield Rd. W7—3A 72
Fairfield Rd. Beck—2C 126
Fairfield Rd. Bexh—2F 101
Fairfield Rd. Brom—7J 113
Fairfield Rd. Croy—3D 134
Fairfield Rd. Ilf—6F 51
Fairfield Rd. King—2E 118
Fairfield Rd. Orp—6H 129
Fairfield Rd. S'hall—6D 54
Fairfield Rd. Wfd G—6D 20
Fairfields Clo. NW9—5J 25
Fairfields Cres. NW9—5J 25
Fairfield S. King—2E 118
Fairfields Rd. Houn—3G 87
Fairfield St. SW18—5K 91
Fairfield Way. Barn—5D 4
Fairfield Way. Eps—5A 130
Fairfield W. King—2E 118
Fairfoot Rd. E3—4C 64
Fairford Av. Bexh—1K 101
Fairford Av. Croy—5K 125
Fairford Clo. Croy—5A 126
Fairford Gdns. Wor Pk—3B 130
Fairgreen. Barn—3J 5
Fairgreen E. Barn—3J 5
Fairgreen Rd. T Hth—5B 124
Fairhaven Av. Croy—6K 125
Fairhazel Gdns. NW6—6K 43
Fairholme Clo. N3—4G 27
Fairholme Gdns. N3—3G 27
Fairholme Rd. W14—5G 75
Fairholme Rd. Croy—7A 124
Fairholme Rd. Harr—5K 23
Fairholme Rd. Ilf—6E 34
Fairholme Rd. Sutt—6H 131
Fairholt Clo. N16—1E 46
Fairholt Rd. N16—1D 46
Fairholt St. SW7
—3C 76 (6D 144)
Fairland Rd. E15—7H 49
Fairlands Av. Buck H—2D 20
Fairlands Av. Sutt—2J 131
Fairlands Av. T Hth—4K 123
Fairlawn. SE7—6A 82
Fairlawn Av. N2—4C 28
Fairlawn Av. W4—4J 73
Fairlawn Av. Bexh—2D 100
Fairlawn Clo. N14—6B 6
Fairlawn Clo. Felt—4D 102
Fairlawn Clo. King—6J 105
Fairlawn Dri. Wfd G—7D 20
Fairlawn Gdns. S'hall—7D 54
Fairlawn Gro. W4—4J 73
Fairlawn Pk. SE26—5A 112
Fairlawn Rd. SW19—7H 107
Fairlawns. Pinn—2B 22
Fairlawns. Twic—6C 88
Fairlea Pl. W5—4C 56
Fairlie Gdns. SE23—7J 95
Fairlight Av. E4—2A 20
Fairlight Av. NW10—2A 58
Fairlight Av. Wfd G—6D 20
Fairlight Clo. E4—2A 20
Fairlight Clo. Wor Pk—4E 130
Fairlight Rd. SW17—4B 108
Fairline Ct. Beck—2E 126
Fairlop Gdns. Ilf—1G 35
Fairlop Pl. NW8—3B 60 (2B 138)
Fairlop Rd. E11—7F 33
Fairlop Rd. Ilf—2G 35
Fairmead. Brom—4D 128
Fairmead Clo. Brom—4D 128
Fairmead Clo. Houn—7B 70
Fairmead Clo. N Mald—3K 119
Fairmead Cres. Edgw—3D 12
Fairmead Gdns. Ilf—5C 34
Fairmead Rd. N19—3J 45
Fairmead Rd. Croy—7K 123
Fairmile Av. SW16—5H 109
Fairmont Clo. Belv—5F 85
Fairmount Rd. SW2—6K 93
Fairoak Clo. Orp—7F 129
Fairoak Dri. SE9—5H 99

Fisons Rd. E16—1J 81
Fitzalan Rd. N3—3G 27
Fitzalan St. SE11
　　　　—4A 78 (8G 147)
Fitzgeorge Av. W14—4G 75
Fitzgeorge Av. N Mald—1K 119
Fitzgerald Av. SW14—3A 90
Fitzgerald Rd. E11—5J 33
Fitzgerald Rd. SW14—3K 89
Fitzgerald Rd. Th Dit—6A 118
Fitzhardinge St. W1
　　　　—6E 60 (7G 139)
Fitzhugh Gro. SW18—6B 92
Fitzjames Av. W14—4G 75
Fitzjames Av. Croy—2G 135
Fitzjohn Av. Barn—5B 4
Fitzjohn's Av. NW3—4A 44
Fitzmaurice Pl. W1
　　　　—1F 77 (2K 145)
Fitzneal St. W12—6B 58
Fitzroy Clo. N6—1D 44
Fitzroy Gdns. SE19—7E 110
Fitzroy Pk. N6—1D 44
Fitzroy Rd. NW1—1E 60
Fitzroy Sq. W1—4G 61 (4L 139)
Fitzroy St. W1—4G 61 (4L 139)
(in two parts)
Fitzstephen Rd. Dag—5B 52
Fitzwarren Gdns. N19—1G 45
Fitzwilliam Av. Rich—2F 89
Fitzwilliam Ho. Rich—4D 88
Fitzwilliam Rd. SW4—3G 93
Fitz Wygram Clo. Hmptn
　　　　—5G 103
Five Acre. NW9—2B 26
Fiveacre Clo. T Hth—6A 124
Five Elms Rd. Brom—3K 137
Five Elms Rd. Dag—3F 53
Fiveways Rd. SW9—2A 94
Fladbury Rd. N15—6D 30
Fladgate Rd. E11—6G 33
Flag Clo. Croy—1K 135
Flambard Rd. Harr—6A 24
Flamborough St. E14—6A 64
Flamingo Gdns. N'holt—3B 54
Flamstead Gdns. Dag—7C 52
Flamstead Rd. Dag—7C 52
Flamsted Av. Wemb—6G 41
Flamsteed Rd. SE7—5C 82
Flanchford Rd. W12—3B 74
Flanders Cres. SW17—7D 108
Flanders Rd. E6—2D 66
Flanders Rd. W4—4A 74
Flanders Way. E9—6K 47
Flank St. E1—7G 63 (9H 143)
Flask Wlk. NW3—4A 44
Flaxley Rd. Mord—7K 121
Flaxman Rd. SE5—2B 94
Flaxman Ter. WC1
　　　　—3H 61 (2B 140)
Flaxton Rd. SE18—7J 83
Flecker Clo. Stan—5E 10
Fleece Rd. Surb—7C 118
Fleece Wlk. N7—6J 45
Fleeming Clo. E17—2B 32
Fleeming Rd. E17—2B 32
Fleet La. EC4—6B 62 (7J 141)
Fleet Rd. NW3—5C 44
Fleet Sq. WC1—3K 61 (2E 140)
Fleet St. EC4—6A 62 (8G 141)
Fleet St. Hill. E1—4G 63 (4J 143)
Fleetway Business Pk. NW2
　　　　—1B 42
Fleetway Business Pk. Gnfd
　　　　—2B 56
Fleetwood Clo. E16—5B 66
Fleetwood Clo. Croy—3F 135
Fleetwood Rd. NW10—5C 42
Fleetwood Rd. King—3H 119
Fleetwood Sq. King—3H 119
Fleetwood St. N16—2E 46
Fleming Ct. Croy—5A 134
Fleming Rd. SE17—6B 78
Fleming Rd. S'hall—6F 55
Fleming Way. SE28—7D 68
Fleming Way. Iswth—3K 87

Flempton Rd. E10—1A 48
Fletcher La. E10—7E 32
Fletcher Path. SE8—7C 80
Fletcher Rd. W4—3J 73
Fletchers Clo. Brom—4K 127
Fletcher St. E1—7G 63 (9H 143)
Fletching Rd. E5—3J 47
Fletching Rd. SE7—6B 82
Fletton Rd. N11—7D 16
Fleur de Lis St. E1
　　　　—4F 63 (4E 142)
Fleur Gates. SW19—7F 91
Flexmere Gdns. N17—1E 30
Flexmere Rd. N17—1D 30
Flight App. NW9—2B 26
Flimwell Clo. Brom—5G 113
Flintmill Cres. SE3—2C 98
Flinton St. SE17—5E 78 (9D 148)
Flint St. SE17—4D 78 (9B 148)
Flitcroft St. WC2
　　　　—6H 61 (8B 140)
Flockton St. SE16
　　　　—2G 79 (5G 149)
Flodden Rd. SE5—1C 94
Flood St. SW3—5C 76
Flood Wlk. SW3—6C 76
Flora Clo. E14—6D 64
Flora Gdns. Romf—6C 36
Floral St. WC2—7J 61 (9C 140)
Flora St. Belv—5F 85
Florence Av. Enf—3H 7
Florence Av. Mord—5A 122
Florence Dri. Enf—3H 7
Florence Gdns. W4—6J 73
Florence Rd. E6—1A 66
Florence Rd. E13—2J 65
Florence Rd. N4—7K 29
Florence Rd. SE2—4C 84
Florence Rd. SE14—1B 96
Florence Rd. SW19—6K 107
Florence Rd. W4—3K 73
Florence Rd. W5—7E 56
Florence Rd. Beck—2A 126
Florence Rd. Brom—1J 127
Florence Rd. Felt—1A 102
Florence Rd. King—7F 105
Florence Rd. S'hall—4B 70
Florence Rd. S Croy—7D 134
Florence St. E16—4H 65
Florence St. N1—7B 46
Florence St. NW4—1E 26
Florence Ter. SE14—1B 96
Florence Ter. SW15—3A 106
Florfield Rd. E8—6H 47
Florian Av. Sutt—4B 132
Florian Rd. SW15—4G 91
Florida Clo. Bush, Wat—2C 10
Florida Rd. T Hth—1B 124
Florida St. E2—3G 63 (2H 143)
Floriston Clo. Stan—1B 24
Floriston Gdns. Stan—1B 24
Floss St. SW15—2E 90
Flower & Dean Wlk. E1
　　　　—5F 63 (6F 142)
Flower La. NW7—5G 13
Flowersmead. SW17—2E 108
Flower Wlk., The. SW7
　　　　—2A 76 (4A 144)
Floyd Rd. SE7—5A 82
Fludyer St. SE13—4G 97
Folair Way. SE16—5H 79
Foley St. W1—5G 61 (6L 139)
Folgate St. E1—5E 62 (5D 142)
Foliot St. W12—6B 58
Folkestone Rd. E6—2E 66
Folkestone Rd. E17—4D 32
Folkestone Rd. N18—4B 18
Folkingham La. NW9—1K 25
Folkington Corner. N12—5C 14
Follett St. E14—6E 64
Folly La. E17—7G 19
Folly Wall. E14—2E 80
Fontaine Rd. SW16—7K 109
Fontarabia Rd. SW11—4E 92
Fontayne Av. Romf—2K 37
Fontenoy Rd. SW12—2F 109

Fonteyne Gdns. Wfd G—2B 34
Fonthill Clo. SE20—2G 125
Fonthill M. N4—2A 46
Fonthill Rd. N4—1K 45
Font Hills. N2—2A 28
Fontley Way. SW15—7C 90
Fontwell Clo. Harr—7D 10
Fontwell Clo. N'holt—6E 38
Fontwell Dri. Brom—5E 128
Football La. Harr—1K 39
Footpath, The. SW15—5C 90
Foots Cray High St. Sidc
　　　　—6C 116
Foots Cray La. Sidc—1C 116
Footscray Rd. SE9—6E 98
Forbes St. E1—6G 63 (8H 143)
Forburg Rd. N16—1G 47
Ford Clo. Harr—7H 23
Ford Clo. T Hth—5B 124
Forde Av. Brom—3A 128
Fordel Rd. SE6—1F 113
Ford End. Wfd G—6E 20
Fordham Clo. Barn—3H 5
Fordham Rd. Barn—3G 5
Fordham St. E1—6G 63 (7H 143)
Fordhook Av. W5—7F 57
Fordingley Rd. W9—3H 59
Fordington Ho. SE26—3H 111
Fordington Rd. N6—5D 28
Fordmill Rd. SE6—2C 112
Ford Rd. E3—2B 64
Ford Rd. Dag—7F 53
Fords Gro. N21—1H 17
Fords Pk. Rd. E16—6J 65
Ford St. E3—1A 64
(in two parts)
Ford St. E16—6H 65
Fordwich Clo. Orp—7K 129
Fordwych Rd. NW2—5G 43
Fordyce Rd. SE13—6E 96
Fordyke Rd. Dag—2F 53
Foreign St. SE5—2B 94
Foreland Ct. NW4—1F 27
Foreland St. SE18—4H 83
Foreman Ct. W6—4E 74
Foreshore. SE8—4B 80
Forest App. E4—1B 20
Forest App. Wfd G—7D 20
Forest Av. E4—1B 20
Forest Av. Chig—5K 21
Forest Business Pk. E10—7K 31
Forest Clo. E11—5J 33
Forest Clo. Chst—1E 128
Forest Clo. Wfd G—3E 20
Forest Ct. E4—1C 20
Forest Ct. E11—4G 33
Forestdale. N14—4C 16
Forestdale Centre, The. Croy
　　　　—7B 136
Forest Dene Ct. Sutt—6A 132
Forest Dri. E12—3B 50
Forest Dri. Wfd G—7A 20
Forest Dri. E. E11—7F 33
Forest Dri. W. E11—7E 32
Forest Edge. Buck H—4F 21
Forest Rd. SE15—3H 95
Foresters Clo. Wall—7H 133
Foresters Cres. Bexh—4H 101
Foresters Dri. E17—4F 33
Foresters Dri. Wall—7H 133
Forest Gdns. N17—2F 31
Forest Ga. NW9—5A 26
Forest Glade. E4—5B 20
Forest Glade. E11—6G 33
Forest Gro. E8—7F 47
Forest Hill Rd.—6H 95
　SE22 3-41 & 2-128
　SE23 remainder
Forestholme Clo. SE23—2J 111
Forest Industrial Pk. Ilf—1J 35
Forest La.—5G 49
　E15 1-91
　E7 remainder
Forest La. Chig—5K 21
Forest Mt. Rd. Wfd G—7A 20
Fore St. EC2—5C 62 (6M 141)

Fore St. N18 & N9—6A 18
Fore St. Av. EC2
　　　　—5D 62 (6A 142)
Forest Ridge. Beck—3C 126
Forest Rise. E17—4F 33
(in three parts)
Forest Rd. E7—4J 49
Forest Rd. E8—6F 47
Forest Rd. E11—7F 33
Forest Rd. E17—4J 31
Forest Rd. N9—1C 18
Forest Rd. Felt—2A 102
Forest Rd. Ilf—2H 35
Forest Rd. Rich—7G 73
Forest Rd. Romf—3H 37
Forest Rd. Sutt—1J 131
Forest Rd. Wfd G—3D 20
Forest Side. E7—2K 49
Forest Side. E7—4K 49
Forest Side. Buck H—1F 21
Forest Side. Wor Pk—1B 130
Forest St. E7—5J 49
Forest View. E4—1B 20
Forest View. E11—7H 33
Forest View Av. E10—5F 33
Forest View Rd. E12—4C 50
Forest View Rd. E17—1E 32
Forest Way. E11—7H 33
Forest Way. N19—2G 45
Forest Way. Orp—5K 129
Forest Way. Sidc—7H 99
Forest Way. Wfd G—4E 20
Forfar Rd. N22—1B 30
Forfar Rd. SW11—1E 92
Forge Clo. Brom—1J 137
Forge La. Felt—5C 102
Forge La. Sutt—7G 131
Forge Pl. NW1—6E 44
Forman Pl. N16—4F 47
Formby Av. Stan—3C 24
Formosa St. W9—4K 59
Formunt Clo. E16—5H 65
Forres Gdns. NW11—6J 27
Forrester Path. SE26—4J 111
Forrest Gdns. SW16—3K 123
Forset St. W1—6C 60 (7D 136)
Forstal Clo. Brom—3J 127
Forster Rd. E17—6A 32
Forster Rd. N17—3F 31
Forster Rd. SW2—7J 93
Forster Rd. Beck—3A 126
Forster Rd. Croy—7C 124
Forsters Clo. Romf—6F 37
Forston St. N1—2C 62
Forsyte Cres. SE19—1E 124
Forsythe Shades Ct. Beck
　　　　—1E 126
Forsyth Gdns. SE17—6B 78
Forsyth Pl. Enf—5K 7
Forterie Gdns. Ilf—4A 52
Fortescue Av. E8—7H 47
(in two parts)
Fortescue Av. Twic—3G 103
Fortescue Rd. SW19—7B 108
Fortescue Rd. Edgw—1K 25
Fortess Gro. NW5—5G 45
Fortess Rd. NW5—5G 45
Fortess Wlk. NW5—5F 45
Forthbridge Rd. SW11—4E 92
Fortis Clo. E16—6A 66
Fortis Grn. N2 & N10—4C 28
Fortis Grn. Av. N2—3D 28
Fortis Grn. Rd. N10—3E 28
Fortismere Av. N10—3E 28
Fortnam Rd. N19—2H 45
Fortnums Acre. Stan—6E 10
Fort Rd. SE1—4F 79 (9F 148)
Fort Rd. N'holt—7E 38
Fortrose Gdns. SW2—1J 109
Fort St. E1—5E 62 (6D 142)
Fort St. E16—1K 81
Fortuna Clo. N7—6K 45
Fortunegate Rd. NW10—1A 58
Fortune Grn. Rd. NW6—4J 43
Fortunes Mead. N'holt—6C 38

201

Fortune St. EC1
—4C 62 (4M 141)
Fortune Way. NW10—3C 58
Forty Acre La. E16—5J 65
Forty Av. Wemb—3F 41
Forty Clo. Wemb—3F 41
Forty Footpath. SW14—3J 89
Forty Hill. Enf—1A 8
Forty La. Wemb—2H 41
Forumside. Edgw—6B 12
Forum Way. Edgw—6B 12
Forval Clo. Mitc—5D 122
Forward Dri. Harr—4K 23
Fosbury M. W2—7K 59
Foscote M. W9—4J 59
Foscote Rd. NW4—6D 26
Foskett Rd. SW6—2H 91
Foss Av. Croy—5A 134
Fossdene Rd. SE7—5K 81
Fossdyke Clo. Hay—5C 54
Fosse Way. W13—5A 56
Fossil Rd. SE13—3C 96
Fossington Rd. Belv—4D 84
Foss Rd. SW17—4B 108
Fossway. Dag—2C 52
Foster La. EC2—6C 62 (7L 141)
Foster Pl. NW4—4E 26
Foster Rd. E13—4J 65
Foster Rd. W3—7A 58
Foster Rd. W4—5K 73
Fosters Clo. E18—1K 33
Fosters Clo. Chst—5D 114
Foster St. NW4—4E 26
Fothergill Rd. E13—2J 65
Fotheringham Rd. Enf—4A 8
Foubert's Pl. W1
—6G 61 (8L 139)
Foulden Rd. N16—4F 47
Foulis Ter. SW7—5B 76 (9B 144)
Foulser Rd. SW17—3D 108
Foulsham Rd. T Hth—3D 124
Founders Gdns. SE19—7C 110
Foundry Clo. SE16—1A 80
Fountain Ct. EC4
—7A 62 (9G 141)
Fountain Dri. SE19—4F 111
Fountain Pl. SW9—1A 94
Fountain Rd. SW17—5B 108
Fountain Rd. T Hth—2C 124
Fountains Av. Felt—3D 102
Fountains Clo. Felt—2D 102
Fountains Cres. N14—7D 6
Fountayne Rd. N15—4G 31
Fountayne Rd. N16—2G 47
Fount St. SW8—7H 77
Fouracres. Enf—1F 9
Fourland Wlk. Edgw—6D 12
Fournier St. E1—5F 63 (5F 142)
Four Seasons Cres. Sutt
—2H 131
Fourth Av. E12—4D 50
Fourth Av. W10—4G 59
Fourth Av. Romf—1K 53
Fourth Cross Rd. Twic—2H 103
Fourth Way. Wemb—4J 41
Four Wents. E4—2A 20
Fowey Av. Ilf—5B 34
Fowey Clo. E1—1H 79 (2J 149)
Fowler Clo. SW11—3B 92
Fowler Rd. E7—4J 49
Fowler Rd. N1—1B 62
Fowler Rd. Mitc—2E 122
Fowler Rd. Sidc—5C 116
Fowler's Wlk. W5—4D 56
Fownes St. SW11—3C 92
Foxberry Rd. SE4—3A 96
Foxborough Gdns. SE4—5C 96
Foxbourne Rd. SW17—2E 108
Foxbury Av. Chst—6H 115
Foxbury Clo. Brom—6K 113
Foxbury Rd. Brom—6J 113
Fox Clo. E1—4J 63 (3M 143)
Fox Clo. E16—5J 65
Foxcombe. Croy—6D 136
(in two parts)
Foxcombe Clo. E6—2B 66
Foxcombe Rd. SW15—1C 106

Foxcroft Rd. SE18—1F 99
Foxearth Spur. S Croy—7J 135
Foxes Dale. SE3—3J 97
Foxes Dale. Brom—3F 127
Foxglove St. W12—7B 58
Foxglove Way. Wall—1F 133
Foxgrove. N14—3D 16
Foxgrove Av. Beck—7D 112
Foxgrove Rd. Beck—7D 112
Foxham Rd. N19—3H 45
Fox Hill. SE19—7F 111
Fox Hill. Kes—5K 137
Fox Hill Gdns. SE19—7F 111
Foxhole Rd. SE9—5C 98
Fox Hollow Dri. Bexh—3D 100
Foxholt Gdns. NW10—7J 41
Foxhome Clo. Chst—6E 114
Fox Ho. Rd. Belv—4H 85
Foxlands Cres. Dag—5J 53
Foxlands La. Dag—5K 53
Foxlands Rd. Dag—5J 53
Fox La. N13—2E 16
Fox La. W5—4E 56
Fox La. Kes—5K 137
Foxleas Ct. Brom—7H 113
Foxlees. Wemb—4A 40
Foxley Clo. E8—5G 47
Foxley Rd. SW9—7A 78
Foxley Rd. T Hth—4B 124
Foxley Sq. SW9—1B 94
Foxmore St. SW11—1D 92
Fox Rd. E16—5H 65
Fox's Path. Mitc—2C 122
Foxwell St. SE4—3A 96
Foxwood Rd. SE3—4H 97
Foyle Rd. N17—1G 31
Foyle Rd. SE3—6H 81
Framfield Clo. N12—3D 14
Framfield Rd. N5—5B 46
Framfield Rd. W7—6K 55
Framfield Rd. Mitc—7E 108
Framlingham Clo. E5—2J 47
Framlingham Cres. SE9
—4C 114
Frampton Clo. Sutt—7J 131
Frampton Pk. Est. E9—7J 47
Frampton Pk. Rd. E9—6J 47
Frampton Rd. Houn—5C 86
Frampton St. NW8
—4B 60 (4B 138)
Francemary Rd. SE4—5C 96
Frances Rd. E4—6H 19
Frances St. SE18—4D 82
Franche Ct. Rd. SW17—3A 108
Francis Av. Bexh—2G 101
Francis Av. Ilf—2H 51
Francis Barber Clo. SW16
—4K 109
Franciscan Rd. SW17—5D 108
Francis Chichester Way. SW11
—1E 92
Francis Clo. E14—4F 81
Francis Gro. SW19—6H 107
Francis Rd. E10—1E 48
Francis Rd. N2—4D 28
Francis Rd. Croy—7B 124
Francis Rd. Gnfd—1C 56
Francis Rd. Harr—5A 24
Francis Rd. Houn—2B 86
Francis Rd. Ilf—2H 51
Francis Rd. Pinn—5A 22
Francis Rd. Wall—6G 133
Francis St. E15—5G 49
Francis St. SW1
—4G 77 (8M 145)
Francis St. Ilf—2H 51
Francis Ter. N19—3G 45
Francis Wlk. N1—1K 61
Francklyn Gdns. Edgw—3B 12
Franconia Rd. SW4—5H 93
Frank Bailey Wlk. E12—6E 50
Frank Dixon Clo. SE21—1E 110
Frank Dixon Way. SE21
—1E 110
Frankel Clo. SW19—6K 107
Frankfurt Rd. SE24—5C 94
Frankham St. SE8—7C 80

Frankland Clo. SE16
—4H 79 (8K 149)
Frankland Clo. Wfd G—5F 21
Frankland Rd. E4—5H 19
Frankland Rd. SW7
—3B 76 (7A 144)
Franklin Clo. N20—7F 5
Franklin Clo. SE27—3B 110
Franklin Clo. King—3G 119
Franklin Cres. Mitc—4G 123
Franklin Industrial Est. SE20
—1J 125
Franklin Pas. SE9—3C 98
Franklin Rd. SE20—7J 111
Franklin Rd. Bexh—1E 100
Franklins Sq. W14—5H 75
Franklin's Row. SW3
—5D 76 (9F 144)
Franklin St. E3—3D 64
Franklin St. N15—6E 30
Franklyn Rd. NW10—6B 42
Franks Av. N Mald—4J 119
Frank St. E13—4J 65
Franks Wood Av. Orp—5G 129
Franlaw Cres. N13—4H 17
Fransfield Gro. SE26—3H 111
Frans Hals Ct. E14—3F 81
Frant Clo. SE20—7J 111
Franthorne Way. SE6—3D 112
Frant Rd. T Hth—5B 124
Fraser Clo. E6—6C 66
Fraser Clo. Bex—1J 117
Fraser Rd. E17—5D 32
Fraser Rd. N9—3C 18
Fraser Rd. Eri—5K 85
Fraser Rd. Gnfd—1C 56
Fraser St. W4—5A 74
Frating Cres. Wfd G—6E 20
Frazer Av. Ruis—5A 38
Frazier St. SE1—2A 78 (5G 147)
Frean St. SE16—3G 79 (6G 149)
Freda Corbett Clo. SE15—7G 79
Frederica Rd. E4—1A 20
Frederica St. N7—7K 45
Frederick Clo. W2
—7C 60 (9D 138)
Frederick Clo. Sutt—4H 131
Frederick Cres. SW9—7B 78
Frederick Cres. Enf—2D 8
Frederick Gdns. Sutt—5H 131
Frederick Pl. SE18—5F 83
Frederick Rd. SE17—6B 78
Frederick Rd. Rain—2K 69
Frederick Rd. Sutt—5H 131
Frederick's Pl. EC2
—6D 62 (8A 142)
Fredericks Pl. N12—4F 15
Frederick's Row. EC1
—3B 62 (1J 141)
Frederick St. WC1
—3K 61 (2E 140)
Frederick Ter. E8—7F 47
Frederic St. E17—5A 32
Freedom St. SW11—2D 92
Freegrove Rd. N7—5J 45
Freehold Industrial Centre.
Houn—5A 86
Freeland Ct. Sidc—3A 116
Freeland Pk. NW4—2G 27
Freeland Rd. W5—7F 57
Freelands Av. S Croy—7K 135
Freelands Gro. Brom—1K 127
Freelands Rd. Brom—1K 127
Freeling St. N1—7J 45
(in two parts)
Freeman Clo. N'holt—7C 38
Freeman Rd. Mord—5B 122
Freemantle Av. Enf—5E 8
Freemasons Rd. E16—5K 65
Freemasons Rd. Croy—1E 134
Freethorpe Clo. SE19—1E 124
Free Trade Wharf. E1
—7K 63 (9M 143)
Freightliner Depot Rd. NW10
—3A 58
Freke Rd. SW11—3E 92

Fremantle Rd. Belve—4G 85
Fremantle Rd. Ilf—2F 35
Fremantle St. SE17
—5E 78 (9C 148)
Fremont St. E9—1J 63
French Pl. E1—3E 62 (2D 142)
Frendsbury Rd. SE4—4A 96
Frensham Clo. S'hall—4D 54
Frensham Dri. SW15—3B 106
Frensham Dri. Croy—7E 136
Frensham Rd. SE9—2H 115
Frensham Rd. Croy—7E 136
Frere St. SW11—2C 92
Freshfield Clo. SE13—3F 97
Freshfield Clo. SE13
Freshfield Dri. N14—7A 6
Freshfields. Croy—1B 136
Freshford St. SW18—3A 108
Freshwater Clo. SW17—6E 108
Freshwater Rd. SW17—6E 108
Freshwater Rd. Dag—1D 52
Freshwell Av. Romf—4C 36
Fresh Wharf Rd. Bark—1F 67
Freshwood Clo. Beck—1D 126
Freshwood Way. Wall—7F 133
Freston Gdns. Barn—5K 5
Freston Pk. N3—2H 27
Freston Rd. W10 & W11—7F 59
Freta Rd. Bexh—5F 101
Frewin Rd. SW18—1B 108
Friar M. SE27—3B 110
Friar Rd. Hay—4B 54
Friar Rd. Orp—5K 129
Friars Av. N20—3H 15
Friars Av. SW15—3B 106
Friars Clo. N'holt—3B 54
Friars Gdns. W3—6K 57
Friarsgate. Wfd G—4D 20
Friars La. Rich—5D 88
Friars Mead. E14—3E 80
Friars M. SE9—5E 98
Friars Pl. La. W3—7K 57
Friars Rd. E6—1B 66
Friars Stile Pl. Rich—6E 88
Friars Stile Rd. Rich—6E 88
Friar St. EC4—6B 62 (8K 141)
Friars Wlk. N14—7A 6
Friars Wlk. SE2—5D 84
Friars Way. W3—6K 57
Friarswood. Croy—7A 136
Friary Clo. N12—5H 15
Friary Est. SE15—6G 79
(in two parts)
Friary La. Wfd G—4D 20
Friary Rd. N12—4G 15
Friary Rd. SE15—7G 79
Friary Rd. W3—6J 57
Friary Way. N12—4H 15
Friday Hill. E4—2B 20
Friday Hill E. E4—3B 20
Friday Hill W. E4—2B 20
Friday Rd. Eri—5K 85
Friday Rd. Mitc—7D 108
Friday St. EC4—7C 62 (9L 141)
Frideswide Pl. NW5—5G 45
Friendly St. SE8—2C 96
Friendly St. M. SE8—2C 96
Friendship Wlk. N'holt—3B 54
Friends Rd. Croy—3D 134
Friend St. EC1—3B 62 (1J 141)
Friern Barnet La.—3G 15
N11 1-71 & 2-80
N20 remainder
Friern Barnet Rd. N11—5J 15
Friern Ct. N20—3G 15
Friern Mt. Dri. N20—7F 5
Friern Pk. N12—5F 15
Friern Rd. SE22—7G 95
Friern Watch Av. N12—4F 15
Frigate M. SE8—6C 80
Frimley Av. Wall—5K 133
Frimley Clo. SW19—2G 107
Frimley Clo. Croy—7E 136
Frimley Ct. Sidc—5C 116
Frimley Cres. Croy—7E 136
Frimley Gdns. Mitc—3C 122
Frimley Rd. Ilf—3J 51

Frimley Way. E1
—4K 63 (4M 143)
Frinsted Rd. Eri—7K 85
Frinton Dri. Wfd G—7A 20
Frinton M. Ilf—6E 34
Frinton Rd. E6—3B 66
Frinton Rd. N15—6E 30
Frinton Rd. SW17—6E 108
Frinton Rd. Sidc—2E 116
Friston St. SW6—2K 91
Friswell Pl. Bexh—4G 101
Fritham Clo. N Mald—6A 120
Frith Ct. NW7—7B 14
Frith La. NW7—7B 14
Frith Rd. E11—4E 48
Frith Rd. Croy—2C 134
Frith St. W1—6H 61 (8A 140)
Frithville Gdns. W12—1E 74
Frizlands La. Dag—2H 53
Frobisher Clo. Pinn—7B 22
Frobisher Ct. NW9—2A 26
Frobisher Rd. E6—5D 66
Frobisher Rd. N8—4A 30
Frobisher St. SE10—6G 81
Frogley Rd. SE22—4F 95
Frogmore. SW18—5J 91
Frogmore Clo. Sutt—3G 131
Frogmore Ct. S'hall—4D 70
Frogmore Gdns. Sutt—4G 131
Frogmore Industrial Est. NW10
—3K 57
Frognal. NW3—5A 44
Frognal Av. Harr—4K 23
Frognal Av. Sidc—6A 116
Frognal Clo. NW3—5A 44
Frognal Ct. NW3—6A 44
Frognal Gdns. NW3—4A 44
Frognal La. NW3—5K 43
Frognal Pde. NW3—6A 44
Frognal Pl. Sidc—6A 116
Frognal Rise. NW3—4A 44
Frognal Way. NW3—4A 44
Froissart Rd. SE9—5B 98
Frome Rd. N15—3B 30
Frome St. N1—2C 62
Fromondes Rd. Sutt—5G 131
Frostic Wlk. E1—5G 63 (6G 143)
Froude St. SW8—2F 93
Fryatt Rd. N17—7J 17
(in two parts)
Fryatt St. E14—6G 65
Fryent Clo. NW9—6G 25
Fryent Cres. NW9—6A 26
Fryent Fields. NW9—6A 26
Fryent Gro. NW9—6A 26
Fryent Way. NW9—5G 25
Frye's Bldgs. N1—2A 62
Fry Rd. E6—7B 50
Fry Rd. NW10—1B 58
Fryston Av. Croy—2G 135
Fuchsia St. SE2—5B 84
Fulbeck Dri. NW9—1A 26
Fulbeck Way. Harr—2G 23
Fulbourne Rd. E17—1E 32
Fulbourne St. E1
—5H 63 (5J 143)
Fulbrook M. N19—4G 45
Fulbrook Rd. N19—4G 45
Fulford Rd. Eps—7A 130
Fulford St. SE16
—2H 79 (5K 149)
Fulham B'way. SW6—7J 75
Fulham High St. SW6—2G 91
Fulham Pal. Rd.—5E 74
W6 55-211 & 2-284
SW6 remainder
Fulham Pk. Gdns. SW6—2H 91
Fulham Pk. Rd. SW6—2H 91
Fulham Rd.—2G 91 (9B 144)
SW3 77-267 & 6-132
SW10 273-459 & 134-366
SW6 remainder
Fullbrooks Av. Wor Pk—1B 130
Fuller Rd. Dag—3B 52
Fullers Av. Wfd G—7C 20
Fullers Clo. Romf—1J 37
Fullers La. Romf—1J 37

Fullers Rd. E18—1H 33
Fuller St. E2—4G 63 (3G 143)
Fuller St. NW4—4E 26
Fuller's Wood. Croy—5C 136
Fullerton Rd. SW18—5A 92
Fullerton Rd. Cars—7C 132
Fullerton Rd. Croy—7F 125
Fullwell Av. Ilf—1D 34
Fullwell Cross. Ilf—2H 35
Fullwoody's M. N1
—3D 62 (1B 142)
Fulmead St. SW6—1K 91
Fulmer Clo. Hmptn—5C 102
Fulmer Rd. E16—5B 66
Fulmer Way. W13—3B 72
Fulready Rd. E10—5F 33
Fulstone Clo. Houn—4D 86
Fulthorp Rd. SE3—2J 97
Fulton Rd. Wemb—3G 41
Fulwell Pk. Av. Twic—2G 103
Fulwell Rd. Tedd—4H 103
Fulwood Av. Wemb—2F 57
Fulwood Gdns. Twic—6K 87
Fulwood Pl. WC1
—5K 61 (6F 140)
Fulwood Wlk. SW19—1G 107
Furber St. W6—3D 74
Furham Field. Pinn—7A 10
Furley Rd. SE15—7G 79
Furlong Clo. Wall—1F 133
Furlong Rd. N7—6A 46
Furmage St. SW18—7K 91
Furneaux Av. SE27—5B 110
Furness Rd. NW10—2C 58
Furness Rd. SW6—2K 91
Furness Rd. Harr—1F 39
Furness Rd. Mord—6K 121
Furnival St. EC4
—6A 62 (7G 141)
Furrow La. E9—5J 47
Fursby Av. N3—6D 14
Further Acre. NW9—2B 26
Furtherfield Clo. Croy—6A 124
Further Grn. Rd. SE6—7G 97
Furzedown Dri. SW17—5F 109
Furzedown Rd. SW17—5F 109
Furzefield Clo. Chst—6F 115
Furzefield Rd. SE3—7K 81
Furze La. T Hth—3C 124
Furze St. E3—5C 64
Fyfe Way. Brom—2J 127
Fyfield Clo. Brom—3F 127
Fyfield Rd. E17—3F 33
Fyfield Rd. SW9—3A 94
Fyfield Rd. Enf—3K 7
Fyfield Rd. Wfd G—7F 21
Fynes St. SW1—4H 77 (8A 146)

Gable Clo. Pinn—1E 22
Gable Ct. SE26—4H 111
Gables Clo. SE12—1J 113
Gabriel Clo. Felt—4C 102
Gabriel Clo. Wemb—3F 41
Gabrielle Ct. NW3—6B 44
Gabriel St. SE23—7K 95
Gaddesden Av. Wemb—6F 41
Gadsbury Clo. NW9—6B 26
Gadwall Way. SE28—2H 83
Gage Rd. E16—5G 65
Gage St. WC1—5J 61 (5D 140)
Gainford St. N1—1A 62
Gainsborough Av. E12—5E 50
Gainsborough Clo. Beck
—7C 112
Gainsborough Ct. N12—5E 14
Gainsborough Gdns. NW3
—3B 44
Gainsborough Gdns. NW11
—7H 27
Gainsborough Gdns. Edgw
—2F 25
Gainsborough Gdns. Gnfd
—5J 39
Gainsborough Gdns. Iswth
—5H 87

Gainsborough M. SE26—3H 111
Gainsborough Rd. E11—7G 33
Gainsborough Rd. E15—3G 65
Gainsborough Rd. N12—5E 14
Gainsborough Rd. W4—4B 74
Gainsborough Rd. Dag—4B 52
Gainsborough Rd. N Mald
—7K 119
Gainsborough Rd. Rich—2F 89
Gainsborough Rd. Wfd G
—6H 21
Gainsborough Sq. Bexh
—3D 100
Gainsford Rd. E17—4B 32
Gainsford St. SE1
—2F 79 (4E 148)
Gairloch Rd. SE5—2E 94
Gaisford St. NW5—6G 45
Gaitskell Rd. SE9—1G 115
Galahad Rd. Brom—4J 113
Galata Rd. SW13—7C 74
Galatea Sq. SE15—3H 95
Galbraith St. E14—3E 80
Galdana Av. Barn—3F 5
Galeborough Av. Wfd G—7A 20
Gale Clo. Hmptn—6C 102
Gale Clo. Mitc—3B 122
Galena Rd. W6—4D 74
Galesbury Rd. SW18—6A 92
Gales Gdns. E2—3H 63 (2K 143)
Gale St. E3—5C 64
Gale St. Dag—5C 52
Gales Way. Wfd G—7H 21
Galgate Clo. SW19—1G 107
Gallants Farm Rd. Barn—7H 5
Galleon Clo. SE16
—2K 79 (4M 149)
Gallery Gdns. N'holt—2B 54
Gallery Rd. SE21—1D 110
Galleywall Rd. SE16
—4H 79 (9K 149)
Galleywall Rd. Trading Est.
SE16—4H 79 (9K 149)
Galliard Clo. N9—6D 8
Galliard Ct. N9—6B 8
Galliard Rd. N9—7B 8
Gallia Rd. N5—5B 46
Gallions Clo. Bark—3A 68
Gallions Entrance. E16—1G 83
Gallions Rd. E16—7F 67
Gallions Rd. SE7—4K 81
Galliver Pl. E5—4H 47
Gallon Clo. SE7—4A 82
Gallop, The. S Croy—7J 135
Gallop, The. Sutt—7B 132
Gallosson Rd. SE18—4J 83
Galloway Rd. W12—1C 74
Gallus Clo. N21—6E 6
Gallus Sq. SE3—3K 97
Galpins Rd. T Hth—5J 123
Galsworthy Av. Romf—6B 36
Galsworthy Clo. SE28—1B 84
Galsworthy Cres. SE3—1A 98
Galsworthy Rd. NW2—4G 43
Galsworthy Rd. King—1H 119
Galsworthy Ter. N16—3E 46
Galton St. W10—3G 59
Galva Clo. Barn—4K 5
Galveston Rd. SW15—5H 91
Galway St. EC1—3C 62 (2M 141)
Gambetta St. SW8—2F 93
Gambia St. SE1—1B 78 (3K 147)
Gambole Rd. SW17—4C 108
Gambra Ct. N13—3D 16
Games Rd. Barn—3J 5
Gamlen Rd. SW15—4F 91
Gamuel Rd. E17—7B 32
Gander Grn. La. Sutt—2G 131
Gandhi Clo. E17—6C 32
Ganton St. W1—7G 61 (9L 139)
Gantshill Cres. Ilf—5E 34
Gants Hill Cross. Ilf—6E 34
Gap Rd. SW19—5J 107
Garage Rd. W3—6G 57
Garbutt Pl. W1—5E 60 (6H 139)
Garden Av. Bexh—3G 101
Garden Av. Mitc—7F 109

Garden City. Edgw—6B 12
Garden Clo. E4—5H 19
Garden Clo. SE12—3K 113
Garden Clo. SW15—7D 90
Garden Clo. Hmptn—5D 102
Garden Clo. N'holt—1C 54
Garden Clo. Wall—5J 133
Garden Ct. Rich—1F 89
Garden Ct. E3—2K 63
Gardeners Rd. Croy—1B 134
Gardenia Rd. Enf—6K 7
Garden La. SW2—1K 109
Garden La. Brom—6K 113
Garden M. W2—7J 59
Garden Rd. NW8
—3A 60 (1A 138)
Garden Rd. SE20—1J 125
Garden Rd. Brom—7K 113
Garden Rd. Rich—3G 89
Garden Row. SE1
—3B 78 (7J 147)
Gardens, The. SE22—4G 95
Gardens, The. Beck—2F 127
Gardens, The. Harr—6G 23
Gardens, The. Pinn—6D 22
Garden St. E1—5K 63
Garden Ter. SW1
—5H 77 (9M 145)
Garden Wlk. EC2
—3E 62 (2C 142)
Garden Wlk. Beck—1B 126
Gardiner Av. NW2—5E 42
Gardiner Av. NW10—5E 42
Gardiner Ct. S Croy—6C 134
Gardiners Rd. N1—7E 46
Gardiner Clo. E11—6K 33
Gardner Gro. Felt—2D 102
Gardner Rd. E13—4K 65
Gardners La. EC4
—7C 62 (9L 141)
Gardnor Rd. NW3—4B 44
Gard St. EC1—3B 62 (1K 141)
Garendon Gdns. Mord—7K 121
Garendon Rd. Mord—7K 121
Garenne Ct. E4—1K 19
Gareth Clo. Wor Pk—2F 131
Gareth Gro. Brom—4J 113
Garfield Rd. E4—1A 20
Garfield Rd. E13—4H 65
Garfield Rd. SW11—3E 92
Garfield Rd. SW19—5A 108
Garfield Rd. Enf—4D 8
Garfield Rd. Twic—1A 104
Garford St. E14—7C 64
Garganey Wlk. SE28—7C 68
Garibaldi St. SE18—4J 83
Garland Rd. SE18—7H 83
Garland Rd. Stan—1E 24
Garlick Hill. EC4
—7C 62 (9M 141)
Garlies Rd. SE23—3A 112
Garlinge Rd. NW2—6H 43
Garman Rd. N17—7D 18
Garnault Pl. EC1
—3A 62 (2H 141)
Garnault Rd. Enf—1A 8
Garner Rd. E17—1E 32
Garner St. E2—2G 63 (1G 143)
Garnet Rd. NW10—6A 42
Garnet Rd. T Hth—4C 124
Garnet St. E1—7J 63 (1L 149)
Garnett Clo. SE9—3D 98
Garnett Rd. NW3—5D 44
Garnet Wlk. E6—5C 66
Garnet Way. E17—1A 32
Garnham Clo. N16—2F 47
Garnham St. N16—2F 47
Garnies Clo. SE15—7F 79
Garrad's Rd. SW16—3H 109
Garrard Clo. Bexh—3G 101
Garrard Clo. Chst—5F 115
Garrard Wlk. NW10—6A 42
Garratt Clo. Croy—4J 133
Garratt La.—6K 91
SW18 1-643 & 2-480
SW17 remainder
Garratts Rd. Bush, Wat—1B 10

Garratt Ter. SW17—4C 108
Garrett Rd. Edgw—7B 12
Garrett St. EC1—4C 62 (3M 141)
Garrick Av. NW11—6G 27
Garrick Clo. W5—4E 56
Garrick Clo. Iswth—3A 88
Garrick Clo. Rich—5D 88
Garrick Cres. Croy—2E 134
Garrick Dri. NW4—2E 26
Garrick Dri. SE28—3H 83
Garrick Pk. NW4—2F 27
Garrick Rd. NW9—6B 26
Garrick Rd. Gnfd—4F 55
Garrick Rd. Rich—2G 89
Garrick St. WC2—7J 61 (9C 140)
Garrick Way. NW4—4F 27
Garrison Clo. SE18—7E 82
Garrowsfield. Barn—5C 4
Garry Way. Romf—1K 37
Garside Clo. SE28—3H 83
Garside Clo. Hmptn—6F 103
Garsington. M.SE4—3B 96
Garth Clo. W4—5K 73
Garth Clo. King—5F 105
Garth Clo. Mord—7F 121
Garth Clo. Ruis—1B 38
Garth Ct. W4—5K 73
Garthorne Rd. SE23—7K 95
Garth Rd. NW2—2H 43
Garth Rd. W4—5K 73
Garth Rd. King—5F 105
Garth Rd. Mord—7F 121
Garthside. Rich—5E 104
Garth, The. Hmptn—6F 103
Garth, The. Harr—6F 25
Garthway. N12—6H 15
Gartmoor Gdns. SW19—1H 107
Gartmore Rd. Ilf—2C 54
Garton Pl. SW18—6A 92
Gartons Way. SW11—3A 92
Garvary Rd. E16—6K 65
Garway Rd. W2—6K 59
Gascoigne Gdns. Wfd G—7B 20
Gascoigne Pl. E2
    —3F 63 (2E 142)
Gascoigne Rd. Bark—1G 67
Gascoigne Rd. Croy—7F 137
Gascony Av. NW6—7J 43
Gascoyne Rd. E9—7K 47
Gaselee St. E14—7E 64
Gasholder Pl. SE11—5K 77
Gaskarth Rd. SW12—6F 93
Gaskarth Rd. Edgw—1J 25
Gaskell Rd. N6—6D 28
Gaskell St. SW4—2J 93
Gaskin St. N1—1B 62
Gaspar M. SW5—4K 75
Gassiot Rd. SW17—4D 108
Gassiot Way. Sutt—3B 132
Gastein Rd. W6—6F 75
Gaston Bell Clo. Rich—3F 89
Gaston Rd. Mitc—3E 122
Gatcombe Ct. Beck—7C 112
Gatcombe Rd. N19—3H 45
Gate Centre. The. Bren—7A 72
Gateforth St. NW8
    —4C 60 (4C 138)
Gatehouse Clo. King—7J 105
Gateley Rd. SW9—3K 93
Gatesborough St. EC2
    —4E 62 (3C 142)
Gates Grn. Rd. W Wick & Kes
    —3H 137
Gateside Rd. SW17—3D 108
Gatestone Rd. SE19—6E 110
Gate St. WC2—6K 61 (7E 140)
Gateway SE17—6C 78
Gateway Trading Est. NW10
    —3B 58
Gatfield Gro. Felt—2E 102
Gathorne Rd. N22—1A 30
Gathorne St. E2—2K 63
Gatliff Rd. SW1—5F 77
Gatling Rd. SE2—5A 84
Gatting Clo. Edgw—7D 12
Gatton Rd SW17—4C 108

Gattons Way. Sidc—4F 117
Gatward Clo. N21—6G 7
Gatward Grn. N9—2A 18
Gatwick Rd. SW18—7H 91
Gauden Clo. SW4—3H 93
Gauden Rd. SW4—2H 93
Gauntlett Clo. N'holt—7C 38
Gauntlett Ct. Wemb—5B 40
Gauntlett Rd. Sutt—5B 132
Gaunt St. SE1—3C 78 (6L 147)
Gautrey Rd. SE15—2J 95
Gautrey Sq. E6—6D 66
Gavel St. SE17—4D 78 (8B 148)
Gaverick St. E14—4C 80
Gavestone Cres. SE12—7K 97
Gavestone Rd. SE12—7K 97
Gavina Clo. Mord—5C 122
Gawber St. E2—3J 63 (1M 143)
Gawsworth Clo. E15—5H 49
Gawthorne Av. NW7—5B 14
Gay Clo. NW2—5D 42
Gaydon La. NW9—1A 26
Gayfere Rd. Eps—5C 130
Gayfere Rd. Ilf—3D 34
Gayfere St. SW1
    —3J 77 (7C 146)
Gayford Rd. W12—2B 74
Gay Gdns. Dag—4J 53
(in two parts)
Gayhurst Rd. E8—7G 47
Gaylor Rd. N'holt—5D 38
Gaynesford Rd. SE23—2K 111
Gaynesford Rd. Cars—7D 132
Gaynes Hill Rd. Wfd G—6H 21
Gay Rd. E15—2F 65
Gaysham Av. Ilf—5E 34
Gaysham Hall. Ilf—3F 35
Gayton Cres. NW3—4B 44
Gayton Rd. NW3—4B 44
Gayton Rd. SE2—3C 84
Gayton Rd. Harr—6K 23
Gayville Rd. SW11—6D 92
Gaywood Clo. SW2—1K 109
Gaywood Rd. E17—3C 32
Gaywood St. SE1
    —3B 78 (7K 147)
Gaza St. SE17—5B 78
Geariesville Gdns. Ilf—4F 35
Geary Rd. NW10—5C 42
Geary St. N7—5K 45
Geddes Pl. Bexh—4G 101
Gedeney Rd. N17—1C 30
Gedling Pl. SE1—3F 79 (6F 148)
Geere Rd. E15—1H 65
Gees Ct. W1—6E 60 (8H 139)
Gee St. EC1—4C 62 (3L 141)
Geffrye Ct. N1—2E 62 (1D 142)
Geffrye St. E2—2F 63 (1E 142)
Geldart Rd. SE15—7H 79
Geldeston Rd. E5—2G 47
Gellatly Rd. SE14—2J 95
Gelsthorpe Rd. Romf—1H 37
Gemini Gro. N'holt—3C 54
General Gordon Pl. SE18—4F 83
General Wolfe Rd. SE10—1F 97
Genesta Rd. SE18—6F 83
Geneva Dri. SW9—4A 94
Geneva Gdns. Romf—5E 36
Geneva Rd. King—4E 118
Geneva Rd. T Hth—5C 124
Genever Clo. E4—5H 19
Genista Rd. N18—5C 18
Genoa Av. SW15—5E 90
Genoa Rd. SE20—1J 125
Genotin Rd. Enf—4J 7
Genotin Ter. Enf—4J 7
Gentian Row. SE13—1E 96
Gentlemans Row. Enf—3H 7
Gentry Gdns. E13—4J 65
Geoffrey Gdns. E6—2C 66
Geoffrey Rd. SE4—3B 96
George & Catherine Wheel All.
    EC2—5E 62 (5D 142)
George Beard Rd. SE8—4B 80
George Comberton Wlk. E12
    —5E 50

George Cres. N10—7K 15
George V Av. Pinn—2D 22
George V Clo. Pinn—3E 22
George V Way. Gnfd—1B 56
George Inn Yd. SE1
    —1D 78 (3A 148)
George La. E18—2J & 3K 33
George La. SE13—6E 96
George La. Brom—1H 137
George Rd. E4—6H 19
George Rd. King—7H 105
George Rd. N Mald—4B 120
George Row SE16
    —2G 79 (5G 149)
George Sq. SW19—3J 121
George's Rd. N7—5K 45
George St. E16—6H 65
George St. W1—6D 60 (7E 138)
George St. W7—1J 71
George St. Bark—7G 51
George St. Croy—2D 134
George St. Houn—2D 86
George St. Rich—5D 88
George St. S'hall—4C 70
George St. Sutt—5K 131
Georgetown Clo. SE19—5E 110
Georgette Pl. SE10—7E 80
Georgeville Gdns. Ilf—4F 35
George Wyver Clo. SW19
    —7G 91
George Yd. EC3—6D 62 (8B 142)
George Yd. W1—7E 60 (9H 139)
Georgiana St. NW1—1G 61
Georgian Clo. Brom—1K 137
Georgian Clo. Stan—7F 11
Georgian Ct. Barn—4F 5
Georgian Ct. Wemb—6H 41
Georgian Way. Harr—2H 39
Georgia Rd. N Mald—4J 119
Georgia Rd. T Hth—1B 124
Georgina Gdns. E2
    —3F 63 (1F 142)
Geraint Rd. Brom—4H 113
Geraldine Rd. SW18—5A 92
Geraldine Rd. W4—6G 73
Geraldine St. SE11
    —3B 78 (7J 147)
Gerald Rd. E16—4H 65
Gerald Rd. SW1—4E 76 (8H 145)
Gerald Rd. Dag—1F 53
Gerard Av. Houn—7E 86
Gerard Gdns. Rain—2K 69
Gerard Rd. SW13—1B 90
Gerard Rd. Harr—6A 24
Gerda Rd. SE9—2G 115
Germander Way. E15—3G 65
Gernon Rd. E3—2A 64
Geron Way. NW2—2D 42
Gerrard Pl. W1—7H 61 (9B 140)
Gerrard Rd. N1—2B 62
Gerrards Clo. N14—5B 6
Gerrards Ct. W5—3D 72
Gerrard St. W1—7H 61 (9B 140)
Gerridge St. SE1
    —3A 78 (6H 147)
Gerry Raffles Sq. E15—7F 49
Gertrude Rd. Belv—4G 85
Gertrude St. SW10—6A 76
Gervase Clo. Wemb—3J 41
Gervase Rd. Edgw—1J 25
Gervase St. SE15—7H 79
Ghent St. SE6—2C 112
Ghent Way. E8—6F 47
Giant Tree Hill. Bush, Wat
    —1C 10
Gibbins Rd. E15—7E 48
Gibbon Rd. SE15—2J 95
Gibbon Rd. W3—7A 58
Gibbon Rd. King—1E 118
Gibbons Rd. NW10—6A 42
Gibbon Wlk. SW15—4C 90
Gibbs Av. SE19—5D 110
Gibbs Clo. SE19—5D 110
Gibbs Grn. W14—5H 75
Gibbs Grn. Edgw—5D 12
Gibb's Rd N18—4D 18
Gibbs Sq. SE19—5D 110

Gibraltar Wlk. E2
    —3F 63 (2F 142)
Gibson Clo. E1—4J 63 (3M 143)
Gibson Clo. Iswth—3J 87
Gibson Gdns. N16—2F 47
Gibson Rd. SE11
    —4K 77 (9F 146)
Gibson Rd. Dag—1C 52
Gibson Rd. Sutt—5K 131
Gibsons Hill. SW16—7A 110
Gibson Sq. N1—1A 62
Gibson St. SE10—5G 81
Gideon Clo. Belv—4H 85
Gideon Rd. SW11—3E 92
Giesbach Rd. N19—2H 45
Giffard Rd. N18—6K 17
Giffin St. SE8—7C 80
Gifford Gdns. W7—5H 55
Gifford St. N1—7J 45
Gift La. E15—1H 65
Giggshill Gdns. Th Dit—7A 118
Giggshill Rd. Th Dit—7A 118
Gilbert Gro. Edgw—1K 25
Gilbert Pl. WC1—5J 61 (6C 140)
Gilbert Rd. SE11
    —4A 78 (9H 147)
Gilbert Rd. SW19—7A 108
Gilbert Rd. Belv—3G 85
Gilbert Rd. Brom—7J 113
Gilbert Rd. Pinn—4B 22
Gilbert St. E15—4G 49
Gilbert St. W1—6E 60 (8H 139)
Gilbert St. Houn—3G 87
Gilbey Rd. SW17—4C 108
Gilbourne Rd. SE18—6K 83
Gilda Av. Enf—5F 9
Gilda Cres. N16—1G 47
Gildea Clo. Pinn—5F 11
Gildea St. W1—5F 61 (6K 139)
Gilden Cres. NW5—5E 44
Gildersome St. SE18—6E 82
Giles Coppice. SE19—4F 111
Gilkes Cres. SE21—6E 94
Gilkes Pl. SE21—6E 94
Gill Av. E16—6J 65
Gillender St.—4E 64
    E14 43-50
    E3 remainder
Gillespie Rd. N5—3A 46
Gillett Av. E6—2C 66
Gillett Rd. T Hth—4D 124
Gillett St. N16—5E 46
Gillham Ter. N17—6B 18
Gillian Grn. Bush, Wat—2B 10
Gillian Pk. Rd. Sutt—1H 131
Gillian St. SE13—5D 96
Gillies St. NW5—5E 44
Gilling Ct. NW3—6C 44
Gillingham M. SW1
    —4G 77 (8L 145)
Gillingham Rd. NW2—3G 43
Gillingham Row. SW1
    —4G 77 (8L 145)
Gillingham St. SW1
    —4G 77 (8L 145)
Gillison Wlk. SE16
    —3G 79 (6H 149)
Gillman Dri. E15—1H 65
Gill St. E14—6B 64
Gillum Clo. Barn—1J 15
Gilmore Ct. N11—5J 15
Gilmore Rd. SE13—4F 97
Gilpin Av. SW14—4K 89
Gilpin Clo. Mitc—2C 122
Gilpin Cres. N18—5A 18
Gilpin Cres. Twic—7F 87
Gilpin Rd. E5—4A 48
Gilsland Rd. T Hth—4D 124
Gilstead Rd. SW6—2K 91
Gilston Rd. SW10—5A 76
Gilton Rd. SE6—3G 113
Giltspur St. EC1—6B 62 (7K 141)
Gilwell Clo. E4—4J 9
Gilwell La. E4—4K 9
Gippeswyck Clo. Pinn—1B 22
Gipsy Corner. W3—5K 57
Gipsy Hill. SE19—5E 110
Gipsy La. SW15—3D 90

Gloucester Rd. N18—5A 18
Gloucester Rd. SW7
   —3A 76 (8A 144)
Gloucester Rd. W3—2J 73
Gloucester Rd. W5—2C 72
Gloucester Rd. Barn—5E 4
Gloucester Rd. Belv—5F 83
Gloucester Rd. Croy—7D 124
Gloucester Rd. Enf—1H 7
Gloucester Rd. Felt—1A 102
Gloucester Rd. Hmptn—7F 103
Gloucester Rd. Harr—5F 23
Gloucester Rd. Houn—4C 86
Gloucester Rd. King—2G 119
Gloucester Rd. Rich—7G 73
Gloucester Rd. Tedd—5J 103
Gloucester Rd. Twic—1G 103
Gloucester Sq. W2
   —6B 60 (8B 138)
Gloucester St. SW1
   —5G 77 (9L 145)
Gloucester Ter. W2
   —6K 59 (8A 138)
Gloucester Wlk. W8—2J 75
Gloucester Way. EC1
   —3A 62 (2H 141)
Glover Rd. Pinn—6B 22
Gloxinia Wlk. Hmptn—6E 102
Glycena Rd. SW11—3D 92
Glyn Av. Barn—4G 5
Glyn Clo. SE25—2E 124
Glynde Rd. Bexh—3D 100
Glynde St. SE4—6B 96
Glyndon Rd. SE18—4G 83
Glyn Dri. Sidc—4B 116
Glynfield Rd. NW10—7A 42
Glynne Rd. N22—2A 30
Glyn Rd. E5—3K 47
Glyn Rd. Enf—4D 8
Glyn Rd. Wor Pk—2F 131
Glyn St. SE11—5K 77
Glynwood Dri. SE23—2J 111
Goat La. Enf—1A 8
Goat Rd. Mitc—7E 122
Goat Wharf. Bren—6E 72
Gobions Av. Romf—1K 37
Godalming Av. Wall—5J 133
Godalming Rd. E14—5D 64
Godbold Rd. E15—3G 65
Goddard Ct. Harr—2A 24
Goddard Rd. Beck—4K 125
Godfrey Av. N'holt—1C 54
Godfrey Av. Twic—7H 87
Godfrey Hill. SE18—4C 82
Godfrey Rd. SE18—4D 82
Godfrey St. E15—2E 64
Godfrey St. SW3
   —5C 76 (9D 144)
Godfrey Way. Houn—7D 86
Goding St. SE11—5K 77
Godley Rd. SW18—1B 108
Godliman St. EC4
   —6C 62 (8L 141)
Godman Rd. SE15—2H 95
Godolphin Pl. W3—7K 57
Godolphin Rd. W12—2D 74
Godric Cres. Croy—7F 137
Godson Rd. Croy—3A 134
Godson St. N1—2A 62
Godstone Rd. Sutt—4A 132
Godstone Rd. Twic—6B 88
Godstow Rd. SE2—2C 84
Godwin Rd. E7—4K 49
Godwin Rd. Brom—3A 128
Goffers Rd. SE3—1G 97
Goidel Clo. Wall—4H 133
Golborne Gdns. W10—4G 59
Golborne M. W10—5G 59
Golborne Rd. W10—5G 59
Golda Clo. Barn—6A 4
Goldbeaters Gro. Edgw—6F 13
Goldcliffe Clo. Mord—7J 121
Goldcrest Clo. E16—5B 66
Goldcrest Clo. SE28—7C 68
Goldcrest M. W5—5D 56
Goldcrest Way. Bush, Wat
   —1B 10

Goldcrest Way. Croy—7F 137
Golden Ct. Rich—5D 88
Golden La. EC1 & EC2
   —4C 62 (3L 141)
Golden La. Est. EC1
   —4C 62 (4L 141)
Golden Mnr. W7—7J 55
Golden M. SE20—1J 125
Golden Sq. W1—7G 61 (9M 139)
Golders Clo. Edgw—5C 12
Golders Gdns. NW11—7G 27
Golders Grn. Cres. NW11
   —7H 27
Golders Grn. Rd. NW11—6G 27
Golders Mnr. Dri. NW11—6F 27
Golders Pk. Clo. NW11—1J 43
Golders Rise. NW4—5F 27
Golders Way. NW11—7H 27
Goldfinch Rd. SE28—3H 83
Goldhawk M. W12—2D 74
Goldhawk Rd.—4B 74
 W12 1-309 & 2-310
 W6 remainder
Goldhaze Clo. Wfd G—7G 21
Gold Hill. Edgw—6E 12
Goldhurst Ter. NW6—7K 43
Golding St. E1—6G 63 (8H 143)
Goldington Cres. NW1—2H 61
Goldington St. NW1—2H 61
Gold La. Edgw—6E 12
Goldman Clo. E2
   —4G 63 (3G 143)
Goldney Rd. W9—4J 59
Goldsborough Cres. E4—2J 19
Goldsborough Rd. SW8—7H 77
Goldsdown Clo. Enf—2F 9
Goldsdown Rd. Enf—2E 8
Goldsmid St. SE18—5J 83
Goldsmith Av. E12—6C 50
Goldsmith Av. NW9—5A 26
Goldsmith Av. W3—7K 57
Goldsmith Av. Romf—7G 37
Goldsmith Clo. W3—1K 73
Goldsmith Clo. Harr—1F 39
Goldsmith La. NW9—4H 25
Goldsmith Rd. E10—1D 48
Goldsmith Rd. E17—2K 31
Goldsmith Rd. N11—5J 15
Goldsmith Rd. SE15—1G 95
Goldsmith Rd. W3—1K 73
Goldsmith's Row. E2—2G 63
Goldsmith's Sq. E2—2G 63
Goldsmith St. EC2
   —6C 62 (7M 141)
Goldsworthy Gdns. SE16
   —5J 79 (9M 149)
Goldwell Rd. T Hth—4K 123
Goldwin Clo. SE14—1J 95
Golf Clo. Stan—7H 11
Golf Club Dri. King—7K 105
Golfe Rd. Ilf—3H 51
Golf Rd. W5—6F 57
Golf Rd. Brom—3E 128
Golf Side. Twic—3H 103
Golfside Clo. N Mald—2A 120
Goliath Clo. Wall—7J 133
Gollogly Ter. SE7—6A 82
Gomer Gdns. Tedd—6A 104
Gomer Pl. Tedd—6A 104
Gomm Rd. SE16
   —3J 79 (7M 149)
Gomshall Av. Wall—5J 133
Gondar Gdns. NW6—5H 43
Gonson St. SE8—6D 80
Gonston Clo. SW19—2G 107
Gonville Cres. N'holt—6F 39
Gonville Rd. T Hth—5K 123
Gonville St. SW6—3G 91
Goodall Rd. E11—3E 48
Gooden Ct. Harr—3J 39
Goodenough Rd. SW19—7H 107
Goodge Pl. W1—5G 61 (6M 139)
Goodge St. W1—5G 61 (6M 139)
Goodhall St. NW10—3B 58
 (in two parts)
Goodhart Way. W Wick
   —7G 127

Goodhew Rd. SE25—6G 125
Gooding Clo. N Mald—4J 119
Goodinge Clo. N7—6J 45
Goodman Cres. SW2—2H 109
Goodman Rd. E10—7E 32
Goodman's Ct. E1
   —7F 63 (9E 142)
Goodmans Ct. Wemb—4D 40
Goodman's Stile. E1
   —6G 63 (7G 143)
Goodman's Yd. E1
   —7F 63 (9E 142)
Goodmayes Av. Ilf—1A 52
Goodmayes La. Ilf—3A 52
Goodmayes Rd. Ilf—1A 52
Goodrich Rd. SE22—6F 95
Goodson Rd. NW10—7A 42
Goods Way. NW1—1H 61
Goodway Gdns. E14—6F 65
Goodwin Clo. SE16
   —3G 79 (7G 149)
Goodwin Clo. Mitc—3B 122
Goodwin Clo. SW19—7C 108
Goodwin Dri. Sidc—3D 116
Goodwin Gdns. Croy—6B 134
Goodwin Rd. N9—1E 18
Goodwin Rd. W12—2C 74
Goodwin Rd. Croy—5B 134
Goodwins Ct. WC2
   —7J 61 (9C 140)
Goodwin St. N4—2A 46
Goodwood Clo. Mord—4J 121
Goodwood Clo. Stan—5H 11
Goodwood Dri. N'holt—6E 38
Goodwood Pde. Beck—4A 126
Goodwood Rd. SE14—7A 80
Goodwyn Av. NW7—5F 13
Goodwyns Vale. N10—1F 29
Goodyear Pl. SE5—6C 78
Goodyers Gdns. NW4—5F 27
Goosander Way. SE26—3H 83
Gooseacre La. Harr—5D 24
Gooseley La. E6—3E 66
Goose Sq. E6—6D 66
Goossens Clo. Sutt—5A 132
Gophir La. EC4—7D 62 (9A 142)
Gopsall St. N1—1D 62
Gordon Av. E4—6B 20
Gordon Av. SW14—4A 90
Gordon Av. Stan—7E 10
Gordon Av. Twic—5A 88
Gordonbrock Rd. SE4—5C 96
Gordon Clo. E17—6C 32
Gordon Clo. N19—2G 45
Gordon Ct. W12—6E 58
Gordon Cres. Croy—1F 135
Gordondale Rd. SW19—2J 107
Gordon Gdns. Edgw—2H 25
Gordon Gro. SE5—2B 94
Gordon Hill. Enf—1H 7
Gordon Ho. Rd. NW5—4E 44
Gordon Pl. W8—2J 75
Gordon Rd. E4—1B 20
Gordon Rd. E11—6J 33
Gordon Rd. E15—4E 48
Gordon Rd. E18—1K 33
Gordon Rd. N3—7C 14
Gordon Rd. N9—2C 18
Gordon Rd. N11—7C 16
Gordon Rd. SE15—2H 95
Gordon Rd. W4—6H 73
Gordon Rd.—7B 56
 W5 1-95 & 2-84
 W13 remainder
Gordon Rd. Bark—1J 67
Gordon Rd. Beck—2K 125
 (Elmers End)
Gordon Rd. Beck—3B 126
 (Eden Park)
Gordon Rd. Belv—4J 85
Gordon Rd. Cars—6D 132
Gordon Rd. Enf—1H 7
Gordon Rd. Harr—3J 23
Gordon Rd. Houn—4G 87
Gordon Rd. Ilf—3H 51
Gordon Rd. King—1F 119
Gordon Rd. Rich—2F 89

Gordon Rd. Romf—6F 37
Gordon Rd. Sidc—5J 99
Gordon Rd. S'hall—4C 70
Gordon Rd. Surb—7F 119
Gordon Sq. WC1
   —4H 61 (3B 140)
Gordon St. E13—3J 65
Gordon St. WC1
   —4H 61 (3A 140)
Gordon Way. Barn—4C 4
Gore Ct. NW9—5G 25
Gorefield Pl. NW6—2J 59
Gore Rd. E9—1J 63
Gore Rd. SW20—2E 120
Goresbrook Rd. Dag—1B 68
Gore St. SW7—3A 76 (6A 144)
Gorham Pl. W11—7G 59
Goring Clo. Romf—1J 37
Goring Gdns. Dag—4C 52
Goring Rd. N11—6D 16
Goring Rd. Dag—6K 53
Goring Way. Gnfd—2G 55
Gorleston Rd. N15—5D 30
Gorleston St. W14—4G 75
Gorman Rd. SE18—4D 82
Gorringe Pk. Av. Mitc—7E 108
Gorse Rise. SW17—5E 108
Gorse Rd. Croy—4C 136
Gorseway. Romf—2K 53
Gorst Rd. NW10—4J 57
Gorst Rd. SW11—6D 92
Gorsuch Pl. E2—3F 63 (1E 142)
Gorsuch St. E2—3F 63 (1E 142)
Gosberton St. SW12—1E 108
Gosfield Rd. Dag—2G 53
Gosfield St. W1—5G 61 (5L 139)
Gosford Gdns. Ilf—5D 34
Goslett Yd. WC2
   —6H 61 (8B 140)
Gosling Clo. Gnfd—3E 54
Gosling Way. SW9—1A 94
Gospatrick Rd. N17—7H 17
Gospel Oak Est. NW5—5D 44
Gosport Rd. E17—5B 32
Gosport Wlk. N17—4H 31
Gosport Way. SE15—7F 79
Gossage Rd. SE18—5H 83
Gosset St. E2—3F 63 (2F 142)
Gosshill Rd. Chst—2E 128
Gossington Clo. Chst—4F 115
Gosterwood St. SE8—6A 80
Gostling Rd. Twic—1E 102
Goston Gdns. T Hth—3A 124
Goswell Rd. EC1—3B 62 (1J 141)
Gothic Rd. Twic—2H 103
Goudhurst Rd. Brom—5G 113
Gough Rd. E15—4H 49
Gough Rd. Enf—2C 8
Gough Sq. EC4—6A 62 (7H 141)
Gough St. WC1—4K 61 (4F 140)
Gough Wlk. E14—6C 64
Gould Rd. Twic—1J 103
Gould Ter. E8—5H 47
Goulston St. E1—6F 63 (7E 142)
Goulton Rd. E5—4H 47
Gourley Pl. N15—5E 30
Gourley St. N15—5E 30
Gourock Rd. SE9—5E 98
Govan St. E2—1G 63
Govier Clo. E15—7G 49
Gowan Av. SW6—1G 91
Gowan Rd. NW10—6D 42
Gower Ct. WC1—4H 61 (3A 140)
Gower M. WC1—5H 61 (6B 140)
Gower Pl. WC1—4H 61 (3A 140)
Gower Rd. E7—6J 49
Gower St. Iswth—6K 71
Gower St. WC1—4G 61 (3M 139)
Gowers Wlk. E1—6G 63 (8G 143)
Gowland Pl. Beck—2B 126
Gowlett Rd. SE15—3G 95
Gowrie Rd. SW11—3E 92
Grace Av. Bexh—2F 101
Gracechurch St. EC3
   —7D 62 (9B 142)
Grace Clo. SE9—3B 114
Grace Clo. Edgw—7D 12

Gt. Maze Pond. SE1
—2D 78 (4B 148)
(in two parts)
Gt. Newport St. WC2
—7J 61 (9C 140)
Gt. New St. EC4—6A 62 (7H 141)
Gt. North Rd.—5C 28
N6 2-66
N2 remainder
Gt. North Rd. Barn—5D 4
(High Barnet)
Gt. North Rd. Barn—2C 4
(New Barnet)
Gt. North Way. NW4—2D 26
Greatorex St. E1
—5G 63 (5G 143)
Gt. Ormond St. WC1
—5J 61 (5D 140)
Gt. Owl Rd. Chig—3K 21
Gt. Percy St. WC1
—3K 61 (1F 140)
Gt. Peter St. SW1
—3H 77 (7B 146)
Gt. Portland St. W1
—4F 61 (4K 139)
Gt. Pulteney St. W1
—7G 61 (9M 139)
Gt. Queen St. WC2
—6J 61 (7D 140)
Gt. Russell St. WC1
—6H 61 (7B 140)
Gt. Saint Helen's. EC3
—6E 62 (7C 142)
Gt. Saint Thomas Apostle. EC4
—7C 62 (9M 141)
Gt. Scotland Yd. SW1
—1J 77 (2C 146)
Gt. Smith St. SW1
—3H 77 (6B 146)
Gt. South West Rd. Felt & Houn
—2A 86
Gt. Spilmans. SE22—5E 94
Gt. Strand. NW9—1B 26
Gt. Suffolk St. SE1
—1B 78 (3K 147)
Gt. Sutton St. EC1
—4B 62 (4K 141)
Gt. Swan All. EC2
—6D 62 (7A 142)
Gt. Thrift. Orp—4G 129
Gt. Titchfield St. W1
—5G 61 (5L 139)
Gt. Tower St. EC3
—7E 62 (1D 148)
Gt. Trinity La. EC4
—7C 62 (9M 141)
Gt. Turnstile. WC1
—5K 61 (6F 140)
Gt. Western Industrial Pk. S'hall
—2F 71
Gt. Western Rd.—5H 59
W9 1-59 & 2-56
W11 remainder
Gt. West Rd. W4 & W6—5B 74
Gt. West Rd. Houn, Iswth & Bren
—2B 86
Gt. West Rd. Trading Est. Bren
—7B 72
Gt. Winchester St. EC2
—6D 62 (7B 142)
Gt. Windmill St. W1
—7H 61 (9A 140)
Greatwood. Chst—7E 114
Greaves Pl. SW17—4C 108
Grecian Cres. SE19—6B 110
Greek Ct. W1—6H 61 (8B 140)
Greek St. W1—6H 61 (8B 140)
Greenacre Clo. Barn—1C 4
Greenacres. SE9—6E 98
Greenacres. Bush, Wat—2C 10
Green Acres. Croy—3F 135
Greenacres Dri. Stan—7G 11
Greenacre Sq. SE16—2K 79
Greenacre Wlk. N14—3C 16
Green Av. NW7—4E 12
Green Av. W13—3B 72
Greenaway Gdns. NW3—4K 43

Green Bank. E1—1G 79 (2H 149)
Green Bank. N12—4E 14
Greenbank Av. Wemb—5A 40
Green Bank Clo. E4—2K 19
Greenbank Cres. NW4—4G 27
Greenbay Rd. SE7—7B 82
Greenberry St. NW8
—2C 60 (1C 138)
Greenbrook Av. Barn—1F 5
Green Clo. NW9—6J 25
Green Clo. N11—7A 28
Green Clo. Brom—3G 127
Green Clo. Cars—2D 132
Green Clo. Felt—5C 102
Greencoat Pl. SW1
—4G 77 (8M 145)
Greencoat Row. SW1
—3G 77 (7M 145)
Greencourt Av. Croy—2H 135
Greencourt Av. Edgw—1H 25
Greencourt Gdns. Croy—2H 135
Greencourt Rd. Orp—5J 129
Greencrest Pl. NW2—3C 42
Greencroft. Edgw—5D 12
Greencroft Av. Ruis—2A 38
Greencroft Clo. E6—5B 66
Greencroft Gdns. NW6—7K 43
Greencroft Gdns. Enf—3K 7
Greencroft Rd. Houn—1D 86
Green Dale. SE22 & SE5—5E 94
Green Dale Clo. SE22—5E 94
Green Dragon La. N21—6F 7
Green Dragon La. Bren—5E 72
Green Dragon Yd. E1
—5G 63 (6G 143)
Green Dri. S'hall—1E 70
Green End. N21—2G 17
Greenend Rd. W4—2A 74
Greenfell St. SE10—3G 81
Greenfield Av. Surb—7H 119
Greenfield Gdns. NW2—2G 43
Greenfield Gdns. Dag—1D 68
Greenfield Gdns. Orp—7H 129
Greenfield Rd. E1
—6G 63 (7H 143)
Greenfield Rd. N15—5E 30
Greenfield Rd. Dag—1C 68
Greenfield Rd. Dart—5K 117
Greenfields. S'hall—6E 54
Greenfield Way. Harr—3F 23
Greenford Av. W7—4J 55
Greenford Av. S'hall—7D 54
Greenford Gdns. Gnfd—3F 55
Greenford Grn. Gnfd—6J 39
Greenford Industrial Est. N'holt
—7F 39
Greenford Rd. S'hall, Gnfd &
Harr—7G 55
Greenford Rd. Sutt—4K 131
Greengate. Gnfd—6B 40
Greengate St. E13—2K 65
Greenhalgh Wlk. N2—4A 28
Greenham Clo. SE1
—2A 78 (5H 147)
Greenham Rd. N10—2E 28
Greenheys Dri. E18—3H 33
Greenhill. NW3—4B 44
Green Hill. SE18—5D 82
Greenhill. Buck H—1F 21
Greenhill. Sutt—2A 132
Greenhill. Wemb—2H 41
Greenhill Gdns. N'holt—2D 54
Greenhill Gro. E12—4C 50
Greenhill Pk. NW10—1A 58
Greenhill Pk. Barn—5E 4
Greenhill Rd. NW10—1A 58
Greenhill Rd. Harr—6J 23
Greenhill's Rents. EC1
—5B 62 (5J 141)
Greenhills Ter. N1—6D 46
Greenhill Ter. N'holt—2D 54
Greenhill Way. Harr—6J 23
Greenhill Way. Wemb—2H 41
Greenhithe Clo. Sidc—7J 99
Greenholm Rd. SE9—5F 99
Green Hundred Rd. SE15—6G 79
Greenhurst Rd. SE27—5A 110

Greening St. SE2—4C 84
Greenland Cres. S'hall—3A 70
Greenland M. SE8—5K 79
Greenland Pl. NW1—1F 61
Greenland Quay. SE16—4K 79
Greenland Rd. NW1—1F 61
Greenland Rd. Barn—6A 4
Greenland St. NW1—1F 61
Green La. NW4—4F 27
Green La. SE9 & Chst—1F 115
Green La. SE20—7K 111
Green La. SW16 & T Hth
—7K 109
Green La. W7—2J 71
Green La. Edgw—4A 12
Green La. Felt—5C 102
Green La. Harr—3J 39
Green La. Houn—3A 86
Green La. Ilf & Dag—2H 51
Green La. Mord—6J 121
Green La. N Mald—5J 119
Green La. Stan—4G 11
Green La. Wor Pk & Mord
—1C 130
Green La. Gdns. T Hth—2C 124
Green Lanes—6E 16
N13 1-615 & 2-604
N21 remainder
Green Lanes—4B 30
N16 1-203 & 2-162
N4 205-531 & 182-430
N8 remainder
Green Lanes. Eps—7A 130
Greenlaw Gdns. N Mald
—7B 120
Green Lawns. Ruis—1A 38
Greenlaw St. SE18—3E 82
Greenleafe Dri. Ilf—3F 35
Greenleaf Rd. E6—1A 66
Greenleaf Rd. E17—3B 32
Greenlea Trading Pk. SW19
—1B 122
Green Man Gdns. W13—7A 56
Green Man La. W13—1A 72
Green Man Pas. W13—7B 72
Greenman St. N1—1C 62
Green Moor Link. N21—7G 7
Greenmoor Rd. Enf—2D 8
Greenoak Way. SW19—4F 107
Greenock Rd. SW16—1H 123
Greenock Rd. W3—3H 73
Greenpark Ct. Gnfd—7C 40
Green Pond Rd. E17—3A 32
Green Rd. N14—6A 6
Green Rd. N20—3F 15
Green's End. SE18—4F 83
Green Shield Industrial Est. E16
—2K 81
Greenside. Bex—1E 116
Greenside. Dag—1C 52
Greenside Rd. W12—3C 74
Greenside Rd. Croy—7A 124
Greenstead Av. Wfd G—6F 21
Greenstead Clo. Wfd G—6F 21
Greenstead Gdns. SW15—5D 90
Greenstead Gdns. Wfd G—6F 21
Greensted Rd. Lou—1H 21
Greenstone M. E11—6J 33
Green St.—6K 49
E7 1-283 & 2-304
E13 remainder
Green St. W1—7E 60 (9G 139)
Green St. Enf—2D 8
Green, The. E4—1A 20
Green, The. E11—6K 33
Green, The. E15—6H 49
Green, The. N9—2B 18
Green, The. N14—3C 16
Green, The. N21—1F 17
Green, The. SW19—5F 107
Green, The. W3—6A 58
Green, The. W5—7D 56
Green, The. Bexh—1G 101
Green, The. Brom—3J 113
(Grove Park)
Green, The. Brom—7J 127
(Hayes)

Green, The. Cars—4E 132
Green, The. Croy—7B 136
Green, The. Houn—6E 70
Green, The. Mord—4G 121
Green, The. N Mald—3J 119
Green, The. Orp—7B 116
(St Paul's Cray)
Green, The. Rich—5D 88
Green, The. Sidc—4A 116
Green, The. S'hall—2D 70
Green, The. Sutt—3K 131
Green, The. Twic—2J 103
Green, The. Well—4J 99
Green, The. Wemb—2A 40
Green, The. Wfd G—5D 20
Green Vale. W5—6F 57
Green Vale. Bexh—5D 100
Greenvale Rd. SE9—4D 98
Green Verges. Stan—7J 11
Greenview Av. Beck—6A 126
Greenview Av. Croy—6A 126
Green Wlk. NW4—5F 27
Green Wlk. SE1—3E 78 (7C 148)
Green Wlk. Hmptn—6D 102
Green Wlk. Lou—1H 5
Green Wlk. S'hall—5E 70
Green Wlk. Wfd G—6H 21
Green Wlk., The. E4—1A 20
Greenway. N14—2D 16
Greenway. N20—2D 14
Green Way. SE9—5B 98
Greenway. SW20—4E 120
Green Way. Brom—6C 128
Greenway. Chst—5E 114
Greenway. Dag—1C 52
Greenway. Harr—5E 24
Greenway. Pinn—2A 22
Green Way. Wall—4G 133
Green Way. Wfd G—5F 21
Greenway Av. E17—4F 33
Greenway Clo. N4—2C 46
Greenway Clo. N11—4K 15
Greenway Clo. N20—2D 14
Greenway Clo. NW9—2K 25
Greenway Gdns. Croy—3B 136
Greenway Gdns. Gnfd—3E 54
Green Way Gdns. Harr—2J 23
Greenways. Beck—2C 126
Greenways Clo. N11—6A 16
Greenways, The. Twic—6A 88
Greenway, The. NW9—2K 25
Green Way, The. Harr—1J 23
Greenway, The. Houn—4D 86
Greenway, The. Pinn—6D 22
Greenwell St. W1
—4F 61 (4K 139)
Greenwich Chu. St. SE10
—6E 80
Greenwich Cres. E6—5C 66
Greenwich High Rd. SE10
—7D 80
Greenwich Mkt. SE10—6E 80
Greenwich Pk. St. SE10—6F 81
Greenwich S. St. SE10—1D 96
Greenwich View Pl. E14—3D 80
Greenwood Av. Dag—4H 53
Greenwood Av. Enf—1F 9
Greenwood Clo. Bush, Wat
—1D 10
Greenwood Clo. Mord—4G 121
Greenwood Clo. Orp—6J 129
Greenwood Clo. Sidc—2A 116
Greenwood Dri. E4—5A 20
Greenwood Gdns. N13—3G 17
Greenwood Gdns. Ilf—1G 35
Greenwood Ho. N22—1A 30
Greenwood La. Hmptn—5F 103
Greenwood Pk. King—7A 106
Greenwood Pl. NW5—5F 45
Greenwood Rd. E8—6G 47
Greenwood Rd. E13—2H 65
Greenwood Rd. Bex—4K 117
Greenwood Rd. Croy—7B 124
Greenwood Rd. Iswth—3K 87
Greenwood Rd. Mitc—3H 123
Greenwood Ter. NW10—2K 57

209

Grummant Rd. SE15—1F 95
Grundy St. E14—6D 64
Gruneisen Rd. N3—7E 14
Gubyon Av. SE24—5B 94
Guerin Sq. E3—3B 64
Guernsey Clo. Houn—7E 70
Guernsey Gro. SE24—7C 94
Guernsey Ho. N1—6C 46
Guernsey Rd. E11—1F 49
Guildersfield Rd. SW16—7J 109
Guildford Gro. SE10—1D 96
Guildford Rd. E6—6D 66
Guildford Rd. E17—1E 32
Guildford Rd. SW8—1G 93
Guildford Rd. Croy—6D 124
Guildford Rd. Ilf—2G 51
Guildford Way. Wall—5J 133
Guildhall Yd. EC2
—6C 62 (7M 141)
Guildhouse St. SW1
—4G 77 (9L 145)
Guildown Av. N12—4E 14
Guild Rd. SE7—5B 82
Guildsway. E17—1B 32
Guilford Av. Surb—5F 119
Guilford Pl. WC1
—4K 61 (4E 140)
Guilford St. WC1
—4J 61 (4D 140)
Guillemot Pl. N22—2K 29
Guilsborough Clo. NW10
—7A 42
Guiness Trust Est. N16—1E 46
Guinness Clo. E9—7A 48
Guinness Ct. NW8—1C 60
Guinness Sq. SE1
—4E 78 (8D 148)
Guion Rd. SW6—2H 91
Gull Clo. Wall—7J 133
Gulliver Clo. N'holt—1D 54
Gulliver Rd. Sidc—2H 115
Gulliver St. SE16—3B 80
Gumleigh Rd. W5—4C 72
Gumley Gdns. Iswth—3A 88
Gundulph Rd. Brom—3A 128
Gunmaker's La. E3—1A 64
Gunner La. SE18—5E 82
Gunnersbury Av.—1F 73
W5 1-119 & 2-114
W3 127-143 & 144-248
W4 remainder
Gunnersbury Clo. W4—5H 73
Gunnersbury Cres. W3—2G 73
Gunnersbury Dri. W5—2F 73
Gunnersbury Gdns. W3—2G 73
Gunnersbury La. W3—2G 73
Gunnersbury M. W4—5H 73
Gunners Gro. E4—3K 19
Gunners Rd. SW18—2B 108
Gunning St. SE18—4J 83
Gunstor Rd. N16—4E 46
Gun St. E1—5F 63 (6E 142)
Gunter Gro. SW10—6A 76
Gunter Gro. Edgw—1K 25
Gunterstone Rd. W14—4G 75
Gunthorpe St. E1
—5F 63 (6F 142)
Gunton Rd. E5—2H 47
Gunton Rd. SW17—6E 108
Gunwhale Clo. SE16—1K 79
Gurdon Rd. SE7—5J 81
Gurnell Gro. W13—4K 55
Gurney Clo. E15—5G 49
Gurney Clo. E17—1K 31
Gurney Clo. Bark—6F 51
Gurney Cres. Croy—1K 133
Gurney Dri. N2—4A 28
Gurney Rd. E15—5G 49
Gurney Rd. Cars—4E 132
Gurney Rd. N'holt—3H 53
Guthrie St. SW3—5B 76 (9B 144)
Gutter La. EC2—6C 62 (7L 141)
Guyatt Gdns. Mitc—2E 122
Guy Rd. Wall—3H 133
Guyscliff Rd. SE13—5E 96
Guys Retreat. Buck H—1F 21

Guy St. SE1—2D 78 (4B 148)
Gwalior Rd. SW15—4F 91
Gwendolen Av. SW15—4F 91
Gwendolen Clo. SW15—5F 91
Gwendoline Av. E13—1K 65
Gwendwr Rd. W14—5G 75
Gwillim Clo. Sidc—5A 100
Gwydor Rd. Beck—3K 125
Gwydyr Rd. Brom—3H 127
Gwyn Clo. SW6—7A 76
Gwynne Av. Croy—7K 125
Gwynne Pk. Av. Wfd G—6J 21
Gwynne Pl. WC1
—3K 61 (2F 140)
Gwynne Rd. SW11—2B 92
Gylcote Clo. SE5—4D 94
Gyles Pk. Stan—1C 24
Gyllyngdune Gdns. Ilf—3K 51

Haarlem Rd. W14—3F 75
Haberdasher Pl. N1
—3D 62 (1B 142)
Haberdasher St. N1
—3D 62 (1B 142)
Haccombe Rd. SW19—6A 108
Hackbridge Grn. Wall—2E 132
Hackbridge Pk. Gdns. Cars
—2D 132
Hackbridge Rd. Wall—2E 132
Hackford Rd. SW9—1K 93
Hackington Cres. Beck—6C 112
Hackney Gro. E8—6H 47
Hackney Rd. E2—3F 63 (1E 142)
Hadden Rd. SE28—3J 83
Hadden Way. Gnfd—6H 39
Haddington Rd. Brom—3F 113
Haddon Clo. Enf—6B 8
Haddon Clo. N Mald—5B 120
Haddonfield. SE8—4K 79
Haddon Gro. Sidc—7A 100
Haddon Rd. Sutt—4K 131
Haddo St. SE10—6E 80
Hadleigh Clo. E1
—4J 63 (3L 143)
Hadleigh Rd. N9—7C 8
Hadleigh St. E2—3J 63 (2M 143)
Hadleigh Wlk. E6—5C 66
Hadley Clo. N21—6F 7
Hadley Comn. Barn—2D 4
Hadley Ct. N16—1G 47
Hadley Gdns. W4—5K 73
Hadley Gdns. S'hall—5D 70
Hadley Grn. Rd. Barn—2C 4
Hadley Grn. W. Barn—2C 4
Hadley Gro. Barn—2B 4
Hadley Highstone. Barn—1C 4
Hadley Ridge. Barn—3C 4
Hadley Rd. Barn—3E 4
Hadley Rd. Barn & Enf—1J 5
Hadley Rd. Belv—4F 85
Hadley Rd. Mitc—4H 123
Hadley St. NW1—6F 45
Hadley Way. N21—6F 7
Hadley Wood Rd. Barn—2G 5
Hadlow Pl. SE19—7G 111
Hadlow Rd. Sidc—4A 116
Hadlow Rd. Well—7C 84
Hadrian Clo. Wall—7J 133
Hadrians Ride. Enf—5A 8
Hadrian St. SE10—5G 81
Hadyn Pk. Rd. W12—2C 74
Hafer Rd. SW11—4D 92
Hafton Rd. SE6—1G 113
Haggard Rd. Twic—7B 88
Haggerston Rd. E8—7F 47
Hague St. E2—3G 63 (2H 143)
Ha Ha Rd. SE18—6D 82
Haig Rd. Stan—5H 11
Haig Rd. E. E13—3A 66
Haig Rd. W. E13—3A 66
Haigville Gdns. Ilf—4F 35
Hailes Clo. SW19—6A 108
Haileybury Av. Enf—6A 8
Hailey Rd. Eri—2G 85
Hailsham Av. SW2—2K 109
Hailsham Clo. Surb—7D 118

Hailsham Dri. Harr—3J 23
Hailsham Rd. SW17—6E 108
Hailsham Ter. N18—4J 17
Haimo Rd. SE9—5B 98
Hainault Ct. E17—4F 33
Hainault Gore. Romf—5E 36
Hainault Rd. E11—1E 48
Hainault Rd. Romf—2J 37
Hainault Rd. Romf—6F 37
(Chadwell Heath)
Hainault St. SE9—1F 115
Hainault St. Ilf—2G 51
Haines St. SW8—7G 77
Haines Wlk. Mord—7K 121
Haining Clo. W4—5H 73
Hainthorpe Rd. SE27—3B 110
Hainton Path. E1
—6H 63 (8K 143)
Halberd M. E5—2H 47
Halbutt Gdns. Dag—3F 53
Halbutt St. Dag—4F 53
Halcomb St. N1—1E 62
Halcot Av. Bexh—5H 101
Halcrow St. E1—5H 63 (6K 143)
Haldane Clo. N10—7A 16
Haldane Pl. SW18—1K 107
Haldane Rd. E6—3B 66
Haldane Rd. SE28—7D 68
Haldane Rd. SW6—7H 75
Haldane Rd. S'hall—6G 55
Haldan Rd. E4—6K 19
Haldon Rd. SW18—6H 91
Hale Clo. E4—3K 19
Hale Clo. Edgw—5D 12
Hale Dri. NW7—6D 12
Hale End Rd.—6A 20
E17 1-197 & 2-148
E4 433-509 & 350-428
Wfd G remainder
Halefield Rd. N17—1H 31
Hale Gdns. N17—3G 31
Hale Gdns. W3—1G 73
Hale Gro. Gdns. NW7—5F 13
Hale La. Edgw & NW7—5C 12
Hale Path. SE27—4B 110
Hale Rd. E6—4C 66
Hale Rd. N17—3G 31
Halesowen Rd. Mord—7K 121
Hales St. SE8—7C 80
Hale St. E14—7D 64
Halesworth Clo. E5—2J 47
Halesworth Rd. SE13—3D 96
Hale, The. E4—7A 20
Hale, The. N17—3G 31
Hale Wlk. W7—5J 55
Haley Rd. NW4—6E 26
Half Acre. Bren—6D 72
Half Moon Cres. N1—2K 61
Half Moon La. SE24—6C 94
Half Moon Pas. E1
—6F 63 (8F 142)
Half Moon St. W1
—1F 77 (3K 145)
Halford Rd. E10—5F 33
Halford Rd. SW6—6J 75
Halford Rd. Rich—5E 88
Halfway St. Sidc—7H 99
Haliburton Rd. Twic—5A 88
Halidon Clo. E9—5J 47
Halifax Rd. Enf—2H 7
Halifax Rd. Gnfd—1F 55
Halifax St. SE26—3H 111
Halifield Dri. Belv—3E 84
Haling Down Pas. Purl & S Croy
—7C 134
Haling Gro. S Croy—7C 134
Haling Pk. Gdns. S Croy
—6B 134
Haling Pk. Rd. S Croy—5B 134
Haling Rd. S Croy—6D 134
Halkin Arc. SW1
—3E 76 (6G 145)
Halkin M. SW1—3E 76 (6G 145)
Halkin Pl. SW1—3E 76 (6G 145)
Halkin St. SW1—2E 76 (5H 145)
Hallam Clo. Chst—5D 114

Hallam Gdns. Pinn—1C 22
Hallam M. W1—5F 61 (5K 139)
Hallam Rd. N15—4B 30
Hallam St. W1—5F 61 (5K 139)
Hall Clo. W5—5E 56
Hall Ct. Tedd—5K 103
Hall Dri. SE26—5J 111
Hall Dri. W7—6J 55
Halley Gdns. SE13—4F 97
Halley Pl. E14—5A 64
Halley Rd.—6A 50
E7 1-207 & 2-188
E12 remainder
Halley St. E14—5A 64
Hall Farm Clo. Stan—4G 11
Hall Farm Dri. Twic—7H 87
Hallfield Est. W2—6A 60
Hall Gdns. E4—4G 19
Hall Ga. NW8—3B 60 (1A 138)
Halliford St. N1—7C 46
Hallingbury Ct. E17—3D 32
Halliwell Rd. SW2—6K 93
Halliwick Rd. N10—1E 28
Hall La. E4—5F 19
Hall La. NW4—1C 26
Hallmead Rd. Sutt—3K 131
Hall Oak Wlk. NW6—6H 43
Hallowell Av. Croy—4J 133
Hallowell Clo. Mitc—3E 122
Hall Pl. W2—4B 60 (4A 138)
Hall Pl. Cres. Bex—5J 101
Hall Rd. E6—1D 66
Hall Rd. E15—4F 49
Hall Rd. NW8—3A 60 (2A 138)
Hall Rd. Iswth—5H 87
Hall Rd. Romf—6C 36
(Chadwell Heath)
Hall Rd. Wall—7F 133
Hallside Rd. Enf—1A 8
Hall St. EC1—3B 62 (1K 141)
Hall St. N12—5F 15
Hallsville Rd. E16—6H 65
Hallswelle Pde. NW1—5H 27
Hallswelle Rd. NW11—5H 27
Hall, The. SE3—3J 97
Hall View. SE9—2B 114
Hallywell Cres. E6—5D 66
Halons Rd. SE9—7E 98
Halpin Pl. SE17—4D 78 (9B 148)
Halsbrook Rd. SE3—3B 98
Halsbury Clo. Stan—4G 11
Halsbury Rd. W12—1D 74
Halsbury Rd. E. Harr—4G 39
Halsbury Rd. W. N'holt—4F 39
Halsey M. SW3—4D 76 (8E 144)
Halsey St. SW3—4D 76 (8E 144)
Halsham Cres. Bark—5K 51
Halsmere Rd. SE5—1B 94
Halstead Gdns. N21—1J 17
Halstead Rd. E11—5J 33
Halstead Rd. N21—1J 17
Halstead Rd. Enf—4K 7
Halston Clo. SW11—6D 92
Halstow Rd. NW10—3F 59
Halstow Rd. SE10—5J 81
Halton Rd. N1—7B 46
Halt Robin La. Belv—4H 85
Halt Robin Rd. Belv—4G 85
Hambalt Rd. SW4—5G 93
Hambleden Pl. SE21—1F 111
Hambledon Gdns. SE25
—3F 125
Hambledon Rd. SW18—7H 91
Hambledown Rd. Sidc—7H 99
Hamble St. SW6—3K 91
Hambridge Way. SW2—7A 94
Hambro Av. Brom—1J 137
Hambrook Rd. SE25—3H 125
Hambro Rd. SW16—6H 109
Hambrough Rd. S'hall—1C 70
Ham Clo. Rich—3C 104
(in two parts)
Hamden Cres. Dag—3H 53
Hamelin St. E14—6E 64
Hameway. E6—4E 66
Ham Farm Rd. Rich—4D 104
Hamfrith Rd. E15—6H 49

Ham Ga. Av. Rich—3D 104
Hamilton Av. N9—7B 8
Hamilton Av. III—4F 35
Hamilton Av. Romf—2K 37
Hamilton Av. Sutt—2G 131
Hamilton Clo. N17—3G 31
Hamilton Clo. NW8
—3B 60 (2A 138)
Hamilton Clo. SE16—2A 80
Hamilton Clo. Barn—4H 5
Hamilton Clo. Stan—2D 10
Hamilton Cres. N13—4F 17
Hamilton Cres. Harr—5D 38
Hamilton Cres. Houn—5F 87
Hamilton Gdns. NW8
—3A 60 (1A 138)
Hamilton La. N5—4B 46
Hamilton M. W1—2F 77 (4J 145)
Hamilton Pk. N5—4B 46
Hamilton Pk. W. N5—4B 46
Hamilton Pl. W1
—1E 76 (3H 145)
Hamilton Rd. E15—3G 65
Hamilton Rd. E17—2A 32
Hamilton Rd. N2—3A 28
Hamilton Rd. N9—7B 8
Hamilton Rd. NW10—5C 42
Hamilton Rd. NW11—7F 27
Hamilton Rd. SE27—4D 110
Hamilton Rd. SW19—7K 107
Hamilton Rd. W4—2A 74
Hamilton Rd. W5—7E 56
Hamilton Rd. Barn—4H 5
Hamilton Rd. Bexh—2E 100
Hamilton Rd. Bren—6D 72
Hamilton Rd. Harr—5J 23
Hamilton Rd. Ilf—4F 51
Hamilton Rd. M. SW19—7K 107
Hamilton Rd. Sidc—4A 116
Hamilton Rd. S'hall—1D 70
Hamilton Rd. T Hth—3D 124
Hamilton Rd. Twic—1J 103
Hamilton Rd. SE8—6C 80
Hamilton Ter. NW8
—2A 60 (2A 138)
Hamilton Way. N3—6D 14
Hamilton Way. N13—4G 17
Hamilton Way. Wall—7F 133
Hamlea Clo. SE12—5J 97
Hamlet Clo. SE13—4G 97
Hamlet Clo. Romf—1G 37
Hamlet Gdns. W6—4C 74
Hamlet Industrial Est. E9
—7C 48
Hamlet Rd. SE19—7F 111
Hamlet Rd. Romf—1G 37
Hamlets Way. E3—4B 64
Hamlet, The. SE5—3D 94
Hamlin Cres. Pinn—5A 22
Hamlyn Clo. Edgw—3K 11
Hamlyn Gdns. SE19—7E 110
Hammelton Grn. SW9—1B 94
Hammelton Rd. Brom—1H 127
Hammers La. NW7—5H 13
Hammersmith Bri. SW13 & W6
—6D 74
Hammersmith Bri. Rd. W6
—4E 74
Hammersmith B'way. W6
—5E 74
Hammersmith Flyover. W6
—5E 74
Hammersmith Gro. W6—3E 74
Hammersmith Rd.—4F 75
W14 1-155 & 2-92
W6 remainder
Hammersmith Ter. W6—5C 74
Hammet Clo. Hay—5B 54
Hammett St. EC3
—7F 63 (9E 142)
Hammond Av. Mitc—2F 123
Hammond Clo. Barn—5B 4
Hammond Clo. Gnfd—5H 39
Hammond Rd. Enf—2C 8
Hammond Rd. S'hall—3C 70
Hammond St. NW5—6G 45
Hamonde Clo Edgw—2C 12

Ham Pk. Rd.—7H 49
E15 1-111 & 2-66
E7 remainder
Hampden Av. Beck—2A 126
Hampden Clo. NW1—2H 61
Hampden Gurney St. W1
—6D 60 (8E 138)
Hampden Ho. SW9—2A 94
Hampden La. N17—1G 31
Hampden Rd. N8—4A 30
Hampden Rd. N10—7K 15
Hampden Rd. N17—1G 31
Hampden Rd. N19—2H 45
Hampden Rd. Beck—2A 126
Hampden Rd. Harr—1G 23
Hampden Rd. King—3G 119
Hampden Rd. Romf—1H 37
Hampden Sq. N14—1A 16
Hampden Way. N14—1A 16
Hampshire Clo. N18—5C 18
Hampshire Hog La. W6—4D 74
Hampshire Rd. N22—7E 16
Hampshire St. NW5—6H 45
Hampson Way. SW8—1K 93
Hampstead Clo. SE28—1B 84
Hampstead Gdns. NW11—4J 27
Hampstead Grn. NW3—5C 44
Hampstead Gro. NW3—3A 44
Hampstead High St. NW3
—4A 44
Hampstead Hill Gdns. NW3
—4B 44
Hampstead La.—1B 44
NW3 50-56
N6 remainder
Hampstead Rd. NW1
—2G 61 (1L 139)
Hampstead Sq. NW3—3A 44
Hampstead Way. NW11—5H 27
Hampton Clo. NW6—3J 59
Hampton Clo. SW20—7E 106
Hampton Ct. N1—6B 46
Hampton Ct. Rd. Hmptn,
E Mol & King—3A 118
Hampton Farm Industrial Est.
Felt—3C 102
Hampton La. Felt—4C 102
Hampton Rise. Harr—6E 24
Hampton Rd. E4—5G 19
Hampton Rd. E7—5K 49
Hampton Rd. E11—1F 49
Hampton Rd. Croy—6C 124
Hampton Rd. Ilf—4G 51
Hampton Rd. Tedd—5H 103
Hampton Rd. Twic—3H 103
Hampton Rd. Wor Pk—2D 130
Hampton Rd. E. Felt—4D 102
Hampton Rd. W. Felt—3C 102
Hampton St. SE17 & SE1
—4C 78 (9L 147)
Ham Ridings. Rich—5F 105
Hamshades Clo. Sidc—3K 115
Ham St. Rich—1B 104
Ham, The. Bren—7C 72
Ham View. Croy—6A 126
Ham Yd. W1—7H 61 (9A 140)
Hanah Ct. SW19—7F 107
Hanameel St. E16—1K 81
Hanbury M. N1—1C 62
Hanbury Rd. N17—2H 31
Hanbury Rd. W3—2H 73
Hanbury St. E1—5F 63 (5F 142)
Hanbury Wlk. Bex—3K 117
Hancock Rd. E3—3E 64
Hancock Rd. SE19—6D 110
Handa Wlk. N1—6D 46
Hand Ct. WC1—5K 61 (6F 140)
Handcroft Rd. Croy—7B 124
Handel Clo. Edgw—6A 12
Handel Pl. NW10—6K 41
Handel St. WC1—4J 61 (3C 140)
Handel Way. Edgw—7B 12
Handen Rd. SE12—5G 97
Handforth Rd. SW9—7A 78
Handforth Rd. Ilf—3F 51
Handley Rd. E9—1J 63
Handside Clo. Wor Pk—1F 131

Hands Wlk. E16—6J 65
Handsworth Av. E4—6A 20
Handsworth Rd. N17—3D 30
Handtrough Way. Bark—2F 67
Hanford Clo. SE4—4K 95
Hanford Clo. SW18—1J 107
Hanford Row. SW19—6E 106
Hanger Grn. W5—4G 57
Hanger La. W5—2E 56
Hanger Vale La. W5—6F 57
Hanger View Way. W3—6G 57
Hankey Pl. SE1—2D 78 (5B 148)
Hankins La. NW7—2F 13
Hanley Rd. N4—1J 45
Hanmer Wlk. N7—2K 45
Hannah Clo. NW10—4J 41
Hannah Mary Way. SE1
—4G 79 (9H 149)
Hannay Wlk. SW16—2H 109
Hannell Rd. SW6—7G 75
Hannen Rd. SE27—3B 110
Hannibal Rd. E1
—5J 63 (5M 143)
Hannibal Way. Croy—5K 133
Hannington Rd. SW4—3F 93
Hanover Clo. Rich—7G 73
Hanover Clo. Sutt—4G 131
Hanover Ct. NW9—3A 26
Hanover Dri. Chst—4G 115
Hanover Est. N22—3K 29
Hanover Gdns. SE11—6A 78
Hanover Gdns. Ilf—1G 35
Hanover Ga. NW1
—3C 60 (2D 138)
Hanover Mead. NW11—5G 27
Hanover Pk. SE15—1G 95
Hanover Pl. WC2
—6J 61 (8D 140)
Hanover Rd. N15—4F 31
Hanover Rd. NW10—7E 42
Hanover Rd. SW19—7A 108
Hanover Sq. W1
—6F 61 (8K 139)
Hanover St. W1—6F 61 (8K 139)
Hanover St. Croy—3B 134
Hanover Ter. NW1
—3D 60 (2E 138)
Hanover Ter. Iswth—1A 88
Hanover Ter. M. NW1
—3D 60 (2E 138)
Hanover Way. Bexh—3D 100
Hanover W. Industrial Est.
NW10—3K 57
Hansard M. W14—2F 75
Hansart Way. Enf—2F 7
Hans Cres. SW1—3D 76 (6E 144)
Hanselin Clo. Stan—5E 10
Hanshawe Dri. Edgw—1K 25
Hansler Rd. SE22—5F 95
Hansol Rd. Bexh—5E 100
Hanson Clo. SW12—7F 93
Hanson Gdns. S'hall—2C 70
Hanson St. W1—5G 61 (5L 139)
Hans Pl. SW1—3D 76 (6F 144)
Hans Rd. SW3—3D 76 (6E 144)
Hans St. SW1—3D 76 (7F 144)
Hanway Pl. W1—6H 61 (7A 140)
Hanway Rd. W7—6H 55
Hanway St. W1—6H 61 (7A 140)
Hanworth Rd. Felt—1A 102
Hanworth Rd. Hmptn—4D 102
Hanworth Rd. Houn—1D 102
Hanworth Ter. Houn—4F 87
Hanworth Trading Est. Felt
—3C 102
Hapgood Clo. Gnfd—5H 39
Harad's Pl. E1—7G 63 (9H 143)
Harben Rd. NW6—7A 44
Harberson Rd. E15—1H 65
Harberson Rd. SW12—1F 109
Harberton Rd. N19—1G 45
Harbet Rd. N18—5E 18
Harbet Rd. W2—5B 60 (6B 138)
Harbex Clo. Bex—7H 101
Harbinger Rd. E14—4D 80
Harbledown Rd. SW6—1J 91
Harbord Clo. SE5—2D 94

Harbord St. SW6—1F 91
Harborough Av. Sidc—7K 99
Harborough Rd. SW16—4K 109
Harbour Av. SW10—1A 92
Harbour Exchange. E14—2D 80
Harbour Exchange Sq. E14
—2D 80
Harbour Quay. E14—1E 80
Harbour Rd. SE5—3C 94
Harbour Yd. SW10—1A 92
Harbridge Av. SW15—7C 90
Harbury Rd. Cars—7C 132
Harbut Rd. SW11—4B 92
Harcombe Rd. N16—3E 46
Harcourt Av. E12—4D 50
Harcourt Av. Edgw—3D 12
Harcourt Av. Sidc—6C 100
Harcourt Av. Wall—4F 133
Harcourt Clo. Iswth—3A 88
Harcourt Field. Wall—4F 133
Harcourt Rd. E15—2H 65
Harcourt Rd. N22—1H 29
Harcourt Rd. SE4—3B 96
Harcourt Rd. SW19—7J 107
Harcourt Rd. Bexh—4E 100
Harcourt Rd. T Hth—6K 123
Harcourt Rd. Wall—4F 133
Harcourt St. W1
—5C 60 (6D 138)
Harcourt Ter. SW10—5K 75
Hardcastle Clo. SE25—6G 125
Hardcourts Clo. W Wick
—3D 136
Hardel Rise. SW2—1B 110
Hardel Wlk. SW2—7A 94
Harden's Mnr. Way. SE7—3B 82
Harders Rd. SE15—1H 95
(in two parts)
Harders Rd. M. SE15—1H 95
Hardess St. SE24—3C 94
Hardie Clo. NW10—5K 41
Hardie Rd. Dag—3J 53
Harding Clo. SE17—6C 78
Hardinge Rd. N18—6K 17
Hardinge Rd. NW10—1D 58
Hardinge St. E1—6J 63 (8M 143)
(in two parts)
Harding Rd. Bexh—2F 101
Hardings La. SE20—6K 111
Hardman Rd. SE7—5K 81
Hardman Rd. King—2E 118
Hardwick Clo. Stan—5H 11
Hardwick Ct. Eri—6K 85
Hardwicke Av. Houn—1E 86
Hardwicke Rd. N13—6D 16
Hardwicke Rd. W4—4K 73
Hardwicke Rd. Rich—4C 104
Hardwicke St. Bark—1G 67
Hardwick Grn. W13—5B 56
Hardwick Pl. EC1
—3A 62 (2H 141)
Hardwicks Way. SW18—5J 91
Hardwidge St. SE1
—2E 78 (4C 148)
Hardy Av. Ruis—5A 38
Hardy Clo. SE16—2K 79
Hardy Clo. Pinn—7B 22
Hardy Rd. SE3—6H 81
Hardy Rd. SW19—7K 107
Hardy Way. Enf—1F 7
Hare & Billet Rd. SE3—1F 97
Harecastle Clo. Hay—4C 54
Hare Ct. EC4—6A 62 (8G 141)
Harecourt Rd. N1—6C 46
Haredale Rd. SE24—4C 94
Haredon Clo. SE23—7K 95
Harefield Grn. NW7—6K 13
Harefield Rd. N8—5H 29
Harefield Rd. SE4—3B 96
Harefield Rd. SW16—7K 109
Harefield Rd. Sidc—3D 116
Hare Marsh. E2—4G 63 (3G 143)
Hare Row. E2—2H 63
Haresfield Rd. Dag—6G 53
Hare St. SE18—3E 82

Hare Wlk. N1—2E 62
Harewood Av. NW1
　　　　—4C 60 (4D 138)
Harewood Av. N'holt—7D 38
Harewood Clo. N'holt—7D 38
Harewood Dri. Ilf—2D 34
Harewood Pl. W1
　　　　—6F 61 (8K 139)
Harewood Rd. SW19—6C 108
Harewood Rd. Iswth—7K 71
Harewood Rd. S Croy—6E 134
Harewood Row. NW1
　　　　—5C 60 (5D 138)
Harewood Ter. S'hall—4D 70
Harfield Gdns. SE5—3E 94
Harford Clo. E4—7J 9
Harford Rd. E4—7J 9
Harford St. E1—4A 64
Harfst Way. Swan—7J 117
Hargood Clo. Harr—6E 24
Hargood Rd. SE3—1A 98
Hargrave Pk. N19—2G 45
Hargrave Pl. N7—5H 45
Hargrave Rd. N19—2G 45
Hargwyne St. SW9—3K 93
Haringey Pk. N8—6J 29
Haringey Rd. N8—4J 29
Harington Ter. N18—3J 17
Harkett Clo. Harr—2K 23
Harland Av. Croy—3G 135
Harland Av. Sidc—3H 115
Harland Rd. SE12—1J 113
Harlech Gdns. Houn—6A 70
Harlech Rd. N14—3D 16
Harlequin Av. Bren—6A 72
Harlequin Av. Tedd—7B 104
Harlequin Centre. S'hall—4A 70
Harlequin Clo. Iswth—5J 87
Harlescott Rd. SE15—4K 95
Harlesden Gdns. NW10—1B 58
Harlesden La. NW10—1C 58
Harlesden Rd. NW10—1C 58
Harleston Clo. E5—2J 47
Harley Clo. Wemb—6D 40
Harley Ct. E11—7J 33
Harley Cres. Harr—4H 23
Harleyford. Brom—1A 128
Harleyford Rd. SE11—6K 77
Harleyford St. SE11—6A 78
Harley Gdns. SW10—5A 76
Harley Gro. E3—3B 64
Harley Pl. W1—5F 61 (6J 139)
Harley Rd. NW3—7B 44
Harley Rd. NW10—2A 58
Harley Rd. Harr—4H 23
Harley St. W1—5F 61 (5J 139)
Harlington Rd. Bexh—3E 100
Harlington Rd. E. Felt—7A 86
Harlington Rd. W. Felt—7A 86
Harlowe Clo. E8—1G 63
Harlow Rd. N13—3J 17
Harman Av. Wfd G—6C 20
Harman Clo. E4—4A 20
Harman Clo. NW2—3G 43
Harman Dri. NW2—3G 43
Harman Dri. Sidc—6K 99
Harman Rd. Enf—5A 8
Harmony Clo. NW11—5G 27
Harmony Clo. Wall—7J 133
Harmony Lodge. S'hall—3E 70
Harmood Gro. NW1—7F 45
Harmood Pl. NW1—7F 45
Harmood St. NW1—6F 45
Harmsworth St. SE17—6B 78
Harmsworth Way. N20—1C 14
Harness Rd. SE28—2A 84
Harold Av. Belv—5F 85
Harold Est. SE1—3E 78 (7D 148)
Harold Pl. SE11—5A 78
Harold Rd. E4—3K 19
Harold Rd. E11—1G 49
Harold Rd. E13—1K 65
Harold Rd. N8—5K 29
Harold Rd. N15—5F 31
Harold Rd. NW10—3K 57
Harold Rd. SE19—7D 110

Harold Rd. Sutt—4B 132
Harold Rd. Wfd G—1J 33
Haroldstone Rd. E17—5A 32
Harold Wilson Ho. SE28—1B 84
Harp All. EC4—6B 62 (7J 141)
Harpenden Rd. E12—2A 50
Harpenden Rd. SE27—2B 110
Harper Rd. E6—6D 66
Harper Rd. SE1—3C 78 (6M 147)
Harp Island Clo. NW2—2K 41
Harpley Sq. E1—4K 63 (3M 143)
Harpour Rd. Bark—6G 51
Harp Rd. W7—4K 55
Harpsden St. SW11—1E 92
Harpur M. WC1—5K 61 (5E 140)
Harpur St. WC1—5K 61 (5E 140)
Harraden Rd. SE3—1A 98
Harrier M. SE28—2H 83
Harriers Clo. W5—7E 56
Harrier Way. E6—5D 66
Harries Rd. Hay—4A 54
Harriet Clo. E8—1G 63
Harriet Gdns. Croy—2G 135
Harriet St. SW1—2D 76 (5F 144)
Harriet Wlk. SW1
　　　　—2D 76 (5F 144)
Harriet Way. Bush, Wat—1C 10
Harringay Gdns. N8—4B 30
Harringay Pas. N8 & N4—4A 30
Harringay Rd. N15—4B 30
Harrington Clo. Croy—2J 133
Harrington Gdns. SW7—4A 76
Harrington Hill. E5—1J 47
Harrington Rd. E11—1G 49
Harrington Rd. SE25—4H 125
Harrington Rd. SW7
　　　　—4B 76 (8A 144)
Harrington Sq. NW1—2G 61
Harrington St. NW1
　　　　—3G 61 (1L 139)
Harrington Way. SE18—3B 82
Harriott Clo. SE10—4H 81
Harris Clo. Enf—1G 7
Harris Clo. Houn—1E 86
Harrison Rd. Dag—6H 53
Harrisons Rise. Croy—3B 134
Harrison St. WC1
　　　　—3J 61 (2D 140)
Harris Rd. Bexh—1F 101
Harris Rd. Dag—5F 53
Harris St. E17—7B 32
Harris St. SE5—7D 78
Harrold Rd. Dag—5B 52
Harrow Av. Enf—6A 8
Harroway Rd. SW11—2B 92
Harrowby St. W1
　　　　—6C 60 (7D 138)
Harrowdene Rd. Wemb—4D 40
Harrowdene Gdns. Tedd
　　　　—7A 104
Harrow Dri. N9—1A 18
Harrowes Meade. Edgw—3B 12
Harrow Fields Gdns. Harr
　　　　—3J 39
Harrowgate Rd. E9—7A 48
Harrow Grn. E11—3G 49
Harrow La. E14—7E 64
Harrow Mnr. Way. SE2—2C 84
Harrow Pk. Harr—2J 39
Harrow Pas. King—2D 118
Harrow Pl. E1—6F 63 (7E 142)
Harrow Rd. E6—1C 66
Harrow Rd. E11—3G 49
Harrow Rd.—30 58
　W2 1-281 & 2-322
　W9 283-421a & 324-570
　W10 421-625 & 572-742
　NW10 remainder
Harrow Rd. Bark—1J 67
Harrow Rd. Cars—6C 132
Harrow Rd. Ilf—4G 51
Harrow Rd. Wemb—4K 39
Harrow Rd. Wemb—5G 41
　(Tokyngton)
Harrow Rd. Bri. W2
　　　　—5A 60 (5A 138)

Harrow View Harr—2G 23
Harrow View Rd. W5—4B 56
Harrow Weald Pk. Harr—6C 10
Harte Rd. Houn—2D 86
Hartfield Av. N'holt—2A 54
Hartfield Cres. SW19—7H 107
Hartfield Cres. W Wick—3J 137
Hartfield Gro. SE20—1H 125
Hartfield Rd. SW19—7H 107
Hartfield Rd. W Wick—4J 137
Hartfield Ter. E3—2C 64
Hartford Av. Harr—3A 24
Hartford Rd. Bex—6G 101
Hart Gro. W5—1G 73
Hart Gro. S'hall—5E 54
Hartham Clo. N7—5J 45
Hartham Clo. Iswth—1A 88
Hartham Rd. N7—5J 45
Hartham Rd. N17—2F 31
Hartham Rd. Iswth—1K 87
Harting Rd. SE9—3C 114
Hartington Clo. Harr—4J 39
Hartington Ct. W4—7H 73
Hartington Rd. E16—6K 65
Hartington Rd. E17—6A 32
Hartington Rd. N17—2G 31
Hartington Rd. SW8—1J 93
Hartington Rd. W4—7H 73
Hartington Rd. W13—7B 56
Hartington Rd. S'hall—3C 70
Hartington Rd. Twic—7B 88
Hartismere Rd. SW6—7H 75
Hartlake Rd. E9—6K 47
Hartland Clo. Edgw—2B 12
Hartland Dri. Edgw—2B 12
Hartland Dri. Ruis—3A 38
Hartland Rd. E15—7H 49
Hartland Rd. N11—5J 15
Hartland Rd. NW1—7F 45
Hartland Rd. NW6—2H 59
Hartland Rd. Hmptn—4F 103
Hartland Rd. Iswth—3A 88
Hartland Rd. Mord—7J 121
Hartland Way. Croy—3A 136
Hartland Way. Mord—7H 121
Hartley Av. E6—1C 66
Hartley Av. NW7—5G 13
Hartley Clo. NW7—5G 13
Hartley Clo. Brom—2D 128
Hartley Rd. E11—1H 49
Hartley Rd. Croy—7C 124
Hartley Rd. Well—7C 84
Hartley St. E2—3J 63 (1M 143)
Hartman Rd. E16—1B 82
Hartnoll St. N7—5K 45
Harton Clo. Brom—1B 128
Harton Rd. N9—2C 18
Harton St. SE8—1C 96
Hartsbourne Av. Bush, Wat
　　　　—2B 10
Hartsbourne Clo. Bush, Wat
　　　　—2C 10
Hartsbourne Rd. Bush, Wat
　　　　—2C 10
Hartshorn Gdns. E6—4E 66
Hart's La. SE14—1A 96
Harts La. Bark—6F 51
Hartslock Dri. SE2—2D 84
Hartsmead Rd. SE9—2D 114
Hart St. EC3—7E 62 (9D 142)
Hartsway. Enf—4D 8
Hartswood Rd. W12—2B 74
Hartsworth Clo. E13—2H 65
Hartville Rd. SE18—4J 83
Hartwell Dri. E4—6K 19
Hartwell St. E8—6F 47
Harvard Hill. W4—6H 73
Harvard La. W4—5J 73
Harvard Rd. SE13—5E 96
Harvard Rd. W4—5H 73
Harvard Rd. Iswth—1J 87
Harvel Cres. SE2—5D 84
Harvest Bank Rd. W Wick
　　　　—3H 137
Harvesters Clo. Iswth—5H 87
Harvest La. Th Dit—6A 118
Harvey Gdns. E11—1H 49

Harvey Gdns. SE7—4B 82
Harvey Rd. E11—1H 49
Harvey Rd. N8—5K 29
Harvey Rd. SE5—1D 94
　(in two parts)
Harvey Rd. Houn—7D 86
Harvey Rd. Ilf—5F 51
Harvey Rd. N'holt—7A 38
Harvey's Bldgs. WC2
　　　　—7J 61 (1D 146)
Harveys La. Romf—2K 53
Harvey St. N1—1D 62
Harvill Rd. Sidc—5E 116
Harvington Wlk. E8—7G 47
Harvist Est. N7—4A 46
Harvist Rd. NW6—2F 59
Harwell Pas. N2—4D 28
Harwood Av. Brom—2K 127
Harwood Av. Mitc—3D 122
Harwood Clo. Wemb—4D 40
Harwood Rd. SW6—7J 75
Harwoods Yd. N21—7F 7
Harwood Ter. SW6—1K 91
Haselbury Rd.—4K 17
　N9 176-306 & 163-279
　N18 remainder
Haseley End. SE23—7J 95
Haselrigge Rd. SW4—4H 93
Haseltine Rd. SE26—4B 112
Haselwood Dri. Enf—4G 7
Haskard Rd. Dag—4D 52
Hasker St. SW3—4C 76 (8D 144)
Haslam Av. Sutt—1G 131
Haslam Clo. N1—7A 46
Haslemere Av. NW4—6F 27
Haslemere Av. SW18—2K 107
Haslemere Av.—3A 72
　W13 1-69 & 2-84
　W7 remainder
Haslemere Av. Barn—1J 15
Haslemere Av. Houn—2A 86
Haslemere Av. Mitc—2B 122
Haslemere Clo. Hmptn—5D 102
Haslemere Clo. Wall—5J 133
Haslemere Gdns. N3—3H 27
Haslemere Rd. N8—7J 29
Haslemere Rd. N21—2G 17
Haslemere Rd. Bexh—2F 101
Haslemere Rd. Ilf—2K 51
Haslemere Rd. T Hth—5B 124
Hasler Clo. SE28—7B 68
Hasluck Gdns. Barn—6E 4
Hassard St. E2—2F 63 (1F 142)
Hassendean Rd. SE3—7K 81
Hassett Rd. E9—6K 47
Hassocks Clo. SE26—3H 111
Hassocks Rd. SW16—1H 123
Hassop Rd. NW2—4F 43
Hassop Wlk. SE9—4C 114
Hasted Rd. SE7—5B 82
Hastings Av. Ilf—4G 35
Hastings Clo. SE15—7G 79
Hastings Clo. Barn—4F 5
Hastings Rd. N11—5C 16
Hastings Rd. N17—3D 30
Hastings Rd. W13—7B 56
Hastings Rd. Brom—7C 128
Hastings Rd. Croy—1F 135
Hastings St. WC1
　　　　—3J 61 (2C 140)
Hastingwood Trading Est. N18
　　　　—6F 19
Hastoe Clo. Hay—4C 54
Hatcham Pk. M. SE14—1K 95
Hatcham Pk. Rd. SE14—1K 95
Hatcham Rd. SE15—6J 79
Hatchard Rd. N19—2H 45
Hatchcroft. NW4—3D 26
Hatch Gro. Romf—4E 36
Hatch La. E4—4A 20
Hatch Pl. King—5F 105
Hatch Rd. SW16—2J 123
Hatch Side. Chig—5K 21
Hatch, The. Enf—1E 8
Hatchwood Clo. Wfd G—4C 20
Hatcliffe Clo. SE3—3H 97

Hatfield Clo. SE14—7K 79
Hatfield Clo. Ilf—3F 35
Hatfield Clo. Mitc—4B 122
Hatfield Mead. Mord—5J 121
Hatfield Rd. E15—5G 49
Hatfield Rd. W4—2K 73
Hatfield Rd. W13—1A 72
Hatfield Rd. Dag—6E 52
Hatfields. SE1—1A 78 (2H 147)
Hathaway Clo. Brom—7D 128
Hathaway Clo. Stan—5F 11
Hathaway Cres. E12—6D 50
Hathaway Gdns. W13—5A 56
Hathaway Gdns. Romf—5D 36
Hathaway Rd. Croy—7B 124
Hatherleigh Clo. Mord—4J 121
Hatherley Cres. Sidc—2A 116
Hatherley Gdns. E6—3B 66
Hatherley Gdns. N8—6J 29
Hatherley Gro. W2—6K 59
Hatherley Rd. E17—4B 32
Hatherley Rd. Rich—1F 89
Hatherley Rd. Sidc—4A 116
Hatherley St. SW1
—4G 77 (9M 145)
Hathern Gdns. SE9—4E 114
Hatherop Rd. Hmptn—7D 102
Hathorne Clo. SE15—2J 95
Hathway St. SE15—2K 95
Hatley Av. Ilf—4G 35
Hatley Clo. N11—5J 15
Hatley Rd. N4—2K 45
Hatteraick St. SE16
—2J 79 (4L 149)
Hattersfield Clo. Belv—4F 85
Hatton Clo. SE18—7H 83
Hatton Garden. EC1
—5A 62 (5H 141)
Hatton Gdns. Mitc—5D 122
Hatton Pl. EC1—5A 62 (5H 141)
Hatton Rd. Croy—1A 134
Hatton St. NW8—4B 60 (4B 138)
Hatton Wall. EC1
—5A 62 (5H 141)
Haunch of Venison Yd. W1
—6F 61 (8J 139)
Havana Rd. SW19—2J 107
Havannah St. E14—2C 80
Havant Rd. E17—3E 32
Havant Way. SE15—7F 79
Havelock Pl. Harr—6J 23
Havelock Rd. N17—2G 31
Havelock Rd. SW19—5A 108
Havelock Rd. Belv—4F 85
Havelock Rd. Brom—4A 128
Havelock Rd. Croy—2F 135
Havelock Rd. Harr—3J 23
Havelock Rd. S'hall—3C 70
Havelock St. N1—1J 61
Havelock St. Ilf—2F 51
Havelock Ter. SW8—1F 93
Havelock Wlk. SE23—1J 111
Haven Clo. SW19—3F 107
Haven Clo. Sidc—6C 116
Haven Ct. Beck—2E 126
Haven Grn. W5—6D 56
Haven Grn. Ct. W5—6D 56
Havenhurst Rise. Enf—2F 7
Haven La. W5—6E 56
Haven M. E3—5B 64
Haven Pl. W5—7D 56
Haven St. NW1—7F 45
Haven, The. Rich—3G 89
Havenwood. Wemb—3H 41
Haverfield Gdns. Rich—6G 73
Haverfield Rd. E3—3A 64
Haverford Way. Edgw—1F 25
Haverhill Rd. E4—1K 19
Haverhill Rd. SW12—1G 109
Havering Dri. Romf—4K 37
Havering Gdns. Romf—5D 36
Havering Rd. Romf—2K 37
Havering St. E1
—6K 63 (8M 143)
Havering Way. Bark—3B 68
Haversham Clo. Twic—6D 88
Haverstock Hill. NW3—5C 44

Haverstock Rd. NW5—5E 44
Haverstock St. N1
—2B 62 (1K 141)
Havil St. SE5—7E 78
Havisham Pl. SE19—7B 110
Hawarden Gro. SE24—7C 94
Hawarden Hill. NW2—3C 42
Hawarden Rd. E17—4K 31
Hawbridge Rd. E11—1F 49
Hawes La. E4—1K 9
Hawes La. W Wick—1E 136
Hawes Rd. N18—6C 18
Hawes Rd. Brom—1K 127
Hawes St. N1—7B 46
Hawgood St. E3—5C 64
Hawkdene. E4—6K 9
Hawke Pk. Rd. N22—3B 30
Hawker Clo. Wall—7J 133
Hawke Rd. SE19—6E 110
Hawkesbury Rd. SW15—5D 90
Hawkesfield Rd. SE23—2A 112
Hawkesley Clo. Twic—4A 104
Hawkesmoor M. E1
—7H 63 (9J 143)
Hawkes Rd. Mitc—1D 122
Hawkhurst Rd. SW16—1H 123
Hawkhurst Way. N Mald
—5K 119
Hawkhurst Way. W Wick
—2D 136
Hawkins Clo. Harr—7H 23
Hawkins Rd. Tedd—6B 104
Hawksley Gdns. SE27—2B 110
Hawkridge Clo. Romf—6C 36
Hawksbrook La. Beck—6D 126
Hawkshaw Clo. SW2—1J 109
Hawkshead Clo. Brom—7G 113
Hawkshead Rd. NW10—7B 42
Hawkshead Rd. W4—2A 74
Hawkslade Rd. SE15—5K 95
Hawksley Rd. N16—3E 46
Hawks M. SE10—7E 80
Hawksmoor Clo. E6—6C 66
Hawksmoor St. W6—6F 75
Hawksmouth. E4—7K 9
Hawks Rd. King—2F 119
Hawkstone Rd. SE16
—4J 79 (8M 149)
Hawkwood Cres. E4—6J 9
Hawkwood La. Chst—1G 129
Hawkwood Mt. E5—1H 47
Hawlands Rd. Pinn—7C 22
Hawley Clo. Hmptn—6D 102
Hawley Cres. NW1—7F 45
Hawley M. NW1—7F 45
Hawley Rd. NW1—7F 45
Hawley St. NW1—7F 45
Hawstead Rd. SE6—6D 96
Hawsted. Buck H—1E 20
Hawthorn Av. N13—5D 16
Hawthorn Av. Rich—2E 88
Hawthorn Centre. Harr—4K 23
Hawthorn Clo. N1—6E 46
Hawthorn Clo. Hmptn—5E 102
Hawthorn Clo. Orp—6H 129
Hawthorndene Clo. Brom
—2H 137
Hawthorndene Rd. Brom
—2H 137
Hawthorn Dri. Harr—6E 22
Hawthorn Dri. W Wick—4G 137
Hawthorne Av. Cars—7E 132
Hawthorne Av. Harr—6A 24
Hawthorne Av. Mitc—2B 122
Hawthorne Av. Ruis—7A 22
Hawthorne Av. T Hth—1B 124
Hawthorne Clo. Brom—3D 128
Hawthorne Clo. Sutt—2A 132
Hawthorne Farm Av. N'holt
—1C 54
Hawthorne Gro. NW9—7J 25
Hawthorne Rd. E17—3C 32
Hawthorne Rd. NW10—7C 42
Hawthorne Rd. Brom—3D 128
Hawthorn Gdns. W5—3D 72
Hawthorn Gro. SE20—1H 125
Hawthorn Gro. Enf—1J 7

Hawthorn Hatch. Bren—7B 72
Hawthorn M. NW7—1G 27
Hawthorn Pl. Eri—5J 85
Hawthorn Rd. N8—3H 29
Hawthorn Rd. N18—5A 18
Hawthorn Rd. Bexh—4F 101
Hawthorn Rd. Bren—7B 72
Hawthorn Rd. Buck H—4G 21
Hawthorn Rd. Sutt—6C 132
Hawthorn Rd. Wall—7F 133
Hawthorns. Wfd G—3D 20
Hawthorn Wlk. W10—4G 59
Hawthorn Way. N9—2A 18
Hawtrey Av. N'holt—2B 54
Hawtrey Rd. NW3—7C 44
Haxted Rd. Brom—1K 127
Hay Clo. E15—7G 49
Haycroft Gdns. NW10—1C 58
Haycroft Rd. SW2—5J 93
Hay Currie St. E14—6D 64
Hayday Rd. E16—5J 65
Hayden's Pl. W11—6H 59
Hayden Way. Romf—2J 37
Haydn's M. W3—6J 57
Haydock Av. N'holt—6E 38
Haydock Grn. N'holt—6E 38
Haydon Clo. NW9—4J 25
Haydon Clo. Enf—5K 7
Haydon Pk. Rd. SW19—5J 107
Haydon Rd. Dag—2C 52
Haydons Rd. SW19—5K 107
Haydon St. EC3—7F 63 (9E 142)
Haydon Wlk. E1—6F 63 (8E 142)
Hayes By-Pass. N'holt & Hay
—3B 54
Hayes Chase. W Wick—6F 127
Hayes Clo. Brom—2J 137
Hayes Cres. NW11—5H 27
Hayes Cres. Sutt—4F 131
Hayesford Pk. Dri. Brom
—5H 127
Hayes Garden. Brom—1J 137
Hayes Hill. Brom—1G 137
Hayes Hill Rd. Brom—1H 137
Hayes La. Beck—3E 126
Hayes La. Brom—5J 127
Hayes Mead. Brom—1G 137
Hayes Metro Centre. Hay
—7A 54
Hayes Pl. NW1—4C 60 (4D 138)
Hayes Rd. Brom—4J 127
Hayes Rd. S'hall—4A 70
Hayes St. Brom—1K 137
Hayes Way. Beck—4E 126
Hayes Wood Av. Brom—1K 137
Hayfield Pas. E1
—4J 63 (4M 143)
Hayfield Yd. E1—4J 63 (4M 143)
Haygarth Pl. SW19—5F 107
Haygreen Clo. King—6H 105
Hay Hill. W1—7F 61 (1K 145)
Hayland Clo. NW9—4K 25
Hay La. NW9—4J 25
Hayles St. SE11—4B 78 (8J 147)
Haylett Gdns. King—4D 118
Hayling Clo. N16—5E 46
Hayman St. N1—7B 46
Haymarket. SW1
—7H 61 (1A 146)
Haymer Gdns. Wor Pk—3C 130
Haymerle Rd. SE15—6G 79
Hayne Rd. Beck—2B 126
Haynes Clo. N17—7C 18
Haynes Clo. SE3—3G 97
Haynes, La. SE19—6E 110
Haynes Rd. Wemb—7E 40
Hayne St. EC1—5B 62 (6C 148)
Haynt Wlk. SW20—3G 121
Hay's Galleria. SE1
—1E 78 (2C 148)
Hay's La. SE1—1E 78 (2C 148)
Haysleigh Gdns. SE20—2G 125
Hay's M. W1—1F 77 (2J 145)
Haysoms Clo. Romf—4K 37
Hay St. E2—1G 63
Hayter Ct. E11—2K 49
Hayter Rd. SW2—5J 93

Hayton Clo. E8—6F 47
Hayward Clo. SW19—1K 121
Hayward Clo. Bex—5K 101
Hayward Gdns. SW15—6E 90
Hayward Rd. N20—2F 15
Hayward's Pl. EC1
—4B 62 (3J 141)
Haywood Clo. Pinn—2B 22
Haywood Rd. Brom—4B 128
Hayworth Clo. Enf—2F 9
Hazelbank Rd. SE6—2F 113
Hazelbourne Rd. SW12—6F 93
Hazelbury Grn. N9—3K 17
Hazelbury La. N9—3K 17
Hazel Clo. N13—3J 17
Hazel Clo. N19—2G 45
Hazel Clo. SE15—2G 95
Hazel Clo. Bren—7B 72
Hazel Clo. Croy—1K 135
Hazel Clo. Mitc—4H 123
Hazel Clo. Twic—7G 87
Hazel Croft. Pinn—6A 10
Hazeldene Dri. Pinn—3A 22
Hazeldene Rd. NW10—7K 41
Hazeldene Rd. Ilf—2B 52
Hazeldene Rd. Well—2C 100
Hazeldon Rd. SE4—5A 96
Hazeleigh Gdns. Wfd G—5H 21
Hazel Gdns. Edgw—4C 12
Hazelgreen Clo. N21—1G 17
Hazel Gro. SE26—4K 111
Hazel Gro. Enf—6B 8
Hazel Gro. Romf—3E 36
Hazel Gro. Wemb—1E 56
Hazelhurst. Beck—1F 127
Hazelhurst Rd. SW17—4B 108
Hazel La. Rich—2E 104
Hazell Cres. Romf—1H 37
Hazellville Rd. N19—7H 29
Hazelmere Clo. N'holt—2D 54
Hazelmere Dri. N'holt—2D 54
Hazelmere Rd. NW6—1H 59
Hazelmere Rd. N'holt—2D 54
Hazelmere Rd. Orp—4G 129
Hazelmere Wlk. N'holt—2D 54
Hazelmere Way. Brom—6J 127
Hazel Rd. E15—5G 49
Hazel Rd. NW10—3E 58
Hazeltree La. N'holt—3C 54
Hazel Wlk. Brom—6E 128
Hazel Way. E4—6G 19
Hazel Way. SE1—4F 79 (8E 148)
Hazelwood Av. Mord—4K 121
Hazelwood Clo. W5—2E 72
Hazelwood Clo. Harr—4F 23
Hazel Wood Ct. NW10—3A 42
Hazelwood Ct. Surb—6E 118
Hazelwood Cres. N13—4F 17
Hazelwood La. N13—4F 17
Hazelwood Rd. E17—5A 32
Hazelwood Rd. Enf—6A 8
Hazlebury Rd. SW6—2K 91
Hazledean Rd. Croy—2D 134
Hazledene Rd. W4—6J 73
Hazlemere Gdns. Wor Pk
—1C 130
Hazlewell Rd. SW15—5E 90
Hazlewood Cres. W10—4G 59
Hazlitt M. W14—3G 75
Hazlitt Rd. W14—3G 75
Headcorn Pl. T Hth—4K 123
Headcorn Rd. N17—7A 18
Headcorn Rd. Brom—5H 113
Headcorn Rd. T Hth—4K 123
Headfort Pl. SW1
—2E 76 (5H 145)
Headington Rd. SW18—2A 108
Headlam Rd. SW4—7H 93
Headlam St. E1—4H 63 (4K 143)
Headley App. Ilf—5F 35
Headley Av. Wall—5K 133
Headley Ct. SE26—5J 111
Headley Dri. Ilf—6F 35
Headley Dri. Croy—7D 136
Head's M. W11—6J 59
Headstone Dri. Harr—3H 23
Headstone Gdns. Harr—4G 23

Herbert St. E13—2J 65
Herbert St. NW5—6E 44
Herbert Ter. SE18—7F 83
Herbrand St. WC1
—4J 61 (3C 140)
Hercules Pl. N7—3J 45
Hercules Rd. SE1
—3K 77 (7F 146)
Hercules St. N7—3J 45
Hereford Av. Barn—1J 15
Hereford Gdns. Ilf—7C 34
Hereford Gdns. Pinn—5C 22
Hereford Gdns. Twic—1G 103
Hereford M. W2—6J 59
Hereford Pl. SE14—7B 80
Hereford Retreat. SE15—7G 79
Hereford Rd. E11—5K 33
Hereford Rd. W2—6J 59
Hereford Rd. W3—7H 57
Hereford Rd. W5—3C 72
Hereford Rd. Felt—1A 102
Hereford Sq.
—4A 76 (9A 144)
Hereford St. E2—4G 63 (3G 143)
Herent Dri. Ilf—3D 34
Hereward Gdns. N13—5F 17
Hereward Rd. SW17—4D 108
Herga Ct. Harr—3J 39
Herga Rd. Harr—4K 23
Heriot Av. E4—2H 19
Heriot Rd. NW4—5E 26
Heriots Clo. Stan—4F 11
Heritage Hill. Kes—5K 137
Heritage View. Harr—3K 39
Herlwyn Gdns. SW17—4D 108
Hermes St. N1—2A 62 (1G 141)
Hermes Wlk. N'holt—2E 54
Hermes Way. Wall—7H 133
Herm Ho. N1—6C 46
Hermiston Av. N8—5J 29
Hermitage Clo. E18—4H 33
Hermitage Clo. Enf—2G 7
Hermitage Ct. E18—4J 33
Hermitage Ct. NW2—3J 43
Hermitage Gdns. SE19—7C 110
Hermitage Gdns. NW2—3J 43
Hermitage Grn. SW16—1J 123
Hermitage La. N18—5J 17
Hermitage La. NW2—3J 43
Hermitage La. SE25 & Croy
—6G 125
Hermitage La. SW16—7K 109
Hermitage Path. SW16—1J 123
Hermitage Rd.—7C 30
N4 1-293 & 2-308
N15 remainder
Hermitage Rd. SE19—7C 110
Hermitage St. W2
—5B 60 (6A 138)
Hermitage, The. SE23—1J 111
Hermitage, The. SW13—1B 90
Hermitage, The. Rich—5E 88
Hermitage Wlk. E18—4H 33
Hermitage Wall. E1
—1G 79 (3H 149)
Hermitage Way. Stan—1A 24
Hermit Pl. NW6—1K 59
Hermit Rd. E16—5H 65
Hermit St. EC1—3B 62 (1J 141)
Hermon Hill.—5J 33
E11 1-47 & 2-88
E18 remainder
Herndon Rd. SW18—5A 92
Herne Clo. NW10—5K 41
Herne Hill. SE24—5C 94
Herne Hill Rd. SE24—3C 94
Herne M. N18—4B 18
Herne Pl. SE24—5B 94
Heron Clo. E17—2B 32
Heron Clo. NW10—6A 42
Heron Clo. Buck H—1D 20
Heron Ct. Brom—4A 128
Heron Cres. Sidc—3J 115
Herondale Av. SW18—1B 108
Herongate Clo. Enf—2A 8
Herongate Rd. E12—2A 50
Heron Hill. Belv—5F 85

Heron Industrial Est. E15
—2D 64
Heron M. Ilf—2F 51
Heron Pl. SE16—1A 80
Heron Quays. E14—1C 80
Heron Quays Development. E14
—1D 80
Heron Rd. SE24—4C 94
Heron Rd. Croy—2E 134
Heron Rd. Twic—4A 88
Heronsforde. W12—6C 56
Herons Ga. Edgw—5B 12
Heronslea Dri. Stan—5K 11
Heron's Pl. Iswth—3B 88
Heron Sq. Rich—5D 88
Herons Rise. Barn—4H 5
Herons, The. E11—6H 33
Heron St. SE17—6B 78
Herrick Rd. N5—3C 46
Herrick St. SW1
—4H 77 (9B 146)
Herries St. W10—3G 59
Herringham Rd. SE7—3A 82
Herring St. SE5—6E 78
Hersant Clo. NW10—1C 58
Herschell Rd. SE23—7A 96
Hersham Clo. SW15—7C 90
Hertford Av. SW14—4A 90
Hertford Clo. Barn—3G 5
Hertford Pl. W1—4G 61 (4L 139)
(in two parts)
Hertford Rd. N1—7E 46
Hertford Rd. N2—3C 28
Hertford Rd. N9, Enf & Wal X
—2C 18
Hertford Rd. Bark—7E 50
Hertford Rd. Barn—3F 5
Hertford Rd. Enf—3D 8
Hertford Rd. Ilf—6J 35
Hertford St. W1—1F 77 (3J 145)
Hertford Wlk. Belv—5G 85
Hertford Way. Mitc—4J 123
Hertslet Rd. N7—3K 45
Hervey Clo. N3—1J 27
Hervey Pk. Rd. E17—4A 32
Hervey Rd. SE3—1K 97
Hervey Way. N3—1J 27
Hesketh Pl. W11—7G 59
Hesketh Rd. E7—3J 49
Heslop Rd. SW12—1D 108
Hesper M. SW5—4K 75
Hesperus Cres. E14—4D 80
Hessel Rd. W13—2A 72
Hessel St. E1—6H 63 (8J 143)
Hestercombe Av. SW6—1G 91
Hester Rd. N18—5B 18
Hester Rd. SW11—7C 76
Heston Av. Houn—6C 70
Heston Garage. Houn—6D 70
Heston Grange La. Houn
—6D 70
Heston Industrial Est. Houn
—6A 70
Heston Industrial Mall. Houn
—7D 70
Heston Rd. Houn—7E 70
Heston St. SE14—1C 96
Hetherington Rd. SW4—4J 93
Hetley Gdns. SE19—7F 111
Hetley Rd. W12—1D 74
Hevelius Clo. SE10—5H 81
Hever Croft. SE9—4E 114
Hever Gdns. Brom—2E 128
Heverham Rd. SE18—4J 83
Heversham Rd. Bexh—2G 101
Hewer St. W10—5F 59
Hewett Clo. Stan—4G 11
Hewett Rd. Dag—5D 52
Hewett Rd. EC2—4E 62 (4D 142)
Hewish Rd. N18—4K 17
Hewitt Av. N22—2B 30
Hewitt Rd. N8—5A 30
Hewlett Rd. E3—2A 64
Hexagon, The. N6—1D 44
Hexal Rd. SE6—3G 113
Hexfam Gdns. Iswth—7A 72

Hexham Rd. SE27—2C 110
Hexham Rd. Barn—4E 4
Hexham Rd. Mord—1K 131
Heybourne Rd. N17—7C 18
Heybridge Av. SW16—7J 109
Heybridge Dri. Ilf—3H 35
Heybridge Way. E10—1B 48
Heyford Av. SW8—7J 77
Heyford Av. SW20—3H 121
Heyford Rd. Mitc—2C 122
Heygate St. SE17
—4C 78 (9L 147)
Heylyn Sq. E3—3B 64
Heynes Pk. Dag—4C 52
Heysham La. NW3—3K 43
Heysham Rd. N15—6D 30
Heythorp St. SW18—1H 107
Heywood Av. NW9—1A 26
Heywood Ct. Stan—5H 11
Heyworth Rd. E5—4H 47
Heyworth Rd. E15—4H 49
Hibbert Rd. E17—7B 32
Hibbert Rd. Harr—2K 23
Hibbert St. SW11—3B 92
Hibernia Gdns. Houn—4E 86
Hibernia Rd. Houn—4E 86
Hichisson Rd. SE15—5J 95
Hickin Clo. SE7—4B 82
Hickin St. E14—3E 80
Hickling Rd. Ilf—5F 51
Hickman Av. E4—6K 19
Hickman Clo. E16—5B 66
Hickman Rd. Romf—7C 36
Hickmore Wlk. SW4—3H 93
Hicks Av. Gnfd—3H 55
Hicks Clo. SW11—3C 92
Hicks St. SE8—5A 80
Hidcote Gdns. SW20—3D 120
Hide Pl. SW1—4H 77 (9A 146)
Hide Rd. Harr—4G 23
Hides St. N7—6K 45
Higham Hill Rd. E17—1A 32
Higham Path. E17—3A 32
Higham Pl. E17—3A 32
Higham Rd. N17—3D 30
Higham Rd. Wfd G—6D 20
Highams Pk. Industrial Est. E4
—6K 19
Higham Sta. Av. E4—6J 19
Higham St. E17—3A 32
Highbanks Clo. Well—7B 84
Highbanks Rd. Pinn—6A 10
Highbarrow Rd. Croy—1G 135
High Beech. S Croy—7E 134
High Beeches. Sidc—5E 116
High Bri. SE10—5F 81
Highbridge Rd. Bark—1F 67
Highbrook Rd. SE3—3B 98
High Broom Cres. W Wick
—7D 126
Highbury Av. T Hth—2A 124
Highbury Clo. N Mald—4J 119
Highbury Clo. W Wick—2D 136
Highbury Cres. N5—5C 46
Highbury Est. N5—5C 46
Highbury Gdns. Ilf—2J 51
Highbury Grange. N5—4C 46
Highbury Gro. N5—5B 46
Highbury Hill. N5—4B 46
Highbury M. N7—6A 46
Highbury New Pk. N5—5C 46
Highbury Pk. N5—4B 46
Highbury Pk. M. N5—4C 46
Highbury Pl. N5—6B 46
Highbury Quadrant. N5—3C 46
Highbury Rd. SW19—5G 107
Highbury Sta. Rd. N1—6A 46
Highbury Ter. N5—5B 46
Highbury Ter. M. N5—5B 46
High Cedar Dri. SW20—7D 106
Highclere Rd. N Mald—3K 119
Highclere St. SE26—4A 112
Highcliffe Dri. SW15—6B 90
Highcliffe Gdns. Ilf—5C 34
Highcombe. SE7—6K 81
Highcombe Clo. SE9—1C 114
High Coombe Pl. King—7K 105

Highcroft. NW9—5A 26
Highcroft Av. Wemb—1G 57
Highcroft Est. N19—7J 29
Highcroft Gdns. NW11—6H 27
Highcroft Rd. N19—7J 29
High Cross Centre. N15—4G 31
High Cross Rd. N17—3G 31
Highcross Way. SW15—1C 106
Highdaun Dri. SW16—4K 123
Highdown. Wor Pk—2B 130
Highdown Rd. SW15—6D 90
High Dri. N Mald—1J 119
High Elms. Wfd G—5D 20
Highfield Av. NW9—5J 25
Highfield Av. NW11—7F 27
Highfield Av. Eri—6H 85
Highfield Av. Gnfd—5J 39
Highfield Av. Pinn—5D 22
Highfield Av. Wemb—3F 41
Highfield Clo. NW9—5J 25
Highfield Clo. Surb—7C 118
Highfield Ct. N14—6B 6
Highfield Cres. NW9—5J 25
Highfield Dri. Brom—4G 127
Highfield Dri. Eps—6B 130
Highfield Dri. W Wick—2D 136
Highfield Gdns. NW11—6G 27
Highfield Hill. SE19—7D 110
Highfield Rd. N21—2G 17
Highfield Rd. NW11—6G 27
Highfield Rd. W3—5H 57
Highfield Rd. Bexh—5F 101
Highfield Rd. Brom—4D 128
Highfield Rd. Chst—3K 129
Highfield Rd. Iswth—1K 87
Highfield Rd. Surb—7J 119
Highfield Rd. Sutt—5C 132
Highfield Rd. Wfd G—7H 21
Highfields Gro. N6—1D 44
Highgate Av. N6—7F 29
Highgate Clo. N6—7E 28
Highgate High St. N6—1E 44
Highgate Hill. N19—1F 45
Highgate Ho. SE26—3G 111
Highgate Rd. NW5—3E 44
Highgate Spinney. N8—6H 29
Highgate W. Hill. N6—2E 44
High Gro. SE18—7H 83
High Gro. Brom—1B 128
Highgrove Clo. Chst—1C 128
Highgrove Ct. Beck—7C 112
Highgrove Rd. Dag—5C 52
High Hill Est. E5—1H 47
High Hill Ferry. E5—1H 47
High Holborn. WC1
—6J 61 (7C 140)
Highland Av. W7—6J 55
Highland Av. Dag—3J 53
Highland Cotts. Wall—4F 133
Highland Ct. E18—1K 33
Highland Croft. Beck—6D 112
Highland Dri. Bush, Wat—1B 10
Highland Rd. SE19—6E 110
Highland Rd. SE26—5K 111
Highland Rd. Bexh—6G 101
Highland Rd. Brom—1H 127
Highlands Av. W3—7J 57
Highlands Clo. N4—7J 29
Highlands Clo. Houn—1F 87
Highlands Gdns. Ilf—1D 50
Highlands Heath. SW15—7E 90
Highlands Rd. Barn—5D 4
Highlands, The. Edgw—2H 25
High La. W7—6H 55
Highlea Clo. NW9—7F 13
High Level Dri. SE26—4G 111
Highlever Rd. W10—5E 58
Highmead. SE18—7K 83
High Mead. Harr—5J 23
High Mead. W Wick—1F 137
Highmead Cres. Wemb—7F 41
High Meadow Clo. Pinn—4A 22
High Meadow Cres. NW9
—5K 25
High Meads Rd. E16—6B 66
Highmore Rd. SE3—7G 81
High Mt. NW4—6C 26
High Oaks. Enf—1E 6
High Pk. Av. Rich—1G 89

High Pk. Rd. Rich—1G 89
High Path. SW19—1K 121
Highpoint. N6—7E 28
High Point. SE9—3F 115
High Rd. Buck H & Lou—2E 20
High Rd. Bushey Heath,
   Bush, Wat—1C 10
High Rd. Chig—5K 21
High Rd. E. Finchley, N2—1B 28
High Rd. Harr—7D 10
High Rd. Ilf & Romf—3F 51
High Rd. Leyton—6D 32
E15 1-185 & 2-164
E10 remainder
High Rd. Leytonstone, E11
   —4G 49
High Rd. New Southgate, N11
   —5A 16
High Rd. N. Finchley, N12
   —4F 15
High Rd. South Woodford, E18
   —1J 33
High Rd. Tottenham—4F 31
N15 1-363 & 2-344
N17 remainder
High Rd. Wemb—5D 40
High Rd. Whetstone, N20—7F 5
High Rd. Willesden, NW10
   —6B 42
High Rd. Wfd G—6C 20
High Rd. Wood Green, N22
   —1K 29
High Sheldon. N6—6D 28
Highshore Rd. SE15—2F 95
Highstead Cres. Eri—1K 101
Highstone Av. E11—6J 33
High St. Acton, W3—1H 73
High St. Barkingside, Ilf—3G 35
High St. Barn—3B 4
High St. Beck—2C 126
High St. Bren—7C 72
High St. Brom—2J 127
High St. Bush, Wat—1A 10
High St. Cars—4E 132
High St. Cheam, Sutt—6G 131
High St. Chst—6F 115
High St. Colliers Wood, SW19
   —7B 108
High St. Cranford, Houn—6A 70
High St. Croy—3C 134
High St. Ealing, W5—7D 56
High St. Edgw—6B 12
High St. Ewell, Eps—7B 130
High St. Hmptn—7G 103
High St. Hampton Hill, Hmptn
   —6G 103
High St. Hampton Wick, King
   —1C 118
High St. Harlesden, NW10
   —2B 58
High St. Harrow on the Hill,
   Harr—1J 39
High St. Hornsey, N8—4J 29
High St. Houn—3F 87
High St. King—3D 118
High St. Mill Hill, NW7—5J 13
High St. N Mald—4A 120
High St. Penge, SE20—6J 111
High St. Pinn—3C 22
High St. Plaistow, E13—2J 65
High St. Ponders End, Enf—5D 8
High St. Romf—5K 37
High St. S'hall—1D 70
High St. Southgate, N14—1C 16
High St. South Norwood, SE25
   —4F 125
High St. Stratford, E15—2E 64
High St. Sutt—4K 131
   (in four parts)
High St. Tedd—5K 103
High St. Th Dit—6A 118
High St. T Hth—4C 124
High St. Walthamstow, E17
   —5A 32
High St. Wanstead, E11—5J 33
High St. Wealdstone, Harr
   —2J 23

High St. Wembley Park, Wemb
   —4F 41
High St. W Wick—1D 136
High St. Whitton, Twic—7G 87
High St. Wimbledon. SW19
   —5F 107
High St. Woolwich, SE18
   —3E 82
High St. M. SW19—5G 107
High St. N.—5C 50
E6 1-239 & 2-226
E12 remainder
High St. S. E6—2D 66
High Timber St. EC4
   —7C 62 (9L 141)
High Tor Clo. Brom—7K 113
High Trees. SW2—1A 110
High Trees. Barn—5H 5
High Trees. Croy—1A 136
High View. Pinn—3A 22
Highview Av. Edgw—4D 12
Highview Av. Wall—5K 133
Highview Gdns. N3—3G 27
Highview Gdns. N11—5B 16
Highview Gdns. Edgw—4D 12
High View Rd. E18—2H 33
Highview Rd. SE19—6D 110
Highview Rd. W13—6A 56
High View Rd. Sidc—4B 116
Highway, The—7K 63 (9M 143)
E1 1-485 & 2-388
E14 remainder
Highway, The. Stan—7F 11
Highway Trading, Centre,
   The. E1—7K 63
Highwood. Brom—3F 127
Highwood Av. N12—4F 15
Highwood Ct. N12—3F 15
Highwood Gdns. Ilf—5D 34
Highwood Gro. NW7—5E 12
Highwood Hill. NW7—2G 13
Highwood Rd. N19—3J 45
Highworth. NW1—2A 94
Hilary Av. Mitc—3E 122
Hilary Clo. E11—5J 33
Hilary Clo. SW6—7K 75
Hilary Clo. Eri—1J 101
Hilary Rd. W12—7B 58
Hilbert Rd. Sutt—3F 131
Hilborough Clo. SW19—7A 108
Hilda Ct. Surb—7D 118
Hilda Rd. E6—7B 50
Hilda Rd. E16—4G 65
   (in two parts)
Hilda Ter. SW9—2A 94
Hildenborough Gdns. Brom
   —6G 113
Hildenlea Pl. Brom—2G 127
Hildreth St. SW12—1F 109
Hildyard Rd. SW6—6J 75
Hiley Rd. NW10—3E 58
Hilgrove Rd. NW6—7A 44
Hiliary Gdns. Stan—2C 24
Hillary Rise. Barn—4D 4
Hillary Rd. S'hall—3E 70
Hillbeck Clo. SE15—7J 79
Hillbeck Way. Gnfd—1H 55
Hillbrook Rd. SW17—3D 108
Hill Brow. Brom—1B 128
Hillbrow. N Mald—3B 120
Hill Brow Clo. Bex—4K 117
Hillbrow Rd. Brom—6G 113
Hillbury Av. Harr—5B 24
Hillbury Rd. SW17—3F 109
Hill Clo. NW2—3D 42
Hill Clo. NW11—6J 27
Hill Clo. Chst—5F 115
Hill Clo. Harr—3J 39
Hill Clo. Stan—4G 11
Hillcote Av. SW16—7A 110
Hillcourt Av. N12—6E 14
Hillcourt Est. N16—1D 46
Hillcourt Rd. SE22—6H 95
Hill Cres. N20—2E 14

Hill Cres. Bex—1J 117
Hill Cres. Harr—5A 24
Hill Cres. Surb—5F 119
Hill Cres. Wor Pk—2E 130
Hillcrest. N6—7E 28
Hillcrest. N21—7F 7
Hillcrest. Sidc—7A 100
Hillcrest Av. NW11—5H 27
Hillcrest Av. Edgw—4C 12
Hillcrest Av. Pinn—4B 22
Hillcrest Clo. SE26—4G 111
Hillcrest Clo. Beck—6B 126
Hillcrest Gdns. N3—4G 27
Hillcrest Gdns. NW2—3C 42
Hillcrest Rd. E17—2F 33
Hillcrest Rd. E18—2J 33
Hillcrest Rd. W3—1H 73
Hillcrest Rd. W5—5E 56
Hillcrest Rd. Brom—5J 113
Hillcrest View. Beck—6B 126
Hillcroft Av. Pinn—6D 22
Hillcroft Cres. W5—6E 56
Hillcroft Cres. Ruis—3B 38
Hillcroft Cres. Wemb—4F 41
Hillcroft Rd. E6—5F 67
Hillcroome Rd. Sutt—6B 132
Hillcross Av. Mord—6F 121
Hilldale Rd. Sutt—4H 131
Hilldown Rd. SW16—7J 109
Hilldown Rd. Brom—1H 137
Hill Dri. NW9—1J 41
Hilldrop Cres. N7—5H 45
Hilldrop Est. N7—4J 45
Hilldrop La. N7—5H 45
Hilldrop Rd. N7—5H 45
Hilldrop Rd. Brom—6J 113
Hilend. SE18—1E 98
Hillersdon Av. SW13—2C 90
Hillersdon Av. Edgw—5A 12
Hillery Clo. SE17
   —4D 78 (9B 148)
Hill Farm Rd. W10—5E 58
Hillfield Av. N8—5J 29
Hillfield Av. NW9—5A 26
Hillfield Av. Mord—6C 122
Hillfield Av. Wemb—7E 40
Hillfield Clo. Harr—4G 23
Hillfield Ct. NW3—5C 44
Hillfield Pk. N10—4F 29
Hillfield Pk. N21—2F 17
Hillfield Pk. M. N10—4F 29
Hillfield Rd. NW6—5H 43
Hillfield Rd. Hmptn—7D 102
Hillfoot Av. Romf—1J 37
Hillfoot Rd. Romf—1J 37
Hillgate Pl. W8—1J 75
Hillgate St. W8—1J 75
Hill Gro. Romf—3K 37
Hill Ho. Av. Stan—7E 10
Hill Ho. Clo. N21—7F 7
Hill Ho. Rd. SW16—5K 109
Hilliards Ct. E1—1J 79 (2L 149)
Hillier Clo. Barn—6E 4
Hillier Gdns. Croy—5A 134
Hillier Rd. SW11—6D 92
Hilliers La. Croy—3J 133
Hillingdon Rd. Bexh—3J 101
Hillingdon St. —6B 78
SE17 1-237 & 2-244
SE5 remainder
Hillington Gdns. Wfd G—2B 34
Hillman St. E8—6H 47
Hillmarton Rd. N7—5J 45
Hillmead Dri. SW9—4B 94
Hillmore Gro. SE26—5A 112
Hill Path. SW16—5K 109
Hillreach. SE18—5D 82
Hill Rise. N6—6C 8
Hill Rise. NW11—4K 27
Hill Rise. SE23—1H 111
Hill Rise. Gnfd—1G 55
Hill Rise. Rich—5D 88
Hillrise Rd. N19—7J 29
Hill Rd. N10—1D 28
Hill Rd. NW8—2A 60 (1A 138)
Hill Rd. Cars—6C 132
Hill Rd. Harr—5A 24

Hill Rd. Mitc—1F 123
Hill Rd. Pinn—5C 22
Hill Rd. Sutt—5K 131
Hill Rd. Wemb—3B 40
Hillsborough Rd. SE22—5E 94
Hillside. NW9—4K 25
Hillside. NW10—7J 41
Hillside. SW19—6F 107
Hillside. Barn—5F 5
Hillside Av. N11—6J 15
Hillside Av. Wemb—4F 41
Hillside Av. Wfd G—6F 21
Hillside Clo. NW8—2K 59
Hillside Clo. Mord—4G 121
Hillside Clo. Wfd G—5F 21
Hillside Cres. Enf—1J 7
Hillside Cres. Harr—1G 39
Hillside Dri. Edgw—6B 12
Hillside Est. N15—6F 31
Hillside Gdns. E17—3F 33
Hillside Gdns. N6—6F 29
Hillside Gdns. N11—6B 16
Hillside Gdns. Barn—4B 4
Hillside Gdns. Edgw—4A 12
Hillside Gdns. Harr—7E 24
Hillside Gdns. Wall—7G 133
Hillside Gro. N14—7C 6
Hillside Gro. NW7—7H 13
Hillside La. Brom—2H 137
Hillside Pas. SW2—2K 109
Hillside Rd. N15—7E 30
Hillside Rd. SW2—2A 110
Hillside Rd. W5—5E 56
Hillside Rd. Brom—3H 127
Hillside Rd. Croy—5B 134
Hillside Rd. N'wald & Pinn—1A 22
Hillside Rd. S'hall—4E 54
Hillside Rd. Surb—4G 119
Hillside Rd. Sutt—7H 131
Hillsleigh Rd. W8—1H 75
Hills M. W5—7E 56
Hills Pl. W1—6G 61 (8L 139)
Hills Rd. Buck H—1E 20
Hillstowe St. E5—3J 47
Hill St. W1—1E 76 (2H 145)
Hill St. Rich—5D 88
Hill Top. NW11—4K 27
Hill Top. Mord—6J 121
Hill Top. Sutt—7H 121
Hill Top. Wfd G—6J 21
Hilltop Gdns. NW4—2D 26
Hilltop Gdns. NW6—7J 43
Hilltop Way. Stan—3F 11
Hillview. SW20—7D 106
Hillview Av. Harr—5E 24
Hill View Cres. Ilf—6D 34
Hillview Gdns. NW4—4F 27
Hillview Gdns. NW9—5K 25
Hillview Gdns. Harr—3E 22
Hill View Rd. NW7—4A 14
Hillview Rd. Chst—5E 114
Hillview Rd. Pinn—1D 22
Hillview Rd. Sutt—3A 132
Hill View Rd. Twic—6A 88
Hillway. N6—2E 44
Hillway. NW9—1A 42
Hillworth Rd. SW2—7A 94
Hillyard Rd. W7—5J 55
Hillyard St. SW9—1A 94
Hillyfield. E17—2A 32
Hilly Fields Cres. SE4—3C 96
Hilsea St. E5—4J 47
Hilton Av. N12—5G 15
Hilversum Cres. SE22—5E 94
Himley Rd. SW17—5C 108
Hinchcliffe Clo. Wall—7K 133
Hinckley Rd. SE15—4G 95
Hind Ct. EC4—6A 62 (8H 141)
Hind Cres. Eri—6K 85
Hindes Rd. Harr—5H 23
Hinde St. W1—6E 60 (7H 139)
Hind Gro. E14—6C 64
Hindhead Clo. N16—1E 46
Hindhead Gdns. N'holt—1C 54
Hindhead Way. Wall—5J 133
Hindmans Rd. SE22—5G 95

Hindmans Way. Dag—4F 69
Hindmarsh Clo. E1
        —7G 63 (9H 143)
Hindrey Rd. E5—5H 47
Hindsley's Pl. SE23—2K 111
Hinkler Clo. Wall—7J 133
Hinkler Rd. Harr—3D 24
Hinksey Path. SE2—2D 84
Hinstock Rd. SE18—7G 83
Hinton Av. Houn—4B 86
Hinton Clo. SE9—1C 114
Hinton Rd. N18—4K 17
Hinton Rd. SE24—3B 94
Hinton Rd. Wall—6G 133
Hippodrome Pl. W11—7G 59
Hitcham Rd. E17—7B 32
Hitchin Sq. E3—2A 64
Hitherfield Rd. SW16—3A 110
Hitherfield Rd. Dag—2E 52
Hither Grn. La. SE13—5E 96
Hitherwell Dri. Harr—1H 23
Hitherwood Dri. SE19—4F 111
Hive Clo. Bush, Wat—2C 10
Hive Rd. Bush, Wat—2C 10
Hoadly Rd. SW16—3H 109
Hobart Clo. N20—2H 15
Hobart Clo. Hay—4B 54
Hobart Dri. Hay—4B 54
Hobart Gdns. T Hth—3D 124
Hobart La. Hay—4B 54
Hobart Pl. SW1—3F 77 (6J 145)
Hobart Pl. Rich—7F 89
Hobart Rd. Dag—4D 52
Hobart Rd. Hay—4B 54
Hobart Rd. Ilf—2G 35
Hobart Rd. Wor Pk—3D 130
Hobbayne Rd. W7—6H 55
Hobbes Wlk. SW15—5D 90
Hobbs Grn. N2—3A 28
Hobbs Pl. N1—2E 62
Hobbs Rd. SE27—4C 110
Hobday St. E14—6D 64
Hobill Wlk. Surb—6F 119
Hoblands End. Chst—6J 115
Hobury St. SW10—6B 76
Hocker St. E2—3F 63 (2E 142)
Hockett Clo. SE8—4A 80
Hockley Av. E6—2C 66
Hocroft Av. NW2—3H 43
Hocroft Ct. NW2—3H 43
Hocroft Rd. NW2—3H 43
Hocroft Wlk. NW2—3H 43
Hodder Dri. Gnfd—2K 55
Hoddesdon Rd. Belv—5G 85
Hodford Rd. NW11—1H 43
Hodgkin Clo. SE28—7D 68
Hodister Clo SE7—5C 78
Hodnet Gro. SE16
        —4K 79 (8M 149)
Hodson Clo. Harr—3D 38
Hoe La. Enf—1B 8
Hoe St. E17—4C 32
Hoever Ho. SE6—4E 112
Hofland Rd. W14—3G 75
Hogan M. W2—5B 60 (5A 138)
Hogan Way. E5—2G 47
Hogarth Clo. E16—5B 66
Hogarth Clo. W5—5E 56
Hogarth Ct. EC3—6E 62 (8D 142)
Hogarth Ct. SE19—4F 111
Hogarth Cres. SW19—1B 122
Hogarth Cres. Croy—7C 124
Hogarth Gdns. Houn—7E 70
Hogarth Hill NW11—4H 27
Hogarth La. W4—6A 74
Hogarth Rd. SW5—4K 75
Hogarth Rd Edgw—2G 25
Hoggin Rd. N9—2K 17
Hog Hill Rd. Romf—1F 37
Hogsden Clo. N1—2C 62
Holbeach Gdns. Sidc—6K 99
Holbeach M. SW12—1F 109
Holbeach Rd. SE6—7C 96
Holbeck Row. SE15—7G 79
Holbein M SW1—5E 76 (9G 145)
Holbein Pl SW1—4E 76 (9G 145)
Holberton Gdns. NW10—3D 58

Holborn. EC1—5A 62 (6G 141)
Holborn Cir. EC1
        —5A 62 (6H 141)
Holborn Rd. E13—5K 65
Holborn Viaduct. EC1
        —5B 62 (6J 141)
Holbrook Clo. N19—1F 45
Holbrook Clo. Enf—1B 8
Holbrooke Ct. N7—3J 45
Holbrooke Pl. Rich—5D 88
Holbrook La. Chst—7H 115
Holbrook Rd. E15—2H 65
Holbrook Way. Brom—6D 128
Holburne Clo. SE3—1A 98
Holburne Gdns. SE3—1B 98
Holburne Rd. SE3—1A 98
Holcombe Hill. NW7—3H 13
Holcombe Rd. N17—3G 31
Holcombe Rd. Ilf—7E 34
Holcombe St. W6—4D 74
Holcote Clo. Belv—3E 84
Holcroft Rd. E9—7J 47
Holden Av. N12—5E 14
Holden Av. NW9—1J 41
Holdenby Rd. SE4—5A 96
Holdenhurst Av. N12—7F 15
Holden Rd. N12—5E 14
Holden St. SW11—2E 92
Holdernesse Rd. SW17—2E 108
Holderness Way. SE27—5B 110
Holder's Hill Av. NW4—2F 27
Holder's Hill Cir. NW7—7B 14
Holder's Hill Cres. NW4—2F 27
Holder's Hill Dri. NW4—3F 27
Holder's Hill Gdns. NW4—2G 27
Holders Hill Rd. NW4 & NW7
        —2F 27
Holdgate St. SE7—3B 82
Holford Pl. WC1—3K 61 (1F 140)
Holford Rd. NW3—3A 44
Holford St. WC1
        —3A 62 (1G 141)
Holgate Av. SW11—3B 92
Holgate Gdns. Dag—6G 53
Holgate Rd. Dag—5G 53
Holland Av. SW20—1B 120
Holland Av. Sutt—7J 131
Holland Clo. N20—7G 5
Holland Clo. Brom—2H 137
Holland Clo. Stan—5G 11
Holland Ct. NW7—6H 13
Holland Ct. Surb—7D 118
Holland Dri. SE23—3A 112
Holland Gdns. W14—3G 75
Holland Gro. SW9—7A 78
Holland La. W14—3H 75
Holland Pk. W11—1G 75
Holland Pk. Av. W11—1G 75
Holland Pk. Av. Ilf—6J 35
Holland Pk. M. W11—1H 75
Holland Pk. Rd. W14—3H 75
Holland Rd. E6—1D 66
Holland Rd. E15—3G 65
Holland Rd. NW10—1C 58
Holland Rd. SE25—5G 125
Holland Rd. W14—2G 75
Holland Rd. Wemb—6D 40
Hollands, The. Felt—4B 86
Hollands, The. Wor Pk—1B 130
Holland St. SE1—1B 78 (2K 147)
Holland St. W8—2J 75
Holland Vs. Rd. W14—2G 75
Holland Wlk. N19—1H 45
Holland Wlk. W8—1H 75
Holland Wlk. Stan—5F 11
Holland Way. Brom—2H 137
Hollar Rd. N16—3F 47
Hollen St. W1—6H 61 (7A 140)
Holles Clo. Hmptn—6E 102
Holles St. W1—6F 61 (7K 139)
Holley Rd. W3—2A 74
Hollick Wood Av. N12—6J 15
Hollidge Way. Dag—7H 53
Hollies Av. Sidc—2K 115
Hollies Clo. SW16—6A 110
Hollies Clo. Twic—2K 103

Hollies End. NW7—5J 13
Hollies Rd. W5—4C 72
Hollies, The. N20—1G 15
Hollies Way. SW12—7E 92
Holligrave Rd. Brom—1J 127
Hollingbourne Av. Bexh
        —1F 101
Hollingbourne Gdns. W13
        —5B 56
Hollingbourne Rd. SE24—5C 94
Hollingsworth Ct. Surb—7D 118
Hollingsworth Rd. Croy
        —6H 135
Hollington Cres. N Mald
        —6B 120
Hollington Rd. E6—3D 66
Hollington Rd. N17—2G 31
Hollingworth Rd. Orp—7F 129
Hollman Gdns. SW16—6B 110
Holloway Rd. E6—3D 66
Holloway Rd. E11—3G 49
Holloway Rd. N7—2H 45
  N7 31-479 & 2-596
  N19 remainder
Holloway St. Houn—3F 87
Hollowfield Wlk. N'holt—7C 38
Hollows, The. Bren—6F 73
Hollow, The. Wfd G—4C 20
Holly Av. Stan—2E 24
Hollybank Clo. Hmptn—5E 102
Holly Berry La. NW3—4A 44
Hollybrake Clo. Chst—7H 115
Hollybush Clo. E11—5J 33
Hollybush Clo. Harr—1J 23
Hollybush Gdns. E2
        —3H 63 (1K 143)
Hollybush Hill. E11—6H 33
Hollybush Hill. NW3—4A 44
Holly Bush La. Hmptn—7D 102
Hollybush Pl. E2
        —3H 63 (1K 143)
Hollybush Rd. King—5E 104
Hollybush St. E13—3K 65
Holly Bush Vale. NW3—4A 44
Holly Clo. NW10—7A 42
Holly Clo. Buck H—3G 21
Holly Clo. Felt—5C 102
Holly Clo. Wall—7F 133
Holly Cres. Beck—5B 126
Holly Cres. Wfd G—7A 20
Hollycroft Av. NW3—3J 43
Hollycroft Av. Wemb—3F 41
Hollydale Rd. SE15—2J 95
Holly Dene. SE15—1H 95
Hollydown Way. E11—3F 49
Holly Dri. E4—7J 9
Hollyfarm Rd. S'hall—5C 70
Hollyfield Av. N11—5J 15
Hollyfield Rd. Surb—7F 119
Holly Gro. NW9—7J 25
Holly Gro. SE15—2F 95
Hollygrove. Bush, Wat—1C 10
Holly Gro. Pinn—1C 22
Holly Hedge Ter. SE13—5F 97
Holly Hill. N21—6E 6
Holly Hill. NW3—4A 44
Holly Hill Rd. Belv & Eri—5H 85
Holly Lodge Gdns. N6—2E 44
Hollymead. Cars—3D 132
Holly Mt. NW3—4A 44
Hollymount Clo. SE10—1E 96
Holly Pk. N3—3H 27
Holly Pk. N4—7K 29
  (in two parts)
Holly Pk. Est. N4—7K 29
Holly Pk. Gdns. N3—3J 27
Holly Pk. Rd. N11—5K 15
Holly Pk. Rd. W7—1K 71
Holly Rd. E11—7H 33
Holly Rd. W4—4K 73
Holly Rd. Hmptn—6G 103
Holly Rd. Houn—4F 87
Holly Rd. Twic—1K 103
Holly St. E8—7F 47
Holly St. Est. E8—7F 47
Holly Ter. N6—1E 44
Holly Ter. N20—2F 15

Holly Tree Clo. SW19—1F 107
Hollyview Clo. NW4—6C 26
Holly Village. N6—2E 44
Holly Wlk. NW3—4A 44
Holly Wlk. Enf—3J 7
Holly Way. Mitc—4H 123
Hollywood M. SW10—6A 76
Hollywood Rd. E4—5F 19
Hollywood Rd. SW10—6A 76
Hollywood Way. Wfd G—7A 20
Holman Rd. SW11—2B 92
Holmbridge Gdns. Enf—4E 8
Holmbrook Dri. NW4—5F 27
Holmbury Clo. Bush, Wat
        —2D 10
Holmbury Ct. SW17—3D 108
Holmbury Ct. S Croy—5E 134
Holmbury Gro. Croy—7B 136
Holmbury Pk. Brom—7C 114
Holmbury View. E5—1H 47
Holmbush Rd. SW15—6G 91
Holmcote Gdns. N5—5C 46
Holmcroft Ho. E17—4D 32
Holmcroft Way. Brom—5D 128
Holmdale Gdns. NW4—5F 27
Holmdale Rd. NW6—5J 43
Holmdale Rd. Chst—5G 115
Holmdale Ter. N15—6E 30
Holmdene Av. NW7—6H 13
Holmdene Av. SE24—5C 94
Holmdene Av. Harr—3F 23
Holmdene Clo. Beck—2E 126
Holmead Rd. SW6—7K 75
Holme Lacey Rd. SE12—6H 97
Holme Rd. E6—1C 66
Holmes Av. E17—3B 32
Holmes Av. NW7—5B 14
Holmesdale Av. SW14—4H 89
Holmesdale Clo. SE25—3F 125
Holmesdale Rd. N6—7F 29
Holmesdale Rd.—5D 124
  SE25 45-387 & 62-326
  Croy remainder
Holmesdale Rd. Bexh—2D 100
Holmesdale Rd. Rich—1F 89
Holmesdale Rd. Tedd—7C 104
Holmesley Rd. SE23—6A 96
Holmes Pl. SW10—6A 76
Holmes Rd. NW5—5F 45
Holmes Rd. SW19—7A 108
Holmes Rd. Twic—2K 103
Holmeswood Ct. N22—2A 30
Holme Way. Stan—6E 10
Holmewood Gdns. SW2—7K 93
Holmewood Rd. SE25—3E 124
Holmewood Rd. SW2—7K 93
Holmfield. NW11—4J 27
Holmfield Av. NW4—5F 27
Holmfield Ct. NW3—6C 44
Holmhurst Rd. Belv—5H 85
Holmleigh Rd. N16—1E 46
Holmoak Clo. SW15—6H 91
Holm Oak M. SW4—5J 93
Holmoaks Ho. Beck—2E 126
Holmshaw Clo. SE26—4A 112
Holmside Rd. SW12—6E 92
Holmsley Clo. N Mald—7B 120
Holmstall Av. Edgw—3J 25
Holm Wlk. SE3—2J 97
Holmwood Clo. Harr—3G 23
Holmwood Clo. N'holt—6F 39
Holmwood Clo. Sutt—7F 131
Holmwood Gdns. N3—2J 27
Holmwood Gdns. Wall—6F 133
Holmwood Gro. NW7—5E 12
Holmwood Rd. Ilf—2J 51
Holmwood Rd. Sutt—7F 131
Holmwood Vs. SE7—5J 81
Holne Chase. N2—6A 28
Holne Chase. Mord—6H 121
Holness Rd. E15—6H 49
Holroyd Rd. SW15—4E 90
Holstein Way. Eri—3D 84
Holstock Rd. Ilf—2G 51
Holsworth Clo. Harr—5G 23
Holt Clo. N10—4E 28
Holt Clo. SE28—7C 68

217

Holt Ct. E15—5E 48
Holt Ho. SW2—6A 94
Holton St. E1—4K 63
Holt Rd. E16—1C 82
Holt Rd. Wemb—3B 40
Holtwhite's Av. Enf—2H 7
Holtwhite's Hill. Enf—1G 7
Holwell Pl. Pinn—4C 22
Holwood Pl. SW4—4H 93
Holybourne Av. SW15—7C 90
Holybush Wlk. SW9—4B 94
Holyhead Clo. E3—3C 64
Holyoake Ct. SE16—2B 80
Holyoake Wlk. N2—3A 28
Holyoake Wlk. W5—4C 56
Holyoak Rd. SE11
—4B 78 (9J 147)
Holyport Rd. SW6—7F 75
Holyrood Av. Harr—4C 38
Holyrood Gdns. Edgw—3H 25
Holyrood Rd. Barn—6F 5
Holyrood St. SE1
—1E 78 (3C 148)
Holywell Clo. SE3—6J 81
Holywell La. EC2
—4E 62 (3D 142)
Holywell Row. EC2
—4E 62 (4C 142)
Homan Ct. N12—4F 15
Homebush Ho. E4—7J 9
Home Clo. Cars—2D 132
Home Clo. N'holt—3D 54
Homecroft Rd. N22—1C 30
Homecroft Rd. SE26—5J 111
Homefarm Rd. W7—6K 55
Home Field. Barn—5C 4
Homefield Av. Ilf—5J 35
Homefield Clo. NW10—7J 41
Homefield Gdns. N2—3B 28
Homefield Gdns. Mitc—2A 122
Homefield Pk. Sutt—6K 131
Homefield Rd. SW19—6G 107
Homefield Rd. W4—5B 74
Homefield Rd. Brom—1A 128
Homefield Rd. Edgw—6E 12
Homefield Rd. Wemb—4B 40
Homefield St. N1
—2E 62 (1C 142)
Homefinch Ho. Sidc—3B 116
Home Gdns. Dag—3J 53
Homeland Dri. Sutt—7K 131
Homelands Dri. SE19—7E 110
Homeleigh Rd. SE15—5K 95
Home Mead. Stan—1C 24
Homemead Rd. Brom—5D 128
Homemead Rd. Croy—6G 123
Home Pk. Rd. SW19—4H 107
Home Pk. Wlk. King—4D 118
Homer Ct. Bexh—1J 101
Home Rd. SW11—2C 92
Homer Rd. E9—6A 48
Homer Rd. Croy—6K 125
Homer Row. W1
—5C 60 (6D 138)
Homersham Rd. King—2G 119
Homer St. W1—5C 60 (6D 138)
Homerton Gro. E9—5K 47
Homerton High St. E9—5K 47
Homerton Rd. E9—5B 48
Homerton Row. E9—5J 47
Homerton Ter. E9—6J 47
(in two parts)
Homesdale Clo. E11—5J 33
Homesdale Rd. Brom—4A 128
Homesdale Rd. Orp—7J 129
Homestall Rd. SE22—5J 95
Homestead Paddock. N14
—5A 6
Homestead Pk. NW2—3B 42
Homestead Rd. SW6—7H 75
Homestead Rd. Dag—2F 53
Homestead, The. N11—4A 16
Homewillow Clo. N21—6G 7
Homewood Clo. Hmptn
—6D 102

Homewood Cres. Chst—6J 115
Homildon Ho. SE26—3G 111
Honduras St. EC1
—4C 62 (3L 141)
Honeybourne Rd. NW6—5K 43
Honeybourne Way. Orp
—7H 129
Honeybrook Rd. SW12—7G 93
Honeyden Rd. Sidc—6E 116
Honeyman Clo. NW6—7F 43
Honeypot Clo. NW9—4F 25
Honeypot La. Stan & NW9
—7J 11
Honeysett Rd. N17—2F 31
Honeysuckle Gdns. Croy
—1K 135
Honeysuckle La. N22—2C 30
Honeywell Rd. SW11—6D 92
Honeywood Rd. NW10—2B 58
Honeywood Rd. Iswth—4A 88
Honeywood Wlk. Cars—4D 132
Honister Clo. Stan—1B 24
Honister Gdns. Stan—7G 11
Honister Pl. Stan—1B 24
Honiton Rd. NW6—2H 59
Honiton Rd. Romf—6K 37
Honiton Rd. Well—2K 99
Honley Rd. SE6—7D 96
Honor Oak Pk. SE23—6J 95
Honor Oak Rise. SE23—6J 95
Honor Oak Rd. SE23—1J 111
Hood Av. N14—6A 6
Hood Av. SW14—5J 89
Hood Clo. Croy—1B 134
Hoodcote Gdns. N21—7G 7
Hood Rd. SW20—7B 106
Hood Wlk. Romf—1H 37
Hookers Rd. E17—3K 31
Hook Farm Rd. Brom—5B 128
Hooking Grn. Harr—5F 23
Hook La. Well—4K 99
Hooks Clo. SE15—1H 95
Hooks Hall Dri. Dag—3J 53
Hookstone Way. Wfd G—7G 21
Hooks Way. SE22—1G 111
Hook, The. Barn—6G 5
Hook Wlk. Edgw—7D 12
Hooper Rd. E16—6J 65
Hooper's Ct. SW3
—2D 76 (5E 144)
Hooper St. E1—6G 63 (8G 143)
Hoop La. NW11—7H 27
Hope Clo. SE12—3K 113
Hope Clo. Sutt—5A 132
Hope Clo. Wfd G—6F 21
Hopedale Rd. SE7—6K 81
Hopefield Av. NW6—2G 59
Hope Pk. Brom—7H 113
Hope St. SW11—3B 92
Hopetown St. E1
—5F 63 (6F 142)
Hopewell St. SE5—7D 78
Hop Gdns. WC2—7J 61 (1C 146)
Hopgood St. W12—1E 74
Hopkinsons Pl. NW1—1E 60
Hopkins St. W1—6G 61 (8M 139)
Hoppers Rd. N21—2F 17
Hoppett Rd. E4—2B 20
Hopping La. N1—6B 46
Hoppingwood Av. N Mald
—3A 120
Hopton Ct. Brom—1J 137
Hopton Gdns. N Mald—6C 120
Hopton Rd. SW16—5J 109
Hopton St. SE1—1B 78 (2K 147)
Hopwood Rd. SE17—6D 78
Hopwood Wlk. E8—7G 47
Horace Av. Romf—1J 53
Horace Rd. E7—4K 49
Horace Rd. Ilf—3G 35
Horace Rd. King—3F 119
Horatio St. E2—2G 63 (1G 143)
Horatius Way. Croy—6K 133
Horbury Cres. W11—7J 59
Horbury M. W11—7H 59
Horder Rd. SW6—1G 91

Hordle Promenade E. SE15
—7F 79
Hordle Promenade N. SE15
—7F 79
Hordle Promenade S. SE15
—7F 79
Hordle Promenade W. SE15
—7E 79
Horizon Way. SE7—4K 81
Horley Clo. Bexh—5G 101
Horley Rd. SE9—4C 114
Hormead Rd. W9—4H 59
Hornbeam Clo. SE11
—4A 78 (8G 147)
Hornbeam Clo. N'holt—5D 38
Hornbeam Cres. Bren—7B 72
Hornbeam Gro. E4—3B 20
Hornbeam La. Bexh—2J 101
Hornbeam Rd. Buck H—3G 21
Hornbeam Rd. Hay—5A 54
Hornbeams Clo. N11—6K 15
Hornbeam Ter. Cars—1C 132
Hornbeam Wlk. Rich—3F 105
Hornbeam Way. Brom—6E 128
Hornblower Clo. SE16—4A 80
Hornbuckle Clo. Harr—2H 39
Hornby Clo. NW3—7C 44
Horncastle Clo. SE12—7J 97
Horncastle Rd. SE12—7J 97
Horndean Clo. SW15—1C 106
Horndon Clo. Romf—1J 37
Horndon Grn. Romf—1J 37
Horndon Rd. Romf—1J 37
Horner La. Mitc—2B 122
Horne Way. SW15—2E 90
Hornfair Rd. SE7—6B 82
Horniman Dri. SE23—1H 111
Horning Clo. SE9—4C 114
Horn La. SE10—4J 81
Horn La. W3—7J 57
Horn La. Wfd G—6D 20
Horn Pk. Clo. SE12—5K 97
Hornpark La. SE12—5K 97
Horns End Pl. Pinn—4A 22
Hornsey La. N6—1G 45
Hornsey La. Est. N19—7H 29
Hornsey La. Gdns. N6—7G 29
Hornsey Pk. Rd. N8—3K 29
Hornsey Rise. N19—7H 29
Hornsey Rise Gdns. N19—7H 29
Hornsey Rd.—2J 45
N7 1-281 & 2-352
N19 remainder
Hornsey St. N7—5K 45
Hornshay St. SE15—6J 79
Horns Rd. Ilf—5G 35
Hornton Pl. W8—2K 75
Hornton St. W8—2J 75
Horsa Clo. Wall—7J 133
Horsa Rd. SE12—7A 98
Horsa Rd. Eri—7J 85
Horsecroft Rd. Edgw—7E 12
Horse Fair. King—2D 118
Horseferry Pl. SE10—6E 80
Horseferry Rd. SW1
—4H 77 (8B 146)
Horseguards Av. SW1
—1J 77 (3C 146)
Horse Guards Rd. SW1
—1H 77 (3B 146)
Horsell Rd. N5—5A 46
Horsell Rd. Orp—7B 116
Horselydown La. SE1
—1F 79 (3E 148)
Horsenden Av. Gnfd—5K 39
Horsenden Cres. Gnfd—5K 39
Horsenden La. N. Gnfd—6J 39
Horsenden La. S. Gnfd—1A 56
Horseshoe Clo. E14—5E 80
Horseshoe Clo. NW2—2D 42
Horse Shoe Cres. N'holt—2E 54
Horse Shoe Grn. Sutt—2K 131
Horseshoe La. N20—1A 14
Horse Shoe La. Enf—3H 7
Horsfeld Gdns. SE9—5C 98
Horsfeld Rd. SE9—5B 98
Horsford Rd. SW2—5K 93

Horsham Av. N12—5H 15
Horsham Rd. Bexh—5G 101
Horsley Dri. Croy—7E 136
Horsley Rd. E4—2K 19
Horsley Rd. Brom—1K 127
Horsley St. SE17—6D 78
Horsman St. SE5—6C 78
Horsmonden Clo. Orp—7K 129
Horsmonden Rd. SE4—6B 96
Hortensia Rd. SW10—7A 76
Horticultural Pl. W4—5K 73
Horton Av. NW2—4G 43
Horton Rd. E8—6H 47
Horton St. SE13—3D 96
Hortus Rd. E4—2K 19
Hortus Rd. S'hall—2D 70
Hosack Rd. SW17—2E 108
Hoser Av. SE12—2J 113
Hosier La. EC1—5B 62 (6K 141)
Hoskins Clo. E16—6A 66
Hoskins St. SE10—5F 81
Hospital Bri. Rd. Twic—7F 87
Hospital La. Iswth—5K 87
Hospital Rd. E9—5J 47
Hospital Rd. Houn—3E 86
Hotham Rd. SW15—3E 90
Hotham Rd. SW19—7A 108
Hotham Rd. M. SW19—7A 108
Hotham St. E15—1G 65
Hothfield Pl. SE16
—3J 79 (7M 149)
Hotspur Rd. N'holt—2E 54
Hotspur St. SE11
—5A 78 (9G 147)
Houblon Rd. Rich—5E 88
Houghton Clo. E8—6F 47
Houghton Clo. Hmptn—6C 102
Houghton Rd. N15—4F 31
Houghton St. WC2
—6K 61 (8F 140)
Houlder Cres. Croy—6B 134
Houndsden Rd. N21—6E 6
Houndsditch. EC3
—6E 62 (7D 142)
Houndsfield Rd. N9—7C 8
Hounslow Av. Houn—5F 87
Hounslow Business Pk. Houn
—4F 87
Hounslow Gdns. Houn—5F 87
Hounslow Rd. Felt—7A 86
Hounslow Rd. Felt—4B 102
(Hanworth)
Hounslow Rd. Twic—6F 87
Housman Way. SE5—7D 78
Houston Rd. SE23—2A 112
Hove Av. E17—5B 32
Hoveden Rd. NW2—5G 43
Hove Gdns. Sutt—1K 131
Hoveton Rd. SE28—6C 68
Howard Av. Bex—1C 116
Howard Clo. N11—2K 15
Howard Clo. NW2—4G 43
Howard Clo. W3—6H 57
Howard Clo. Bush, Wat—1D 10
Howard Clo. Hmptn—7G 103
Howard M. N5—4B 46
Howard Pl. SW1
—3G 77 (7L 145)
Howard Rd. E6—2D 66
Howard Rd. E11—3G 49
Howard Rd. E17—3D 32
Howard Rd. N15—6E 30
Howard Rd. N16—4D 46
Howard Rd. NW2—4F 43
Howard Rd. SE20—1J 125
Howard Rd. SE25—5G 125
Howard Rd. Bark—1H 67
Howard Rd. Brom—7J 113
Howard Rd. Ilf—4F 51
Howard Rd. Iswth—3K 87
Howard Rd. N Mald—3A 120
Howard Rd. S'hall—6F 55
Howard Rd. Surb—6F 119
Howards Clo. Pinn—2A 22
Howards Crest Clo. Beck
—2E 126

Imperial Way. Harr—6E 24
Inca Dri. SE9—7F 99
Inchmery Rd. SE6—2D 112
Inchwood. Croy—4D 136
Independents Rd. SE3—3H 97
Inderwick Rd. N8—5K 29
Indescon Ct. E14—2D 80
India St. EC3—6F 63 (8E 142)
India Way. W12—7D 58
Indus Rd. SE7—7A 82
Industry Ter. SW9—3A 94
Ingal Rd. E13—4J 65
Ingate Pl. SW8—1F 93
Ingatestone Rd. E12—1A 50
Ingatestone Rd. SE25—4H 125
Ingatestone Rd. Wfd G—7E 20
Ingelow Rd. SW8—2F 93
Ingersoll Rd. W12—1D 74
Ingersoll Rd. Enf—1D 8
Ingestre Pl. W1—6G 61 (8M 139)
Ingestre Rd. E7—4J 49
Ingestre Rd. NW5—4F 45
Ingham Clo. S Croy—7K 135
Ingham Rd. NW6—4J 43
Ingham Rd. S Croy—7J 135
Inglebert St. EC1
—3A 62 (1G 141)
Ingleborough Ct. N17—3F 31
Ingleborough St. SW9—2A 94
Ingleby Dri. Harr—3H 39
Ingleby Rd. N7—3J 45
Ingleby Rd. Dag—6H 53
Ingleby Rd. Ilf—1F 51
Ingleby Way. Chst—5E 114
Ingleby Way. Wall—7H 133
Ingle Clo. Pinn—3C 22
Ingledew Rd. SE18—5H 83
Inglehurst Gdns. Ilf—5D 34
Inglemere Rd. SE23—3K 111
Inglemere Rd. Mitc—7D 108
Inglesham Wlk. E9—6B 48
Ingleside Clo. Beck—7C 112
Ingleside Gro. SE3—6H 81
Inglethorpe St. SW6—1F 91
Ingleton Av. Well—5A 100
Ingleton Rd. N18—6B 18
Ingleton Rd. Cars—7C 132
Ingleton St. SW9—2A 94
Ingleway. N12—6G 15
Inglewood. Croy—7A 136
Inglewood Clo. E14—4C 80
Inglewood Copse. Brom
—2D 128
Inglewood Rd. NW6—5J 43
Inglewood Rd. Bexh—4K 101
Inglis Rd. W5—7F 57
Inglis Rd. Croy—1F 135
Inglis St. SE5—1B 94
Ingram Av. NW11—7A 28
Ingram Clo. SE11
—4K 77 (8F 146)
Ingram Clo. Stan—5H 11
Ingram Rd. N2—4C 28
Ingram Rd. T Hth—1C 124
Ingram Way. Gnfd—1H 55
Ingrave Rd. Romf—4K 37
Ingrave St. SW11—3B 92
Ingress St. W4—5A 74
Inigo Jones Rd. SE7—7C 82
Inkerman Rd. NW5—6F 45
Inkerman Ter. W8—3J 75
Inks Grn. E4—5K 19
Inman Rd. NW10—1A 58
Inman Rd. SW18—7A 92
Inmans Row. Wfd G—4D 20
Inner Circ. NW1—3E 60 (2G 139)
Inner Pk. Rd. SW19—2F 107
Inner Temple La. EC4
—6A 62 (8G 141)
Innes Clo. SW20—2G 121
Innes Gdns. SW15—6D 90
Inniskilling Rd. E13—2A 66
Innis Yd. Croy—3C 134
Inskip Clo. E10—2D 48
Inskip Rd. Dag—1D 52
Institute Pl. E8—5H 47
Instone Clo. Wall—7J 133

Insurance St. WC1
—3A 62 (2G 141)
Integer Gdns. E11—7F 33
International Av. Houn—5A 70
International Trading Est.
S'hall—3A 70
Inverary Pl. SE18—6H 83
Inver Clo. E5—2J 47
Inverclyde Gdns. Romf—4D 36
Inver Ct. W2—6K 59
Inveresk Gdns. Wor Pk—3C 130
Inverforth Clo. NW3—2A 44
Inverforth Rd. N11—5A 16
Inverine Rd. SE7—5K 81
Invermore Pl. SE18—4G 83
Inverness Gdns. W8—1K 75
Inverness M. W2—7K 59
Inverness Pl. W2—7K 59
Inverness Rd. N18—5C 18
Inverness Rd. Houn—4D 86
Inverness Rd. S'hall—4C 70
Inverness Rd. Wor Pk—1F 131
Inverness St. NW1—1F 61
Inverness Ter. W2—6K 59
Inverton Rd. SE15—4K 95
Invicta Clo. Chst—5E 114
Invicta Gro. N'holt—3D 54
Invicta Rd. SE3—7J 81
Inville Rd. SE17—5D 78
Inville Wlk. SE17—5D 78
Inwood Av. Houn—3G 87
Inwood Business Centre Houn
—4F 87
Inwood Clo. Croy—2A 136
Inwood Rd. Houn—4F 87
inworth St. SW11—2C 92
Iona Clo. SE6—7C 96
Ion Sq. E2—2G 63 (1G 143)
Ipswich Rd. SW17—6E 108
Ireland Yd. EC4—6B 62 (8K 141)
Irene Rd. SW6—1J 91
Irene Rd. Orp—7K 129
Ireton Ho. SW9—2A 94
Ireton Rd. N19—2H 45
Iris Av. Bex—5E 100
Iris Clo. Croy—1K 135
Iris Clo. Surb—7F 119
Iris Ct. Pinn—3A 22
Iris Cres. Bexh—6F 85
Iris Way. E4—6G 19
Irkdale Av. Enf—1A 8
Iron Mill Pl. SW18—6K 91
Iron Mill Rd. SW18—6K 91
Ironmonger La. EC2
—6D 62 (8A 142)
Ironmonger Row. EC1
—3C 62 (2M 141)
Ironmongers Pl. E14—4C 80
Ironside Clo. SE16
—2K 79 (4M 149)
Irons Way. Romf—1J 37
Irvine Av. Harr—3A 24
Irvine Clo. N20—2H 15
Irvine Way. Orp—7K 129
Irving Av. N'holt—1B 54
Irving Gro. SW9—2K 93
Irving Rd. W14—3F 75
Irving St. WC2—7H 61 (1B 146)
Irving Way. NW9—6B 26
Irwin Av. SE18—7J 83
Irwin Gdns. NW10—1D 58
Isabella Rd. E9—5J 47
Isabella St. SE1—1B 78 (3J 147)
Isabel St. SW9—1K 93
Isambard M. E14—3E 80
Isambard Pl. SE16
—1J 79 (3M 149)
Isard Ho. Brom—1K 137
Isel Way. SE22—5E 94
Isham Rd. SW16—2J 123
Isis Clo. SW15—4E 90
Isis St. SW18—2A 108
Island Quay. E14—1C 80
Island Rd. Mitc—7D 108
Island Row. E14—6B 64
Island, The. Th Dit—6A 118

Isla Rd. SE18—6G 83
Islay Gdns. Houn—5B 86
Islay Wlk. N1—6C 46
Isledon Rd. N7—3A 46
Islehurst Clo. Chst—1E 128
Isleworth Business Complex
Iswth—2K 87
Isleworth Promenade. Twic
—4B 88
Islington Grn. N1—1B 62
Islington High St. N1—2A 62
(in two parts)
Islington Pk. St. N1—7A 46
Islip Gdns. Edgw—7E 12
Islip Gdns. N'holt—7C 38
Islip Mnr. Rd. N'holt—7C 38
Islip St. NW5—5G 45
Ismailia Rd. E7—7K 49
Isom Clo. E13—3K 65
Ivanhoe Dri. Harr—3A 24
Ivanhoe Rd. SE5—3F 95
Ivanhoe Rd. Houn—3B 86
Ivatt Pl. W14—5H 75
Ivatt Way. N17—3B 30
Iveagh Av. NW10—2G 57
Iveagh Clo. E9—1K 63
Iveagh Clo. NW10—2G 57
Iveagh Ct. Beck—3E 126
Ivedon Rd. Well—2C 100
Ive Farm Clo. E10—2C 48
Ive Farm La. E10—2C 48
Iveley Rd. SW4—2G 93
Ivere Dri. Barn—6E 4
Iverhurst Clo. Bexh—5D 100
Iverna Ct. W8—3J 75
Iverna Gdns. W8—3J 75
Iverson Rd. NW6—6H 43
Ivers Way. Croy—7D 136
Ives Rd. E16—5G 65
Ives St. SW3—4C 76 (8D 144)
Ivestor Ter. SE23—7J 95
Ivimey St. E2—3G 63 (1H 143)
Ivinghoe Clo. Enf—1K 7
Ivinghoe Rd. Dag—5B 52
Ivor Gro. SE9—1F 115
Ivor Pl. NW1—4D 60 (4E 138)
Ivor St. NW1—7G 45
Ivorydown. Brom—4J 113
Ivory Ho. E1—1F 79 (2E 148)
Ivory Sq. SW11—3A 92
Ivybridge Clo. Twic—7A 88
Ivybridge La. WC2
—7J 61 (1D 146)
Ivychurch Clo. SE20—7J 111
Ivychurch La. SE17
—5F 79 (9E 148)
Ivy Clo. Harr—4D 38
Ivy Clo. Pinn—7A 22
Ivy Cotts. E14—7D 64
Ivy Cres. W4—4J 73
Ivydale Rd. SE15—3K 95
Ivydale Rd. Cars—2D 132
Ivyday Gro. SW16—3K 109
Ivydene Clo. Sutt—4A 132
Ivy Gdns. N8—6J 29
Ivy Gdns. Mitc—3H 123
Ivyhouse Rd. Dag—6D 52
Ivy La. Houn—4D 86
Ivymount Rd. SE27—3A 110
Ivy Rd. E16—6J 65
Ivy Rd. E17—6C 32
Ivy Rd. N14—7B 6
Ivy Rd. NW2—4E 42
Ivy Rd. SE4—4B 96
Ivy Rd. Houn—4F 87
Ivy St. N1—2E 62
Ivy Wlk. Dag—6E 52
Ixworth Pl. SW3
—5C 76 (9C 144)
Izane Rd. Bexh—4F 101

Jackass La. Kes—5K 137
Jack Barnett Way. N22—2K 29
Jack Cornwell St. E12—4E 50
Jacklin Grn. Wfd G—4D 20
Jackman M. NW10—3A 42

Jackman St. E8—1H 63
Jackson Rd. N7—4K 45
Jackson Rd. Bark—1H 67
Jackson Rd. Barn—6H 5
Jackson Rd. Brom—7D 128
Jacksons La. N6—7F 29
Jackson's Pi. Croy—1E 134
Jackson St. SE18—6E 82
Jack Walker Ct. N5—4B 46
Jacob St. SE1—2G 79 (4G 149)
Jacob's Well M. W1
—6E 60 (7H 139)
Jacqueline Clo. N'holt—1C 54
Jade Clo. E16—6B 66
Jade Clo. Dag—1C 52
Jade Clo. NW11—6G 27
Jaffray Rd. Brom—4B 128
Jaggard Way. SW12—7D 92
Jago Clo. SE18—6G 83
Jago Wlk. SE5—7D 78
Jamaica Rd. SE1 & SE16
—2F 79 (5F 148)
Jamaica Rd. T Hth—6B 124
Jamaica St. E1—5J 63 (6M 143)
James Av. NW2—5E 42
James Av. Dag—1F 53
James Bedford Clo. Pinn
—2A 22
James Boswell Clo. SW16
—4A 110
James Clo. E13—2J 65
James Clo. NW11—6G 27
James Collins Clo. W9—4H 59
James Ct. NW9—2A 26
James Gdns. N22—6H 17
James La. —7E 32
E11 27-55
E10 remainder
Jameson St. W8—1J 75
James Pl. N17—1F 31
James's Cotts. Rich—7G 73
James St. W1—6E 60 (8H 139)
James St. WC2—7J 61 (9D 140)
James St. Bark—7G 51
James St. Enf—5A 8
James St. Houn—3H 87
Jamestown Rd. NW1—1F 61
James Yd. E4—6A 20
Jane St. E1—6H 63 (7K 143)
Janet St. E14—3C 80
Janeway Pl. SE16
—2H 79 (5J 149)
Janeway St. SE16
—2G 79 (5H 149)
Jansen Wlk. SW11—3B 92
Janson Clo. E15—5G 49
Janson Clo. NW10—3K 41
Janson Rd. E15—5G 49
Jansons Rd. N15—3E 30
Japan Cres. N4—7K 29
Japan Rd. Romf—6D 36
Jarrett Clo. SW2—1B 110
Jarrow Clo. Mord—5K 121
Jarrow Rd. N17—4H 31
Jarrow Rd. SE16
—4J 79 (9L 149)
Jarrow Rd. Romf—6C 36
Jarrow Way. E9—4B 48
Jarvis Clo. Barn—5A 4
Jarvis Rd. SE22—4E 94
Jarvis Rd. S Croy—6D 134
Jasmine Ct. SW19—5J 107
Jasmine Gdns. Croy—3D 136
Jasmine Gdns. Harr—2E 38
Jasmine Gro. SE20—1H 125
Jason Wlk. SE9—4E 114
Jasper Clo. Enf—1D 8
Jasper Pas. SE19—6F 111
Jasper Rd. E16—6B 66
Jasper Rd. SE19—6F 111
Javelin Way. N'holt—3B 54
Jaycroft. Enf—1F 7
Jay M. SW7—2A 76 (5A 144)
Jebb Av. SW2—6J 93
Jebb St. E3—2C 64
Jedburgh Rd. E13—3A 66
Jedburgh St. SW11—4E 92
Jeddo Rd. W12—2B 74

Jefferson Clo. W13—3B 72
Jefferson Clo. Ilf—5F 35
Jeffrey Row. SE12—5K 97
Jeffreys Rd. SW4—2J 93
Jeffreys Rd. Enf—4F 9
Jeffrey's St. NW1—7G 45
Jeffreys Wlk. SW4—2J 93
Jeffs Clo. Hmptn—6F 103
Jeffs Rd. Sutt—4H 131
Jeken Rd. SE9—4A 98
Jelf Rd. SW2—5A 94
Jellicoe Gdns. Stan—6F 11
 (in two parts)
Jellicoe Rd. E13—4J 65
Jellicoe Rd. N17—7J 17
Jengar Clo. Sutt—4K 131
Jenkins La. Bark—2G 67
Jenkins Rd. E13—4K 65
Jenner Pl. SW13—6D 74
Jenner Rd. N16—3F 47
Jennett Rd. Croy—3A 134
Jennifer Rd. Brom—3H 113
Jennings Rd. SE22—6F 95
Jennings Way. Barn—3A 4
Jenningtree Way. Belv—2J 85
Jenson Way. SE19—7F 111
Jenton Av. Bexh—2E 100
Jephson Rd. E7—7A 50
Jephson St. SE5—1D 94
Jephtha Rd. SW18—6J 91
Jeppos La. Mitc—4D 122
Jerdan Pl. SW6—7J 75
Jeremiah St. E14—6D 64
Jeremy's Grn. N18—4C 18
Jermyn St. SW1—1G 77 (2L 145)
Jerningham Av. Ilf—2F 35
Jerningham Rd. SE14—2A 96
Jerome Cres. NW8
          —4C 60 (3C 138)
Jerome St. E1—4F 63 (4E 142)
Jerrard St. SE13—3D 96
Jerrold St. N1—2E 62 (1D 142)
Jersey Av. Stan—2C 24
Jersey Dri. Orp—6H 129
Jersey Ho. N1—6C 46
Jersey Rd. E11—1F 49
Jersey Rd. E16—6K 65
Jersey Rd. SW17—6F 109
Jersey Rd. W7—2A 72
Jersey Rd. Houn & Iswth—1F 87
Jersey Rd. Ilf—4F 51
Jersey St. E2—3H 63 (1J 143)
Jerusalem Pas. EC1
          —4B 62 (4J 141)
Jerviston Gdns. SW16—6A 110
Jesmond Av. Wemb—6F 41
Jesmond Rd. Croy—7F 125
Jesmond Way. Stan—5K 11
Jessam Av. E5—1H 47
Jessamine Rd. W7—1K 71
Jesse Rd. E10—1E 48
Jessica Rd. SW18—6A 92
Jessop Av. S'hall—4D 70
Jessop Rd. SE24—4C 94
Jessop Sq. E14—1C 80
Jessops Way. Croy—6G 123
Jessup Clo. SE18—4G 83
Jetstar Way. N'holt—3E 54
Jevington Way. SE12—1K 113
Jewel Rd. E17—3C 32
Jewry St. EC3—6F 63 (8E 142)
Jew's Row. SW18—4A 92
Jews Wlk. SE26—4H 111
Jeymer Av. NW2—5D 42
Jeymer Dri. Gnfd—1G 55
 (in two parts)
Jeypore Pas. SW18—6A 92
Jeypore Rd. SW18—6A 92
Jillian Clo. Hmptn—7E 102
Jim Bradley Clo. SE18—4E 82
Joan Cres. SE9—7B 98
Joan Gdns. Dag—2E 52
Joan Rd. Dag—2E 52
Joan St. SE1—1B 78 (3J 147)
Jocelyn Rd. Rich—3E 88

Jockey's Fields. WC1
          —5K 61 (5F 140)
Jodrell Rd. E3—1B 64
Joe Hunte Ct. SE27—5B 110
Johanna St. SE1
          —2A 78 (5G 147)
John Adam St. WC2
          —7J 61 (1D 146)
John Ashby Clo. SW2—6J 93
John Baird Ct. SE26—4K 111
John Barnes Wlk. E15—6H 49
John Bradshaw Rd. N14—1C 16
John Burns Dri. Bark—7J 51
John Campbell Rd. N16—5E 46
John Carpenter St. EC4
          —7B 62 (9J 141)
John Felton Rd. SE16
          —2G 79 (5G 149)
John Fisher St. E1
          —7G 63 (9G 143)
John Gooch Dri. Enf—1G 7
John Islip St. SW1
          —4H 77 (9B 146)
John McKenna Wlk. SE16
          —3G 79 (6H 149)
John Newton Ct. Well—3B 100
John Parker Clo. Dag—7H 53
John Parker Sq. SW11—3B 92
John Penn St. SE13—1D 96
John Perrin Pl. Harr—7E 24
John Prince's St. W1
          —6F 61 (7K 139)
John Rennie Wlk. E1
          —1H 79 (2K 149)
John Roll Way. SE16
          —3G 79 (6H 149)
John Ruskin St. SE5—7B 78
John's Av. NW4—4E 26
Johns La. Mord—5A 122
John's M. WC1—4K 61 (4F 140)
Johnson Clo. E8—1G 63
Johnson Rd. Brom—5B 128
Johnson Rd. Croy—7D 124
Johnson Rd. Houn—7A 70
Johnsons Clo. Cars—2D 132
Johnson's Ct. EC4
          —6A 62 (8H 141)
Johnson's Pl. SW1—5G 77
Johnson St. E1—7J 63 (9M 149)
Johnson St. S'hall—3A 70
Johnsons Way. NW10—4H 57
John Spencer Sq. N1—6B 46
John's Pl. E1—6H 63 (7K 143)
John's Ter. Croy—1E 134
Johnstone Rd. E6—3D 66
Johnston Rd. Wfd G—6D 20
Johnston Ter. NW2—3F 43
John St. E15—1H 65
John St. SE25—4G 125
John St. WC1—4K 61 (4F 140)
John St. Enf—5A 8
John St. Houn—2C 86
John Wilson St. SE18—3E 82
John Woolley Clo. SE13—4F 97
Joiner St. SE1—1D 78 (3B 148)
Jollys La. Harr—1H 39
Jolly's La. Hay—5B 54
Jonathan St. SE11
          —5K 77 (9E 146)
Jones Rd. E13—4K 65
Jones St. W1—7F 61 (1J 145)
Jones Wlk. Rich—6F 89
Jonquil Gdns. Hmptn—6E 102
Jonson Clo. Mitc—4F 123
Joram Way. SE16—5H 79
Jordan Clo. Dag—4H 53
Jordan Clo. Harr—3D 38
Jordan Rd. Gnfd—1B 56
Jordans Clo. Iswth—1J 87
Joseph Av. W3—6K 57
Josephine Av. SW2—5K 93
Joseph Powell Clo. SW12
          —6F 93
Joseph St. E3—4B 64
Joshua St. E14—6E 64
Joubert St. SW11—2D 92

Jowett St. SE15—7F 79
Joyce Av. N18—5A 18
Joyce Dawson Way. SE28
          —7A 68
Joyce Page Clo. SE7—6B 82
Joydens Wood Rd. Bex—4K 117
Joydon Dri. Romf—6B 36
Joyners Clo. Dag—4F 53
Jubb Powell Ho. N15—6E 30
Jubilee Av. E4—6K 19
Jubilee Av. Romf—5H 37
Jubilee Av. Twic—1G 103
Jubilee Clo. NW9—6K 25
Jubilee Clo. Pinn—2A 22
Jubilee Clo. Romf—5H 37
Jubilee Cres. E14—3E 80
Jubilee Dri. Ruis—4B 38
Jubilee Gdns. S'hall—5E 54
Jubilee Pl. SW3—5C 76 (9D 144)
Jubilee Rd. Gnfd—1B 56
Jubilee Rd. Sutt—7F 131
Jubilee St. E1—6J 63 (7L 143)
Jubilee Ter. N1—2D 62
Jubilee Way. SW19—1K 121
Jubilee Way. Sidc—2A 116
Judd St. WC1—3J 61 (2C 140)
Jude St. E16—6H 65
Judges Wlk. NW3—3A 44
Juer St. SW11—7C 76
Julia Gdns. Bark—2D 68
Julian Av. W3—7H 57
Julian Clo. Barn—3E 4
Julian Hill. Harr—2J 39
Julian Pl. E14—5D 80
Julia St. NW5—4E 44
Julien Rd. W5—3C 72
Junction App. SE13—3E 96
Junction App. SW11—3C 92
Junction M. W2—6C 60 (7C 138)
Junction Rd. E13—2K 65
Junction Rd. N9—1B 18
Junction Rd. N17—3G 31
Junction Rd. N19—3G 45
Junction Rd. W5—4C 72
Junction Rd. Harr—6J 23
Junction Rd. S Croy—5D 134
Junction Rd. E. Romf—7E 36
Junction Rd. W. Romf—7E 36
Juniper Clo. Wemb—5F 41
Juniper Ct. Harr—1K 23
Juniper Gdns. SW16—1G 123
Juniper La. E6—5C 66
Juniper Rd. Ilf—3E 50
Juniper St. E1—7J 63 (9L 143)
Juno Way. SE14—6K 79
Jupiter Way. N7—6K 45
Jupp Rd. E15—7F 49
Jupp Rd. W. E15—1F 65
Justin Clo. Bren—7D 72
Justin Rd. E4—7H 19
Jute La. Enf—3F 9
Jutland Clo. N19—1J 45
Jutland Rd. E13—4J 65
Jutland Rd. SE6—7E 96
Jutsums Av. Romf—6H 37
Jutsums La. Romf—6H 37
Juxon Clo. Harr—1F 23
Juxon St. SE11—4K 77 (8F 146)

Kale Rd. Eri—3E 84
Kambala Rd. SW11—3B 92
Kangley Bri. Rd. SE26—5B 112
Karen Ct. Brom—1H 127
Kashgar Rd. SE18—4K 83
Kashmir Rd. SE7—7B 82
Kassala Rd. SW11—1D 92
Katherine Gdns. SE9—4B 98
Katherine Rd. E6—4A 50
 E6 1-239 & 2-224
 E7 remainder
Katherine Rd. Twic—1A 104
Katherine St. Croy—3C 134
Kathleen Av. W3—5J 57
Kathleen Av. Wemb—7E 40
Kathleen Rd. SW11—3D 92

Kayemoor Rd. Sutt—6B 132
Kay Rd. SW9—2J 93
Kay St. E2—2G 63 (1G 143)
Kay St. E15—7F 49
Kay St. Well—1B 100
Kean St. WC2—6K 61 (8E 140)
Kearsley M. SW11—1D 92
Keats Clo. NW3—4C 44
Keats Clo. SE19—6B 108
Keat's Gro. NW3—4C 44
Keats Rd. Belv—3J 85
Keats Rd. Well—1J 99
Keats Way. Croy—6J 125
Keats Way. Gnfd—5F 55
Keble Clo. N'holt—5G 39
Keble Clo. Wor Pk—1B 130
Keble St. SW17—4A 108
Kechill Gdns. Brom—7J 127
Kedleston Dri. Orp—5K 129
Kedleston Wlk. E2
          —3H 63 (1K 143)
Keedonwood Rd. Brom—5G 113
Keel Clo. SE16—1K 79
Keeley Rd. Croy—2C 134
Keeley St. WC2—6K 61 (8E 140)
Keeling Rd. SE9—5B 98
Keely Clo. Barn—5H 5
Keemor Clo. SE18—7E 82
Keens Rd. Croy—4C 134
Keen's Yd. N1—6B 46
Keep, The. SE3—2J 97
Keep, The. King—7F 105
Keeton's Rd. SE16
          —3H 79 (6J 149)
Keevil Dri. SW19—7F 91
Keighley Clo. N7—4J 45
Keightley Dri. SE9—1G 115
Keildon Rd. SW11—4D 92
Keir Hardie Way. Bark—7A 52
Keith Connor Clo. SW8—3F 93
Keith Gro. W12—2C 74
Keith Rd. E17—1B 32
Keith Rd. Bark—2H 67
Kelbrook Rd. SE3—2C 98
Kelby Path. SE9—3F 115
Kelceda Clo. NW2—2C 42
Kelfield Gdns. W10—6E 58
Kelfield M. W10—6F 59
Kelland Rd. E13—4J 65
Kellaway Rd. SE3—2B 98
Kellerton Rd. SE13—5G 97
Kellett Rd. SW2—4A 94
Kelling Gdns. Croy—7B 124
Kellino St. SW17—4D 108
Kellner Rd. SE28—3K 83
Kell St. SE1—3B 78 (6K 147)
Kelly Rd. NW7—6B 14
Kelly St. NW1—6F 45
Kelly Way. Romf—6E 36
Kelman Clo. SW4—2H 93
Kelmore Gro. SE22—4G 95
Kelmscott Clo. E17—1B 32
Kelmscott Gdns. W12—3C 74
Kelmscott Rd. SW11—5C 92
Kelross Rd. N5—4C 46
Kelsall Clo. SE3—2K 97
Kelsey La. Beck—2C 126
Kelsey Pk. Av. Beck—3D 126
Kelsey Pk. Rd. Beck—2C 126
Kelsey Sq. Beck—2C 126
Kelsey St. E2—4G 63 (3H 143)
Kelsey Way. Beck—3C 126
Kelso Pl. W8—3K 75
Kelso Rd. Cars—7A 122
Kelston Rd. Ilf—2F 35
Kelvedon Clo. King—6G 105
Kelvedon Rd. SW6—7H 75
Kelvedon Way. Wfd G—6J 21
Kelvin Av. N13—6E 16
Kelvin Av. Tedd—6J 103
Kelvin Cres. Harr—7D 10
Kelvin Dri. Twic—6B 88
Kelvin Gdns. S'hall—6E 54
Kelvin Gro. SE26—3H 111
Kelvington Clo. Croy—7A 126
Kelvington Rd. SE15—5K 95
Kelvin Rd. N5—4C 46

221

223

Lady Booth Rd. King—2E 118
Ladycroft Rd. SE13—3D 96
Ladycroft Wlk. Stan—1D 24
Lady Dock Wlk. SE16—2A 80
Lady Hay. Wor Pk—2B 130
Lady Margaret Rd.—5G 45
NW5 1-83 & 2-70
N19 remainder
Lady Margaret Rd. S'hall
—7D 54
Lady Shaw Ct. N13—2E 16
Ladyship Ter. SE22—7G 95
Ladysmith Av. E6—2C 66
Ladysmith Av. Ilf—7J 35
Ladysmith Rd. E16—3H 65
Ladysmith Rd. N17—2G 31
Ladysmith Rd. N18—5C 18
Ladysmith Rd. SE9—6E 98
Ladysmith Rd. Enf—3K 7
Ladysmith Rd. Harr—2J 23
Lady Somerset Rd. NW5—4F 45
Ladywell Rd. SE13—5C 96
Ladywell St. E15—1H 65
Ladywood Av. Orp—5J 129
Lafone Av. Felt—2A 102
Lafone St. SE1—2F 79 (4E 148)
Lagado M. SE16—1K 79
Laing Dean. N'holt—1A 54
Laings Av. Mitc—2D 122
Lainlock Pl. Houn—1F 87
Lainson St. SW18—7J 91
Lairdale Clo. SE21—1C 110
Lairs Clo. N7—5J 45
Laitwood Rd. SW12—1F 109
Lake Av. Brom—6J 113
Lake Business Centre. N17
—7B 18
Lakedale Rd. SE18—6J 83
Lakefield Rd. N22—2B 30
Lake Footpath. SE2—2D 84
Lake Gdns. Dag—5G 53
Lake Gdns. Rich—2B 104
Lake Gdns. Wall—3F 133
Lakehall Gdns. T Hth—5B 124
Lakehall Rd. T Hth—5B 124
Lake Ho. Rd. E11—3J 49
Lakehurst Rd. Eps—5A 130
Lakeland Clo. Harr—6C 10
Lakenheath. N14—5C 6
Lake Rd. SW19—5H 107
Lake Rd. Croy—2B 136
Lake Rd. Romf—4D 36
Laker Pl. SW15—6G 91
Lakeside. N3—2K 27
Lakeside. N13—6C 56
Lakeside. Beck—3D 126
Lakeside. Enf—4C 6
Lakeside. Eps—6A 130
Lakeside. Wall—4F 133
Lakeside Av. Ilf—4B 34
Lakeside Clo. SE25—2G 125
Lakeside Clo. Sidc—5C 100
Lakeside Ct. N4—2C 46
Lakeside Cres. Barn—5J 5
Lakeside Rd. N13—4E 16
Lakeside Rd. W14—3F 75
Lakeside Way. Wemb—4G 41
Lake, The. Bush, Wat—1C 10
Lake View. Edgw—5A 12
Lakeview Rd. SE27—5A 110
Lake View Rd. Well—4B 100
Lakewood Rd. Orp—6F 129
Lakis Clo. NW3—4A 44
Laleham Av. NW7—3E 12
Laleham Rd. SE6—7E 96
Lalor St. SW6—2G 91
Lambarde Av. SE9—4E 114
Lamberhurst Rd. SE27—4A 110
Lamberhurst Rd. Dag—1F 53
Lambert Av. Rich—3G 89
Lambert Rd. E16—6K 65
Lambert Rd. N12—5F 15
Lambert Rd. SW2—5J 93
Lamberts Pl. Croy—1D 134
Lamberts Rd. Surb—5F 119
Lambert St. N1—7A 46
Lambert Wlk. Wemb—3D 40

Lambert Way. N12—5F 15
Lambeth Bri. SW1 & SE1
—4J 77 (8D 146)
Lambeth High St. SE1
—4K 77 (8E 146)
Lambeth Hill. EC4
—7C 62 (9L 141)
Lambeth Pal. Rd. SE1
—3K 77 (7E 146)
Lambeth Rd. SE1
—3K 77 (7F 146)
Lambeth Rd. Croy—1A 134
Lambeth Wlk. SE11
—4K 77 (8F 146)
(in two parts)
Lamb La. E8—7H 47
Lamble St. NW5—5E 44
Lambley Rd. Dag—6B 52
Lambolle Pl. NW3—6C 44
Lambolle Rd. NW3—6C 44
Lambourne Av. SW19—4H 107
Lambourne Gdns. E4—2H 19
Lambourne Gdns. Bark—7K 51
Lambourne Gdns. Enf—2A 8
Lambourne Pl. SE3—1K 97
Lambourne Rd. E11—7E 32
Lambourne Rd. Bark—7J 51
Lambourne Rd. Ilf—2J 51
Lambourn Gro. King—2H 119
Lambourn Rd. SW4—3F 93
Lamb Pas. Bren—6F 73
Lambrook Ter. SW6—1G 91
Lamb's Bldgs. EC1
—4D 62 (4A 142)
Lambs Clo. N9—2B 18
Lamb's Conduit Pas. WC1
—5K 61 (5E 140)
Lamb's Conduit St. WC1
—4K 61 (4E 140)
Lambscroft Av. SE9—3A 114
Lambs Meadow. Wfd G—2B 34
Lamb's M. N1—1B 62
Lamb's Pas. EC1
—4D 62 (4A 142)
Lambs Ter. N9—2J 17
Lamb St. E1—5F 63 (5E 142)
Lamb's Wlk. Enf—2H 7
Lambton Pl. W11—7H 59
Lambton Rd. N19—1J 45
Lambton Rd. SW20—1E 120
Lamb Wlk. SE1—2E 78 (5C 148)
Lamerock Rd. Brom—4H 113
Lamerton Rd. Ilf—2F 35
Lamerton St. SE8—6C 80
Lamford Clo. N17—7J 17
Lamington St. W6—4D 74
Lamlash St. SE11
—4B 78 (8J 147)
Lammas Av. Mitc—2E 122
Lammas Grn. SE26—3H 111
Lammas Pk. Gdns. W5—1C 72
Lammas Pk. Rd. W5—2D 72
Lammas Rd. E9—7K 47
Lammas Rd. E10—2A 48
Lammas Rd. Rich—4C 104
Lammermoor Rd. SW12—7F 93
Lamont Rd. SW10—6A 76
Lamorbey Clo. Sidc—2K 115
Lamorna Clo. Orp—7K 129
Lamorna Gro. Stan—1D 24
Lampard Gro. N16—1F 47
Lampern Sq. E2—3G 63 (1H 143)
Lampeter Sq. W6—6G 75
Lamplighter Clo. E1
—4J 63 (4L 143)
Lampmead Rd. SE12—5H 97
Lamport Clo. SE18—4D 82
Lampton Av. Houn—1F 87
Lampton Ho. Clo. SW19
—4F 107
Lampton Pk. Rd. Houn—2F 87
Lampton Rd. Houn—2F 87
Lanacre Av. NW9—1A 26
Lanark Clo. W5—5C 56
Lanark Pl. W9—4A 60 (3A 138)
Lanark Rd. W9—2K 59 (3A 138)

Lanark Sq. E14—3D 80
Lanbury Rd. SE15—4K 95
Lancaster Av. E18—4K 33
Lancaster Av. SE27—2B 110
Lancaster Av. SW19—5F 107
Lancaster Av. Bark—7J 51
Lancaster Av. Barn—1G 5
Lancaster Av. Mitc—5J 123
Lancaster Clo. N1—7E 46
Lancaster Clo. N17—7B 18
Lancaster Clo. SE27—2B 110
Lancaster Clo. Brom—4H 127
Lancaster Clo. Croy—2J 133
Lancaster Clo. King—5D 104
Lancaster Cotts. Rich—6E 88
Lancaster Ct. SW6—7H 75
Lancaster Dri. E14—1E 80
Lancaster Dri. NW3—6C 44
Lancaster Gdns. SW19—5G 107
Lancaster Gdns. W13—2B 72
Lancaster Gdns. King—5D 104
Lancaster Ga. W2
—7A 60 (9A 138)
Lancaster Gro. NW3—6B 44
Lancaster M. W2
—7A 60 (9A 138)
Lancaster M. Rich—6E 88
Lancaster Pk. Rich—6E 88
Lancaster Pl. SW19—5F 107
Lancaster Pl. WC2
—7K 61 (1E 146)
Lancaster Pl. Houn—2B 86
Lancaster Pl. Twic—6A 88
Lancaster Rd. E7—7J 49
Lancaster Rd. E11—2G 49
Lancaster Rd. E17—2K 31
Lancaster Rd. N4—7A 30
Lancaster Rd. N11—6C 16
Lancaster Rd. N18—5A 18
Lancaster Rd. NW10—5C 42
Lancaster Rd. SE25—2F 125
Lancaster Rd. SW19—5F 107
Lancaster Rd. W11—6G 59
Lancaster Rd. Barn—6G 5
Lancaster Rd. Enf—1J 7
Lancaster Rd. Harr—5E 22
Lancaster Rd. N'holt—6G 39
Lancaster Rd. S'hall—7C 54
Lancaster Stables. NW3—6C 44
Lancaster St. SE1
—2B 78 (5K 147)
Lancaster Ter. W2
—7B 60 (9A 138)
Lancaster Wlk. W2 & SW7
—1A 76 (2A 144)
Lancefield St. W10—3H 59
(in two parts)
Lancell St. N16—2E 46
Lancelot Av. Wemb—4D 40
Lancelot Cres. Wemb—4D 40
Lancelot Gdns. Barn—7K 5
Lancelot Pl. SW7
—2D 76 (5E 144)
Lancelot Rd. Well—4A 100
Lancelot Rd. Wemb—5D 40
Lance Rd. Harr—7G 23
Lancey Clo. SE7—4C 82
Lanchester Rd. N6—5D 28
Lancing Gdns. N9—1A 18
Lancing Rd. W13—7B 56
Lancing Rd. Croy—7K 123
Lancing Rd. Ilf—6H 35
Lancing St. NW1
—3H 61 (2A 140)
Landau Way. Eri—5H 77
Landcroft Rd. SE22—5F 95
Landells Rd. SE22—6F 95
Landford Rd. SW15—3E 90
Landgrove Rd. SW19—5J 107
Landmann Way. SE14—5K 79
Landon Pl. SW1—3D 76 (6E 144)
Landon's Clo. E14—1E 80
Landon Wlk. E14—7D 64
Landor Rd. SW9—3J 93
Landor Wlk. W12—2C 74
Landport Way. SE15—7F 79
Landra Gdns. N21—6G 7

Landridge Rd. SW6—2H 91
Landrock Rd. N8—6K 29
Landscape Rd. Wfd G—7E 20
Landseer Av. E12—5E 50
Landseer Clo. SW19—1A 122
Landseer Clo. Edgw—2G 25
Landseer Rd. N19—3J 45
Landseer Rd. Enf—5B 8
Landseer Rd. N Mald—7K 119
Landseer Rd. Sutt—6J 131
Landstead Rd. SE18—7H 83
Lane App. NW7—5B 14
Lane Clo. NW2—3D 42
Lane End. Bexh—3H 101
Lane Gdns. Bush, Wat—1D 10
Lanercost Clo. SW2—2A 110
Lanercost Gdns. N14—7D 6
Lanercost Rd. SW2—2A 110
Laneside. Chst—5G 115
Laneside. Edgw—5D 12
Laneside Av. Dag—7F 37
Lane, The. NW8—2A 60
Lane, The. SE3—3J 97
Laneway. SW15—5D 90
Lanfranc Rd. E3—2A 64
Lanfrey Pl. W14—5H 75
Langbourne Av. N6—2E 44
Langbrook Rd. SE3—3B 98
Langcroft Clo. Cars—3D 132
Langdale Av. Mitc—3D 122
Langdale Clo. SE17—6C 78
Langdale Cres. Bexh—7G 85
Langdale Gdns. Gnfd—3B 56
Langdale Rd. SE10—7E 80
Langdale Rd. T Hth—4A 124
Langdale St. E1—6H 63 (8J 143)
Langdon Ct. NW10—1A 58
Langdon Cres. E6—2E 66
Langdon Dri. NW9—1J 41
Langdon Pk. Rd. N6—7G 29
Langdon Pl. SW14—3J 89
Langdon Rd. E6—1E 66
Langdon Rd. Brom—3K 127
Langdon Rd. Mord—5A 122
Langdons Ct. S'hall—3E 70
Langdon Shaw. Sidc—5K 115
Langdon Wlk. Mord—5A 122
Langdon Way. SE1
—4G 79 (9H 149)
Langford Clo. E8—5G 47
Langford Clo. N15—6E 30
Langford Clo. NW8—2A 60
Langford Cres. Barn—4J 5
Langford Grn. SE5—3E 94
Langford Pl. NW8—2A 60
Langford Pl. Sidc—3A 116
Langford Rd. SW6—2K 91
Langford Rd. Barn—4J 5
Langford Rd. Wfd G—6F 21
Langfords. Buck H—2G 21
Langham Dri. Romf—6B 36
Langham Gdns. W13—7B 56
Langham Gdns. Edgw—7D 12
Langham Gdns. Rich—4C 104
Langham Gdns. Wemb—2C 40
Langham Ho. NW4—5D 27
Langham Ho. Clo. Rich—4D 104
Langham Pl. N15—3B 30
Langham Pl. W1
—5F 61 (6K 139)
Langham Rd. N15—3B 30
Langham Rd. SW20—1E 120
Langham Rd. Edgw—6D 12
Langham Rd. Tedd—5B 104
Langham St. W1
—5F 61 (6K 139)
Langhedge Clo. N18—6A 18
Langhedge La. N18—6A 18
Langhedge La. Industrial Est.
N18—6A 18
Langholm Clo. SW12—7H 93
Langholme. Bush, Wat—1B 10
Langhorne Rd. Dag—7G 53
Langland Cres. E. Stan—2D 24
Langland Cres. W. Stan—2D 24

225

Langland Dri. Pinn—1C 22
Langland Gdns. NW3—5K 43
Langland Gdns. Croy—2B 136
Langler Rd. NW10—2E 58
Langley Av. Ruis—2A 38
Langley Av. Surb—7D 118
Langley Av. Wor Pk—2F 131
Langley Ct. WC2
—7J 61 (9C 140)
Langley Cres. E11—7A 34
Langley Cres. Dag—7C 52
Langley Cres. Edgw—3D 12
Langley Dri. E11—7K 33
Langley Dri. W3—2H 73
Langley Gdns. Brom—4A 128
Langley Gdns. Dag—7D 52
Langley Gdns. Orp—6F 129
Langley Gro. N Mald—2A 120
Langley Pk. NW7—6F 13
Langley Pk. Rd. Sutt—6A 132
Langley Rd. SW19—1H 121
Langley Rd. Beck—4A 126
Langley Rd. Iswth—2K 87
Langley Rd. Surb—7E 118
Langley Rd. Well—6C 84
Langley St. WC2
—6J 61 (8C 140)
Langley Way. W Wick—1F 137
—1D 10
Langmead Dri. Bush, Wat
Langmead St. SE27—4C 110
Langmore Ct. Bexh—3D 100
Langroyd Rd. SW17—2D 108
Langside Av. SW15—4C 90
Langside Cres. N14—3C 16
Lang St. E1—4J 63 (3L 143)
Langthorn Ct. EC2
—6D 62 (7A 142)
Langthorne Rd. E11—3E 48
Langthorne St. SW6—7F 75
Langton Av. E6—3E 66
Langton Av. N20—7F 5
Langton Clo. WC1
—4K 61 (3F 140)
Langton Rise. SE23—7H 95
Langton Rd. NW2—3E 42
Langton Rd. SW9—7B 78
Langton Rd. Harr—7B 10
Langton St. SW10—6A 76
Langton Way. SE3—1J 97
Langton Way. Croy—4E 134
Langtry Rd. NW8—1K 59
Langtry Rd. N'holt—2B 54
Langtry Wlk. NW8—1A 60
Langwood Chase. Tedd
—6C 104
Lanhill Rd. W9—4J 59
Lanier Rd. SE13—6F 97
Lankaster Gdns. N2—1B 28
Lankers Dri. Harr—6D 22
Lankton Clo. Beck—1E 126
Lanrick Rd. E14—6F 65
Lanridge Rd. SE2—3D 84
Lansbury Av. N18—5J 17
Lansbury Av. Bark—7A 52
Lansbury Av. Felt—6A 86
Lansbury Av. Romf—5E 36
Lansbury Clo. NW10—5J 41
Lansbury Est. E14—6D 64
Lansbury Gdns. E14—6F 65
Lansbury Rd. Enf—1E 8
Lansbury Way. N18—5K 17
Lanscombe Wlk. SW8—1J 93
Lansdell Rd. Mitc—2E 122
Lansdowne Av. Bexh—7D 84
Lansdowne Clo. SW20—7F 107
Lansdowne Clo. Twic—1K 103
Lansdowne Ct. Wor Pk—2C 130
Lansdowne Cres. W11—7G 59
Lansdowne Dri. E8—7G 47
Lansdowne Gdns. SW8—1J 93
Lansdowne Gro. NW10—4A 42
Lansdowne Hill. SE27—3B 110
Lansdowne La. SE7—5B 82
Lansdowne M. SE7—5B 82

Lansdowne M. W11—1H 75
Lansdowne Pl. SE1
—3D 78 (6B 148)
Lansdowne Pl. SE19—7F 111
Lansdowne Rise. W11—7G 59
Lansdowne Rd. E4—2H 19
Lansdowne Rd. E11—2H 49
Lansdowne Rd. E17—6C 32
Lansdowne Rd. E18—3J 33
Lansdowne Rd. N3—7D 14
Lansdowne Rd. N10—2G 29
Lansdowne Rd. N17—1G 31
Lansdowne Rd. SW20—7E 106
Lansdowne Rd. W11—7G 59
Lansdowne Rd. Brom—7J 113
Lansdowne Rd. Croy—2D 134
Lansdowne Rd. Harr—7J 23
Lansdowne Rd. Houn—3F 87
Lansdowne Rd. Ilf—1K 51
Lansdowne Rd. Stan—6H 11
Lansdowne Row. W1
—1F 77 (2K 145)
Lansdowne Ter. WC1
—4J 61 (4D 140)
Lansdowne Wlk. W11—1H 75
Lansdowne Way. SW8—1H 93
Lansdowne Wood. SE27
—3B 110
Lansdown Rd. E7—7A 50
Lansdown Rd. Sidc—3B 116
Lansfield Av. N18—4B 18
Lantern Clo. SW15—4C 90
Lantern Clo. Wemb—5D 40
Lanterns Ct. E14—3D 80
Lant St. SE1—2C 78 (4L 147)
Lanvanor Rd. SE15—2J 95
Lapford Clo. W9—4B 59
Lapponum Wlk. Hay—4B 54
Lapse Wood Wlk. SE23—2H 111
Lapstone Gdns. Harr—6C 24
Lara Clo. SE13—6E 96
Larbert Rd. SW16—7G 109
Larch Av. W3—1A 74
Larch Clo. N11—7K 15
Larch Clo. SE8—6B 80
Larch Clo. SW12—2F 109
Larch Cres. Hay—5A 54
Larch Dri. W4—5G 73
Larches Av. SW14—4K 89
Larches, The. N13—3H 17
Larch Grn. NW9—1A 26
Larch M. N19—2G 45
Larch Rd. NW2—4E 42
Larch Tree Way. Croy—3C 136
Larchvale Ct. Sutt—7K 131
Larch Way. Brom—7E 128
Larchwood Rd. SE9—2F 115
Larcombe Clo. Croy—4F 135
Larcom St. SE17
—4C 78 (9M 147)
Larden Rd. W3—2A 74
Larkbere Rd. SE26—4A 112
Larken Dri. Bush, Wat—1B 10
Larkfield Av. Harr—3B 24
Larkfield Clo. Brom—2H 137
Larkfield Rd. Rich—4E 88
Larkfield Rd. Sidc—3K 115
Larkhall La. SW4—2H 93
Larkhall Rise. SW4—3G 93
Lark Row. E2—1J 63
Larksfield Gro. Enf—1C 8
Larks Gro. Bark—7J 51
Larkshall Ct. Romf—2J 37
Larkshall Cres. E4—4K 19
Larkshall Rd. E4—5K 19
Larkspur Clo. E6—5C 66
Larkspur Clo. N17—7J 17
Larkspur Lodge. Sidc—3B 116
Larkswood Ct. E4—5A 20
Larkswood Rise. Pinn—4A 22
Larkswood Rd. E4—4H 19
Larkway Clo. NW9—4K 25
Larnach Rd. W6—6F 75
Larpent Av. SW15—5E 90
Larwood Clo. Gnfd—5H 39
Lascelles Av. Harr—7H 23
Lascelles Clo. E11—2F 49

Lascotts Rd. N22—6E 16
Lassa Rd. SE9—5C 98
Lassell St. SE10—5F 81
Latchett Rd. E18—1K 33
Latchingdon Ct. E17—4K 31
Latchingdon Gdns. Wfd G
—6H 21
Latchmere Clo. Rich—5E 104
Latchmere La. King & Rich
—6F 105
Latchmere Pas. SW11—2D 92
Latchmere Rd. SW11—2D 92
Latchmere Rd. King—7E 104
Latchmere St. SW11—2D 92
Lateward Rd. Bren—6D 72
Latham Clo. E6—5C 66
Latham Clo. Twic—7A 88
Latham Rd. Bexh—5G 101
Latham Rd. Twic—7K 87
Latham's Way. Croy—1J 133
Lathkill Clo. Enf—7B 8
Lathom Rd. E6—7C 50
Latimer Av. E6—1D 66
Latimer Clo. Pinn—1A 22
Latimer Clo. Wor Pk—4D 130
Latimer Gdns. Pinn—1A 22
Latimer Pl. W10—6E 58
Latimer Rd. E7—4K 49
Latimer Rd. N15—6E 30
Latimer Rd. SW19—6K 107
Latimer Rd. W10—5E 58
Latimer Rd. Barn—3E 4
Latimer Rd. Croy—3B 134
Latimer Rd. Tedd—5K 103
Latimer St. E1—5K 63 (6M 143)
Latona Rd. SE15—6G 79
Latymer Ct. W6—4F 75
Latymer Gdns. N3—2G 27
Latymer Rd. N9—1A 18
Latymer Way. N9—2K 17
Lauder Clo. N'holt—2B 54
Lauder Ct. N14—7D 6
Lauderdale Dri. Rich—3D 104
Lauderdale Rd. W9—3K 59
Laud St. SE11—5K 77
Laud St. Croy—3C 134
Laughton Rd. N'holt—1B 54
Launcelot Rd. Brom—4J 113
Launcelot St. SE1
—2A 78 (5G 147)
Launceston Gdns. Gnfd—7C 40
Launceston Pl. W8—3A 76
Launceston Rd. Gnfd—1C 56
Launch St. E14—3E 80
Laundry Rd. W6—6G 75
Laura Clo. E11—5A 34
Laura Clo. Enf—5K 7
Lauradale Rd. N2—4D 28
Laura Pl. E5—4J 47
Laurel Av. Twic—1K 103
Laurel Bank Gdns. SW6—2H 91
Laurel Bank Rd. Enf—1J 7
Laurelbrook. SE6—3G 113
Laurel Clo. N19—2G 45
Laurel Clo. Sidc—3A 116
Laurel Cres. Croy—3C 136
Laurel Cres. Romf—1K 53
Laurel Dri. N21—7F 7
Laurel Gdns. E4—7J 9
Laurel Gdns. NW7—3E 12
Laurel Gdns. W7—1J 71
Laurel Gdns. Houn—4C 86
Laurel Gro. SE20—7J 111
Laurel Gro. SE26—4K 111
Laurel Pk. Harr—7E 10
Laurel Rd. SW13—2C 90
Laurel Rd. SW20—1D 120
Laurel Rd. Tedd—5H 103
Laurel St. E8—6F 47
Laurel View. N12—3E 14
Laurel Way. E18—4H 33
Laurel Way. N20—3D 14
Laurence M. W12—2C 74
Laurence Pountney Hill. EC4
—7D 62 (9A 142)
Laurence Pountney La. EC4
—7D 62 (9A 142)

Laurie Gro. SE14—1A 96
Laurie Rd. W7—5J 55
Laurier Rd. NW5—3F 45
Laurier Rd. Croy—7F 125
Laurimel Clo. Stan—6G 11
Lauriston Rd. E9—7J 47
Lauriston Rd. SW19—6F 107
Lausanne Rd. N8—4A 30
Lausanne Rd. SE15—1J 95
Lavell St. N16—4D 46
Lavender Av. NW9—1J 41
Lavender Av. Mitc—1C 122
Lavender Av. Wor Pk—3E 130
Lavender Clo. SW3—6B 76
Lavender Clo. Cars—4F 133
Lavender Gdns. SW11—4D 92
Lavender Gdns. Enf—1G 7
Lavender Gro. E8—7G 47
Lavender Hill. SW11—3D 92
Lavender Hill. Enf—1F 7
Lavender Rd. SE16—1A 80
Lavender Rd. SW11—3B 92
Lavender Rd. Cars—4E 132
Lavender Rd. Croy—6K 123
Lavender Rd. Enf—1J 7
Lavender Rd. Sutt—4B 132
Lavender St. E15—6G 49
Lavender Sweep. SW11—4D 92
Lavender Ter. SW11—3C 92
Lavender Vale. Wall—6H 133
Lavender Wlk. SW11—4D 92
Lavender Wlk. Mitc—1E 122
Lavender Way. Croy—6K 125
Lavengro Rd. SE27—2C 110
Lavenham Rd. SW18—2H 107
Lavernock Rd. Bexh—2G 101
Lavers Rd. N16—3E 46
Laverstoke Gdns. SW15—7B 90
Laverton M. SW5—4K 75
Laverton Pl. SW5—4K 75
Lavidge Rd. SE9—2C 114
Lavina Gro. N1—2K 61
Lavington Rd. W13—1B 72
Lavington Rd. Croy—3K 133
Lavington St. SE1
—1B 78 (3K 147)
Lawdons Gdns. Croy—4B 134
Lawford Clo. Wall—7J 133
Lawford Rd. N1—7E 46
Lawford Rd. NW5—6G 45
Lawford Rd. W4—7J 73
Lawless St. E14—7D 64
Lawley Rd. N14—7A 6
Lawley St. E5—4J 47
Lawn Clo. N9—7A 8
Lawn Clo. Brom—7K 113
Lawn Clo. N Mald—2A 120
Lawn Cres. Rich—2G 89
Lawn Farm Gro. Romf—4E 36
Lawn Gdns. W7—1J 71
Lawn La. SW8—6K 77
Lawn Rd. NW3—5D 44
Lawn Rd. Beck—7B 112
Lawnside. SE3—4H 97
Lawns, The. E4—5H 19
Lawns, The. SE3—3H 97
Lawns, The. SE19—1D 124
Lawns, The. Pinn—7A 10
Lawns, The. Sidc—4C 116
Lawns, The. Sutt—5G 131
Lawnsway. Romf—1J 37
Lawn Ter. SE3—3G 97
Lawn, The. S'hall—5E 70
Lawn Vale. Pinn—2C 22
Lawrence Av. E12—4E 50
Lawrence Av. E17—1K 31
Lawrence Av. N13—4G 17
Lawrence Av. NW7—4F 13
Lawrence Av. N Mald—6K 119
Lawrence Bldgs. N16—3F 47
Lawrence Campe Clo. N20
—3G 15
Lawrence Clo. E3—3C 64
Lawrence Clo. N15—3E 30
Lawrence Ct. NW7—5F 13
Lawrence Cres. Dag—3H 53

Lawrence Cres. Edgw—2G 25
Lawrence Gdns. NW7—3G 13
Lawrence Hill. E4—2H 19
Lawrence La. EC2
 —6C 62 (7M 141)
Lawrence Rd. E6—1C 66
Lawrence Rd. E13—1K 65
Lawrence Rd. N15—4E 30
Lawrence Rd. N18—4C 18
Lawrence Rd. SE25—4F 125
Lawrence Rd. W5—4D 72
Lawrence Rd. Hmptn—7D 102
Lawrence Rd. Houn—4A 86
Lawrence Rd. Pinn—5B 22
Lawrence Rd. Rich—4C 104
Lawrence Rd. W Wick—4J 137
Lawrence St. E16—5H 65
Lawrence St. NW7—5G 13
Lawrence St. SW3—6C 76
Lawrence Weaver Clo. Mord
 —6J 121
Lawrence Wharf Development.
 SE16—1B 80
Lawrence Yd. N15—4E 30
Lawrie Pk. Av. SE26—5H 111
Lawrie Pk. Cres. SE26—5H 111
Lawrie Pk. Gdns. SE26—4H 111
Lawrie Pk. Rd. SE26—6H 111
Lawson Clo. E16—5A 66
Lawson Clo. SW19—3F 107
Lawson Ct. Surb—7D 118
Lawson Gdns. Pinn—3A 22
Lawson Rd. Enf—1D 8
Lawson Rd. S'hall—4E 54
Law St. SE1—3D 78 (6B 148)
Lawton Rd. E3—3A 64
Lawton Rd. E10—1E 48
Lawton Rd. Barn—3G 5
Laxcon Clo. NW10—5K 41
Laxley Clo. SE5—7B 78
Laxton Pl. NW1—4F 61 (3K 139)
Layard Rd. SE16
 —4H 79 (8K 149)
Layard Rd. Enf—1A 8
Layard Rd. T Hth—2D 124
Layard Sq. SE16
 —4H 79 (8K 149)
Laybrook Lodge. E18—4H 33
Laycock St. N1—6A 46
Layer Gdns. W3—7G 57
Layfield Clo. NW4—7D 26
Layfield Cres. NW4—7D 26
Layfield Rd. NW4—7D 26
Layhams Rd. W Wick, Kes &
 Warl—4J 137
Laymarsh Clo. Belv—3F 85
Laymead Clo. N'holt—6C 38
Laystall St. EC1
 —4A 62 (4G 141)
Layton Cres. Croy—5A 134
Layton Rd. N1—2A 62
Layton Rd. Bren—5D 72
Layton Rd. Houn—4F 87
Layton's Bldgs. SE1
 —2D 78 (4A 148)
Layzell Wlk. SE9—1B 114
Lazar Wlk. N7—2K 45
Leabank Clo. Harr—3J 39
Leabank View. N15—6G 31
Leabourne Rd. N16—7G 31
Lea Bri. Rd.—3J 47
 E5 1-49 & 2-148
 E10 51-713 & 150-738
 E17 remainder
Lea Ct. E4—2K 19
Leacroft Av. SW12—7D 92
Leadale Av. E4—2H 19
Leadale Rd.—6G 31
 N16 1-81 & 2-46
 N15 remainder
Leadenhall Pl. EC3
 —6E 62 (8C 142)
Leadenhall St. EC3
 —6E 62 (8C 142)
Leadenham Ct. E3—4C 64
Leader Av. E12—5E 50
Leadings, The. Wemb—3J 41

Leaf Gro. SE27—5A 110
Leafield Clo. SW16—6B 110
Leafield La. Sidc—3F 117
Leafield Rd. SW20—3H 121
Leafield Rd. Sutt—1J 131
Leafy Gro. Kes—5K 137
Leafy Oak Rd. SE12—4A 114
Leafy Wlk. Croy—2F 135
Lea Gdns. Wemb—4E 40
Leagrave St. E5—3J 47
Lea Hall Rd. E10—1C 48
Leahurst Rd. SE13—5F 97
Leake Ct. SE1—2K 77 (5F 146)
Leake St. SE1—2K 77 (4F 146)
Lealand Rd. N15—6F 31
Lealand Rd. W13—1A 72
Leamington Av. E17—5C 32
Leamington Av. Brom—5A 114
Leamington Av. Mord—4G 121
Leamington Clo. E12—5C 50
Leamington Clo. Brom—5A 114
Leamington Clo. Houn—5G 87
Leamington Cres. Harr—3C 38
Leamington Gdns. Ilf—2K 51
Leamington Pk. W3—5K 57
Leamington Rd. S'hall—4B 70
Leamington Rd. Vs. W11
 —5H 59
Leamore St. W6—4E 74
Leamouth Rd. E6—5C 66
Leamouth Rd. E14—7F 65
Leander Ct. SE8—1C 96
Leander Ct. SE16—1B 80
Leander Ct. Surb—7D 118
Leander Rd. SW2—6K 93
Leander Rd. N'holt—2E 54
Leander Rd. T Hth—4K 123
Lea Rd. Beck—2C 126
Lea Rd. Enf—1J 7
Lea Rd. S'hall—4C 70
Learoyd Gdns. E6—7E 66
Leas Dale. SE9—3E 114
Leas Grn. Chst—6K 115
Leaside Av. N10—3E 28
Leaside Rd. E5—1J 47
Leasowes Rd. E10—1C 48
Leatherbottle Grn. Eri—3F 85
Leather Bottle La. Belv—4E 84
Leather Clo. Mitc—2E 122
Leatherdale St. E1
 (in two parts)—4J 63 (3M 143)
Leather Gdns. E15—1G 65
Leatherhead Clo. N16—1F 47
Leather La. EC1—5A 62 (5G 141)
Leathermarket St. SE1
 —2E 78 (5C 148)
Leathsail Rd. Harr—3F 39
Leathwaite Rd. SW11—4D 92
Leathwell Rd. SE8—2D 96
Lea Vale. Dart—4K 101
Lea Valley Rd. Enf & E4—5F 9
Lea Valley Viaduct. N18 & E4
 —5E 18
Leaveland Clo. Beck—4C 126
Leaver Gdns. Gnfd—2H 55
Leavesden Rd. Stan—6F 11
Leaway. E10—1K 47
Lebanon Av. Felt—5B 102
Lebanon Gdns. SW18—6J 91
Lebanon Pk. Twic—7B 88
Lebanon Rd. SW18—5J 91
Lebanon Rd. Croy—1E 134
Lebrun Sq. SE3—4K 97
Lechmere App. Wfd G—2B 34
Lechmere Av. Wfd G—2B 34
Lechmere Rd. NW2—6D 42
Leckford Rd. SW18—2A 108
Leckwith Av. Bexh—6E 84
Lecky St. SW7—5B 76
Leconfield Av. SW13—3B 90
Leconfield Rd. N5—4D 46
Leda Av. Enf—1E 8
Leda Rd. SE18—3D 82
Ledbury M. N. W11—7J 59
Ledbury M. W. W11—7J 59

Ledbury Pl. Croy—4D 134
Ledbury Rd. W11—6H 59
Ledbury Rd. Croy—4D 134
Ledbury St. SE15—7G 79
Ledrington Rd. SE19—6G 111
Ledway Dri. Wemb—7F 25
Lee Av. Romf—6E 36
Lee Bri. SE13—3E 96
Leechcroft Av. Sidc—5K 99
Leechcroft Rd. Wall—3E 132
Lee Chu. St. SE13—4G 97
Lee Clo. E17—1K 31
Lee Conservancy Rd. E9—5B 48
Leecroft Rd. Barn—5B 4
Leeds Pl. N4—1K 45
Leeds Rd. Ilf—1H 51
Leeds St. N18—5B 18
Leefern Rd. W12—2C 74
Lee Ga. SE12—5H 97
Lee Grn. SE12—5H 97
Lee Gro. Chig—2K 21
Lee High Rd.—3E 96
 SE13 1-231 & 2-332
 SE12 remainder
Leeke St. WC1—3K 61 (1E 140)
Leeland Rd. W13—1A 72
Leeland Ter. W13—1A 72
Leeland Way. NW10—4B 42
Lee Pk. SE3—4H 97
Lee Pk. Way. E4, N18 & N9
 —5E 18
Leerdam Rd. E14—3E 80
Lee Rd. NW7—7A 14
Lee Rd. SE3—3H 97
Lee Rd. SW19—1K 121
Lee Rd. Enf—6B 8
Lee Rd. Gnfd—1C 56
Leeside. Barn—5B 4
Leeside Cres. NW11—6G 27
Leeside Rd. N17—6C 18
Leeson Rd. SE24—4A 94
Leeson's Hill. Chst & Orp
 —3J 129
Leeson's Way. Orp—2K 129
Lees Pl. W1—7E 60 (9B 139)
Lees, The. Croy—2B 136
Lee St. E8—1F 63
Lee Ter. SE3—3G 97
Lee View. Enf—1G 7
Leeward Gdns. SW19—5G 107
Leeway. SE8—5B 80
Leeway Clo. Pinn—1D 22
Lefevre Wlk. E3—1B 64
Lefroy Rd. W12—2B 74
Legard Rd. N5—3B 46
Legatt Rd. SE9—5B 98
Leggatt Rd. E15—2E 64
Legge St. SE13—5E 96
Leghorn Rd. NW10—2B 58
Leghorn Rd. SE18—5H 83
Legion Clo. N1—7A 46
Legion Ct. Mord—6J 121
Legion Rd. Gnfd—2H 55
Legion Way. N12—7H 15
Legon Av. Romf—1J 53
Legrace Av. Houn—2B 86
Leicester Av. Mitc—4J 123
Leicester Clo. Wor Pk—4E 130
Leicester Gdns. Ilf—7J 35
Leicester Pl. WC2
 —7H 61 (9B 146)
Leicester Rd. E11—5K 33
Leicester Rd. N2—3C 28
Leicester Rd. Barn—5E 4
Leicester Rd. Croy—7E 124
Leicester Sq. WC2
 —7H 61 (9B 146)
Leicester St. WC2
 —7H 61 (9B 146)
Leigham Av. SW16—3J 109
Leigham Ct. Rd. SW16—2J 109
Leigham Dri. Iswth—7J 71
Leigham Vale—3K 109
 SW16 8-91
 SW2 remainder
Leigh Av. Ilf—4B 34
Leigh Clo. N Mald—4K 119

Leigh Ct. Harr—1J 39
Leigh Cres. Croy—7D 136
Leigh Gdns. NW10—2E 58
Leigh Hunt St. SE1
 —2C 78 (4L 147)
Leigh Orchard Clo. SW16
 —3K 109
Leigh Pl. EC1—5A 62 (5G 141)
Leigh Pl. Well—2A 100
Leigh Rd. E6—6E 50
Leigh Rd. E10—7E 32
Leigh Rd. N5—4B 46
Leigh Rd. Houn—4H 87
Leigh St. WC1—3J 61 (2C 140)
Leighton Av. E12—5E 50
Leighton Av. Pinn—3C 22
Leighton Clo. Edgw—2G 25
Leighton Cres. NW5—5G 45
Leighton Gdns. NW10—2D 58
Leighton Gro. NW5—5G 45
Leighton Pl. NW5—5G 45
Leighton Rd. NW5—5G 45
Leighton Rd. W13—2A 72
Leighton Rd. Enf—5A 8
Leighton Rd. Harr—2H 23
Leighton St. Croy—1B 134
Leinster Av. SW14—3J 89
Leinster Gdns. W2—6A 60
Leinster M. W2—7A 60
Leinster Pl. W2—6A 60.
Leinster Rd. N10—4F 29
Leinster Rd. NW6—3J 59
Leinster Sq. W2—6K 59
Leinster Ter. W2—7A 60
Leith Clo. NW9—1K 41
Leithcote Gdns. SW16—4K 109
Leithcote Path. SW16—3K 109
Leith Hill. Orp—1K 129
Leith Hill Grn. Orp—1K 129
Leith Rd. N22—1B 30
Lela Av. Houn—2A 86
Lelitia Clo. E8—1G 63
Leman St. E1—6F 63 (8F 142)
Lemark Clo. Stan—5H 11
Le May Av. SE12—3K 113
Lemmon Rd. SE10—6G 81
Lemna Rd. E11—7G 33
Lemonwell Dri. SE9—6G 99
Lemsford Clo. N15—6G 31
Lemuel St. SW18—6A 92
Lena Gdns. W6—3E 74
Lena Kennedy Clo. E4—6K 19
Lendal Ter. SW4—3H 93
Lenelby Rd. Surb—7G 119
Lenham Rd. SE12—4H 97
Lenham Rd. Bexh—6F 85
Lenham Rd. Sutt—4K 131
Lenham Rd. T Hth—2D 124
Lennard Av. W Wick—2G 137
Lennard Clo. W Wick—2G 137
Lennard Rd.—6K 111
 SE20 1-89 & 2-98
 Beck remainder
Lennard Rd. Brom—7D 128
Lennard Rd. Croy—1C 134
Lennon Rd. NW2—5E 42
Lennox Gdns. NW10—4B 42
Lennox Gdns. SW1
 —4D 76 (8E 144)
Lennox Gdns. Croy—4B 134
Lennox Gdns. Ilf—1D 50
Lennox Gdns. M. SW1
 —4D 76 (8E 144)
Lennox Rd. E17—6B 32
Lennox Rd. N4—2K 45
Lenor Clo. Bexh—4E 100
Lensbury Way. SE2—3C 84
Lens Rd. E7—7A 50
Lenthall Rd. E8—7G 47
Lenthorp Rd. SE10—4H 81
Lentmead Rd. Brom—3H 113
Lenton Rise. Rich—3E 88
Lenton St. SE18—4H 83
Lenton Ter. N4—2A 46
Lenville Way. SE16—5G 79
Leof Cres. SE6—5D 112
Leominster Rd. Mord—6A 122

Leominster Wlk. Mord—6A 122
Leonard Av. Mord—5A 122
Leonard Av. Romf—1K 53
Leonard Rd. E4—6H 19
Leonard Rd. E7—4J 49
Leonard Rd. N9—3A 18
Leonard Rd. SW16—1G 123
Leonard Rd. S'hall—4B 70
Leonard St. E16—1C 82
Leonard St. EC2
—4D 62 (3B 142)
Leontine Clo. SE15—7G 79
Leopold Av. SW19—5H 107
Leopold Rd. E17—5C 32
Leopold Rd. N2—3B 28
Leopold Rd. N18—5C 18
Leopold Rd. NW10—7A 42
Leopold Rd. SW19—4H 107
Leopold Rd. W5—1F 73
Leopold St. E3—5B 64
Leo St. SE15—7H 79
Leppoc Rd. SW4—5H 93
Leroy St. SE1—4E 78 (8C 148)
Lerwick Ct. Enf—5K 7
Lescombe Clo. SE23—3A 112
Lescombe Rd. SE23—3A 112
Lesley Clo. Bex—7H 101
Leslie Gdns. Sutt—7J 131
Leslie Gro. Croy—1E 134
Leslie Gro. Pl. Croy—1E 134
Leslie Pk. Rd. Croy—1E 134
Leslie Rd. E11—4E 48
Leslie Rd. E16—6K 65
Leslie Rd. N2—3B 28
Leslie Smith Sq. SE18—6E 82
Lesney Farm Est. Eri—7K 85
Lesney Pk. Eri—6K 85
Lesney Pk. Rd. Eri—6K 85
Lessar Av. SW4—6G 93
Lessingham Av. SW17—4D 108
Lessingham Av. Ilf—3E 34
Lessing St. SE23—7A 96
Lessington Av. Romf—6J 37
Lessness Av. Bexh—7D 84
Lessness Pk. Belv—5G 85
Lessness Rd. Belv—6G 85
Lessness Rd. Mord—6A 122
Lester Av. E15—3G 65
Leswin Pl. N16—3F 47
Leswin Rd. N16—3F 47
Letchford Gdns. NW10—3C 58
Letchford M. NW10—3C 58
Letchford Ter. Harr—1F 23
Letchworth Clo. Brom—5J 127
Letchworth Dri. Brom—5J 127
Letchworth St. SW17—4D 108
Lethbridge Clo. SE13—1E 96
Letterstone Rd. SW6—7H 75
Lettice St. SW6—1H 91
Lett Rd. E15—7F 49
Lettsom St. SE5—2E 94
Lettsom Wlk. E13—2J 65
Leucha Rd. E17—5A 32
Levana Clo. SW19—1G 107
Levehurst Way. SW4—2J 93
Levendale Rd. SE23—2A 112
Leven Rd. E14—5E 64
Leverett St. SW3
—4C 76 (8D 144)
Leverholme Gdns. SE9—4E 114
Leverson St. SW16—6G 109
Lever St. EC1—3B 62 (2K 141)
Leverton Pl. NW5—5G 45
Leverton St. NW5—5G 45
Levett Gdns. Ilf—4K 51
Levett Rd. Bark—6J 51
Levine Gdns. Bark—2D 68
Levison Way. N19—1H 45
Lewes Clo. N'holt—6E 38
Lewesdon Clo. SW19—1F 107
Lewes Rd. N12—5H 15
Lewes Rd. Brom—2B 128
Leweston Pl. N16—7F 31
Lewgars Av. NW9—6J 25
Lewin Rd. SW14—3K 89
Lewin Rd. SW16—6H 109
Lewin Rd. Bexh—4E 100
Lewis Av. E17—1C 32

Lewis Cres. NW10—5K 41
Lewis Gdns. N2—2B 28
Lewis Gro. SE13—3E 96
Lewisham High St. SE13
—6D 96
Lewisham Hill. SE13—2E 96
Lewisham Pk. SE13—5E 96
Lewisham Rd. SE13—1D 96
Lewisham St. SW1
—2H 77 (5B 146)
Lewisham Way. SE14 1-169 & 2-158a
SE4 remainder
Lewis Rd. Mitc—2B 122
Lewis Rd. Rich—5D 88
Lewis Rd. Sidc—3C 116
Lewis Rd. S'hall—2C 70
Lewis Rd. Sutt—4K 131
Lewis Rd. Well—3C 100
Lewis St. NW1—7F 45
(in two parts)
Lexden Dri. Romf—6B 36
Lexden Rd. W3—1H 73
Lexden Rd. Mitc—4H 123
Lexham Gdns. W8—4J 75
Lexham Gdns. M. W8—3K 75
Lexham M. W8—4J 75
Lexington St. W1
—7G 61 (9M 139)
Lexington Way. Barn—4A 4
Lexton Gdns. SW12—1H 109
Leyborne Av. W13—2B 72
Leyborne Pk. Rich—1G 89
Leybourne Clo. Brom—6J 127
Leybourne Rd. E11—1H 49
Leybourne Rd. NW1—7F 45
(in two parts)
Leybourne Rd. NW9—5G 25
Leybourne St. NW1—7F 45
Leybridge Ct. SE12—5J 97
Leyburn Clo. E17—4D 32
Leyburn Gdns. Croy—2E 134
Leyburn Gro. N18—6B 18
Leyburn Rd. N18—6B 18
Leydenhatch La. Swan—7J 117
Leyden St. E1—5F 63 (6E 142)
Leydon Clo. SE16—1K 79
Leyes Rd. E16—6A 66
Leyfield. Wor Pk—1A 130
Leyland Av. Enf—2F 9
Leyland Gdns. Wfd G—5F 21
Leyland Rd. SE12—5J 97
Leylang Rd. SE14—7K 79
Leys Av. Dag—1J 69
Leys Clo. Dag—7J 53
(in two parts)
Leys Clo. Harr—5H 23
Leysdown Av. Bexh—4J 101
Leysdown Rd. SE9—2C 114
Leysfield Rd. W12—3C 74
Leys Gdns. Barn—5K 5
Leyspring Rd. E11—1H 49
Leys Rd. E. Enf—1F 9
Leys Rd. W. Enf—1F 9
Leys Sq. N3—1K 27
Leys, The. N2—4A 28
Leys, The. Harr—6F 25
Ley St. Ilf—2F 51
Leyswood Dri. Ilf—5J 35
Leythe Rd. W3—2J 73
Leyton Business Centre. E10
—2C 48
Leyton Ct. SE23—1J 111
Leyton Grange Est. E10—1D 48
Leyton Grn. Rd. E10—5E 32
Leyton Industrial Village. E10
—7K 31
Leyton Pk. Rd. E10—3E 48
Leyton Rd. E15—5E 48
Leyton Rd. SW19—7A 108
Leytonstone Rd. E15—5G 49
Leyton Way. E11—7G 33
Leywick St. E15—2G 65
Liardet St. SE14—6A 80
Liberia Rd. N5—6B 46
Liberty Av. SW19—1B 122
Liberty M. SW12—6F 93

Liberty St. SW9—1K 93
Libra Rd. E3—2B 64
Libra Rd. E13—2J 65
Library Pl. E1—7H 63 (9K 143)
Library St. SE1—2B 78 (5J 147)
Lichfield Gdns. Rich—4E 88
Lichfield Gro. N3—1J 27
Lichfield Rd. E3—3A 64
Lichfield Rd. E6—3B 66
Lichfield Rd. N9—2B 18
Lichfield Rd. NW2—4G 43
Lichfield Rd. Dag—4B 52
Lichfield Rd. Houn—3A 86
Lichfield Rd. Rich—1F 89
Lichfield Rd. Wfd G—4B 20
Lidbury Rd. NW7—6B 14
Lidcote Gdns. SW9—2A 94
Liddell Gdns. NW10—2E 58
Liddell Rd. NW6—6J 43
Lidding Rd. Harr—5D 24
Liddington Rd. E15—1H 65
Liddon Rd. E13—3K 65
Liddon Rd. Brom—3A 128
Lidell Clo. Harr—3D 24
Liden Clo. E17—7B 32
Lidfield Rd. N16—4D 46
Lidiard Rd. SW18—2A 108
Lidlington Pl. NW1—2G 61
Lidyard Rd. N19—1G 45
Liffler Rd. SE18—5J 83
Liffords Pl. SW13—2B 90
Lifford St. SW15—4F 91
Lightcliffe Rd. N13—4F 17
Lightermans Rd. E14—2C 80
Lightfoot Rd. N8—5J 29
Lightley Clo. Wemb—1E 56
Ligonier St. E2—4F 63 (3E 142)
Lilac Clo. E4—6G 19
Lilac Gdns. W5—3D 72
Lilac Gdns. Croy—3C 136
Lilac Gdns. Romf—1K 53
Lilac Pl. SE11—4K 77 (9E 146)
Lilac St. W12—7C 58
Lilburne Gdns. SE9—5C 98
Lilburne Rd. SE9—5C 98
Lilburne Wlk. NW10—6J 41
Lile Cres. W7—5J 55
Lilestone St. NW8
—4C 60 (3D 138)
Lilford Rd. SE5—2B 94
Lilian Board Way. Gnfd—5H 39
Lilian Clo. N16—3E 46
Lilian Gdns. Wfd G—1K 33
Lilian Rd. SW16—1G 123
Lillechurch Rd. Dag—6B 52
Lilley La. NW7—5E 12
Lillian Av. W3—2G 73
Lillian Rd. SW13—6D 74
Lillie Rd. SW6—6G 75
Lillieshall Rd. SW4—3F 93
Lillieshall Rd. Mord—6B 122
Lillie Yd. SW6—6J 75
Lillington Gdns. Est. SW1
—4G 77 (9M 145)
Lilliput Av. N'holt—1C 54
Lilliput Ct. SE12—5K 97
Lilliput Rd. Romf—7K 37
Lillyville Rd. SW6—1H 91
Lily Clo. W14—4F 75
Lily Gdns. Wemb—2C 56
Lily Pl. EC1—5A 62 (5H 141)
Lily Rd. E17—6C 32
Limbourne Av. Dag—7F 37
Limburg Rd. SW11—4C 92
Lime Clo. E1—1G 79 (2H 149)
Lime Clo. Buck H—2G 21
Lime Clo. Cars—2D 132
Lime Clo. Romf—4J 37
Lime Ct. E17—5E 32
Lime Ct. Harr—6K 23
Lime Ct. Mitc—2B 122
Limecroft Clo. Eps—7A 130
Limedene Clo. Pinn—1B 22
Lime Gro. N20—1C 14
Lime Gro. W12—2E 74
Lime Gro. N Mald—3K 119

Lime Gro. Sidc—6K 99
Lime Gro. Twic—5K 87
Limeharbour. E14—3D 80
Limeharbour Ct. E14—3D 80
Limehouse Causeway. E14
—7B 64
Limehouse Fields Est. E14
—5A 64
Limerick Clo. SW12—7G 93
Lime Row. Eri—3F 85
Limerston St. SW10—6A 76
Limes Av. E11—4K 33
Limes Av. N12—4F 15
Limes Av. NW7—6F 13
Limes Av. NW11—7G 27
Limes Av. SE20—7H 111
Limes Av. SW13—2B 90
Limes Av. Cars—1D 132
Limes Av. Croy—3A 134
Limes Av., The. N11—5B 16
Limesdale Gdns. Edgw—2J 25
Limes Field Rd. SW14—3A 90
Limesford Rd. SE15—4K 95
Limes Gdns. SW18—6J 91
Limes Gro. SE13—4E 96
Limes Pl. Croy—7D 124
Limes Rd. Beck—2D 126
Limes Rd. Croy—7D 124
Limestone Wlk. Eri—2D 84
Lime St. E17—4A 32
Lime St. EC3—7E 62 (9C 142)
Lime St. Pas. EC3
—6E 62 (8C 142)
Limes Wlk. SE15—4J 95
Limes Wlk. W5—2D 72
Limer Ter. W7—7J 55
Limetree Clo. SW2—1K 109
Lime Tree Gro. Croy—3B 136
Lime Tree Pl. Mitc—1F 123
Lime Tree Rd. Houn—1F 87
Lime Tree Wlk. Bush, Wat
—1D 10
Lime Tree Wlk. Enf—1H 7
Lime Tree Wlk. W Wick—4H 137
Lime Wlk. E15—1G 65
Limewood Clo. W13—6B 56
Limewood Rd. Eri—7J 85
Limpsfield Av. SW19—2F 107
Limpsfield Av. T Hth—5K 123
Linacre Rd. NW2—6D 42
Linberry Wlk. SE8—4B 80
Linchmere Rd. SE12—7H 97
Lincoln Av. N14—3B 16
Lincoln Av. SW19—3F 107
Lincoln Av. Romf—1K 53
Lincoln Av. Twic—2G 103
Lincoln Clo. Gnfd—1G 55
Lincoln Clo. Harr—5D 22
Lincoln Cres. Enf—5K 7
Lincoln Gdns. Ilf—7C 34
Lincoln Grn. Rd. Orp—5K 129
Lincoln M. NW6—1H 59
Lincoln M. SE21—2D 110
Lincoln Rd. E7—6B 50
Lincoln Rd. E13—4K 65
Lincoln Rd. E18—1J 33
Lincoln Rd. N2—3C 28
Lincoln Rd. SE25—3H 125
Lincoln Rd. Enf—4K 7
Lincoln Rd. Felt—3D 102
Lincoln Rd. Harr—5D 22
Lincoln Rd. Mitc—5J 123
Lincoln Rd. N Mald—3J 119
Lincoln Rd. Sidc—5B 116
Lincoln Rd. Wemb—6D 40
Lincoln Rd. Wor Pk—1D 130
Lincoln's Inn Fields. WC2
—6K 61 (7E 140)
Lincolns, The. NW7—3G 13
Lincoln St. E11—2G 49
Lincoln St. SW3—4D 76 (9F 144)
Lincoln Way. Enf—5C 8
Lincombe Rd. Brom—3H 113
Lindal Cres. Enf—4D 6
Lindal Rd. SE4—5B 96
Lindbergh Rd. Wall—7J 133

Linden Av. NW10—2F 59
Linden Av. Enf—1B 8
Linden Av. Houn—5F 87
Linden Av. Ruis—1A 38
Linden Av. T Hth—4B 124
Linden Av. Wemb—5F 41
Linden Clo. N14—6B 6
Linden Clo. Stan—5G 11
Linden Clo. Th Dit—7A 118
Linden Ct. W12—1E 74
Linden Ct. Sidc—4J 115
Linden Cres. Gnfd—6K 39
Linden Cres. King—2F 119
Linden Cres. Wfd G—6E 20
Lindenfield. Chst—2F 129
Linden Gdns. W2—7J 59
Linden Gdns. Enf—1B 8
Linden Gdns. W4—5A 74
Linden Gro. SE15—3H 95
Linden Gro. SE26—6J 111
Linden Gro. N Mald—3A 120
Linden Gro. Tedd—5K 103
Linden Lea. N2—5A 28
Linden Leas. W Wick—2F 137
Linden M. W2—7J 59
Linden Rd. N10—4F 29
Linden Rd. N11—2J 15
Linden Rd. N15—4C 30
Linden Rd. Hmptn—7E 102
Lindens Lawns. Wemb—4F 41
Lindens, The. W4—1J 89
Lindens, The. Croy—6E 136
Linden St. Romf—4K 37
Linden Wlk. N19—2G 45
Lindeth Clo. Stan—6G 11
Lindfield Gdns. NW3—5A 44
Lindfield Rd. W5—4C 56
Lindfield Rd. Croy—6F 125
Lindfield St. E14—6C 64
Lindisfarne Rd. SW20—7C 106
Lindisfarne Rd. Dag—3C 52
Lindisfarne Way. E9—4A 48
Lindley Est. SE15—7G 79
Lindley Rd. E10—2E 48
Lindley St. E1—5J 63 (5L 143)
Lindore Rd. SW11—4D 92
Lindores Rd. Cars—1A 132
Lind Rd. Sutt—5A 132
Lindrop St. SW6—2A 92
Lindsay Dri. Harr—6E 24
Lindsay Rd. Hmptn—4F 103
Lindsay Rd. Wor Pk—2D 130
Lindsay Sq. SW1—5H 77
Lindsell St. SE10—1E 96
Lindsey Clo. Brom—3C 128
Lindsey Clo. Mitc—4J 123
Lindsey M. N1—7C 46
Lindsey Rd. Dag—4C 52
Lindsey St. EC1—5B 62 (5K 141)
Lind St. SE8—2C 96
Lindum Rd. Tedd—7C 104
Lindway. SE27—5B 110
Linford Rd. E17—3E 32
Linford St. SW8—1G 93
Lingards Rd. SE13—4E 96
Lingey Clo. Sidc—2K 115
Lingfield Av. King—4E 118
Lingfield Clo. Enf—6K 7
Lingfield Cres. SE9—4H 99
Lingfield Gdns. N9—7C 8
Lingfield Rd. SW19—5F 107
Lingfield Rd. Wor Pk—3E 130
Lingham St. SW9—2J 93
Lingholm Way. Barn—5A 4
Ling Rd. E16—5J 65
Ling Rd. Eri—6J 85
Lingrove Gdns. Buck H—2E 20
Lings Coppice. SE21—2D 110
Lingwell Rd. SW17—3C 108
Lingwood. Bexh—2H 101
Lingwood Gdns. Iswth—7J 71
Lingwood Rd. E5—7G 31
Linhope St. NW1
—4D 60 (4E 138)
Linkfield. Brom—6J 127
Linkfield Rd. Iswth—2K 87

Link La. Wall—6H 133
Linklea Clo. NW9—7F 13
Link Rd. N8—3A 30
Link Rd. N11—4K 15
Link Rd. Dag—2H 69
Link Rd. Wall—1E 132
Links Av. Mord—4J 121
Links Dri. N20—1D 14
Links Gdns. SW16—7A 110
Linkside. N12—6D 14
Linkside. N Mald—2A 120
Linkside Clo. Enf—3F 7
Linkside Gdns. Enf—3E 6
Links Rd. NW2—2B 42
Links Rd. SW17—6E 108
Links Rd. W3—6G 57
Links Rd. W Wick—1E 136
Links Rd. Wfd G—5D 20
Links Side. Enf—3F 7
Links, The. E17—4A 32
Link St. E9—6J 47
Links View. N3—7C 14
Links View Clo. Stan—6F 11
Links View Rd. Croy—3C 136
Links View Rd. Hmptn—5G 103
Linksway. NW4—2F 27
Links Way. Beck—6C 126
Link, The. W3—6H 57
Link, The. Enf—1F 9
Link, The. N'holt—5D 38
Link, The. Pinn—7A 22
Link, The. Wemb—1C 40
Linkway. N4—7C 30
Linkway. SW20—3D 120
Linkway. Dag—4G 52
Link Way. Pinn—1B 22
Linkway. Rich—2B 104
Linkway, The. Barn—6E 4
Linley Cres. Romf—3H 37
Linley Rd. N17—2E 30
Linnell Clo. NW11—6K 27
Linnell Dri. NW11—6K 27
Linnell Rd. N18—5B 18
Linnell Rd. SE5—2E 94
Linnet Clo. SE28—7C 68
Linnet Clo. Bush, Wat—1B 10
Linnet M. SW12—7E 92
Linnett Clo. E4—4K 19
Linom Rd. SW4—4J 93
Linscott Rd. E5—4J 47
Linsdell Rd. Bark—1G 67
Linsey St. SE16—4G 79 (8G 149)
(in two parts)
Linslade Clo. Houn—5C 86
Linstead St. NW6—7J 43
Linstead Way. SW18—7G 91
Lintaine Clo. W6—6G 75
Linthorpe Av. Wemb—6C 40
Linthorpe Rd. N16—7E 30
Linthorpe Rd. Barn—3H 5
Linton Clo. Well—1B 100
Linton Ct. Romf—2K 37
Linton Gdns. E6—5C 66
Linton Gro. SE27—5C 110
Linton Rd. Bark—7G 51
Linton St. N1—1C 62
Linver Rd. SW6—2J 91
Linwood Clo. E6—5D 66
Linwood Clo. SE5—2F 95
Linzee Rd. N8—4J 29
Lion Av. Twic—1K 103
Lionel Gdns. SE9—5B 98
Lionel M. W10—5G 59
Lionel Rd. SE9—5B 98
Lionel Rd. Bren—3E 72
(in two parts)
Lion Ga. Gdns. Rich—3F 89
Liongate. M. E Mol—3A 118
Lion Rd. E6—5D 66
Lion Rd. N9—2B 18
Lion Rd. Bexh—4E 100
Lion Rd. Croy—5C 124
Lion Rd. Twic—1K 103
Lions Clo. SE9—3B 114
Lion Way. Bren—7D 72
Lion Wharf Rd. Iswth—3B 88

Liphook Cres. SE23—7J 95
Lipton Clo. SE28—7C 68
Lipton Rd. E1—6K 63
Lisbon Av. Twic—2G 103
Lisburne Rd. NW3—4D 44
Lisford St. SE15—1F 95
Lisgar Ter. W14—4H 75
Liskeard Clo. Chst—6G 115
Liskeard Gdns. SE3—1J 97
Lisle St. WC2—7H 61 (9B 140)
Lismore Clo. Iswth—2A 88
Lismore Rd. N17—3D 30
Lismore Rd. S Croy—6E 134
Lissenden Gdns. NW5—4E 44
Lisson Gro.—4B 60 (3B 138)
NW1 1-135 & 2-116
NW8 remainder
Lisson St. NW1—5C 60 (5C 138)
Liss Way. SE15—7F 79
Lister Gdns. N18—5H 17
Listergate Ct. SW15—4E 90
Lister M. N7—4K 45
Lister Rd. E11—1G 49
Lister St. E13—3J 65
Lister Wlk. SE28—7D 68
Liston Rd. N17—1G 31
Liston Rd. SW4—3G 93
Liston Way. Wfd G—7F 21
Listowel Clo. SW9—7B 78
Listowel Rd. Dag—3G 53
Listria Pk. N16—2E 46
Litchfield Av. E15—6G 49
Litchfield Av. Mord—7H 121
Litchfield Gdns. NW10—6C 42
Litchfield Rd. Sutt—4A 132
Litchfield St. WC2
—7H 61 (9B 140)
Litchfield Way. NW11—5K 27
Lithos Rd. NW3—6K 43
Lit. Acre. Beck—3C 126
Lit. Argyll St. W1
—6G 61 (8L 139)
Lit. Birches. Sidc—2J 115
Lit. Boltons, The. SW10—5K 75
Lit. Bornes. SE21—4E 110
Lit. Britain. EC1—5B 62 (6K 141)
Littlebrook Clo. Croy—6K 125
Lit. Brownings. SE23—2H 111
Littlebury Rd. SW4—3H 93
Lit. Bury St. N9—7K 7
Lit. Bushey La. Bush, Wat
—1C 10
Lit. Cedars. N12—4F 15
Lit. Chester St. SW1
—3F 77 (6J 145)
Lit. College St. SW1
—3J 77 (6C 146)
Littlecombe. SE7—6K 81
Littlecombe Clo. SW15—6F 91
Littlecote Clo. SW19—7G 91
Littlecote Pl. Pinn—1C 22
Little Ct. W Wick—2G 137
Lit. Cottage St. E14—7B 64
Littledale. SE2—6A 84
Lit. Dimocks. SW12—2F 109
Lit. Dorrit Ct. SE1
—2C 78 (4M 147)
Lit. Ealing La. W5—4C 72
Lit. Edward St. NW1
—3F 61 (1K 139)
Lit. Ferry Rd. Twic—1B 104
Lit. Friday Hill. E4—2B 20
Lit. Gearies. Ilf—4F 35
Lit. George St. SW1
—2J 77 (5C 146)
Lit. Grange. Gnfd—3A 56
Lit. Green. Rich—4D 88
Lit. Green St. NW5—4F 45
Littlegrove. Barn—6H 5
Lit. Heath. SE7—6C 82
Lit. Heath. Romf—4B 36
Lit. Heath Rd. Bexh—1F 101
Littleheath Rd. S Croy—7H 135
Lit. Holt. E11—5J 33

Lit. Ilford La. E12—4D 50
Lit. John Rd. W7—6K 55
Littlemede. SE9—3D 114
Littlemore Rd. SE2—2A 84
Lit. Moss La. Pinn—2C 22
Lit. Newport St. WC2
—7H 61 (9B 140)
Lit. New St. EC4
—6A 62 (7H 141)
Lit. Orchard Clo. Pinn—2C 22
Lit. Park Dri. Felt—2C 102
Lit. Park Gdns. Enf—3J 7
Lit. Pluckett's Way. Buck H
—1G 21
Lit. Portland St. W1
—6G 61 (7L 139)
Lit. Potters. Bush, Wat—1C 10
Lit. Queen's Rd. Tedd—6K 103
Lit. Redlands. Brom—2C 128
Littlers Clo. SW19—1B 122
Lit. Russell St. WC1
—5J 61 (6C 140)
Lit. Saint James's St. SW1
—1G 77 (3L 145)
Lit. Saint Leonard's. SW14
—3J 89
Lit. Sanctuary. SW1
—2H 77 (5B 146)
Lit. Smith St. SW1
—3H 77 (6B 146)
Lit. Somerset St. E1
—6F 63 (8E 142)
Littlestone Clo. Beck—6C 112
Lit. Strand. NW9—2B 26
Lit. Thrift. Orp—4G 129
Lit. Titchfield St. W1
—5G 61 (6L 139)
Littleton Av. E4—1C 20
Littleton Cres. Harr—2K 39
Littleton Rd. Harr—2K 39
Littleton St. SW18—2A 108
Lit. Trinity La. EC4
—7C 62 (9M 141)
Lit. Turnstile. WC1
—5K 61 (6E 140)
Lit. Venice. W2—5A 60
Littlewood. SE13—6E 96
Littlewood Clo. W13—3B 72
Livermere Rd. E8—1F 63
Liverpool Gro. SE17—5D 78
Liverpool Rd. E10—6E 32
Liverpool Rd. E16—5G 65
Liverpool Rd.—6A 46
N1 1-393 & 2-296
N7 remainder
Liverpool Rd. W5—2D 72
Liverpool Rd. King—7G 105
Liverpool Rd. T Hth—3C 124
Liverpool St. EC2
—5E 62 (6C 142)
Livesey Pl. SE15—6G 79
Livingstone College Towers.
E10—6E 32
Livingstone Ct. E10—6E 32
Livingstone Pl. E14—5E 80
Livingstone Rd. E15—1E 64
Livingstone Rd. E17—6D 32
Livingstone Rd. N13—6D 16
Livingstone Rd. SW11—3B 92
Livingstone Rd. Houn—4G 87
Livingstone Rd. S'hall—7B 54
Livingstone Rd. T Hth—2D 124
Livonia St. W1—6G 61 (8M 139)
Lizard St. EC1—3C 62 (2M 141)
Lizban St. SE3—7K 81
Llanelly Rd. NW2—2H 43
Llanover Rd. SE18—6E 82
Llanover Rd. Wemb—3D 40
Llanthony Rd. Mord—5B 122
Llanvanor Rd. NW2—2H 43
Llewellyn St. SE16
—2G 79 (5H 149)
Lloyd Av. SW16—1J 123
Lloyd Baker St. WC1
—3A 62 (2G 141)
Lloyd Ct. Pinn—5B 22

229

Lloyd Pk. Av. Croy—4F 135
Lloyd Rd. E6—1D 66
Lloyd Rd. E17—4K 31
Lloyd Rd. Dag—7F 53
Lloyd Rd. Wor Pk—3E 130
Lloyd's Av. EC3—6E 62 (8D 142)
Lloyd's Pl. SE3—2G 97
Lloyd Sq. WC1—3A 62 (1G 141)
Lloyd's Row. EC1
—3A 62 (2H 141)
Lloyd St. WC1—3A 62 (1G 141)
Lloyds Way. Beck—5A 126
Loampit Hill. SE13—2C 96
Loampit Vale. SE13—3D 96
Loanda Clo. E8—1F 63
Loats Rd. SW2—6J 93
Lobelia Clo. E6—5C 66
Locarno Rd. W3—1J 73
Locarno Rd. Gnfd—4H 55
Lochaber Rd. SE13—4G 97
Lochaline St. W6—6E 74
Lochan Clo. Hay—4C 54
Lochinvar St. SW12—7F 93
Lochmere Clo. Eri—6H 85
Lock Chase. SE3—3G 97
Lockesfield Pl. E14—5D 80
Lockesley Dri. Orp—6K 129
Lockesley Sq. Surb—6D 118
Locke's Wharf Development.
E14—5D 80
Locket Rd. Harr—3J 23
Lockfield Av. Enf—2F 9
Lockhart Clo. N7—6K 45
Lockhart St. E3—4B 64
Lockhurst St. E5—4K 47
Lockington Rd. SW8—1F 93
Lockmead Rd. N15—6G 31
Lockmead Rd. SE13—3E 96
Lock Rd. Rich—4C 104
Locks La. Mitc—1E 122
Locksley Est. E14—6B 64
Locksley St. E14—5B 64
Locksmeade Rd. Rich—4C 104
Lockwood Clo. SE26—4K 111
Lockwood Industrial Pk. N17
—3H 31
Lockwood Sq. SE16
—3H 79 (6J 149)
Lockwood Way. E17—2K 31
Lockyer St. SE1—2D 78 (5B 148)
Loddiges Rd. E9—7J 47
Loder St. SE15—7J 79
Lodge Av. SW14—3A 90
Lodge Av. Croy—3A 134
Lodge Av. Dag—1A 68
Lodge Av. Harr—4E 24
Lodge Clo. N18—5H 17
Lodge Clo. Edgw—6A 12
Lodge Clo. Iswth—1B 88
Lodge Clo. Wall—1E 132
Lodge Dri. N13—4F 17
Lodge Gdns. Beck—5B 126
Lodge Hill. Ilf—4C 34
Lodge Hill. Well—7B 84
Lodgehill Pk. Clo. Harr—2F 39
Lodge La. N12—5F 15
Lodge La. Bex—6D 100
Lodge La. Croy—6C 136
Lodge La. Romf—1G 37
Lodge Pl. Sutt—5K 131
Lodge Rd. NW4—4E 26
Lodge Rd. NW8—3B 60 (2B 138)
Lodge Rd. Brom—7A 114
Lodge Rd. Croy—6B 124
Lodge Rd. Wall—5F 133
Lodge Vs. Wfd G—7C 20
Lodore Gdns. NW9—5A 26
Lodore St. E14—6E 64
Loftie St. SE16—2G 79 (5H 149)
Lofting Rd. N1—7A 46
Loftus Rd. W12—1D 74
Logan Clo. Enf—1E 8
Logan Clo. Houn—3D 86
Logan M. W8—4J 75
Logan Pl. W8—4J 75

Logan Rd. N9—2C 18
Logan Rd. Wemb—2D 40
Loggetts. SE21—2E 110
Logs Hill. Chst—7C 114
Logs Hill Clo. Chst—1C 128
Lolesworth Clo. E1
—5F 63 (6F 142)
Lollard St. SE11—4K 77 (8F 146)
(in two parts)
Loman St. SE1—2B 78 (4K 147)
Lomas Clo. Croy—7E 136
Lomas St. E1—5G 63 (5H 143)
Lombard Av. Enf—1D 8
Lombard Av. Ilf—1J 51
Lombard Business Centre, The.
SW11—2B 92
Lombard Ct. EC3
—7D 62 (9B 142)
Lombard La. EC4
—6A 62 (8H 141)
Lombard Rd. N11—5A 16
Lombard Rd. SW11—2B 92
Lombard Rd. SW19—2K 121
Lombard St. EC3
—6D 62 (8B 142)
Lombard Wall. SE7—3K 81
(in two parts)
Lombardy Pl. W2—7K 59
Lomond Clo. N15—5E 30
Lomond Clo. Wemb—7F 41
Lomond Gro. SE5—7D 78
Lomond Ho. SE5—7F 79
Loncroft Rd. SE5—6E 78
Londesborough Rd. N16—4E 46
London Bri. SE1 & EC4
—1D 78 (2B 148)
London Bri. St. SE1
—1D 78 (3B 148)
London Fields E. Side. E8
—7H 47
London Fields W. Side. E8
—7G 47
London Industrial Pk., The. E6
—5F 67
London La. E8—7H 47
London La. Brom—7H 113
London M. W2—6B 60 (8B 138)
London Rd. E13—2J 65
London Rd. SE1—3B 78 (6J 147)
London Rd. SE23—1H 111
London Rd.—1K 123
SW16 1102-1544 & 1109-1599
T Hth & Croy remainder
London Rd. Bark—7F 51
London Rd. Brom—7H 113
London Rd. Dart—5K 101
London Rd. Enf—5J 7
London Rd. Eps & Wor Pk
—7C 130
London Rd. Harr—2J 39
London Rd. Houn, Iswth & Bren
—3G 87
London Rd. King—2F 119
London Rd.—5C 122
Mitc 85-479 & 80-522
SW17 remainder
London Rd. Mitc & Wall
(Hackbridge)—7E 122
London Rd. Mord—5J 121
London Rd. Romf—6G 37
London Rd. Stan—5H 11
London Rd. Twic—7A 88
London Rd. Wemb—5E 40
London Stile. W4—5G 73
London Rd. EC3—7E 62 (9D 142)
London St. W2—6B 60 (7A 138)
London Ter. E2—2G 63 (1G 143)
London Wall. EC2
—5C 62 (6M 141)
Long Acre. WC2—7J 61 (9C 140)
Longacre Pl. Cars—6E 132
Longacre Rd. E17—1F 33
Longbeach Rd. SW11—3D 92
Longberrys. NW2—3H 43
Longboat Row. S'hall—6D 54
Longbridge Rd. Bark & Dag
—6H 51

Longbridge Way. SE13—5E 96
Longcroft. SE9—3D 114
Longcrofte Rd. Edgw—7J 11
Long Deacon Rd. E4—1B 20
Longdown Rd. SE6—4C 112
Long Dri. W3—6A 58
Long Dri. Gnfd—1F 55
Long Dri. Ruis—4A 38
Long Elmes. Harr—1F 23
Longfellow Rd. E3—3A 64
Longfellow Rd. E17—6B 32
Longfellow Rd. Wor Pk—1C 130
Long Field. NW9—7F 13
Longfield. Brom—1H 127
Longfield Av. E17—4A 32
Longfield Av. NW7—7H 13
Longfield Av. W5—7C 56
Longfield Av. Wall—1E 132
Longfield Av. Wemb—1E 40
Longfield Cres. SE26—3J 111
Longfield Dri. SW14—5H 89
Longfield Est. SE1
—4F 79 (9F 148)
Longfield Rd. W5—6C 56
Longfield St. SW18—7J 91
Longfield Wlk. W5—6C 56
Longford Av. S'hall—7F 55
Longford Clo. Hmptn—4E 102
Longford Clo. Hay—7B 54
Longford Gdns. Hay—7B 54
Longford Gdns. Sutt—2A 132
Longford Rd. Twic—1F 103
Longford St. NW1
—4F 61 (3K 139)
Longford Wlk. SW2—7A 94
Longhayes Av. Romf—4D 36
Longheath Gdns. Croy—5J 125
Long Hedges. Houn—1E 86
Longhedge St. SW11—2E 92
Longhill Rd. SE6—2F 113
Longhope Clo. SE15—6E 78
Longhope Gdns. SE15—6E 78
Longhurst Rd. SE13—5F 97
Longhurst Rd. Croy—6H 125
Longland Ct. SE1
—5G 79 (9G 149)
Longland Dri. N20—3E 14
Longlands Pk. Cres. Sidc
—3J 115
Longlands Rd. Sidc—3J 115
Long La. EC1—5B 62 (6K 141)
Long La.—1K 27
N3 1-223 & 2-280
N2 remainder
Long La. SE1—2D 78 (5A 148)
Long La. Bexh—7D 84
Long La. Croy—6J 125
Longleat Rd. Enf—5K 7
Longleigh La. SE2 & Bex H
—6C 84
Longley Av. Wemb—1F 57
Longley Rd. SW17—6C 108
Longley Rd. Croy—7B 124
Longley Rd. Harr—5G 23
Long Leys. E4—6K 19
Longley St. SE1—4G 79 (9G 149)
Longley Way. NW2—3E 42
Long Mark Rd. E16—5B 66
Long Mead. NW9—1B 26
Longmead. Chst—2E 128
Longmead Dri. Sidc—2D 116
Longmead Ho. SE27—5C 110
Long Meadow. NW5—5H 45
Long Meadow Clo. W Wick
—7E 126
Longmeadow Rd. Sidc—1J 115
Longmead Rd. SW17—5D 108
Longmoore St. SW1
—4G 77 (9L 145)
Longmore Av. Barn—6F 5
Longnor Est. E1—3K 63
Longnor Rd. E1—3K 63
Long Pond Rd. SE3—1G 97
Longreach Ct. Bark—2H 67
Long Reach Rd. Bark—4K 67
Longridge La. S'hall—6F 55
Longridge Rd. SW5—4J 75

Long Rd. SW4—4G 93
Longs Ct. Rich—4F 89
Longshaw Rd. E4—3A 20
Longshore. SE8—4B 80
Longstaff Cres. SW18—7J 91
Longstaff Rd. SW18—6J 91
Longstone Av. NW10—7B 42
Longstone Rd. SW17—5F 109
Long St. E2—3F 63 (1E 142)
(in two parts)
Longthornton Rd. SW16
—2G 123
Longton Av. SE26—4G 111
Longton Gro. SE26—4H 111
Longview Way. Romf—1K 37
Longville Rd. SE11
—4B 78 (8K 147)
Long Wlk. SE1—3E 78 (6D 148)
Long Wlk. SE18—6F 83
Long Wlk. SW13—2B 90
Long Wlk. N Mald—3J 119
Long Wall. E15—3F 65
Longwood Dri. SW15—6C 90
Longwood Gdns. Ilf—4D 34
Longworth Clo. SE28—6D 68
Long Yd. WC1—4K 61 (4E 140)
Loning, The. NW9—4B 26
Lonsdale Av. E6—4B 66
Lonsdale Av. Romf—6J 37
Lonsdale Av. Wemb—5E 40
Lonsdale Clo. E6—4C 66
Lonsdale Clo. SE9—3B 114
Lonsdale Clo. Pinn—1C 22
Lonsdale Ct. Surb—7D 118
Lonsdale Cres. Ilf—6F 35
Lonsdale Dri. Enf—4C 6
Lonsdale Gdns. T Hth—4K 123
Lonsdale M. Rich—1G 89
Lonsdale Pl. N1—7A 46
Lonsdale Rd. E11—7H 33
Lonsdale Rd. NW6—1H 59
Lonsdale Rd. SE25—4H 125
Lonsdale Rd. SW13—1B 90
Lonsdale Rd. W4—4B 74
Lonsdale Rd. W11—6H 59
Lonsdale Rd. Bexh—2F 101
Lonsdale Rd. S'hall—3B 70
Lonsdale Sq. N1—7A 46
Lonsdale Yd. W11—7J 59
Loobert Rd. N15—3E 30
Looe Gdns. Ilf—3F 35
Loop Rd. Chst—6G 115
Lopen Rd. N18—4K 17
Loraine Clo. Enf—5D 8
Loraine Rd. N7—4K 45
Loraine Rd. W4—6H 73
Lord Av. Ilf—4D 34
Lord Chancellor Wlk. King
—1J 119
Lorden Wlk. E2—3G 63 (2G 143)
Lord Gdns. Ilf—4C 34
Lord Hills Bri. W2—5K 59
Lord Hill's Rd. W2—5K 59
Lord Holland La. SW9—2A 94
Lord Napier Pl. W6—5C 74
Lord North St. SW1
—3J 77 (7C 146)
Lord Roberts M. SW6—7K 75
Lord Roberts Ter. SE18—5E 82
Lord's Clo. SE21—2C 110
Lords Clo. Felt—2C 102
Lordship Gro. N16—2D 46
Lordship La.—2A 30
N17 1-421 & 2-470
N22 remainder
Lordship La. SE22—5F 95
Lordship La. Est. SE22—1G 111
Lordship Pk. N16—2C 46
Lordship Pk. M. N16—2C 46
Lordship Pl. SW3—6C 76
Lordship Rd. N16—1D 46
Lordship Rd. N'holt—7C 38
Lordship Ter. N16—2D 46
Lordsmead Rd. N17—2E 30
Lord St. E16—1C 82
Lords View. NW8
—3C 60 (2C 138)

230

Lord Warwick St. SE18—3D 82
Lorenzo St. WC1
—3K 61 (1E 140)
Loretto Gdns. Harr—4E 24
Lorian Clo. N12—4E 14
Loring Rd. N20—2H 15
Loring Rd. Iswth—2K 87
Loris Rd. W6—3E 74
Lorn Ct. SW9—1A 94
Lorne Av. Croy—7K 125
Lorne Clo. NW8—3C 60 (2D 138)
Lorne Gdns. E11—4A 34
Lorne Gdns. W11—2G 75
Lorne Gdns. Croy—7K 125
Lorne Rd. E7—4K 49
Lorne Rd. E17—5C 32
Lorne Rd. N4—1K 45
Lorne Rd. Harr—2K 23
Lorne Rd. Rich—5F 89
Lorne Ter. N3—2H 27
Lorn Rd. SW9—2K 93
Lorraine Pk. Harr—7D 10
Lorrimore Rd. SE17—6B 78
Lorrimore Sq. SE17—6B 78
Losberne Way. SE16—5G 79
Lothair Rd. N4—7B 30
Lothair Rd. W5—2D 72
Lothair Rd. N. N4—6B 30
Lothbury. EC2—6D 62 (7A 142)
Lothian Av. Hay—5A 54
Lothian Clo. Wemb—4A 40
Lothian Rd. SW9—1B 94
Lothrop St. W10—3G 59
Lots Rd. SW10—7A 76
Loubet St. SW17—6D 108
Loudoun Av. Ilf—5F 35
Loudoun Rd. NW8—1A 60
Loughborough Est. SW9
—3B 94
Loughborough Pk. SW9—4B 94
Loughborough Rd. SW9—2A 94
Loughborough St. SE11—5K 77
Lough Rd. N7—5K 45
Loughton Way. Buck H & Lou
—1G 21
Louisa Gdns. E1
—4K 63 (4M 143)
Louisa St. E1—4K 63 (4M 143)
Louise Ct. N22—1A 30
Louise Rd. E15—6G 49
Louisville Rd. SW17—3E 108
Louvaine Rd. SW11—4B 92
Lovage App. E6—5C 66
Lovat Clo. NW2—3B 42
Lovat Clo. Edgw—6C 12
Lovat La. EC3—7E 62 (1C 148)
Lovat Wlk. Houn—7C 70
Loveday Rd. W13—2B 72
Lovegrove St. SE1—5G 79
Lovegrove Wlk. E14—1E 80
Lovekyn Clo. King—2E 118
Lovelace Av. Brom—6E 128
Lovelace Gdns. Bark—4A 52
Lovelace Gdns. Surb—7D 118
Lovelace Grn. SE9—3D 98
Lovelace Rd. SE21—2C 110
Lovelace Rd. Barn—7H 5
Lovelace Rd. Surb—7C 118
Love La. EC2—6C 62 (7M 141)
Love La. N17—7A 18
Love La. SE18—4E 82
Love La. SE25—3H 125
Love La. Bex—6F 101
Love La. Brom—1K 127
Love La. Mitc—3C 122
Love La. Mord—7J 121
Love La. Pinn—3C 22
Love La. Sutt—6G 131
(in two parts)
Love La. Wfd G—6J 21
Lovel Av. Well—2A 100
Lovelinch Clo. SE15—6J 79
Lovell Pl. SE16—3A 80
Lovell Rd. Rich—3C 104
Lovell Rd. S'hall—6F 55
Loveridge M. NW6—6H 43
Loveridge Rd. NW6—6H 43

Lovers Wlk. NW7—6C 14
Lovers Wlk. SE10—6F 81
Lovett Dri. Cars—7A 122
Lovett Way. NW10—5J 41
Love Wlk. SE5—2D 94
Lowbrook Rd. Ilf—4F 51
Low Cross Wood La. SE21
—3F 111
Lowden Rd. N9—1C 18
Lowden Rd. SE24—4B 94
Lowden Rd. S'hall—7C 54
Lowe Av. E16—5J 65
Lowell St. E14—6A 64
Lowen Rd. Rain—2K 69
Lwr. Addiscombe Rd. Croy
—1E 134
Lwr. Addison Gdns. W14
—2G 75
Lwr. Belgrave St. SW1
—3F 77 (7J 145)
Lwr. Boston Rd. W7—1J 71
Lwr. Broad St. Dag—1G 69
Lwr. Camden. Chst—7D 114
Lwr. Church St. Croy—2B 134
Lwr. Clapton Rd. E5—3H 47
Lwr. Common S. SW15—3D 90
Lwr. Coombe St. Croy—4C 134
Lwr. Downs Rd. SW20—1F 121
Lwr. Drayton Pl. Croy—2B 134
Lwr. George St. Rich—5D 88
Lwr. Gravel Rd. Brom—7D 128
Lwr. Green W. Mitc—3C 122
Lwr. Grosvenor Pl. SW1
—3F 77 (6K 145)
Lwr. Grove Rd. Rich—6F 89
Lwr. Hall La. E4—5F 19
Lwr. Ham Rd. King—6D 104
Lwr. James St. W1
—7G 61 (9M 139)
Lwr. John St. W1
—7G 61 (9M 139)
Lwr. Kenwood Av. Enf—5D 6
Lwr. Maidstone Rd. N11—6B 16
Lwr. Mall. W6—5D 74
Lwr. Mardyke Av. Rain—2J 69
Lwr. Marsh. SE1
—2A 78 (5G 147)
Lwr. Marsh La. King—4F 119
Lwr. Merton Risc. NW3—7C 44
Lwr. Morden La. Mord—6F 121
Lwr. Mortlake Rd. Rich—4E 88
Lwr. Park Rd. N11—5A 16
Lwr. Park Rd. Belv—4G 85
Lwr. Queen's Rd. Buck H—2G 21
Lwr. Richmond Rd. SW15
—3D 90
Lwr. Richmond Rd. Rich &
SW14—3G 89
Lower Rd.—3J 79 (7M 149)
SE16 1-245 & 2-196
SE8 remainder
Lower Rd. Belv & Eri—3H 85
Lower Rd. Harr—1H 39
Lower Rd. Sutt—4A 132
Lwr. Sloane St. SW1
—4E 76 (9G 145)
Lower Sq., The. Sutt—5K 131
Lwr. Strand. NW9—2B 26
Lwr. Sydenham Industrial Est.
SE26—5B 112
Lwr. Teddington Rd. King
—1D 118
Lower Ter. NW3—3A 44
Lwr. Thames St. EC3
—7E 62 (1D 148)
Loweswater Clo. Wemb—2D 40
Lowfield Rd. NW6—7J 43
Lowfield Rd. W3—6J 57
Low Hall Clo. E4—7J 9
Lowhall La. E17—6A 32
Lowick Rd. Harr—4J 23
Lowlands Gdns. Romf—6H 37
Lowlands Rd. Harr—7J 23
Lowlands Rd. Pinn—6A 22
Lowman Rd. N7—4K 45
Lowndes Clo. SW1
—3E 76 (7H 145)

Lowndes Ct. SW1
—3D 76 (6F 144)
Lowndes Pl. SW1
—3E 76 (7G 145)
Lowndes Sq. SW1
—2D 76 (5F 144)
Lowndes St. SW1
—3E 76 (6G 145)
Lowood St. E1—7H 63 (9K 143)
Lowry Cres. Mitc—2C 122
Lowshoe La. Romf—1H 37
Lowther Dri. Enf—4D 6
Lowther Gdns. SW7
—3B 76 (6B 144)
Lowther Hill. SE23—7A 96
Lowther Rd. E17—2A 32
Lowther Rd. N7—5A 46
Lowther Rd. SW13—1B 90
Lowther Rd. King—1F 119
Lowther Rd. Stan—3F 25
Lowth Rd. SE5—2C 94
Loxford Av. E6—2B 66
Loxford La. Ilf—5G 51
Loxford Rd. Bark—6F 51
Loxham Rd. E4—7J 19
Loxham St. WC1
—3J 61 (2D 140)
Loxley Clo. SE26—5K 111
Loxley Rd. SW18—1B 108
Loxley Rd. Hmptn—4D 102
Loxton Rd. SE23—1K 111
Loxwood Rd. N17—3E 30
Lubbock Rd. Chst—7D 114
Lubbock St. SE14—7J 79
Lucan Pl. SW3—4C 76 (9D 144)
Lucan Rd. Barn—3B 4
Lucas Av. E13—1K 65
Lucas Av. Harr—2E 38
Lucas Rd. SE20—6J 111
Lucas Sq. NW11—6J 27
Lucas St. SE8—1C 96
Lucerne Clo. N13—3D 16
Lucerne Ct. Eri—3E 84
Lucerne Gro. E17—4F 33
Lucerne M. W8—1J 75
Lucerne Rd. N5—4B 46
Lucerne Rd. Orp—7K 129
Lucerne Rd. T Hth—4C 124
Lucey Rd. SE16—3G 79 (7G 149)
Lucey Way. SE16
—3G 79 (7H 149)
Lucien Rd. SW17—4E 108
Lucien Rd. SW19—2K 107
Lucinda Ct. Enf—4K 7
Lucorn Clo. SE12—6H 97
Luctons Av. Buck H—1F 21
Lucy Cres. W3—5J 57
Lucy Gdns. Dag—3F 53
Luddesdon Rd. Eri—7G 85
Ludford Clo. NW9—2A 26
Ludford Clo. Croy—4B 134
Ludgate B'way. EC4
—6B 62 (8J 141)
Ludgate Cir. EC4
—6B 62 (8J 141)
Ludgate Hill. EC4
—6B 62 (8J 141)
Ludgate Sq. EC4
—6B 62 (8K 141)
Ludham Clo. SE28—6C 68
Ludlow Clo. Brom—3J 127
Ludlow Clo. Harr—4D 38
Ludlow Rd. W5—4C 56
Ludlow St. EC1—4C 62 (3L 141)
Ludlow Way. N2—4A 28
Ludovick Wlk. SW15—4A 90
Ludwick M. SE14—7A 80
Luffield Rd. SE2—3B 84
Luffman Rd. SE12—3K 113
Lugard Rd. SE15—2H 95
Luke St. EC2—4E 62 (3C 142)
Lukin Cres. E4—3A 20
Lukin St. E1—6J 63 (8M 143)
Lullingstone Clo. Orp—7B 116
Lullingstone Cres. Orp—7A 116
Lullingstone Rd. Belv—6F 85

Lullington Garth. N12—5C 14
Lullington Garth. Brom—7G 113
Lullington Rd. SE20—7G 111
Lullington Rd. Dag—7E 52
Lulot Gdns. N19—2F 45
Lulworth Av. Houn—7G 71
Lulworth Av. Wemb—7C 24
Lulworth Clo. Harr—3D 38
Lulworth Dri. Pinn—7B 22
Lulworth Gdns. Harr—2C 38
Lulworth Rd. SE9—2C 114
Lulworth Rd. SE15—2H 95
Lulworth Rd. Well—2K 99
Lulworth Waye. Hay—6A 54
Lumley Clo. Belv—5G 85
Lumley Ct. WC2—7J 61 (1D 146)
Lumley Gdns. Sutt—5G 131
Lumley Rd. Sutt—5G 131
Lumley St. W1—6E 60 (8H 139)
Luna Rd. T Hth—3C 124
Lundy Wlk. N1—6C 46
Lunham Rd. SE19—6E 110
Lupin Clo. SW2—2B 110
Lupin Clo. Croy—1K 135
Lupton Clo. SE12—3K 113
Lupton St. NW5—4G 45
Lupus St. SW1—5F 77
Luralda Gdns. E14—5F 81
Lurgan Av. W6—6F 75
Lurline Gdns. SW11—1E 92
Luscombe Ct. Brom—2G 127
Luscombe Way. SW8—7J 77
Lushington Rd. NW10—2D 58
Lushington Rd. SE6—5D 112
Lushington Ter. E8—5G 47
Luther Clo. Edgw—2D 12
Luther King Clo. E17—6A 32
Luther Rd. Tedd—5K 103
Luton Pl. SE10—7E 80
Luton Rd. E13—4J 65
Luton Rd. E17—3B 32
Luton Rd. Sidc—3C 116
Luton St. NW8—4B 60 (4B 138)
Luttrell Av. SW15—5D 90
Lutwyche Rd. SE6—2B 112
Luxborough La. Chig—3H 21
Luxborough St. W1
—5E 60 (5G 139)
Luxemburg Gdns. W6—4F 75
Luxfield Rd. SE9—1C 114
Luxford St. SE16
—4K 79 (9M 149)
Luxmore Gdns. SE4—2B 96
Luxmore St. SE4—1B 96
Luxor St. SE5—3C 94
Lyall Av. SE21—4E 110
Lyall M. SW1—3E 76 (7G 145)
Lyall M. W. SW1
—3E 76 (7G 145)
Lyall St. SW1—3E 76 (7G 145)
Lyal Rd. E3—2A 64
Lycett Pl. W12—2C 74
Lyconby Gdns. Croy—7A 126
Lydd Clo. Sidc—3J 115
Lydden Gro. SW18—7K 91
Lydden Rd. SW18—7K 91
Lydeard Rd. E6—7D 50
Lydford Rd. N15—5D 30
Lydford Rd. NW2—6F 43
Lydford Rd. W9—4H 59
Lydhurst Av. SW2—2K 109
Lydney Clo. SE15—7E 78
Lydney Clo. SW19—2G 107
Lydon Rd. SW4—3G 93
Lydstep Rd. Chst—4E 114
Lyford Rd. SW18—7B 92
Lygon Pl. SW1—3F 77 (7J 145)
Lyham Clo. SW2—6J 93
Lyham Rd. SW2—5J 93
Lyle Clo. Mitc—7E 122
Lyme Farm Rd. SE12—4J 97
Lyme Gro. E9—7J 47
Lymer Av. SE19—5F 111
Lyme Rd. Well—1B 100
Lymescote Gdns. Sutt—2J 131
Lyme St. NW1—7G 45

231

Lyme Ter. NW1—7G 45
Lyminge Clo. Sidc—4K 115
Lyminge Gdns. SW18—1C 108
Lymington Av. N22—2A 30
Lymington Clo. SW16—2H 123
Lymington Gdns. Eps—5B 130
Lymington Rd. NW6—6K 43
Lymington Rd. Dag—1D 52
Lympstone Gdns. SE15—7G 79
Lynbridge Gdns. N13—4G 17
Lynbrook Clo. SE15—7E 78
Lynbrook Clo. Rain—2K 69
Lynch Wlk. SE8—6B 80
Lyncott Cres. SW4—4F 93
Lyncroft Av. Pinn—5C 22
Lyncroft Gdns. NW6—5J 43
Lyncroft Gdns. W13—2C 72
Lyncroft Gdns. Houn—5G 87
Lyndale. NW2—4H 43
Lyndale Av. NW2—3H 43
Lyndale Clo. SE3—6H 81
Lyndhurst Av. N12—6J 15
Lyndhurst Av. NW7—6F 13
Lyndhurst Av. SW16—2H 123
Lyndhurst Av. Pinn—1A 22
Lyndhurst Av. S'hall—1F 71
Lyndhurst Av. Surb—7H 119
Lyndhurst Av. Twic—1D 102
Lyndhurst Clo. NW10—3K 41
Lyndhurst Clo. Bexh—3H 101
Lyndhurst Clo. Croy—3F 135
Lyndhurst Ct. E18—1J 33
Lyndhurst Dri. E10—7E 32
Lyndhurst Dri. N Mald—7A 120
Lyndhurst Gdns. N3—1G 27
Lyndhurst Gdns. NW3—5B 44
Lyndhurst Gdns. Bark—6J 51
Lyndhurst Gdns. Enf—4K 7
Lyndhurst Gdns. IIf—6H 35
Lyndhurst Gdns. Pinn—1A 22
Lyndhurst Gro. SE15—2E 94
Lyndhurst Rise. Chig—4K 21
Lyndhurst Rd. E4—7K 19
Lyndhurst Rd. N18—4B 18
Lyndhurst Rd. N22—6F 17
Lyndhurst Rd. NW3—5B 44
Lyndhurst Rd. Bexh—3H 101
Lyndhurst Rd. Gnfd—4F 55
Lyndhurst Rd. T Hth—4A 124
Lyndhurst Sq. SE15—1F 95
Lyndhurst Ter. NW3—5B 44
Lyndhurst Way. SE15—1F 95
Lyndhurst Way. Sutt—7J 131
Lyndon Av. Sidc—5K 99
Lyndon Av. Wall—3E 132
Lyndon Rd. Belv—4G 85
Lyne Cres. E17—1B 32
Lyneham Wlk. E5—5A 48
Lynette Av. SW4—6G 93
Lynett Rd. Dag—2D 52
Lynford Clo. Edgw—7D 12
Lynford Gdns. Edgw—3C 12
Lynford Gdns. IIf—2K 51
Lynford Ter. N9—7A 8
Lynmere Rd. Well—2B 100
Lynmouth Av. Enf—6A 8
Lynmouth Av. Mord—7F 121
Lynmouth Gdns. Gnfd—1B 56
Lynmouth Gdns. Houn—7B 70
Lynmouth Rd. E17—6A 32
Lynmouth Rd. N2—4D 28
Lynmouth Rd. N16—1F 47
Lynmouth Rd. Gnfd—1B 56
Lynn Clo. Harr—2H 23
Lynne Way. NW10—6A 42
Lynne Way. N'holt—2B 54
Lynn Rd. E11—2G 49
Lynn Rd. SW12—7F 93
Lynn Rd. IIf—7H 35
Lynn St. Enf—1J 7
Lynscott Way. S Croy—7B 134
Lynsted Clo. Bexh—5H 101
Lynsted Clo. Brom—2A 128
Lynsted Ct. Beck—2A 126
Lynsted Gdns. SE9—4B 98
Lynton Av. N12—4G 15
Lynton Av. NW9—4B 26

Lynton Av. W13—6A 56
Lynton Av. Romf—1H 37
Lynton Clo. Iswth—4K 87
Lynton Cres. IIf—6F 35
Lynton Gdns. Enf—7K 7
Lynton Mead. N20—3D 14
Lynton Rd. E4—5J 19
Lynton Rd. N8—5H 29
Lynton Rd. N11—6C 16
Lynton Rd. NW6—2H 59
Lynton Rd. SE1—4F 79 (9F 148)
Lynton Rd. W3—7G 57
Lynton Rd. Croy—6A 124
Lynton Rd. Harr—2C 38
Lynton Rd. N Mald—5K 119
Lynwood Clo. E18—1A 34
Lynwood Clo. Harr—3C 38
Lynwood Ct. King—2H 119
Lynwood Dri. Wor Pk—2C 130
Lynwood Gdns. Croy—4K 133
Lynwood Gdns. S'hall—6D 54
Lynwood Gro. N21—1F 17
Lynwood Gro. Orp—7J 129
Lynwood Rd. SW17—4D 108
Lynwood Rd. W5—3E 56
Lyon Industrial Est. NW2
—2D 42
Lyon Meade. Stan—1C 24
Lyon Pk. Av. Wemb—6E 40
(in two parts)
Lyon Rd. SW19—1A 122
Lyon Rd. Harr—6K 23
Lyonsdown Av. Barn—6F 5
Lyonsdown Rd. Barn—6F 5
Lyons Pl. NW8—4B 60 (4A 138)
Lyon St. N1—7K 45
Lyons Wlk. W14—4G 75
Lyon Way. Gnfd—1J 55
Lyric Dri. Gnfd—4F 55
Lyric Rd. SW13—1B 90
Lysander Gro. N19—1H 45
Lysander Rd. Croy—6K 133
Lysias Rd. SW12—6F 93
Lysia St. SW6—7F 75
Lysons Wlk. SW15—4C 90
Lytcott Gro. SE22—5F 95
Lytham Gro. W5—3F 57
Lytham St. SE17—5D 78
Lyttelton Clo. NW3—7C 44
Lyttelton Rd. E10—3D 48
Lyttleton Rd. N2—5A 28
Lyttleton Rd. N8—3A 30
Lytton Av. N13—2F 17
Lytton Av. Enf—1F 9
Lytton Clo. N2—5B 28
Lytton Clo. N'holt—7D 38
Lytton Gdns. Wall—4H 133
Lytton Gro. SW15—5F 91
Lytton Rd. E11—7G 33
Lytton Rd. Barn—4F 5
Lytton Rd. Pinn—1C 22
Lytton Strachey Path. SE28
—7B 68
Lyveden Rd. SE3—7K 81
Lyveden Rd. SW17—6D 108

Maberley Cres. SE19—7G 111
Maberley Rd. SE19—1F 125
Maberley Rd. Beck—3K 125
Mabledon Pl. WC1
—3H 61 (2B 140)
Mablethorpe Rd. SW6—7G 75
Mabley St. E9—5A 48
McAdam Dri. Enf—2G 7
Macaret Clo. N20—7F 5
Macarthur Ter. SE7—6B 82
Macaulay Rd. E6—2B 66
Macaulay Rd. SW4—3F 93
Macaulay Sq. SW4—4F 93
Macaulay Way. SE28—1B 84
McAuley Clo. SE1
—3A 78 (6G 147)

Macauley M SE13—2E 96
Macbean St SE18—3F 83
Macbeth St. W6—5D 74
McCall Clo. SW4—2J 93
McCall Cres. SE7—5C 82
McCarthy Rd Felt—5B 102
Macclesfield Rd. EC1
—3C 62 (1L 141)
Macclesfield Rd. SE25—5J 125
Macclesfield St. W1
—7H 61 (9B 140)
MacCoid Way SE1
—2C 78 (5L 147)
McCrone M NW3—6B 44
McCullum Rd. E3—2B 64
McDermott Clo SW11—3C 92
McDermott Rd. SE15—3G 95
Macdonald Av. Dag—3H 53
Macdonald Rd. E7—4J 49
Macdonald Rd. E17—2E 32
Macdonald Rd. N11—5J 15
Macdonald Rd. N19—2G 45
McDowall Clo. E16—5H 65
McDowall Rd. SE5—1C 94
Macduff Rd. SW11—1E 92
Mace Clo. E1—1H 79 (2J 149)
McEntee Av. E17—1A 32
Mace St. E2—2K 63 (1M 143)
McEwan Way. E15—1F 65
Macfarlane La. Iswth—6K 71
Macfarlane Rd W12—1E 74
Macfarren Pl. NW1
—4E 60 (4H 139)
McGrath Rd E15—6H 49
Macgregor Rd E16—5A 66
McGregor Rd W11—5H 59
Machell Rd. SE15—3J 95
McIntosh Clo. Romf—3K 37
McIntosh Clo Wall—7J 133
McIntosh Rd Romf—3K 37
Mackay Rd SW4—3F 93
McKay Rd. SW20—7D 106
McKellar Clo. Bush, Wat—2B 10
Mackennal St. NW8—2C 60
Mackenzie Rd. N7—6K 45
Mackenzie Rd Beck—2J 125
McKerrell Rd. SE15—1G 95
Mackeson Rd. NW3—4D 44
Mackie Rd. SW2—7A 94
Mackintosh La. E9—5K 47
Macklin St. WC2
—6J 61 (7D 140)
Mackrow Wlk. E14—7E 64
Mack's Rd SE16
—4G 79 (8H 149)
Mackworth St. NW1
—3G 61 (1L 139)
Maclean Rd. SE23—6A 96
McLeod Rd. SE2—4B 84
McLeod's M. SW4—7K 75
McLeod's Ter. SE17—5C 78
Maclise Rd. W14—3G 75
McMillan St. SE8—6C 80
McNeil Rd. SE5—2E 94
Macoma Rd. SE18—6H 83
Macoma Ter. SE18—6H 83
Macquarie Way. E14—4D 80
Macready Pl. N7—4J 45
Macroom Rd. W9—3H 59
Maddams St. E3—4D 64
Maddison Clo. Tedd—6K 103
Maddocks Clo. Sidc—5E 116
Maddock Way. SE17—6B 78
Maddox St. W1—7F 61 (9K 139)
Madeira Av. Brom—7G 113
Madeira Gro. Wfd G—6F 21
Madeira Rd. E11—1F 49
Madeira Rd. N13—3G 17
Madeira Rd. SW16—5J 109
Madeira Rd. Mitc—4D 122
Madeley Rd. W5—6E 56
Madeline Rd. SE20—7G 111
Madison Cres. Bexh—7C 84
Madison Gdns. Bexh—7C 84
Madison Gdns. Brom—3H 127
Madras Pl. N7—6A 46
Madras Rd. IIf—4F 51

Madrid Rd SW13—1C 90
Madron St SE17
—5E 78 (9D 148)
Mafeking Av. E6—2C 66
Mafeking Av. Bren—6E 72
Mafeking Av. IIf—7H 35
Mafeking Rd. E16—4H 65
Mafeking Rd. N17—2G 31
Mafeking Rd Enf—3A 8
Magdala Av N19—2G 45
Magdala Rd Iswth—3A 88
Magdala Rd S Croy—7D 134
Magdalene Clo. SE15—2H 95
Magdalene Gdns. E6—4E 66
Magdalen Pas. E1
—7F 63 (9F 142)
Magdalen Rd SW18—1A 108
Magdalen St. SE1
—1E 78 (3C 148)
Magee St. SE11—6A 78
Magnaville Rd. Bush, Wat
—1D 10
Magnin Clo E8—1G 63
Magnolia Clo. King—6H 105
Magnolia Ct. SW4—5J 93
Magnolia Ct. Harr—7F 25
Magnolia Rd W4—6H 73
Magpie All. EC4
—6A 62 (8H 141)
Magpie Hall Clo. Brom—6C 128
Magpie Hall La. Brom—7C 128
Magpie Hall Rd Bush, Wat
—2D 10
Magri Wlk E1—5J 63 (6L 143)
Maguire Dri Rich—4C 104
Maguire St SE1—2F 79 (4F 148)
Mahatma Gandhi Industrial
Est. SE24—4B 94
Mahlon Av Ruis—5A 38
Mahogany Clo. SE16—1A 80
Mahone Clo Enf—1A 8
Maida Av. E4—7J 9
Maida Av W2—5A 60 (5A 138)
Maida Rd. Belv—3G 85
Maida Vale. W9—2K 59 (3A 138)
Maida Way. E4—7J 9
Maiden Erlegh Av. Bex—1E 116
Maiden La. NW1—7H 45
Maiden La. WC2
—7J 61 (9D 140)
Maiden Rd. E15—7G 49
Maidenstone Hill. SE10—1E 96
Maids of Honour Row. Rich
—5D 88
Maidstone Av Romf—2J 37
Maidstone Bldgs SE1
—1C 78 (3M 147)
Maidstone Rd. N11—6C 16
Maidstone Rd. Sidc—6D 116
Mail Coach Yd N1
—3E 62 (1D 142)
Main Av. Enf—5A 8
Mainridge Rd. Chst—4E 114
Main Rd. Sidc—3H 115
Main St. Felt—5B 102
Maismore St. SE15—7G 79
Maitland Clo Houn—3D 86
Maitland Pk. Est. NW3—6D 44
Maitland Pk. Rd. NW3—6D 44
Maitland Pk. Vs. NW3—6D 44
Maitland Pl. E5—4H 47
Maitland Rd. E15—6H 49
Maitland Rd. SE26—6K 111
Maize Row. E14—7B 64
Majendie Rd. SE18—5H 83
Majestic Way. Mitc—2D 122
Major Rd. E15—5F 49
Major Rd. SE16—3G 79 (6H 149)
Makepeace Av. N6—2E 44
Makepeace Rd. N'holt—2C 54
Makins St. SW3—4C 76 (9D 144)
Malabar St. E14—2C 80
Malam Gdns. E14—7D 64
Malbrook Rd. SW15—4D 90
Malcolm Ct. E7—6H 49
Malcolm Ct. Stan—5H 11
Malcolm Cres. NW4—6C 26

Malcolm Dri. Surb—7D 118
Malcolm Pl. E2—4J 63 (3L 143)
Malcolm Rd. E1—4J 63 (3L 143)
Malcolm Rd. SE20—7J 111
Malcolm Rd. SE25—6G 125
Malcolm Way. E11—4J 33
Malden Av. SE25—3H 125
Malden Av. Gnfd—5J 39
Malden Ct. N Mald—3D 120
Malden Cres. NW1—6E 44
Malden Grn. Av. Wor Pk
—1B 130
Malden Hill. N Mald—3B 120
Malden Hill Gdns. N Mald
—3B 120
Malden Pk. N Mald—6B 120
Malden Pl. NW5—5E 44
Malden Rd. NW5—5E 44
Malden Rd. N Mald & Wor Pk
—5A 120
Malden Rd. Sutt—4F 131
Malden Way. Surb & N Mald
—7J 119
Maldon Clo. N1—1C 62
Maldon Clo. SE5—3E 94
Maldon Rd. N9—3A 18
Maldon Rd. W3—7J 57
Maldon Rd. Romf—7J 37
Maldon Rd. Wall—5F 133
Maldon Wlk. Wfd G—6F 21
Malet Pl. WC1—4H 61 (4A 140)
Malet St. WC1—4H 61 (4A 140)
Maley Av. SE27—2B 110
Malford Ct. E18—2J 33
Malford Gro. E18—4H 33
Malfort Rd. SE5—3E 94
Malham Rd. SE23—1K 111
Malham Rd. Industrial Centre.
SE23—1K 111
Mallams M. SW9—3B 94
Mallard Clo. E9—6B 48
Mallard Clo. Barn—6G 5
Mallard Clo. Twic—7E 86
Mallard Pl. N22—2K 29
Mallard Pl. Twic—3A 104
Mallards Rd. Wfd G—7E 20
Mallard Wlk. Sidc—6C 116
Mallard Way. NW9—7J 25
Mallet Dri. N'holt—5D 38
Mallet Rd. SE13—6F 97
Malling Clo. Croy—6J 125
Malling Gdns. Mord—6A 122
Malling Way. Brom—7H 127
Mallinson Rd. SW11—5C 92
Mallinson Rd. Croy—3H 133
Mallord St. SW3—6B 76
Mallory Clo. SE4—4A 96
Mallory Gdns. Barn—7K 5
Mallory St. NW8
—4C 60 (3D 138)
Mallow Clo. Croy—1K 135
Mallow Mead. NW7—7B 14
Mallow St. EC1—4D 62 (3A 142)
Mall Rd. W6—5D 74
Mall, The. E15—7F 49
Mall, The. N14—2D 16
Mall, The. SW1—1H 77 (3B 146)
Mall, The. SW14—5J 89
Mall, The. W5—7E 56
Mall, The. Bexh—4G 101
Mall, The. Brom—3J 127
Mall, The. Croy—2C 134
Mall, The. Dag—6G 53
Mall, The. Harr—6F 25
Mall, The. Surb—6D 118
Malmains Clo. Beck—4F 127
Malmains Way. Beck—4E 126
Malmesbury Rd. E3—3B 64
Malmesbury Rd. E16—5G 65
Malmesbury Rd. E18—1H 33
Malmesbury Rd. Mord—7A 122
Malmesbury Ter. E16—5H 65
Malpas Dri. Pinn—5B 22
Malpas Rd. E8—5H 47
Malpas Rd. SE4—2B 96
Malpas Rd. Dag—6D 52

Malta Rd. E10—7C 32
Malta St. EC1—4B 62 (3K 141)
Maltby Clo. Orp—7K 129
Maltby Dri. Enf—1C 8
Maltby St. SE1—2F 79 (5E 148)
Malthouse Dri. Felt—5B 102
Malthus Path. SE28—1C 84
Maltings Clo. SW13—2B 90
Maltings M. Sidc—3A 116
Maltings Pl. SW6—1K 91
Malton M. W10—6G 59
Malton Rd. W10—6G 59
Malton St. SE18—6J 83
Maltravers St. WC2
—7K 61 (9F 140)
Malt St. SE1—6G 79
Malva Clo. SW18—5K 91
Malvern Av. E4—7A 20
Malvern Av. Bexh—7E 84
Malvern Av. Harr—3C 38
Malvern Clo. SE20—2G 125
Malvern Clo. W10—5H 59
Malvern Clo. Mitc—3G 123
Malvern Dri. Felt—5B 102
Malvern Dri. Ilf—4K 51
Malvern Dri. Wfd G—5F 21
Malvern Gdns. NW2—2G 43
Malvern Gdns. NW6—2H 59
Malvern Gdns. Harr—4E 24
Malvern Ho. N16—1F 47
Malvern M. NW6—3J 59
Malvern Pl. NW6—3H 59
Malvern Rd. E6—1C 66
Malvern Rd. E8—7G 47
Malvern Rd. E11—2G 49
Malvern Rd. N8—3A 30
Malvern Rd. N17—3G 31
Malvern Rd. NW6—3J 59
Malvern Rd. Hmptn—7E 102
Malvern Rd. T Hth—4A 124
Malvern Ter. N1—1A 62
Malvern Ter. N9—1A 18
Malvern Way. W13—5B 56
Malwood Rd. SW12—6F 93
Malyons Rd. SE13—5D 96
Malyons Ter. SE13—5D 96
Managers St. E14—1E 80
Manaton Clo. SE15—3H 95
Manaton Cres. S'hall—6E 54
Manbey Gro. E15—6G 49
Manbey Pk. Rd. E15—6G 49
Manbey Rd. E15—6G 49
Manbey St. E15—6G 49
Manbre Rd. W6—6E 74
Manbrough Av. E6—3E 66
Manchester Dri. W10—4G 59
Manchester Gro. E14—5E 80
Manchester Rd. E14—5E 80
Manchester Rd. N15—6D 30
Manchester Rd. T Hth—3C 124
Manchester Sq. W1
—6E 60 (7H 139)
Manchester St. W1
—5E 60 (6G 139)
Manchester Way. Dag—4H 53
Manchuria Rd. SW11—6E 92
Manciple St. SE1
—2D 78 (5A 148)
Manconochies Rd. E14—5D 80
Mandalay Rd. SW4—5G 93
Mandarin St. E14—7C 64
Mandela Clo. NW10—7J 41
Mandela Rd. E16—6J 65
Mandela St. NW1—1G 61
Mandela St. SW9—7A 78
Mandela Way. SE1
—4E 78 (8D 148)
Mandeville Clo. SE3—7J 81
Mandeville Clo. SW20—1G 121
Mandeville Pl. W1
—6E 60 (7H 139)
Mandeville Rd. N14—2A 16
Mandeville Rd. Iswth—2A 88
Mandeville Rd. N'holt—7E 38
Mandeville St. E5—3A 48
Mandrake Rd. SW17—3D 108
Mandrell Rd. SW2—5J 93

Manette St. W1—6H 61 (8B 140)
Manfred Rd. SW15—5H 91
Manger Rd. N7—6J 45
Mangold Way. Eri—3D 84
Manilla St. E14—2C 80
Manister Rd. SE2—3A 84
Manley Ct. N16—3F 47
Manley St. NW1—1E 60
Manning Av. SW4—4J 93
Manningford Clo. EC1
—3B 62 (1J 141)
Manning Gdns. Harr—7D 24
Manning Rd. E17—5A 32
Manning Rd. Dag—6G 53
Manningtree Clo. SW19
—1G 107
Manningtree Rd. Ruis—4A 38
Manningtree St. E1
—6G 63 (7G 143)
Mannin Rd. Romf—7B 36
Mannock Rd. N22—3B 30
Mann's Clo. Iswth—5K 87
Manns Rd. Edgw—6B 12
Manoel Rd. Twic—2G 103
Manor Av. SE4—2B 96
Manor Av. Houn—3B 86
Manor Av. N'holt—7D 38
Manor Brook. SE3—4J 97
Manor Clo. NW7—5E 12
Manor Clo. NW9—5H 25
Manor Clo. SE28—6C 68
Manor Clo. Barn—4B 4
Manor Clo. Dag—6K 53
Manor Clo. Dart—4K 101
(Crayford)
Manor Clo. Wor Pk—1A 130
Manor Cotts. App. N2—2A 28
Manor Ct. SW6—1K 91
Manor Ct. Twic—2G 103
Manor Ct. Rd. W7—7J 55
Manor Cres. Surb—6G 119
Manor Dene. SE28—6C 68
Manor Dri. N14—1A 16
Manor Dri. N20—4H 15
Manor Dri. NW7—5E 12
Manor Dri. Eps—6A 130
Manor Dri. Felt—5B 102
Manor Dri. Surb—6F 119
Manor Dri. Wemb—4F 41
Manor Dri. N. N Mald & Wor Pk
—7K 119
Manor Dri., The. Wor Pk
—1B 130
Manor Est. SE16
—4H 79 (9J 149)
Manor Farm Dri. E4—3B 20
Manor Farm Rd. SW16—2A 124
Manor Farm Rd. Wemb—2D 56
Manor Fields. SW15—6F 91
Manor Gdns. N7—3J 45
Manor Gdns. SW20—2H 121
Manor Gdns. W3—4G 73
Manor Gdns. W4—5A 74
Manor Gdns. Hmptn—7F 103
Manor Gdns. Rich—4F 89
Manor Gdns. Ruis—5A 38
Manor Gdns. S Croy—6F 135
Manor Ga. N'holt—7C 38
Manorgate Rd. King—1G 119
Manor Gro. SE15—6J 79
Manor Gro. Beck—2D 126
Manor Gro. Rich—4G 89
Manor Hall Av. NW4—2F 27
Manor Hall Dri. NW4—2F 27
Manorhall Gdns. E10—1C 48
Manor Ho. Dri. NW6—7F 43
Manor Ho. Way. Iswth—3B 88
Manor La. SE12—7H 97
SE13 1-59 & 2-86
SE12 remainder
Manor La. Sutt—5A 132
Manor La. Ter. SE13—5G 97
Manor Mt. SE23—1J 111
Manor Pk. SE13—4F 97
Manor Pk. Chst—2H 129

Manor Pk. Rich—4F 89
Manor Pk. Clo. W Wick—1D 136
Manor Pk. Cres. Edgw—6B 12
Manor Pk. Dri. Harr—3F 23
Manor Pk. Gdns. Edgw—5B 12
Manor Pk. Rd. E12—4B 50
Manor Pk. Rd. N2—3A 28
Manor Pk. Rd. NW10—1B 58
Manor Pk. Rd. Chst—1G 129
Manor Pk. Rd. Sutt—5A 132
Manor Pk. Rd. W Wick—1D 136
Manor Pl. SE17—5B 78 (9L 147)
Manor Pl. Chst—2H 129
Manor Pl. Mitc—3G 123
Manor Pl. Sutt—4K 131
Manor Rd. E10—7C 32
Manor Rd.—4G 65
E15 1-347 & 2-118
E16 remainder
Manor Rd. E17—2A 32
Manor Rd. N16—1E 46
Manor Rd. N17—1G 31
Manor Rd. N22—6D 16
Manor Rd. SE25—4G 125
Manor Rd. SW20—2H 121
Manor Rd. W13—7A 56
Manor Rd. Bark—6K 51
Manor Rd. Barn—4B 4
Manor Rd. Beck—2D 126
Manor Rd. Bex—1H 117
Manor Rd. Dag—6J 53
Manor Rd. Dart—4K 101
Manor Rd. Enf—2H 7
Manor Rd. Harr—6A 24
Manor Rd. Mitc—4G 123
Manor Rd. Rich—4G 89
Manor Rd. Romf—6D 36
(Chadwell Heath)
Manor Rd. Sidc—3A 116
Manor Rd. Sutt—7H 131
Manor Rd. Tedd—5A 104
(in two parts)
Manor Rd. Twic—2G 103
Manor Rd. Wall—4F 133
Manor Rd. W Wick—2D 136
Manor Rd. Wfd G & Chig—6J 21
Manor Rd. N. Wall—4F 133
Manorside. Barn—4B 4
Manorside Clo. SE2—4C 84
Manor Sq. Dag—2D 52
Manor Vale. Bren—5C 72
Manor View. N3—2K 27
Manor Way. E4—4A 20
Manor Way. NW9—4A 26
Manor Way. SE3—4H 97
Manor Way. Beck—2C 126
Manor Way. Bex—1G 117
Manor Way. Bexh—3K 101
Manor Way. Brom—6C 128
Manorway. Enf—7K 7
Manor Way. Harr—4F 23
Manor Way. Mitc—3G 123
Manor Way. Orp—6G 129
Manor Way. Rain—6K 69
Manor Way. S'hall—4B 70
Manor Way. S Croy—6E 134
Manor Way. Wfd G—5F 21
Manor Way. Wor Pk—1A 130
Manorway Gdns. SE28—7C 68
Manor Way, The. Wall—4F 133
Manresa Rd. SW3—5C 76
Mansard Beeches. SW17
—5E 108
Mansard Clo. Pinn—3B 22
Mansel Gro. E17—1C 32
Mansell Rd. W3—2K 73
Mansell Rd. Gnfd—5F 55
Mansell St. E1—6F 63 (8F 142)
Mansel Rd. SW19—6G 107
Mansergh Clo. SE18—7C 82
Manse Rd. N16—3F 47
Manser Rd. Rain—3K 69
Mansfield Av. N15—4D 30
Mansfield Av. Barn—6J 5
Mansfield Clo. N9—6B 8
Mansfield Hill. E4—1J 19

Mansfield M. W1
—5F 61 (6J 139)
Mansfield Pl. NW3—4A 44
Mansfield Rd. E11—6K 33
Mansfield Rd. E17—4B 32
Mansfield Rd. NW3—5D 44
Mansfield Rd. W3—4H 57
Mansfield Rd. Ilf—2E 50
Mansfield Rd. S Croy—6D 134
Mansfield St. W1
—5F 61 (6J 139)
Mansford St. E2
—2G 63 (1H 143)
Manship Rd. Mitc—7E 108
Mansion Gdns. NW3—3K 43
Mansion Ho. Pl. EC4
—6D 62 (8A 142)
Manson M. SW7
—4A 76 (9A 144)
Manson Pl. SW7
—4B 76 (9A 144)
Mansted Gdns. Romf—7C 36
Manston Av. S'hall—4E 70
Manston Clo. SE20—1J 125
Manstone Rd. NW2—5G 43
Manthorp Rd. SE18—5G 83
Mantilla Rd. SW17—4E 108
Mantle Rd. SE4—3A 96
Manton Av. W7—2K 71
Manton Rd. SE2—4A 84
Mantua St. SW11—3B 92
Mantus Clo. E1—4J 63 (3M 143)
Mantus Rd. E1—4J 63 (3L 143)
Manus Way. N20—2F 15
Manville Gdns. SW17—3F 109
Manville Rd. SW17—2E 108
Manwood Rd. SE4—5B 96
Manwood St. E16—1D 82
Manygates. SW12—2F 109
Mapesbury Rd. NW2—7G 43
Mape St. E2—4H 63 (3J 143)
Maple Av. E4—5G 19
Maple Av. W3—1A 74
Maple Av. Harr—2F 39
Maple Clo. N16—6G 31
Maple Clo. SW4—6H 93
Maple Clo. Buck H—3G 21
Maple Clo. Mitc—1F 123
Maple Clo. Orp—5H 129
Maple Ct. N Mald—3K 119
Maple Cres. Sidc—6A 100
Maplecroft Clo. E6—6B 66
Mapledale Av. Croy—2G 135
Mapledene. Chst—5G 115
Mapledene Rd. E8—7G 47
Maple Gdns. Edgw—7F 13
Maple Gro. NW9—7J 25
Maple Gro. W5—3D 72
Maple Gro. Bren—7B 72
Maple Gro. S'hall—5D 54
Maplehurst Clo. King—4E 118
Mapleleaf Dri. Sidc—1K 115
Mapleleafe Gdns. Ilf—3F 35
Maple Leaf Sq. SE16—2K 79
Maple M. NW6—2K 59
Maple M. SW16—5K 109
Maple Pl. W1—5G 61 (5M 139)
Maple Rd. E11—6G 33
Maple Rd. SE20—1H 125
Maple Rd. Hay—3A 54
Maple Rd. Surb—6D 118
Maples Pl. E1—5H 63 (5K 143)
Maplestead Rd. SW2—7K 93
Maplestead Rd. Dag—1B 68
Maple St. W1—5G 61 (5L 139)
Maple St. Romf—4J 37
Maplethorpe Rd. T Hth—4B 124
Mapleton Clo. Brom—6J 127
Mapleton Cres. SW18—6K 91
Mapleton Cres. Enf—1D 8
Mapleton Rd. E4—3K 19
Mapleton Rd. Enf—2C 8
Maple Wlk. W10—3F 59
Maplin Clo. N21—6E 6
Maplin Rd. E16—6J 65
Maplin St. E3—4B 64

Mapperley Dri. Wfd G—7B 20
Maran Way. Eri—3D 84
Marban Rd. W9—3H 59
Marble Arch. W1
—7D 60 (9E 138)
Marble Clo. W3—1H 73
Marble Hill Clo. Twic—7B 88
Marble Hill Gdns. Twic—7B 88
Marble Quay. E1
—1G 79 (2G 149)
Marbrook Ct. SE12—3A 114
Marchant Rd. E11—2F 49
Marchbank Rd. W14—6H 75
Marchmont Rd. Rich—5F 89
Marchmont Rd. Wall—7G 133
Marchmont St. WC1
—4J 61 (3C 140)
March Rd. Twic—7A 88
Marchside Clo. Houn—1B 86
Marchwood Clo. SE5—7E 78
Marchwood Cres. W5—6D 56
Marcia Rd. SE1—4E 78 (9D 148)
Marcilly Rd. SW18—5B 92
Marcon Pl. E8—5H 47
Marco Rd. W6—3E 74
Marcourt Lawns. W5—4E 56
Marcus St. E15—1G 65
Marcus Garvey Way. SE24
—4A 94
Marcus St. E15—1G 65
Marcus St. SW18—6K 91
Marcus Ter. SW18—6K 91
Mardale Dri. NW9—5K 25
Mardell Rd. Croy—5K 125
Marden Av. Brom—6J 127
Marden Clo. SE8—6B 80
Marden Cres. Bexh—5J 101
Marden Cres. Croy—6K 123
Marden Rd. N17—2E 30
Marden Rd. Croy—6K 123
Marden Sq. SE16
—3H 79 (7J 149)
Marder Rd. W13—2A 72
Marechal Niel Av. Sidc—3H 115
Mares Field. Croy—3E 134
Maresfield Gdns. NW3—5A 44
Mare St. E8—1H 63
Margaret Av. E4—6J 9
Margaret Bondfield Av. Bark
—7A 52
Margaret Bldgs. N16—1F 47
Margaret Ct. Barn—4G 5
Margaret Rd. N16—1F 47
Margaret Rd. Barn—4G 5
Margaret Rd. Bex—6D 100
Margaret St. W1
—6G 61 (7L 139)
Margaretta Ter. SW3—6C 76
Margaretting Rd. E12—1A 50
Margaret Way. Ilf—6C 34
Margate Rd. SW2—5J 93
Margery Pk. Rd. E7—6J 49
Margery Rd. Dag—3D 52
Margery St. WC1
—3A 62 (2G 141)
Margin Dri. SW19—5F 107
Margravine Gdns. W6—5F 75
Margravine Rd. W6—5F 75
Marham Gdns. SW18—1C 108
Marham Gdns. Mord—6A 122
Marian Clo. Hay—4B 54
Marian Ct. Sutt—5K 131
Marian Pl. E2—2H 63
Marian Rd. SW16—1G 123
Marian St. E2—2H 63
Marian Way. NW10—7B 42
Maria Ter. E1—5K 63 (5M 143)
Maria Theresa Clo. N Mald
—5K 119
Maricas Av. Harr—1H 23
Marie Lloyd Gdns. N19—7J 29
Marie Lloyd Wlk. E8—6G 47
Mariette Way. Wall—7J 133
Marigold St. SE16
—2H 79 (5J 149)
Marigold Way. E4—6G 19

Marigold Way. Croy—1K 135
Marina Av. N Mald—5D 120
Marina Clo. Brom—3J 127
Marina Dri. Well—2J 99
Marina Gdns. Romf—5J 37
Marina Way. Tedd—7D 104
Marine Dri. SE18—4D 82
Marinefield Rd. SW6—2K 91
Mariner Gdns. Rich—3C 104
Mariner Rd. E12—4E 50
Mariners M. E14—4F 81
Marine St. SE16—3G 79 (6G 149)
Marion Gro. Wfd G—4B 20
Marion Rd. NW7—5H 13
Marion Rd. T Hth—5C 124
Marion Sq. E2—2H 63
Marischal Rd. SE13—3F 97
Maritime St. E3—4B 64
Marius Pas. SW17—2E 108
Marius Rd. SW17—2E 108
Market Centre, The. S'hall
—4A 70
Market Entrance. SW8—7G 77
Market Hill. SE18—3E 82
Market La. Edgw—1J 25
Market Link. Romf—4K 37
Market M. W1—1F 77 (3J 145)
Market Pl. N2—3C 28
Market Pl. NW11—4K 27
Market Pl. SE16—4G 79 (8H 149)
Market Pl. W1—6G 61 (7L 139)
Market Pl. W3—1J 73
Market Pl. Bexh—4G 101
Market Pl. Bren—7C 72
Market Pl. Enf—3J 7
Market Pl. King—2D 118
Market Pl. S'hall—1E 70
Market Rd. N7—6J 45
Market Rd. Rich—3G 89
Market Sq. E14—6D 64
Market Sq. N9—3B 18
Market Sq. Brom—2J 127
Market St. E6—2D 66
Market St. SE18—4E 82
Market Way. E14—6D 64
Markfield Gdns. E4—7J 9
Markfield Rd. N15—4G 31
Markham Pl.—5D 76 (9E 144)
Markham Sq. SW3
—5D 76 (9E 144)
Markham St. SW3
—5C 76 (9D 144)
Markhole Clo. Hmptn—7D 102
Markhouse Av. E17—6A 32
Markhouse Rd. E17—6B 32
Mark La. EC3—7E 62 (9D 142)
Markmanor Av. E17—7A 32
Mark Rd. N22—2B 30
Marksbury Av. Rich—3G 89
Marks Rd. Romf—5J 37
Mark St. E15—7G 49
Mark St. EC2—4E 62 (3C 142)
Markwell Clo. SE26—4H 111
Markyate Rd. Dag—5B 52
Marlands Rd. Ilf—3C 34
Marlborough Av. E8—1G 63
(in three parts)
Marlborough Av. N14—3B 16
Marlborough Av. Edgw—3C 12
Marlborough Clo. N20—3J 15
Marlborough Clo. SE17
—4C 78 (9L 147)
Marlborough Clo. SW19
—6C 108
Marlborough Clo. Orp—7K 129
Marlborough Ct. Enf—5K 7
Marlborough Cres. W4—3A 74
Marlborough Dri. Ilf—3C 34
Marlborough Gdns. N20—3J 15
Marlborough Gdns. Surb
—7D 118
Marlborough Gro. SE1—5G 79
Marlborough Hill. NW8—1A 60

Marlborough Hill. Harr—4J 23
Marlborough La. SE7—7A 82
Marlborough Pk. Av. Sidc
—7A 100
Marlborough Pl. NW8—2A 60
Marlborough Rd. E4—6J 19
Marlborough Rd. E7—7A 50
Marlborough Rd. E15—4G 49
Marlborough Rd. E18—2J 33
Marlborough Rd. N9—1A 18
Marlborough Rd. N19—2H 45
Marlborough Rd. N22—7E 16
Marlborough Rd. SW1
—1G 77 (3M 145)
Marlborough Rd. SW19
—6C 108
Marlborough Rd. W4—5J 73
Marlborough Rd. W5—2D 72
Marlborough Rd. Bexh—3D 100
Marlborough Rd. Brom
—4A 128
Marlborough Rd. Dag—4B 52
Marlborough Rd. Felt—2B 102
Marlborough Rd. Hmptn
—6E 102
Marlborough Rd. Iswth—1B 88
Marlborough Rd. Rich—6F 89
Marlborough Rd. Romf—4G 37
Marlborough Rd. S'hall—3A 70
Marlborough Rd. S Croy
—7C 134
Marlborough Rd. Sutt—2J 131
Marlborough St. SW3
—4C 76 (9D 144)
Marlborough Yd. N19—2H 45
Marler Rd. SE23—1A 112
Marley Av. Bexh—6D 84
Marley Clo. Gnfd—3E 54
Marley Wlk. NW2—5E 42
Marlingdene Clo. Hmptn
—6E 102
Marlings Clo. Chst—4J 129
Marlings Pk. Av. Chst—4J 129
Marlins Clo. Sutt—5A 132
Marloes Clo. Wemb—4D 40
Marloes Rd. W8—3K 75
Marlow Clo. SE20—3H 125
Marlow Ct. NW9—3B 26
Marlow Cres. Twic—6K 87
Marlow Dri. Sutt—2F 131
Marlowe Clo. Chst—6H 115
Marlowe Clo. Ilf—1G 35
Marlowe Gdns. SE9—6E 98
Marlowe Rd. E17—4E 32
Marlowe Sq. Mitc—4G 123
Marlowes, The. NW8—1B 60
Marlowes, The. Dart—4K 101
Marlow Rd. E6—3D 66
Marlow Rd. SE20—3H 125
Marlow Rd. S'hall—3D 70
Marlow Way. SE16—2K 79
Marl Rd. SW18—4K 91
Marlton St. SE10—5H 81
Marmadon Rd. SE18—4K 83
Marmion App. E4—4H 19
Marmion Av. E4—4H 19
Marmion Clo. E4—4G 19
Marmion M. SW11—3E 92
Marmion Rd. SW11—4E 92
Marmont Rd. SE15—1G 95
Marmora Rd. SE22—6J 95
Marmot Rd. Houn—3B 86
Marne Av. N11—4A 16
Marne Av. Well—3A 100
Marnell Way. Houn—3B 86
Marne St. W10—3G 59
Marney Rd. SW11—4E 92
Marnham Av. NW2—4G 43
Marnham Cres. Gnfd—3H 55
Marnock Rd. SE4—5B 96
Maroon St. E14—5A 64
Maroons Way. SE6—5C 112
Marquess Rd. N1—6D 46
Marquis Clo. Wemb—7F 41
Marquis Rd. N4—1K 45
Marquis Rd. N22—6E 16

234

Marquis Rd. NW1—6H 45
Marrick Clo. SW15—4C 90
Marriett Ho. SE6—4E 112
Marrilyne Av. Enf—1G 9
Marriots Clo. NW9—6B 26
Marriott Rd. E15—1G 65
Marriott Rd. N4—1K 45
Marriott Rd. N10—1D 28
Marriott Rd. Barn—3A 4
Marryat Pl. SW19—4G 107
Marryat Rd. SW19—5F 107
Marsala Rd. SE13—4D 96
Marsden Rd. N9—2C 18
Marsden Rd. SE15—3F 95
Marsden St. NW5—6E 44
Marshall Clo. SW18—6A 92
Marshall Clo. Harr—7H 23
Marshall Clo. Houn—5D 86
Marshall Path. SE28—7B 68
Marshall Rd. N17—1D 30
Marshalls Clo. N11—4A 16
Marshalls Dri. Romf—3K 37
Marshall's Gro. SE18—4C 82
Marshall's Pl. SE16
    —3F 79 (7F 148)
Marshalls Rd. Romf—4K 37
Marshall's Rd. Sutt—4K 131
Marshall St. W1
    —6G 61 (8M 139)
Marshalsea Rd. SE1
    —2C 78 (4M 147)
Marsham Clo. Chst—5F 115
Marsham Ct. SW1
    —4H 77 (8B 146)
Marsham St. SW1
    —3H 77 (7B 146)
Marsh Av. Mitc—2D 122
Marshbrook Clo. SE3—3B 98
Marsh Clo. NW7—3G 13
Marsh Ct. E8—7G 47
Marsh Dri. NW9—6B 26
Marshfield St. E14—3E 80
Marshgate La. E15—1D 64
Marshgate Path. SE18—3G 83
Marsh Grn. Rd. Dag—1G 69
Marsh Hill. E9—5A 48
Marsh La. E10—2B 48
Marsh La. N17—1H 31
Marsh La. NW7—3F 13
Marsh La. Stan—5H 11
Marsh Rd. Pinn—4C 22
Marsh Rd. Wemb—3D 56
Marsh St. E14—4D 80
Marsh Wall. E14—1C 80
Marsh Way. Rain—5K 69
Marsland Clo. SE17—5B 78
Marston Av. Dag—2G 53
Marston Clo. NW6—7A 44
Marston Clo. Dag—3G 53
Marston Ho. SW9—2A 94
Marston Rd. Ilf—1C 34
Marston Rd. Tedd—5B 104
Marston Way. SE19—7C 110
Marsworth Av. Pinn—1B 22
Martaban Rd. N16—2F 47
Martello St. E8—7H 47
Martello Ter. E8—7H 47
Martell Rd. SE21—3D 110
Martel Pl. E8—6F 47
Marten Rd. E17—2C 32
Martens Av. Bexh—4H 101
Martens Clo. Bexh—4J 101
Martha Ct. E2—2H 63
Martham Clo. SE28—7D 68
Martha Rd. E15—6G 49
Martha St. E1—6J 63 (8L 143)
Marthorne Cres. Harr—2H 23
Martinau Est. E1
    —6J 63 (8M 143)
Martinau St. E1—6J 63 (8M 143)
Martin Bowes Rd. SE9—4D 114
Martinbridge Trading Est. Enf
    —5B 8
Martin Cres. Croy—1A 134
Martindale. SW14—5J 89

Martin Dale Industrial Est. Enf
    —3B 8
Martindale Rd. SW12—7F 93
Martindale Rd. Houn—3C 86
Martin Dene. Bexh—5F 101
Martin Dri. N'holt—5D 38
Martineau Rd. N5—4B 46
Martingales Clo. Rich—3D 104
Martin Gdns. Dag—4D 52
Martin Gro. Mord—3J 121
Martin La. EC4—7D 62 (9B 142)
Martin Rise. Bexh—5F 101
Martin Rd. Dag—4C 52
Martins Mt. Barn—4D 4
Martins Rd. Brom—2H 127
Martins Wlk. N10—1E 28
Martin Way—3G 121
    SW20 267-347 & 274-358
    Mord remainder
Martlet Gro. N'holt—3B 54
Martlett Ct. WC2
    —6J 61 (8D 140)
Martley Dri. Ilf—5F 35
Martock Clo. Harr—4A 24
Marton Clo. SE6—3C 112
Marton Rd. N16—3E 46
Mart St. WC2—7J 61 (9D 140)
Marvels Clo. SE12—2K 113
Marvels La. SE12—2K 113
Marville Rd. SW6—7H 75
Marvin St. E8—6H 47
Marwell Clo. W Wick—2H 137
Marwood Clo. Well—3B 100
Marwood Way. SE16—5H 79
Mary Adelaide Clo. SW15
    —4A 106
Mary Ann Gdns. SE8—6C 80
Maryatt Av. Harr—2F 39
Mary Bank. SE18—4D 82
Mary Clo. Stan—4F 25
Mary Datchelor Clo. SE5
    —1D 94
Maryfield Clo. Bex—3K 117
Mary Gardner Clo. SE9—2D 114
Maryland Pk. E15—5G 49
(in two parts)
Maryland Rd. E15—5F 49
Maryland Rd. N22—6F 17
Maryland Rd. T Hth—1B 124
Maryland Sq. E15—5G 49
Marylands Rd. W9—4J 59
Maryland St. E15—5F 49
Mary Lawrenson Pl. SE3—7J 81
Marylebone Fly-over. W2 &
    NW1—5C 60 (6C 138)
Marylebone High St. W1
    —5E 60 (6H 139)
Marylebone La. W1
    —6E 60 (7H 139)
Marylebone M. W1
    —5F 61 (6J 139)
Marylebone Pas. W1
    —6G 61 (7M 139)
Marylebone Rd. NW1
    —5C 60 (5D 138)
Marylebone St. W1
    —5E 60 (6H 139)
Marylee Way. SE11
    —4K 77 (9F 146)
Maryon Gro. SE7—4C 82
Maryon M. NW3—4C 44
Maryon Rd. SE7 & SE18—4C 82
Mary Peters Dri. Gnfd—5H 39
Mary Pl. W11—7G 59
Mary Rose Mall. E6—5D 66
Maryrose Way. N20—1G 15
Mary Seacole Clo. E8—1F 63
Mary's Ter. Twic—7A 88
(in two parts)
Mary St. E16—5H 65
Mary St. N1—1C 62
Mary Ter. NW1—1G 61
Maryville. Well—2K 99
Masbro Rd. W14—3F 75
Mascalls Rd. SE7—6A 82
Mascotte Rd. SW15—4F 91
Mascotts Clo. NW2—3D 42

Masefield Av. S'hall—7E 54
Masefield Av. Stan—5E 10
Masefield Ct. Surb—7D 118
Masefield Cres. N14—5A 6
Masefield Gdns. E6—4E 66
Masefield La. Hay—4A 54
Masefield Rd. Hmptn—4D 102
Mashie Rd. W3—6A 58
Mashiters Hill. Romf—1K 37
Maskell Clo. SW2—1A 110
Maskell Rd. SW17—3A 108
Maskelyne Clo. SW11—1C 92
Mason Clo. E16—7J 65
Mason Clo. Bexh—3H 101
Mason Rd. Wfd G—4B 20
Mason's Arms M. W1
    —6F 61 (8K 139)
Mason's Av. EC2
    —6D 62 (7A 142)
Masons Av. Croy—3C 134
Masons Av. Harr—4K 23
Masons Grn. La. W5 & W3
    —4G 57
Masons Hill. SE18—4F 83
Masons Hill. Brom—3K 127
Mason's Pl. EC1—3C 62 (1L 141)
Masons Pl. Mitc—1D 122
Mason St. SE17—4D 78 (8B 148)
Mason's Yd. SW1
    —1G 77 (2M 145)
Mason's Yd. SW19—5F 107
Massey Clo. N11—5A 16
Massie Rd. E8—6G 47
Massinger St. SE17
    —4E 78 (9C 148)
Massingham St. E1
    —4H 63 (3M 143)
Masson Av. Ruis—6A 38
Master Gunners Pl. SE18
    —7C 82
Masterman Rd. E6—3C 66
Master's St. E1—5K 63
Mast Ho. Ter. E14—4C 80
Masthouse Ter. Development.
    E14—4C 80
Mastmaker Ct. E14—2C 80
Mastmaker Rd. E14—2C 80
Maswell Pk. Cres. Houn—5G 87
Maswell Pk. Rd. Houn—5F 87
Matcham Rd. E11—3G 49
Matchless Dri. SE18—7E 82
Matfield Clo. Brom—5J 127
Matfield Rd. Belv—6G 85
Matham Gro. SE22—4F 95
Matheson Rd. W14—4H 75
Mathew Ct. E17—3E 32
Mathews Av. E6—2E 66
Mathews Pk. Av. E15—6H 49
Mathews Yd. WC2
    —6J 61 (8C 140)
Matilda St. N1—1K 61
Matlock Clo. SE24—4C 94
Matlock Cres. Sutt—4G 131
Matlock Gdns. Sutt—4G 131
Matlock Pl. Sutt—4G 131
Matlock Rd. E10—6E 32
Matlock St. E14—6A 64
Matlock Way. N Mald—1K 119
Matrimony Pl. SW4—2G 93
Matthew Clo. W10—4F 59
Matthew Ct. Mitc—5H 123
Matthew Parker St. SW1
    —2H 77 (5B 146)
Matthews Rd. Gnfd—5H 39
Matthews St. SW11—2D 92
Matthias Rd. N16—5E 46
Mattison Rd. N4—6A 30
Mattock La.—1B 72
    W13 37-81
    W5 remainder
Maude Rd. E17—5A 32
Maude Rd. SE5—1E 94
Maude Ter. E17—5A 32
Maud Gdns. E13—2H 65
Maud Gdns. Bark—2K 67
Maudlin's Grn. E1
    —1G 79 (2G 149)

Maud Rd. E10—3E 48
Maud Rd. E13—2H 65
Maudslay Rd. SE9—3D 98
Maud St. E16—5H 65
Maudsville Cotts. W7—1J 71
Mauleverer Rd. SW2—5J 93
Maundeby Wlk. NW10—6A 42
Maunder Rd. W7—1K 71
Maunsel St. SW1
    —4H 77 (8A 146)
Maureen Ct. Beck—2K 125
Maurice Av. N22—2B 30
Maurice Brown Clo. NW7
    —5A 14
Maurice St. W12—6D 58
Maurice Wlk. NW11—4A 28
Maurier Clo. N'holt—1A 54
Mauritius Rd. SE10—6G 81
Maury Rd. N16—3G 47
Mavelstone Clo. Brom—1C 128
Mavelstone Rd. Brom—1C 128
Maverton Rd. E3—1C 64
Mavis Av. Eps—5A 130
Mavis Clo. Eps—5A 130
Mavis Wlk. E6—5C 66
Mawbey Pl. SE1—5F 79
Mawbey Rd. SE1—5F 79
Mawbey St. SW8—7J 77
Mawney Clo. Romf—2H 37
Mawney Rd. Romf—2H 37
Mawson Clo. SW20—2G 121
Mawson La. W4—6B 74
Maxey Gdns. Dag—4E 52
Maxey Rd. SE18—4G 83
Maxey Rd. Dag—4E 52
Maxilla Wlk. W10—6F 59
Maximfeldt Rd. Eri—5K 85
Maxim Rd. N21—6F 7
Maxim Rd. Eri—4K 85
Maxted Pk. Harr—7J 23
Maxted Rd. SE15—3F 95
Maxwell Rd. SW6—7K 75
Maxwell Rd. Well—3K 99
Maxwelton Av. NW7—5E 12
Maxwelton Clo. NW7—5E 12
Mayall Rd. SE24—5B 94
Maya Rd. N2—4A 28
Maybank Av. E18—2K 33
Maybank Av. Wemb—5A 40
Maybank Rd. E18—1K 33
Mayberry Pl. Surb—7F 119
Maybourne Clo. SE26—6H 111
Maybury Clo. Orp—5F 129
Maybury Ct. Harr—6H 23
Maybury Gdns. NW10—6D 42
Maybury M. N6—7G 29
Maybury Rd. E13—4A 66
Maybury Rd. Bark—2K 67
Maybury St. SW17—5C 108
Maychurch Clo. Stan—7J 11
Maycross Av. Mord—3H 121
Mayday Gdns. SE3—2C 98
Mayday Rd. T Hth—6B 124
Mayerne Rd. SE9—5B 98
Mayesbrook Rd. Bark—1K 67
Mayesbrook Rd. Ilf & Dag
    —3A 52
Mayesford Rd. Romf—7C 36
Mayes Rd. N22—2K 29
Mayeswood Rd. SE12—4A 114
Mayfair Av. Bexh—1D 100
Mayfair Av. Ilf—2D 50
Mayfair Av. Romf—6D 36
Mayfair Av. Twic—7G 87
Mayfair Av. Wor Pk—1C 130
Mayfair Clo. Beck—1D 126
Mayfair Clo. Surb—7E 118
Mayfair Gdns. N17—6J 17
Mayfair Gdns. Wfd G—7D 20
Mayfair Pl. W1—1F 77 (2K 145)
Mayfair Ter. N14—7C 6
Mayfield. Bexh—3F 101
Mayfield Av. N12—4F 15
Mayfield Av. N14—2C 16
Mayfield Av. W4—4A 74
Mayfield Av. W13—2B 72
Mayfield Av. Harr—5B 24

235

Mayfield Av. Orp—7K 129
Mayfield Av. Wfd G—6D 20
Mayfield Clo. E8—7F 47
Mayfield Clo. SE20—1H 125
Mayfield Clo. SW4—5H 93
Mayfield Cres. N9—6C 8
Mayfield Cres. T Hth—4K 123
Mayfield Dri. Pinn—4D 22
Mayfield Gdns. NW4—6F 27
Mayfield Gdns. W7—6H 55
Mayfield Rd. E4—2K 19
Mayfield Rd. E8—7F 47
Mayfield Rd. E13—4H 65
Mayfield Rd. E17—2A 32
Mayfield Rd. N8—5K 29
Mayfield Rd. SW19—1H 121
Mayfield Rd. W3—7H 57
Mayfield Rd. W12—2A 74
Mayfield Rd. Belv—4J 85
Mayfield Rd. Brom—5C 128
Mayfield Rd. Dag—1C 52
Mayfield Rd. Enf—2E 8
Mayfield Rd. S Croy—7D 134
Mayfield Rd. Sutt—6B 132
Mayfield Rd. T Hth—4K 123
Mayfield Rd. Flats. N8—6K 29
Mayfields. Wemb—2G 41
Mayfields Clo. Wemb—2G 41
Mayflower Clo. SE16—4K 79
Mayflower Ct. SE16
—2J 79 (5K 149)
Mayflower Rd. SW9—3J 93
Mayflower St. SE16
—2J 79 (5L 149)
Mayfly Gdns. N'holt—3B 54
Mayford Clo. SW12—7D 92
Mayford Clo. Beck—3K 125
Mayford Rd. SW12—7D 92
May Gdns. Wemb—3C 56
Maygood St. N1—2A 62
Maygrove Rd. NW6—6H 43
Mayhew Clo. E4—3H 19
Mayhill Rd. SE7—6K 81
Mayhill Rd. Barn—6B 4
Maylands Dri. Sidc—3D 116
Maynard Clo. SW6—7K 75
Maynard Rd. E17—5E 32
Maynards Quay. E1
—7J 63 (1L 149)
Mayo Ct. W13—3B 72
Mayola Rd. E5—4J 47
Mayo Rd. NW10—6A 42
Mayo Rd. Croy—5D 124
Mayow Rd.—4K 111
SE23 1-69 & 2-24
SE26 remainder
Mayplace Clo. Bexh—3H 101
Mayplace La. SE18—7F 83
Mayplace Rd. E. Bexh—3H 101
Mayplace Rd. W. Bexh—4G 101
May Rd. E4—6H 19
May Rd. E13—2J 65
May Rd. Twic—1J 103
Mays Ct. WC2—7J 61 (1C 146)
Mays Hill Rd. Brom—2G 127
Mays La. Barn—6A 4
Maysoule Rd. SW11—4B 92
Mays Rd. Tedd—5H 103
May St. W14—5H 75
Mayswood Gdns. Dag—6J 53
Mayton St. N7—3K 45
Maytree Clo. Edgw—3D 12
Maytree Ct. N'holt—3C 54
May Tree La. Stan—7F 11
May Tree Wlk. SW2—2A 110
Mayville Est. N16—5E 46
Mayville Rd. E11—2G 49
(in two parts)
Mayville Rd. Ilf—5F 51
May Wlk. E13—2K 65
Maywood Clo. Beck—7D 112
Maze Hill—6G 81
SE10 1-119 & 2-40
SE3 remainder
Mazenod Av. NW6—7J 43
Maze Rd. Rich—7G 73
Mead Clo. Harr—1H 23
Mead Ct. NW9—5K 25

Mead Cres. E4—4K 19
Mead Cres. Sutt—3C 132
Meadcroft Rd. SE11—6B 78
Meadcroft Rd. SE17—6B 78
Meade Clo. W4—6G 73
Meader Ct. SE14—7K 79
Meadfield. Edgw—2C 12
Meadfield Grn. Edgw—2C 12
Meadfoot Rd. SW16—7G 109
Meadgate Av. Wfd G—5H 21
Mead Gro. Romf—3D 36
Meadlands Dri. Rich—2D 104
Meadow Av. Croy—6K 125
Meadow Bank. N21—6E 6
Meadow Bank. SE3—3H 97
Meadowbank. NW3—7D 44
Meadowbank. SE3—3H 97
Meadowbank Clo. SW6—7E 74
Meadowbank Rd. NW9—7K 25
Meadow Clo. E4—1J 19
Meadow Clo. SE6—5C 112
Meadow Clo. SW20—4E 120
Meadow Clo. Barn—6C 4
Meadow Clo. Chst—5F 115
Meadow Clo. Enf—1G 9
Meadow Clo. Houn—6E 86
Meadow Clo. N'holt—2E 54
Meadow Clo. Rich—1E 104
Meadow Clo. Sutt—2A 132
Meadowcourt Rd. SE3—4H 97
Meadowcroft. Brom—3D 128
Meadowcroft Clo. N13—2G 17
Meadowcroft Rd. N13—2F 17
Meadow Dri. N10—2F 29
Meadow Dri. NW4—2E 26
Meadow Gdns. Edgw—6C 12
Meadow Garth. NW10—6J 41
Meadow Hill. N Mald—6A 120
Meadow M. SW8—6K 77
Meadow Pl. SW8—7J 77
Meadow Rd. SW8—7K 77
Meadow Rd. SW19—7A 108
Meadow Rd. Bark—7K 51
Meadow Rd. Brom—2G 127
Meadow Rd. Dag—6F 53
Meadow Rd. Felt—2C 102
Meadow Rd. Pinn—4B 22
Meadow Rd. Romf—1J 53
Meadow Rd. S'hall—7D 54
Meadow Rd. Sutt—4C 132
Meadow Row. SE1
—3C 78 (7L 147)
Meadows Clo. E10—2C 48
Meadows Ct. Sidc—6B 116
Meadowside. SE9—4A 98
Meadow Stile. Croy—3C 134
Meadowsweet Clo. E16—5B 66
Meadow, The. Chst—6G 115
Meadow View. Sidc—7B 100
Meadowview Rd. SE6—1C 112
Meadowview Rd. Bex—6E 100
Meadowview Rd. Eps—7A 130
Meadow View Rd. T Hth
—5B 124
Meadow Wlk. E18—4J 33
Meadow Wlk. Dag—6F 53
Meadow Wlk. Eps—6A 130
Meadow Wlk. Wall—3F 133
Meadow Way. NW9—5K 25
Meadow Way. Ruis—6A 22
Meadow Way. Wemb—4D 40
Meadow Way. Houn—6C 70
Meadow Way, The. Harr—1J 23
Mead Path. SW17—4A 108
Mead Pl. E9—6J 47
Mead Pl. Croy—1C 134
Mead Plat. NW10—6J 41
Mead Rd. Chst—6G 115
Mead Rd. Edgw—6B 12
Mead Rd. Rich—3C 104
Mead Row. SE1—3A 78 (6G 147)
Meads Ct. E15—6H 49
Meads La. Ilf—7J 35
Meads Rd. N22—2B 30
Meads Rd. Enf—1F 9
Meads, The. Edgw—6E 12
Meads, The. Sutt—3G 131

Mead, The. N2—2A 28
Mead, The. W13—5B 56
Mead, The. Beck—1E 126
Mead, The. Wall—6H 133
Mead, The. W Wick—1F 137
Meadvale Rd. W5—4B 56
Meadvale Rd. Croy—7F 125
Meadway. N14—2D 16
Meadway. NW11—6K 27
Meadway. SW20—4E 120
Meadway. Barn—4D 4
Meadway. Beck—1E 126
Mead Way. Brom—6H 127
Mead Way. Croy—2A 136
Meadway. Ilf—4J 51
Meadway. Twic—1H 103
Mead Way. Wfd G—5F 21
Meadway Clo. NW11—6K 27
Meadway Clo. Barn—4D 4
Meadway Clo. Pinn—6A 10
Meadway Ct. Dag—2F 53
Meadway Ga. NW11—6J 27
Meadway, The. SE3—7F 80
Meadway, The. Buck H—1G 21
Meaford Way. SE20—7H 111
Meakin Est. SE1
—3E 78 (6C 148)
Meanley Rd. E12—4C 50
Meard St. W1—6H 61 (8A 140)
Meath Rd. E15—2H 65
Meath Rd. Ilf—3G 51
Meath St. SW11—1F 93
Mechanic's Path. SE18—7C 80
Mecklenburgh Pl. WC1
—4K 61 (3E 140)
Mecklenburgh Sq. WC1
—4K 61 (3E 140)
Mecklenburgh St. WC1
—4K 61 (3E 140)
Medburn St. NW1—2H 61
Medcalfe Pl. N1—2A 62 (1H 141)
Medcroft Gdns. SW14—4J 89
Medebourne Clo. SE3—3J 97
Medesenge Way. N13—6G 17
Medfield St. SW15—7D 90
Medhurst Clo. E3—2A 64
Median Rd. E5—5J 47
Medina Gro. N7—3A 46
Medina Rd. N7—3A 46
Mediand Clo. Wall—1E 132
Medlar Clo. N'holt—2B 54
Medlar St. SE5—1C 94
Medley Rd. NW6—6J 43
Medora Rd. SW2—7K 93
Medora Rd. Romf—4K 37
Medusa Rd. SE6—6D 96
Medway Clo. Croy—6J 125
Medway Clo. Ilf—5G 51
Medway Dri. Gnfd—2K 55
Medway Gdns. Wemb—4A 40
Medway M. E3—2A 64
Medway Pde. Gnfd—2K 55
Medway Rd. E3—2A 64
Medway St. SW1
—3H 77 (7B 146)
Medwin St. SW4—4K 93
Meerbrook Rd. SE3—3A 98
Meeson Rd. E15—7H 49
Meeson St. E5—4A 48
Meeting Field Path. E9—6J 47
Meetinghouse All. E1
—1H 79 (2K 149)
Meeting Ho. La. SE15—1H 95
Mehetabel Rd. E9—5J 47
Melancholy Wlk. Rich—2C 104
Melanda Clo. Chst—5D 114
Melanie Clo. Bexh—1E 100
Melba Way. SE13—1D 96
Melbourne Av. N13—6E 16
Melbourne Av. W13—1A 72
Melbourne Av. Pinn—3F 23
Melbourne Clo. SE20—7G 111
Melbourne Clo. Orp—7J 129
Melbourne Clo. Wall—5G 133
Melbourne Gdns. Romf—5E 36
Melbourne Gro. SE22—4E 94
Melbourne M. SE6—7E 96

Mead, The. N2—2A 28
Melbourne M. SW9—1A 94
Melbourne Pl. WC2
—6K 61 (8F 140)
Melbourne Rd. E6—2D 66
Melbourne Rd. E10—7D 32
Melbourne Rd. E17—4A 32
Melbourne Rd. SW19—1J 121
Melbourne Rd. Ilf—1F 51
Melbourne Rd. Tedd—6C 104
Melbourne Rd. Wall—5F 133
Melbourne Sq. SW9—1A 94
Melbourne Way. Enf—6A 8
Melbury Av. S'hall—3F 71
Melbury Clo. Chst—6D 114
Melbury Ct. W8—3J 75
Melbury Dri. SE5—7E 78
Melbury Gdns. SW20—1D 120
Melbury Rd. W14—3H 75
Melbury Rd. Harr—5F 25
Melbury Ter. NW1
—4C 60 (4D 138)
Melcombe Gdns. Harr—6F 25
Melcombe Pl. NW1
—5D 60 (5E 138)
Melcombe St. NW1
—4D 60 (4F 138)
Meldon Clo. SW6—1K 91
Meldrum Rd. Ilf—2A 52
Melfield Gdns. SE6—5E 112
Melford Av. Bark—6J 51
Melford Rd. E6—3D 66
Melford Rd. E11—2G 49
Melford Rd. E17—4B 32
Melford Rd. SE22—7G 95
Melford Rd. Ilf—2H 51
Melfort Av. T Hth—3B 124
Melfort Rd. T Hth—3B 124
Melgund Rd. N5—5A 46
Melina Ct. SW15—3C 90
Melina Pl. NW8—3B 60 (2A 138)
Melina Rd. W12—2D 74
Melior Pl. SE1—2E 78 (4C 148)
Melior St. SE1—2E 78 (4C 148)
Meliot Rd. SE6—2F 113
Meller Clo. Croy—3J 133
Melling St. SE18—6J 83
Mellish Clo. Bark—1K 67
Mellish St. E14—3C 80
Mellison Rd. SW17—5C 108
Mellitus St. W12—6B 58
Mellows Rd. Ilf—3D 34
Mellows Rd. Wall—5H 133
Mells Cres. SE9—4D 114
Mell St. SE10—5G 81
Melody Rd. SW18—5A 92
Melon Pl. W8—2J 75
Melon Rd. SE15—1G 95
Melrose Av. N22—1B 30
Melrose Av. NW2—5D 42
Melrose Av. SW16—3A 124
Melrose Av. SW19—1H 107
Melrose Av. Gnfd—2F 55
Melrose Av. Mitc—7F 109
Melrose Av. Twic—7F 87
Melrose Clo. SE12—1J 113
Melrose Clo. Gnfd—2F 55
Melrose Dri. S'hall—1E 70
Melrose Gdns. W6—3E 74
Melrose Gdns. Edgw—2H 25
Melrose Gdns. N Mald—3K 119
Melrose Rd. SW13—2B 90
Melrose Rd. SW18—6H 91
Melrose Rd. SW19—2J 121
Melrose Rd. W3—3J 73
Melrose Rd. Pinn—4D 22
Melrose Ter. W6—5E 74
Melsa Rd. Mord—6A 122
Meltham Way. SE16—5H 79
Melthorne Dri. Ruis—3A 38
Melthorpe Gdns. SE13—1G 98
Melton Clo. Ruis—1A 38
Melton Ct. SW7—4B 76 (9B 144)
Melton St. NW1—3H 61 (2A 140)
Melville Av. SW20—7C 106
Melville Av. Gnfd—5K 39
Melville Av. S Croy—7F 135
Melville Gdns. N13—5G 17

Melville Ho. Barn—6G 5
Melville Rd. E17—3B 32
Melville Rd. NW10—7K 41
Melville Rd. SW13—1C 90
Melville Rd. Romf—1H 37
Melville Rd. Sidc—2C 116
Melville St. N1—7C 46
Melvin Rd. SE20—1J 125
Melyn Clo. N7—4G 45
Memel St. EC1—4C 62 (4L 141)
Memess Path. SE18—6E 82
Memorial Av. E15—3G 65
Memorial Clo. Houn—6D 70
Mendip Clo. SE26—4J 111
Mendip Clo. SW19—2G 107
Mendip Dri. NW2—2G 43
Mendip Rd. SW11—3A 92
Mendip Rd. Bexh—1K 101
Mendip Rd. Ilf—5J 35
Mendora Rd. SW6—7G 75
Menelik Rd. NW2—4G 43
Menlo Gdns. SE19—7D 110
Menotti St. E2—4G 63 (3H 143)
Mentmore Clo. Harr—6C 24
Mentmore Ter. E8—7H 47
Meon Ct. Iswth—2J 87
Meon Rd. W3—2J 73
Meopham Rd. Mitc—1G 123
Mepham Cres. Harr—7B 10
Mepham Gdns. Harr—7B 10
Mepham St. SE1—1A 78 (3G 147)
Mera Dri. Bexh—4G 101
Merantun Way. SW19—1K 121
Merbury Clo. SE13—5E 96
Mercator Rd. SE13—4F 97
Mercer Clo. Th Dit—7A 118
Merceron St. E1—4H 63 (4K 143)
Mercers Clo. SE10—4H 81
Mercers Pl. W6—4E 74
Mercers Rd. N19—3H 45
Mercer St. WC2—6J 61 (8C 140)
Merchant Industrial Ter. NW10—4J 57
Merchant St. E3—3B 64
Merchiston Rd. SE6—2F 113
Merchland Rd. SE9—1G 115
Mercia Gro. SE13—4E 96
Mercier Rd. SW15—5G 91
Mercury Rd. Bren—5C 72
Mercury Way. SE14—6K 79
Mercy Ter. SE13—5D 96
Merebank La. Croy—5K 133
Mere Clo. SW15—7F 91
Meredith Av. NW2—5E 42
Meredith Clo. Pinn—1B 22
Meredith St. E13—3J 65
Meredith St. EC1—3B 62 (2J 141)
Meredyth Rd. SW13—2C 90
Mere End. Croy—7K 125
Meretone Clo. SE4—4A 96
Merevale Cres. Mord—6A 122
Mereway Rd. Twic—1H 103
Merewood Clo. Brom—2E 128
Merewood Rd. Bexh—2J 101
Mereworth Clo. Brom—5H 127
Mereworth Dri. SE18—7F 83
Merganser Gdns. SE28—3H 83
Meriden Clo. Brom—7B 114
Meriden Clo. Ilf—1G 35
Meridian Ga. E14—2E 80
Meridian Rd. SE7—7B 82
Meridian Wlk. N17—6K 17
Merifield Rd. SE9—4A 98
Merino Pl. Sidc—6A 100
Merivale Rd. SW15—4G 91
Merivale Rd. Harr—7G 23
Merlewood Dri. Chst—1D 128
Merlewood Pl. SE9—6D 98
Merley Ct. NW9—1J 41
Merlin Clo. Croy—4E 134
Merlin Clo. N'holt—3A 54
Merlin Ct. Brom—4H 127

Merlin Cres. Edgw—1F 25
Merlin Gdns. Brom—3J 113
Merlin Gro. Beck—4B 126
Merlin Rd. E12—2B 50
Merlin Rd. Well—4A 100
Merlin Rd. N. Well—4A 100
Merlins Av. Harr—3D 38
Mermaid Ct. SE1—2D 78 (4A 148)
Merredene St. SE9—6K 93
Merrick Rd. S'hall—3D 70
Merrick Sq. SE1—3D 78 (6A 148)
Merridene. N21—6G 7
Merrielands Cres. Dag—2F 69
Merrilands Rd. Wor Pk—1E 130
Merrilees Rd. Sidc—7J 99
Merriman Rd. SE3—1A 98
Merrington Rd. SW6—6J 75
Merrion Av. Stan—5J 11
Merritt Rd. SE4—5B 96
Merrivale. N14—6C 6
Merrivale Av. Ilf—4B 34
Merrow Rd. Sutt—7F 131
Merrow St. SE17—5D 78
Merrow Wlk. SE17—5D 78 (9B 148)
Merrow Way. Croy—6E 136
Merrydown Way. Chst—1C 128
Merryfield. SE3—2H 97
Merryfield Gdns. Stan—5H 11
Merryhill Clo. E4—7J 9
Merry Hill Mt. Bush. Wat—1A 10
Merry Hill Rd. Bush, Wat—1A 10
Merryhills Ct. N14—5B 6
Merryhills Dri. Enf—4C 6
Merryweather Ct. N19—3G 45
Mersey Rd. E17—3B 32
Mersham Dri. NW9—5G 25
Mersham Pl. SE20—1H 125
Mersham Rd. T Hth—2D 124
Merten Rd. Romf—7E 36
Merton Av. W4—4B 74
Merton Av. N'holt—5G 39
Merton Gdns. Orp—5F 129
Merton Hall Gdns. SW20—1G 121
Merton Hall Rd. SW19—1G 121
Merton High St. SW19—7K 107
Merton La. N6—2D 44
Merton Mans. SW20—2F 121
Merton Pk. Industrial Est. SW19—1K 121
Merton Rise. NW3—7C 44
Merton Rd. E17—5E 32
Merton Rd. SE25—5G 125
Merton Rd. SW18—6J 91
Merton Rd. SW19—7K 107
Merton Rd. Bark—7K 51
Merton Rd. Enf—1J 7
Merton Rd. Harr—1G 39
Merton Rd. Ilf—7K 35
Merttins Rd. SE15—5K 95
Mervan Rd. SW2—4A 94
Mervyn Av. SE9—3G 115
Mervyn Rd. W13—3A 72
Messaline Av. W3—6J 57
Messent Rd. SE9—5A 98
Messeter Pl. SE9—6E 98
Messina Av. NW6—7J 43
Metcalfe Wlk. Felt—4C 102
Meteor St. SW11—4E 92
Meteor Way. Wall—7J 133
Metheringham Way. NW9—1A 26
Methley St. SE11—5A 78
Methuen Clo. Edgw—7B 12
Methuen Pk. N10—3F 29
Methuen Rd. Belv—4H 85
Methuen Rd. Bexh—4F 101
Methuen Rd. Edgw—7B 12
Methwold Rd. W10—5F 59
Metro Centre. Iswth—2J 87

Mews Pl. Wfd G—4D 20
Mews St. E1—1G 79 (2G 149)
Mews, The. N1—1C 62
Mews, The. Ilf—5B 34
Mews, The. Romf—4K 37
Mews, The. Twic—6B 88
Mexfield Rd. SW15—5H 91
Meyer Gro. Enf—1B 8
Meyer Rd. Eri—6K 85
Meymott St. SE1—1B 78 (3J 147)
Meynell Cres. E9—7K 47
Meynell Gdns. E9—7K 47
Meynell Rd. E9—7K 47
Meyrick Rd. NW10—6C 42
Meyrick Rd. SW11—3B 92
Miall Wlk. SE26—4A 112
Micawber St. N1—3C 62 (1M 141)
Michael Gaynor Clo. W7—1K 71
Michael Rd. E11—1H 49
Michael Rd. SE25—3E 124
Michael Rd. SW6—1K 91
Michael's Clo. SE13—4G 97
Micheldever Rd. SE12—6H 97
Michelham Gdns. Twic—3K 103
Michel's Row. Rich—4E 88
Michigan Av. E12—4C 50
Michigan Ho. E14—3C 80
Michleham Down. N12—4C 14
Mickleham Clo. Orp—2K 129
Mickleham Gdns. Sutt—6G 131
Mickleham Rd. Orp—1K 129
Mickleham Way. Croy—7F 137
Micklethwaite Rd. SW6—6J 75
Midas Metropolitan Industrial Est. Mord—1F 131
Middle Dene. NW7—3E 12
Middle Field. NW8—1B 60
Middlefielde. W13—5B 56
Middlefields. Croy—7A 136
Middle Grn. Clo. Surb—6F 119
Middleham Gdns. N18—6B 18
Middleham Rd. N18—6B 18
Middle La. N8—5J 29
Middle La. Tedd—6K 103
Middle La. M. N8—5J 29
Middle Pk. Av. SE9—6B 98
Middle Path. Harr—1H 39
Middle Rd. E13—2J 65
Middle Rd. SW16—2H 123
Middle Rd. Barn—6H 5
Middle Rd. Harr—2H 39
Middle Row. W10—4G 59
Middlesborough Rd. N18—6B 18
Middlesex Ct. W4—5B 74
Middlesex Rd. Mitc—5J 123
Middlesex St. E1—5E 62 (6D 142)
Middlesex Wharf. E5—2J 47
Middle St. EC1—5C 62 (5L 141)
Middle St. Croy—2C 134
Middle Temple La. EC4—6A 62 (8G 141)
Middleton Av. E4—4G 19
Middleton Av. Gnfd—2H 55
Middleton Av. Sidc—6C 116
Middleton Clo. E4—3G 19
Middleton Dri. SE16—2K 79
Middleton Gdns. Ilf—6F 35
Middleton Gro. N7—5J 45
Middleton M. N7—5J 45
Middleton Rd. E8—7F 47
Middleton Rd. NW11—7J 27
Middleton Rd. Mord & Cars—6K 121
Middleton St. E2—3H 63 (1J 143)
Middleton Way. SE13—4F 97
Middleway. NW11—5K 27
Middle Way. SW16—2H 123
Middle Way. Hay—4A 54
Middle Way, The. Harr—2K 23
Middle Yd. SE1—1E 78 (2C 148)
Midfield Av. Bexh—3J 101
Midfield Pde. Bexh—3J 101

Midfield Way. Orp—7B 116
Midford Pl. W1—4G 61 (4M 139)
Midholm. NW11—4K 27
Midholm. Wemb—1G 41
Midholm Clo. NW11—4K 27
Midholm Rd. Croy—2A 136
Midhope St. WC1—3J 61 (2D 140)
Midhurst Av. N10—3E 28
Midhurst Av. Croy—7A 124
Midhurst Hill. Bexh—6G 101
Midhurst Rd. W13—2A 72
Midland Pl. E14—5E 80
Midland Rd. E10—7E 32
Midland Rd. NW1—2H 61 (1B 140)
Midland Ter. NW2—3F 43
Midland Ter. NW10—4A 58
Midleton Rd. N Mald—2J 119
Midlothian Rd. E3—4B 64
Midmoor Rd. SW12—1G 109
Midmoor Rd. SW19—1G 121
Midship Clo. SE16—1K 79
Midstrath Rd. NW10—4A 42
Midsummer Av. Houn—4D 86
Midway. Sutt—7H 121
Midwood Clo. NW2—3D 42
Miers Clo. E6—1E 66
Mighell Av. Ilf—5B 34
Milborne Gro. SW10—5A 76
Milborne St. E9—6J 47
Milborough Cres. SE12—6G 97
Milcote St. SE1—2B 78 (5J 147)
Mildenhall Rd. E5—4J 47
Mildmay Av. N1—6D 46
Mildmay Gro. N1—5D 46 (in two parts)
Mildmay Pk. N1—5D 46
Mildmay Rd. N1—5D 46
Mildmay Rd. Ilf—3F 51
Mildmay Rd. Romf—5J 37
Mildmay St. N1—6D 46
Mildred Av. N'holt—5F 39
Mildred Rd. Eri—5K 85
Mile End Pl. E1—4K 63
Mile End Rd. E1-357 & 2-510
Mile End Rd. E3 remainder
E1 1-357 & 2-510
Mile End, The. E17—1K 31
Mile Rd. Wall—1F 133
Milespit Hill. NW7—5J 13
Miles Pl. Surb—4F 119
Miles Rd. N8—3J 29
Miles Rd. Mitc—3C 122
Miles St. SW8—6J 77 (in two parts)
Milestone Clo. Sutt—7B 132
Milestone Rd. SE19—6F 111
Miles Way. N20—2H 15
Milfoil St. W12—7C 58
Milford Clo. SE2—6E 84
Milford Gdns. Edgw—7B 12
Milford Gdns. Wemb—5D 40
Milford Gro. Sutt—4A 132
Milford La. WC2—7A 62 (9G 141)
Milford M. SW16—3K 109
Milford Rd. W13—1B 72
Milford Rd. S'hall—1E 54
Milford Towers. SE6—7D 96
Milford Way. SE15—1F 95
Milk St. E16—1F 83
Milk St. EC2—6C 62 (8M 141)
Milk St. Brom—6K 113
Milkwell Gdns. Wfd G—7E 20
Milkwell Yd. SE5—1D 94
Milkwood Rd. SE24—5B 94
Milk Yd. E1—7J 63 (1L 149)
Millais Av. E12—5E 50
Millais Gdns. Edgw—2G 25
Millais Rd. E11—4E 48
Millais Rd. Enf—5A 8
Millais Rd. N Mald—7A 120
Millard Clo. N16—5E 46
Millard Ter. Dag—6G 53
Millbank. SW1—4J 77 (9C 146)
Millbank Way. SE12—5J 97

237

Millbourne Rd. Felt—4C 102
Mill Bridge. Barn—6C 4
Millbrook Av. Well—4H 99
Millbrook Gdns. Romf—6F 37
(Chadwell Heath)
Millbrook Rd. N9—1C 18
Millbrook Rd. SW9—3B 94
Mill Clo. Cars—2E 132
Mill Corner. Barn—1C 4
Mill Ct. E10—3E 48
Mill Dri. SW16—3K 123
Millender Wlk. SE16
—4J 79 (9M 149)
Miller Clo. Pinn—2A 22
Miller Rd. SW19—6B 108
Miller Rd. Croy—1K 133
Millers Av. E8—5F 47
Miller's Ct. W6—5B 74
Millers Grn. Clo. Enf—3G 7
Millers Ter. E8—5F 47
Miller St. NW1—2G 61
Millers Way. W6—2F 75
Millet Rd. Gnfd—3F 55
Mill Farm Clo. Pinn—2A 22
Mill Farm Cres. Houn—1C 102
Millfield Av. E17—1A 32
Millfield La. N6—2D 44
Millfield Pl. N6—2E 44
Millfield Rd. Edgw—2J 25
Millfield Rd. Houn—1C 102
Millfields Rd. E5—4J 47
Mill Gdns. SE26—3H 111
Mill Grn. Rd. Mitc—7E 122
Millgrove St. SW11—2E 92
Millharbour. E14—3D 80
Millhaven Clo. Romf—6B 36
Mill Hill Cir. NW7—5G 13
Mill Hill Gro. W3—1H 73
Mill Hill Rd. SW13—2C 90
Mill Hill Rd. W3—2H 73
Mill Hill Ter. W3—1H 73
Millhouse Pl. SE27—4B 110
Millicent Rd. E10—1B 48
Milligan St. E14—7B 64
Milling Rd. Edgw—7E 12
Mill La. E4—3J 9
Mill La. NW6—5H 43
Mill La. SE18—5E 82
Mill La. Cars—4D 132
Mill La. Croy—3K 133
Mill La. Eps—7B 130
Mill La. Romf—6E 36
(Chadwell Heath)
Mill La. Wfd G—5C 20
Millman M. WC1
—4K 61 (4E 140)
Millman St. WC1
—4K 61 (4E 140)
Millmark Gro. SE14—2A 96
Millmarsh La. Enf—2G 9
Millmead Industrial Centre. N17
—3H 31
Mill Mead Rd. N17—3H 31
Mill Pl. E14—6A 64
Mill Pl. Chst—1F 129
Mill Pl. King—3F 119
Mill Plat. Iswth—2A 88
Mill Plat Av. Iswth—2A 88
Mill Quay Development. E14
—4D 80
Mill Ridge. Edgw—5A 12
Mill Rd. E16—1K 81
Mill Rd. SE13—3E 96
Mill Rd. SW19—7A 108
Mill Rd. Eri—7J 85
Mill Rd. Ilf—3E 50
Mill Rd. Twic—2G 103
Mill Row. N1—1E 62
Mills Gro. E14—6E 64
Mills Gro. NW4—3F 27
Mill Shot Clo. SW6—1B 92
Millside. Cars—2D 132
Millside Pl. Iswth—2B 88
Millson Clo. N20—2G 15
Mills Rd. W4—4K 73
Mills Row. W4—4K 73

Millstream Rd. SE1
—2F 79 (5E 148)
Mill St. SE1—2F 79 (5F 148)
Mill St. W1—7G 61 (9L 139)
Mill St. King—3E 118
Mill Vale. Brom—2H 127
Mill View Gdns. Croy—3K 135
Millwall Dock Rd. E14—3C 80
Millwall Wharf Development.
E14—3F 81
Mill Way. NW7—4F 13
Mill Way. Felt—5A 86
Millway Gdns. N'holt—6D 38
Millwood Rd. Houn—5G 87
Millwood St. W10—5G 59
Milman Clo. Pinn—3B 22
Milman Rd. NW6—2G 59
Milman's St. SW10—6B 76
Milne Est. SE18—4D 82
Milne Feild. Pinn—7A 10
Milne Gdns. SE9—5C 98
Milner Dri. Twic—7H 87
Milner Pl. N1—1B 62
Milner Pl. Cars—4E 132
Milner Rd. E15—3G 65
Milner Rd. SW19—1K 121
Milner Rd. Dag—2C 52
Milner Rd. King—3D 118
Milner Rd. Mord—5B 122
Milner Rd. T Hth—3D 124
Milner Sq. N1—7B 46
Milner St. SW3—4D 76 (8E 144)
Milner Wlk. Sidc—1H 115
Milnthorpe Rd. W4—6K 73
Milo Rd. SE22—6F 95
Milroy Wlk. SE1—1B 78 (2J 147)
Milson Rd. W14—3F 75
Milton Av. E6—7B 50
Milton Av. N6—7G 29
Milton Av. NW9—3J 25
Milton Av. NW10—1J 57
Milton Av. Barn—5C 4
Milton Av. Croy—7D 124
Milton Av. Sutt—3B 132
Milton Clo. N2—5A 28
Milton Clo. Sutt—3B 132
Milton Ct. EC2—5D 62 (5A 142)
Milton Ct. Rd. SE14—6A 80
Milton Cres. Ilf—7G 35
Milton Garden Est. N16—4E 46
Milton Gro. N11—5B 16
Milton Gro. N16—4E 46
Milton Pk. N6—7G 29
Milton Pl. N7—5A 46
Milton Rd. E17—4C 32
Milton Rd. N6—7G 29
Milton Rd. N15—4B 30
Milton Rd. NW7—5H 13
Milton Rd. NW9—7C 26
Milton Rd. SE24—5B 94
Milton Rd. SW14—3K 89
Milton Rd. SW19—6A 108
Milton Rd. W3—1K 73
Milton Rd. W7—7K 55
Milton Rd. Belv—4G 85
Milton Rd. Croy—7D 124
Milton Rd. Hmptn—7E 102
Milton Rd. Harr—4J 23
Milton Rd. Mitc—7F 108
Milton Rd. Sutt—3J 131
Milton Rd. Wall—6G 133
Milton Rd. Well—1K 99
Milton St. EC2—5D 62 (5A 142)
Milverton Gdns. Ilf—2K 51
Milverton Rd. NW6—7E 42
Milverton St. SE11—5A 78
Milverton Way. SE9—4E 114
Milward St. E1—5H 63 (6K 143)
Milward Wlk. SE18—6E 82
Mimosa Rd. Hay—5A 54
Mimosa St. SW6—1H 91
Minard Rd. SE6—7G 97
Mina Rd. SE17—5E 78
Mina Rd. SW19—1J 121
Minchenden Cres. N14—3C 16
Mincing La. EC3
—7E 62 (9C 142)

Minden Rd. SE20—1H 125
Minden Rd. Sutt—2H 131
Minehead Rd. SW16—5K 109
Minehead Rd. Harr—3E 38
Mineral St. SE18—4J 83
Minera M. SW1—4E 76 (8H 145)
Minerva Clo. SW9—7A 78
Minerva Clo. Sidc—4J 115
Minerva Rd. E4—7J 19
Minerva Rd. NW10—4J 57
Minerva Rd. King—2F 119
Minerva St. E2—2H 63 (1J 143)
Minet Av. NW10—2A 58
Minet Gdns. NW10—2A 58
Minet Rd. SW9—2B 94
Minford Gdns. W14—2F 75
Mingard Wlk. N7—2K 45
Ming St. E14—7C 64
Ministry Way. SE9—2D 114
Mink Ct. Houn—2A 86
Minniedale. Surb—5F 119
Minnow Wlk. SE17
—4E 78 (9D 148)
Minories. EC3—6F 63 (8E 142)
Minshull St. SW8—1H 93
Minson Rd. E9—1K 63
Minstead Gdns. SW15—7B 90
Minstead Way. N Mald—6A 120
Minster Av. Sutt—2J 131
Minster Dri. Croy—4E 134
Minster Rd. NW2—5G 43
Minster Rd. Brom—7K 113
Minster Wlk. N8—4J 29
Minstrel Gdns. Surb—4F 119
Mintern Clo. N13—3G 17
Minterne Av. S'hall—4E 70
Minterne Rd. Harr—5F 25
Minterne Waye. Hay—6A 54
Mintern St. N1—2D 62
Minton M. NW6—6K 43
Mint Rd. Wall—4F 133
Mint St. SE1—2C 78 (4H 147)
Mint Wlk. Croy—3C 134
Mirabel Rd. SW6—7H 75
Miranda Rd. N19—1G 45
Mirfield St. SE7—4B 82
Miriam Rd. SE18—5J 83
Mirren Clo. Harr—3D 38
Mirror Path. SE9—3A 114
Missenden Gdns. Mord
—6A 122
Mission Gro. E17—5A 32
Mission Pl. SE15—1G 95
Mission Sq. Bren—6E 72
Mistletoe Clo. Croy—1K 135
Mitcham Garden Village. Mitc
—5E 122
Mitcham La. SW16—6F 109
Mitcham Pk. Mitc—4C 122
Mitcham Rd. E6—3C 66
Mitcham Rd. SW17—5D 108
Mitcham Rd. Croy—6J 123
Mitcham Rd. Ilf—7K 35
Mitchellbrook Way. NW10
—6K 41
Mitchell Clo. SE2—4C 84
Mitchell Rd. N13—5H 17
Mitchell St. EC1—4C 62 (3L 141)
Mitchell Way. NW10—6J 41
Mitchell Way. Brom—1J 127
Mitchison Rd. N1—6D 46
Mitchley Rd. N17—3G 31
Mitford Rd. N19—2J 45
Mitre Clo. Sutt—7A 132
Mitre Ct. EC4—6A 62 (8H 141)
Mitre Rd. E15—2G 65
Mitre Rd. SE1—2A 78 (4H 147)
Mitre Sq. EC3—6E 62 (8D 142)
Mitre St. EC3—6E 62 (8D 142)
Mitre, The. E14—7B 64
Mitre Way. NW10—5D 58
Moat Cres. N3—3K 27
Moat Croft. Well—3C 100
Moat Dri. E13—2A 66
Moat Dri. Harr—4G 23
Moat Farm Rd. N'holt—6D 38
Moat Pl. SW9—3K 93

Moat Pl. W3—6H 57
Moatside. Enf—4E 8
Moatside. Felt—4A 102
Moberley Rd. SW4—7H 93
Modbury Gdns. NW5—6E 44
Modder Pl. SW15—4F 91
Model Cotts. SW14—4J 89
Model Cotts. W13—2B 72
Model Farm Clo. SE9—3C 114
Moelwyn Hughes Ct. N7—5H 45
Moelyn M. Harr—5A 24
Moffat Gdns. Mitc—3C 122
Moffat Rd. N13—6D 16
Moffat Rd. SW17—4D 108
Moffat Rd. T Hth—2C 124
Mogden La. Iswth—5K 87
Moiety Rd. E14—2C 80
Moira Clo. N17—2E 30
Moira Rd. SE9—4D 98
Mokswell Ct. N10—1E 28
Moland Mead. SE16
—5K 79 (9M 149)
Molasses Row. SW11—3A 92
Molescroft. SE9—3G 115
Molesey Dri. Sutt—2G 131
Molesford Rd. SW6—1J 91
Molesworth St. SE13—3E 96
Moliner Ct. Beck—7C 112
Mollison Av. Enf—4F 9
Mollison Dri. Wall—7H 133
Mollison Way. Edgw—2F 25
Molly Huggins Clo. SW12
—7G 93
Molyneux St. W1
—5C 60 (6D 138)
Monarch Clo. W Wick—4H 137
Monarch Dri. E16—5B 66
Monarch M. SW16—5A 110
Monarch Rd. Belv—3G 85
Mona Rd. SE15—2J 95
Monastery Gdns. Enf—2J 7
Mona St. E16—5H 65
Monck St. SW1—3H 77 (7B 146)
Monclar Rd. SE5—4D 94
Moncorvo Clo. SW7
—2C 76 (5C 144)
Moncrieff Clo. E6—6C 66
Moncrieff St. SE15—2G 95
(in two parts)
Monega Rd.—6A 50
E7 1-203 & 2-204
E12 remainder
Monica Ct. Enf—5K 7
Monica James Ho. Sidc
—3A 116
Monier Rd. E3—7C 48
Monivea Rd. Beck—7B 112
Monk Dri. E16—7J 65
Monkfrith Av. N14—6A 6
Monkfrith Clo. N14—7A 6
Monkfrith Way. N14—7K 5
Monkham's Av. Wfd G—5E 20
Monkham's Dri. Wfd G—5E 20
Monkham's La. Buck H—3E 20
Monkham's La. Wfd G—4E 20
Monkleigh Rd. Mord—3G 121
Monks Av. Barn—6F 5
Monks Clo. SE2—4D 84
Monks Clo. Enf—2H 7
Monks Clo. Harr—2F 39
Monks Clo. Ruis—4B 38
Monksdene Gdns. Sutt—3K 131
Monks Dri. W3—5G 57
Monks Orchard Rd. Beck
—1C 136
Monks Pk. Wemb—6H 41
Monks Pk. Gdns. Wemb—7H 41
Monks Rd. Enf—2H 7
Monk St. SE18—4E 82
Monks Way. NW11—4H 27
Monks Way. Beck—6C 126
Monks Way. Orp—7G 129
Monkswood Gdns. Ilf—3E 34
Monkton Rd. Well—2K 99
Monkton St. SE11
—4A 78 (8H 147)

Monkville Av. NW11—4H 27
Monkwell Sq. EC2
—5C 62 (6M 141)
Monmouth Av. E18—3K 33
Monmouth Av. King—7C 104
Monmouth Clo. Mitc—4J 123
Monmouth Clo. Well—4A 100
Monmouth Gro. W5—4E 72
Monmouth Rd. E6—3D 66
Monmouth Rd. N9—2C 18
Monmouth Rd. W2—6J 59
Monmouth Rd. Dag—5F 53
Monmouth St. WC2
—6J 61 (8C 140)
Monnery Rd. N19—3G 45
Monnow Rd. SE1
—4G 79 (9G 149)
Monoux Gro. E17—1C 32
Monroe Cres. Enf—1C 8
Monroe Dri. SW14—5H 89
Monro Gdns. Harr—7D 10
Monsell Rd. N4—3B 46
Monson Rd. NW10—2C 58
Monson Rd. SE14—7K 79
Mons Way. Brom—6C 128
Montacute Rd. SE6—7B 96
Montacute Rd. Bush, Wat
—1D 10
Montacute Rd. Croy—7E 136
Montacute Rd. Mord—6B 122
Montagu Cres. N18—4C 18
Montague Av. SE4—4B 96
Montague Av. W7—1K 71
Montague Clo. SE1
—1D 78 (2A 148)
Montague Gdns. W3—7G 57
Montague Pl. WC1
—5H 61 (5B 140)
Montague Rd. E8—5G 47
Montague Rd. E11—2H 49
Montague Rd. N8—5K 29
Montague Rd. N15—4G 31
Montague Rd. W7—2K 71
Montague Rd. W13—6B 56
Montague Rd. Croy—1B 134
Montague Rd. Houn—3F 87
Montague Rd. Rich—6E 88
Montague Rd. S'hall—4C 70
Montague Rd. Industrial Est.
N18—4D 18
Montague Sq. SE15—7J 79
Montague St. WC1
—5J 61 (5C 140)
Montague Way. S'hall—3C 70
Montagu Gdns. N18—4C 18
Montagu Gdns. Wall—4G 133
Montagu Mans. W1
—5D 60 (5F 138)
Montagu M. N. W1
—5D 60 (6F 138)
Montagu M. S. W1
—6D 60 (7F 138)
Montagu M. W. W1
—6D 60 (7F 138)
Montagu Pl. W1—5D 60 (6E 138)
Montagu Rd. NW4—6C 26
Montagu Row. W1
—5D 60 (6F 138)
Montagu Sq. W1
—5D 60 (6F 138)
Montagu St. W1—6D 60 (7F 138)
Montaft Rd. Wfd G—5C 20
Montana Rd. SW17—3E 108
Montana Rd. SW20—1E 120
Montbelle Rd. SE9—3F 115
Montcalm Clo. Brom—6J 127
Montcalm Ho. E14—4C 80
Montcalm Rd. SE7—7B 82
Montclare St. E2
—4F 63 (3E 142)
Monteagle Av. Bark—6G 51
Monteagle Ct. N1—2E 62
Monteagle Way. E5—3G 47

Monteagle Way. SE15—3H 95
Montefiore St. SW8—2F 93
Monteith Rd. E3—1B 64
Montem Rd. SE23—7B 96
Montem Rd. N Mald—4A 120
Montem St. N4—1K 45
Montenotte Rd. N8—5G 28
Monterey Clo. Bex—2J 117
Montesole Ct. Pinn—2A 22
Montford Pl. SE11—5A 78
Montford St. Pinn—1F 107
Montgolfier Wlk. N'holt—3C 54
Montgomery Clo. Mitc—4J 123
Montgomery Clo. Sidc—6K 99
Montgomery Rd. W4—4J 73
Montgomery Rd. Edgw—6A 12
Montholme Rd. SW11—6D 92
Monthope Rd. E1
—5G 63 (6G 143)
Montolieu Gdns. SW15—5D 90
Montpelier Av. W5—5C 56
Montpelier Av. Bex—7D 100
Montpelier Gdns. E6—3B 66
Montpelier Gdns. Romf—7C 36
Montpelier Gro. NW5—5G 45
Montpelier M. SW7
—3C 76 (6D 144)
Montpelier Pl. SW7
—3C 76 (6D 144)
Montpelier Rise. NW11—7G 27
(in two parts)
Montpelier Rise. Wemb—1D 40
Montpelier Rd. N3—1A 28
Montpelier Rd. SE15—1H 95
Montpelier Rd. W5—5D 56
Montpelier Rd. Sutt—4A 132
Montpelier Row. SE3—2H 97
Montpelier Row. Twic—7C 88
Montpelier Sq. SW7
—2C 76 (5D 144)
Montpelier St. SW7
—3C 76 (6D 144)
Montpelier Ter. SW7
—2C 76 (5D 144)
Montpelier Vale. SE3—2H 97
Montpelier Wlk. SW7
—3C 76 (6D 144)
Montpelier Way. NW11—7G 27
Montrave Rd. SE20—6J 111
Montreal Pl. WC2
—7K 61 (9E 140)
Montreal Rd. Ilf—7G 35
Montrell Rd. SW2—1J 109
Montrose Av. NW6—2G 59
Montrose Av. Edgw—2J 25
Montrose Av. Sidc—7A 100
Montrose Av. Twic—7F 87
Montrose Av. Well—3H 99
Montrose Clo. Well—3K 99
Montrose Clo. Wfd G—4D 20
Montrose Ct. SW7
—2B 76 (5B 144)
Montrose Cres. N12—6F 15
Montrose Cres. Wemb—6E 40
Montrose Gdns. Mitc—2D 122
Montrose Gdns. Sutt—2K 131
Montrose Ho. E14—3C 80
Montrose Pl. SW1
—2E 76 (5H 145)
Montrose Rd. Harr—2J 23
Montrose Rd. SW19—1K 111
Montserrat Av. Wfd G—7A 20
Montserrat Clo. SE19—5D 110
Montserrat Rd. SW15—4G 91
Monument Gdns. SE13—5E 96
Monument St. EC3
—7D 62 (9B 142)
Monument Way. N17—3F 31
Monza Rd. E1—7J 63 (1L 149)
Moodkee St. SE16
—3J 79 (6M 149)
Moody St. E1—3K 63
Moon La. Barn—3C 4
Moon St. N1—1B 62
Moorcroft Rd. SW16—3J 109
Moorcroft Way. Pinn—5C 22
Moordown. SE18—1F 99

Moore Clo. SW14—3J 89
Moore Clo. Mitc—2F 123
Moore Clo. Wall—7J 133
Moore Cres. Dag—1B 68
Moorehead Way. SE3—3K 97
Moorehead Rd. Brom—7H 113
Moor End Rd. Twic—6A 88
Moor Pk. Rd. SW6—7K 75
Moore Rd. SE19—6C 110
Moore St. SW3—4D 76 (8E 144)
Moore Wlk. E7—4J 49
Moore Way. SE22—1G 111
Moore Way. Sutt—7J 131
Moorey Clo. E15—1H 65
Moorfield Av. W5—4D 56
Moorfield Rd. N17—2F 31
Moorfield Rd. Enf—1D 8
Moorfields. EC2
—5D 62 (6A 142)
Moorgate. EC2—6D 62 (7A 142)
Moorhouse Rd. W2—6J 59
Moorhouse Rd. Harr—3D 24
Moorland Clo. Romf—1H 37
Moorland Clo. Twic—7E 86
Moorland Rd. SW9—4B 94
Moorlands. N'holt—1C 54
Moorlands Av. NW7—6J 13
Moor La. EC2—5D 62 (6A 142)
Moormead Dri. Eps—5A 130
Moor Mead Rd. Twic—6A 88
Moor Pl. EC2—5D 62 (6A 142)
Moorside Rd. Brom—3G 113
Moot Ct. NW9—5G 25
Morant Pl. N22—1K 29
Morant St. E14—7C 64
Mora Rd. NW2—4E 42
Mora St. EC1—3C 62 (2M 141)
Morat St. SW9—1K 93
Moravian Pl. SW10—6B 76
Moravian St. E2—3J 63 (1L 143)
Moray Clo. Romf—1K 37
Moray M. N7—2K 45
Moray Rd. N4—2K 45
Moray Way. Romf—1K 37
Mordaunt Gdns. Dag—7E 52
Mordaunt Rd. NW10—1K 57
Mordaunt St. SW9—3K 93
Morden Ct. Mord—4K 121
Morden Ct. Pde. Mord—4K 121
Morden Gdns. Gnfd—5K 39
Morden Gdns. Mitc—4B 122
Morden Hall Rd. Mord—3K 121
Morden Hill. SE13—2E 96
Morden La. SE13—1E 96
Morden Rd. SE3—2J 97
Morden Rd. SW19—1K 121
Morden Rd. Mord & Mitc
—4A 122
Morden Rd. Romf—7E 36
Morden Rd. M. SE3—2J 97
Morden St. SE13—1D 96
Morden Way. Sutt—7J 121
Morden Wharf Rd. SE10—3G 81
Mordon Rd. Ilf—7K 35
Mordred Rd. SE6—2G 113
Morecambe Clo. E1
—5K 63 (5M 143)
Morecambe Gdns. Stan—4J 11
Morecambe St. SE17
—5C 78 (9M 147)
Morecambe Ter. N18—4J 17
More Clo. E16—6H 65
More Clo. W14—4F 75
Morecoombe Clo. King—7H 105
Moree Way. N18—4B 18
Moreland Clo. NW11—1K 43
Moreland St. EC1
—3B 62 (1K 141)
Moreland Way. E4—3K 19
Morella Rd. SW12—7D 92
Moremead Rd. SE6—4B 112
Morena St. SE6—7D 96
Moresby Av. Surb—7H 119
Moresby Rd. E5—1H 47
Moresby Wlk. SW8—2G 93
Moreton Av. Iswth—1J 87

Moreton Clo. E5—2H 47
Moreton Clo. N15—6D 30
Moreton Gdns. Wfd G—5H 21
Moreton Pl. SW1
—5G 77 (9M 145)
Moreton Rd. N15—6D 30
Moreton Rd. S Croy—5D 134
Moreton Rd. Wor Pk—2C 130
Moreton St. SW1
—5G 77 (9A 146)
Moreton Ter. SW1—5G 77
Moreton Ter. M. N. SW1
—5G 77 (9M 145)
Moreton Ter. M. S. SW1—5G 77
Morford Clo. Ruis—7A 22
Morford Way. Ruis—7A 22
Morgan Av. E17—4F 33
Morgan Clo. Dag—7G 53
Morgan Rd. N7—5A 46
Morgan Rd. W10—5H 59
Morgan Rd. Brom—7J 113
Morgan's La. SE1
—1E 78 (3C 148)
Morgan St. E3—3A 64
Morgan St. E16—5H 65
Morgan Way. Wfd G—6H 21
Morie St. SW18—5K 91
Morieux Rd. E10—1B 48
Moring Rd. SW17—4E 108
Morkyns Wlk. SE21—3E 110
Morland Av. Croy—1E 134
Morland Clo. Hmptn—5D 102
Morland Clo. Mitc—3C 122
Morland Gdns. NW10—7K 41
Morland Gdns. S'hall—1F 71
Morland M. N1—7A 46
Morland Rd. E17—5K 31
Morland Rd. SE20—6K 111
Morland Rd. Croy—1E 134
Morland Rd. Dag—7G 53
Morland Rd. Harr—5E 24
Morland Rd. Ilf—2F 51
Morland Rd. Sutt—5A 132
Morley Av. E4—7A 20
Morley Av. N18—4B 18
Morley Av. N22—2A 30
Morley Clo. Ruis—2A 38
Morley Ct. Brom—4H 127
Morley Cres. Edgw—2D 12
Morley Cres. E. Stan—2C 24
Morley Cres. W. Stan—3C 24
Morley Hill. Enf—1J 7
Morley Ho. N16—2G 47
Morley Rd. E10—1E 48
Morley Rd. E15—2H 65
Morley Rd. SE13—4E 96
Morley Rd. Bark—1H 67
Morley Rd. Chst—1G 129
Morley Rd. Romf—5E 36
Morley Rd. Sutt—1H 131
Morley Rd. Twic—6D 88
Morley St. SE1—3A 78 (6H 147)
Morna Rd. SE5—2C 94
Morning La. E9—6J 47
Morningside Rd. Wor Pk
—2E 130
Mornington Av. W14—4H 75
Mornington Av. Brom—3A 128
Mornington Av. Ilf—7E 34
Mornington Clo. Wfd G—4D 20
Mornington Ct. Bex—1K 117
Mornington Cres. NW1—2G 61
Mornington Cres. Houn—1A 86
Mornington Gro. E3—3C 64
Mornington M. SE5—1C 94
Mornington Pl. NW1—2G 61
Mornington Rd. E4—7K 9
Mornington Rd. E11—7H 33
Mornington Rd. SE8—7B 80
Mornington Rd. Gnfd—5F 55
Mornington Rd. Wfd G—4C 20
Mornington St. NW1—2F 61
Mornington Ter. NW1—2F 61
Mornington Wlk. Rich—4C 104
Morocco St. SE1
—2E 78 (5C 148)

Morpeth Gro. E9—1K 63
Morpeth Rd. E9—1K 63
Morpeth St. E2—3K 63 (1M 143)
Morpeth Ter. SW1
    —3G 77 (7L 145)
Morpeth Wlk. N17—7C 18
Morrab Gdns. Ilf—3K 51
Morrell Clo. Barn—3F 5
Morris Av. E12—5D 50
Morris Gdns. SW18—7J 91
Morrish Rd. SW2—7J 93
Morrison Av. N17—3E 30
Morrison Rd. Bark—2E 68
Morrison St. SW11—3E 92
Morris Pl. N4—2A 46
Morris Rd. E14—5D 64
Morris Rd. E15—4G 49
Morris Rd. Dag—2F 53
Morris Rd. Iswth—3K 87
Morris St. E1—6H 63 (8K 143)
Morse Clo. E13—3J 65
Morshead Rd. W9—3J 59
Morston Gdns. SE9—4D 114
Morten Clo. SW4—6H 93
Morteyne Rd. N17—1D 30
Mortham St. E15—1G 65
Mortimer Av. E17—2H 33
Mortimer Clo. NW2—2H 43
Mortimer Clo. SW16—2H 109
Mortimer Cres. NW6—1K 59
Mortimer Dri. Enf—5K 7
Mortimer Mkt. WC1
    —4G 61 (4M 139)
Mortimer Pl. NW6—1K 59
Mortimer Rd. E6—3D 66
Mortimer Rd. N1—7E 46
Mortimer Rd. NW10—3E 58
Mortimer Rd. W13—6C 56
Mortimer Rd. Eri—6K 85
Mortimer Rd. Mitc—1D 122
Mortimer Sq. W11—7F 59
Mortimer St. W1
    —5G 61 (6L 139)
Mortimer Ter. NW5—4F 45
Mortlake Clo. Croy—3J 133
Mortlake High St. SW14—3K 89
Mortlake Rd. E16—6K 65
Mortlake Rd. Ilf—4G 51
Mortlake Rd. Rich—7G 73
Mortlock Clo. SE15—1H 95
Mortlock Ct. E12—4B 50
Morton Cres. N14—4C 16
Morton Gdns. Wall—5G 133
Morton M. SW5—4K 75
Morton Pl. SE1—3A 78 (7G 147)
Morton Rd. E15—7H 49
Morton Rd. N1—7C 46
Morton Rd. Mord—5B 122
Morton Way. N14—3B 16
Morvale Clo. Belv—4F 85
Morval Rd. SW2—5A 94
Morven Rd. SW17—3D 108
Morville St. E3—2C 64
Morwell St. WC1
    —5H 61 (6A 140)
Moscow Pl. W2—7K 59
Moscow Rd. W2—7J 59
Moselle Av. N22—2A 30
Moselle Clo. N8—3K 29
Moselle St. N17—7A 18
Mossborough Clo. N12—6E 14
Mossbury Rd. SW11—3C 92
Moss Clo. E1—5G 63 (5H 143)
Moss Clo. Pinn—2D 22
Mossdown Clo. Belv—4G 85
Mossford Ct. Ilf—3F 35
Mossford Grn. Ilf—3F 35
Mossford La. Ilf—2F 35
Mossford St. E3—4B 64
Moss Gdns. S Croy—7K 135
Moss Hall Ct. N12—6E 14
Moss Hall Cres. N12—6E 14
Moss Hall Gro. N12—6E 14
Mossington Gdns. SE16
    —4J 79 (9L 149)
Moss La. Pinn—1C 22
Mosslea Rd. SE20—6J 111

Mosslea Rd. Brom—5B 128
Mossop St. SW3
    —4C 76 (8D 144)
Moss Rd. Dag—7G 53
Mossville Gdns. Mord—3H 121
Mostyn Av. Wemb—5F 41
Mostyn Gdns. NW10—3F 59
Mostyn Gro. E3—2C 64
Mostyn Rd. SW9—1A 94
Mostyn Rd. SW19—1H 121
Mostyn Rd. Edgw—7F 13
Mosul Way. Brom—6C 128
Motcomb St. SW1
    —3E 76 (6G 145)
Motley St. SW8—2G 93
Motspur Pk. N Mald—6B 120
Mottingham Gdns. SE9—1B 114
Mottingham La.—1A 114
  SE12 2-48
  SE9 remainder
Mottingham Rd. N9—6E 8
Mottingham Rd. SE9—2C 114
Mottisfont Rd. SE2—3A 84
Mott St. E4 & Lou—1K 9
Moulins Rd. E9—7K 47
Moulton Av. Houn—2C 86
Moundfield Rd. N16—6G 31
Mound, The. SE9—3E 114
Mountacre Clo. SE26—4G 111
Mt. Adon Pk. SE22—7G 95
Mountague Pl. E14—7E 64
Mt. Angelus Rd. SW15—7B 90
Mt. Ararat Rd. Rich—5E 88
Mt. Ash Rd. SE26—3H 111
Mount Av. E4—3H 19
Mount Av. W5—5C 56
Mount Av. S'hall—6E 54
Mountbatten Clo. SE18—6J 83
Mountbatten Clo. SE19—5E 110
Mountbatten M. SW18—7A 92
Mountbel Rd. Stan—2A 24
Mount Clo. W5—5C 56
Mount Clo. Barn—4K 5
Mount Clo. Brom—1C 128
Mount Clo. Cars—7E 132
Mountcombe Clo. Surb—7E 118
Mount Ct. SW15—3G 91
Mount Ct. W Wick—2G 137
Mt. Culver Av. Sidc—6D 116
Mount Dri. Bexh—5E 100
Mount Dri. Harr—5D 22
Mount Dri. Wemb—2J 41
Mountearl Gdns. SW16—3K 109
Mt. Echo Av. E4—1J 19
Mt. Echo Dri. E4—1J 19
Mt. Ephraim La. SW16—3H 109
Mt. Ephraim Rd. SW16—3H 109
Mountfield Rd. E6—2E 66
Mountfield Rd. N3—3H 27
  (in two parts)
Mountfield Rd. W5—6D 56
Mountford St. E1
    —6G 63 (7G 143)
Mountfort Cres. N1—7A 46
Mountfort Ter. N1—7A 46
Mount Gdns. SE26—3H 111
Mount Gro. Edgw—3D 12
Mountgrove Rd. N5—3C 46
Mounthurst Rd. Brom—7H 127
Mountington Pk. Clo. Harr
    —6D 24
Mountjoy Clo. SE2—2B 84
Mt. Mills. EC1—3B 62 (2K 141)
Mt. Nod Rd. SW16—3K 109
Mount Pk. Cars—7E 132
Mount Pk. Av. Harr—2H 39
Mount Pk. Av. S Croy—7C 134
Mount Pk. Cres. W5—6D 56
Mount Pk. Rd. W5—5D 56
Mount Pk. Rd. Harr—3H 39
Mt. Pleasant. SE27—4C 110
Mt. Pleasant. WC1
    —4A 62 (4G 141)
Mt. Pleasant. Barn—4J 5
Mt. Pleasant. Ruis—2A 38
Mt. Pleasant. Wemb—1E 56
Mt. Pleasant Cres. N4—7K 29

Mt. Pleasant Hill. E5—2J 47
Mt. Pleasant La. E5—2H 47
Mt. Pleasant Rd. E17—2A 32
Mt. Pleasant Rd. N17—2E 30
Mt. Pleasant Rd. NW10—7E 42
Mt. Pleasant Rd. SE13—6D 96
Mt. Pleasant Rd. W5—4C 56
Mt. Pleasant Rd. N Mald
    —3J 119
Mt. Pleasant Vs. N4—7K 29
Mt. Pleasant Wlk. Bex—5J 101
Mount Rd. NW2—3E 42
Mount Rd. NW4—6C 26
Mount Rd. SW19—2J 107
Mount Rd. Barn—5H 5
Mount Rd. Bexh—5D 100
Mount Rd. Dag—1F 53
Mount Rd. Felt—3C 102
Mount Rd. Ilf—5F 51
Mount Rd. Mitc—2B 122
Mount Rd. N Mald—3K 119
Mount Row. W1—7F 61 (1J 145)
Mountsfield Ct. SE13—6F 97
Mountside. Stan—1A 24
Mounts Pond Rd. SE3—2F 97
  (in two parts)
Mount Sq., The. NW3—3A 44
Mt. Stewart Av. Harr—7D 24
Mount St. W1—7E 60 (1G 145)
Mount Ter. E1—5H 63 (6J 143)
Mount, The. N20—2F 15
Mount, The. NW3—4A 44
Mount, The. W3—1J 73
Mount, The. N Mald—3B 120
Mount, The. Wemb—2J 41
Mount, The. Wor Pk—4D 130
Mt. Vernon. NW3—4A 44
Mount View. NW7—3E 12
Mount View. W5—4D 56
Mount View. Enf—1E 6
Mountview Ct. N15—4B 30
Mt. View Rd. E4—7K 9
Mt. View Rd. N4—7J 29
Mt. View Rd. NW9—5K 25
Mountview Rd. Orp—7K 129
Mount Vs. SE27—3B 110
Mount Way. Cars—7E 132
Movers La. Bark—1H 67
Mowatt Clo. N19—2H 45
Mowbray Ct. SE19—1F 125
Mowbray Pde. Edgw—4B 12
Mowbray Rd. SE19—1F 125
Mowbray Rd. Barn—5F 5
Mowbray Rd. Edgw—4B 12
Mowbray Rd. Rich—3C 104
Mowbrays Clo. Romf—1J 37
Mowbrays Rd. Romf—2J 37
Mowlem St. E2—2H 63
Mowlem Trading Est. N17
    —7D 18
Mowll St. SW9—7A 78
Moxon Clo. E13—2H 65
Moxon St. W1—5E 60 (6H 139)
Moxon St. Barn—3C 4
Moye Clo. E2—2G 63
Moyers Rd. E10—7E 32
Moylan Rd. W6—6G 75
Moyne Pl. NW10—2G 57
Moyser Rd. SW16—5F 109
Mozart St. W10—3H 59
Muchelney Rd. Mord—6A 122
Mudlarks Way. SE10 & SE7
    —3H 81
Muggeridge Rd. Dag—4H 53
Muirdown Av. SW14—4K 89
Muirfield. W3—6A 58
Muirkirk Rd. SE6—1E 112
Muir Rd. E5—4G 47
Muir St. E16—1C 82
  (in two parts)
Mulberry Business Centre.
    SE16—2K 79 (5M 149)
Mulberry Business Pk. SE16
    —2K 79
Mulberry Clo. E4—2H 19
Mulberry Clo. NW3—4B 44

Mulberry Clo. NW4—3E 26
Mulberry Clo. SW16—4G 109
Mulberry Clo. Barn—4G 5
Mulberry Clo. N'holt—2C 54
Mulberry Ct. Bark—7K 51
Mulberry Ct. Surb—7D 118
Mulberry Cres. Bren—7C 72
Mulberry La. Croy—1F 135
Mulberry M. Wall—6G 133
Mulberry Pl. W6—5C 74
Mulberry St. E1—6G 63 (7G 143)
Mulberry Wlk. SW3—6B 76
Mulberry Way. E18—2K 33
Mulberry Way. Belv—2J 85
Mulberry Way. Ilf—4G 35
Mulgrave Rd. NW10—4B 42
Mulgrave Rd. SW6—6H 75
Mulgrave Rd. W5—4D 56
Mulgrave Rd. Croy—3D 134
Mulgrave Rd. Harr—2A 40
Mulgrave Rd. Sutt—7H 131
Mulholland Clo. Mitc—2F 123
Mulkern Rd. N19—1H 45
Muller Rd. SW4—6H 93
Mullet Gdns. E2—3G 63 (1H 143)
Mullins Path. SW14—3K 89
Mullion Clo. Harr—1F 23
Mulready St. NW8
    —4C 60 (4C 138)
Multi Way. W3—2A 74
Multon Rd. SW18—7B 92
Mulvaney Way. SE1
    —2D 78 (5B 148)
Mumford Ct. EC2
    —6C 62 (7M 141)
Mumford Rd. SE24—5B 94
Muncaster Rd. SW11—5D 92
Muncies M. SE6—2E 112
Mundania Rd. SE22—6H 95
Munday Rd. E16—7J 65
Munden St. W14—4G 75
Mundford Rd. E5—2J 47
Mundon Gdns. Ilf—1H 51
Mund St. W14—5H 75
Mundy St. N1—3E 62 (1C 142)
Mungo Pk. Clo. Bush, Wat
    —2B 10
Munnings Gdns. Iswth—5H 87
Munro Dri. N11—6B 16
Munro M. W10—5G 59
Munro Ter. SW10—6B 76
Munster Av. Houn—5C 86
Munster Gdns. N13—4G 17
Munster Rd. SW6—7G 75
Munster Rd. Tedd—6C 104
Munster Sq. NW1
    —4F 61 (3K 139)
Munton Rd. SE17
    —4C 78 (8M 147)
Murchison Av. Bex—1D 116
Murchison Rd. E10—2E 48
Murdock Clo. E16—6H 65
Murdock St. SE15—6H 79
Murfett Clo. SW19—2G 107
Muriel St. N1—2K 61
  (in two parts)
Murillo Rd. SE13—4F 97
Murphy St. SE1—2A 78 (5G 147)
Murray Av. Brom—3K 127
Murray Av. Houn—5F 87
Murray Ct. Twic—1H 103
Murray Cres. Pinn—1B 22
Murray Gro. N1—2C 62 (1M 141)
Murray M. NW1—7H 45
Murray Rd. SW19—6F 107
Murray Rd. W5—4C 72
Murray Rd. Rich—2C 104
Murray Sq. E16—6J 65
Murray St. NW1—7H 45
Murray Ter. NW3—4B 44
Mursell Est. SW8—1K 93
Musard Rd. W6—6G 75
Musbury St. E1—6J 63 (7M 143)
Muscatel Pl. SE5—1E 94
Muschamp Rd. SE15—3F 95
Muschamp Rd. Cars—2C 132

Muscovy St. EC3
—7E 62 (9D 142)
Museum Pas. E2
—3J 63 (1L 143)
Museum St. WC1
—5J 61 (6C 140)
Musgrave Clo. Barn—1F 5
Musgrave Cres. SW6—1J 91
Musgrave Rd. Iswth—1K 87
Musgrove St. SE14—1K 95
Musjid Rd. SW11—2B 92
Musquash Way. Houn—2A 86
Muston Rd. E5—2H 47
Mustow Pl. SW6—2H 91
Muswell Av. N10—1F 29
Muswell Hill. N10—3F 29
Muswell Hill B'way. N10—3F 29
Muswell Hill Pl. N10—4F 29
Muswell Hill Rd.—6E 28
N6 1 & 2-40
N10 remainder
Muswell M. N10—3F 29
Muswell Rd. N10—3F 29
Mutrix Rd. NW6—1J 59
Mutton Pl. NW1—6E 44
Muybridge Rd. N Mald—2J 119
Myatt Rd. SW9—1B 94
Mycenae Rd. SE3—7J 81
Myddelton Av. Enf—1K 7
Myddelton Clo. Enf—1A 8
Myddelton Gdns. N21—7H 7
Myddelton Pk. N20—3G 15
Myddelton Pas. EC1
—3A 62 (1H 141)
Myddelton Rd. N8—4J 29
Myddelton Sq. EC1
—3A 62 (1H 141)
Myddelton St. EC1
—3A 62 (2H 141)
Myddleton Rd. N22—7D 16
Mylis Clo. SE26—4H 111
Mylne St. EC1—3A 62 (1H 141)
Myra St. SE2—4A 84
Myrdle St. E1—5G 63 (6H 143)
Myrna Clo. Mitc—7C 108
Myron Pl. SE13—3E 96
Myrtle Clo. Barn—1J 15
Myrtledene Rd. SE2—5A 84
Myrtle Gdns. W7—1J 71
Myrtle Gro. Enf—1J 7
Myrtle Gro. N Mald—2J 119
Myrtle Rd. E6—1C 66
Myrtle Rd. E17—6A 32
Myrtle Rd. N13—3H 17
Myrtle Rd. W3—1J 73
Myrtle Rd. Croy—3C 136
Myrtle Rd. Hmptn—6G 103
Myrtle Rd. Houn—2G 87
Myrtle Rd. Ilf—2F 51
Myrtle Rd. Sutt—5A 132
Myrtle Wlk. N1—2E 62 (1C 142)
Mysore Rd. SW11—4D 92
Myton Rd. SE21—3D 110

Nadine St. SE7—5A 82
Nagle Clo. E17—2F 33
Nags Head La. Well—3B 100
Nags Head Rd. Enf—4D 8
Nairne Gro. SE24—5D 94
Nairn Rd. Ruis—6A 38
Nairn St. E14—5E 64
Naish Ct. N1—1J 61
Naldera Gdns. SE3—6J 81
Nallhead Rd. Felt—5A 102
Namton Dri. T Hth—4K 123
Nan Clark's La. NW7—2G 13
Nankin St. E14—6C 64
Nansen Rd. SW11—3E 92
Nansen Village. N12—4E 14
Nantes Clo. SW18—4A 92
Nantes Pas. E1—5F 63 (5E 142)
Nant Rd. NW2—2H 43
Nant St. E2—3H 63 (1K 143)
Napier Av. E14—5C 80
Napier Av. SW6—3H 91
Napier Clo. SE8—7B 80

Napier Clo. W14—3H 75
Napier Gro. N1—2C 62
Napier Pl. W14—3H 75
Napier Rd. E6—1E 66
Napier Rd. E11—4G 49
Napier Rd. E15—2G 65
Napier Rd. N17—3E 30
Napier Rd. NW10—3D 58
Napier Rd. SE25—4H 125
Napier Rd. W14—3H 75
Napier Rd. Belv—4F 85
Napier Rd. Brom—4K 127
Napier Rd. Enf—5E 8
Napier Rd. Iswth—4A 88
Napier Rd. S Croy—7D 134
Napier Rd. Wemb—6D 40
Napier Ter. N1—7B 46
Napoleon Rd. E5—3H 47
Napoleon Rd. Twic—7B 88
Napton Clo. Hay—4C 54
Narbonne Av. SW4—5G 93
Narborough St. SW6—2K 91
Narcissus Rd. NW6—5J 43
Naresby Fold. Stan—6H 11
Narford Rd. E5—3G 47
Narrow St. E14—7A 64
Narrow St. W3—1H 73
Narrow Way. Brom—6C 128
Nascot St. W12—6E 58
Naseby Clo. NW6—7A 44
Naseby Clo. Iswth—1J 87
Naseby Rd. SE19—6D 110
Naseby Rd. Dag—3G 53
Naseby Rd. Ilf—1D 34
Nash Grn. Brom—6J 113
Nash La. Kes—7J 137
Nash Rd. N9—2D 18
Nash Rd. SE4—5A 96
Nash Rd. Romf—4D 36
Nash St. NW1—3F 61 (1K 139)
Nasmyth St. W6—3D 74
Nassau Path. SE28—1C 84
Nassau Rd. SW13—1B 90
Nassau St. W1—5G 61 (6L 139)
Nassington Rd. NW3—4D 44
Natal Rd. N11—6D 16
Natal Rd. NW6—6H 109
Natal Rd. Ilf—4F 51
Natal Rd. T Hth—3D 124
Nathaniel Clo. E1
—5F 63 (6F 142)
Nathans Rd. Wemb—1C 40
Nathan Way. SE28, Eri & Belv
—4J 83
Nation Way. E4—1K 19
Naval Row. E14—7E 64
Naval Wlk. Brom—2J 127
Navarino Gro. E8—6G 47
Navarino Rd. E8—6G 47
Navarre Rd. E6—2C 66
Navarre St. E2—4F 63 (3E 142)
Navenby Wlk. E3—4C 64
Navestock Clo. E4—3K 19
Navestock Cres. Wfd G—7F 21
Navy St. SW4—3H 93
Naylor Gro. Enf—5E 8
Naylor Rd. N20—2F 15
Naylor Rd. SE15—7H 79
Nazrul St. E2—3F 63 (1E 142)
Neal Av. S'hall—4D 54
Nealden St. SW9—3K 93
Neale Clo. N2—3A 28
Neal St. WC2—6J 61 (8C 140)
Neal's Yd. WC2—6J 61 (8C 140)
Near Acre. NW9—1B 26
Neasden Clo. NW10—5A 42
Neasden La. NW10—4A 42
(in two parts)
Neasden La. N. NW10—3K 41
Neasham Rd. Dag—5B 52
Neate St. SE5—6E 78
Neath Gdns. Mord—6A 122
Neathouse Pl. SW1
—4G 77 (8L 145)
Neatscourt Rd. E6—5B 66
Nebraska St. SE1
—2D 78 (5A 148)

Neckinger. SE1—3F 79 (6F 148)
Neckinger St. SE1
—2F 79 (5F 148)
Nectarine Way. SE13—2D 96
Needham Rd. W11—6J 59
Needham Ter. NW2—3F 43
Needleman St. SE16
—2K 79 (5M 149)
Neeld Cres. NW4—5D 26
Neeld Cres. Wemb—5G 41
Nelgarde Rd. SE6—7C 96
Nella Rd. W6—6F 75
Nelldale Rd. SE16
—4J 79 (8L 149)
Nello James Gdns. SE27
—4D 110
Nelson Clo. Croy—1B 134
Nelson Clo. Romf—1H 37
Nelson Gdns. E2
—3G 63 (1H 141)
Nelson Gdns. Houn—6E 86
Nelson Gro. Rd. SW19—1A 122
Nelson Industrial Est. SW19
—1K 121
Nelson Mandela Clo. N10
—2E 28
Nelson Mandela Rd. SE3
—3A 98
Nelson Pas. EC1
—3C 62 (2M 141)
Nelson Pl. N1—2B 62 (1K 141)
Nelson Pl. W3—1H 73
Nelson Pl. Sidc—4A 116
Nelson Rd. E4—6J 19
Nelson Rd. E11—4J 33
Nelson Rd. N8—5K 29
Nelson Rd. N9—2C 18
Nelson Rd. N15—4E 30
Nelson Rd. SE10—6E 80
Nelson Rd. SW19—7A 108
Nelson Rd. Belv—5F 85
Nelson Rd. Brom—4A 128
Nelson Rd. Enf—6E 8
Nelson Rd. Harr—1J 39
Nelson Rd. Houn & Twic—6E 86
Nelson Rd. N Mald—5K 119
Nelson Rd. Sidc—4A 116
Nelson Rd. Stan—6H 11
Nelson Sq. SE1—2B 78 (4J 147)
Nelson's Row. SW4—4H 93
Nelson St. E1—6H 63 (7J 143)
Nelson St. E6—2D 66
(in two parts)
Nelson St. E16—7H 65
(in two parts)
Nelson Ter. N1—2B 62 (1K 141)
Nelson Wlk. SE16—1A 80
Nemoure Rd. W3—7J 57
Nene Gdns. Felt—2D 102
Nepaul Rd. SW11—3C 92
Nepean St. SW15—6C 90
Neptune Rd. Harr—6H 23
Neptune St. SE16
—3J 79 (6M 149)
Nesbit Clo. SE3—3G 97
Nesbit Rd. SE9—4B 98
Nesbitts All. Barn—3C 4
Nesbitt Sq. SE19—7E 110
Nesham St. E1—7G 63 (1G 149)
Ness St. SE16—3G 79 (6G 149)
Nesta Rd. Wfd G—6B 20
Nestor Av. N21—6G 7
Netheravon Rd. W7—1K 71
Netheravon Rd. N. W4—4B 74
Netheravon Rd. S. W4—5B 74
Netherbury Rd. W5—3D 72
Netherby Gdns. Enf—4D 6
Netherby Rd. SE23—7J 95
Nether Clo. N3—7D 14
Nethercourt Av. N3—6D 14
Netherfield Gdns. Bark—7H 51
Netherfield Rd. N12—5E 14
Netherfield Rd. SW17—3E 108
Netherford Rd. SW4—2G 93
Netherhall Gdns. NW3—6A 44
Netherhall Way. NW3—5A 44

Netherlands Rd. Barn & N20
—6G 5
Netherleigh Clo. N6—1G 45
Nether St.—1J 27
N12 1-175 & 2-124
N3 remainder
Netherton Gro. SW10—6A 76
Netherton Rd. N15—6D 30
Netherton Rd. Twic—5A 88
Netherwood. N2—2B 28
Netherwood Rd. W14—3F 75
Netherwood St. NW6—7H 43
Netley Clo. Croy—7E 136
Netley Clo. Sutt—5F 131
Netley Gdns. Mord—7A 122
Netley Rd. E17—5B 32
Netley Rd. Bren—6E 72
Netley Rd. Ilf—5H 35
Netley Rd. Mord—7A 122
Netley St. NW1—3G 61 (2L 139)
Nettleden Av. Wemb—6G 41
Nettlefold Pl. SE27—3B 110
Nettlestead Clo. Beck—7B 112
Nettleton Rd. SE14—1K 95
Nettlewood Rd. SW16—7H 109
Neuchatel Rd. SE6—2B 112
Nevada Clo. N Mald—4J 119
Nevada St. SE10—6E 80
Nevern Pl. SW5—4J 75
Nevern Rd. SW5—4J 75
Nevern Sq. SW5—4J 75
Neville Av. N Mald—1K 119
Neville Clo. E11—3H 49
Neville Clo. NW1
—2H 61 (1B 140)
Neville Clo. NW6—2H 59
Neville Clo. SE15—1G 95
Neville Clo. W3—2J 73
Neville Clo. Houn—2F 87
Neville Clo. Sidc—4K 115
Neville Dri. N2—6A 28
Neville Gdns. Dag—3D 52
Neville Gill Clo. SW18—6J 91
Neville Pl. N22—1K 29
Neville Rd. E7—7J 49
Neville Rd. NW6—2H 59
Neville Rd. W5—4D 56
Neville Rd. Croy—7D 124
Neville Rd. Dag—3D 52
Neville Rd. Ilf—1G 35
Neville Rd. King—2G 119
Neville Rd. Rich—3C 104
Nevilles Ct. NW2—3C 42
Neville St. SW7—5B 76 (9B 144)
Neville Ter. SW7
—5B 76 (9A 144)
Neville Wlk. Cars—7C 122
Nevill Rd. N16—4E 46
Nevin Dri. E4—1J 19
Nevis Rd. SW17—2E 108
Newark Cres. NW10—3K 57
Newark Rd. S Croy—6D 134
Newark St. E1—5H 63 (6J 143)
(in two parts)
Newark Way. NW4—4C 26
New Ash Clo. N2—3B 28
New Barn Rd. Swan—7K 117
New Barns Av. Mitc—4H 123
New Barn St. E13—4J 65
New Barns Way. Chig—3K 21
Newbolt Av. Sutt—5E 130
Newbolt Rd. Stan—5E 10
New Bond St. W1
—6F 61 (8J 139)
Newborough Grn. N Mald
—4K 119
New Brent St. NW4—5E 26
New Bri. St. EC4—6B 62 (8J 141)
New Broad St. EC2
—5E 62 (6C 142)
New B'way. W5—7D 56
Newburgh Rd. W3—1J 73
Newburgh St. W1
—6G 61 (8M 139)
New Burlington M. W1
—7G 61 (9L 139)

241

New Burlington Pl. W1
—7G 61 (9L 139)
New Burlington St. W1
—7G 61 (9L 139)
Newburn St. SE11
—5K 77 (9F 146)
Newbury Clo. N'holt—6D 38
Newbury Gdns. Eps—4B 130
Newbury M. NW5—6E 44
Newbury Rd. E4—6K 19
Newbury Rd. Brom—3J 127
Newbury Rd. Ilf—6J 35
Newbury St. EC1
—5C 62 (5L 141)
Newbury Way. N'holt—6C 38
New Butt La. SE8—7C 80
Newby Clo. Enf—2K 7
Newby St. E14—7E 64
Newby St. SW8—3F 93
New Caledonian Wharf. SE16
—3B 80
Newcastle Clo. EC4
—6B 62 (7J 141)
Newcastle Pl. W2
—5B 60 (5B 138)
Newcastle Row. EC1
—4A 62 (3H 141)
New Cavendish St. W1
—5E 60 (6H 139)
New Change. EC4
—6C 62 (8L 141)
New Chu. Rd. SE5—7D 78
(in two parts)
New City Rd. E13—3A 66
New Clo. SW19—3A 122
New Clo. Felt—5C 102
New College M. N1—7A 46
Newcombe Gdns. SW16
—4J 109
Newcombe Pk. NW7—5F 13
Newcombe Pk. Wemb—1F 57
Newcombe St. W8—1J 75
Newcomen Rd. E11—3H 49
Newcomen Rd. SW11—3B 92
Newcomen St. SE1
—2D 78 (4A 148)
New Compton St. WC2
—6H 61 (8B 140)
Newcourt St. NW8
—2C 60 (1C 138)
New Coventry St. W1
—7H 61 (1B 146)
New Cross Rd. SE14—7K 79
Newdales Clo. N9—2B 18
Newdene Av. N'holt—2B 54
Newell St. E14—6B 64
New End. NW3—3A 44
New End Sq. NW3—4B 44
Newent Clo. SE15—7E 78
Newent Clo. Cars—1D 132
New Farm Av. Brom—4J 127
New Fetter La. EC4
—6A 62 (7H 141)
Newfield Clo. Hmptn—7E 102
Newfield Rise. NW2—3D 42
New Forest La. Chig—6K 21
Newgale Gdns. Edgw—1F 25
Newgate. Croy—1C 134
Newgate Clo. Felt—3C 102
Newgate St. E4—3B 20
Newgate St. EC1
—6B 62 (7K 141)
New Goulston St. E1
—6F 63 (7E 142)
Newham's Row. SE1
—2E 78 (5D 148)
Newham Way—5H 65
E16 55-413
E6 remainder
Newhaven Gdns. SE9—4B 98
Newhaven Rd. SE25—5D 124
New Heston Rd. Houn—7D 70
Newhouse Av. Romf—3D 36
Newhouse Clo. N Mald—7A 120
Newhouse Wlk. Mord—7A 122
Newick Clo. Bex—6H 101
Newick Rd. E5—4H 47

Newing Grn. Brom—7B 114
Newington Barrow Way. N7
—3K 45
Newington Butts
—4B 78 (9K 147)
SE1 2-22
SE11 remainder
Newington Causeway. SE1
—3C 78 (7L 147)
Newington Grn. N1 & N16
—5D 46
Newington Grn. Rd. N1—5D 46
Newington Industrial Est. SE17
—4C 78 (9L 147)
New Inn B'way. EC2
—4E 62 (3D 142)
New Inn St. EC2—4E 62 (3D 142)
New Inn Yd. EC2
—4E 62 (3D 142)
New Kent Rd. SE1
—4C 78 (8M 147)
New Kings Rd. SW6—2H 91
New King St. SE8—6C 80
Newland Dri. Enf—1C 8
Newland Gdns. W13—2A 72
Newland Rd. N8—3J 29
Newlands Clo. Edgw—3K 11
Newlands Clo. S'hall—5C 70
Newlands Clo. Wemb—6C 40
Newlands Ct. SE9—6E 98
Newlands Pk. SE26—6J 111
Newlands Pl. Barn—5A 4
Newlands Quay. E1
—7J 63 (1L 149)
Newlands Rd. SW16—2J 123
Newlands Rd. Wfd G—2C 20
Newlands, The. Wall—7H 133
Newland St. E16—1C 82
Newlands Wood. Croy—7B 136
Newling Clo. E6—6D 66
New Lydenburgh St. SE7
—3A 82
New Lyndenburgh Commercial
Est. SE7—3A 82
Newlyn Gdns. Harr—7D 22
Newlyn Rd. N17—1F 31
Newlyn Rd. Barn—4C 4
Newlyn Rd. Well—2K 99
Newman Pas. W1
—5G 61 (6M 139)
Newman Rd. E13—3K 65
Newman Rd. E17—5K 31
Newman Rd. Brom—1J 127
Newman Rd. Croy—1K 133
Newmans La. Surb—6D 118
Newman's Row. WC2
—5K 61 (6F 140)
Newman St. W1
—5G 61 (6M 139)
Newman Yd. W1
—6H 61 (7A 140)
Newmarket Av. N'holt—5E 38
Newmarket Grn. SE9—7B 98
Newminster Rd. Mord—6A 122
New Mount St. E15—7F 49
Newnes Path. SW15—4D 90
Newnham Av. Ruis—1A 38
Newnham Clo. N'holt—6G 39
Newnham Clo. T Hth—2C 124
Newnham Gdns. N'holt—6G 39
Newnham M. N22—1A 30
Newnham Rd. N22—1K 29
Newnhams Clo. Brom—3D 128
Newnham Ter. SE1
—3A 78 (6G 147)
Newnham Way. Harr—5E 24
New North Pl. EC2
—4E 62 (3C 142)
New North Rd. N1
—7C 46 (1B 142)
New North St. WC1
—5K 61 (5E 140)
Newnton Clo. N4—7D 30
(in two parts)
New Oak Rd. N2—2B 28
New Orleans Wlk. N19—7H 29

New Oxford St. WC1
—6H 61 (7B 140)
New Pk. Av. N13—3H 17
New Pk. Clo. N'holt—6C 38
New Pk. Rd. SW2—1H 109
New Pl. Croy—6C 136
New Pl. Sq. SE16
—3H 79 (6J 149)
New Plaistow Rd. E15—1G 65
Newport Av. E13—4K 65
Newport Ct. WC2
—7H 61 (9B 140)
Newport Pl. WC2
—7H 61 (9B 140)
Newport Rd. E10—2E 48
Newport Rd. E17—4A 32
Newport Rd. SW13—1C 90
Newport St. SE11
—4K 77 (9E 146)
Newquay Cres. Harr—2C 38
Newquay Rd. SE6—2D 112
New Quebec St. W1
—6D 60 (8F 138)
New River Cres. N13—4G 17
New River Wlk. N1—6C 46
New Rd. E1—5H 63 (6J 143)
New Rd. E4—4J 19
New Rd. N8—5J 29
New Rd. N9—3B 18
New Rd. N17—1F 31
New Rd. N22—1C 30
New Rd. NW7—7B 14
(Bittacy Hill)
New Rd. SE2—4D 84
New Rd. Bren—6D 72
New Rd. Dag & Bans—2G 69
New Rd. Felt—5C 102
(Hanworth)
New Rd. Harr—4K 39
New Rd. Houn—4F 87
New Rd. Ilf—2J 51
New Rd. King—7G 105
New Rd. Mitc—1E 1322
New Rd. Rich—4C 104
New Rd. Well—2B 100
New Rochford St. NW5—5D 44
New Row. WC2—7J 61 (9C 140)
Newry Rd. Twic—5A 88
Newsam Av. N15—5D 30
New Southgate Industrial Est.
N11—5B 16
New Spring Gdns. Wlk. SE11
—5J 77
New Sq. WC2—6A 62 (7G 141)
Newstead Rd. SE12—7H 97
Newstead Wlk. Cars—7A 122
Newstead Way. SW19—4G 107
New St. EC2—5E 62 (6D 142)
New St. Hill. Brom—5K 113
New St. Sq. EC4
—6A 62 (7H 141)
Newton Av. N10—1E 28
Newton Av. W3—2J 73
Newton Gro. W4—4A 74
Newton Rd. E15—5F 49
Newton Rd. N15—5G 31
Newton Rd. NW2—4E 42
Newton Rd. SW19—7G 107
Newton Rd. W2—6K 59
Newton Rd. Harr—2J 23
Newton Rd. Iswth—2K 87
Newton Rd. Well—3A 100
Newton Rd. Wemb—7F 41
Newton St. WC2—6J 61 (7D 140)
Newton's Yd. SW18—5J 91
Newton Wlk. Edgw—1H 25
Newton Way. N18—5H 17
Newtown St. SW11—1F 93
(in two parts)
New Trinity Rd. N2—3B 28
New Union Clo. E14—3E 80
New Union St. EC2
—5D 62 (5A 142)
New Wanstead. E11—6H 33
New Way Rd. NW9—4A 26
New Wharf Rd. N1—2J 61
New Zealand Way. W12—7D 58

Niagara Av. W5—4C 72
Nibthwaite Rd. Harr—5J 23
Nicholas Clo. Gnfd—2F 55
Nicholas Gdns. W5—2D 72
Nicholas La. EC4
—7D 62 (9B 142)
Nicholas Rd. E1—4J 63 (4M 143)
Nicholas Rd. Croy—4J 133
Nicholas Rd. Dag—2F 53
Nicholay Rd. N19—1H 45
Nichol Clo. N14—1C 16
Nicholes Rd. Houn—4E 86
Nichol La. Brom—7J 113
Nichollsfield Wlk. N7—5K 45
Nicholl St. E2—1G 63
Nichols Grn. W5—5E 56
Nicholson Rd. Croy—1F 135
Nicholson St. SE1
—1B 78 (3J 147)
Nichol's Sq. E2—2F 63 (1E 142)
Nickelby Clo. SE28—6C 68
Nicola Clo. Harr—2H 23
Nicola Clo. S Croy—6C 134
Nicol Clo. Twic—6B 88
Nicoll Pl. NW4—6D 26
Nicoll Rd. NW10—1A 58
Nicolson Dri. Bush, Wat—2B 10
Nicosia Rd. SW18—7C 92
Niederwald Rd. SE26—4A 112
Nigel Clo. N'holt—1C 54
Nigel M. Ilf—4F 51
Nigel Rd. E7—5A 50
Nigel Rd. SE15—3G 95
Nigeria Rd. SE7—7B 82
Nightingale Clo. E4—5B 20
Nightingale Clo. W4—6J 73
Nightingale Clo. Cars—2E 132
Nightingale Clo. Pinn—5A 22
Nightingale Gro. SE13—5F 97
Nightingale La. E11—5K 33
Nightingale La. N8—4J 29
Nightingale La.—7D 92
SW4 1-25
SW12 remainder
Nightingale La. Brom—2A 128
Nightingale La. Rich—7E 88
Nightingale Pl. SE18—6E 82
Nightingale Rd. E5—3H 47
Nightingale Rd. N9—6D 8
Nightingale Rd. N22—7D 16
Nightingale Rd. NW10—2B 58
Nightingale Rd. W7—1K 71
Nightingale Rd. Cars—3D 132
Nightingale Rd. Hmptn—5E 102
Nightingale Rd. Orp—6G 129
Nightingale Rd. SW12—7E 92
Nightingale Vale. SE18—6E 82
Nightingale Wlk. SW4—6F 93
Nightingale Way. E6—5C 66
Nile Path. SE18—6E 82
Nile Rd. E13—2A 66
Nile St. N1—3D 62 (1A 142)
Nile Ter. SE15—5F 79
Nimegan Way. SE22—5E 94
Nimmo Dri. Bush, Wat—1C 10
Nimrod Clo. N'holt—3B 54
Nimrod Rd. SW16—6F 109
Nine Acres Clo. E12—5C 50
Nine Elms La. SW8—7G 77
Nineteenth Rd. Mitc—4J 123
Nithdale Rd. SE18—7F 83
Niton Clo. Barn—6A 4
Niton Rd. Rich—3G 89
Niton St. SW6—7F 75
Nobel Ct. Mitc—2B 122
Nobel Rd. N18—5D 18
Noble St. EC2—6C 62 (7L 141)
Noel Pk. Rd. N22—2A 30
Noel Rd. E6—4C 66
Noel Rd. N1—2B 62
Noel Rd. W3—7G 57
Noel Sq. Dag—4C 52
Noel St. W1—6G 61 (8M 139)
Nolan Way. E5—4G 47
Nolton Pl. Edgw—1F 25

Northumberland Av. Enf—1C 8
Northumberland Av. Iswth
　—1K 87
Northumberland Av. Well
　—3J 99
Northumberland Clo. Eri—7J 85
Northumberland Gdns. N9
　—3A 18
Northumberland Gdns. Iswth
　—7A 72
Northumberland Gdns. Mitc
　—5H 123
Northumberland Gro. N17
　—7C 63
Northumberland Pk. N17
　—7B 18
Northumberland Pk. Eri—7J 85
Northumberland Pl. W2—6J 59
Northumberland Pl. Rich
　—5D 88
Northumberland Rd. E6—5C 66
Northumberland Rd. E17
　—7C 32
Northumberland Rd. Barn
　—6F 5
Northumberland Rd. Harr
　—5D 22
Northumberland Row. Twic
　—1J 103
Northumberland St. WC2
　—1J 77 (2C 146)
Northumberland Way. Eri
　—1J 101
Northumbria St. E14—6C 64
N. Verbena Gdns. W6—5C 74
North View. SW19—5E 106
North View. W5—4C 56
North View. Ilf—1A 36
North View. Pinn—7A 22
N. View Cres. NW10—4B 42
N. View Dri. Wfd G—2B 34
N. View Rd. N8—3H 29
North Vs. NW1—6H 45
North Wlk. Croy—6D 136
(in two parts)
North Way. N9—2E 18
North Way. N11—6B 16
North Way. NW9—3H 25
Northway. NW11—5K 27
Northway. Mord—4G 121
North Way. Pinn—4B 22
Northway. Wall—4G 133
Northway Cir. NW4—4E 12
Northway Cres. NW7—4E 12
Northway Gdns. NW11—5K 27
Northway Rd. SE5—3C 94
Northway Rd. Croy—6E 125
N. West Pier. E1—1H 79 (3J 149)
Northwest Pl. N1—2A 62
N. Wharf Rd. W2
　—5B 60 (6A 138)
Northwick Av. Harr—6A 24
Northwick Circ. Harr—6C 24
Northwick Clo. NW8
　—4B 60 (3A 138)
Northwick Pk. Rd. Harr—6K 23
Northwick Rd. Wemb—1D 56
Northwick Ter. NW8
　—4B 60 (3A 138)
Northwick Wlk. Harr—7K 23
Northwold Dri. Pinn—2A 22
Northwold Est. E5—2G 47
Northwold Rd.—2F 47
N16 1-67 & 2-34
E5 remainder
N. Wood Ct. SE25—3G 125
Northwood Gdns. N12—5G 15
Northwood Gdns. Gnfd—5K 39
Northwood Gdns. Ilf—4E 34
Northwood Pl. Eri—3F 85
Northwood Rd. N6—7F 29
Northwood Rd. SE23—1B 112
Northwood Rd. Cars—6E 132
Northwood Rd. T Hth—2C 124
Northwood Way. SE19—6D 110
N. Woolwich Rd. E16—1K 81
(in two parts)

N. Worple Way. SW14—3K 89
Norton Av. Surb—7H 119
Norton Clo. E4—5H 19
Norton Clo. Enf—2C 8
Norton Folgate. E1
　—5E 62 (5D 142)
Norton Gdns. SW16—2J 123
Norton Rd. E10—1B 48
Norton Rd. Dag—6K 53
Norton Rd. Wemb—6D 40
Norval Rd. Wemb—2B 40
Norway Ga. SE16—3A 80
Norway Pl. E14—6B 64
Norway St. SE10—6D 80
Norwich M. Ilf—1A 52
Norwich Pl. Bexh—4G 101
Norwich Rd. E7—5J 49
Norwich Rd. Dag—2G 69
Norwich Rd. Gnfd—1F 55
Norwich Rd. T Hth—3C 124
Norwich St. EC4
　—6A 62 (7G 141)
Norwich Wlk. Edgw—7D 12
Norwood Av. Romf—7K 37
Norwood Av. Wemb—1F 57
Norwood Clo. S'hall—4E 70
Norwood Dri. Harr—6E 22
Norwood Gdns. Hay—4A 54
Norwood Gdns. S'hall—4D 70
Norwood Grn. Rd. S'hall—4E 70
Norwood High St. SE27
　—3B 110
Norwood Pk. Rd. SE27—5C 110
Norwood Rd.—1B 110
SE24 1-339 & 2-150
SE27 remainder
Norwood Rd. S'hall—3C 70
Notley St. SE5—7D 78
Notson Rd. SE25—4H 125
Notting Barn Rd. W10—4F 59
Nottingham Av. E16—5A 66
Nottingham Ct. WC2
　—6J 61 (8C 140)
Nottingham Pl. W1
　—5E 60 (5G 139)
Nottingham Rd. E10—6E 32
Nottingham Rd. SW17—1D 108
Nottingham Rd. Iswth—2K 87
Nottingham Rd. S Croy—2K 87
Nottingham St. W1
　—5E 60 (5G 139)
Notting Hill Ga. W11—1J 75
Nova M. Sutt—1G 131
Novar Clo. Orp—7K 129
Nova Rd. Croy—7B 124
Novar Rd. SE9—1G 115
Novello St. SW6—1J 91
Nowell Rd. SW13—6C 74
Nower Hill. Pinn—4D 22
Noyna Rd. SW17—3D 108
Nuding Clo. SE13—3C 96
Nuffield Lodge. W6—6F 29
Nugent Rd. N19—1J 45
Nugent Rd. SE25—3F 125
Nugents Pk. Pinn—1C 22
Nugent Ter. NW8
　—2A 60 (1A 138)
Nuneaton Rd. Dag—7E 52
Nunhead Cres. SE15—3H 95
Nunhead Grn. SE15—3H 95
Nunhead Gro. SE15—3J 95
Nunhead La. SE15—3H 95
Nunnington Clo. SE9—3C 114
Nunns Rd. Enf—2H 7
Nupton Dri. Barn—6A 4
Nursery App. N12—6H 15
Nursery Av. N3—2A 28
Nursery Av. Bexh—3F 101
Nursery Av. Croy—2K 135
Nursery Clo. SW15—4F 91
Nursery Clo. Croy—2K 135
Nursery Clo. Enf—1E 8
Nursery Clo. Orp—7K 129
Nursery Clo. Romf—6D 36
Nursery Clo. Wfd G—5E 20
Nursery Ct. N17—7A 18
Nursery Gdns. Enf—1E 8

Nursery La. E7—6J 49
Nursery La. W10—5E 58
Nursery Rd. E9—6J 47
Nursery Rd. N2—1B 28
Nursery Rd. N14—7B 6
Nursery Rd. SW9—4K 93
Nursery Rd. SW19—2K 121
(Merton)
Nursery Rd. SW19—7G 107
(Wimbledon)
Nursery Rd. Sutt—4A 132
Nursery Rd. T Hth—4D 124
Nursery Row. Barn—3B 4
Nursery St. N17—7A 18
Nursery Wlk. NW4—3E 26
Nursery Wlk. Romf—7K 37
Nurstead Rd. Eri—7G 85
Nutbourne St. W10—3G 59
Nutbrook St. SE15—3G 95
Nutbrowne Rd. Dag—1F 69
Nutcroft Rd. SE15—7H 79
Nutfield Clo. N18—6B 18
Nutfield Clo. Cars—3C 132
Nutfield Gdns. Ilf—2A 52
Nutfield Gdns. N'holt—2A 54
Nutfield Rd. E15—4E 48
Nutfield Rd. NW2—3C 42
Nutfield Rd. SE22—4F 95
Nutfield Rd. T Hth—4B 124
Nutford Pl. W1—6D 60 (7E 138)
Nuthatch Gdns. SE28—2H 83
(in two parts)
Nuthurst Av. SW2—2K 109
Nutley Ter. NW3—6A 44
Nutmead Clo. Bex—1J 117
Nutmeg La. E14—6F 65
Nuttall St. N1—2E 62
Nutter La. E11—6A 34
Nutt Gro. Edgw—2J 11
Nutt St. SE15—7F 79
Nutwell St. SW17—5C 108
Nuxley Rd. Belv—6F 85
Nyanza St. SE18—6H 83
Nylands Av. Rich—2G 89
Nymans Gdns. SW20—3D 120
Nynehead St. SE14—7A 80
Nyon Gro. SE6—2B 112
Nyssia Clo. Wfd G—6J 21
Nyton Clo. N19—1J 45

Oak Av. N8—4J 29
Oak Av. N10—7A 16
Oak Av. N17—7J 17
Oak Av. Croy—2C 136
Oak Av. Enf—1E 6
Oak Av. Hmptn—5C 102
Oak Av. Houn—7B 70
Oak Bank. Croy—6E 136
Oakbank Gro. SE24—4C 94
Oakbrook Clo. Brom—4K 113
Oakbury Rd. SW6—2K 91
Oak Clo. N14—7A 6
Oak Clo. Sutt—2A 132
Oakcombe Clo. N Mald—1A 120
Oak Cottage Clo. SE6—1H 113
Oak Cotts. W7—2J 71
Oak Cres. E16—5G 65
Oakcroft Clo. Pinn—2A 22
Oakcroft Rd. SE13—2F 97
Oakdale. N14—1A 16
Oakdale Av. Harr—5E 24
Oakdale Rd. E7—7K 49
Oakdale Rd. E11—2F 49
Oakdale Rd. E18—2K 33
Oakdale Rd. N4—6C 30
Oakdale Rd. SE15—3J 95
Oakdale Rd. SW16—5J 109
Oakdale Rd. Eps—2A 130
Oakdale Way. Wall—7E 122
Oak Dene. SE15—1H 95
Oak Dene. W13—5B 56
Oakdene Av. Chst—5E 114
Oakdene Av. Eri—6J 85
Oakdene Av. Th Dit—7A 118
Oakdene Clo. Pinn—1D 22

Oakdene Dri. Surb—7J 119
Oakdene Pk. N3—7C 14
Oakdene Rd. Orp—5K 129
Oakden St. SE11
　—4A 78 (8H 147)
Oake Ct. SW15—5G 91
Oakenshaw Clo. Surb—7E 118
Oakes Clo. E6—6D 66
Oakeshott Av. N6—2E 44
Oakey La. SE1—3A 78 (6G 147)
Oakfield. E4—5J 19
Oakfield Av. Harr—3B 24
Oakfield Clo. N Mald—5B 120
Oakfield Ct. N8—7J 29
Oakfield Ct. NW11—7F 27
Oakfield Gdns. N18—4K 17
Oakfield Gdns. SE19—5F 111
(in two parts)
Oakfield Gdns. Beck—5D 126
Oakfield Gdns. Cars—1C 132
Oakfield Gdns. Gnfd—4H 55
Oakfield Rd. E6—1C 66
Oakfield Rd. E17—2A 32
Oakfield Rd. N3—1K 27
Oakfield Rd. N4—6A 30
Oakfield Rd. N14—2D 16
Oakfield Rd. SE20—7H 111
Oakfield Rd. SW19—3F 107
Oakfield Rd. Croy—1C 134
Oakfield Rd. Ilf—3F 51
Oakfield Rd. Th Dit—5A 118
Oakfields Rd. NW11—6G 27
Oakfield St. SW10—6A 76
Oakford Rd. NW5—4G 45
Oak Gdns. Croy—2C 136
Oak Gdns. Edgw—2H 25
Oak Gro. NW2—4G 43
Oak Gro. Ruis—7A 22
Oak Gro. W Wick—1E 136
Oak Gro. Rd. SE20—1J 125
Oak Hall Rd. E11—6K 33
Oakham Clo. SE6—2B 112
Oakhampton Rd. NW7—7A 14
Oak Hill. Surb—7E 118
Oak Hill. Wfd G—7A 20
Oakhill Av. NW3—4K 43
Oakhill Av. Pinn—2C 22
Oak Hill Clo. Wfd G—7A 20
Oakhill Ct. E11—6K 33
Oakhill Cres. Surb—7E 118
Oak Hill Cres. Wfd G—7A 20
Oakhill Dri. Surb—7E 118
Oak Hill Gdns. Wfd G—1G 33
Oakhill Gro. Surb—6E 118
Oak Hill Pk. NW3—4K 43
Oak Hill Pk. M. NW3—4A 44
Oakhill Path. Surb—6E 118
Oakhill Pl. SW15—5J 91
Oakhill Rd. SW15—5H 91
Oakhill Rd. SW16—1K 123
Oakhill Rd. Beck—2E 126
Oakhill Rd. Surb—6E 118
Oakhill Rd. Sutt—3K 131
Oak Hill Way. NW3—4K 43
Oakhouse Rd. Bexh—5G 101
Oakhurst Av. Barn—7H 5
Oakhurst Av. Bexh—7E 84
Oakhurst Clo. E17—4G 33
Oakhurst Clo. Tedd—5J 103
Oakhurst Gdns. E4—1C 20
Oakhurst Gdns. E17—4G 33
Oakhurst Gdns. Bexh—7E 84
Oakhurst Gro. SE22—4G 95
Oakington Av. Harr—7E 22
Oakington Av. Wemb—3F 41
Oakington Mnr. Dri. Wemb
　—5G 41
Oakington Rd. W9—4J 59
Oakington Way. N8—7J 29
Oaklands. N21—2E 16
Oaklands. Beck—1D 126
Oaklands Av. N9—6C 8
Oaklands Av. Iswth—6K 71
Oaklands Av. Sidc—7K 99
Oaklands Av. T Hth—4A 124
Oaklands Av. W Wick—3D 136

244

Oaklands Clo. Bexh—5F 101
Oaklands Clo. Orp—6J 129
Oaklands Clo. Wemb—5D 40
Oaklands Ct. Wemb—5D 40
Oaklands Dri. Twic—7G 87
Oaklands Est. SW4—6G 93
Oaklands Gro. W12—1C 74
Oaklands Pk. Av. Ilf—2G 51
Oaklands Pl. SW4—4G 93
Oaklands Rd. N20—7C 4
Oaklands Rd. NW2—4F 43
Oaklands Rd. SW14—3K 89
Oaklands Rd. W7—2K 71
Oaklands Rd. Bexh—4F 101
Oaklands Rd. Brom—7G 113
Oaklands Way. Wall—7H 133
Oakland Way. Eps—6A 130
Oak La. E14—7B 64
Oak La. N2—2B 28
Oak La. N11—6C 16
Oak La. Iswth—4J 87
Oak La. Twic—7A 88
Oak La. Wfd G—4C 20
Oakleafe Gdns. Ilf—3F 35
Oaklea Pas. King—3D 118
Oakleigh Av. N20—2G 15
Oakleigh Av. Edgw—2H 25
Oakleigh Clo. N20—3J 15
Oakleigh Ct. Edgw—2J 25
Oakleigh Cres. N20—3H 15
Oakleigh Gdns. N20—3H 15
Oakleigh Gdns. Edgw—5A 12
Oakleigh M. N20—1F 15
Oakleigh Pk. Av. Chst—1E 128
Oakleigh Pk. N. N20—1G 15
Oakleigh Pk. S. N20—1H 15
Oakleigh Rd. N. N20—2G 15
Oakleigh Rd. S. N11—3K 15
Oakleigh Way. Mitc—1F 123
Oakley Av. W5—7G 57
Oakley Av. Bark—7K 51
Oakley Av. Croy—4K 133
Oakley Clo. E4—3K 19
Oakley Clo. E6—6C 66
Oakley Clo. W7—7J 55
Oakley Clo. Iswth—1H 87
Oakley Cres. EC1
—2B 62 (1K 141)
Oakley Dri. SE9—1H 115
Oakley Gdns. N8—5K 29
Oakley Gdns. SW3—6C 76
Oakley Grange. Harr—3H 39
Oakley Pk. Bex—7C 100
Oakley Pl. SE1—5F 79
Oakley Rd. N1—7D 46
Oakley Rd. SE25—5H 125
Oakley Rd. Brom—7C 128
Oakley Rd. Harr—6J 23
Oakley Sq. NW1—2G 61
Oakley St. SW3—6C 76
Oakley Wlk. W6—6F 75
Oak Lodge. E11—6J 33
Oak Lodge Clo. Stan—5H 11
Oak Lodge Dri. W Wick—7D 126
Oakmead Av. Brom—6J 127
Oak Meade. Pinn—6A 10
Oakmead Gdns. Edgw—4E 12
Oakmead Rd. SW12—1F 109
Oakmead Rd. Croy—6H 123
Oakmede. Barn—4A 4
Oakmere Rd. SE2—6A 84
Oakmont Pl. Orp—7H 129
Oak Pk. Gdns. SW19—1F 107
Oak Pl. SW18—5K 91
Oakridge Dri. N2—3B 28
Oakridge Rd. Brom—4G 113
Oak Rise. Buck H—3G 21
Oak Rd. W5—7D 56
Oak Rd. Eri—7J 85
(Northumberland Heath)
Oak Rd. N Mald—2K 119
Oak Row. SW6—2G 123
Oaks Av. SE19—5E 110
Oaks Av. Felt—2C 102
Oaks Av. Romf—2J 37
Oaks Av. Wor Pk—3D 130
Oaksford Av. SE26—3H 111

Oaks Gro. E4—2B 20
Oakshade Rd. Brom—4F 113
Oakshaw Rd. SW18—7K 91
Oaks La. Croy—3J 135
Oaks La. Ilf—5J 35
Oaks Rd. Croy—5H 135
Oaks, The. N12—4E 14
Oaks, The. SE18—5G 83
Oaks, The. Wfd G—7B 20
Oak St. Romf—5J 37
Oaks Way. Cars—7D 132
Oakthorpe Pk. Est. N13—5H 17
Oakthorpe Rd. N13—5F 17
Oaktree Av. N13—3G 17
Oak Tree Clo. W5—6C 56
Oak Tree Clo. Stan—7H 11
Oak Tree Ct. N'holt—2B 54
Oak Tree Dell. NW9—5K 25
Oak Tree Dri. N20—1E 14
Oak Tree Gdns. Brom—5K 113
Oak Tree Rd. NW8
—3C 60 (2C 138)
Oakview Gdns. N2—4B 28
Oakview Gro. Croy—1A 136
Oakview Rd. SE6—5D 112
Oak Village. NW4—4E 44
Oak Way. N14—7A 6
Oakway. SW20—4E 120
Oak Way. W3—1A 74
Oakway. Brom—2F 127
Oak Way. Croy—6K 125
Oakway Clo. Bex—6E 100
Oakways. SE9—6F 99
Oakwood Av. N14—7C 6
Oakwood Av. Beck—2E 126
Oakwood Av. Brom—3K 127
Oakwood Av. Mitc—2B 122
Oakwood Av. S'hall—7E 54
Oakwood Clo. N14—6B 6
Oakwood Clo. Chst—6D 114
Oakwood Clo. Wfd G—6H 21
Oakwood Ct. W14—3H 75
Oakwood Cres. N21—6D 6
Oakwood Cres. Gnfd—6A 40
Oakwood Dri. SE19—6D 110
Oakwood Dri. Bexh—4J 101
Oakwood Dri. Edgw—6D 12
Oakwood Gdns. Ilf—2K 51
Oakwood Gdns. Sutt—2J 131
Oakwood La. W14—3H 75
Oakwood Pde. Enf—5A 8
Oakwood Pk. Rd. N14—6D 6
Oakwood Pl. Croy—6A 124
Oakwood Rd. NW11—5J 27
Oakwood Rd. SW20—1C 120
Oakwood Rd. Croy—6A 124
Oakwood View. N14—6C 6
Oakworth Rd. W10—5F 59
Oates Clo. Brom—3F 127
Oatfield Rd. Orp—7K 129
Oatland Rise. E17—2A 32
Oatlands Rd. Enf—1D 8
Oat La. EC2—6C 62 (7H 141)
Oban Rd. E13—3A 66
Oban Rd. SE25—4D 124
Oban St. E14—6F 65
Oberstein Rd. SW11—4B 92
Oborne Clo. SE24—5B 94
Observatory Gdns. W8—2J 75
Observatory Rd. SW14—4J 89
Occupation La. SE18—1F 99
Occupation La. W5—4D 72
Occupation Rd. SE17
—5C 78 (9L 147)
Occupation Rd. W13—2B 72
Ocean Est. E1—5A 64
(in two parts)
Ocean St. E1—5K 63
Ocean Wharf Development. E14
—2C 80
Ockendon Rd. N1—6D 46
Ockham Dri. Orp—7A 116
Ockley Rd. SW16—4J 109
Ockley Rd. Croy—7K 123
Octagon Arc. EC2
—5E 62 (6C 142)

Octavia Clo. Mitc—5C 122
Octavia Rd. Iswth—3J 87
Octavia St. SW11—1C 92
Octavia Way. SE28—7B 68
Octavius St. SE8—7C 80
Odessa Rd. E7—4H 49
Odessa Rd. NW10—2C 58
Odessa St. SE16—2B 80
Odger St. SW11—2D 92
Odhams Wlk. W1
—6J 61 (8D 140)
Offa's Mead. E9—4B 48
Offenham Rd. SE9—4D 114
Offerton Rd. SW4—3G 93
Offham Slope. N12—5C 14
Offley Rd. SW9—7A 78
Offord Clo. N17—6B 18
Offord Rd. N1—7K 45
Offord St. N1—7K 45
Ogilby St. SE18—4D 82
Oglander Rd. SE15—3F 95
Ogle St. W1—5G 61 (5L 139)
Oglethorpe Rd. Dag—3G 53
Ohio Rd. E13—4H 65
Oil Mill La. W6—5C 74
Okeburn Rd. SW17—5E 108
Okehampton Clo. N12—5G 15
Okehampton Cres. Well
—1B 100
Okehampton Rd. NW10—1E 58
Olaf St. W11—7F 59
Oldacre M. SW12—7F 93
Old Bailey. EC4—6B 62 (8K 141)
Old Barn Clo. Sutt—7G 131
Old Barn Way. Bexh—4K 101
Old Barrack Yd. SW1
—2E 76 (5G 145)
Old Barrowfield. E15—1G 65
Oldberry Rd. Edgw—6E 12
Old Bethnal Grn. Rd. E2
—3G 63 (1H 143)
Old Bexley La. Bex & Dart
—2K 117
Old Bond St. W1—7G 61 (1L 145)
Oldborough Rd. Wemb—3C 40
Old Brewer's Yd. WC2
—6J 61 (8C 140)
Old Brewery M. NW3—4B 44
Old Bri. Clo. N'holt—2E 54
Old Bri. St. King—2D 118
Old Broad St. EC2
—6D 62 (7B 142)
Old Bromley Rd. Brom—5F 113
Old Brompton Rd.
—5K 75 (9A 144)
SW7 1-125 & 2-146
SW5 remainder
Old Burlington St. W1
—7G 61 (1L 145)
Oldbury Pl. W1—5E 60 (5H 139)
Oldbury Rd. Enf—2B 8
Old Castle St. E1
—6F 63 (7E 142)
Old Cavendish St. W1
—6F 61 (8J 139)
Old Chelsea M. SW3—6B 76
Old Church Gdns. Romf—7K 37
Old Chu. La. NW9—2K 41
Old Chu. La. Gnfd—3A 56
Old Chu. La. Stan—5G 11
Oldchurch Rise. Romf—7K 37
Old Chu. Rd. E1—6K 63
Old Chu. Rd. E4—4H 19
Oldchurch Rd. Romf—7K 37
Old Chu. St. SW3—5B 76
Old Compton St. W1
—7H 61 (9A 140)
Old Cote Dri. Houn—6E 70
Old Ct. Pl. W8—2K 75
Old Deer Pk. Gdns. Rich—3E 88
Old Devonshire Rd. SW12
—7F 93
Old Dock Clo. Rich—6G 73
Old Dover Rd. SE3—7J 81
Oldenhurst Av. N12—7F 15
Old Farm Av. N14—7B 6
Old Farm Av. Sidc—1H 115

Old Farm Clo. Houn—4D 86
Old Farm Rd. N2—1B 28
Old Farm Rd. Hmptn—6D 102
Old Farm Rd. E. Sidc—2A 116
Old Farm Rd. W. Sidc—2K 115
Oldfield Clo. Brom—4D 128
Oldfield Clo. Gnfd—5J 39
Oldfield Clo. Stan—5F 11
Oldfield Farm Gdns. Gnfd
—1H 55
Oldfield Gro. SE16
—4K 79 (9M 143)
Oldfield La. N. Gnfd—1H 55
Oldfield La. S. Gnfd—3G 55
Oldfield M. N6—7G 29
Oldfield Rd. N16—3E 46
Oldfield Rd. NW10—7B 42
Oldfield Rd. SW19—6G 107
Oldfield Rd. W3—2B 74
Oldfield Rd. Bexh—2E 100
Oldfield Rd. Brom—4D 128
Oldfield Rd. Hmptn—7D 102
Oldfields Cir. N'holt—6G 39
Oldfields Rd. Sutt—3H 131
Old Fold Clo. Barn—1C 4
Old Fold La. Barn—1C 4
Old Fold View. Barn—4A 4
Old Ford Rd. E2—2J 63 (1L 143)
E2 1-211 & 2-232
E3 remainder
Old Forge Clo. Stan—4F 11
Old Forge M. W12—2D 74
Old Forge Rd. Enf—1A 8
Old Forge Way. Sidc—4B 116
Old Gloucester St. WC1
—5J 61 (5D 140)
Old Hall Clo. Pinn—1C 22
Old Hall Dri. Pinn—1C 22
Oldhams Ter. W3—2J 73
Oldhill St. N16—1G 47
Old Homesdale Rd. Brom
—4A 128
Old Ho. Clo. SW19—5G 107
Old Ho. Gdns. Twic—6C 88
Old Jamaica Rd. SE16
—3G 79 (6G 149)
Old James St. SE15—3H 95
Old Jewry. EC2—6D 62 (8A 142)
Old Kenton La. NW9—5H 25
Old Kent Rd. SE1
—4E 78 (9D 148)
Old Lodge Pl. Twic—6B 88
Old Lodge Way. Stan—5F 11
Old Maidstone Rd. Sidc—7F 117
Old Malden La. Wor Pk—2A 130
Old Mnr. Dri. Iswth—6G 87
Old Mnr. Way. SE9—5D 114
Old Mnr. Way. Bexh—2K 101
Old Mnr. Yd. SW5—4K 75
Old Marylebone Rd. NW1
—5C 60 (6D 138)
Old. M. Harr—5J 23
Old Mill Clo. E18—3A 34
Old Mill Rd. SE18—6H 83
Old Montague St. E1
—5G 63 (6G 143)
Old Nichol St. E2
—4F 63 (3E 142)
Old Oak Common La.—5A 58
W3 51-189 & 82-240
NW10 remainder
Old Oak La. NW10—3A 58
Old Oak Rd. W3—7B 58
Old Orchard, The. NW3—4D 44
Old Pal. La. Rich—5C 88
Old Pal. Rd. Croy—3C 134
Old Pal. Ter. Rich—5D 88
Old Pal. Yd. SW1
—3J 77 (6C 146)
Old Pal. Yd. Rich—5D 88
Old Paradise St. SE11
—4K 77 (8E 146)
Old Pk. Av. SW12—6E 92
Old Pk. Av. Enf—4H 7
Old Pk. Gro. Enf—4H 7
Old Pk. La. W1—1F 77 (3J 145)

Old Pk. M. Houn—7D 70
Old Pk. Ridings. N21—6G 7
Old Pk. Rd. N13—4E 16
Old Pk. Rd. SE2—5A 84
Old Pk. Rd. Enf—3G 7
Old Pk. Rd. S. Enf—4G 7
Old Pk. View. Enf—3F 7
Old Perry St. Chst—6J 115
Old Pye St. SW1
    —3H 77 (6A 146)
Old Quebec St. W1
    —6D 60 (8F 138)
Old Queen St. SW1
    —2H 77 (5B 146)
Old Rectory Gdns. Edgw—6B 12
Old Redding. Harr—5A 10
Oldridge Rd. SW12—7E 92
Old Rd. SE13—4G 97
Old Rd. Dart—5K 101
Old Rd. Enf—1D 8
Old Ruislip Rd. N'holt—2A 54
  (in two parts)
Old School Clo. SW19—2J 121
Old Schools La. Eps—7B 130
Old Seacoal La. EC4
    —6B 62 (7J 141)
Old Sq. WC2—6A 62 (7G 141)
Oldstead Rd. Brom—4F 113
Old St. E13—2A 66
Old St. EC1—4C 62 (3L 141)
Old Swan Yd. Cars—4D 132
Old Town. SW4—3G 93
Old Town. Croy—3B 134
Old Woolwich Rd. SE10—6F 81
Old York Rd. SW18—5K 91
O'Leary Sq. E1—5J 63 (5L 143)
Olga St. E3—2A 64
Olinda Rd. N16—6F 31
Oliphant St. W10—3F 59
Oliver Av. SE25—3F 125
Oliver Clo. E10—2D 48
Oliver Clo. W4—6H 73
Oliver Ct. SE18—4G 83
Oliver Gdns. E6—5C 66
Oliver Goldsmith Est. SE15
    —1G 95
Oliver Gro. SE25—4F 125
Olive Rd. E13—3A 66
Olive Rd. NW2—4E 42
Olive Rd. SW19—7A 108
Olive Rd. W5—3D 72
Oliver Rd. E10—2D 48
Oliver Rd. E17—5E 32
Oliver Rd. N Mald—2J 119
Oliver Rd. Sutt—4B 132
Olivers Yd. EC1—4D 62 (3B 142)
Olive St. Romf—5K 37
Olivette St. SW15—4F 91
Ollerton Grn. E3—1B 64
Ollerton Rd. N11—5C 16
Olley Clo. Wall—7J 133
Ollgar Clo. W12—1B 74
Olliffe St. E14—3E 80
Olmar St. SE1—6G 79
Olney Rd. SE17—6B 78
Olron Cres. Bexh—5D 100
Olven Rd. SE18—6G 83
Olveston Wlk. Cars—6B 122
Olwen M. Pinn—2B 22
Olyffe Av. Well—2A 100
Olyffe Dri. Beck—1E 126
Olympia M. W2—7K 59
Olympia Way. W14—3G 75
Olympic Industrial Est. Wemb
    —4H 41
Olympic Way. Gnfd—1G 55
Olympic Way. Wemb—3G 41
Olympus Sq. E5—3G 47
Oman Av. NW2—4D 42
O'Meara St. SE1
    —1C 78 (3M 147)
Omega St. SE14—1C 96
Ommaney Rd. SE14—1K 95
Ondine Rd. SE15—4F 95
Onega Ga. SE16—3A 80

O'Neill Path. SE18—6E 82
One Tree Clo. SE23—4B 95
Ongar Clo. Romf—5C 36
Ongar Rd. SW6—6J 75
Onra Rd. E17—7C 32
Onslow Av. Rich—5E 88
Onslow Clo. E4—2K 19
Onslow Cres. Chst—1F 129
Onslow Dri. Sidc—2D 116
Onslow Gdns. E18—3K 33
Onslow Gdns. N10—5F 29
Onslow Gdns. N21—5F 7
Onslow Gdns. SW7
    —5B 76 (9A 144)
Onslow Gdns. Wall—6G 133
Onslow M. E. SW7
    —4B 76 (9A 144)
Onslow M. W. SW7
    —4B 76 (9A 144)
Onslow Rd. Croy—7A 124
Onslow Rd. N Mald—4C 120
Onslow Rd. Rich—5E 88
Onslow Sq. SW7
    —4B 76 (9B 144)
Onslow St. EC1—5B 78 (9J 147)
Ontario St. SE1—3B 78 (7K 147)
Opal Clo. E16—6B 66
Opal St. SE11—5B 78 (9J 147)
Opel M. Ilf—2F 51
Openshaw Rd. SE2—4B 84
Openview. SW18—1A 108
Ophir Ter. SE15—1G 95
Opossum Way. Houn—3A 86
Oppidans M. NW3—7D 44
Oppidans Rd. NW3—7D 44
Orange Ct. E1—1G 79 (3H 149)
Orange Hill Rd. Edgw—7D 12
Orange Pl. SE16
    —3J 79 (7M 149)
Orangery La. SE9—5D 98
Orangery, The. Rich—2C 104
Orange St. WC2—7H 61 (1B 146)
Orbain Rd. SW6—7G 75
Orbel St. SW11—1C 92
Orb St. SE17—4D 78 (9A 148)
Orchard Av. N3—3J 27
Orchard Av. N14—7B 6
Orchard Av. N20—2G 15
Orchard Av. Belv—6E 84
Orchard Av. Croy—1A 136
Orchard Av. Houn—7C 70
Orchard Av. Mitc—1E 132
Orchard Av. N Mald—3A 120
Orchard Av. S'hall—1D 70
Orchard Clo. E4—4H 19
Orchard Clo. E11—4K 33
Orchard Clo. NW2—3C 42
Orchard Clo. SE23—6J 95
Orchard Clo. SW20—4E 120
Orchard Clo. W10—5H 59
Orchard Clo. Bexh—1E 100
Orchard Clo. Bush, Wat—1C 10
Orchard Clo. Edgw—6K 11
Orchard Clo. N'holt—6G 39
Orchard Clo. Surb—7B 118
Orchard Clo. Wemb—1E 56
Orchard Ct. Twic—2G 103
Orchard Ct. Wor Pk—1C 130
Orchard Cres. Croy—7A 126
Orchard Cres. Edgw—5D 12
Orchard Cres. Enf—1A 8
Orchard Dri. SE3—2F 97
Orchard Dri. Edgw—5A 12
Orchard Gdns. Sutt—5J 131
Orchard Ga. NW9—4A 26
Orchard Ga. Gnfd—6B 40
Orchard Gro. SE20—7G 111
Orchard Gro. Edgw—1G 25
Orchard Gro. Harr—5F 25
Orchard Hill. SE13—2D 96
Orchard Hill. Cars—5D 132
Orchard Hill. Dart—5K 101
Orchard La. SW20—2D 120
Orchard La. Wfd G—4F 21
Orchardleigh Av. Enf—2D 8
Orchardmede. N21—6J 7
Orchard M. N1—7D 46

Orchard Pl. E14—7G 65
Orchard Pl. N17—7A 18
Orchard Rise. Croy—1A 136
Orchard Rise. King—1J 119
Orchard Rise. Rich—4H 89
Orchard Rise E. Sidc—5K 99
Orchard Rise W. Sidc—5J 99
Orchard Rd. N6—7F 29
Orchard Rd. SE3—2G 97
Orchard Rd. SE18—4H 83
Orchard Rd. Barn—4C 4
Orchard Rd. Belv—6G 85
Orchard Rd. Bren—6C 72
Orchard Rd. Brom—1A 128
Orchard Rd. Dag—6G 53
Orchard Rd. Enf—5D 8
Orchard Rd. Hmptn—7D 102
Orchard Rd. Houn—5D 86
Orchard Rd. King—2E 118
Orchard Rd. Mitc—1E 132
Orchard Rd. Rich—3G 89
Orchard Rd. Romf—1H 37
Orchard Rd. Sidc—4J 115
Orchard Rd. Sutt—5J 131
Orchard Rd. Twic—5A 88
Orchard Rd. Well—3B 100
Orchardson St. NW8
    —4B 60 (4A 138)
Orchard St. E17—4A 32
Orchard St. W1—6E 60 (8G 139)
Orchard Ter. Enf—6B 8
Orchard Ter. King—1G 119
Orchard, The. N14—5A 6
Orchard, The. N21—6J 7
Orchard, The. NW11—5J 27
Orchard, The. SE3—2F 97
Orchard, The. W4—4K 73
Orchard, The. Houn—2G 87
Orchard Way. Croy & Beck
    —7A 126
Orchard Way. Enf—3K 7
Orchard Way. Sutt—4B 132
Orchid Clo. E6—5C 66
Orchid Rd. N14—7B 6
Orchid St. W12—7C 58
Orde Hall St. WC1
    —5K 61 (5E 140)
Ordell Rd. E3—2B 64
Ordnance Cres. SE10—2G 81
Ordnance Hill. NW8—1B 60
Ordnance M. NW8—2B 60
Ordnance Rd. E16—5H 65
Ordnance Rd. SE18—6E 82
Oregon Av. E12—4D 50
Oregon Clo. N Mald—4J 119
Orestes M. NW6—5J 43
Orford Gdns. Twic—2K 103
Orford Rd. E17—5D 32
Orford Rd. E18—4K 33
Organ La. E4—2K 19
Oriel Clo. Mitc—4H 123
Oriel Ct. NW3—4A 44
Oriel Ct. Croy—1D 134
Oriel Gdns. Ilf—3D 34
Oriel Rd. E9—6K 47
Oriel Way. N'holt—7F 39
Oriental Rd. E16—1B 82
Orient Industrial Pk. E10—2C 48
Orient St. SE11—4B 78 (8J 147)
Orient Way. E5—3K 47
Oriole Way. SE28—7B 68
Orissa Rd. SE18—5J 83
Orkney St. SW11—2E 92
Orlando Rd. SW4—3G 93
Orleans Rd. SE19—6D 110
Orleans Rd. Twic—7B 88
Orleston M. N7—6A 46
Orleston Rd. N7—6A 46
Orley Farm Rd. Harr—3J 39
Orlop St. SE10—5G 81
Ormanton Rd. SE26—4G 111
Orme Ct. W2—7K 59
Orme La. W2—7K 59
Ormeley Rd. SW12—1F 109
Orme Rd. King—2H 119
Ormerod Gdns. Mitc—2E 122
Ormesby Clo. SE28—7D 68

Ormesby Way. Harr—6F 25
Orme Sq. W2—7K 59
Ormiston Gro. W12—1D 74
Ormiston Rd. SE10—5J 81
Ormond Av. Hmptn—7F 103
Ormond Clo. WC1
    —5J 61 (5D 140)
Ormond Cres. Hmptn—7F 103
Ormond Dri. Hmptn—7F 103
Ormonde Ga. SW3—5D 76
Ormonde Pl. SW1
    —4E 76 (9G 145)
Ormonde Rise. Buck H—1F 21
Ormonde Rd. SW14—3J 89
Ormonde Ter. NW8—1D 60
Ormond M. WC1—4J 61 (4D 140)
Ormond Rd. N19—1J 45
Ormond Rd. Rich—5D 88
Ormond Yd. SW1
    —1G 77 (2M 145)
Ormsby Gdns. Gnfd—2G 55
Ormsby Pl. N16—3F 47
Ormsby St. E2—2F 63
Ormside St. SE15—6J 79
Ornan Rd. NW3—5C 44
Oronsay Wlk. N1—7C 46
Orpen Wlk. N16—3E 46
Orpheus St. SE5—1D 94
Orpington Gdns. N18—3K 17
Orpington Rd. N21—1G 17
Orpington Rd. Chst—3J 129
Orpwood Clo. Hmptn—6D 102
Orsett St. SE11—5K 77 (9F 146)
Orsett Ter. W2—6A 60
Orsett Ter. Wfd G—7F 21
Orsman Rd. N1—1E 62
Orton St. E1—1G 79 (3G 149)
Orville Rd. SW11—2B 92
Orwell Clo. Rain—5K 69
Orwell Rd. E13—2A 66
Osbaldeston Rd. N16—2G 47
Osberton Rd. SE12—5J 97
Osbert St. SW1—4H 77 (9A 146)
Osborn Clo. E8—1G 63
Osborne Clo. Beck—4A 126
Osborne Clo. Felt—5B 102
Osborne Gdns. T Hth—2C 124
Osborne Gro. E17—4B 32
Osborne Gro. N4—1A 46
Osborne Pl. Sutt—5B 132
Osborne Rd. E7—5K 49
Osborne Rd. E9—6B 48
Osborne Rd. E10—2D 48
Osborne Rd. N4—1A 46
Osborne Rd. N13—3F 17
Osborne Rd. NW2—6D 42
Osborne Rd. W3—3H 73
Osborne Rd. Belv—5F 85
Osborne Rd. Buck H—1E 20
Osborne Rd. Dag—5F 53
Osborne Rd. Enf—2F 9
Osborne Rd. Houn—3D 86
Osborne Rd. King—7E 104
Osborne Rd. S'hall—6G 55
Osborne Rd. T Hth—2C 124
Osborne Sq. Dag—4F 53
Osborn Gdns. NW7—7A 14
Osborn La. SE23—7A 96
Osborn St. E1—5F 63 (6F 142)
Osborn Ter. SE3—4H 97
Oscar St. SE8—1C 96
Oseney Cres. NW5—5G 45
O'Shea Gro. E3—1B 64
Osidge La. N14—1K 15
Osiers Rd. SW18—4J 91
Osier St. E1—4J 63 (4M 143)
Osier Way. E10—3D 48
Oslo Sq. SE16—3A 80
Osman Rd. N9—3B 18
Osman Rd. W6—3E 74
Osmond Clo. Harr—2G 39
Osmond Gdns. Wall—5G 133
Osmund St. W12—5B 58
Osnaburgh St. NW1
    —4F 61 (3K 139)

Osnaburgh Ter. NW1
—4F 61 (3K 139)
Osney Wlk. Cars—6B 122
Osprey Clo. E6—5C 66
Osprey Est. SE16—4K 79
Osprey M. Enf—5C 8
Ospringe Clo. SE20—7J 111
Ospringe Rd. NW5—4G 45
Ossian Rd. N4—7K 29
Ossington Bldgs. W1
—5E 60 (6G 139)
Ossington Clo. W2—7J 59
Ossington St. W2—7K 59
Ossory Rd. SE1—6G 79
Ossulston St. NW1
—2H 61 (1B 140)
Ossulton Pl. N2—3A 28
Ossulton Way. N2—4A 28
Ostade Rd. SW2—7K 93
Osten M. SW7—3K 75
Osterley Av. Iswth—7H 71
Osterley Clo. Orp—1K 129
Osterley Cres. Iswth—1K 87
Osterley Gdns. T Hth—2C 124
Osterley La. S'hall & Iswth
—5E 70
Osterley Pk. Rd. S'hall—3D 70
Osterley Pk. View Rd. W7
—2J 71
Osterley Rd. N16—4E 46
Osterley Rd. Iswth—7J 71
Oswald Rd. S'hall—1C 70
Oswald's Mead. E9—4A 48
Oswald St. E5—3K 47
Osward Pl. N9—2C 18
Osward Rd. SW17—2D 108
Oswin St. SE11—4B 78 (8K 147)
Oswyth Rd. SE5—2E 94
Otford Clo. Bex—6H 101
Otford Clo. Brom—3E 128
Otford Cres. SE4—6B 96
Othello Clo. SE11
—5B 78 (9J 147)
Otis St. E3—3E 64
Otley App. Ilf—6F 35
Otley Dri. Ilf—6F 35
Otley Rd. E16—6A 66
Otley Ter. E5—3K 47
Ottawa Gdns. Dag—7K 53
Ottaway Ct. E5—3G 47
Ottaway St. E5—3G 47
Otterbourne Rd. E4—3A 20
Otterbourne Rd. Croy—2C 134
Otterburn Gdns. Iswth—7A 72
Otterburn St. SW17—6D 108
Otterden St. SE6—4C 112
Otter Rd. Gnfd—4G 55
Otto Clo. SE26—3H 111
Otto St. SE17—6B 78
(in two parts)
Oulton Clo. E5—2J 47
Oulton Clo. SE28—6C 68
Oulton Cres. Bark—6K 51
Oulton Rd. N15—5D 30
Ousley Rd. SW12—1D 108
Outer Circ. NW1—2C 60 (2E 138)
Outgate Rd. NW10—7B 42
Outram Pl. N1—1J 61
Outram Rd. E6—1C 66
Outram Rd. N22—1H 29
Outram Rd. Croy—2F 135
Oval Pl. SW8—7K 77
Oval Rd. NW1—1F 61
Oval Rd. Croy—1E 134
Oval Rd. N. Dag—1H 69
Oval Rd. S. Dag—2H 69
Oval, The. E2—2H 63
Oval, The. Sidc—7A 100
Oval Way. SE11—5K 77
Overbrae. Beck—5C 112
Overbrook Wlk. Edgw—7B 12
Overbury Av. Beck—3D 126
Overbury Rd. N15—6D 30
Overbury St. E5—4K 47
Overcliff Rd. SE13—3C 96
Overcourt Clo. Sidc—6B 100
Overdale Av. N Mald—2K 119

Overdale Rd. W5—3C 72
Overdown Rd. SE6—4C 112
Overhill Rd. SE22—7G 95
Overhill Way. Beck—5F 127
Overlea Rd. E5—7G 31
Overmead. Sidc—7H 99
Overstand Clo. Beck—5C 126
Overstone Gdns. Croy—7B 126
Overstone Rd. W6—4E 74
Overton Clo. NW10—6J 41
Overton Clo. Iswth—1K 87
Overton Ct. E11—7J 33
Overton Dri. E11—7J 33
Overton Dri. Romf—7C 36
Overton Rd. E10—1A 48
Overton Rd. N14—5D 6
Overton Rd. SE2—3C 84
Overton Rd. SW9—2A 94
Overton Rd. Sutt—7J 131
Overton Rd. E. SE2—3D 84
Overtons Yd. Croy—3C 134
Ovesdon Av. Harr—1D 38
Ovett Clo. SE19—6E 110
Ovex Clo. E14—2E 80
Ovington Gdns. SW3
—3C 76 (7D 144)
Ovington Sq. SW3
—3C 76 (7D 144)
Ovington St. SW3
—4C 76 (8D 144)
Owen Clo. SE28—1C 84
Owen Gdns. Wfd G—6H 21
Owenite St. SE2—4B 84
Owen Rd. N13—4H 17
Owen Rd. Hay—3A 54
Owen's Row. EC1
—3B 62 (1J 141)
Owen St. EC1—2B 62 (1J 141)
Owens Way. SE23—7A 96
Owen Wlk. SE20—1G 125
Owen Way. NW10—5J 41
Owgan Clo. SE5—7D 78
Oxberry Av. SW6—2G 91
Oxendon St. SW1
—7H 61 (1A 146)
Oxenford St. SE15—3F 95
Oxenpark Av. Wemb—1E 40
Oxestall's Rd. SE8—5A 80
Oxford Av. NW10—3E 58
Oxford Av. SW20—2G 121
Oxford Av. Houn—5E 70
Oxford Cir. Av. W1
—6G 61 (8L 139)
Oxford Clo. N9—2C 18
Oxford Clo. Mitc—3G 123
Oxford Ct. W3—6G 57
Oxford Ct. Felt—4B 102
Oxford Cres. N Mald—6K 119
Oxford Dri. Ruis—2A 38
Oxford Gdns. N20—1G 15
Oxford Gdns. N21—7H 7
Oxford Gdns. W4—5H 73
Oxford Gdns. W10—6F 59
Oxford Ga. W6—4F 75
Oxford M. Bex—7G 101
Oxford Rd. E15—6F 49
(in two parts)
Oxford Rd. N4—1A 46
Oxford Rd. N9—2C 18
Oxford Rd. NW6—2J 59
Oxford Rd. SE19—6D 110
Oxford Rd. SW15—4G 91
Oxford Rd. W5—7D 56
Oxford Rd. Cars—6C 132
Oxford Rd. Enf—5C 8
Oxford Rd. Harr—3K 23
(Wealdstone)
Oxford Rd. Harr—6G 23
(West Harrow)
Oxford Rd. Ilf—5G 51
Oxford Rd. Sidc—5B 116
Oxford Rd. Tedd—5H 103
Oxford Rd. Wall—5G 133
Oxford Rd. Wfd G—5G 21
Oxford Rd. N. W4—5H 73
Oxford Rd. S. W4—5H 73
Oxford Sq. W2—6C 60 (8C 138)

Oxford St. W1—6E 60 (8G 139)
Oxford Wlk. S'hall—1D 70
Oxford Way. Felt—4B 102
Oxgate Gdns. NW2—3D 42
Oxgate La. NW2—2D 42
Oxhawth Cres. Brom—6E 128
Oxhey La. Wat & Pinn—5A 10
Oxleas Clo. Well—2H 99
Oxleay Rd. Harr—1E 38
Oxleigh Clo. N Mald—5A 120
Oxleys Rd. NW2—3D 42
Oxlip Clo. Croy—1K 135
Oxlow La. Dag—4F 53
Oxonian St. SE22—4F 95
Oxted Clo. Mitc—3B 122
Oxtoby Way. SW16—1H 123
Ozolins Way. E16—6J 65

Pacific Rd. E16—6J 65
Packington Rd. W3—3J 73
Packington Sq. N1—1C 62
Packington St. N1—1B 62
Packmores Rd. SE9—5H 99
Padbury Ct. E2—3F 63 (2F 142)
Paddenswick Rd. W6—3C 74
Paddington Clo. Hay—4B 54
Paddington Grn. W2
—5B 60 (5A 138)
Paddington St. W1
—5E 60 (5G 139)
Paddock Clo. SE3—3J 97
Paddock Clo. SE26—4K 111
Paddock Clo. Harr—4F 39
Paddock Clo. N'holt—2E 54
Paddock Clo. Wor Pk—1A 130
Paddock Gdns. SE19—6E 110
Paddock Rd. NW2—3C 42
Paddock Rd. Bexh—4E 100
Paddock Rd. Ruis—3B 38
Paddocks, The. Barn—3J 5
Paddocks, The. Croy—6C 136
Paddocks, The. Wemb—2H 41
Paddock Way. Chst—7H 115
Padfield Rd. SE5—3C 94
Padnall Rd. Romf—3D 36
Padstow Rd. Enf—2G 7
Padua Rd. SE20—1J 125
Pagden St. SW8—1F 93
Pageant Wlk. Croy—3E 134
Page Clo. Dag—5E 52
Page Clo. Hmptn—6C 102
Page Cres. Croy—5B 134
Page Grn. N15—5F 31
Page Grn. Rd. N15—5G 31
Page Heath La. Brom—3B 128
Page Heath Vs. Brom—3B 128
Pagehurst Rd. Croy—7H 125
Page Meadow. NW7—7H 13
Page Pl. E1—6H 63 (8K 143)
Pages Hill. N10—2E 28
Pages La. N10—2E 28
Page St. NW7—1C 26
Page St. SW1—4H 77 (8B 146)
Page's Wlk. SE1—4E 78 (8C 148)
Pages Yd. W4—6A 74
Paget Av. Sutt—3B 132
Paget Clo. Hmptn—4H 103
Paget Gdns. Chst—1F 129
Paget La. Iswth—3H 87
Paget Pl. King—6J 105
Paget Rise. SE18—6E 82
Paget Rd. N16—1D 46
Paget Rd. Ilf—4F 51
Paget St. EC1—3B 62 (1J 141)
Paget Ter. SE18—6F 83
Pagnell St. SE14—7B 80
Pagoda Av. Rich—3F 89
Pagoda Gdns. SE3—2F 97
Pagoda Vista. Rich—1F 89
Paignton Rd. N15—6E 30
Paines Clo. Pinn—3C 22
Paines La. Pinn—1C 22
Pain's Clo. Mitc—2F 123
Painsthorpe Rd. N16—3E 46
Painters Rd. Ilf—3K 35

Paisley Rd. N22—1B 30
Paisley Rd. Cars—1B 132
Pakeman St. N7—3K 45
Pakenham Clo. SW12—1E 108
Pakenham St. WC1
—4K 61 (3F 140)
Palace Av. W8—2K 75
Palace Ct. NW3—5K 43
Palace Ct. W2—7K 59
Palace Ct. Harr—6E 24
Palace Ct. Gdns. N10—3G 29
Palace Gdns. Buck H—1G 21
Palace Gdns. Enf—4J 7
Palace Gdns. M. W8—1K 75
Palace Gdns. Ter. W8—1J 75
Palace Ga. W8—2A 76
Palace Grn. Croy—7B 136
Palace Grn. Croy—7B 136
Palace Gro. SE19—7F 111
Palace Gro. Brom—1K 127
Palace M. SW6—7H 75
Palace M. Enf—3J 7
Palace Pl. SW1—3G 77 (6L 145)
Palace Rd. N8—5H 29
(in two parts)
Palace Rd. N11—7D 16
Palace Rd. SE19—7F 111
Palace Rd. SW2—1K 109
Palace Rd. Brom—1K 127
Palace Rd. King—4D 118
Palace Rd. Ruis—4C 38
Palace Sq. SE19—7F 111
Palace St. SW1—3G 77 (6L 145)
Palace View. SE12—2J 113
Palace View. Brom—3K 127
Palace View. Croy—4B 136
Palace View Rd. E4—5J 19
Palamos Rd. E10—1C 48
Palatine Av. N16—4E 46
Palatine Rd. N16—4E 46
Palermo Rd. NW10—2C 58
Palestine Gro. SW19—1B 122
Palewell Comn. Dri. SW14
—5K 89
Palewell Pk. SW14—5K 89
Palfrey Pl. SW8—7K 77
Palgrave Av. S'hall—7E 54
Palgrave Rd. W12—3B 74
Palissy St. E2—3F 63 (2E 142)
(in two parts)
Pallet Way. SE18—1C 98
Palliser Rd. W14—5G 75
Pall Mall. SW1—1G 77 (3M 145)
Pall Mall E. SW1
—1H 77 (2B 146)
Palmar Cres. Bexh—3G 101
Palmar Rd. Bexh—2G 101
Palm Av. Sidc—6D 116
Palmeira Rd. Bexh—3D 100
Palmer Av. Sutt—4E 130
Palmer Clo. Houn—1E 86
Palmer Gdns. Barn—5A 4
Palmer Pl. N7—5A 46
Palmer Rd. E13—4K 65
Palmer Rd. Dag—1D 52
Palmers La. Enf—1C 8
Palmers Pas. SW14—3J 89
Palmer's Rd. E2—2K 63
Palmer's Rd. N11—5B 16
Palmers Rd. SW14—3J 89
Palmers Rd. SW16—7J 123
Palmerston Ct. Surb—7D 118
Palmerston Cres. N13—5E 16
Palmerston Cres. SE18—6G 83
Palmerston Gro. SW19—7J 107
Palmerston Rd. E7—6K 49
Palmerston Rd. E17—4B 32
Palmerston Rd. N22—7E 16
Palmerston Rd. NW6—7H 43
(in two parts)
Palmerston Rd. SW14—4J 89
Palmerston Rd. SW19—7J 107
Palmerston Rd. W3—3J 73
Palmerston Rd. Buck H—2E 20
Palmerston Rd. Cars—4D 132

Parkside. Sutt—6G 131
Parkside Av. SW19—5F 107
Parkside Av. Bexh—2K 101
Parkside Av. Brom—4C 128
Parkside Av. Romf—3K 87
Parkside Cres. Surb—6J 119
Parkside Cross. Bexh—2K 101
Parkside Dri. Edgw—3B 12
Parkside Gdns. SW19—4F 107
Parkside Gdns. Barn—1J 15
Parkside Rd. SW11—1E 92
Parkside Rd. Belv—4H 85
Parkside Rd. Houn—5F 87
Parkside Ter. N18—4J 17
Parkside Way. Harr—4F 23
Park Sq. E. NW1—4F 61 (3J 139)
Park Sq. W. NW1
    —4F 61 (4J 139)
Parkstead Rd. SW15—5D 90
Parkstone Av. N18—5A 18
Parkstone Rd. E17—3E 32
Parkstone Rd. SE15—2G 95
Park St. SE1—1C 78 (2L 147)
Park St. Croy—2C 134
Park St. W1—7E 60 (9G 139)
Park St. Tedd—6J 103
Park Ter. Enf—1F 9
Park Ter. Wor Pk—1C 130
Park, The. N6—6E 28
Park, The. NW11—1K 43
Park, The. SE19—7E 110
Park, The. SE23—1J 111
Park, The. W5—1D 72
Park, The. Cars—6D 132
Park, The. Sidc—4A 116
Parkthorne Clo. Harr—6F 23
Parkthorne Dri. Harr—6E 22
Parkthorne Rd. SW12—7H 93
Park Towers. W2—7A 60
Park View. N21—7E 6
Park View. W3—5J 57
Park View. N Mald—3B 120
Park View. Pinn—1D 22
Park View. Wemb—5H 41
Park View Cres. N11—4A 16
Park View Est. E2—2K 63
Park View Gdns. N22—1A 30
Park View Gdns. NW4—5E 26
Park View Gdns. Bark—2J 67
Park View Gdns. Ilf—4D 34
Park View Rd. N3—1K 27
Park View Rd. N17—3G 31
Park View Rd. NW10—4B 42
Parkview Rd. SE9—2F 115
Park View Rd. W5—5E 56
Park View Rd. Croy—1G 135
Park View Rd. S'hall—1E 70
Park View Rd. Well—3C 100
Park Village E. NW1
    —2F 61 (1K 139)
Park Village W. NW1—2F 61
Park Vs. Romf—6D 36
Parkville Rd. SW6—7H 75
Park Vista. SE10—6F 81
Park Wlk. N6—7E 28
Park Wlk. SW10—6A 76
Park Wlk. Barn—3G 5
Parkway. N14—2D 16
Park Way. N20—4J 15
Parkway. NW1—1F 61
Park Way. NW11—5G 27
Park Way. SW20—4F 121
Park Way. Edgw—1H 25
Park Way. Enf—2F 7
Parkway. Eri—3E 84
Park Way. Felt—7A 86
Park Way. Ilf—3K 51
Park Way. Wfd G—5F 21
Parkway, The. Houn & S'hall
    —2A 86
Parkway Trading Est. Houn
    —6A 70
Parkwood. N20—3K 15
Parkwood. Beck—7C 112
Parkwood M. N6—6F 29
Parkwood Rd. SW19—5H 107

Park Wood Rd. Bex—7F 101
Parkwood Rd. Iswth—1K 87
Parliament Hill. NW3—4C 44
Parliament Sq. SW1
    —2J 77 (5C 146)
Parliament St. SW1
    —2J 77 (5C 146)
Parluke Clo. SE7—5B 82
Parma Cres. SW11—4D 92
Parmiter St. E2—2H 63 (1J 143)
Parnell Clo. Edgw—4C 12
Parnell Rd. E3—1B 64
Parnham St. E14—6A 64
Parolles Rd. N19—1G 45
Paroma Rd. Belv—3G 85
Parr Clo. N9—4C 18
Parr Ct. Felt—4A 102
Parr Rd. E6—1B 66
Parr Rd. Stan—1E 24
Parrs Clo. S Croy—7D 134
Parrs Pl. Hmptn—7E 102
Parr St. N1—2D 62
Parry Av. E6—6D 66
Parry Clo. Eps—7D 130
Parry Pl. SE18—4F 83
Parry Rd. SE25—3E 124
Parry St. SW8—6J 77
Parsifal Rd. NW6—5J 43
Parsley Gdns. Croy—1K 135
Parsloes Av. Dag—4D 52
Parsonage Gdns. Enf—2H 7
Parsonage La. Enf—2J 7
Parsonage La. Sidc—4F 117
Parsonage Manorway. Belv
    —6G 85
Parsonage St. E14—4E 80
Parson's Cres. Edgw—3B 12
Parson's Grn. SW6—2J 91
Parson's Grn. La. SW6—1J 91
Parson's Gro. Edgw—3B 12
Parsons Mead. Croy—1B 134
Parson's Rd. E13—2A 66
Parson St. NW4—4E 26
Parthenia Rd. SW6—1J 91
Partingdale La. NW7—5A 14
Partington Clo. N19—1H 45
Partridge Clo. E16—5B 66
Partridge Clo. Bush, Wat
    —1A 10
Partridge Grn. SE9—3E 114
Partridge Rd. Hmptn—6D 102
Partridge Rd. Sidc—3J 115
Partridge Sq. E6—5C 66
Partridge Way. N22—1J 29
Parvin St. SW8—1H 93
Pascal St. SW8—7H 77
Pascoe Rd. SE13—5F 97
Pasley Clo. SE17—5C 78
Pasquier Rd. E17—3A 32
Passey Pl. SE9—6D 98
Passfield Dri. E14—5D 64
Passfield Path. SE28—7B 68
Passmore Gdns. N11—6C 16
Passmore St. SW1
    —5E 76 (9G 145)
Pasteur Clo. NW9—2A 26
Pasteur Gdns. N18—5G 17
Paston Cres. SE12—7K 97
Pastor St. SE11—4B 78 (8K 147)
Pasture Clo. Wemb—3B 40
Pasture Rd. SE6—1H 113
Pasture Rd. Dag—5F 53
Pasture Rd. Wemb—2B 40
Pastures, The. N20—1C 14
Patcham Ter. SW8—1F 93
Patch, The. E4—1C 20
Paternoster Row. EC4
    —6C 62 (8L 141)
Paternoster Sq. EC4
    —6B 62 (8K 141)
Pater St. W8—3J 75
Pathfield Rd. SW16—6H 109
Path, The. SW19—1K 121
Patience Rd. SW11—2C 92
Patio Clo. SW4—6H 93
Patmore Est. SW8—1G 93

Patmore St. SW8—1G 93
Patmos Rd. SW9—7B 78
Paton Clo. E3—3C 64
Patricia Ct. Chst—1H 129
Patricia Ct. Well—7B 84
Patrick Connolly Gdns. E3
    —3D 64
Patrick Pas. SW11—2C 92
Patrick Rd. E13—3A 66
Patriot Sq. E2—2J 63 (1L 143)
Patrol Pl. SE6—6D 96
Patshull Pl. NW5—6G 45
Patshull Rd. NW5—6G 45
Patten All. Rich—5D 88
Pattenden Rd. SE6—1B 112
Patten Rd. SW18—7C 92
Patterdale Clo. Brom—6H 113
Patterdale Rd. SE15—7J 79
Patterson Ct. SE19—7F 111
Patterson Rd. SE19—6F 111
Pattison Rd. NW2—3J 43
Pattison Wlk. SE18—5G 83
Paul Clo. E15—7G 49
Paulet Rd. SE5—2B 94
Paul Gdns. Croy—2F 135
Paulhan Rd. Harr—4D 24
Paulin Dri. N21—7F 7
Pauline Cres. Twic—1G 103
Paul St. E15—1G 65
Paul St. EC2—4D 62 (4B 142)
Paul's Wlk. EC4—7C 62 (9L 141)
Paultons Sq. SW3—6B 76
Paultons St. SW3—6B 76
Pauntley St. N19—1G 45
Paved Ct. Rich—5D 88
Paveley Dri. SW11—7C 76
Paveley St. NW8
    —3C 60 (2C 138)
Pavement M. Romf—7D 36
Pavement Sq. Croy—1G 135
Pavement, The. SW4—4G 93
Pavement, The. W5—3E 72
Pavet Clo. Dag—6H 53
Pavilion Rd. SW1
    —3D 76 (6F 144)
Pavilion Rd. Ilf—7D 34
Pavilion St. SW1
    —3D 76 (7F 144)
Pavilion Ter. Ilf—5J 35
Pavilion Way. Edgw—7C 12
Pavilion Way. Ruis—2A 38
Pawleyne Clo. SE20—7J 111
Pawsey Clo. E13—1K 65
Pawsons Rd. Croy—6C 124
Paxford Rd. Wemb—2B 40
Paxton Clo. Rich—2F 89
Paxton Pl. SE27—4E 110
Paxton Rd. N17—7B 18
Paxton Rd. W4—6A 74
Paxton Rd. Brom—7J 113
Paynell Ct. SE3—3G 97
Payne Rd. E3—2D 64
Paynesfield Av. SW14—3K 89
Paynesfield Rd. Bush, Wat
    —1E 10
Payne St. SE8—7B 80
Paynes Wlk. W6—6G 75
Payne Way. Edgw—3G 25
Peabody Av. SW1—5F 77
Peabody Bldgs. EC1
    —4C 62 (4M 141)
Peabody Clo. SE10—1D 96
Peabody Cotts. N17—1E 30
Peabody Est. SE24—7B 94
Peabody Est. W6—5E 74
Peabody Hill. SE21—1B 110
Peabody Sq. SE1
    —2B 78 (5J 147)
Peabody Yd. N1—1C 62
Peace Clo. N14—6A 6
Peace Gro. Wemb—2H 41
Peace St. SE18—6E 82
Peaches Clo. Sutt—7G 131
Peach Rd. W10—3F 59
Peachum Rd. SE3—6H 81
Peacock St. SE17
    —4B 78 (9K 147)

Peaketon Av. Ilf—4B 34
Peak Hill. SE26—4J 111
Peak Hill Av. SE26—4J 111
Peak Hill Gdns. SE26—4J 111
Peak, The. SE26—3J 111
Peal Gdns. W13—4A 56
Peall Rd. Croy—6K 123
Pearcefield Av. SE23—1J 111
Pear Clo. NW9—4K 25
Pear Clo. SE14—7A 80
Pearcroft Rd. E11—2F 49
Peardon St. SW8—2F 93
Pearestree Clo. Eri—1K 101
Pearfield Rd. SE23—3A 112
Pearl Clo. E6—6E 66
Pearl Rd. E17—3C 32
Pearl St. E1—1H 79 (2K 149)
Pearman St. SE1
    —3A 78 (6H 147)
Pear Pl. SE1—2A 78 (4G 147)
Pearscroft Ct. SW6—1K 91
Pearscroft Rd. SW6—1K 91
Pearson's Av. SE14—1C 96
Pearson St. E2—2F 63
Pears Rd. Houn—3G 87
Peartree Clo. Eri—1K 101
Peartree Clo. Mitc—2C 122
Pear Tree Ct. E18—1K 33
Pear Tree Ct. EC1
    —4A 62 (4H 141)
Peartree Gdns. Dag—4B 52
Peartree Gdns. Romf—2H 37
Peartree La. E1—7J 63 (1M 149)
Peartree Rd. Enf—3K 7
Peartree St. EC1
    —4C 62 (3L 141)
Peary Pl. E2—3J 63 (1M 143)
Peas Mead Ter. E4—4K 19
Peatfield Clo. Sidc—3J 115
Pebworth Rd. Harr—2A 40
Peckarmans Wood. SE26
    —3G 111
Peckett Sq. N5—4C 46
Peckford Clo. SW9—2A 94
Peckford Pl. SW9—2A 94
Peckham Gro. SE15—7E 78
Peckham High St. SE15—1G 95
Peckham Hill St. SE15—7G 79
Peckham Pk. Rd. SE15—7G 79
Peckham Rd.—1E 94
    SE5 1-93 & 2-84
    SE15 remainder
Peckham Rye—3G 95
    SE15 1-261 & 2-132
    SE22 remainder
Peckwater St. NW5—5G 45
Pedhoulas. N14—3D 16
Pedlars Wlk. N7—5K 45
Pedley Rd. Dag—1C 52
Pedley St. E1—4F 63 (4F 142)
Pedro St. E5—3K 47
Pedworth Gdns. SE16
    —4J 79 (9L 149)
Peek Cres. SW19—5F 107
Peel Dri. NW9—3B 26
Peel Dri. Ilf—3C 34
Peel Gro. E2—2J 63 (1L 143)
Peel Pl. Ilf—2C 34
Peel Precinct. NW6—2J 59
Peel Rd. E18—1H 33
Peel Rd. NW6—3H 59
Peel Rd. Harr—3K 23
Peel Rd. Wemb—3D 40
Peel St. W8—1J 75
Peerless St. EC1
    —3D 62 (2A 142)
Pegamoid Rd. N18—3D 18
Pegasus Ct. King—3D 118
Pegasus Pl. SE11—6A 78
Pegasus Rd. Croy—6A 134
Pegg Rd. Houn—7B 70
Pegley Gdns. SE12—2J 113
Pegwell St. SE18—7J 83
Pekin St. E14—6C 64
Peldon Ct. Rich—5F 89
Peldon Pas. Rich—4F 89
Pelham Av. Bark—1K 67

Pelham Clo. SE5—3E 94
Pelham Ct. Sidc—3A 116
Pelham Cres. SW7
—4C 76 (9C 144)
Pelham Pl. SW7—4C 76 (9C 144)
Pelham Rd. E18—3K 33
Pelham Rd. N15—4F 31
Pelham Rd. N22—2A 30
Pelham Rd. SW19—7J 107
Pelham Rd. Beck—2J 125
Pelham Rd. Bexh—3G 101
Pelham Rd. Ilf—2H 51
Pelham St. SW7—4B 76 (8B 144)
Pelican Est. SE15—1F 95
Pelican Pas. E1—4J 63 (3L 143)
Pelican Wlk. SW9—4B 94
Pelier St. SE17—6C 78
Pelinore Rd. SE6—2G 113
Pellant Rd. SW6—7G 75
Pellatt Gro. N22—1A 30
Pellatt Rd. SE22—5F 95
Pellerin Rd. N16—5E 46
Pelling St. E14—6C 64
Pellipar Clo. N13—3F 17
Pellipar Gdns. SE18—5D 82
Pelly Rd. E13—1J 65
Pelter St. E2—3F 63 (1E 142)
Pelton Rd. SE10—5G 81
Pembar Av. E17—3A 32
Pember Rd. NW10—3F 59
Pemberton Gdns. N19—3G 45
Pemberton Gdns. Romf—5E 36
Pemberton Pl. E9—7J 47
Pemberton Rd. N4—5A 30
Pemberton Row. EC4
—6A 62 (7H 141)
Pemberton Ter. N19—3G 45
Pembridge Av. Twic—1D 102
Pembridge Cres. W11—7J 59
Pembridge Gdns. W2—7J 59
Pembridge M. W11—7J 59
Pembridge Pl. W2—7J 59
Pembridge Rd. W11—7J 59
Pembridge Sq. W2—7J 59
Pembridge Vs. W11—7J 59
Pembroke Av. Enf—1C 8
Pembroke Av. Harr—3A 24
Pembroke Av. Surb—5H 119
Pembroke Clo. SW1
—2E 76 (5H 145)
Pembroke Gdns. W8—4H 75
Pembroke Gdns. Dag—3H 53
Pembroke Gdns. Clo. W8—3J 75
Pembroke M. N10—1E 28
Pembroke M. W8—3J 75
Pembroke Pl. Edgw—7B 12
Pembroke Pl. Iswth—2J 87
Pembroke Rd. E6—5D 66
Pembroke Rd. E17—5D 32
Pembroke Rd. N8—4J 29
Pembroke Rd. N10—1E 28
Pembroke Rd. N13—3H 17
Pembroke Rd. N15—5F 31
Pembroke Rd. SE25—4E 124
Pembroke Rd. W8—4J 75
Pembroke Rd. Brom—2A 128
Pembroke Rd. Eri—5J 85
Pembroke Rd. Gnfd—4F 55
Pembroke Rd. Ilf—1K 51
Pembroke Rd. Mitc—2E 122
Pembroke Rd. Wemb—3D 40
Pembroke Sq. W8—3J 75
Pembroke St. N1—7J 45
Pembroke Vs. W8—4J 75
Pembroke Vs. Rich—4D 88
Pembroke Wlk. W8—4J 75
Pembury Av. Wor Pk—1C 130
Pembury Clo. Brom—7H 127
Pembury Cres. Sidc—2E 116
Pembury Pl. E5—5H 47
Pembury Rd. E5—5H 47
Pembury Rd. N17—1F 31
Pembury Rd. SE25—4G 125
Pembury Rd. Bexh—7E 84
Pemdevon Rd. Croy—7A 124
Pemell Clo. E1—4J 63 (3M 143)

Penally Pl. N1—1D 62
Penang St. E1—1H 79 (2K 149)
Penarth St. SE15—6J 79
Penberth Rd. SE6—2E 112
Penbury Rd. S'hall—5D 70
Pencombe M. W11—7H 59
Pencraig Way. SE15—6H 79
Penda Rd. Eri—7H 85
Pendarves Rd. SW20—1E 120
Penda's Mead. E9—4A 48
Pendennis Rd. N17—3D 30
Pendennis Rd. SW16—4J 109
Penderel Rd. Houn—5E 86
Penderry Rise. SE6—2F 113
Penderyn Way. N7—4H 45
Pendle Ho. SE26—3G 111
Pendle Rd. SW16—6F 109
Pendlestone Rd. E17—5D 32
Pendragon Rd. Brom—3H 113
Pendragon Wlk. NW9—6A 26
Pendrell Rd. SE4—2A 96
Pendrell St. SE18—6H 83
Pendula Dri. Hay—4B 54
Penerley Rd. SE6—1D 112
Penfold Clo. Croy—3A 134
Penfold La. Bex—2D 116
Penfold Pl. NW1—5C 60 (5C 138)
Penfold Rd. N9—1E 18
Penfold St. —4B 60 (4B 138)
NW1 1-11 & 2-28
NW8 remainder
Penford Gdns. SE9—3B 98
Penford St. SE5—2B 94
Pengarth Rd. Bex—6D 100
Penge La. SE20—7J 111
Penge Rd. E13—1A 66
Penge Rd.—3G 125
SE25 1-81 & 2-70
SE20 remainder
Penhall Rd. SE7—4B 82
Penhill Rd. Bex—6C 100
Penhurst Rd. Ilf—1F 35
Penifather La. Gnfd—3H 55
Penistone Rd. SW16—7J 109
Penketh Dri. Harr—3H 39
Penmon Rd. SE2—3A 84
Pennack Rd. SE15—6F 79
Pennant M. W8—4K 75
Pennant Ter. E17—2B 32
Pennard Rd. W12—2E 74
Penn Clo. Gnfd—2F 55
Penn Clo. Harr—4C 24
Penner Clo. SW19—2G 107
Pennethorne Clo. E9—1J 63
Pennethorne Rd. SE15—7H 79
Penn Gdns. Chst—2F 129
Penn Gdns. Romf—1G 37
Pennine Dri. NW2—2F 43
Pennine La. NW2—2G 43
Pennine Way. Bexh—1K 101
Pennington Clo. SE27—4D 110
Pennington St. N1
—7H 63 (1J 149)
Penn La. Bex—6D 100
Penn Rd. N7—5J 45
Penn St. N1—1D 62
Pennycroft. Croy—7A 136
Pennyfields. E14—7C 64
Pennymoor Wlk. W9—3H 59
Penny Rd. NW10—3H 57
Pennyroyal Av. E6—6E 66
Penpoll Rd. E8—6H 47
Penpool La. Well—3B 100
Penrhyn Av. E17—1C 32
Penrhyn Cres. E17—1C 32
Penrhyn Cres. SW14—4J 89
Penrhyn Gro. E17—1C 32
Penrhyn Rd. King—4E 118
Penrith Clo. SW15—5G 91
Penrith Clo. Beck—1D 126
Penrith Pl. SE27—2B 110
Penrith Rd. N15—5D 30
Penrith Rd. N Mald—4K 119
Penrith Rd. T Hth—2C 124
Penrith St. SW16—6G 109
Penrose Gro. SE17—5C 78
Penrose St. SE17—5C 78

Penryn St. NW1—2H 61
Penry St. SE1—4E 78 (9D 148)
Pensbury Pl. SW8—2G 93
Pensbury St. SW8—2G 93
Pensford Av. Rich—2G 89
Penshurst Av. Sidc—6A 100
Penshurst Gdns. Edgw—5C 12
Penshurst Grn. Brom—5H 127
Penshurst Rd. E9—7K 47
Penshurst Rd. N17—7A 18
Penshurst Rd. Bexh—1F 101
Penshurst Rd. T Hth—5B 124
Penshurst Wlk. Brom—5H 127
Penshurst Way. Sutt—7J 131
Pentagon, The. W13—7A 56
Pentire Rd. E17—1F 33
Pentland Clo. NW11—2G 43
Pentland Gdns. SW18—6A 92
Pentland Pl. N'holt—1C 54
Pentlands Clo. Mitc—3F 123
Pentland St. SW18—6A 92
Pentlow St. SW15—3E 90
Pentlow Way. Buck H—1H 21
Pentney Rd. E4—1A 20
Pentney Rd. SW12—1G 109
Pentney Rd. SW19—1G 121
Penton Gro. N1—2A 62
Penton Pl. SE17—5B 78 (9K 147)
Penton Rise. WC1
—3K 61 (1F 140)
Penton St. N1—2A 62 (1G 141)
Pentonville Rd. N1
—2K 61 (1E 140)
Pentrich Av. Enf—1B 8
Pentridge St. SE15—7F 79
Pentyre Av. N18—5J 17
Penwerris Av. Iswth—7G 71
Penwith Rd. SW18—2K 107
Penwortham Ct. N22—2K 29
Penwortham Rd. SW16—6G 109
Penylan Pl. Edgw—7B 12
Penywern Rd. SW5—5J 75
Penzance Pl. W11—1G 75
Penzance St. W11—1G 75
Peony Ct. Wfd G—7B 20
Peony Gdns. W12—7C 58
Poploe Rd. NW6—2F 59
Pepper Clo. E6—5D 66
Peppermint Clo. Croy—7J 123
Pepper St. SE1—2C 78 (4L 147)
Pepys Cres. Barn—5A 4
Pepys Rd. SE14—1K 95
Pepys Rd. SW20—1E 120
Pepys St. EC3—7E 62 (9D 142)
Perceval Av. NW3—5C 44
Perch St. E8—4F 47
Percival Ct. N17—7A 18
Percival Gdns. Romf—6D 36
Percival Rd. SW14—4J 89
Percival Rd. Enf—4A 8
Percival St. EC1—4B 62 (3J 141)
Percy Cir. WC1—3K 61 (1F 140)
Percy Gdns. Enf—5E 8
Percy Gdns. Iswth—3A 88
Percy Gdns. Wor Pk—1A 130
Percy Rd. E11—7G 33
Percy Rd. E16—5G 65
Percy Rd. N12—5F 15
Percy Rd. N21—7H 7
Percy Rd. NW6—3J 59
Percy Rd. SE20—1K 125
Percy Rd. SE25—5G 125
Percy Rd. W12—2C 74
Percy Rd. Bexh—2E 100
Percy Rd. Dag—4G 69
Percy Rd. Hmptn—7E 102
Percy Rd. Ilf—7A 36
Percy Rd. Iswth—4A 88
Percy Rd. Mitc—7E 122
Percy Rd. Romf—3H 37
Percy Rd. Twic—1F 103
Percy St. W1—5H 61 (6A 140)
Percy Way. Twic—1G 103
Percy Yd. WC1—3K 61 (1F 140)
Peregrine Ct. SW16—4K 109
Peregrine Way. SW19—7E 106
Perham Rd. W14—5G 75

Peridot St. E6—5C 66
Perifield. SE21—1C 110
Perimeade Rd. Gnfd—2C 56
Periton Rd. SE9—4B 98
Perivale Gdns. W13—4B 56
Perivale Industrial Pk. Gnfd
—1B 56
Perivale La. Gnfd—3A 56
Perkin Clo. Wemb—5B 40
Perkin's Rents. SW1
—3H 77 (7A 146)
Perkins Rd. Ilf—5H 35
Perks Clo. SE3—3G 97
Perpins Rd. SE9—6J 99
Perran Rd. SW2—1B 110
Perran Wlk. Bren—5E 72
Perren St. NW5—6F 45
Perrers Rd. W6—4D 74
Perrin Rd. Wemb—4B 40
Perrins Ct. NW3—4A 44
Perrin's La. NW3—4A 44
Perrin's Wlk. NW3—4A 44
Perrott St. SE18—4G 83
Perry Av. W3—6K 57
Perry Clo. Rain—2K 69
Perry Ct. N15—6E 30
Perryfield Way. NW9—6B 26
Perryfield Way. Rich—3B 104
Perry Gdns. N9—3J 17
Perry Garth. N'holt—1A 54
Perry Hall Rd. Orp—6K 129
Perry Hill. SE6—3B 112
Perry How. Wor Pk—1B 130
Perrymans Farm Rd. Ilf—6H 35
Perry Mead. Enf—2G 7
Perrymead St. SW6—1K 91
Perryn Rd. SE16—3H 79 (6J 149)
Perryn Rd. W3—1K 73
Perry Rise. SE23—3A 112
Perry's Pl. W1—6H 61 (7A 140)
Perry St. Chst—6H 115
Perry St. Dart—4K 101
Perry St. Gdns. Chst—6J 115
Perry St. Shaw. Chst—7J 115
Perry Vale. SE23—2J 111
Persant Rd. SE6—2G 113
Perseverance Pl. SW9—7A 78
Perseverance Pl. Rich—4E 88
Pershore Clo. Ilf—5F 35
Pershore Gro. Cars—6B 122
Pert Clo. N10—6A 16
Perth Av. NW9—7K 25
Perth Av. Hay—4A 54
Perth Clo. SW20—2C 120
Perth Rd. E10—1A 48
Perth Rd. E13—2K 65
Perth Rd. N4—1A 46
Perth Rd. N22—1B 30
Perth Rd. Bark—1H 67
Perth Rd. Beck—2E 126
Perth Rd. Ilf—6E 34
Perth Ter. Ilf—7G 35
Perwell Av. Harr—1D 38
Peter Av. NW10—7D 42
Peterboat Clo. SE10—4G 81
Peterborough Ct. EC4
—6A 62 (8H 141)
Peterborough Gdns. Ilf—7C 34
Peterborough M. SW6—2J 91
Peterborough Rd. E10—5E 32
Peterborough Rd. SW6—2J 91
Peterborough Rd. Cars—6C 122
Peterborough Rd. Harr—1J 39
Peterborough Vs. SW6—1K 91
Petergate. SW11—4A 92
Peter James Enterprise Centre.
NW10—3J 57
Peterley Business Centre. E2
—2H 63
Peters Clo. Dag—1D 52
Peters Clo. Stan—6J 11
Peters Clo. Well—2J 99
Petersfield Clo. N18—5H 17
Petersfield Rise. SW15—1D 106
Petersfield Rd. W3—2J 73
Petersham Clo. Rich—2D 104
Petersham Clo. Sutt—5J 131

Petersham Dri. Orp—2K 129
Petersham Gdns. Orp—2K 129
Petersham M. SW7—3A 76
Petersham Pl. SW7—3A 76
Petersham Rd. Rich—6D 88
Peters Hill. EC4—7C 62 (9L 141)
Peter's La. EC1—5B 62 (5K 141)
Peter's Path. SE26—4H 111
Peterstone Rd. SE2—2B 84
Peterstow Clo. SW19—2G 107
Petherton Rd. N5—5C 46
Petley Rd. W6—6F 75
Peto Pl. NW1—4F 61 (3K 139)
Peto St. N. E16—6H 65
Peto St. S. E16—7H 65
Petrie Clo. NW2—6G 43
Petticoat La. E1—5E 62 (6D 142)
Petticoat Sq. E1—6F 63 (7E 142)
Pettits Clo. Romf—2K 37
Pettits La. N. Romf—1K 37
Pettits Pl. Dag—5G 53
Pettits Rd. Dag—5G 53
Pettiward Clo. SW15—4E 90
Pettley Gdns. Romf—5K 37
Pettman Cres. SE28—3H 83
Pettsgrove Av. Wemb—5C 40
Pett's Hill. N'holt—5F 39
Pett St. SE18—4C 82
Petts Wood Rd. Orp—5H 129
Petty France. SW1
—3G 77 (6M 145)
Petworth Clo. N'holt—7D 38
Petworth Gdns. SW20—3D 120
Petworth Rd. N12—5H 15
Petworth Rd. Bexh—5G 101
Petworth St. SW11—1C 92
Petyt Pl. SW3—6C 76
Petyward. SW3—4C 76 (9D 144)
Pevensey Av. N11—5C 16
Pevensey Av. Enf—2K 7
Pevensey Clo. Iswth—7G 71
Pevensey Rd. E7—4H 49
Pevensey Rd. SW17—4B 108
Pevensey Rd. Felt—1C 102
Peverett Clo. N11—5A 16
Peveril Dri. Tedd—5H 103
Pewsey Clo. E4—5H 19
Peyton Pl. SE10—7E 80
Phelp St. SE17—6D 78
Phene St. SW3—6C 76
Philbeach Gdns. SW5—5J 75
Philchurch Pl. E1
—6G 63 (8H 143)
Philip Av. Romf—1K 53
Philip Clo. Romf—1K 53
Philip Gdns. Croy—2B 136
Philip La. N15—4D 30
Philipot Path. SE9—6D 98
Philippa Gdns. SE9—5B 98
Philip St. E13—4J 65
Philip Wlk. SE15—3G 95
Phillimore Gdns. NW10—1E 58
Phillimore Gdns. W8—2J 75
Phillimore Gdns. Clo. W8
—3J 75
Phillimore Pl. W8—2J 75
Phillimore Ter. W8—3J 75
Phillimore Wlk. W8—3J 75
Phillipp St. N1—1E 62
Philpot La. EC3—7E 62 (9C 142)
Philpot Path. Ilf—3G 51
Philpot Sq. SW6—3K 91
Philpot St. E1—6H 63 (7K 143)
(in two parts)
Phineas Pett Rd. SE9—3C 98
Phipps Bri. Rd.—2A 122
SW19 97-273 & 84-176
Mitc remainder
Phipps Hatch La. Enf—1H 7
Phipp's M. SW1—4F 77 (8J 145)
Phipp St. EC2—4E 62 (3C 142)
Phoebeth Rd. SE4—5C 96
Phoenix Clo. E8—1F 63
Phoenix Clo. W Wick—2F 137

Phoenix Pl. WC1
—4K 61 (3F 140)
Phoenix Rd. NW1
—3H 61 (1A 140)
Phoenix Rd. SE20—6J 111
Phoenix St. WC2
—6H 61 (8B 140)
Phoenix Trading Pk. Bren
—5D 72
Phoenix Way. Houn—6B 70
Phyllis Av. N Mald—5D 120
Physic Pl. SW3—6D 76
Picardy Manorway. Belv
—3H 85
Picardy Rd. Belv—5G 85
Picardy St. Belv—3G 85
Piccadilly. W1—1F 77 (3K 145)
Piccadilly Cir. W1
—7H 61 (1A 146)
Pickard St. EC1—3B 62 (1K 141)
Pickering Av. E6—2E 66
Pickering M. W2—6K 59
Pickering St. N1—1B 62
Pickets Clo. Bush, Wat—1C 10
Pickets St. SW12—7F 93
Pickett Croft. Stan—1D 24
Picketts Lock La. N9—2E 18
Picketts Lock La. Industrial
Est. N9—2F 19
Pickford Clo. Bexh—2E 100
Pickford La. Bexh—2E 100
Pickford Rd. Bexh—3E 100
Pickfords Yd. N17—6A 18
Pickhurst Grn. Brom—7H 127
Pickhurst La. W Wick & Brom
—5G 127
Pickhurst Mead. Brom—7H 127
Pickhurst Pk. Brom—5G 127
Pickhurst Rise. W Wick—1F 137
Pickwick Clo. Houn—5C 86
Pickwick M. N18—5K 17
Pickwick Pl. Harr—7J 23
Pickwick Rd. SE21—7D 94
Pickwick St. SE1
—2C 78 (5L 147)
Pickwick Way. Chst—6G 115
Pickworth Clo. SW8—7J 77
Picton Pl. W1—6E 60 (8H 139)
Picton St. SE5—7D 78
Piedmont Rd. SE18—5H 83
Piermont Rd. SE22—5H 95
Pierrepoint Rd. W3—7H 57
Pier Rd. E16—2E 82
Pier St. E14—4E 80
Pier Ter. SW18—4K 91
Pier Way. SE28—3H 83
Pigeon La. Hmptn—4E 102
Pigott St. E14—6C 64
Pike Clo. Brom—5K 113
Pike Rd. NW7—4E 12
Pikestone Clo. Hay—4C 54
Pilgrimage St. SE1
—2D 78 (5A 148)
Pilgrim Hill. SE27—4C 110
Pilgrims Clo. N13—4G 16
Pilgrims Clo. N'holt—5G 39
Pilgrim's La. NW3—4B 44
Pilgrim's Pl. NW3—4B 44
Pilgrims Rise. Barn—5H 5
Pilgrim St. EC4—6B 62 (8J 141)
Pilgrims Way. N19—1H 45
Pilgrims Way. S Croy—5F 135
Pilgrim's Way. Wemb—1H 41
Pilkington Rd. SE15—2H 95
Pillmans Clo. Sidc—6C 116
Pilot Industrial Centre. NW10
—4K 57
Pilsdon Clo. SW19—1F 107
Pimlico Rd. SW1
—5E 76 (9G 145)
Pimlico Wlk. N1—3E 62 (1C 142)
Pinchin St. E1—7G 63 (9H 143)
Pincott Rd. SW19—7A 108
Pincott Rd. Bexh—5G 101
Pindar St. EC2—5E 62 (5C 142)
Pindock M. W9—4K 59
Pine Av. E15—5F 49

Pine Av. W Wick—1D 136
Pine Clo. N14—7B 6
Pine Clo. N19—2G 45
Pine Clo. Stan—4G 11
Pine Coombe. Croy—4K 135
Pine Ct. E4—6G 19
Pine Ct. N'holt—4C 54
Pinecroft Ct. Well—7A 84
Pine Dene. SE15—1H 95
Pinefield Clo. E14—7C 64
Pine Gdns. Ruis—1A 38
Pine Gdns. Surb—6G 119
Pine Gro. N4—2J 45
Pine Gro. N20—1C 14
Pine Gro. SW19—5H 107
Pine Ridge. Cars—7E 132
Pine Rd. N11—2K 15
Pine Rd. NW2—4E 42
Pines Rd. Brom—2C 128
Pines, The. N14—5B 6
Pines, The. SE19—7B 110
Pines, The. Wfd G—3D 20
Pine St. EC1—4A 62 (3G 141)
Pine Wlk. Surb—6G 119
Pinewood Av. Pinn—6A 10
Pinewood Av. Sidc—1J 115
Pinewood Clo. Croy—3A 136
Pinewood Clo. Pinn—6A 10
Pinewood Gro. W5—6C 56
Pinewood Lodge. Bush, Wat
—1C 10
Pinewood Rd. SE2—6D 84
Pinewood Rd. Brom—4J 127
Pinewood Rd. Felt—3A 102
Pinfold Rd. SW16—4J 109
Pinkerton Pl. SW16—4H 109
Pinkham Way. N11—7K 15
Pinley Gdns. Dag—1B 68
Pinnacle Hill. Bexh—4H 101
Pinnacle Hill N. Bexh—4H 101
Pinnell Rd. SE9—4B 98
Pinner Grn. Pinn—2A 22
Pinner Gro. Pinn—4C 22
Pinner Hill Rd. Pinn—1A 22
Pinner Pk. Av. Harr—3F 23
Pinner Pk. Gdns. Harr—2G 23
Pinner Rd. Pinn & Harr—4D 22
Pinner View. Harr—4G 23
Pintail Clo. E6—5C 66
Pintail Rd. Wfd G—7E 20
Pinto Way. SE3—4K 97
Pioneer Way. W12—6D 58
Piper Clo. N7—5K 45
Piper Rd. King—3G 119
Piper's Gdns. Croy—7A 126
Pipers Grn. NW9—5J 25
Pipers Grn. La. Edgw—3K 11
Pipewell Rd. Cars—6C 122
Pippin Clo. Croy—1B 136
Piquet Rd. SE20—2J 125
Pirbright Cres. Croy—6E 136
Pirbright Rd. SW18—1H 107
Pirie St. E16—1K 81
Pitcairn Clo. Romf—4G 37
Pitcairn Rd. Mitc—7D 108
Pitchford St. E15—7F 49
Pitfield Cres. SE28—1A 84
Pitfield St. N1—3E 62 (1C 142)
Pitfield St. N1—3E 62 (2C 142)
Pitfield Way. NW10—6J 41
Pitfield Way. Enf—1D 8
Pitfold Clo. SE12—6K 97
Pitfold Rd. SE12—6J 97
Pitlake. Croy—2B 134
Pitman St. SE5—7C 78
Pitsea Pl. E1—6K 63
Pitsea St. E1—6K 63
Pitshanger La. W5—4B 56
Pitt Cres. SW19—4K 107
Pittman Gdns. Ilf—5G 51
Pitt Rd. Harr—2G 39
Pitt Rd. T Hth—5C 124
Pitt's Head M. W1
—1E 76 (3H 145)
Pittsmead Av. Brom—7J 127
Pitt St. SE15—1F 95

Pitt St. W8—2J 75
Pittville Gdns. SE25—3G 125
Pixley St. E14—6B 64
Pixton Way. Croy—7A 136
Place Farm Av. Orp—7H 129
Plaistow Gro. E15—1H 65
Plaistow Gro. Brom—7K 113
Plaistow La. Brom—7K 113
Plaistow Pk. Rd. E13—2K 65
Plaistow Rd. E15—1H 65
Plane St. SE26—3H 111
Plane Tree Wlk. SE19—6E 110
Plantagenet Clo. Wor Pk
—4A 130
Plantagenet Gdns. Romf—7D 36
Plantagenet Pl. Romf—7D 36
Plantagenet Rd. Barn—4F 5
Plantain Pl. SE1—2D 78 (4A 148)
Plantation, The. SE3—2J 97
Plashet Gro. E6—1A 66
Plashet Rd. E13—1J 65
Plassy Rd. SE6—7D 96
Plato Rd. SW2—4J 93
Platt's La. NW3—3J 43
Platts Rd. Enf—1D 8
Platt St. NW1—2H 61
Platt, The. SW15—3F 91
(in two parts)
Plawsfield Rd. Beck—1K 125
Plaxtol Clo. Brom—1A 128
Plaxtol Rd. Eri—7G 85
Playfair St. W6—5E 74
Playfield Av. Romf—1J 37
Playfield Cres. SE22—5F 95
Playfield Rd. Edgw—2J 25
Playford Rd. N4—2K 45
(in two parts)
Playgreen Way. SE6—3C 112
Playhouse Yd. EC4
—6B 62 (8K 141)
Pleasance Rd. SW15—5D 90
Pleasance, The. SW15—4D 90
Pleasant Gro. Croy—3B 136
Pleasant Pl. N1—7B 46
Pleasant Pl. Harr—2H 39
Pleasant Row. NW1—1F 61
Pleasant View. Eri—5K 85
Pleasant Way. Wemb—2C 56
Plender St. NW1—1G 61
Pleshey Rd. N7—4H 45
Plesman Way. Wall—7J 133
Plevna Cres. N15—6E 30
Plevna Rd. N9—3B 18
Plevna St. E14—3E 80
Pleydell Av. SE19—7F 111
Pleydell Av. W6—4B 74
Plimsoll Clo. E14—6D 64
Plimsoll Rd. N4—3B 46
Plough Ct. EC3—7D 62 (9B 142)
Plough La. SE22—6F 95
Plough La.—5K 107
SW19 2-56
SW17 remainder
Plough La. Wall—4J 133
Plough La. Clo. Wall—5J 133
Ploughmans Clo. NW1—1F 61
Ploughmans End. Iswth—5H 87
Plough Pl. EC4—6A 62 (7H 141)
Plough Rd. SW11—3B 92
Plough Rd. Eps—7A 130
Plough Ter. SW11—4B 92
Plough Way. SE16—4K 79
Plough Yd. EC2—4E 62 (4D 142)
Plover Way. SE16—3A 80
Plowman Way. Dag—1C 52
Plumber's Row. E1
—6G 63 (7H 143)
Plumbridge St. SE10—1E 96
Plum Garth. Bren—4D 72
Plum La. SE18—7F 83
Plummer La. Mitc—2D 122
Plummer Rd. SW4—7H 93
Plumpton Clo. N'holt—6E 38
Plumpton Way. Cars—3C 132
Plumstead Comn. Rd. SE18
—6F 83

Plumstead High St. SE18
—4H 83
Plumstead Rd. SE18—4F 83
Plumtree Clo. Wall—7H 133
Plumtree Ct. EC4
—6B 62 (7J 141)
Plybrook Rd. Sutt—3J 131
Plymouth Rd. E16—5J 65
Plymouth Rd. Brom—1K 127
Plymouth Wharf. E14—4F 81
Plympton Av. NW6—7H 43
Plympton Clo. Belv—3E 84
Plympton Pl. NW8
—4C 60 (4C 138)
Plympton Rd. NW6—7H 43
Plympton St. NW8
—4C 60 (4C 138)
Plymstock Rd. Well—7C 84
Pocklington Clo. NW9—2A 26
Pocock St. SE1—2B 78 (4J 147)
Podmore Rd. SW18—4A 92
Poets' Corner. SW1
—3J 77 (6C 146)
Poet's Rd. N5—5D 46
Poets Way. Harr—4J 23
Pointalls Clo. N3—2A 28
Point Clo. SE10—1E 96
Pointer Clo. SE28—6D 68
Pointers Clo. E14—5D 80
Pointers Cotts. Rich—2C 104
Point Hill. SE10—1E 96
Point Pleasant. SW18—4J 91
Poland St. W1—6G 61 (8M 139)
Polebrook Rd. SE3—3A 98
Pole Cat All. Brom—2H 137
Polecroft La. SE6—2B 112
Pole Hill Rd. E4—7K 9
Polesden Gdns. SW20—2D 120
Polesworth Rd. Dag—7D 52
Police Sta. La. Bush, Wat
—1A 10
Pollard Clo. E16—7J 65
Pollard Clo. N7—4K 45
Pollard Rd. N20—2H 15
Pollard Rd. Mord—5B 122
Pollard Row. E2—3G 63 (1H 143)
Pollards Cres. SW16—3J 123
Pollards Hill E. SW16—3J 123
Pollards Hill N. SW16—3J 123
Pollards Hill S. SW16—3J 123
Pollards Hill W. SW16—3K 123
Pollard St. E2—3G 63 (1H 143)
Pollards Wood Rd. SW16
—3J 123
Pollard Wlk. Sidc—6C 116
Pollen St. W1—6G 61 (8L 139)
Pollitt Dri. NW8—4B 60 (3B 138)
Polperro Clo. Orp—6K 129
Polsted Rd. SE6—7B 96
Polthorne Gro. SE18—4H 83
Polworth Rd. SW16—5J 109
Polygon Rd. NW1
—2H 61 (1A 140)
Polygon, The. SW4—4G 93
Polytechnic St. SE18—4E 82
Pomell Way. E1—6F 63 (7F 142)
Pomeroy St. SE14—7J 79
Pomfret Rd. SE5—3C 94
Pond Clo. SE3—2H 97
Pond Cottage La. Beck—1C 136
Pond Cotts. SE21—1E 110
Ponders End Industrial Est. Enf
—5F 9
Ponder St. N7—7K 45
Pondfield Ho. SE27—5C 110
Pondfield Rd. Brom—1G 137
Pondfield Rd. Dag—5H 53
Pond Hill Gdns. Sutt—6G 131
Pond Mead. SE21—6D 94
Pond Pl. SW3—4C 76 (9C 144)
Pond Pl. E15—2G 65
Pond St. NW3—5C 44
Pond Rd. SE3—2H 97
Pond Sq. N6—1E 44
Pond Way. Chst—6F 115
Pond Way. Tedd—6C 104
Pondwood Rise. Orp—7J 129

Ponler St. E1—6H 63 (8J 143)
Ponsard Rd. NW10—3D 58
Ponsford St. E9—6J 47
Ponsonby Pl. SW1
—5H 77 (9B 146)
Ponsonby Rd. SW15—7D 90
Ponsonby Ter. SW1
—5H 77 (9B 146)
Pontefract Rd. Brom—5H 113
Ponton Rd. SW8—7H 77
Pont St. SW1—3D 76 (7E 144)
Pont St. M. SW1—3D 76 (7E 144)
Pontypool Pl. SE1
—2B 78 (4J 147)
Pool Clo. Beck—5C 112
Poole Ct. Rd. Houn—2C 86
Poole Rd. E9—6K 47
Poole Rd. Eps—7A 130
Pooles Cotts. Rich—2D 104
Pooles La. SW10—7A 76
Pooles La. Dag—2E 68
Pooles Pk. N4—2A 46
Poole St. N1—1D 62
Poolmans St. SE16—2K 79
Pool Rd. Harr—7H 23
Poolsford Rd. NW9—4A 26
Poonah St. E1—6J 63 (8M 143)
Pope Clo. SW19—6B 108
Pope Rd. Brom—5B 128
Popes Av. Twic—2J 103
Pope's Dri. N3—1J 27
Popes Gro. Croy—3B 136
Popes Gro. Twic—2K 103
Pope's Head All. EC3
—6D 62 (8B 142)
Popes La. W5—3D 72
Pope's Rd. SW9—3A 94
Pope St. SE1—2E 78 (5D 148)
Popham Clo. Felt—3D 102
Popham Gdns. Rich—3G 89
Popham Rd. N1—1C 62
Poplar Av. Mitc—1D 122
Poplar Av. S'hall—3F 71
Poplar Bath St. E14—7D 64
Poplar Business Pk. E14—7E 64
Poplar Clo. Pinn—1B 22
Poplar Ct. SW19—5J 107
Poplar Gdns. SE28—6C 68
Poplar Gro. N11—6K 15
Poplar Gro. W6—2E 74
Poplar Gro. N Mald—2K 119
Poplar Gro. Wemb—3J 41
Poplar High St. E14—7D 64
Poplar Mt. Belv—4J 85
Poplar Pl. SE28—1C 84
Poplar Pl. W2—7K 59
Poplar Rd. SE24—4C 94
Poplar Rd. SW19—2J 121
Poplar Rd. Sutt—1H 131
Poplar Rd. S. SW19—3J 121
Poplars Av. NW2—6E 42
Poplars Rd. E17—6D 32
Poplars, The. N14—5A 6
Poplar St. Romf—4J 37
Poplar Wlk. SE24—4C 94
Poplar Wlk. Croy—1C 134
Poplar Way. Ilf—4G 35
Poppins Ct. EC4—6B 62 (8J 141)
Poppleton Rd. E11—6G 33
Poppy Clo. Wall—1E 132
Poppy La. Croy—1J 135
Porchester Clo. SE5—4D 94
Porchester Gdns. W2—7K 59
Porchester Gdns. M. W2—6K 59
Porchester Mead. Beck
—6C 112
Porchester M. W2—6K 59
Porchester Pl. W2
—6C 60 (8D 138)
Porchester Rd. W2—6K 59
Porchester Rd. King—2H 119
Porchester Sq. W2—6K 59
Porchester Ter. W2—7A 60
Porchester Ter. N. W2—6K 59
Porch Way. N20—3J 15
Porcupine Clo. SE9—2C 114

Porden Rd. SW2—4K 93
Porlock Av. Harr—1G 39
Porlock Ho. SE26—3G 111
Porlock Rd. W10—4F 59
Porlock Rd. Enf—7A 8
Porlock St. SE1—2D 78 (4B 148)
Porrington Clo. Chst—1E 128
Portal Clo. SE27—3A 110
Portbury Clo. SE15—1G 95
Port Cres. E13—4K 65
Portcullis Lodge Rd. Enf—3J 7
Portelet Rd. E1—3K 63 (2M 143)
Porten Rd. W14—3G 75
Porter Rd. E6—6D 66
Porters Av. Dag—6B 52
Porter St. W1—5D 60 (5F 138)
Porteus Rd. W2—5A 60 (5A 138)
Portgate Clo. W9—4H 59
Porthcawe Rd. SE26—4K 112
Porthkerry Av. Well—4A 100
Portia Way. E3—4B 64
Portinscale Rd. SW15—5G 91
Portland Av. N16—7F 31
Portland Av. N Mald—7B 120
Portland Av. Sidc—6A 100
Portland Clo. Romf—5E 36
Portland Cres. SE9—2C 114
Portland Cres. Gnfd—5F 55
Portland Cres. Stan—2D 25
Portland Gdns. N4—6B 30
Portland Gdns. Romf—5D 36
Portland Gro. SW8—1K 93
Portland M. W1—6G 61 (8M 139)
Portland Pl. W1—5F 61 (5J 139)
Portland Rise. N4—1B 46
Portland Rise Est. N4—1C 46
Portland Rd. N15—4F 31
Portland Rd. SE9—2C 114
Portland Rd. SE25—4G 125
Portland Rd. W11—7G 59
Portland Rd. Brom—4A 114
Portland Rd. King—3E 118
Portland Rd. Mitc—2C 122
Portland Rd. S'hall—3D 70
Portland Sq. E1—1H 79 (2J 149)
Portland St. SE17—5D 78
Portland Ter. Rich—4D 88
Portman Av. SW14—3K 89
Portman Clo. W1
—6E 60 (7G 139)
Portman Clo. Bex—1K 117
Portman Clo. Bexh—3E 100
Portman Dri. Wfd G—2B 34
Portman Gdns. NW9—2K 25
Portman M. S. W1
—6E 60 (8G 139)
Portman Pl. E2—3J 63 (2M 143)
Portman Rd. King—2F 119
Portman Sq. W1
—6E 60 (7G 139)
Portman St. W1—6E 60 (8G 139)
Portmeadow Wlk. SE2—2D 84
Portmeers Clo. E17—6B 32
Portnall Rd. W9—3H 59
Portnoi Clo. Romf—2K 37
Portobello M. W11—7J 59
Portobello Rd. W10—5G 59
W11 1-275 & 2-262
W10 remainder
Portpool La. EC1
—5A 62 (5G 141)
Portree Clo. N22—7E 16
Portree St. E14—6F 65
Portsdown Av. NW11—6H 27
Portsdown M. NW11—6H 27
Portsea Pl. W2—6C 60 (8D 138)
Portslade Rd. SW8—2G 93
Portsmouth Av. Th Dit—7A 118
Portsmouth Rd. SW15—7D 90
Portsmouth Rd. Esh, Th Dit,
Surb & King—7A 118
Portsmouth St. WC2
—6K 61 (8F 140)
Portsoken St. E1
—7F 63 (9E 142)
Portswood Pl. SW15—7B 90

Portugal Gdns. Twic—2G 103
Portugal St. WC2
—6K 61 (8F 140)
Portway. E15—1H 65
Portway Gdns. SE18—7B 82
Postern Grn. Enf—3F 7
Post La. Twic—1H 103
Post Office App. E7—5K 49
Post Office Way. SW8—6H 77
Postway M. Ilf—3F 51
(in two parts)
Potier St. SE1—3D 78 (7B 148)
Potter Clo. Mitc—2F 123
Potterne Clo. SW19—7F 91
Potters Clo. Croy—1A 136
Potters' Fields. SE1
—1E 78 (3D 148)
Potters Gro. N Mald—4J 119
Potter's La. SW16—6H 109
Potters La. Barn—4D 4
Potters La. Barn—4E 4
Potter St. N'wd & Pinn—1A 22
Pottery La. W11—1G 75
Pottery Rd. Bex—2J 117
Pottery Rd. Bren—6E 72
Pottery St. SE16
—2H 79 (5J 149)
Pott St. E2—3H 63 (2K 143)
Poulett Gdns. Twic—1A 104
Poulett Rd. E6—2D 66
Poulner Way. SE15—7F 79
Poulton Av. Sutt—3B 132
Poulton Clo. E8—6H 47
Poultry. EC2—6D 62 (8A 142)
Pound Clo. Surb—7C 118
Pound La. NW10—6C 42
Pound Pk. Rd. SE7—4B 82
Pound Pl. SE9—6E 98
Pound St. Cars—5D 132
Pountney Rd. SW11—3E 92
Poverest Rd. Orp—5K 129
Powder Mill La. Twic—7D 86
Powell Clo. Edgw—6A 12
Powell Clo. Wall—7J 133
Powell Gdns. Dag—4G 53
Powell Rd. E5—3H 47
Powell Rd. Buck H—1F 21
Powell's Wlk. W4—6A 74
Power Rd. W4—4G 73
Powers Ct. Twic—7D 88
Powerscroft Rd. E5—4J 47
Powerscroft Rd. Sidc—6C 116
Powis Gdns. NW11—7H 27
Powis Gdns. W11—6H 59
Powis M. W11—6H 59
Powis Pl. WC1—4J 61 (4D 140)
Powis Rd. E3—3D 64
Powis Sq. W11—6H 59
Powis St. SE18—3E 82
Powis Ter. W11—6H 59
Powlett Pl. NW1—7F 45
Pownall Gdns. Houn—4F 87
Pownall Rd. E8—1G 63
Pownall Rd. Houn—4F 87
Powster Rd. Brom—5J 113
Powys Clo. Bexh—6D 84
Powys La. N13—5D 16
Powys La.—4D 16
N14 2-46
N13 remainder
Poynders Gdns. SW4—7G 93
Poynders Rd. SW4—6G 93
Poynings Rd. N19—3G 45
Poynings Way. N12—5D 14
Poyntell Cres. Chst—1H 129
Poynter Rd. Enf—5B 8
Poynton Rd. N17—2G 31
Poyntz Rd. SW11—2D 92
Poyser St. E2—2H 63 (1K 143)
Praed M. W2—6B 60 (7B 138)
Praed St. W2—6B 60 (7B 138)
Pragel St. E13—2A 66
Pragnell Rd. SE12—2K 113
Prague St. SW2—5J 93
Prah Rd. N4—2A 46
Prairie St. SW8—2F 93
Pratt M. NW1—1G 61

Pratts Pas. King.—2E 118
Pratt St. NW1—1G 61
Pratt Wlk. SE11—4K 77 (8F 146)
Prayle Gro. NW2—1F 43
Prebend Gdns.—4B 74
W4 1-37 & 2-40
W6 remainder
Prebend St. N1—1C 62
Prendergast Rd. SE3—3G 97
Prentis Rd. SW16—4H 109
Prentiss Ct. SE7—4B 82
Presburg Rd. N Mald—5A 120
Prescelly Pl. Edgw—1F 25
Prescot St. E1—7F 63 (9F 142)
Prescott Av. Orp—6F 129
Prescott Clo. SW16—7J 109
Prescott Pl. SW4—4H 93
Preshaw Cres. Mitc—3C 122
Presidents Dri. E1
—1H 79 (2J 149)
Press Rd. NW10—3K 41
Prestbury Rd. E7—7A 50
Prestbury Sq. SE9—4D 114
Prested Rd. SW11—4C 92
Preston Av. E4—6A 20
Preston Clo. SE1
—4E 78 (8C 148)
Preston Clo. Twic—3J 103
Preston Dri. E11—5A 34
Preston Dri. Bexh—1D 100
Preston Dri. Eps—6A 130
Preston Gdns. NW10—6A 42
Preston Gdns. Ilf—6C 34
Preston Hill. Harr—7E 24
Preston Pl. NW2—6C 42
Preston Rd. Rich—5E 88
Preston Rd. E11—6G 33
Preston Rd. SE19—6B 110
Preston Rd. SW20—7B 106
Preston Rd. Wemb & Harr
—2E 40
Preston's Rd. E14—7E 64
Prestons Rd. Brom—3J 137
Preston Waye. Harr—1E 40
Prestwick Clo. S'hall—5C 70
Prestwood Av. Harr—4B 24
Prestwood Clo. Harr—4B 24
Prestwood Gdns. Croy—7C 124
Prestwood St. N1
—2C 62 (1M 141)
Pretoria Av. E17—4A 32
Pretoria Clo. N17—7A 18
Pretoria Cres. E4—1K 19
Pretoria Rd. E4—1K 19
Pretoria Rd. E11—1F 49
Pretoria Rd. E16—4H 65
Pretoria Rd. N17—7A 18
Pretoria Rd. SW16—6F 109
Pretoria Rd. Ilf—5F 51
Pretoria Rd. Romf—4J 37
Pretoria Rd. N. N18—6A 18
Prevost Rd. N11—2K 15
Price Clo. NW7—6B 14
Price Clo. SW17—3D 108
Price Rd. Croy—5B 134
Price's St. SE1—1B 78 (3K 147)
Price's Yd. N1—1K 61
Price Way. Hmptn—6C 102
Pricklers Hill. Barn—6E 4
Prickley Wood. Brom—1H 137
Priddy's Yd. Croy—2C 134
Prideaux Pl. WC1
—3K 61 (1F 140)
Prideaux Rd. SW9—3J 93
Pridham Rd. E . T Hth—4D 124
Priestfield Rd. SE23—3A 112
Priestlands Pk. Rd. Sidc
—3K 115
Priestley Clo. N16—7F 31
Priestley Gdns. Romf—6B 36
Priestley Rd. Mitc—2E 122
Priestley Way. E17—3K 31
Priestley Way. NW2—1C 42
Priest Pk. Av. Harr—2E 38
Priests Av. Romf—2K 37

Priests Bri.—3A 90
SW15 2-20
SW14 remainder
Prima Rd. SW9—7A 78
Primrose Av. Enf—1K 7
Primrose Av. Romf—7B 36
Primrose Clo. SE6—5E 112
Primrose Clo. Harr—3D 38
Primrose Clo. Wall—1F 133
Primrose Gdns. NW3—6C 44
Primrose Gdns. Bush, Wat
—1A 10
Primrose Gdns. Ruis—5A 38
Primrose Hill. EC4
—6A 62 (8H 141)
Primrose Hill. NW3—7D 44
Primrose La. Croy—1K 135
Primrose Rd. E10—1D 48
Primrose Rd. E18—2K 33
Primrose St. EC2
—5E 62 (5D 142)
Primrose Way. Wemb—2D 56
Primula St. W12—6C 58
Prince Albert Rd.
—2C 60 (1C 138)
NW1 1-23
NW8 remainder
Prince Arthur M. NW3—4A 44
Prince Arthur Rd. NW3—5A 44
Prince Charles Dri. NW4—7E 26
Prince Charles Rd. SE3—2H 97
Prince Charles Way. Wall
—3F 133
Prince Consort Dri. Chst
—1H 129
Prince Consort Rd. SW7
—3B 76 (6A 144)
Princedale Rd. W11—1G 75
Prince Edward Rd. E9—6B 48
Prince George Av. N14—5C 6
Prince George Rd. N16—4E 46
Prince George's Av. SW20
—2E 120
Prince George's Rd. SW19
—1B 122
Prince Henry Rd. SE7—7B 82
Prince Imperial Rd. SE18
—1D 98
Prince Imperial Rd. Chst
—7F 115
Prince John Rd. SE9—5C 98
Princelet St. E1—5F 63 (5F 142)
Prince of Orange La. SE10
—7E 80
Prince of Wales Clo. NW4
—4D 26
Prince of Wales Dri. SW11 &
SW8—1D 92
Prince of Wales Rd. E16—6A 66
Prince of Wales Rd. NW5
—6E 44
Prince of Wales Rd. SE3—1H 97
Prince of Wales Rd. Sutt
—2B 132
Prince of Wales Ter. W4—5A 74
Prince of Wales Ter. W8—2K 75
Prince Regent La.—3K 65
E13 1-279 & 2-250
E16 remainder
Prince Regent Rd. Houn—3G 87
Prince Rd. SE25—5E 124
Prince Rupert Rd. SE9—4D 98
Princes Av. N3—1J 27
Princes Av. N10—3F 29
Princes Av. N13—5F 17
Princes Av. N22—1H 29
Princes Av. NW9—4G 25
Princes Av. W3—3G 73
Princes Av. Cars—7D 132
Prince's Av. Gnfd—6F 55
Princes Av. Orp—5J 129
Princes Av. Wfd G—4E 20
Princes Clo. NW9—4G 25
Princes Clo. Edgw—5B 12
Princes Clo. Sidc—3D 116
Prince's Clo. Tedd—4H 103
Princes Ct. Wemb—5E 40

Princes Dri. Harr—3J 23
Prince's Gdns. SW7
—3B 76 (6B 144)
Princes Gdns. W3—5G 57
Princes Gdns. W5—4C 56
Prince's Ga. SW7
—2B 76 (5B 144)
(in three parts)
Prince's Ga. Ct. SW7
—2B 76 (5B 144)
Prince's Ga. M. SW7
—3B 76 (6B 144)
Princes La. N10—3F 29
Prince's M. W2—7K 59
Prince's Pl. SW7—1G 75
Prince's Pl. W11—1G 75
Prince's Plain. Brom—7C 128
Prince's Rise. SE13—2E 96
Princes Rd. N18—4D 18
Princes Rd. SE20—6K 111
Princes Rd. SW14—3K 89
Prince's Rd. SW19—6J 107
Princes Rd. W13—1B 72
Prince's Rd. Buck H—2F 21
Princes Rd. Ilf—4H 35
Princes Rd. King—7G 105
Princes Rd. Rich—5F 89
Princes Rd. Rich—1F 89
(Kew)
Prince's Rd. Tedd—4H 103
Princes Av. Wemb—2E 40
Princess Ct. N6—7G 29
Princess Ct. SE16—3B 80
Princess Cres. N4—2B 46
Princess May Rd. N16—4E 46
Princess M. NW3—5B 44
Prince's Sq. W2—7K 59
Princess Rd. NW1—1E 60
Princess Rd. NW6—2J 59
Princess Rd. Croy—6C 124
Princess St. SE1
—3B 78 (7K 147)
Princes St. N17—6K 17
Princes St. W1—6F 61 (8K 139)
Princes St. Bexh—4F 101
Princes St. Rich—4E 88
Princes St. Sutt—4B 132
Princes Ter. E13—1K 65
Prince St. SE8—6B 80
Princes Way. SW19—7F 91
Princes Way. Buck H—2F 21
Princes Way. Croy—5K 133
Princes Way. Ruis—4C 38
Princes Way. W Wick—4H 137
Princethorpe Rd. SE26—4K 111
Princeton St. WC1
—5K 61 (5E 140)
Pringle Gdns. SW16—4G 109
(in two parts)
Printer St. EC4—6A 62 (7H 141)
Printing Ho. Yd. E2
—3E 62 (1D 142)
Priolo Rd. SE7—5A 82
Prior Av. Sutt—7C 132
Prior Bolton St. N1—6B 46
Prioress Rd. SE27—3B 110
Prioress St. SE1—3E 78 (7C 148)
Prior Rd. Ilf—3E 50
Priors Croft. E17—2A 32
Priors Field. N'holt—6C 38
Priors Gdns. Ruis—5A 38
Priors Mead. Enf—1K 7
Prior St. SE10—7E 80
Priory Av. E4—3G 19
Priory Av. E17—5C 32
Priory Av. N8—4H 29
Priory Av. W4—4A 74
Priory Av. Orp—6H 129
Priory Av. Sutt—4F 131
Priory Av. Wemb—4K 39
Priory Clo. E4—3G 19
Priory Clo. E18—1J 33
Priory Clo. N3—1H 27
Priory Clo. N14—5A 6
Priory Clo. N20—1C 14
Priory Clo. SW19—1K 121

Priory Clo. Beck—3A 126
Priory Clo. Chst—1D 128
Priory Clo. Hmptn—7D 102
Priory Clo. Stan—8E 10
Priory Clo. Wemb—4K 39
Priory Ct. E17—2B 32
Priory Ct. SW8—1H 93
Priory Ct. Bush, Wat—1B 10
Priory Ct. Eps—7B 130
Priory Ct. Est. E17—2B 32
Priory Cres. SE19—7C 110
Priory Cres. Sutt—4F 131
Priory Cres. Wemb—3A 40
Priory Dri. SE2—5D 84
Priory Dri. Stan—3E 10
Prioryfield Dri. Edgw—4C 12
Priory Gdns. N6—6F 29
Priory Gdns. SW13—3B 90
Priory Gdns. W4—4A 74
Priory Gdns. W5—3E 56
Priory Gdns. Hmptn—7D 102
Priory Gdns. Wemb—4A 40
Priory Grn. Est. N1—2K 61
Priory Gro. SW8—1J 93
Priory Hill. Wemb—4A 40
Priory La. SW15—6A 90
Priory La. Rich—7G 73
Priory M. SW8—1H 93
Priory Pk. SE3—3H 97
Priory Pk. Rd. NW6—1H 59
Priory Pk. Rd. Wemb—4A 40
Priory Rd. E6—1B 66
Priory Rd. N8—4H 29
Priory Rd. NW6—1K 59
Priory Rd. SW19—7B 108
Priory Rd. W4—3K 73
Priory Rd. Bark—7H 51
Priory Rd. Croy—7A 124
Priory Rd. Hmptn—7D 102
Priory Rd. Houn—5G 87
Priory Rd. Rich—6G 73
Priory Rd. Sutt—4F 131
Priory St. E3—3D 64
Priory Ter. NW6—1K 59
Priory, The. SE3—4H 97
Priory View. Bush, Wat—1D 10
Priory Wlk. SW10—5A 76
Priory Way. Harr—4F 23
Priory Way. S'hall—3B 70
Pritchard's Rd. E2
—2G 63 (1G 143)
Priter Rd. SE16—3G 79 (7H 149)
Priter Way. SE16
—3G 79 (7H 149)
Private Rd. Enf—5J 7
Probert Rd. SW2—5A 94
Probyn Rd. SW2—2B 110
Procter St. WC1—5K 61 (6E 140)
Progress Way. N22—1A 30
Progress Way. Croy—2K 133
Progress Way. Enf—5B 8
Promenade App. Rd. W4—7A 74
Promenade, The. W4—1A 90
Prospect Clo. SE26—4H 111
Prospect Clo. Belv—4G 85
Prospect Clo. Houn—1D 86
Prospect Clo. Ruis—7B 22
Prospect Cotts. SW18—4J 91
Prospect Cres. Twic—6F 87
Prospect Hill. E17—4D 32
Prospect Pl. E1—1J 79 (2L 149)
(in two parts)
Prospect Pl. N2—4B 28
Prospect Pl. N17—7K 17
Prospect Pl. NW2—3H 43
Prospect Pl. NW3—4A 44
Prospect Pl. W4—5K 73
Prospect Pl. Brom—3K 127
Prospect Pl. Romf—2J 37
Prospect Ring. N2—3B 28
Prospect Rd. NW2—3H 43
Prospect Rd. Barn—4D 4
Prospect Rd. Surb—6C 118
Prospect Rd. Wfd G—6F 21
Prospect St. SE16
—3H 79 (6K 149)
Prospect Vale. SE18—4C 82

Queen St. Bexh—3F 101
Queen St. Croy—4C 134
Queen St. Romf—6K 37
Queen St. Pl. EC4
—7C 62 (9M 141)
Queensville Rd. SW12—7H 93
Queens Wlk. E4—1A 20
Queens Wlk. NW9—2J 41
Queen's Wlk. SW1
—1G 77 (3L 145)
Queen's Wlk. W5—4C 56
Queens Wlk. Harr—4J 23
Queens Wlk. Ruis—2A 38
Queens Wlk. Ter. Ruis—3A 38
Queen's Way. NW4—5E 26
Queensway. Croy—5K 133
Queensway. Enf—4C 8
Queensway. Felt—4A 102
Queensway. Orp—5G 129
Queensway. W Wick—4H 137
Queensway Industrial Est. Enf
—4D 8
Queenswell Av. N20—4H 15
Queenswood Av. E17—1E 32
Queenswood Av. Hmptn
—6F 103
Queenswood Av. Houn—2D 86
Queenswood Av. T Hth—5A 124
Queenswood Av. Wall—4H 133
Queenswood Ct. SE27—4D 110
Queenswood Gdns. E11—1K 49
Queens Wood Pk. N3—2G 27
Queens Wood Rd. N10—6F 29
Queenswood Rd. SE23—3K 111
Queenswood Rd. Sidc—6K 99
Queen Victoria Av. Wemb
—7D 40
Queen Victoria St. EC4
—7B 62 (9K 141)
Quemerford Rd. N7—5K 45
Quentin Pl. SE13—3G 97
Quentin Rd. SE13—3G 97
Quernmore Clo. Brom—6J 113
Quernmore Rd. N4—6A 30
Quernmore Rd. Brom—6J 113
Querrin St. SW6—2A 92
Quex M. NW6—1J 59
Quex Rd. NW6—1J 59
Quick Pl. N1—1B 62
Quick Rd. W4—5A 74
Quicksilver Pl. N22—2K 29
Quicks Rd. SW19—7K 107
Quick St. N1—2B 62
Quickswood. NW3—7C 44
Quill La. SW15—4F 91
Quilp St. SE1—2C 78 (4L 147)
Quilter St. E2—3G 63 (1G 143)
Quinta Dri. Barn—5A 4
Quintin Av. SW20—1H 121
Quinton Clo. Beck—3E 126
Quinton Clo. Wall—4F 133
Quinton Rd. Th Dit—7A 118
Quinton St. SW18—2A 108
Quixley St. E14—7F 65
Quorn Rd. SE22—4E 94

Rabbit Row. W8—1J 75
Rabbits Rd. E12—4C 50
Rabournmead Dri. N'holt
—5C 38
Raby Rd. N Mald—4K 119
Raby St. E14—6A 64
Raccoon Way. Houn—2A 86
Racton Rd. SW6—6J 75
Radbourne Av. W5—4C 72
Radbourne Clo. E5—4K 47
Radbourne Cres. E17—3F 33
Radbourne Rd. SW12—7G 93
Radcliffe Av. NW10—2C 58
Radcliffe Av. Enf—1H 7
Radcliffe Gdns. Cars—7C 132
Radcliffe Rd. N21—1G 17
Radcliffe Rd. Croy—2F 135
Radcliffe Rd. Stan—2A 24
Radcliffe Sq. SW15—6F 91

Radcliffe Way. N'holt—3B 54
Radcot St. SE11—5A 78
Raddington Rd. W10—5G 59
Radfield Way. Sidc—7H 99
Radford Rd. SE13—6E 96
Radford Way. Bark—3K 67
Radipole Rd. SW6—1H 91
Radland Rd. E16—6H 65
Radlet Av. SE26—2H 111
Radlett Clo. E7—6H 49
Radlett Pl. NW8—1C 60
Radley Av. Ilf—4A 52
Radley Ct. SE16—2K 79
Radley Gdns. Harr—4E 24
Radley M. W8—3K 75
Radley Rd. N17—2E 30
Radley's La. E18—2J 33
Radleys Mead. Dag—6H 53
Radley Sq. E5—2J 47
Radlix Rd. E10—1C 48
Radnor Av. Harr—5J 23
Radnor Av. Well—5B 100
Radnor Clo. Chst—6J 115
Radnor Clo. Mitc—4J 123
Radnor Cres. Ilf—5D 34
Radnor Gdns. Enf—1K 7
Radnor Gdns. Twic—2K 103
Radnor M. W2—6B 60 (8B 138)
Radnor Pl. W2—6C 60 (8C 138)
Radnor Rd. NW6—1G 59
Radnor Rd. SE15—7G 79
Radnor Rd. Harr—5H 23
Radnor Rd. Twic—2K 103
(in two parts)
Radnor St. EC1—3C 62 (2M 141)
Radnor Ter. W14—4H 75
Radnor Wlk. SW3—5C 76
Radnor Wlk. Croy—6B 126
Radnor Way. NW10—4H 57
Radstock Av. Harr—3A 24
Radstock St. SW11—7C 76
Raeburn Av. Surb—7H 119
Raeburn Clo. NW11—6A 28
Raeburn Clo. King—7D 104
Raeburn Rd. Edgw—1G 25
Raeburn Rd. Sidc—6A 84
Raeburn St. SW2—4J 93
Rafford Way. Brom—2K 127
Raggleswood. Chst—1E 128
Raglan Clo. Houn—5C 86
Raglan Ct. SE12—5J 97
Raglan Ct. S Croy—5B 134
Raglan Rd. E17—5E 32
Raglan Rd. SE18—5G 83
Raglan Rd. Belv—4F 85
Raglan Rd. Brom—4A 128
Raglan Rd. Enf—7A 8
Raglan St. NW5—6F 45
Raglan Ter. Harr—4F 39
Raglan Way. N'holt—6G 39
Ragley Clo. W3—2J 73
Raider Clo. Romf—1H 37
Railey M. NW5—5G 45
Railshead Rd. Twic—4B 88
Railton Rd. SE24—4A 94
Railway App. SE1
—1D 78 (2B 148)
Railway App. Harr—4K 23
Railway App. Twic—7A 88
Railway App. Wall—5F 133
Railway Av. SE16
—2J 79 (4M 149)
Railway Cotts. Houn—6E 86
Railway Gro. SE14—7B 80
Railway M. W10—6G 59
Railway Pas. Tedd—6A 104
Railway Pl. Belv—3G 85
Railway Rise. SE22—4E 94
Railway Rd. Tedd—4K 103
Railway Side. SW13—3B 90
Railway St. N1—2J 61
Railway St. Romf—7C 36
Railway Ter. E17—1E 32
Railway Ter. SE13—5D 96
Rainborough Clo. NW10—6J 41
Rainbow Av. E14—5D 80
Rainbow St. SE5—7E 78

Raine St. E1—1H 79 (2K 149)
Rainham Clo. SE9—6J 99
Rainham Clo. SW11—6C 92
Rainham Rd. NW10—3E 58
Rainham Rd. N. Dag—2H 53
Rainham Rd. S. Dag—4H 53
Rainhill Way. E3—3D 64
Rainsborough Av. SE8—4A 80
Rainsford Clo. Stan—4H 11
Rainsford Rd. NW10—2H 57
Rainton Rd. SE7—5J 81
Rainville Rd. W6—6E 74
Raisins Hill. Pinn—3A 22
Raith Av. N14—3C 16
Raleana Rd. E14—1E 80
Raleigh Av. Hay—5A 54
Raleigh Av. Wall—4H 133
Raleigh Clo. NW4—5E 26
Raleigh Clo. Pinn—7B 22
Raleigh Ct. Beck—1D 126
Raleigh Ct. Wall—6F 133
Raleigh Dri. N20—3H 15
Raleigh Dri. Surb—7J 119
Raleigh Gdns. SW2—6K 93
Raleigh Gdns. Mitc—3D 122
Raleigh Rd. N8—4A 30
Raleigh Rd. SE20—7K 111
Raleigh Rd. Enf—4J 7
Raleigh Rd. Rich—3F 89
Raleigh Rd. S'hall—5C 70
Raleigh St. N1—1B 62
Raleigh Way. N14—1C 16
Raleigh Way. Felt—5A 102
Ralston St. SW3—5D 76
Rama Ct. Harr—2J 39
Ramac Way. SE7—5K 81
Rambler Clo. SW16—4G 109
Ramillies Clo. SW2—6J 93
Ramillies Pl. W1
—6G 61 (8L 139)
Ramillies Rd. NW7—2F 13
Ramillies Rd. W4—4K 73
Ramillies Rd. Sidc—6B 100
Ramillies St. W1
—6G 61 (8L 139)
Rampart St. E1—6H 63 (8J 143)
Rampayne St. SW1
—5H 77 (9A 146)
Ram Pl. E9—6J 47
Rampton Clo. E4—3H 19
Ramsay Rd. E7—4G 49
Ramscroft Clo. N9—7K 7
Ramsdale Rd. SW17—5E 108
Ramsden Dri. Romf—1G 37
Ramsden Rd. N11—5J 15
Ramsden Rd. SW12—6E 92
Ramsden Rd. Eri—7K 85
Ramsey Clo. NW9—6B 26
Ramsey Clo. Gnfd—5H 39
Ramsey Pl. Harr—1J 39
Ramsey Rd. W3—3J 73
Ramsey Rd. T Hth—6K 123
Ramsey St. E2—4G 63 (3H 143)
Ramsey Wlk. N1—6D 46
Ramsey Way. N14—7B 6
Ramsgate St. E8—6F 47
Ramsgill App. Ilf—4K 35
Ramsgill Dri. Ilf—5K 35
Rams Gro. Romf—4E 36
Ram St. SW18—5K 91
Ramulis Dri. Hay—4C 54
Rancliffe Gdns. SE9—4C 98
Rancliffe Rd. E6—2C 66
Randall Av. NW2—2A 42
Randall Clo. SW11—1C 92
Randall Clo. Eri—6J 85
Randall Ct. NW7—7H 13
Randall Pl. SE10—7E 80
Randall Rd. SE11
—4K 77 (9E 146)
Randall Row. SE11
—4K 77 (9E 146)
Randell's Rd. N1—1J 61
Randisbourne Gdns. SE6
—3D 112
Randle Rd. Rich—4C 104

Randlesdown Rd. SE6—4C 112
Randolph App. E16—6A 66
Randolph Av. W9
—3K 59 (5A 138)
Randolph Clo. Bexh—3J 101
Randolph Clo. King—5J 105
Randolph Cres. W9—4A 60
Randolph Gdns. NW6—2K 59
Randolph Gro. Romf—5C 36
Randolph M. W9
—4A 60 (4A 138)
Randolph Rd. E17—5D 32
Randolph Rd. W9—4A 60
Randolph Rd. S'hall—2D 70
Randolph St. NW1—7G 45
Randon Clo. Harr—2F 23
Ranelagh Av. SW6—3H 91
Ranelagh Av. SW13—2C 90
Ranelagh Bri. W2—5K 59
Ranelagh Clo. Edgw—4B 12
Ranelagh Dri. Edgw—4B 12
Ranelagh Dri. Twic—5B 88
Ranelagh Gdns. E11—5A 34
Ranelagh Gdns. SW6—3G 91
Ranelagh Gdns. W4—7J 73
Ranelagh Gdns. W6—3B 74
Ranelagh Gdns. Ilf—1D 50
Ranelagh Gro. SW1
—5E 76 (9H 145)
Ranelagh M. W5—2D 72
Ranelagh Pl. N Mald—5A 120
Ranelagh Rd. E6—1E 66
Ranelagh Rd. E11—4G 49
Ranelagh Rd. E15—2G 65
Ranelagh Rd. N17—3E 30
Ranelagh Rd. N22—1K 29
Ranelagh Rd. NW10—2B 58
Ranelagh Rd. SW1—5G 77
Ranelagh Rd. W5—2D 72
Ranelagh Rd. S'hall—1B 70
Ranelagh Rd. Wemb—6D 40
Ranfurly Rd. Sutt—2J 131
Rangefield Rd. Brom—5G 113
Rangemoor Rd. N15—5F 31
Rangers Rd. E4 & Lou—1C 20
Rangers Sq. SE10—1F 97
Rangeworth Pl. Sidc—3K 115
Rankin Clo. NW9—3A 26
Ranleigh Gdns. Bexh—7F 85
Ranmere St. SW12—1F 109
Ranmoor Clo. Harr—4H 23
Ranmoor Gdns. Harr—4H 23
Ranmore Av. Croy—3F 135
Ranmore Path. Orp—4K 129
Ranmore Rd. Sutt—7F 131
Rannoch Rd. W6—6E 74
Rannock Av. NW9—7K 25
Ransom Rd. SE7—5A 82
Ransom Wlk. SE7—4A 82
Ranston St. NW1
—5C 60 (5C 138)
Ranulf Rd. NW2—4H 43
Ranwell Clo. E3—1B 64
Ranworth Rd. N9—2D 18
Raphael St. SW7
—2D 76 (5E 144)
Rashleigh St. SW8—3F 93
Rasper Rd. N20—2F 15
Rastell Av. SW2—1H 109
Ratcliffe Cross St. E1—6K 63
Ratcliffe La. E14—6A 64
Ratcliffe Orchard. E1—7K 63
Ratcliff Gro. EC1
—3C 62 (2M 141)
Ratcliff Rd. E7—5A 50
Rathbone Pl. W1
—5G 61 (7A 140)
Rathbone St. E16—6H 65
Rathbone St. W1
—5G 61 (6M 139)
Rathcoole Av. N8—5K 29
Rathcoole Gdns. N8—5K 29
Rathfern Rd. SE6—1B 112
Rathgar Av. W13—1B 72
Rathgar Clo. N3—2H 27
Rathgar Rd. SW9—3B 94
Rathmell Dri. SW4—6H 93

Rathmore Rd. SE7—5K 81
Rattray Rd. SW2—4A 94
Raul Rd. SE15—2G 95
Raveley St. NW5—4G 45
Ravenet St. SW11—1F 93
Ravenfield Rd. SW17—3D 108
Ravenhill Rd. E13—2A 66
Ravenna Rd. SW15—5F 91
Ravenor Pk. Rd. Gnfd—3F 55
Raven Rd. E18—2A 34
Raven Row. E1—5H 63 (5K 143)
Ravensbourne Av. Brom
—7F 113
Ravensbourne Gdns. W13
—5B 56
Ravensbourne Gdns. Ilf—1E 34
Ravensbourne Pk. SE6—7C 96
Ravensbourne Pk. Cres. SE6
—7B 96
Ravensbourne Pl. SE13—2D 96
Ravensbourne Rd. SE6—7B 96
Ravensbourne Rd. Brom
—3J 127
Ravensbourne Rd. Twic—6C 88
Ravensbury Av. Mord—5A 122
Ravensbury Gro. Mitc—4B 122
Ravensbury La. Mitc—4B 122
Ravensbury Path. Mitc—4B 122
Ravensbury Rd. SW18—2K 107
Ravensbury Rd. Orp—4K 129
Ravensbury Ter. SW18—1K 107
Ravenscar Rd. Brom—4G 113
Ravens Clo. Brom—2H 127
Ravens Clo. Enf—2K 7
Ravenscourt Av. W6—4C 74
Ravenscourt Gdns. W6—4C 74
Ravenscourt Pk. W6—4C 74
Ravenscourt Pl. W6—4D 74
Ravenscourt Rd. W6—4D 74
Ravenscourt Sq. W6—3C 74
Ravenscraig Rd. N11—4B 16
Ravenscroft Av. NW11—7H 27
Ravenscroft Av. Wemb—1E 40
Ravenscroft Clo. E16—5J 65
Ravenscroft Pk. Barn—3A 4
Ravenscroft Rd. E16—5J 65
Ravenscroft Rd. W4—4J 73
Ravenscroft Rd. Beck—2J 125
Ravenscroft St. E2
—2F 63 (1F 142)
Ravensdale Av. N12—4F 15
Ravensdale Gdns. SE19
—7D 110
Ravensdale Rd. N16—7F 31
Ravensdale Rd. Houn—3C 86
Ravensdon St. SE11—5A 78
Ravensfield. Dag—4D 52
Ravensfield Gdns. Eps—5A 130
Ravenshaw St. NW6—5H 43
Ravenshill. Chst—1F 129
Ravenshurst Av. NW4—4E 26
Ravenside Clo. N18—5E 18
Ravenside Retail Pk. N18
—5E 18
Ravenslea Rd. SW12—7D 92
Ravensmead Rd. Brom—7F 113
Ravensmede Way. W4—4B 74
Ravens M. SE12—5J 97
Ravenstone Rd. N8—3A 30
Ravenstone Rd. NW9—6B 26
Ravenstone St. SW12—1E 108
Ravens Way. SE12—5J 97
Ravenswood. Bex—1E 116
Ravenswood Av. W Wick
—1E 136
Ravenswood Ct. King—6H 103
Ravenswood Cres. Harr—2D 38
Ravenswood Cres. W Wick
—1E 136
Ravenswood Gdns. Iswth
—1J 87
Ravenswood Rd. E17—4E 32
Ravenswood Rd. SW12—7F 93
Ravenswood Rd. Croy—3B 134
Ravensworth Rd. NW10—3D 58
Ravensworth Rd. SE9—4D 114

Ravent Rd. SE11
—4K 77 (8F 146)
Ravey St. EC2—4E 62 (3C 142)
Ravine Gro. SE18—6J 83
Rawchester Clo. SW18—1H 107
Rawlings St. SW3
—4D 76 (8E 144)
Rawlins Clo. N3—3G 27
Rawlins Clo. S Croy—7B 136
Rawlinson Ter. N17—3F 31
Rawnsley Av. Mitc—5B 122
Rawson St. SW11—1E 92
Rawstone Wlk. E13—2J 65
Rawstorne Pl. EC1
—3B 62 (1J 141)
Rawstorne St. EC1
—3B 62 (1J 141)
Raybell Ct. Iswth—2K 87
Raydean Rd. Barn—5E 4
Raydene Rd. SE18—6J 83
Raydons Gdns. Dag—5E 52
Raydons Rd. Dag—5E 52
Raydon St. N19—2F 45
Ray Edwards Vs. N'holt—2A 54
Rayfield Clo. Brom—6C 128
Rayford Av. SE12—7H 97
Ray Gdns. Bark—2A 68
Ray Gdns. Stan—5G 11
Rayleas Clo. SE18—1F 99
Rayleigh Av. Tedd—6J 103
Rayleigh Clo. N13—3J 17
Rayleigh Ct. King—2G 119
Rayleigh Rise. S Croy—6E 134
Rayleigh Rd. N13—3H 17
Rayleigh Rd. SW19—1H 121
Rayleigh Rd. Wfd G—6F 21
Ray Lodge Rd. Wfd G—6F 21
Raymead. NW4—4E 26
Raymead Av. T Hth—5A 124
Raymere Gdns. SE18—7H 83
Raymond Av. E18—3H 33
Raymond Av. W13—3A 72
Raymond Bldgs. WC1
—5K 61 (5F 140)
Raymond Clo. SE26—5J 111
Raymond Postgate Ct. SE28
—7B 68
Raymond Rd. E13—1A 66
Raymond Rd. SW19—6G 107
Raymond Rd. Beck—4A 126
Raymond Rd. Ilf—7H 35
Raymouth Rd. SE16
—4H 79 (8K 149)
Rayne Ct. E18—4H 33
Rayners Clo. Wemb—5D 40
Rayners La. Pinn & Harr—5D 22
to 3F 39
Rayners Rd. SW15—5G 91
Raynes Av. E11—7A 34
Raynham Av. N18—6B 18
Raynham Rd. N18—5B 18
Raynham Rd. W6—4D 74
Raynham Ter. N18—5B 18
Raynor Clo. S'hall—1D 70
Raynor Pl. N1—7C 46
Raynton Clo. Harr—1C 38
Rays Av. N18—4D 18
Rays Rd. N18—4D 18
Rays Rd. W Wick—7E 126
Ray St. EC1—4A 62 (4H 141)
Ray Wlk. N7—2K 45
Reachview Clo. NW1—7G 45
Reade Wlk. NW10—7A 42
Reading La. E8—6H 47
Reading Rd. N'holt—5F 39
Reading Rd. Sutt—5A 132
Reading Way. NW7—5A 14
Reads Clo. Ilf—3E 50
Reapers Clo. NW1—1H 61
Reapers Way. Iswth—5H 87
Reardon Path. E1
—1H 79 (3K 149)
Reardon St. E1—1H 79 (2J 149)
Reaston St. SE14—7K 79
Rebecca Ter. SE16
—3J 79 (7M 149)
Reckitt Rd. W4—5A 74

Record St. SE15—6J 79
Recovery St. SW17—5C 108
Recreation Av. Romf—5J 37
Recreation Rd. SE26—4K 111
Recreation Rd. Brom—2H 127
Recreation Rd. Sidc—3K 115
Recreation Rd. S'hall—4C 70
Recreation Way. Mitc—3J 123
Rector St. N1—1C 62
Rectory Clo. E4—3H 19
Rectory Clo. N3—1H 27
Rectory Clo. SW20—3E 120
Rectory Clo. Sidc—4B 116
Rectory Clo. Stan—5G 11
Rectory Cres. E11—6A 34
Rectory Field Cres. SE7—7A 82
Rectory Gdns. N8—4J 29
Rectory Gdns. SW4—3G 93
Rectory Gdns. N'holt—1D 54
Rectory Grn. Beck—1B 126
Rectory Gro. SW4—3G 93
Rectory Gro. Croy—3B 134
Rectory Gro. Hmptn—4D 102
Rectory La. SW17—5E 108
Rectory La. Edgw—6B 12
Rectory La. Sidc—4B 116
Rectory La. Stan—5G 11
Rectory La. Surb—7C 118
Rectory La. Wall—4G 133
Rectory Orchard. SW19
—4G 107
Rectory Pk. Av. N'holt—3D 54
Rectory Pl. SE18—4E 82
Rectory Rd. E12—5D 50
Rectory Rd. E17—4D 32
Rectory Rd. N16—3F 47
Rectory Rd. SW13—2C 90
Rectory Rd. W3—1H 73
Rectory Rd. Beck—1C 126
Rectory Rd. Dag—7H 53
Rectory Rd. Houn—2A 86
Rectory Rd. S'hall—3D 70
Rectory Rd. Sutt—3J 131
Rectory Sq. E1—5K 63
Reculver M. N18—4B 18
Reculver Rd. SE16
—5K 79 (9M 149)
Red Anchor Clo. SW3—6B 76
Redan Pl. W2—6K 59
Redan St. W14—3F 75
Redan Ter. SE5—2B 94
Red Barracks Rd. SE18—4D 82
Redberry Gro. SE26—3J 111
Redbourne Av. N3—1J 27
Redbridge Gdns. SE5—7E 78
Redbridge La. E. Ilf—6B 34
Redbridge La. W. E11—6K 33
Redburn Industrial Est. Enf
—6E 8
Redburn St. SW3—6D 76
Redcar Clo. N'holt—5F 39
Redcar St. SE5—7C 78
Redcastle Clo. E1
—7J 63 (9M 143)
Red Cedars Rd. Orp—7J 129
Redchurch St. E2
—4F 63 (3E 142)
Redcliffe Gdns. SW10—5K 75
Redcliffe Gdns. Ilf—1E 50
Redcliffe M. SW10—5K 75
Redcliffe Pl. SW10—6A 76
Redcliffe Rd. SW10—6A 76
Redcliffe Sq. SW10—5K 75
Redcliffe St. SW10—6K 75
Redclose Av. Mord—5J 121
Redclyffe Rd. E6—1A 66
Redcourt. Croy—3E 134
Redcroft Rd. S'hall—7G 55
Redcross Way. SE1
—2C 78 (4M 147)
Reddings Clo. NW7—4G 13
Reddings, The. NW7—3G 13
Reddins Rd. SE15—7G 79
Reddons Rd. Beck—7A 112
Rede Pl. W2—6J 59
Redesdale Gdns. Iswth—7A 72
Redesdale St. SW3—6D 76

Redfern Av. Houn—7E 86
Redfern Rd. NW10—7A 42
Redfern Rd. SE6—7E 96
Redfield La. SW5—4J 75
Redford Av. T Hth—4K 123
Redford Av. Wall—6J 133
Redgates Dri. Brom—2K 137
Redgate Ter. SW15—6F 91
Redgrave Clo. SE25—6F 125
Redgrave Rd. SW15—3F 91
Red Hill. Chst—5F 115
Redhill Ct. SW2—2A 110
Redhill Dri. Edgw—2J 25
Redhill St. NW1—2F 61 (1K 139)
Red Ho. La. Bexh—4E 100
Redhouse Rd. Croy—6H 123
Redington Gdns. NW3—4K 43
Redington Rd. NW3—3K 43
Redlands. N15—4D 30
Redlands Ct. Brom—7H 113
Redlands Rd. Enf—1F 9
Redlands Way. SW2—7K 93
Redlaw Way. SE16—5G 79
Redleaf Clo. Belv—6G 85
Redlees Clo. Iswth—4A 88
Red Lion Ct. EC4
—6A 62 (8H 141)
Red Lion Hill. N2—2B 28
Red Lion La. SE18—1E 98
Red Lion Pl. SE18—1E 98
Red Lion Rd. Surb—7G 119
Red Lion Sq. WC1
—5K 61 (6E 140)
Red Lion Sq. WC1
—5K 61 (6E 140)
Red Lion St. Rich—5D 88
Red Lion Way. SE17—6C 78
Red Lodge Cres. Bex—3K 117
Red Lodge Rd. Bex—3K 117
Red Lodge Rd. W Wick—7E 126
Redman Clo. N'holt—2A 54
Redman's Rd. E1
—5J 63 (5M 143)
Redmead La. E1
—1G 79 (2H 149)
Redmore Rd. W6—4D 74
Red Path. E9—6B 48
Red Pl. W1—7E 60 (9G 139)
Redpoll Way. Eri—3D 84
Red Post Hill—4D 94
SE21 1-9 & 2-12
SE24 remainder
Redriffe Rd. E13—1H 65
Redriff Rd. SE16—3K 79
Redriff Rd. Romf—2H 37
Redruth Clo. N22—7E 16
Redruth Rd. E9—1J 63
Redstart Clo. E6—5C 66
Redstart Clo. SE14—7A 80
Redston Rd. N8—4H 29
Redvers Rd. N22—2A 30
Redvers St. N1—3E 62 (1D 142)
Redwald Rd. E5—4K 47
Redway Dri. Twic—7G 87
Redwing Path. SE28—3H 83
Redwood Clo. N14—7C 6
Redwood Clo. SE16—1A 80
Redwood Ct. N'holt—3C 54
Redwood Ct. Surb—7D 118
Redwood Est. Houn—6A 70
Redwoods. SW15—1C 106
Redwood Way. Barn—5A 4
Reece M. SW7—4B 76 (9A 144)
Reed Clo. E16—5J 65
Reed Clo. SE12—5J 97
Reede Gdns. Dag—5H 53
Reede Rd. Dag—6G 53
Reede Way. Dag—6H 53
Reedham Clo. N17—4H 31
Reedham St. SE15—3G 95
Reedholm Vs. N16—4D 46
Reed Rd. N17—2F 31
Reed's Pl. NW1—7G 45
Reedworth St. SE11
—4A 78 (9H 147)
Reenglass Rd. Stan—4J 11
Rees Gdns. Croy—6F 125

Reesland Clo. E12—6E 50
Rees St. N1—1C 62
Reets Farm Clo. NW9—6A 26
Reeves Av. NW9—7K 25
Reeves Corner. Croy—2B 134
Reeves M. W1—7E 60 (1H 145)
Reeves Rd. SE18—6F 83
Reform Row. N17—2F 31
Reform St. SW11—2D 92
Regal Clo. E1—5G 63 (5H 143)
Regal Clo. W5—5D 56
Regal Ct. N18—5A 18
Regal Cres. Wall—3F 133
Regal La. NW1—1E 60
Regal Way. Harr—6E 24
Regan Way. N1—2E 62 (1C 142)
Regency Clo. W5—6E 56
Regency Clo. Hmptn—5D 102
Regency Ct. Enf—5J 7
Regency M. Iswth—5J 87
Regency Pl. SW1
—4H 77 (8B 146)
Regency St. SW1
—4H 77 (8A 146)
Regency Wlk. Croy—6B 126
Regency Way. Bexh—3D 100
Regent Clo. N12—5F 15
Regent Clo. Harr—6E 24
Regent Clo. Houn—1A 86
Regent Ct. N20—2F 15
Regent Pl. W1—7G 61 (9M 139)
Regent Pl. Croy—1F 135
Regent Rd. SE24—5B 94
Regent Rd. Surb—5F 119
Regents Av. N13—5F 17
Regents Av. Industrial Est. N13
—5F 17
Regent's Bri. Gdns. SW8—7J 77
Regents Clo. S Croy—6E 134
Regents Ct. Edgw—4K 11
Regents M. NW8—2A 60
Regent's Pk. Gdns. M. NW1
—1E 60
Regents Pk. Rd. N3—3H 27
Regent's Pk. Rd. NW1—1D 60
Regent's Pk. Ter. NW1—1F 61
Regent's Pl. SE3—2J 97
Regent Sq. E3—3D 64
Regent Sq. WC1—3J 61 (2D 140)
Regent Sq. Belv—4H 85
Regent's Row. E8—1G 63
Regent St. NW10—3F 59
Regent St.—6F 61 (7K 139)
SW1 1-37 & 2-36
W1 remainder
Regent St. W4—5G 73
Regina Clo. Barn—3A 4
Reginald Rd. E7—6J 49
Reginald Rd. SE8—7C 80
Reginald Sq. SE8—7C 80
Regina Rd. N4—1K 45
Regina Rd. SE25—3G 125
Regina Rd. W13—1A 72
Regina Rd. S'hall—4C 70
Regina Ter. W13—1B 72
Regis Rd. NW5—5F 45
Reidhaven Rd. SE18—4J 83
Reigate Av. Sutt—1J 131
Reigate Rd. Brom—3H 113
Reigate Rd. Ilf—2K 51
Reigate Way. Wall—5J 133
Reighton Rd. E5—3G 47
Relay Rd. W12—1E 74
Relf Rd. SE15—3G 95
Relko Gdns. Sutt—5B 132
Relton M. SW7—3C 76 (6D 144)
Rembrandt Clo. E14—3E 80
Rembrandt Rd. SE13—4G 97
Rembrandt Rd. Edgw—2G 25
Remington Rd. E6—6C 66
Remington Rd. N15—6D 30
Remington St. N1
—2B 62 (1K 141)
Remnant St. WC2
—6K 61 (7E 140)
Rempstone M. N1—2D 62
Remus Rd. E3—7C 48

Rendlesham Rd. E5—4G 47
Rendlesham Rd. Enf—1G 7
Renforth St. SE16
—2J 79 (5M 149)
Renfrew Clo. E6—7E 66
Renfrew Ct. Houn—2C 86
Renfrew Rd. SE11
—4B 78 (9J 147)
Renfrew Rd. Houn—2C 86
Renfrew Rd. King—7H 105
Renmuir St. SW17—6D 108
Rennell St. SE13—3E 96
Rennels Way. Iswth—2J 87
Renness Rd. E17—3A 32
Rennets Clo. SE9—5J 99
Rennets Wood Rd. SE9—5H 99
Rennie Est. SE16
—4H 79 (9K 149)
Rennie St. SE1—1B 78 (2J 147)
Renown Clo. Croy—1B 134
Renown Clo. Romf—1G 37
Rensburg Rd. E17—6K 31
Renshaw Clo. Belv—6F 85
Renters Av. NW4—6E 26
Renwick Rd. Bark—4B 68
Repens Way. Hay—4B 54
Rephidim St. SE1
—3E 78 (7C 148)
Replingham Rd. SW18—1H 107
Reporton Rd. SW6—7G 75
Repository Rd. SE18—6D 82
Repton Av. Wemb—4C 40
Repton Clo. Cars—5C 132
Repton Ct. Beck—1D 126
Repton Ct. Ilf—1D 34
Repton Gro. Ilf—1D 34
Repton Rd. Harr—4F 25
Repton St. E14—6A 64
Repulse Clo. Romf—1G 37
Reservoir Rd. N14—5B 6
Reservoir Rd. SE4—2A 96
Resolution Wlk. SE18—3D 82
Restell Clo. SE3—6G 81
Reston Pl. SW7—2A 76
Restons Cres. SE9—6H 99
Restormel Clo. Houn—5E 86
Retcar Clo. N19—2F 45
Retford St. N1—2E 62 (1D 142)
Retingham Way. E4—2J 19
Retreat Clo. Harr—5C 24
Retreat Pl. E9—6J 47
Retreat Rd. Rich—5D 88
Retreat, The. NW9—5K 25
Retreat, The. SW14—3A 90
Retreat, The. Harr—7E 22
Retreat, The. Surb—6F 119
Retreat, The. T Hth—4D 124
Retreat, The. Wor Pk—3D 130
Reveley Sq. SE16—2A 80
Revell Rise. SE18—6K 83
Revell Rd. King—2H 119
Revell Rd. Sutt—6H 131
Revelon Rd. SE4—3A 96
Revelstoke Rd. SW18—2H 107
Reventlow Rd. SE9—1G 115
Reverdy Rd. SE1
—4G 79 (9G 149)
Reverend Clo. Harr—3F 39
Revesby Rd. Cars—6C 122
Review Rd. NW2—2B 42
Review Rd. Dag—7H 69
Rewell St. SW6—7A 76
Rewley Rd. Cars—6B 122
Rex Clo. Romf—1H 37
Rex Pl. W1—7E 60 (1H 145)
Reydon Av. E11—6A 34
Reynard Clo. Brom—3D 128
Reynard Dri. SE19—7F 111
Reynardson Rd. N17—7H 17
Reynolds Av. E12—5E 50
Reynolds Av. Romf—7C 36
Reynolds Clo. NW11—7K 27
Reynolds Clo. SW19—1B 122
Reynolds Clo. Cars—1D 132
Reynolds Dri. Edgw—3F 25
Reynold's Pl. SE3—7K 81
Reynolds Pl. Rich—6F 89

Reynolds Rd. SE15—4J 95
Reynolds Rd. W4—3J 73
Reynolds Rd. Hay—4A 54
Reynolds Rd. N Mald—7K 119
Reynolds Way. Croy—4E 134
Rheidol M. N1—2C 62
Rheidol Ter. N1—1F 31
Rheingold Way. Wall—7J 133
Rheola Clo. N17—1F 31
Rhoda St. E2—4F 63 (3F 142)
Rhodes Av. N22—1G 29
Rhodesia Rd. E11—2F 49
Rhodesia Rd. SW9—2J 93
Rhodesmoor Ho. Ct. Mord—6J 121
Rhodes St. N7—5K 45
Rhodeswell Rd. E14—6B 64
Rhondda Gro. E3—3A 64
Rhyl Rd. Gnfd—2K 55
Rhyl St. NW5—6E 44
Rhys Av. N11—7C 16
Rialto Rd. Mitc—2E 122
Ribble Clo. Wfd G—6F 21
Ribblesdale Av. N'holt—6F 39
Ribblesdale Rd. N8—4K 29
Ribblesdale Rd. SW16—6F 109
Ribchester Av. Gnfd—3K 55
Ricardo Path. SE28—1C 84
Ricardo St. E14—6D 64
Ricards Rd. SW19—5H 107
Richard Clo. SE18—4C 82
Richard Foster Clo. E17—7B 32
Richards Av. Romf—6J 37
Richards Clo. Bush, Wat—1C 10
Richards Clo. Harr—5A 24
Richardson Clo. E8—1F 63
Richardson Rd. E15—2G 65
Richards Pl. E17—3C 32
Richard's Pl. SW3
—4C 76 (8D 144)
Richard St. E1—6H 63 (8J 143)
(in two parts)
Richbell Pl. WC1
—5K 61 (5E 140)
Richborne Ter. SW8—7K 77
Richborough Rd. NW2—4G 43
Riches Rd. Ilf—2G 51
Richfield Rd. Bush, Wat—1B 10
Richford Rd. E15—1H 65
Richford St. W6—2E 74
Richlands Av. Eps—4C 130
Rich La. SW5—5K 75
Richmond Av. E4—5A 20
Richmond Av. N1—1K 61
Richmond Av. NW10—6E 42
Richmond Av. SW20—1G 121
Richmond Bri. Twic & Rich
—6D 88
Richmond Bldgs. W1
—6H 61 (8A 140)
Richmond Clo. E17—6B 32
Richmond Cres. E4—5A 20
Richmond Cres. N1—1A 62
Richmond Cres. N9—1B 18
Richmond Gdns. NW4—5C 26
Richmond Gdns. Harr—7E 10
Richmond Grn. Croy—3J 133
Richmond Gro. N1—7B 46
Richmond Gro. Surb—6F 119
Richmond Hill. Rich—6E 88
Richmond Hill Ct. Rich—6E 88
Richmond M. W1
—6H 61 (8A 140)
Richmond M. Tedd—5K 103
Richmond Pk. Rd. SW14—5J 89
Richmond Pk. Rd. King—7E 104
Richmond Pl. SE18—4G 83
Richmond Rd. E4—1A 20
Richmond Rd. E7—5K 49
Richmond Rd. E8—7F 47
Richmond Rd. E11—2F 49
Richmond Rd. N2—2A 28
Richmond Rd. N11—6D 16
Richmond Rd. N15—6E 30
Richmond Rd. SW20—1D 120
Richmond Rd. W5—2E 72
Richmond Rd. Barn—5E 4
Richmond Rd. Croy—3J 133

Richmond Rd. Ilf—3G 51
Richmond Rd. Iswth—3A 88
Richmond Rd. King—5D 104
Richmond Rd. T Hth—3B 124
Richmond Rd. Twic—7B 88
Richmond St. E13—2J 65
Richmond Ter. SW1
—2J 77 (4C 146)
Richmond Ter. M. SW1
—2J 77 (4C 146)
Richmond Way. E11—2J 49
Richmond Way—2F 75
W12 1-15 & 2-52
W14 remainder
Richmount Gdns. SE3—3J 97
Rich St. E14—7B 64
Rickard Clo. SW2—1A 110
Rickett St. SW6—6J 75
Rickman St. E1—4J 63 (3M 143)
Rickmansworth Rd. Pinn
—2A 22
Rickthorne Rd. N19—2J 45
Rickyard Path. SE9—4C 98
Ridding La. Gnfd—5K 39
Riddons Rd. SE12—3A 114
Rideout St. SE18—4D 82
Rider Clo. Sidc—6J 99
Ride, The. Bren—5B 72
Ride, The. Enf—4E 8
Ridge Av. N21—7H 7
Ridgebrook Rd. SE3—3B 98
Ridge Clo. NW4—2F 27
Ridge Clo. NW9—4K 25
Ridge Crest. Enf—1E 6
Ridgecroft Clo. Bex—1J 117
Ridgedale St. E3—2D 64
Ridge Hill. NW11—1G 43
Ridgemont Gdns. Edgw—4D 12
Ridgemount Av. Croy—1K 135
Ridgemount Clo. SE20—7H 111
Ridgemount Gdns. Enf—2G 7
Ridge Rd. N8—6K 29
Ridge Rd. N21—1H 17
Ridge Rd. NW2—3H 43
Ridge Rd. Mitc—7F 109
Ridge Rd. Sutt—1G 131
Ridge, The. Barn—5C 4
Ridge, The. Bex—7F 101
Ridge, The. Surb—5G 119
Ridge, The. Twic—7H 87
Ridgeview Clo. Barn—6A 4
Ridgeview Rd. N20—3E 14
Ridge Way. SE19—6E 110
Ridgeway. Brom—2J 137
Ridge Way. Felt—3C 102
Ridgeway. Wfd G—4F 21
Ridgeway Av. Barn—6J 5
Ridgeway Dri. Brom—5H 113
Ridgeway E. Sidc—5K 99
Ridgeway Gdns. N6—7G 29
Ridgeway Gdns. Ilf—5C 34
Ridgeway Rd. Iswth—7J 71
Ridgeway Rd. N. Iswth—7J 71
Ridgeway, The. E4—1K 19
Ridgeway, The. N3—7E 14
Ridgeway, The. N11—4J 15
Ridgeway, The. N14—2D 16
Ridgeway, The. NW7—4J 13
Ridgeway, The. NW9—4K 25
Ridgeway, The. NW11—1H 43
Ridgeway, The. W3—3G 73
Ridgeway, The. Croy—3K 133
Ridgeway, The. Enf & Pott B
—2G 7
Ridgeway, The. Harr—6C 24
(Kenton)
Ridgeway, The. Harr—5D 22 &
(North Harrow)   7F 23
Ridgeway, The. Stan—8H 11
Ridgeway, The. Sutt—5B 132
Ridgeway W. Sidc—5J 99
Ridgewell Clo. N1—1C 62
Ridgewell Clo. Dag—1H 69
Ridgmount Gdns. WC1
—5H 61 (5A 140)
Ridgmount Pl. WC1
—5H 61 (5A 140)

Rockhampton Clo. SE27
—4A 110
Rockhampton Rd. SE27
—4A 110
Rockhampton Rd. S Croy
—6E 134
Rock Hill. SE26—4F 111
Rockingham Clo. SW15—4B 90
Rockingham St. SE1
—3C 78 (7L 147)
Rockland Rd. SW15—4G 91
Rocklands Dri. Stan—2B 24
Rockley Rd. W14—2F 75
Rockmount Rd. SE18—5K 83
Rockmount Rd. SE19—6D 110
Rocks La. SW13—3C 90
Rock St. N4—2A 46
Rockware Av. Gnfd—1H 55
Rockwell Rd. Dag—5H 53
Rockwells Gdns. SE19—5E 110
Rockwood Pl. W12—2E 74
Rocliffe St. N1—2B 62
Rocombe Cres. SE23—7J 95
Rocque La. SE3—3H 97
Rodborough Rd. NW11—1J 43
Roden Gdns. Croy—6E 124
Rodenhurst Rd. SW4—6G 93
Roden St. N7—3K 45
Roderick Rd. NW3—4D 44
Roding Av. Wfd G—6H 21
Roding La. Buck H & Chig
—1H to 1K 21
Roding La. N. Wfd G—2B 34
Roding La. S. Ilf & Wfd G—4B 34
Roding M. E1—1G 79 (2H 149)
Roding Rd. E5—4K 47
Roding Rd. E6—5F 67
Rodings, The. Wfd G—6F 21
Roding Trading Est. Bark
—7F 51
Roding View. Buck H—1G 21
Rodmarton St. W1
—5D 60 (6F 138)
Rodmell Clo. Hay—4C 54
Rodmell Slope. N12—5C 14
Rodmere St. SE10—5G 81
Rodmill La. SW2—7J 93
Rodney Clo. Croy—1B 134
Rodney Clo. N Mald—5A 120
Rodney Clo. Pinn—7C 22
Rodney Ct. Barn—3C 4
Rodney Gdns. Pinn—5A 22
Rodney Gdns. W Wick—4J 137
(in two parts)
Rodney Pl. E17—2A 32
Rodney Pl. SE17
—4C 78 (8M 147)
Rodney Pl. SW19—1A 122
Rodney Rd. E11—4K 33
Rodney Rd. SE17
—4D 78 (9A 148)
Rodney Rd. Mitc—3C 122
Rodney Rd. N Mald—5A 120
Rodney Rd. Twic—6E 86
Rodney St. N1—2K 61 (1F 140)
Rodney Way. Romf—1H 37
Rodsley St. SE1—6G 79
Rodway Rd. SW15—7C 90
Rodway Rd. Brom—1K 127
Rodwell Clo. Ruis—1A 38
Rodwell Rd. SE22—6F 95
Roebourne Way. E16—1E 82
Roebuck La. N17—6A 18
Roebuck La. Buck H—1F 21
Roedean Av. Enf—1D 8
Roedean Clo. Enf—1D 8
Roedean Cres. SW15—6A 90
Roe End. NW9—4J 25
Roe Grn. NW9—5J 25
Roehampton Clo. SW15—4C 90
Roehampton Dri. Chst—6G 115
Roehampton Ga. SW15—6A 90
Roehampton High St. SW15
—7C 90
Roehampton La. SW15—4C 90
Roehampton Vale. SW15
—3B 106

Roe La. NW9—4H 25
Roe Way. Wall—6J 133
Roffey St. E14—2E 80
Rogers Gdns. Dag—5G 53
Rogers Rd. E16—6H 65
Rogers Rd. SW17—4B 108
Roger St. WC1—4K 61 (4F 140)
Rogers Wlk. N12—3E 14
Rojack Rd. SE23—1K 111
Rokeby Gdns. Wfd G—1J 33
Rokeby Pl. SW20—7D 106
Rokeby Rd. SE4—2B 96
Rokeby Rd. Harr—3H 23
Rokeby St. E15—1G 65
Rokesby Clo. Well—2H 99
Rokesby Pl. Wemb—5D 40
Rokesly Av. N8—5J 29
Roland Gdns. SW7
—5A 76 (9A 144)
Roland M. E1—5K 63 (5M 143)
Roland Rd. E17—4F 33
Roland Way. SE17—5D 78
Roland Way. SW7
—5A 76 (9A 144)
Roland Way. Wor Pk—2B 130
Roles Gro. Romf—4D 36
Rolfe Clo. Barn—4H 5
Rollesby Way. SE28—6C 68
Rolleston Av. Orp—6F 129
Rolleston Clo. Orp—7F 129
Rolleston Rd. S Croy—7D 134
Roll Gdns. Ilf—5E 34
Rollins St. SE15—6J 79
Rollit Cres. Houn—5E 86
Rollit St. N7—5A 46
Rolls Bldgs. EC4
—6A 62 (7G 141)
Rolls Pk. Av. E4—5H 19
Rolls Pk. Rd. E4—5J 19
Rolls Rd. SE1—5F 79 (9F 148)
Rolt St. SE8—6A 80
Rolvenden Gdns. Brom—7B 114
Rolvenden Pl. N17—1G 31
Roman Clo. W3—2H 73
Roman Clo. Felt—5A 86
Roman Clo. Rain—2K 69
Romanhurst Av. Brom—4G 127
Romanhurst Gdns. Brom
—4G 127
Roman Industrial Est. Croy
—7E 124
Roman Rise. SE19—6D 110
Roman Rd.—3J 63 (1M 143)
E2 1-229 & 2-256
E3 remainder
Roman Rd. E6—4C 66
Roman Rd. N10—7A 16
Roman Rd. W4—4B 74
Roman Rd. Ilf—6F 51
Roman Sq. SE28—1A 84
Roman Way. N7—6K 45
Roman Way. SE15—7J 79
Roman Way. Croy—2B 134
Roman Way. Enf—5A 8
Romany Gdns. E17—1A 32
Romany Gdns. Sutt—7J 121
Roma Read Clo. SW15—7D 90
Roma Rd. E17—3A 32
Romberg Rd. SW17—3E 108
Romborough Gdns. SE13
—5E 96
Romborough Way. SE13—5E 96
Romero Clo. SW9—3K 93
Romero Sq. SE3—4A 98
Romeyn Rd. SW16—3K 109
Romford Rd.—6G 49
E15 1-191 & 2-166a
E7 193-607 & 168-544
E12 remainder
Romford Rd. Chig & Romf
—1F 37
Romilly Rd. N4—2B 46
Romilly St. W1—7H 61 (9B 140)
Romily Ct. SW6—2H 91
Rommany Rd. SE27—4D 110

Romney Clo. N17—1H 31
Romney Clo. NW11—1A 44
Romney Clo. SE14—7J 79
Romney Clo. Harr—7E 22
Romney Dri. Brom—7B 114
Romney Dri. Harr—7E 22
Romney Gdns. Bexh—1F 101
Romney Rd. SE10—6F 81
Romney Rd. N Mald—6K 119
Romney St. SW1
—3J 77 (7C 146)
Romola Rd. SE24—1B 110
Romsey Gdns. Dag—1D 68
Romsey Rd. W13—7A 56
Romsey Rd. Dag—1D 68
Ronald Av. E15—3G 65
Ronald Clo. Beck—5B 126
Ronalds Rd. N5—5A 46
Ronalds Rd. Brom—1J 127
Ronaldstone Rd. Sidc—6J 99
Ronald St. E1—6J 63 (8M 143)
Rona Rd. NW3—4E 44
Ronart St. Harr—3K 23
Rondu Rd. NW2—5G 43
Ronver Rd. SE12—1H 113
Rood La. EC3—7E 62 (9C 142)
Rookby Ct. N21—2G 17
Rookeries Clo. Felt—3A 102
Rookery Clo. NW9—5B 26
Rookery Cres. Dag—7H 53
Rookery Dri. Chst—1E 128
Rookery La. Brom—6B 128
Rookery Rd. SW4—4G 93
Rookery Way. NW9—5B 26
Rooke Way. SE10—5H 81
Rookfield Av. N10—4G 29
Rookfield Clo. N10—4G 29
Rookstone Rd. SW17—5D 108
Rook Wlk. E6—6B 66
Rookwood Av. N Mald—4C 120
Rookwood Av. Wall—4H 133
Rookwood Gdns. E4—2C 20
Rookwood Rd. N16—7G 31
Roosevelt Way. Dag—6K 53
Ropemaker Rd. SE16—3A 80
Ropemakers' Fields. E14
—7B 64
Ropemaker St. EC2
—5D 62 (5A 142)
Roper La. SE1—2E 78 (5D 148)
Ropers Av. E4—5J 19
Roper St. SE9—6D 98
Ropers Wlk. SW2—7A 94
Roper Way. Mitc—2E 122
Ropery St. E3—4B 64
Rope St. SE16—4A 80
Rope Wlk. Gdns. E1
—6G 63 (7H 143)
Ropley St. E2—2G 63 (1G 143)
Rosa Alba M. N5—4C 46
Rosaline Rd. SW6—7G 75
Rosamond St. SE26—3H 111
Rosary Clo. Houn—2C 86
Rosary Gdns. SW7
—4A 76 (9A 144)
Rosaville Rd. SW6—7H 75
Rosbery Rd. N9—3B 18
Roscoe St. EC1—4C 62 (3M 141)
Roscoe St. Edgw—1J 25
Roseacre Clo. W13—5B 56
Roseacre Rd. Well—3B 100
Rose All. SE1—1C 78 (2M 147)
Rose & Crown Pas. Iswth
—1A 88
Rose & Crown Yd. SW1
—1G 77 (3M 145)
Rose Av. E18—2K 33
Rose Av. Mitc—1D 122
Rose Av. Mord—5A 122
Rosebank. SE20—7H 111
Rosebank Av. Wemb—4K 39
Rose Bank Clo. N12—5H 15
Rosebank Gdns. E3—2B 64
Rosebank Gro. E17—3B 32
Rosebank Rd. E17—6D 32
Rosebank Rd. W7—2J 71

Rosebank Vs. E17—4C 32
Rosebank Wlk. NW1—7H 45
Rosebank Way. W3—6K 57
Rose Bates Dri. NW9—4G 25
Roseberry Av. N Mald—2B 120
Roseberry Gdns. N4—6B 30
Roseberry Pl. E8—6F 47
Roseberry St. SE16
—4H 79 (9J 149)
Rosebery Av. E12—6C 50
Rosebery Av. EC1
—4A 62 (4G 141)
Rosebery Av. N17—2G 31
Rosebery Av. Harr—4C 38
Rosebery Av. Sidc—7J 99
Rosebery Av. T Hth—2C 124
Rosebery Clo. Mord—6F 121
Rosebery Gdns. N8—5J 29
Rosebery Gdns. W13—6A 56
Rosebery Gdns. Sutt—4K 131
Rosebery M. N10—2G 29
Rosebery Rd. N10—2G 29
Rosebery Rd. SW2—6J 93
Rosebery Rd. Bush, Wat—1A 10
Rosebery Rd. Houn—5G 87
Rosebery Rd. King—2H 119
Rosebery Rd. Sutt—6H 131
Rosebery Sq. King—2H 119
Rosebine Av. Twic—7H 87
Rosebury Rd. SW6—2K 91
Rose Ct. Pinn—3A 22
Rosecourt Rd. Croy—6K 123
Rosecroft Av. NW3—3J 43
Rosecroft Gdns. NW2—3C 42
Rosecroft Gdns. Twic—1H 103
Rosecroft Rd. S'hall—4E 54
Rosecroft Wlk. Pinn—5B 22
Rosecroft Wlk. Wemb—5D 40
Rosedale Clo. SE2—3B 84
Rosedale Clo. W7—2K 71
Rosedale Clo. Stan—6G 11
Rosedale Ct. N5—4B 46
Rosedale Gdns. Dag—7B 52
Rosedale Rd. E7—5A 50
Rosedale Rd. SE21—1C 110
Rosedale Rd. Dag—7B 52
Rosedale Rd. Eps—5C 130
Rosedale Rd. Rich—4E 88
Rosedale Rd. Romf—3J 37
Rosedene Av. SW16—3K 109
Rosedene Av. Croy—7J 123
Rosedene Av. Gnfd—3E 54
Rosedene Av. Mord—5J 121
Rosedene Gdns. Ilf—4E 34
Rosedene Ter. E10—2D 48
Rosedew Rd. W6—6F 75
Rose End. Wor Pk—1F 131
Rosefield Gdns. E14—7C 64
Rose Garden Clo. Edgw—6K 11
Rose Gdns. W5—3D 72
Rose Gdns. S'hall—6E 54
Rose Glen. NW9—4K 25
Rose Glen. Romf—1K 53
Rosehart M. W11—6J 59
Rosehatch Av. Romf—3D 36
Roseheath Rd. Houn—5D 86
Rose Hill. Sutt—3K 131
Rosehill Av. Sutt—1A 132
Rosehill Gdns. Gnfd—5K 39
Rosehill Gdns. Sutt—2K 131
Rosehill Pk. W. Sutt—1A 132
Rosehill Rd. SW18—6A 92
Roseland Clo. N17—7J 17
Rose La. Romf—3D 36
Rose Lawn. Bush, Wat—1B 10
Roseleigh Av. N5—4B 46
Roseleigh Clo. Twic—6D 88
Rosemary Av. N3—2K 27
Rosemary Av. N9—1C 18
Rosemary Av. Enf—1K 7
Rosemary Av. Houn—2B 86
Rosemary Dri. Ilf—5B 34
Rosemary Gdns. Dag—1F 53
Rosemary La. SW14—3J 89
Rosemary Rd. SE15—7F 79
Rosemary Rd. SW17—3A 108
Rosemary Rd. Well—1K 99

Rosemary St. N1—1D 62
Rosemead. NW9—7B 26
Rosemead Av. Mitc—3G 123
Rosemead Av. Wemb—5E 40
Rosemont Av. N12—6F 15
Rosemont Rd. NW3—6A 44
Rosemont Rd. W3—7H 57
Rosemont Rd. N Mald—3J 119
Rosemont Rd. Rich—6E 88
Rosemont Rd. Wemb—1E 56
Rosemoor St. SW3
—4D 76 (9E 144)
Rosemount Clo. Wfd G—6J 21
Rosemount Dri. Brom—4D 128
Rosemount Rd. W13—6A 56
Rosenau Cres. SW11—1D 92
Rosenau Rd. SW11—1C 92
Rosendale Rd. SE21—7C 94
  SE21 1-245 & 2-248
  SE24 remainder
Roseneath Av. N21—1G 17
Roseneath Rd. SW11—6E 92
Roseneath Wlk. Enf—4K 7
Rosen's Wlk. Edgw—3C 12
Rosenthal Rd. SE6—6D 96
Rosenthorpe Rd. SE15—5K 95
Roserton St. E14—2E 80
Rosery, The. Croy—6K 125
Roses, The. Wfd G—7C 20
Rose St. WC2—7J 61 (9C 140)
Rosethorn Clo. SW12—7H 93
Rosetta Clo. SW8—7J 77
Roseveare Rd. SE12—4A 114
Roseville Av. Houn—5E 86
Rosevine Rd. SW20—1E 120
Rose Wlk. Surb—5H 119
Rose Wlk. W Wick—2E 136
Rose Way. SE12—5J 97
Roseway. SE21—6D 94
Rosewood Av. Gnfd—5A 40
Rosewood Clo. Sidc—3C 116
Rosewood Ct. Brom—1B 128
Rosewood Gdns. SE13—2E 96
Rosewood Gro. Sutt—2A 132
Rosewood Sq. W12—6C 58
Rosher Clo. E15—7F 49
Rosina St. E9—6K 47
Roskell Rd. SW15—3F 91
Roslin Rd. W3—3H 73
Roslin Way. Brom—5J 113
Roslyn Clo. Mitc—2B 122
Roslyn Rd. N15—5D 30
Rosmead Rd. W11—7G 59
Rosoman Pl. EC1
—4A 62 (3H 141)
Rosoman St. EC1
—3A 62 (2H 141)
Rossall Cres. NW10—3F 57
Ross Av. NW7—5B 14
Ross Av. Dag—1F 53
Ross Clo. Harr—7B 10
Ross Ct. NW9—3A 26
Rossdale. Sutt—5C 132
Rossdale Dri. N9—6D 8
Rossdale Dri. NW9—1J 41
Rossdale Rd. SW15—4E 90
Rossdale Way. NW1—7G 45
Rosse M. SE3—1K 97
Rossendale St. E5—2H 47
Rossindel Rd. Houn—5E 86
Rossington St. E5—2G 47
Rossiter Rd. SW12—1F 109
Rossland Clo. Bexh—5H 101
Rosslyn Av. E4—2C 20
Rosslyn Av. SW13—3A 90
Rosslyn Av. Barn—6H 5
Rosslyn Av. Dag—7F 37
Rosslyn Clo. W Wick—3H 137
Rosslyn Cres. Harr—4K 23
Rosslyn Cres. Wemb—4E 40
Rosslyn Hill. NW3—4B 44
Rosslyn M. NW3—4B 44
Rosslyn Pk. M. NW3—5B 44
Rosslyn Rd. Bark—7H 51
Rosslyn Rd. E17—4E 32
Rosslyn Rd. Twic—6C 88

Rossmore Rd. NW1
—4C 60 (4D 138)
Ross Pde. Wall—6F 133
Ross Rd. SE25—3D 124
Ross Rd. Twic—1F 103
Ross Rd. Wall—5G 133
Ross Way. SE9—3C 98
Rosswood Gdns. Wall—6G 133
Rostella Rd. SW17—4B 108
Rostrevor Av. N15—6F 31
Rostrevor Gdns. S'hall—5C 70
Rostrevor M. SW6—1H 91
Rostrevor Rd. SW6—1H 91
Rostrevor Rd. SW19—5J 107
Rotary St. SE1—3B 78 (6K 147)
Rothbury Gdns. Iswth—7A 72
Rothbury Rd. E9—7B 48
Rothbury Wlk. N17—7B 18
Rotherfield Rd. Cars—5E 132
Rotherfield St. N1—7C 46
Rotherhill Av. SW16—6H 109
Rotherhithe New Rd. SE16
—5H 79 (9K 149)
Rotherhithe Old Rd. SE16
—4K 79 (8M 149)
Rotherhithe St. SE16
—2J 79 (4L 149)
Rotherhithe Tunnel. SE16
—2J 79 (5M 149)
Rothermere Rd. Croy—5K 133
Rotherwick Hill. W5—4F 57
Rotherwick Rd. NW11—7J 27
Rotherwood Clo. SW20—1G 121
Rotherwood Rd. SW15—3F 91
Rothesay Av. SW20—2G 121
Rothesay Av. Gnfd—6G 39
Rothesay Av. Rich—4H 89
Rothesay Rd. SE25—4D 124
Rothsay Rd. E7—7A 50
Rothsay St. SE1—3E 78 (6C 148)
Rothschild Rd. W4—3J 73
Rothschild St. SE27—4B 110
Roth Wlk. N7—2K 45
Rothwell Gdns. Dag—7C 52
Rothwell Rd. Dag—1C 68
Rothwell St. NW1—1D 60
Rotten Row. NW3—1A 44
Rotterdam Dri. E14—3E 80
Rouel Rd. SE16—3G 79 (7G 149)
Rougemont Av. Mord—6J 121
Roundacre. SW19—2F 107
Roundaway Rd. Ilf—2D 34
Round Gro. Croy—7K 125
Roundhay Clo. SE23—2K 111
Round Hill. SE26—3J 111
Roundhill Dri. Enf—4E 6
Roundtable Rd. Brom—3H 113
Roundtree Rd. Wemb—5B 40
Roundway, The. N17—1D 30
Roundwood Rd. NW10—6B 42
Rounton Rd. E3—4C 64
Roupell Rd. SW2—1K 109
Roupell St. SE1—1A 78 (3H 147)
Rousden St. NW1—7G 45
Rouse Gdns. SE21—4E 110
Rous Rd. Buck H—1H 21
Routh Rd. SW18—7C 92
Routh St. E6—5D 66
Routledge Clo. N19—1H 45
Rovel Rd. SE16—4G 79 (8G 149)
Rowallan Rd. SW6—7G 75
Rowan Av. E4—6G 19
Rowan Clo. SW16—1G 123
Rowan Clo. W5—2E 72
Rowan Clo. N Mald—2A 120
Rowan Clo. Wemb—3A 40
Rowan Cres. SW16—1G 123
Rowan Dri. NW9—3C 26
Rowan Gdns. Croy—3F 135
Rowan Rd. SW16—2G 123
Rowan Rd. W6—4F 75
Rowan Rd. Bexh—3E 100
Rowan Rd. Bren—7B 72
Rowans, The. N13—3H 17
Rowantree Clo. N21—1J 17

Rowantree Rd. N21—1J 17
Rowantree Rd. Enf—2G 7
Rowan Wlk. N2—5A 28
Rowan Wlk. N19—2G 45
Rowan Wlk. W10—4G 59
Rowan Way. Romf—3C 36
Rowben Clo. N20—1E 14
Rowberry Clo. SW6—7E 74
Rowcross St. SE1
—5F 79 (9F 148)
Rowdell Rd. N'holt—1E 54
Rowden Rd. E4—6J 19
Rowden Rd. Beck—1A 126
Rowditch La. SW11—2E 92
Rowdon Av. NW10—7D 42
Rowdown Cres. Croy—7F 137
Rowdowns Rd. Dag—1F 69
Rowe Gdns. Bark—2K 67
Rowe La. E9—5J 47
Rowena Cres. SW11—2C 92
Rowe Wlk. Harr—3E 38
Rowfant Rd. SW17—1E 108
Rowhill Rd. E5—4H 47
Rowington Clo. W2—5K 59
Rowland Av. Harr—3C 24
Rowland Ct. E16—4H 65
Rowland Gro. SE26—3H 111
Rowland Hill Av. N17—7H 17
Rowland Hill St. NW3—5C 44
Rowlands Av. Pinn—6A 10
Rowlands Clo. N6—6E 28
Rowlands Clo. NW7—7H 13
Rowlands Rd. Dag—2F 53
Rowland Way. SW19—1K 121
Rowley Av. Sidc—7B 100
Rowley Clo. Wemb—7F 41
Rowley Gdns. N4—7C 30
Rowley Industrial Pk. W3
—3H 73
Rowley Rd. N15—5C 30
Rowley Way. NW8—1K 59
Rowlls Rd. King—3F 119
Rowney Gdns. Dag—6C 52
Rowney Rd. Dag—6B 52
Rowntree Path. SE28—1B 84
Rowntree Rd. Twic—1J 103
Rowse Clo. E15—1E 64
Rowsley Av. NW4—3E 26
Rowstock Gdns. N7—5H 45
Rowton Rd. SE18—7G 83
Roxborough Av. Harr—7J 23
Roxborough Av. Iswth—7K 71
Roxborough Pk. Harr—7J 23
Roxborough Rd. Harr—6H 23
Roxbourne Clo. N'holt—6C 38
Roxburgh Rd. SE27—5B 110
Roxby Pl. SW6—6J 75
Roxeth Grn. Av. Harr—3F 39
Roxeth Gro. Harr—4F 39
Roxeth Hill. Harr—2H 39
Roxley Rd. SE13—6D 96
Roxton Gdns. Croy—5C 136
Roxwell Rd. W12—2C 74
Roxwell Rd. Bark—2A 68
Roxwell Trading Pk. E10
—7A 32
Roxwell Way. Wfd G—7F 21
Roxy Av. Romf—7C 36
Royal Albert Dock Spine Rd.
E16—7B 66
Royal Av. SW3—5D 76 (9E 144)
Royal Av. Wor Pk—2A 130
Royal Cir. SE27—3A 110
Royal Clo. Wor Pk—2A 130
Royal College St. NW1—7G 45
Royal Ct. SE16—3B 80
Royal Cres. W11—1F 75
Royal Cres. Ruis—4C 38
Royal Cres. M. W11—1F 75
Royal Gdns. W7—3A 72
Royal Hill. SE10—7E 80
Royal Hospital Rd. SW3—6D 76
Royal London Est. N17—6C 18
Royal London Industrial Est.
NW10—2K 57
Royal Mint Pl. E1
—7F 63 (9F 142)

Royal Mint St. E1
—7F 63 (9F 142)
Royal Naval Pl. SE14—7B 80
Royal Oak Pl. SE22—6H 95
Royal Oak Rd. E8—6H 47
Royal Oak Rd. Bexh—4F 101
Royal Opera Arc. SW1
—1H 77 (2A 146)
Royal Pde. SE3—2H 97
Royal Pde. SW6—7G 75
Royal Pde. W5—3E 56
Royal Pde. Chst—7G 115
Royal Pde. M. Chst—7G 115
Royal Pl. SE10—7E 80
Royal Rd. E16—6A 66
Royal Rd. SE17—6B 78
Royal Rd. Sidc—3D 116
Royal Rd. Tedd—5H 103
Royal Route. Wemb—4G 41
Royal St. SE1—3K 77 (6F 146)
Royal Victoria Patriotic
Building. SW18—6B 92
Royal Victor Pl. E3—2K 63
Royal Wlk. Wall—2F 133
Roycraft Av. Bark—2K 67
Roycroft Clo. E18—1K 33
Roycroft Clo. SW2—1A 110
Roydene Rd. SE18—6J 83
Roydon Clo. Lou—1H 21
Roy Gdns. Ilf—4J 35
Roy Gro. Hmptn—6F 103
Royle Cres. W13—4A 56
Roy Sq. E14—7B 64
Royston Av. E4—5H 19
Royston Av. Sutt—3B 132
Royston Av. Wall—4H 133
Royston Ct. SE24—6C 94
Royston Ct. Rich—1F 89
Royston Gdns. Ilf—6B 34
Royston Pde. Ilf—6B 34
Royston Pk. Rd. Pinn—5A 10
Royston Rd. SE20—1K 125
Royston Rd. Rich—5E 88
Roystons, The. Surb—5H 119
Royston St. E2—2J 63 (1M 143)
Rozel Rd. SW4—3G 93
(in two parts)
Rubastic Rd. S'hall—3A 70
Rubens Rd. N'holt—2A 54
Rubens St. SE6—2B 112
Ruberoid Rd. Enf—3G 9
Ruby M. E17—3C 32
Ruby Rd. E17—3C 32
Ruby St. SE15—6H 79
Ruby Triangle. SE15—6H 79
Ruckholt Clo. E10—3D 48
Ruckholt Rd. E10—4D 48
Rucklidge Av. NW10—2B 58
Rudall Cres. NW3—4B 44
Ruddstreet Clo. SE18—4F 83
Ruddy Way. NW7—6G 13
Rudland Rd. Bexh—3H 101
Rudloe Rd. SW12—7G 93
Rudolf Pl. E13—2H 65
Rudolph Rd. NW6—2J 59
Rudyard Gro. NW7—6D 12
Ruffetts Clo. S Croy—7H 135
Ruffetts, The. S Croy—7H 135
Rufford Clo. Harr—6A 24
Rufford St. N1—1J 61
Rufus Clo. Ruis—3C 38
Rufus St. N1—3E 62 (2C 142)
Rugby Av. N9—1A 18
Rugby Av. Gnfd—6H 39
Rugby Av. Wemb—5B 40
Rugby Clo. Harr—4J 23
Rugby Gdns. Dag—6C 52
Rugby Rd. NW9—4H 25
Rugby Rd. W4—2A 74
Rugby Rd. Dag—7B 52
Rugby Rd. Twic & Iswth—6J 87
Rugby St. WC1—4K 61 (4E 140)
Rugg St. E14—7C 64
Ruislip Clo. Gnfd—4F 55
Ruislip Rd. N'holt & Gnfd
—1A 54

Ruislip Rd. E.—4H 55
  W13 1-33 & 80-82
  W7 101-165
  Gnfd remainder
Ruislip St. SW17—4D 108
Rumbold Rd. SW6—7K 75
Rum Clo. E1—7J 63 (1L 149)
Rumsey Clo. Hmptn—6D 102
Rumsey Rd. SW9—3K 93
Runbury Circ. NW9—2K 41
Runcorn Clo. N17—4H 31
Runcorn Pl. W11—7G 59
Rundell Cres. NW4—5D 26
Runnel Field. Harr—3J 39
Running Horse Yd. Bren—6E 72
Runnymede. SW19—1B 122
Runnymede Clo. Twic—6F 87
Runnymede Ct. SW15—1C 106
Runnymede Cres. SW16
    —1H 123
Runnymede Gdns. Gnfd—2J 55
Runnymede Gdns. Twic—6F 87
Runnymede Rd. Twic—6F 87
Runway, The. Ruis—5A 38
Rupack St. SE16
    —2J 79 (5L 149)
Rupert Av. Wemb—5E 40
Rupert Ct. W1—7H 61 (9A 140)
Rupert Gdns. SW9—2B 94
Rupert Rd. N19—3H 45
(in two parts)
Rupert Rd. NW6—2H 59
Rupert Rd. W4—3A 74
Rupert St. W1—7H 61 (9A 140)
Rural Way. SW16—7F 109
Ruscoe Rd. E16—6H 65
Rusham Rd. SW12—6D 92
Rushbrook Cres. E17—1B 32
Rushbrook Rd. SE9—2G 115
Rushcroft Rd. E4—7J 19
Rushcroft Rd. SW2—4A 94
Rushden Clo. SE19—7D 110
Rushdene. SE2—3D 84
Rushdene Av. Barn—7H 5
Rushdene Clo. N'holt—2A 54
Rushdene Cres. N'holt—2A 54
Rushdene Rd. Pinn—6B 22
Rushden Gdns. NW7—6K 13
Rushden Gdns. Ilf—3E 34
Rushen Wlk. Cars—1B 132
Rushett Clo. Th Dit—7B 118
Rushett Rd. Th Dit—7B 118
Rushey Clo. N Mald—4K 119
Rushey Grn. SE6—7D 96
Rushey Hill. Enf—4E 6
Rushey Mead. SE4—5C 96
Rushford Rd. SE4—6B 96
Rush Grn. Gdns. Romf—1J 53
Rush Grn. Rd. Romf—1J 53
Rushgrove Av. NW9—5A 26
Rushgrove Pde. NW9—5A 26
Rushgrove St. SE18—4D 82
Rush Hill Rd. SW11—3E 92
Rushmead. E2—3H 63 (2J 143)
Rushmead. Rich—3B 104
Rushmead Clo. Croy—4F 135
Rushmead Clo. Edgw—2C 12
Rushmoor Clo. Pinn—4A 22
Rushmore Clo. Brom—3C 128
Rushmore Ct. Wor Pk—2C 130
Rushmore Rd. E5—4J 47
Rusholme Av. Dag—3G 53
Rusholme Gro. SE19—5E 110
Rusholme Rd. SW15—6F 91
Rushout Av. Harr—6B 24
Rushton St. N1—2D 62
Rushworth Av. NW4—3C 26
Rushworth Gdns. NW4—4C 26
Rushworth St. SE1
    —2B 78 (4K 147)
Ruskin Av. E12—6C 50
Ruskin Av. Rich—7G 73
Ruskin Av. Well—2A 100
Ruskin Clo. NW11—6K 27
Ruskin Dri. Well—3A 100
Ruskin Dri. Wor Pk—2D 130
Ruskin Gdns. W5—4D 56

Ruskin Gdns. Harr—5F 25
Ruskin Gro. Well—2A 100
Ruskin Pk. Ho. SE5—3D 94
Ruskin Rd. N17—1F 31
Ruskin Rd. Belv—4G 85
Ruskin Rd. Cars—5E 132
Ruskin Rd. Croy—2B 134
Ruskin Rd. Iswth—3K 87
Ruskin Rd. S'hall—7C 54
Ruskin Wlk. N9—2B 18
Ruskin Wlk. SE24—5C 94
Ruskin Wlk. Brom—6D 128
Ruskin Way. SW19—1B 122
Rusland Pk. Rd. Harr—4J 23
Rusper Clo. NW2—3E 42
Rusper Clo. Stan—4H 11
Rusper Rd. N22—3C 30
Rusper Rd. Dag—6C 52
Russell Av. N22—2B 30
Russell Clo. NW10—7J 41
Russell Clo. SE7—7A 82
Russell Clo. Beck—3E 126
Russell Clo. Bexh—4G 101
Russell Clo. Ruis—2A 38
Russell Ct. N14—6C 6
Russell Gdns. N20—2H 15
Russell Gdns. NW11—6G 27
Russell Gdns. W14—3G 75
Russell Gdns. Ilf—7H 35
Russell Gdns. Rich—2C 104
Russell Gdns. M. W14—3G 75
Russell Gro. NW7—4F 13
Russell Gro. SW9—7A 78
Russell Kerr Clo. W4—7K 73
Russell La. N20—2H 15
Russell Pl. NW3—5C 44
Russell Pl. SE16—3A 80
Russell Rd. E4—4G 19
Russell Rd. E10—6D 32
Russell Rd. E16—6J 65
Russell Rd. E17—3B 32
Russell Rd. N8—6H 29
Russell Rd. N13—6E 16
Russell Rd. N15—5E 30
Russell Rd. N20—2H 15
Russell Rd. NW9—6B 26
Russell Rd. SW19—7J 107
Russell Rd. W14—3G 75
Russell Rd. Buck H—1F 21
Russell Rd. Enf—1A 8
Russell Rd. Mitc—3C 122
Russell Rd. N'holt—5G 39
Russell Rd. Twic—6K 87
Russell's Footpath. SW16
    —5J 109
Russell Sq. WC1
    —5J 61 (5C 140)
Russell St. WC2—7J 61 (9D 140)
Russell Wlk. Rich—6F 89
Russell Way. Sutt—5K 131
Russet Cres. N7—5K 45
Russets Clo. E4—4A 20
Russett Way. SE13—2D 96
Russia Dock Rd. SE16—1A 80
Russia La. E2—2J 63 (1L 143)
Russia Row. EC2
    —6C 62 (8M 141)
Russia Wlk. SE16—2A 80
Rusthall Av. W4—4K 73
Rusthall Clo. Croy—6J 125
Rustic Av. SW16—7F 109
Rustic Pl. Wemb—4D 40
Rustington Wlk. Mord—7H 121
Ruston Av. Surb—7H 119
Ruston M. W11—6G 59
Ruston St. E3—1B 64
Rust Sq. SE5—7D 78
Rutford Rd. SW16—5J 109
Ruth Clo. Stan—4F 25
Ruth Ct. E3—2A 64
Rutherford Clo. Sutt—6B 132
Rutherford St. SW1
    —4H 77 (8A 146)
Rutherford Way. Bush, Wat
    —1C 10
Rutherford Way. Wemb—4G 41
Rutherglen Rd. SE2—6A 84

Rutherwyke Clo. Eps—6C 130
Ruthin Rd. SE3—6J 81
Ruthven St. E9—1K 63
Rutin Clo. NW9—6A 26
Rutland Av. Sidc—7A 100
Rutland Clo. SW14—3J 89
Rutland Clo. SW19—7C 108
Rutland Clo. Bex—1D 116
Rutland Ct. W3—6G 57
Rutland Ct. Enf—5C 8
Rutland Dri. Mord—6H 121
Rutland Dri. Rich—1E 104
Rutland Gdns. N4—6B 30
Rutland Gdns. SW7
    —2C 76 (5D 144)
Rutland Gdns. W13—5A 56
Rutland Gdns. Croy—4E 134
Rutland Gdns. Dag—5C 52
Rutland Gdns. M. SW7
    —2C 76 (5D 144)
Rutland Ga. SW7
    —2C 76 (5C 144)
Rutland Ga. Belv—5H 85
Rutland Gro. W6—5D 74
Rutland M. NW8—1K 59
Rutland Pk. NW2—6E 42
Rutland Pk. SE6—2D 112
Rutland Pl. EC1—5B 62 (5K 141)
Rutland Pl. Bush, Wat—1C 10
Rutland Rd. E7—7B 50
Rutland Rd. E9—1K 63
Rutland Rd. E11—5K 33
Rutland Rd. E17—6C 32
Rutland Rd. SW19—7C 108
Rutland Rd. Harr—6G 23
Rutland Rd. Ilf—3F 51
Rutland Rd. S'hall—5E 54
Rutland Rd. Twic—2H 103
Rutland St. SW7
    —3C 76 (6D 144)
Rutland Wlk. SE6—2B 112
Rutley Clo. SE17—6B 78
Rutlish Rd. SW19—1J 121
Rutter Gdns. Mitc—4A 122
Rutt's Ter. SE14—1K 95
Rutts, The. Bush, Wat—1C 10
Ruvigny Gdns. SW15—3F 91
Ruxley Clo. Sidc—6E 116
Ruxley Corner Industrial Est.
    Sidc—6D 116
Ruxley La. Eps—4A 130
Ryall Ct. N20—3J 15
Ryan Clo. SE3—4A 98
Rycott Path. SE22—7G 95
Rycroft Way. N17—3F 31
Ryculf Sq. SE3—2H 97
Rydal Clo. NW4—2F 27
Rydal Cres. Gnfd—3B 56
Rydal Dri. Bexh—1G 101
Rydal Gdns. NW9—5A 26
Rydal Gdns. SW15—5A 106
Rydal Gdns. Houn—6F 87
Rydal Gdns. Wemb—1C 40
Rydal Rd. SW16—4H 109
Rydal Way. Enf—6D 8
Rydal Way. Ruis—4A 38
Ryder Clo. Brom—5K 113
Ryders Ter. NW8—2A 60
Ryder St. SW1—1G 77 (2M 145)
Ryder Yd. SW1—1G 77 (2M 145)
Ryde Vale Rd. SW12—2G 109
Rydons Clo. SE9—3C 98
Rydon St. N1—1C 62
Rydston Clo. N7—7J 45
Rye Clo. Bex—6H 101
Ryecotes Mead. SE21—1E 110
Ryecroft Av. Ilf—2F 35
Ryecroft Av. Twic—1F 103
Ryecroft Rd. SE13—5E 96
Ryecroft Rd. SW16—6A 110
Ryecroft Rd. Orp—6H 129
Ryecroft St. SW6—1K 91
Ryedale. SE22—6H 95
Ryefield Path. SW15—1C 106
Ryefield Rd. SE19—6C 110
Rye Hill Pk. SE15—4J 95

Ryelands Cres. SE12—6A 98
Rye La. SE15—2G 95
Rye Pas. SE15—3G 95
Rye Rd. SE15—4K 95
Rye, The. N14—7B 6
Rye Wlk. SW15—5F 91
Rye Way. Edgw—6A 12
Ryfold Rd. SW19—3J 107
Ryhope Rd. N11—4A 16
Rylandes Rd. NW2—3C 42
Ryland Rd. NW5—6F 45
Rylett Cres. W12—3B 74
Rylett Rd. W12—2B 74
Rylston Rd. N13—3J 17
Rylston Rd. SW6—6H 75
Rymer Rd. Croy—7E 124
Rymer St. SE24—6B 94
Rymill St. E16—1E 82
Rysbrack St. SW3
    —3D 76 (6E 144)
Rythe Ct. Th Dit—7A 118

Sabbarton St. E16—6H 65
Sabella Ct. E3—2B 64
Sabine Rd. SW11—3D 92
Sable Clo. Houn—3A 86
Sable St. N1—7B 46
Sach Rd. E5—2H 47
Sackville Av. Brom—1J 137
Sackville Clo. Harr—3H 39
Sackville Gdns. Ilf—1D 50
Sackville Rd. Sutt—7J 131
Sackville St. W1
    —7G 61 (1M 145)
Sackville Way. SE22—1G 111
Saddlers Clo. Pinn—6A 10
Saddlers M. Wemb—4K 39
Saddlescombe Way. N12
    —5D 14
Sadler Clo. Mitc—2D 122
Saffron Clo. NW11—5H 27
Saffron Hill. EC1
    —5A 62 (5H 141)
Saffron Rd. Romf—2K 37
Saffron St. EC1—5A 62 (5H 141)
Sage St. E1—7J 63 (9L 143)
Saigasso Clo. E16—6B 66
Sail St. SE11—4K 77 (8F 146)
Sainfoin Rd. SW17—2E 108
Sainsbury Rd. SE19—5E 110
St Agatha's Dri. King—6F 105
St Agatha's Gro. Cars—1D 132
St Agnes Clo. E9—1J 63
St Agnes Pl. SE11—6B 78
St Aidan's Rd. SE22—6H 95
St Aidan's Rd. W13—2B 72
St Alban's Av. E6—3E 66
St Alban's Av. W4—3K 73
St Alban's Av. Felt—5B 102
St Albans Clo. NW11—1J 43
St Alban's Cres. N22—1A 30
St Alban's Cres. Wfd G—7D 20
St Alban's Gdns. Tedd—5A 104
St Alban's Gro. W8—3K 75
St Alban's Gro. Cars—7C 122
St Albans La. NW11—1J 43
St Alban's M. W2
    —5B 60 (5B 138)
St Alban's Pl. N1—1B 62
St Alban's Rd. NW5—3E 44
St Albans Rd. NW10—1A 58
St Alban's Rd. Barn—1A 4
St Albans Rd. Ilf—1K 51
St Alban's Rd. King—6E 104
St Alban's Rd. Sutt—4H 131
St Alban's Rd. Wfd G—7D 20
St Alban's St. SW1
    —7H 61 (1A 146)
St Alban's Ter. W6—6G 75
St Alfege Pas. SE10—6E 80
St Alfege Rd. SE7—6B 82
St Alphage Garden. EC2
    —5C 62 (6M 141)
St Alphage Wlk. Edgw—2J 25
St Alphege Rd. N9—7D 64
St Alphonsus Rd. SW4—4G 93

St Amunds Clo. SE6—4C 112
St Andrew's Av. Wemb—4A 40
St Andrew's Clo. N12—4F 15
St Andrew's Clo. NW2—3D 42
St Andrew's Clo. Iswth—1J 87
St Andrew's Clo. Ruis—2B 38
St Andrew's Clo. Stan—2C 24
St Andrew's Ct. SW18—2A 108
St Andrew's Dri. Stan—1C 24
St Andrew's Gro. N16—1D 46
St Andrew's Hill. EC4
—6B 62 (8K 141)
St Andrew's M. N16—1E 46
St Andrew's M. SE3—7J 81
St Andrew's Pl. NW1
—4F 61 (3J 139)
St Andrew's Rd. E11—6G 33
St Andrew's Rd. E13—3K 65
St Andrew's Rd. E17—2K 31
St Andrew's Rd. N9—7D 8
St Andrew's Rd. NW9—1K 41
St Andrew's Rd. NW10—6D 42
St Andrew's Rd. NW11—6H 27
St Andrew's Rd. W3—7A 58
St Andrew's Rd. W7—2J 71
St Andrew's Rd. W14—6G 75
St Andrew's Rd. Cars—3C 132
St Andrew's Rd. Croy—4C 134
St Andrew's Rd. Enf—3J 7
St Andrew's Rd. Ilf—7D 34
St Andrew's Rd. Romf—6K 37
St Andrew's Rd. Sidc—3D 116
St Andrew's Rd. Surb—6D 118
St Andrew's Sq. W11—6G 59
St Andrew's Sq. Surb—6D 118
St Andrew St. EC4
—5A 62 (6H 141)
St Anne's Clo. N6—3E 44
St Anne's Ct. W1
—6H 61 (8A 140)
St Anne's Ct. W Wick—4G 137
St Anne's Pas. E14—6B 64
St Anne's Rd. E11—2F 49
St Anne's Rd. Wemb—5D 40
St Anne's Row. E14—6B 64
St Anne St. E14—6B 64
St Ann's. Bark—1G 67
St Ann's Cres. SW18—6A 92
St Ann's Gdns. NW5—6E 44
St Ann's Gdns. NW10—3F 57
St Ann's Hill. SW18—6K 91
St Ann's La. SW1
—3H 77 (6B 146)
St Ann's Pk. Rd. SW18—6A 92
St Ann's Pas. SW13—3A 90
St Ann's Rd. N9—1A 18
St Ann's Rd. N15—5C 30
St Ann's Rd. SW13—2B 90
St Ann's Rd. W11—7F 59
St Ann's Rd. Bark—1G 67
St Ann's Rd. Harr—6J 23
St Ann's St. SW1
—3H 77 (6B 146)
St Ann's Ter. NW8—2B 60
St Ann's Vs. W11—1F 75
St Ann's Way S Croy—6B 134
St Anselm's Pl. W1
—7F 61 (9J 139)
St Anthony's Av. Wfd G—6F 21
St Anthony's Clo. E1
—1G 79 (2G 149)
St Anthony's Clo. SW17
—2C 108
St Antony's Rd. E7—7K 49
St Arvan's Clo. Croy—3E 134
St Asaph Rd. SE4—3K 95
St Aubyn's Av. SW19—5H 107
St Aubyn's Av. Houn—5E 86
St Aubyn's Rd. SE19—6F 111
St Audrey Av. Bexh—2G 101
St Augustine's Av. Brom
—5C 128
St Augustine's Av. S Croy
—7C 134
St Augustine's Av. Wemb
—3E 40
St Augustine's Av. W5—2E 56

St Augustine's Rd. NW1—7H 45
St Augustine's Rd. Belv—4F 85
St Austell Clo. Edgw—2F 25
St Austell Rd. SE13—2E 96
St Awdry's Rd. Bark—7H 51
St Awdry's Wlk. Bark—7G 51
St Barnabas Clo. Beck—2E 126
St Barnabas Ct. Harr—1G 23
St Barnabas Rd. E17—6C 32
St Barnabas Rd. Mitc—7E 108
St Barnabas Rd. Sutt—5B 132
St Barnabas Rd. Wfd G—1K 33
St Barnabas St. SW1
—5E 76 (9H 145)
St Barnabas Ter. E9—5K 47
St Barnabas Vs. SW8—1J 93
St Bartholomew's Clo. SE26
—4J 111
St Bartholomew's Rd. E6
—2D 66
St Benedict's Clo. SW17
—5E 108
St Benet's Clo. SW17—2C 108
St Benet's Gro. Cars—7A 122
St Benet's Pl. EC3
—7E 62 (9C 142)
St Bernards. Croy—3E 134
St Bernard's Clo. SE27—4D 110
St Bernard's Rd. E6—1B 66
St Blaise Av. Brom—2K 127
St Botolph Row. EC3
—6F 63 (8E 142)
St Botolph St. EC3
—6F 63 (7E 142)
St Bride's Av. Edgw—1F 25
St Bride's Clo. Eri—2D 84
St Bride Rd. EC4—6B 62 (7J 141)
St Catherine's Clo. SW17
—2C 108
St Catherine's Dri. SE14—2K 95
St Catherines M. SW3
—4D 76 (8E 144)
St Catherine's Rd. E4—2H 19
St Chad's Gdns. Romf—7E 36
St Chad's Pl. WC1
—3K 61 (1E 140)
St Chad's Rd. Romf—7E 36
St Chad's St. WC1
—3J 61 (1D 140)
St Charles Pl. W10—5G 59
St Charles Sq. W10—5G 59
St Christopher's Clo. Iswth
—1J 87
St Christopher's Gdns. T Hth
—3A 124
St Christopher's M. Wall
—5G 133
St Christopher's Pl. W1
—6E 60 (8H 139)
St Clair Dri. Wor Pk—3D 130
St Claire Clo. Ilf—2D 34
St Clair Rd. E13—2K 65
St Clair's Rd. Croy—2E 134
St Clare Business Pk. Hmptn
—6G 103
St Clare St. EC3—6F 63 (8E 142)
St Clements Heights. SE26
—3G 111
St Clement's La. WC2
—6K 61 (8F 140)
St Clement St. N7—7A 46
St Cloud Rd. SE27—4C 110
St Crispin Clo. NW3—4C 44
St Crispin's Clo. S'hall—6D 54
St Cross St. EC1
—5A 62 (5H 141)
St Cuthbert's Rd. NW2—6H 43
St Cuthbert's Wlk. NW6—6H 43
St Cyprian's St. SW17—4D 108
St David's Clo. Wemb—3J 41
St David's Clo. W Wick—7D 126
St David's Dri. Edgw—1F 25
St David's Pl. NW4—7D 26
St Denis Rd. SE27—4D 110
St Dionis Rd. SW6—2H 91
St Donatt's Rd. SE14—1B 96

St Dunstan's Av. W3—7K 57
St Dunstan's Ct. EC4
—6A 62 (8H 141)
St Dunstan's Gdns. W3—7K 57
St Dunstan's Hill. EC3
—7E 62 (1C 148)
St Dunstan's Hill. Sutt—6G 131
St Dunstan's La. EC3
—7E 62 (1C 148)
St Dunstan's La. Beck—6E 126
St Dunstan's Rd. E7—6A 50
St Dunstan's Rd. SE25—4F 125
St Dunstan's Rd. W6—5F 75
St Dunstan's Rd. W7—2J 71
St Dunstan's Rd. Houn—2A 86
St Edmund's Clo. NW8—1D 60
St Edmund's Clo. SW17
—2C 108
St Edmund's Clo. Eri—2D 84
St Edmund's Dri. Stan—1A 24
St Edmund's La. Twic—7F 87
St Edmund's Rd. N9—7B 8
St Edmund's Rd. Ilf—6D 34
St Edmund's Ter. NW8—1C 60
St Edward's Clo. NW11—6J 27
St Edward's Way. Romf—5K 37
St Egbert's Way. E4—1K 19
St Elmo Rd. W12—2B 74
St Elmos Rd. SE16—2A 80
St Erkenwald Rd. Bark—1H 67
St Ervan's Rd. W10—5H 59
St Faith's Clo. Enf—1H 7
St Faith's Rd. SE21—1B 110
St Fidelis Rd. Eri—4K 85
St Fillans Rd. SE6—1E 112
St Francis Clo. Orp—6J 129
St Francis Rd. SE22—4E 94
St Francis Rd. Eri—4K 85
St Gabriel's Clo. E11—1K 49
St Gabriel's Rd. NW2—5F 43
St George's Av. E7—7K 49
St George's Av. N7—4H 45
St George's Av. NW9—4K 25
St George's Av. W5—2D 72
St George's Av. S'hall—7D 54
St George's Bldgs. SE1
—2C 78 (4M 147)
St George's Cir. SE1
—3B 78 (6J 147)
St George's Clo. NW11—6H 27
St George's Clo. Wemb—3A 40
St George's Ct. E6—4D 66
St George's Dri. SW1
—4F 77 (9K 145)
St George's Fields. W2
—6C 60 (8D 138)
St George's Gro. SW17—3B 108
St Georges Industrial Est. N17
—7G 17
St George's M. NW1—7D 44
St George's Rd. E7—7K 49
St George's Rd. E10—3E 48
St George's Rd. N9—3B 18
St George's Rd. N13—2E 16
St George's Rd. NW11—6H 27
St George's Rd. SE1
—3B 78 (7J 147)
St George's Rd. SW19—6H 107
St George's Rd. W4—2K 73
St George's Rd. W7—1K 71
St George's Rd. Beck—1D 126
St George's Rd. Brom—2D 128
St George's Rd. Dag—5E 52
St George's Rd. Enf—1A 8
St George's Rd. Felt—4B 102
St George's Rd. Ilf—7D 34
St George's Rd. King—7G 105
St George's Rd. Mitc—3F 123
St George's Rd. Orp—6H 129
St George's Rd. Rich—3F 89
St George's Rd. Sidc—6D 116
St George's Rd. Twic—5B 88
St George's Rd. Wall—5F 133
St George's Rd. W. Brom
—2C 128
St George's Sq. E7—7K 49
St Georges Sq. E14—7A 64

St Georges Sq. SE8—4B 80
St George's Sq. SW1
—5H 77 (9A 146)
St George's Sq. N Mald—3A 120
St George's Sq. M. SW1—5H 77
St George's Ter. NW1—7D 44
St George St. W1
—7F 61 (9K 139)
St George's Wlk. Croy—3C 134
St George's Way. SE15—6E 78
St Gerard's Clo. SW4—5G 93
St German's Pl. SE3—1J 97
St German's Rd. SE23—1A 112
St Giles Av. Dag—7H 53
St Giles Cir. W1, WC1 & WC2
—6H 61 (7B 140)
St Giles Clo. Dag—7H 53
St Giles High St. WC2
—6H 61 (7B 140)
St Giles Rd. SE5—7E 78
St Gothard Rd. SE27—4D 110
St Gregory Clo. Ruis—4A 38
St Helena Rd. SE16
—4K 79 (9M 149)
St Helena St. WC1
—3A 62 (2G 141)
St Helen's Cres. SW16—1K 123
St Helen's Gdns. W10—6F 59
St Helen's Pl. EC3
—6E 62 (7C 142)
St Helen's Rd. SW16—1K 123
St Helen's Rd. W13—1C 72
St Helen's Rd. Eri—2D 84
St Helen's Rd. Ilf—6D 34
St Helier Av. Mord—7A 122
St Helier's Av. Houn—5E 86
St Helier's Rd. E10—6E 32
St Hilda's Clo. NW6—1F 59
St Hilda's Clo. SW17—2C 108
St Hilda's Rd. SW13—6D 74
St Hughe's Clo. SW17—2C 108
St Hughes Rd. SE20—1H 125
St James Av. N20—3H 15
St James Av. W13—1A 72
St James Av. Sutt—5J 131
St James Clo. N20—3H 15
St James Clo. SE18—5G 83
St James Clo. N Mald—5B 120
St James Clo. Ruis—2A 38
St James Ct. SW1
—3G 77 (6M 145)
St James Gdns. Wemb—7E 40
St James Ga. NW1—7H 45
St James Gro. SW11—2D 92
St James M. E14—3E 80
St James' Rd. E15—5H 49
St James' Rd. N9—2C 18
St James Rd. Cars—3C 132
St James Rd. King—2D 118
St James Rd. Mitc—7E 108
St James Rd. Surb—6D 118
St James Rd. Sutt—5J 131
St James's. SE14—1A 96
St James's Av. E2—2J 63
St James's Av. Hmptn—5G 103
St James's Clo. SW17—2D 108
St James's Cotts. Rich—5D 88
St James's Cres. SW9—3A 94
St James's Dri. SW17—1D 108
St James's Gdns. W11—1G 75
St James's La. N10—4F 29
St James's Mkt. SW1
—7H 61 (1A 146)
St James's Pk. Croy—7C 124
St James's Pl. SW1
—1G 77 (3L 145)
St James's Rd. SE1—3G 79 (6H 149)
SE16 1-167 & 2-144
SE1 remainder
St James's Rd. Croy—7C 124
St James's Rd. Hmptn—5F 103
St James's Row. EC1
—4B 62 (3J 141)
St James's Sq. SW1
—1G 77 (2M 145)

St James's St. SW1
—1G 77 (2L 145)
St James's Ter. M. NW8—1D 60
St James St. E17—5A 32
St James St. W6—5E 74
St James's Wlk. EC1
—4B 62 (3J 141)
St James Way. Sidc—5E 116
St Joan's Rd. N9—2A 18
St John's Av. N11—5J 15
St John's Av. NW10—1B 58
St John's Av. SW15—5F 91
St John's Chu. Rd. E9—5J 47
St John's Clo. SW6—7J 75
St John's Clo. Wemb—5E 40
St John's Cotts. SE20—7J 111
St Johns Ct. N5—4B 46
St John's Ct. Buck H—1E 20
St John's Ct. Eri—5K 85
St John's Ct. Iswth—2K 87
St John's Cres. SW9—3A 94
St John's Dri. SW18—1K 107
St John's Est. N1
—2D 62 (1B 142)
St John's Gdns. W11—7H 59
St John's Gro. N19—2G 45
St Johns Gro. SW13—2B 90
St John's Gro. Rich—4E 88
St John's Hill. SW11—4B 92
St John's Hill Gro. SW11—4B 92
St John's La. EC1
—4B 62 (4J 141)
St John's M. W11—6J 59
St John's Pk. SE3—7H 81
St John's Pas. SW19—6G 107
St Johns Pathway. SE23
—1J 111
St John's Pl. EC1
—4B 62 (4J 141)
St John's Rd. E4—4J 19
St John's Rd. E6—1C 66
St John's Rd. E16—6J 65
St John's Rd. E17—2D 32
St John's Rd. N15—6E 30
St John's Rd. NW11—6H 27
St John's Rd. SE20—6J 111
St John's Rd. SW11—4C 92
St John's Rd. SW19—7G 107
St John's Rd. Bark—1J 67
St John's Rd. Cars—3C 132
St John's Rd. Croy—3B 134
St John's Rd. Eri—5K 85
St John's Rd. Felt—4C 102
St John's Rd. Harr—6K 23
St John's Rd. Ilf—7J 35
St John's Rd. Iswth—2K 87
St John's Rd. King—2C 118
St John's Rd. N Mald—3J 119
St John's Rd. Orp—6H 129
St John's Rd. Rich—4E 88
St John's Rd. Sidc—4B 116
St John's Rd. S'hall—3C 70
St John's Rd. Sutt—2K 131
St John's Rd. Well—3B 100
St John's Rd. Wemb—4D 40
St John's Sq. EC1
—4B 62 (4J 141)
St John's Ter. E7—6K 49
St John's Ter. SE18—6G 83
St John's Ter. W10—4F 59
St John St. EC1—3B 62 (1J 141)
St John's Vale. SE8—2C 96
St John's Vs. N19—2H 45
St John's Way. N19—2G 45
St John's Wood High St. NW8
—2C 60 (1C 138)
St John's Wood Pk. NW8
—1B 60
St John's Wood Rd. NW8
—4B 60 (3A 138)
St John's Wood Ter. NW8
—2C 60
St John's Yd. N17—7A 18
St Joseph's Clo. W10—5G 59
St Joseph's Dri. S'hall—1C 70
St Joseph's Rd. N9—7C 8
St Joseph's St. SW8—1F 93

St Joseph's Vale. SE3—3F 97
St Jude's Rd. E2—2H 63 (1K 143)
St Jude St. N16—5E 46
St Julian's Clo. SW16—4A 110
St Julian's Farm Rd. SE27
—4A 110
St Julian's Rd. NW6—1J 59
St Katharine's Precinct. NW1
—2F 61
St Katharine's Way. E1
—1F 79 (2F 148)
St Katherine's Rd. Eri—2D 84
St Keverne Rd. SE9—4C 114
St Kilda Rd. W13—2A 72
St Kilda Rd. Orp—7K 129
St Kilda's Rd. N16—1D 46
St Kilda's Rd. Harr—6J 23
St Kitts Ter. SE19—5E 110
St Laurence's Clo. NW6—1F 59
St Lawrence Clo. Edgw—7A 12
St Lawrence Dri. Pinn—5A 22
St Lawrence St. E14—1E 80
St Lawrence Ter. W10—5G 59
St Lawrence Way. SW9—2A 94
St Leonard's Av. E4—6A 20
St Leonard's Av. Harr—5C 24
St Leonard's Clo. Well—3A 100
St Leonard's Gdns. Houn
—1C 86
St Leonard's Gdns. Ilf—5G 51
St Leonard's Rd. E14—5D 64
(in two parts)
St Leonard's Rd. NW10—4K 57
St Leonard's Rd. SW14—3J 89
St Leonard's Rd. W13—7C 56
St Leonard's Rd. Croy—3B 134
St Leonard's Rd. Surb—5D 118
St Leonard's Rd. Th Dit—7A 118
St Leonard's Sq. NW5—6E 44
St Leonard's Sq. Surb—5D 118
St Leonard's St. E3—3D 64
St Leonard's Ter. SW3—5D 76
St Leonard St. NW5—6E 44
St Leonard's Wlk. SW16
—7K 109
St Loo Av. SW3—6C 76
St Louis Rd. SE27—4D 110
St Loy's Rd. N17—2E 30
St Luke's Av. SW4—4H 93
St Luke's Av. Enf—1J 7
St Luke's Av. Ilf—5F 51
St Luke's Clo. EC1
—4C 62 (3M 141)
St Luke's Clo. SE25—6H 125
St Luke's Est. EC1
—3D 62 (2A 142)
St Luke's M. W11—6H 59
St Luke's Pas. King—1F 119
St Luke's Path. Ilf—5F 51
St Luke's Rd. W11—5H 59
St Luke's Sq. E16—6H 65
St Luke's St. SW3
—5C 76 (9D 144)
St Luke's Yd. W9—2H 59
St Malo Av. N9—3D 18
St Margaret's. Bark—1H 67
St Margaret's Av. N15—4B 30
St Margaret's Av. N20—1F 15
St Margaret's Av. Harr—3G 39
St Margaret's Av. Sidc—3H 115
St Margaret's Av. Sutt—3G 131
St Margaret's Ct. N11—4K 15
St Margaret's Ct. SE1
—1D 78 (3A 148)
St Margaret's Cres. SW15
St Margaret's Dri. Twic—5B 88
St Margaret's Gro. SE18—6G 83
St Margaret's Gro. Twic—6A 88
St Margaret's Pas. SE13—3G 97
St Margaret's Rd. E12—2A 50
St Margaret's Rd. N17—3E 30
St Margaret's Rd. NW10—3E 58
St Margaret's Rd. SE4—4B 96
St Margaret's Rd. W7—2J 71
St Margaret's Rd. Beck—4K 125
St Margaret's Rd. Edgw—5C 12

St Margaret's Rd. Twic—4B 88
St Margaret's Sq. SE4—4B 96
St Margaret's Ter. SE18—5G 83
St Margaret St. SW1
—2J 77 (5C 146)
St Mark's Clo. SE10—7E 80
St Mark's Clo. W11—6G 59
St Mark's Clo. Barn—3E 4
St Mark's Cres. NW1—1E 60
St Mark's Ga. E9—7B 48
St Mark's Gro. SW10—6K 75
St Mark's Hill. Surb—6E 118
St Mark's Industrial Est. E16
—1B 82
St Mark's Pl. SW19—6H 107
St Mark's Pl. W11—6G 59
St Mark's Rise. E8—5F 47
St Mark's Rd. SE25—4G 125
St Mark's Rd. W5—1E 72
St Mark's Rd. W7—2J 71
St Mark's Rd. W10—5F 59
W11 1-53a & 2-22
W10 remainder
St Mark's Rd. Brom—3K 127
St Mark's Rd. Enf—6A 8
St Mark's Rd. Mitc—2D 122
St Mark's Rd. Tedd—7B 104
St Mark's Sq. NW1—1E 60
St Mark St. E1—6F 63 (8F 142)
St Martin's Av. E6—2B 66
St Martin's Clo. NW1—1G 61
St Martin's Clo. Enf—1C 8
St Martin's Clo. Eri—2D 84
St Martin's Ct. WC2
—7J 61 (9C 140)
St Martin's Est. SW2—1A 110
St Martin's La. WC2
—7J 61 (9C 140)
St Martin's le Grand. EC1
—6C 62 (7L 141)
St Martin's Pl. WC2
—7J 61 (1C 146)
St Martin's Rd. N9—2C 18
St Martin's Rd. SW9—2K 93
St Martin's St. WC2
—7H 61 (1B 146)
St Martin's Way. SW17—3A 108
St Mary Abbot's Pl. W8—3H 75
St Mary Abbot's Ter. W14
—3H 75
St Mary at Hill. EC3
—7E 62 (1C 148)
St Mary Av. Wall—3F 133
St Mary Axe. EC3
—6E 62 (8C 142)
St Marychurch St. SE16
—2J 79 (5L 149)
St Mary Graces Ct. EC3
—7F 63 (1F 148)
St Mary Rd. E17—4C 32
St Mary's. Bark—1H 67
St Mary's App. E12—5D 50
St Mary's Av. E11—7K 33
St Mary's Av. N3—2G 27
St Mary's Av. Brom—3G 127
St Mary's Av. S'hall—4F 71
(in two parts)
St Mary's Av. Tedd—6K 103
St Mary's Clo. N17—1G 31
St Mary's Clo. Eps—7K 131
St Mary's Ct. E6—4D 66
St Mary's Ct. SE7—7B 82
St Mary's Ct. W5—2D 72
St Mary's Cres. NW4—3D 26
St Mary's Cres. Iswth—7H 71
St Mary's Gdns. SE11
—4A 78 (8H 147)
St Mary's Grn. N2—2A 28
St Mary's Gro. N1—6B 46
St Mary's Gro. SW13—3D 90
St Mary's Gro. W4—6H 73
St Mary's Gro. Rich—4F 89
St Mary's Mans. W2
—5B 60 (5A 138)
St Mary's M. NW6—7K 43
St Mary's Path. N1—1B 62
St Mary's Pl. SE9—6E 98

St Mary's Rd. E10—3E 48
St Mary's Rd. E13—2K 65
St Mary's Rd. N8—4J 29
St Mary's Rd. N9—1C 18
St Mary's Rd. NW10—1A 58
St Mary's Rd. NW11—7G 27
St Mary's Rd. SE15—1J 95
St Mary's Rd. SE25—3E 124
St Mary's Rd. SW19—5G 107
St Mary's Rd. W5—2D 72
St Mary's Rd. Barn—7J 5
St Mary's Rd. Bex—1J 117
St Mary's Rd. Ilf—2H 51
St Mary's Rd. Surb—6D 118
St Mary's Rd. Surb—7C 118
(Long Ditton)
St Mary's Rd. Wor Pk—2A 130
St Mary's Sq. W2
—5B 60 (5A 138)
St Mary's Sq. W5—2D 72
St Mary's Ter. W2
—5B 60 (5A 138)
St Mary St. SE18—4D 82
St Mary's View. Harr—5C 24
St Mary's Wlk. SE11
—4A 78 (8H 147)
St Mary's Way. Chig—5K 21
St Matthew's Av. Surb—7E 118
St Matthew's Dri. Brom
—3D 128
St Matthew's Rd. SW2—5K 93
St Matthew's Rd. W5—1E 72
St Matthew's Row. E2
—4G 63 (3G 143)
St Matthew St. SW1
—3H 77 (7A 146)
St Matthias Clo. NW9—5B 26
St Maur Rd. SW6—1H 91
St Merryn Clo. SE18—7H 83
St Merryn Ct. Beck—7C 112
St Michael's All. EC3
—6D 62 (8B 142)
St Michael's Av. N9—7D 8
St Michael's Av. Wemb—6G 41
St Michael's Clo. E16—5B 66
St Michael's Clo. N3—2H 27
St Michael's Clo. N12—5H 15
St Michael's Clo. Brom—3C 128
St Michael's Clo. Eri—2D 84
St Michael's Cres. Pinn—6C 22
St Michael's Gdns. W10—5G 59
St Michael's Rise. Well—1B 100
St Michael's Rd. NW2—4E 42
St Michael's Rd. SW9—2K 93
St Michael's Rd. Croy—1C 134
St Michael's Rd. Wall—6G 133
St Michael's Rd. Well—3B 100
St Michael's St. W2
—6B 60 (7B 138)
St Michael's Ter. N22—1J 29
St Mildred's Ct. EC2
—6D 62 (8A 142)
St Mildred's Rd. SE12—7H 97
St Nicholas Glebe. SW17
—5E 108
St Nicholas Rd. SE18—5K 83
St Nicholas Rd. Sutt—5K 131
St Nicholas St. SE8—1B 96
St Nicholas Way. Sutt—4K 131
St Nicolas La. Chst—1C 128
St Ninian's Ct. N20—3J 15
St Norbert Grn. SE4—5A 96
St Norbert Rd. SE4—5K 95
St Olaf's Rd. SW6—7G 75
St Olave's Ct. EC2
—6D 62 (8A 142)
St Olave's Gdns. SE11
—4A 78 (8G 147)
St Olave's Rd. E6—1E 66
St Olave's Wlk. SW16—2G 123
St Oswald's Pl. SE11—5K 77
St Oswald's Rd. SW16—1B 124
St Pancras Ct. N2—2B 28
St Pancras Way. NW1—7G 45
St Patrick's Ct. Wfd G—7B 20
St Paul's Av. NW2—6E 42
St Paul's Av. SE16—1K 79

264

Sandringham Dri. Well—2J 99
Sandringham Gdns. N8—6J 29
Sandringham Gdns. N12

—6G 15
Sandringham Gdns. Ilf—3G 35
Sandringham M. W5—7D 56
Sandringham Rd. E7—5A 50
Sandringham Rd. E8—5F 47
Sandringham Rd. E10—6F 33
Sandringham Rd. N22—2C 30
Sandringham Rd. NW2—6D 42
Sandringham Rd. NW11—7G 27
Sandringham Rd. Bark—6K 51
Sandringham Rd. Brom

—5J 113
Sandringham Rd. N'holt—7E 38
Sandringham Rd. T Hth

—5C 124
Sandringham Rd. Wor Pk

—3C 130
Sandrock Pl. Croy—4K 135
Sandrock Rd. SE13—3C 96
Sand's End La. SW6—1K 91
Sandstone Pl. N19—2F 45
Sandstone Rd. SE12—2K 113
Sands Way. Wfd G—6J 21
Sandtoft Rd. SE7—6K 81
Sandwell Cres. NW6—6J 43
Sandwich St. WC1

—3J 61 (2C 140)
Sandycombe Rd. Rich—3G 89
Sandycombe Rd. Twic—6C 88
Sandycroft. SE2—6A 84
Sandy Hill Av. SE18—5F 83
Sandy Hill Rd. SE18—5F 83
Sandyhill Rd. Ilf—4F 51
Sandy Hill Rd. Wall—7G 133
Sandy La. Harr—6F 25
Sandy La. Mitc—1E 122
Sandy La. Orp—7K 129
Sandy La. Orp & Sidc—7D 116
Sandy La. Rich—2C 104
Sandy La. Sutt—7G 131
Sandy La. Tedd & King—7A 104
Sandy La. N. Wall—5H 133
Sandy La. S. Wall—7G 133
Sandymount Av. Stan—5H 11
Sandy Ridge. Chst—6E 114
Sandy Rd. NW3—2K 43
Sandys Row. E1

—5E 62 (6D 142)
Sandy Way. Croy—3B 136
Sanford La. N16—2F 47
Sanford St. SE14—6A 80
Sanford Ter. N16—3F 47
Sanford Wlk. N16—2F 47
Sanford Wlk. SE14—6A 80
Sangley Rd. SE6—7D 96
Sangley Rd. SE25—4E 124
Sangora Rd. SW11—4B 92
Sansom Rd. E11—2H 49
Sansom St. SE5—1D 94
Sans Wlk. EC1—4A 62 (3H 141)
Santley St. SW4—4K 93
Santos Rd. SW18—5J 91
Santway, The. Stan—5D 10
Sapcote Trading Est. NW10

—6B 42
Sapphire Clo. E6—6E 66
Sapphire Clo. Dag—1C 52
Sapphire Rd. SE8—4A 80
Saracen Clo. Croy—6D 124
Saracen St. E14—6C 64
Sarah St. N1—3E 62 (1D 142)
Saratoga Rd. E5—4J 47
Sardinia St. WC2

—6K 61 (7E 140)
Sarita Clo. Harr—2H 23
Sark Clo. Houn—7E 70
Sark Wlk. E16—6K 65
Sarnesfield Rd. Enf—4J 7
Sarre Rd. NW2—5H 43
Sarsen Av. Houn—2E 86
Sarsfeld Rd. SW12—1D 108
Sarsfield Rd. Gnfd—2B 56
Sartor Rd. SE15—4K 95
Satanita Clo. E16—6B 66

Satchell Mead. NW9—1B 26
Satchwell Rd. E2

—3G 63 (2G 143)
Sauls Grn. E11—3G 49
Saunders Ness Rd. E14—5E 80
Saunders Rd. SE18—5K 83
Saunders St. SE11

—4K 77 (8F 146)
Saunders Way. SE28—7B 68
Saunderton Rd. Wemb—5B 40
Savage Gdns. E6—6D 66
Savage Gdns. EC3

—7E 62 (9D 142)
Savernake Rd. N9—6B 8
Savernake Rd. NW3—4D 44
Savile Clo. N Mald—5A 120
Savile Gdns. Croy—2F 135
Savile Row. W1—7G 61 (9L 139)
Saville Rd. E16—1C 82
Saville Rd. W4—3K 73
Saville Rd. Romf—6F 37
Saville Rd. Twic—1K 103
Saville Row. Enf—2C 8
Savill Gdns. SW20—3C 120
Savill Row. Wfd G—6C 20
Savona Clo. SW19—7F 107
Savona St. SW8—7G 77
Savoy Clo. E15—1G 65
Savoy Clo. Edgw—5B 12
Savoy Ct. NW3—3K 43
Savoy Ct. WC2—7K 61 (1E 146)
Savoy Hill. WC2

—7K 61 (1E 146)
Savoy Pde. Enf—3K 7
Savoy Row. WC2—7J 61 (1D 146)
Savoy St. WC2—7K 61 (1E 146)
Sawkins Clo. SW19—2G 107
Sawley Rd. W12—1C 74
Sawtry Clo. Cars—7C 122
Sawyers Clo. Dag—6J 53
Sawyer's Hill. Rich—7F 89
Sawyers Lawn. W13—6A 56
Sawyer St. SE1—2C 78 (4L 147)
Saxby Rd. SW2—7J 93
Saxham Rd. Bark—1J 67
Saxlingham Rd. E4—3A 20
Saxon Av. Felt—2C 102
Saxonbury Clo. Mitc—3B 122
Saxonbury Gdns. Surb—7C 118
Saxon Clo. Surb—6E 118
Saxon Dri. W3—6G 57
Saxon Gdns. S'hall—7C 54
Saxon Rd. E3—2B 64
Saxon Rd. E6—4D 66
Saxon Rd. N22—1B 30
Saxon Rd. SE25—5D 124
Saxon Rd. Brom—7H 113
Saxon Rd. Ilf—6F 51
Saxon Rd. S'hall—7C 54
Saxon Rd. Wemb—3J 41
Saxon Wlk. Sidc—6C 116
Saxon Way. N14—6C 6
Saxton Clo. SE13—3F 97
Sayer's Wlk. Rich—7F 89
Sayes Ct. SE8—5B 80
Sayes Ct. St. SE8—6B 80
Scads Hill Clo. Orp—6K 129
Scala St. W1—5G 61 (5M 139)
Scales Rd. N17—3G 31
Scampston M. W10—6F 59
Scandrett St. E1

—1H 79 (3J 149)
Scarborough Rd. E11—1F 49
Scarborough Rd. N4—1A 46
Scarborough Rd. N9—7D 8
Scarborough St. E1

—6F 63 (8F 142)
Scarbrook Rd. Croy—3C 134
Scarle Rd. Wemb—6D 40
Scarlet Rd. SE6—3G 113
Scarlette Mnr. Way. SW2

—7A 94
Scarsbrook Rd. SE3—3B 98
Scarsdale Pl. W8—3K 75
Scarsdale Rd. Harr—3G 39
Scarsdale Vs. W8—3J 75
Scarth Rd. SW13—3B 90

Scawen Rd. SE8—5A 80
Scawfell St. E2—2F 63 (1F 142)
Sceau Gdns. SE5—1E 94
Sceptre Rd. E2—3J 63 (2M 143)
Sceynes Link. N12—4D 14
Schofield Wlk. SE3—7K 81
Scholars Rd. E4—1A 20
Scholars Rd. SW12—1G 109
Scholefield Rd. N19—2H 45
School All. Twic—1A 104
School App. E2—3E 62 (1D 142)
Schoolbell M. E3—2A 64
School Ho. La. E1

—7K 63 (9M 143)
School Ho. La. Tedd—7B 104
School La. SE23—2H 111
School La. Bush, Wat—1A 10
School La. Dag—3C 52
School La. King—1C 118
School La. Pinn—4C 22
School La. Well—3B 100
School Pas. King—2F 119
School Pas. S'hall—7D 54
School Rd. E12—4D 50
School Rd. NW10—4K 57
School Rd. Chst—1G 129
School Rd. Dag—1G 69
School Rd. Hmptn—6G 103
School Rd. Houn—3G 87
School Rd. King—1C 118
School Rd. Av. Hmptn—6G 103
School Way. N12—6G 15
Schooner Clo. SE16

—2K 79 (4M 149)
Schubert Rd. SW15—5H 91
Sclater St. E1—4F 63 (3F 142)
Scoble Pl. N16—4F 47
Scoles Cres. SW2—1A 110
Scoresby St. SE1

—1B 78 (3J 147)
Scorton Av. Gnfd—2A 56
Scotch Comn. W13—5A 56
Scoter Clo. Wfd G—7E 20
Scotland Grn. N17—2G 31
Scotland Grn. Rd. Enf—5E 8
Scotland Grn. Rd. N. Enf—4F 9
Scotland Pl. SW1

—1J 77 (2C 146)
Scotland Rd. Buck H—1F 21
Scotsdale Clo. Orp—4J 129
Scotsdale Clo. Sutt—7G 131
Scotsdale Rd. SE12—5K 97
Scotswood St. EC1

—4A 62 (3H 141)
Scotswood Wlk. N17—7B 18
Scott Clo. SW16—1K 123
Scott Cres. Harr—1F 39
Scott Ellis Gdns. NW8

—3B 60 (2A 138)
Scottes La. Dag—1D 52
Scott Farm Clo. Th Dit—7B 118
Scott Gdns. Houn—7B 70
Scott Gro. Pinn—1B 22
Scott Lidgett Cres. SE16

—2G 79 (5H 149)
Scotts Av. Brom—2F 127
Scotts Dri. Hmptn—7F 103
Scotts La. Brom—3F 127
Scott's Rd. E10—1E 48
Scotts Rd. W12—2D 74
Scotts Rd. Brom—7J 113
Scott's Rd. S'hall—3A 70
Scott St. E1—4H 63 (4J 143)
Scoulding Rd. E16—6J 65
Scout App. NW10—4A 42
Scout La. SW4—3G 93
Scout Way. NW7—4E 12
Scovell Rd. SE1—2C 78 (5L 147)
Scrattons Ter. Bark—1D 68
Scriven St. E8—1F 63
Scrooby St. SE6—6D 96
Scrubs La. NW10—3C 58
Scrutton Clo. SW12—7H 93
Scrutton St. EC2

—4E 62 (4C 142)
Scudamore La. NW9—4J 25
Scutari Rd. SE22—5J 95

Scylla Rd. SE15—3H 95
(in two parts)
Seabright St. E2

—3H 63 (2J 143)
Seabrook Dri. W Wick—2G 137
Seabrook Gdns. Romf—7G 37
Seabrook Rd. Dag—3D 52
Seaburn Clo. Rain—3K 69
Seacoal La. EC4—6B 62 (8J 141)
Seacourt Rd. SE2—2D 84
Seafield Rd. N11—4C 16
Seaford Rd. E17—3D 32
Seaford Rd. N15—5D 30
Seaford Rd. W13—1B 72
Seaford Rd. Enf—4K 7
Seaford St. WC1

—3J 61 (2D 140)
Seaforth Av. N Mald—5D 120
Seaforth Cres. N5—5C 46
Seaforth Gdns. N21—7E 6
Seaforth Gdns. Eps—4B 130
Seaforth Gdns. Wfd G—5F 21
Seager Pl. E3—5B 64
Seagrave Rd. SW6—6J 75
Seagry Rd. E11—6J 33
Sealand Wlk. N'holt—3B 54
Seal St. E8—4F 47
Searle Pl. N4—1K 45
Searles Clo. SW11—7C 76
Searles Rd. SE1—4D 78 (8B 148)
Sears St. SE5—7D 78
Seasprite Clo. N'holt—3B 54
Seaton Av. Ilf—5K 51
Seaton Clo. E13—4J 65
Seaton Clo. SE11

—5A 78 (9H 147)
Seaton Clo. SW15—1D 106
Seaton Clo. Twic—6H 87
Seaton Rd. Mitc—2C 122
Seaton Rd. Twic—6G 87
Seaton Rd. Well—7C 84
Seaton Rd. Wemb—2E 56
Seaton St. N18—5B 18
Sebastian St. EC1

—3B 62 (2K 141)
Sebastopol Rd. N9—4B 18
Sebbon St. N1—7B 46
Sebert Rd. E7—5K 49
Sebright Pas. E2

—2G 63 (1G 143)
Sebright Rd. Barn—2A 4
Secker Cres. Harr—1G 23
Secker St. SE1—1A 78 (3G 147)
Second Av. E12—4C 50
Second Av. E13—3J 65
Second Av. E17—5C 32
Second Av. N18—4D 18
Second Av. NW4—4F 27
Second Av. SW14—3A 90
Second Av. W3—1B 74
Second Av. W10—4G 59
Second Av. Dag—2H 69
Second Av. Enf—5A 8
Second Av. Romf—5C 36
Second Av. Wemb—2D 40
Second Cross Rd. Twic—2J 103
Second Way. Wemb—4H 41
Sedan Way. SE17

—5E 78 (9C 148)
Seddon Rd. Mord—5B 122
Seddon St. WC1—3K 61 (2F 140)
Sedgebrook Rd. SE3—3B 98
Sedgecombe Av. Harr—5C 24
Sedgeford Rd. W12—1B 74
Sedgehill Rd. SE6—4C 112
Sedgemere Av. N2—3A 28
Sedgemere Rd. SE2—3C 84
Sedgemoor Dri. Dag—4G 53
Sedgeway. SE6—1H 113
Sedgewood Clo. Brom—7H 127
Sedgmoor Pl. SE5—7E 78
Sedgwick Rd. E10—2E 48
Sedgwick St. E9—5K 47

265

Sedleigh Rd. SW18—6H 91
Sedlescombe Rd. SW6—6J 75
Sedley Pl. W1—6F 61 (8J 139)
Seeley Dri. SE21—4E 110
Seelig Av. NW9—7C 26
Seely Rd. SW17—6E 108
Seething La. EC3
—7E 62 (9D 142)
Seething Wells La. Surb
—6C 118
Sefton Av. NW7—5E 12
Sefton Av. Harr—1H 23
Sefton Clo. Orp—4K 129
Sefton Rd. Croy—1G 135
Sefton Rd. Orp—4K 129
Sefton St. SW15—3E 90
Segal Clo. SE23—7A 96
Sekforde St. EC1
—4B 62 (3J 141)
Selah Dri. Swan—7J 117
Selbie Av. NW10—5B 42
Selborne Av. E12—4E 50
Selborne Av. Bex—1E 116
Selborne Gdns. NW4—4C 26
Selborne Gdns. Gnfd—2A 56
Selborne Rd. E17—5B 32
Selborne Rd. N14—3D 16
Selborne Rd. N22—1K 29
Selborne Rd. SE5—2D 94
Selborne Rd. Croy—3E 134
Selborne Rd. Ilf—2E 50
Selborne Rd. N Mald—2A 120
Selborne Rd. Sidc—4B 116
Selborne Wlk. E17—4B 32
Selby Clo. E6—5C 66
Selby Clo. Chst—6E 114
Selby Gdns. S'hall—4E 54
Selby Grn. Cars—7C 122
Selby Rd. E11—3G 49
Selby Rd. E13—5K 65
Selby Rd. N17—7K 17
Selby Rd. SE20—2G 125
Selby Rd. W5—4B 56
Selby Rd. Cars—7C 122
Selby St. E1—4G 63 (4H 143)
Selden Rd. SE15—2J 95
Selden Wlk. N7—2K 45
Selhurst New Rd. SE25—6E 124
Selhurst Pl. SE25—6E 124
Selhurst Rd. N9—3K 17
Selhurst Rd. SE25—6E 124
Selinas La. Dag—7E 36
Selkirk Rd. SW17—4C 108
Selkirk Rd. Twic—2G 103
Sellers Hall Clo. N3—7D 14
Sellincourt Rd. SW17—5C 108
Sellindge Clo. Beck—7B 112
Sellon M. SE11—4K 77 (9F 146)
Sellons Av. NW10—1B 58
Sellwood Dri. Barn—5A 4
Selsdon Av. S Croy—6D 134
Selsdon Clo. Romf—1J 37
Selsdon Clo. Surb—5E 118
Selsdon Pk. Rd. S Croy & Croy
—7K 135
Selsdon Rd. E11—7J 33
Selsdon Rd. E13—1A 66
Selsdon Rd. NW2—2B 42
Selsdon Rd. SE27—3A 110
Selsdon Rd. S Croy—5D 134
Selsea Pl. N16—5E 46
Selsey Cres. Well—1D 100
Selsey St. E14—5C 64
Selvage La. NW7—5B 12
Selway Clo. Pinn—3A 22
Selwood Pl. SW7
—5B 76 (9A 144)
Selwood Rd. Croy—2H 135
Selwood Rd. Sutt—1H 131
Selwood Ter. SW7
—5B 76 (9A 144)
Selworthy Clo. E11—5J 33
Selworthy Rd. SE6—3B 112
Selwyn Av. E4—6K 19
Selwyn Av. Ilf—6K 35
Selwyn Av. Rich—3E 88
Selwyn Clo. Houn—4C 86

Selwyn Ct. Edgw—7C 12
Selwyn Cres. Well—3B 100
Selwyn Rd. E3—2B 64
Selwyn Rd. E13—1K 65
Selwyn Rd. NW10—7A 42
Selwyn Rd. N Mald—5K 119
Semley Ga. E9—6B 48
Semley Pl. SW1—4E 76 (9H 145)
Semley Rd. SW16—2J 123
Senate St. SE15—2J 95
Senator Wlk. SE28—3H 83
Seneca Rd. T Hth—4C 124
Senga Rd. Wall—1E 132
Senhouse Rd. Sutt—3F 131
Senior St. W2—5K 59
Senlac Rd. SE12—1K 113
Sennen Rd. Enf—7A 8
Senrab St. E1—6K 63 (7M 143)
Sentinel Clo. N'holt—4C 54
Sentinel Sq. NW4—4E 26
September Way. Stan—6G 11
Septimus Pl. Enf—5B 8
Sequoia La. Bush, Wat—1C 10
Sequoia Gdns. Orp—7K 129
Sequoia Pk. Pinn—6A 10
Serbin Clo. E10—7E 32
Serjeant's Inn. EC4
—6A 62 (8H 141)
Serle St. WC2—6K 61 (7F 140)
Serpentine Rd. W2
—1C 76 (3C 144)
Serviden Dri. Brom—1B 128
Setchell Rd. SE1
—4F 79 (8E 148)
Setchell Way. SE1
—4F 79 (8E 148)
Seth St. SE16—2J 79 (5M 149)
Seton Gdns. Dag—7C 52
Settle Rd. E13—2J 65
Settles St. E1—5G 63 (6H 143)
Settrington Rd. SW6—2K 91
Seven Dials. WC2
—6J 61 (8C 140)
Seven Kings Rd. Ilf—2K 51
Sevenoaks Clo. Bexh—4H 101
Sevenoaks Rd. SE4—4A 96
Sevenoaks Way. Orp & Sidc
—7C 116
Seven Sisters Rd.—3K 45
N7 1a-163 & 2-188a
N4 165-437 & 190-486
N15 remainder
Seventh Av. E12—4D 50
Severnake Clo. E14—4C 80
Severn Way. NW10—5B 42
Severus Rd. SW11—4C 92
Seville St. SW1—2D 76 (5F 144)
Sevington Rd. NW4—6D 26
Sevington St. W9—4K 59
Seward Rd. W7—2A 72
Seward Rd. Beck—2K 125
Sewardstone Gdns. E4—5J 9
Sewardstone Rd. E2—2J 63
Sewardstone Rd. E4 & Wal A
—7J 9
Seward St. EC1—3C 62 (1J 141)
Sewdley St. E5—4K 47
Sewell Rd. SE2—3A 84
Sewell St. E13—3J 65
Sextant Av. E14—4F 81
Sexton Clo. Rain—2E 68
Seymer Rd. Romf—3K 37
Seymour Av. N17—2G 31
Seymour Av. Eps—7D 130
Seymour Av. Mord—7F 121
Seymour Clo. EC1
—4B 62 (4J 141)
Seymour Clo. Pinn—1D 22
Seymour Ct. E4—2C 20
Seymour Ct. NW2—2D 42
Seymour Dri. Brom—7D 128
Seymour Gdns. SE4—3A 96
Seymour Gdns. Felt—4A 102
Seymour Gdns. Ilf—1D 50
Seymour Gdns. Ruis—1B 40
Seymour Gdns. Surb—5F 119
Seymour Gdns. Twic—7B 88

Seymour M. W1—6E 60 (7G 139)
Seymour Pl. SE25—4H 125
Seymour Pl. W1—50 60 (6E 138)
Seymour Rd. E4—1J 19
Seymour Rd. E6—2B 66
Seymour Rd. E10—1B 48
Seymour Rd. N3—7E 14
Seymour Rd. N8—5A 30
Seymour Rd. N9—2C 18
Seymour Rd. SW18—6H 91
Seymour Rd. SW19—3F 107
Seymour Rd. W4—4J 73
Seymour Rd. Cars—5E 132
Seymour Rd. Hmptn—5G 103
(Hampton Hill)
Seymour Rd. King—1D 118
(Hampton Wick)
Seymour Rd. Mitc—7E 122
Seymour St.—6D 60 (8E 138)
W1 1-61 & 2-68
W2 remainder
Seymour Ter. SE20—1H 125
Seymour Vs. SE20—1H 125
Seymour Wlk. SW10—6A 76
Seyssel St. E14—4E 80
Shaa Rd. W3—7K 57
Shacklegate La. Tedd—4J 103
Shackleton Clo. SE23—2H 111
Shackleton Rd. S'hall—7D 54
Shackleton Grn. E8—4F 47
Shacklewell La. E8—5F 47
Shacklewell Rd. N16—4F 47
Shacklewell Row. E8—4F 47
Shacklewell St. E2
—3F 63 (2F 142)
Shadbolt Clo. Wor Pk—2B 130
Shad Thames. SE1
—2F 79 (4F 148)
Shadwell Dri. N'holt—3D 54
Shadwell Pierhead. E1
—7J 63 (1M 149)
Shadwell Pl. E1—7J 63 (9L 143)
Shadybush Clo. Bush, Wat
—1B 10
Shaef Way. Tedd—7A 104
Shafter Rd. Dag—6J 53
Shaftesbury Av.
—7H 61 (9A 140)
W1 1-111 & 2-136
WC2 remainder
Shaftesbury Av. Barn—4F 5
Shaftesbury Av. Enf—2E 8
Shaftesbury Av. Harr—1F 39
Shaftesbury Av. Harr—5D 24
(Kenton)
Shaftesbury Av. S'hall—3E 70
Shaftesbury Rd. E4—1A 20
Shaftesbury Rd. E7—7A 50
Shaftesbury Rd. E10—1C 48
Shaftesbury Rd. E17—6D 32
Shaftesbury Rd. N18—6K 17
Shaftesbury Rd. N19—1J 45
Shaftesbury Rd. Beck—2B 126
Shaftesbury Rd. Cars—7B 122
Shaftesbury Rd. Rich—3E 88
Shaftesburys, The. Bark
—2G 67
Shaftesbury St. N1—2C 62
Shaftesbury Way. Twic
—3H 103
Shaftesbury Waye. Hay—6A 54
Shafto M. SW1—3D 76 (7F 144)
Shafton Rd. E9—1K 63
Shafts Ct. EC3—6E 62 (8C 142)
Shakespeare Av. N11—5B 16
Shakespeare Av. NW10—1K 57
Shakespeare Av. Hay—4A 54
(in two parts)
Shakespeare Ct. Barn—3E 4
Shakespeare Cres. E12—6D 50
Shakespeare Cres. NW10
—1K 57
Shakespeare Dri. Harr—6F 25
Shakespeare Gdns. N2—4D 28
Shakespeare Rd. E17—2K 31
Shakespeare Rd. N3—1J 27
Shakespeare Rd. NW7—4H 13

Shakespeare Rd. SE24—5B 94
Shakespeare Rd. W3—1J 73
Shakespeare Rd. W7—7K 55
Shakespeare Rd. Bexh—1E 100
Shakespeare Way. Felt
—4A 102
Shakspeare Wlk. N16—4E 46
Shalcomb St. SW10—6A 76
Shaldon Dri. Mord—5G 121
Shaldon Dri. Ruis—3A 38
Shaldon Rd. Edgw—2F 25
Shalfleet Dri. W10—7F 59
Shalimar Gdns. W3—7J 57
Shalimar Rd. W3—7J 57
Shallons Rd. SE9—4F 115
Shalstone Rd. SW14—3H 89
Shalston Vs. Surb—6F 119
Shamrock Rd. Croy—6K 123
Shamrock St. SW4—3H 93
Shamrock Way. N14—1A 16
Shandon Rd. SW4—6G 93
Shand St. SE1—2E 78 (4D 148)
Shandy St. E1—5K 63
Shanklin Rd. N8—5H 29
Shanklin Rd. N15—4G 31
Shanklin Way. SE15—7F 79
Shannon Clo. S'hall—5B 70
Shannon Gro. SW9—4K 93
Shannon Pl. NW8—2C 60
Shannon Way. Beck—6D 112
Shap Cres. Cars—1D 132
Shap St. E2—2F 63
(in two parts)
Shardcroft Av. SE24—5B 94
Shardeloes Rd. SE14—2B 96
Shard's Sq. SE15—6G 79
Sharman Ct. Sidc—4A 116
Sharnbrooke Clo. Well—3C 100
Sharon Clo. Surb—7D 118
Sharon Gdns. E9—1J 63
Sharon Rd. W4—5K 73
Sharon Rd. Enf—2F 9
Sharp Clo. W7—5K 55
Sharpleshall St. NW1—7D 44
Sharpness Clo. Hay—5C 54
Sharratt St. SE15—6J 79
Sharsted St. SE17—5B 78
Sharvel La. N'holt—1A 54
Shaw Av. Bark—2E 68
Shawbrooke Rd. SE9—5B 98
Shawbury Rd. SE22—5F 95
Shaw Clo. SE28—1B 84
Shaw Clo. Bush, Wat—2D 10
Shawfield Pk. Brom—2B 128
Shawfield St. SW3—5C 76
Shawford Ct. SW15—7C 90
Shaw Gdns. Bark—2E 68
Shaw Rd. Brom—3H 113
Shaw Rd. Enf—1E 8
Shaw Sq. E17—1A 32
Shaw Way. Wall—7J 133
Shearing Dri. Cars—7A 122
Shearling Way. N7—6J 45
Shearman Rd. SE3—4H 97
Sheaveshill Av. NW9—4A 26
Sheba St. E1—4F 63 (4F 142)
Sheen Comn. Dri. Rich—4G 89
Sheen Ct. Rich—4G 89
Sheendale Rd. Rich—4F 89
Sheenewood. SE26—4H 111
Sheen Ga. Gdns. SW14—4J 89
Sheen Gro. N1—1A 62
Sheen La. SW14—5J 89
Sheen Pk. Rich—4F 89
Sheen Rd. Orp—4K 129
Sheen Rd. Rich—5E 88
Sheen Way. Wall—5K 133
Sheen Wood. SW14—5J 89
Sheepcote La. SW11—2D 92
Sheepcote Rd. Harr—6K 23
Sheepcotes Rd. Romf—4E 36
Sheephouse Way. N Mald
—7A 120
Sheep La. E8—1H 63
Sheep Wlk. M. SW19—6G 107
Sheerwater Rd. E16—5B 66
Sheffield Sq. E3—3B 64

Sheffield St. WC2

  —6K 61 (8E 140)

Sheffield Ter. W8—1J 75

Shelbourne Clo. Pinn—3D 22

Shelbourne Rd. N17—1H 31

Shelburne Rd. N7—4K 45

Shelbury Clo. Sidc—3A 116

Shelbury Rd. SE22—5H 95

Sheldon Av. N6—7C 28

Sheldon Av. Ilf—2F 35

Sheldon Clo. SE12—5K 97

Sheldon Clo. SE20—1H 125

Sheldon Rd. N18—4K 17

Sheldon Rd. NW2—4F 43

Sheldon Rd. Bexh—1F 101

Sheldon Rd. Dag—7E 52

Sheldon St. Croy—3C 134

Sheldrake Pl. W8—2J 75

Sheldrick Clo. Mitc—2B 122

Sheldwich Ter. Brom—6C 128

Shelford Pl. N16—3D 46

Shelford Rise. SE19—7F 111

Shelford Rd. Barn—6A 4

Shelgate Rd. SW11—5C 92

Shell Clo. Brom—6C 128

Shelley Av. E12—6C 50

Shelley Av. Gnfd—3H 55

Shelley Clo. Edgw—4B 12

Shelley Clo. Gnfd—3H 55

Shelley Cres. Houn—1B 86

Shelley Cres. S'hall—6D 54

Shelley Dri. Well—1J 99

Shelley Gdns. Wemb—2C 40

Shelley Way. SW19—6B 108

Shellness Rd. E5—5H 47

Shell Rd. SE13—3D 96

Shellwood Rd. SW11—2D 92

Shelmerdine Clo. E3—5C 64

Shelton Rd. SW19—1J 121

Shelton St. WC2—6J 61 (8C 140)

(in two parts)

Shenfield Rd. Wfd G—7E 20

Shenfield St. N1—2E 62 (1D 142)

Shenley Rd. SE5—1E 94

Shenley Rd. Houn—1C 86

Shenstone Clo. Dart—4K 101

Shepherdess Pl. N1

  —3D 62 (1A 142)

Shepherdess Wlk. N1

  —2C 62 (1M 141)

Shepherd Mkt. W1

  —1F 77 (2J 145)

Shepherd's Bush Centre. W12

Shepherd's Bush Grn. W12

  —2E 75

Shepherd's Bush Mkt. W12

  —2E 75

Shepherd's Bush Pl. W12

  —2F 75

Shepherd's Bush Rd. W6—4E 74

Shepherd's Clo. N6—6F 29

Shepherds Clo. Romf—5D 36

Shepherds Grn. Chst—7H 115

Shepherd's La. E9—6K 47

Shepherds Pl. W1

  —7E 60 (9G 139)

Shepherd St. W1

  —1F 77 (3J 145)

Shepherds Wlk. NW2—2C 42

Shepherd's Wlk. NW3—5B 44

Shepherds Wlk. Bush, Wat

  —2C 10

Shepherds Way. S Croy

  —7K 135

Shepley Clo. Cars—3E 132

Sheppard Clo. Enf—1C 8

Sheppard Clo. King—4E 118

Sheppard St. E16—4H 65

Shepperton Rd. N1—1D 62

Shepperton Rd. Orp—6G 129

Sheppey Gdns. Dag—7C 52

Sheppey Rd. Dag—7B 52

Sheppey Wlk. N1—6C 46

Sherard Rd. SE9—5C 98

Sheraton St. W1

  —6H 61 (8A 140)

Sherborne Av. Enf—2D 8

Sherborne Av. S'hall—4E 70

Sherborne Cres. Cars—7C 122

Sherborne Gdns. NW9—3G 25

Sherborne Gdns. W13—5B 56

Sherborne La. EC4

  —7D 62 (9A 142)

Sherborne Rd. Orp—5K 129

Sherborne Rd. Sutt—2J 131

Sherborne St. N1—1D 62

Sherbrooke Clo. Bexh—4G 101

Sherbrooke Rd. SW6—7G 75

Sherbrook Gdns. N21—7G 7

Shereboro Rd. N15—6F 31

Sheredan Rd. E4—5B 20

Shere Rd. Ilf—5E 34

Sherfield Gdns. SW15—6B 90

Sheridan Ct. Harr—6H 23

Sheridan Ct. Houn—5C 86

Sheridan Cres. Chst—2F 129

Sheridan Gdns. Harr—6D 24

Sheridan Pl. SW13—3B 90

Sheridan Pl. Hmptn—7F 103

Sheridan Rd. E7—3H 49

Sheridan Rd. E12—5C 50

Sheridan Rd. SW19—1H 121

Sheridan Rd. Belv—4G 85

Sheridan Rd. Bexh—3E 100

Sheridan Rd. Rich—3C 104

Sheridan St. E1—6H 63 (8K 143)

Sheridan Ter. N'holt—5F 39

Sheridan Wlk. NW11—6J 27

Sheridan Wlk. Cars—5D 132

Sheridan Way. Beck—1B 126

Sheringham Av. E12—4D 50

Sheringham Av. N14—5C 6

Sheringham Av. Romf—6J 37

Sheringham Av. Twic—1E 102

Sheringham Dri. Bark—5K 51

Sheringham Rd. N7—6A 46

Sheringham Rd. SE20—3J 125

Sheringham Tower. S'hall

  —7F 55

Sherington Av. Pinn—7A 10

Sherington Rd. SE7—6K 81

Sherland Rd. Twic—1K 103

Sherlock M. W1—5E 60 (5G 139)

Sherman Rd. Brom—1J 127

Shernhall St. E17—3E 32

Sherrard Rd. —6A 50

  E7 1-195 & 2-210

  E12 remainder

Sherrards Way. Barn—5D 4

Shorrick Grn. Rd. NW10—5D 42

Sherriff Rd. NW6—6J 43

Sherringham Av. N17—2G 31

Sherrock Gdns. NW4—4C 26

Sherwin Rd. SE14—1K 95

Sherwood Av. E18—3K 33

Sherwood Av. SW16—7H 109

Sherwood Av. Gnfd—6J 39

Sherwood Clo. SW13—1B 72

Sherwood Clo. W13—1B 72

Sherwood Clo. Bex—6C 100

Sherwood Gdns. E14—4C 80

Sherwood Gdns. Bark—7H 51

Sherwood Pk. Av. Sidc—7A 100

Sherwood Pk. Rd. Mitc—4G 123

Sherwood Pk. Rd. Sutt—5J 131

Sherwood Rd. NW4—3E 26

Sherwood Rd. SW19—7H 107

Sherwood Rd. Croy—7H 125

Sherwood Rd. Hmptn—5G 103

Sherwood Rd. Harr—2G 39

Sherwood Rd. Ilf—4H 35

Sherwood Rd. Well—2J 99

Sherwood St. N20—3G 15

Sherwood St. W1

  —7G 61 (9M 139)

Sherwood Ter. N20—3G 15

Sherwood Way. W Wick

  —2E 136

Shetland Rd. E3—2B 64

Shield Dri. Bren—6A 72

Shieldhall St. SE2—4C 84

Shillingford St. N1—7B 46

Shillitoe Rd. N13—5H 17

Shinfield St. W12—6E 58

Shinford Path. SE23—3K 111

Shingle End. Bren—7C 72

Shinglewell Rd. Eri—7G 85

Shinners Clo. SE25—5G 125

Ship & Half Moon Pas. SE18

  —3F 83

Ship & Mermaid Row. SE1

  —2D 78 (4B 148)

Shipka Rd. SW12—1F 109

Shipman Rd. E16—6K 65

Shipman Rd. SE23—2K 111

Ship St. SE8—1C 96

Ship Tavern Pas. EC3

  —7E 62 (9C 142)

Shipton Clo. Dag—3D 52

Shipton Pl. NW5—6E 44

Shipton St. E2—3F 63 (1F 142)

Shipway Ter. N16—3F 47

Shipwright Rd. SE16—2A 80

Shirburn Clo. SE23—7J 95

Shirbutt St. E14—7D 64

Shirebrook Rd. SE3—3B 98

Shirehall Clo. NW4—6F 27

Shirehall Gdns. NW4—6F 27

Shirehall La. NW4—6F 27

Shirehall Rd. NW4—6F 27

Shires, The. Rich—4E 104

Shirland M. W9—3H 59

Shirland Rd. W9—3H 59

Shirley Av. Bex—7D 100

Shirley Av. Croy—1J 135

Shirley Av. Sutt—4B 132

Shirley Chu. Rd. Croy—3K 135

Shirley Clo. E17—5D 32

Shirley Clo. Houn—5G 87

Shirley Cres. Beck—4A 126

Shirley Dri. Houn—5G 87

Shirley Gdns. W7—1K 71

Shirley Gdns. Bark—6J 51

Shirley Gro. N9—7E 8

Shirley Gro. SW11—3E 92

Shirley Heights. Wall—7G 133

Shirley Hills Rd. Croy—5J 135

Shirley Ho. Dri. SE7—7A 82

Shirley Oaks Rd. Croy—1K 135

Shirley Pk. Rd. Croy—1H 135

Shirley Rd. E15—7G 49

Shirley Rd. W4—2K 73

Shirley Rd. Croy—7H 125

Shirley Rd. Enf—3H 7

Shirley Rd. Sidc—3J 115

Shirley Rd. Wall—7G 133

Shirley St. E16—6H 65

Shirley Way. Croy—3A 136

Shirlock Rd. NW3—4D 44

Shobden Rd. N17—1D 30

Shoebury Rd. E6—7D 50

Shoe La. EC4—6A 62 (7H 141)

Shooters Av. Harr—4C 24

Shooters Hill. SE18 & Well

  —1E 98

Shooters Hill Rd.—1F 97

  SE3 1-311 & 2-238

  SE18 remainder

Shooters Rd. Enf—1G 7

Shoot up Hill. NW2—5G 43

Shore Clo. Hmptn—6C 102

Shoreditch High St. E1

  —4E 62 (4D 142)

Shore Gro. Felt—2E 102

Shoreham Clo. SW18—5K 91

Shoreham Clo. Bex—1D 116

Shoreham Clo. Croy—5J 125

Shoreham Way. Brom—6J 127

Shore Pl. E9—7J 47

Shore Rd. E9—7J 47

Shorncliffe Rd. SE1—5F 79

Shorndean St. SE6—1E 112

Shorne Clo. Sidc—6B 100

Shornefield Clo. Brom—3E 128

Shornells Way. SE2—5C 84

Shorrold's Rd. SW6—7H 75

Shortcroft Rd. Eps—7B 130

Shortcrofts Rd. Dag—6F 53

Shorter St. E1—7F 63 (9F 142)

Short Ga. N12—4C 14

Short Hedges. Houn—1E 86

Short Hill. Harr—1J 39

Shortlands. W6—4F 75

Shortlands Clo. N18—3J 17

Shortlands Gdns. Brom

  —2G 127

Shortlands Gro. Brom—3F 127

Shortlands Ho. E17—5B 32

Shortlands Rd. E10—7D 32

Shortlands Rd. Brom—3F 127

Shortlands Rd. King—7F 105

Short Path. SE18—6F 83

Short Rd. E11—2G 49

Short Rd. E15—1F 65

Short Rd. W4—6A 74

Shorts Croft. NW9—4H 25

Shorts Gdns. WC2

  —6J 61 (8C 140)

Shorts Rd. Cars—4C 132

Short St. NW4—4E 26

Short St. SE1—2A 78 (4H 147)

Short Wall. E15—3E 64

Short Way. N12—6H 15

Short Way. SE9—3C 98

Short Way. Twic—7G 87

Shotfield. Wall—6F 133

Shotfield Av. SW14—4A 90

Shott Clo. Sutt—5A 132

Shottendane Rd. SW6—1J 91

Shottery Clo. SE9—3C 114

Shoulder of Mutton All. E14

  —7A 64

Shouldham St. W1

  —5C 60 (6D 138)

Shrapnel Clo. SE18—7C 82

Shrapnel Rd. SE9—3D 98

Shrewsbury Av. SW14—4K 89

Shrewsbury Av. Harr—4E 24

Shrewsbury Cres. NW10

  —1K 57

Shrewsbury La. SE18—1F 99

Shrewsbury Rd. E7—5B 50

Shrewsbury Rd. N11—6C 16

Shrewsbury Rd. W2—6J 59

Shrewsbury Rd. Beck—3A 126

Shrewsbury Rd. Cars—7C 122

Shrewsbury Wlk. Iswth—3A 88

Shrewton Rd. SW17—7D 108

Shroffold Rd. Brom—4G 113

Shropshire Clo. Mitc—4J 123

Shropshire Pl. WC1

  —4G 61 (4M 139)

Shropshire Rd. N22—7E 16

Shroton St. NW1

  —5C 60 (5D 138)

Shrubberies, The. E18—2J 33

Shrubbery Gdns. N21—7G 7

Shrubbery Rd. N9—3B 18

Shrubbery Rd. SW16—4J 109

Shrubbery Rd. S'hall—1E 70

Shrubland Gro. Wor Pk—3E 130

Shrubland Rd. E8—1G 63

Shrubland Rd. E10—7C 32

Shrubland Rd. E17—5C 32

Shrublands Av. Croy—3C 136

Shrublands Clo. N20—1G 15

Shuna Wlk. N1—6D 46

Shurland Av. Barn—6G 5

Shurland Gdns. SE15—7F 79

Shuttle Clo. Sidc—7K 99

Shuttlemead. Bex—7F 101

Shuttle St. E1—4G 63 (4G 143)

Shuttleworth Rd. SW11—2C 92

Sibella Rd. SW4—2H 93

Sibley Clo. Bexh—5E 100

Sibley Gro. E12—7C 50

Sibthorpe Rd. SE12—7K 97

Sibthorp Rd. Mitc—2D 122

Sibton Rd. Cars—7C 122

Sickert Ct. N1—7C 46

Sickle Corner. Dag—4H 69

Sidbury St. SW6—1G 91

Sidcup By-Pass. Sidc—3H 115

Sidcup High St. Sidc—4A 116

267

Sidcup Hill. Sidc—4B 116
Sidcup Hill Gdns. Sidc—5C 116
Sidcup Rd.—6A 98
 SE12 1-59 & 2-188
 SE9 remainder
Siddons La. NW1
—4D 60 (4F 138)
Siddons Rd. N17—1G 31
Siddons Rd. SE23—2A 112
Siddons Rd. Croy—3A 134
Side Rd. E17—5B 32
Sidewood Rd. SE9—1H 115
Sidford Pl. SE1—3A 78 (7G 147)
Sidings, The. E11—1F 49
Sidmouth Av. Iswth—2J 87
Sidmouth Rd. E10—3E 48
Sidmouth Rd. NW2—7E 42
Sidmouth Rd. SE15—1F 95
Sidmouth Rd. Well—7C 84
Sidmouth St. WC1
—3K 61 (2E 140)
Sidney Av. N13—5E 16
Sidney Elson Way. E6—2E 66
Sidney Est. E1—5J 63 (6L 143)
 (in two parts)
Sidney Gdns. Bren—6D 72
Sidney Gro. EC1—2B 62 (1J 141)
Sidney Rd. E7—3J 49
Sidney Rd. N22—7E 16
Sidney Rd. SE25—5G 125
Sidney Rd. SW9—2K 93
Sidney Rd. Beck—2A 126
Sidney Rd. Harr—3G 23
Sidney Rd. Twic—6A 88
Sidney Sq. E1—5J 63 (6L 143)
Sidney St. E1—5J 63 (5L 143)
Sidworth St. E8—7H 47
Siebert Rd. SE3—6J 81
Siemens Rd. SE18—3B 82
Sigdon Rd. E8—5G 47
Sigers, The. Pinn—5K 21
Silbury Ho. SE26—3G 111
Silbury St. N1—3D 62 (1A 142)
Silchester Rd. W10—6F 59
Silecroft Rd. Bexh—1G 101
Silesia Bldgs. E8—7H 47
Silex St. SE1—2B 78 (5K 147)
Silicon Business Centre. Gnfd
—2C 56
Silk Clo. SE12—5J 97
Silkfield Rd. NW9—5A 26
Silk Mills Path. SE13—2E 96
Silks Ct. E11—1G 49
Silkstream Rd. Edgw—1J 25
Silk St. EC2—5C 62 (5M 141)
Silsoe Rd. N22—2K 29
Silver Birch Av. E4—6G 19
Silverbirch Clo. N11—6K 15
Silver Birch Clo. Dart—4K 117
Silvercliffe Gdns. Barn—4H 5
Silver Clo. SE14—7A 80
Silver Clo. Harr—7C 10
Silver Cres. W4—4H 73
Silverdale. SE26—4J 111
Silverdale. Enf—4D 6
Silverdale Av. Ilf—5J 35
Silverdale Clo. W7—1K 71
Silverdale Clo. N'holt—5D 38
Silverdale Clo. Sutt—4H 131
Silverdale Dri. SE9—2C 114
Silverdale Rd. E4—6A 20
Silverdale Rd. Bexh—2H 101
Silverdale Rd. Croy—3B 134
Silverdale Rd. Orp—4G 129
 (Petts Wood)
Silverhall St. Iswth—3A 88
Silverholme Clo. Harr—7E 24
Silverland St. E16—1D 82
Silver La. W Wick—2F 137
Silverleigh Rd. T Hth—4K 123
Silvermere Rd. SE6—7D 96
Silver Pl. W1—7G 61 (9M 139)
Silver Rd. W12—7F 59
Silver Spring Clo. Eri—6H 85
Silverston Way. Stan—6H 11
Silver St. N18—4A 17
Silver St. Enf—3J 7

Silverthorne Gdns. E4—2H 19
Silverthorne Rd. SW8—2F 93
Silverton Rd. W6—6F 75
Silvertown By-Pass. E16
—1B 82
Silvertown Way. E16—6H 65
Silvertree La. Gnfd—3H 55
Silver Wlk. SE16—1B 80
Silver Way. Romf—3H 37
Silverwood Clo. Beck—7C 112
Silverwood Clo. Croy—7B 136
Silvester Rd. SE22—5F 95
Silvester St. SE1
—2D 78 (5A 148)
Silwood Est. SE16
—4J 79 (9M 149)
Silwood St. SE16
—4J 79 (9M 149)
Simla Clo. SE14—6A 80
Simmons La. N20—2H 15
Simmons La. E4—2A 20
Simmons Rd. SE18—5F 83
Simmons Way. N20—2H 15
Simms Clo. Cars—2C 132
Simms Rd. SE1—4G 79 (9H 149)
Simnel Rd. SE12—7K 97
Simon Clo. W11—7H 59
Simonds Rd. E10—2C 48
Simone Clo. Brom—1C 128
Simon Peter Ct. Enf—2F 7
Simons Wlk. E15—5F 49
Simpson Rd. Houn—6D 86
Simpson Rd. Rich—4C 104
Simpson's Rd. E14—7D 64
Simpsons Rd. Brom—3J 127
Simpson St. SW11—2C 92
Simrose Ct. SW18—5J 91
Sims Wlk. SE3—4H 97
Sinclair Ct. Croy—2F 135
Sinclair Dri. Sutt—7K 131
Sinclair Gdns. W14—2F 75
Sinclair Rd. NW11—6F 27
Sinclair Rd. E4—5G 19
Sinclair Rd. W14—2F 75
Sinclare Clo. Enf—1A 8
Singapore Rd. W13—1A 72
Singer St. EC2—3D 62 (2B 142)
Singleton Clo. SW17—7D 108
Singleton Clo. Croy—7C 124
Singleton Rd. Dag—5F 53
Singleton Scarp. N12—5D 14
Sinnott Rd. E17—1K 31
Sion Rd. Twic—1B 104
Sir Alexander Clo. W3—1B 74
Sir Alexander Rd. W3—1B 74
Sirdar Rd. N22—3B 30
Sirdar Rd. W11—7F 59
Sirdar Rd. Mitc—6E 108
Sisley Rd. Bark—1J 67
Sispara Gdns. SW18—6H 91
Sissinghurst Rd. Croy—7G 125
Sister Mabel's Way. SE15
—7G 79
Sisters Av. SW11—3D 92
Sistova Rd. SW12—1F 109
Sisulu Pl. SW9—3A 94
Sittingbourne Av. Enf—6J 7
Sitwell Gro. Stan—5E 10
Siverst Clo. N'holt—6F 39
Siviter Way. Dag—7H 53
Siward Rd. N17—1D 30
Siward Rd. SW17—3A 108
Siward Rd. Brom—3K 127
Six Acres Est. N4—2A 46
Sixth Av. E12—4D 50
Sixth Av. W10—3G 59
Sixth Cross Rd. Twic—3G 103
Skardu Rd. NW2—5G 43
Skeena Hill. SW18—7G 91
Skeffington Rd. E6—1D 66
Skelbrook St. SW18—2A 108
Skelgill Rd. SW15—4H 91
Skelley Rd. E15—7H 49
Skelton Clo. E8—6F 47
Skelton Rd. E7—6J 49
Skelton's La. E10—7D 32
Skelwith Rd. W6—6E 74

Sketchley Gdns. SE16
—5K 79 (9M 149)
Sketty Rd. Enf—3A 8
Skiers St. E15—1G 65
Skiffington Clo. SW2—1A 110
Skinner Ct. E2—2H 63 (1J 143)
Skinners La. EC4
—7C 62 (9M 141)
Skinners La. Houn—1F 87
Skinner's Row. SE10—1D 96
Skinner St. EC1—4A 62 (3H 141)
Skipsey Av. E6—3D 66
Skipton St. SE1—3B 78 (7K 147)
Skipworth Rd. E9—1J 63
Skomer Wlk. N1—6C 46
Skylines. E14—2D 80
Sky Peals Rd. Wfd G—7A 20
Sladebrook Rd. SE3—3B 98
Sladedale Rd. SE18—5J 83
Sladen Pl. E5—4H 47
Slades Clo. Enf—3F 7
Slades Dri. Chst—4G 115
Slades Gdns. Enf—3F 7
Slades Hill. Enf—3F 7
Slades Rise. Enf—3F 7
Slade, The. SE18—6J 83
Slade Wlk. SE17—6C 78
Slagrove Pl. SE13—5C 96
Slaidburn St. SW10—6A 76
Slaithwaite Rd. SE13—4E 96
Slaney Pl. N7—5A 46
Sleaford St. SW8—7G 77
Slievemore Clo. SW4—3H 93
Slindon Ct. N16—3F 47
Slingsby Pl. WC2
—7J 61 (9C 140)
Slippers Pl. SE16
—3H 79 (6K 149)
Sloane Av. SW3
—4C 76 (9D 144)
Sloane Ct. E. SW3
—5E 76 (9G 145)
Sloane Ct. W. SW3—5E 76
Sloane Gdns. SW1
—4E 76 (9G 145)
Sloane Sq. SW1—4D 76 (9F 144)
Sloane St. SW1—3D 76 (6F 144)
Sloane Ter. SW1
—4E 76 (8G 145)
Sloane Wlk. Croy—6B 126
Slocum Clo. SE28—7C 68
Slough La. NW9—5J 25
Sly St. E1—6H 63 (8J 143)
Smallberry Av. Iswth—2K 87
Smallbrook M. W2
—6B 60 (8A 138)
Smalley Clo. N16—3F 47
Smallwood Rd. SW17—4B 108
Smarden Clo. Belv—5G 85
Smarden Gro. SE9—4D 114
Smart's Pl. WC2—6J 61 (7D 140)
Smart St. E2—3K 63 (1M 143)
Smeaton Rd. SW18—7J 91
Smeaton Rd. Wfd G—5J 21
Smeaton St. E1—1H 79 (2J 149)
Smedley St.—2H 93
 SW8 1-3
 SW4 remainder
Smeed Rd. E3—7C 48
Smith Clo. SE16—1K 79
Smithfield St. EC1
—5B 62 (6J 141)
Smithies Ct. E15—5E 48
Smithies Rd. SE2—4B 84
Smithson Rd. N17—1D 30
Smith Sq. SW1—3J 77 (7C 146)
Smith St. SW3—5D 76
Smith St. Surb—6F 119
Smiths Way. NW2—2C 42
Smiths Yd. SW18—2A 108
Smith Ter. SW3—5D 76
Smithwood Clo. SW19—1G 107
Smithy St. E1—5J 63 (5H 143)
Smock Wlk. Croy—6C 124
Smoothfield. Houn—4E 86
Smugglers Way. SW18—4K 91
Smyrk's Rd. SE17—5E 78

Smyrna Rd. NW6—7J 43
Smythe St. E14—7D 64
Snakes La. Barn—3A 6
Snakes La. E Wfd G—6F 21
Snakes La. W. Wfd G—6D 20
Snaresbrook Dri. Stan—4J 11
Snaresbrook Rd. E11—4G 33
Snarsgate St. W10—5F 59
Sneath Av. NW11—7H 27
Snells Pk. N18—6A 18
Sneyd Rd. NW2—5E 42
Snowbury Rd. SW6—2K 91
Snowden St. EC2
—4E 62 (4C 142)
Snowdon Dri. NW9—6A 26
Snowdrop Clo. Hmptn—6E 102
Snow Hill. EC1—5B 62 (6J 141)
Snow Hill Ct. EC1
—6B 62 (7K 141)
Snowsfields. SE1
—2D 78 (4B 148)
Snowshill Rd. E12—5C 50
Snowy Fielder Waye. Iswth
—2B 88
Soames St. SE15—3F 95
Soames Wlk. N Mald—1A 120
Socket La. Brom—6K 127
Soho Sq. W1—6H 61 (7A 140)
Soho St. W1—6H 61 (7A 140)
Solebay St. E1—4A 64
Solent Rd. NW6—5J 43
Soley M. WC1—3A 62 (1G 141)
Solna Av. SW15—5E 90
Solna Rd. N21—1J 17
Solomon's Pas. SE15—4H 95
Solon New Rd. SW4—4J 93
Solon New Rd. Est. SW4—4J 93
Solon Rd. SW2—4J 93
Solway Clo. Houn—3C 86
Solway Rd. N22—1B 30
Solway Rd. SE22—4G 95
Somaford Gro. Barn—6G 5
Somali Rd. NW2—5H 43
Somerby Rd. Bark—7H 51
Somercoates Clo. Barn—3H 5
Somerfield Rd. N4—2B 46
Somerford Est. N16—4F 47
Somerford Gro. N16—4F 47
Somerford Gro. N17—7B 18
Somerford St. E1
—4H 63 (4J 143)
Somerford Way. SE16—2A 80
Somerhill Av. Sidc—7B 100
Somerhill Rd. Well—2B 100
Somerleyton Rd. SW9—4A 94
Somersby Gdns. Ilf—5D 34
Somers Clo. NW1—2H 61
Somers Cres. W2
—6C 60 (8C 138)
Somerset Av. SW20—2D 120
Somerset Av. Well—4K 99
Somerset Clo. N Mald—6A 120
Somerset Clo. Wfd G—1J 33
Somerset Est. SW11—1C 92
Somerset Gdns. N6—7E 28
Somerset Gdns. SE13—2D 96
Somerset Gdns. SW16—3K 123
Somerset Gdns. Tedd—5J 103
Somerset Rd. E17—6C 32
Somerset Rd. N17—3F 31
Somerset Rd. N18—5A 18
Somerset Rd. NW4—4E 26
Somerset Rd. SW19—3F 107
Somerset Rd. W4—3K 73
Somerset Rd. W13—1C 72
Somerset Rd. Barn—5E 4
Somerset Rd. Bren—6C 72
Somerset Rd. Harr—5G 23
Somerset Rd. King—2F 119
Somerset Rd. S'hall—5E 54
Somerset Rd. Tedd—5J 103
Somerset Sq. W14—2G 75
Somerset Waye. Houn—6C 70
Somersham Rd. Bexh—2E 100
Somers M. W2—6C 60 (8C 138)
Somers Pl. SW2—7K 93
Somers Rd. E17—4B 32

Somers Rd. SW2—6K 93
Somers Way. Bush Wat—1B 10
Somerton Av. Rich—3H 89
Somerton Rd. NW2—3G 43
Somerton Rd. SE15—4H 95
Somertrees Av. SE12—2K 113
Somervell Rd. Harr—5D 38
Somerville Rd. SE20—7K 111
Somerville Rd. Romf—6C 36
Sonderburg Rd. N7—2K 45
Sondes St. SE17—6D 78
Sonia Ct. Harr—6K 23
Sonia Gdns. N12—4F 15
Sonia Gdns. NW10—4B 42
Sonia Gdns. Houn—7E 70
Sonning Gdns. Hmptn—6C 102
Sonning Rd. SE25—6G 125
Soper Clo. E4—5G 19
Sophia Clo. N7—6K 45
Sophia Rd. E10—1D 48
Sophia Rd. E16—6K 65
Sopwith Rd. Houn—7A 70
Sopwith Way. Wall—7H 95
Sopwith Way. King—1E 118
Sorrel Clo. SE28—1A 84
Sorrel Gdns. E6—5C 66
Sorrell Clo. SE14—7A 80
Sorrell Clo. SW9—2A 94
Sorrento Rd. Sutt—3K 131
Sotheby Rd. N5—3B 46
Sotheron Rd. SW6—7K 75
Soudan Rd. SW11—1D 92
Souldern Rd. W14—3F 75
S. Access Rd. E17—7A 32
South Acre. NW9—2B 26
Southacre Way. Pinn—1A 22
S. Africa Rd. W12—1D 74
Southall Ct. S'hall—7E 54
Southall La. Houn & S'hall
　　　　　　　　　—6A 70
Southall Pl. SE1
　　　　　　—2D 78 (5A 148)
Southampton Bldgs. WC2
　　　　　　—5A 62 (6A 141)
Southampton Gdns. Mitc
　　　　　　　　　—5J 123
Southampton Pl. WC1
　　　　　　—5J 61 (6D 140)
Southampton Rd. NW5—5D 44
Southampton Row. WC1
　　　　　　—5J 61 (5D 140)
Southampton St. WC2
　　　　　　—7J 61 (9D 140)
Southampton Way. SE5—7D 78
Southam St. W10—4G 59
S. Audley St. W1
　　　　　　—7E 60 (1H 145)
South Av. E4—7J 9
South Av. Cars—7E 132
South Av. Rich—2G 89
South Av. S'hall—7D 54
South Av. Gdns. S'hall—7D 54
South Bank. Chst—4G 115
South Bank. Surb—6E 118
Southbank. Th Dit—7B 118
S. Bank Ter. Surb—6E 118
S. Birkbeck Rd. E11—3F 49
S. Black Lion La. W6—5C 74
S. Bolton Gdns. SW5—5A 76
Southborough Clo. Surb
　　　　　　　　　—7D 118
Southborough La. Brom
　　　　　　　　　—5C 128
Southborough Rd. E9—1K 63
Southborough Rd. Brom
　　　　　　　　　—3C 128
Southborough Rd. Surb
　　　　　　　　　—7E 118
Southbourne. Brom—7J 127
Southbourne Av. NW9—2J 25
Southbourne Clo. Pinn—7C 22
Southbourne Cres. NW4—4G 27
Southbourne Gdns. SE12
　　　　　　　　　—5K 97
Southbourne Gdns. Ilf—5G 51
Southbourne Gdns. Ruis
　　　　　　　　　—1A 38

Southbridge Pl. Croy—4C 134
Southbridge Rd. Croy—4C 134
Southbridge Way. S'hall
　　　　　　　　　—2C 70
Southbrook M. SE12—6H 97
Southbrook Rd. SE12—6H 97
Southbrook Rd. SW16—1J 123
Southbury Av. Enf—4B 8
Southbury Rd. Enf—3K 7
S. Carriage Dri. SW7 & SW1
　　　　　　—2B 76 (5B 144)
Southchurch Rd. E6—2D 66
South Clo. N6—6F 29
South Clo. Barn—3C 4
South Clo. Bexh—4D 100
South Clo. Dag—1G 69
South Clo. Mord—6J 121
South Clo. Pinn—1B 22
　(Pinner Green)
South Clo. Pinn—7D 22
　(Rayners Lane)
South Clo. Twic—3E 102
Southcombe St. W14—4G 75
Southcote Av. Surb—7H 119
Southcote Rd. E17—5K 31
Southcote Rd. N19—4G 45
Southcote Rd. SE25—6H 125
S. Countess Rd. E17—3B 32
South Cres. WC1
　　　　　　—5H 61 (6A 140)
Southcroft Av. Well—3J 99
Southcroft Av. W Wick—2E 136
Southcroft Rd.—6E 108
　SW17 1-161 & 2-248
　SW16 remainder
S. Cross Rd. Ilf—5G 35
S. Croxted Rd. SE21—3D 110
Southdean Gdns. SW19
　　　　　　　　　—2H 107
South Dene. NW7—3E 12
Southdown Av. W7—3A 72
Southdown Cres. Harr—1G 39
Southdown Cres. Ilf—5J 35
Southdown Dri. SW20—7F 107
Southdown Rd. SW20—1F 121
Southdown Rd. Cars—7E 132
S. Ealing Rd. W5 & Bren—2D 72
S. Eastern Av. N9—3A 18
S. Eaton Pl. SW1
　　　　　　—4E 76 (8H 145)
S. Eden Pk. Rd. Beck—6D 126
S. Edwardes Sq. W8—3J 75
South End. W8—3K 75
South End. Croy—4C 134
S. End Clo. NW3—4C 44
S. End Grn. NW3—4C 44
Southend Clo. SE9—6F 99
Southend Cres. SE9—6F 99
S. End Grn. NW3—4C 44
Southend La.—4B 112
　SE6 1-299 & 2-298
　SE26 remainder
Southend Rd. E6—7D 50
Southend Rd. E17—1F 33
Southend Rd. E18—1J 33
S. End Rd. NW3—4C 44
Southend Rd. Beck—1C 126
Southend Rd. Wfd G—2B 34
S. End Row. W8—3K 75
Southern Av. SE25—3F 125
Southern Clo. E8—1G 63
Southerngate Way. SE14
　　　　　　　　　—7A 80
Southern Gro. E3—3B 64
Southern Rd. E13—2K 65
Southern Rd. N2—4D 28
Southern Row. W10—4G 59
Southern St. N1—2K 61
Southern Way. Romf—6G 37
Southerton Rd. W6—4E 74
S. Esk Rd. E7—6A 50
Southey Rd. N15—5E 30
Southey Rd. SE20—7K 111
Southey Rd. SW9—1A 94
Southey Rd. SW19—7J 107
Southfield. Barn—6A 4
Southfield Cotts. W7—2K 71
Southfield Ct. E11—3F 49

Southfield Gdns. Twic—4K 103
Southfield Pk. Harr—4F 23
Southfield Rd. N17—2E 30
Southfield Rd. W4—2K 73
Southfield Rd. Chst—3K 129
Southfields. NW4—3D 26
Southfields. SW18—6J 91
Southfields Rd. SW18—6J 91
South Gdns. SW19—7B 108
South Gdns. Wemb—2G 41
Southgate Cir. N14—1C 16
Southgate Gro. N1—7D 46
Southgate Industrial Est. N14
　　　　　　　　　—1B 16
Southgate Rd. N1—1D 62
S. Gipsy Rd. Well—3D 100
South Glade, The. Bex—1F 117
South Grn. NW9—1A 26
South Gro. E17—5B 32
South Gro. N6—1E 44
South Gro. N15—5D 30
South Hill. Chst—6D 114
S. Hill Av. Harr—3G 39
S. Hill Gro. Harr—4J 39
S. Hill Pk. NW3—4C 44
S. Hill Rd. Brom—3G 127
Southholme Clo. SE19—1E 124
Southhill Rd. Chst—7C 114
Southill St. E14—6D 64
S. Island Pl. SW9—7A 78
S. Lambeth Pl. SW8—6J 77
S. Lambeth Rd. SW8—6J 77
Southland Rd. SE18—7K 83
Southlands Gro. Brom—3C 128
Southlands Rd. Brom—4B 128
Southland Way. Houn—5H 87
South La. King—3D 118
South La. N Mald—4K 119
South La. W. N Mald—4K 119
S. Lodge Av. Mitc—4J 123
S. Lodge Cres. Enf—4C 6
　(in two parts)
S. Lodge Dri. N14—4C 6
Southly Clo. Sutt—3J 131
South Mall, The. N9—3B 18
South Mead. NW9—1B 26
South Mead. Eps—7B 130
S. Meadows. Wemb—5F 41
Southmead Rd. SW19—1G 107
S. Molton La. W1
　　　　　　—7F 61 (9J 139)
S. Molton Rd. E16—6J 65
S. Molton St. W1
　　　　　　—6F 61 (8J 139)
Southmoor Way. E9—6B 48
S. Norwood Hill. SE25—1E 124
S. Oak Rd. SW16—4K 109
Southold Rise. SE9—3D 114
Southolm St. SW11—1F 93
Southover. N12—3D 14
Southover. Brom—5J 113
South Pde. SW3—5B 76 (9B 144)
South Pde. W4—4J 73
S. Park Cres. SE6—1H 113
S. Park Cres. Ilf—3H 51
S. Park Dri. Bark & Ilf—5J 51
S. Park Gro. N Mald—4J 119
S. Park Hill Rd. S Croy—5D 134
S. Park M. SW6—3K 91
S. Park Rd. SW19—6J 107
S. Park Ter. Ilf—3J 51
S. Park Way. Ruis—6A 38
South Pl. Enf—5D 8
South Pl. Surb—7F 119
South Pl. M. EC2
　　　　　　—5D 62 (6B 142)
Southport Rd. SE18—4H 83
S. Quay Plaza. E14—2D 80
Southridge Pl. SW20—7F 107
South Rise. Cars—7C 132
South Rd. N9—1B 18
South Rd. SE23—2K 111
South Rd. SW19—6A 108
South Rd. W5—4D 72

South Rd. Edgw—1H 25
South Rd. Felt—5B 102
South Rd. Hmptn—6C 102
South Rd. Romf—6E 36
　(Chadwell Heath)
South Rd. Romf—5C 36
　(Little Heath)
South Rd. S'hall—2D 70
South Rd. Twic—3H 103
South Row. SE3—2H 97
Southsea Rd. King—4E 118
S. Sea St. SE16—3B 80
South Side. W6—3B 74
Southside Comn. SW19
　　　　　　　　　—6E 106
Southspring. Sidc—7H 99
South Sq. NW11—6K 27
South Sq. WC1—5A 62 (6G 141)
South St. W1—1E 76 (2H 145)
South St. Brom—2J 127
South St. Enf—5D 8
South St. Iswth—3A 88
South St. Rain—2J 69
South St. Romf—5K 37
South St. Industrial Est. Enf
　　　　　　　　　—5E 8
S. Tenter St. E1—7F 63 (9F 142)
South Ter. SW7—4C 76 (8C 144)
South Ter. Surb—6E 118
South Vale. SE19—6E 110
South Vale. Harr—4J 39
Southvale Rd. SE3—2G 97
Southview. Brom—2A 128
Southview Av. NW10—5B 42
Southview Clo. Bex—6F 101
Southview Cres. Ilf—6F 35
S. View Dri. E18—3K 33
Southview Gdns. Wall—7G 133
S. View Rd. N8—3H 29
Southview Rd. Brom—4F 113
S. View Rd. Pinn—1A 22
South Vs. NW1—6H 45
Southville. SW8—1H 93
Southville Clo. Eps—7A 130
Southville Rd. Th Dit—7B 118
Southville Rd. EC4
　　　　　　—7C 62 (1M 147)
Southwark Bri. SE1 & EC4
　　　　　　—2C 78 (5L 147)
Southwark Bri. Rd. SE1
　　　　　　—1C 78 (3L 147)
Southwark Gro. SE1
　　　　　　—1C 78 (3L 147)
Southwark Pk. Rd. SE16
　　　　　　—4F to 3H 79 (8F 148)
Southwark Pl. Brom—3D 128
Southwark St. SE1
　　　　　　—1B 78 (2K 147)
Southwater Clo. E14—6B 64
Southwater Clo. Beck—7D 112
South Way. N9—2D 18
South Way. N11—6B 16
Southway. N20—2D 14
Southway. NW11—6K 27
Southway. SW20—4E 120
South Way. Brom—7J 127
South Way. Croy—3A 136
South Way. Harr—4E 22
Southway. Wall—4G 133
South Way. Wemb—5G 41
Southwell Av. N'holt—6F 39
Southwell Gdns. SW7—3A 76
Southwell Rd. SE5—3C 94
Southwell Rd. Croy—6A 124
Southwell Rd. Harr—6D 24
S. Western Rd. Twic—6A 88
S. W. India Dock Entrance. E14
　　　　　　　　　—2E 80
Southwest Rd. E11—1F 49
S. Wharf Rd. W2
　　　　　　—6B 60 (7A 138)
Southwick M. W2
　　　　　　—6B 60 (7B 138)
Southwick Pl. W2
　　　　　　—6C 60 (8C 138)
Southwick St. W2
　　　　　　—6C 60 (7C 138)

269

Southwold Dri. Bark—5A 52
Southwold Rd. E5—2H 47
Southwold Rd. Bex—6H 101
Southwood Av. N6—7F 29
Southwood Av. King—1J 119
Southwood Clo. Brom—4D 128
Southwood Clo. Wor Pk
—1F 131
Southwood Ct. NW11—5K 27
Southwood Dri. Surb—7J 119
Southwood Gdns. Ilf—4F 35
Southwood Hall. N6—6F 29
Southwood La. N6—7E 28
Southwood Lawn Rd. N6
—7F 29
Southwood Pk. N6—7E 28
Southwood Rd. SE9—2F 115
Southwood Rd. SE28—1B 84
S. Worple Av. SW14—3A 90
S. Worple Way. SW14—3K 89
Sovereign Clo. W5—5C 56
Sovereign M. E2—2F 63
Sowerby Clo. SE9—5D 98
Spa Clo. SE25—1E 124
Spa Ct. SW16—4K 109
Spafield St. EC1
—4A 62 (3G 141)
Spa Hill. SE19—1D 124
Spalding Rd. NW4—7E 26
Spalding Rd. SW17—5F 109
Spanby Rd. E3—4C 64
Spaniards Clo. NW11—1B 44
Spaniards End. NW3—1A 44
Spaniards Rd. NW3—2A 44
Spanish Pl. W1—6E 60 (7H 139)
Spanish Rd. SW18—5A 92
Spanswick Lodge. N15—4B 30
Sparkbridge Rd. Harr—4J 23
Sparks Clo. W3—6K 57
Sparks Clo. Hmptn—6C 102
Spa Rd. SE16—3F 79 (7E 148)
Sparrick's Row. SE1
—2D 78 (4B 148)
Sparrow Clo. Hmptn—5C 102
Sparrow Dri. Orp—7H 129
Sparrow Farm Dri. Felt—7A 86
Sparrow Farm Rd. Eps—4C 130
Sparrow Grn. Dag—3H 53
Sparrows Herne. Bush, Wat
—1A 10
Sparrows La. SE9—1G 115
Sparrows Way. Bush, Wat
—1B 10
Sparsholt Rd. N19—1K 45
Sparsholt Rd. Bark—1J 67
Sparta St. SE10—1E 96
Spearman St. SE18—6E 82
Spear M. SW5—4J 75
Spearpoint Gdns. Ilf—5K 35
Spears Rd. N19—1J 45
Speart La. Houn—7C 70
Spedan Clo. NW3—3A 44
Speedwell St. SE8—7C 80
Speirs Clo. N Mald—6B 120
Speke Hill. SE9—3D 114
Speke Rd. T Hth—2D 124
Speldhurst Clo. Brom—5H 127
Speldhurst Rd. E9—7K 47
Speldhurst Rd. W4—3K 73
Spellbrook Wlk. N1—1C 62
Spelman St. E1—5G 63 (5G 143)
Spencer Av. N13—6E 16
Spencer Clo. N3—2J 27
Spencer Clo. NW10—3F 57
Spencer Clo. Croy—7D 124
Spencer Clo. Wfd G—5F 21
Spencer Dri. N2—6A 28
Spencer Gdns. SE9—5D 98
Spencer Gdns. SW14—5J 89
Spencer Hill. SW19—6G 107
Spencer Ho. NW4—6G 75
Spencer M. W6—6G 75
Spencer Pk. SW18—5B 92
Spencer Rise. NW5—3F 45
Spencer Rd. E6—1B 66
Spencer Rd. E17—2E 32

Spencer Rd. N8—5K 29
(in two parts)
Spencer Rd. N11—4A 16
Spencer Rd. N17—1G 31
Spencer Rd. SW18—5B 92
Spencer Rd. SW20—1D 120
Spencer Rd. W3—1J 73
Spencer Rd. W4—7J 73
Spencer Rd. Brom—7H 113
Spencer Rd. Harr—2J 23
Spencer Rd. Ilf—1K 51
Spencer Rd. Iswth—6E 71
Spencer Rd. Mitc—3E 122
Spencer Rd. Mitc—7E 122
(Beddington Corner)
Spencer Rd. Rain—3K 69
Spencer Rd. S Croy—5E 134
Spencer Rd. Twic—3J 103
Spencer St. EC1—3B 62 (2J 141)
Spencer St. S'hall—2B 70
Spencer Wlk. SW15—4F 91
Spenser Gro. N16—4E 46
(in two parts)
Spenser Rd. SE24—5B 94
Spenser St. SW1
—3G 77 (6M 145)
Spensley Wlk. N16—3D 46
Speranza St. SE18—5K 83
Sperling Rd. N17—2E 30
Spert St. E14—7A 64
Spey Side. N14—6B 6
Spey St. E14—5E 64
Spey Way. Romf—1K 37
Spezia Rd. NW10—2C 58
Spicer Clo. SW9—2B 94
Spice's Yd. Croy—4C 134
Spigurnell Rd. N17—1D 30
Spikes Bri. Rd. S'hall—7C 54
Spilsby Clo. NW9—1A 26
Spindlewood Gdns. Croy
—4E 134
Spindrift Av. E14—4C 80
Spinel Clo. SE18—5K 83
Spinnells Rd. Harr—1D 38
Spinney Clo. N Mald—5A 120
Spinney Gdns. SE19—5F 111
Spinney Oak. Brom—2C 128
Spinneys, The. Brom—2D 128
Spinney, The. N21—7F 7
Spinney, The. SW16—3G 109
Spinney, The. Barn—2E 4
Spinney, The. Sidc—5E 116
Spinney, The. Stan—4K 11
Spinney, The. Sutt—4E 130
Spinney, The. Wemb—3A 40
Spires Shopping Centre, The.
Barn—3B 4
Spirit Quay. E1—1G 79 (2H 149)
Spital Sq. E1—5E 62 (5D 142)
Spital St. E1—5G 63 (5G 143)
Spital Yd. E1—5E 62 (5D 142)
Spitfire Way. Houn—5A 70
Spode Wlk. NW6—5K 43
Spondon Rd. N15—4G 31
Spooner Wlk. Wall—5J 133
Sportsbank St. SE6—7E 96
Spottons Gro. N17—1C 30
Spout Hill. Croy—5C 136
Spratt Hall Rd. E11—6J 33
Spray La. Twic—6J 87
Spray St. SE18—4F 83
Sprimont Pl. SW3
—4D 76 (9E 144)
Springall St. SE15—7H 79
Spring Bank. N21—6E 6
Springbank Rd. SE13—6F 97
Springbank Wlk. NW1—7H 45
Springbourne Ct. Beck—1E 126
Spring Bri. M. W5—7D 56
Springbridge Rd. W5—7D 56
Spring Clo. Dag—1D 52
Spring Clo. La. Sutt—6G 131
Spring Cotts. Surb—5D 118
Spring Ct. NW6—6H 43
Spring Ct. Eps—7B 130

Spring Ct. Rd. Enf—1F 7
Springcroft Av. N2—4D 28
Springdale Rd. N16—4D 46
Springfield. E5—1H 47
Springfield. Bush, Wat—1C 10
Springfield Av. N10—3G 29
Springfield Av. SW20—3H 121
Springfield Av. Hmptn—6F 103
Springfield Clo. N12—5E 14
Springfield Clo. Stan—3F 11
Springfield Dri. Ilf—5G 35
Springfield Gdns. E5—1H 47
Springfield Gdns. NW9—5K 25
Springfield Gdns. Brom
—4D 128
Springfield Gdns. Ruis—1A 38
Springfield Gdns. W Wick
—2D 136
Springfield Gdns. Wfd G—7F 21
Springfield Gro. SE7—6A 82
Springfield La. NW6—1K 59
Springfield Mt. NW9—5A 26
Springfield Rise. SE26—3H 111
Springfield Rd. E4—1B 20
Springfield Rd. E6—7D 50
Springfield Rd. E15—3G 65
Springfield Rd. E17—6B 32
Springfield Rd. N11—5A 16
Springfield Rd. N15—4G 31
Springfield Rd. NW8—1A 60
Springfield Rd. SE26—5H 111
Springfield Rd. SW19—5H 107
Springfield Rd. W7—1J 71
Springfield Rd. Bexh—4H 101
Springfield Rd. Brom—4D 128
Springfield Rd. Harr—6J 23
Springfield Rd. Hay—1A 70
Springfield Rd. King—3E 118
Springfield Rd. Tedd—5A 104
Springfield Rd. T Hth—1C 124
Springfield Rd. Twic—1E 102
Springfield Rd. Wall—5F 133
Springfield Rd. Well—3B 100
Springfield Wlk. NW6—1K 59
Spring Gdns. N5—5C 46
Spring Gdns. SW1
—1H 77 (2B 146)
Spring Gdns. Romf—5J 37
Spring Gdns. Wall—5G 133
Spring Gdns. Wfd G—7F 21
Spring Gro. SE19—7F 111
Spring Gro. W4—5G 73
Spring Gro. Mitc—1E 122
Spring Gro. Cres. Houn—1G 87
Spring Gro. Rd. Houn & Iswth
—1F 87
Spring Gro. Rd. Rich—5F 89
Spring Hill. E5—7G 31
Spring Hill. SE26—4J 111
Springhill Clo. SE5—3D 94
Springhurst Clo. Croy—4B 136
Spring Lake. Stan—4G 11
Spring La. E5—7H 31
Spring La. SE25—6H 125
Spring M. W1—5D 60 (5F 138)
Spring Pk. Av. Croy—4K 135
Spring Pk. Dri. N4—1C 46
Springpark Dri. Beck—3E 126
Spring Pk. Rd. Croy—2K 135
Spring Path. NW3—5B 44
Spring Pl. NW5—5F 45
Springpond Rd. Dag—5E 52
Springrice Rd. SE13—6F 97
Spring St. W2—6B 60 (8A 138)
Spring Ter. Rich—5E 88
Spring Vale. Bexh—4H 101
Springvale Av. Bren—5E 72
Spring Vale Ter. W14—3F 75
Springvilla Rd. Edgw—7B 12
Springwater Clo. SE18—1E 98
Springwell Av. NW10—1B 58
Springwell Clo. SW16—4K 109
Springwell Ct. Houn—2B 86
Springwell Rd. SW16—4A 110
Springwell Rd. Houn—1B 86
Springwood Ct. S Croy—4E 134

Springwood Cres. Edgw—2C 12
Sprowston M. E7—6J 49
Sprowston Rd. E7—5J 49
Spruce Ct. E4—6G 19
Sprucedale Gdns. Croy—4K 135
Spruce Hills Rd. E17—2E 32
Spruce Pk. Brom—4H 127
Sprules Rd. SE4—2A 96
Spurgeon Av. SE19—1D 124
Spurgeon Rd. SE19—1D 124
Spurgeon St. SE1
—3D 78 (6A 148)
Spurling Rd. SE22—4F 95
Spurling Rd. Dag—6F 53
Spurrell Av. Bex—4K 117
Spur Rd. N15—4D 30
Spur Rd. SW1—2G 77 (5L 145)
Spur Rd. Edgw—4K 11
Spur Rd. Felt—4A 86
Spur Rd. Iswth—7B 72
Spurstowe Rd. E8—5H 47
Spurstowe Ter. E8—6H 47
Square Rigger Row. SW11
—3A 92
Square, The. W6—5E 74
Square, The. Cars—5E 132
Square, The. Ilf—7E 34
Square, The. Rich—5D 88
Square, The. Wfd G—5D 20
Squarey St. SW17—3A 108
Squires Ct. SW19—4J 107
Squires La. N3—2K 27
Squires Mt. NW3—3B 44
Squires Way. Bex—4K 117
Squires Wood Dri. Chst
—7C 114
Squirrel Clo. Houn—3A 86
Squirrel M. W13—7A 56
Squirrels Clo. N12—4F 15
Squirrels Grn. Wor Pk—2B 130
Squirrel's La. Buck H—3G 21
Squirrels, The. SE13—3F 97
Squirrels, The. Pinn—3D 22
Squirries St. E2—3G 63 (2H 143)
Stable Clo. N'holt—2E 54
Stable M. SE27—5C 110
Stables, The. Buck H—1F 21
Stables Way. SE11—5A 78
Stable Wlk. N2—1B 28
Stable Way. W10—6E 58
Stable Yd. SW9—2K 93
Stable Yd. Rd. SW1
—2G 77 (4M 145)
Stacey Av. N18—4D 18
Stacey Clo. E10—5F 33
Stacey St. WC2—6H 61 (8B 140)
Stacy Path. SE5—7E 78
Stadium Rd. NW4—7C 26
Stadium Rd. SE18—7D 82
Stadium St. SW10—7A 76
Stadium Way. Wemb—4G 41
Staffa Rd. E10—1A 48
Stafford Clo. N14—5B 6
Stafford Clo. NW6—3J 59
Stafford Clo. Sutt—6G 131
Stafford Gdns. Croy—5K 133
Stafford M. Rich—7F 89
Stafford Pl. SW1
—3G 77 (6L 145)
Stafford Rd. E3—2B 64
Stafford Rd. E7—6B 50
Stafford Rd. NW6—3J 59
Stafford Rd. Harr—7B 10
Stafford Rd. N Mald—3J 119
Stafford Rd. Sidc—4J 115
Stafford Rd. Wall & Croy
—6G 133
Staffordshire St. SE15—1G 95
Stafford St. W1—1G 77 (2L 145)
Stafford Ter. W8—2J 75
Staff St. EC1—3D 62 (2B 142)
Stag Clo. Edgw—2H 25
Stag La. SW15—3B 106
Stag La. Buck H—2E 20
Stag La. Edgw—2H 25
Stag Pl. SW1—3G 77 (6L 145)
Stags Way. Iswth—6K 71

Stainbank Rd. Mitc—3F 123
Stainby Rd. N15—4F 31
Stainer St. SE1—1D 78 (3B 148)
Staines Av. Sutt—2F 131
Staines Rd. Felt & Houn—5A 86
Staines Rd. Ilf—5G 51
Staines Rd. Twic—3F 103
Staines Rd. E. Sun—7A 102
Staines Wlk. Sidc—6C 116
Stainforth Rd. E17—4C 32
Stainforth Rd. Ilf—7H 35
Staining La. EC2
　　　　　　—6C 62 (7M 141)
Stainmore Clo. Chst—1H 129
Stainsbury St. E2
　　　　　　—2J 63 (1M 143)
Stainsby Pl. E14—6C 64
Stainsby Rd. E14—6C 64
Stainton Rd. SE6—6F 97
Stainton Rd. Enf—1D 8
Stalbridge St. NW1
　　　　　　—5C 60 (5D 138)
Stalham St. SE16
　　　　　　—3H 79 (7K 149)
Stambourne Way. SE19
　　　　　　—7E 110
Stambourne Way. W Wick
　　　　　　—2E 136
Stamford Brook Av. W6—3B 74
Stamford Brook Rd. W6—3B 74
Stamford Clo. N15—5G 31
Stamford Clo. Harr—7D 10
Stamford Clo. S'hall—7E 54
Stamford Dri. Brom—4H 127
Stamford Gdns. Dag—7C 52
Stamford Gro. E. N16—1G 47
Stamford Gro. W. N16—1G 47
Stamford Hill. N16—2F 47
Stamford Rd. E6—1C 66
Stamford Rd. N1—7E 46
Stamford Rd. N15—5G 31
Stamford Rd. Dag—1B 68
Stamford St. SE1
　　　　　　—1A 78 (3G 147)
Stamp Pl. E2—2F 63 (1F 142)
Stanborough Clo. Hmptn
　　　　　　—6D 102
Stanborough Pas. E8—6F 47
Stanborough Rd. Houn—3H 87
Stanbridge Rd. SW15—3E 90
Stanbrook Rd. SE2—2B 84
Stanbury Rd. SE15—2H 95
(in two parts)
Stancroft. NW9—5A 26
Standard Clo. N16—7E 30
Standard Industrial Est. E16
　　　　　　—2D 82
Standard Rd. NW10—4J 57
Standard Rd. Belv—5G 85
Standard Rd. Bexh—4E 100
Standard Rd. Houn—3C 86
Standen Rd. SW18—7H 91
Standfield Gdns. Dag—6G 53
Standfield Rd. Dag—5G 53
Standish Rd. W6—4C 74
Stane Clo. SW19—7K 107
Stane Pas. SW16—5J 109
Stane Way. SE18—7B 82
Stanfield Rd. E3—2A 64
Stanford Clo. Hmptn—6D 102
Stanford Clo. Romf—6H 37
Stanford Clo. Wfd G—5H 21
Stanford Ct. SW6—1K 91
Stanford Pl. SE17
　　　　　　—4E 78 (9C 148)
Stanford Rd. N11—5J 15
Stanford Rd. SW16—2H 123
Stanford Rd. W8—3K 75
Stanford St. SW1
　　　　　　—4H 77 (9A 146)
Stanford Way. SW16—2H 123
Stangate Gdns. Stan—4G 11
Stanger Rd. SE25—4G 125
Stanhope Av. N3—3H 27
Stanhope Av. Brom—1J 137
Stanhope Av. Harr—1H 23
Stanhope Clo. SE16—2K 79

Stanhope Gdns. N4—6B 30
Stanhope Gdns. N6—6G 29
Stanhope Gdns. NW7—5G 13
Stanhope Gdns. SW7
　　　　　　—4A 76 (8A 144)
Stanhope Gdns. Dag—3F 53
Stanhope Gdns. Ilf—1D 50
Stanhope Ga. W1
　　　　　　—1E 76 (2H 145)
Stanhope Gro. Beck—5B 126
Stanhope M. E. SW7
　　　　　　—4A 76 (8A 144)
Stanhope M. S. SW7
　　　　　　—4A 76 (9A 144)
Stanhope M. W. SW7
　　　　　　—4A 76 (8A 144)
Stanhope Pk. Rd. Gnfd—4G 55
Stanhope Pl. W2
　　　　　　—7D 60 (9E 138)
Stanhope Rd. E17—5D 32
Stanhope Rd. N6—6G 29
Stanhope Rd. N12—5F 15
Stanhope Rd. Barn—6A 4
Stanhope Rd. Bexh—2E 100
Stanhope Rd. Cars—7E 132
Stanhope Rd. Croy—3E 134
Stanhope Rd. Dag—2F 53
Stanhope Rd. Gnfd—5G 55
Stanhope Rd. Sidc—4A 116
Stanhope Row. W1
　　　　　　—1F 77 (3J 145)
Stanhope St. NW1
(in two parts)—3G 61 (1L 139)
Stanhope Ter. W2
　　　　　　—7B 60 (9B 138)
Stanier Clo. W14—5H 75
Stanlake M. W12—1E 74
Stanlake Rd. W12—1E 74
Stanlake Vs. W12—1E 74
Stanley Av. Bark—2K 67
Stanley Av. Beck—3E 126
Stanley Av. Dag—1F 53
Stanley Av. Gnfd—1G 55
Stanley Av. N Mald—5C 120
Stanley Av. Wemb—7E 40
Stanley Clo. SW8—6K 77
Stanley Clo. Wemb—7E 40
Stanley Cres. W11—7H 59
Stanleycroft Clo. Iswth—1J 87
Stanley Gdns. NW2—5E 42
Stanley Gdns. W3—2A 74
Stanley Gdns. W11—7H 59
Stanley Gdns. Mitc—6E 108
Stanley Gdns. Wall—4G 133
Stanley Gdns. Rd. Tedd—5J 103
Stanley Gro. N17—7A 18
Stanley Gro. SW8—2E 92
Stanley Gro. Croy—6A 124
Stanley Pk. Dri. Wemb—1F 57
Stanley Pk. Rd. Cars—7D 132
Stanley Pk. Rd. Wall—6F 133
Stanley Pas. NW1
　　　　　　—2J 61 (1C 140)
Stanley Rd. E4—1A 20
Stanley Rd. E10—6D 32
Stanley Rd. E12—5C 50
Stanley Rd. E15—1F 65
Stanley Rd. E18—1H 33
Stanley Rd. N2—3B 28
Stanley Rd. N9—2A 18
Stanley Rd. N10—7A 16
Stanley Rd. N11—6C 16
Stanley Rd. N15—4B 30
Stanley Rd. NW9—7C 26
Stanley Rd. SW14—4H 89
Stanley Rd. SW19—6J 107
Stanley Rd. W3—3J 73
Stanley Rd. Brom—4A 128
Stanley Rd. Cars—7E 132
Stanley Rd. Croy—7A 124
Stanley Rd. Enf—3K 7
Stanley Rd. Harr—2G 39
Stanley Rd. Houn—4G 87
Stanley Rd. Ilf—2H 51
Stanley Rd. Mitc—7E 108
Stanley Rd. Mord—4J 121
Stanley Rd. Orp—7K 129

Stanley Rd. Sidc—3A 116
Stanley Rd. S'hall—7C 54
Stanley Rd. Sutt—6K 131
Stanley Rd. Twic & Tedd
　　　　　　—3H 103
Stanley Rd. Wemb—6F 41
Stanley Sq. Cars—7D 132
Stanley St. SW11—2C 92
Stanley Ter. N19—2J 45
Stanmer St. SW11—2C 92
Stanmore Gdns. Rich—3F 89
Stanmore Gdns. Sutt—3A 132
Stanmore Hill. Stan—3F 11
Stanmore Pl. NW1—1F 61
Stanmore Rd. E11—1H 49
Stanmore Rd. N15—4B 30
Stanmore Rd. Belv—4J 85
Stanmore Rd. Rich—3F 89
Stanmore St. N1—1K 61
Stanmore Ter. Beck—2C 126
Stannard Rd. E8—6G 47
Stannary St. SE11—6A 78
Stansfeld Rd. E16 & E6—5B 66
Stansfield Rd. SW9—3K 93
Stansfield Rd. Houn—2A 86
Stansgate Rd. Dag—3G 53
Stanstead Clo. Brom—6H 127
Stanstead Cres. Bex—1D 116
Stanstead Gro. SE6—1B 112
Stanstead Mnr. Sutt—6J 131
Stanstead Rd. E11—5K 33
Stanstead Rd. SE6—1K 111
Stanstead Rd. SE23
SE23 1-319 & 2-302
SE6 remainder
Stanswood Gdns. SE5—7E 78
Stanthorpe Clo. SW16—5J 109
Stanthorpe Rd. SW16—5J 109
Stanton Av. Tedd—6J 103
Stanton Clo. Wor Pk—1F 131
Stanton Rd. SE26—4B 112
Stanton Rd. SW13—2B 90
Stanton Rd. SW20—1F 121
Stanton Rd. Croy—7C 124
Stanton St. SE15—1G 95
Stanton Way. SE26—4B 112
Stanway Ct. N1—2E 62
Stanway Gdns. W3—1G 73
Stanway Gdns. Edgw—5D 12
Stanway St. N1—2E 62 (1D 142)
Stanwick Rd. W14—4H 75
Stanworth St. SE1
　　　　　　—3F 79 (6E 148)
Stapenhill Rd. Wemb—3B 40
Staple Clo. Bex—3H 117
Staplefield Clo. SW2—1J 109
Stapleford Av. Ilf—5J 35
Stapleford Clo. E4—3K 19
Stapleford Clo. SW19—7G 91
Stapleford Clo. King—2G 119
Stapleford Rd. Wemb—7D 40
Stapleford Way. Bark—3B 68
Staplehurst Rd. SE13—5G 97
Staplehurst Rd. Cars—7C 132
Staple Inn Bldgs. WC1
　　　　　　—5A 62 (6G 141)
Staples Clo. SE16—1A 80
Staples Corner. NW2—1D 42
Staple St. SE1—2D 78 (5B 148)
Stapleton Gdns. Croy—5A 134
Stapleton Hall Rd. N4—7K 29
Stapleton Rd. SW17—3E 108
Stapleton Rd. Bexh—7F 85
Stapley Rd. Belv—5G 85
Stapylton Rd. Barn—3B 4
Star & Garter Hill. Rich—1E 104
Starboard Way. E14—3C 80
Starch Ho. La. Ilf—2H 35
Starcross St. NW1
　　　　　　—3G 61 (2M 139)
Starfield Rd. W12—2C 74
Star Hill. Dart—5K 101
Starkleigh Way. SE16—5H 79
Star La. E16—4G 65
Starling Clo. Buck H—1D 20
Starling Clo. Pinn—3A 22
Starling M. SE28—2H 83
Starling Wlk. Hmptn—5C 102

Star Rd. W14—6H 75
Star Rd. Iswth—2H 87
Star St. E16—5H 65
Star St. W2—6C 60 (7C 138)
Star Yd. WC2—6A 62 (7G 141)
Staten Gdns. Twic—1K 103
Statham Gro. N16—4D 46
Statham Gro. N18—5K 17
Station App. E7—4K 49
Station App. E11—5J 33
Station App. N11—5A 16
Station App. N12—4E 14
Station App. NW10—3B 58
Station App. SE3—3K 97
Station App. SE26—4J 111
Station App. SW6—3G 91
Station App. SW16—5H 109
Station App. W7—1J 71
Station App. Barn—4F 5
Station App. Bex—1G 117
Station App. Bexh—2J 101
(Barnehurst)
Station App. Bexh—2E 100
(Bexleyheath)
Station App. Brom—1J 137
Station App. Buck H—4G 21
Station App. Chst—1E 128
Station App. Chst—6C 114
(Elmstead Woods)
Station App. Eps—7B 130
(Ewell West)
Station App. Eps—5C 130
(Stoneleigh)
Station App. Gnfd—7H 39
Station App. Hmptn—7E 102
Station App. Harr—7J 23
Station App. King—2G 119
Station App. Pinn—3C 22
Station App. Rich—1G 89
Station App. Ruis—5A 38
(South Ruislip)
Station App. S Croy—7D 134
Station App. Sutt—7G 131
Station App. Well—2A 100
Station App. Wemb—6B 40
Station App. W Wick—1F 136
Station App. N. Sidc—2A 116
Station App. Rd. W4—7J 73
Station Av. SW9—3B 94
Station Av. Eps—7A 130
Station Av. N Mald—3A 120
Station Av. Rich—1G 89
Station Clo. N3—1J 27
Station Clo. N12—4E 14
Station Clo. Hmptn—7F 103
Station Cres. N15—4D 30
Station Cres. SE3—5J 81
Station Cres. Wemb—6B 40
Stationer's Hall Ct. EC4
　　　　　　—6B 62 (8K 141)
Station Est. Beck—4K 125
Station Garage M. SW16
　　　　　　—6H 109
Station Gdns. W4—7J 73
Station Gro. Wemb—6E 40
Station Hill. Brom—2J 137
Station Pde. E11—5J 33
Station Pde. N14—1C 16
Station Pde. NW2—6E 42
Station Pde. Bark—7G 51
Station Pde. Rich—1G 89
Station Pl. N4—2A 46
Station Rise. SE27—2B 110
Station Rd. E4—1A 20
Station Rd. E7—4J 49
Station Rd. E10—3E 48
Station Rd. E12—4C 50
Station Rd. E17—6A 32
Station Rd. N3—1J 27
Station Rd. N11—5A 16
Station Rd. N17—3G 31
Station Rd. N18—5A 18
Station Rd. N19—3G 45
Station Rd. N21—1G 17
Station Rd. N22—7D 16
(Bowes Park)

271

Sunbury Gdns. NW7—5E 12
Sunbury La. SW11—1B 92
Sunbury Rd. Sutt—3G 131
Sunbury St. SE18—3D 82
Sunbury Way. Felt—5A 102
Suncroft Pl. SE26—3J 111
Sunderland Rd. SE23—1K 111
Sunderland Rd. W5—3D 72
Sunderland Ter. W2—6K 59
Sunderland Way. E12—2B 50
Sundew Av. W12—7C 58
Sundial Av. SE25—3F 125
Sundorne Rd. SE7—5A 82
Sundra Wlk. E1—4K 63 (4M 143)
Sundridge Av. Brom & Chst
—1B 128
Sundridge Av. Well—2H 99
Sundridge Pl. Croy—1G 135
Sundridge Rd. Croy—1F 135
Sunfields Pl. SE3—7K 81
Sunkist Way. Wall—7J 133
Sunland Av. Bexh—4E 100
Sun La. SE3—7K 81
Sunleigh Rd. Wemb—1E 56
Sunley Gdns. Gnfd—1A 56
Sunningdale. N14—5C 16
Sunningdale Av. W3—7A 58
Sunningdale Av. Bark—7H 51
Sunningdale Av. Felt—2C 102
Sunningdale Av. Ruis—1A 38
Sunningdale Clo. Stan—7F 11
Sunningdale Gdns. NW9—5J 25
Sunningdale Rd. Brom—4C 128
Sunningdale Rd. Sutt—4H 131
Sunningfields Cres. NW4
—2D 26
Sunningfields Rd. NW4—3D 26
Sunninghill Rd. SE13—2D 96
Sunny Bank. SE25—3G 125
Sunny Cres. NW10—7J 41
Sunnycroft Rd. SE25—4G 125
Sunnycroft Rd. Houn—2F 87
Sunnycroft Rd. S'hall—5E 54
Sunnydale Gdns. NW7—6E 12
Sunnydale Rd. SE12—5K 97
Sunnydene Av. E4—5A 20
Sunnydene Gdns. Wemb
—6C 40
Sunnydene St. SE26—4A 112
Sunnyfield. NW7—4G 13
Sunnyfield Rd. Chst—3K 129
Sunny Gdns. Rd. NW4—2D 26
Sunny Hill. NW4—3D 26
Sunnyhill Rd. SW16—4J 109
Sunnyhurst Clo. Sutt—3J 131
Sunnymead Av. Mitc—3H 123
Sunnymead Rd. NW9—7K 25
Sunnymead Rd. SW15—5D 90
Sunnymede Av. Eps—7A 130
Sunnymede Dri. Ilf—4F 35
Sunny Nook Gdns. S Croy
—6D 134
Sunny Rise, The. Enf—1E 8
Sunnyside. NW2—3H 43
Sunnyside. SW19—6G 107
Sunnyside Dri. E4—7K 9
Sunnyside Pas. SW19—6G 107
Sunnyside Rd. E10—1C 48
Sunnyside Rd. N19—7H 29
Sunnyside Rd. W5—1D 72
Sunnyside Rd. Ilf—3G 51
Sunnyside Rd. Tedd—4H 103
Sunnyside Rd. E. N9—3B 18
Sunnyside Rd. N. N9—3B 18
Sunnyside Rd. S. N9—3A 18
Sunny View. NW9—5K 25
Sunny Way. N12—7H 15
Sunray Av. SE24—4D 94
Sunray Av. Brom—6C 128
Sunrise Clo. Felt—3D 102
Sun Rd. W14—5H 75
Sunset Av. E4—1J 19
Sunset Av. Wfd G—4C 20
Sunset Gdns. SE25—2F 125
Sunset Rd. SE5—4C 94
Sunset View. Barn—2B 4
Sunshine Way. Mitc—2D 122

Sun St. EC2—5D 62 (5B 142)
Sunwell Clo. SE15—1H 95
Surbiton Ct. Surb—6D 118
Surbiton Cres. King—4E 118
Surbiton Hall Clo. King—4E 118
Surbiton Hill Pk. Surb—5F 119
Surbiton Hill Rd. Surb—5E 118
Surbiton Rd. King—4D 118
Surlingham Clo. SE28—7D 68
Surrendale Pl. W9—4J 59
Surrey Canal Rd. SE15 & SE14
—6J 79
Surrey Cres. W4—5G 73
Surrey Gro. SE17—5E 78
Surrey Gro. Sutt—3B 132
Surrey La. SW11—1C 92
Surrey La. Est. SW11—1C 92
Surrey M. SE27—4E 110
Surrey Mt. SE23—1H 111
Surrey Quays Retail Centre.
SE16—3K 79 (6M 149)
Surrey Quays Rd. SE16
—3J 79 (6M 149)
Surrey Rd. SE15—5K 95
Surrey Rd. Bark—7J 51
Surrey Rd. Dag—5H 53
Surrey Rd. Harr—5G 23
Surrey Rd. W Wick—1D 136
Surrey Row. SE1
—2B 78 (4J 147)
Surrey Sq. SE17
—5E 78 (9C 148)
Surrey St. E13—3K 65
Surrey St. WC2—7K 61 (9F 140)
Surrey St. Croy—3C 134
Surrey Ter. SE17
—5E 78 (9D 148)
Surrey Water Rd. SE16—1K 79
Surridge Gdns. SE19—6D 110
Surr St. N7—5J 45
Susan Clo. Romf—3J 37
Susannah St. E14—6D 64
Susan Rd. SE3—2K 97
Susan Wood. Chst—1E 128
Sussex Av. Iswth—3J 87
Sussex Clo. N19—2J 45
Sussex Clo. Ilf—5D 34
Sussex Clo. N Mald—4A 120
Sussex Clo. Twic—6B 88
Sussex Cres. N'holt—6E 38
Sussex Gdns. N4—5C 30
Sussex Gdns. N6—5D 28
Sussex Gdns. W2
—6B 60 (8B 138)
Sussex M. W. W2
—7B 60 (9B 138)
Sussex Pl. NW1—4D 60 (3E 138)
Sussex Pl. W2—6B 60 (8B 138)
Sussex Pl. W6—5E 74
Sussex Pl. Eri—7H 85
Sussex Pl. N Mald—4A 120
Sussex Ring. N12—5D 14
Sussex Rd. E6—1E 66
Sussex Rd. Cars—6D 132
Sussex Rd. Eri—7H 85
Sussex Rd. Harr—5G 23
Sussex Rd. Mitc—5J 123
Sussex Rd. N Mald—4A 120
Sussex Rd. Sidc—5B 116
Sussex Rd. S'hall—3B 70
Sussex Rd. S Croy—6D 134
Sussex Rd. W Wick—1D 136
Sussex Sq. W2—7B 60 (9B 138)
Sussex St. E13—3K 65
Sussex St. SW1—5F 77
Sussex Wlk. SW9—4B 94
Sussex Way—1J 45
N7 1-131 & 2-130
N19 remainder
Sussex Way. Barn—5A 6
Sutcliffe Clo. NW11—5K 27
Sutcliffe Rd. SE18—6J 83
Sutcliffe Rd. Well—2C 100
Sutherland Av. W9—4J 59
Sutherland Av. W13—6B 56
Sutherland Av. Orp—6K 129
Sutherland Av. Well—4J 99

Sutherland Clo. Barn—4B 4
Sutherland Ct. NW9—5H 25
Sutherland Dri. SW19—1B 122
Sutherland Gdns. SW14—3A 90
Sutherland Gdns. Wor Pk
—1D 130
Sutherland Gro. SW18—6G 91
Sutherland Gro. Tedd—5J 103
Sutherland Pl. W2—6J 59
Sutherland Rd. E3—2B 64
Sutherland Rd. E17—3K 31
Sutherland Rd. N9—1C 18
Sutherland Rd. N17—1G 31
Sutherland Rd. W4—6A 74
Sutherland Rd. W13—6A 56
Sutherland Rd. Belv—3G 85
Sutherland Rd. Croy—7A 124
Sutherland Rd. Enf—6E 8
Sutherland Rd. S'hall—6D 54
Sutherland Rd. Path. E17
—3K 31
Sutherland Row. SW1
—5F 77 (9K 145)
Sutherland Sq. SE17—5C 78
Sutherland St. SW1
—5F 77 (9J 145)
Sutherland Wlk. SE17—5C 78
Sutlej Rd. SE7—7A 82
Sutterton St. N7—6K 45
Sutton Arc. Sutt—5K 131
Sutton Clo. Beck—1D 126
Sutton Clo. Lou—1H 21
Sutton Comn. Rd. Sutt—7H 121
Sutton Ct. W4—6J 73
Sutton Ct. Cars—4A 132
Sutton Ct. Rd. E13—3A 66
Sutton Ct. Rd. W4—7J 73
Sutton Ct. Rd. Sutt—6A 132
Sutton Cres. Barn—5A 4
Sutton Dene. Houn—1F 87
Sutton Est. W10—5E 58
Sutton Est., The. N1—7B 46
Sutton Est., The. SW3
—5C 76 (9C 144)
Sutton Gdns. Bark—1J 67
Sutton Gdns. Croy—5F 125
Sutton Gro. Sutt—5B 132
Sutton Hall Rd. Houn—7E 70
Sutton La. Houn—2D 86
Sutton La. N. W4—5J 73
Sutton La. S. W4—6J 73
Sutton Pk. Rd. Sutt—6K 131
Sutton Pl. E9—5J 47
Sutton Rd. E13—4H 65
Sutton Rd. E17—1K 31
Sutton Rd. N10—1E 28
Sutton Rd. Bark—1J 67
Sutton Rd. Houn—1E 86
Sutton Row. W1
—6H 61 (7B 140)
Sutton Sq. E9—5J 47
Sutton Sq. Houn—1D 86
Sutton St. E1—7J 63 (9L 143)
Sutton's Way. EC1
—4C 62 (4M 141)
Sutton Way. W10—4E 58
Sutton Way. Houn—1D 86
Swaby Rd. SW18—1A 108
Swaffham Way. N22—7G 17
Swaffield Rd. SW18—7K 91
Swain Rd. T Hth—5C 124
Swain's La. N6—3E 44
Swainson Rd. W3—2B 74
Swains Rd. SW17—7D 108
Swalecliffe Rd. Belv—5H 85
Swallands Rd. SE6—4D 112
(in two parts)
Swallow Clo. SE14—1K 95
Swallow Clo. Bush, Wat—1A 10
Swallow Ct. SE12—7J 97
Swallow Ct. Ilf—5F 35
Swallow Ct. Ruis—1A 38
Swallow Dri. N'holt—2E 54
Swallow Dri. NW10—6J 41
Swallowfield Rd. SE7—5K 81
Swallow Pl. W1—6F 61 (8K 139)
Swallow St. E6—5C 66

Swallow St. W1
—7G 61 (1M 145)
Swanage Rd. E4—7K 19
Swanage Rd. SW18—6A 92
Swanage Waye. Hay—6A 54
Swan App. E6—5C 66
Swanbridge Rd. Bexh—1G 101
Swan Clo. Felt—4C 102
Swandon Way. SW18—4K 91
Swanfield St. E2
—3F 63 (2E 142)
Swan La. EC4—7D 62 (1B 148)
Swan La. N20—3F 15
Swanley Rd. Well—1C 100
Swan Mead. SE1
—3E 78 (7C 148)
Swan M. SW9—1K 93
Swan Pl. SW13—2B 90
Swan Rd. SE16—2J 79 (4M 149)
Swan Rd. SE18—3B 82
Swan Rd. Felt—5C 102
Swan Rd. S'hall—6F 55
Swanscombe Rd. W4—5A 74
Swanscombe Rd. W11—1F 75
Swansea Rd. Enf—4D 8
Swansland Gdns. E17—1A 32
Swan St. SE1—3C 78 (6M 147)
Swan St. Iswth—3B 88
Swanton Gdns. SW19—1F 107
Swanton Rd. Eri—7G 85
Swan Wlk. SW3—6D 76
Swan Way. Enf—2C 8
Swanwick Clo. SW15—7B 90
Swan Yd. N1—6B 46
Sward Rd. Orp—6K 129
Swaton Rd. E3—4C 64
Swaylands Rd. Belv—6G 85
Swedenborg Gdns. E1
—7H 63 (9J 143)
Sweden Ga. SE16—3A 80
Swedish Quays Development
SE16—3A 80
Sweeney Cres. SE1
—2F 79 (5F 148)
Sweet Briar Grn. N9—3A 18
Sweet Briar Gro. N9—3A 18
Sweet Briar Wlk. N18—4A 18
Sweetland Ct. Dag—6B 52
Sweetmans Av. Pinn—3B 22
Sweets Way. N20—2G 15
Swetenham Wlk. SE18—5G 83
Swete St. E13—2J 65
Sweyn Pl. SE3—2J 97
Swift Clo. Harr—2F 39
Swift Ct. Sutt—7K 131
Swift Rd. Felt—4B 102
Swift Rd. S'hall—3E 70
Swiftsden Way. Brom—6G 113
Swift St. SW6—1H 91
Swift Way. Wall—7H 133
Swinbrook Rd. W10—5G 59
Swinburne Cres. Croy—6J 125
Swinburne Rd. SW15—4C 90
Swinderby Rd. Wemb—6E 40
Swindon Clo. Ilf—2J 51
Swindon St. W12—1E 74
Swinfield Clo. Felt—3C 102
Swinford Gdns. SW9—3B 94
Swingate La. SE18—6J 83
Swinnerton St. E9—5A 48
Swinton Clo. Wemb—1H 41
Swinton Pl. WC1
—3K 61 (1E 140)
Swinton St. WC1
—3K 61 (1E 140)
Swiss Ter. NW6—7B 44
Swithland Gdns. SE9—4E 114
Swyncombe Av. W5—4B 72
Sybil M. N4—6B 30
Sybourn St. E17—7B 32
Sycamore Av. W5—3D 72
Sycamore Av. Sidc—6K 99
Sycamore Clo. E16—5G 65
Sycamore Clo. N9—4A 18
Sycamore Clo. SE9—2C 114
Sycamore Clo. Barn—6G 5

274

Sycamore Clo. Cars—4D 132
Sycamore Clo. N'holt—1C 54
Sycamore Ct. E4—6G 19
Sycamore Gdns. W6—3D 74
Sycamore Gdns. Mitc—2B 122
Sycamore Gro. NW9—7J 25
Sycamore Gro. SE6—6E 96
Sycamore Gro. SE20—1G 125
Sycamore Gro. N Mald—3K 119
Sycamore Hill. N11—6A 16
Sycamore Rd. SW19—6E 106
Sycamore St. EC1
    —4C 62 (4L 141)
Sycamore Wlk. W10—4G 59
Sycamore Wlk. Ilf—4G 35
Sycamore Way. T Hth—5A 124
Sydcote. SE21—1C 110
Sydenham Av. SE26—5H 111
Sydenham Cotts. SE12—2A 114
Sydenham Hill—4F 111
  SE26 1-135 & 2-48
  SE23 remainder
Sydenham Pk. SE26—3J 111
Sydenham Pk. Rd. SE26
    —3J 111
Sydenham Pl. SE27—3B 110
Sydenham Rise. SE23—2H 111
Sydenham Rd. SE26—4J 111
Sydenham Rd. Croy—1D 134
Sydmons Ct. SE23—7J 95
Sydner M. N16—4F 47
Sydner Rd. N16—4F 47
Sydney Clo. SW3
    —4B 76 (9B 144)
Sydney Gro. NW4—5E 26
Sydney M. SW3—4B 76 (9B 144)
Sydney Pl. SW7—4B 76 (9B 144)
Sydney Rd. E11—6K 33
Sydney Rd. N8—4A 30
Sydney Rd. N10—1F 29
Sydney Rd. SE2—3D 84
Sydney Rd. SW20—2F 121
Sydney Rd. W13—1A 72
Sydney Rd. Bexh—4D 100
Sydney Rd. Enf—4J 7
Sydney Rd. Ilf—2G 35
Sydney Rd. Rich—4E 88
Sydney Rd. Sidc—4J 115
Sydney Rd. Sutt—4J 131
Sydney Rd. Tedd—5K 103
Sydney Rd. Wfd G—4D 20
Sydney St. SW3
    —5C 76 (9C 144)
Sylvan Av. N3—2J 27
Sylvan Av. N22—7E 16
Sylvan Av. NW7—6G 13
Sylvan Av. Romf—6F 37
Sylvan Ct. N12—3E 14
Sylvan Est. SE19—1F 125
Sylvan Gro. SE15—6H 79
Sylvan Gdns. Surb—7D 118
Sylvan Hill. SE19—1E 124
Sylvan Rd. E7—6J 49
Sylvan Rd. E11—5J 33
Sylvan Rd. E17—5C 32
Sylvan Rd. SE19—1F 125
Sylvan Way. Dag—4B 52
Sylvan Way. W Wick—4G 137
Sylvester Av. Chst—6D 114
Sylvester Path. E8—6H 47
Sylvester Rd. E8—6H 47
Sylvester Rd. E17—7B 32
Sylvester Rd. N2—2B 28
Sylvester Rd. Wemb—5C 40
Sylvestrus Clo. King—1G 119
Sylvia Gdns. Wemb—7H 41
Symes M. NW1—2G 61
Symons St. SW3
    —4D 76 (9F 144)
Syon Ga. Way. Bren—7A 72
Syon La. Iswth—6K 71
Syon Pk. Gdns. Iswth—7K 71
Syon Vista. Rich—1E 88

Tabard Garden Est. SE1
    —3D 78 (6A 148)

Tabard St. SE1—2D 78 (5A 148)
Tabernacle Av. E13—4J 65
Tabernacle St. EC2
    —4D 62 (4B 142)
Tableer Av. SW4—5H 93
Tabley Rd. N7—4J 45
Tabor Gdns. Sutt—6H 131
Tabor Gro. SW19—7H 107
Tabor Rd. W6—3D 74
Tachbrook Est. SW1—5H 77
Tachbrook M. SW1
    —4G 77 (8L 145)
Tachbrook Rd. S'hall—4B 70
Tachbrook St. SW1
    —4G 77 (9M 145)
Tack M. SE4—3C 96
Tadema Rd. SW10—7A 76
Tadmor St. W12—1F 75
Tadworth Av. N Mald—5B 120
Tadworth Rd. NW2—2C 42
Taeping St. E14—4D 80
Taffy's How. Mitc—3C 122
Taft Way. E3—3D 64
Tait Rd. Croy—7E 124
Takeley Clo. Romf—2K 37
Talacre Rd. NW5—6E 44
Talbot Av. N2—3B 28
Talbot Clo. N15—4F 31
Talbot Cres. NW4—5C 26
Talbot Gdns. Ilf—2A 52
Talbot Pl. SE3—2G 97
  (in two parts)
Talbot Rd. E6—2E 66
Talbot Rd. E7—4J 49
Talbot Rd. N6—6E 28
Talbot Rd. N15—4F 31
Talbot Rd. N22—2G 29
Talbot Rd.—6H 59
  W2 1-97 & 2-102
  W11 remainder
  (in two parts)
Talbot Rd. W13—1A 72
Talbot Rd. Brom—3H 127
Talbot Rd. Cars—5E 132
Talbot Rd. Dag—6F 53
Talbot Rd. Harr—2K 23
Talbot Rd. Iswth—4A 88
Talbot Rd. S'hall—4C 70
Talbot Rd. T Hth—4D 124
Talbot Rd. Twic—1J 103
Talbot Rd. Wemb—6D 40
Talbot Sq. W2—6B 60 (8B 138)
Talbot Wlk. NW10—6A 42
Talbot Yd. SE1—1D 78 (3A 148)
Talcott Path. SW2—1A 110
Talfourd Pl. SE15—1F 95
Talfourd Rd. SE15—1F 95
Talgarth Rd.—5F 75
  W14 1-155
  W6 remainder
Talisman Sq. SE26—4G 111
Talisman Way. Wemb—3F 41
Tallack Clo. Harr—7D 10
Tallack Rd. E10—1B 48
Tall Elms Clo. Brom—5H 127
Tallis Gro. SE7—6K 81
Tallis St. EC4—7A 62 (9H 141)
Tallis View. NW10—6K 41
Tall Trees. SW16—3K 123
Talma Gdns. Twic—6J 87
Talmage Clo. SE23—7J 95
Talman Gro. Stan—6J 11
Talma Rd. SW2—4A 94
Talwin St. E3—3D 64
Tamarind Yd. E1
    —1G 79 (2H 149)
Tamarisk Sq. W12—7B 58
Tamar Sq. Wfd G—6E 20
Tamar Way. N17—3G 31
Tamesis Gdns. Wor Pk—2A 130
Tamian Way. Houn—4A 86
Tamworth Av. E4—6B 20
Tamworth La. Mitc—2F 123
Tamworth Pk. Mitc—3F 123
Tamworth Pl. Croy—2C 134
Tamworth Rd. Croy—2B 134
Tamworth St. SW6—6J 75

Tamworth Vs. Mitc—4G 123
Tancred Rd. N4—6B 30
Tandridge Dri. Orp—7H 129
Tandridge Pl. Orp—7H 129
Tanfield Av. NW2—4A 42
Tanfield Rd. Croy—4C 134
Tangier Rd. Rich—4G 89
Tangleberry Clo. Brom—4D 128
Tanglewood Clo. Croy—3J 135
Tanglewood Clo. Stan—7D 10
Tangley Gro. SW15—6B 90
Tangley Pk. Rd. Hmptn—5D 102
Tangmere Gdns. N'holt—2A 54
Tangmere Way. NW9—2A 26
Tanhurst Wlk. SE2—3D 84
Tankerton St. WC1
    —3J 61 (2D 140)
Tankerville Rd. SW16—7H 109
Tankridge Rd. NW2—2D 42
Tanners End La. N18—5K 17
Tanner's Hill. SE8—1B 96
Tanners La. Ilf—3G 35
Tanner St. SE1—2E 78 (5D 148)
Tanner St. Bark—6G 51
Tannery Clo. Beck—5K 125
Tannery Clo. Dag—3H 53
Tannsfeld Rd. SE26—5K 111
Tansley Clo. N7—5H 45
Tansy Clo. E6—6E 66
Tantallon Rd. SW12—1E 108
Tant Av. E16—6H 65
Tantony Gro. Romf—3D 36
Tanworth Gdns. Pinn—2A 22
Tanyard La. Bex—7G 101
Tanza Rd. NW3—4D 44
Tapestry Clo. Sutt—7K 131
Taplow St. N1—2C 62 (1M 141)
Tappesfield Rd. SE15—3J 95
Tapp St. E1—4H 63 (3J 143)
Tapster St. Barn—4C 4
Tarbert Rd. SE22—5E 94
Tarbert Wlk. E1—7J 63 (9L 143)
Tariff Rd. N17—6B 18
Tarleton Ct. N22—2A 30
Tarleton Gdns. SE23—2H 111
Tarling Clo. Sidc—3B 116
Tarling Rd. E16—6H 65
Tarling Rd. N2—2A 28
Tarling St. E1—6J 63 (8L 143)
Tarling St. Est. E1
    —6J 63 (8L 143)
Tarn Bank. Enf—5D 6
Tarn St. SE1—3C 78 (7L 147)
Tarnwood Pk. SE9—1D 114
Tarrington Clo. SW16—3H 109
Tarry La. SE8—4A 80
Tarver Rd. SE17—5B 78
Tarves Way. SE10—7D 80
Tash Pl. N11—5A 16
Tasker Rd. NW3—5D 44
Tasmania Ter. N18—6H 17
Tasman Rd. SW9—3J 93
Tasman Wlk. E16—6B 66
Tasso Rd. W6—6G 75
Tatam Rd. NW10—7K 41
Tate Rd. E16—1D 82
Tate Rd. Sutt—5J 131
Tatnell Rd. SE23—6A 96
Tattersall Clo. SE9—5C 98
Tatton Cres. N16—7F 31
Tatum St. SE17—4D 78 (9B 148)
Taunton Av. SW20—2D 120
Taunton Av. Houn—2G 87
Taunton Clo. Bexh—2K 101
Taunton Clo. Sutt—1J 131
Taunton Dri. Enf—3F 7
Taunton M. NW1
    —4D 60 (4E 138)
Taunton Pl. NW1
    —4D 60 (3E 138)
Taunton Rd. SE12—5G 97
Taunton Rd. Gnfd—1F 55
Taunton Way. Stan—2E 24
Taverners Clo. W11—1G 75
Taverner Sq. N5—4C 46
Taverners Way. E4—1B 20
Tavern La. SW9—2A 94

Tavistock Av. E17—3K 31
Tavistock Av. Gnfd—2A 56
Tavistock Clo. N16—5E 46
Tavistock Cres. W11—5H 59
Tavistock Cres. Mitc—4J 123
Tavistock Gdns. Ilf—4A 51
Tavistock Gro. Croy—7D 124
Tavistock Ho. WC1
    —4H 61 (3B 140)
Tavistock M. E18—3J 33
Tavistock M. W11—6H 59
Tavistock Pl. E18—3J 33
Tavistock Pl. N14—7A 6
Tavistock Pl. WC1
    —4J 61 (3C 140)
Tavistock Rd. E7—4H 49
Tavistock Rd. E15—6H 49
Tavistock Rd. E18—3J 33
Tavistock Rd. N4—6D 30
Tavistock Rd. NW10—2B 58
Tavistock Rd. W11—6H 59
Tavistock Rd. Brom—4H 127
Tavistock Rd. Cars—1B 132
Tavistock Rd. Croy—1D 134
Tavistock Rd. Edgw—1G 25
Tavistock Rd. Well—1C 100
Tavistock Sq. WC1
    —4H 61 (3B 140)
Tavistock St. WC2
    —7J 61 (9D 140)
Tavistock Ter. N19—3H 45
Tavistock Tower. SE16—3A 80
Tavistock Wlk. Cars—1B 132
Taviton St. WC1
    —4H 61 (3A 140)
Tavy Bri. SE2—2C 84
Tavy Bri. Centre. SE2—2C 84
Tawney Rd. SE28—7B 68
Tawny Way. SE16—4K 79
Tayben Av. Twic—6J 87
Taybridge Rd. SW11—3E 92
Tayburn Clo. E14—6E 64
Taylor Av. Rich—2H 89
Taylor Clo. N17—7B 18
Taylor Clo. Hmptn—5G 103
Taylor Ct. E15—5E 48
Taylor Rd. Mitc—7C 108
Taylor Rd. Wall—5F 133
Taylors Bldgs. SE18—4F 83
Taylors Clo. Sidc—4K 115
Taylors Grn. W3—6A 58
Taylors La. NW10—7A 42
Taylor's La. SE26—4H 111
Taylors La. Barn—1C 4
Taylor St. SE18—4F 83
Taymount Rise. SE23—2J 111
Tayport Clo. N1—7K 45
Taywood Rd. N'holt—3D 54
Teak Clo. SE16—1A 80
Teal Clo. E16—5B 66
Teale St. E2—2G 63
Teasel Clo. Croy—1K 135
Teasel Way. E15—3G 65
Tebworth Rd. N17—7A 18
Tedder Rd. S Croy—7K 135
Teddington Pk. Tedd—5K 103
Teddington Pk. Rd. Tedd
    —4K 103
Tedworth Sq. SW3—5D 76
Tees Av. Gnfd—2K 55
Teesdale Av. Iswth—1A 88
Teesdale Clo. E2
    —2H 63 (1H 143)
Teesdale Gdns. SE25—2E 124
Teesdale Gdns. Iswth—1A 88
Teesdale Rd. E11—7H 33
Teesdale St. E2—2H 63 (1J 143)
Tee, The. W3—6A 58
Teevan Clo. Croy—7G 125
Teevan Rd. Croy—7G 125
Teignmouth Clo. SW4—4H 93
Teignmouth Clo. Edgw—2F 25
Teignmouth Gdns. Gnfd—2A 56
Teignmouth Rd. NW2—5F 43
Teignmouth Rd. Well—2C 100
Telcote Way. Ruis—7A 22
Telegraph Hill. NW3—3K 43

Telegraph M. Ilf—1A 52
Telegraph Rd. SW15—7D 90
Telegraph St. EC2
—6D 62 (7A 142)
Teleman Sq. SE3—4K 97
Telephone Pl. SW6—6H 75
Telfer Clo. W3—2J 73
Telferscot Rd. SW12—1H 109
Telford Clo. SE19—6F 111
Telford Av. SW2—1H 109
Telford Rd. N11—5B 16
Telford Rd. SE9—2H 115
Telford Rd. W10—5G 59
Telford Rd. S'hall—7F 55
Telford Rd. Twic—7E 86
Telfords Yd. E1—7G 63 (1H 109)
Telford Way. W3—5A 58
Telford Way. Hay—5C 54
Telham Rd. E6—2E 66
Tell Gro. SE22—4F 95
Tellson Av. SE18—1B 98
Temeraire St. SE16
—2J 79 (5M 149)
Temperley Rd. SW12—7E 92
Templar Dri. SE28—6D 68
Templar Ho. NW2—6H 43
Templar Pl. Hmptn—7E 102
Templars Av. NW11—6H 27
Templars Cres. N3—2J 27
Templars Dri. Harr—6C 10
Templars Ho. E15—5D 48
Templar St. SE5—2B 94
Temple Av. EC4—7A 62 (9H 141)
Temple Av. N20—7G 5
Temple Av. Croy—2B 136
Temple Av. Dag—1G 53
Temple Clo. E11—7G 33
Temple Clo. N3—2H 27
Temple Clo. SE28—2G 83
Templecombe Rd. E9—1J 63
Templecombe Way. Mord
—5G 121
Temple Fortune Hill. NW11
—5J 27
Temple Fortune La. NW11
—6J 27
Temple Fortune Pde. NW11
—5H 27
Temple Gdns. N21—2G 17
Temple Gdns. NW11—6H 27
Temple Gdns. Dag—3D 52
Temple Gro. NW11—6J 27
Temple Gro. Enf—3G 7
Temple Hall Ct. E4—2A 20
Templehof Av. NW4—7E 26
Templeman Rd. W7—5K 55
Templemead Clo. W3—6A 58
Temple Mead Clo. Stan—6G 11
Temple Mill La. E15—4D 48
Temple Mills Rd. E15—4C 48
Temple Pl. WC2—7K 61 (9F 140)
Temple Rd. E6—1C 66
Temple Rd. N8—4K 29
Temple Rd. NW2—4E 42
Temple Rd. W4—3J 73
Temple Rd. W5—3D 72
Temple Rd. Croy—4D 134
Temple Rd. Houn—4F 87
Temple Rd. Rich—2F 89
Temple Sheen. SW14—5J 89
Temple Sheen Rd. SW14—4H 89
Temple St. E2—2H 63 (1J 143)
Templeton Av. E4—4H 19
Templeton Clo. N15—6D 30
Templeton Clo. N16—5E 46
Templeton Clo. SE19—1D 124
Templeton Pl. SW5—4J 75
Templeton Rd. N15—6D 30
Temple Way. Sutt—3B 132
Templewood. W13—5B 56
Templewood Av. NW3—3K 43
Templewood Gdns. NW3
—3K 43
Tempsford Clo. Enf—3H 7
Temsford Clo. Harr—2G 23
Tenbury Clo. E7—5B 50

Tenbury Ct. SW2—1H 109
Tenby Av. Harr—2B 24
Tenby Clo. N15—4F 31
Tenby Clo. Romf—6E 36
Tenby Gdns. N'holt—6E 38
Tenby Rd. E17—5A 32
Tenby Rd. Edgw—1F 25
Tenby Rd. Enf—4D 8
Tenby Rd. Romf—6E 36
Tenby Rd. Well—1D 100
Tench St. E1—1H 79 (3J 149)
Tenda Rd. SE16—4H 79 (9J 149)
Tendring Way. Romf—5C 36
Tenham Av. SW2—2H 109
Tenison Ct. W1—7G 61 (9L 139)
Tenison Way. SE1
—1A 78 (3G 147)
Tenniel Clo. W2—7A 60
Tennison Rd. SE25—4F 125
Tennis St. SE1—2D 78 (4A 148)
Tenniswood Rd. Enf—1K 7
Tennyson Av. E11—7J 33
Tennyson Av. E12—7C 50
Tennyson Av. NW9—3J 25
Tennyson Av. N Mald—5D 120
Tennyson Av. Twic—1K 103
Tennyson Av. Well—1J 99
Tennyson Rd. E10—1D 48
Tennyson Rd. E15—7G 49
Tennyson Rd. E17—6B 32
Tennyson Rd. NW6—1H 59
Tennyson Rd. NW7—5H 13
Tennyson Rd. SE20—7K 111
Tennyson Rd. SW19—6A 108
Tennyson Rd. W7—7K 55
Tennyson Rd. Houn—2G 87
Tennyson St. SW8—2F 93
Tensing Rd. S'hall—3E 70
Tentelow La. S'hall—5E 70
Tenterden Clo. NW4—3F 27
Tenterden Clo. SE9—4D 114
Tenterden Dri. NW4—3F 27
Tenterden Gdns. NW4—3F 27
Tenterden Gdns. Croy—7G 125
Tenterden Gro. NW4—3F 27
Tenterden Rd. N17—7A 18
Tenterden Rd. Croy—7G 125
Tenterden Rd. Dag—2F 53
Tenterden St. W1
—6F 61 (8K 139)
Tenter Ground. E1
—5F 63 (6E 142)
Tent St. E1—4H 63 (3J 143)
Terborch Way. SE22—5E 94
Teresa M. E17—4C 32
Teresa Wlk. N10—5F 29
Terling Clo. E11—3H 49
Terling Rd. Dag—2G 53
Terminus Pl. SW1
—3F 77 (7K 145)
Terrace Gdns. SW13—2B 90
Terrace La. Rich—6E 88
Terrace Rd. E9—7K 47
Terrace Rd. E13—1J 65
Terrace, The. N3—2H 27
Terrace, The. NW6—1J 59
Terrace, The. SW1
—2J 77 (5D 146)
Terrace, The. SW13—2A 90
Terrace, The. Wfd G—6D 20
Terrace Wlk. Dag—5E 52
Terrapin Rd. SW17—3F 109
Terretts Pl. N1—7B 46
Terrick Rd. N22—1J 29
Terrick St. W12—6D 58
Terrilands. Pinn—3D 22
Terront Rd. N15—4C 30
Tessa Sanderson Pl. SW8
—3F 93
Tessa Sanderson Way. Gnfd
—5H 39
Testerton Wlk. W11—7F 59
Tetbury Pl. N1—1B 62
Tetcott Rd. SW10—7A 76
Tetherdown. N10—2E 28
Tetterby Way. SE16—5G 79
Tetty Way. Brom—2J 127

Teversham La. SW8—1J 93
Teviot Clo. Well—1B 100
Teviot St. E14—5E 64
Tewkesbury Av. SE23—7H 95
Tewkesbury Av. Pinn—5C 22
Tewkesbury Gdns. NW9—3H 25
Tewkesbury Rd. N15—6D 30
Tewkesbury Rd. W13—1A 72
Tewkesbury Rd. Cars—1B 132
Tewkesbury Ter. N11—6B 16
Tewson Rd. SE18—5J 83
Teynham Av. Enf—6J 7
Teynham Grn. Brom—5J 127
Teynton Ter. N17—1C 30
Thackeray Av. N17—2G 31
Thackeray Clo. SW19—7F 107
Thackeray Clo. Harr—1E 38
Thackeray Dri. Romf—7A 36
Thackeray Rd. E6—2B 66
Thackeray Rd. SW8—2F 93
Thackeray St. W8—3K 75
Thackrah Clo. N2—2A 28
Thakeham Clo. SE26—5H 111
Thalia Clo. SE10—6F 81
Thame Rd. SE16—2K 79
Thames Av. SW10—1A 92
Thames Av. Dag—4H 69
Thames Av. Gnfd—2K 55
Thames Bank. SW14—2J 89
Thamesbank Pl. SE28—6C 68
Thamesgate Clo. Rich—4B 104
Thameshill Av. Romf—2J 37
Thameside. Tedd—7D 104
Thameside Industrial Est. E16
—2B 82
Thameside Wlk. SE28—6A 68
Thamesmere Dri. SE28—7A 68
Thames Pl. E14—7B 64
Thames Quay. E14—2D 80
Thames Rd. E16—1B 82
Thames Rd. W4—6G 73
Thames Rd. Bark—3K 67
Thames Rd. Industrial Est. E16
—1B 82
Thames Side. King—1D 118
Thames St. SE10—6D 80
Thames St. King—2D 118
Thamesvale Clo. Houn—2E 86
Thames Village. W4—1J 89
Thanescroft Gdns. Croy
—3E 134
Thanet Ct. W3—6G 57
Thanet Pl. Croy—4C 134
Thanet Rd. Bex—7G 101
Thanet St. WC1—3J 61 (2C 140)
Thane Vs. N7—3K 45
Thant Clo. E10—3D 48
Tharp Rd. Wall—5H 133
Thatcham Gdns. N20—7F 5
Thatchers Way. Iswth—5H 87
Thatches Gro. Romf—4E 36
Thavies Inn. EC1
—6A 62 (7H 141)
Thaxted Ho. Dag—7H 53
Thaxted Pl. SW20—7F 107
Thaxted Rd. SE9—2G 115
Thaxted Rd. Buck H—1H 21
Thaxton Rd. W14—6H 75
Thayers Farm Rd. Beck
—1A 126
Thayer St. W1—6E 60 (7H 139)
Theatre St. SW11—3D 92
Theberton St. N1—1A 62
Theed St. SE1—1A 78 (3H 147)
Thelma Gdns. SE3—1B 98
Thelma Gro. Tedd—6A 104
Theobald Cres. Harr—1G 23
Theobald Rd. E17—7C 32
Theobald Rd. Croy—2B 134
Theobalds Av. N12—4F 15
Theobald's Rd. WC1
—5K 61 (5E 140)
Theodore Ct. SE13—6F 97
Theodore Rd. SE13—6F 97
Therapia La. Croy—7H 123
(in two parts)
Therapia Rd. SE22—6J 95

Theresa Rd. W6—4C 74
Thermopylae Ga. E14—4D 80
Thesiger Rd. SE20—7K 111
Thessaly Rd. SW8—7G 77
Thetford Clo. N13—6G 17
Thetford Gdns. Dag—7E 52
Thetford Rd. Dag—7D 52
Thetford Rd. N Mald—6K 119
Thetis Ter. Rich—6G 73
(in two parts)
Theydon Gro. Wfd G—6F 21
Theydon Rd. E5—2J 47
Theydon St. E17—7B 32
Thicket Cres. Sutt—4A 132
Thicket Gro. SE20—7J 111
Thicket Gro. Dag—6C 52
Thicket Rd. SE20—7G 111
Thicket Rd. Sutt—4A 132
Third Av. E12—4C 50
Third Av. E13—3J 65
Third Av. E17—5C 32
Third Av. W3—1B 74
Third Av. W10—3G 59
Third Av. Dag—1H 69
Third Av. Enf—5A 8
Third Av. Romf—6C 36
Third Av. Wemb—2D 40
Third Cross Rd. Twic—2H 103
Third Way. Wemb—4H 41
Thirleby Rd. SW1
—3G 77 (7M 145)
Thirleby Rd. Edgw—1K 25
Thirlmere Av. Gnfd—3C 56
Thirlmere Gdns. Wemb—1C 40
Thirlmere Rise. Brom—6H 113
Thirlmere Rd. N10—1F 29
Thirlmere Rd. SW16—4H 109
Thirlmere Rd. Bexh—1J 101
Thirsk Clo. N'holt—6E 38
Thirsk Rd. SE25—4D 124
Thirsk Rd. SW11—3E 92
Thirsk Rd. Mitc—7E 108
Thistlebrook.SE2—2C 84
Thistlecroft Gdns. Stan—2D 24
Thistledene Av. Harr—3C 38
Thistle Gro. SW10
—5A 76 (9A 144)
Thistlemead. Chst—2F 129
Thistlewaite Rd. E5—3H 47
Thistlewood Clo. N7—2K 45
Thistleworth Clo. Iswth—7H 71
Thomas a' Beckett Clo. Wemb
—4K 39
Thomas Baines Rd. SW11
—3B 92
Thomas Doyle St. SE1
—3B 78 (6K 147)
Thomas La. SE6—7C 96
Thomas Mcre St. E1
—1G 79 (2G 149)
Thomas More Way. N2—3A 28
Thomas Rd. E14—6B 64
Thomas St. SE18—4F 83
Thompson Av. Rich—3G 89
Thompson Clo. Ilf—2G 51
Thompson Rd. SE22—6F 95
Thompson Rd. Dag—3F 53
Thompson's Av. SE5—7C 78
Thomson Cres. Croy—1A 134
Thomson Rd. Harr—3J 23
Thorburn Sq. SE1
—4G 79 (9G 149)
Thorburn Way. SW19—1B 122
Thoresby St. N1
—3C 62 (1M 141)
Thorkhill Gdns. Th Dit—7A 118
Thorkhill Rd. Th Dit—7A 118
Thornaby Gdns. N18—5B 18
Thorn Av. Bush, Wat—1B 10
Thornbury Av. Iswth—7H 71
Thornbury Rd. SW2—6J 93
Thornbury Rd. Iswth—7H 71
Thornby Rd. E5—3J 47
Thorncliffe Rd. SW2—6J 93
Thorncliffe Rd. S'hall—5D 70
Thorn Clo. Brom—6E 128
Thorn Clo. N'holt—3D 54

Thorncombe Rd. SE22—5E 94
Thorncroft Rd. Sutt—5K 131
Thorncroft St. SW8—7J 77
Thorndean St. SW18—2A 108
Thorndene. SE28—7C 68
Thorndene Av. N11—1K 15
Thorndike Av. N'holt—1B 54
Thorndike Clo. SW10—7A 76
Thorndon Clo. Orp—2K 129
Thorndon Gdns. Eps—5A 130
Thorndon Rd. Orp—2K 129
Thorne Clo. E11—4G 49
Thorne Clo. E16—6J 65
Thorne Clo. Eri—6H 85
Thorneloe Gdns. Croy—5A 134
Thorne Pas. SW13—2A 90
Thorne Rd. SW8—7J 77
Thornes Clo. Beck—3E 126
Thorne St. SW13—3A 90
Thornet Wood Rd. Brom
—3E 128
Thorney Cres. SW11—7B 76
Thorney Hedge Rd. W4—4H 73
Thorney St. SW1
—4J 77 (8C 146)
Thornfield Av. NW7—1G 27
Thornfield Rd. W12—2D 74
Thornford Rd. SE13—5E 96
Thorngate Rd. W9—4J 59
Thorngrove Rd E13—1K 65
Thornham Gro. E15—5F 49
Thornham St. SE10—6D 80
Thornhaugh M. WC1
—4H 61 (4B 140)
Thornhaugh St. WC1
—4H 61 (4B 140)
Thornhill Av. SE18—7J 83
Thornhill Cres N1—7K 45
Thornhill Gdns. E10—2D 48
Thornhill Gdns. Bark—7J 51
Thornhill Gro. N1—7K 45
Thornhill Rd. E10—2D 48
Thornhill Rd. N1—7A 46
Thornhill Rd. Croy—7C 124
Thornhill Sq. N1—7K 45
Thornlaw Rd. SE27—4A 110
Thornley Clo. N17—7C 18
Thornley Dri Harr—2F 39
Thornley Pl. SE10—5G 81
Thornsbeach Rd. SE6—1E 112
Thornsett Pl. SE20—2H 125
Thornsett Rd. SE20—2H 125
Thornsett Rd. SW18—1K 107
Thornton Av. SW2—1H 109
Thornton Av. W4—4A 74
Thornton Av. Croy—6K 123
Thornton Dene Beck—2C 126
Thornton Gdns. SW12—1H 109
Thornton Hill. SW19—7G 107
Thornton Rd. E11—2F 49
Thornton Rd. SW12—7H 93
Thornton Rd. SW14—4K 89
Thornton Rd. SW19—6F 107
Thornton Rd. Barn—3B 4
Thornton Rd. Belv—4H 85
Thornton Rd. Brom—5J 113
Thornton Rd. Cars—1B 132
Thornton Rd. Croy & T Hth
—6K 123
Thornton Rd. Ilf—4F 51
Thornton Rd. E. SW19—6F 107
Thornton Row. T Hth—5A 124
Thornton's Farm Av. Romf
—1K 53
Thornton St. SW9—2A 94
Thornton Way. NW11—5H 27
Thorn Tree Ct. W5—5E 56
Thorntree Rd. SE7—5B 82
Thornville St. SE8—1C 96
Thornwood Clo. E18—2K 33
Thornwood Rd. SE13—5G 97
Thorogood Gdns. E15—5G 49
Thorogood Way. Rain—1K 69
Thorold Rd. N22—7D 16
Thorold Rd. Ilf—2F 51
Thorparch Rd. SW8—1H 93

Thorpebank Rd. W12—1C 74
Thorpe Clo. W10—6G 59
Thorpe Cres. E17—2B 32
Thorpedale Gdns. Ilf—4E 34
Thorpedale Rd. N4—1J 45
Thorpe Hall Rd. E17—1E 32
Thorpe Rd. E6—1D 66
Thorpe Rd. E7—4H 49
Thorpe Rd. E17—2E 32
Thorpe Rd. N15—6E 30
Thorpe Rd. Bark—7H 51
Thorpe Rd. King—7E 104
Thorpewood Av. SE26—2H 111
Thorsden Way. SE19—5E 110
Thorverton Rd. NW2—3G 43
Thoydon Rd. E3—2A 64
Thrale Rd. SW16—5G 109
Thrale St. SE1—1C 78 (3M 147)
Thrasher Clo. E8—1F 63
Thrawl St. E1—5F 63 (6F 142)
Threadneedle St. EC2
—6D 62 (8B 142)
Three Colts La. E2
—4H 63 (3K 143)
Three Colt St. E14—6B 64
Three Corners. Bexh—2H 101
Three Kings Rd. Mitc—3E 122
Three Kings Yd. W1
—7F 61 (9J 139)
Three Mill La. E3—3E 64
Three Oak La. SE1
—2F 79 (4E 148)
Threshers Pl. W11—7G 59
Thriffwood. SE26—3K 111
Thrisk Rd. SW11—3E 92
Throckmorten Rd. E16—6K 65
Throgmorton Av. EC2
—6D 62 (7B 142)
Throgmorton St. EC2
—6D 62 (7B 142)
Throwley Clo. SE2—3C 84
(in two parts)
Throwley Rd. Sutt—5K 131
Throwley Way. Sutt—4K 131
Thrupp Clo. Mitc—2F 123
Thrush Grn. Harr—4E 22
Thrush St. SE17—5C 78 (9L 147)
Thruxton Way. SE15—7F 79
Thurbarn Rd. SE6—5D 112
Thurland Rd. SE16
—3G 79 (6H 149)
Thurlby Clo. Harr—6A 24
Thurlby Clo. Wfd G—5J 21
Thurlby Rd. SE27—4A 110
Thurlby Rd. Wemb—6D 40
Thurleigh Av. SW12—6E 92
Thurleigh Rd. SW12—6D 92
Thurlestone Av. Mord—5G 121
Thurlestone Av. N12—6J 15
Thurlestone Rd. Ilf—4K 51
Thurlestone Rd. SE27—4A 110
Thurloe Clo. SW7
—4C 76 (8C 144)
Thurloe Pl. SW7—4B 76 (8B 144)
Thurloe Sq. SW7
—4B 76 (8C 144)
Thurloe St. SW7
—4B 76 (8B 144)
Thurlow Clo. E4—6J 19
Thurlow Gdns. Wemb—5D 40
Thurlow Hill. SE21—1C 110
Thurlow Pk. Rd. SE21—2B 110
Thurlow Rd. NW3—5B 44
Thurlow Rd. W7—2A 72
Thurlow St. SE17
—5D 78 (9B 148)
Thurlow Ter. NW5—5E 44
Thurlow Wlk. SE17—5E 78
Thursland Rd. Sidc—5E 116
Thursley Cres. Croy—7F 137
Thursley Gdns. SW19—2F 107
Thursley Rd. SE9—3D 114
Thurso St. SW17—4B 108
Thurstan Rd. SW20—7D 106
Thurston Rd. SE13—2D 96
Thurston Rd. S'hall—6D 54
Thurtle Rd. E2—2F 63

Thwaite Clo. Eri—6J 85
Thyra Gro. N12—6E 14
Tibbenham Wlk. E13—2H 65
Tibberton Sq. N1—7C 46
Tibbet's Clo. SW19—1F 107
Tibbet's Corner. SW19—1F 107
Tibbet's Ride. SW15—7F 91
Tiber Gdns. N1—1J 61
Ticehurst Clo. Orp—7A 116
Ticehurst Rd. SE23—2A 112
Tickford Clo. SE2—2C 84
Tidal Basin Rd. E16—7H 65
Tidenham Gdns. Croy—3E 134
Tideswell Rd. SW15—4E 90
Tideswell Rd. Croy—3C 136
Tideway Clo. Rich—4B 104
Tideway Wlk. SW8—6G 77
Tidey St. E3—5C 64
Tidford Rd. Well—2K 99
Tidworth Rd. E3—4C 64
Tiepigs La. W Wick—2G 137
Tierney Ct. Croy—2F 135
Tierney Rd. SW2—1J 109
Tiger La. Brom—4K 127
Tiger Way. E5—4H 47
Tilbrook Rd. SE3—3A 98
Tilbury Clo. SE15—7F 79
Tilbury Rd. E6—2D 66
Tilbury Rd. E10—7E 32
Tildesley Rd. SW15—6E 90
Tilehurst Rd. SW18—1B 108
Tilehurst Rd. Sutt—5G 131
Tile Kiln La. N6—1G 45
Tile Kiln La. N13—5H 17
Tile Kiln La. Bex—2J 117
(in two parts)
Tile Kiln Studios. N6—1G 45
Tile Yd. E14—6B 64
Tileyard Rd. N7—7J 45
Tilford Av. Croy—7E 136
Tilford Gdns. SW19—1F 107
Tilia Rd. E5—4H 47
Tiller Rd. E14—3C 80
Tillet Clo. NW10—6J 41
Tillett Sq. SE16—2A 80
Tillet Way. E2—3G 63 (1G 143)
Tillingbourne Gdns. N3—3H 27
Tillingbourne Grn. Orp—4K 129
Tillingbourne Way. N3—4H 27
Tillingham Way. N12—4D 14
Tilling Rd. NW4—1E 42
Tillman St. E1—6H 63 (8K 143)
Tilloch St. N1—7K 45
Tillotson Rd. N9—2A 18
Tillotson Rd. Harr—7A 10
Tillotson Rd. Ilf—7E 34
Tillotson St. E1—5K 63 (6M 143)
Tilney Ct. EC1—4C 62 (3M 141)
Tilney Dri. Buck H—2D 20
Tilney Gdns. N1—6D 46
Tilney Rd. Dag—6F 53
Tilney Rd. S'hall—4A 70
Tilney St. W1—1E 76 (2H 145)
Tilson Gdns. SW2—7J 93
Tilson Rd. N17—1G 31
Tilton St. SW6—6G 75
Tiltwood, The. W3—7J 57
Tilt Yd. App. SE9—6D 98
Timber Clo. Chst—2E 128
Timbercroft. Eps—4A 130
Timbercroft La. SE18—6J 83
Timberdene. NW4—2F 27
Timberland Rd. E1
—6H 63 (8K 143)
Timber Mill Way. SW4—3H 93
Timber Pond Rd. SE16—1K 79
Timberslip Dri. Wall—7H 133
Timber St. EC1—4C 62 (3L 141)
Timberwharf Rd. N16—6G 31
Times Sq. Sutt—5K 131
Timothy Clo. SW4—5G 93
Timothy Rd. E3—5B 64
Timsbury Wlk. SW15—1C 106
Tindal St. SW9—1B 94
Tinderbox All. SW14—3K 89
Tinsley Rd. E1—5J 63 (5M 143)
Tintagel Cres. SE22—4F 95

Tintagel Dri. Stan—4J 11
Tintern Av. NW9—3H 25
Tintern Clo. SW15—5G 91
Tintern Clo. SW19—6A 108
Tintern Gdns. N14—7D 6
Tintern Rd. N22—1C 30
Tintern Rd. Cars—1B 132
Tintern St. SW4—4J 93
Tintern Way. Harr—1F 39
Tinto Rd. E16—4J 65
Tinworth St. SE11
—5J 77 (9D 146)
Tippetts Clo. Enf—1H 7
Tipthorpe Rd. SW11—3E 92
Tipton Dri. Croy—4E 134
Tiptree Clo. E4—3K 19
Tiptree Cres. Ilf—3E 34
Tiptree Dri. Enf—4J 7
Tiptree Rd. Ruis—4A 38
Tirlemont Rd. S Croy—7C 134
Tirrell Rd. Croy—6C 124
Tisbury Rd. SW16—2J 123
Titchborne Row. W2
—6C 60 (8C 138)
Titchfield Rd. NW8—2D 60
Titchfield Rd. Cars—1B 132
Titchfield Wlk. Cars—7B 122
Titchwell Rd. SW18—1B 108
Tite St. SW3—6D 76
Tithe Barn Clo. King—1F 119
Tithe Barn Way. N'holt—2A 54
Tithe Clo. NW7—1C 26
Tithe Farm Av. Harr—3E 38
Tithe Farm Clo. Harr—3E 38
Tithe Wlk. NW7—1C 26
Titian Av. Bush, Wat—1D 10
Titley Clo. E4—5H 19
Titmuss Av. SE28—7B 68
Titmuss St. W12—2D 74
Tiverton Av. Ilf—3E 34
Tiverton Dri. SE9—1G 115
Tiverton Rd. N15—6D 30
Tiverton Rd. N18—5K 17
Tiverton Rd. NW10—1F 59
Tiverton Rd. Edgw—2F 25
Tiverton Rd. Houn—2G 87
Tiverton Rd. T Hth—5A 124
Tiverton Rd. Wemb—2E 56
Tiverton St. SE1
—3C 78 (6L 147)
Tivoli Gdns. SE18—4C 82
Tivoli Rd. N8—5H 29
Tivoli Rd. SE27—5C 110
Tivoli Rd. Houn—4C 86
Tobacco Dock. E1
—7H 63 (1J 149)
Tobago St. E14—2C 80
Tobin Clo. NW3—7C 44
Toby La. E1—4A 64
Todds Wlk. N7—2K 45
Tokenhouse Yd. EC2
—6D 62 (7A 142)
Tokyngton Av. Wemb—6G 41
Toland Sq. SW15—5C 90
Tolcarne Dri. N'wd—3A 22
Toley Av. Wemb—7E 24
Tollbridge Clo. W10—4H 59
Tollesbury Gdns. Ilf—3H 35
Tollet St. E1—4K 63 (3M 143)
Tollgate Dri. SE21—2E 110
Tollgate Gdns. NW6—2K 59
Tollgate Rd.—5A 66
E16 1-153 & 2-130
E6 remainder
Tollgate Sq. E6—5D 66
Tollhouse Way. N19—2G 45
Tollington Pk. N4—2K 45
Tollington Pl. N4—2K 45
Tollington Rd. N7—4K 45
Tollington Way. N7—3J 45
Tolmers Sq. NW1
—4G 61 (3M 139)
Tolpuddle St. N1—2A 62
Tolsford Rd. E5—5H 47
Tolson Rd. Iswth—3A 88
Tolverne Rd. SW20—1E 120
Tolworth Gdns. Romf—5D 36

277

Tolworth Rise. N. Surb—7J 119
Tolworth Rise. S. Surb—7J 119
Tomahawk Gdns. N'holt—3B 54
Tom Coombs Clo. SE9—4C 98
Tom Cribb Rd. SE28—3G 83
Tomlins All. Twic—1A 104
Tomlin's Gro. E3—3C 64
Tomlinson Clo. E2
—3F 63 (2F 142)
Tomlinson Clo. W4—5H 73
Tomlins Orchard. Bark—1G 67
Tomlins Ter. E14—6A 64
Tomlins Wlk. N7—2K 45
Tom Mann Clo. Bark—1J 67
Tompion St. EC1
—3B 62 (2K 141)
Tom Smith Clo. SE10—6G 81
Tomswood Ct. Ilf—1G 35
Tomswood Hill. Ilf—1F 35
Tomswood Rd. Chig—6K 21
Tonbridge Cres. Harr—4E 24
Tonbridge St. WC1
—3J 61 (1C 140)
Tonfield Rd. Sutt—1H 131
Tonge Clo. Beck—5C 126
Tonsley Hill. SW18—5K 91
Tonsley Pl. SW18—5K 91
Tonsley Rd. SW18—5K 91
Tonsley St. SW18—5K 91
Tonstall Rd. Mitc—2E 122
Tony Law Ho. SE20—1H 125
Tooke Clo. Pinn—1C 22
Took's Ct. EC4—6A 62 (7G 141)
Tooley St. SE1—1E 78 (3C 148)
Toorack Rd. Harr—2H 23
Tooting Bec Gdns. SW16
(in two parts)—4H 109
Tooting Bec Rd. SW17 & SW16
—3E 108
Tooting B'way. SW17—5D 108
Tooting Gro. SW17—5C 108
Tooting High St. SW17—5C 108
Tootswood Rd. Brom—5G 127
Topham Sq. N17—1C 30
Topham St. EC1
—4A 62 (3G 141)
Topiary Sq. Rich—3F 89
Topley St. SE9—4A 98
Top Pk. Beck—5G 127
Topp Wlk. NW2—2E 42
Topsfield Rd. N8—5J 29
Topsham Rd. SW17—3D 108
Torbay Rd. NW6—7H 43
Torbay Rd. Harr—2C 38
Torbay St. NW1—7F 45
Torbridge Clo. Edgw—7K 11
Torbrook Clo. Bex—6E 100
Torcross Dri. SE23—2J 111
Torcross Rd. Ruis—3A 38
Tor Gdns. W8—2J 75
Tor Ho. N6—6F 29
Tormead Clo. Sutt—6J 131
Tormount Rd. SE18—6J 83
Toronto Av. E12—4D 50
Toronto Rd. E11—4F 49
Toronto Rd. Ilf—1F 51
Torquay Gdns. Ilf—4B 34
Torquay St. W2—5K 59
Torrens Rd. E15—6H 49
Torrens Rd. SW2—5K 93
Torrens Sq. E15—6H 49
Torrens St. EC1—2B 62
Torre Wlk. Cars—1C 132
Torriano Av. NW5—5H 45
Torriano Cotts. NW5—5G 45
Torriano M. NW5—5G 45
Torridge Gdns. SE15—4J 95
Torridge Rd. T Hth—5B 124
Torridon Rd.—7F 97
SE13 1 & 3
SE6 remainder
Torrington Av. N12—5G 15
Torrington Clo. N2—4G 15
Torrington Dri. Harr—3F 39
Torrington Gdns. N11—6B 16
Torrington Gdns. Gnfd—7C 40

Torrington Gro. N12—5H 15
Torrington Pk. N12—5F 15
Torrington Pl. E1—1G 79 (2H 149)
Torrington Pl. WC1
—5H 61 (5A 140)
Torrington Rd. E18—3J 33
Torrington Rd. Dag—1F 53
Torrington Rd. Gnfd—1C 56
Torrington Sq. WC1
—4H 61 (4B 140)
Torrington Sq. Croy—7D 124
Torrington Way. Mord—6J 121
Tor Rd. Well—1C 100
Torr Rd. SE20—7K 111
Torver Rd. Harr—4J 23
Torwood Rd. SW15—5C 90
Tothill St. SW1—2H 77 (5A 148)
Totnes Rd. Well—7B 84
Totnes Wlk. N2—4B 28
Tottenhall Rd. N13—6F 17
Tottenham Ct. Rd. W1
—4G 61 (4M 139)
Tottenham Grn. E. N15—4F 31
Tottenham Grn. E. S. Side. N15
—4F 31
Tottenham La. N8—5J 29
Tottenham M. W1
—5G 61 (5M 139)
Tottenham Rd. N1—6E 46
Tottenham St. W1
—5G 61 (5M 139)
Totterdown St. SW17—4D 108
Totteridge Comn. N20—2H 13
Totteridge Grn. N20—2D 14
Totteridge La. N20—2D 14
Totteridge Village. N20—1B 14
Totternhoe Clo. Harr—5C 24
Totton Rd. T Hth—3A 124
Totty St. E3—2A 64
Toulmin St. SE1—2C 78 (5L 147)
Toulon St. SE5—7C 78
Tournay Rd. SW6—7H 75
Toussaint Wlk. SE16
—3G 79 (6H 149)
Tovil Clo. SE20—2H 125
Towcester Rd. E3—4E 64
Tower Bri. SE1 & E1
—1F 79 (3E 148)
Tower Bri. Wharf E1
—1G 79 (3G 149)
Tower Bri. App. E1
—7F 63 (1E 148)
Tower Bri. Rd. SE1
—3E 78 (7C 148)
Tower Clo. NW3—5B 44
Tower Clo. SE20—7H 111
Tower Ct. E5—7F 31
Tower Gdns. Rd. N17—1C 30
Tower Hamlets Rd. E7—4H 49
Tower Hamlets Rd. E17—3C 32
Tower Hill. EC3—7F 63 (1E 148)
Tower M. E17—4C 32
Tower Rise. Rich—3E 88
Tower Rd. NW10—7C 42
Tower Rd. Belv—4J 85
Tower Rd. Bexh—4G 101
Tower Rd. Twic—3K 103
Tower Royal. EC4
—7D 62 (9A 142)
Towers Pl. Rich—5E 88
Towers Rd. Pinn—1C 22
Towers Rd. S'hall—4E 54
Tower St. WC2—6J 61 (8C 140)
Tower Ter. N22—2K 29
Tower View. Croy—7A 126
Tower Yd. Rich—5F 89
Towfield Rd. Felt—2D 102
Towgar Ct. N20—7F 5
Towncourt Cres. Orp—5G 129
Towncourt La. Orp—6H 129
Towncourt Path. N14—1C 46
Towney Mead. N'holt—2D 54
Town Hall App. Rd. N15—4F 31
Town Hall Av. W4—5K 73
Town Hall Rd. SW11—3D 92
Townholm Cres. W7—3K 71
Townley Ct. E15—6H 49

Townley Rd. SE22—5E 94
Townley Rd. Bexh—5F 101
Townley St. SE17
—5D 78 (9A 148)
(in two parts)
Town Mead. Bren—6D 72
Townmead Rd. SW6—3K 91
Townmead Rd. Rich—2H 89
Town Quay. Bark—1F 67
Town Rd. N9—2C 18
Townsend Av. N14—4C 16
Townsend Industrial Est. NW10
—2J 57
Townsend La. NW9—7K 25
Townsend Rd. N15—5F 31
Townsend Rd. S'hall—1C 70
Townsend St. SE17
—4E 78 (8C 148)
Townsend Yd. N6—1F 45
Townshend Rd. NW8—1C 60
Townshend Rd. Rich—4F 89
Townshend Ter. Rich—4F 89
Town, The. Enf—3J 7
Town Wharf. Iswth—3B 88
Towpath, The. SW10—1A 92
Towton Rd. SE27—2C 110
Toynbee Clo. Chst—4F 115
Toynbee Rd. SW20—1G 121
Toynbee St. E1—5F 63 (6E 142)
Toyne Way. N6—6D 28
Tracey Av. NW2—5E 42
Tracy Ct. Stan—7H 11
Tradescant Rd. SW8—7J 77
Trading Est. Rd. NW10—4J 57
Trafalgar Av. N17—6K 17
Trafalgar Av. SE15—5F 79
Trafalgar Av. Wor Pk—1F 131
Trafalgar Clo. SE16—4A 80
Trafalgar Gdns. E1—5K 63
Trafalgar Gro. SE10—6F 81
Trafalgar Pl. E11—4J 33
Trafalgar Pl. N18—5B 18
Trafalgar Rd. SE10—6F 81
Trafalgar Rd. SW19—7A 108
Trafalgar Rd. Twic—2H 103
Trafalgar Sq. WC2 & SW1
—1H 77 (2B 146)
Trafalgar St. SE17—5D 78
Trafalgar Ter. Harr—1J 39
Trafalgar Way. Croy—2A 134
Trafford Clo. E15—5D 48
Trafford Rd. T Hth—5K 123
Tramway Av. E15—7F 49
Tramway Av. N9—7D 8
Tramway Path. Mitc—4C 122
(in two parts)
Tranley M. NW3—4C 44
Tranmere Rd. N9—7A 8
Tranmere Rd. SW18—2A 108
Tranmere Rd. Twic—7F 87
Tranquil Pas. SE3—2H 97
Tranquil Vale. SE3—2G 97
Transay Wlk. N1—6D 46
Transept St. NW1
—5C 60 (6D 138)
Transmere Clo. Orp—6G 129
Transmere Rd. Orp—6G 129
Transport Av. Bren—5B 72
Transwell St. SE1
—2A 78 (5G 147)
Tranton Rd. SE16
—3G 79 (6H 149)
Traps La. N Mald—1A 120
Travellers Way. Houn—2A 86
Travers Clo. E17—1K 31
Travers Rd. N7—3A 46
Treacy Clo. Bush, Wat—2B 10
Treadgold St. W11—7F 59
Treadway St. E2
—2H 63 (1J 143)
Treaty Centre. Houn—3F 87
Treaty St. N1—1K 61
Trebeck St. W1—1F 77 (2J 145)
Trebovir Rd. SW5—5J 75
Treby St. E3—4B 64
Trecastle Way. N7—4H 45

Tredegar M. E3—3B 64
Tredegar Rd. E3—2B 64
Tredegar Rd. N11—7C 16
Tredegar Sq. E3—3B 64
Tredegar Ter. E3—3B 64
Trederwen Rd. E8—1G 63
Tredown Rd. SE26—5J 111
Tredwell Clo. Brom—4C 128
Tredwell Rd. SE27—4B 110
Tree Clo. Rich—1D 104
Treen Av. SW13—3B 90
Tree Rd. E16—6A 66
Treetops Clo. SE2—5E 84
Treeview Clo. SE19—1E 124
Treewall Gdns. Brom—4K 113
Trefgarne Rd. Dag—2G 53
Trefil Wlk. N7—4J 45
Trefoil Rd. SW18—5A 92
Tregaron Av. N8—6J 29
Tregaron Gdns. N Mald
—4A 120
Tregarvon Rd. SW11—4E 92
Tregenna Av. Harr—4E 38
Tregenna Clo. N14—5B 6
Trego Rd. E9—7C 48
Tregothnan Rd. SW9—3J 93
Tregunter Rd. SW10—6A 76
Trehearn Rd. Ilf—1H 35
Treherne Ct. SW9—1B 94
Treherne Ct. SW17—4E 108
Trehern Rd. SW14—3K 89
Trehurst St. E5—5A 48
Trelawney Est. E9—6J 47
Trelawney Rd. Ilf—1H 35
Trelawn Rd. E10—3E 48
Trelawn Rd. SW2—5A 94
Trellis Sq. E3—3B 64
Treloar Gdns. SE19—6D 110
Tremadoc Rd. SW4—4H 93
Tremaine Clo. SE4—2C 96
Tremaine Rd. SE20—2H 125
Tremlett Gro. N19—3G 45
Tremlett M. N19—3G 45
Trenance Gdns. Ilf—3A 52
Trenchard Clo. Stan—6F 11
Trenchard Ct. NW4—5C 26
Trenchard Ct. Mord—6J 121
Trenchard St. SE10—5F 81
Trenchold St. SW8—6J 77
Trenholme Clo. SE20—7H 111
Trenholme Rd. SE20—7H 111
Trenholme Ter. SE20—7H 111
Trenmar Gdns. NW10—3D 58
Trent Av. W5—3C 72
Trent Gdns. N14—6A 6
Trentham St. SW18—1J 107
Trent Rd. SW2—5K 93
Trent Rd. Buck H—1E 20
Trent Way. Wor Pk—3E 130
Trentwood Side. Enf—3E 6
Treport St. SW18—7K 91
Tresco Clo. Brom—6G 113
Trescoe Gdns. Harr—7C 22
Tresco Gdns. Ilf—2A 52
Tresco Rd. SE15—4H 95
Tresham Cres. NW8
—4C 60 (3C 138)
Tresham Rd. Bark—7K 51
Tresham Wlk. E9—5J 47
Tressell Clo. N1—7B 46
Tressillian Cres. SE4—3C 96
Tressillian Rd. SE4—4B 96
Trestis Clo. Hay—4B 54
Treswell Rd. Dag—1E 68
Tretawn Gdns. NW7—4F 13
Tretawn Pk. NW7—4F 13
Trevanion Rd. W14—5G 75
Treve Av. Harr—7H 23
Trevelyan Av. E12—4D 50
Trevelyan Cres. Harr—7D 24
Trevelyan Gdns. NW10—1E 58
Trevelyan Rd. E15—4H 49
Trevelyan Rd. SW17—6C 108
Treveris St. SE1
—1B 78 (3K 147)
Treverton St. W10—4F 59
Treville St. SW15—7D 90

Treviso Rd. SE23—2K 111
Trevithick St. SE8—6C 80
Trevone Gdns. Pinn.—6C 22
Trevor Clo. Barn—6G 5
Trevor Clo. Brom—7H 127
Trevor Clo. Harr—7E 10
Trevor Clo. Iswth—5K 87
Trevor Clo. N'holt—2A 54
Trevor Gdns. Edgw—1K 25
Trevor Gdns. N'holt—2A 54
Trevor Pl. SW7—2C 76 (5D 144)
Trevor Rd. SW19—7G 107
Trevor Rd. Edgw—1K 25
Trevor Rd. Wfd G—7D 20
Trevor Sq. SW7—2D 76 (5E 144)
Trevor St. SW7—2C 76 (5D 144)
Trevose Rd. E17—1F 33
Trewince Rd. SW20—1E 120
Trewint St. SW18—2A 108
Trewsbury Rd. SE26—5K 111
Triandra Way. Hay—5B 54
Triangle Ct. E16—5B 66
Triangle Pas. Barn—4F 5
Triangle Pl. SW4—4H 93
Triangle Rd. E8—1H 63
Triangle, The. E8—1H 63
Triangle, The. N13—4F 17
Triangle, The. Bark—6G 51
Triangle, The. King—2J 119
Trident Gdns. N'holt—3B 54
Trident St. SE16—4K 79
Trident Way. S'hall—3A 70
Trigon Rd. SW8—7K 77
Trilby Rd. SE23—2K 111
Trimmer Wlk. Bren—6E 72
Trinder Gdns. N19—1J 45
Trinder Rd. N19—1J 45
Trinder Rd. Barn—5A 4
Tring Av. W5—1F 73
Tring Av. S'hall—6D 54
Tring Av. Wemb—6G 41
Tring Clo. Ilf—5H 35
Trinidad Gdns. Dag—7K 53
Trinidad St. E14—7B 64
Trinity Av. N2—3B 28
Trinity Av. Enf—6A 8
Trinity Business Centre. SE16
—2B 80
Trinity Business Pk. E4—6H 19
Trinity Church Pas. SW13
—6D 74
Trinity Chu. Rd. SW13—6D 74
Trinity Chu. Sq. SE1
—3C 78 (6M 147)
Trinity Clo. E11—2G 49
Trinity Clo. NW3—4B 44
Trinity Clo. SE13—4F 97
Trinity Clo. Houn—4C 86
Trinity Clo. S Croy—7E 134
Trinity Cotts. Rich—3F 89
Trinity Ct. N1—1E 62
Trinity Ct. SE28—6E 124
Trinity Ct. W2—6A 60
Trinity Ct. Croy—2C 134
Trinity Cres. SW17—2D 108
Trinity Gdns. E16—5H 65
Trinity Gdns. SW9—4K 93
Trinity Gro. SE10—1E 96
Trinity M. W10—6F 59
Trinity Pl. EC3—7F 63 (9E 142)
Trinity Pl. Bexh—4F 101
Trinity Rise. SW2—1A 110
Trinity Rd. N2—3B 28
Trinity Rd. N22—7D 16
Trinity Rd.—4A 92
  SW17 1-259 & 4-226
  SW18 remainder
Trinity Rd. SW19—6J 107
Trinity Rd. Ilf—3G 35
Trinity Rd. Rich—3F 89
Trinity Rd. S'hall—1C 70
Trinity Sq. EC3—7F 63 (9E 142)
Trinity St. E16—5H 65
Trinity St. SE1—2C 78 (5M 147)
Trinity St. Enf—2H 7
Trinity Wlk. NW3—6A 44
Trinity Way. W3—7A 58

Trinity Wharf Business Centre.
  SE16—2B 80
Trio Pl. SE1—2C 78 (5M 147)
Tristan Sq. SE3—3G 97
Tristram Clo. E17—3F 33
Tristram Rd. Brom—4H 113
Triton Sq. NW1—4G 61 (3L 139)
Tritton Av. Croy—4J 133
Tritton Rd. SE21—3D 110
Triumph Rd. E6—5D 66
Trojan Way. Croy—3K 133
Troon St. E1—6A 64
Trosley Rd. Belv—6G 85
Trossachs Rd. SE22—5E 94
Trothy Rd. SE1—4G 79 (9H 149)
Trott Rd. N10—7J 15
Trott St. SW11—1C 92
Troughton Rd. SE7—5K 81
Troutbeck Rd. SE14—1A 96
Trouville Rd. SW4—6G 93
Trowbridge Rd. E9—6B 48
Trowlock Av. Tedd—6C 104
Trowlock Way. Tedd—6D 104
Troy Rd. SE19—6D 110
Troy St. SE18—4F 83
Troy Town. SE15—3G 95
Truesdale Rd. E6—6D 66
Trulock Rd. N17—7B 18
Truman Clo. Edgw—7C 12
Truman's Rd. N16—5E 46
Trumble Gdns. T Hth—4B 124
Trumpers Way. W7—3J 71
Trumpington Rd. E7—4H 49
Trump St. EC2—6C 62 (8M 141)
Trundlers Way. Bush, Wat
  —1D 10
Trundley's Rd. SE8—5K 79
Trundley's Ter. SE8—4K 79
Truro Gdns. Ilf—7C 34
Truro Rd. E17—4B 32
Truro Rd. N22—7D 16
Truro St. NW5—6E 44
Truslove Rd. SE27—5A 110
Trussley Rd. W6—3E 74
Trust Wlk. SE21—1B 110
Tryfan Clo. Ilf—5B 34
Tryon St. SW3—5D 76 (9E 144)
Tuam Rd. SE18—6H 83
Tubbs Rd. NW10—2B 58
Tuckton Wlk. SW15—7B 90
Tudor Av. Hmptn—7E 102
Tudor Av. Wor Pk—3D 130
Tudor Clo. N6—7G 29
Tudor Clo. NW3—5C 44
Tudor Clo. NW7—6H 13
Tudor Clo. NW9—2J 41
Tudor Clo. Chig—4K 21
Tudor Clo. Chst—1D 128
Tudor Clo. Sutt—5F 131
Tudor Clo. Wall—7G 133
Tudor Clo. Wfd G—5E 20
Tudor Ct. E17—7B 32
Tudor Ct. Felt—4A 102
Tudor Ct. Sidc—3A 116
Tudor Ct. N. Wemb—5G 41
Tudor Ct. S. Wemb—5G 41
Tudor Cres. Enf—1H 7
Tudor Dri. King—5D 104
Tudor Dri. Mord—6F 121
Tudor Est. NW10—2H 57
Tudor Gdns. NW9—2J 41
Tudor Gdns. SW13—3A 90
Tudor Gdns. W3—5G 57
Tudor Gdns. Harr—2H 23
Tudor Gdns. Twic—1K 103
Tudor Gdns. W Wick—3E 136
Tudor Gro. E9—7J 47
Tudor Pl. Mitc—7C 108
Tudor Rd. E4—6J 19
Tudor Rd. E6—1A 66
Tudor Rd. E9—1H 63
Tudor Rd. N9—7C 8
Tudor Rd. SE19—7F 111
Tudor Rd. SE25—5H 125
Tudor Rd. Bark—1K 67
Tudor Rd. Barn—3D 4
Tudor Rd. Beck—3E 126

Tudor Rd. Hmptn—7E 102
Tudor Rd. Harr—2H 23
Tudor Rd. Houn—4H 87
Tudor Rd. King—7G 105
Tudor Rd. Pinn—2A 22
Tudor Rd. S'hall—7C 54
Tudor St. EC4—7A 62 (9H 141)
Tudor Wlk. Bex—6E 100
Tudor Way. N14—1C 16
Tudor Way. W3—2G 73
Tudor Way. Orp—6H 129
Tudor Well Clo. Stan—5G 11
Tudway Rd. SE3—3K 97
Tufnell Pk. Rd.—4G 45
  N7 1-217 & 2-210
  N19 remainder
Tufton Rd. E4—4H 19
Tufton St. SW1—3J 77 (7C 146)
Tugela Rd. Croy—6D 124
Tugela St. SE6—2B 112
Tulip Clo. Croy—1K 135
Tulip Clo. Hmptn—6D 102
Tulip Ct. Pinn—3A 22
Tuliptree Av. Rich—1E 88
Tulse Clo. Beck—3E 126
Tulse Hill. SW2—6A 94
Tulse Hill. SW2—6A 94
Tulse Hill Est. SW2—6A 94
Tulsemere Rd. SE27—2C 110
Tummons Gdns. SE25—2E 124
Tuncombe Rd. N18—4K 17
Tunis Rd. W12—1E 74
Tunley Grn. E14—5B 64
Tunley Rd. NW10—1A 58
Tunley Rd. SW17—2E 108
Tunmarsh La. E13—3A 66
Tunnel App. E14—7A 64
Tunnel App. SE10—2G 81
Tunnel Av. SE10—2F 81
  (in two parts)
Tunnel Gdns. N11—7B 16
Tunnel Rd. SE16—2J 79 (4L 149)
Tunstall Rd. SW9—4K 93
Tunstall Rd. Croy—1E 134
Tunstall Wlk. Bren—6E 72
Tunstock Way. Belv—7F 85
Tunworth Clo. NW9—6J 25
Tunworth Cres. SW15—6B 90
Turenne Clo. SW18—4A 92
Turin Rd. N9—1D 18
Turin St. E2—3G 63 (2G 143)
Turkey Oak Clo. SE19—1E 124
Turk's Head Yd. EC1
  —5B 62 (5J 141)
Turks Row. SW3
  —5D 76 (9F 144)
Turle Rd. N4—2K 45
Turle Rd. SW16—2J 123
Turlewray Clo. N4—1K 45
Turley Clo. E15—1G 65
Turnage Rd. Dag—1E 52
Turnberry Quay. E14—3D 80
Turnberry Way. Orp—7H 129
Turnchapel M. SW4—3F 93
Turner Av. N15—4E 30
Turner Av. Mitc—1D 122
Turner Av. Twic—3G 103
Turner Clo. NW11—6K 27
Turner Dri. NW11—6K 27
Turner Rd. E17—3E 32
Turner Rd. Edgw—2E 24
Turner Rd. N Mald—7K 119
Turner's All. EC3
  —7E 62 (9C 142)
Turners Meadow Way. Beck
  —1B 126
Turner's Rd. E3—5B 64
Turner St. E1—5H 63 (6J 143)
Turner St. E16—6H 65
Turners Wood. NW11—7A 28
Turneville Rd. W14—6H 75
Turney Rd. SE21—7C 94
Turnham Grn. Ter. W4—4A 74
Turnham Grn. Ter. M. W4
  —4A 74
Turnham Rd. SE4—5A 96

Turnmill St. EC1—5B 62 (5J 141)
Turnpike Clo. SE8—7B 80
Turnpike La. N8—4K 29
Turnpike La. Sutt—5A 132
Turnpike Link. Croy—2E 134
Turnpin La. SE10—6E 80
Turnstone Clo. E13—3J 65
Turpentine La. SW1—5F 77
Turpington Clo. Brom—7C 128
Turpington La. Brom—7C 128
Turpin's La. Wfd G—5J 21
Turpin Way. N19—2H 45
Turpin Way. Wall—7F 133
Turquand St. SE17
  —4C 78 (9M 147)
Turret Gro. SW4—3G 93
Turton Rd. Wemb—5E 40
Turville St. E2—4F 63 (3E 142)
Tuscan Rd. SE18—6H 83
Tuskar St. SE10—6G 81
Tustin Est. SE15—6J 79
Tuttlebee La. Buck H—2D 20
Tweedale Ct. E15—5E 48
Tweeddale Rd. Cars—1B 132
Tweed Glen. Romf—1K 37
Tweed Grn. Romf—1K 37
Tweedmouth Rd. E13—2K 65
Tweed Way. Romf—1K 37
Tweedy Rd. Brom—1J 127
Twelvetrees Cres. E3—4E 64
Twentyman Clo. Wfd G—5D 20
Twickenham Bri. Twic & Rich
  —5C 88
Twickenham Clo. Croy—3K 133
Twickenham Gdns. Gnfd
  —5A 40
Twickenham Gdns. Harr
  —7D 10
Twickenham Rd. E11—2F 49
Twickenham Rd. Felt—3D 102
Twickenham Rd. Iswth—5A 88
Twickenham Rd. Rich—4C 88
Twickenham Rd. Tedd—4A 104
  (in two parts)
Twickenham Trading Est. Iswth
  —6K 87
Twigg Clo. Eri—7K 85
Twilley St. SW18—7K 91
Twine Ct. E1—7J 63 (9L 143)
Twineham Grn. N12—4D 14
Twining Av. Twic—3G 103
Twinn Rd. NW7—6B 14
Twisden Rd. NW5—4F 45
Twybridge Way. NW10—7J 41
Twyford Abbey Rd. NW10
  —3F 57
Twyford Av. N2—3D 28
Twyford Av. W3—7G 57
Twyford Cres. W3—1G 73
Twyford Pl. WC2
  —6K 61 (7E 140)
Twyford Rd. Cars—1B 132
Twyford Rd. Harr—1F 39
Twyford Rd. Ilf—5G 51
Twyford St. N1—1K 61
Tyas Rd. E16—4H 65
Tybenham Rd. SW19—3J 121
Tyberry Rd. Enf—3D 8
Tyburn La. Harr—7K 23
Tyburn Way. W1
  —7D 60 (9F 138)
Tyers Ga. SE1—2E 78 (5C 148)
Tyers St. SE11—5K 77 (9E 146)
Tyers Ter. SE11—5K 77
Tyeshurst Clo. SE2—5E 84
Tylecroft Rd. SW16—2J 123
Tyler Clo. E2—2F 63
Tylers Ga. Harr—6E 24
Tylers Path. Cars—4D 132
Tyler St. SE10—5G 81
Tylney Av. SE19—5F 111
Tylney Rd. E7—4A 50
Tylney Rd. Brom—2B 128
Tyndale La. N1—7B 46
Tyndale Ter. N1—7B 46
Tyndall Rd. E10—2E 48

Tyndall Rd. Well—3K 99
Tyneham Clo. SW11—3E 92
Tyneham Rd. SW11—2E 92
Tynemouth Dri. Enf—1B 8
Tynemouth Rd. N15—4F 31
Tynemouth Rd. Mitc—7E 108
Tynemouth St. SW6—2A 92
Tyne St. E1—6F 63 (7F 142)
Tynwald Ho. SE26—3G 111
Type St. E2—2K 63 (1M 143)
Tyrawley Rd. SW6—1K 91
Tyrell Clo. Harr—4J 39
Tyrell Ct. Cars—4D 132
Tyrone Rd. E6—2D 66
Tyron Way. Sidc—4J 115
Tyrrell Rd. SE22—4G 95
Tyrrel Way. NW9—7B 26
Tyrwhitt Rd. SE4—3C 96
Tysoe St. EC1—3A 62 (2G 141)
Tyson Gdns. SE23—7J 95
Tyson Rd. SE23—7J 95
Tyssen Pas. E8—6F 47
Tyssen Rd. N16—3F 47
Tyssen St. E8—6F 47
Tytherton Rd. N19—3H 45

Uamvar St. E14—5D 64
Uckfield Gro. Mitc—1E 122
Udall St. SW1—4G 77 (9M 145)
Udney Pk. Rd. Tedd—6A 104
Uffington Rd. NW10—1C 58
Uffington Rd. SE27—4A 110
Ufford Clo. Harr—7A 10
Ufford Rd. Harr—7A 10
Ufford St. SE1—2A 78 (4H 147)
Ufton Gro. N1—7D 46
Ufton Rd. N1—7E 46
Ujima Ct. SW16—4J 109
Ullathorne Rd. SW16—4G 109
Ulleswater Rd. N14—3D 16
Ullin St. E14—5E 64
Ullswater Clo. SW15—4K 105
Ullswater Clo. Brom—7G 113
Ullswater Cres. SW15—4K 105
Ullswater Rd. SE27—2B 110
Ullswater Rd. SW13—7C 74
Ulster Gdns. N13—4H 17
Ulster Pl. NW1—4F 61 (4J 139)
Ulundi Rd. SE3—6G 81
Ulva Rd. SW15—5F 91
Ulverscroft Rd. SE22—5G 95
Ulverstone Rd. SE27—2B 110
Ulverston Rd. E17—2F 33
Ulysses Rd. NW6—5H 43
Umberston St. E1
　　　　　—6G 63 (7H 143)
Umbria St. SW15—6C 90
Umfreville Rd. N4—6B 30
Underbridge Way. Enf—3F 9
Undercliff Rd. SE13—3C 96
Underhill. Barn—5D 4
Underhill Rd. SE22—5G 95
Underhill St. NW1—1F 61
Underne Av. N14—2A 16
Undershaft. EC3
　　　　　—6E 62 (8C 142)
Undershaw Rd. Brom—3H 113
Underwood. Croy—5E 136
Underwood Rd. E1
　　　　　—4G 63 (4G 143)
Underwood Rd. E4—5J 19
Underwood. Wfd G—7F 21
Underwood Row. N1
　　　　　—3C 62 (1M 141)
Underwood St. N1
　　　　　—3C 62 (1M 141)
Underwood, The. SE9—3D 114
Undine Rd. E14—4D 80
Undine St. SW17—5D 108
Uneeda Dri. Gnfd—1H 55
Unicorn Pas. SE1
　　　　　—1E 78 (3D 148)
Union Cotts. E15—7G 49
Union Ct. Rich—5E 88
Union Dri. E1—4A 64

Union Gro. SW8—2H 93
Union Rd. N11—6C 16
Union Rd.—2H 93
　SW4 1-93 & 2-102
　SW8 remainder
Union Rd. Brom—5B 128
Union Rd. Croy—7C 124
Union Rd. N'holt—2E 54
Union Rd. Wemb—6E 40
Union Sq. N1—1C 62
Union St. E15—1E 64
Union St. SE1—1B 78 (3K 147)
Union St. Barn—3B 4
Union St. King—2D 118
Union Wlk. E2—3E 62 (1D 142)
Union Yd. W1—6F 61 (8K 139)
Unity Way. SE18—3B 82
University Clo. NW7—7G 13
University Pl. Eri—7J 85
University Rd. SW19—6B 108
University St. WC1
　　　　　—4G 61 (4M 139)
Unwin Clo. SE15—6G 79
Unwin Rd. SW7—3B 76 (6B 144)
Unwin Rd. Iswth—3J 87
Upbrook M. W2—6A 60 (8A 138)
Upcerne Rd. SW10—7A 76
Upchurch Clo. SE20—7H 111
Upcroft Av. Edgw—5D 12
Updale Rd. Sidc—4K 115
Upfield. Croy—3H 135
Upfield Rd. W13—5K 55
Upgrove Mnr. Way. SW2
　　　　　—7A 94
Uphall Rd. Ilf—5F 51
Upham Pk. Rd. W4—4A 74
Uphill Dri. NW7—5F 13
Uphill Dri. NW9—5J 25
Uphill Gro. NW7—4F 13
Uphill Rd. NW7—4F 13
Upland Rd. E13—4J 65
Upland Rd. SE22—7G 95
Upland Rd. Bexh—3F 101
Upland Rd. S Croy—5D 134
Upland Rd. Sutt—7B 132
Uplands. Beck—2C 126
Uplands Av. E17—2K 31
Uplands Clo. SW14—5H 89
Uplands End. Wfd G—7H 21
Uplands Pk. Rd. Enf—2F 7
Uplands Rd. N8—5K 29
Uplands Rd. Barn—1K 15
Uplands Rd. Romf—3D 36
Uplands Rd. Wfd G—7H 21
Uplands Trading Est. E17
　　　　　—3K 31
Uplands Way. N21—5F 7
Upney La. Bark—6J 51
Upnor Way. SE17—5E 78
Uppark Dri. Ilf—6G 35
Up. Abbey Rd. Belv—4F 85
Up. Addison Gdns. W14—2G 75
Up. Belgrave St. SW1
　　　　　—3E 76 (6H 145)
Up. Berkeley St. W1
　　　　　—6D 60 (8E 138)
Up. Beulah Hill. SE19—1E 124
Up. Brighton Rd. Surb—6D 118
Up. Brockley Rd. SE4—2B 96
Up. Brook St. W1
　　　　　—7E 60 (9G 139)
Up. Butts. Bren—6C 72
Up. Cavendish Av. N3—3J 27
Up. Cheyne Row. SW3—6C 76
Up. Clapton Rd. E5—2H 47
Up. Elmers End Rd. Beck
　　　　　—4A 126
Up. Green E. Mitc—3D 122
Up. Green W. Mitc—2D 122
Up. Grosvenor St. W1
　　　　　—7E 60 (1G 145)
Up. Grotto Rd. Twic—2K 103
Up. Ground. SE1
　　　　　—1A 78 (2G 147)
Upper SE25—4F 125
Up. Grove Rd. Belv—6F 85
Up. Ham Rd. Rich—4D 104

Up. Harley St. NW1
　　　　　—4E 60 (4H 139)
Up. Holly Hill Rd. Belv—5H 85
Up. James St. W1
　　　　　—7G 61 (9M 139)
Up. John St. W1
　　　　　—7G 61 (9M 139)
Up. Mall. W6—5C 74
Up. Marsh. SE1—3K 77 (6F 146)
Up. Montagu St. W1
　　　　　—5D 60 (5E 138)
Up. Mulgrave Rd. Sutt—7G 131
Up. North St. E14—5C 64
Up. Park Rd. N11—5B 16
Up. Park Rd. NW3—5D 44
Up. Park Rd. Belv—4H 85
Up. Park Rd. Brom—1K 127
Up. Park Rd. King—6G 105
Up. Phillimore Gdns. W8—2J 75
Up. Richmond Rd. SW15—4B 90
Up. Richmond Rd. W. Rich &
　　　　　SW14—4G 89
Upper Rd. E13—3J 65
Upper Rd. Wall—5H 133
Up. Saint Martin's La. WC2
　　　　　—7J 61 (9C 140)
Up. Selsdon Rd. S Croy—7F 135
Up. Sheridan Rd. Belv—4G 85
Up. Shirley Rd. Croy—2J 135
Upper Sq. Iswth—3A 88
Upper St. N1—2B 62
Up. Sutton La. Houn—1E 86
Up. Tachbrook St. SW1
　　　　　—4G 77 (9M 145)
Up. Teddington Rd. King
　　　　　—1C 118
Upper Ter. NW3—3A 44
Up. Thames St. EC4
　　　　　—7B 62 (9K 141)
Up. Tollington Pk. N4—1A 46
(in two parts)
Upperton Rd. Sidc—5K 115
Upperton Rd. E. E13—3A 66
Upperton Rd. W. E13—3A 66
Up. Tooting Pk. SW17—2D 108
Up. Tooting Rd. SW17—4D 108
Up. Town Rd. Gnfd—4F 55
Up. Tulse Hill. SW2—7K 93
Up. Vernon Rd. Sutt—5B 132
Upper Wlk., The. Sutt—5K 131
Up. Walthamstow Rd. E17
　　　　　—3F 33
Up. Wickham La. Well—2B 100
Up. Wimpole St. W1
　　　　　—5E 60 (5H 139)
Up. Woburn Pl. WC1
　　　　　—3H 61 (2B 140)
Uppingham Av. Stan—1B 24
Upsdell Av. N13—6F 17
Upstall St. SE5—1B 94
Upton Av. E7—7J 49
Upton Clo. Bex—6F 101
Upton Dene. Sutt—7K 131
Upton Gdns. Harr—5B 24
Upton La. E7—7J 49
Upton Lodge Clo. Bush, Wat
　　　　　—1B 10
Upton Pk. Rd. E7—7K 49
Upton Rd. N18—5C 18
Upton Rd. SE18—6G 83
Upton Rd. Bexh & Bex—4E 100
Upton Rd. Houn—3E 86
Upton Rd. T Hth—2D 124
Upton Rd. S. Bex—6F 101
Upway. N12—6H 15
Upwood Rd. SE12—6J 97
Upwood Rd. SW16—1J 123
Urlwin St. SE5—6C 78
Urlwin Wlk. SW9—1A 94
Urmston Dri. SW19—1G 107
Ursula St. SW11—1C 92
Urswick Gdns. Dag—7E 52
Urswick Rd. E9—5J 47
Urswick Rd. Dag—7D 52
Usborne M. SW8—7K 77
Usher Rd. E3—2B 64
(in two parts)

Usk Rd. SW11—4A 92
Usk St. E2—3K 63 (1M 143)
Uvedale Rd. Dag—3G 53
Uvedale Rd. Enf—5J 7
Uverdale Rd. SW10—7A 76
Uxbridge Rd. W5 & W3—7E 56
Uxbridge Rd. W12—1C 74
Uxbridge Rd. W13 & W5—1B 72
Uxbridge Rd. Felt—2A 102
Uxbridge Rd. Hmptn—4E 102
Uxbridge Rd. King—4D 118
Uxbridge Rd. Pinn, Harr & Stan
　　　　　—2B 22
Uxbridge Rd. S'hall—1E 70
Uxbridge Rd. Uxb & Hay—7A 54
Uxbridge St. W8—1J 75
Uxendon Cres. Wemb—1E 40
Uxendon Hill. Wemb—1F 41

Valance Av. E4—1B 20
Valan Leas. Brom—3G 127
Vale Clo. W9—3A 60
Vale Cres. SW15—4A 106
Vale Croft. Pinn—5C 22
Vale Dri. Barn—4C 4
Vale End. SE22—4F 95
Vale Gro. N4—7C 30
Vale Gro. W3—2K 73
Vale La. W3—5G 57
Valence Av. Dag—1D 52
Valence Cir. Dag—3E 52
Valence Rd. Eri—7K 85
Valence Wood Rd. Dag—3D 52
Valencia Rd. Stan—4H 11
Valentia Pl. SW9—4A 94
Valentine Av. Bex—1E 116
Valentine St. SE23—2K 111
Valentine Pl. SE1
　　　　　—2B 78 (4J 147)
Valentine Rd. E9—6K 47
Valentine Rd. Harr—3F 39
Valentine Row. SE1
　　　　　—2B 78 (5J 147)
Valentines Rd. Ilf—1F 51
Valentine's Way. Romf—2K 53
Vale of Health. NW3—3A 44
Valerian Way. E15—3G 65
Vale Rise. NW11—1H 43
Vale Rd. E7—6K 49
Vale Rd. N4—7C 30
Vale Rd. Brom—1E 128
Vale Rd. Mitc—4H 123
Vale Rd. Sutt—4K 131
Vale Rd. Wor Pk & Eps—3B 130
Vale Row. N5—3B 46
Vale Royal. N7—7J 45
Vale St. SE27—3D 110
Valeswood Rd. Brom—5H 113
Vale Ter. N4—6C 30
Vale, The. N10—1E 28
Vale, The. N14—6E 6
Vale, The. NW11—2G 43
Vale, The. SW3—6B 76
Vale, The. W3—1B 74
Vale, The. Croy—2K 135
Vale, The. Felt—6A 86
Vale, The. Houn—6C 70
Vale, The. Ruis—4A 38
Vale, The. Wfd G—7D 20
Valetta Gro. E13—2J 65
Valetta Rd. W3—2A 74
Valette St. E9—6J 47
Valiant Clo. N'holt—3B 54
Valiant Clo. Romf—2H 37
Valiant Way. E6—5D 66
Vallance Rd.—4G 63 (3G 143)
　E1 1-121 & 2-168
　E2 remainder
Vallance Rd. N22—2G 29
Vallentin Rd. E17—4E 32
Valley Av. N12—4G 15
Valley Dri. NW9—6G 25
Valleyfield Rd. SW16—5K 109
Valley Fields Cres. Enf—2F 7
Valley Gdns. SW19—7B 108
Valley Gdns. Wemb—7F 41

Valley Gro. SE7—5A 82
Valley M. Twic—2K 103
Valley Rd. SW16—5K 109
Valley Rd. Belv—4H 85
Valley Rd. Brom—2G 127
Valley Rd. Eri—4K 85
Valley Rd. Orp—7B 116
Valley Side. E4—2H 19
Valley View. Barn—6B 4
Valley Wlk. Croy—2J 135
Valliere Rd. NW10—3C 58
Valliers Wood Rd. Sidc—1J 115
Vallis Way. W13—5A 56
Valmar Rd. SE5—1C 94
Valmar Trading Est. SE5
—1C 94
Valnay St. SW17—5D 108
Valognes Av. E17—1A 32
Valonia Gdns. SW18—6H 91
Vambery Rd. SE18—6G 83
Vanbrough Cres. N'holt—1A 54
Vanbrugh Clo. E16—5B 66
Vanbrugh Fields. SE3—7H 81
Vanbrugh Hill—5H 81
  SE3 1-31 & 2-44
  SE10 remainder
Vanbrugh Pk. SE3—7H 81
Vanbrugh Pk. Rd. SE3—7H 81
Vanbrugh Pk. Rd. W. SE3
—7H 81
Vanbrugh Rd. W4—3K 73
Vanbrugh Ter. SE3—1H 97
Vanburgh Clo. Orp—7J 129
Vancouver Rd. SE23—2A 112
Vancouver Rd. Edgw—1H 25
Vancouver Rd. Rich—4C 104
Vanderbilt Rd. SW18—1A 108
Vandome Clo. E16—6K 65
Vandon Pas. SW1
—3G 77 (6M 145)
Vandon St. SW1
—3G 77 (6M 145)
Van Dyck Av. N Mald—7K 119
Vandyke Clo. SW15—6F 91
Vandyke Cross. SE9—5C 98
Vandy St. EC2—4E 62 (4C 142)
Vane Clo. NW3—4B 44
Vane Clo. Harr—6F 25
Vanessa Clo. Belv—5G 85
Vanessa Way. Bex—3K 117
Vane St. SW1—4G 77 (8M 145)
Van Gogh Ct. E14—3F 81
Vanguard Clo. Croy—1B 134
Vanguard Clo. Romf—2H 37
Vanguard St. SE8—1C 96
Vanguard Way. Wall—7J 133
Vanoc Gdns. Brom—4J 113
Vansittart Rd. E7—4H 49
Vansittart St. SE14—6A 80
Vanston Pl. SW6—7J 75
Vant Rd. SW17—5D 108
Varcoe Rd. SE16—5H 79
Vardens Rd. SW11—4B 92
Varden St. E1—6H 63 (7J 143)
Vardon Clo. N3—1G 27
Varley Pde. NW9—4A 26
Varley Rd. E16—6K 65
Varley Way. Mitc—2B 122
Varna Rd. SW6—7G 75
Varndell St. NW1
—3G 61 (2L 139)
Vartry Rd. N15—6D 30
Vassall Rd. SW9—7A 78
Vauban Est. SE16
—3F 79 (7F 148)
Vauban St. SE16
—3F 79 (7F 148)
Vaughan Av. NW4—5C 26
Vaughan Av. W6—4B 74
Vaughan Clo. Hmptn—6C 102
Vaughan Gdns. Ilf—7D 34
Vaughan Rd. E15—6H 49
Vaughan Rd. SE5—2C 94
Vaughan Rd. Harr—7G 23
Vaughan Rd. Th Dit—7B 118
Vaughan Rd. Well—2K 99
Vaughan Way. E1
—1G 79 (1G 149)

Vaughan Williams Clo. SE8
—7C 80
Vauxhall Bri. SW1 & SE1—5J 77
Vauxhall Bri. Rd. SW1
—4G 77 (8L 145)
Vauxhall Cross. SE1—5J 77
Vauxhall Gdns. S Croy—6C 134
Vauxhall Gro. SW8—6K 77
Vauxhall St. SE11
—5K 77 (9F 146)
Vauxhall Wlk. SE11
—5K 77 (9E 146)
Vawdrey Clo. E1
—4J 63 (4L 143)
Vectis Gdns. SW17—6F 109
Vectis Rd. SW17—6F 109
Veda Rd. SE13—4C 96
Vega Rd. Bush, Wat—1B 10
Veldene Way. Harr—3D 38
Velde Way. SE22—5E 94
Vellum Dri. Cars—3E 132
Venables St. NW8
—4B 60 (4B 138)
Vencourt Pl. W6—4C 74
Venetian Rd. SE5—2C 94
Venetia Rd. N4—6B 30
Venetia Rd. W5—2D 72
Venner Rd. SE26—6J 111
Venn St. SW4—4G 93
Ventnor Av. Stan—1B 24
Ventnor Dri. N20—3E 14
Ventnor Gdns. Bark—6J 51
Ventnor Rd. SE14—7K 79
Ventnor Rd. Sutt—7K 131
Venture Clo. Bex—7E 100
Venue St. E14—5E 64
Venus Rd. SE18—3D 82
Vera Av. N21—5F 7
Vera Lynn Clo. E7—4J 49
Vera Rd. SW6—1G 91
Verbena Gdns. W6—5C 74
Verdant La. SE6—7G 97
Verdayne Av. Croy—2K 135
Verdun Rd. SE18—6A 84
Verdun Rd. SW13—6C 74
Vereker Rd. W14—5G 75
Vere St. W1—6F 61 (8J 139)
Verity Clo. W11—7G 59
Ver Meer Ct. E14—3F 81
Vermont Rd. SE19—6E 110
Vermont Rd. SW18—6K 91
Vermont Rd. Sutt—3K 131
Verney Gdns. Dag—4E 52
Verney Rd. SE16—5H 79
Verney Rd. Dag—4E 52
  (in two parts)
Verney St. NW10—3K 41
Verney Way. SE16—5H 79
Vernham Rd. SE18—6G 83
Vernon Av. E12—4D 50
Vernon Av. SW20—2F 121
Vernon Av. Wfd G—7E 20
Vernon Ct. W5—7C 56
Vernon Ct. Stan—1B 24
Vernon Cres. Barn—6K 5
Vernon Dri. Stan—1A 24
Vernon Pl. WC1—5J 61 (6D 140)
Vernon Rise. WC1
—3K 61 (1F 140)
Vernon Rise. Gnfd—5H 39
Vernon Rd. E3—2B 64
Vernon Rd. E11—2G 49
Vernon Rd. E15—7G 49
Vernon Rd. E17—5B 32
Vernon Rd. N8—3A 30
Vernon Rd. SW14—3K 89
Vernon Rd. Ilf—1K 51
Vernon Rd. Sutt—5B 132
Vernon Sq. WC1
—3K 61 (1F 140)
Vernon St. W14—4G 75
Vernon Yd. W11—7H 59
Veroan Rd. Bexh—2E 100
Verona Rd. E7—7J 49
Veronica Gdns. SW16—1G 123
Veronica Rd. SW17—2F 109
Veronique Gdns. Ilf—5G 35

Verran Rd. SW12—7F 93
Versailles Rd. SE20—7G 111
Verulam Av. E17—7B 32
Verulam Rd. Gnfd—4E 54
Verulam St. WC1
—5A 62 (5G 141)
Verwood Rd. Harr—2G 23
Vesey Path. E14—6D 64
Vespan Rd. W12—2C 74
Vesta Rd. SE4—2A 96
Vestris Rd. SE23—2K 111
Vestry M. SE5—1E 94
Vestry Rd. E17—4D 32
Vestry Rd. SE5—1E 94
Vestry St. N1—3D 62 (1A 142)
Vevey St. SE6—2B 112
Veysey Gdns. Dag—3G 53
Viaduct Bldgs. EC1
—5A 62 (6H 141)
Viaduct Pl. E2—3H 63 (2J 143)
Viaduct St. E2—3H 63 (2J 143)
Viaduct, The. E18—2K 33
Vian St. SE13—3D 96
Vibart Gdns. SW2—7K 93
Vicarage Av. SE3—7J 81
Vicarage Clo. Eri—6J 85
Vicarage Clo. N'holt—7D 38
Vicarage Ct. W8—2K 75
Vicarage Ct. Beck—3A 126
Vicarage Ct. Ilf—5F 51
Vicarage Cres. SW11—1B 92
Vicarage Dri. SW14—5K 89
Vicarage Dri. Bark—7G 51
Vicarage Farm Rd. Houn
—2C 86
Vicarage Field Shopping
  Centre. Bark—7G 51
Vicarage Gdns. W8—1J 75
Vicarage Gdns. Mitc—3C 122
Vicarage Ga. W8—1K 75
Vicarage Gro. SE5—1D 94
Vicarage La. E6—3D 66
Vicarage La. E15—7G 49
Vicarage La. Eps—7C 130
Vicarage La. Ilf—1H 51
Vicarage M. NW9—2K 41
Vicarage Pk. SE18—5G 83
Vicarage Path. N8—7H 29
Vicarage Rd. E10—7C 32
Vicarage Rd. E15—7H 49
Vicarage Rd. N17—1G 31
Vicarage Rd. NW4—6C 26
Vicarage Rd. SE18—5G 83
Vicarage Rd. SW14—5K 89
Vicarage Rd. Bex—1H 117
Vicarage Rd. Croy—3A 134
Vicarage Rd. Dag—7H 53
Vicarage Rd. King—2D 118
Vicarage Rd. King—1C 118
  (Hampton Wick)
Vicarage Rd. Sutt—3K 131
Vicarage Rd. Tedd—5A 104
Vicarage Rd. Twic—2J 103
Vicarage Rd. Twic—6G 87
  (Whitton)
Vicarage Rd. Wfd G—7H 21
Vicarage Wlk. SW11—1B 92
Vicarage Way. NW10—3K 41
Vicarage Way. Harr—7E 22
Vicars Bri. Clo. Wemb—2E 56
Vicar's Clo. E9—1J 63
Vicars Clo. E15—1J 65
Vicars Clo. Enf—2K 7
Vicar's Hill. SE13—4D 96
Vicars Moor La. N21—7G 7
Vicars Oak Rd. SE19—6E 110
Vicar's Rd. NW5—5E 44
Vicars Wlk. Dag—3B 52
Viceroy Clo. N2—4C 28
Viceroy Ct. Croy—1D 134
Viceroy Rd. SW8—1J 93
Vickers Rd. Eri—5K 85
Victor Gro. Wemb—7E 40
Victoria Av. E6—1B 66
Victoria Av. EC2
—5E 62 (6D 142)

Victoria Av. N3—1H 27
Victoria Av. Barn—4G 5
Victoria Av. Houn—5E 86
Victoria Av. Surb—6D 118
Victoria Av. Wall—3E 132
Victoria Av. Wemb—6H 41
Victoria Clo. Barn—4G 5
Victoria Cotts. Rich—1F 89
Victoria Ct. SE26—6J 111
Victoria Ct. Wemb—6G 41
Victoria Cres. N15—5E 30
Victoria Cres. SE19—6E 110
Victoria Cres. SW19—7H 107
Victoria Dock Rd. E16—6G 65
Victoria Dri. SW19—7F 91
Victoria Embkmt. SW1, WC2 &
  EC4—2J 77 (4D 146)
Victoria Gdns. W11—1J 75
Victoria Gdns. Houn—1C 86
Victoria Gro. N12—5G 15
Victoria Gro. W8—3A 76
Victoria Gro. M. W2—7J 59
Victoria Industrial Est., The
  NW10—4A 58
Victoria La. Barn—4C 4
Victoria M. NW6—1J 59
Victoria M. SW4—4F 93
Victorian Gro. N16—3E 46
Victorian Rd. N16—3F 47
Victoria Pk. Rd. E9—1J 63
Victoria Pk. Sq. E2
—3J 63 (1L 143)
Victoria Pl. Rich—5D 88
Victoria Rise. SW4—3F 93
Victoria Rd. E4—1B 20
Victoria Rd. E11—4G 49
Victoria Rd. E13—2J 65
Victoria Rd. E17—2E 32
Victoria Rd. E18—3K 33
Victoria Rd. N4—7K 29
Victoria Rd. N15—4G 31
Victoria Rd.—4A 18
  N18 1-55
  N9 remainder
Victoria Rd. N22—1G 29
Victoria Rd. NW4—4E 26
Victoria Rd. NW6—2H 59
Victoria Rd. NW7—5G 13
Victoria Rd. SW14—3K 89
Victoria Rd. W3 & NW10—5K 57
Victoria Rd. W5—5B 56
Victoria Rd. W8—3A 76
Victoria Rd. Bark—6F 51
Victoria Rd. Barn—4G 5
Victoria Rd. Bexh—6G 101
Victoria Rd. Brom—5B 128
Victoria Rd. Buck H—2G 21
Victoria Rd. Bush, Wat—1A 10
Victoria Rd. Chst—5E 114
Victoria Rd. Dag—5H 53
Victoria Rd. Eri—6K 85
Victoria Rd. King—2F 119
Victoria Rd. Mitc—7C 108
Victoria Rd. Sidc—3K 115
Victoria Rd. S'hall—3D 70
Victoria Rd. Surb—6D 118
Victoria Rd. Sutt—5B 132
Victoria Rd. Tedd—6K 103
Victoria Rd. Twic—7B 88
Victoria Sq. SW1
—3F 77 (6K 145)
Victoria St. E15—7G 49
Victoria St. SW1
—3G 77 (7L 145)
Victoria St. Belv—5F 85
Victoria Ter. N4—1A 46
Victoria Ter. Harr—1J 39
Victoria Vs. Rich—4F 89
Victoria Way. SE7—5K 81
Victor Rd. NW10—3D 58
Victor Rd. SE20—7K 111
Victor Rd. Harr—3G 23
Victor Rd. Tedd—4J 103
Victors Dri. Hmptn—6C 102
Victors Way. Barn—3C 4
Victor Vs. N9—3J 17
Victory Av. Mord—5A 122

281

Victory Business Centre Iswth
—4K 87
Victory Pl. SE17
—4D 78 (8A 148)
Victory Pl. SE19—7E 110
Victory Rd. SW19—7A 108
Victory Sq. SE5—6D 78
Victory Wlk. SE8—1C 96
Victory Way. SE16—2A 80
Victory Way. Houn—5A 70
Victory Way. Romf—2H 37
Vienna Clo. Ilf—2C 34
View Clo. N6—7D 28
View Clo. Harr—4H 23
Viewfield Clo. Harr—7E 24
Viewfield Rd. SW18—6H 91
Viewfield Rd. Bex—1C 116
Viewland Rd. SE18—5K 83
View Rd. N6—7D 28
View, The. SE2—5E 84
Viga Rd. N21—6F 7
Vigilant Clo. SE26—4G 111
Vignoles Rd. Romf—7G 37
Vigo Rd. W1—7G 61 (1L 145)
Viking Ct. SW6—6J 75
Viking Rd. S'hall—7C 54
Villacourt Rd. SE18—7A 84
Village Arc. E4—1A 20
Village Clo. E4—5K 19
Village Rd. N3—2G 27
Village Rd. Enf—7J 7
Village Row. Sutt—7J 131
Village, The. SE7—6B 82
Village Way. NW10—4K 41
Village Way. SE21—6D 94
Village Way. Beck—2C 126
Village Way. Pinn—7C 22
Village Way E. Harr—7E 22
Villa Rd. SW9—3A 94
Villas Rd. SE18—4G 83
(in two parts)
Villa St. SE17—5D 78
Villa Wlk. SE17—5D 78
Villiers Av. Surb—5F 119
Villiers Av Twic—1D 102
Villiers Clo. E10—2C 48
Villiers Clo. Surb—4F 119
Villiers Path. Surb—5E 118
Villiers Rd. NW2—6C 42
Villiers Rd. Beck—2K 125
Villiers Rd. Iswth—2J 87
Villiers Rd. King—4F 119
Villiers Rd. S'hall—1D 70
Villiers St. WC2—1J 77 (2D 146)
Vincam Clo. Twic—7E 86
Vincent Clo. SE16—2A 80
Vincent Clo. Barn—3E 4
Vincent Clo. Brom—4K 127
Vincent Clo. Sidc—1J 115
Vincent Ct. N4—1J 45
Vincent Gdns. NW2—3B 42
Vincent Rd. E4—6A 20
Vincent Rd. N15—4C 30
Vincent Rd. N22—2A 30
Vincent Rd. SE18—4F 83
Vincent Rd. W3—3J 73
Vincent Rd. Croy—7E 124
Vincent Rd. Dag—7E 52
Vincent Rd. Houn—3B 86
Vincent Rd. Iswth—1H 87
Vincent Rd. King—3G 119
Vincent Rd. Wemb—7F 41
Vincent Row. Hmptn—6G 103
Vincent Sq. SW1
—4H 77 (8A 146)
Vincent St. E16—5H 65
Vincent St. SW1
—4H 77 (8A 146)
Vincent Ter. N1—2B 62
Vince St. EC1—3D 62 (2B 142)
Vine Clo. Surb—6F 119
Vine Clo. Sutt—3A 132
Vine Ct. E1—5G 63 (6H 143)
Vine Ct. Harr—6E 24
Vinegar All. E17—4D 32
Vine Gdns. Ilf—5G 51
Vinegar St. E1—1H 79 (2J 149)

Vine Hill EC1—4A 62 (4G 141)
Vine La. SE1—1E 78 (3D 148)
Vine Pl. Houn—4F 87
Vineries Bank. NW7—5J 13
Vineries Clo. Dag—6F 53
Vineries, The. N14—6B 6
Vineries, The. SE16—1C 112
Vineries, The. Enf—3K 7
Vine Rd. E15—7H 49
Vine Rd. SW13—3B 90
Vines Av. N3—1K 27
Vine St. EC3—7F 63 (9E 142)
(in two parts)
Vine St. W1—7G 61 (1M 145)
Vine St. Romf—4J 37
Vine St. Bri. EC1
—4A 62 (4H 141)
Vineyard Av. NW7—7B 14
Vineyard Clo. SE6—1C 112
Vineyard Hill Rd. SW19—4J 107
Vineyard Pas. Rich—5E 88
Vineyard Path. SW14—3K 89
Vineyard Row. King—1C 118
Vineyard, The. Rich—5E 88
Vineyard Wlk. EC1
—4A 62 (3G 141)
Viney Bank. Croy—7B 136
Viney Rd. SE13—3D 96
Vining St. SW9—4A 94
Vinson Clo. Orp—7K 129
Vintners Pl. EC4
—7C 62 (9M 141)
Viola Av. SE2—4B 84
Viola Av. Felt—6A 86
Viola Sq. W12—7B 58
Violet Av. Enf—1J 7
Violet Clo. Wall—1E 132
Violet Gdns. Croy—5B 134
Violet Hill. NW8—2A 60
Violet La. Croy—5B 134
Violet Rd. E3—4D 64
Violet Rd. E17—6C 32
Violet Rd. E18—2K 33
Violet St. E2—4H 63 (3K 143)
Virgil Pl. W1—5D 60 (6E 138)
Virgil St. SE1—3K 77 (6F 146)
Virginia Clo. N Mald—4J 119
Virginia Gdns. Ilf—2H 35
Virginia Rd. E2—3F 63 (2E 142)
Virginia Rd. T Hth—1B 124
Virginia St. E1—7G 63 (1H 149)
Virginia Wlk. SW2—6K 93
Viscount Dri. E6—5D 66
Viscount Gro. N'holt—3B 54
Viscount St. EC1
—4C 62 (4L 141)
Vista Av. Enf—2E 8
Vista Dri. Ilf—5B 34
Vista, The. SE9—6B 98
Vista, The. Sidc—5K 115
Vista Way. Harr—6E 24
Vivian Av. NW4—5D 26
Vivian Av. Wemb—5G 41
Vivian Gdns. Wemb—5G 41
Vivian Rd. E3—2A 64
Vivian Sq. SE15—3H 95
Vivian Way. N2—5B 28
Vivienne Clo. Twic—6D 88
Voce Rd. SE18—7H 83
Voewood Clo. N Mald—6B 120
Voltaire Rd. SW4—3H 93
Voluntary Pl. E11—6J 33
Vorley Rd. N19—2G 45
Voss Ct. SW16—6J 109
Voss St. E2—3G 63 (2H 143)
Vulcan Clo. Wall—7K 133
Vulcan Ga. Enf—2F 7
Vulcan Rd. SE4—2B 96
Vulcan Ter. SE4—2B 96
Vulcan Way. N7—6K 45
Vyner Rd. W3—7K 57
Vyner St. E2—1H 63
Vyne, The. Bexh—3H 101

Wadding St. SE17
—4D 78 (9A 148)

Waddington Rd. E15—5F 49
Waddington St. E15—6F 49
Waddington Way. SE19
—7C 110
Waddon Clo. Croy—3A 134
Waddon Ct. Rd. Croy—3A 134
Waddon Marsh Way. Croy
—1K 133
Waddon New Rd. Croy—3B 134
Waddon Pk. Av. Croy—4A 134
Waddon Rd. Croy—3A 134
Waddon Way. Croy—6A 134
Wade Ho. Enf—5K 7
Wade Rd. E16—6A 66
Wades Gro. N21—7F 7
Wades Hill. N21—6F 7
Wades La. Tedd—5A 104
Wadeson St. E2—2H 63
Wade's Pl. E14—7D 64
Wadeville Av. Romf—7F 37
Wadeville Clo. Belv—5G 85
Wadham Av. E17—7J 19
Wadham Gdns. NW3—7C 44
Wadham Gdns. Gnfd—6H 39
Wadham Rd. E17—1D 32
Wadham Rd. SW15—4G 91
Wadhurst Clo. SE20—2H 125
Wadhurst Rd. SW8—1G 93
Wadhurst Rd. W4—3K 73
Wadley Rd. E11—7G 33
Wadsworth Clo. Enf—5E 8
Wadsworth Clo. Gnfd—2C 56
Wadsworth Rd. Gnfd—2B 56
Wager St. E3—4B 64
Waggon La. N17—6B 18
Waggon M. N14—1B 16
Waghorn Rd. E13—1A 66
Waghorn Rd. Harr—3D 24
Waghorn St. SE15—3G 95
Wagner St. SE15—7J 79
Waights Ct. King—1E 118
Wainfleet Av. Romf—2J 37
Wainford Clo. SW19—1F 107
Wainwright Gro. Iswth—4H 87
Waite Davies Rd. SE12—7H 97
Waite St. SE15—6F 79
Wakefield Gdns. SE19—7E 110
Wakefield Gdns. Ilf—6C 34
Wakefield M. WC1
—3J 61 (2D 140)
Wakefield Rd. N11—5C 16
Wakefield Rd. N15—5F 31
Wakefield Rd. Rich—5D 88
Wakefield St. E6—1B 66
Wakefield St. N18—5B 18
Wakefield St. WC1
—4J 61 (3D 140)
Wakehams Hill. Pinn—3D 22
Wakeham St. N1—6D 46
Wakehurst Rd. SW11—5C 92
Wakeling Rd. W7—5K 55
Wakeling St. E14—6A 64
Wakelin Rd. E15—2G 65
Wakeman Rd. NW10—3E 58
Wakemans Hill Av. NW9
—5K 25
Wakering Rd. Bark—6G 51
Wakerley Clo. E6—6D 66
Wakley St. EC1—3B 62 (1J 141)
Walberswick St. SW8—7J 77
Walbrook. EC4—7D 62 (9A 142)
Walburgh St. E1
—6H 63 (8J 143)
Walcorde Av. SE17
—4C 78 (9M 147)
Walcot Rd. Enf—2G 9
Walcot Sq. SE11
—4A 78 (8H 147)
Walcott St. SW1
—4G 77 (8M 145)
Waldeck Gro. SE27—3B 110
Waldeck Rd. N15—4B 30
Waldeck Rd. SW14—3J 89
Waldeck Rd. W4—6G 73
Waldeck Rd. W13—6B 56
Waldegrave Av. Tedd—5K 103

Waldegrave Gdns. Twic
—3K 103
Waldegrave Pk. Twic—4K 103
Waldegrave Rd. N8—3A 30
Waldegrave Rd. SE19—7F 111
Waldegrave Rd. W5—7F 57
Waldegrave Rd. Brom—4C 128
Waldegrave Rd. Dag—2C 52
Waldegrave Rd. Twic & Tedd
—4K 103
Waldegrove. Croy—4F 135
Waldemar Av. SW6—1G 91
Waldemar Av. W13—1C 72
Waldemar Rd. SW19—5J 107
Walden Av. N13—4H 17
Walden Av. Chst—4D 114
Walden Av. Rain—2K 69
Walden Clo. Belv—5F 85
Walden Gdns. T Hth—3K 123
Walden Rd. N17—1D 30
Walden Rd. Chst—6D 114
Waldenshaw Rd. SE23—1J 111
Walden St. E1—6H 63 (7J 143)
Walden Way. NW7—6A 14
Waldo Clo. SW4—5G 93
Waldo Pl. Mitc—7C 108
Waldorf Clo. S Croy—7B 134
Waldo Rd. NW10—3C 58
Waldo Rd. Brom—3B 128
Waldram Cres. SE23—1J 111
Waldram Pk. Rd. SE23—1K 111
Waldram Rd. SE23—1J 111
Waldrist Way. Eri—2F 85
Waldron Gdns. Brom—3F 127
Waldronhyrst. S Croy—4B 134
Waldron M. SW3—6B 76
Waldron Rd. SW18—3A 108
Waldron Rd. Harr—1J 39
Waldron's Path. S Croy
—4C 134
Waldrons, The. Croy—4B 134
Waldrons Yd. Harr—2H 39
Waleran Clo. Stan—5E 10
Walerand Rd. SE13—2E 96
Wales Av. Cars—5C 132
Wales Farm Rd. W3—5K 57
Waley St. E1—5A 64
Walfield Av. N20—7E 4
Walford Rd. N16—4E 46
Walfrey Gdns. Dag—7E 52
Walham Gro. SW6—7J 75
Walham Rise. SW19—6G 107
Walham Yd. SW6—7J 75
Walkden Rd. Chst—5E 114
Walker Clo. N11—4B 16
Walker Clo. SE18—4G 83
Walker Clo. W7—1J 71
Walker Clo. Hmptn—6D 102
Walkerscroft Mead. SE21
—1C 110
Walkers Pl. SW15—4G 91
Walkford Way. SE15—7F 79
Wallace Clo. SE28—7D 68
Wallace Cres. Cars—5D 132
Wallace Rd. N1—6C 46
Wallcote Av. NW2—1F 43
Wall End Rd. E6—7E 50
Waller Rd. SE14—1K 95
Wallers Clo. Wfd G—6J 21
Wallflower St. W12—7B 58
Wallgrave Rd. SW5—4K 75
Wallingford Av. W10—6F 59
Wallington Rd. Ilf—7K 35
Wallington Sq. Wall—6G 133
Wallis Clo. SW11—3B 92
Wallis Rd. E9—6B 48
Wallis Rd. S'hall—5F 55
Wallorton Gdns. SW14—4K 89
Wall St. N1—6D 46
Wallwood Rd. E11—7F 33
Wallwood St. E14—5B 64
Walmer Clo. Barn—1G 5
Walmer Clo. Romf—2H 37
Walmer Gdns. W13—2A 72
Walmer Rd. W11—7G 59
Walmer St. W1—5D 60 (5E 138)

282

Walmer Ter. SE18—4G 83
Walmgate Rd. Gnfd—1B 56
Walmington Fold. N12—6D 14
Walm La. NW2—6E 42
Walney Wlk. N1—6C 46
Walnut Clo. SE8—6B 80
Walnut Clo. Cars—5D 132
Walnut Clo. Ilf—4G 35
Walnut Ct. W5—2E 72
Walnut Fields. Eps—7B 130
Walnut Gdns. E15—5G 49
Walnut Gro. Enf—5J 7
Walnut M. Sutt—7A 132
Walnut Tree Av. Mitc—3C 122
Walnut Tree Clo. SW13—1B 90
Walnut Tree Clo. Chst—1H 129
Walnut Tree Cotts. SW19
—5G 107
Walnut Tree Rd. SE10—5G 81
(in two parts)
Walnut Tree Rd. Bren—6E 72
Walnut Tree Rd. Dag—2E 52
Walnut Tree Rd. Houn—6D 70
Walnut Tree Wlk. SE11
—4A 78 (8G 147)
Walnut Way. Buck H—3G 21
Walnut Way. Ruis—6A 38
Walpole Av. Rich—2F 89
Walpole Clo. W13—2C 72
Walpole Cres. Tedd—5K 103
Walpole Gdns. W4—5J 73
Walpole Gdns. Twic—2J 103
Walpole Pl. SE18—4F 83
Walpole Pl. Tedd—5K 103
Walpole Rd. E6—7A 50
Walpole Rd. E17—4B 32
Walpole Rd. E18—1H 33
Walpole Rd. N17—3C 30
(in two parts)
Walpole Rd. SE14—7B 80
Walpole Rd. SW19—6B 108
Walpole Rd. Brom—5B 128
Walpole Rd. Croy—2D 134
Walpole Rd. Surb—6E 118
Walpole Rd. Tedd—5K 103
Walpole Rd. Twic—2J 103
Walpole St. SW3
—5D 76 (9F 144)
Walrond Av. Wemb—5E 40
Walsham Clo. N16—1G 47
Walsham Clo. SE28—7D 68
Walsham Rd. SE14—2K 95
Walsham Rd. Felt—7A 86
Walsingham Gdns. Eps
—4A 130
Walsingham Pk. Chst—2H 129
Walsingham Rd. E5—3G 47
Walsingham Rd. W13—1A 72
Walsingham Rd. Enf—5J 7
Walsingham Rd. Mitc—5D 122
Walsingham Wlk. Belv—6G 85
Walters Rd. SE25—4E 124
Walters Rd. Enf—4D 8
Walter St. E2—3K 63 (2M 143)
Walter St. King—1E 118
Walters Way. SE23—6K 95
Walters Yd. Brom—2J 127
Walter Ter. E1—6K 63
Walterton Rd. W9—4H 59
Walter Wlk. Edgw—6D 12
Waltham Av. NW9—6G 25
Waltham Dri. Edgw—2G 25
Waltham Pk. Way. E17—1C 32
Waltham Rd. Cars—7B 122
Waltham Rd. S'hall—3C 70
Waltham Rd. Wfd G—6H 21
Walthamstow Av. E4—6F 19
Waltham Way. E4—3G 19
Waltheof Av. N17—1D 30
Waltheof Gdns. N17—1D 30
Walton Av. Harr—5D 38
Walton Av. N Mald—4B 120
Walton Av. Sutt—3H 131
Walton Clo. E5—3K 47
Walton Clo. NW2—2D 42
Walton Clo. SW8—7J 77
Walton Clo. Harr—4H 23

Walton Dri. NW10—6K 41
Walton Dri. Harr—4H 23
Walton Gdns. W3—5H 57
Walton Gdns. Wemb—2E 40
Walton Grn. Croy—7E 136
Walton Pl. SW3—3D 76 (6E 144)
Walton Rd. E12—4E 50
(in two parts)
Walton Rd. E13—2A 66
Walton Rd. N15—4F 31
Walton Rd. Harr—4H 23
Walton Rd. Romf—1F 37
Walton Rd. Sidc—3B 116
Walton St. SW3—4C 76 (8D 144)
Walton St. Enf—1J 7
Walton Way. W3—5H 57
Walton Way. Mitc—4G 123
Walworth Pl. SE17—5C 78
Walworth Rd.—4C 78 (9L 147)
SE1 2-96
SE17 remainder
Walwyn Av. Brom—3B 128
Wanborough Dri. SW15
—1D 106
Wandle Bank. SW19—7B 108
Wandle Bank. Croy—3J 133
Wandle Ct. Gdns. Croy—3J 133
Wandle Pk. Trading Est. Croy
—1A 134
Wandle Rd. SW17—2C 108
Wandle Rd. Croy—3C 134
Wandle Rd. Croy—3J 133
(Beddington)
Wandle Rd. Mord—4A 122
Wandle Rd. Wall—2F 133
Wandle Side. Croy—3K 133
Wandle Side. Wall—3F 133
Wandle Way. SW18—1K 107
Wandle Way. Mitc—5D 122
Wandon Rd. SW6—7K 75
Wandsworth Bri. SW6 & SW18
—3K 91
Wandsworth Bri. Rd. SW6
—1K 91
Wandsworth Comn. N. Side.
SW18—5B 92
Wandsworth Comn. W. Side.
SW18—5A 92
Wandsworth High St. SW18
—5J 91
Wandsworth Plain. SW18
—5K 91
Wandsworth Rd. SW8—3F 93
Wangye Rd. Romf—7D 36
Wanless Rd. SE24—3C 94
Wanley Rd. SE5—4D 94
Wanlip Rd. E13—4K 65
Wannock Gdns. Ilf—1F 35
Wansbeck Rd. E9—7B 48
Wansdown Pl. SW6—7K 75
Wansey St. SE17
—4C 78 (9M 147)
Wansford Rd. Wfd G—1A 34
Wanstead Clo. Brom—2A 128
Wanstead Gdns. Ilf—6B 34
Wanstead La. Ilf—6C 34
Wanstead Pk. Av. E12—2B 50
Wanstead Pk. Rd. Ilf—7C 34
Wanstead Pl. E11—6J 33
Wanstead Rd. Brom—2A 128
Wansunt Rd. Bex—1J 117
Wantage Rd. SE12—5H 97
Wantz Rd. Dag—4H 53
Wapping Dock St. E1
—1H 79 (3K 149)
Wapping High St. E1
—1G 79 (3H 149)
Wapping La. E1—7H 63 (1K 149)
Wapping Wall. E1
—1J 79 (2L 149)
Warbank La. King—7B 106
Warbeck Rd. W12—2D 74
Warberry Rd. N22—1K 29
Warboys App. King—6H 105
Warboys Cres. E4—5K 19
Warboys Rd. King—6H 105
Warburton Clo. Harr—6C 10

Warburton Rd. E8—1H 63
Warburton Rd. Twic—1F 103
Warburton Ter. E17—2D 32
Wardale Clo. SE16
—3H 79 (7K 149)
Wardalls Clo. SE14—7J 79
Ward Clo. Eri—6K 85
Wardell Clo. NW7—7F 13
Wardell Field. NW9—1A 26
Warden Av. Harr—1D 38
Warden Rd. NW5—6E 44
Wardens Gro. SE1
—1C 78 (3L 147)
Wardle St. E9—5K 47
Wardley St. SW18—7K 91
Wardo Av. SW6—1G 91
Wardour St. W1
—6G 61 (8M 139)
Ward Rd. E15—1F 65
Ward Rd. N19—3G 45
Wards Rd. SW19—1A 122
Wards Rd. Ilf—7H 35
Ware Ct. Sutt—4H 131
Wareham Ho. Houn—4F 87
Waremead Rd. Ilf—5F 35
Warfield Rd. NW10—3F 59
Warfield Rd. Hmptn—7F 103
Wargrave Av. N15—6F 31
Wargrave Rd. Harr—3G 39
Warham Rd. N4—5A 30
Warham Rd. Croy & S Croy
—5B 134
Warham Rd. Harr—2K 23
Warham St. SE5—7B 78
(in two parts)
Waring Rd. Sidc—6C 116
Waring St. SE27—4C 110
Warkworth Gdns. Iswth—7A 72
Warkworth Rd. N17—7J 17
Warland Rd. SE18—7H 83
Warley Av. Dag—7F 37
Warley Clo. E10—1B 48
Warley Rd. N9—2D 18
Warley Rd. Ilf—1E 34
Warley Rd. Wfd G—7E 20
Warley Rd. E2—3K 63 (2M 143)
Warlingham Rd. T Hth—4B 124
Warlock Rd. W9—4H 59
Warlters Clo. N7—4J 45
Warlters Rd. N7—4J 45
Warltersville Rd. N19—7J 29
Warmington Rd. SE24—6C 94
Warminster Gdns. SE25
—2G 125
Warminster Rd. SE25—3G 125
Warminster Sq. SE25—2G 125
Warminster Way. Mitc—1F 123
Warndon St. SE16
—4K 79 (9M 149)
Warneford Rd. Harr—3D 24
Warneford St. E9—1H 63
Warner Av. Sutt—2G 131
Warner Clo. E15—5G 49
Warner Clo. NW9—7B 26
Warner Clo. Wfd G—5D 20
Warner Pl. E2—2G 63 (1H 143)
Warner Rd. E17—4H 32
Warner Rd. N8—4H 29
Warner Rd. SE5—1C 94
Warner Rd. Brom—7H 113
Warners La. Rich & King
—4D 104
Warners Path. Wfd G—5D 20
Warner St. EC1—4A 62 (4G 141)
Warnham Ct. Rd. Cars—7D 132
Warnham Rd. N12—5H 15
Warple Way. W3—2A 74
Warren Av. E10—3E 48
Warren Av. Brom—7G 113
Warren Av. Rich—4H 89
Warren Av. S Croy—7K 135
Warren Clo. N9—7E 8
Warren Clo. SE21—7C 94
Warren Clo. Bexh—5G 101
Warren Clo. Wemb—2D 40
Warren Ct. Beck—7C 112
Warren Cres. N9—7A 8

Warren Cutting. King—7K 105
Warrender Rd. N19—4G 45
Warren Dri. Gnfd—4F 55
Warren Dri. Ruis—7B 22
Warren Dri. N. Surb—7H 119
Warren Dri. S. Surb—7J 119
Warren Dri., The. E11—7A 34
Warren Footpath. Twic
—1C 104
Warren Gdns. E15—5F 49
Warren La. SE18—3F 83
Warren La. Stan—2F 11
Warren M. W1—4G 61 (4L 139)
Warren Pk. King—6J 105
Warren Pk. Rd. Sutt—6C 132
Warren Pond Rd. E4—1C 20
Warren Rise. N Mald—1K 119
Warren Rd. E4—2K 19
Warren Rd. E10—3E 48
Warren Rd. E11—6A 34
Warren Rd. NW2—2B 42
Warren Rd. SW19—6C 108
Warren Rd. Bexh—5G 101
Warren Rd. Brom—2J 137
Warren Rd. Bush, Wat—1B 10
Warren Rd. Croy—1F 135
Warren Rd. Ilf—5H 35
Warren Rd. King—6J 105
Warren Rd. Sidc—3C 116
Warren Rd. Twic—5G 87
Warrens Shawe La. Edgw
—2C 12
Warren St. W1—4G 61 (4L 139)
Warren Ter. Romf—4D 36
Warren, The. E12—4C 50
Warren, The. Houn—7D 70
Warren, The. Wor Pk—3A 130
Warren Wlk. SE7—6A 82
Warren Way. NW7—6B 14
Warren Wood Clo. Brom
—2H 137
Warriner Gdns. SW11—1D 92
Warrington Cres. W9—4A 60
Warrington Gdns. W9—4A 60
Warrington Rd. Croy—3B 134
Warrington Rd. Dag—2D 52
Warrington Rd. Harr—5J 23
Warrington Rd. Rich—5D 88
Warrington Sq. Dag—2D 52
Warrior Sq. E12—4E 50
Warsaw Clo. Ruis—6A 38
Warspite Rd. SE18—3C 82
Warton Rd. E15—7E 48
Warwick Av.—4K 59
W2 1-5a & 2-16
W9 remainder
Warwick Av. Edgw—3C 12
Warwick Av. Harr—4D 38
Warwick Clo. Barn—5G 5
Warwick Clo. Bush, Wat—1D 10
Warwick Clo. Hmptn—7G 103
Warwick Ct. WC1
—5K 61 (6F 140)
Warwick Ct. Barn—5E 4
Warwick Cres. W2—5A 60
Warwick Dene. W5—1E 72
Warwick Dri. SW15—3D 90
Warwick Est. W2—5K 59
Warwick Gdns. N4—5C 30
Warwick Gdns. W14—4H 75
Warwick Gdns. Ilf—1F 51
Warwick Gdns. T Hth—4A 124
Warwick Gro. E5—1H 47
Warwick Gro. Surb—7F 119
Warwick Ho. St. SW1
—1H 77 (2B 146)
Warwick La. EC4
—6B 62 (7K 141)
Warwick Pl. W5—2D 72
Warwick Pl. W9—5A 60
Warwick Pl. N. SW1
—4G 77 (9L 145)
Warwick Rd. E4—5H 19
Warwick Rd. E11—5K 33
Warwick Rd. E12—5C 50
Warwick Rd. E15—6H 49
Warwick Rd. E17—1B 32

Warwick Rd. N11—6C 16
Warwick Rd. N18—4K 17
Warwick Rd. SE20—3H 125
Warwick Rd.—4H 75
SW5 1-133 & 2-76
W14 remainder
Warwick Rd. W5—2D 72
Warwick Rd. Barn—4E 4
Warwick Rd. Houn—3A 86
Warwick Rd. King—1C 118
Warwick Rd. N Mald—3J 119
Warwick Rd. Sidc—5B 116
Warwick Rd. S'hall—3D 70
Warwick Rd. Sutt—4A 132
Warwick Rd. T Hth—3A 124
Warwick Rd. Twic—1J 103
Warwick Rd. Well—3C 100
Warwick Row. SW1
—3G 77 (6L 145)
Warwickshire Path. SE8—7B 80
Warwick Sq. EC4
—6B 62 (7K 141)
Warwick Sq. SW1
—5G 77 (9L 145)
Warwick Sq. M. SW1
—4G 77 (9L 145)
Warwick St. W1
—7G 61 (9M 139)
Warwick Ter. SE18—6H 83
Warwick Way. SW1
—5F 77 (9K 145)
Warwick Yd. EC1
—4C 62 (4M 141)
Washington Av. E12—4C 50
Washington Rd. E6—7A 50
Washington Rd. E18—2H 33
Washington Rd. SW13—7C 74
Washington Rd. King—2G 119
Washington Rd. Wor Pk
—2D 130
Wastdale Rd. SE23—1K 111
Watchfield Ct. W4—5J 73
Watcombe Cotts. Rich—6G 73
Watcombe Pl. Croy—4H 125
Watcombe Rd. SE25—5H 125
Waterbank Rd. SE6—4E 112
Waterbeach Dri. NW9—2A 26
Waterbeach Rd. Dag—6C 52
Water Brook La. NW4—5E 26
Waterdale Rd. SE2—6A 84
Waterden Rd. E15—5C 48
Waterer Ho. SE6—4E 112
Waterer Rise. Wall—6H 133
Waterfall Clo. N14—3B 16
Waterfall Cotts. SW19—6B 108
Waterfall Rd.—4A 16
N11 1-27 & 2-46
N14 remainder
Waterfall Rd. SW19—6B 108
Waterfall Ter. SW17—6C 108
Waterfall Wlk. N14—1A 16
Waterfield Clo. SE28—1B 84
Waterfield Gdns. SE28—1B 84
Waterflow Rd. N19—1G 45
Waterford Rd. SW6—7K 75
Water Gdns. Stan—6G 11
Watergardens, The. King
—6J 105
Watergate. EC4—7B 62 (9J 141)
Watergate. SE8—6C 80
Watergate Wlk. WC2
—1J 77 (2D 146)
Waterglade Centre, The. W5
—7D 56
Waterhall Av. E4—4B 20
Waterhall Clo. E17—1K 31
Waterhouse Clo. E16—5B 48
Waterhouse Clo. NW3—5B 44
Waterhouse Clo. W6—4F 75
Water La. E15—6G 49
Water La. NW1—7F 45
Water La. Ilf—3K 51
Water La. King—1D 118
Water La. Rich—5D 88
Water La. Sidc—3F 117
Water La. Twic—1A 104

Waterloo Bri. WC2 & SE1
—7K 61 (1F 146)
Waterloo Clo. E9—5J 47
Waterloo Gdns. E2—2J 63
Waterloo Gdns. Romf—6K 37
Waterloo Pas. NW6—7H 43
Waterloo Pl. SW1
—1H 77 (2A 146)
Waterloo Pl. Rich—4E 88
Waterloo Rd. E6—7A 50
Waterloo Rd. E7—5H 49
Waterloo Rd. E10—7C 32
Waterloo Rd. NW2—1C 42
Waterloo Rd. SE1
—2A 78 (4H 147)
Waterloo Rd. Ilf—2G 35
Waterloo Rd. Romf—6K 37
Waterloo Rd. Sutt—5B 132
Waterlow Ter. N1—7B 46
Waterlow Rd. N19—1G 45
Watermans Clo. King—7E 104
Waterman's Sq. SE20—7J 111
Watermans St. SW15—3F 91
Watermans Wlk. SE16—3A 80
Waterman Way. E1
—1H 79 (2J 149)
Watermead La. Cars—7D 122
Watermead Rd. SE6—4E 112
Watermill Clo. Rich—3C 104
Watermill La. N18—5K 17
Watermill Way. Felt—2D 102
Watermint Quay. N16—6G 31
Water Rd. Wemb—1F 57
Watersfield Way. Edgw—7J 11
Waters Gdns. Dag—5G 53
Waterside. Beck—1B 126
Waterside Clo. SE16
—2G 79 (5H 149)
Waterside Clo. N'holt—3D 54
Waterside Pl. NW1—1E 60
Waterside Point. SW11—7C 76
Waterside Rd. S'hall—3E 70
Waterside Way. SW17—4A 108
Watersmeet Way. SE28—6D 68
Waterson St. E2—3F 63 (1E 142)
Watersplash Clo. King—3E 118
Waters Rd. SE6—3G 113
Waters Rd. King—2H 119
Waters Sq. King—3H 119
Water Tower Hill. Croy—4D 134
Waterville Rd. N17—1C 30
Waterworks La. E5—2K 47
Waterworks Rd. SW2—6K 93
Waterworks Yd. Croy—3C 134
Watery La. SW20—2H 121
Watery La. N'holt—2A 54
Watery La. Sidc—6B 116
Wates Way. Mitc—6D 122
Watford By-Pass. Borwd
—1G 11
Watford By-Pass. Edgw—2K 11
Watford Clo. SW11—1C 92
Watford Rd. E16—5J 65
Watford Rd. Harr & Wemb
—7A 24
Watford Way—4F 13
NW4 1-103, 171-487 &
2-46, 190-402
NW7 remainder
Watkin Rd. Wemb—3H 41
Watkinson Rd. N7—6K 45
Watling Av. Edgw—1J 25
Watling Farm Clo. Stan—1H 11
Watling Gdns. NW2—6G 43
Watling St. EC4
—6C 62 (8M 141)
Watling St. Bexh—4H 101
Watlington Gro. SE26—5A 112
Watney Mkt. E1—6H 63 (8K 143)
Watney Rd. SW14—3J 89
Watney's Rd. Mitc—5H 123
Watney St. E1—6H 63 (8K 143)
Watson Av. E6—7E 50
Watson Av. Sutt—2G 131
Watson Clo. N16—5D 46
Watson Clo. SW19—6C 108

Watson's M. W1
—5C 60 (6D 138)
Watsons Rd. N22—1K 29
Watson's St. SE8—7C 80
Watson St. E13—2K 65
Watsons Yd. NW2—2C 42
Wattisfield Rd. E5—3J 47
Watts Gro. E3—5D 64
Watts La. Chst—1F 129
Watts La. Tedd—5A 104
Watts Rd. Th Dit—7A 118
Watts St. E1—1H 79 (2K 149)
Wat Tyler Rd. SE10—2E 96
Wauthier Clo. N13—5G 17
Wavell Dri. Sidc—6J 99
Wavel M. N8—4H 29
Wavel M. NW6—7K 43
Wavel Pl. SE26—5F 111
Wavendon Av. W4—5K 73
Waveney Av. SE15—4H 95
Waveney Clo. E1
—1G 79 (2H 149)
Waverley Av. E4—4G 19
Waverley Av. E17—3F 33
Waverley Av. Surb—6H 119
Waverley Av. Sutt—2K 131
Waverley Av. Twic—1D 102
Waverley Av. Wemb—5F 41
Waverley Clo. E18—1A 34
Waverley Clo. Brom—5B 128
Waverley Ct. SE26—5J 111
Waverley Cres. SE18—5H 83
Waverley Gdns. E6—5C 66
Waverley Gdns. NW10—2F 57
Waverley Gdns. Bark—2J 67
Waverley Gdns. Ilf—2G 35
Waverley Gro. N3—3F 27
Waverley Pl. N4—1B 46
Waverley Pl. NW8—2B 60
Waverley Rd. E17—3E 32
Waverley Rd. E18—1A 34
Waverley Rd. N8—6J 29
Waverley Rd. N17—7C 18
Waverley Rd. SE18—5H 83
Waverley Rd. SE25—4H 125
Waverley Rd. Enf—3G 7
Waverley Rd. Eps—5D 130
Waverley Rd. Harr—1C 38
Waverley Rd. S'hall—7E 54
Waverley Vs. N17—2F 31
Waverley Way. Cars—6C 132
Waverton Rd. SW18—7A 92
Waverton St. W1
—1F 77 (2J 145)
Wavertree Rd. E18—2J 33
Wavertree Rd. SW2—1K 109
Waxlow Cres. S'hall—6E 54
Waxlow Rd. NW10—2J 57
Waxwell Clo. Pinn—3B 22
Waxwell La. Pinn—2B 22
Waxwell Ter. SE1
—2K 77 (5F 146)
Wayfarer Rd. N'holt—4B 54
Wayfield Link. SE9—6H 99
Wayford St. SW11—2C 92
Wayland Av. E8—5G 47
Waylands Mead. Beck—1D 126
Waylett Pl. SE27—3B 110
Waylett Pl. Wemb—4D 40
Wayneflete Av. Croy—3B 134
Wayneflete Sq. W10—7F 59
Wayneflete St. SW18—2A 108
Wayside. NW11—1G 43
Wayside. SW14—5J 89
Wayside. Croy—6D 136
Wayside Clo. N14—6B 6
Wayside Clo. Romf—3G 37
Wayside Ct. Twic—6C 88
Wayside Ct. Wemb—3G 41
Wayside Gdns. SE9—4D 114
Wayside Gdns. Dag—5G 53
Wayside Gro. SE9—4D 114
Wayside M. Ilf—5E 34
Weald La. Harr—2H 23
Weald Rise. Harr—7E 10
Weald Sq. E5—2H 47
Wealdstone Rd. Sutt—2H 131
Weald, The. Chst—6D 114

Weald Way. Romf—6H 37
Wealdwood Gdns. Pinn—6A 10
Weale Rd. E4—3A 20
Weardale Gdns. Enf—1J 7
Weardale Rd. SE13—4F 97
Wear Pl. E2—3H 63 (2J 143)
Wearside Rd. SE13—4D 96
Weatherley Clo. E3—5B 64
Weavers Clo. Iswth—4J 87
Weaver's La. SE1
—1E 78 (3D 148)
Weavers Ter. SW6—6J 75
Weaver St. E1—4G 63 (4G 143)
Weavers Way. NW1—1H 61
Weaver Wlk. SE27—4C 110
Webber Row. SE1
—2B 78 (5J 147)
Webber St. SE1—2A 78 (4H 147)
Webb Est. E5—7G 31
Webb Gdns. E13—4J 65
Webb Pl. NW10—3B 58
Webb Rd. SE3—6H 81
Webb's Rd. SW11—5D 92
Webb St. SE1—3E 78 (7C 148)
Webster Gdns. W5—1D 72
Webster Rd. E11—3E 48
Webster Rd. SE16
—3G 79 (7H 149)
Wedderburn Rd. NW3—5B 44
Wedderburn Rd. Bark—1J 67
Wedgewood Way. SE19
—7C 110
Wedgwood M. W1
—6H 61 (8B 140)
Wedlake St. W10—4G 59
Wedmore Av. Ilf—1E 34
Wedmore Gdns. N19—2H 45
Wedmore M. N19—3H 45
Wedmore Rd. Gnfd—3H 55
Wedmore St. N19—3H 45
Weech Rd. NW6—4J 43
Weedington Rd. NW5—5E 44
Weekley Sq. SW11—3B 92
Weigall Rd. SE12—5J 97
Weighhouse St. W1
—6E 60 (8H 139)
Weighton M. SE20—2H 125
Weighton Rd. SE20—2H 125
Weighton Rd. Harr—1H 23
Weihurst Gdns. Sutt—5B 132
Weimar St. SW15—3G 91
Weirdale Av. N20—2J 15
Weir Hall Av. N18—6J 17
Weir Hall Gdns. N18—5J 17
Weir Hall Rd.—5J 17
N17 1-35 & 2-34
N18 remainder
Weir Rd. SW12—7G 93
Weir Rd. SW19—3K 107
Weir Rd. Bex—7H 101
Weir's Pas. NW1
—3H 61 (1B 140)
Weiss Rd. SW15—3F 91
Welbeck Av. Brom—4J 113
Welbeck Av. Sidc—1A 116
Welbeck Clo. N12—5G 15
Welbeck Clo. Eps—7C 130
Welbeck Clo. N Mald—5B 120
Welbeck Rd. E6—3B 66
Welbeck Rd. Barn—6H 5
Welbeck Rd. Harr—1F 39
Welbeck Rd. Sutt & Cars
—2B 132
Welbeck St. W1—5E 60 (6H 139)
Welbeck Wlk. Cars—1B 132
Welbeck Way. W1
—6F 61 (7J 139)
Welbourne Rd. N17—3F 31
Welby St. SE5—1B 94
Welch Pl. Pinn—1A 22
Weldon Clo. Ruis—6A 38
Weld Pl. N11—5A 16
Welfare Rd. E15—7G 49
Welford Clo. E5—3K 47
Welford Pl. SW19—4G 107

284

Westcoombe Av. SW20
—1B 120
Westcote Rd. SW16—5G 109
West Cotts. NW6—5J 43
Westcott Clo. N15—6F 31
Westcott Clo. Brom—5C 128
Westcott Clo. Croy—7D 136
Westcott Cres. W7—6J 55
Westcott Rd. SE17—6B 78
West Ct. Wemb—2C 40
Westcroft Clo. NW2—4G 43
Westcroft Clo. Enf—1D 8
Westcroft Gdns. Mord—3H 121
Westcroft Rd. Cars & Wall
—4E 132
Westcroft Sq. W6—4C 74
Westcroft Way. NW2—4G 43
W. Cromwell Rd.—5H 75
SW5 1-87 & 2-94
W14 remainder
W. Cross Centre. Bren—6B 72
W. Cross Route.—7F 59
W. Cross Way. Bren—6B 72
Westdale Pas. SE18—6F 83
Westdale Rd. SE18—6F 83
Westdean Av. SE12—1K 113
Westdean Clo. SW18—6K 91
West Dene. Sutt—6G 131
Westdown Rd. E15—4E 48
Westdown Rd. SE6—7C 96
West Dri. SW16—4G 109
West Dri. Harr—6C 10
West Dri. Sutt—7F 131
West Dri. Gdns. Harr—6C 10
W. Eaton Pl. SW1
—4E 76 (8G 145)
W. Ella Rd. NW10—7A 42
W. End Av. E10—5F 33
W. End Av. Pinn—4B 22
W. End Ct. Pinn—4B 22
W. End Gdns. N'holt—2A 54
W. End La. NW6—5J 43
W. End La. Barn—4A 4
W. End La. Pinn—3B 22
W. End Rd. S'hall—1C 70
Westerdale Rd. SE10—5J 81
Westerfield Rd. N15—5F 31
Westergate Rd. SE2—6E 84
Westerham Av. N9—3J 17
Westerham Rd. E10—7D 32
Westerley Cres. SE26—5B 112
Western Av. NW11—6F 27
Western Av. Dag—6J 53
Western Av.—7A 38 to 7A 58
Ruis—7A 38
N'holt—7B 38
Gnfd—1F 55
W5—3D 56
W3—4G 57
Western Ct. N3—6D 14
Western Gdns. W5—7G 57
Western La. SW12—7E 92
Western Pde. Barn—5D 4
Western Pl. SE16
—2J 79 (4M 149)
Western Rd. E13—2A 66
Western Rd. E17—5E 32
Western Rd. N2—4D 28
Western Rd. N22—2K 29
Western Rd. NW10—4J 57
Western Rd. SW9—3A 94
Western Rd.—1B 102
SW19 193-231 & 278-340
Mitc remainder
Western Rd. W5—7D 56
Western Rd. S'hall—4A 70
Western Rd. Sutt—5J 131
Westernville Gdns. Ilf—7G 35
Western Way. SE28—2J 83
Western Way. Barn—6E 4
W. Ferry Rd. E14—1C 80
Westfield Clo. Enf—3F 9
Westfield Clo. Sutt—4G 131
Westfield Dri. Harr—4D 24
Westfield Gdns. Harr—4D 24
Westfield La. Harr—4D 24

Westfield Pk. Pinn—1D 22
Westfield Rd. NW7—3F 13
Westfield Rd. W13—1A 72
Westfield Rd. Beck—2B 126
Westfield Rd. Bexh—3J 101
Westfield Rd. Croy—2B 134
Westfield Rd. Dag—4E 52
Westfield Rd. Mitc—2D 122
Westfield Rd. Surb—5D 118
Westfield Rd. Sutt—4H 131
Westfields. SW13—3B 90
Westfields Av. SW13—3A 90
Westfields Rd. W3—5H 57
Westfield St. SE18—3B 82
W. Garden Pl. W2
—6C 60 (8D 138)
West Gdns. E1—7H 63 (1K 149)
West Gdns. SW17—6C 108
Westgate. W5—3E 56
Westgate Rd. SE25—4H 125
Westgate Rd. Beck—1E 126
Westgate St. E8—1H 63
Westgate Ter. SW10—6K 75
Westglade Ct. Harr—5D 24
W. Green Rd. N15—4B 30
West Gro. SE10—1E 96
West Gro. Wfd G—6F 21
Westgrove La. SE10—1E 96
W. Halkin St. SW1
—3E 76 (6G 145)
W. Hallowes. SE9—1C 114
W. Hall Rd. Rich—1H 89
W. Ham La. E15—7G 49
W. Hampstead M. NW6—6K 43
W. Harding St. EC4
—6A 62 (7H 141)
Westhay Gdns. SW14—5H 89
W. Heath Av. NW11—1J 43
W. Heath Clo. NW3—3J 43
W. Heath Dri. NW11—1J 43
W. Heath Gdns. NW3—3J 43
W. Heath Rd. NW3—2J 43
W. Heath Rd. SE2—6D 84
West Hill—7F 91
SW18 1-61 & 2-70
SW15 remainder
West Hill. Harr—2J 39
West Hill. S Croy—7E 134
West Hill. Wemb—1F 41
W. Hill Ct. N6—3E 44
Westhill Pk. N6—2D 44
(in two parts)
W. Hill Rd. SW18—6H 91
W. Hill Way. N20—1E 14
Westholm. NW11—4K 27
West Holme. E1—1J 101
Westholme. Orp—7K 129
Westhorne Av.—7J 97
SE12 1-421 & 2-320
SE9 remainder
Westhorpe Gdns. NW4—3E 26
Westhorpe Rd. SW15—3E 90
W. House Clo. SW19—1G 107
Westhurst Dri. Chst—5F 115
W. India Dock Pier
Development. E14—2C 80
W. India Dock Rd. E14—7C 64
Westlake Clo. Hay—4C 54
Westland Dri. Brom—2H 137
Westland Pl. N1—3D 62 (1A 142)
Westlands Ter. SW12—6G 93
Westland Way. Wall—7H 133
West La. SE16—2H 79 (5J 149)
Westlea Rd. W7—3A 72
Westleigh Av. SW15—5D 90
Westleigh Ct. E11—5J 33
Westleigh Dri. Brom—1C 128
Westleigh Gdns. Edgw—1G 25
W. Lodge Av. W3—1G 73
Westmead. SW15—6D 90
West Mead. Eps—6A 130
West Mead. Ruis—4A 38
Westmead Rd. Sutt—4B 132
Westmere Dri. NW7—3E 12
West M. N17—6C 18
Westminster Av. T Hth—2B 124

Westminster Bri. SW1 & SE1
—2J 77 (5D 146)
Westminster Bri. Rd. SE1
—3A 78 (6G 147)
Westminster Clo. Ilf—2H 35
Westminster Clo. Tedd—5A 104
Westminster Dri. N13—5D 16
Westminster Gdns. Bark—2J 67
Westminster Gdns. Ilf—2G 35
Westminster Industrial Est.
SE18—3B 82
Westminster Rd. N9—1C 18
Westminster Rd. W7—1J 71
Westminster Rd. Sutt—2B 132
Westmoat Clo. Beck—7E 112
Westmoor Gdns. Enf—2E 8
Westmoor Rd. Enf—2E 8
Westmoor St. SE7—3B 82
Westmoreland Av. Well—4J 99
Westmoreland Dri. Sutt
—7K 131
Westmoreland Pl. SW1—5F 77
Westmoreland Pl. W5—5D 56
Westmoreland Rd. NW9—3F 25
Westmoreland Rd. SE17—6D 78
Westmoreland Rd. SW13
—1B 90
Westmoreland Rd. Brom
—5G 127
Westmoreland St. W1
—5E 60 (6H 139)
Westmoreland Ter. SW1—5F 77
Westmorland Clo. E12—2B 50
Westmorland Clo. Twic—6B 88
Westmorland Ct. Surb—7D 118
Westmorland Pl. Brom—3J 127
Westmorland Rd. E17—6C 32
Westmorland Rd. Harr—5F 23
Westmorland Way. Mitc
—5J 123
Westmount Rd. SE9—2D 98
West Oak. Beck—1F 127
Westoe Rd. N9—2C 18
Weston Dri. Stan—1B 24
Weston Grn. Dag—4F 53
Weston Gro. Brom—1H 127
Weston Pk. N8—6J 29
Weston Pk. King—2E 118
Weston Rise. WC1
—3K 61 (1F 140)
Weston Rd. W4—3J 73
Weston Rd. Brom—7H 113
Weston Rd. Dag—4E 52
Weston Rd. Enf—2J 7
Weston St. SE1—2E 78 (5C 146)
Westover Hill. NW3—2J 43
Westover Rd. SW18—7A 92
Westow Hill. SE19—6E 110
Westow St. SE19—6E 110
West Pk. SE9—2C 114
W. Park Av. Rich—1H 89
W. Park Rd. Romf—5D 36
W. Park Rd. Rich—1G 89
West Pier. E1—1H 79 (3J 149)
Westpoint. Pk SW19—5E 106
Westpole Trading Est. W3
—5G 57
Westpole Av. Barn—4K 5
Westport Rd. E13—4K 65
Westport St. E1—6K 63
W. Poultry Av. EC1
—5B 62 (6J 141)
W. Quarters. W12—6C 58
West Quay. SW10—1A 92
W. Ridge Gdns. Gnfd—2G 55
West Rd. E15—1H 65
West Rd. N17—6C 18
West Rd. SW3—6D 76
West Rd. SW4—5H 93
West Rd. W5—5E 56
West Rd. Barn—1K 15
West Rd. King—1J 119
West Rd. Romf—6D 36
(Chadwell Heath)
West Rd. Romf—7K 37
(Rush Green)

Westrow. SW15—6E 90
West Row. W10—4G 59
Westrow Dri. Bark—6K 51
Westrow Gdns. Ilf—2K 51
W. Sheen Vale. Rich—4F 89
West Side. NW4—2D 26
W. Side Comn. SW19—5E 106
W. Smithfield. EC1
—5B 62 (6J 141)
West Sq. SE11—3B 78 (7J 147)
West St. E2—2H 63 (1K 143)
West St. E11—3G 49
West St. E17—5D 32
West St. WC2—6H 61 (8B 140)
West St. Bexh—3F 101
West St. Bren—6C 72
West St. Brom—1J 127
West St. Cars—3D 132
West St. Croy—4C 134
West St. Eri—4K 85
West St. Harr—1H 39
West St. Sutt—5K 131
West St. La. Cars—4D 132
W. Temple Sheen SW14—5H 89
W. Tenter St. E1—7F 63 (9F 142)
West Towers. Pinn—6B 22
West View. NW4—4E 26
W. View Clo. NW10—5B 42
Westview Clo. W7—6J 55
W. View Cres. N9—7K 7
Westview Dri. Wfd G—2B 34
Westville Rd. W12—2C 74
Westville Rd. Th Dit—7A 118
West Wlk. W5—5E 56
West Wlk. Barn—7K 5
W. Walkway, The. Sutt—5K 131
Westward Rd. E4—5G 19
Westward Way. Harr—6E 24
W. Warwick Pl. SW1
—4G 77 (9L 145)
Westway. N18—4J 17
West Way. NW10—3K 41
Westway. SW20—4D 120
Westway. W12, W10, W9 & W2
—7B 58
West Way. Croy—2A 136
West Way. Edgw—6C 12
West Way. Houn—1D 86
Westway. Orp—5H 129
West Way. Pinn—4B 22
West Way. W Wick—6C 127
Westway Clo. SW20—3D 120
W. Way Gdns. Croy—2K 135
Westways. Eps—4B 130
Westwell M. SW16—6J 109
Westwell Rd. SW16—6J 109
Westwell Rd. App. SW16
—6J 109
Westwick Gdns. W14—2F 75
Westwood Av. SE19—7D 110
Westwood Av. Harr—4F 39
Westwood Clo. Brom—3B 128
Westwood Gdns. SW13—3B 90
Westwood Hill. SE26—5G 111
Westwood La. Well & Sidc
—3K 99
Westwood Pk. SE23—7H 95
Westwood Rd. E16—1K 81
Westwood Rd. SW13—3B 90
Westwood Rd. Ilf—1K 51
W. Woodside. Bex—1E 119
Wetharal Dri. Stan—1B 24
Wetherby Clo. N'holt—6F 39
Wetherby Gdns. SW5—4A 76
Wetherby M. SW5—5K 75
Wetherby Pl. SW7—4A 76
Wetherby Rd. Enf—1H 7
Wetherden St. E17—7B 32
Wetherell Rd. 9—1K 63
Wetherill Rd. N10—1E 28
Wexford Rd. SW12—7D 92
Weybourne St. SW18—2A 108
Weybridge Rd. T Hth—4A 124
Weydown Clo. SW19—1G 107
Weyhill Rd. E1—6G 63 (7H 143)
Weylond Rd. Dag—3F 53
Weyman Rd. SE3—1A 98

286

Weymouth Av. NW7—5F 13
Weymouth Av. W5—3C 72
Weymouth Ct. Sutt—7J 131
Weymouth M. W1
—5F 61 (5J 139)
Weymouth St. W1
—5E 60 (5H 139)
Weymouth Ter. E2
(in two parts)—2F 63 (1F 142)
Weymouth Wlk. Stan—6F 11
Whadcoat St. N4—2A 46
Whalebone Av. Romf—6F 37
Whalebone Gro. Romf—6F 37
Whalebone La. E15—7G 49
Whalebone La. S. Romf & Dag
—7F 37
Wharfdale Rd. N1—2J 61
Wharfedale Gdns. T Hth
—4K 123
Wharfedale St. SW10—5K 75
Wharf La. Twic—1A 104
Wharf Pl. E2—1H 63
Wharf Rd. E15—1F 65
Wharf Rd. N1—2C 62 (1L 141)
Wharf Rd. Enf—6F 9
Wharf Rd. Industrial Est. Enf
—6F 9
Wharfside Rd. E16—6G 65
Wharf St. E16—5G 65
Wharncliffe Dri. S'hall—1H 71
Wharncliffe Gdns. SE25
—2E 124
Wharncliffe Rd. SE25—2E 124
Wharton Clo. NW10—6A 42
Wharton Cotts. WC1
—3K 61 (2F 140)
Wharton Rd. Brom—1K 127
Wharton St. WC1
—3K 61 (2F 140)
Whateley Rd. SE20—7K 111
Whateley Rd SE22—5F 95
Whatley Av. SW20—3F 121
Whatman Rd. SE23—7K 95
Wheatfields. Enf—1F 9
Wheatfield Way. King—2E 118
Wheathill Rd. SE20—3H 125
Wheatlands. Houn—6E 70
Wheatlands Rd. SW17—3E 108
Wheatley Clo. NW4—2C 26
Wheatley Gdns. N9—2K 17
Wheatley Rd. Iswth—3K 87
Wheatley St. W1
—5E 60 (6H 139)
Wheatsheaf Clo N'holt—5E 38
Wheatsheaf La. SW6—7E 74
Wheatsheaf La. SW8—7J 77
Wheatsheaf Ter. SW6—7H 75
Wheelers Cross Bark—2H 67
Wheel Farm Dri. Dag—3J 53
Wheelwright St. N7—7K 45
Whelan Way. Wall—3H 133
Wheler St. E1—4F 63 (4E 142)
Whellock Rd. W4—3A 74
Whenman Av. Bex—3J 117
Whernside Clo. SE28—7C 68
Whetstone Clo. N20—2G 15
Whetstone Pk. WC2
—6K 61 (7E 140)
Whetstone Rd. SE3—2A 98
Whewell Rd. N19—2J 45
Whidborne Clo. SE8—2C 96
Whidborne St. WC1
—3J 61 (2D 140)
Whimbrel Clo. SE28—7C 68
Whinchat Rd. SE28—3H 83
Whinfell Clo. SW16—5H 109
Whinyates Rd. SE9—3C 98
Whipps Cross. E17—5F 33
Whipps Cross Rd. E17—5F 33
Whiskin St. EC1—3B 62 (2J 141)
Whisperwood Clo. Harr—1J 23
Whistler Gdns. Edgw—2F 25
Whistlers Av. SW11—7B 76
Whistler St. N5—5B 46
Whistler Wlk. SW10—7B 76
Whiston Rd. E2—1F 63
Whitbread Clo. N17—1G 31

Whitbread Rd. SE4—4A 96
Whitburn Rd. SE13—4E 96
Whitby Av. NW10—3H 57
Whitby Ct. N7—4J 45
Whitby Gdns. NW9—3G 25
Whitby Gdns. Sutt—2B 132
Whitby Rd. SE18—4D 82
Whitby Rd. Harr—3G 39
Whitby Rd. Ruis—3A 38
Whitby Rd. Sutt—2B 132
Whitby St. E1—4F 63 (3E 142)
Whitcher Clo. SE14—6A 80
Whitcher Pl. NW1—6G 45
Whitchurch Av. Edgw—7A 12
Whitchurch Clo. Edgw—6A 12
Whitchurch Gdns. Edgw—6A 12
Whitchurch La. Edgw—7J 11
Whitchurch Rd. W11—7F 59
Whitcomb St. WC2
—7H 61 (1B 146)
White Acre. NW9—2A 26
Whiteadder Way. E14—4D 80
Whitear Wlk. E15—6F 49
Whitebarn La. Dag—1G 69
Whitebeam Av. Brom—7E 128
Whitebeam Clo. SW9—7K 77
White Bear Pl. NW3—4B 44
White Butts Rd. Ruis—3B 38
Whitechapel High St. E1
—6F 63 (7F 142)
Whitechapel Rd. E1
—5G 63 (6G 143)
White Chu. La. E1
—6G 63 (7G 143)
White City Clo W12—7E 58
White City Est. W12—7D 58
White City Rd. W12—7D 58
White Conduit St. N1—2A 62
Whitecote Rd. S'hall—6G 55
White Craig Clo. Pinn—5A 10
Whitecroft Clo. Beck—4F 127
Whitecroft Way. Beck—4E 126
Whitecross Pl. EC2
—5D 62 (5B 142)
Whitecross St. EC1 & EC2
—4C 62 (3M 141)
Whitefield Av NW2—1E 42
Whitefield Clo SW18—6G 91
Whitefoot La Brom—4E 112
Whitefoot Ter Brom—3H 113
Whitefriars Av. Harr—2J 23
Whitefriars Dri. Harr—2J 23
Whitefriars St. EC4
—6A 62 (8H 141)
White Gdns Dag—6G 53
Whitegate Gdns. Harr—7E 10
Whitehall. SW1—1J 77 (3C 146)
Whitehall Ct. SW1
—1J 77 (3D 148)
Whitehall Gdns. E4—1B 20
Whitehall Gdns. W3—6G 73
Whitehall Gdns. W4—6H 73
Whitehall La. Buck H—2D 20
Whitehall Pk. N19—1G 45
Whitehall Pk. Rd. W4—6H 73
Whitehall Pl. E7—5J 49
Whitehall Pl. SW1
—1J 77 (3C 146)
Whitehall Pl. Wall—4F 133
Whitehall Rd. E4 & Wfd G
—2B 20
Whitehall Rd. W7—2A 72
Whitehall Rd. Brom—5B 128
Whitehall Rd. Harr—7J 23
Whitehall Rd. T Hth—5A 124
Whitehall St. N17—7A 18
White Hart La. N17—7H 17
White Hart La. N22—1A 30
White Hart La. NW10—6B 42
White Hart La. SW13—3A 90
White Hart La. Romf—1G 37
White Hart Rd. SE18—4J 83
White Hart Slip. Brom—2J 127
White Hart St. SE11
—5A 78 (9H 147)
White Hart Yd. SE1
—1D 78 (3A 148)

Whitehaven Clo. Brom—4J 127
Whitehaven St. NW8
—4C 60 (4C 138)
Whitehead Clo. SW18—7A 92
Whitehead's Gro. SW3
—4C 76 (9D 144)
White Horse Hill. Chst—4E 114
White Horse La. E1—5K 63
Whitehorse La. SE25—4D 124
Whitehorse M. SE1
—3A 78 (6H 147)
White Horse Rd. E1—6A 64
(in two parts)
White Horse Rd. E6—3D 66
Whitehorse Rd Croy & T Hth
—7C 124
White Horse St W1
—1F 77 (3K 145)
White Horse Yd. EC2
—6D 62 (7A 142)
White Ho. Dri. Stan—4H 11
White Ho. Dri Wfd G—6C 20
Whitehouse La. Enf—1H 7
Whitehouse Way. N14—2A 16
White Kennett St E1
—6F 63 (7E 142)
Whiteledges. W13—6C 56
Whitelegg Rd. E13—2H 65
Whiteley Rd. SE19—5D 110
Whiteley's Cotts. W14—4H 75
Whiteley's Way. Felt—3E 102
White Lion Hill. EC4
—7B 62 (9K 141)
White Lion St. N1—2A 62
White Lodge. SE19—7B 110
White Lodge Clo. N2—6B 28
White Lodge Clo. Sutt—7A 132
Whiteoak Ct. Chst—6E 114
White Oak Dri. Beck—2E 126
White Oak Gdns. Sidc—7K 99
Whiteoaks La. Gnfd—3H 55
White Orchards. N20—7C 4
White Orchards. Stan—5F 11
White Post La. E9—6C 48
Whitepost La. SE13—3C 96
White Post St. SE15—7J 79
Whites Av. Ilf—6J 35
Whites Dri. Brom—7H 127
White's Grounds. SE1
—2E 78 (5D 148)
White's Row E1—5F 63 (6E 142)
White's Sq. SW4—4H 93
Whitestile Rd Bren—5C 72
Whitestone La. NW3—3A 44
Whitestone Wlk. NW3—3A 44
White St. S'hall—2B 70
White Swan M. W4—6A 74
Whitethorn Gdns Croy—2H 135
Whitethorn Gdns Enf—5J 7
Whitethorn St. E3—5C 64
Whitewebbs Way. Orp—1K 129
Whitfield Rd. E6—7A 50
Whitfield Rd. SE3—1F 97
Whitfield Rd. Bexh—7F 85
Whitfield St. W1
—4G 61 (4M 139)
Whitford Gdns. Mitc—3D 122
Whitgift Av. S Croy—5C 134
Whitgift Centre. Croy—2C 134
Whitgift Sq. Croy—2C 134
Whitgift St. SE11
—4K 77 (8E 146)
Whitgift St. Croy—3C 134
Whiting Av. Bark—7F 51
Whitings Rd. Barn—5A 4
Whitings Way. E6—5E 66
Whitland Rd. Cars—1B 132
Whitley Rd. N17—2E 30
Whitlock Dri. SW19—7G 91
Whitman Rd. E3—4A 64
Whitmead Clo. S Croy—6E 134
Whitmore Clo. N11—5A 16
Whitmore Gdns. NW10—2E 58
Whitmore Rd. N1—1E 62
Whitmore Rd. Beck—3B 126
Whitmore Rd. Harr—7G 23

Whitnell Way. SW15—5E 90
Whitney Av. Ilf—4B 34
Whitney Rd. E10—7D 32
Whitney Wlk. Sidc—6E 116
Whitstable Clo. Beck—1B 126
Whittaker Av. Rich—5D 88
Whittaker Rd. E6—7B 50
Whittaker Rd. Sutt—3H 131
Whittaker St. SW1
—4E 76 (9G 145)
Whittaker Way. SE1
—4G 79 (9H 149)
Whitta Rd. E12—4B 50
Whittell Gdns. SE26—3J 111
Whittingstall Rd. SW6—1H 91
Whittington Av. EC3
—6E 62 (8C 142)
Whittington Rd. N22—7D 16
Whittington Way. Pinn—5C 22
Whittlebury Clo. Cars—7D 132
Whittle Clo S'hall—6F 55
Whittle Rd. Houn—7A 70
Whittlesea Clo. Harr—7B 10
Whittlesea Path. Harr—1G 23
Whittlesea Rd. Harr—1G 23
Whittlesey St. SE1
—1A 78 (3H 147)
Whitton Av. E. Gnfd—5K 39
Whitton Av. W. N'holt & Gnfd
—5F 39
Whitton Clo. Gnfd—6B 40
Whitton Dene Houn & Iswth
—5G 87
Whitton Dene Iswth—6H 87
Whitton Dri. Gnfd—6A 40
Whitton Mnr. Rd. Iswth—6H 87
Whitton Rd. Houn—4F 87
Whitton Rd. Twic—6J 87
Whitton Wlk. E3—3C 64
Whitton Waye. Houn—6E 86
Whitwell Rd. E13—3J 65
Whitworth Rd. SE18—7E 82
Whitworth Rd. SE25—3E 124
Whitworth St. SE10—5G 81
Whorlton Rd. SE15—3H 95
Whymark Av. N22—3B 30
Whytecliffe Rd. E7—6K 49
Whytecroft. Houn—7B 70
Whyteville Rd. E7—6K 49
Wickersley Rd. SW11—2E 92
Wickers Oake. SE19—4F 111
Wicker St. E1—6H 63 (8J 143)
Wicket, The. Croy—5C 136
Wickford St. E1—4J 63 (3L 143)
Wickford Way. E17—4K 31
Wickham Av. Croy—2A 136
Wickham Av. Sutt—5E 130
Wickham Chase. W Wick
—1F 137
Wickham Clo. Enf—3D 8
Wickham Clo. N Mald—5B 120
Wickham Ct. Rd. W Wick
—2E 136
Wickham Cres. W Wick
—2E 136
Wickham Gdns. SE4—3B 96
Wickham La. SE2—5A 84
Wickham M. SE4—2B 96
Wickham Rd. E4—7K 19
Wickham Rd. SE4—3B 96
Wickham Rd. Beck—2D 126
Wickham Rd. Croy—2K 135
Wickham Rd. Harr—2H 23
Wickham St. SE11
—5K 77 (9E 146)
Wickham St. Well—2J 99
Wickham Way. Beck—4E 126
Wick La. E3—1C 64
(in two parts)
Wickliffe Av. N3—2G 27
Wickliffe Gdns. Wemb—2H 41
Wicklow St. WC1
—3K 61 (1E 140)
Wick Rd. E9—6K 47
Wick Rd. Tedd—7B 104
Wicks Clo. SE9—4B 114
Wick Sq. E9—6B 48
Wicksteed Clo. Bex—3K 117

287

Wickwood St. SE5—2B 94
Widdecombe Av. Harr—2C 38
Widdenham Rd. N7—4K 45
Widdin St. E15—7G 49
Widecombe Gdns. Ilf—4C 34
Widecombe Rd. SE9—3C 114
Widecombe Way. N2—4B 28
Widegate St. E1—5E 62 (6D 142)
Widenham Clo. Pinn—5A 22
Wide Way. Mitc—3H 123
Widley Rd. W9—3J 59
Widmore Lodge Rd. Brom
—2B 128
Widmore Rd. Brom—2J 127
Wigan Ho. E5—1H 47
Wigeon Path. SE28—3H 83
Wiggington Av. Wemb—6H 41
Wiggins Mead. NW9—7G 13
Wightman Rd. N8—4A 30
Wigley Rd. Felt—2B 102
Wigmore Pl. W1—6F 61 (7J 139)
Wigmore Rd. Cars—2B 132
Wigmore St. W1
—6E 60 (7H 139)
Wigmore Wlk. Cars—2B 132
Wigram Rd. E11—6A 34
Wigram Sq. E17—3E 32
Wigston Rd. E13—4K 65
Wigton Gdns. Stan—1E 24
Wigton Pl. SE11—5A 78
Wigton Rd. E17—1B 32
Wilberforce Rd. N4—2B 46
Wilberforce Rd. NW9—6C 26
Wilberforce Way. SW19
—6F 107
Wilbraham Pl. SW1
—4D 76 (8F 144)
Wilbury Way. N18—5J 17
Wilby M. W11—1H 75
Wilcox Clo. SW8—7J 77
Wilcox Pl. SW1—3G 77 (7M 145)
Wilcox Rd. SW8—7J 77
Wilcox Rd. Sutt—4K 131
Wilcox Rd. Tedd—4H 103
Wild Ct. WC2—6K 61 (7E 140)
Wildcroft Gdns. Edgw—6J 11
Wildcroft Mnr. SW15—7E 90
Wildcroft Rd. SW15—7E 90
Wilde Clo. E8—1G 63
Wilde Pl. N13—6G 17
Wilde Pl. SW18—7B 92
Wilderness Rd. Chst—7F 115
Wilderness, The. Hmptn
—4F 103
Wilderton Rd. N16—7E 30
Wildfell Rd. SE6—7D 96
Wild Goose Dri. SE14—1J 95
Wild Hatch. NW11—6J 27
Wild's Rents. SE1
—3E 78 (6C 148)
Wild St. WC2—6J 61 (8D 140)
Wildwood Clo. SE12—7H 97
Wildwood Gro. NW3—1A 44
Wildwood Rise. NW11—1A 44
Wildwood Rd. NW11—6A 28
Wilford Clo. Enf—3J 7
Wilford Owen Clo. SW19
—6A 108
Wilfred St. SW1—3G 77 (6L 145)
Wilfrid Gdns. W3—5J 57
Wilkes St. E1—5F 63 (5F 142)
(in two parts)
Wilkie Way. SE22—1G 111
Wilkinson Ct. SW17—4B 108
Wilkinson Rd. E16—6A 66
Wilkinson St. SW8—7K 77
Wilkinson Way. W4—2K 73
Wilkin St. NW5—6F 45
Wilkin St. M. NW5—6F 45
Wilks Pl. N1—2E 62
Willan Rd. N17—2E 30
Willan Wall. E16—7H 65
Willard St. SW8—3F 93
Willcott Rd. W3—1H 73
Will Crooks Gdns. SE9—4B 98
Willenhall Av. Barn—6F 5
Willenhall Rd. SE18—5F 83

Willersley Av. Sidc—1K 115
Willersley Clo. Sidc—1K 115
Willesden La.—6E 42
NW6 1-221 & 2-218
NW2 remainder
Willes Rd. NW5—6F 45
Willet Clo. N'holt—3A 54
Willett Clo. Orp—6J 129
Willett Pl. T Hth—5A 124
Willett Rd. T Hth—5A 124
Willett Way. Orp—5H 129
Willett Way. SE16—5H 79
William Barefoot Dri. SE9
—4E 114
William Bonney Est. SW4
—4H 93
William Booth Rd. SE20
—1G 125
William Carey Way. Harr
—6J 23
William Clo. Romf—1K 37
William Ct. W5—5C 56
William Covell Clo. Enf—1E 6
William Ellis Way. SE16
—3G 79 (7H 149)
William Gdns. SW15—5D 90
William Gunn Ho. NW3—5C 44
William Guy Gdns. E3—3D 64
William Margrie Clo. SE15
—2G 95
William M. SW1—2D 76 (5F 144)
William Morley Clo. E6—1B 66
William Morris Clo. E17—3B 32
William Rd. NW1
—3G 61 (2L 139)
William Rd. SW19—7G 107
William Rd. Sutt—5A 132
Williams Av. E17—1B 32
William's Bldgs. E2
—4J 63 (3L 143)
Williams Clo. N8—6H 29
Williams Gro. N22—1A 30
Williams La. SW14—3J 89
Williams La. Mord—5A 122
Williamson Clo. SE10—5H 81
Williamson Rd. N4—6B 30
Williamson St. N7—4J 45
Williamson Way. NW7—6B 14
Williams Rd. W13—1A 72
Williams Rd. S'hall—4C 70
Williams Ter. Croy—6A 134
William St. E10—6D 32
William St. N17—7A 18
William St. SW1
—2D 76 (5F 144)
William St. Bark—7G 51
William St. Cars—3C 132
Willifield Way. NW11—4H 27
Willingale Clo. Wfd G—6F 21
Willingdon Rd. N22—2B 30
Willingham Clo. NW5—5G 45
Willingham Ter. NW5—5G 45
Willingham Way. King—3G 119
Willington Rd. SW9—3J 93
Willis Av. Sutt—6C 132
Willis Rd. E15—2H 65
Willis Rd. Croy—7C 124
Willis Rd. Eri—4K 85
Willis St. E14—6D 64
Willmore End. SW19—1K 121
Willoughby Av. Croy—4K 133
Willoughby Gro. N17—7C 18
Willoughby La. N17—6C 18
Willoughby Pk. Rd. N17—7C 18
Willoughby Rd. N8—3A 30
Willoughby Rd. NW3—4B 44
Willoughby Rd. King—1F 119
Willoughby Rd. Rain—7K 53
Willoughby Rd. Twic—5C 88
Willoughby Way. SE7—4K 81
Willow Av. SW13—2B 90
Willow Av. Sidc—6A 100
Willow Bank. SW6—3G 91
Willow Bank. Rich—3B 104
Willow Bri. Rd. N1—6C 46

Willowbrook Rd. SE15—6F 79
Willowbrook Rd. S'hall—3E 70
Willow Clo. Bex—6F 101
Willow Clo. Bren—6C 72
Willow Clo. Brom—5D 128
Willow Clo. Buck H—3G 21
Willow Cotts. N16—2F 47
Willow Cotts. Rich—6G 73
Willow Ct. Edgw—4K 11
Willowcourt Av. Harr—5A 24
Willowdene. N6—7D 28
Willow Dene. Bush, Wat—1D 10
Willow Dene. Pinn—2B 22
Willowdene Clo. Twic—7G 87
Willow Dri. Barn—4B 4
Willow End. N20—2D 14
Willow End. Surb—7E 118
Willow Gdns. Houn—1E 86
Willow Grange. Sidc—3B 116
Willow Grn. NW9—1A 26
Willow Gro. E13—2J 65
Willow Gro. Chst—6E 114
Willowhayne Gdns. Wor Pk
—4E 130
Willow La. Mitc—5D 122
Willow La. Industrial Est. Mitc
—6D 122
Willow Lodge. SW6—1F 91
Willowmead Clo. W5—5D 56
Willow Mt. Croy—3E 134
Willow Pl. SW1—4G 77 (8M 145)
Willow Rd. NW3—4B 44
Willow Rd. W5—2E 72
Willow Rd. Enf—3K 7
Willow Rd. N Mald—4J 119
Willow Rd. Romf—6E 36
Willow Rd. Wall—7F 133
Willows Av. Mord—5K 121
Willows Clo. Pinn—2A 22
Willow St. E4—1A 20
Willow St. EC2—4E 62 (3C 142)
Willow St. Romf—4J 37
Willow Tree Clo. SW18—1K 107
Willowtree Clo. Hay—4A 54
Willow Tree La. Hay—4A 54
Willow Tree Wlk. Brom—1K 127
Willow Vale. W12—1C 74
Willow Vale. Chst—6F 115
Willow View. SW19—1B 122
Willow Wlk. E17—5B 32
Willow Wlk. N2—2B 28
Willow Wlk. N15—4B 30
Willow Wlk. N21—6E 6
Willow Wlk. SE1
—4E 78 (8D 148)
Willow Wlk. Ilf—2E 51
Willow Wlk. Sutt—3H 131
Willow Way. N3—7E 14
Willow Way. SE26—3J 111
Willow Way. W11—7F 59
Willow Way. Twic—2F 103
Willow Way. Wemb—3A 40
Willow Wood Cres. SE25
—6E 124
Willrose Cres. SE2—5B 84
Wills Cres. Houn—6F 87
Wills Gro. NW7—5H 13
Wilman Gro. E8—7G 47
Wilmar Gdns. W Wick—1D 136
Wilmer Clo. King—5F 105
Wilmer Cres. King—5F 105
Wilmer Gdns. N1—1E 62
(in two parts)
Wilmer Lea Clo. E15—7F 49
Wilmer Way. N14—5C 16
Wilmington Av. W4—7K 73
Wilmington Gdns. Bark—6H 51
Wilmington Sq. WC1
—3A 62 (2G 141)
Wilmington St. WC1
—3A 62 (2G 141)
Wilmot Clo. N2—2A 28
Wilmot Clo. SE15—7G 79
Wilmot Pl. NW1—7G 45
Wilmot Pl. W7—1J 71
Wilmot Rd. E10—2D 48
Wilmot Rd. N17—3D 30

Wilmot Rd. Cars—5D 132
Wilmot St. E2—4H 63 (3J 143)
Wilmount St. SE18—4F 83
Wilna Rd. SW18—7A 92
Wilsham St. W11—1G 75
Wilshaw St. SE14—1C 96
Wilsmere Dri. Harr—7D 10
Wilsmere Dri. Ruis—5C 38
Wilson Av. Mitc—1C 122
Wilson Clo. Wemb—7F 25
Wilson Dri. Wemb—7F 25
Wilson Gdns. Harr—7G 23
Wilson Gro. SE16
—2H 79 (5J 149)
Wilson Rd. E6—3B 66
Wilson Rd. SE5—1E 94
Wilson Rd. Ilf—7D 34
Wilson's Pl. E14—6B 64
Wilson's Rd. W6—5F 75
Wilson St. E17—5E 32
Wilson St. EC2—5D 62 (5B 142)
Wilson St. N21—7F 7
Wilstone Clo. Hay—4C 54
Wilthorne Gdns. Dag—7H 53
Wilton Av. W4—5A 74
Wilton Cres. SW1
—2E 76 (5G 145)
Wilton Cres. SW19—1H 121
Wilton Dri. Romf—1J 37
Wilton Gro. SW19—1H 121
Wilton Gro. N Mald—6B 120
Wilton M. SW1—3E 76 (6H 145)
Wilton Pl. SW1—2E 76 (5G 145)
Wilton Rd. N10—2E 28
Wilton Rd. SE2—4C 84
Wilton Rd. SW1—4G 77 (8L 145)
Wilton Rd. SW19—7C 108
Wilton Rd. Barn—4J 5
Wilton Rd. Houn—3B 86
Wilton Row. SW1
—2E 76 (5G 145)
Wilton Sq. N1—1D 62
Wilton St. SW1—3F 77 (6J 145)
Wilton Ter. SW1
—3E 76 (6G 145)
Wilton Way. E8—6G 47
Wiltshire Clo. SW3
—4D 76 (9E 144)
Wiltshire Ct. Ilf—6G 51
Wiltshire Gdns. Twic—1G 103
Wiltshire Rd. SW9—3A 94
Wiltshire Rd. Orp—7K 129
Wiltshire Rd. T Hth—3A 124
Wiltshire Row. N1—1D 62
Wilverley Cres. N Mald—6A 120
Wimbart Rd. SW2—7K 93
Wimbledon Bri. SW19—6H 107
Wimbledon Hill Rd. SW19
—6G 107
Wimbledon Pk. Rd.—2G 107
SW18 1-257 & 2-218
SW19 remainder
Wimbledon Pk. Side. SW19
—2F 107
Wimbledon Rd. SW17—4A 108
Wimbledon Stadium Business
Centre. SW17—3K 107
Wimbolt St. E2—3G 63 (1G 143)
Wimborne Av. Hay—6A 54
Wimborne Av. Orp & Chst
—4K 129
Wimborne Av. S'hall—4E 70
Wimborne Clo. SE12—5H 97
Wimborne Clo. Buck H—2E 20
Wimborne Clo. Wor Pk—1E 130
Wimborne Dri. NW9—3G 25
Wimborne Dri. Pinn—7B 22
Wimborne Gdns. W13—5B 56
Wimborne Rd. N9—2B 18
Wimborne Rd. N17—2E 30
Wimborne Way. Beck—3K 125
Wimbourne Ct. SW12—3G 109
Wimbourne St. N1—2D 62
Wimpole Clo. King—2F 119
Wimpole M. W1—5F 61 (6J 139)
Wimpole St. W1—5F 61 (6J 139)
Winans Wlk. SW9—2A 94

Wincanton Cres. N'holt—5E 38
Wincanton Gdns. Ilf—2F 35
Wincanton Rd. SW18—7H 91
Winchcombe Rd. Cars—7B 122
Winchcomb Gdns. SE9—3B 98
Winchelsea Av. Bexh—7F 85
Winchelsea Clo. SW15—5F 91
Winchelsea Rd. E7—4J 49
Winchelsea Rd. N17—3E 30
Winchelsea Rd. NW10—1K 57
Winchelsey Rise. S Croy
—6F 135
Winchendon Rd. SW6—1H 91
Winchendon Rd. Tedd—4H 103
Winchester Av. NW6—1G 59
Winchester Av. NW9—3G 25
Winchester Av. Houn—6D 70
Winchester Clo. E6—6D 66
Winchester Clo. SE17
—4B 78 (9K 147)
Winchester Clo. Brom—3H 127
Winchester Clo. Enf—6K 7
Winchester Clo. King—7H 105
Winchester Dri. Pinn—5B 22
Winchester Pk. Brom—3H 127
Winchester Pl. E8—5F 47
Winchester Pl. N6—1F 45
Winchester Rd. E4—7K 19
Winchester Rd. N6—7F 29
Winchester Rd. N9—1A 18
Winchester Rd. NW3—7B 44
Winchester Rd. Bexh—2D 100
Winchester Rd. Brom—3H 127
Winchester Rd. Felt—3D 102
Winchester Rd. Harr—4E 24
Winchester Rd. Ilf—3H 51
Winchester Rd. Twic—6B 88
Winchester Sq. SE1
—1D 78 (2A 148)
Winchester St. SW1
—5F 77 (9K 145)
Winchester St. W3—2J 73
Winchester Wlk. SE1
—1D 78 (2A 148)
Winchet Wlk. Croy—6J 125
Winchfield Clo. Harr—6C 24
Winchfield Rd. SE26—5A 112
Winchmore Hill Rd.—1C 16
N14 1-173 & 2-136
N21 remainder
Winckley Clo. Harr—5F 25
Wincott St. SE11
—4A 78 (9H 147)
Wincrofts Dri. SE9—4H 99
Windborough Rd. Cars—7E 132
Windermere Av. N3—3J 27
Windermere Av. NW6—1G 59
Windermere Av. SW19—3K 121
Windermere Av. Ruis—7A 22
Windermere Av. Wemb—7C 24
Windermere Gdns. Ilf—5C 34
Windermere Gro. Wemb—1C 40
Windermere Ho. Barn—4E 4
Windermere Rd. N10—1F 29
Windermere Rd. N19—2G 45
Windermere Rd. SW15—4A 106
Windermere Rd. SW16—1G 123
Windermere Rd. W5—3C 72
Windermere Rd. Bexh—2J 101
Windermere Rd. Croy—1F 135
Windermere Rd. S'hall—5D 54
Windermere Rd. W Wick
—2G 137
Winders Rd. SW11—2C 92
Windfield Clo. SE26—4K 111
Windham Rd. Rich—3F 89
Winding Way. Dag—3C 52
Winding Way. Harr—4J 39
Windlass Pl. SE8—4A 80
Windlesham Gro. SW19
—1F 107
Windley Clo. SE23—2J 111
Windmill Clo. Surb—7C 118
Windmill Ct. NW2—6G 43
Windmill Dri. SW4—5F 93
Windmill Gdns. Enf—3F 7
Windmill Gro. Croy—6C 124

Windmill Hill. NW3—3A 44
Windmill Hill. Enf—3G 7
Windmill La. E15—6F 49
Windmill La. Bush, Wat—1D 10
Windmill La. Gnfd—5G 55
Windmill La. S'hall & Iswth
—2G 71
Windmill La. Surb—7B 118
Windmill M. W4—4A 74
Windmill Pas. W4—4A 74
Windmill Rise. King—7H 105
Windmill Rd. N18—4J 17
Windmill Rd. SW18—6B 92
Windmill Rd. SW19—2D 106
Windmill Rd. W4—4A 74
Windmill Rd.—4C 72
W5 143a-245 & 158-366
Bren remainder
Windmill Rd. Croy—7C 124
Windmill Rd. Hmptn—5F 103
Windmill Rd. Mitc—5G 123
Windmill Row. SE11—5A 78
Windmill St. W1
(in two parts)—5H 61 (6A 140)
Windmill St. Bush, Wat—1D 10
Windmill Wlk. SE1
—1A 78 (3H 147)
Windover Av. NW9—4K 25
Windrose Clo. SE16
—2K 79 (4M 149)
Windrush. SE28—1B 84
Windrush Clo. SW11—4B 92
Windrush Clo. W4—1J 89
Windrush La. SE23—3K 111
Windsor Av. E17—2A 32
Windsor Av. SW19—1A 122
Windsor Av. Edgw—4C 12
Windsor Av. N Mald—5J 119
Windsor Av. Sutt—3G 131
Windsor Clo. N3—2G 27
Windsor Clo. SE27—4C 110
Windsor Clo. Bren—6B 72
Windsor Clo. Chst—5F 115
Windsor Clo. Harr—3E 38
Windsor Ct. N14—7B 6
Windsor Ct. SW11—2B 92
Windsor Cres. Harr—3E 38
Windsor Cres. Wemb—3H 41
Windsor Dri. Barn—6J 5
Windsor Gdns. W9—5J 59
Windsor Gro. SE27—4C 110
Windsor Pl. SW1
—4G 77 (8M 145)
Windsor Rd. E4—4J 19
Windsor Rd. E7—5K 49
Windsor Rd. E10—2D 48
Windsor Rd. E11—2J 49
Windsor Rd. N3—2G 27
Windsor Rd. N7—3J 45
Windsor Rd. N13—3F 17
Windsor Rd. N17—2G 31
Windsor Rd. NW2—6D 42
Windsor Rd. W5—7E 56
Windsor Rd. Barn—6A 4
Windsor Rd. Bexh—4E 100
Windsor Rd. Dag—3E 52
Windsor Rd. Harr—1H 23
Windsor Rd. Houn—2A 86
Windsor Rd. Ilf—4F 51
Windsor Rd. King—7E 104
Windsor Rd. Rich—2F 89
Windsor Rd. Sidc—6B 116
Windsor Rd. S'hall—3D 70
Windsor Rd. Tedd—5H 103
Windsor Rd. T Hth—2B 124
Windsor Rd. Wor Pk—2C 130
Windsors, The. Buck H—2H 21
Windsor St. N1—1B 62
Windsor Ter. N1
—3C 62 (1M 141)
Windsor Wlk. SE5—2D 94
Windsor Way. W14—4G 75
Windspoint Dri. SE15—6H 79
Windus Rd. N16—1F 47
Windus Wlk. N16—1F 47
Windy Ridge. Brom—1C 128

Windy Ridge Clo. SW19
—5F 107
Wine Clo. E1—7J 63 (1L 149)
Wine Office Ct. EC4
—6A 62 (8H 141)
Winforton St. SE10—1E 96
Winfred Gro. SW11—4D 92
Winfrith Rd. SW18—1A 108
Wingate Cres. Croy—6J 123
Wingate Rd. W6—3D 74
Wingate Rd. Ilf—5F 51
Wingate Rd. Sidc—6C 116
Wingfield Rd. E15—4G 49
Wingfield Rd. E17—5D 32
Wingfield Rd. King—6G 105
Wingfield St. SE15—3G 95
Wingfield Way. Ruis—6A 38
Wingford Rd. SW2—6J 93
Wingmore Rd. SE24—3C 94
Wingrave Rd. W6—6E 74
Wingrove Rd. SE6—2G 113
Winifred Rd. SW19—1J 121
Winifred Rd. Dag—2E 52
Winifred Rd. Eri—5K 85
Winifred Rd. Hmptn—4E 102
Winifred St. E16—1D 82
Winifred Ter. Enf—7A 8
Winkfield Rd. E13—2K 65
Winkfield Rd. N22—1A 30
Winkley St. E2—2H 63 (1J 143)
Winkley's Wharf Development.
E14—4C 80
Winlaton Rd. Brom—4F 113
Winmill Rd. Dag—3F 53
Winnett St. W1—7H 61 (9A 140)
Winnington Clo. N2—6B 28
Winnington Rd. N2—6B 28
Winn Rd. SE12—1J 113
Winns Av. E17—3B 32
Winns Comm. Rd. SE18—6J 83
Winns M. N15—4E 30
Winns Ter. E17—3C 32
Winsbeach. E17—2F 33
Winscombe Cres. W5—4D 56
Winscombe St. N19—2F 45
Winscombe Way. Stan—5F 11
Winsford Rd. SE6—3B 112
Winsford Ter. N18—5J 17
Winsham Gro. SW11—5E 92
Winslade Rd. SW2—5J 93
Winslade Way. SE6—7D 96
Winsland M. W2
—6B 60 (7A 138)
Winsland St. W2
—6B 60 (7A 138)
Winsley St. W1—6G 61 (7L 139)
Winslow Clo. NW10—3A 42
Winslow Clo. Pinn—6A 22
Winslow Gro. E4—2B 20
Winslow Rd. W6—6E 74
Winslow Way. Felt—3C 102
Winsor Ter. E6—5E 66
Winstanley Est. SW11—3B 92
Winstanley Rd. SW11—3B 92
Winstead Gdns. Dag—5J 53
Winston Av. NW9—7A 26
Winston Clo. Harr—6E 10
Winston Clo. Romf—4H 37
Winston Ct. Harr—7A 10
Winston Rd. N16—4D 46
Winston Wlk. W4—4K 73
Winston Way. Ilf—3F 51
Winter Av. E6—1C 66
Winterbourne Rd. SE6—1B 112
Winterbourne Rd. Dag—2C 52
Winterbourne Rd. T Hth
—4A 124
Winter Box Wlk. Rich—5F 89
Winterbrook Rd. SE24—6C 94
Winterfold Clo. SW19—2G 107
Wintergreen Clo. E6—5C 66
Winters Rd. Th Dit—7B 118
Winterstoke Gdns. NW7—5H 13
Winterstoke Rd. SE6—1B 112
Winterton Ct. SE20—2G 125
Winterton Pl. SW10—6A 76
Winterwell Rd. SW2—5J 93

Winthorpe Rd. SW15—4G 91
Winthrop St. E1—5H 63 (5J 143)
Winthrop Wlk. Wemb—3E 40
Winton Av. N11—7B 16
Winton Clo. N9—7E 8
Winton Gdns. Edgw—7A 12
Winton Way. SW16—5A 110
Wirrall Ho. SE26—3G 111
Wisbeach Rd. Croy—5D 124
Wisborough Rd. S Croy
—7F 135
Wisdons Clo. Dag—1H 53
Wise La. NW7—5H 13
Wiseman Rd. E10—2C 48
Wise Rd. E15—1F 65
Wiseton Rd. SW17—1C 108
Wishart Rd. SE3—2B 98
Wisley Rd. SW11—5E 92
Wisley Rd. Orp—7A 116
Wisteria Rd. SE13—4F 97
Witan St. E2—3H 63 (2K 143)
Witham Ct. E10—3D 48
Witham Rd. SE20—3J 125
Witham Rd. W13—1A 72
Witham Rd. Dag—5G 53
Witham Rd. Iswth—1H 87
Witherby Clo. Croy—4E 134
Witherfield Way. SE16—5H 79
Witheringtn Rd. N5—5A 46
Withers Mead. NW9—1B 26
Withers Pl. EC1—4C 62 (3M 141)
Witherston Way. SE9—2E 114
Withycombe Rd. SW19—7F 91
Withy Mead. E4—3A 20
Witley Cres. Croy—6E 136
Witley Gdns. S'hall—4D 70
Witley Rd. N19—2G 45
Witney Path. SE23—3K 111
Wittenham Way. E4—3A 20
Wittersham Rd. Brom—5H 113
Wivenhoe Clo. SE15—3H 95
Wivenhoe Ct. Houn—4D 86
Wivenhoe Rd. Bark—2A 68
Wiverton Rd. SE26—6J 111
Wix Rd. Dag—1D 68
Wix's La. SW4—3F 93
Woburn Clo. SW19—6A 108
Woburn Pl. WC1—4J 61 (4C 140)
Woburn Rd. Cars—1C 132
Woburn Rd. Croy—1C 134
Woburn Sq. WC1
—4H 61 (4B 140)
Woburn Wlk. WC1
—3H 61 (2B 140)
Woffington Clo. King—1C 118
Woking Clo. SW15—4B 90
Woldham Rd. Brom—4A 128
Wolfe Clo. Brom—6J 127
Wolfe Cres. SE7—5B 82
Wolfe Cres. SE16—2K 79
Wolfe Gdns. E15—6H 49
Wolferton Rd. E12—4D 50
Wolfington Rd. SE27—4B 110
Wolfram Clo. SE13—5G 97
Wolftencroft Clo. SW11—3C 92
Wollaston Clo. SE1
—4C 78 (8L 147)
Wolmer Clo. Edgw—4B 12
Wolmer Gdns. Edgw—3B 12
Wolseley Av. SW19—2J 107
Wolseley Gdns. W4—6H 73
Wolseley Rd. E7—7K 49
Wolseley Rd. N8—6H 29
Wolseley Rd. N22—1K 29
Wolseley Rd. W4—4J 73
Wolseley Rd. Harr—3J 23
Wolseley Rd. Mitc—7E 122
Wolseley Rd. Romf—7K 37
Wolseley St. SE1
—2G 79 (5G 149)
Wolsey Av. E6—3E 66
Wolsey Av. E17—3B 32
Wolsey Clo. SW20—7D 106
Wolsey Clo. Houn—4G 87
Wolsey Clo. King—1H 119
Wolsey Clo. S'hall—3G 71
Wolsey Clo. Wor Pk—4C 130

Wolsey Cres. Croy—7E 136
Wolsey Cres. Mord—7G 121
Wolsey Dri. King—5E 104
Wolsey Gro. Edgw—7E 12
Wolsey M. NW5—6G 45
Wolsey Rd. N1—5D 46
Wolsey Rd. Enf—2C 8
Wolsey Rd. Hmptn—6F 103
Wolsey St. E1—5J 63 (6L 143)
Wolstonbury. N12—5D 14
Wolvercote Rd. SE2—2D 84
Wolverley St. E2
　　　　　　—3H 63 (1J 143)
Wolverton. SE17
　　　　　　—5E 78 (9C 148)
Wolverton Av. King—1G 119
Wolverton Gdns. W5—7F 57
Wolverton Gdns. W6—4F 75
Wolverton Rd. Stan—6G 11
Wolverton Way. N14—5B 6
Wolves La.—7F 17
　N13 1-37 & 2-40
　N22 remainder
Womersley Rd. N8—6K 29
Wonersh Way. Sutt—7F 131
Wonford Clo. King—1A 120
Wontner Rd. SW17—2D 108
Woodall Rd. Enf—6E 8
Woodbank Rd. Brom—3H 113
Woodbastwick Rd. SE26
　　　　　　　　—5K 111
Woodberry Av. N21—2F 17
Woodberry Av. Harr—4G 23
Woodberry Cres. N10—3F 29
Woodberry Down. N4—7C 30
Woodberry Down Est. N4
　　　　　　　　—7C 30
Woodberry Gdns. N12—6F 15
Woodberry Gro. N4—7C 30
Woodberry Gro. N12—6F 15
Woodberry Gro. Bex—3K 117
Woodberry Way. E4—7K 9
Woodberry Way. N12—6F 15
Woodbine Clo. Twic—2H 103
Woodbine Gro. SE20—7H 111
Woodbine Gro. Enf—1J 7
Woodbine La. Wor Pk—3E 130
Woodbine Pl. E11—6J 33
Woodbine Rd. Sidc—1J 115
Woodbines Av. King—3D 118
Woodbine Ter. E9—6J 47
Woodborough Rd. SW15
　　　　　　　　—4D 90
Woodbourne Av. SW16
　　　　　　　　—3H 109
Woodbourne Gdns. Wall
　　　　　　　　—7F 133
Woodbridge Clo. N7—2K 45
Woodbridge Ct. Wfd G—7H 21
Woodbridge Rd. Bark—5K 51
Woodbridge St. EC1
　　　　　　—4B 62 (3J 141)
Woodbrook Rd. SE2—6A 84
Woodburn Clo. NW4—5F 27
Woodbury Clo. E11—4K 33
Woodbury Clo. Croy—2F 135
Woodbury Ho. SE26—3G 111
Woodbury Pk. Rd. W13—4B 56
Woodbury Rd. E17—4D 32
Woodbury St. SW17—5C 108
Woodchester Sq. W2—5K 59
Woodchurch Clo. Sidc—3J 115
Woodchurch Dri. Brom—7B 114
Woodchurch Rd. NW6—7K 43
Wood Clo. E2—4G 63 (3G 143)
Wood Clo. NW9—7K 25
Wood Clo. Harr—7H 23
Woodclyffe Dri. Chst—2E 128
Woodcock Ct. Harr—7E 24
Woodcock Dell Av. Harr—7D 24
Woodcock Hill. Harr—5C 24
Woodcombe Cres. SE23
　　　　　　　　—1J 111
Woodcote Av. NW7—6K 13
Woodcote Av. T Hth—4B 124
Woodcote Av. Wall—7F 133
Woodcote Clo. Enf—6D 8

Woodcote Clo. King—5F 105
Woodcote Dri. Orp—7H 129
Woodcote Grn. Wall—7G 133
Woodcote M. Wall—6F 133
Woodcote Pl. SE27—5B 110
Woodcote Rd. E11—7J 33
Woodcote Rd. Wall & Purl
　　　　　　　　—6F 133
Woodcroft. N21—1F 17
Woodcroft. SE9—3D 114
Woodcroft. Gnfd—6A 40
Woodcroft Av. NW7—6F 13
Woodcroft Av. Stan—1A 24
Woodcroft Rd. T Hth—5B 124
Wood Dri. Chst—6C 114
Woodedge Clo. E4—1C 20
Woodend. SE19—6C 110
Woodend. Sutt—2A 132
Wood End Av. Harr—4F 39
Wood End Clo. N'holt—5G 39
Woodend Gdns. Enf—4D 6
Wood End Gdns. N'holt—5G 39
Wood End La. N'holt—5F 39
Woodend Rd. E17—2E 32
Wood End Rd. Harr—4H 39
Woodend, The. Wall—7F 133
Woodend Way. Mord—4H 121
Wood End Way. N'holt—5G 39
Wooder Gdns. E7—4J 49
Wooderson Clo. SE25—4E 124
Woodfall Av. Barn—5C 4
Woodfall Rd. N4—2A 46
Woodfall St. SW3—5D 76
Woodfarrs. SE5—4D 94
Woodfield Av. NW9—4A 26
Woodfield Av. SW16—3H 109
Woodfield Av. W5—4C 56
Woodfield Av. Cars—6E 132
Woodfield Av. Wemb—3C 40
Woodfield Clo. SE19—7C 110
Woodfield Cres. W5—4D 56
Woodfield Dri. Barn—1K 15
Woodfield Gdns. W9—5J 59
Woodfield Gdns. N Mald
　　　　　　　　—5B 120
Woodfield Gro. SW16—3H 109
Woodfield La. SW16—3H 109
Woodfield Pl. W9—4H 59
Woodfield Rise. Bush, Wat
　　　　　　　　—1C 10
Woodfield Rd. W5—4C 56
Woodfield Rd. W9—5H 59
Woodfield Rd. Houn—2A 86
Woodfield Way. N11—7C 16
Woodford Av. Ilf—3C 34
Woodford Bri. Rd. Ilf—3B 34
Woodford Cres. Pinn—2A 22
Woodford New Rd. E17, E18 &
　　　　　　　　Wfd G—4G 33
Woodford Pl. Wemb—1E 40
Woodford Rd. E7—4K 49
Woodford Rd. E18—4J 33
Woodford Trading Est. Wfd G
　　　　　　　　—3B 34
Woodger Rd. W12—2E 74
Woodget Clo. E6—6C 66
Woodgrange Av. N12—6G 15
Woodgrange Av. W5—1G 73
Woodgrange Av. Enf—6B 8
Woodgrange Av. Harr—5C 24
Woodgrange Clo. Harr—5D 24
Woodgrange Gdns. Enf—6B 8
Woodgrange Rd. E7—6K 49
Woodgrange Ter. Enf—6B 8
Wood Green Shopping City. N22
　　　　　　　　—2A 30
Woodhall Av. SE21—3F 111
Woodhall Av. Pinn—1C 22
Woodhall Dri. SE21—3F 111
Woodhall Dri. Pinn—1B 22
Woodhall Ga. Pinn—1B 22
Woodham Ct. E18—4H 33
Woodham Rd. SE6—3E 112
Woodhatch Clo. E6—5C 66
Woodhaven Gdns. Ilf—4G 35
Woodhayes Rd. SW19—7E 106
Woodheyes Rd. NW10—5K 41

Woodhill. SE18—4C 82
Woodhill Cres. Harr—6D 24
Woodhouse Av. Gnfd—2K 55
Woodhouse Clo. Gnfd—2K 55
Woodhouse Gro. E12—6G 55
Woodhouse Rd. E11—3H 49
Woodhouse Rd. N12—6G 15
Woodhurst Av. Orp—6G 129
Woodhurst Rd. SE2—5A 84
Woodhurst Rd. W3—7J 57
Woodington Clo. SE9—6E 98
Woodin St. E14—5D 64
Woodison St. E3—4A 64
Woodknoll Dri. Chst—1D 128
Woodland App. Gnfd—6A 40
Woodland Clo. NW9—6J 25
Woodland Clo. SE19—6E 110
Woodland Clo. Eps—6A 130
Woodland Clo. Wfd G—3E 20
Woodland Cres. SE10—6G 81
Woodland Gdns. N10—5F 29
Woodland Gdns. Iswth—3J 87
Woodland Gro. SE10—5G 81
Woodland Hill. SE19—6E 110
Woodland Rise. N10—4F 29
Woodland Rise. Gnfd—6A 40
Woodland Rd. E4—1K 19
Woodland Rd. N11—5A 16
Woodland Rd. SE19—5E 110
Woodland Rd. T Hth—4A 124
Woodlands. NW11—5G 27
Woodlands. SW20—4E 120
Woodlands. Harr—4E 22
Woodlands Av. E11—1K 49
Woodlands Av. N3—7F 15
Woodlands Av. W3—1H 73
Woodlands Av. N Mald—1J 119
Woodlands Av. Romf—7E 36
Woodlands Av. Ruis—7A 22
Woodlands Av. Sidc—1J 115
Woodlands Av. Wor Pk—2C 130
Woodlands Clo. NW11—5G 27
Woodlands Clo. Brom—2D 128
Woodlands Ct. SE22—7H 95
Woodlands Dri. Stan—6E 10
Woodlands Gro. Iswth—2J 87
Woodlands Pk. Bex—4K 117
Woodlands Pk. Rd. N15—5C 30
Woodlands Pk. Rd. SE10
　　　　　　　　—6G 81
Woodlands Rd. E11—2G 49
Woodlands Rd. E17—3E 32
Woodlands Rd. N9—1D 18
Woodlands Rd. SW13—3B 90
Woodlands Rd. Bexh—3E 100
Woodlands Rd. Brom—2C 128
Woodlands Rd. Enf—1J 7
Woodlands Rd. Harr—5K 23
Woodlands Rd. Ilf—3G 51
Woodlands Rd. Iswth—3H 87
Woodlands Rd. S'hall—1B 70
Woodlands Rd. Surb—7D 118
Woodlands St. SE13—7F 97
Woodlands, The. N14—1A 16
Woodlands, The. SE13—7F 97
Woodlands, The. SE19—7C 110
Woodlands, The. Iswth—2K 87
Woodlands, The. Wall—7F 133
Woodland St. E8—6F 47
Woodlands Way. SW15—5H 91
Woodland Ter. SE7—4C 82
Woodland Wlk. NW3—5C 44
Woodland Wlk. SE10—5G 81
Woodland Wlk. Brom—6A 113
　(in two parts)
Woodland Way. N21—2F 17
Woodland Way. NW7—6G 13
Woodland Way. SE2—4D 84
Woodland Way. Croy—1A 136
Woodland Way. Mitc—7E 108
Woodland Way. Mord—4H 121
Woodland Way. Orp—4G 129
Woodland Way. W Wick
　　　　　　　　—4D 136
Woodland Way. Wfd G—3E 20
Wood La. N6—6F 29
Wood La. NW9—7K 25

Wood La. W12—6E 58
Wood La. Dag—4D 52
Wood La. Iswth—6J 71
Wood La. Stan—3F 11
Wood La. Wfd G—5B 20
Woodlawn Clo. SW15—4K 105
　(Kingston Vale)
Woodlawn Clo. SW15—5H 91
　(Wandsworth)
Woodlawn Cres. Twic—2F 103
Woodlawn Dri. Felt—2B 102
Woodlawn Rd. SW6—7F 75
Woodlea Dri. Brom—5G 127
Woodlea Rd. N16—3E 46
Woodleigh Av. N12—6H 15
Woodleigh Gdns. SW16—3J 109
Woodley Clo. SW17—7D 108
Woodley La. Sutt—3C 132
Wood Lodge Gdns. Brom
　　　　　　　　—7C 114
Wood Lodge La. W Wick
　　　　　　　　—3E 136
Woodman's M. W12—5D 58
Woodmansterne Rd. SW16
　　　　　　　　—1H 123
Woodmansterne Rd. Cars
　　　　　　　　—7C 132
Woodman St. E16—1E 82
Woodmere. SE9—1D 114
Woodmere Av. Croy—7K 125
Woodmere Clo. SW11—3E 92
Woodmere Clo. Croy—7K 125
Woodmere Gdns. Croy—7K 125
Woodmere Way. Beck—5F 127
Woodnook Rd. SW16—5F 109
Woodpecker Clo. N9—6C 8
Woodpecker Clo. Bush, Wat
　　　　　　　　—1B 10
Woodpecker Mt. Croy—7A 136
Woodpecker Rd. SE14—6A 80
Woodpecker Rd. SE28—7C 68
Woodquest Av. SE24—5C 94
Wood Ride. Barn—1G 5
Wood Ride. Orp—4H 129
Woodridge Clo. NW2—3D 42
Woodridge Clo. Enf—2F 7
Woodridings Av. Pinn—1D 22
Woodridings Clo. Pinn—1D 22
Woodriffe Rd. E11—7F 33
Woodrow. SE18—4D 82
Woodrow Clo. Gnfd—7B 40
Woodrow Ct. N17—7C 18
Woodrush Clo. SE14—7A 80
Woodrush Way. Romf—4D 36
Woodseer St. E1
　　　　　　—5F 63 (5F 142)
Woodsford Sq. W14—2G 75
Woodshire Rd. Dag—3H 53
Wood Side. NW11—5J 27
Woodside. SW19—5H 107
Woodside. Buck H—2F 21
Woodside Av.—5D 28
　N6 1-37 & 2-68
　N10 remainder
Woodside Av. N12—4E 14
Woodside Av. SE25—6H 125
Woodside Av. Chst—5G 115
Woodside Av. Wemb—1E 56
Woodside Clo. Bexh—4K 101
Woodside Clo. Stan—5G 11
Woodside Clo. Surb—7J 119
Woodside Clo. Wemb—1E 56
Woodside Ct. N12—4F 15
Woodside Ct. Rd. Croy—7G 125
Woodside Cres. Sidc—3J 115
Woodside Dri. Dart—4K 177
Woodside End. Wemb—1E 56
Woodside Gdns. E4—6J 19
Woodside Gdns. N17—2F 31
Woodside Grange Rd. N12
　　　　　　　　—4E 14
Woodside Grn. SE25—6G 125
Woodside Gro. N12—3F 15
Woodside La. N12—3F 15
Woodside La. Bex—6D 100
Woodside Pk. SE25—6H 125
Woodside Pk. Av. E17—4F 33

290

Woodside Pk. Rd. N12—4E 14
Woodside Pl. Wemb—1E 56
Woodside Rd. E13—4A 66
Woodside Rd. N22—7E 16
Woodside Rd. SE25—6H 125
Woodside Rd. Bexh—4K 101
Woodside Rd. Brom—5C 128
Woodside Rd. King—7E 104
Woodside Rd. N Mald—4K 119
Woodside Rd. Sidc—3J 115
Woodside Rd. Sutt—3A 132
Woodside Rd. Wfd G—4D 20
Woodside Way. Croy—6J 125
Woodside Way. Mitc—1G 123
Woods M. W1—7E 60 (9G 139)
Woodsome Rd. NW5—3F 45
Wood's Pl. SE1—3E 78 (7D 148)
Woodspring Rd. SW19—2G 107
Woods Rd. SE15—1H 95
Woodstead Gro. Edgw—6K 11
Woodstock Av. NW11—7G 27
Woodstock Av. W13—3A 72
Woodstock Av. Iswth—5A 88
Woodstock Av. S'hall—3D 54
Woodstock Av. Sutt—7H 121
Woodstock Clo. Bex—1F 117
Woodstock Clo. Stan—2E 24
Woodstock Ct. SE12—6J 97
Woodstock Cres. N9—6C 8
Woodstock Gdns. Beck
—1D 126
Woodstock Gdns. Ilf—2A 52
Woodstock Gro. W12—2F 75
Woodstock Rise. Sutt—7H 121
Woodstock Rd. E7—7A 50
Woodstock Rd. E17—2F 33
Woodstock Rd. N4—1A 46
Woodstock Rd. NW11—7H 27
Woodstock Rd. W4—3A 74
Woodstock Rd. Bush, Wat
—1D 10
Woodstock Rd. Cars—5D 132
Woodstock Rd. Croy—3D 134
Woodstock Rd. Wemb—1F 57
Woodstock St. E16—6H 65
Woodstock St. W1
—6F 61 (8J 139)
Woodstock Ter. E14—7D 64
Woodstock Way. Mitc—2F 123
Woodstone Av. Eps—5C 130
Wood St. E16—7K 65
Wood St. E17—3E 32
Wood St. EC2—6C 62 (7M 141)
Wood St. W4—5A 74
Wood St. King—2D 118
Wood St. Mitc—7E 122
Woodsyre. SE26—4F 111
Woodthorpe Rd. SW15—4D 90
Woodtree Clo. NW4—2E 26
Wood Vale. N10—5G 29
Wood Vale. SE23—1H 111
Wood Vale Est. SE23—6J 95
Woodvale Wlk. SE27—5C 110
Woodview Av. E4—4K 19
Woodview Clo. N4—7B 30
Woodville Clo. SE12—5J 97
Woodville Clo. Tedd—4A 104
Woodville Ct. SE19—1F 125
Woodville Gdns. NW11—7F 27
Woodville Gdns. W5—6E 56
Woodville Gdns. Ilf—4F 35
Woodville Gro. Well—3A 100
Woodville Rd. E11—1H 49
Woodville Rd. E17—4B 32
Woodville Rd. E18—2K 33
Woodville Rd. N16—5E 46
Woodville Rd. NW6—2H 59
Woodville Rd. NW11—7F 27
Woodville Rd. W5—6D 56
Woodville Rd. Barn—3E 4
Woodville Rd. Mord—4J 121
Woodville Rd. Rich—3B 104
Woodville Rd. T Hth—4C 124
Woodville St. SE18—4C 82
Woodward Av. NW4—5C 26

Woodwarde Rd. SE22—6E 94
Woodward Gdns. Dag—7C 52
Woodward Gdns. Stan—7E 10
Woodward Rd. Dag—7B 52
Woodward's Footpath. Twic
—6H 87
Woodway Cres. Harr—6A 24
Woodwell St. SW18—5A 92
Wood Wharf Business Pk. E14
—1E 80
Woodyard Clo. NW5—5E 44
Woodyard La. SE21—7E 94
Woodyates Rd. SE12—6J 97
Wooler St. SE17—5D 78
Woolf Clo. SE28—1B 84
Woollaston Rd. N4—6B 30
Woolmead Av. NW9—7C 26
Woolmer Gdns. N18—5B 18
Woolmer Rd. N18—5B 18
Woolmore St. E14—7E 64
Woolneigh St. SW6—3K 91
Wool Rd. SW20—6D 106
Woolstaplers Way. SE16
—4G 79 (8G 149)
Woolston Clo. E17—2K 31
Woolstone Rd. SE23—2A 112
Woolwich Chu. St. SE18—3C 82
Woolwich Comn. SE18—6E 82
Woolwich Dockyard Industrial
Est. SE18—3C 82
Woolwich Industrial Est. SE28
—3J 83
Woolwich Mnr. Way. E16
—5E 66
Woolwich New Rd. SE18—5E 82
Woolwich Rd.—6D 84
SE2 75-303 & 120-324
Belv remainder
Woolwich Rd.—5H 81
SE10 1-265 & 2-160
SE7 remainder
Woolwich Rd. Bexh—4G 101
Wooster Gdns. E14—6F 65
Woosters M. Harr—3G 23
Wootton Gro. N3—1J 27
Wootton St. SE1
—1A 78 (3H 147)
Worbeck Rd. SE20—2J 125
Worcester Av. N17—7B 18
Worcester Clo. Croy—2C 136
Worcester Clo. Mitc—3F 123
Worcester Cres. NW7—3F 13
Worcester Cres. Wfd G—4F 21
Worcester Gdns. Gnfd—6H 39
Worcester Gdns. Ilf—7C 34
Worcester Gdns. Wor Pk
—3A 130
Worcester M. NW6—6K 43
Worcester Pk. Rd. Wor Pk
—3A 130
Worcester Pl. EC4
—7C 62 (9M 141)
Worcester Rd. E12—4D 50
Worcester Rd. E17—2K 31
Worcester Rd. SW19—5H 107
Worcester Rd. Sutt—7J 131
Worcesters Av. Enf—1B 8
Wordsworth Av. E12—7C 50
Wordsworth Av. E18—3H 33
Wordsworth Av. Gnfd—3H 55
Wordsworth Ct. Harr—7H 23
Wordsworth Dri. Sutt—4E 130
Wordsworth Pde. N8—4B 30
Wordsworth Rd. N16—4E 46
Wordsworth Rd. SE20—7K 111
Wordsworth Rd. Hmptn
—4D 102
Wordsworth Rd. Wall—6G 133
Wordsworth Rd. Well—1J 99
Wordsworth Wlk. NW11—4J 27
Wordsworth Rd. SW11—7C 76
Worgan St. SE11
—5K 77 (9E 146)
Worland Rd. E15—7G 49
World's End La. N21 & Enf
—5E 6

World's End Pas. SW10—7B 76
Worlidge St. W6—5E 74
Worlingham Rd. SE22—4F 95
Wormholt Rd. W12—7C 58
Wormwood St. EC2
—6E 62 (7C 142)
Wornington Rd. W10—4G 59
Woronzow Rd. NW8—1B 60
Worple Av. SW19—7F 107
Worple Av. Iswth—5A 88
Worple Clo. Harr—1D 38
Worple Rd.—1F 121
SW19 1-95 & 2-140
SW20 remainder
Worple Rd. Iswth—4A 88
Worple Rd. M. SW19—6H 107
Worple St. SW14—3K 89
Worple Way. Harr—1D 38
Worple Way. Rich—5E 88
Worship St. EC2
—4D 62 (4B 142)
Worslade Rd. SW17—4B 108
Worsley Bri. Rd. SE26 & Beck
—4B 112
Worsley Rd. E11—4G 49
Worsopp Dri. SW4—5G 93
Worthfield Clo. Eps—7A 130
Worthing Clo. E15—1G 65
Worthing Rd. Houn—6D 70
Worthington Rd. Surb—7F 119
Wortley Rd. E6—7B 50
Wortley Rd. Croy—7A 124
Worton Gdns. Iswth—2H 87
Worton Hall Est. Iswth—4J 87
Worton Rd. Iswth—4H 87
Worton Way. Houn & Iswth
—2H 87
Wotton Rd. NW2—3E 42
Wotton Rd. SE8—6B 80
Wouldham Rd. E16—6H 65
Wragby Rd. E11—3G 49
Wrampling Pl. N9—1B 18
Wrangthorn Wlk. Croy—4A 134
Wray Av. Ilf—3E 34
Wray Cres. N4—2K 45
Wrayfield Rd. Sutt—3F 131
Wray Rd. Sutt—7H 131
Wraysbury Clo. Houn—5C 86
Wrekin Rd. SE18—7G 83
Wren Av. NW2—5E 42
Wren Av. S'hall—4D 70
Wren Clo. E16—6H 65
Wren Cres. Bush, Wat—1B 10
Wren Gdns. Dag—5D 52
Wren Path. SE28—3H 83
Wren Rd. SE5—1D 94
Wren Rd. Dag—5D 52
Wren Rd. Sidc—4C 116
Wrens Pk. Rd. E5—2H 47
Wren St. WC1—4K 61 (3F 140)
Wrentham Av. NW10—2F 59
Wrenthorpe Rd. Brom—4G 113
Wrenwood Way. Pinn—4A 22
Wrexham Rd. E3—2C 64
Wricklemarsh Rd. SE3—1A 98
Wrigglesworth St. SE14—7K 79
Wright Rd. N1—6E 46
Wright Rd. Houn—7A 70
Wrights All. SW19—6E 106
Wrights Clo. SE13—4F 97
Wright's Grn. SW4—4H 93
Wrights La. W8—3K 75
Wrights Pl. NW10—6J 41
Wright's Rd. E3—2B 64
Wrights Rd. SE25—2E 124
Wrights Row. Wall—4F 133
Wright's Wlk. SW14—3K 89
Wrigley Clo. E4—5A 20
Wrotham Rd. NW1—7G 45
Wrotham Rd. W13—1C 72
Wrotham Rd. Barn—2B 4
Wrotham Rd. Well—1C 100
Wrottesley Rd. NW10—2C 58
Wrottesley Rd. SE18—6G 83
Wroughton Rd. SW11—6D 92
Wroughton Ter. NW4—4D 26
Wroxall Rd. Dag—6C 52

Wroxham Gdns. N11—7C 16
Wroxham Rd. SE28—7D 68
Wroxton Rd. SE15—2J 95
Wrythe Grn. Rd. Cars—3D 132
Wrythe Grn. Rd. Cars—3D 132
Wrythe La. Cars—1A 132
Wulfstan St. W12—5B 58
Wyatt Pk. Rd. SW2—2K 109
Wyatt Rd. E7—6J 49
Wyatt Rd. N5—3C 46
Wyatts La. E17—3E 32
Wybert St. NW1—4G 61 (3L 139)
Wyborne Way. NW10—7J 41
Wyburn Av. Barn—3C 4
Wyche Gro. S Croy—7D 134
Wych Elm Pas. King—7F 105
Wycherley Clo. SE3—7H 81
Wycherley Cres. Barn—6E 4
Wychwood Av. Edgw—6J 11
Wychwood Av. T Hth—3C 124
Wychwood Clo. Edgw—6J 11
Wychwood End. N6—7G 29
Wychwood Gdns. Ilf—4D 34
Wychwood Way. SE19—6D 110
Wycliffe Clo. Well—1K 99
Wycliffe Rd. SW11—2E 92
Wycliffe Rd. SW19—6K 107
Wyclif St. EC1—3B 62 (2J 141)
Wycombe Gdns. NW11—2J 43
Wycombe Rd. N17—1G 31
Wycombe Rd. Ilf—5D 34
Wycombe Rd. Wemb—1G 57
Wydehurst Rd. Croy—7G 125
Wydell Clo. Mord—6F 121
Wydeville Mnr. Rd. SE12
—4K 113
Wye Clo. Orp—7K 129
Wyemead Cres. E4—2B 20
Wye St. SW11—2B 92
Wyfields. Ilf—1F 35
Wyfold Rd. SW6—7G 75
Wyhill Wlk. Dag—7J 53
Wyke Clo. Iswth—6K 71
Wyke Gdns. W7—3A 72
Wykeham Grn. Dag—6C 52
Wykeham Hill. Wemb—1F 41
Wykeham Rise. N20—1B 14
Wykeham Rd. NW4—4E 26
Wykeham Rd. Harr—4B 24
Wyke Rd. E3—7C 48
Wyke Rd. SW20—2E 120
Wyldes Clo. NW11—1A 44
Wyldfield Gdns. N9—2A 18
Wyld Way. Wemb—6H 41
Wyleu St. SE23—7A 96
Wylie Rd. S'hall—3E 70
Wyllen Clo. E1—4J 63 (4L 143)
Wymering Rd. W9—3J 59
Wymond St. SW15—3E 90
Wynan Rd. E14—5D 80
Wynaud Ct. N22—6E 16
Wyncham Av. Sidc—1J 115
Wynchgate—1D 16
N14 1-119 & 2-108
N21 remainder
Wynchgate. Harr—7D 10
Wynchgate. N'holt—5D 38
Wyncroft Clo. Brom—3D 128
Wyndale Av. NW9—6G 25
Wyndcliffe Rd. SE7—6K 81
Wyndcroft Clo. Enf—3G 7
Wyndham Clo. Sutt—7J 131
Wyndham Cres. N19—3G 45
Wyndham Cres. Houn—6E 86
Wyndham Est. SE5—7C 78
Wyndham M. W1
—5D 60 (6E 138)
Wyndham Pl. W1
—5D 60 (6E 138)
Wyndham Rd. E6—7B 50
Wyndham Rd. SE5—7C 78
Wyndham Rd. W13—3B 72
Wyndham Rd. Barn—1J 15
Wyndham Rd. King—7F 105
Wyndham St. W1
—5D 60 (5E 138)

Wyndham Yd. W1
—5D 60 (6E 138)
Wyneham Rd. SE24—5D 94
Wynell Rd. SE23—3K 111
Wynford Pl. Belv—6G 85
Wynford Rd. N1—2K 61
Wynford Way. SE9—3D 114
Wynlie Gdns. Pinn—2A 22
Wynndale Rd. E18—1K 33
Wynne Rd. SW9—2A 94
Wynns Av. Sidc—5A 100
Wynnstay Gdns. W8—3J 75
Wynter St. SW11—4A 92
Wynton Gdns. SE25—5F 125
Wynton Pl. W3—6H 57
Wynyard Ter. SE11—5K 77
Wynyatt St. EC1
—3B 62 (1J 141)
Wyre Gro. Edgw—3C 12
Wyresdale Cres. Gnfd—3K 55
Wythburn Pl. W1
—6D 60 (8E 138)
Wythenshawe Rd. Dag—3G 53
Wythens Wlk. SE9—6F 99
Wythes Clo. Brom—2D 128
Wythes Rd. E16—1C 82
Wythfield Rd. SE9—6D 98
Wyvenhoe Rd. Harr—4G 39
Wyvil Rd. SW8—6J 77
Wyvis St. E14—5D 64

Yabsley St. E14—1E 80
Yalding Rd. SE16
—3G 79 (7G 149)
Yale Clo. Houn—5D 86
Yarborough Rd. SW19—1B 122
Yardley Clo. E4—5J 9
Yardley La. E4—5J 9
Yardley St. WC1
—3A 62 (2G 141)
Yarmouth Cres. N17—5H 31
Yarmouth Pl. W1
—1F 77 (3J 145)
Yarnfield Sq. SE15—1G 95
Yarnton Way. SE2 & Eri—2D 84
Yarrow Cres. E6—5C 66
Yately St. SE18—3B 82

Yeading Av. Harr—2C 38
Yeading Fork. Hay—5A 54
Yeading Gdns. Hay—6A 54
Yeading La. Hay & N'holt
—6A 54
Yeading Wlk. Harr—5D 22
Yeames Clo. W13—6A 56
Yeate St. N1—7D 46
Yeatman Rd. N6—6D 28
Yeats Clo. SE13—2F 97
Yeldham Rd. W6—5F 75
Yelverton Rd. SW11—2B 92
Yenston Clo. Mord—6J 121
Yeoman Clo. SE27—3B 110
Yeoman Rd. N'holt—7C 38
Yeomans M. Iswth—6H 87
Yeoman's Row. SW3
—3C 76 (7D 144)
Yeoman St. SE8—4A 80
Yeomans Way. Enf—2D 8
Yeo St. E3—5D 64
Yerbury Rd. N19—3H 45
Yester Dri. Chst—7C 114
Yester Pk. Chst—7D 114
Yester Rd. Chst—7C 114
Yew Clo. Buck H—2G 21
Yew Ct. E4—6G 19
Yewdale Clo. Brom—6G 113
Yewfield Rd. NW10—6B 42
Yew Gro. NW2—4F 43
Yew Tree Clo. N21—7F 7
Yewtree Clo. N22—1G 29
Yew Tree Clo. Well—1A 100
Yew Tree Clo. Wor Pk—1A 130
Yew Tree Gdns. Romf—5K 37
Yew Tree Gdns. Romf—5E 36
(Chadwell Heath)
Yew Tree Rd. W12—7B 58
Yewtree Rd. Beck—3B 126
Yew Tree Way. Croy—7B 136
Yew Wlk. Harr—1J 39
Yoakley Rd. N16—2E 46
Yoke Clo. N7—6J 45
Yolande Gdns. SE9—5C 98
Yonge Pk. N4—3A 46
York Av. SW14—5J 89
York Av. W7—1J 71

York Av. Sidc—2J 115
York Av. Stan—1B 24
York Bri. NW1—4E 60 (3G 139)
York Bldgs. WC2
—7J 61 (1D 146)
York Clo. E6—6D 66
York Clo. W7—1J 71
York Clo. Mord—4K 121
York Ct. N13—3D 16
York Ga. N14—7D 6
York Ga. NW1—4E 60 (4G 139)
York Gro. SE15—1J 95
York Hill. SE27—3B 110
York Ho. Pl. W8—2K 75
York M. NW5—5F 45
York M. Ilf—2E 50
York Pde. Bren—5D 72
York Pl. SW11—3B 92
York Pl. Dag—6J 53
York Pl. Ilf—2E 50
York Rise. NW5—3F 45
York Rd. E4—4H 19
York Rd. E7—6J 49
York Rd. E10—3E 48
York Rd. E17—5K 31
York Rd. N11—6C 16
York Rd. N18—5C 18
York Rd. N21—7J 7
York Rd. SE1—2K 77 (4F 146)
York Rd. SW11—4A 92
York Rd. SW19—6A 108
York Rd. W3—6J 57
York Rd. W5—3C 72
York Rd. Barn—5F 5
York Rd. Bren—5D 72
York Rd. Croy—7A 124
York Rd. Houn—3F 87
York Rd. Ilf—3E 50
York Rd. King—7F 105
York Rd. Rain—7K 53
York Rd. Rich—5F 89
York Rd. Sutt—6J 131
York Rd. Tedd—4J 103
Yorkshire Clo. N16—3E 46
Yorkshire Gdns. N18—5C 18
Yorkshire Grey Pl. NW3—4A 44
Yorkshire Pl. E14—6A 64

Yorkshire Rd. E14—6A 64
Yorkshire Rd. Mitc—4J 123
York Sq. E14—6A 64
York St. W1—5D 60 (6E 138)
York St. Bark—1G 67
York St. Mitc—7E 122
York St. Twic—1A 104
York Ter. Enf—1H 7
York Ter. Eri—1J 101
York Ter. E. NW1
—4E 60 (4H 139)
York Ter. W. NW1
—4E 60 (4G 139)
Yorkton St. E2—2G 63
York Way—6H 45
N1 1-7 & 2-178
N7 remainder
York Way. N20—3J 15
York Way. Felt—3D 102
(in two parts)
York Way Ct. N1—1J 61
Young Ct. NW6—7G 43
Youngmans Clo. Enf—1H 7
Young Rd. E16—6A 66
Youngs Rd. Ilf—5H 35
Young St. W8—2K 75
Yoxley App. Ilf—6G 35
Yoxley Dri. Ilf—6G 35
Yukon Rd. SW12—7F 93
Yuletide Clo. NW10—7A 42
Yunus Khan Clo. E17—5C 32

Zampa Rd. SE16—5J 79
Zander Ct. E2—3G 63 (1H 143)
Zangwill Rd. SE3—1B 98
Zealand Rd. E3—2A 64
Zennor Rd. SW12—1G 109
Zenoria St. SE22—4F 95
Zermatt Rd. T Hth—4C 124
Zetland St. E14—5E 64
Zion Pl. T Hth—4D 124
Zion Rd. T Hth—4D 124
Zoar St. SE1—1C 78 (2L 147)
Zoffany St. N19—2H 45

Every possible care has been taken to ensure that the information given
in this atlas is accurate and whilst the publishers would be grateful to
learn of any errors, they regret they can accept no responsibility for any
expense or loss thereby caused.

The representation on the maps of a road, track, or footpath is no
evidence of the existence of a right of way.

NOTES

NOTES

NOTES

Printed and bound in Great Britain by BPCC Hazell Books Ltd,
Member of BPCC Ltd, Aylesbury, Bucks, England